THE LATE MEDIEVAL BALKANS

The Late Medieval Balkans

*A Critical Survey from the
Late Twelfth Century
to the Ottoman Conquest*

JOHN V. A. FINE, JR.

*Ann Arbor
The University of Michigan Press*

First paperback edition 1994
Copyright © by the University of Michigan 1987
All rights reserved
Published in the United States of America by
The University of Michigan Press
Manufactured in the United States of America

2000   1999   1998   1997   6   5   4   3

Library of Congress Cataloging-in-Publication Data

Fine, John V. A. (John Van Antwerp), 1939–
   The late medieval Balkans.

   Bibliography: p.
   Includes index.
   1. Balkan Peninsula—History.   I. Title.
DR39.F57   1987   949.6   86-16120
ISBN 0-472-10079-3 (alk. paper). — ISBN 0-472-08260-4
(pbk. : alk. paper).

To the inspiring teachers under whom
I studied the medieval Balkans
at Harvard and Sarajevo
With deep gratitude to
  Albert Lord
  Vlajko Palavestra
and to the memory of
  Ante Babić
  Georges Florovsky
  Robert Lee Wolff

Acknowledgments

The decision to write this work began when the American Council of Learned Societies (ACLS) Committee on Eastern Europe asked me to produce a major regional history of medieval southeastern Europe, as part of a series for which they hoped to receive outside funding. When their funding efforts proved unsuccessful, I decided to go ahead with my part anyway, because there had long been a need for a book such as this one. I divided the project in half, first surveying the period from the late sixth century to the 1180s. That volume, entitled *The Early Medieval Balkans: A Critical Survey from the Sixth to the Late Twelfth Century* was published by the University of Michigan Press in 1983. The present volume is that work's continuation. And to prevent this already long volume from becoming any longer, I have kept the background material to a bare minimum. Thus readers seeking a more thorough background about the state of the Balkans in the 1180s than this work provides are referred to the earlier volume.

Like its predecessor, this volume is to a large extent based upon lectures for the course on the medieval Balkans that I have been giving for the past fifteen years at the University of Michigan. I owe a debt to my students' responses to these lectures; their comments and questions have compelled me constantly to rethink and clarify my thoughts.

A grant from the John Simon Guggenheim Foundation combined with a University of Michigan sabbatical semester gave me the academic year 1982–83 to devote entirely to writing. By the end of the year I had completed a first draft, which became the basis for a semester's lectures in the winter term 1984. I then carried out the revisions I felt the work required. It is a pleasure to recognize here the various people and institutions that have assisted in this work's preparation. First the John Simon Guggenheim Foundation, in addition to supporting my time to write, also provided funds for travel—which enabled me to go to London and utilize the magnificent British Library of the British Museum and to visit Yugoslavia to use the Narodna Biblioteka in Sarajevo and to discuss various questions with Yugoslav scholars—as well as funds for typing and preparation of maps. The Horace H. Rackham School of Graduate Studies at the University of Michigan generously provided a subvention to facilitate the book's publication. The Center for Russian and East

European Studies at the University of Michigan, encouraging me to have the manuscript prepared on a word processor, assumed the responsibility for printing what appeared on my many disks. The Center also provided funds for me to hire a research assistant, Michael Oyserman, who could read Hebrew texts and scholarship; this enabled me to expand my discussion of Jewish communities in the medieval Balkans. I also owe a debt to Michael, whose enthusiasm for the project equaled my own. My debt to my friend and typist, Mary Ann Rodgers, is enormous. Not only did she do a fabulous typing job, but she also introduced me to the world of computers and went well beyond the call of duty by producing dictionaries of terms, which made the production of maps and glossaries much easier. I also want to thank my friends Professor Thomas Trautmann and Marion Hoyer, both of the University of Michigan, who generously assisted me in proofreading the galleys, and my nephew Ljubiša Mladenović, who created the computer program to do the index and whose enthusiasm for every aspect of my project was unflagging.

I am very grateful to Professor R. V. Burks of Wayne State University and to Dr. Duncan M. Perry and Professor George Majeska, both of the University of Maryland, whose careful reading and detailed suggestions have greatly improved the work. I am also indebted to Professor Sima Ćirković of the University of Beograd and to Professor Desanka Kovačević of the University of Sarajevo for their thorough and careful responses to various questions I put to them. None of the individuals named, of course, bears any responsibility for the errors of fact and interpretation that may remain in the work.

I am also most grateful to my family, to my wife, Gena, and sons, Alexander (Sasha) and Paul, who all suffered at times from the loss of my attention. They not only bore this deprivation with good spirit but also provided encouragement and a great deal of time in the thankless job of proofreading.

Note on Transliteration and Names

Serbo-Croatian is a single language (with, of course, dialectical differences) written with two alphabets, Latin for Croatian and Cyrillic for Serbian. Thus the Croatian Latin scheme is a natural one to use for transliterating Serbian names. Furthermore, it seems to me a better system than any other now being used to transliterate Bulgarian and Russian as well. Thus, following Croatian, the following transliteration scheme is used:

c = *ts* (except in words already accepted into English such as *tsar*)
$ć$ = *ch* (soft)
$č$ = *ch* (hard)
h = guttural *kh* (though I have left the *kh,* since it is standard, for Turkic names such as Khazars, khagan, Isperikh)
j = *y* (as in *yes*)
$š$ = *sh*
$ž$ = *zh*
The Slavic softsign is indicated by a single apostrophe (').
The Bulgarian hardsign has been rendered with a double apostrophe ('').

Greek was undergoing evolution at this time with the *b* coming to be pronounced as a *v*. However, I have consistently stuck with the *b* in transliterating names, thus *Bardas* rather than *Vardas*. The same thing was happening to *u,* with its pronunciation shifting from *u* to *v*. I have almost always stuck to the *u;* thus *Staurakios* rather than *Stavrakios*. A major problem with Greek names is also the fact that their latinization has already become standard in English. Thus *k* tends to be rendered as *c* rather than *k*. I have reverted to the less ambiguous *k* in all cases (Kastoria, Nikopolis, etc.) unless names have already become commonplace in English: e.g., Nicephorus, Lecapenus, etc. In the same way the Greek *os* tends to be latinized to *us*. In names already commonplace in the English literature I have stuck with the *us*, otherwise I have used the *os*.

Since control of particular territories in the Balkans has changed over time from Romans or Greeks to different Slavic people to Turks, it is not surprising that there are many different names for some cities. On the whole, I have chosen the name used in the Middle Ages by the power that controlled that place most. Upon first mention (and also in the index) I give the variant names for each place (e.g., Philippopolis [modern Plovdiv], or Durazzo [Dyrrachium, Durres], etc.).

Personal names have presented an insoluble problem, at least to an author making an attempt at consistency. Originally I intended in all cases to use Slavic names; however, how could I say Ivan Alexander when his Greek counterpart was John Cantacuzenus? I then tried to make a distinction between ultimate rulers and nobles, so that I could at least retain the Slavic flavor with the nobility. However, should we then suddenly change the name of Djuradj Branković to George when he became the ruler? As a result I threw up my hands and anglicized all first names, merely providing the Slavic forms on first mention. The only exception is Stephen (a name with various spellings in English as well as Slavic) whose significance on occasions went beyond that of a mere name. Its adoption by Serbian rulers came close to being part of a title, and its subsequent adoption by the Bosnian rulers—after Tvrtko's 1377 coronation—indicates the Serbian origin of Bosnia's kingship. Thus I have used the forms Stefan and Stjepan as they are appropriate.

Contents

CHAPTER 1

The Balkans in the Late Twelfth Century

By 1172 Manuel I Comnenus had recovered for the Byzantine Empire all the Balkans except for what is now Slovenia and the Croatian territory north of the Krka River, which Hungary retained. But the Hungarian presence was not a major danger to Byzantium because the Hungarian throne was then occupied by King Bela III (1172–96), an imperial in-law (having married the step-sister of Manuel's wife) who after a long residence at the imperial court had been allowed to return to Hungary to take its throne after having sworn allegiance to Manuel. In the warfare against Hungary, prior to Bela's assumption of power, the empire had recovered from Hungary Dalmatia, Croatia, Bosnia, and Srem. Probably in Croatia and Bosnia little or no direct imperial rule existed, which would have left these lands in the hands of local nobles who only nominally accepted Byzantine suzerainty. Closer to imperial centers, the Serbian lands of Raška, Zeta, and Hum were under vassal princes at the time loyal to the empire, while Bulgaria and Macedonia were still annexed and under regular Byzantine administration. These last two regions, Bulgaria and Macedonia, were divided into three themes (i.e., militarized provinces under military governors entitled strategoi). However, although the empire seemed to be in a strong position with direct control over much of the Balkans and indirect control (through vassal princes) over the rest, seeds of destruction existed that threatened the maintenance of this situation.

First, as we saw in the previous volume,[1] the theme administration was in decline. No longer did the military governor have sufficient forces directly under his command to control and defend his province. Provincial magnates had been increasing their estates and building up large private armies. In order to carry out its military needs when it found its thematic army (i.e., the state troops directly under the strategos) insufficient, the state had had to turn to these magnates and award them additional lands as fiefs (called pronoias) in order to obtain military service from them. The pronoiar (or pronoia holder) owed for his fief military service accompanied by a given number (depending on the size of the fief) of retainers. By Manuel's time in most provinces the retainers of the pronoiars plus mercenaries made up over half of a province's armed forces. Thus in a time of weakness at the center, the strategos might well have been unable to force obedience from the magnates; as a result more and more local authority was falling into the hands of local magnates, setting the stage for separatism. We shall soon return to this problem when we turn to the imperial Balkans (especially Greece and Thrace) in the period after Manuel's death. Second, the vassal princes, though cowed by Manuel's successful military campaigns against them, culminating in his forcing submission from Stefan Nemanja of Serbia (Raška) in 1172, were not necessarily happy with this situation. Thus the people in the border regions were more or less waiting for Manuel's death to re-assert themselves. This was particularly true of Serbia.

Stefan Nemanja Acquires Power in Serbia

The previous volume traced the course of events in Serbia under Vukan, Uroš I, Uroš II, and Desa through the mid-1160s. It discussed the large number of Serbian revolts (often aided by Hungary) for full independence. Each time, the Byzantines were able sooner or later to suppress these uprisings, but Serbia never remained pacified for long. Even when Byzantium changed rulers in Serbia—as it did upon occasion—it could not prevent new rebellions from breaking out. Finally in about 1166 a major change occurred in Serbia. The old dynasty was replaced by a new one headed at first by a certain Tihomir who was quickly replaced by his brother Stefan Nemanja. This new dynasty was to reign in Serbia until 1371.

Where the founders of this new dynasty came from and what—if any— connection they had to the preceding dynasty is a matter of great controversy. Unfortunately, very little is really known about the subject. In the years prior to 1165/66 Serbia had been ruled by a family related to the dynasty of Duklja or Zeta (what is now Montenegro). This Serbian or Raškan branch of the family traced its descent to a certain Vukan, a nephew of Constantine Bodin of Duklja, who had been appointed governor of Raška by Bodin in 1083/84. After Vukan's death, succession went to his son Uroš I who was then succeeded by his son Uroš II. With a brief interruption when the Byzantines ousted him in favor of his brother Desa in 1155, Uroš II ruled Serbia until 1161/62, when the Byzantines intervened again and restored Desa. Desa, under pressure, supported Byzantium in its campaign of 1163 or 1164 against Hungary.

In the late 1160s Uroš and Desa disappear from the scene and four brothers (Tihomir, Stracimir, Miroslav, and Stefan Nemanja) came to rule Serbia. Who were they and where did they come from? Most scholars have concluded that the four were somehow related to the preceding dynasty. Later Serbian and Dalmatian sources from the sixteenth and seventeenth centuries state Nemanja was the son of Desa. A relationship to the previous dynasty is also suggested by the fact that both Nemanja's charter issued to Hilandar in 1198 and the biographies of him written by his sons state that he came to power in his grandfather's patrimony, implying he had a right to inherit it. They also state that Nemanja's great-grandfather and grandfather had ruled the land but make no such claims about his father. The natural inference from this is that Desa could not have been his father. Also militating against Desa as his father is an inscription written in a Gospel by Nemanja's brother Miroslav that states Miroslav was the son of Zavid. Nothing else is known about Zavid, but he might well have been an otherwise unknown son of Uroš I. Also suggesting descent from Uroš I is the fact that several of Nemanja's descendants who were to rule Serbia bore the name Stefan Uroš.[2]

The life of Nemanja by his son Stefan states that Stefan Nemanja, the youngest son of a man whose name is not given, was born in Zeta near Podgorica (modern Titograd) after his father, having involved himself in a power struggle with his brothers, had fled Raška for Zeta. There Nemanja received a Catholic baptism, for that region was under Catholic jurisdiction. This statement reflects the strength of Catholicism in western Zeta and shows that that faith was not limited to Zeta's coastal cities. When the family returned to Raška, Nemanja was re-baptized in an Orthodox ceremony. The father presumably had either tried to oust Uroš II or Desa or else had tried to acquire an appanage of his own and, failing in his attempt, had then fled. Subsequently when this father, presumably named Zavid, eventually died at an unknown date, each son received a hereditary appanage. Thus his lands were divided among his sons with precedence going to the eldest, Tihomir. Nemanja's appanage lay in the region of the Ibar River and included Toplica. Though no dates are given in any source as to when Nemanja received this appanage, it was probably about 1166, the approximate date when the four brothers replaced Desa as joint rulers of Serbia, with seniority belonging to Tihomir.

In fact, it seems likely that this family was installed by Manuel, and one would expect him to turn to the existing ruling family, for its members would be more likely to gain acceptance from the Serbs than would leaders from an entirely new family. Manuel's role and the approximate date of 1166 for the change of ruler find support in a Byzantine oration published by Robert Browning and referring to events of about 1166. The oration states that Manuel easily reduced the Serbs to submission; they repented and accepted the change of ruler that Manuel imposed on them. Thus quite possibly Desa did something to displease Manuel, leading once again to Byzantine intervention and a change on the Serbian throne. Or possibly since a major war with Hungary had flared up in 1166, Desa's ties with Hungary simply made his continued presence as leader of Serbia seem too dangerous. Since 1166 is about the date other sources give for Tihomir's coming to power, it makes sense to conclude that Tihomir was the ruler appointed in that year over the Serbs by Manuel. From the start of Tihomir's reign Serbian territory was divided among the four brothers: Tihomir, Stracimir, Miroslav, and Stefan Nemanja. Tihomir, the eldest, bore the title Grand župan.

Now, with Tihomir on the throne, we can turn to the Serbian sources, which unfortunately provide no dates for events. The near contemporary ones are two lives of Stefan Nemanja (each in the form of a saint's life) written by two of his sons early in the thirteenth century, after Nemanja's death. One was written by Stefan Prvovenčani (the First-Crowned), his successor on the throne of Serbia (1196–1227), and the other was written by his youngest son Sava, who became a monk and later, in 1219, the first Archbishop of Serbia.

These biographies state that Nemanja received his inherited lands from his father. As noted, these consisted of the Ibar region with Toplica. Whether he received this territory before or after Tihomir acquired the throne is not known. We are told that Nemanja also received Dubočica as an appanage from Manuel. Most scholars believe that the Dubočica appanage was the same as the appanage of Dendra near Niš, which Manuel had assigned to Desa previously when he deposed him and restored Uroš II to the throne in 1155 or 1156. As a result Nemanja was not only the vassal of his elder brother Tihomir but was also a direct vassal of Manuel for Dubočica. This direct tie to Byzantium probably alarmed Tihomir, who must have seen it as a threat to his own rule. Stefan Prvovenčani's biography also states that Nemanja built a church to the Virgin at Toplica and a second church dedicated to Saint Nicholas on the near-by River Banja without seeking Tihomir's approval, as Tihomir believed Nemanja should have. Nemanja, on the other hand, considered himself free to erect churches on his own initiative. Thus it seems Nemanja was, or Tihomir at least thought he was, trying to assert his own independence, possibly through an alliance with the Byzantines.

Tihomir summoned Nemanja, and when he came had him thrown in jail in chains. He then seized Nemanja's lands. Nemanja's supporters made Tihomir's actions appear to be a response to Nemanja's church building, and thus the Church was mobilized against Tihomir, be it at the time or subsequently, by using this issue to justify the revolt that won Nemanja the throne. Nemanja prayed to Saint George, who effected his escape. He fled to his own province. Since a clash was inevitable, Nemanja began mobilizing an army. Warfare followed, and through the help of God and of Saint George Nemanja triumphed and expelled his brothers. The other two brothers presumably suffered expulsion for continued support of Tihomir. Very likely the real miracle behind Nemanja's victory was Byzantine help. Manuel may well have been displeased with Tihomir for acting on his own against Nemanja, who was also Manuel's vassal. By depicting Nemanja's victory as a miracle, Stefan Prvovenčani was able to imply God's favor for Nemanja. Moreover, having Nemanja do it alone (or with God's help) was more in keeping with Serbian pride than an admission that he needed Byzantine help. Nemanja's expulsion of Tihomir and assumption of the throne probably occurred in 1167 or 1168. Niketas Choniates refers to Nemanja as being Grand župan in 1168 but does not give the date he assumed the title.

Nemanja, having acquired all Raška after the expulsion of his brothers, had quickly become a powerful figure. Presumably his success had made him stronger than Manuel liked. In any case, Manuel soon gave his support to

Tihomir and the two other brothers, who had all fled to Byzantium. After all, the Byzantines had initially installed Tihomir and presumably did not like his expulsion; surely they wanted to see Serbia divided among several princes to keep it weak. When Nemanja was the weaker figure, they had been willing to support him, but they had not sought his total triumph. So, claiming that Nemanja had acted against the legal rulers of Serbia, the Byzantines provided Tihomir with an army. Choniates describes the background of this new campaign as follows:

> Then the emperor [Manuel] turned west to Philippopolis, for he had learned that the Serbian satrap, who was Stefan Nemanja, had become bolder than he should have, and being a man who evilly used his free time and who was filled with unsated desires, he strove to expand his authority over all the neighboring provinces, cruelly attacking his own family, and not knowing any limit he tried to take Croatia [?] and Kotor.

This Byzantine force, as well as the Serbian troops collected by the brothers, invaded Raška from Skopje. This attack posed a serious danger to Nemanja; not only was he worried about the size of the armies against him, but he also found himself for the first time fighting against the troops of his suzerain Manuel. Possibly, however, the presence of Byzantine troops tarnished Tihomir's cause in the eyes of the independent-minded Serbs. In any case, Nemanja was able to raise a large army. The two armies met at the village of Pantino near Zvečan on the Sitnica River. Nemanja won a major victory, again with Saint George's help, and Tihomir was killed, drowning in the Sitnica. The two remaining brothers, Stracimir and Miroslav, made peace with Nemanja and recognized him as Grand župan of Serbia and as their suzerain. Nemanja allowed them appanages, presumably restoring to them their former holdings. Miroslav obtained Hum, and Stracimir a territory in northern Raška on the West Morava River centered near modern Čačak. The two brothers were allowed broad autonomy in ruling their lands; they remained loyal to Nemanja thereafter. Then, if not later, Tihomir's son Prvoslav submitted to Nemanja and seems to have been allowed a small appanage, Budimlje (near modern Ivangrad) on the Lim, in which he built the well-known church of Djurdjevi Stupovi, the seat of the subsequent Bishop of Budimlje. The important battle of Pantino occurred between 1168 and 1171; most scholars now accept a date nearer to 1168.

At this time Hungary, still under the anti-Byzantine Stephen III, and Venice, angry at Manuel's massive arrest of the Venetians residing in the empire in 1171, were trying to create an anti-Byzantine coalition. A Venetian embassy visited Nemanja, who was probably expecting further Byzantine action against himself for his resistance against the Byzantine army that had supported Tihomir. Thus he willingly joined the coalition. His troops moved against Kotor while those of Miroslav attacked Omiš. The Serbs were also active against various Byzantine forts along the Niš-Beograd (Belgrade) route. When a domestic naval revolt ended the Venetians' participation and the death of Stephen III in Hungary made it possible for Manuel's candidate, Bela III, to mount the Hungarian throne, Stefan Nemanja was left high and dry. Manuel, now free to turn against him, marched into Raška. Nemanja, seeing that resistance against a major Byzantine force was hopeless, went forth to surrender and submit to the emperor. The emperor made him go through a humiliating ceremony at the imperial camp and then took him back to Constantinople for another humiliating ceremony there that featured long orations celebrating his submission. Some wall-paintings depicting Nemanja at this ceremony bareheaded, barefooted, and with a rope around his neck were painted. Then, as a sworn loyal vassal, Nemanja was allowed to return to Serbia as its Grand župan. Nemanja remained loyal to the oath he took to the emperor for the next eight years, the duration of Manuel's life. During this period Nemanja, though a Byzantine vassal, firmly established himself as ruler of Raška.

Byzantine Difficulties in the Balkans under Andronicus I

Manuel died in 1180, and a brief and unsuccessful regency for his minor son, Alexius II, followed. What had held Bela III of Hungary and Nemanja loyal had been personal ties to Manuel. Now those ties were broken, and in 1181 Bela recovered Srem, Dalmatia, and most probably Croatia as well. It seems this was a bloodless recovery; perhaps the Byzantines even acquiesced in it. It was a time of anarchy and intrigue at home, and Byzantium was in no position to send troops to Dalmatia. Presumably it seemed better to lose Dalmatia to friendly Hungary than to Venice, with which Byzantium was at war. Venice had in fact already seized Zadar (Zara), and the Hungarians had to take it by force in February 1181. Meanwhile, the regency for the young Alexius was unpopular, and an elderly cousin named Andronicus Comnenus, who had long been a dissident against Manuel and had been exiled all over the map, appeared with an army in Asia Minor. At first he seemed appealing to the population of Constantinople. He was willing to pose as being anti-Western (for the Westerners under Manuel's widow, a Latin princess, held great influence) and anti-rich. And he was to ride to power on the coattails of a riot in which hundreds of Westerners in the city of Constantinople were massacred. He awaited the end of the bloodbath and then entered the city, whose gates were opened to him. He became regent for the little boy in 1183. He quickly had Alexius' mother strangled, then made himself co-emperor, and finally had Alexius strangled. As a result he became the sole emperor. These murders gave Bela the opportunity to step forward to avenge the victims. Bela's wife was the step-sister of Manuel's murdered widow. Bela moved at once and occupied Beograd and Braničevo. Then, picking up the Serbs as allies, he headed down the main invasion route (the modern Orient Express route), driving out imperial garrisons from Niš and Sardika (modern Sofija) and sacking them both. Six years later, passing crusaders spoke of the two towns as being deserted and partly in ruins. The Hungarians were to keep control of this highway and the towns along it for the next three years.

At home Andronicus was fighting corruption, but he also seems to have been intent on eliminating any and all powerful and rich figures who might conceivably have sought his overthrow and on avenging himself on those who had opposed him earlier. Falling victim to a persecution mania, he unleashed a reign of terror in the capital, which led to various plots against him. The Hungarians, who occupied much of the central and eastern Balkans, were in Thrace and threatened to attack the capital. Then in June 1185 the Normans from southern Italy launched an attack on Durazzo (Dyrrachium, Durrës). The commander of Durazzo, Alexius Branas, immediately surrendered the city to them, for he was opposed to Andronicus. The Norman army then moved across the Balkans toward Thessaloniki (Salonica), while the Norman fleet, having occupied Corfu (Kerkira, Corcyra), sailed around into the Aegean and occupied various other islands. In August 1185 this fleet finally reached Thessaloniki. The army arrived there at about the same time, and after a brief siege the Normans took Thessaloniki on 24 August and sacked it, massacring large numbers of its citizens. Part of the Norman army then moved toward Serres and took that city; other Normans went off plundering into Thessaly, while still others headed for Constantinople.

Serbian Expansion and Military Activities, 1180–90

Stefan Nemanja took advantage of this chaos to assert Serbia's independence and expand his territory. Between 1180 and 1190, when a partially recovered Byzantium was able to take action against Serbia, Nemanja made considerable gains. The dates that he acquired particular territories are often not certain. However, taking advantage of the internal disorders under Andronicus, of the Hungarian attack launched in 1183 with which Nemanja was allied, of the 1185 Norman invasion, and of the Third Crusade in 1189, Nemanja, during those ten years, was able to conquer Kosovo and Metohija, including Prizren, and penetrate into northern Macedonia, taking Skopje and the upper Vardar (Axios). He also moved northeast, acquiring most of the towns along the Morava. By 1188 Niš on the Morava was functioning as his capital. His armies then pressed further east and reached the upper Timok River. In the 1180s he also pushed into Zeta and in the course of that decade took it all. The conquest of Zeta was completed by 1189, when Desislava, widow of Michael, the last ruler of independent Zeta, appeared as an exile in Dubrovnik (Ragusa). No territory remained under the former Dukljan dynasty; Zeta was incorporated into Nemanja's state of Raška. Soon he assigned Zeta to his eldest son, Vukan. Having reached the coast, he acquired southern Dalmatia, including the towns of Kotor, Ulcinj (Dulcigno), and Bar (Antibari). From Zeta he also advanced into northern Albania, obtaining the region of Pilot lying between Prizren and Lake Skadar.

Nemanja's activities in southern Dalmatia brought him into conflict with

Dubrovnik. Fighting seems to have broken out in 1184. The issues of dispute seem to have been both territorial and ecclesiastical. As Nemanja acquired Hum (formerly Zahumlje) and Zeta, which as principalities had controlled much of the territory around Dubrovnik, Nemanja and Dubrovnik laid over-lapping claims to certain borderlands. Furthermore, Nemanja had acquired Bar, whose bishop had been made an independent archbishop by the pope in 1089. Since this change had meant a considerable loss of territory for Dubrov-nik's archbishop, Dubrovnik had protested long and hard against it. Finally in 1142 Dubrovnik had triumphed when the pope reduced Bar's archbishop to a bishop and again subordinated Bar to Dubrovnik. Outraged by this reversal of policy, Bar was still protesting when Nemanja acquired Bar in the 1180s. Furthermore Hum had now been annexed by Raška and assigned as the holding of Nemanja's brother Miroslav. Having as its capital the coastal city of Ston, Hum was oriented toward coastal affairs and had economic and territorial ambitions that clashed with Dubrovnik's. One such ambition was to control the island of Korčula.

In 1184 Nemanja's brother Stracimir, presumably with Nemanja's bless-ing, launched an attack against Korčula. The action failed as the islanders, aided by Dubrovnik, repelled the invaders, and Hum was soon forced to give up its claim to Korčula. Dubrovnik's support of the islanders of Korčula rankled with the Serbs. It is not clear whether Nemanja had already gone to war against Dubrovnik, making its support of Korčula part of its war against Nemanja, or whether Dubrovnik's assistance to Korčula was the last straw leading Nemanja to initiate his war against Dubrovnik. But in any case in 1185 Nemanja attacked the city of Dubrovnik itself and laid siege to it. Later chronicles from Dubrovnik (written three hundred or more years later) state that the siege failed. However, a Church document prepared for the pope in the 1250s (probably in 1255) in connection with the Dubrovnik-Bar Church quarrel, explaining the loss of certain documents, states that Nemanja cap-tured Dubrovnik. Although most historians have accepted the statements made by the chronicles, Foretić argues plausibly that the city fell.[3] After all, the 1255 document was prepared only seventy years after the event and is far older than the chronicles. Foretić thinks Nemanja penetrated into the town or at least into part of it. For the 1255 document states he plundered part of the city, including the archives, which as a result lost certain documents. The archival losses were not wanton theft, but included the calculated removal of certain materials that argued against Bar's claims.

The Serbs were unable to hold the town. Did a Ragusan counter-attack force them out, or did Dubrovnik receive outside help? Since Dubrovnik in 1186 is found under Norman suzerainty, it seems likely that the town received Norman assistance. Either the threat of Norman intervention or even an actual Norman campaign may well have forced the Serbs to depart. By autumn 1186, for whatever reason, but most probably one related to Ragusan negotia-tions with the Normans, Nemanja had given up the idea of conquering and retaining Dubrovnik. He made peace with the city. The treaty was signed 27

September 1186 in the city of Dubrovnik "in the lands of lord King William," the Norman ruler of Sicily, and before his representative, thereby showing the existence of Norman suzerainty. The treaty was also signed in the name of all three Serbian brothers by two of them, Nemanja and Miroslav, showing that their rule was a family enterprise and that Nemanja as Grand župan, though senior, was obliged to consult his brothers.

The treaty ended the war. Both sides agreed not to seek damages for destruction occurring during the fighting. It re-established the pre-war borders, enabling Dubrovnik to retain rights to its "patrimony," which had been under dispute (presumably to Rožat and Kurilo mentioned in the document). Dubrovnik received the right to trade duty-free in Nemanja's and Miroslav's lands, particularly along the Neretva and at the customs station at Drijeva. Dubrovnik also received the right to carry out other economic activities (including chopping wood and grazing flocks) without hindrance in Serbian lands in the vicinity of Dubrovnik, according to former custom. The tribute that Dubrovnik had formerly rendered partly in wine and partly in cash to the princes of Hum and Trebinje, presumably in return for these economic privileges, would henceforth be paid entirely in cash. Joint courts were to be established; thus legal disputes between Serbs and Ragusans were to be settled by a court composed of an equal number of Serbs and Ragusans. Hum renounced its claims to the islands of Korčula and Vis. Each party to the treaty received the right to give asylum to the enemies of the other but was obliged to see that such enemies did not use this asylum as a base to attack the other.

Isaac Angelus Assumes Power in Byzantium and Expels the Normans[4]

On 12 September 1185 Andronicus ordered the arrest of a Constantinopolitan nobleman, Isaac Angelus. Isaac resisted arrest, and since his family stood jointly responsible for the correct behavior of all its members, his resistance threatened the whole Angelus clan. The Angeli began stirring up mob action. This was not difficult to do, for there was much popular dissatisfaction with the reign of terror unleashed by Andronicus and there was widespread belief that he was doing nothing to resist the Normans who were rapidly approaching the city. The uprising was made easier by Andronicus' being outside the city at that moment. The revolution succeeded. Isaac Angelus, a cousin of the Comneni, obtained the throne. He was to rule for the next decade, 1185–95. Andronicus was seized and tortured to death.

Isaac's first task was to expel the Normans from the Balkans. He quickly mobilized a large force and sent it out against them under the able commander Alexius Branas. Unaware of Andronicus' overthrow and in considerable disorder—for they were out plundering in small bands—the Normans were quickly defeated. Thessaloniki was recovered and then the Byzantine forces pushed west to regain Durazzo and Corfu. Isaac also made peace with the Hungarians, whose justification for their action had been to avenge Manuel's family. Isaac's elimination of Andronicus had resolved this issue. Isaac agreed to marry Bela's nine-year-old daughter, Margaret. For her dowry the Byzantines recovered at least certain cities along the Morava–Orient Express route. Beograd, Braničevo, and probably Niš were returned. Various other cities along the middle and upper Morava may not have reverted to the Byzantines at once since they were in the possession of the Serbs. In exchange for this territory and Bela's agreement to withdraw all his troops beyond the Danube, the Byzantines recognized Hungarian possession of the Dalmatian cities. The royal wedding took place, probably in November 1185.

Bulgarian Uprising, 1185–88

In the interim, when the Byzantine campaign against the Normans was still underway, Isaac had gone to the fortress of Kypsela (modern Ipsala) near the mouth of the Marica. Over the previous weeks he had been actively recruiting troops to fight the Normans and granting pronoias (fiefs) in large numbers for service. By the early fall he had raised a large enough force for his present needs, and his troops under Branas were rapidly clearing the Normans out of the Balkans. Thus, Isaac was no longer seeking recruits and granting pronoias for that purpose.

At that moment, in the fall of 1185, two brothers named Theodore (soon to take the name of Peter) and Asen, from the region of Trnovo in Bulgaria, arrived at Kypsela to seek audience with the emperor. They hoped to obtain a mountain district in the Balkan (Haemus) Mountains—one, according to Choniates, of little value—as a pronoia for service to the emperor. Not needing more troops, the emperor refused. Asen tried to argue his case and became quite heated in his words. At that point Isaac's uncle, Sebastocrator John, ordered Asen struck across the face. The two brothers withdrew in a huff and, returning to their region of Trnovo, immediately began to raise a rebellion. Before turning to that rebellion, I want to draw attention to two odd features of this story noticed by Mutafčiev.[5] First, it had not been necessary for the brothers to go directly to the emperor for a pronoia of little value; these were usually distributed by relevant bureaucrats. Thus, Mutafčiev wonders, could the brothers in fact have been seeking something considerably more significant, like a provincial governorship? Second, Asen's insolent manner of protesting to the emperor was most unusual behavior. That he dared to behave in this manner and also that he was not immediately pitched into prison or worse suggest to Mutafčiev that the brothers must have been people of considerable stature. Whatever the explanations for these two oddities, it is also strange that, having refused their request and insulted them in the bargain, Isaac and his officials allowed the brothers to return freely to Bulgaria.

Bulgaria at the time was not calm. Choniates mentions that Bulgarians, holding small fortresses in inaccessible places, were already acting uppity toward the Romans. Dujčev thus sees the first stirrings of revolt in Bulgaria as occurring even prior to the Theodore and Asen incident. These stirrings,

Dujčev believes, were probably spontaneous and quite disorganized, carried out by small, scattered groups of peasants and shepherds and lacking unified leadership or even any defined goals. The Bulgarians were dissatisfied with taxes, which increased rapidly in the first months under Isaac, who sought cash to award his followers and to establish the luxurious court he was to maintain. At the time, taxes also included a special wedding tax to finance the elaborate ceremonies for his wedding with the Hungarian princess. Presumably other Bulgarians sought independence as well. Memories of the First Bulgarian State, which existed from the late seventh century until the second decade of the eleventh, were not dead. Subsequent Byzantine administration had weighed heavily upon the Bulgarians. Furthermore, the success of the Serbs in winning their independence surely whetted some appetites for a similar liberation of Bulgaria. Thus Dujčev argues that a revolutionary situation, including a number of small groups up in arms, already existed in Bulgaria when in the fall of 1185 Theodore and Asen returned to Bulgaria. The wedding tax had been announced by then and was being met with widespread opposition.

The two brothers called for a full rebellion. Still, many hesitated. The brothers then made use of a major catalyst. When Thessaloniki had been under siege from the Normans, some Bulgarians had saved, by bringing back to Bulgaria, several miracle-working icons of Saint Demetrius, the patron saint and long-time savior of Thessaloniki. They had set up a chapel to Saint Demetrius to house these icons in Trnovo. The brothers now procured some Vlach shamans, who at a gathering of many Vlachs went into a trance and prophesied the success of the forthcoming Bulgarian rebellion. Saint Demetrius had deserted Thessaloniki, as was clearly shown by the city's fall to the Normans. But the saint had come to Trnovo, and the success of their uprising with the great saint as its patron was assured. According to Choniates, this persuaded the doubtful, and crowds flocked to the standard of the brothers. Thus now and in the weeks that followed they managed to coordinate the various small dissident groups into a coherent force, while at the same time mobilizing new support.

They were also able to mobilize many Cumans. These nomads had a loose state in the Steppes extending into what is now Wallachia in southern Rumania. Cumans had also come to settle in Bulgaria, some of whom had received large pronoias from the Byzantines to defend the Danube frontier or to garrison various interior regions. By the late twelfth century many of these Cumans in Bulgaria had become Christians. Friendly contacts were maintained between the Cumans in Bulgaria and those beyond the Danube. Now large numbers of these Cumans, both from within Bulgaria and from beyond the Danube, flocked to Asen's standard; they were probably as interested in booty as anything else. They provided a key element in the Bulgarian rebel army. That the rebellion was to succeed was probably owing in great part to Cuman participation. The close relations with the Cumans also meant that Bulgarian fugitives could flee across the Danube for asylum and there regroup for subsequent offensives that would often be more effective than the preceding one owing to increased manpower from further recruitment among the Cumans.

Recently there has been much dispute over the ethnicity of the rebels. The Byzantine sources almost exclusively call the rebels Vlachs. And in the early thirteenth century, the Western historians of the Fourth Crusade, which took Constantinople and established the Latin Empire (1204–61), also usually refer to the Bulgarians, who by then had established their independent state, as Vlachs. Bulgarian sources from the early thirteenth century as well as Serb and Ragusan sources refer to the new state and its people as Bulgarian. The term *Vlach* refers to an ethnic group related to the modern Rumanians. The Vlachs seem to have been descended from the pre-Slavic Dacians, who took to the mountains and other security zones during the Slavic invasions of the mid-sixth and seventh centuries. For several centuries thereafter nothing is heard of Dacians or Vlachs. Then in the eleventh century the sources begin to have quite a lot to say about Vlachs. So many Vlachs were to be found in Thessaly that Thessaly was called Valachia or Great Valachia in the late eleventh century. A century later the Jewish traveler Benjamin of Tudela describes the Vlachs of Thessaly as descending nimble as deer from the mountains into the plains of Greece, committing robberies and taking booty. Nobody, Benjamin states, ventured to make war upon them, nor could any king bring them to submission. He adds, accurately or not we cannot say, that they also did not profess the Christian faith. Sources of the late eleventh and twelfth century also begin to mention Vlachs in Bulgaria. Since many of these mountain Vlachs were shepherds, the term *Vlach* came in time also to denote a shepherd. Were they emphasized in the Byzantine and Crusader sources because they had a major role in directing or manning the uprising? Was the Bulgarian state created after the successful revolt primarily Vlach, Bulgarian, or both? Modern Bulgarian historians have tended to downplay or even deny the role of Vlachs in the uprising, finding various ways to explain away the term used in these sources. Rumanian historians, not surprisingly, have tended to insist that the leadership of the uprising was in the hands of Vlachs and to make them the creators of this Bulgarian state.

Though it is impossible to resolve the problem on the basis of the surviving sources, it is worth pointing out that the issue is not as important as many twentieth-century scholars think. The twelfth century was not a period of nationalism. Bulgarians and Vlachs had been living together amicably in Bulgaria, Macedonia, and northern Thessaly for years. They had jointly participated in a revolt in 1076 in Thessaly against the Byzantines. They jointly inhabited Bulgaria, where the Bulgarian Slavs, the largest element in the population, were chiefly peasants farming the lowlands, while the Vlachs with their flocks dominated the mountains. They do not seem to have been in competition for land, and trade by which each obtained the other's produce surely benefited both groups. Both groups also would have suffered similar annoyances from the Byzantine authorities. Thus one would expect them to come together in common cause and would expect people from either group to follow an impressive leader who seemed likely to succeed regardless of which "race" he belonged to. There is no evidence of any "national" conflict or rivalry between these two people at this time. Thus the modern academic controversy, being over an issue of little relevance to the Middle Ages, is probably best dropped.

What is important is that Bulgarians and Vlachs flocked to the standard of Theodore and Asen. The brothers may well have been Vlachs, and they clearly were associated with the Vlach population of the mountainous regions around Trnovo. The prophets who went into trances to call for revolt exhibited behavior in keeping with Vlach shamans and surely were Vlachs, as Choniates states. What followed was a Bulgarian-Vlach-Cuman uprising that produced a state in which all three peoples participated. The state called itself Bulgaria, and both Vlachs and Bulgarians belonged to the revived Bulgarian Church. The name Bulgaria for the state may be derived as much from historic Bulgaria, the territory on which it was established, as from its largest ethnic group. When documents from this state begin to appear in the thirteenth century, their authors write in Slavic and consider themselves Bulgarians. Why the Byzantine and Crusader sources emphasize Vlachs is not clear. The possible Vlach origin of the ruling house may be the explanation. Another possibility is that the term *Vlach* had for these foreign authors a more derogatory connotation, and they stressed the term *Vlach* for that reason. In any case, the rebellion was clearly a joint venture and we should not become bogged down in a senseless nationalist polemic that reflects nineteenth- and twentieth-century rivalries rather than the feelings of the twelfth- and thirteenth-century actors.

Having mobilized this support, the brothers began to attack and take various fortresses in the vicinity of Trnovo. The uprising broke out at a considerable distance from imperial centers, at a time when many troops had presumably been withdrawn to repel the Normans; thus there seem to have been few loyal imperial troops north of the Balkan Mountains. So the revolt grew quickly. The chronology of the revolt is not secure. Many scholars believe that substantial fighting began only early in 1186. Dujčev argues persuasively that significant fighting had broken out by November 1185. In the discussion of the early phases of the uprising that follows, I have basically employed Dujčev's dating of these events.[6] Other scholars have given dates from six months to a year later.

The rebels benefited from the shortage of Byzantine garrison troops in Bulgaria, for until the end of November 1185 the Byzantine armies were actively completing their action against the Normans and at first Byzantine officials did not realize the seriousness of the uprising. Thus the revolt was given time to grow, and by the end of the year raiders were crossing the Balkan Mountains into Thrace, both plundering and recruiting more rebels. With their successes the rebels' ambitions grew, and they soon began to dream of full independence. One of the brothers, Theodore, put on the purple boots, a symbol worn by an emperor—in this case Emperor (Tsar) of Bulgaria—and was proclaimed Tsar. He took the name of Peter, after the canonized Tsar Peter I who had ruled Bulgaria in the middle of the tenth century; Theodore's assumption of this name shows that the subsequently much maligned Peter still had a good reputation in late twelfth-century Bulgaria. I shall hereafter call Theodore, Peter. Peter attacked Preslav, once the capital of the First Bulgarian State, but its walls and garrison held out. So, for their capital the brothers then settled on the naturally well-fortified settlement of Trnovo in the region from which they themselves came and where presumably they had their own power base. They strengthened Trnovo's fortifications and erected a church to Saint Demetrius.

At the very end of 1185 (or during the first days of 1186) Emperor Isaac was finally prepared to take action. He dispatched an army under his own uncle, Sebastocrator John Ducas, the official who had ordered Asen struck in the face at Kypsela. But before this force had had time to achieve anything Isaac became worried that John might revolt; so, he quickly recalled him. Isaac then sent out John Cantacuzenus, his brother-in-law, who being blind (probably blinded by Andronicus) was ineligible for the throne and thus not a threat to Isaac. But by now the rebels had established themselves in the Balkan Mountains, the natural fortifications that separated the rebellious Bulgarian territory from imperial Thrace. Cantacuzenus did not take proper precautions and fell into an ambush, losing a large number of soldiers. Cantacuzenus was recalled and a third army under Alexius Branas was dispatched.

Dujčev believes the sending of the first two armies and the appointment of Branas occurred between the end of November 1185 and February 1186. Unknown to Isaac, Branas already had ambitions for the throne. Having penetrated rebel territory, probably reaching the vicinity of Jambol, Branas decided not to pursue the campaign but to utilize the army in his own interests. He led the troops to his own hometown of Adrianople (modern Edirne), where they proclaimed him emperor. By this time he had added to his force various Bulgarians and Cumans. Branas then marched on Constantinople. While he was laying siege to the city, soldiers loyal to Emperor Isaac emerged from the city and put Branas' troops to flight. In the course of the fighting Branas was killed. Isaac offered broad amnesties to the rebels, but some of their leaders, either still disgruntled and ambitious or distrusting the proffered amnesty, fled to Bulgaria. After Branas' revolt was suppressed, Isaac decided to lead the armies against the Bulgarian rebels himself.

Dujčev argues persuasively that the whole Branas rebellion lasted no more than three months, from Branas' appointment as commander in early February 1186 to its demise. Branas' defeat probably occurred in late April 1186. Thus Isaac's attack on Bulgaria, which followed Branas' defeat, probably began in late May or early June 1186. Still, all these Byzantine troubles meant that the rebels had had at least six months to organize themselves, to mobilize more troops, and to establish themselves in better defensive positions. Isaac seems to have been a fairly effective commander, however. He successfully drove the rebel armies, including Peter and Asen, across the Danube. To have subdued all the remaining fortresses in the mountains of Bulgaria, some of which still had rebel garrisons inside, would have been a major task that the emperor, still not taking the revolt very seriously, did not feel was worth the effort. He returned to his capital without even leaving new garrisons in Bulgaria. Meanwhile, across the Danube the two brothers had been recruiting more Cumans and soon, probably in the fall of 1186, returned to Bulgaria and regained control over it, while Cuman armies poured through Bulgaria to raid Byzantine territory both in Thrace and along the Black Sea.

Isaac was thus forced to take action against the Bulgarians again. Once more he chose to lead his troops himself. His second campaign probably began in September 1187. His forces marched first to Adrianople, which was under siege from a Cuman force. There they almost fell into a trap, for upon their appearance the Cumans fled in apparent disorder, hoping the Byzantines would break ranks in pursuit. However, when the Cumans wheeled around for the counter-attack, Isaac just barely managed to regroup his forces and win the day. The Cumans retreated beyond the Balkan Mountains. As it was already late in the season, Isaac did not think it sensible to pursue them or to make any effort against Bulgaria itself. So, he dispatched part of his army to winter at Sardika, while he returned to Constantinople.

During these Byzantine-Bulgarian conflicts, Stefan Nemanja of Serbia was expanding his state in all directions at Byzantine expense as noted earlier. In 1188 he is found in possession of Niš. Whether he had acquired it from the Hungarians before their peace with Isaac in the fall of 1185 or whether the Byzantines had regained it as part of Margaret's dowry only to lose it subsequently to Nemanja is not known.

In 1188 Asen directed further raids into imperial territory and thereby amassed considerable booty. Isaac crossed the Balkan Mountains into Bulgaria but failed to force an engagement with Bulgarian forces. In general the Bulgarians, Vlachs, and Cumans tried to avoid major battles with the Byzantines, preferring to carry out raids against places with weak defenses or else to ambush smaller units. But though he failed to engage Asen's main forces, Isaac did manage to capture Asen's wife. To get her back Asen had to enter into treaty negotiations. He did so from a position of considerable strength, however, as is seen from the fact that he came out of the negotiations with a very advantageous treaty. The treaty recognized the existence of an independent Bulgarian state that included the territory between the Balkan Mountains and the Danube. Thus the empire recognized that this region was no longer imperial. Asen regained his wife, but he was obliged to send a third brother, Kalojan or Ioanica, to Constantinople as a hostage. In spite of the treaty, raids continued over the next years, although the brothers were not necessarily responsible. They very likely had little control over many of the Cuman and other local leaders who surely found such incursions profitable. Thus much of the raiding during this period should probably be seen as small-scale private enterprise.

Trnovo was retained as the capital of the newly recognized state. The brothers decided that it should have an archbishop. Previously Trnovo had had a bishopric under the major autocephalous Bulgarian Archbishop of Ohrid. However, the liberation of Bulgaria had not included Macedonia and so Ohrid had remained Byzantine. The new Bulgarian leadership, not surprisingly, did not want its Church to be under a Byzantine archbishop, so the brothers unilaterally removed Bulgaria from Ohrid's authority and placed all Bulgaria under the Bishop of Trnovo, whose rank they now raised to archbishop. And in 1187 they appointed one of Asen's close supporters, a certain Basil, to that office. However, all these actions violated Church canons. So, when the brothers ordered the Greek Bishop of Vidin, whom they had brought to Trnovo, to install Basil, he refused and fled, only to be re-captured and executed. Basil, who thus remained unrecognized by the Byzantine Church, took up his duties nevertheless. Shortly after assuming office, he crowned one of the brothers tsar in a splendid church coronation. One account has the archbishop crowning Peter, who, as noted, had already been proclaimed tsar by his followers. According to this version, shortly thereafter Peter turned the rule over to Asen and departed for Preslav, over which he took control. A second account states that it was Asen whom the archbishop crowned. The conflicting stories should not bother us too much, for both accounts agree that shortly thereafter, and certainly by early 1190, Asen had become the senior ruler. But the two brothers continued to rule as colleagues, with Asen in Trnovo and Peter in Preslav.

After nearly two centuries of Byzantine rule many former Bulgarian institutions had become extinct. They had been replaced by the Byzantine administrative and landholding system. Mutafčiev argues, though he does not prove, that the leaders of the rebellion, Peter and Asen, and presumably some of their chief lieutenants as well, acquired their positions of leadership because they were already leaders—magnates and pronoia holders—in their regions prior to the rebellion. Thus Mutafčiev argues that the existing landed aristocracy provided the leadership first for the rebellion and then for the new state. Inheriting the Byzantine system, the rulers of the Second Bulgarian Empire, as the newly liberated state came to be called, retained it and modeled their state institutions and court ceremony on those of Byzantium. Yet despite the model, institutionally the Bulgarians were never to achieve a truly nation-wide, Byzantine-style bureaucracy. The boyars (nobles) in the new state were no longer from ancient Bulgar families dating back to the previous Bulgarian empire. The boyars in the revived state rose to prominence from their role in the liberation struggle or from royal appointment. Thus, many boyar families began as service nobility, with certain figures gaining their eminence because they were relatives of Peter and Asen. In time, however, some boyars, either through building upon lands held under the Byzantines or else through acquiring landed power from royal grant, accumulated vast estates and with them considerable local authority, enabling them to become in times of central government instability autonomous rulers in their provinces. In this period, and continuing throughout the thirteenth century, many important boyars were of Cuman origin. It has even been argued that *Asen* is a Cuman name, and one theory, though unproven, has Asen descended from a Cuman prince on his mother's side.

The overwhelming majority of the Bulgarian population remained peasant. Our limited sources suggest that most of these peasants were serfs on royal, boyar, or monastic estates. The liberation from Byzantium did not bring social liberation. Conditions on the land did not change; the peasants simply continued to work the estates of their masters, whether new ones or, in the case of those on estates of landlords who had supported the rebellion, the same.

Bosnia and Hum to ca. 1198

Meanwhile, late in the twelfth century, sources begin to speak more of Bosnia and Hum (formerly Zahumlje). Bosnia had long been a very obscure area. It had nominally gone over to Hungary in 1102 when Koloman annexed Croatia. In 1167 a Bosnian ban named Borić had, as a Hungarian vassal, provided troops for the Hungarian armies defeated by the Byzantines at the major battle of Zemun. After that defeat Bosnia was recognized as Byzantine. Byzantium's role in Bosnia was probably only nominal during the brief period of imperial rule, 1167 to ca. 1180. After all, Bosnia was distant and, owing to its mountainous terrain, possessed of a poor communications system. Probably the various nobles in Bosnia simply continued to manage their own local affairs. After 1180/81, when Hungary reoccupied Dalmatia and southern Croatia, it also laid claim to Bosnia. And in 1185 Emperor Isaac Angelus recognized Hungary's claim to Bosnia. Bosnia was mentioned in the title of the King of Hungary, and some of the nobles in the northern parts of Bosnia probably even recognized his suzerainty. There is no evidence, however, that the Hungarians actually occupied any part of Bosnia. And the regions of central Bosnia, including the župa (county) of Bosnia—the Visoko-Zenica-Sutjeska-Vrhbosna (Sarajevo) area—seem, despite Hungarian claims to the contrary, to have been in fact independent. In the 1180s Bosnia was ruled by a Ban named Kulin.

Under Kulin in the 1180s and 1190s there is no sign of direct Hungarian influence within Bosnia, be it the presence there of any Hungarian officials or of any Bosnian troops from Kulin's banate (or banovina) aiding the Hungarians in their campaigns. Hungary probably had more influence over the rulers, also often called bans, in the north of greater Bosnia.

Bosnia's location put it between East and West, and it is often referred to as a meeting ground between the two worlds. But, owing to its mountainous terrain and poor communications, it was more a no-man's-land than a meeting ground between the two worlds, until the fifteenth century when increased trade opened it up to greater Western cultural influences. The mountainous terrain encouraged localism. Bosnia was divided into various large regions, e.g., the Po-Drina (the region of the Drina River), Bosnia (the central region), Soli (Tuzla), Usora, the Donji Kraji, and eventually, after its annexation in 1326, Hum (more or less corresponding to modern Hercegovina). Each region had its own local traditions and its own hereditary nobility. A region was divided into župas, each ruled by the most important local family, whose head often bore the title of župan. The Bosnian tendency to form local units that resisted control from the center, which we shall see throughout Bosnia's subsequent history, was already in existence in Kulin's time. It is highly doubtful that Kulin had much control over regions away from the center of his state or even much knowledge of what was happening in these distant parts. This tradition of local rule, which lasted throughout the Middle Ages, made the ban's task of centralizing Bosnia difficult. And periods of expansion were regularly followed by separatism. Regionalism was expressed in cultural phenomena (e.g., gravestone motifs, folk-songs, folk-costumes) and later was to be intensified by uneven economic development and differing foreign influences. Different religious faiths prevailed in different areas; the Orthodox predominated in the east near Serbia and the Drina and in most of Hum, while Catholics predominated in the west, the north, and also in central Bosnia, until an independent Bosnian Church emerged in the central region in the middle of the thirteenth century. From that time Catholicism was eclipsed in the center until it began a revival there in the middle of the fourteenth century.

As this volume opens, in the late twelfth century, when Hum was still separate from Bosnia, Bosnia was nominally Catholic and under the jurisdiction of the Archbishop of Dubrovnik. The Bosnians then had a single bishop entitled the Bishop of Bosnia, whose diocese stretched beyond Kulin's banate all the way to the Sava River. This bishop was a local cleric, who was chosen locally and then sent to Dubrovnik to be consecrated. Thus Dubrovnik interfered very little in Bosnian affairs and was content to simply consecrate as bishop the man chosen by the Bosnians themselves. Bosnian Catholics—even though they were under the pope who elsewhere insisted on Latin as the language of Church services—used the Slavic liturgy. A later chronicle (here based on earlier documents subsequently lost) reports that in 1189 the Archbishop of Dubrovnik consecrated Radigost (note the vernacular name) as Bishop of Bosnia. Radigost "knew no Latin, nor other language, except the Slavic; so, when he swore his oath of faith and obedience to his Metropolitan, he swore it in the Slavic language."[7] Kulin had good relations with Dubrovnik and issued a charter in 1189 granting Ragusan merchants the right to trade throughout his banate duty-free.

To Bosnia's south and southwest, and less isolated than Bosnia, was Hum. Like Bosnia Hum was mountainous. However, it was a rockier, more arid region and its valleys were less fertile. Thus transhumant pastoralism (with sheep the predominant animal) played a major role in Hum's economy. In addition to its Slavic, Serbo-Croatian, speaking population, Hum had a large number of Vlachs. The Vlachs, as noted, were descended from the pre-Slavic population of the northeastern Balkans that had migrated into mountainous regions and adopted a pastoral way of life at the time of the Slavic migrations. Related to the Rumanians and originally speaking a language related to Rumanian, the Vlachs of what was Hum are today Slavic speaking. When they ceased to be Vlach speaking is unknown. The main evidence we have on this subject for the later Middle Ages is drawn from Vlach gravestone inscriptions and names. These inscriptions are all in medieval Serbo-Croatian, suggesting the Vlachs were already Slavic speakers. This evidence is not conclusive, however, for Vlach was not then a written language; thus even if these individuals spoke Vlach, they (or the stone-carvers who wrote the inscriptions) would still probably have written in Slavic. However, since many, or even most, of them also had Slavic names, it seems likely that their linguistic assimilation was well under way, if not completed. By the end of the medieval period, as noted, the term Vlach was coming to have a second, non-ethnic meaning—that of shepherd. So some non-ethnic Vlachs probably acquired this label. Nevertheless, the profession or occupation of shepherd seems to have been dominated in Hum by ethnic Vlachs, and we find that, despite their linguistic assimilation, they have retained to the present a variety of special customs (in dress, death rituals, etc.) derived from their pre-Slavic, pre-Christian heritage. Since they had horses, the Vlachs of Hum came to dominate the carrying trade and caravans across the Balkans. Hired by the coastal merchants, they led and protected the caravans from brigands who were common in the area, many of whom were also Vlachs. Through this role some Vlachs became extremely rich, built up large estates, and came to dominate whole regions of Hum.

Partly as a result of its mountains Hum, like Bosnia, developed as a series of lesser regions, each under a local noble family, whether Slavic or Vlach. Thus regionalism was strong and little feeling existed for the broad region or for being a Hum-ite. These nobles feuded with one another. Increasing its own lands and independence by supporting and relying upon first one neighboring power and then upon another, a particular family might build up a large principality within Hum. But such creations were usually short-lived, until the end of the fourteenth century when one family, the Kosače, began expanding and subduing its neighbors permanently. By early in the following century this family had absorbed most of Hum and created what for all practical purposes was an independent state.

From about 1166 (i.e., when Tihomir assumed power in Serbia) to 1326, Hum was ruled by princes from the Serbian dynasty. From this starting point until ca. 1190, excluding a brief expulsion by Nemanja when he overthrew Tihomir, Hum was ruled by Nemanja's brother Miroslav. Between 1190 and 1192 part or even most of Hum may have been removed from Miroslav's jurisdiction and assigned to Nemanja's youngest son Rastko, the future Saint Sava. However, after Rastko ran away to Mount Athos to become a monk in

1192 Miroslav may well have regained all Hum, though our sources do not allow us certainty about this. Miroslav was married to Ban Kulin's sister. He was to die in about 1198. Hum then extended from the Lim River to the Adriatic coast. Most of Hum's interior was settled by Serbs and belonged to the Eastern Church (under the Archbishop of Ohrid until 1219 when Hum was subordinated to the new independent Serbian Church). The coastal region of Hum, including its capital Ston, had a mixed population of Catholics and Orthodox. Miroslav was Orthodox himself and built a major church dedicated to Saints Peter and Paul on the Lim River, for whose support he gave over twenty villages.

The existence of two Churches and the favor of Miroslav toward the Orthodox caused a certain amount of tension in the coastal area of Hum. This tension came to a head in about 1180 when Rainer, the Archbishop of Split, was murdered and robbed "on the Neretva." This phrasing is vague, and while it could refer to any place along the course of this major river, it almost certainly refers to the region of the river's mouth controlled by the Kačić family, whose members were prominent pirates. Only nominally Catholic, these pirates probably had little respect for the archbishop and saw him simply as a rich target for predation. Since Rainer was a zealous champion of the rights of Split, it is also possible that he brought his fate upon himself by visiting the area to force submission and Church tithes upon its independent-minded people. Since Miroslav was the region's overlord, the pope complained to him and demanded that he punish the murderers and restore to the Church the sum taken. We know nothing about Miroslav's relations with the Kačići and their retainers, but regardless of whether or not he approved of their action, to have forced them to cough up their plunder would have required considerable military action, which Miroslav might well have been reluctant to take. So, Miroslav refused the pope's demand. When the dispute escalated, Miroslav expelled the Catholic Bishop of Ston from his capital. The pope then excommunicated Miroslav. This act does not seem to have troubled Miroslav particularly. He simply allowed Orthodox priests to take over various Catholic Church buildings in the vicinity of Ston.

Miroslav, as noted, as an ally of his brother Stefan Nemanja, was also at war with Dubrovnik in about 1185. However, peace was concluded in 1186 and each party allowed the merchants of the other to trade in its own territory. As far as is known cordial relations existed between Miroslav and Dubrovnik from 1186 until his death.

In both Bosnia and Hum the traditional patterns of Slavic family structure remained strong and retained more archaic forms than elsewhere in the Balkans. Families regularly retained their lands under collective leadership, with an elder dominant but managing the lands in the name of his whole family. Frequently, charters were signed, "N. and brothers." In these regions the rulers were not able to enforce conditional landholding and link possession of land to service obligations as rulers were in the Greek lands, Bulgaria, and Serbia. In Bosnia and Hum lands were held unconditionally with the noble in full possession. The ruler did not have the right to confiscate the land in the event of a noble's failure to render services demanded of him. Only out-and-out betrayal provided justification for an estate's confiscation, and even then a council of nobles had to approve such action. This meant families could feel secure about their landed possessions; for dispossessing them was so difficult, it rarely happened. This secure landed base in its turn provided the foundation of the nobles' great strength and independence. Thus the Bosnian ruler, unable to create ties between land and service, was relatively weak militarily, whether against an outside enemy (unless the great nobles shared the ruler's enmity against that enemy) or against the great nobles within his state. Only Stjepan Kotromanić and Tvrtko I in the fourteenth century overcame this disadvantage. And neither of them was able to institutionalize his temporary assertion of authority. By the end of the fourteenth century this weakness was to necessitate, as we shall see, the frequent convocation of councils on military matters in order to procure in advance both the nobles' assent to an action and agreement to participate in it.

Croatia

The previous volume discussed the annexation of Croatia by Hungary. In 1102 King Koloman of Hungary had marched against Croatia and, if we can believe later sources, was met by a delegation of Croatian nobles interested in retaining their own local power. The two sides negotiated a settlement, by which a dual monarchy was created. The King of Hungary also became King of Croatia, for which he needed a second coronation in Croatia. The Croatian nobles kept their local power, retaining their lands plus local administrative and judicial authority, and were freed of taxes. They lost independence in foreign affairs and owed the King of Hungary military service. But if they had to cross the Drava (into Hungary), they were paid for it. Moreover, the king assumed the obligation to defend Croatia. Thus the Kingdom of Croatia continued to exist. And despite the new Hungarian dynasty, it was to be little altered, for matters continued more or less as they had prior to 1102, with the same noble families on top and the peasantry, with unchanged obligations, still subjected to them.

What could be called "Croatia" had previously been divided into three parts: Dalmatian Croatia (excluding the Roman-Byzantine cities in Dalmatia), Pannonian Croatia (the interior region between Hungary, Bosnia, and Dalmatia), and Bosnia (which sometimes was under the Croatian state and had a mixed population of Serbs and Croats). By 1107 the Hungarians had annexed most of Dalmatia (including the Byzantine cities) and come to conceive of Dalmatia as part of what it called Croatia. Owing to Dalmatia's importance, however, Hungary was regularly involved in a struggle, often unsuccessful, with Venice and Byzantium for this region. Thus for much of the period after 1107 much of Dalmatia was not Hungarian. Furthermore, as noted, Bosnia also was a special case. Acquired by Hungary in the 1130s, it was surrendered to Byzantium in 1167. After Manuel's death in 1180, though in theory it reverted to Hungary, in fact it was administered by its own rulers and became more or less independent. Hungary, however, was able to retain Pannonian (interior) Croatia throughout the rest of the Middle Ages (except for the brief surrender of Croatia south of the Krka River to Byzantium from 1167 to 1180, which region, as we saw, was regained for Hungary by Bela III immediately after Manuel's death). The Hungarians divided what we call Croatia into two parts: Croatia (including whatever parts of Dalmatia Hungary held) and Slavonia. Croatia was the territory bounded to the west by the Dalmatian coast (from the headland of the Gulf of Kvarner in the north to the mouth of the Neretva in the south), bounded to the east by the courses of the Vrbas and Neretva rivers, to the south by the lower Neretva, and to the north by the Gvozd Mountain and Kupa River. The territory between Dalmatia and the Neretva, western Hum, was not always in Croatia's possession. Slavonia was the region east and north of the Gvozd Mountain, extending north to the Drava River, east to Srem, and south to the Sava (and sometimes extending beyond the Sava to include the lower Una, Vrbas, and Bosna rivers).

Croatia and Slavonia were ruled by a deputy for the king, a governor called a ban. Then in 1196 after the succession of Imre (Emeric), his younger brother Andrew demanded Croatia and Dalmatia as an appanage. When Imre refused, Andrew in 1197 revolted successfully and by early 1198 obtained his demands from his brother. He became Duke of Croatia and Dalmatia. Andrew and his successors ran their duchy as independent rulers, though usually as close associates, vassal-allies, of the king. They provided the monarch with military forces and were supposed to (and usually did) refrain from conducting independent foreign policy. The dukes installed bishops, settled disputes among the great nobles, warred with the states on their borders, and issued charters of privilege and land grants.

Thus from the late 1190s Croatia and Slavonia were under the Duke of Croatia. This office was usually filled by a son or brother of the Hungarian king. The dukes coined their own money and, as the king's deputies, ran their duchy (which was also still known as the Kingdom of Croatia) like kings, presiding over a court and entourage modelled on the Hungarian royal court. The duke had residences in Zagreb, Knin, Zadar (when Hungary held it), and later also in Bihać. Under the duke there also stood a ban or governor. The ban was generally a major nobleman, sometimes of Croatian origin, sometimes Hungarian. From 1225, though possibly regularly only from the 1260s, the duke divided the territory between two bans: the Ban of Croatia and Dalmatia and the Ban of Slavonia. We shall also meet other bans in this general region, including those of Bosnia and of Mačva (the territory south of the Sava between the Drina and Kolubara rivers).

Slavonia was to be much more a part of Hungary than was Croatia. A considerable number of Hungarian nobles settled in Slavonia, and Western-style fiefs were granted here to the nobility (both Hungarian and Croatian). Thus Slavonia's nobility was ethnically mixed. Moreover, the exemption from taxes granted to the nobility of Croatia was not in effect in Slavonia, whose nobles paid a land tax unless they received a special charter of exemption. Furthermore, the courts of Slavonia were run according to Hungarian law. Finally, the Church in Slavonia (divided into three dioceses), like Bosnia after 1252, was subjected to the Hungarian Archbishop of Kalocsa. In contrast, the Croatian bishops remained under Split, while Croatia's nobles were exempt from the land tax and managed their law courts under the customary law of Croatia. Furthermore, there was no Hungarian settlement in Croatia. The king himself seems to have acquired certain estates of the previous Croatian kings within Croatia, but it is evident that his lands there were not extensive. As a result he had little land to grant there to acquire the loyalty of local nobles. He could merely grant titles or confirm these nobles in the lands they already held. Such grants were not very enticing; thus lacking lands in Croatia to grant, the king lacked the leverage to assert himself in Croatia. So, his authority, and that of the Duke of Croatia, was chiefly felt in Slavonia. Moreover, the Dalmatians and Croatians identified far less with the king's administration than the Slavonians; N. Klaić has noted in this connection that the former frequently referred to the Hungarian king as the King of Hungary rather than the King of Croatia.

The territory of both regions (Croatia and Slavonia) was divided into counties (županijas), each under a župan (count). Once again there was a difference: in Croatia the župans were local nobles in hereditary succession ruling as they had before 1102; in Slavonia the župans were royal appointees. Occasionally, instead of appointing a župan as temporary administrator of a Slavonian county, the king made the individual an out-and-out hereditary grant of a county. In this case, instead of being a župan the holder became a hereditary prince (knez) or grof.

The merger with Hungary brought about various changes, to a greater extent in Slavonia than Croatia. Commerce with Hungary increased, which increased the overall volume of trade, expanded the monetary economy, and furthered the development of towns. As a result, particularly in Slavonia, the merchant class grew rapidly, aided in its growth by the arrival of a certain number of Germans, Hungarians, and Jews in these towns. The Church of Croatia, particularly that of Slavonia, increased its ties with international Catholicism. The nobles, in preserving their privileges and local authority, were clearly satisifed; for though they participated in civil strife as members of factions, not once in the Middle Ages did a single Croatian nobleman (I do not include Bosnians) revolt against Hungary to separate Croatia from the Hungarian state.

The Third Crusade (1189)

In 1187 a Saracen counter-crusade under Saladin recovered Jerusalem. The fall of this holy city resulted in a new Christian campaign, the Third Crusade, led by the German Emperor Frederick I Barbarossa. In 1189 he led his army through Hungary and reached the Byzantine border at Braničevo on the junction of the Danube and Mlava rivers. Having had various differences with the Byzantine authorities in Braničevo, he moved on to Beograd and then proceeded down the Orient Express route toward Niš. Accounts describe the thick forests then existing in this area, part of which is still known as Šumadija (derived from the word *šuma,* "forest"); along the route the army was troubled by the bandits who infested the forests and skirmished with peasants, described as people of Serbian, Greek, Bulgarian, and Vlach nationality, who resented and resisted crusaders foraging in their fields. Eventually the crusaders captured some of the bandits who had been making hit-and-run attacks upon them. The captives stated that they had been acting under the orders of the governor of Braničevo. This information incited the ire of Frederick against the Byzantine authorities.

Finally, in late July, Frederick reached Niš, recently taken from the Byzantines and then the main residence of Stefan Nemanja. Nemanja had previously sent envoys to Germany, offering Frederick free passage through Raška. Now Nemanja received the emperor with great ceremony. Bulgarian-Vlach envoys from Tsar Peter had also come to Niš. That only Peter's name is mentioned in crusader reports suggests that in 1189 he was still the dominant figure in Bulgaria. The Bulgarians were clearly on good terms with the Serbs; in fact, a Western chronicle states they were allied. The Slavs sought to persuade Frederick to create a joint alliance against the Byzantine empire and expressed their willingness to recognize Frederick as their suzerain. Nemanja offered Frederick twenty thousand troops while the Bulgarians offered forty thousand archers. Frederick was tempted. However, he was seriously interested in his crusade and in the recovery of Jerusalem and did not want to be diverted against Byzantium, with which he was not certain he needed to remain on bad terms. So, he turned down the offer. But to seal good relations with the Serbs, a marriage was arranged between the daughter of a German nobleman, Duke Berthold of Andechs, and a certain "Tohu," called in the Western source Vojvoda of Dalmatia, on the condition that Tohu inherit his father's land before his other brothers; this phrasing suggests that Tohu was not an eldest son. Jireček has convincingly shown that Tohu was in fact Toljen, a son of Nemanja's brother Miroslav. It seems that the marriage never actually took place.

The Byzantines, hearing reports of the meeting between Frederick and the two Slavic states but not knowing the results of their talks, became alarmed. As Frederick moved along the Orient Express route beyond Niš, he and the Byzantines each grew more worried and suspicious of the other. Afraid of an attack from Frederick, the Byzantines made peace with Frederick's main enemy, Saladin. Word of this reached Frederick, who was still angry about the bandits sent against him by the governor of Braničevo. Next, when the first crusading armies reached imperial Thrace, the Byzantines, fearing an alliance of crusaders and Slavs, took hostages, including the Bishop of Munster. Frederick demanded their release. Then the two emperors began quarreling over the use of the title emperor, to which each side claimed its ruler had sole right. So, when Frederick reached Philippopolis (modern Plovdiv), he took the town. Many of its inhabitants fled, but the Armenians, who had long resided there, remained and, according to Greek sources, got along well with Frederick. While Frederick rested in this city, further angry letters were exchanged between the two emperors. Frederick then allowed his men to plunder imperial territory in Thrace, particularly in the vicinity of Philippopolis. He also entered into negotiations with the Sultan of Iconium (Konya). This figure, who controlled a large state in central Anatolia bordering on Byzantium there, was Byzantium's leading enemy in the East. Though Frederick seems only to have been trying to arrange free passage for his armies overland through the sultan's state and to assure the sultan he had no hostile intent toward him, the Byzantines had no way to know this and feared Frederick was arranging an alliance that might result in simultaneous attacks against Byzantium's eastern and western borders.

Frederick, whose letters to Isaac continued to threaten, then moved on to Adrianople, only a five-days' march from Constantinople. He took this city and established his winter quarters there. Again Serbian and Bulgarian envoys visited him, still hoping to form an alliance to attack Byzantium. Isaac, finally realizing the magnitude of the danger, yielded; he now recognized Frederick's title and agreed to arrange Frederick's passage through imperial territory. After the two emperors made peace, Frederick once again turned down the Slavs' offer, explaining to them that his aim was to recover the Holy Land. Receiving supplies and transport across the straits, Frederick and his army began marching across Anatolia. They were never to reach the Holy Land, however, for Frederick fell into a river in his heavy armor and drowned. Harried by attacks from Anatolian Muslims and suffering considerable losses, his crusaders became disillusioned and the movement broke up.

Serbs and Bulgarians, 1190–95

While Frederick was in Adrianople, many Byzantine troops had been withdrawn from Thrace to the capital in case they were needed to defend it. In their absence much of Thrace had been occupied by Bulgarians and Vlachs. But early in 1190, having seen the crusaders out of the Balkans and on their way through Anatolia, Isaac was free to turn against his Slavic neighbors. He led his army against the Bulgarians; he failed to take Trnovo, and the Bulgarians successfully avoided meeting his forces until late summer. Then en route home Isaac's army fell into a Bulgarian ambush in the Balkan Mountains and suffered a major defeat. Probably fewer Greeks were killed than Niketas Choniates (an author hostile to Isaac) claimed, for the following month the Byzantines were able to win a victory over the Serbs. After their victory, however, the Bulgarians found themselves relatively unopposed and sent raiding parties both south into Thrace and east against various Byzantine cities on the shore of the Black Sea. Varna, Anchialos, and Sardika all suffered pillaging.

Stefan Nemanja had also been active that summer raiding into imperial territory, so in September Isaac ordered his Thracian troops to move against the Serbs. The Byzantines won what they described as a major victory on the

Morava River. After the battle the two sides concluded a peace treaty. Since Nemanja emerged from the negotiations with a considerable portion of his conquests intact and recognized, it appears that the Byzantine victory was not as complete as Byzantine sources claim. The Byzantines recognized Serbian independence; thus they had been forced to recognize the independence of both their Slavic neighbors, the Bulgarians in 1188 and the Serbs in 1190. The Byzantines regained the territory they had lost along the Morava (or Orient Express route), including Niš and Ravno (modern Ćuprije), and thus regained control over the overland route to Beograd, which along with Braničevo was recognized by the Serbs as being Byzantine. The Byzantines also regained their northern Macedonian losses, the territory along the upper Struma (Strymon) and upper Vardar, including Skopje. Further they recovered part of Kosovo-Metohija, including Prizren, as well as the territory between the Morava and Timok rivers. However, Nemanja was recognized as the ruler of the territory between the South Morava and West Morava rivers, most of Kosovo-Metohija, Zeta, part of northern Albania (including the region of Pilot), southern Dalmatia, Trebinje, and Hum. Thus Serbia ended up with a consolidated territory bordering Hungary along the low mountain range on the north side of the West Morava River and extending south well into Kosovo and Metohija and west to the coast, including Zeta, Trebinje, Hum, and southern Dalmatia. The Byzantines were clearly on the defensive, although Braničevo, Niš, and Velbužd (modern Kjustendil) were to remain Byzantine for almost a decade, being documented as imperial in 1198. It also seems that the Serbian-Byzantine treaty was sealed by the marriage of Nemanja's second son, Stefan, with Isaac's niece Eudocia, though some scholars believe this event occurred earlier, in 1187. Eudocia was the daughter of Alexius Angelus, who was to depose Isaac and become emperor in 1195.

Following his peace with the Serbs, late in 1190 or early in 1191, Isaac went north to Beograd where he met with King Bela of Hungary. The two had a cordial meeting though Isaac was unable to obtain a commitment from Bela for joint action against Bulgaria. Byzantine-Serbian relations remained friendly after the 1190 treaty. In 1192 Bela attacked Serbia and occupied some territory south of the West Morava River. This Hungarian action against Serbia distressed Isaac, who sent the Serbs some military aid and also appealed to the pope. The pope effected a Hungarian withdrawal from Serbia that seems to have again left the Serbian-Hungarian border north of the West Morava River.

During 1193, after the Byzantines had successfully repelled a Cuman raid against the region of Philippopolis, the empire received word of a split between the two Bulgarian leaders, Peter and Asen. Some court orators report that Peter had been won over to the Byzantine side, and soon Asen would also be won over or else he would suffer destruction. Whether there was any truth to the rumor is not known; later in 1193 Niketas Choniates, in reporting Byzantine successes against some Vlachs who had been raiding in the vicinity of Berrhoia and Philippopolis, states these raids had been ordered by Peter and Asen. If Choniates is accurate in attributing the order to both brothers, then any quarrel that may have arisen between them seems to have been quickly patched up.

Next Isaac's cousin Constantine Angelus was sent at the head of an army to invade Bulgaria. He revolted, hoping to acquire the throne, thus ending the planned offensive. To suppress Constantine's revolt Isaac employed the troops who had remained to defend Thrace. Their removal enabled the Bulgarians to plunder the regions of Philippopolis, Sardika, and Adrianople. To face these regular and increasingly larger raids, Isaac next brought a large number of troops from Anatolia to attack the Bulgarians. The Bulgarians met this army near Arcadiopolis and annihilated it. As a result the Bulgarians were free to pour into central Thrace, part of which they annexed. Until this time the Balkan Mountains had formed the Byzantine-Bulgarian border; but after the victory near Arcadiopolis the Bulgarians and Vlachs began assuming control over and stepping up their settlements in territory to the south of this range. The future conflict zone was to be southern Thrace, the Rhodope region, and Macedonia.

In deep trouble, Isaac patched up his quarrel over Serbia with Bela and sought his aid. Bela agreed to attack the Bulgarians from the north in conjunction with a Byzantine attack from the south. This joint action was scheduled for 1195. In that year Isaac assembled a new army to replace the experienced regulars he had lost at Arcadiopolis and left the capital, accompanied by his brother Alexius. The army reached near-by Kypsela near the mouth of the Marica. While camped there, Isaac went hunting. Alexius, claiming not to feel well, remained in camp. Upon Isaac's departure, Alexius met with a group of conspirators who had been scattered throughout the army; they won over a significant portion of the camped army and then declared Alexius emperor. Hearing what had happened, Isaac fled; however, he was soon captured by his brother's men and blinded. So ended what was to have been Isaac's sixth personal campaign against the Bulgarians. After ten years of warfare, the situation was still deteriorating; Bulgaria, having achieved its independence, was now expanding successfully beyond the Balkan Mountains. Furthermore, this warfare was sapping the strength of the Byzantine empire both in manpower and financially at a dangerous time when the empire was threatened from the West. Byzantium had escaped the dangers of being conquered by the Third Crusade but the empire was to prove no match for the crusaders of the Fourth. Part of its weakness in 1204 must be attributed to losses incurred in the Bulgarian wars.

To solidify his position in the capital, Alexius immediately called off the campaign and returned to Constantinople. His policy at first was to buy support; he distributed large land grants and numerous gifts. To pay for these he had to increase taxes. Yet to obtain support he also had to grant various tax exemptions to rich and important figures; so the tax burden fell increasingly on the overtaxed poor. Though Isaac had been no great statesman, he had at least been brave and a relatively able military commander. Alexius lacked those saving graces. The splendor at the imperial court and the sale of offices increased; and such abuses had clearly already been serious under Isaac who, we are told, had sold offices like vegetables at the market. Under Alexius positions were auctioned off and a larger number of posts and honors were assigned to relatives and in-laws.

After the overthrow of his daughter's husband (which probably resulted in Margaret entering a convent) Bela's relations with the empire cooled considerably. Shortly thereafter the Hungarians occupied Beograd. The Byzantines were able to retain Braničevo a little longer; it was still theirs as late as 1198. But soon thereafter, in any case by 1203, Hungary had regained Braničevo.

Alexius sought to solve the empire's difficulties with Bulgaria by negotiation. However, Asen's terms were so demanding that Alexius was unable to reach agreement with him. So, the Bulgarian raiding continued. In the fall of 1195 the Bulgarians overran the region south of the Rhodopes and reached the environs of Thessaloniki. They defeated the garrisons of various fortresses, including that of Serres, which they captured. A Byzantine relief force dispatched under Isaac Comnenus, Alexius' son-in-law, ran into a Cuman raiding force on the Struma River. The Cumans defeated the Byzantine army and captured Isaac, who was sent to Trnovo where, bound in chains and pitched into prison, he soon died.

Ivanko and Dobromir Chrysos

That fall Asen discovered that one of his boyars, a Vlach named Ivanko, was having an affair with Asen's wife's sister. Considering this an insult to the royal family, Asen wanted to have the woman executed. Not surprisingly, the Bulgarian queen objected and argued that instead of her sister, Ivanko should be killed. Asen was persuaded, and late one evening he summoned Ivanko to his tent. Sensing danger, Ivanko secreted a knife under his robes. The two men quarreled; tempers soon flared, and Ivanko stabbed Asen to death. Ivanko then succeeded in winning enough support to take over in Trnovo.

Upon receiving news of his brother's murder, Peter raised an army from his Preslav lands, marched on Trnovo, and laid siege to it. Unable to disperse the besieging troops, Ivanko managed to slip an envoy through Peter's lines to Constantinople to seek Byzantine aid. The envoy claimed that Ivanko had murdered Asen because he had been called on to do so by Isaac Comnenus, the emperor's son-in-law who had died in Asen's prison shortly before. He added that, as a reward for this act, Isaac had promised his own daughter as a bride for Ivanko. Alexius, faced with a fine opportunity, dispatched an army for Trnovo. But when it reached the Balkan Mountains, the army mutinied and refused to proceed further. Byzantium's chance was lost, and so was Ivanko's, for without military help he had no chance to break Peter's siege of Trnovo. Realizing that he was doomed if he remained, Ivanko secretly slipped out of Trnovo and fled to Constantinople. Well received by the emperor, he was at once offered Isaac's daughter (who was also Alexius' granddaughter) as a bride. Upon seeing the girl, Ivanko claimed she was too young and expressed a preference for her mother, Alexius' daughter. Annoyed, Alexius forced Ivanko to betroth the younger princess. Then he dispatched Ivanko to Philippopolis, which seems to have been an isolated Byzantine outpost in the midst of hostile territory. Having established himself there, Ivanko was very successful for a time in repelling Bulgarian and Vlach raids and in restoring imperial rule over various settlements in the area.

Meanwhile, a Vlach named Dobromir Chrysos (in Slavic Hrs) with a personal retinue of about five hundred Vlachs joined the ranks of imperial opponents. He had originally fought for Byzantium against Peter and Asen, but at some point, probably in about 1194, he had been captured by the Bulgarians and, having agreed to switch sides, been released. Unaware of his changed allegiances, the Byzantines had allowed him and his men to assume control of the important fortress of Strumica. Once in control of the fortress, Chrysos showed his new colors and began to extend his authority over the surrounding countryside, which was inhabited by large numbers of Bulgarians and Vlachs. The emperor marched against him, besieged him unsuccessfully for two months, and then returned to the capital.

Kalojan Assumes Power in Bulgaria, 1197

Upon Ivanko's depature, Peter took over in Trnovo. His rule was short, however, as he died in 1197, allegedly slain by a relative. He was succeeded by the third brother, Kalojan. Kalojan had been sent as a hostage to Constantinople after the 1188 treaty. Having soon thereafter escaped back to Bulgaria, he had then taken up a career of leading raids against imperial territory. He was the ablest warrior of the three brothers. Under his rule the number of raids against the empire increased as did the amount of plunder procured by the raiders. This helped him not only to retain the loyalty of the boyars but also to recruit further manpower. The increasing ineffectiveness of Byzantine defenses also contributed to his successes.

The demoralization of the Byzantine army is seen clearly in the following incident recounted by Choniates: A fair was held in a certain Thracian village on Saint George's Day, every year. The local governor, knowing he would be unable to protect the fair-goers from raiders who would be likely to attack the fair, ordered the fair canceled. However, a near-by monastery that had a right to collect a sales-tax on goods sold at the fair, not wanting to lose its income, suppressed the order. The fair was duly held and the Cumans duly swept down upon it. However, the peasants fortified the fair-grounds by encircling it with carts and beat off the attack. Discouraged, the Cumans departed, finding captives and booty elsewhere in the vicinity. A near-by Byzantine garrison, which had made no effort to protect the fair, realizing that the raiding party was small, emerged from its fortress, overtook the Cumans, and relieved them of their booty and captives. However, instead of returning the loot, which had been acquired from their own neighborhood, the Byzantine soldiers began to quarrel among themselves over the division of spoils. At this point the Cumans regrouped, attacked the Byzantines, defeated them, and regained their booty. If this Byzantine unit was typical in its corruption and lack of discipline, it is hardly surprising that Byzantine armies were so often unsuccessful during this period.

Meanwhile in 1197, Alexius decided to launch a new campaign against Dobromir Chrysos, who had by this time also occupied the fortress of Prosek (Prosakon, modern Demir Kapija) on an inaccessible cliff overlooking the Vardar River. Chrysos' forces were well supplied at this fortress since his flocks were housed inside the walls. Alexius' army contained many Turkish mercenaries and, as they moved through Thrace, the Turks continually broke discipline to plunder and take captives, many of whom were Vlachs.

The siege of Prosek was a fiasco. The weather was hot, little drinking water was to be found outside the walls, and Chrysos' men launched surprise raids on the Byzantine camp at night. With morale growing worse among his men and with no chance of success, the emperor almost immediately sought to negotiate a treaty. Alexius must have felt great need for concluding peace at the time, for his terms were most generous. He allowed Chrysos to retain all the fortresses he then held and offered him an imperial in-law as a bride, the daughter of a general named Kamytzes. Chrysos, though married at the time, agreed to dispose of his wife and accepted the terms. When Alexius returned to the capital, he actually sent the girl to Chrysos, who married her despite his dislike of her dainty manners and her refusal to drink heavily at the wedding feast. That the emperor and his armies were unable to expel a brigand chief with only five hundred men from a key fortress and in the end felt the threat from him was of such magnitude that it necessitated concluding a humiliating treaty with him illustrates vividly the decline of the Byzantine Empire.

The Byzantine Triumph over Ivanko

Until 1199 Ivanko, holding a Byzantine command post at Philippopolis, had been very useful to the empire. He had been successful in stopping raids, had recovered a number of small fortresses in the area, and had trained his troops well. By 1199, having organized a disciplined army loyal to him personally, Ivanko decided to use his army for his own ends. His army included many Vlachs and Bulgarians. Whether these individuals were among the Byzantine troops assigned to him or whether they had been recruited recently by Ivanko is not known. Alexius had by then received a number of warnings that Ivanko was not to be trusted. It is possible these warnings had a basis in fact, but it is also possible that they originated from Greeks jealous of Ivanko who were simply trying to turn the emperor against him. Thus it is possible that Ivanko was driven to revolt not because he wanted to but from fear that the emperor might believe this slander and take action against him.

In any event, whether from ambition or from fear, Ivanko revolted. Imperial missions failed to dissuade him because Ivanko supposedly interpreted the emperor's willingness to negotiate as a sign of weakness. Byzantine troops sent against him began picking off certain of Ivanko's lesser fortresses. Ivanko decided to trap these forces. He dispatched a large herd of cattle and a collection of captives across a plain near the Byzantine camp, while placing his men in ambush along the route. The bait worked, as the Byzantines rushed out in disorder to loot the procession. The Byzantine troops were routed, though most succeeded in fleeing to Philippopolis (which shows that the empire, despite the revolt, had succeeded in retaining or regaining this city). However, the Byzantine commander Kamytzes was captured. Ivanko sent him to Kalojan as a gift. In need of allies against Byzantium, Ivanko was probably seeking to restore himself to the good graces of Kalojan, who undoubtedly had no love for the murderer of his brother Asen. Ivanko then proceeded to raid along the Struma River down to the Aegean coast. Next, moving east he took various towns including Xantheia and Mosynopolis. He also took much booty and many prisoners. Choniates reports that, when drunk, Ivanko for amusement liked to have Greek captives torn apart alive before him, while he ransomed off other nationalities, except for the Vlach prisoners, whom he encouraged to join him by offering them land. This is the only sign of ethnic-national feeling in this period that I have come across; other leaders, whether Byzantine or Bulgarian, seem to have favored no particular ethnic group in administering multi-ethnic states.

Ivanko thus seems to have been trying to build up local support from the Vlachs to establish a principality near the coast between the Struma and Marica rivers. In 1200 Alexius en route to oppose him had reached Adrianople when he heard a rumor that Ivanko had begun to wear purple boots, an emperor's insignia. If true, did this mean that this petty chief had actually begun to dream of becoming the Byzantine emperor? Alexius sent an embassy to Ivanko, suggesting a meeting. Oaths of safe conduct were exchanged and Ivanko, stupidly not insisting on an exchange of hostages, came. Upon his arrival, Ivanko was at once seized and executed by order of Alexius. The Byzantines immediately recovered all Ivanko's fortresses, expelling Ivanko's brother who had tried unsuccessfully to retain Ivanko's holdings on the Struma. Thus, briefly, central Thrace and the southern Rhodopes were restored to the empire.

The Byzantine Treaty with Kalojan

Kalojan's Bulgarians, however, continued to raid. In 1201, on Good Friday, Kalojan took Varna; ignoring the season, he put all his captives into the moat and filled it in with earth. He spent Easter Sunday leveling the walls of the city. He then departed. Unlike many of the petty brigand leaders of his time, Kalojan was a master of siege-craft. He employed huge wooden towers on wheels to take Varna. But soon thereafter conditions declined for Kalojan and improved for the empire, for in 1201 the Russians of Galicia and Volynia attacked the Cuman lands in south Russia. This caused many Cumans to leave

Bulgarian service and return beyond the Danube to defend their homeland. Thus for several years the number of Cumans available for service in the Balkans was reduced, which in turn diminished the size, and thereby the effectiveness, of the Bulgarian armies. As a result, in late 1201 or early 1202 on the eve of a Byzantine expedition, Kalojan agreed to a peace with Byzantium that re-established the Balkan Mountains as the Byzantine-Bulgarian border. This allowed the Byzantines to recover whatever territory they had lost to the Bulgarians in Thrace. Kalojan also promised to put a stop to the raiding of Thrace. Dujčev and Nikov accept 1201 as the date for this important treaty, while Zlatarski dates it 1202.

Chrysos and Kamytzes

While this was occurring, Alexius was also able, after considerable difficulty, to more-or-less tame Chrysos. When Kalojan acquired General Kamytzes as a gift from Ivanko, he had demanded a large ransom from Alexius for his return. Alexius not only refused to pay it, but took advantage of Kamytzes' absence to seize his estates. Kamytzes was the father of Chrysos' recent bride, so Chrysos then paid the ransom and acquired Kamytzes. However, he refused to release the general until he was reimbursed for the ransom money he had paid. The two jointly sought the money from Alexius, who once again refused to pay it. Angry, the two decided to avenge themselves on the emperor and recoup Chrysos' investment from the neighboring Byzantine territory, which they began to raid. They seized a major monastery in Prilep and then raided into Thessaly, part of which they took control of, allowing Kamytzes to establish a more-or-less independent principality in northern Thessaly. Chrysos then returned to Prosek.

Alexius dispatched a force against the two trouble-makers but ahead of these troops he sent envoys to split the two rebels' alliance. He offered Chrysos a new bride, Ivanko's fiancée or (if the marriage had ever taken place) his widow. (She was the emperor's granddaughter, thus of better family than Chrysos' present wife, Kamytzes' daughter.) In turn, Chrysos would have to send away Kamytzes' daughter, who, unless she had changed her habits and taken to drink, probably still was not appreciated by her husband. Presumably a dowry was also offered. Chrysos agreed to change wives. Alexius sent to Constantinople for his granddaughter, who was duly dispatched and married to Chrysos. In this way the Chrysos-Kamytzes alliance was broken and Chrysos agreed to restore Pelagonia (the region around modern Bitola) and Prilep to Byzantium. Alexius then sent his armies into Thessaly. They expelled Kamytzes, who fled into the Rhodopes. Imperial troops pursued him thither and drove him out of that region as well. Nothing more is heard of him; if he did not die, presumably he fled to Kalojan.

Before he returned to Constantinople, the emperor used his troops to pick off various fortresses belonging to his new ally, Chrysos. He then forced Chrysos to accept a new treaty that recognized these losses and also gave the

Byzantines Strumica. However, Chrysos remained in control of Prosek, which the Byzantines again had besieged without success.

Thus during the years 1200–02 the empire had had considerable success. It had put an end to Ivanko's attempts to establish a principality first in the Philippopolis region and subsequently along the Struma. It had also recovered northern Thessaly from Kamytzes. Chrysos' power was reduced and a number of his forts, including Strumica, had been recovered. At the same time a Byzantine magnate and general named Spiridanakis had tried to carve out an independent principality for himself at Smolena; imperial troops had driven him out and recovered his territory. And most importantly, a peace that again pushed the boundaries of the Bulgarian state back to the Balkan Mountains had been established with a temporarily weakened Kalojan. Thus Thrace and Macedonia south of the Balkan Mountains, except for Chrysos' small holding on the Vardar, were all Byzantine again.

Greece at the End of the Twelfth Century[8]

While imperial Greece was spared from most of the raids by various Slavs, Vlachs, and Cumans, it was not spared from abuses by imperial authority or separatism by magnates. By the first half of the eleventh century, excluding the region west of the Pindus range (Acarnania and Epirus), which continued as the separate theme of Nikopolis, most of Greece—the themes of the Peloponnesus and the Helladikoi (central Greece: Thessaly, Attica, Aetolia, Euboea, and the island of Aegina)—had been combined into one theme.

The theme's governor, generally now called a praitor, was a non-local appointed from Constantinople who generally held office for about three years. Many of these governors, who were drawn from Constantinopolitan court circles, did not actually go to their post but remained in Constantinople, sending memos and orders to the lesser administrators who were present. The main task of the governor was to collect taxes, a task which was often turned over to tax farmers—individuals who at the start of their tenure paid the sum sought by the state and then went to their "farm" and tried to extract not only the taxes actually owed but a healthy profit for themselves as well. Since the governors also often purchased their office at court, they too, either acting for themselves or through their agents in Greece, tried to recover their investments. There was a long tradition of raising money from the populace for the support of governors; since the introduction of the theme system the earlier military governors (the strategoi) of the Helladikoi and of the Peloponnesus had never received government salaries but had had to support themselves by raising their salaries from the local population. Thus Greece suffered from excessive taxation.

The governor's residence, when a governor actually took up residence in Greece, was in Thebes, where he assembled a huge court in imitation of the imperial court in Constantinople. The governor also frequently traveled around Greece with a huge entourage, expecting to be maintained by the unwilling towns that had to host him. Michael Choniates, Archbishop of Athens (1182–1205) and brother of the historian Niketas Choniates, speaks of the plague of government officials oppressing the city of Athens. The governor, though his position had arisen centuries earlier as a military commander (the strategos who had been assigned the province to defend and administer), had by now become chiefly a civil official. He had only a small number of troops under his command, little more than a body guard which, though worthless to provide defense from raiders and pirates, was sufficient for him to extract and extort the hospitality and funds he demanded from the townspeople.

Within Greece there were also a small number of garrisons that guarded certain important castles on key routes or key mountain passes. It was difficult to find the manpower to maintain them, for here too there was corruption. Volunteers were needed to man them, but volunteers were few since the peasants who entered such service—voluntarily or under compulsion when volunteers were not forthcoming—frequently found their lands expropriated in their absence by local landlords or even by the government official who had recruited them. Illegal occupation of peasant land was a common abuse in Greece in the twelfth century.

The chief official under the governor, the praktor, was a financial official responsible for the assessment and collection of regular taxes, land taxes, and irregular services. When a governor chose to remain in Constantinople, the praktor tended to become the de facto governor. The praitor and/or praktor, living at a considerable distance from Constantinople, enjoyed freedom from imperial supervision and thus exercised more-or-less unrestricted authority in Greece. Appeals made by local citizens to the emperor about abuses tended to be ignored. After all, the individuals against whom they complained were court favorites.

Many locals must have dreamed of resistance. But only a few were able to act upon this dream. They tended to be the powerful local magnates who had amassed large estates with large retinues of armed men. Governors, with their limited forces, were not able to challenge the most powerful of these warlords, so they tended to ignore them and concentrate their extortion on the militarily unprotected towns. When the governors were absentees, the warlords were able to increase their local authority even more easily. Thus in various provinces of Greece powerful local figures emerged, patrons and protectors of large numbers of locals, with sizeable armies. Since they were strong enough to resist the governor, they tended to be left alone by him. In their localities such magnates, depending on their proclivities, could exploit and rob or protect the rural population.

Since the governor had become mainly a civil official, military affairs were transferred to a second figure, the megaduke. This official's role in Greece was more theoretical than actual, however. As a grand admiral responsible for maritime affairs throughout the empire, the megaduke had a zone of responsibility far broader than just the Greek themes of the Helladikoi and Peloponnesus. And though he was in theory the supreme military commander for Greece, he was in fact almost never present and thus exercised almost no actual authority. Though in some areas (Crete, Cyprus, the Adriatic) the megaduke appointed a subordinate to be resident and supervise defense, he appointed no such resident subordinate for Greece. Each area of Greece was to be taxed to support local naval defense under the overall authority of this commander. By the early twelfth century, however, more and more of the money, though raised throughout the empire in areas needing naval protection, was being diverted to Constantinople, where a large portion of it ended up in the pockets of the megaduke and his associates.

After Manuel's death, the actual number of ships and sailors under the megaduke had declined significantly, and the sailors tended to consist of unreliable foreigners. Indigenous fleets in Byzantine harbors were frequently allowed to decline to almost nothing. Thus any port was at the mercy of an attack from an effective fleet, be it Norman, Venetian, or Genoese. Ports were also at the mercy of pirates, some of whom were local Greeks while others were Italians. The islands off the coast, particularly Salamis, Aegina, and Makronisos (Makronesi), were pirate strongholds. The government was unable to defend Attica from them. Even though they were Christians, many of the pirates plundered churches. The Genoese pirates Vetrano and Caffaro also ravaged the coasts and isles of the Aegean. Finally in 1197 or 1198 an ex-pirate, John Steiriones, was sent with thirty ships against Caffaro, who was based in Calabria, and rid the Aegean of him. While this was occurring, however, the megaduke of the fleet, a certain Michael Stryphnos, whose wife was the sister of Alexius III's wife, enriched himself by sharing in the plunder of pirates and privately pillaging on his own the ships and dockyards of the Aegean whose duty it was for him to defend.

Thus the two major officials responsible for the administration and defense of Greece were almost always (in the case of the megaduke) or frequently (in the case of the praitor) absentees. They did almost nothing for the benefit or defense of their area of responsibility but drained its resources for their own benefit. Not surprisingly, a major role in protecting the population and sending appeals to the emperor about abuses fell to the Church. The ecclesiastical organization was spread throughout Greece, and the bishops, holding sees for life, were in office for long terms and actually resided in the areas of their responsibility.

The worthlessness of the imperial government's local defenses, as Herrin points out, is illustrated by the lack of provincial resistance against the crusaders when they appeared in Greece in 1205 and the ease with which they conquered Greece. No opposition was offered by any provincial military or naval force under the praitor's or the megaduke's command. The only opposition to the crusaders came from independent locals, most frequently landlords supported by their own retinues.

While the number of garrison soldiers, unwillingly serving the state, was small, and the forces making up local harbor patrols disintegrated as funds meant for their maintenance were drained off and sent to Constantinople, imperial authority weakened. As a result local landlords began taking matters more and more into their own hands until eventually some of the more powerful ones began hacking out independent principalities.

The Greece dominated by such provincial warlords not surprisingly had become, in the eyes of the few intellectuals present (namely, certain of the higher clergy) a cultural backwater. Michael Choniates complains that whereas once the Athenians had spoken classical Attic, now their language was barbaric; only with the greatest difficulty had he achieved an understanding of the language which they spoke. In fact, he claims, it had taken him three years to learn the Attic dialect of the twelfth century. Unless the whole statement is simply exaggerated rhetoric, one might conclude this reflects more on Michael's inability to learn languages than on the actual speech of the locals. He bemoans the fact, if it truly was a fact, that there were no longer any philosophers and that most of the clergy was uneducated. The ignorance of the Athenians shocks Michael. They attended church but rarely, and when they did so it was chiefly to chatter among themselves. The city was in ruins; weeds and grass grew in the streets and animals grazed about in them. The women and children were ill-fed and ill-clothed. There were even few ordinary workmen. Michael claims there were no sword-makers, iron-workers, or brass-workers in Athens. He could not even have a carriage built in Athens but had to have it ordered from a town on the Gulf of Corinth. Agriculture was in decline; the fertility of the soil had become poor and local agricultural implements were poor. Though the olive and vine still flourished, Athenian wine was poor, sharp, and bitter (possibly, if the suggestion is not anachronistic, it was retsina, to which he was not accustomed) and there were frequent shortages of wheat. The ordinary bread was wretched. However, the Athenians did make soap, and the local honey from Mount Hymettus was still famous.

Presumably to some extent Michael is exaggerating when he speaks of the decline of Athens. Some towns in Greece were clearly prosperous then. Thebes, Corinth, and Patras seem to have been rich by any standard. All three had flourishing silk industries. Though the Normans had captured many Theban silk-makers and carted them off to Palermo to establish the industry there in 1147, Thebes' industry had quickly revived. When Benjamin of Tudela visited Thebes in the 1160s he raved about its silk industry, many of whose leading practitioners were Jews. In fact, Benjamin states that there were two thousand Jewish inhabitants in Thebes. "Among them are many eminent Talmudic scholars and men as famous as any of the present generation. No scholars like them are to be found in the whole Greek empire, except at Constantinople." The northern regions (Thessaly, Macedonia, and Thrace), when spared from raids, were rich in wheat, and Euboea and the islands of Chios and Rhodes were famous for their wine.

However, the magnates and warlords, often called archons, were the dominant figures in Greece. At the same time that Kamytzes was trying with the help of Chrysos to carve out his own principality in northern Thessaly, several magnates in the Peloponnesus asserted their independence and put an end to all imperial authority south of the Isthmus of Corinth. The Chamaretos family, under Leo, its head, took over in Laconia, the region of ancient Sparta. Three families parceled out the region of Monemvasia: the Mamonas family, which was to be prominent for the next 250 years, along with the Sophianos and the Eudaimonoioannes families. And most important of all was the revolt of Leo Sgouros (Sguras), hereditary archon of Nauplia. By seizing Argos and Corinth, he gained control over the Isthmus of Corinth. Then in about 1201 he launched an attack against Athens. The city, led by Michael Choniates, its bishop, resisted until an imperial general arrived with an army to relieve the siege. Choniates would have had little to hope for should his city have fallen. Sgouros had already murdered the Bishop of Argos. He had also invited the Archbishop of Corinth to dinner, only to blind him before pitching him to his death from the heights of Acrocorinth.

Soon Sgouros attacked Athens again and, according to Choniates, also waged naval war against the city's port. As a result, in 1202 communications were cut off between Athens and Constantinople. While Sgouros left troops to carry on the siege, other "brigands" under his command began raiding to the north, subduing various other towns including Thebes. His men then moved north into southern Thessaly. Only Athens seems to have held out, frequently under siege. When the knights of the Fourth Crusade reached Attica on their way to the Peloponnesus, they found Athens encircled by the brigands of Sgouros. Sgouros thus succeeded in creating an independent principality centered in the northeastern Peloponnesus that extended well into Attica and Boeotia, which the Byzantine state was in no position to oppose. Quite likely, it was only the arrival of the crusaders that prevented it from becoming a lasting affair. Not only did these warlords resist orders from the central government, but they also quarrelled and fought with each other, squeezed the rural population, and blackmailed the towns.

A fitting final example of a warlord robber baron is Alexius Kapandrites. He captured the widow of an archon from Durazzo who, to escape a grasping imperial tax collector who had been trying to enforce an extremely high inheritance tax, had packed up her valuables and tried to flee to her relatives. En route, however, she had fallen into the clutches of Kapandrites, who forcibly married her and thus acquired her valuables. He and his private army so completely dominated his part of western Macedonia that he had no trouble in obtaining a certificate from the local Bishop of Devol attesting that no force had been used to carry out the marriage.

Thus on the eve of the Fourth Crusade the trend for magnates to build up huge estates supporting private armies had increased to the extent that they were setting up independent principalities that frequently ceased recognizing Constantinople's authority; in some cases, owing to distance or the strength of certain of these warlords, Constantinople was helpless to oppose them. Alexius III had contributed to this situation; for to obtain support after his seizure of the throne he had increased the privileges and exemptions of such figures, who then took advantage of the power gained thereby to bring about the secession of whole districts. This type of revolt was very different from the rebellions the empire had been familiar with earlier. For previous rebels had declared themselves emperors and then marched on Constantinople to try to seize the capital and realize their claim. Though rebellions of that sort did still occur from time to time, now for the first time, this new type of revolt, by separatism, had become endemic, causing the empire to disintegrate from within.

Abdication of Stefan Nemanja

On 23 or 24 March 1196 Stefan Nemanja abdicated at a sabor (council) of nobles and people that he had convoked at the Church of Saint Peter at Ras. Presumably he called the council and acquired its agreement in order to guarantee a smooth succession, particularly since his heir was to be Stefan, his second son, rather than Vukan, the eldest. And by abdicating in his lifetime, when he was still influential, Nemanja was in a position to secure the succession as he wanted it. Then, on the 25th, he was tonsured as a monk, taking the name Simeon. His wife became a nun. Nemanja first entered Studenica, the magnificent monastery he had built. By 1198 he had joined his youngest son, Sava, on Mount Athos.

Sava, born Rastko, had run away from home to Athos in 1191 or 1192 as a teenager. He first entered the Russian monastery Saint Panteleimon there, where he was tonsured and took the name of Sava. Nemanja's arrival attracted considerable notice since it was not common for rulers to become monks on the Holy Mountain. By that time various nations, such as the Russians and Georgians, had their own monasteries there. Nemanja and Sava dreamed of a monastery for the Serbs. Nemanja also had the resources behind him to carry out this dream. The council of monks for Athos quickly approved the plan to build a new monastery. Then Sava went to Constantinople, where in 1198 the Emperor, Alexius III, granted the Serbs Hilandar, an abandoned monastery on the mountain that had fallen into disrepair. Sava and Nemanja restored it and made various additions to create a magnificent monastery church and complex. For its support Nemanja gave it considerable lands back in Serbia. He also obtained for it other lands nearer by in the Chalcidic area. Sava drew up the monastery's typikon (rule or charter), which was his privilege as ktitor (founder) of the institution. He based his Rule on that of the monastery of the Virgin Benefactress (Evergetis) in Constantinople. Hilandar grew rapidly. When Nemanja died in February 1199 it had fourteen monks. By the time Sava returned to Serbia bearing Nemanja's body, probably in 1207, it had two hundred. Under the guidance of Sava and various other Serb intellectuals who resided there during the following centuries, Hilandar rose to become the cultural center of the Serbs.

Athos, over the previous two centuries the center of Byzantine monasticism, was becoming international with its Russian and Georgian houses. Now it had become more so with the establishment of a Serbian monastery. Soon it was to acquire a Bulgarian one. Before the 1220s the Bulgarians acquired ownership of an older monastery, founded back in the tenth century, known as Zographou. Thus Athos became a center for international Orthodoxy. However, it should be stressed, as one might expect for an international faith, that monasteries, though acquiring national labels as rulers established, endowed, and showered with gifts their own special houses, did not become purely national. Membership cut across national lines; Serbs did not limit themselves to Hilandar but also resided in various Greek monasteries as well as in the Russian Panteleimon and the Bulgarian Zographou, and various non-Serbs dwelt in Hilandar.

Athos, under its protos (first chief elder), was administered by a central council composed of representatives from different monasteries. The council had a prescribed number of members; thus as new monasteries were created the number of council members did not change. As a result, some monasteries did not acquire representation. In the early thirteenth century, for example, neither Hilandar nor Zographou had delegates on the central council.

For the Slavic lands Athos served as a model of how monasteries should be organized and how monks should ideally live. Its ideals of the Christian life also penetrated into Slavic societies. Scholars frequently speak of an Orthodox synthesis being created on Athos, since there alone monks from all over the Orthodox world gathered, exchanging ideas. Generally, Greek ideas predominated on the mountain, and they were then carried back from Athos to the other Orthodox lands, for it was common for monks, after spending a period on Athos, to return home to monasteries in their native land. Thus Athos was a major source for the spread of manuscripts, texts, and theological ideas, as texts were copied and translated on the mountain and then carried back to the different Orthodox lands. Athos was also the source from which the Slavs drew ideas about Church law and Church organization. For example, as we shall see, Byzantine Canon Law was to reach Serbia via Athos. Athos was also a center from which various political ideas and Byzantine secular legal texts spread to the Orthodox world. Byzantine charter forms came to the Slavic lands via Athos because monasteries, receiving grants from Slavic rulers, expected them to be couched in traditional form. The earliest Serbian and Bulgarian charters in existence today were those issued by their rulers to monasteries on Athos. Soon the Slavic rulers were issuing their own charters to native monasteries and to their nobility using the same form.

Stefan Nemanja, now Simeon, died in February 1199. His body was brought back to Serbia by Sava, probably early in 1207, and buried at his monastery of Studenica. He was canonized, and his sons Stefan, the ruler of Serbia, and Sava each wrote a life of him, couched as a saint's life in which he was called by his monastic name Simeon. Nemanja and Sava forged the close ties between Church and state that were to continue in Serbia thereafter. Serbian rulers were to be very generous to the Church. Each built at least one major monastery church, an obligation for the salvation of his soul. Most rulers were also generous in donating lands and cash to the Church. As a result of this generosity and the Church's gratitude, Nemanja and several of his successors were to be canonized. In appreciation, and from the time of Nemanja, the Church supported the dynasty. Following the lead of Sava, who of course was the dominant Serbian Church figure of his time, the Church depicted Nemanja as the founder of Serbia. Its previous history faded into a fog.

The Nemanja depicted, however, differs in the two biographies. Sava's, written before Nemanja was canonized, emphasizes him as a good man and good Christian monk. It speaks little of his secular life and focuses on two moments in his life: his abdication to become a monk and his death. It was probably intended to advance his candidacy as a saint while also serving as a model for others to imitate. Nemanja's successor Stefan the First-Crowned, on the other hand, wrote a longer life, which emphasizes his deeds as a ruler: Nemanja as a military leader, his conquests, his actions against heretics. Stefan presents him as the founder of a state and a dynasty. Nemanja, by then already canonized, is depicted as a patron saint for Serbia (akin to Saint Demetrius for Thessaloniki) who after his death had become the protector of the state. And since Nemanja was effective in this role, his ability to protect showed God's favor for Serbia and for its dynasty. Such a depiction thus re-enforced the dynasty's right to rule Serbia, and, of course, it also advanced Stefan's own claims to rule, not only over rivals from other families, but also (since Nemanja had personally selected Stefan over his older son Vukan to be Grand župan of Serbia) against Vukan. And Stefan found it easy to insert a great deal about himself and his successes in the life he wrote, making this relevant by seeing Nemanja's supernatural help behind his own successes. At the same time, to bolster the ruler, himself and his successors, Stefan also moralizes about the duty of subjects to obey their ruler and to render services and taxes to him.

The cult of Nemanja, developed from the start by his sons Stefan and Sava, proved useful to his heirs. All his reigning descendants until the last Serbian Nemanjić, who died in 1371, benefited from being descended from a saint, for descent from the holy king strengthened their right to rule. Nemanja also became a protector for the state whose miraculous intervention from time to time either saved the state or proved useful to explain certain events, like the death of Strez (whom we shall meet soon) who was on the verge of attacking Serbia. A miraculous intervention by Nemanja provided a more pleasing, less embarrassing explanation than what was probably the true one: that Stefan, if not Saint Sava himself, hired someone from Strez's own entou-rage to murder him. On the subject of cults, it is interesting to note that Saints Cyril and Methodius, the Apostles to the Slavs and the creators of Slavic letters, who were very popular saints and cult figures in Bulgaria and Mac-edonia, received little notice in Serbia. There they rarely were mentioned in literary works and seldom appeared on frescoes.

No source gives a reason for Nemanja's abdication. Since this act followed immediately upon the succession of Alexius III in Byzantium in 1195, and since Alexius was the father of Stefan's wife, various scholars have tried to connect the two events. However, the abdication need not be linked to Alexius' succession. Nemanja seems to have been genuinely religious. He had long been active in Church affairs and church building. In fact his church building had been an issue between him and his brother Tihomir back in the 1160s. He had continued to build churches in the decades that followed. He also donated land and gifts not only to Orthodox churches but also to Catholic churches on the coast, in Bar and Dubrovnik. Further, he held a large Church council in about 1170 that had condemned a heresy about which we learn only that the heretics did not teach that Christ was the Son of God. The heretical leaders were branded and exiled. Most scholars believe these heretics were Bogomils; however, though quite possible, we cannot be certain about this conclusion since the information about their beliefs is much too scanty to permit any conclusions to be drawn. We shall find very little about heretics thereafter in Serbia, though Dušan's law code from 1349 does contain a couple of articles against heresy.

Therefore I do not agree that Nemanja's abdication in 1196 was a result of Alexius' succession in 1195. However, that Stefan, the second son, rather than Vukan, the eldest, succeeded to the throne of Raška may well be owing to the fact that Stefan's wife was the emperor's daughter. In fact it could easily have been agreed at the time of the marriage arrangements—as Sava actually reports—that Stefan was to succeed. The emperor, then Isaac, might have agreed to give his niece to Stefan only on that condition. But by 1196 Byzantium was too weak for Serbia to gain any advantage from having a Byzantine princess sharing its throne. Hungary and the papacy were to have far more influence than Byzantium in Serbia during the years that followed.

Rivalry between Stefan and Vukan in Serbia

Vukan, the eldest son, was given Zeta, Trebinje, and the coast (southern Dalmatia) to rule.[9] This territory had been assigned to him several years before the abdication—by 1190, when Vukan is referred to in a charter to Split as ruling in this region. Some scholars believe that Vukan's possession of this territory during his father's reign indicates that at the time of his appointment he had been the intended heir to the throne and had been given this territory in order to acquire experience and prestige for his subsequent rule. This was to be the case for intended heirs later on toward the end of the thirteenth and into the fourteenth century. However, others have seen Vukan's appointment as being similar to Hungary's policy in the twelfth century of granting a banate (the banate of Croatia and Dalmatia) to a younger son not in line for the throne, as compensation. If this Hungarian model applies to Nemanja's Serbia, then Stefan's succession should not be seen as a post-1190 policy change. In any case, regardless of when and why, Nemanja decided that Stefan rather than Vukan should become Serbia's Grand župan. The granting to Vukan of a large appanage reflects the typical South Slavic custom of dividing an inheritance among the various heirs rather than having the whole realm devolve upon a single heir. If Vukan had by then acquired a large number of associates and supporters, the grant of an appanage to him may also have been made to avoid rebellion. However, though the territory was divided, Nemanja expected the unity of the state to continue. He did not visualize Zeta becoming a separate kingdom under Vukan. His final instructions were for his sons to co-operate in brotherly love and peace.

Scholars have debated on how much independence Zeta actually had under Raškan rule. However, it must be stressed that there are theoretical and practical aspects to this question. Sava states that Stefan was to have suzerainty; he adds that Nemanja made Vukan "Great Prince," gave him sufficient land, and asked him to obey Stefan, who was ordered to hold his brother Vukan in honor and not to offend him. Presumably in theory, then, Vukan was to have internal autonomy and the right to his territory's income, but as a subordinate prince he owed military service when Raška was at war and did not have the right to carry on independent foreign affairs.

However, regardless of the theory, what is of importance is what actually happened. And Vukan at once asserted himself as an independent ruler. Thus even though it may have violated the "constitution" or spirit of his assignment, Vukan carried on his own foreign policy. He did this not because of a right to do so, but because he was strong enough to get away with it. He immediately began calling himself king and was called king by the pope. In fact a dated inscription from 1195, before Nemanja's abdication, from the Church of Saint Luke in Kotor calls Vukan King of Duklja. Since Stefan Nemanja at his abdication shortly thereafter called Vukan "Great Prince" it is evident that Nemanja did not give Vukan, or agree to his having, a royal title. Thus we can conclude that Vukan was a self-styled king. Most probably Nemanja was not aware that Vukan was doing this. Probably Vukan simply assumed the title of the former rulers of Zeta (Duklja), who had been kings until about 1146. He may well have found it convenient to claim that this title went with the territory he had been assigned. Furthermore, since the previous Dukljan and Serbian dynasties were related (and if, as seems evident, Nemanja was related to the previous Serbian dynasty), then Nemanja and Vukan were descendants of the former Dukljan royal house, enabling Vukan to advance a family claim to the title as well. By calling Vukan king, the pope, with whom Vukan had cordial relations (for there were many Catholics in the western parts of Zeta, particularly along the coast), provided support for Vukan's use of the title. He may eventually have sent him a crown. If Vukan was using this title in 1195, however, he clearly was using it prior to any grant he may have had from the pope, who would not have granted a crown when Nemanja still ruled all Serbia.

From the above it is evident that since Vukan's title was self-taken and against Nemanja's wishes, it cannot be used to argue, as some scholars have in the past, that Nemanja had tried to divide his realm into two independent principalities, each under its own dynasty, with Stefan and his descendants ruling Serbia and Vukan and his heirs ruling Zeta. However, even though Nemanja did not want this, it was what Vukan sought to realize. It has also been stated that Vukan played upon Zetan feelings of separateness to create a second state. This is an anachronistic theory. Both Raška and Zeta were populated by Serbs. But the loyalty of most people then was to a far more local unit than a region like Zeta. It was to a village, or possibly to a county or to a family. Few, if any, would have had strong awareness that they were Zetans. Those Zetan nobles who supported Vukan (and as far as we know most of them did) surely did so for the personal advantages they saw in this policy, and not because of any Zetan consciousness. The localism within Raška and Zeta makes it hard to speak of these regions as states. In fact the term frequently used for them was *država,* which now means a state but is derived from the verb *to hold* and meant a holding, one's patrimony. Under Vukan stood a whole series of Zetan nobles holding their smaller county patrimonies to which their interests were attached. Each noble with his family and retainers gave service to the prince when he had to or wanted to and avoided such service when he saw it to be in his own interests and if he felt strong enough to get away with it.

Vukan, then, was clearly dissatisfied with being excluded from the succession in Raška and felt he, not Stefan, should rule there. In order to realize his ambitions and assert his independence from Stefan in his own territory, he began to seek assistance. Presumably, though we know nothing about this process, he carried out a policy to win the support of the nobles of Zeta. He also opened up cordial relations with foreign powers, especially with the papacy and Hungary. The result of Vukan's policy, despite Nemanja's wish that his sons co-operate and jointly manage their realms as two parts of one state, was to divide the state into two independent realms. Each ruler, though, dreamed of a united Serbia, but one under himself at the expense of his brother.

Alliances and Church Policy Involving Zeta and Bosnia

Vukan sought to advance his cause by involving himself in the wrangling over Church jurisdiction then going on in the western Balkans. In 1190 Dubrovnik's archbishop stood over all the churches under the pope in Bosnia and southern Dalmatia. Split's archbishop stood over all the central and northern Dalmatian churches. Thus the Catholics of Zeta and Bosnia were under Dubrovnik. Dubrovnik, as noted, tolerated Bosnia's local customs, allowing Bosnia to use Slavic in its liturgy and to choose its own bishop who simply went to Dubrovnik for consecration. Hungary was the overlord of the town of

Split, and the Archbishop of Split, though directly under the pope, had close ties to the Hungarian court and higher clergy. Hungary was in theory also the overlord over the state of Bosnia. However, Bosnia under Kulin had, for all practical purposes, made itself into an independent state. Thus Hungary was seeking a chance to reassert its authority over Bosnia.

In 1192 the Hungarian king succeeded in persuading the pope that Bosnia should be removed from the jurisdiction of Dubrovnik and placed under the Archbishop of Split. Bosnia, wanting to retain its independence and seeing the pope's decision as a means to extend Hungarian influence, seems simply to have ignored the change. At least, if we can believe later Ragusan chronicles, throughout the 1190s Bosnia continued to send its bishops to Dubrovnik, not Split, to be consecrated. And an Archbishop of Dubrovnik traveled to Bosnia to consecrate two churches in 1194. Dubrovnik, wishing to retain its jurisdiction over Bosnia and objecting to the growth of Split's authority, thus supported Bosnia in resisting subordination to Split. Needless to say, the behavior of Bosnia and Dubrovnik annoyed both Hungary and the Archbishop of Split.

Vukan also had reason to oppose Dubrovnik. In his realm lay the important Catholic bishopric of Bar. With great effort the earlier Dukljan (Zetan) rulers had persuaded the pope to remove Bar and various other bishoprics in Zeta from the jurisdiction of Dubrovnik's archbishop. They met with success in 1089 when the pope removed Bar from the jurisdiction of Dubrovnik and made Bar into an independent archbishopric standing over a series of southern Dalmatian suffragan bishoprics that had also been taken from Dubrovnik. Dubrovnik protested this change vehemently. Eventually, as the state of Zeta declined, Dubrovnik was able in 1142 to persuade the pope to rescind this reform. In that year Bar was reduced again to a bishopric and, along with its former suffragans, was restored to Dubrovnik's jurisdiction. Now it was Bar's turn to protest. In the 1170s Bar even entered into the scheming of Archbishop Rainer of Split. Rainer was then trying to restore Split to the position it had held in the tenth century when all Dalmatia, including Dubrovnik, had been subordinate to Split. Bishop Gregory of Bar, angry at Dubrovnik, had thrown his support behind the intrigues of Rainer and had agreed to recognize Split as Bar's suzerain. However, this plan petered out when, as we saw earlier, Rainer was murdered by the Kačići in about 1180. Soon thereafter Zeta was annexed by Nemanja, who took up Bar's cause. We noted earlier that in the course of a war with Dubrovnik, Nemanja had pilfered documents supporting Dubrovnik's claims to Bar from the Ragusan archives. However, as an Orthodox ruler, rather than a papal subject, Nemanja was not able to effect a change.

But then in the 1190s Vukan assumed power in Zeta. To assert his independence from Raška he needed allies, in case his policies led to war. As a power and one bordering on Serbia, Hungary was a valuable ally to gain. Vukan soon entered into negotiations with Hungary and the papacy. Both these rulers recognized his title of king and his independence from Raška. In fact he may have eventually received a crown from the pope. It was natural for him to turn to the pope; it would get him into the good graces of Hungary. In addition there were many Catholics in his realm, not only along the coast but also inland as far as Podgorica, whose support he wanted. As a result of the negotiations that established his alliance with the pope and brought him recognition as king, Vukan accepted papal supremacy and became a Catholic. As a Catholic he was now also in a better position to fight for Bar's cause. Hostile to Dubrovnik and forging closer ties with Hungary, not surprisingly he soon came to support Hungary against Bosnia and involved himself in plots against that state. Vukan's relations with Hungary seem to have become closer after 1198 when Andrew, brother of King Imre and now Duke of Croatia and Dalmatia, conquered part of Hum, probably western Hum down to the Neretva. If Andrew's conquests extended that far, it would have brought Andrew and his officials physically into the proximity of Vukan's Zeta. The Hungarian presence in Hum may well have encouraged Vukan to enter into a more active and aggressive policy.

At this time Split had ulterior motives to criticize matters in Bosnia, to show that Dubrovnik was managing Bosnia's Church affairs badly and that Bosnia's ruler was lax or even worse on Church matters. Vukan, to support his Hungarian allies and to discredit Dubrovnik as a means to advance Bar's cause, had similar motives. Thus in 1199 Vukan wrote the pope that Ban Kulin of Bosnia, his wife, his sister (the widow of Miroslav of Hum who had been living at Kulin's court since Miroslav's death in ca. 1198), various other relatives, and ten thousand other Christians had been seduced by heresy. He gives no description of this so-called heresy, and the emphasis on the alleged involvement of these political leaders makes one think Vukan had ulterior motives for writing his letter. In the years immediately following, the Archbishop of Split, whose ulterior motives are obvious, began to complain about heretics in Bosnia as did Split's supporter the King of Hungary. The pope also took an interest. Thus Bosnia was faced with an impressive array of opponents, all concerned with its internal affairs. We shall return to Bosnia's reaction shortly. Dubrovnik, accused of laxness, however, also found itself under considerable pressure. And it seems that the combination of Vukan, Hungary, and Split were sufficient to persuade the pope once again to remove Bar and its former suffragans—the most important of which were the Bishops of Ulcinj and Drivast—from Dubrovnik's jurisdiction. Bar's bishop was again raised to archbishop. This change occurred in 1199.

Bar's restored status was announced at a Church synod held at Bar in the summer of 1199 and attended by bishops from Vukan's lands. The decisions of the council were binding only on those lands and reflect the degeneracy of Catholicism in southern Dalmatia at the time. The council banned various forms of simony and forbade priests to undergo judicial ordeals—showing that the ordeal to decide legal quarrels was then practiced in Zeta. The synod also insisted that priests shave their beards and be celibate; these last two demands suggest that certain Orthodox Church practices may have been adopted by Zeta's Catholic clergy. The council also forbade laymen to expel their wives without a Church hearing.

The reforms do not seem to have improved Church conditions. Throughout the early thirteenth century we find it was the practice for citizens to loot the homes of bishops on their deaths which frequently led to brawls, some of which even took place inside churches. Such looting was a widespread practice; in fifteenth-century Rome it was still customary to plunder the house of a cardinal when it was announced he had been elected pope. The citizens of Drivast on one occasion murdered their bishop. And in 1249 when the Archbishop of Bar tried to suspend a suffragan bishop until he had been cleared by the pope, the bishop ignored his superior's orders and continued to serve mass. Finally the pope suspended all the bishops of the archdiocese until they appeared before him in Rome. Only the Archbishop of Bar was excluded from this order, for he was said to have been too elderly to travel to Rome.

Needless to say, Dubrovnik protested Bar's restored status, and the issue remained under heated discussion throughout the first half of the thirteenth century. Each time an Archbishop of Bar died, Dubrovnik tried to prevent the selection of a new archbishop. Dubrovnik regularly sent protests to the pope and issued frequent appeals to Bar's suffragans to try to steal their recognition from Bar. At times Dubrovnik's attempts were met with violence. According to a later chronicle, when early in the thirteenth century an Archbishop of Dubrovnik tried to visit Bar officially he was driven away with stones. At other times Dubrovnik achieved small successes such as occurred in the 1240s, when the Bishop of Ulcinj, with the consent of local authorities, decided to submit to Dubrovnik. The fight was to continue until 1255 when Dubrovnik finally gave up the struggle.

Presumably Stefan of Serbia also felt threatened by Vukan's alliances, for in 1198 Stefan entered into negotiations with the pope. Evidently he hoped that if he created ties with the papacy, the pope would restrain Vukan and the Hungarians from acting against Raška. Indicating his willingness to submit to Rome, Stefan also sought a crown from the pope. He had expectations of success until King Imre of Hungary got wind of the plan and persuaded the pope to drop it. In 1200 or 1201 (previously scholars had dated it 1198) Stefan accused his queen, the emperor's daughter Eudocia, of adultery. He chased her from Raška. She left on foot with only the clothes on her back. This action provides another example of the decline of Byzantium's prestige. It is evident that Stefan had no fear of antagonizing the empire and also no hope that the empire could supply him with effective support should his conflict with Vukan result in war. The ousting of the Byzantine princess may also reflect Stefan's attempts to align himself more closely with the pope, from whom he was then still hoping to receive a crown. The lady fled to Zeta, where Vukan befriended her, feeding and clothing her until, recovered, she went to Durazzo where a Byzantine ship arrived to take her home.

The Bosnian Church Council of 1203

Meanwhile between 1199 and 1202 the verbal attacks continued against Ban Kulin of Bosnia. He was accused of warmly receiving heretics (the heresy unspecified) who had been expelled from Dalmatia. His accusers claimed that many Bosnians, and possibly even Bosnia's ruler, had become tainted with heresy, if not out and out heretics themselves. Kulin wrote to the pope that he thought these refugees were good Christians, and he sent some to Rome to be examined. Whether or not they were really heretics is not stated in any surviving source. But one could not have expected the uneducated Bosnian ruler to have discerned the difference. He clearly considered himself a faithful Catholic; he maintained ties with the Archbishop of Dubrovnik, sent gifts to the pope, and built Catholic churches. But Bosnia was clearly in a vulnerable position. Split, Hungary's tool, was seeking to assert its ecclesiastical control over Bosnia, which would increase Hungarian influence in Bosnia and threaten Bosnia's independence. And furthering Hungary's ambitions, the pope, probably incited by Hungary, was calling on Hungary to take action against heresy in Bosnia. Clearly a crusade against heretics would serve as a fine excuse for Hungary to assert its overlordship over Bosnia.

Kulin, however, defused the threat against himself by calling a Church council. It was held on 6 April 1203 at Bolino Polje. The Catholic Church was represented by an archdeacon from Dubrovnik rather than a representative of the Archbishop of Split. Thus Kulin was able to stand fast, ignore the papal order to change his Church's suzerain bishop, and continue to deal with Dubrovnik. Presumably his clear loyalty to the pope, at a time when heresy was threatening so much of southern Europe including (at least so the pope feared) Bosnia, led the pope to look the other way and not insist on the jurisdictional change. For though it might be lax, Dubrovnik was a zealously Catholic city.

The Bosnians at the council renounced a whole series of errors (mostly errors in practice) that probably arose through ignorance of how practices should be carried out. Few, if any, seemed related to the doctrines and practices of any known heresy. They promised to reform their Church, recognized the pope as head of the Church, and reaffirmed their loyalty to Rome. Kulin also reaffirmed his allegiance to Hungary and sent envoys to the Hungarian court to confirm this and swear again to uphold the decisions of the Council of Bolino Polje. Despite these verbal assurances, however, Hungary's authority in Bosnia remained nominal. Kulin seems to have died the following year; the name of his successor is not known.

Vukan Seizes Raška

In the spring of 1202 Vukan, with Hungarian aid, attacked Raška and deposed Stefan, who fled. Vukan took over in Raška, taking also the title Grand župan and recognizing Hungarian suzerainty. The Hungarian king added "Serbia" to his title. Hungarian kings were to retain the name "Serbia" in their title throughout the Middle Ages, even though they usually held no Serbian territory to base this title upon. An inscription from 1202 describes Vukan's holdings as follows: the Serbian land (i.e., Raška), the Zeta region, the coastal towns, and the Niš region. Such a description reflects the unintegrated character of this territory and shows that Niš, recently regained by Raška, still retained a special identity.

In November 1202 Ban Kulin of Bosnia attacked some "Hungarian lands." Since it is unlikely that he would have launched an attack against the strong Hungarian monarch, it seems probable that he had actually attacked Vukan, who had been trying to make trouble for Kulin earlier and whose submission to the King of Hungary would explain the reference to "Hungarian lands." Whether Kulin attacked Vukan in Raška or in Zeta is not known, nor do we know whether he attacked him for his own reasons or in an attempt to support Stefan. We do not know what, if anything, resulted from Kulin's attack. Finally we also do not know where Stefan fled from Raška; it is usually claimed that he fled to Bulgaria. This is perfectly possible, but he might also have fled to Bosnia.

In March 1203 the pope ordered a Hungarian bishop, the Archbishop of Kalocsa, to go to Serbia to strengthen the position of the Catholic faith there. Presumably, then, with Vukan in power there, the pope aimed with Vukan's help to win Raška over to the Catholic Church. There is no evidence that the bishop actually made this trip. And no information exists about Church affairs in Raška during Vukan's brief reign. Kalojan of Bulgaria, however, was surely alarmed at the strengthening of his Hungarian rival's position in Serbia along Bulgaria's western border. In the summer of 1203 Bulgaria attacked Vukan's Serbia, plundering Raška and annexing the Niš region. Whether Kalojan's attack was made to support Stefan or simply to take advantage of the unstable situation to benefit Bulgaria is not known. In any case Bulgaria did take advantage of matters to annex the Niš region. Kalojan established a Bulgarian bishop in that city. The pope now found himself caught in the middle between his Hungarian friends and Kalojan, whom he was trying to woo. In September 1203 he wrote to Kalojan asking him to make peace with Vukan. The letter seems to have had no effect.

It is often stated that Stefan was returned to his throne in 1203 and his restoration was a result of Kalojan's attack. This view is mere speculation, however. First, no source states that Kalojan had any role in restoring Stefan. In fact, no source provides any information at all on how Stefan regained his throne. His restoration could easily have been the result of Bulgarian aid, but he also could have regained his throne with Bosnian help or even through the support of local Raškans. Furthermore, it is not at all clear when Stefan regained his throne.

There certainly is no evidence that Stefan returned to his throne during the summer of 1203, though this is often stated. In fact, in the autumn of 1203 the pope wrote Kalojan to make peace with Vukan. This suggests that a state of enmity still existed between the two after Kalojan's attack in the summer and that the pope wanted peace between them to secure Vukan from danger. That Vukan could be in danger from Kalojan suggests the two still had a common border. If Stefan had by then regained Raška, then his lands would have separated Vukan's from Kalojan's and Kalojan would not have threatened Vukan except possibly as an ally of Stefan. Next, early in 1204, the pope wrote King Imre of Hungary about arranging a coronation for Vukan. Since Vukan was already crowned King of Zeta, this presumably referred to a coronation for Raška. Unless this was to be an empty ceremony that would award a meaningless title for propagandistic purposes, this statement suggests that Vukan was still in Raška.

If these two imprecise statements are to be interpreted in the most obvious way, then Vukan was still in power in Raška early in 1204. Stefan's return, about which we have no information, then would have followed this date, presumably coming later in 1204 or early in 1205. In any case, Stefan was back in Raška and the brothers were still in a state of war when Sava returned to Serbia with Nemanja's body and mediated peace between them. Exactly when between late 1204 and April 1207 Sava arrived in Serbia is not certain either, though early 1207 has long been accepted as the most reasonable date.

The view that was formerly popular among scholars, that Stefan was restored to power by Kalojan in the summer of 1203, attributes the pope's continued interest in Vukan after that date to slow communications and ignorance. It was argued that the pope had not received information as to what was happening in Raška and thus still believed Vukan was in power there after he had actually been deposed.

Raška and Zeta, 1206/07 to ca. 1216

Stefan retained Raška from the time of his return to power until his death in 1227. Vukan returned to Zeta, and tensions continued between the two brothers, breaking out in skirmishes from time to time, until about 1206/07 (an argument can be made for February 1206 or February 1207) when their brother Sava returned from Athos with their father's body and mediated peace. This peace restored the pre-war status quo of two separate realms. Sava's mediation almost certainly preceded an April 1207 Kotor-Dubrovnik treaty since that document refers to Stefan and Vukan together, suggesting that at least officially the two were then at peace and recognized one another. Sava then settled down in Serbia as abbot of Studenica. Vukan seems to have abdicated in his lifetime, for his son George is referred to as king in 1208, while Vukan is referred to as alive, interestingly enough as "Great Prince," in an inscription from 1209 at Studenica. His reduced title may not reflect Vukan's view of matters but rather how Sava or other Raškans regarded him. We do not know why he abdicated. Possibly he wanted to secure his son's succession when he was still alive and able to play a role, perhaps fearing that if he died before George's installation, Stefan might take advantage of an interregnum to gain Zeta for himself. Vukan seems to have died in 1209 or shortly thereafter.

The struggle between the two branches of the family continued, however, under Vukan's son George. In order to procure further security for his lands against any threat from Stefan, George accepted, probably in 1208, Venetian suzerainty. Though this submission may well reflect tensions between George and Stefan, his acceptance of Venetian suzerainty need not have been from that cause. Venice at that time, right after the Fourth Crusade (which it had played a major role in), was trying to assert its control over many Balkan ports. For example, in 1205 Venice had obtained submission from Dubrovnik, which was allowed to retain its own autonomy and customary civil government but had assumed the obligation to provide Venice with ships for military needs when called on to do so. George may well have submitted to Venice to prevent Venice from taking over his own ports in southern Dalmatia.

George of Zeta, bearing the title king, was soon allied militarily with Venice against a second, theoretically Venetian vassal, an Albanian named Dimitri who from his mountain stronghold at Kroja (Krujë) dominated that part of Albania toward the end of the first decade of the thirteenth century. George promised military support to Venice should Dimitri attack Venetian territory. This alliance and conflict may have been related to the Raškan-Zetan struggle, for Dimitri had close ties with Raška, having married Stefan's daughter. After concluding the alliance George temporarily disappears from the sources, and by 1216 Stefan had obtained control, probably through military action, over Zeta. Thus he finally put an end to Zeta's separatism and independent kingship. He may eventually have assigned Zeta to his own son Radoslav. Recently, however, this assignment has been questioned by scholars who believe that Stefan retained Zeta for himself. In either case, Stefan seems to have been making an effort to make Zeta the patrimony of his own family rather than that of Vukan's heirs. Until Dušan's death in 1355, Zeta remained part of Raška with no special privileges. Frequently it was administered by the heir to the Raškan throne, who bore a title connected not with Zeta but with his position at the Raškan court. Agreements and grants made by the young holder of Zeta generally had to be confirmed by the ruler of Raška. However, though Zeta retained no special legal position, its nobles tended to be unruly. They frequently revolted or supported revolts by the holder of Zeta against the ruler of Raška.

Vukan's descendant George was to continue the struggle beyond 1216, as we shall see, but his descendants of the next generation had no special positions and they are found as common župans (county lords) lost in the crowd of Zeta's nobility. Then Zeta, with its special dynasty eliminated, became juridically no different from the rest of the Serbian state, except in its frequently being managed by a special governor from the reigning family, whose presence may be explained by the need to keep closer supervision over this unruly area and whose actions, in turn, remained under the close supervision of the Grand župan, later King, of Raška.

The Region of Albania in the Late Twelfth and Early Thirteenth Centuries

The Albanians were not to create any structure resembling a state until the fifteenth century. However, organized in tribes under their own chieftains, the Albanians dominated the mountains of most of what we today think of as Albania. The Albanians were and are divided into speakers of two distinct dialects: the Ghegs in the north and the Tosks in the south. The Shkumbi (Vrego) River marks the approximate boundary between the two linguistic groups. The second major boundary within Albania is the Drin River. The territory to its north was oriented toward Serbia and/or Zeta. One or the other of these two Serb entities frequently ruled this territory and Serbian influence had a major impact on its political organization, commercial affairs, and culture. At the close of the twelfth century the Serbs held the town of Skadar (Scutari, Shkodër, Scodra) and presumably controlled, possibly only loosely, the territory to the Drin.

South of the Drin (and increasingly so the further south one went) Greek influence was strong. This territory had been incorporated into the Byzantine theme of Durazzo, and the Greek Church organization, headed by the Metropolitan of Durazzo, had authority over it. Along the coast, including in Durazzo, Latin peoples were also to be found, and the Roman Church worked actively to maintain and improve the position of its institutions in Durazzo and other coastal cities. Despite the rivalry between Orthodox and Catholic institutions, the local Durazzans of both rites seem to have coexisted peacefully and were to continue to do so. Durazzo had long been a major trade center, the point of arrival or departure for goods to and from Macedonia, Thrace, Constantinople, and points further east, as the via Egnatia (from Constantinople through Thessaloniki and Ohrid) ended in Durazzo. Though Durazzo had an active citizenry that participated in local affairs—as we saw in the first volume of our history—the Byzantines (and their various successors who were to hold Durazzo during the later Middle Ages) were usually able to keep the local citizenry under control and manage the town. Thus Durazzo was not to achieve the level of local autonomy that was found in the towns of Dalmatia. In fact, no town south of Bar was able to create an autonomous commune or city-state governed under its own law code and by its own local council.

At the close of the twelfth century, excluding the tribesmen in the mountains, many of whom functioned freely regardless of which state they owed theoretical submission to, the only known Albanian political entity was that of Kroja. A certain Progon seems to have gained possession of this castle and come to control the territory around it. Possession of the fortress remained in his family, and by 1208 his son or grandson Dimitri, against whom, as we have just seen, Venice and Zeta formed an alliance, had become lord of Kroja.

Hum at the End of the Twelfth and the Beginning of the Thirteenth Centuries

The history of Hum in this period is almost impossible to unravel. In about 1190 part or even most of Hum had been assigned to Nemanja's youngest son Rastko. However, after this grant Miroslav, who prior to 1190 had held all Hum, continued to hold at least the region of the Lim River with Bijelo Polje, where he built his church dedicated to Saints Peter and Paul. Since Rastko was only a teen-ager at the time it is not certain that he actually occupied his appanage. Perhaps Nemanja was chiefly planning for the future, hoping to prevent Hum from breaking away under Miroslav's heirs. Soon thereafter, probably in 1192, Rastko decided to become a monk and fled to Mount Athos where he realized that ambition, being tonsured and taking the name Sava. Whether Nemanja then allowed his brother to regain his former Hum holdings or whether these were assigned to some appointee of Nemanja is not known. Miroslav continued to manage at least part of Hum until his death in about 1198, after which, according to various poor and unusually unspecific sources, most of which were written considerably later, various claimants struggled over Hum. Usually it is not stated how much of Hum any of them held or which parts they were seeking to gain.

Hungary immediately laid claim to Hum, considering it part of the Bosnian lands it claimed. Imre, King of Hungary, appointed his brother Andrew Duke of Croatia, Dalmatia, and Hum in 1198. Whether he was ever able to obtain actual control over any part of Hum is not certain. However, it seems likely that he acquired some of Hum, for a Hungarian charter refers to a military victory over Raška *and Hum.* Thus it seems he obtained part of Hum, presumably the region north and west of the Neretva extending up to the Cetina River. It is inconceivable that he acquired any of the region stretching east from the Neretva to the Serbian border.

If we can believe Orbini, who wrote a history of the Slavs in 1601, using an unknown source now lost, a ten-year-old son of Miroslav named Andrew (Andrej) succeeded Miroslav. No mention is made of Toljen, who was to have been Miroslav's heir back in 1189 when the marriage was negotiated between Toljen and the German crusader's daughter. Presumably this Andrew held Hum east of the Neretva while the Hungarians held the western part. Soon after Andrew's succession, according to Orbini, the nobles of Hum rose up and chose as their lord a prince born in Hum named Peter. Though Orbini does not make Peter a descendant of Miroslav, most scholars think he was actually Andrew's brother. When Peter came to power, Andrew and Miroslav's widow were exiled. And we have noted that Miroslav's widow did take up residence outside of Hum at the court of her brother, Ban Kulin of Bosnia. Andrew fled to Nemanja. Here Orbini's chronology is wrong and he shows this clearly when he proceeds to discuss Nemanja's war of 1190 with Byzantium. If, as seems reasonable, we place Andrew's flight after the deaths of Miroslav and Nemanja, then it was Nemanja's son Stefan who gave Andrew asylum.

Then Orbini, clearly allowing for a considerable passage of time, continues his narration by reporting that Peter controlled all of Hum and frequently fought successfully with the ruler of Bosnia and his Croatian neighbors, the latter presumably residing around and beyond the Cetina River. Next, after his accession to the throne Stefan of Raška took up Andrew's cause and attacked Peter in Hum. Peter was defeated, crossed the Neretva, and took control of that part of Hum beyond (west and north of) the Neretva. This, of course, is the part of Hum that Duke Andrew of Hungary would have held if he had assumed actual control over any part of Hum. Possibly Duke Andrew had held this territory only briefly and lost control over it when he became involved in a war with his brother, King Imre, in 1203. If Duke Andrew had been forced to withdraw from affairs in Hum, then Peter may have stepped into the power vacuum and assumed control over this part of Hum as well. This could explain Orbini's statement about Peter's fighting with his Bosnian and Croatian neighbors.

Having defeated Peter, Stefan gave most of Hum to his own son Radoslav; to his "nephew" (actually, his cousin) Andrew he gave only the district of Popovo and the coastal lands of Hum, including Ston. Soon thereafter, according to Orbini, when Radoslav died, this Andrew, with Stefan's agreement, took control of all Hum. Since in fact Radoslav did not die then but lived to succeed Stefan, something is clearly wrong here. Whether the statement is completely erroneous or whether Stefan for some other reason removed Radoslav from Hum and turned over all eastern Hum (i.e., up to the Neretva) to Andrew is not known.

Then, Orbini continues, some nobles and župans of Nevesinje revolted and placed themselves under the protection of the Ban of Bosnia, leaving Andrew only the coast with Ston and Popovo. Later Orbini returns to this event to say that the Bosnian ruler also acquired Dabar and Gacko. Whether Bosnia really acquired any of this territory at this time is unknown. Orbini also states that Peter retained the territory of Hum beyond the Neretva. Late in the second decade of the thirteenth century other sources mention a Peter as Prince of Hum, presumably the same figure Orbini spoke of. By then Peter seems to have had cordial relations with Serbia. How much of Hum Peter then controlled is not certain. Whether Andrew was still alive then is also unknown.

How much of Orbini's account can be believed is difficult to determine. One would expect Miroslav's heirs, supported by various of Miroslav's courtiers, to have tried to retain power. That two sons should have struggled over the inheritance would not have been strange either. Furthermore, Stefan of Raška, then striving to retain control over Zeta, could well have tried to step in to secure Raška's control over Hum and prevent it from seceding under its own dynasty of Miroslav's descendants. But it is unknown whether Stefan actually made any efforts in this direction and, if he did so, whether he at first supported one weak heir of Miroslav (to make into a pupper ruler) and subsequently, after he had installed his "legitimate" puppet, turned against him and put most of eastern Hum under closer Raškan control by installing there his own son Radoslav.

However, the establishment of his own son as ruler of Hum does seem the sort of policy we might expect Stefan to have aimed for, if he had had the power to carry it out. Thus we may conclude that what happened in Hum after Miroslav's death in about 1198 was roughly as follows: The Hungarian Duke Andrew tried to seize Hum. He won a victory over some Serbs in Hum in about 1198 and acquired that part of Hum lying northwest of the Neretva. He was either pushed out of this territory by Peter, probably a son of Miroslav who was supported by local nobles, or else was forced to withdraw his men from this part of Hum when war broke out in 1203 between him and his brother King Imre. In the second alternative, Peter probably simply assumed control of western Hum after Andrew's withdrawal. Next, Peter expelled his brother Andrew, who had succeeded in eastern Hum, from his lands. In this Peter was supported by various local nobles. Stefan of Raška then intervened on behalf of the expelled Andrew and regained Hum to the Neretva. This intervention may not have occurred until considerably later, possibly in about 1216. Stefan campaigned in the name of Andrew, thereby presumably acquiring support from some nobles of Hum, and, upon achieving victory, established him as a puppet prince. Then later, either because he then felt strong enough to do so or else because he felt the puppet arrangement was not going to succeed in closely binding Hum to Raška, Stefan removed Andrew from the lands of eastern Hum bordering on Serbia and installed his own governor there, quite possibly his son Radoslav. Andrew was left with only Popovo and Hum's coast. Whether Bosnia also intervened to pick off part of Hum is not known. Presumably Serbia retained control of this eastern territory thereafter, though we may imagine actual authority was in the hands of the local nobility. Soon Andrew disappeared from the scene, and Peter acquired Andrew's coastal and Popovo holdings, which he added to his holding between the Neretva and Cetina rivers. And it is there that we find Peter in about 1218.

Kalojan on the Eve of the Fourth Crusade

Kalojan, who, as we saw, annexed Niš from Serbia in 1203, was reaching the height of his power. Thus the Serbs were in no position to object to this annexation. Even after Stefan regained power, Raška probably remained in a position of some dependence upon Bulgaria until Kalojan died in 1207. Kalojan's armies were strong again. The Cumans' difficulties with the Russians were over and once again they were free to join Kalojan's armies, and many of them did so.

Soon Bulgarian troops moved north where they clashed with the Hungarians near the junction of the Danube and Morava. In 1202 they failed to take Braničevo. In 1203 Kalojan wrote to Pope Innocent III that Hungary held territory belonging to his state, surely a reference to Srem, Beograd, and Braničevo, which had belonged to the First Bulgarian State. That year Hungary found itself embroiled in a civil war, when Duke Andrew revolted against his brother, King Imre. It seems Kalojan took advantage of the Hungarians' difficulties to regain for Bulgaria Beograd, Braničevo, and Vidin, since all three fortresses are found in his possession in 1204. Kalojan installed a Bulgarian bishop in Braničevo. The Hungarian king protested to the pope about Kalojan's conquest of Beograd and Braničevo, but the pope, in the midst of discussions with Kalojan, in which he promised the Bulgarian a crown if he would recognize papal suzerainty, wanted to do nothing to threaten these delicate negotiations. Thus he showed little sympathy for Imre and in a letter of October 1204 ordered him to take no action against Bulgaria over these cities. The pope stated that he would consider mediating the problem later, but only after Kalojan's coronation. Imre complied and called off military preparations against Kalojan. The delay gained for him by the pope was useful to Kalojan, for it enabled him to consolidate his power in the region just south of the Danube.

Unlike the First Bulgarian State, Kalojan's state did not extend beyond the Danube, which he sought to establish as the border with Hungary. Thus it was important for him to possess and fortify strongly these major fortresses on the south side of the Danube. In the thirteenth century Vidin also rose to importance as a border fortress. Throughout the thirteenth century Bulgaria and Hungary were to remain rivals for these major cities on the south shore of the Danube, and were to fight a series of wars over them.

On 30 November 1204 King Imre of Hungary died. He tried to leave the throne to his five-year-old son, Ladislas. But within a year his brother Andrew had ousted the infant and established himself as king. Earlier that year, as we shall see, the Fourth Crusade had taken Constantinople. Kalojan took advantage of the chaos that followed this conquest to pick off much Byzantine territory in Macedonia and Thrace. In most of the towns he took he expelled the Greek bishops and replaced them with Slavs. Various Greeks in these cities whose loyalty he doubted found themselves transferred from their homes and resettled in Kalojan's Danubian lands. In this case, Kalojan was following a centuries-old Byzantine practice.

During the years just before the Fourth Crusade, Kalojan seems to have begun worrying whether the self-claimed crown he received from the hands of his own Archbishop of Trnovo really had legitimacy. The great powers (the papacy and Byzantium) believed that to have legitimacy a tsar's crown had to be granted by one or the other of them. Kalojan seems to have felt a need to have his crown confirmed by one of these two and to have decided the means to achieve this end was to play Byzantium and the papacy off against each other. He held out to the pope his willingness to recognize the pope as suzerain over the Bulgarian Church if he would send Kalojan a tsar's crown and award Bulgaria a patriarch; he also threatened the empire that if it did not recognize the titles he claimed, he would turn to Rome. Finally, after prolonged negotiations and after the crusaders' conquest of Constantinople, on 7 November 1204 Kalojan received a crown from a papal legate, a cardinal; at the time he officially recognized papal supremacy. However, following papal orders, the cardinal crowned Kalojan king and consecrated the Archbishop of Trnovo, whose autocephaly was recognized, as a "primate." Kalojan was told that the titles king and primate were more or less the same as the tsarist and patriarchal titles that he was seeking. Kalojan, slightly rebuffed, certainly not fooled, and by then on the verge of joining an anti-Latin coalition, ignored the fine distinctions explained by the cardinal and simply continued to call himself tsar and his bishop patriarch anyway.

The papacy seemed on the brink of phenomenal success: Bosnia had submitted and re-affirmed its loyalty to the pope in 1203. The ruler of Zeta had converted to Catholicism and had now conquered Raška, giving the pope optimism about converting that land. Bulgaria now seemed added to his fold. Furthermore, in 1204 the crusaders had taken Constantinople and established a Latin patriarch there, and during 1204 and particularly 1205 a Latin Church was being established throughout most of Greece in the wake of successful crusading armies. Thus the pope had reason to hope for the submission of the Greeks as well. It might well have seemed to optimists at the papacy that the Greeks and Orthodox South Slavs were on the verge of recognizing papal supremacy, and that the Schism of 1054 was about to be ended. Appearances, however, were misleading. Despite Kalojan's assurances, events soon swung the Bulgarian tsar into opposition to the crusaders and the whole Latin cause. And his submission to Rome faded from being nominal to becoming a dead letter. However, even had Kalojan's relations with the crusaders been cordial, it is unlikely that the papacy would have achieved any actual authority in Bulgaria. The Bulgarians were attached to their traditions and Kalojan was not a ruler to be dictated to. Presumably he would have resisted at the first sign of papal interference in the management of the Bulgarian state or Church. Moreover, as we shall see, it would take much more than the establishment of a Latin hierarchy in Greece to bring about the conversion of the Greeks. And finally, as seen, the Catholic candidate, Vukan, did not last as ruler of Raška. He was soon replaced by the Orthodox Stefan. Yet, even this change did not necessarily doom papal hopes for Raška's conversion, as Stefan remained for a considerable time (until 1219) quite willing to negotiate with Rome.

GENERAL NOTES

Certain general histories of medieval states and regions contributed in a major way to this chapter and the subsequent chapters of this work. It seems fitting to acknowledge their contribution once at the outset and thereafter cite them only if specific reference is relevant to a discussion of a controversial point.

Albania
A. Ducellier, *La Façade maritime de l'Albanie au moyen âge: Durazzo et Valona du XIᵉ au XVᵉ siècle* (Thessaloniki, 1981).

Bosnia
S. Ćirković, *Istorija srednjovekovne bosanske države* (Beograd, 1964).
D. Kovačević-Kojić, *Gradska naselja srednjovekovne bosanske države* (Sarajevo, 1978).

Bulgaria
K. Jireček, *Istorija na B"lgarite* (1876; reprint, Sofija, 1978).
P. Mutafčiev, *Istorija na b"lgarskija narod*, pt. 2 (Sofija, 1944). Mutafčiev died before completing the work and I. Dujčev wrote the concluding section, covering the period 1323–93.

Byzantine Empire
D. Nicol, *The Last Centuries of Byzantium, 1261–1453* (New York, 1972).
G. Ostrogorsky, *History of the Byzantine State*, 3d ed. (New Brunswick, N.J., 1969).

Croatia
N. Klaić, *Povijest Hrvata u razvijenom srednjem vijeku* (Zagreb, 1976).
V. Klaić, *Povijest Hrvata*, 5 vols. (1899–1911; reprint, Zagreb, 1982).
F. Šišić, *Pregled povijesti hrvatskoga naroda* (1920; reprint, Zagreb, 1975).

Greece (as a whole)
N. Cheetham, *Mediaeval Greece* (New Haven, 1981).
G. Finlay, *A History of Greece*, rev. ed., vols. 3–4 (Oxford, 1877).
W. Miller, *The Latins in the Levant: A History of Frankish Greece (1204–1566)* (London, 1908).
W. Miller, *Essays on the Latin Orient* (Cambridge, 1921).

Epirus
D. Nicol, *The Despotate of Epirus* (Oxford, 1957).
D. Nicol, *The Despotate of Epiros, 1267–1479* (Cambridge, 1984).

The Peloponnesus (Morea)
D. Zakythinos, *Le Despotat Grec de Morée*, 2 vols. (Athens, 1932, 1953).

Thessaly
B. Ferjančić, *Tesalija u XIII i XIV veku*, Serbian Academy of Sciences (SAN) Vizantološki institut, Monograph no. 15 (Beograd, 1974).

Hum (to 1326 see histories of Serbia; after 1326 see histories of Bosnia)

Serbia
Istorija srpskog naroda, vols. 1–2 (Beograd, 1981–82). A collective work published by Srpska književna zadruga.
K. Jireček, *Istorija Srba*, trans. into Serbo-Croatian and updated by J. Radonić, 2 vols. (Beograd, 1952).

Zeta (Duklja, Montenegro)
Istorija Crne Gore, vol. 2, pts. 1–2 (Titograd, 1970). A collective work. Vol. 2
covers the period from the end of the twelfth to the end of the fifteenth century.

NOTES TO CHAPTER 1

1. For the period to the 1180s, see J. Fine, *The Early Medieval Balkans* (Ann Arbor,
Mich., 1983).
2. D. N. Anastasijević (*Otac Nemanjin* [Beograd, 1914]) makes the best case against
the view presented above. Arguing that the term *brat* (brother) can also mean a cousin,
he suggests that Miroslav and Nemanja may have been first cousins. In that case Zavid
need not have been Nemanja's father but instead could have been his uncle. Then he
turns to Stefan the First-Crowned's *Life of Saint Simeon* (i.e., Nemanja), which, after
describing Nemanja's father's flight from Raška to Zeta, states that after Nemanja's
birth in Zeta the father returned to the "stol'noje mesto" (literally, "the place of the
throne"). Anastasijević believes that this phrase refers to the throne itself and thus that
Nemanja's father returned to rule. Thus he in fact had been a ruler of Serbia. He then
concludes that Nemanja's father was Desa. However, it seems to me that this statement could just as well mean that he returned to the capital as a place and need not
imply he returned to become the actual ruler. Moreover, if Nemanja's father had been
Desa (or any other Serbian Grand župan) one would expect one of our sources to have
stated it directly.
3. V. Foretić, "Ugovor Dubrovnika sa Srpskim Velikim županom Stefanom Nemanjom i stara Dubrovačka djedina," *Rad* (JAZU) 283 (1951): 51–118.
4. This section—and subsequent sections on Byzantine politics and Byzantine relations with Bulgaria and with various Bulgarian and Vlach chieftains in Thrace—is
indebted to C. Brand, *Byzantium Confronts the West, 1180–1204* (Cambridge, Mass.,
1968).
5. P. Mutafčiev, "Proizhod"t na Asenovci," in P. Mutafčiev, *Izbrani proizvedenija,*
vol. 2 (Sofija, 1973), pp. 150–94.
6. I. Dujčev, "V"stanieto v 1185 g. i negovata hronologija," *Izvestija na Instituta za
B"lgarska istorija* (BAN) 6 (1956): 327–56.
7. J. Resti, *Chronica Ragusina ab origine urbis usque ad annum 1451,* ed. S. Nodilo,
JAZU, MSHSM 25, Scriptores 2 (Zagreb, 1893), p. 63.
8. This section is greatly indebted to J. Herrin, "Realities of Byzantine Provincial
Government: Hellas and Peloponnesos, 1180–1205," *Dumbarton Oaks Papers* 29
(1975): 255–84.
9. In the early Middle Ages the region we are calling Zeta and which subsequently
became Montenegro was called Duklja (derived from Dioclea). Vukan, possibly to
justify his royal title from possession of the former kingdom of Duklja, called his state
Dalmatia and Duklja (Dioclea). And the name Duklja-Dioclea lasted for some time
among intellectuals. However, the name Zeta, originally referring to a county within
Zeta, came more and more in this period to be used for the whole area that had been

Duklja. Zeta, though occasionally still used for the county, had become the regular term used for the region in Serbian and Ragusan/Dalmatian documents. Thus I shall use the name Zeta for this region throughout my work, unless a different term is relevant to a particular moment, event, or claim.

CHAPTER 2

The Fourth Crusade and its Aftermath

Background for the Fourth Crusade

During the last decades of the twelfth century tensions had increased between East and West. They resulted from increased contacts as greater numbers of Westerners appeared in the East, including crusaders, Western mercenaries, and Venetian and other Italian merchants. These tensions led to various incidents that in turn led to more serious major events: the 1171 mass arrest of Venetians throughout the empire followed by over a decade of war between Venice and Byzantium; the 1182 massacre of Westerners (particularly Italians) residing in Constantinople by the local population preceding Andronicus' takeover; the 1185 massacre-sack of Thessaloniki by the Normans; and the near assault on Constantinople by Frederick Barbarossa's Third Crusade in 1189. Increased contacts engendered feelings of hostility over differences in customs and among Greeks produced jealousy of the Westerners who were favored by the last Comnenus emperors and of the Italians who had acquired dominance over Byzantine commerce and naval defense. Thus friction was common between foreign and local merchants as well as between Greek and Latin priests over differences in ritual. Rome, moreover, applied steady pressure on the East to accept Church Union under an autocratic pope. It seemed probable that it was only a matter of time before the West attacked schismatic and (probably more important) wealthy Constantinople.

After Isaac II was overthrown and blinded in 1195, Frederick's successor Henry VI threatened to intervene to avenge Isaac, with whom Frederick had been bound by treaty. It was necessary to buy Henry off; to do so Alexius III had had to levy a special "German" tax, which still failed to raise the exorbitant amount Henry was demanding. Henry began preparing to attack Constantinople; the pope sought to dissuade him since he preferred a campaign to recover Jerusalem that would be indefinitely delayed should the crusaders attack Constantinople instead. Henry then died in 1197, and the empire was spared from his threatened attack. Innocent III, who became pope in 1198, however, immediately upon his succession began pressing for a full-scale crusade to the East. His objective too was Jerusalem. But he also wanted the Byzantine Empire to submit to the papacy and recognize papal supremacy on his terms and thereby unite the Churches, after which the Eastern and Western Christians could mount a joint crusade against Muslim-held Jerusalem.

The Venetian doge Dandolo, over eighty and blind, became one of the prime movers for the crusade, but one who never lost sight of Venice's material interests. He hated the Byzantines and felt that Venetian trade was in danger as long as the empire survived. He feared that at any time some emperor might repeat the 1171 arrests and property seizures. Furthermore, in an attempt to escape from Venice's stranglehold on its economy, trade, and naval defense, the empire had been granting privileges to other Italian cities—Genoa and Pisa, Venice's rivals. A conquest of Constantinople by a Venetian-led crusade could give Venice a monopoly over Eastern trade. Thus the Germans, Normans, and Venetians, the manpower being mobilized for the new crusade, were all hostile to Byzantium.

Venice rapidly acquired a leading role in the crusade through its role in transport. After the failures of recent crusades that had taken the overland route across Anatolia, a territory divided between the empire and various Muslim states, it made sense to travel to the Holy Land by sea. Venice, however, expected the other crusaders to pay their passage. Not surprisingly, the crusaders did not have the cash to pay Venice's high prices; so, unknown to the pope, Venice sought services in lieu of the debt. The first service demanded was the recovery of Zadar from Hungary for Venice. The Hungarians had retaken this Dalmatian city from Venice in 1181. That the King of Hungary was a Catholic who had already agreed to go as a crusader to the Holy Land himself was immaterial. So, the crusaders, aboard Venetian ships, sailed up to the walls of Zadar. Its citizens, also Catholic (though some accounts try to give the impression that Zadar was a hotbed of heresy—a heresy whose nature is not specified) hung their walls with crosses. In November 1202 the crusaders took Zadar, turned the city over to Venice, and spent winter 1202–03 there.

Meanwhile, in 1201 the son of the blinded Isaac II Angelus, named Alexius (and referred to as the Young Alexius to distinguish him from his uncle who then ruled the empire) had escaped from Constantinople. He headed west, trying to mobilize support to restore his father and himself to the throne. He talked to the German emperor, who was non-committal, and to the pope, who was opposed because he did not want any diversion to delay the campaign for Jerusalem. In fact, Innocent forbade any action by the crusaders against Constantinople. But the Doge of Venice jumped at the chance; he agreed to restore Isaac and Young Alexius to the throne in exchange for a huge cash pay-off to be delivered upon their restoration. Furthermore, to placate the pope the doge insisted that Young Alexius agree to reunite the Churches and then to add Byzantine forces to the crusading armies when they moved on to the Holy Land. The crusaders, easily persuaded by the huge pay-off, sailed to Constantinople, arriving there in July 1203. Having bungled the city's defenses,

Alexius III panicked and fled on 17 July 1203, taking most of the state treasury and crown jewels with him. A coup in the city hauled Isaac out of prison and put him back on the throne.

The Conquest of Constantinople by the Crusaders

The Young Alexius (now Alexius IV) and his blind, and it seems also senile, father Isaac mounted the throne as co-emperors. The crusaders remained camped outside the walls waiting for their puppet to deliver the goods. Soon it became clear that Alexius IV's looted treasury did not contain the amount promised. The crusaders refused to reduce their price. Moreover, the population of Constantinople was still strongly anti-Latin and had no desire to unite the Churches. Having reached an impasse, the crusaders issued an ultimatum that Alexius deliver on his promises immediately or else they would re-take the city. The populace got wind of the situation and, already angry at Alexius IV for bringing the crusaders thither, in January 1204 engineered a counter-revolution. They murdered Alexius IV, and the anti-Latin party came to power installing its leader Alexius V Murtzuphlus as the new emperor. Various incidents followed between Greeks and Latins, including the murder of some Latins in the city, until finally matters came to a head and the crusaders took the city on 13 April 1204. They massacred a large portion of its population and thoroughly looted the city, whose treasures, accumulated over nearly a thousand years, were seized and many of which were taken back west.

The conquest followed an agreement among the crusaders as to how they were to partition the empire. Having taken Constantinople, the crusaders then set about carrying out its terms. However, most of the empire was still in the hands of the Byzantines. Thus a man awarded a given territory usually had to capture it. In some instances, when this proved impossible, various adjustments of the treaty had to be made.

The crusader agreement divided both the empire and the city of Constantinople into eighths. The new Latin emperor was to obtain a fourth of the city and a fourth of the empire, including eastern Thrace, vital for the defense of the capital. Venice acquired a fourth of Constantinople and three-eighths of the empire, including most of Epirus. Venice immediately adjusted its acquisitions, trading most of its inland territories for a series of islands and ports. Thus acquiring dominance over ports throughout the empire, Venice came to control the waterway between Venice and Constantinople. It also gained a trade monopoly in these ports. The other Italian cities were excluded from trade with the empire, now called by scholars the Latin Empire of Constantinople. The final three-eighths was divided into fiefs assigned to the leading knights. Needless to say, many of these fiefs existed only on paper, because most of this territory remained—and was to remain—in the hands of Greeks or was to be picked off by Kalojan of Bulgaria.

The negotiators consisted of two parties, the Venetians and the knights. They agreed that whichever party did not obtain the throne should have the patriarchate. Since the knights obtained the throne for one of their number,

Baldwin of Flanders, the Venetians received control of the Church. They appointed Thomas Morosini as Patriarch of Constantinople. To try to placate the pope, Thomas immediately declared the Union of the Churches. This policy was to be enforced in Constantinople and wherever else the crusaders were able to acquire control. Needless to say, the Greeks throughout the East did not recognize this union, and though some in conquered cities grudgingly accepted it, many others did not.

Boniface of Montferrat, the most powerful knight, had hoped to become emperor. To advance his claims he had, after the conquest, married Margaret, the daughter of Bela III of Hungary and the widow of Isaac II. Opposed by Venice and a minority of the knights, he lost the throne to Baldwin who then assigned Boniface a large fief in Anatolia. However, Boniface wanted a fief in Europe and demanded Thessaloniki, which he claimed as a family right: His brother Renier, having served Emperor Manuel Comnenus, had married the emperor's daughter; as a result Manuel had granted Renier the title caesar and a large estate in the territory of Thessaloniki. At first Baldwin agreed, but soon he reconsidered and took Thessaloniki before Boniface could arrive there. Furious, Boniface took Demotika (Didymotichus), one of Baldwin's cities, and besieged Adrianople. Peace was soon mediated and Baldwin exchanged Thessaloniki for Demotika. Now, as King of Thessaloniki Boniface set about creating his own state in the region of Thessaloniki, which he extended northward into Macedonia and southward into Thessaly.

Many knights received fiefs in Anatolia. Some set out to try to obtain them; others, annoyed and pessimistic about their chances of acquiring them, simply remained in Constantinople and griped. The Latins practiced subinfeudation; this meant that many knights did not obtain their fiefs from, and therefore owe their service to, the emperor directly, but instead received fiefs from, and owed service to, intermediate lords like Boniface. As a result, the Latin Empire was to be weak militarily. For if the intermediate lord did not answer a call from the emperor, then the lord's knights did not either. Baldwin immediately suffered from this system. For Boniface and his men, no longer in the capital, were not available either to defend it or to contribute to Baldwin's campaigns to expand his or his knights' holdings in Thrace or Anatolia. Baldwin was obliged to campaign in Anatolia to win the lands assigned to his knights, but without the help of Boniface and his men Baldwin's chances of success were slight. And Boniface, angry at being passed over for emperor, was not to be the most faithful vassal and moreover had no interest in Anatolia. His ambition was to acquire Thessaly and the regions south of it and attach these lands to his own kingdom as fiefs for his own servitors. So instead of helping Baldwin acquire Bithynia across the straits from Constantinople in Anatolia, vitally important for the security of Latin rule in Constantinople, Boniface mobilized his men and marched south into Thessaly leaving his wife to govern Thessaloniki.

Meanwhile, after the fall of Constantinople in April 1204, the former emperor Alexius III eventually made his way to eastern Thessaly where his wife Evrosina's family had large estates. Presumably he hoped to establish a base of resistance in this region. At Larissa he came into contact with Leo Sgouros, who, having taken Thebes and most of Attica and Boeotia, was pressing north into Thessaly. The two formed an alliance, probably early in 1205, and Sgouros married Alexius' daughter Eudocia, the former wife of Stefan of Serbia.

Boniface's Conquests and his Vassals

In the fall of 1204 Boniface and his knights advanced through Thessaly without meeting any opposition to speak of. And since the cities did not resist, none suffered sacks or massacres as Constantinople had. Sgouros, realizing he was no match for the crusading army, fell back before it, eventually establishing a short-lived defense at the Isthmus of Corinth. In the course of his southward march Boniface captured Alexius III, who had been with Sgouros' army. In October and November 1204 Boniface overran and conquered Boeotia, Euboea, and Attica. He took Thebes (probably Greece's largest city at the time) and Athens, which until then, under the command of its archbishop Michael Choniates, had been under constant pressure and siege from Sgouros. Athens was surrendered by Michael. Boniface turned its churches over to the Latin clergy, who established a Latin archbishopric there. Michael soon left his city for an island exile. Boniface installed a garrison in Athens and then launched his offensive against the Isthmus of Corinth, which was defended by Sgouros, who drove back Boniface's first attack. Boniface's second attack, however, broke through, and soon—probably by January 1205—he had taken most of the northeastern corner of the Peloponnesus, except for the cities of Argos, Nauplia, and Corinth, all of which he besieged. The siege of Corinth, defended by Sgouros, was to last five years. When it finally fell neither Boniface nor Sgouros was alive any longer. Boniface, as we shall see, was to be killed in 1207, and in 1208 Sgouros, losing all hope, was to make a suicidal leap on horseback at full gallop from the heights of Acrocorinth.

As he marched through Thessaly, Boniface expanded his own kingdom and assigned most of the lands he captured in central Greece as fiefs to his followers.[1] Thus he succeeded in hacking out an independent, self-supporting kingdom that needed no help from Baldwin; moreover, being involved in his own affairs, he had little time for or interest in giving Baldwin the assistance he needed. With his Greek ties Boniface made serious efforts to attract the support of the Greek population. As he marched through Thessaly he won acceptance from various Greeks of good family.

Most scholars believe that Boniface assigned Boeotia (including Thebes), Attica (including Athens), the region of Opuntian Lokris to the north of Boeotia, and the Megarid to one of his leading knights, Othon de la Roche of Burgundy. Othon took the title Lord of Athens and paid homage to Boniface for his extensive fief. By the end of the century Othon's descendants had acquired the title of duke. This Burgundian duchy was to survive for over a century until conquered by the Catalans in 1311. Though usually called the

Duchy of Athens, the state's capital was Thebes throughout both the Burgundian and Catalan periods.[2] This feudal state, having a large Jewish commercial colony, was a rich center of industry (particularly textiles) and of commerce. Othon soon was to grant privileges to the Genoese, who thus obtained a foothold in Greece, most of which was then falling under Venetian dominance, if not monopoly. In addition, the plain of Boeotia was a fertile grain-growing region. Othon expelled the Greek bishops and supported the newly established Latin archbishops in Athens and Thebes. The major churches and monasteries, together with their estates, were turned over to the Catholics. The famous monastery church of Daphne was granted to the Cistercians. Most of the major fiefs that Othon assigned within his principality were granted to his own relatives. Thus he had more authority over his state than the Villehardouins—whom we shall soon meet—in the Morea (Peloponnesus), whose prince had to govern in association with the leading barons.

Euboea was assigned by Boniface to three noblemen of Verona to hold in fief. Of the three Ravano dalle Carceri was the most prominent. Thus all Greece east of the Pindus range and north of the Gulf of Corinth recognized Boniface's overlordship.

The Greek State of Epirus

While the Latins were moving from success to success and taking control of eastern Greece, the Greeks were to succeed in maintaining themselves in western Greece, where they established a strong state. Usually referred to as Epirus, which made up the bulk of the state, its territory for most of its existence also included Acarnania and Aetolia to the south of Epirus. Thus it comprised most of western Greece. This state was established by a certain Michael Comnenus Ducas. He seems to have been a son of Sebastocrator John, who was an uncle of Isaac II Angelus. John, as noted, had played a major role at court. Michael had risen to fairly high positions in the military administration under Isaac but then had fallen on hard times under Alexius and, having tried unsuccessfully to lead an uprising against Alexius, had fled to the Sultan of Iconium. In 1204 he seems to have been in Constantinople and amenable to co-operating with the Latin conquerors. Thus when Boniface left the capital to assert control over Thessaloniki, Michael had joined his suite. He then, according to the historian Villehardouin, joined Boniface in his march through Thessaly. In the course of this campaign Michael deserted and went to Arta in Epirus, where the Byzantine governor, not wanting to submit to the crusaders, was preparing Arta's defense. Michael then, according to this account, married the governor's daughter. Almost immediately the governor died, and Michael succeeded to his territory. Soon his authority was recognized in western Greece from Durazzo (though not including the city itself, which had been taken by Venice in July 1205) down to Naupaktos (Lepanto) on the Gulf of Corinth. Thus he succeeded in creating a Greek state in this region before any crusaders had tried to take Epirus.

A second account, from the end of the thirteenth century (the *Life of*

Saint Theodora Petraliphina of Arta), states that Alexius III sent Michael to govern the Peloponnesus. At that time the provinces north of the Gulf of Corinth, Aetolia and the Theme of Nikopolis (including Epirus), had been assigned to a governor named Senacherim. He and Michael had married first cousins, girls from the Melissenos family. After the fall of Constantinople in 1204 some locals revolted against Senacherim, who appealed to Michael. Michael responded, but before he could reach Arta the rebels had killed Senacherim. Michael arrived, put down the rebellion, punished the murderers, and, being by then a widower, married Senacherim's widow. As a result he inherited Senacherim's domains, which, with the fall of the Greek empire, seem to have become the private holding of Senacherim. Thus Michael obtained the government of Epirus. Soon he ransomed off—from a Genoese to whom he had been turned over—Alexius III, who had been taken captive by Boniface in his Thessalian campaign. Alexius supposedly then confirmed Michael in his rule over western Greece. Much of this account—that Michael was imperially appointed to govern the Peloponnesus, came to Epirus to aid a second imperially appointed governor, and was confirmed in his rule of Epirus by Alexius III—may well be fiction invented to provide Michael and his family with a legitimate claim to rule this region. Thus probably the first and earlier account by Villehardouin is the more reliable one, though it seems likely that Michael did in fact pay the ransom for Alexius.

Having acquired control of western Greece, Michael left the existing local Byzantine administration in office and the local Greeks in possession of their lands. Then he built up the armed forces of the region. He thus established a principality of considerable size and strength in which life continued much as it had previously under the empire. In fact life probably improved, for the region's taxes, no longer siphoned off to Constantinople, remained to be used at home. The rugged mountains of the region helped Michael to prepare the defense of his lands against crusader attack. He maintained good relations with the Albanian and Vlach chieftains in the area, and their men provided able troops for his army.

Shortly after Michael achieved control of Epirus, the Greeks of Sparta and Arcadia were attacked by the crusader forces of Villehardouin and William of Champlitte, whom we shall meet next. It is usually stated by scholars that these Greeks then sought aid from Michael, who in 1205 led an army under his own command into the Peloponnesus, suffered a defeat, and returned to Epirus, leaving the crusaders to overcome the remnants of Greek resistance in the Peloponnesus and take the whole peninsula. Recently Loenertz has raised doubts about this commonly held view.[3] Loenertz believes that Michael would not have gone to the Peloponnesus then, since in 1205 he still had not established himself securely in control of Epirus. Furthermore, had he at that time left Epirus with his army, it would have been an open invitation for Boniface to attack Epirus. Boniface, whom Michael had just deserted, presumably would have borne a strong grudge against Michael and have been waiting for such a chance to attack him. Michael of Epirus may have intervened in the Peloponnesus later, at some time between the fall of

1207 and May 1209. Loenertz thus wonders whether the account of the 1205 intervention, which was written later, either pushed up the date of that intervention or confused a different Michael who was a Greek leader in 1205 with Michael of Epirus. In any case Loenertz concludes that the Michael who led the opposition to Villehardouin in 1205 was a local Peloponnesian; Michael of Epirus, he argues, did not intervene then at all, though he may have launched a brief and unsuccessful attack (to be discussed below) against the Peloponnesus several years later.

Loenertz also believes that the Theodore who was to lead the defense of Acrocorinth after Sgouros' suicide was not, as is usually held, Michael of Epirus' brother Theodore, but a second individual of that name. For, he argues, evidence exists to show that Michael's brother Theodore remained in Anatolia until 1205, when Michael of Epirus summoned him. It would make no sense for Theodore to leave Anatolia to answer this call only to shut himself up for several years in a doomed fortress which had no connection with Michael's holdings.

Thus if Loenertz is correct, Michael spent the first years of his reign in Epirus actively consolidating control over his own principality. His major concern had to be Venice, which had been assigned all Epirus in the 1204 partition treaty. The existence of this Venetian threat would have supplied a further reason for Michael not to have left Epirus for the Peloponnesus in 1205. In 1205 Venice also had acquired possession of Durazzo, the chief port for the northern Epirote-Albanian hinterland. To try to secure himself from attack by either the Latin Empire or Venice, Michael entered into negotiations with the pope, seeking papal protection by declaring himself willing to discuss Church Union. In this way he bought time.[4]

Eventually, in the summer of 1209, Michael made a treaty with the Latin Empire, sealed with a marriage between Michael's daughter and the brother of Emperor Henry (Baldwin's successor). This obligation was to mean little to Michael, for later, probably in 1210, when Henry went to war against the Greeks of the Nicean empire in Anatolia, Michael attacked Thessaloniki; his action angered Henry because Thessaloniki was then ruled by a government installed by and loyal to Henry. Henry soon was to attack Michael, forcing Michael to retreat. Loenertz wonders if Henry might not have had some Peloponnesian vassals in the army with which he relieved Thessaloniki. If so, this could explain a reference in the letter of Pope Innocent III of 31 October 1210 to Moreots (Peloponnesians) fighting Michael. If this should be the true explanation, then Michael may never have attacked the Peloponnesus and Innocent's reference to Moreots fighting Michael may have referred to them acting against him elsewhere. Otherwise, we should probably accept the commonly held view that Michael attacked the Peloponnesus without success at some time between 1207 and 1209, after the Franks had established themselves there.

The pope excommunicated Michael for this attack on Thessaloniki; the pope's action had little effect, however, because the two Churches were not united in Michael's state. And even though Michael employed various Westerners in his army, they did not seem troubled by the excommunication either.

Shortly thereafter Michael entered into negotiations with Venice, and on 20 June 1210 he concluded a treaty with Venice that recognized Venetian overlordship over his lands—an overlordship which was to remain nominal— and granted Venice the right of free trade throughout his realm. This right was of course Venice's primary concern. In this way Michael eliminated any cause that Venice might have had to attack him and thus gained for Epirus security from that potential danger.

In 1212 Michael invaded Thessaly and captured Larissa, thereby cutting off the Kingdom of Thessaloniki from the Burgundian state of Athens. Taking much of central Thessaly and expelling various Lombard fief-holders, Michael acquired a firm foothold in Thessaly. Then in 1213 he violated his agreement with Venice and captured Durazzo. In 1214 he conquered Corfu from Venice, whose forces had taken the island in 1207 after overcoming stout resistance by the Corfiots. Soon Michael began pressing northward into southern Macedonia and Albania. He conquered Kroja, and its lord Dimitri, having lost his lands, is heard of no more in surviving sources. Michael then tried to push up the coast into Zeta. He succeeded in taking Skadar, but his attempt to press beyond Skadar was stopped by the Serbs and by his own death. For late in 1214 or in 1215 Michael was murdered by a servant whose motives are not known. He was succeeded by his half-brother Theodore who had originally fled from Byzantium to Nicea but subsequently, in 1205, had come to Epirus at Michael's request. The Niceans had permitted his departure after extracting from him an oath of loyalty to Theodore Lascaris of Nicea. Once he took power in Epirus Theodore soon forgot his oath. Theodore's rule in Epirus will be discussed in the next chapter.

Thus in the last years of his reign Michael had significantly expanded the boundaries of his state. Theodore was to increase them still further. Epirus had considerable vitality and good prospects for the future. Many Greeks came thither to serve him. Thus his state was coming to be a serious threat to the ambitions of Nicea and a second potential base from which the Greeks might hope to recover Constantinople. However, under Michael no serious rivalry developed with Nicea. Only under Michael's successor Theodore, who dreamed of obtaining Constantinople and becoming its emperor, did Epirus begin to question the theoretical foundations of the Nicean state, i.e., Nicea's claims to have transferred to itself the empire, the patriarchate, and the right of jurisdiction over the Greek churches in western Greece.

Though modern historians frequently call Michael a despot and his state the Despotate of Epirus, this nomenclature is wrong. Only Western sources— and none earlier than the fourteenth century—refer to Michael as a despot. They claim Michael received the despot's title from Alexius III when he came to Epirus after Michael ransomed him. Since the title despot must be granted by an emperor, Michael could have obtained the title in this way. However, no contemporary source ever calls Michael a despot; he seems to have called himself simply governor or lord of his principality. In fact no ruler of Epirus was to bear the title of despot until the 1230s when Michael II of Epirus received the title, probably from Manuel of Thessaloniki. Soon after, in 1242, Thessaloniki's Greek ruler John submitted to Nicea and received the title of despot from the Emperor John Vatatzes. This title reflected John's submission and his rank in the Nicean court hierarchy and had nothing to do with his position as ruler of any territory. Thus there never was a despot of Epirus and the state was never a despotate. Even after 1236 and 1242 when some rulers in western Greece bore the title despot, it still would be incorrect to call them despots *of* Epirus. This fact has been demonstrated clearly by Ferjančić's fine study on Byzantine and Balkan despots[5] which appeared after Nicol's excellent major work on Epirus was published. Nicol's work, unfortunately written prior to the clarification of this title, not only erred in its discussion on the use of titles but even bore the incorrect title, *The Despotate of Epirus.*[6]

Villehardouin in the Morea

Meanwhile Geoffrey Villehardouin, the nephew of the chronicler, was in Syria as part of the crusading force. Hearing of the capture of Constantinople, he decided to sail west to get in on the spoils. He was blown off course and landed in November 1204 at Modon (Methone) in the southern Peloponnesus. He and his followers at once began to hack out their own state. At first Geoffrey's efforts were made easier by his entering into an alliance with a Greek archon (nobleman) from Messenia in the same general region, whose name has not survived but who had similar ambitions. Finlay believes the initiative was the Greek's and Geoffrey and his retinue were first hired as retainers by the Greek. Almost immediately afterward the Greek died; his son, not partial to the Latins and not wishing to share the territory they were subduing, broke off the alliance.

   Geoffrey, meanwhile, hearing of Boniface's arrival in the northeastern Peloponnesus, rode up early in 1205 to join him at his siege of Nauplia. Boniface greeted him warmly. Geoffrey soon persuaded him that even though the northeastern part of the Peloponnesus was offering resistance the rest of the peninsula was ripe for the picking. Boniface thereupon appointed one of his leading vassals, William (Guillaume) de Champlitte, to hold the Peloponnesus as a fief from Boniface. Villehardouin then paid homage to William and the two, with one hundred knights given them by Boniface plus each leader's own personal retinue, set off to conquer the rest of the Peloponnesus. They took Patras easily, then moved west along the north coast and then south along the west coast of the peninsula, obtaining submission from the Greek lords of Elis and Messenia, who, having submitted, were allowed to keep their lands, probably as fiefs from the new conquerors. William went out of his way to assure the Greek landlords that he was not opposed to them and that if they submitted, they could retain their lands and privileges. Thus the conquerors met with very little resistance from the Greeks.

   Only in Arcadia were the crusaders resisted. This opposition was led by landlords from Arcadia and Laconia (particularly the Chamaretos family) allied to the Slavic Melingi tribe. The resistance was soon joined by a certain Michael who, though most scholars believe he was, may or may not have been the Michael who was then creating his own principality in Epirus. The opposing forces met at Koundoura in northeast Messenia where the well-armed, well-disciplined Franks won an overwhelming victory over the much more numerous Greek forces. Villehardouin, the historian, claims the Greeks outnumbered the Latins ten to one. After this William and Geoffrey met no more serious resistance. Michael ceased to be a factor in Peloponnesian politics. If in fact he was Michael of Epirus, his disappearance is explained by the fact that he returned home. William subdued the rest of Arcadia, while Geoffrey took Kalamata. William then assigned Kalamata and Messenia to Geoffrey as a fief. By the end of the fall of 1205 William, having taken almost all the Peloponnesus, had assumed with Boniface's blessing the title Prince of Achaea. The name was derived from the region of Achaea in the northwestern part of the peninsula, one of the first regions they had subdued. The Achaea in the prince's title, however, was to refer to the whole Peloponnesus, and subsequently to whatever parts of the peninsula were held by William's and Geoffrey's successors.

In all these conquests in Greece, whether Boniface's or William's and Geoffrey's, no opposition was met from any official Byzantine governor or force. The limited resistance that was offered came from certain Greek magnates and their private retinues. The majority of the landlords, however, preferred to submit and thus retain their lands and privileges as semi-autonomous vassals of the conquerors rather than resist and risk losing everything. Having only limited manpower, the Franks were quite willing to receive them. William and Geoffrey endeavored to discipline their followers to prevent pillaging and to maintain order, which encouraged the local Greeks to accept them. The crusaders lost nothing by guaranteeing these Greeks in their possessions, for there was plenty of other land for the Franks to take for themselves, including imperial lands, the lands of Greeks who had fled or refused to submit, and the land of absentee Greek landlords. Among the important Greek families who were not present to deal with the crusaders when they arrived and who prior to 1204 had possessed huge estates in the Peloponnesus were the Cantacuzenus and Branas families. By making many Greeks into allies the Franks were spared a prolonged state of war. The co-opting of Greek leaders not only prevented them from leading revolts but also increased the forces available to carry out further conquests under crusader command and to suppress the resistance that did exist. But it should be stressed that the small number of crusaders could not have taken the Peloponnesus so easily, if at all, had the Greeks put up serious resistance. However, most of the native population seems not to have involved itself and thus allowed the crusaders to take over by default. The Byzantine policy of preventing revolts and secession by not arming or recruiting the local population for military service aided the Franks in their conquest.

Finlay concludes: "Under such circumstances, it need not surprise us to learn that the little army of Champlitte subdued the Greeks with as much ease as the band of Cortes conquered the Mexicans; for the bravest men, not habituated to the use of arms, and ignorant how to range themselves on the field of battle or behind the leaguered rampart, can do little to avert the catastrophe of their country's ruin."[7] And on the Franks' positive contribution to the local populace Finlay states,

> Anarchy and civil war had commenced. Champlitte assured the inhabitants of the Peloponnesus that he came among them as a prince determined to occupy the vacant sovereignty [vacant from the fall of Constantinople] and not as a passing conqueror bent on pillage. He offered terms of peace that put an end to all grounds of hostility; while the continuance of war would expose them to certain ruin, as the invading army must then be maintained by plunder. The Greek people, destitute of military leaders, freed from alarm by the small number of the French troops, and confiding in the strict military discipline that prevailed in their camp, submitted to a domination which did not appear likely to become very burdensome.[8]

Early in 1206 the Venetians, in a move to secure control of the key ports between Italy and Constantinople, seized Modon and Coron (Korone), expelling the Frankish garrisons and demanding that their right to the ports—granted to them by the 1204 partition treaty—be recognized. Since the garrisons were referred to as "pirates," Loenertz wonders if they were not manned by Genoese who had been allied with Geoffrey; their support of him could well have been suppressed by subsequent writers, leading to their being so labeled owing to Venice's hostility toward Genoa. Geoffrey, realizing that it made no sense to involve himself in a war with Venice, acquiesced, and William compensated Geoffrey by assigning him Arcadia. Geoffrey paid homage to the doge for the parts of the Morea he still held that the partition treaty had assigned to Venice. He also gave Venice the right to free trade throughout the Morea. Though Geoffrey's relations with Venice may have been basically settled in 1206, Setton believes the actual treaty that legally established these relations was not signed by Venice and Geoffrey until June 1209.

Late in 1208, William de Champlitte heard of the death of his older brother in Burgundy and returned home to France to claim the family lands. He left Geoffrey as acting bailiff (bailie) to administer Achaea (i.e., the whole principality) until William's nephew Hugh should arrive to replace Geoffrey as bailiff. Thus Geoffrey took over the actual administration of the Peloponnesus. William, however, died en route home and Hugh died shortly thereafter, so Geoffrey became the titular bailiff. According to the story, the new Champlitte heir, named Robert, had a year and a day to travel to the Peloponnesus and claim his inheritance. Most of the Peloponnesian knights, it seems, preferred Geoffrey, who knew the area, over a newcomer unfamiliar with Greece. Geoffrey was also ambitious to become the Prince of Achaea. All sorts of ruses, we are told, were used to cause delays in Robert's trip east, and when he finally arrived in the Peloponnesus Geoffrey kept moving from place to place with the leading knights until the time had elapsed. Geoffrey then held an assembly that declared that the heir had forfeited his rights and elected Geoffrey hereditary Prince of Achaea. Setton and Runciman think the whole story is fictitious and Runciman even believes that Robert probably never existed. In any case, Geoffrey was recognized in the Morea as prince in the fall of 1209 and was recognized as such by both the pope and the Latin emperor in 1210. By then the Peloponnesus was coming more and more frequently to be called the Morea.

Geoffrey was to be succeeded by his son Geoffrey II. Since no source notes Geoffrey I's death and since his heir bore the same name, resulting in documents that simply speak of the prince as "Geoffrey" into the 1240s, it is very difficult to determine when Geoffrey II succeeded Geoffrey I. Traditionally scholars have accepted 1218; recently, however, Longnon has advanced sound reasons to date Geoffrey II's succession to 1228.[9]

The prince governed the Peloponnesus through a high court on which he and twenty other members sat. The first ten members of the court were the holders of ten major fiefs. The whole Peloponnesus had been divided into a total of twelve major fiefs, but two, Kalamata and Arcadia, were held by Prince Geoffrey himself.[10] Thus the prince kept a large parcel of territory as his own direct holding. Besides the ten great secular noblemen holding the ten great fiefs, the other ten members of the court were the Archbishop of Patras (the major Latin cleric on the peninsula), the six bishops subordinate to him, and the local masters of the three military orders which were present in the area, the Templars, the Hospitalers, and the Teutonic knights. All the territory of the Peloponnesus was under the prince or one of the ten great barons. Each lesser knight was subordinate to one or another of these eleven lords; thus once again subinfeudation existed. These lesser knights included the Greeks who had submitted and been allowed to retain their lands. No lesser knight could construct a castle without authorization from the prince or relevant baron. Only the prince and great barons could freely build castles.

A commission of Frankish barons, Greek archons, and Latin clerics was established by William of Champlitte to assign the fiefs. It kept a register of these fiefs and what specific services were owed from each one.

The above-mentioned great council of twenty had political, judicial, and military duties. It had the obligation to manage the state in conjunction with the prince and to defend the state. Its armies were based on the retinues of the prince and the ten great barons (whose retinues included all their vassals). In theory, the council only advised the prince, but in fact major decisions were made jointly. Thus the council, presided over by the prince, made the major political decisions and served as the highest court, dealing with fiefs, the obligations of their holders, and issues of inheritance. Only the council could impose the death penalty. Each vassal owed four months service a year in the field and four more on garrison duty and was on call at all times in emergencies. Each town had a local council that was under the supervision either of the prince or of the great baron who held as his fief the region in which the town lay.

Two different laws operated in the Peloponnesus and two different societies existed, overlapping only in places. The highest authority was the prince and his council. Relations among the Westerners were guided by feudal customs eventually codified in the *Assizes of Romania*.[11] The conquerors took over existing castles or built new ones throughout the Morea and assumed control of the citadels of major towns, which they supervised and in which they established garrisons. Thus we may say they took over the functions of the now defunct Byzantine military structure. And as noted, the lands made into the Franks' fiefs were chiefly centered around rural castles and in general consisted of the former lands of the Byzantine emperor and of the magnates who had fled. The towns remained chiefly inhabited by Greeks, who retained their previous status and for whom, on the whole, day-to-day life remained as it had been. They simply rendered their former tax obligations to the new rulers and had their civil relations (civil suits, inheritance, marriages, contractual obligations, etc.) administered or judged by their own urban officials still operating under the laws of the former Byzantine Empire. The Greek landlords who remained also continued to enjoy their lands; they retained, as guaranteed by law, their former privileges and obligations but now owed the taxes and other obligations that had existed under Byzantine rule to the new prince or to the relevant baron. Only for a new fief would a Greek acquire Western-style obligations. The peasants also remained in much the same position as before, fulfilling their traditional obligations to their Greek lord or to a new Frankish lord.

It is often stated that pronoias (Byzantine fiefs) had been widespread in the Peloponnesus prior to the Frankish conquest; thus the new order under the Franks was more or less a continuation of the feudal order existing prior to the conquest. It is thus said that the Greek lords simply changed their suzerains; the only significant difference, it is said, was that all the Byzantine pronoia holders had held their fiefs directly from the emperor, whereas after the Latin conquest they held them from a variety of different lords. Thus subinfeudation and a feudal hierarchy were post-1204 innovations. This view was generally held until it was recently questioned by Jacoby, who expresses doubts that pronoias existed in the Peloponnesus in 1204.[12] He argues that the feudalization of the Morea occurred as a result of the Frankish conquest.

Assuming the absence of pronoias in the Peloponnesus, Jacoby then contends that since the Greeks retained their holdings according to Byzantine (Greek) custom these lands remained freeholdings, owing no service. He also notes that Greek lands, as specified in the Assizes of Romania, continued to be inherited according to the Greek custom of equal shares for all male heirs.

Thus the lands retained by Greeks from the days of the empire did not change their character or legal status. Military service in exchange for land as well as the Frankish custom of primogeniture in the inheritance of lands applied only to estates granted as fiefs after the conquest. Jacoby then argues that, by granting to the Greek landlords additional lands as Frankish-type fiefs, the conquerors were able to win the loyalty of Greeks and also to demand service from them, with that service being owed only from the new fief. It is not certain, however, when Greeks began receiving fiefs, as opposed to confirmations of their patrimonial estates.

Jacoby points out that when the Greek archons at first submitted they were admitted only to the lowest stratum of the feudal hierarchy, the equivalent of the French mounted sergeants who were not of noble descent. By the mid-thirteenth century, documentation mentions that Greeks were receiving new lands as fiefs. Possibly the awarding of fiefs to Greeks began earlier, perhaps even at the time of the conquest; if so, however, no evidence of such early grants has survived. Also found for the first time in the 1260s is documentation of Greeks' being dubbed knights. But even though some Greeks were to be admitted to knighthood, none became barons.

In either case, whether the Greeks' estates had all been freeholdings as Jacoby argues, or whether some had been pronoia fiefs, the sources make it clear that the Greek holders retained the same lands on the same terms as they had held them under the Byzantines. If some had actually been pronoias, the Greeks would have continued to hold them as fiefs with the only difference being a changed service obligation. In all cases they would have retained the same peasants on their lands who would have continued to render the same obligations to the lords as had existed earlier. Thus life on an estate would have been unchanged.

We do not know how many Greeks came to serve the Achaean or Morean state, or who they were, or what proportion of the Morean army they constituted, or what proportion of the land of the principality they held. Neither do we know whether Greek magnates were permitted to retain private armies, nor, if they were, whether limitations were imposed upon the size of their retinues. We do not know what, if any, role the Greeks had in the overall Morean government or even in local decision making. We are told that Greek estate holders were given equal status with the Latin knights; this clearly means the lesser knights, for no Greeks were to be found among the ten great barons. We also know that by law no greater demands were to be placed upon them than those imposed by the Byzantine emperor earlier.

Except for the Church issue, to which we shall next turn, there seems to have been little Frankish interference in the lives of the Greeks who submitted. However, though they were secure in their landed possessions, presumably they suffered some loss of influence in regional affairs. Moreover, they did face problems in religious matters. The Orthodox hierarchy, except for those willing to accept papal supremacy, which most bishops were not, was expelled. After its expulsion, the vacated Greek cathedral churches were assigned to Latin priests, and Latin services were carried out in them. Most monasteries were also taken over by Latin orders. However, though the higher level Orthodox clergy was removed, the Orthodox parish priests were usually allowed to remain. Geoffrey did not interfere with them and willingly allowed parishes to retain their Church services unchanged.

Thus, two ways of life co-existed in the Morea. For while the Greeks followed their accustomed ways, the upper-class Westerners retained their own languages and customs. The Frankish elite, excluding a small number of German speakers, continued to speak French. In fact the Villehardouin court prided itself on speaking better French than that spoken in Paris. And troubadours appeared at the Morean courts as well. Therefore the Morea has been described as a bit of France transferred to Greece.

Though some nobles also learned Greek, they tended to feel themselves socially and culturally superior to the Greek population. They frequently lived in separate communities, or quarters, with other Westerners. And they usually imported their brides from Western Europe. Thus it was common to find a Latin quarter in a town's citadel or acropolis. Others lived in a Western style in isolated castles or fortified rural mansions, maintaining an existence separate from Greek society and its activities.

Few Peloponnesian Greeks converted to Catholicism. However, many became bi-lingual, particularly those who entered military service. Greeks also remained important figures in the administration and bureaucracy, carrying out the state's relations with the local population. Since many Byzantine laws and customs, including the Byzantine financial system, continued in practice, with Byzantine land lists still being used into the fourteenth century, it was necessary that the bureaucrats understand Greek. Thus native Greeks retained many administrative posts.

After 1212 this state included the whole Peloponnesus except for the isolated Greek outpost of Monemvasia and the two ports obtained by Venice, with which the principality of the Morea had good relations. The principality's only other neighbor by land was the Burgundian principality of Athens, with which the Morean ruler also usually had excellent relations. Thus the Morean state enjoyed considerable security. However, despite the peace and security, matters were not entirely smooth. Dislikes and hostility sprang up frequently between Latins and Greeks. Close contact brought their differences in custom to the fore; and each side felt with certainty the superiority of its own ways. The Franks had also, as noted, proclaimed the Union of the Churches, and even when secular leaders tried to be tolerant of their Greek subjects the Latin clerics often were not. Thus when the Latins expelled the Greek hierarchy, replacing it with a Latin one, and tried to enforce Church Union, various Greeks resisted. Even some who had submitted and been confirmed in their lands became disgruntled over the attack upon their Church and emigrated to territory still under Greek control, either in Epirus or in Anatolia. Thus emigration of Greeks from the Peloponnesus, and from other Frankish-held lands in Greece, was a feature of this period.

Latin Religious Policy in the Conquered Greek Lands

The conquest of Constantinople presented Pope Innocent III with a dilemma. The crusaders had violated his express orders when they sailed to Constantinople. Thus he was angered by their disobedience in taking the city; he was also displeased at the violence that accompanied the conquest. The crusaders' declaration of Church Union was not sufficient to pacify his wrath, and he excommunicated the crusaders. However, the potential gains for Catholicism were so great that, although he condemned much about it, Innocent soon "showed a determination to profit by the crime" and accepted the conquest, on condition that Church affairs in the East were settled according to his wishes. His wishes, though, were frequently disregarded. After all, the distance between Rome and Constantinople was great and the Venetians were never obedient subjects of any foreign authority. Innocent first objected that, adhering to the partition treaty, the Venetians had appointed one of their own men as Patriarch of Constantinople and were claiming the right to control the appointment of future patriarchs. Innocent believed the appointment of the patriarch of the second see of Christendom should be a papal prerogative. Though he was to fulminate over this, he and his less dynamic successors found they could not alter this Venetian prerogative. So, to make the situation more palatable and to assert his rights, Innocent issued his own appointment of the Venetian Morosini to the patriarchate.

The existing Greek ecclesiastical hierarchical system was retained under Latin rule. But to keep his post a Greek incumbent had to accept Church Union and submit to Rome. Almost none of them did. Thus the Greek bishops were replaced by Latins. Miller claims that the Latin hierarchs had the same titles, diocesan territories, and suffragan bishops under them as had their Greek predecessors at the time of the conquest. Wolff, however, has demonstrated that the Latins made major changes in every one of the above-mentioned aspects of ecclesiastical organization.[13]

After the conquest, swarms of Catholic clerics entered the dominions of the Latin conquerors: Constantinople, Thessaly, Attica, and the Peloponnesus. They wanted to share in the spoils, and Innocent supported their claims. He and they both wanted for the Roman Catholic Church all lands that had belonged to the Orthodox Church. And these included the vast holdings of the Greek monasteries. Since fighting men were scarce, it was important for the Latin princes and dukes to award land to their followers and to use land as a means of attracting further support. Particularly in the Peloponnesus, where the Prince of Achaea was trying to maintain the good will of the Greeks by allowing those who submitted to retain their lands, it was important to make use of the lands of the Greek Church as fiefs for the Latin troops who had effected the conquest. Thus the disposition of land became a bone of contention between the pope (and the clergy on the ground) and the barons. The Latin emperor, in need of fighting men to defend Constantinople and unable to conquer enough territory in Anatolia to assign a significant number of fiefs there, also found himself dependent on utilizing land of the Greek Church. He too was determined that no further land should fall into the hands of the Church.

In 1209 Emperor Henry, supported by his barons, issued an edict prohibiting the granting or willing of land to the Church or to monasteries. He permitted only donations of moveable property to the Church. Thus a would-be donor had to sell his land and then give the proceeds from the sale to the Church. In Achaea it was decreed that the prince alone could donate land to the Church; his vassals could make only temporary donations valid just for the lifetime of the donor. The pope regularly protested against these policies concerning the disposition of land; generally his protests did not have much effect. Three times between 1210 and 1233 popes excommunicated Geoffrey I Villehardouin, his successor Geoffrey II, and Othon de la Roche of Athens.

The excommunications of the Villehardouins also touched on a second issue, the prince's demand that the Church hierarchy and the military orders should share in the cost of the principality's defense. Thus at times the prince and other lords demanded and seized Church revenues to contribute to the cost of building fortresses, claiming that the clergy owed the land tax still in force from the Byzantine period. Geoffrey I (if Longnon's dating of his reign is correct, otherwise Geoffrey II) had a major clash with the Church in about 1218 on this issue. For when he summoned his vassals for a major campaign to conquer Monemvasia, the clergy, who by then may have held as many as a third of the fiefs, refused to provide troops, claiming their fiefs were from the pope and not from Villehardouin. Geoffrey then seized the fiefs, providing subsistence pensions for those clerics with no other income. Geoffrey was excommunicated but after two or three years negotiated his way back into the papacy's good graces; he expressed his willingness to restore the fiefs if the clerical holders would provide men for military service.

Further difficulties between crusaders and Church arose because the knights were very lax in paying their Church tithes. In fact the Venetians throughout adamantly refused to pay tithes. Geoffrey also did not pay tithes and made no effort to force his vassals to do so either. The pope, furthermore, insisted that the clergy and religious orders, and their lands and tenants, were to be exempt from civil jurisdiction; this in theory created a state within a state. Emperor Henry gave verbal assent to this last demand. But Geoffrey continually pressured clergy to be tried before secular tribunals.

The papacy, actively supported by the Latin clergy on the ground, demanded a policy to force the Greek population to accept Church Union. Needless to say the Greeks resisted. In order to keep their sees Greek bishops were required to accept papal supremacy, *Filioque* (the "and the Son" addition to the Nicene Creed), and unleavened bread for communion wafers. Few did. In fact the only known bishop from Greece proper to accept these terms was Theodore of Euboea. That is why most of the Greek hierarchy was expelled and replaced by Latins. The great monasteries and their lands were assigned to Catholic orders. In Constantinople the Greek population sought to resist by establishing a separate Orthodox Church in the city under its own Greek patriarch. When the pre-conquest Patriarch of Constantinople died in exile in 1206, the Greeks sought to elect a successor to him as Greek Patriarch of Constantinople. They expressed their willingness, if this request were granted, to recognize the political authority of the Latin emperor. The Latins refused, insisting there could be only one Patriarch of Constantinople, the Catholic one. In 1208, after two years of fruitless negotiations and bickering, the Greek leaders of Constantinople turned to Theodore Lascaris in Nicea and agreed to support his plans to create a new Ecumenical Greek patriarchate in Nicea.

But while these negotiations between the Greek leaders and the new crusader establishment continued, the Latins stepped up pressure upon the Greeks to accept Union, increasing the Greeks' anger. To support the Roman Catholic clergy a tithe was instituted and levied on the whole population. The Greeks resisted this measure. Then the pope became impatient, ordering Emperor Henry to take strong measures, particularly against those Greek monks who opposed adopting the Catholic liturgy or resisted recognizing papal supremacy. The Cardinal legate Pelagius was sent to Constantinople to enforce the pope's wishes. Various Orthodox churches were closed for resisting papal policy and large numbers of monks were imprisoned. These acts only increased the anger of the population. As the Greeks continued to refuse to pay the tithe, the pope ordered Henry to threaten the Greeks with direr penalties, including death.

Henry became increasingly unhappy with the situation. Faced with considerable dissent from his population and with a relatively popular Greek empire across the Straits, centered in Nicea, to which he did not want to lose the loyalty of his population (and a steady flow of emigrants from Constantinople to Nicea was already taking place), he realized that some sort of accommodation with the Greeks was necessary. In 1213 a delegation of Greek aristocrats from the capital presented Henry with a petition. It expressed the Greeks' loyalty to Henry yet also stated they recognized him as the master of their bodies, but not of their souls. Promising continued loyalty to Henry, they requested religious freedom, which meant specifically the re-opening of their churches and an end to pressure upon them to accept Church Union and Catholic rites. Should their request be rejected, they asked for permission to depart freely to Nicea. Henry gave in and, in defiance of the legate Pelagius, ordered the Greek churches of the city re-opened and the many jailed Orthodox monks released. Thereafter he followed a policy of appeasing the Greeks. In this way he avoided an uprising but, of course, this did not put an end to the bitterness. And the bitterness was constantly stirred up by incidents between the Greek population and the Westerners, especially the Western clerics.

From the middle of the tenth century Mount Athos had been the center of Greek monasticism and a leading center of Orthodox spiritual life. It lay on the Chalcidic peninsula, which belonged to Boniface of Montferrat. Saint Sava, the Serbian monk then at Hilandar, mentions that disorders reached even Mount Athos at the time of the conquest. Many scholars believe that these disorders were the cause of his leaving the Holy Mountain, for he returned to Serbia with Nemanja's body during a winter, either in 1205–06 or 1206–07.

Since Athos was a major Orthodox center, Catholic leaders realized that its acceptance of Union was particularly important and would have profound impact on the attitudes of Greeks elsewhere. Considerable pressure was therefore put on the monks. A special papal legate, Benedict, whose assignment was to effect Church Union, arrived in near-by Thessaloniki in the summer of 1206. In response to this threat Greek clerics held a synod at Ohrid, presided over by Demetrius Chomatianus, Chancellor (Chartophylax) for the Archbishop of Ohrid, who later acquired prominence as Ohrid's archbishop himself. An Athonite monk named Gregory Ikodomopoulos came to Ohrid to describe to the synod the efforts of Italian clerics, including a Latin cardinal (who probably was the above-mentioned Benedict), to pressure the Athonite monasteries to accept papal supremacy, insert the pope's name in their services, and adopt various Latin rites. Despite this pressure, Gregory stated, the whole mountain remained firm, except for the monks of Iveron (the Georgian monastery). Iveron's submission to Rome was the cause of Gregory's appearance at Ohrid. The synod at Ohrid condemned such apostasy and concluded the other Athonite monasteries should break off relations with Iveron. No references exist to other monasteries' yielding at this time, so scholars on the whole have concluded that, despite pressure, the other monasteries remained firm and rejected Union.

Needless to say, problems continued for the Orthodox monasteries on Athos. The mountain had been assigned to the jurisdiction of a Latin bishop, whose seat was in Sevastia or Samaria, near Thessaloniki. The bishop's authority seems to have been recognized only by Iveron. Sources also mention that Latin "brigands" (crusaders? Italian pirates?) had sacked the monasteries. As a result the monasteries lost considerable wealth and also many documents from their archives. These archival losses meant the monasteries lost proof of their titles to various estates and in time caused confusion as to which monastery had rights to what. This led to many subsequent quarrels, in the course of which various forgeries were drawn up to replace lost charters that had supposedly demonstrated the rights of particular monasteries to particular lands.

Unable to defend themselves against the brigands, the monks appealed to Emperor Henry who, after Boniface's death in 1207, had asserted himself as the dominant secular figure in the area. Henry had already reached the conclusion that he must reach some accommodation with the Greeks. They clearly were not going to accept Union; pressure from him to make them do so would only lead to greater disorder in his realm and further emigration of his subjects to Nicea or Epirus. Surrounded by two powerful Orthodox states, Bulgaria and Nicea, he needed not only to avoid a fifth column within his realm but also to obtain the active support of his subjects. And so, as noted, he responded positively to the petition of the Constantinopolitan aristocrats and in 1213 granted them freedom of worship. From 1213 Henry also adopted an active policy of conciliation toward the Greeks, confirming both Greek nobles and monasteries in the possession of their lands and working to diminish the aggressive Unionist policy of the Venetian Patriarch of Constantinople.

In keeping with this policy, Henry also intervened on behalf of the Athonite monks. To try to restrain the brigands—the worst of whom at the time seem to have been Lombards, many of whom had come to serve the Montferrats in Thessaloniki—Henry extended imperial protection over Mount Athos. The exact date he took this action is uncertain; but it clearly occurred between 1210 and 1213. Most scholars place it nearer the later date. He expressed interest not only in the monks' physical security, but also in their spiritual welfare. To promote the latter, he ordered an end to pressure on the monks to convert and removed the monasteries from the jurisdiction of the Latin Bishop of Sevastia. The monasteries were to be placed directly under the jurisdiction of the emperor, who in exchange demanded an oath of loyalty from the monks.

Imperial protection did not put an end to the looting of the monasteries, so in late 1213 some monks sought the protection of the pope, which was granted in 1214. Živojinović argues that if the monasteries received papal protection, they must have submitted to the pope—a fact which they clearly would have covered up subsequently.[14] Papal letters also imply that papal protection was extended only to those monasteries that accepted Union. Protected monasteries included the Great Lavra, the largest and most important Greek monastery. The pope confirmed the submitting monasteries in possession of their lands and privileges. He stated that he wanted an end to violence, for the Latins who carried out such acts made a bad impression on the Greeks and thus were not acting in the interests of Church Union. Whether submission to the pope had been enough to satisfy the pope, or whether these monasteries had to adopt Latin customs (*Filioque* and unleavened bread), is unknown. Also unknown is whether all or only some of the monasteries submitted and which, if any, held out. This situation did not last long beyond the death of the zealous Innocent III in 1216. Honorius III (1216–27) took less interest in the Greek world and was ineffective in asserting his wishes in the lands of the Latin East. The Athonite monks who had submitted soon dropped any recognition of Church Union or papal primacy and entered into relations with the Ecumenical (Greek) Patriarch in Nicea. With the restoration of Orthodoxy (and also a reduction in brigandage), Sava felt able to return to Mount Athos in 1217.

Baldwin and Kalojan in Thrace

After the conquest of Constantinople many Greeks fled from the city and its environs to Anatolia, where they joined the Greek population already living there. Several small Greek political centers sprang up, the most important of which was to develop in Nicea under the Constantinopolitan nobleman Theodore Lascaris, a son-in-law of Alexius III, who after a brief residence in Bursa (Brusa) established himself in Nicea. He soon was to claim the title emperor. As noted, western Anatolia had been parceled out on paper as fiefs for various knights in the partition treaty drawn up on the eve of the conquest. At the end of 1204 or early 1205, before Nicea or any other Greek center had had time to consolidate itself or prepare its defenses, the Latins invaded Anatolia to claim their fiefs. The crusaders had achieved various successes, and Nicea itself was threatened, when the Greeks of Anatolia were saved by events in the Balkans.

In Thrace the Latin barons had refused to confirm the lands (probably in many cases pronoias) of a large number of Greek landlords. The barons had wanted these estates in the vicinity of the capital for themselves and their followers. Their refusal set off a revolt by the Greeks of Thrace. Meanwhile Kalojan of Bulgaria was also interesting himself in Thrace. He had been taking advantage of the chaos following the events of April 1204 to expand into Thrace at the expense of the Thracian Greeks. He had occupied considerable Thracian territory before the crusaders had appeared there to seek their Thracian fiefs. About to receive a crown from the pope, with whom he was establishing good relations, Kalojan believed himself a natural ally of the crusaders against the Greeks. He sought to form an alliance with the crusaders, probably expecting to conclude a treaty defining a division of Thrace between the Latin Empire and Bulgaria. Seeing Kalojan annexing territory they believed should belong to the Latin Empire and thus threatening their ambitions, the crusaders turned down Kalojan's proposal.

Rebuffed by the crusaders, the hot-tempered Kalojan was receptive to the request for help that came from the rebelling Greek lords of Thrace. He immediately (in February 1205) dispatched further Bulgarian forces to Thrace. Seeing this attack as a major threat to the new Latin Empire, Emperor Baldwin immediately ordered the recall of the crusading armies from Anatolia to campaign against Kalojan. Determined to expel Kalojan from Thrace and to suppress the Greek rebellion in Thrace, Baldwin then, without awaiting the arrival of the armies from Anatolia, set out at once for Adrianople, whose Greek population had already driven out its crusader garrison and, having submitted to Kalojan's suzerainty, was flying his flag. Baldwin laid siege to Adrianople. Kalojan soon arrived to relieve the siege.

The two armies met in a fierce battle on 14 April 1205 before the walls of Adrianople. Kalojan's Bulgarians and Cumans not only won but also captured the emperor and carried him off to Bulgaria as a prisoner. Different stories about Baldwin's fate are told: Greek sources (Niketas Choniates and Acropolites) state that Baldwin was killed after suffering great tortures on the orders of Kalojan. Niketas states that Baldwin was thrown over a precipice and his body left to the dogs and birds. However, Baldwin's successor Henry, seeking papal intervention for Baldwin's release, had written the pope in 1205 stating that the Latin prisoners were being treated with respect. Kalojan in his 1206 reply to the pope stated he could not release Baldwin because he had already died in jail; Kalojan gives no details as to when and how he died. One Frankish chronicle reports that Baldwin had died from his battle wounds.

The defeat at Adrianople, together with Baldwin's capture, threw the Latin Empire into a major crisis. Months were to pass without word about Baldwin; was he alive or dead? Should they await word or should they elect a new emperor? The Latins also found themselves now with almost no territory in Thrace. Most of what they had conquered in 1204 was now annexed by the powerful Kalojan, and the territory assigned as fiefs by the treaty but not yet occupied was no longer in the hands of petty and disunited Greek lords but also belonged to the strong Bulgarian state. Thus acquisition and recovery would be difficult. The Anatolian campaign had been called off, leaving the crusaders only a small foothold there while a strong Greek state was beginning to take form around Nicea. Thus one year after the conquest of Constantinople, the Latin Empire was on the verge of collapse. It basically consisted of Constantinople itself, an island behind powerful walls, but surrounded by hostile states—Nicea, Bulgaria, and groups of hostile Greeks in Thrace—having only maritime communications with friendly powers. The other crusader states were distant. The closest one, that of Boniface of Montferrat in Thessaloniki and Thessaly, was not only far away but also had a leader hostile to Baldwin and thus could not be counted on. After Boniface's death in 1207 this state was to become weaker and divided by factions until the Greeks of Epirus completed its conquest in 1224. The Morea (or Achaea) was at an even greater distance and like Thessaloniki had direct contact with the Latin Empire only by sea.

Furthermore, the number of Latins in the East was small. As Finlay observes,

> The Franks formed a small dominant class of foreign warriors, many of whom were constantly returning to the lands of their birth, where they had ancestral estates and honors, while many died without leaving posterity. Their numbers consequently required to be perpetually recruited by new bodies of immigrants.[15]

Recruiting these new bodies entailed a constant effort by the Latin emperors, who often were unsuccessful in their attempts. Their weakness required them to be on the defensive rather than expanding—and thereby acquiring new territory to award as fiefs—and made the recruitment of new warriors from the West difficult. As a result the Latins in Achaea initiated a policy of making heirs to Achaean fiefs pay homage in person in Achaea. The requirement of personal appearance precluded possession of fiefs by heirs residing in the West who would provide no service. To make this policy more effective a second rule was instituted, namely, that no vassal could leave the principality without the prince's permission. Thus if the vassal appeared to claim his fief, he could not then depart and escape the service obligation.

The Adrianople campaign, followed by the Latin defeat that encouraged increased Bulgarian activity in Thrace near the capital, required the presence of every able-bodied Latin in the capital or Thrace to oppose the Bulgarians. Thus Nicea was saved. For by the time the crusaders were able to turn back to Anatolia again, the town of Nicea was well fortified and Lascaris had secured his hold over the other Greek centers in western Anatolia and had created a major state—in relative terms for that region at that time—that was growing rapidly in population as Greeks from Constantinople and other Latin-held parts of southeastern Europe migrated to it. Thus Kalojan's victory at Adrianople and his activities in Thrace after that victory were crucial for the survival of the Greek state in Nicea, the state that in 1261 was to regain Constantinople.

Kalojan's Activities after April 1205

Thrace was the meeting- and hence battle-ground among (1) the local Greek lords who had had estates there, (2) Kalojan, who had begun to annex as much of Thrace as he could immediately after the conquest of Constantinople, and (3) the Latin emperor and knights of Constantinople who wanted to add this region to the Latin Empire and award it as fiefs to the knights who had participated in the conquest of Constantinople. The Latins immediately alienated the Greeks there. Not only did they seize the lands of the Greek landed aristocracy but their religious policy antagonized Greeks of all classes. For upon conquest the Latins immediately expelled from Thrace the Greek hierarchy, replacing it with a Latin one and sending Latin priests into conquered areas to effect Church Union. Thus from the start many Greeks in Thrace preferred submission to Kalojan who, though he might replace Greek bishops with Bulgarian ones, was Orthodox and did not interfere with Orthodox beliefs and practices. Thus early in 1205 many Greeks in Thrace were already lined up with Kalojan and serving in his armies. Furthermore, Greek leaders in various crusader-held cities in Thrace, held by small garrisons, began in one city after another to organize revolts that expelled the Latin garrisons. In this way Demotika, Adrianople, and other towns were liberated. The leaders of such rebellions early in 1205 usually then acknowledged Kalojan's suzerainty. Needless to say, such behavior caused great insecurity among the crusaders still in possession of other Thracian cities, for they constituted a small minority in cities with substantial Greek populations.

To isolate Constantinople as much as possible, Kalojan had decided on eastern Thrace as a battle zone and dispatched his armies into this region early in 1205. They took many fortresses, including the important Arcadiopolis, either from Greeks before the crusaders could obtain them or from the Latins before they had a chance to strengthen town defenses. This attack had led

Baldwin to call off the Anatolian campaign and to march into Thrace. His attempt to regain the major city of Adrianople, as noted, led to his defeat and capture on 14 April 1205. After this victory Kalojan's armies were active throughout much of Thrace.

When a Bulgarian force moved into the vicinity of Constantinople, the crusaders elected Baldwin's brother Henry as regent. A second Bulgarian force led by Kalojan himself moved toward Thessaloniki. On its way this army stopped in June 1205 to besiege Serres, which was held by a vassal of Boniface. This vassal surrendered the city after the Bulgarians had agreed to a treaty that promised the population's safe departure together with their moveable property. However, Kalojan broke his word immediately afterward and seized a large number of captives. He executed certain leaders and then sent the rest, numbered in the hundreds, off to Bulgaria as captives. Kalojan's behavior at Serres was to have considerable influence on the attitude of the Greeks thereafter and caused many of them to become disillusioned with Kalojan and desert him as a result.

As Kalojan's forces, led by the tsar himself, marched south beyond Serres, word that they were approaching Thessaloniki reached Boniface in the Peloponnesus. Leaving troops to carry on the siege of the three Peloponnesian cities, Boniface hurried back north to defend his capital. Meanwhile Kalojan split up his forces, leading a major force toward Philippopolis himself while sending the rest against Thessaloniki. The latter plundered the environs of Thessaloniki and seem to have taken the lower town briefly. Unable to take the city's citadel and realizing that they were no match for Boniface, the Bulgarians departed before Boniface's arrival. Having returned home and having, it seems, put down some sort of unrest in his city, Boniface thought to march out against the Bulgarians; but word of Baldwin's fate apparently caused him to reconsider this plan and remain in his capital.

Early in 1205, meanwhile, the crusader Renier de Trit had succeeded in capturing the important city, assigned to him by treaty, of Philippopolis. When Kalojan appeared in Thrace part of the town's population (including, according to Villehardouin, many Paulicians) hostile to Renier sent envoys to Kalojan inviting him to come and promising to assist him to take the town. Knowing that Kalojan was in the vicinity, and feeling insecure, Renier withdrew to a second fortress, Stanimaka (Stanimachus, Stenimachus), so as to avoid falling into Kalojan's hands should he, as seemed likely, capture Philippopolis. However, word then reached Philippopolis of the Serres events, and a Greek party led by Alexius Aspietes and Theodore Branas seized control of Philippopolis. They, acting in their own interests, did not trust Kalojan and put an end to the plans to surrender the city to him. Kalojan, changing his plans (which may well have included an assault on Thessaloniki), marched north from Serres against Philippopolis. Overcoming the resistance of the local Greek leaders, he took the city and sacked it, destroying many palaces and executing those Greek leaders he was able to capture, who included

Aspietes and the town's archbishop. He then established a Bulgarian administration in the town.

Next, the sources report, a revolt broke out against Kalojan in Trnovo, his capital. It is not certain whether the revolt coincided with the Philippopolis events or took place subsequently. In any case, Kalojan suppressed the Trnovo rising after his conquest of Philippopolis. This revolt in Trnovo, the exact date and causes of which are unknown, is usually dated by scholars to the second half of 1205 or even early in 1206. After dealing with the rebels brutally, according to the sources, Kalojan began to make war on the "treacherous" Greeks. And the sources list a whole series of Greek towns in Thrace, some nominally loyal to Kalojan, taken and destroyed by him in the fall of 1205 and during the winter that followed. Taking large numbers of prisoners, Kalojan generally executed the leaders while sending the rest as captives to Bulgaria.

Because Greek sources depict Kalojan's actions against the Greeks as following upon his suppression of the Trnovo rebellion, some scholars have suggested that Greeks were somehow involved in, if not even leaders of, the Trnovo uprising. Other than the time sequence, having one event following the other, no evidence exists of Greek participation in the rebellion in the Bulgarian capital. In the absence of specific evidence, it makes more sense to associate Kalojan's anti-Greek policy with the behavior of the Greek leaders in Philippopolis and in other Thracian cities that may have turned against him. In fact Niketas Choniates states that after the Philippopolis events, Kalojan, feeling great anger at the Greek nobles whom he had in prison in Trnovo, condemned them to death.

And the events in Philippopolis were scarcely unique. In the fall of 1205 and the winter that followed various Greek leaders of Thracian towns under Kalojan's suzerainty, presumably in response to Kalojan's actions in Serres and Philippopolis, turned against him and voluntarily submitted to the Latins. In early 1206 some Greek leaders from Adrianople and Demotika sent envoys to Theodore Branas, then in Constantinople, asking him to mediate their submission to Henry. Henry accepted their proffered loyalty and entrusted the two cities to Theodore Branas, who had been an ally of the Latins. The son of Alexius Branas, whom we met earlier, Theodore had been a leader of the Greek party in Philippopolis that opposed Kalojan. Having escaped when that city fell, he had returned to his family home in Adrianople. A leader of the anti-Bulgarian Greeks, he had close ties with the Latins. He was the husband of Agnes, the sister of King Philip Augustus II of France; left a widow in Constantinople by Alexius II and Andronicus, she had subsequently married Branas. Presumably he had had ties with the pro-Latin party in Adrianople prior to his departure from there to Constantinople; very likely he had gone to the capital to arrange with the Latin leaders the smooth transfer of authority over the town prior to the arrival of the official delegation.

Thus Kalojan's ruthlessness should be seen as a major cause of Greek desertions and of the loss of some of his Thracian cities, particularly those held by indirect rule under Greeks who, having submitted to him, continued to govern their towns.

As a result of the defection of these cities, Kalojan sent his forces back into Thrace in the spring of 1206. Many Greeks in his armies deserted during the campaign. The Bulgarians destroyed a number of smaller fortresses, while Kalojan himself directed sieges of Adrianople and Demotika. Emperor Henry led an army to the relief of Demotika, causing Kalojan to lift his siege and withdraw. Adrianople also held out. In the course of 1206 it became more and more common to find the Greeks of Thrace allied with the Latins against Kalojan. Kalojan responded to this development by unleashing greater and more brutal reprisals.

By the middle of 1206 the crusaders came to realize that the rumors they had heard about Baldwin's death were true. So, they proceeded to elect Henry as emperor; he was crowned 20 August 1206.

Shortly after Henry's coronation, Kalojan launched a new attack against Demotika, which was defended by Theodore Branas. This time the Bulgarians took the city, which suffered considerable destruction; large numbers of captives (the sources say, probably with exaggeration, twenty thousand) were taken. Emperor Henry marched out and, catching up with the Bulgarian armies en route home, procured the captives' release. Kalojan did not try to hold Demotika. Instead he destroyed the fortifications to such an extent that they would be worthless in the future. He succeeded, for Henry concluded that the town could not be refortified with the resources at his command. By late 1206 Kalojan's policy (presumably owing to the hostility, and hence unreliability, of the local populations) was not to try to hold eastern Thrace, but to sack its urban centers, destroy their fortifications, and then withdraw with as much booty and as many captives as possible. Thus he seems to have written off the conquest and retention of this area. In this way the Latin Empire secured eastern Thrace for itself, while Kalojan regarded the region as a raiding ground. His destruction of these cities' fortifications left them vulnerable to subsequent raids, especially by the Cumans. The Adrianople region in particular suffered from their plundering. Large numbers of Thracians were killed, taken off to Bulgaria as captives, or forced to flee elsewhere. While Kalojan and his clients particularly ravaged the Adrianople region, the crusaders' plundering was concentrated on the region of Philippopolis held by Kalojan. Near-by Berrhoia and its environs also suffered greatly from the activities of Henry's men. Thus Thrace as a whole suffered great devastation and depopulation. Furthermore, all this activity disrupted the agriculture of Thrace, which was a fertile region and had long been a leading granary for Constantinople and Thessaloniki.

Meanwhile, Kalojan between 1204 and 1207 also procured control of most of Macedonia. The Bulgarian tsar, probably in 1205, established a governor named Eciismen in Prosek. Dobromir Chrysos, the previous holder of Prosek, is not mentioned in any source from this period. Whether he submitted to Kalojan or whether Kalojan took Prosek by storm is not known. In any case Chrysos lost his fortress, and Prosek—and presumably any other territory he held as well—became Bulgarian.

In the winter of 1206–07, when Kalojan was active around Demotika, Boniface recovered Serres and repaired its fortifications. He also erected new and stronger fortifications for his town of Drama. In February 1207 Henry married Boniface's daughter Agnes. Meanwhile, the Niceans concluded an alliance with Kalojan, who again marched into Thrace in March or April 1207, once again besieging Adrianople. But when summer approached without success, his Cumans refused to remain any longer, forcing Kalojan to lift the siege. At this time the Niceans were besieging various Latin-held fortresses in the northwest corner of Anatolia. Henry, torn between the necessity of campaigning in both Anatolia and Thrace, finally made peace with the Niceans, surrendering further Anatolian forts to them. That summer, after concluding this peace, Henry returned to Thrace. He arranged a meeting with Boniface, which took place at Kypsela, near the mouth of the Marica River; at it Boniface submitted to him.

Then, on his return to Thessaloniki from this meeting, Boniface and his small entourage were attacked on 4 September by a small Bulgarian raiding party. In the skirmish that followed Boniface was killed. After his knights were put to flight, Boniface's head was recovered by the Bulgarians and sent to Kalojan. This unexpected encounter eliminated the strongest Latin warrior in the area. A power struggle for control of Thessaloniki followed, leading to the decline of what had probably been the strongest crusading state. Kalojan immediately brought his armies to besiege Thessaloniki. Despite the existence of factions and rivalries inside the city, however, all those inside did at least agree they did not want to fall to Kalojan; so an effective defense of the city was maintained until Kalojan died unexpectedly in October 1207. This brought the siege to an end. We shall turn shortly to the different rumors about the causes of Kalojan's death and the succession question it created in Bulgaria.

The Kingdom of Thessaloniki after Boniface's Death

Boniface's heir in Thessaloniki was his infant son Demetrius, who, to acquire local support for the Montferrats, had been named for the patron saint of Thessaloniki. Boniface's widow Margaret, also known as Maria, was to be regent for Demetrius. Opposition to Margaret immediately developed, and the leading local nobles and military types elected a Lombard count, Hubert of Biandrate, long a retainer of the Montferrat family, as bailiff and guardian to manage the kingdom. The count had no interest in recognizing the suzerainty of Emperor Henry and seems to have sought to tighten Thessaloniki's ties to the Montferrats of Italy, possibly hoping to create an independent state that would include most of Greece. Hubert was accused by the court in Constantinople (and many scholars accept the accusation) of also not supporting little Demetrius but of aiming instead to replace him with Demetrius' much older half-brother William, who was then living in Italy. Though most scholars have accepted the accusation, over a century and a half ago Finlay plausibly argued that Hubert's plans do not appear to have really extended beyond effecting a close union between the dominions of the two half-brothers—Thessaloniki and those in Italy—and recruiting more Lombards from Italy to garrison various fortresses in the Kingdom of Thessaloniki.

A large percentage of the Lombards in the kingdom supported Hubert. The revolt soon spread throughout much of northeastern Greece into Thessaly, Boeotia, Attica, and Euboea, and Hubert tried to assert his own direct control over certain cities assigned by Boniface to various vassals. These cities included Thebes, which Hubert's supporters managed to gain and make into a center for his operations.

Either as a matter of principle or as a means to obtain allies, Demetrius' mother Margaret was willing to establish closer ties with the emperor in Constantinople as long as the emperor supported the succession of Demetrius. Count Hubert made no move to recognize Henry as his suzerain and, in fact, did not respond when Henry summoned him to Constantinople to pay homage. So, in December 1208 Henry marched for Thessaloniki. In the cold of winter he and his army arrived at Kavalla (Christopolis), whose Lombard garrison refused to open its gates, leaving Henry to camp outside. The Lombards also refused to admit the emperor to Philippi. Henry, learning that Serres had also been ordered closed against him, avoided it and marched to Thessaloniki itself. The count refused to allow Henry to enter unless he recognized the ruler of Thessaloniki's right to govern not only Thessaloniki but also the lands to the south—Thessaly, Boeotia, Attica, and Euboea—that had been conquered by Boniface. Thus Othon de la Roche and Ravano, Boniface's former vassals who had received their fiefs from Boniface, would remain feudatories of Thessaloniki's ruler and not be directly subject to the emperor. Henry apparently had had other plans for these fiefs in central Greece. Since it was winter and he, not expecting this resistance, had not brought a large army, Henry found himself in an uncomfortable position. However, his entourage urged him to accept the count's terms since his clergy promised to absolve him whenever it suited him from any agreement he might conclude with Hubert. The agreement was duly concluded and Henry entered the city.

Henry was soon in touch with Margaret and her supporters. What exactly occurred is not certain, but Henry and Margaret's faction seem to have quickly gained the upper hand. On 6 January 1209, Henry personally crowned little Demetrius king. As Thessaloniki submitted to Henry, Count Hubert and his leading supporters made their way south through Thessaly into Boeotia. Deciding to secure Thessaloniki's northern possessions before moving against Thessaly and Boeotia, Henry sent his troops against Serres, which was taken. Then his troops moved against Drama. Near it they defeated a Lombard army and put its survivors to flight.

Having restored his and little Demetrius' authority in the north and, presumably, having summoned more troops to re-enforce his army, Henry marched south in the spring of 1209 through Thessaly down to Athens, confirming in their fiefs the followers of Boniface who submitted to him. And it seems that many of these southern barons preferred Henry's suzerainty to that of a Lombard ruler. These barons—including Othon de la Roche, the lord of Athens who held Attica and part of Boeotia, and Geoffrey Villehardouin, the bailiff of the Morea—came to a great parliament of feudal grandees which Henry held on 1–2 May 1209 at Ravennika near Lamia (Zeitounion) where they all paid homage to Henry.

The Lombard leaders were not present; they and their supporters, based in Thebes, still refused submission. Thebes, the last center of resistance, withstood an assault from Henry but then, as a result of negotiations and mediation, yielded a week later. Those surrendering at Thebes included Ravano, the leading triarch of Euboea. Thus Euboea now submitted to Henry. Henry allowed the rebels who paid homage to retain their fiefs. And Henry, it is generally believed, restored Thebes to Othon de la Roche, whom Henry invested also with Athens. Thus, according to the traditional view, the Kingdom of Thessaloniki was deprived of direct sovereignty over these southern lands—Boeotia, Attica, and Euboea—conquered by Boniface and over the Morea conquered by Boniface's vassal; for the lords holding these lands submitted directly to Henry.

Longnon does not accept the traditional view, just presented, of Othon's position. First, as noted earlier, he believes that Othon acquired Thebes for the first time only in 1211; thus anything occurring in 1209 affected only Attica and whatever other parts of Boeotia Othon may have held. Second, Longnon believes that Othon did not submit to the emperor's direct suzerainty at Ravennika in 1209 but remained under that of the King of Thessaloniki. Since at this time Thessaloniki was weak, if Longnon is correct, then Othon's choice of suzerain would reflect his own wishes and strength; thus Henry, deciding not to tangle with him, had to be content with having him only as an ally. Thereafter, as a result of Thessaloniki's weakness, Othon was to enjoy considerable independence. Longnon believes that Othon accepted the direct suzerainty of the Latin emperor only after the fall of the Kingdom of Thessaloniki to Theodore of Epirus in 1224.

Count Hubert was captured in Euboea shortly after Henry's conquest of Thebes and persuaded to submit to Henry; he then retired to Italy, leaving Thessaloniki under Margaret. She maintained close ties with Henry, who named Thessaloniki's military commander and also concerned himself with Thessaloniki's defenses.

At this time Michael of Epirus, realizing that Henry, supported by a large force of Greece's barons, was now free to move against him, forestalled this threat by sending envoys to offer his submission. This was stipulated in the treaty, mentioned previously, concluded between Michael and Henry in the summer of 1209.

In 1210 Acrocorinth, which by this time was being besieged by Villehardouin, finally surrendered. Shortly thereafter—though possibly as late as 1212—Nauplia did so as well. And in 1212 Argos finally followed suit. Since Othon de la Roche had played a major role in the capture of these cities, Geoffrey granted him Argos and Nauplia as fiefs. Othon held these two cities from the Prince of Achaea. At the same time his other, and major, holdings (Attica-Boeotia) were held most probably from the Latin emperor or, as Longnon would have it, from the King of Thessaloniki. In Geoffrey's Corinth, a Latin archbishop was installed. Monemvasia, behind its massive fortifications on the southern tip of the Peloponnesus, was now the only city in the Peloponnesus to hold out against the Latins.

Nicea Proclaims Imperial Status

As the state of Nicea expanded and consolidated its rule in northwestern Anatolia more Greeks left Europe to settle there. Lascaris soon drove the Latins from most of the little territory they had occupied in western Anatolia. He then erected, to the best of his ability, a duplicate of the Byzantine Empire, establishing a court modeled on that of the fallen empire and awarding to his courtiers the full array of Byzantine court titles. In the spring of 1205, after the crusaders' withdrawal from their Anatolian invasion, Theodore Lascaris began calling himself emperor; however, many Greeks, including some in Anatolia, did not accept his claim. Theodore realized he needed a stronger foundation for his claim. He tried to persuade John Kamateros, who had been Patriarch of Constantinople at the time the city fell, to come to Nicea and carry on as patriarch. However, being elderly, John refused. He died shortly thereafter, in the spring of 1206, in Adrianople.

After much preparation, Theodore Lascaris convoked a Church Council in Holy Week 1208 in Nicea which elected a new Ecumenical Patriarch, Michael IV Autorianos. Then, on Easter Sunday 1208, this patriarch crowned Theodore Lascaris Emperor of the Romans. This, of course, was the title borne by the Greek emperors who had ruled in Constantinople; patriarchs of that city had borne the title Ecumenical Patriarch. Thus Lascaris had ceremonially sanctioned his claim that his state was the continuation of the Roman Empire, which had acquired a new seat in Nicea while its former capital of Constantinople was under temporary foreign occupation. Thus the Empire of the Romans was still held by the Greeks; in holding Constantinople, Henry was an illegal usurper. Theodore the legitimate emperor and Michael the legitimate Ecumenical Patriarch were now resident in Nicea.

Since most Greeks did not want to recognize the usurping crusaders in Constantinople as emperors and patriarchs, many were willing to accept Lascaris' actions and claims and recognize his state as the direct continuation of the pre–April 1204 empire. However, there were legal problems. There had been a definite break after the conquest, and it had taken Lascaris over a year to emerge from being an exile leader to the head of a consolidated state.

Moreover, he had not been crowned in Constantinople. It was also necessary that the patriarch perform the coronation. Furthermore, a legitimate patriarch had to have been elected by an established procedure—by the resident synod of Constantinople and by the legitimate emperor. Thus a vicious circle existed, for it required a patriarch to create an emperor and an emperor to create a patriarch, but after the death of Patriarch John in 1206 the Greeks had neither. Not only was there no existing emperor to appoint the new patriarch to succeed John but also the entire resident synod had not moved to Nicea. The council convoked by Lascaris in 1208 in Nicea to create the new patriarch was large, but it was in fact only a random collection of bishops. Thus objections could be made, and were to be made, that the patriarch chosen in Holy Week 1208 was not legally elected, and, of course, if he was not legally elected, then his crowning of Lascaris could not be valid, and Lascaris could not be a true emperor. The Niceans replied that exceptional circumstances necessitated a flexible interpretation of the laws and even certain modifications in them. The right to do this was well established, Niceans would claim, by the Church's established principle of Economy, which allowed flexibility in interpreting the law when emergencies required it as long as the spirit of the faith was retained.

Boril in Bulgaria and Balkan Affairs, 1207–13

The death of Kalojan before the walls of Thessaloniki in October 1207 is shrouded in mystery. According to Acropolites he died of pleurisy. However, legend has it that Saint Demetrius had returned to his city and brought about the death of its enemy through the hand of "Manastras" (?). This legend has caused various scholars to conclude that Kalojan was murdered. Some scholars suspect the Greeks, a group that clearly had reason to dislike Kalojan, though one with limited access to him. Other scholars place the blame closer to home, accusing his boyars. Clearly Bulgarian opposition did exist; the rebellion that had broken out the year before in Trnovo reflects such dissent. That rebellion had been repressed brutally, which could have stirred up further hatred. Of specific possible candidates for murderer the name Boril is frequently advanced, mainly because he profited and gained the succession.

However, other than his benefiting and his subsequent somewhat unprincipled behavior, there is no evidence against Boril. In fact there is no evidence to suggest he was even in the vicinity of Thessaloniki at the time of Kalojan's death—though the possibility of his having hired a killer cannot be ruled out. Thus once again we must admit our ignorance. In any case, Kalojan's heir should have been Asen's minor son John Asen, then about eleven years old. But a quarrel erupted at once and Kalojan's nephew Boril emerged as tsar. John Asen's supporters, fearing for the boy's safety, smuggled him out of the country, first to the Cumans and shortly thereafter to Galicia among the Russians. Boril is usually depicted as a usurper. But given the unstable conditions in Bulgaria, it is possible that he acted primarily to keep the family in power by providing an adult for the throne. In any case, his actions do not prove he was involved in Kalojan's death; he may well have simply taken advantage of the opportunity it provided. But whatever his initial reasons for assuming power, once in possession of power Boril decided to retain it. He married Kalojan's widow, a Cuman princess, which not only enhanced his legitimacy but also presumably gained for him at least some Cuman military support. However, he was never to gain the support of the whole aristocracy or even that of his whole family.

Boril's reign was to be marked by uprisings against him and by the secession of peripheral territories from what had been Kalojan's Bulgaria. It is evident that Kalojan's state lacked strong central institutions; it had been a federation of units (each under a local chief, be he a royal appointee or a local) that had supported Kalojan either for the booty to be gained from his campaigns or from fear of punitive attack. After Kalojan's death there was little to hold the state together unless a successor were able to win boyar support and assert control over the outlying provinces. In fact, the frequency and ease with which outlying territories split away from Trnovo's rulers in Bulgaria, as well as from the rulers of other medieval Balkan states, show that these territories were not parts of anything resembling truly integrated national states (even though they are sometimes treated as such by modern scholars).

In fact it is hard to speak of any of the broader Balkan entities as states, for the population seems to have been loyal chiefly to its own locality, and localities under given warlords tended to break away whenever a profitable opportunity arose. If the risks from secession seemed too great or if the profits from staying loyal seemed worth their while, they stayed. Counties dominated by local notables existed in all Balkan states; a federation of these units, willing or otherwise, composed the state. Great war chiefs like Kalojan, having subdued or won the loyalty of a sufficient number of these local warlords, were then able to force the rest into the fold. But after gaining their submission, Kalojan, like other great medieval war chiefs, created no apparatus or bureaucracy to retain control of them. Thus, little state control existed over the boyars, be it from state officials or from an independent state army; for the army continued to be made up chiefly of regional units, each composed of a major boyar leading his own local retinue. Even when Kalojan placed one of his own appointees over a province as governor, as he did when he acquired Prosek, this figure did not have sufficient troops or staff to truly control the region; the local boyars continued to dominate in their counties. Thus a state like Kalojan's was bound to be ephemeral; under a weak tsar or during a period when a new tsar was establishing himself, these counties could, if they chose, cease to render obligations, which further weakened the center, or even secede completely. Boril was immediately faced with this situation; and overnight Bulgaria ceased to be a major power.

Boril's difficulties were compounded by considerable domestic opposition to his rule. First, there were the supporters of the legitimate heir, John

Asen. Acropolites claims that they besieged Trnovo, the capital, for seven years before taking it in 1218. This is difficult to believe; Jireček may be right when he suggests Acropolites meant seven *months*. But possibly Acropolites meant that the capital was threatened with attack throughout this period, or that actual attacks occurred sporadically during it. In any case opposition from Asen's supporters existed from the start, becoming more serious later (possibly from 1211) until finally they were to bring Asen to power in 1218. Second, Boril was opposed by two cousins (possibly one of whom was actually Boril's brother)—Strez and Alexius Slav—who felt they had an equal or even better right to rule than Boril. The circumstances behind their opposition are unknown. For it is not known whether they initiated revolts to satisfy their own ambitions or whether, innocent of such ambitions, they were driven to rebellion by Boril's distrust of them and his attempts to seize them. In any case, each led a rebellion that resulted in the secession of large chunks of territory from Bulgaria.

In his last year and a half Kalojan, hoping to conquer Thessaloniki, had shifted the emphasis of Bulgaria's military activities from eastern Thrace to eastern Macedonia. This policy change, as we have seen, allowed various Greek aristocrats of eastern Thrace, hostile to Kalojan, to secede and seek alliance with the Latin Empire; recognition by these Greeks allowed the Latin Empire to penetrate deeply into eastern Thrace without much difficulty. Thus the Latin Empire came to hold eastern Thrace, chiefly by indirect rule with Greeks holding various towns as fiefs from the emperor. Unhappy with this situation, Boril's first goal seems to have been to reassert Bulgarian authority in eastern Thrace.

Boril attacked Thrace in 1208. The Latin emperor, Henry, marched out to meet him. Reaching Adrianople, Henry sent envoys to seek the aid of a Bulgarian nobleman, Alexius Slav, who, though a first cousin of Boril, was "at war" with Boril, who "had taken his lands through deceit." Since these negotiations were to have no immediate effect, though they were to have implications shortly, we shall return to Alexius Slav later. However, it is worth mentioning his resistance to Boril here, for it reveals that Boril, while trying to carry out his Thracian campaign, was simultaneously experiencing internal difficulties. If Alexius' being "at war" with Boril indicates active fighting, then Boril clearly had to divide his manpower between two fronts, for Alexius had by then established himself in the Rhodope Mountains.

The Bulgarian and Latin armies then met at Berrhoia in Stara Zagora. Though the fighting was indecisive, Boril was able to prevent further Latin advance toward the Balkan Mountains. The Latins then withdrew in a southwesterly direction toward Philippopolis. Although Philippopolis was taken by Bulgaria in 1205, it is not clear who held the town at this moment. Quite possibly the local Greek aristocrats had reasserted their control over it after Kalojan's death. Boril's armies, pursuing the Latins, caught up with them at Philippopolis. A major battle followed, resulting in a complete Latin triumph.

Presumably after this battle, the Latins took Philippopolis. They were to hold it until 1230. Soon after its acquisition it was given as a fief to Gerard de Stroem.

Thus the result of this 1208 campaign was that Bulgaria lost manpower and more (this time western) Thracian territory. Soon, as a result of Latin activity and secession (particularly that of Strez, whom we shall meet shortly), Bulgaria had lost all its territory south of the Balkan Mountains. The separatists bear particular responsibility for these losses. Taking advantage of the freedom of action afforded by Boril's campaign in 1208 against the Latins, the separatists Alexius Slav and Strez asserted their independence and then began expanding their territories at the expense of the Bulgarian state. These territorial losses also, of course, lost for Boril the manpower that could be raised from these regions. Thus Bulgaria's military strength suffered further reductions; it was to be diminished even further in the clashes between Boril and the separatists.

Let us turn first to Alexius Slav. Weaker than Boril and needing support, Alexius Slav made an alliance with Emperor Henry shortly after Henry's victory at Philippopolis in 1208. Alexius accepted imperial suzerainty and married an illegitimate daughter of Henry. Alexius is referred to as despot, the second title in the imperial hierarchy. Acropolites states that Alexius received this title from Henry, presumably obtaining it at the time of his treaty with Henry, when he became an imperial in-law. However, as scholars have pointed out, it is always possible that he had already acquired this title from Kalojan, who, as a tsar and one who asserted all imperial prerogatives, could also have granted it. If he had obtained this title from Kalojan, then it would indicate that under Kalojan Alexius had been the second figure in Bulgaria, and one can well see why Alexius regarded Boril as a usurper and why it was said that Boril had taken "his lands." Either because he was angry at his deprivation or because Boril threatened his person, Alexius had seceded, establishing his own state in the Rhodope Mountains, now re-enforced by his alliance with Henry. This state, with certain border changes, was to exist until 1230.

The second separatist figure was Strez. He too was a nephew of Kalojan, but whether this makes him a first cousin or brother to Boril is not known. Possibly he also had more right to the throne than Boril, for the Serbian monk Theodosius states that Strez as the tsar's relative had been at the Bulgarian court at the time Kalojan died. Boril had then ordered Strez hunted down and killed. As a result Strez had fled at the very end of 1207 or the very beginning of 1208 to the Serbian court, where Grand župan Stefan received him warmly, refusing Boril's requests for extradition despite Boril's proffered bribes and gifts. However, the honor given Strez by Stefan soon excited the jealousy of various Serbian nobles. Realizing this and fearing Stefan would side with his nobles and possibly send him back to Bulgaria, Strez planned to flee. Learning of Strez's plans, Stefan reassured Strez of his continued favor and proved it by becoming a blood brother with Strez.

Kalojan had gained for Bulgaria Beograd, Braničevo, Niš, Skopje, and Prizren, all towns and regions claimed by the Serbs. The death of Kalojan and the difficulties ensuing under his successor resulted in the weakening of Bulgaria and presented the Serbs with an opportunity to acquire some of these towns. Strez's arrival at the Serbian court provided Stefan with a marvellous means to carry out his plans, a means important enough to make it worth risking the jealousy of Serbian nobles. For even though Bulgaria was weaker, Serbia was still not a great power; moreover, a Serbian attack upon Bulgarian territory might be expected to rally many Bulgarians around Boril in the defense of that territory. However, to march against Bulgarian territories with a Bulgarian claimant to the throne might be expected to divide the Bulgarians and allow Serbia to obtain the submission of various cities and regions for the Serbian-supported claimant. As a result Boril would be weakened still further and Serbian influence in these border regions would be strengthened.

The first attack was to be aimed at the Vardar valley in Macedonia, a region recently acquired by Kalojan, probably in 1205, whose population probably did not feel closely bound to Trnovo and which might be expected to support Strez. It is not known whether Stefan would have remained satisfied in having this territory in the hands of an ally or puppet, thus limiting himself to increasing Serbian influence in the area, or whether he saw this as a first step toward Serbian annexation.

Whatever Stefan's long-range motives, Strez with Serbian troops invaded Bulgarian territory. The attack occurred in 1208, presumably when Boril was campaigning in Thrace. Strez established himself, at first as a Serb vassal, in the fortress of Prosek on a high cliff overlooking the Vardar River and on the main Niš-Skopje-Thessaloniki route. This was the fortress previously held by Dobromir Chrysos. Some scholars, seeing the similarity of Chrysos' name (in Slavic, Hrs) to Strez, have argued that the two names in fact refer to one individual. However, this does not seem to have been the case. First, Strez was clearly a close relative of Kalojan. Had Chrysos had such a connection presumably Choniates would have mentioned it. Second, as noted above, when Kalojan took Prosek he established a second individual as governor there; thus there is no question of any direct continuity between Chrysos and Strez. Thus most scholars now believe that the two were entirely different individuals.

Once Strez had acquired an initial territory, presumably at first the region between the Vardar and Struma rivers on the Bulgarian border, many Bulgarians came to join him, increasing his strength and proportionally weakening Boril's. Then, with continued Serbian support, Strez expanded westward across Macedonia, eventually reaching at least Bitola. One Serbian source, presumably with considerable exaggeration, says Stefan and Strez took half of Bulgaria. Theodosius, the Serbian monk, asserts they conquered the territory from Thessaloniki (clearly not including the city) to Ohrid (some scholars feel Ohrid was taken, others do not).[16] This territory was not necessarily all taken in one campaign. They could have conquered most of it in 1208 and then added further territory early the following year. In any case, Church documents indicate that within a year or so Strez held territory extending from and including Veria (Veroia, Berrhoia, Ber)[17] in the south to and including Skopje on the Vardar in the north, and from the Struma River in the east to Bitola (if not Ohrid) in the west. As a result of this Boril's rule in Macedonia was brought to an end. Either his officials were ousted or, as probably was frequently the case, they entered Strez's service. Presumably since Strez's conquest was rapid, many towns at once opened their gates to Strez, be it owing to his own dynastic connections and popularity, or to Boril's unpopularity, or to opportunism based on their evaluation of the balance of forces and the difficulty of resisting the combined forces of Strez and Stefan.

Stefan then ordered many Serbian troops to remain in Strez's realm. Whether Stefan was satisfied with the situation and simply wanted the troops there to guarantee Strez's continued loyalty to Serbia and prevent his breaking away or whether they were intended to overthrow Strez and annex his lands is not known. Strez presumably was unhappy with their presence, particularly if he suspected they might sooner or later be used to overthrow him. Strez, by then holding strong fortresses like Prosek (documented as his in 1208), was in a position to assert considerable independence, provided he could remove the Serbs from his fortresses and surround himself with loyal supporters. And regardless of any earlier agreements, Strez surely was out for himself and would not have remained satisfied with being a Serbian puppet for long.

Serb sources report that next, as a result of the devil's actions, Strez turned against Stefan and soon made peace with the "Greeks" (i.e., Michael of Epirus) and then later even with Boril. The biased Serbian sources depict Strez as a bloodthirsty, ungrateful sadist who turned against a patron and bloodbrother who harbored no evil intentions against him. Clearly the ambitions of the two princes overlapped. And even if Stefan's intentions were honorable, Strez could never have been certain of them; moreover, the presence of Serbian troops and nobles in his fortresses could well have seemed to him a threat, an effort to control rather than aid him. Thus rightly or wrongly Strez may well have come to feel that he was being used by Serbia as a tool for it to sooner or later gain Macedonia. Tensions grew, and Serb sources report that Strez tortured some Serbian nobles and then hurled them from his fort (presumably Prosek) into the Vardar. Strez thus seems to have been making an effort to gain security and also independence by eliminating troops he could not trust.

Meanwhile, having secured his empire's control of Thrace and secured Alexius Slav as a vassal in the Rhodopes able to defend against renewed Bulgarian penetration into western Thrace, Henry at the end of 1208 marched on Thessaloniki to secure the position of little Demetrius and the pro-imperial party against the Lombard count's attempt to seize power there. (This action was described above.) Meanwhile the Greeks of Serres were hostile to the Latins, who, as noted, had regained that fortress in 1207. The city had been assigned in 1207 to a vassal of Boniface, and in 1208 was held by a garrison loyal to Count Hubert in Thessaloniki. These Greeks sent a deputation to Boril's deputy in Melnik (proof that Boril then held this city) offering Serres to Boril because they preferred the Bulgarians to the Franks. Henry, having gained control of Thessaloniki for his allies there, as we recall, then turned north in early 1209 to oust the Lombard's supporters and assert his control over Serres and the other cities of Macedonia belonging to Thessaloniki. His presence in this area may also have been intended to deter Boril from trying to assume power in Serres or intervene in this area. Henry presumably turned south into Thessaly and Attica only in March or April 1209, when he felt certain that Boril was not going to attack Thessaloniki's territory.

In 1209 Boril concluded agreements with Theodore Lascaris of Nicea and Michael of Epirus. If he tried to take any action in 1209 against Thessaloniki (and it is not certain whether or not he did), he certainly achieved nothing. However, he does seem to have moved against Strez's territory during that year, probably in the spring. If a spring date for Boril's move is correct, knowledge of this action would then have reached Henry in time to free him for his march south into Greece. At the time Boril moved against Strez (if we can believe the chronology implied in the Serb sources), Strez was trying to shed his vassalage to Stefan. Strez was too weak to achieve this entirely on his own, however. Thus if he saw the Serbs as a danger to himself and wanted to break with them, he needed a new ally. If he could negotiate a workable arrangement with Boril, he could at the same time solve his difficulties with the Serbs and secure himself from the ever-present danger of Bulgarian attack.

Boril, heading a weak and declining state and realizing his weakness after the previous year's failure against the Latins, also needed help. Strez's Macedonian territory could provide considerable manpower. Boril clearly would have liked to regain Macedonia, but he could not have been certain that he could do so militarily. However, if through negotiations he could persuade Strez to submit to his suzerainty, he could at least acquire loose control over Macedonia, possibly utilize, through Strez, some of its manpower, and keep the region in the hands of a Bulgarian rather than allow its annexation by the Serbs.

Thus it seems Boril advanced upon Macedonia. Most probably he and Strez, instead of fighting, negotiated their differences; Boril recognized Strez's rights to his lands and the two then formed an alliance. It is also possible that Boril attacked Strez and, though not powerful enough to defeat him completely, was sufficiently successful to force Strez to drop the Serbian connection and accept a Bulgarian alliance. In the latter case, Strez's actions against Serbian nobles within his lands may have followed a military clash between Strez and Boril in which Boril emerged the victor. Making the first alternative seem the more likely, however, are the absence of any evidence of Serbian military aid to Strez, which might have been expected had Strez still been Stefan's vassal, and also the statements in Serbian sources that Strez, through the devil's actions, turned against Stefan (making it appear Strez acted on his own) and then, after that, entered into negotiations with Michael and Boril.

In any case, Strez became a Bulgarian ally and an opponent of Serbia from 1209 until his death in 1214. A document from a Church synod held in 1211 refers to Strez as sevastocrator, a title just below despot. Possibly he received this title in 1209, at the time of his agreement with Boril, in which case it reflected Strez's submission and his admission to the Bulgarian court hierarchy. If the title dated back to Kalojan's time, as is also possible, its use in the Church document of 1211 would show that Boril at least recognized Strez's right to the title.

That Strez was able to obtain such favorable terms, rather than be conquered by Boril, as one might expect him to have been without Serbian support, shows that Strez had become a fairly powerful figure in his own right. He clearly had military ability and was able to acquire the loyalty of the regions he came to rule, whether because he was a member of the Bulgarian dynasty able to attract popular acceptance for that reason or because he appointed able and loyal deputies to rule his towns. In fact, no source mentions any disloyalty toward him until his demise during a campaign against Serbia in 1214. Strez appointed officials entitled "sevasts" in his major towns; each also ruled over the surrounding province. References exist, for example, to a "sevast" in Veria. Presumably his whole realm was divided into territorial units, each of which was governed by a sevast.

Michael of Epirus had allied himself with both Boril and Strez in 1209. That same year, in the summer, Michael had submitted to Henry, only to attack, probably at the end of the summer, Thessaloniki, which had also recognized Henry's suzerainty. Michael was clearly out for himself and took none of these alliances seriously. Shortly thereafter, late in 1209 or more probably early in 1210, Henry took action against Michael, which not only drove him away from Thessaloniki but also, according to a letter of Henry's, won some of their best land from Michael and Strez. Thus it seems likely that Strez had participated as an ally in Michael's attack upon Thessaloniki late in 1209 and had suffered along with Michael Henry's retaliation shortly thereafter. By 1211 Michael had come to reconsider his policy. He probably came to the conclusion that the allied forces of Boril and Strez based in the vicinity of Thessaloniki constituted a greater threat to Epirus' long-range interests (i.e., the eventual acquisition of Thessaloniki) than the town's remaining under the administration of the Latin barons. Thus in 1211 Michael disassociated himself from his Bulgarian alliances and concluded an agreement with the Latins. Soon he was to attack Strez.

At that time, in the spring of 1211, Nicean troops had crossed into Europe to lay siege to Constantinople. Henry, who had been at Thessaloniki, hurried back to defend his capital. Boril, then allied to the Niceans, thought this a golden opportunity and prepared an ambush to waylay Henry. However, Henry was able to avoid it and reach Constantinople safely. He then dispatched an army against Boril, who seems again to have been operating in some part of Thrace. As far as we can tell, Boril's activities in Thrace early in 1211 were without any significant result. After Henry's departure from Thessaloniki in the spring of 1211, Strez directed an attack against the Latins there; Michael of Epirus came to the aid of the barons, and together they expelled Strez from the city's environs. Michael then acquired further troops from his new allies, the barons of Thessaloniki, and pursued Strez's retreating forces, penetrating into Strez's western Macedonian territory. Boril immediately sent troops to support his new ally Strez. The combined Bulgarian armies met those of Michael and his Latin allies in early summer 1211 at Pelagonia (modern Bitola) and suffered a major defeat. However, as far as we know, Michael did not acquire any Macedonian territory to speak of at this time. Thus we may presume his losses were heavy enough to prevent him from pursuing the campaign.

Meanwhile Henry had persuaded the Seljuk Sultan of Iconium to attack Nicea. This attack forced the Niceans to raise their siege of Constantinople and return to Anatolia to defend their state from the Seljuks. The Niceans rapidly drove out the Turks. Henry, in the meantime, had launched troops into Anatolia hoping to catch the Niceans in a two-front war. When he learned the Turkish invaders had been repelled, he realized that he had no chance now of acquiring territory in Anatolia, so he withdrew his forces. However, during Henry's brief foray into Anatolia against Nicea, Boril had tried to take advantage of his absence to attack Thessaloniki in October 1211. The Latin barons, this time with help from Alexius Slav, defeated Boril's forces and drove them away.

The Bulgarian cause was sputtering. Strez was surely weaker after his defeat at Pelagonia; and having the barons and Michael lined up against him probably forced him to give up his goal of southward expansion, though his men probably still carried out sporadic raids in that region. For his part, Boril had also met with failure; he had proved unable to regain the territory lost in Thrace and had had no success against Thessaloniki. Thus these two territorial goals, which he had fought against the Latins to achieve from 1207 to 1211, had not been realized, and there seemed little chance that he would realize them in the future. In fact, Boril's attempts to realize them had brought about further territorial losses for Bulgaria. In 1208 his attempt to regain eastern Thrace had ended in Bulgaria's losing all Thrace. And in 1211 when he had attacked the Latins he had suffered further losses in Bulgaria, as Henry's ally Alexius Slav had not only helped expel Boril from Thessaloniki but had also taken advantage of the absence from Bulgaria of Boril's troops on that campaign to take Boril's town of Melnik, which then became Alexius' main residence.

Perhaps Boril's failures stirred up dissatisfaction at home. A revolt in Vidin, whose date is unknown, has often been dated by scholars to 1211 and associated with such discontent. However, a recent redating of this Vidin uprising to 1213 (to be discussed below) seems more plausible. But even if the revolt occurred as late as 1213, popular dissatisfaction with his reign may still have existed as early as 1211 and caused Boril to make efforts to rally Church support for his regime. For in 1211 Boril convoked a Church synod whose main stated purpose was to condemn the Bogomil heretics and demand their persecution.

Many scholars have argued that the existence of the synod at this time suggests the Bogomils were increasing in number and becoming a threat to Orthodoxy in Bulgaria; hence the synod was summoned to meet an actual threat. Some scholars have claimed that dissatisfaction over the military failures and internal chaos of the time had encouraged Bulgarians to turn against the establishment and join the heresy. However, we actually know almost nothing about Bogomils at this time. No other sources refer to Bogomils in Bulgaria during this period. And one might expect Greek or Crusader sources, written at a time when both Greeks and Latins were warring against Kalojan and then Boril, to have used the presence of heretics to smear the Bulgarians, if heretics had actually been numerous. Moreover, after the synod of 1211 nothing more is said about Bogomils for the duration of Boril's reign. We also have no evidence that any actual persecutions followed the synod. Thus I do not believe we can conclude that Bogomils were numerous in Bulgaria at the time. It seems more likely that the Orthodox Church wanted state action taken against what was still a small sect, and Boril, to acquire Church support, obliged by holding the synod.

Certain recent Bulgarian scholars have tried to differentiate between the religious policies of Kalojan and Boril. They have depicted Kalojan as a leader having broad religious tolerance—or possibly it is more accurate to say indifference—who was willing to negotiate and ally with the pope and other Catholics and who even seemed tolerant to the Paulicians of Philippopolis who wanted to surrender their town to him. They describe Boril as a more narrow and zealous Orthodox Churchman, who condemned heresy and made alliances primarily with Orthodox states. However, this is reading a great deal into a few specific items; and, as we shall soon see, a little more than a year after Boril's anti-Bogomil synod Boril was to enter into alliances and close relations with both the Catholic Latin emperor and the Catholic King of Hungary.

Boril's 1213 Alliance with the Latins and the Conclusion of his Reign

It was clearly in Henry's interests to make peace with Bulgaria and end the Bulgarian threat to Thrace and Thessaloniki, so as to allow a greater concentration of his limited resources against the Nicean danger. The papacy approved this plan, for it would provide greater security for the lands of the Latin East. So in 1213 a papal legate traveled to Bulgaria to offer Boril peace and an alliance.

Since he could not gain Thessaloniki or the Thracian territory he sought, but only suffered losses in men and territory by trying, it made sense for Boril to re-orient his policy. Peace with the Latins made sense; for if he could not wrest territory away from them, peace and their support would enable him to retain what he still had. So, Boril accepted the offer. To seal the alliance Henry, a widower, married Boril's "daughter" (in fact she was Kalojan's daughter whom Boril had adopted when he married Kalojan's widow). The wedding probably occurred also in 1213. Soon thereafter Boril married Henry's niece, the daughter of Henry's sister. To facilitate the arrangement, Kalojan's widow—Boril's wife up to this time—was probably packed off to a convent. In 1213 Henry also married off two other nieces, daughters of the same sister, one to King Andrew II of Hungary and the other to Theodore Lascaris of Nicea. Henry's alliance with Bulgaria remained firm until Henry's death in 1216.

Meanwhile a revolt broke out in Vidin that is generally attributed by scholars to popular dissatisfaction with Boril's failures. The uprising, undated in our sources, is usually dated to 1211. Recently Dančeva-Vasileva has argued that the uprising probably broke out in 1213 after the Bulgarian and Hungarian rulers married the two sisters, for the King of Hungary came to Boril's aid.[18] Dančeva-Vasileva believes this marriage created the ties that led to Hungarian support of Boril. For before Boril's Latin alliance, during which time Boril had been carrying out a staunch anti-Latin policy, such co-opera-tion from the zealous Catholic King of Hungary would have been unlikely. The argument is sound, but not conclusive. In any case, between 1211 and 1213 an uprising led by three Cuman officers and supported by other Cumans broke out in Vidin. It soon spread throughout northwestern Bulgaria. Boril could not put it down. Since the province of Vidin lay on the Danube, the border with Hungary, Boril sought aid from the King of Hungary. The king willingly sent it. Hungarian troops defeated the main rebel army on the River Ogosta, where many rebels were killed and many others taken prisoner. Then the Hungarians marched on Vidin and after a siege took the town and finally the rebellion was ended.

The causes of the rebellion, as noted, are not known. Possibly it was simply another manifestation of local separatism; supporting this theory is the fact that Vidin frequently followed a separatist course later on. Possibly it reflected disillusionment with Boril's military failures, or, if it did take place in 1213, opposition to his alliance with the Latins and to his relinquishing claims to Thrace. Since Cumans led it, it might even have reflected anger at Boril for divorcing his Cuman wife. Possibly these Cumans in Vidin were her relatives. Finally, the rebellion could well have been initiated on behalf of young John Asen. Cumans were to support him when he regained the throne in 1218. That support might have begun earlier, since Acropolites reports that seven years of action preceded his restoration. Possibly the Vidin revolt was part of that action. Nonetheless, to link Cuman support for the Vidin revolt to later Cuman support for John Asen is a weak argument. There were Cumans throughout Bulgaria. They were involved in most major events and were often to be found divided in any given conflict, some supporting one side and some the other. Thus one should neither expect there to have been a single "Cuman policy" nor treat the Cumans as if they were a monolithic group.

It has been suggested that at this time Hungary, as the price for its aid to Boril, regained Beograd and Braničevo, taken from Hungary by Kalojan. It seems to me, however, that since the Hungarians felt so strongly about regaining these cities, they probably had retaken them immediately when conditions became unsettled after Kalojan's death. Not only was Boril struggling then to secure his position against domestic rivals, but he was occupied on the opposite frontier fighting the Latins in Thrace during 1208. Thus one should probably date Bulgaria's loss of these two cities to 1207 or 1208. Quite possibly, however, Boril in 1213 (or in 1211 if the revolt occurred then) to obtain Hungarian aid did relinquish his claim to them and recognize Hungarian possession. Relations between Bulgaria and Hungary remained cordial. In 1214 Hungarian envoys came to Bulgaria to arrange the engagement of King Andrew's oldest son (the future Bela IV) to Boril's daughter.

Boril's alliance with Henry made things difficult for the separatists. For until then Alexius Slav had been allied with Henry against Boril. Moreover by this time, 1213, Alexius' position had become much weaker, since his main bond with Henry, his marriage to Henry's daughter, had been broken by the lady's death. Needing new allies, Alexius Slav soon entered into a close association with Epirus sealed by his marriage in 1216 to the niece of the wife of Theodore, Michael of Epirus' successor.

Strez's options were also reduced, for he too could no longer campaign against Henry or Thessaloniki since this would bring him into conflict with Henry's new ally and Strez's own suzerain, Boril. Not surprisingly, Strez was soon drawn into the Bulgarian-Latin alliance. This was to be appealing to Strez, for almost immediately that alliance was directed against the Serbs, and Strez presumably had been expecting Serbian retaliation for his defection.

That the Bulgarian-Latin alliance was to be directed against Serbia also suggests that Boril was not the weak incompetent he often is said to have been. This verdict, though often seen, could well be doubted on the basis of the evidence already presented; for Henry was not likely to have pressed for an alliance with Boril and concluded two marriages with his family had Boril not been a worrisome adversary. Boril's influence is further shown by the fact that the alliance was almost immediately directed against the Serbs. The Serbs were neighbors of, and problems for, Boril but should have been a matter of indifference for Henry. In no way did the Serbs threaten any imperial possessions, nor had they as yet warred against or even supported a war against the Latin Empire. That the alliance was directed against them, clearly in Boril's interests, shows that he was influential enough to guide the alliance's policies toward the fulfillment of his own aims.

The 1214 War, the End of Strez, and the Division
of his Lands

In 1214 the new allies planned a two-pronged attack. The Latins' and Boril's troops were to advance upon Serbia from the east while Strez invaded from the south. It has been argued that Michael of Epirus also participated in this alliance. However, this does not appear to have been the case. Michael intervened only later and seems simply to have been taking advantage of the opportunity created by the others. It has also been suggested by scholars that Henry's and Boril's ally, the King of Hungary, participated in the campaign. Whereas the Serbs may have feared this would occur, and though there may even have been some discussion along these lines between the Hungarians and the allies, there is no mention in the sources of any actual Hungarian action.

The Latin and Bulgarian armies reached Niš, while Strez moved up the Vardar valley and probably made camp at or near Polog (modern Tetovo) on the Vardar. Serbia was faced with what seemed a desperate situation, with a two-front war against a coalition which, if it had brought the large armies it was capable of mobilizing, should have had far stronger forces than anything Serbia, alone and without allies, could have raised. Grand župan Stefan sent envoys to try to negotiate peace with Strez while he mobilized an army to oppose Strez's attack. When Stefan's negotiators failed, Stefan's brother the monk Sava, abbot of Studenica (the monastery where Nemanja's body was interred) went as an envoy to Strez's camp, which was pitched on Serbia's border and from which Strez's men had been plundering the Serbian border region. Sava's words, we are told by the Serbian sources, made a great impression on some of Strez's leading followers but not on Strez himself. So, Sava's efforts also failed. Sava departed, but that very night Strez died. Immediately thereafter many of Strez's leading associates deserted to the Serbs, and his army disintegrated, and so ended the danger to the Serbs. The mysterious death of Strez is depicted as a miracle by the Serbian sources. According to Theodosius' *Life of Saint Sava*, a member of Strez's entourage reported that Strez had suffered an attack in his sleep that had made it difficult for him to breathe. Then, waking up, Strez had gasped out that a terrible youth, at the command of Sava, had attacked him while he slept, using Strez's own sword to stab his innards.

Whereas the Serbs depict Strez's death as a miracle and claim that Sava's prayers to Nemanja caused an angel to kill Strez, it seems more likely that Strez was the victim of a murder plot, which the miraculous tales were trying to cover up. Clearly Sava, who had already departed, did not actually stab Strez. But Sava's presence immediately beforehand and the fact he had proposed terms that had impressed many of Strez's courtiers suggest that Sava had not only made contacts but might also have found allies at the camp. Thus when Sava realized he could not get Strez to call off the campaign, he could have hired or persuaded some of Strez's followers to kill him. Strez's claim that the terrible youth had stabbed him at Sava's command suggests Sava's involvement, and the desertion to the Serbian camp of many of Strez's leading associates suggests at least the existence of a pro-Serb party at Strez's camp, if not the participation of some of its members in the actual murder. Their guilt would have explained their flight, for they may well not have been sure which faction would get the upper hand upon Strez's death. In any case, with or without Sava's involvement, it seems probable that a pro-Serbian party in Strez's entourage killed him.

The Latin and Bulgarian allies at Niš, however, took no action. Perhaps their inactivity was owing to Serbian defensive actions on this front, actions not mentioned in any surviving source. Or perhaps news of Strez's death, which made it possible for Stefan to meet any attack they might make with his entire force, discouraged them. In any case, the Serbian sources simply state that disorders occurred in the allies' camp, after which they withdrew and Serbia was spared. However, Serbia did not capitalize on Strez's death to acquire any of his lands. This suggests that at least some of the allied troops had remained at Niš or that Stefan feared their return to Niš, and thus he kept his armies in Serbia to defend Serbia rather than sending them south to pick off Strez's lands.

The fate of Strez's territory is also obscure. Some scholars believe that Boril occupied the bulk of this Macedonian territory, either by a campaign— which may explain why he took no action against Serbia, preferring to use his men to recover Macedonia—or by the submission to him of Strez's deputies who might well have preferred rule by Boril to rule by Serbia or Epirus. If Boril did in fact acquire some or all of Strez's Macedonia, he retained it only briefly, for by 1217 all the Macedonian towns for which documentation exists were under the rule of Theodore, Michael of Epirus' successor. Thus one must postulate either a short-lived annexation of territory by Boril that was soon taken by Theodore or else visualize the immediate conquest of some or all of these towns by Michael himself late in 1214, which gave them to Theodore when he inherited the Epirote state. It also is possible that in 1214 both Bulgaria and Epirus were active in Macedonia, with each obtaining territory, but with Bulgaria keeping what it acquired only briefly. Moreover, it has been argued that some of Strez's southeastern holdings bordering on the Kingdom of Thessaloniki may have been grabbed by the Latin barons of Thessaloniki. If the barons did annex part of Strez's lands, their possession was to be short-lasting also.

In any case, after the failure of the invading forces to attack Serbia and while Stefan, for whatever reason, took no action beyond his own borders, Michael of Epirus went on the offensive. Though Theodosius' *Life of Sava* implies Michael was an ally of Strez, Boril, and Henry, most scholars think Michael had not joined the alliance but, simply seeing a good chance to add territory to his state, had gone into action for himself upon Strez's death. He seems to have acquired at least some of western Macedonia (and, as noted, it is possible he annexed even more of Macedonia than that) and then marched into the region of Albania. Soon he turned northward, taking Skadar, and then made plans to march on Zeta. Threatened by this new enemy, Stefan dispatched his forces for Zeta. Whether Zeta was at the time more-or-less under his authority or still under George, whom the sources do not mention in connection with these events, is not clear. Whether the two armies actually clashed in Zeta or not is also not known. However, once again Stefan was saved by what seemed a miracle. In late 1214 or early 1215, while stationed at Berat in Albania, Michael was murdered by a servant. Nemanja's intercession is said to have played a role here too. This ended the Epirote threat to Serbia, because Michael's heir Theodore was much more interested in the lands to Serbia's south, Macedonia and Thessaly, including Thessaloniki, and even Constantinople itself.

Thus Stefan was able to recover southern Zeta, including Skadar and any other fortresses Michael might have taken in that region. It is not clear exactly when Stefan recovered Skadar from Epirus. However, since Stefan had troops in Zeta and Theodore does not seem to have been interested in contesting Zeta, Stefan probably recovered whatever losses the Serbs had sustained in Zeta promptly. Furthermore, one may assume that, if he had not done so already, Stefan must now have used the armies he had in Zeta to assert his own control over that region. Thus if George had been able to maintain his independent appanage—or part of it—up to this time, he would have lost it to Stefan now.

Since Theodore's interests lay to his east, as noted, he did not want to quarrel with Serbia over Zeta. In fact, to avoid a two-front war when he moved against the Latin territories in the east, it was important to him to be assured of good relations with Serbia. So, he concluded a treaty with Stefan. In this he renounced his claims to the northern Albanian-Zetan area, thereby taking pressure off Serbia from the south. If he still possessed any Zetan fortresses, presumably he relinquished them after the treaty was signed. Theodore thereupon married Stefan's sister, and shortly thereafter Stefan's eldest son Radoslav, who was officially declared to be Stefan's heir by 1220, married Theodore's daughter Anna. Their marriage probably occurred in 1219 or 1220.

In 1215 Serbia found itself threatened again. This time, Serb sources claim, the Latins and Hungarians were preparing an attack on Serbia. Other than these preparations, whatever they were, there seems to have been no Hungarian action. Nor is there this time any sign of action by Boril against the Serbs, though this might have been expected in order to prevent the Serbs from moving into Strez's former lands. We would also expect Henry to have pressured his ally Boril into action, for why would Henry have been preparing to attack the Serbs at all unless it was to aid Boril? One certainly would not expect Henry to have been planning to put his armies in the field in such a situation if Boril was remaining on the sidelines. If any action did occur, which is not certain, there is no evidence that it had any results of importance. In 1216, a later Serb source claims, the Hungarians again prepared for war against Serbia. It seems this attack was forestalled by negotiations. In any case we learn where the Serbian-Hungarian border then lay, because the negotiations that took place on the common border between the two rulers occurred at Ravno (modern Ćuprije) on the Morava, mid-way between Beograd and Niš. Thus the Hungarians evidently still held, as would be expected, Beograd and Braničevo. Since Vidin stood as the Bulgarian province bordering on Hungary, Hungary's eastern border with Bulgaria must have lain somewhere between the Morava and Timok rivers.

John Asen Overthrows Boril

Boril seems to have found himself in an increasingly weak position in his last years, though he maintained the Latin alliance until the end. In June 1216 his ally Emperor Henry died. The following year his second ally, the King of Hungary, went east to crusade. Possibly because Boril now lacked outside support, his enemies decided the time had come to strike. In any case, in 1218 John Asen's supporters summoned him back from Russia. The young prince was now an adult of about twenty. They marched on Trnovo, whose citizens opened the gates to him. Boril was blinded and John Asen II (1218–41) became tsar. During the decade of Boril's rule, even though he may have been less incompetent than earlier historians have tended to think, Bulgaria clearly suffered considerable decline. It lost all its territory south of the Balkan Mountains, and two large chunks of southwestern territory seceded under Alexius Slav and Strez respectively. After Strez's death Epirus, and possibly also Thessaloniki (though only briefly)—not Bulgaria—acquired Strez's lands. And even if Boril had at first occupied some of Strez's territory, as certain scholars believe, he still was not able to retain it. During the decade that Boril ruled, 1207–18, the initiative in the Balkans had passed from Bulgaria to Epirus, ruled from 1215 by the vigorous Theodore. It was to take John Asen twelve years to restore Bulgaria to sufficient strength to reverse the balance.

Serbia in the Second Decade of the Thirteenth Century

Grand župan Stefan's main concern in the second decade of the thirteenth century, after he had overcome the threats from Strez and Michael of Epirus, seems to have been directed toward the west, and in particular to securing his control over Zeta. By 1216 he seems to have temporarily eliminated Vukan's son George and to have annexed Zeta. Scholars have long claimed that having annexed Zeta, Stefan assigned it—along with Trebinje—to his eldest son Radoslav to administer. This action, by establishing in Zeta as governor the heir to the throne, might have facilitated the binding of this newly gained area more tightly to Serbia and have hindered a reassertion of separatism. Recently, however, some scholars have argued that Stefan, fearing to do anything that might encourage Zeta's tradition of separateness and independence, did not want to give Zeta the special status of an appanage and thus continued to rule Zeta directly.

As noted in the last chapter, at some point Stefan intervened on behalf of Miroslav's son Andrew of Hum against Andrew's brother Peter, who had expelled Andrew and taken over most of Hum. Some scholars would date this intervention to 1216, believing that as soon as Stefan had annexed Zeta and was free to turn to other problems, he intervened in Hum, which bordered on Zeta. Whether he then assigned much of Hum to his son Radoslav, as Orbini claims, is uncertain. In any case, he probably would have tried to assert direct Raškan control, be it his own or his son's, over as much of Hum as possible. And Orbini insists that Andrew, in whose name Stefan acted, received only a small part of Hum, just Popovo Polje and the coast. Peter seems to have withdrawn across the Neretva, retaining only the territory between that river and the Cetina.

With so much of his attention directed to the western Serbian lands where the Catholic Church enjoyed considerable support, particularly in the coastal regions (western Zeta as far inland as Podgorica and western Hum with Trebinje), Stefan naturally came to have considerable contact with Catholic leaders, both noblemen and churchmen. He also entered into closer relations with Venice. According to a later Venetian chronicle, in 1216 or 1217 (some scholars believe it actually was earlier) Stefan married Anna, the granddaughter of the Venetian doge Henry Dandolo. Venetian influence seems to have increased in Serbia from this time. Thus Catholic influence within the state presumably increased. Stefan, as we have seen, had long wanted to assume the title king. In 1217 a papal legate at last appeared in Serbia and carried out the royal coronation. Stefan has gone down in history as Stefan the "First-Crowned" (Prvovenčani) to distinguish him from the many other Stefans who ruled Serbia. The frequency of this name resulted from the fact that Serbia's patron saint was Stephen the First Martyr.

It has been argued that since the only crown and kingship then recognized in the Serbian lands was that of Duklja (Zeta), Stefan must have been crowned with the crown of Duklja. Since George had been eliminated, no one was then wearing that crown; thus Stefan, as the conqueror of Zeta, had acquired the right to it. While this is a perfectly plausible hypothesis, it should be noted that there was nothing to prevent the pope from using his own authority to create new kingships. What promises Stefan made to the pope and what role, if any, the Catholic Church consequently obtained in Raška itself are not known.

However, either owing to actual promises made by Stefan to the pope or to their fears that concessions to Rome and Church Union were likely to be the next logical step, many of the Serbian Church hierarchs seem to have opposed the coronation and closer relations with Rome. Stefan's brother Sava, abbot of Studenica and the most influential churchman in Serbia, expressed his protest by leaving Serbia. He returned in 1217 to Mount Athos. Since he seems to have left Athos previously owing to the influence of Catholicism on the Holy Mountain, his return is often seen as evidence that conditions for the Orthodox there had by this time improved and that the privileges Emperor Henry had granted to the Orthodox monasteries had actually been implemented.

In any case, the Catholic Church seems to have been making progress inside Serbia. However, as we shall see in the next chapter, these gains were not to be lasting. It should also be stressed that, whereas some Serbian clerics saw the Church schism as a burning issue, most secular leaders seem to have been indifferent to it and quite prepared to deal with either Church to secure their own advantage.

These relations with Rome were also to particularly bother later Serbian churchmen. Whereas Domentian in his *Life of Sava* mentions the papal coronation of Stefan, the more elaborate *Life of Sava* written by Theodosius at the turn of the thirteenth-fourteenth century, which utilized Domentian's work, ignored the papal role and claimed that Stefan had been crowned by Saint Sava. This contradiction has caused considerable controversy among scholars, including some Serbian scholars who also were troubled by the papal coronation, resulting in the theory that after he established an autocephalous Serbian Church in 1219 Sava gave Stefan a second coronation. This view has by now largely been discarded. It is generally accepted by modern scholars that Stefan had just one coronation, that from the papal legate.

The Serbian clerics were not alone in protesting Stefan's coronation. The King of Hungary did so as well, for he saw the crowning as a contravention of his own rights held ever since 1202 when, after he had helped install Vukan in Raška, he had added "Serbia" to his own title. Claiming that he alone possessed the right to the Serbian kingship, he argued that a second ruler could not be entitled King of Serbia. Serbian sources claim that the Hungarians planned military action, and some scholars believe an attack was actually launched. Stanojević, however, argues that no Hungarian attack occurred at this time.[19]

The Serbian sources, Domentian and Theodosius, state that immediately after Stefan's coronation the Hungarian king in protest began to mobilize for war, but then Sava traveled to Hungary and talked the king out of it, astonishing the monarch by miraculously procuring ice in the midst of a hot summer. As Stanojević points out, neither source states that the Hungarian king did more than prepare for war; and neither source mentions any actual fighting. Stanojević also notes that the story as given cannot be accurate; for if Theodosius is correct in stating that the Hungarian king *immediately* prepared for action, the king was not even present to take action. For in August 1217 the Hungarian king, Andrew II, had set sail from Split for Palestine as a crusader, not to return until the end of 1218. Furthermore, Sava could not have participated in negotiations at that time, as the sources claim, for immediately after the coronation he had left Serbia for Athos only to return in 1219/20. Stanojević suggests the story of Sava's negotiations with the Hungarians is actually a distorted version of the negotiations between the two states that took place in 1216, discussed above, when Stefan met Andrew at Ravno on their common border. Stanojević proceeds to describe the economic and political difficulties that then burdened Hungary and argues that for the ensuing decade Hungary was in no position to carry out a war against Serbia.

The only existing evidence from the time that suggests some fighting occurred between Hungarians and Serbs is a Hungarian charter from 1229 granted to a Hungarian nobleman which thanks him for service in a war against Serbia. If this reference to a Serbian war does not refer to some skirmish taking place between 1214 and 1216, when Hungary was allied to the members of the anti-Serbian coalition, this statement presumably refers to some small encounter against some Serbs that occurred after 1217. However, it seems safe to assume that though Hungary did protest the coronation, it took no major action. Whether action was prevented by diplomacy or by Hungary's inability to launch a campaign at the time is not known.

NOTES

1. For a list of major fiefs established by Boniface on his march through Thessaly to Boeotia, see W. Miller, *Essays on the Latin Orient* (Cambridge, 1921), pp. 62–63.

2. Longnon ("Problèmes de l'histoire de la principauté de Morée," *Journal des savants,* 1946, pp. 88–93) argues that Othon de la Roche acquired Thebes for the first time in 1211. Longnon believes Thebes was held from late 1204 or early 1205 until about 1211 by a certain Albertino of Canossa, another vassal of Boniface; Albertino seems to have supported Hubert of Biandrate's faction after Boniface's death. Setton remains on the fence on this question: "Although there is some reason to believe that Thebes was first granted to Albertino . . . , the city . . . was certainly being ruled after 1211 by Othon" (*Cambridge Medieval History,* vol. 4, pt. 1 [Cambridge, 1966], p. 389). A second controversy concerning the de la Roche holding centers around the date the de la Roche lords acquired the title duke, enabling the holding to be called a duchy. It is commonly stated that the ducal title was granted to Guy de la Roche in about 1259. However, many scholars have come to believe that the story in the *Chronicle of the Morea,* the source for this date, is pure legend. And scholars have noted that the title duke was used off and on before 1259. For example, Pope Innocent III, who usually called Othon "lord," in one letter of July 1208 called him "duke." The ducal title came into regular use, however, only in the last quarter of the thirteenth century. In any case, when, by whom, and under what circumstances the title was granted remain a mystery.

3. R.-J. Loenertz, "Aux origines du despotat d'Épire et la principauté d'Achaie," *Byzantion* 43 (1973):360–94.

4. Ducellier argues that Venice was not in a position to pose a major threat to Michael's state and would not have launched a serious war over what to it would have been relatively low priority territory. He argues the greatest threat to Epirus came initially from Thessaloniki and then after 1209 from the Latin Empire itself (Ducellier, *La façade maritime de l'Albanie au moyen âge* [Thessaloniki (Institute for Balkan

Studies), 1981], pp. 136–38). In any case, regardless of which enemy seemed most dangerous to Michael, the arguments presented above on Michael's policies and the motives for them still remain relevant.

5. B. Ferjančić, *Despoti u Vizantiji i južnoslovenskim zemljama,* SAN, Posebna izdanja, 336 (Beograd, 1960), pp. 49–58.

6. D. Nicol, *The Despotate of Epirus* (Oxford, 1957).

7. G. Finlay, *A History of Greece,* rev. ed. (Oxford, 1877), vol. 4, p. 175.

8. Finlay, *History of Greece,* vol. 4, p. 180.

9. Longnon, "Problèmes de l'histoire de la principauté de Morée," pp. 157–59.

10. For a list of the baronies, see K. M. Setton, "The Latins in Greece and the Aegean . . ." *Cambridge Medieval History,* vol. 4, pt. 1, 1966 ed., pp. 393–94. Also in Finlay, *History of Greece,* vol. 4, p. 186, n. 4. Finlay also provides a description of each baron's military and defensive role and the effect this had on determining the fiefs' locations, vol. 4, pp. 183–86.

11. For a translation of text, see P. Topping, *Feudal Institutions as Revealed in the Assizes of Romania, The Law Code of Frankish Greece* (Philadelphia, 1949). Reprinted in Topping, *Studies on Latin Greece:* A.D. *1205–1715,* Variorum reprint (London, 1977). Topping's extensive commentary to the Assizes provides a valuable essay on feudal institutions, relationships, laws, and usages in the Morea.

12. D. Jacoby, "The Encounter of Two Societies: Western Conquerors and Byzantines in the Peloponnesus after the Fourth Crusade," *American Historical Review* 78, no. 4 (October 1973): 873–906.

13. R. L. Wolff, "The Organization of the Latin Patriarchate of Constantinople, 1204–1261: Social and Administrative Consequences of the Latin Conquest," *Traditio* 6 (1948): 44–60.

14. M. Živojinović, "Sveta Gora u doba Latinskog carstva," *Zbornik radova Vizantološkog Instituta* (hereafter cited as *ZRVI*) *(Serbian Academy of Sciences)* 17 (1976): 77–90.

15. Finlay, *History of Greece,* vol. 4, p. 105.

16. E. Savčeva ("Sevastokrator Strez," *Godišnik na Sofijskija universitet* (Istoričeski fakultet) 68 [1974]:67–97) argues that at some point Strez did acquire Ohrid itself. He then sought to make Ohrid a bishopric for the territory of his state and presumably succeeded in subjecting all the towns of his realm to that archbishop. At this time Skopje, which Strez held, was transferred from the jurisdiction of Trnovo to Ohrid. This transfer would make no sense if Strez did not hold Ohrid. Though many Bulgarians received episcopal and clerical appointments at this time in towns under Strez, the major figures at Ohrid's archbishop's court remained Greek. But cf. F. Barišić and B. Ferjančić, " Vesti Dimitrija Homatijana o'vlasti Druguvita'," *ZRVI* 20 (1981): 41–55.

17. The reader should be aware that two different towns bore the name Berrhoia/Veroia (with beta's *b* sound changing to that of *v* in the course of the Middle Ages). One lay in southern Bulgaria/northern Thrace. The other, Strez's town, lay in Macedonia just north of Thessaly. The Slavs often called the latter Ber, which should not be confused with a third town Bera/Vera which lay in southern Thrace on the via Egnatia near the mouth of the Marica River. To avoid confusion I shall refer to the three places by different forms, calling the first, the southern Bulgarian town, Berrhoia; the second, the Macedonian town, Veria; and the third, the southern Thracian town, Bera.

18. A. Dančeva-Vasileva, "B"lgarija i Latinskata Imperija, 1207–1218," *Istoričeski pregled* 33, no. 1 (1977): 35–51.

19. St. Stanojević, "O napadu ugarskog Kralja Andrije II na Srbiju zbog proglasa kraljevstva," *Glas* (SKA) 161 (1934): 109–30.

CHAPTER 3

The First Half of the
Thirteenth Century

Theodore of Epirus' First Decade, 1215–24

Michael of Epirus, as we saw in the last chapter, was murdered in late 1214 or
early 1215. His murderer was a servant; whether he was hired to do the act
and, if so, by whom is not known. Michael was succeeded by his half-brother
Theodore. Theodore immediately exiled Michael's son Michael, to secure his
own authority, and then set about expanding his state. As we shall see,
Theodore rapidly doubled the size of Epirus and came to consider himself the
heir to the Byzantine Empire. This posture sharpened the rivalry between
Epirus and Nicea, for clearly they could not both regain Constantinople and
re-establish the empire. The rivalry was exacerbated still more by the increasing weakness of the Latin Empire; particularly after Emperor Henry's death in
1216, its collapse must have seemed only a matter of time. And owing to
Theodore's territorial expansion Epirus' borders moved ever nearer to Constantinople, making the possibility of Epirus' achieving this goal ever more
likely and thus an ever increasing worry for Nicea. Yet though Theodore was
a great military planner and commander, he was a fairly poor administrator
and did not consolidate his conquests well or administratively integrate them
into his state. Instead he was ever pushing on for further conquests.

Because his goal was Constantinople, Theodore willingly gave up
Michael's idea of northern expansion into Zeta and made peace with the Serbs.
To seal this peace, Theodore married Grand župan Stefan's sister. Though
relinquishing Skadar and whatever other northern Albanian-Zetan territory
Michael may have occupied, Theodore retained possession of the southern-
central Albanian lands including Durazzo. Theodore worked diligently to
assure himself of the loyalty and support of various Albanian chieftains.

Durazzo and Theodore's position in Albania were threatened almost
immediately. As noted, Emperor Henry died in 1216 without an heir. The
barons elected as his successor his brother-in-law Peter of Courtenay. Peter
was crowned by the pope in Rome. He then had to travel east to assume
control of his domain. Since the Venetians had recently lost Durazzo to

Epirus, they sought Peter's help to recover it. He agreed, deciding to land in Durazzo, recover the city, and then march overland to Constantinople, his capital. Scholars have long believed that Theodore's defenses held out, causing Peter's attack in 1217 on Durazzo to fail. Ducellier, however, following three Western chronicles, argues that Peter was successful and, having taken the city, received submission from Theodore and then, presumably leaving a garrison to hold Durazzo, proceeded to follow his original plan and march overland across Albania, Macedonia, and Thrace to Constantinople.[1] In either case, Peter left Durazzo and proceeded east overland. Not surprisingly, Theodore ambushed and captured him. For our purposes, it is not important which version is correct; for if Theodore had lost Durazzo to Peter, he quickly regained it after Peter was eliminated from the scene. Peter was subsequently executed by Theodore.

For a long time, however, Peter's fate remained a mystery; thus the administrators of the Latin Empire had to await confirmation of his death before they could elect a new emperor. At first they created a regency under Henry's sister and Peter's widow, Yolande, who had reached Constantinople safely by sea in 1217; soon after her arrival she gave birth to a son, Baldwin (II). Her regency continued until her death in 1219. Needing an adult to rule, the barons then turned the empire over to Yolande's elder son, Robert of Courtenay, who came to Constantinople and was crowned emperor in 1221.

Meanwhile, having secured himself in Epirus, Theodore pressed into Macedonia and quickly overran most of it. By the summer of 1215 he possessed Prosek and by 1216 Ohrid, where in 1216 or 1217 he installed Demetrius Chomatianus, one of his leading supporters, as archbishop. Demetrius, as we saw in the last chapter, had previously served as chancellor to that archbishopric. By 1217 Theodore held Prilep. These documented dates merely show Theodore to be in possession but do not necessarily reflect the order of conquest; for it is likely that he started in the west, gained Ohrid, and then moved straight across Macedonia through Prilep to Prosek. If such was the case, then (to the degree that Macedonia had not already been acquired by Michael in the second half of 1214 after Strez's demise) he acquired all this territory in 1215, when he is found holding Prosek. To what extent Theodore's conquests involved warfare with Boril's Bulgaria depends on the extent, if any, to which Boril had been able to recover Strez's territory. And as noted in the last chapter, some scholars believe Boril had been very successful in acquiring most of it, while others argue that Boril got little or nothing and believe Michael of Epirus had obtained the lion's share of it while the barons of Thessaloniki, taking some of Strez's eastern lands, had taken the rest. In any case, regardless of how much credit Michael and Theodore respectively should receive for these conquests, by 1217 Theodore was in possession of Macedonia at least as far east as the Vardar if not beyond it to the Struma.

As Theodore expanded toward the Struma he threatened the holdings of Alexius Slav in the vicinity of Melnik, stretching into the Rhodopes. Alexius had become isolated first when his wife, Henry's illegitimate daughter, had died and then further in 1213 when Henry allied himself with Boril, Alexius' major enemy. Needing support and finding Theodore threatening his lands from the west, Alexius realized he needed either to make peace with Boril to guarantee his borders from Theodore's expansion or else to seek an alliance with Theodore to prop himself up against Boril. If Theodore was then at war with Boril over Strez's former Macedonian holdings, as seems likely, then an alliance with Alexius would have proved useful to Theodore. Thus in 1216 Theodore concluded a treaty with Alexius, who married the niece of Theodore's wife.

Theodore, in the meantime, having obtained Macedonia, pressed into Thessaly and, over the next five or so years, conquered it all. In Thessaly he assigned pronoias to various Greeks of aristocratic families. At the same time he reduced most of the fortresses in the vicinity of Thessaloniki. Thus by about 1220 Theodore held all Greece west of the Pindus Mountains together with southern Albania, Macedonia, and Thessaly except for Thessaloniki itself, which, after Theodore's capture of Serres in 1221, had become more or less an island in the midst of Theodore's possessions. This city, all that was left of Boniface's once relatively strong kingdom, now held out under an ineffective regency for the little Demetrius headed by his mother, Boniface's widow.

Thus it seemed only a matter of time before Theodore would obtain Thessaloniki. There was no power able to come to the city's relief and Theodore faced no serious enemy on any of his borders. The Duchy of Athens, bordering him in Thessaly, was taking care not to provoke Theodore into attacking it; Asen, a novice ruler, was still trying to assert himself over his central lands; and Serbia enjoyed good relations with Theodore. By this time a serious Church dispute had erupted between Serbia and the Archbishop of Ohrid. But, as we shall see, though Serbia's policy incensed Theodore's leading bishop Demetrius Chomatianus, it did not affect Theodore's policy of maintaining cordial political relations with Serbia. For his eastern goals necessitated his maintaining a peaceful border with Serbia to prevent it from attacking him in the rear when he was involved in the east. Thus in 1219 or 1220, in the midst of the Church quarrel, to be described shortly, Theodore's daughter married Stefan's son Radoslav.

Quarrel between the Churches of Epirus and Nicea

In these years the Greek Church found itself in a complex situation. Since the Latin Empire would not allow the election of a Greek Patriarch of Constantinople and permitted the existence only of its own Latin patriarch in that city, the Greeks of Nicea in 1208 had convoked a council and created a new Ecumenical Patriarch (the title of their former Patriarch of Constantinople) who established his residence in Nicea. This new patriarch then crowned Theodore Lascaris emperor. As noted, the manner in which this patriarch was created—by the convocation of a synod of bishops who happened to be present rather than by a body properly constituted according to Church canons—gave a basis for any opponent of the new patriarch or of Nicea to reject his claims to patriarchal status and also to reject the validity of the coronation he performed for Theodore Lascaris and therefore the legitimacy of Theodore's title. Nicea argued that both expediency and the critical situation faced by the Greek Church, as it fought to preserve Orthodoxy against the serious Latin threat to it, justified a very loose interpretation of canons. If the Greeks wanted to preserve their Church hierarchy, some action had to be taken, and it was impossible to take action if the letter of the law had to be followed.

Meanwhile in Epirus, it became necessary to replace bishops as they died. Furthermore, as Theodore expanded into territory that had been under the Latins, he expelled those Latin bishops he found in office. So, when the former Greek bishops were not available to be restored to office, new Greek bishops had to be appointed. In 1213 a regular standing synod of Epirote bishops had been created to carry out this task, in that year appointing new bishops for Durazzo and Larissa. Soon two such synods existed for western Greece, one for the south centered in Naupaktos and one for the north centered in Ohrid. And since Archbishop Demetrius of Ohrid was younger, abler, more ambitious, and more wholehearted in his loyalty to Theodore's political aims, Theodore turned more and more to Demetrius, who with his synod soon obtained greater influence than did John Apocaucus, Metropolitan of Naupaktos and his synod.

In view of his own ambitions to regain Constantinople and become emperor, it is not surprising that Theodore did not want to recognize Lascaris' title. He had a sound basis for refusal if he rejected the legality of the 1208 events. At the same time Theodore's leading bishop, Demetrius, was ambitious as well. An excellent and serious canonist, he probably really did harbor doubts about the legality of the 1208 synod at Nicea. Furthermore, it was in the interest of his own authority to reject that synod. For if the Epirotes recognized the legality of the 1208 synod and the patriarch's claims, they would have to recognize that patriarch's actions—which would have meant recognizing Lascaris as emperor. Furthermore, if they recognized the legitimacy of the Nicean patriarch, they would also have to concede him the right to appoint bishops in Epirus, which could lead to the appointment of pro-Lascaris bishops there.

Thus Demetrius argued that Epirus should have ecclesiastical autonomy: namely, the right to administer Church affairs for its territorial state. Nicea, of course, argued that despite state boundaries the Ecumenical Patriarch should have jurisdiction over the whole Greek Church; things eternal should not be governed by a temporary secular situation. Demetrius' party might admit the principle stated, but would deny that the bishop in Nicea was really the Ecumenical Patriarch. In 1213, Michael of Epirus, who had not entered into the theoretical issue, had sought recognition from the patriarch for his two new bishops of Larissa and Durazzo appointed by the newly created Epirote synod out of the practical need to fill vacant sees. Already worried about principles and precedents, the Nicean patriarch had simply ignored his request. Under Theodore the Epirote synods continued to fill an increasing number of ecclesiastical vacancies with their own appointees. It seems they ceased informing or seeking confirmation from Nicea for these. Nicea began to protest, claiming the right to appoint or at least confirm episcopal appointees. And Nicea now began to appoint men to fill the Epirote sees, whom the Epirotes refused to accept, claiming, plausibly enough, that Nicea did not understand enough about local conditions to intervene in Epirote Church affairs. Thus frequently—as in the cases just cited—the reasons given by Epirus for refusing to accept Nicea's appointees remained practical rather than canonical-theoretical.

However, regardless of the nature of Epirote objections, Nicea's patriarch, Manuel I Sarantenos (1215–22), convinced of his right as patriarch to exercise jurisdiction over Epirus, was bent on asserting that right. In 1222 Manuel convoked a synod at which he insisted on his authority to appoint bishops for Epirus. He stated that though he was willing to compromise and recognize any bishops in Epirus now in office, he would tolerate no further uncanonical ordinations of bishops by the Epirotes. His synod rubber-stamped his position. Manuel died later that year, but his successor Germanos II was equally adamant and maintained Manuel's policies firmly.

Creation of an Autocephalous Serbian Church, 1219

Meanwhile, as the Nicean-Epirote dispute began to heat up, Sava decided the Serbs could profit from it by obtaining an independent Church. At that time Sava was on Athos in protest of Stefan's closer ties with the pope, from whom Stefan had received a royal crown. Presumably Sava hoped to draw Stefan away from his Western ties by obtaining Byzantine (i.e., Nicean) recognition of his royal title and at the same time winning an independent Serbian Church. Nothing is known about the preparations preceding Sava's actions. Did Sava act entirely on his own, or had he been in touch with his brother and obtained some sort of agreement from him? In any case, in 1219 Sava left Athos for Nicea.

At that time the Serbian bishopric was a suffragan of Ohrid, the chief bishopric in Theodore's state and Nicea's main opponent in the developing Church dispute. In Nicea, Sava agreed to recognize the patriarch in Nicea as the Ecumenical Patriarch in exchange for Nicea's granting Serbia's Church autocephalous (autonomous) status. The Nicean patriarch was happy to do so, for at one stroke of the pen he was able to reduce by almost half the size of his rival's (Demetrius of Ohrid's) territory. And since Serbia had not even recognized Nicea before, Nicea lost nothing by recognizing Serbian autonomy. In fact, through Serbia's recognition Nicea gained support for its claims and was brought into closer and friendlier relations with the Serbs. The Patriarch of Nicea appointed Sava as Archbishop of Serbia to head the new Church.

Thereafter the Serbs were to manage their own Church, and autocephalous status allowed the Serbs henceforth to choose their own archbishop.

Sava returned to Serbia; he was to head its Church until he abdicated in 1233. He was well received by King Stefan, who was pleased by the arrangement and threw his support wholeheartedly behind his brother, the new archbishop. His ties with the Catholic Church dwindled. Serbia was never to fall under strong Catholic influence thereafter. Sava's first task was to place all Serbian territory under the jurisdiction of its new archbishop. This necessitated the ousting in 1220 of Greek bishops from the recently acquired towns of Prizren and Lipljan. Sava then proceeded to construct Serbia's Church administration, dividing all Serbia's territory (including Zeta and Hum) up into about ten bishoprics. The inclusion of Zeta and Hum contributed to the binding of these previously separate Serbian regions more tightly to Raška by helping their populations to identify themselves as Serbs and to perceive a commonality of interest with the Serbs of Raška. Sava then appointed bishops to fill these sees. The sees had jurisdiction over the following regions: Raška, Hum (with its seat in Ston), Zeta (with its seat at Prevlaka on the Gulf of Kotor), the Coast (Primorje), Hvosno (the Metohija), Budimlje (modern Ivangrad), Dabar, Morava, Toplica, and Prizren-Lipljan.

The establishment of these dioceses necessitated the employment of many more priests, but there were not enough available; thus certain regions were to be almost entirely priestless. A life of Sava notes, for example, that he sent priests on tours of the countryside to at last marry many old, middle-aged, and young people who had long lived together without the Church's blessing. The Church leaders also hoped to reduce the role of the Catholic Church in Serbia's western regions, including the coast. However, they did not expel Catholic bishops, as they did Greek ones. Thus in the west the Catholic organization continued to exist parallel to the Serbian Church, with each confession having in the same town its own church buildings, clergy, and occasionally even bishops. The Catholic hierarchy along the coast and its organizational problems will be treated later. In the years that followed a certain number of conversions from Catholicism to Orthodoxy occurred in western Zeta and in southern Dalmatia, where the Catholic Church had been strong.

As Catholic influence declined, the alliance between Church and dynasty was reasserted, and both ruler and Church worked to make the Church a strong national institution closely tied to the holy dynasty. The Church was to have a major role in medieval Serbia. Its leaders participated in state affairs, side by side with the aristocracy. High clerics were frequently drawn from the greatest families, including the royal family, which played a dominant role in the Church as well as in the state. The Church, through its canons, was to provide the foundations of the state's legal order until the following century. When the state created chancelleries it needed literate officials, and the clergy provided many of these. Not only did clerics witness and draw up charters, but they also were to play a major role in diplomacy. Each ruler stuck to the pattern established by Nemanja and built at least one major monastery, his zadužbina (obligation), for the salvation of his soul. Many of these magnificent monasteries are still standing and a few are even active to the present. Many rulers built other churches as well and gave these and other monasteries lavish gifts including large landed estates and whole villages. They also continued to endow Hilandar on Athos with villages inside Serbia.

As new churches built by the rulers spread through Serbia, they played a role in Christianizing the populace—converting pagans or further Christianizing many peasants who had been only nominal Christians. The wealthier monasteries also provided schools, some of which probably taught only monks and young men destined to be clerics; these schools increased the number of literate Serbs, especially clerics and monks. Major monasteries also kept libraries containing Byzantine works translated into Slavic from the Greek (translated either at the monasteries themselves in Serbia or at Hilandar on Mount Athos and then brought to Serbia) as well as original Serbian works which began to appear in the thirteenth century. Sava played a major role in translations, doing some himself and encouraging others. Sava also produced original works such as his monastic rule and his biography of Simeon (Nemanja) couched as a saint's life. For furthering education, literacy, translations, and original writing, Sava earned the popular epithet of Illuminator (enlightener) of the Serbs.

In 1221, the year after Sava's major organizing efforts, Sava convoked a Church council at Žiča, the monastery built by Stefan and the first seat of the Serbian archbishop. This Council endorsed the new administrative structure of the Church and also endorsed Sava's episcopal appointees. Sava also presented at the Council a translation of the Byzantine Nomocanon that he had worked on for over ten years.

Perhaps as early as 1208 Sava had begun translating Greek Canon laws into Serbian for the use of the Serbian state and its churches. He had used as his basic text the *Byzantine Nomocanon of Fourteen Titles* (from the seventh century) which he modified with the canonical commentaries of Aristinos (from the third quarter of the twelfth century) and, when Aristinos' interpretations did not suit what Sava saw as Serbia's needs, Sava turned to the canonical commentaries of John Zonaras. Sava completed his work in 1220 in Thessaloniki where presumably he was able to find the texts he needed. He intended his translation to become, as it now officially did in 1221, the legal basis of the Serbian Church. His version made the Church and state equal partners; to achieve this he had to omit those Byzantine legal texts (the *Ecloga,* the *Epanagoge,* and Balsamon's commentaries from the twelfth century) that subordinated the Church to the state. Since Church canons also devoted much attention to how Christians were to live, Sava's compilation also was to have considerable impact on what we might consider civil law.

The 1221 council endorsed Sava's text which, as seen, was basically a translation drawn from the three Byzantine texts, but whose articles were carefully selected to fit what Sava saw as Serbia's needs. Sava's Nomocanon became the main legal code for the Serbian state which was to have no other official statewide law code until it was supplemented in the fourteenth century by a secular code.[2] Arguments can be advanced that a secular code was first issued by Milutin (1282–1321). If his legislative efforts, most of which have not survived, did not comprise what one would call a code, then Serbia had to await Dušan's code, issued in 1349, as its first secular law code. (The Nomocanon was also translated from Greek and introduced into Bulgaria early in the thirteenth century.)

The Žiča council also endorsed the Sinodik of Orthodoxy, a ninth-century affirmation of Orthodoxy that condemned a variety of earlier heresies. To it were regularly appended anathemas of subsequent heresies. Sava not only conveyed to Serbia his translation of Byzantine Canon Law texts but also brought translations of monastic rules from Athos to be used in, or adapted for, Serbian monasteries. Sava brought as well translations of other Greek texts (sermons, saints' lives) to Serbia and encouraged ties between Serbia and Athos, where an increasing number of Serbs were to go as monks. There, in contact with the Greek cultural world and Athos' fine libraries, more and more Serbs came into contact with the Greek theological heritage. And, as noted, Serbs did not limit themselves to Hilandar but also resided in various of the Greek institutions on Athos. New translations followed over the next centuries and the Serbian Church acquired through them, as well as through oral contacts between Serbs and monks of other nationalities on Athos, many of the fruits of the ancient heritage of Orthodoxy.

Needless to say, Demetrius of Ohrid was infuriated by the agreement between Sava and Nicea. He denied its legality, arguing that the Nicean patriarch was not the true patriarch; moreover, he further argued that even if he were the true patriarch he still did not have a canonical right to remove territory from Ohrid's archdiocese. For Emperor Basil II in 1018 had removed Ohrid from the jurisdiction of the Patriarch of Constantinople and made it an autocephalous archbishopric directly under the emperor; thus no patriarch had any right to interfere in the affairs of Ohrid's diocese. And Demetrius went on to point out that prior to the disaster of 1204 Patriarchs of Constantinople had recognized both Ohrid's autocephaly and Ohrid's jurisdiction over Serbia. Demetrius also launched a personal attack against Sava.

However, though Theodore was probably unhappy with Sava's action, he could not afford to break off his Serbian alliance. Thus he seems to have tolerated what had occurred, allowing his daughter to marry Radoslav, Stefan's heir, in 1219 or 1220, at the very height of the crisis—surely a gesture of good will designed to allay any alarm Stefan might have felt about the possibility of Theodore going to war against him.

Theodore Acquires Thessaloniki and Coronation

In December 1224 after a long siege, Theodore conquered Thessaloniki, putting an end to that Latin state. In the West there was talk about a new crusade for its recovery, but nothing was to come of it. Theodore ousted the Latin bishop of the city and restored the exiled Greek metropolitan.

Having conquered the second city of Byzantium, Theodore felt his claims to Constantinople were as strong as those of Nicea's ruler. Thus he, too, was justified in taking the title emperor. He put on the purple boots, dress worn only by an emperor, and began planning his coronation. Constantine Mesopotamites, the Metropolitan of Thessaloniki, restored to his see by Theodore, doubted Theodore's right to the title, however. For though a majority of Epirote bishops supported Theodore and Demetrius' position on Church autonomy for Epirus, a minority of Epirote bishops had recognized the legitimacy of the Nicean council of 1208 and Nicea's reasoning to justify its legitimacy; this minority therefore accepted the council's decision that gave patriarchal status to Nicea and also the patriarch's action in crowning Lascaris emperor. When Thessaloniki's bishop refused to participate in Theodore's coronation and went back into exile, Theodore convoked an assembly at Arta in Epirus to approve his imperial claims. Then, with that approval obtained, his loyal supporter Demetrius of Ohrid, possessor of the state's second ranking see after Thessaloniki, crowned Theodore Emperor of the Romans (the official title of the Byzantine emperor). This coronation occurred between December 1224 and 1227, most probably in 1225.

Nicea's horror at and condemnation of Theodore's coronation intensified the Church quarrel. What right did a Bulgarian bishop (for Ohrid not only lay in a Slavic area but had also been the chief bishopric for Bulgaria under Samuel [976–1014]) have to crown an Emperor of the Romans? demanded Germanos, Patriarch of Nicea. Trying at first to avoid a fight with Theodore, the Niceans tried to place the blame for this "illegal action" on the irresponsible and ambitious Demetrius. At the same time, since the see of Durazzo had recently fallen vacant again, the Nicean patriarch, to assert his prerogatives, appointed a new bishop for that see. The Epirotes, not surprisingly, rejected the appointment. The Epirote synod in fact named a close friend of Demetrius to fill the see and announced as a matter of principle that Epirus would accept no Nicean appointees to sees in Epirus. Then Theodore expelled from Durazzo the Nicean candidate, asking on what authority could the Bishop of Nicea appoint bishops in Europe. Demetrius, moreover, argued that, on the basis of pre-1204 rankings, his see of Ohrid (as the successor of the important and ancient see of Justiniana Prima) ranked higher than the see of Nicea. Indeed, through much of this dispute Demetrius treated the patriarch in Nicea as if he were only the regular Bishop of Nicea. For, it could be argued, after the death of the last Greek Patriarch of Constantinople in 1206 the Ecumenical Patriarchate had ceased to exist.

In about 1227 Theodore convoked a new council at Arta to discuss the deteriorating relations between the Churches of Nicea and Epirus. Though some, led by Demetrius, felt strongly enough about the autonomy of the Epirote Church to risk schism over it, many other Epirote bishops were disturbed by the situation that was developing. These moderates, who may well have been in the majority, did not want a schism but instead sought a united Greek Church to better face the Latin threat. For practical reasons they were willing to resist the encroachment of the Nicean patriarch into Epirus, but if the patriarch were willing to go half way, they, in order to unite the Greek Church, would be willing to accept him as the nominal head of the Greek Church. As a result the Arta council put forward a compromise, which it persuaded Theodore to accept. Noting that their ruler, Theodore, would not permit Nicean nominees to occupy Epirote sees, they requested the patriarch to grant them autonomy by allowing the Epirote assembly to name local bishops. They emphasized that it was administrative autonomy they were seeking and insisted that since they had no intention of making doctrinal changes, they were quite willing to leave doctrinal authority to the patriarch. If the Nicean patriarch were to agree to this request, then Theodore would allow the patriarch's name to be mentioned in church services and recognize the right of Epirotes to appeal to the patriarch. Thus in the compromise the Epirotes went so far as to recognize the Nicean bishop as Ecumenical Patriarch, demanding only administrative autonomy for themselves. The patriarch was called upon to reply in three months. This offer was accompanied by the threat that if the patriarch refused, Theodore might consider submitting to Rome.

The patriarch, however, wanting all or nothing, refused to take the olive branch offered him. A whole year passed before he sent envoys to refuse the demands and once again to protest over the uncanonical election of the bishops of Durazzo and Thessaloniki. The patriarch's message was delivered to an assembly of Epirote bishops at Arta which, obedient to Theodore, rejected the message. Moreover, since Theodore had involved himself in the dispute, the Nicean clergy had begun to attack Theodore. Thus, not surprisingly, a full-scale schism between the two branches of the Greek Church followed. The schism was to last until 1232–33.

In 1224 or 1225 Theodore also occupied the Chalcidic peninsula, including Mount Athos. After Pope Innocent III's death in 1216, various of the monasteries that seem to have submitted to Rome soon broke away again, as Innocent's successor Honorius III (1216–27) was unable to effect his will on the mountain. As noted, Sava felt free to return to Athos as an Orthodox center as early as 1217. A few years later some of the monasteries were in regular contact with the patriarch in Nicea. Hence Honorius in 1223 referred to the Athos monks as disobedient rebels. Then in 1224–25, after the monasteries had again come under the jurisdiction of an Orthodox ruler Theodore, all pressure from the Catholic Church was ended. Theodore does not seem to have pressured the monks on Athos to involve themselves in his dispute with Nicea. One may presume that he knew, or at least suspected, that various, possibly even many, important monastic figures recognized the Nicean patriarch as the Ecumenical Patriarch and would, if pressed, come out against Theodore and damage his cause.

Theodore's Ambitions and Actions, 1225–30

After Theodore's coronation in 1225 there were four rulers in the region of Constantinople who claimed the title emperor, one of whom held Constantinople while the other three sought to gain it. They were the Latin emperor, who possessed Constantinople and hoped to retain it; the emperor in Nicea; Theodore of Epirus-Thessaloniki; and Tsar John Asen II of Bulgaria. By now Asen had greatly strengthened his position, having built up his armies and consolidated his hold over the central Bulgarian territory; thus Bulgaria was a considerable Balkan power again. Even so, Asen did not yet feel strong enough to challenge Theodore over Macedonia or to assert himself against Alexius Slav in the Rhodopes. Each of the three have-not emperors possessed strong armies and stood, given a bit of luck, a realistic chance of gaining Constantinople. And after the fall of Thessaloniki, Constantinople truly stood alone.

Excluding island possessions, the Westerners retained in Greece only Attica-Boeotia and the Morea (Peloponnesus). By this time a new generation governed these two duchies. Othon de la Roche had returned to France in 1225, and his nephew Guy had succeeded him in Athens. Geoffrey Villehardouin had died, probably in about 1228, to be succeeded by his son Geoffrey II. The new Morean ruler was to enjoy a peaceful reign, and under him the Morea achieved considerable economic prosperity. However, despite the strength and prosperity of these two Latin states, they lay at too great a distance from Constantinople to provide effective aid for it in the event of an emergency. The chief reason that Constantinople was to remain Latin until 1261 was the rivalry among its enemies, whose warfare against one another prevented any of them from taking the city.

After acquiring Thessaloniki, Theodore began to think seriously about Constantinople. Nicea, aware of this interest and realizing all northern Greece, with western Thrace, was in Theodore's hands, felt it had to act quickly. So, in 1225, responding to the appeals of the Greek population of Latin-ruled Adrianople, Nicea, under John Vatatzes, who had succeeded to the throne on Theodore Lascaris' death in 1222, launched its forces into Europe. The gates of Adrianople were opened to the Niceans. Surrounded by Nicean forces on all sides, Constantinople seemed about to fall to Nicea. To prevent this from happening, Theodore quickly led his army into Thrace toward Adrianople. Threatened by a larger army, the Niceans immediately yielded, agreeing to vacate both Adrianople and the rest of Thrace. Theodore, having occupied Adrianople, then provided ships to ferry the Niceans back to Asia Minor.

Theodore, moving from victory to victory, now after this campaign, held Thrace comprehensively as far east as Mosynopolis and also Adrianople. As a result he seemed even nearer success than Vatatzes had been. Theodore realized, however, that taking Constantinople would require a long siege for which he was not at the moment prepared. In particular he feared being hit in the rear by the Bulgarians, who could thereby trap his men between their attacking forces and the walls of Constantinople. Thus Theodore understood that before he could attack the capital, he must conclude an agreement with John Asen. The alliance between Epirus-Thessaloniki and Bulgaria was soon concluded, sealed by a marriage between Theodore's brother Manuel and a daughter of Asen. Then, late in 1225, Theodore brought his armies to Constantinople, but neither being technically prepared nor having the time for the long siege he saw would be needed, he withdrew.

Expecting an attack from Theodore and thus needing allies, the Latin Empire turned to Nicea, which also was interested in preventing Theodore from obtaining Constantinople. Nicea and the Latins had been skirmishing in Anatolia; now after a Nicean military victory, the two sides ended their state of war and reached an agreement. In exchange for an alliance and for support against Theodore, the Latin Empire agreed to give up its last holdings in Anatolia to Nicea. This agreement was carried out; Nicea now held all northwestern Anatolia, and the Latin Empire was now more-or-less limited to the city of Constantinople itself and its immediate environs.

At this point a major question forces itself upon us. Now that Theodore had concluded his Bulgarian alliance, freeing him to attack Constantinople, why did he not do so in 1226 or in the years immediately following? Not only are we unable to answer this question, but we have no information on what he did concern himself with over the next few years. In 1228 his chances of success seem to have improved further when Emperor Robert died, leaving his eleven-year-old half-brother, Baldwin II, as heir. An interregnum or rule by regency would seem to have provided an ideal time for an attack. But Theodore still took no action.

Seeing the weakness of the Latin Empire and the probability of its fall if it received no outside help, Asen, it seems, offered the Latins in 1228 a solution that would provide such aid. He offered a marriage between his daughter Helen and the young Latin emperor Baldwin II. As father-in-law of the emperor he could then have assumed direction of the regency and drawn from Bulgaria sufficient troops to defend Constantinople from Theodore's attack. The Latins, presumably seeing this scheme as a revival of Symeon's plans from the tenth century which would have ended up delivering the city to the Bulgarians, did not want to accept this offer. But it seems they did not actually turn Asen down, but strung out negotiations with him—possibly even agreeing to an engagement between his daughter Helen and Baldwin— to keep his hopes up and prevent him from participating in any action by his nominal ally Theodore. Possibly they even hoped to procure Bulgarian troops from him to use against Theodore, if they could get them without actually agreeing to make Asen regent or letting him enter the city.[3]

Meanwhile, the barons and papacy decided to offer the regency, together with the title of emperor, to an aged but able Western knight, John of Brienne. John accepted the offer in an agreement concluded, with papal confirmation, in April 1229 at Perugia. The agreement seems to have been kept secret for a time from the non-Latin actors in the East. It was agreed that Brienne would go east, be crowned emperor, and assume command of the defense of Constantinople. If Brienne, who in 1229 was already over eighty, should still be alive when Baldwin reached his majority, at age twenty in 1237, then the two would rule as co-emperors. Brienne had various affairs to settle in the West; thus he did not arrive in Constantinople until 1231, when the major threat, as we shall see, was over. Upon his arrival Brienne was crowned and assumed control of the Latin Empire.

Meanwhile, in 1230 Theodore finally decided to march on Constantinople. But suddenly, his armies changed course en route and entered Bulgaria. Evidence about his motives has not survived. Had he received word of the Latin-Bulgar negotiations of 1228, which may well have continued during 1229, and come to believe the two states were on the verge of concluding, or even had concluded, an alliance against him? In any case, we may presume that for some reason Theodore had concluded he could not trust Asen not to attack him during the siege of Constantinople, which clearly was going to be a long one. If Theodore felt himself faced with that eventuality, he had to reduce Bulgaria first in order to protect his rear.

The Battle of Klokotnica (1230) and its Results for Bulgaria

John Asen II seemed surprised by Theodore's attack and played the role of an injured innocent who found himself attacked perfidiously by an ally with whom he had had a treaty. He quickly put together an army, said to have been assembled on the spur of the moment and thus considerably smaller than the forces with which Theodore was invading Bulgaria. He marched out to meet Theodore, with a copy of their treaty, including Theodore's seal and oath, affixed to his standard. The two armies met in April 1230 at the village of Klokotnica on the Marica River, close to Philippopolis on the route between that city and Adrianople. The Bulgarians enjoyed a massive victory and Theodore was captured.

A recently discovered letter in Hebrew, which discusses Jewish affairs in southeastern Europe, reports that Asen, having decided to blind Theodore so as to put an end to him imperial pretensions, ordered two Jews to carry out the deed. (Jews were frequently used as executioners in medieval eastern Europe.) It appears that he also expected them to carry out the act willingly, for the letter reports that Theodore had been persecuting the Jews in his territories as an excuse to confiscate their wealth, which he needed for his campaigns. (The persecution of Jews in Thessaloniki was not a new phenomenon under Theodore. Benjamin of Tudela, a rabbi who had traveled through the Balkans in the 1160s, reports that in his day there were about five hundred Jewish inhabitants in Thessaloniki who were much oppressed.) Theodore was flung to the ground and the Jews were ordered to blind "their enemy," but Theodore begged so piteously for mercy that the Jews refused to carry out the order. As a result Asen lost his temper with them and had them thrown to their deaths from a high cliff. This did not save Theodore, who was blinded anyway and then pitched into a Bulgarian prison where he languished for the next seven years.

Once again the Latin Empire was saved by the rivalry between its enemies. Asen next mobilized a larger army and marched through Macedonia into Albania, taking one after the other most of Theodore's Macedonian and Albanian fortresses, including Serres, Prilep, and Ohrid. He also acquired more of Thrace, including Philippopolis with the Marica valley, Demotika, and Adrianople. As Kalojan had done earlier, Asen consistently replaced Greek bishops in the towns he conquered with Bulgarian ones.

It is often stated that Asen also took Durazzo. The evidence for this claim comes from an inscription, to be discussed below, that states Asen held all the land from Adrianople to Durazzo. However, as Ducellier notes, "to" does not necessarily mean "and including." He points out that in 1230, after the battle, Asen issued a charter of trading privileges to Dubrovnik in which were listed Asen's major towns; Durazzo is not to be found among them. Durazzo was a major commercial town; had Asen possessed it, one would expect it to be mentioned. Thus Ducellier concludes that though Asen's forces reached Durazzo, they did not take the town itself, which remained under the rule of Theodore's brother and successor Manuel.[4] Thus in one stroke at Klokotnica Asen had shattered the might of Theodore's state. The speed with which its northern holdings fell and its remaining territory fragmented shows how poorly Theodore had organized his administration and integrated his territories.

Klokotnica also spelled the end for Alexius Slav's principality in the Rhodopes. Presumably all that had prevented Asen from absorbing Alexius' principality previously was Alexius' alliance with Theodore. Having lost this prop, Alexius was clearly no match for the powerful Bulgarian ruler. Whether Asen had to carry out a military campaign against Alexius or whether Alexius surrendered on demand to receive a court position and lands elsewhere, as most scholars think, is not known. In any case Alexius' lands once again were incorporated into the Bulgarian state and Alexius himself disappears from the sources.

A contemporary inscription survives that expresses Asen's view of the situation:

> I waged war in Romania, defeated the Greek army, and captured the Lord Emperor Theodore Comnenus himself and all his boyars. And I occupied all the land from Adrianople to Durazzo, Greek, Serbian, and Albanian alike. The Franks hold only the cities in the vicinity of Constantinople itself. But even they [these cities] are under the authority of my empire since they have no other emperor but me, and only thanks to me do they survive, for thus God has decreed.

Asen, however, did not yet have Constantinople. But he still seems to have been thinking of obtaining the regency over little Baldwin—as is seen when he asserts that the Latins "have no emperor but me." This suggests that the Latins had been stringing out negotiations with him and that he was unaware of the Perugia agreement of 1229 that had already awarded the throne to Brienne. To have kept Perugia secret would have been sensible policy on the Latins' part to prevent Asen from co-operating with Theodore. But now after Theodore's defeat, the Latins had no further need of Asen. So they broke off negotiations with him. Soon Asen learned that John of Brienne had been invited to govern Constantinople, and, as noted, John arrived there in 1231. Burning for revenge, Asen at once opened negotiations with Nicea for a joint attack on Constantinople.

Thessaloniki-Epirus after Klokotnica

After Klokotnica, Thessaloniki-Epirus was a shell of what it had recently been; the weakness of Theodore's administration is shown by the speed with which the kingdom collapsed after his capture. The northern territory, Macedonia and Albania, as noted, went to Bulgaria. Theodore's brother Manuel took the throne in Thessaloniki; he was also at first ruler of Thessaly, Epirus, the isle of Corfu, and probably Durazzo. However, he was far weaker than Theodore had been, and Thessaloniki-Epirus was for the moment out of the running for Constantinople. After the battle, not surprisingly, Manuel found himself more or less a client of the victorious Asen. (Since 1225 Manuel had also been married to Asen's daughter.) As Asen's client, Manuel seems to have been allowed control over internal affairs in the territory he retained but not to have enjoyed independence in foreign affairs. In the struggle for Constantinople, to be discussed below, among the Latin Empire, Nicea, and Bulgaria, Manuel was unable to capitalize on their rivalries to advance any claim of his own for Constantinople, to recover territory, or to reassert to any extent his freedom of action. It also seems that none of the three rivals involved, Latins, Niceans, or Bulgarians, thought it worth their while to seek his aid.

In Church matters Manuel also found himself hemmed in. Asen, as noted, was installing Bulgarians as bishops in the Macedonian territory he occupied, expelling the Greek incumbents. Having conquered the Chalcidic peninsula, later in 1230, Asen also visited Mount Athos (situated near the tip of this peninsula) and announced his protection over the monasteries; his charters make it appear that the monasteries had sought this protection. Asen gave the monasteries rich gifts and confirmed their earlier charters as well. He was especially generous to the Zographou monastery which by now had become a Bulgarian house. Though the monastery dated back to the late tenth century, it had become a center for Bulgarian monks only in the early thirteenth century, probably around 1220. Asen then tried to give his bishop in Trnovo jurisdiction over Mount Athos. The monasteries protested, as they always did when attempts were made to place urban bishops over them. Apparently Asen backed down on this issue; at least he does not seem to have taken any action to facilitate his bishop's acquiring actual control over Athos.

At the same time, however, Asen did successfully acquire for Trnovo's hierarch jurisdiction over the various bishoprics he had conquered from Epirus. He also attempted to place his Trnovo bishop over various bishoprics in the territory retained by Manuel. To do this he tried to subordinate the Metropolitan of Thessaloniki to the hierarch in Trnovo and named a loyal clergyman to occupy the Thessaloniki metropolitanate. This was considered an even more unacceptable violation of canons and traditions than Nicea's earlier attempts to subordinate the bishops of Epirus to the hierarch in Nicea. Not only did the clergy of Thessaloniki and Epirus express strong objections, but the Athonite monks protested to the patriarch in Nicea about it.

To prevent the Bulgarians from achieving domination over his Church, Manuel sent envoys to negotiate with Nicea. He expressed his willingness to recognize the patriarch there as ecumenical and to submit to him. Thus to escape from an even more unpleasant situation, a weakened Epirus submitted to Nicea. And thus the schism between the two branches of the Greek Church was brought to an end. Manuel, in negotiating his submission, had tried to maintain a certain amount of autonomy for his Church. By emphasizing the difficulties of transportation and the time required to travel between Greece and Nicea, he hoped to avoid sending his bishops to Nicea for ordination. And he sought for western Greece freedom to elect its own bishops, as it had been doing since 1213.

Germanos II, patriarch in Nicea, however, would have none of this. His reply blamed past difficulties entirely on Epirus. Problems in communication, he declared, were irrelevant and merely a pretext to prolong the schism. In fact, the issue could easily be resolved, he claimed, if Nicea were to send thither a legate as plenipotentiary to carry out ordinations and supervise western Greek Church affairs. Germanos then proceeded to realize his suggestion by sending west as his legate Christopher, Bishop of Ancyra (Ankara). Manuel, though presumably not happy with this turn of events, received Christopher cordially. Christopher then convoked a synod of western bishops in 1233 at which Germanos' letter was read. The western Greeks thereupon renounced all claims to ecclesiastical independence, and the schism was officially proclaimed at an end. The legate also received complaints from the Athonite monks concerning Bulgarian interference in the administration of Athos and of the diocese of Thessaloniki.

In the years that followed, the Niceans regularly sent Church officials west to assert and implement the authority their patriarch claimed. Demetrius Chomatianus remained defiant to the end. But by this time his influence in politics was greatly reduced. He was not only older and less energetic, but his see, Ohrid, was no longer even part of the Thessaloniki-Epirus state but belonged to Asen's Bulgaria; moreover, his ally and protector Theodore was no longer in power in Thessaloniki. Thus the border changes and the Bulgarian threat altered the issues of conflict and made Demetrius' concerns considerably less relevant to Manuel and his prelates. Demetrius died soon thereafter, in about 1234.

Asen seems to have taken no action to prevent the Nicean-Epirote negotiations. At that time he himself was trying to enter into closer relations with Nicea, which included obtaining Nicea's recognition of patriarchal rank for his bishop in Trnovo. Presumably Asen thought it best to obtain his main goals rather than risk them by starting a quarrel with Nicea over the Epirote Church, which while a secondary issue for Bulgaria was a major one for Nicea.

Manuel's weakened state continued to decline. By 1236 northern Greece found itself divided among members of the ruling family. Michael of Epirus' son Michael II, who had fled to the Morea when Theodore took over in 1215, returned and established himself in his father's old capital of Arta in Epirus. He seems to have received considerable local Epirote support. His return may well have occurred immediately after the Battle of Klokotnica, when Theodore was out of the picture and Manuel was in no position to oppose him. Manuel seems to have recognized him shortly thereafter, in exchange for Michael's recognition of Manuel's suzerainty. That this submission occurred is suggested by the fact that in his charters Michael II called himself "despot." This title is documented for Michael from 1236, but it may well have been taken a few years before. This title, second in the Byzantine court hierarchy after emperor (basileus), could be bestowed only by an emperor. When Theodore assumed the title emperor in 1225, he had made his brothers Manuel and Constantine despots. Subsequently, when Manuel succeeded Theodore, he had assumed the imperial title for himself. Then, soon thereafter, Manuel as emperor had apparently granted this title to Michael in exchange for Michael's recognition of Manuel's suzerainty. It should be stressed, however, that this was a ceremonial court title, not a functional one. Thus Michael was a ruler of Epirus who happened to be a despot. Michael was not despot *of* Epirus and thus Epirus was not a despotate.

As Manuel's actual power did not increase during the next few years while Michael's did, Michael became more and more independent. He also expanded his authority over the rest of Epirus, and by 1236 he also had Corfu. By 1236 whatever suzerainty Manuel might have claimed had become entirely nominal. Michael II clearly managed his territory as he saw fit, as if it were an independent state. In 1237, as an independent prince, and without seeking confirmation from Manuel, Michael issued a charter granting commercial privileges in his realm to the merchants of Dubrovnik. While the 1230s were years of decline for Thessaloniki and its territories, they were years of prosperity for Epirus.

Bulgarian-Hungarian Relations

The Bulgarian negotiations with Nicea, opened after John of Brienne's assumption of power in Constantinople in 1231 (to be discussed shortly), affected Bulgaria's relations with Hungary. As noted above, Boril had entered into close and somewhat dependent relations with Hungary in 1213, and Hungary, probably in that same year, had helped him put down the Vidin rebellion. Returning from his crusade in late 1218, the Hungarian king Andrew II appeared on Bulgaria's border, intending to return home by crossing Bulgaria. Instead of finding his client and friend Boril in power, he found John Asen II. Asen seized Andrew and allowed him to proceed on his journey only after he had agreed to a marriage between Asen and Andrew's daughter Maria. The wedding occurred early in 1221. Presumably, a major reason for Asen's insistence upon the marriage was his determination to regain Beograd and Braničevo. For he seems to have procured these cities and their provinces as the princess' dowry. These two cities were still Bulgarian in 1230, for in Asen's charter of privilege granted to Dubrovnik in that year they are mentioned as Bulgarian cities in which Ragusan merchants were to enjoy free trade.

Presumably the Hungarians were not happy about the loss of these cities, which they felt were rightfully theirs. Presumably they also disapproved of Asen's breaking off negotiations with the Latin Empire and entering into an alliance, in 1232, with Nicea against the Latin Empire. Hungary, as a zealous Catholic power, regularly maintained good relations with the Latin Empire. Thus Bulgaria's break with Constantinople and the threat it now posed to it—leading Brienne to call upon Hungary to attack Bulgaria—provided an additional excuse for the Hungarians to break with Bulgaria. So, in 1232, when Asen was involved in affairs to his south, the Hungarians attacked northwestern Bulgaria and took Beograd and Braničevo. They also laid siege to Vidin. Alexander, Asen's brother, led a Bulgarian army to relieve that siege. He suffered a defeat before its walls, but the defenders within Vidin held out successfully, so the Hungarians did not capture Vidin itself. After withdrawing from Vidin, the Hungarian troops crossed the Danube into Wallachia, where they occupied the Severin region, creating a special banate there in 1233.

Bulgarian-Nicean Relations

Asen was unable to respond to the Hungarian provocation because of his increasing involvement in affairs concerning Constantinople. Angry at the Latins, Asen established closer relations with Nicea. In 1234 an engagement between his daughter and the Nicean heir was agreed upon. Then in the spring of 1235 the Niceans crossed the Dardanelles and occupied Gallipoli. Asen and his family arrived there to meet with Vatatzes and his court. At this meeting their differences on Church questions were resolved. The Trnovo bishopric renounced its claims of suzerainty over Thessaloniki. In response to complaints made to the Nicean patriarch by the Mount Athos monks it was also agreed that the Trnovo bishop had no authority over Mount Athos. Furthermore Asen and his bishop recognized that the Patriarch of Nicea had jurisdiction over eastern Thrace. Finally the Bulgarians recognized the patriarch in Nicea as the Ecumenical Patriarch. In exchange the Nicean patriarch recognized the bishop in Trnovo as a patriarch and the Bulgarian Church as autocephalous. The Athos monks, relieved of Trnovo's interference, gave their support to Trnovo's newly recognized status.

To be sure, the Bulgarian Church had been claiming patriarchal status ever since the time of Kalojan; until 1235, however, Byzantium (i.e., Nicea) had not recognized these claims. This recognition for his Church was useful to Asen, particularly in his relations with the Greeks in the territory he had annexed. The status of the Bulgarian Church was officially recognized in a formal ceremony in 1235 at which Asen's daughter Helen married Theodore (II) Lascaris, heir to the Nicean throne. Each child was then about ten years old. The frontier between the two states was also formally established. The treaty recognized as Bulgarian everything northwest of the lower Marica, which incidentally established the Bulgarian-Nicean border along the line of the present Greek-Turkish border.

Shortly thereafter the Nicean patriarch asserted his newly recognized authority by installing a new metropolitan in Thessaloniki. On this occasion he pleased the monks of Athos by asserting that Thessaloniki also was to have no authority over Athos. The monasteries, he decreed, were to be independent of all episcopal control.

From Gallipoli Vatatzes moved north, taking from the Latins a chunk of eastern Thrace including Tzurulum. From there he moved to the coast and occupied the coast of eastern Thrace as far west as the mouth of the Marica. The two allies, the Bulgarians and Niceans, then laid siege to Constantinople. The capital, defended by the aged John of Brienne, a small garrison of knights, the Venetian fleet, and in 1236 also by some troops provided by Geoffrey II Villehardouin of the Morea, heroically held out; but the situation was so critical that Constantinople's fall seemed but a matter of time. So in 1236, the young emperor Baldwin II was sent west by ship to seek further aid for his beleaguered capital. While involved in this effort Asen clearly could not take action against Hungary.

Meanwhile, as the Nicean-Bulgarian siege of Constantinople continued into 1236, it finally became clear to Asen that a victory for their coalition would simply give Constantinople to the Niceans; and a Greek empire centered there under the Nicean dynasty would be a greater impediment to a future Bulgarian conquest of Constantinople and also a greater danger to the state of Bulgaria in general than the continued rule of the weak Latins. So, once again Constantinople was saved by a quarrel between two of its enemies. Asen unilaterally broke off his alliance with Nicea and, it seems, sent an envoy to demand the return of his daughter. He then recruited a number of Cumans and declared war on Nicea.

Cumans were then appearing in the Balkans in large numbers. Displaced from their Steppe homes by the Mongols or Tatars who were in the process of conquering south Russia, large numbers of Cumans migrated across the Danube, some settling in Bulgaria, others moving on into Thrace. Both regions suffered considerable plundering. Though both Bulgarians and Latins enrolled soldiers from their ranks, it appears that in the long run Vatatzes of Nicea recruited the largest number. He was to settle many in his lands, both in the parts of Thrace he held and in Anatolia.

Asen next concluded an alliance with the Latins and they—having been joined by a large number of Cuman refugees who had fled the Mongol conquest of the Steppes—jointly laid siege to the important fortress of Tzurulum in Thrace, which had recently been taken by the Niceans. Hardly had the siege begun when an epidemic of plague struck Trnovo, killing among others Asen's wife, his eldest son and heir, and the newly recognized Bulgarian patriarch. Supposedly interpreting this tragedy as a reflection of God's anger at his breaking his oath of alliance with Nicea, Asen repented, called off his siege of Tzurulum—thereby leaving the Frankish contingent high and dry and forcing the end of the siege—and made peace with Vatatzes. Once again they concluded a treaty, later in 1237.

At roughly the same time, also in 1237, some Western knights, recruited by Baldwin on his trip west and by the pope, appeared in Constantinople as crusaders and joined the garrison defending the city. However, their arrival could not compensate for the defection of Asen and the death that year of John of Brienne.

Continued Nicean pressure and Asen's defection from the Latins—which created the possibility that he might rejoin the Nicean attack on the capital—caused considerable worry for the leaders of the Latin Empire and the pope. The pope, in an attempt to take pressure off Constantinople, called on the Hungarians to attack Bulgaria from the north, hoping this would cause the Bulgarians to withdraw their troops from Thrace to defend their homeland. Thus in February 1238, Pope Gregory IX called on the King of Hungary to mobilize a crusade against the "heretical" Bulgarians. Since there were Bogomils, who were heretics, in Bulgaria, this statement is often taken as evidence by Church historians, who often take little notice of the general historical situation, that Bogomil activity had increased in Bulgaria to such an extent as to become a threat to Christendom, therefore necessitating the calling of a crusade. However, the date of this letter makes it seem more probable that the pope, as part of the Catholic alliance, was simply seeking justification for calling on Hungary to aid the Catholic-held city of Constantinople by attacking Bulgaria. The pope would also surely have been happy to see Bulgaria suffer a Hungarian attack. For back in 1204 Rome had received from Kalojan Bulgaria's submission to Rome, and not only had nothing come of it, but now Bulgaria had allied itself with the Greeks of Nicea and, breaking its nominal papal ties, had concluded an agreement with the schismatic patriarch in Nicea. Thus, with such clear political motives behind the pope's call for a crusade, we should not see this letter as evidence for an increase in Bogomil activity. The Bogomils were probably nothing more than a nominal excuse to justify a war against Bulgaria or, better put, to justify calling a politically motivated war a religious crusade to make it more popular.

As far as we know, the Hungarians did not take action against Bulgaria at this time. They were then busy carrying out another so-called crusade, one directed against Bosnia, a war, we shall discuss shortly, which also, like the call to action against Bulgaria, was as much, if not more, politically motivated as religious.

Even so, Asen does not seem to have participated further in the action around Constantinople; possibly he remained at home to defend Bulgaria should a crusading effort from Hungary materialize. And, in fact, he was threatened by an assault from the northwest in 1239—though not from the Hungarians themselves. In the summer of that year Baldwin II, having mobilized a large number of crusaders in the West (estimates vary from thirty to sixty thousand) marched east with them overland. Having crossed Hungary, Baldwin and these crusaders appeared at the Bulgarian border. Not wishing to fight them, Asen, in violation of his treaty with Nicea, allowed them to pass freely across Bulgaria. The crusaders reached Thrace and once there re-opened the siege on the Nicean Thracian fortress of Tzurulum. Nicea's attempt to relieve the siege failed, and the fortress fell to the crusaders in 1240. A large contingent of Cumans participated in the Latin victory. These crusaders then disappear into obscurity. Presumably most soon returned to their homes in the West, while a few may have remained to supplement the garrison of Constantinople. However, their arrival at this opportune moment surely did contribute to the Latin Empire's escape from disaster once again.

It has been argued that the fact Asen permitted the crusaders to pass through his realm to support the Latin Empire against Nicea shows that Asen had reverted to the Western alliance. It seems, however, that he did not actually break his alliance with Nicea but merely stood on the sidelines. Unwilling to support Nicea for fear that Nicea would make further gains that could cost Bulgaria its dominant position in the Balkans, he did not, however, go so far as to conclude an alliance with the Latins. But, he does seem to have worked to improve his relations with Hungary, a state which supported the Latin Empire. Scholars have called this policy a defensive one, designed to dissuade the Hungarians from responding to the papal call for a crusade against Bulgaria.

Though this concern may have had some influence on Asen's thinking, the main reason, it seems to me, for a Bulgarian-Hungarian alliance at this juncture was the danger posed by the appearance in the Steppes of the Tatars, who destroyed the Cuman state in 1238/39 and conquered Kiev in December 1240.[5] Both Bulgaria and Hungary now had the Tatars on their borders and reason to fear that the Tatars would continue their expansion further west at their expense. There was thus every reason for Hungary and Bulgaria to forget their relatively small differences and plan a joint defense against this danger.

And in fact a Bulgarian envoy visited Hungary between January and May 1240 and was well received by King Bela. Thus at the end of Asen's reign there occurred an improvement in Bulgarian-Hungarian relations, which was accompanied by smoother relations between the Latin Empire and Bulgaria. These improved relations with Catholic states continued into the opening years of the reign of Asen's successor Koloman.

It has been argued by various Bulgarian scholars that once Asen had withdrawn from his involvement of 1235–37 around Constantinople and Thrace, he had turned against Hungary and recovered Beograd and Braničevo. Whereas this theory is entirely possible, we have no contemporary source to support it. The main reason behind the assertion, it seems to me, is the belief of these scholars that Asen was powerful enough, when not involved elsewhere, to have achieved this; therefore, if he could have, then he would have. Such a recovery, in any case, would have been brief, for shortly after his death, when Bulgaria was ruled by successive weak regencies for Asen's minor sons, the Hungarians are documented as possessing these cities. Whether they held them straight through from 1232 or whether they had lost them only to regain them again after Asen's death is unknown.

Greek Affairs, 1237–42

Meanwhile in 1237 Asen, a widower, fell in love with the daughter of Theodore, his blinded captive since 1230. He married the lady and then released Theodore, allowing him to depart wherever he wished. Ambitious to regain his lost dominions, Theodore secretly arrived in Thessaloniki and assembled a group of supporters who then seized, dethroned, and briefly imprisoned his brother Manuel. Theodore then crowned his own son John. Thus he observed the Byzantine custom denying the blind the right to rule. Theodore remained at John's side, however, and was the actual decision-maker. Manuel, soon released, escaped to Nicea. Once there Manuel paid homage to Vatatzes and then received Nicean aid to regain his kingdom. After all, the Niceans had no love for Theodore and saw him as a dangerous opponent of their main goals.

In 1239 Manuel returned on a Nicean ship to Greece, landing in Thessaly where he began to assemble an army. He soon conquered Larissa. At this point Theodore decided it was best to negotiate with Manuel. He was probably concerned over the possibility that Manuel might receive subsequent reinforcements from Nicea. Manuel was receptive and agreed to break off his Nicean alliance in exchange for the division of the realm of Thessaloniki into three parts: Manuel was to keep Thessaly, Theodore and John were to keep Thessaloniki and its environs, and a third brother, Constantine, was to have Aetolia and Acarnania. Constantine was actually ensconced there already. Having been granted these regions as an appanage by Theodore before Klokotnica, Constantine had held them through the 1230s. Epirus, the most important province of the former state, remained in the hands of Michael II, who was not a party to the agreement and whose territory was not mentioned in it. When Manuel died in the summer of 1241 his territory in Thessaly was taken over by Michael, who seems simply to have occupied it.

In about 1240 Theodore, offered a safe-conduct, accepted an invitation to visit Nicea. Once there, he was detained while Nicea began to prepare for a new campaign against Constantinople. Vatatzes clearly wanted Theodore out of the way so he could not intrigue against this attempt. In early 1242 the Nicean army embarked, with Theodore brought along as an honorary prisoner; but instead of advancing on Constantinople for the expected siege, the troops marched on to Thessaloniki, devastating the region up to its walls. Inside, John ruled.

At this moment Vatatzes received word that the Mongols had invaded Anatolia; they were then in the eastern part, but Vatatzes realized they might well overrun the whole region. Thus he needed to return home at once to prepare his defenses. John, inside Thessaloniki, was unaware of this development. Thus not knowing that the Nicean army had to depart immediately and wishing to avoid a long siege if not the loss of his city (for the brave Vatatzes was popular with many groups in Thessaloniki), John was willing to negotiate to secure his continued rule. Theodore, also ignorant of the Mongol invasion, was allowed to participate in the talks. Vatatzes agreed to call off his attack and leave John and Theodore in possession of Thessaloniki if John would renounce his imperial title and submit to Nicean overlordship. In exchange for renouncing the title basileus, Vatatzes granted John the second title in the empire, despot.

This is the first time that the title despot was to be held by the dominant ruler in Greece and holder of Thessaloniki. We have seen that it was already held by Michael II of Epirus in the 1230s, probably having been granted him by the ruler of Thessaloniki. Despot, as noted, is an honorary court title, not a functional one. It made John part of the Byzantine (Nicean) court hierarchy and reflected his ceremonial place in that hierarchy. Thus John became a despot who also happened to be ruler of Thessaloniki, but he was not despot of Thessaloniki.

Having made this peace, receiving John's submission and permitting Theodore's return to Thessaloniki, Vatatzes marched back to Nicea. However, as Nicol points out, Vatatzes had only eliminated a title. Thessaloniki under a despot was as strong as it had been under an emperor. If Vatatzes had had time to capture and annex Thessaloniki on this occasion, he would have saved himself and his successors considerable future effort.

Back in Nicea, Vatatzes prepared his state's defenses against the anticipated Mongol attack. However, the Great Khan died suddenly in Karakorum, causing the withdrawal of the invading Mongols, who returned east to participate in the election of the new khan; thus Nicea was spared attack. In fact, by defeating and plundering the Seljuk state in central Anatolia, the Mongols contributed to Nicea's betterment, for it made Nicea that much more the strongest state in Anatolia. And by having less reason to worry about a Seljuk attack from the east, Nicea was left in a better position to attack Constantinople. At the same time the western developments, just described, that culminated in John's submission, took Thessaloniki temporarily out of the running for Constantinople. Michael's state in Epirus, though prosperous, was too distant to threaten the imperial capital at this time. And since Asen had died in June 1241, leaving his seven-year-old son Koloman under a regency, within which various factions soon emerged, Bulgaria, too, declined rapidly. Thus in 1242 Vatatzes in Nicea stood alone without rivals—excluding the incumbent Latins—for the conquest of Constantinople.

Bulgaria's decline after Asen's death proves that he too, though a great conqueror, had been unable to create an administrative apparatus capable of sustaining a lasting state. Božilov argues that, despite Asen's many great and obvious contributions, he made one capital blunder in foreign affairs. Failing to recognize the danger posed to Bulgaria by Nicea, for much of his reign he had been allied to and supportive of the Niceans. This resulted in the firm establishment of Nicea in Europe, the consequences of which could be seen immediately after Asen's death when Bulgaria, ruled by minors and incompetent regencies, suffered great losses to the Niceans in Thrace, the Rhodopes, and Macedonia, losses that contributed substantially to Bulgaria's decline.[6]

Though Božilov's point is basically true, it should be noted in Asen's defense that he seems to have come to a realization of this danger from Nicea in 1236. Thereafter he did not make any serious contribution to the Nicean cause. In fact, his support of Nicea was limited to the brief period 1234/35–36. And in that time he contributed to only a few Nicean acquisitions in eastern Thrace, the major one of which, Tzurulum, was regained by the Latins in 1240. His major contribution to the Nicean cause was his destruction of Theodore as a power, but this he did in his own interests and in self-defense, for Theodore had attacked him. Thus if one wishes to criticize Asen, one should not focus on his contributions to Nicea's cause, but rather on his failure to concentrate a major offensive against the Niceans, after 1230, to expel them from Thrace. Yet even had he done this, had he not then also destroyed their state in Anatolia (which he was not strong enough to do), his gains could have been only temporary. After his death, upon Bulgaria's ensuing decline, the Niceans would simply have returned to Thrace as strong as they had been in the 1230s. Thus I believe there was really nothing that Asen could have done to prevent Nicean success in the long run.

Serbia under Radoslav and Vladislav

Meanwhile Stefan, the King of Serbia, having fallen ill, became a monk and died in 1227. He was succeeded by his eldest son, Radoslav, who was crowned king at Žiča by Archbishop Sava. The younger sons of Stefan, Vladislav and Uroš, received appanages. Stefan's youngest son, who had become a monk and had also taken the name Sava, was shortly thereafter appointed Bishop of Hum and was to be Archbishop of Serbia from 1263 to

1270. The same family thus dominated both Church and state. And the close ties between dynasty and Church as well as the dynasty's role within the Church continued.

At first Radoslav, according to the biographer and monk Theodosius, was a good ruler, but then he fell under the influence of his wife. She, of course, was Greek—the daughter of Theodore of Thessaloniki-Epirus. And scholars have indeed detected a degree of Byzantine (Greek) influence on Radoslav. For example, when in exile in Dubrovnik after he was overthrown, Radoslav issued on 4 February 1234 a charter to Dubrovnik, valid upon his restoration to his throne, in which he gave himself the Byzantine royal name of Ducas. Whether Radoslav derived this name from his mother Eudocia, the daughter of Alexius III Angelus, whose family had intermarried with the Ducas family, or from his wife, whose father Theodore frequently used the last name Ducas, is not certain. Radoslav also referred to himself as Ducas on his coins.

Radoslav, in the interest of maintaining friendly relations with Epirus, seems to have wanted to improve his ties with Demetrius, the Archbishop of Ohrid, who, of course, was furious at the Serbs for their defection from his archdiocese. Radoslav corresponded with Demetrius about certain canonical issues, albeit those that did not directly touch upon Serbia's status; however, the very existence of this correspondence and the relationship it reflected may well have made Serbian churchmen uneasy. They may even have seen in it a threat to the newly won independence of the Serbian Church. Radoslav was probably safe from domestic rebellion as long as his neighbor Theodore remained strong. However, Radoslav's position seems to have weakened after Theodore's defeat and capture by John Asen II in 1230. Opposition against Radoslav grew, and in the fall of 1233 some of his nobles revolted. Radoslav fled from Serbia at some time between 1 September 1233 and 4 February 1234; for on the latter date he is found in Dubrovnik issuing to that city a charter of privileges whose validity depended upon Radoslav regaining his kingdom, something he was never able to do. Radoslav eventually returned to Serbia to become a monk.

Radoslav was succeeded by his brother Vladislav. Archbishop Sava, not part of the plot against Radoslav, was unhappy, but he eventually agreed to crown Vladislav. Then, upset by the dissensions among his nephews, Sava abdicated, taking a pilgrimage to Palestine. On his way home in 1235, Sava died during a visit to the Bulgarian court. The Bulgarians then buried him with honor in Trnovo. By this time Vladislav was married to John Asen's daughter Belisava. Their marriage seems to have occurred after Vladislav's coronation. As relations were fairly cordial between the two states, the Serbs were able, after a series of requests, to persuade the Bulgarians to return Sava's body. It was then buried in the monastery of Mileševo, built by Vladislav. Sava was soon canonized and his relics worked many miracles. His cult was to remain important throughout the rest of the medieval and Turkish periods.

At this time the Hungarians were exerting pressure on the lands south of the Danube. We discussed their conquest of Braničevo and Beograd from Bulgaria and the threat of their attacking Bulgaria in response to a papal summons in the late 1230s. At the same time, between 1235 and 1241, as we shall see, they were campaigning as crusaders against Bosnia. These policies posed a threat to the Serbs, now broken with Catholicism and once again fully in the Orthodox camp. This threat may have been a contributing factor to the marriage alliance Vladislav concluded with Bulgaria, then under the powerful Asen, who also was threatened by Hungary. Some scholars have speculated that under Vladislav Serbia accepted Bulgarian suzerainty. Whether or not it did is not known.

Serbia, though possibly feeling threatened, was not directly attacked by the Hungarians. However, the Hungarian crusaders, as we shall see, did threaten Serbian Hum directly. In fact, they may even have occupied some of it. Documents refer to Hungarian action in Hum, though it is not made clear whether the Hungarians had penetrated the parts of Hum under Serbian control or whether all their activity occurred in western Hum between the Neretva and Cetina rivers, where the Serbs had no role. In any case, once faced with this situation, the Serbs asserted their right to Hum and Vladislav added "Hum" to his title.

In the spring of 1243 the "inhabitants" of Serbia rose up and ousted Vladislav; they put Uroš, the third brother, on the throne. Many scholars have argued that Bulgarian influence had been strong and unpopular in Serbia under Vladislav, causing domestic opposition to him that was able to break out and bring about Vladislav's deposition after the death of his powerful father-in-law John Asen II in June 1241. It is impossible to prove that Radoslav and Vladislav were representatives of pro-Epirote and pro-Bulgarian parties in Serbia. But at least Asen's death did remove a powerful prop who might have aided Vladislav and prevented Uroš' successful coup.

Though overthrown, Vladislav did not retire from state affairs. He maintained good relations with his brother Uroš and was still referred to as king with his name linked to Uroš' in some official documents. Whether he had any special position or territorial responsibility is not known. However, since, as we shall see, Uroš seems to have opposed appanages, it seems likely that Vladislav was not given one.

Zeta in the Second Quarter of the Thirteenth Century

Under Radoslav Vukan's son George re-emerged as governor of Zeta under Radoslav's suzerainty. Whether he had remained there throughout the latter half of Stefan's reign, possibly surrendering his kingship in exchange for an appanage within Zeta, or whether he had re-asserted himself, with local support, upon Stefan's death is unknown. In any case, whether the arrangement was based on a more ancient agreement or on one he and his supporters were able to wrench from Radoslav, George seems to have guaranteed his position by a negotiated settlement. He clearly ruled with Radoslav's permission, be it happily or unhappily granted, and with recognition of Radoslav's suzerainty, because the charters George issued needed confirmation by Radoslav. How much of Zeta George held is not known. He continued to hold onto an appanage in Zeta under Vladislav. He is then found associated with the coastal town of Ulcinj, whose bishop was negotiating submission to the Archbishop of Dubrovnik and thus acting against the claims of the Archbishop of Bar, whose interests both Vukan and Nemanja had supported. The Ragusan records refer to George as Prince of Duklja, son of "Župan" Vukan. The mention of his being Vukan's son shows that this George is in fact George of Zeta. Not only was his title reduced from "king" to "prince," (or at least that is how Dubrovnik, probably interested in maintaining good relations with Serbia, spoke of him), but he or the town also posthumously deflated Vukan's title.

In 1242, a letter of the Bishop of Ulcinj, confirming the agreement with Dubrovnik, refers to "our king." Did this usage reflect local patriotism or was it instead evidence that George was again trying to claim that title, perhaps taking advantage of the chaos caused by the Tatars' passing through Serbia and of the disorders at home that were to lead to Vladislav's deposition in 1243?

In 1243 Uroš came to the throne and George disappears from the sources. There is no evidence that any other member of the family ruled Zeta thereafter, though George's brother Stefan, who built the Morača monastery in 1251 or 1252, is spoken of as king in a seventeenth-century fresco (thought to be a redoing of an older, possibly contemporary, one). A third brother, Dmitri, who built a church at Brodarevo on the Lim in 1281, called himself only župan and soon thereafter became a monk. Thereafter no more is heard of Vukan's descendants in Zeta.

The different locations—scattered widely apart across Zeta—in which the three brothers left evidence suggest that perhaps each brother was given a small appanage by one of the Kings of Raška: George's along the coast, including Ulcinj; Stefan's on the Morača River; and Dmitri's on the Lim. The local populations of their appanages (or at least the Bishop of Ulcinj and the fresco painter of Morača) honored George and Stefan with the traditional royal title, even though that title was not recognized by foreign states, as is seen when Dubrovnik referred to George as prince rather than king.

In any case, regardless of what territory Vukan's descendants controlled, Zeta was under Serbian (Raškan) suzerainty. When Vladislav granted Ragusan merchants free-trade privileges in his realm, in listing the regions under his rule Vladislav included Zeta and made no reference to George or any other descendant of Vukan.

The documents, examined above, showing that George and the Bishop of Ulcinj recognized the Archbishop of Dubrovnik and gave up recognition of Zeta's Archbishop of Bar, are curious, for the secular rulers of Zeta, including George's father Vukan, were regularly strong partisans of Bar's claims. Since in the 1240s Uroš of Serbia—and perhaps Vladislav before him as well—was also a strong advocate of Bar's claims, could George's relations with Dubrovnik have been an attempt to build up other alliances as a first step toward separating himself and his holding from Serbian rule? In any case, whatever George's motives for opposing the Church policy of his cousins ruling Serbia and of Zeta's archbishop, George's actions came at a moment when the quarrel between Dubrovnik and Bar had reached crisis proportions.

In 1247, after the death of an Archbishop of Bar had created a vacancy in that see, an envoy of the Archbishop of Dubrovnik came to Bar to read a letter expressing Dubrovnik's rights. The Serbian-appointed prince (or mayor) in Bar tried to be agreeable and neutral. But the leading cleric in Bar at the time, the archdeacon, could not find the time to meet the envoy. The archdeacon refused the first summons because he had to have lunch and the second because he had to go hunting; so eventually the Ragusan archbishop's letter was read to an assembly demanded by the envoy and convoked by the prince, but attended only by the lay population, with the clerics prominent by their absence. The citizens shouted down the envoy, and when he suggested that the pope supported Dubrovnik's claim, they cried, "What is the pope? Our lord, King Uroš, is our pope!" After this failure the embassy, on the verge of departing, heard rumors that it was to be attacked on the road. So, the prince gave it an escort, including his own son, to see it safely along its route.

The Archbishop of Dubrovnik then turned to the pope to protest. The pope seemed willing to listen, but at the same time, much to Dubrovnik's disappointment, he appointed a new archbishop—giving him the disputed higher rank—for Bar, John de Plano Carpini, a Franciscan famous for his earlier mission to the Mongols. Carpini began by being conciliatory. On his way to Bar he stopped in Dubrovnik, where he agreed that each side should gather all the evidence it could about the rights of each Church, after which both sides should meet, bringing their documents for discussion, at the neutral site of Kotor. (Kotor was neutral because it, alone among Dalmatian sees, was subordinated to the Archbishop of Bari in Italy.) Then, Carpini proposed, after the meeting and within four months, each side should take its documents to the pope for judgment. John promised to excommunicate anyone in Bar who should try to prevent the meeting in Kotor and promised not to use any Church discipline against Ulcinj, Bar's suffragan then recognizing Dubrovnik. Ulcinj soon thereafter, in 1249 or 1250, returned in its allegiance to Bar. Once in Bar, however, Archbishop John became a strong partisan of the rights of his see. And it seems that the proposed meeting in Kotor never took place. At one point in the ensuing dispute John was seized and imprisoned by Dubrovnik and had to purchase his release, for which humiliation he then excommunicated the Ragusans.

In any case the two contending archbishops finally presented their cases to the pope in 1252. Dubrovnik objected to the title archbishop for Bar and insisted that Bar and all its suffragans should be subjected to Dubrovnik. Bar claimed its see was older than Dubrovnik's. Originally, Bar claimed, there were only two archbishops in Dalmatia: Salona (now Split) and Dioclea (succeeded to by Bar). Dubrovnik was a newcomer, at first only a bishopric, whose jurisdiction extended only over the town of Dubrovnik itself, under the supervision of the archbishop in Split. Dubrovnik insisted that in the eighth century Pope Zacharias had installed a certain Andrew as Archbishop of Dubrovnik and had placed him over a whole series of territories and towns, including Bar and its present suffragans. However, this letter—almost certainly a forgery—could not be produced, Dubrovnik claimed, because seventy years before a Serbian king [Stefan Nemanja] had stolen it when he occupied Dubrovnik. Dubrovnik also cited a series of submissions to its archbishop by various southern Dalmatian bishoprics, such as Ulcinj's in 1189 and 1242; pointed out that Pope Alexander III (1159–81) had recognized an excommunication of Bar and Ulcinj for disobedience by the Ragusan archbishop; and finally claimed that Bar had been recognized as an archbishopric only owing to an error; for Innocent III had given this recognition, it was claimed, at a time when the see of Dubrovnik was vacant and thus unable to protest. For its part, Bar denied its see had been created in this manner and stated that a whole series of documents presented by Dubrovnik to support its claims of jurisdiction over neighboring territories had nothing whatsoever to do with Duklja (Zeta). Bar supported its case with a series of documents from the previous century and a half, showing its archbishop exercising jurisdiction over its diocese with the approval of the pope.

While the pope and the agent he had appointed to supervise the case, the Archbishop of Ancona, heard the conflicting testimony, rumors circulated that King Uroš, a supporter of Bar, planned to attack Dubrovnik. Shortly thereafter, as we shall see, he in fact did. Meanwhile, to obtain further information a papal commission, accompanied by the two feuding bishops, left Italy to visit the two cities. After a visit to Dubrovnik, they were scheduled to visit Bar. But the Archbishop of Dubrovnik did not dare go there, for word was out that Uroš had ordered his capture and intended to skin him alive. Rumor also circulated to the effect that Uroš did not care what the pope should decide, for the pope had no authority in his kingdom, which had its own archbishop [the Orthodox Archbishop of Serbia] honored alike by Slavs and Latins.

On 1 August 1252, Archbishop John of Bar died, and despite Dubrovnik's protests, the pope again appointed a new archbishop for Bar. At the same time, in 1252, Dubrovnik, now involved in a war with Serbia, signed a treaty of alliance with Bulgaria, in which the Bulgarian ruler Michael promised that if he succeeded in his ambition to expel Uroš and Vladislav from Serbia and extend his conquests to the coast, he would turn over to the Church of Dubrovnik the coastal cities it had a right to. The Bulgarians, however, produced little more than a raid against Serbia and obtained no significant results.

The Church dispute continued to drag on without solution. In 1254, at the death of the new Archbishop of Bar, the pope confirmed a successor; at the same time Dubrovnik concluded peace with Uroš. Finally, in 1255, Dubrovnik's representative to the papacy wrote home saying he could achieve nothing and sought permission to return home. Permission was granted, and in the absence of further pressure the papacy seems to have tabled the whole issue. Thus no final decision was given, and Bar won by default.

Stanojević argues that Dubrovnik simply gave up the fight. It was costing the town considerable money to maintain a lobbyist in Rome and his efforts were getting nowhere. The Serb ruler, in whose territory the disputed suffragans lay, was insistent that these sees be under Bar. Thus Dubrovnik's attempts to reassert the authority of its archbishop were bringing about bad relations with its powerful Serbian neighbor; in fact this issue may have been a major cause for Serbia's recent attack on Dubrovnik and the war that followed. So, when the pope, who was becoming tired of the whole quarrel, confirmed Bar's new archbishop, Dubrovnik recalled its lobbyist.[7] Thus Bar won a full victory, keeping its archbishopric and all its suffragans, and Serbia was not forced to see any of its Catholic coastal cities subordinated to an archbishop resident outside of the Serbian state.

Throughout this lengthy dispute, Kotor had remained neutral. Though its Church was listed in various papal bulls as being subject to the Archbishop of Dubrovnik, Kotor had made its own submission to the Archbishop of Bari in Italy in the eleventh century and remained under Bari thereafter. As Kotor was Serbia's major coastal city, its bishop received special honor from Serbia's rulers, and all Catholics living in the interior of Serbia (privileged foreigners granted the right to reside there whose religious freedom was guaranteed by charter, they included the Sasi [Saxon] miners and the Dalmatian merchants) were placed under the jurisdiction of the Bishop of Kotor. The Bishop of Kotor was also given jurisdiction over the Catholics in Serbia's Hum (east of the Neretva) and later, after Serbia acquired it, over Catholics in Mačva. Kotor's privileged position no doubt emerged naturally. In the late twelfth and thirteenth centuries in Serbia merchants from Kotor outnumbered those from any other Catholic center; they established colonies with churches, in Serbia, and (presumably) naturally recognized the authority of their own bishop. Their wishes in this coincided with those of Serbia's rulers who maintained throughout cordial and close ties with Kotor and certainly would have preferred Catholics in Serbia to be governed by a bishop in a town that recognized Serbian suzerainty rather than by a bishop located in an independent town like Dubrovnik.

Bar, needless to say, was not happy about this. And in the second half of the thirteenth century Bar was to quarrel with Kotor over which bishop had jurisdiction over the Catholic church, built by the Sasi, in Brskovo in Serbia. Early in the fourteenth century Bar temporarily won out, obtaining from the papacy the right to administer Catholics in Brskovo, Rudnik, Trepča, Gračanica, and around Mount Rogozna. But this victory seems to have remained a dead letter; for in the middle of the fourteenth century Pope Clement V was calling upon the relevant Slavic rulers to help the Bishop of Kotor collect his tithes in these and other places.

Kotor's bishop was to retain his jurisdiction over Catholics in Serbia thereafter, even though Dubrovnik, which by the middle of the fourteenth century had more merchants in Serbia than Kotor did, presumably would have liked to have had its colonists in Serbia under the Archbishop of Dubrovnik. Even Kotor's political submission to Venice in 1420 did not change jurisdictional matters, though in practice the bishop may well have had more difficulty in exercising his authority thereafter. However, despite various differences with Venice, Serbia's rulers desired good relations with Venice and were not going to disrupt these relations over what to them was a relatively unimportant issue. Thus one clause in the Serbian-Venetian treaty of 1435 specifically recognized Kotor's jurisdiction over all Roman Catholic property in Serbia.

Hum in the Second Quarter of the Thirteenth Century

Very little is known about Hum at this time. In the last chapter we saw that in ca. 1216 Raška occupied most of Hum east of the Neretva, leaving only a small appanage (Popovo Polje and the coast) for Andrew (Andrej), Miroslav's son and Stefan of Raška's client. Peter, probably Andrew's brother, who had expelled Andrew earlier, retreated beyond the Neretva where he continued to rule in western Hum, styling himself Prince (Knez) of Hum. Shortly thereafter, probably in 1220, a Serbian bishopric for Hum was established by Sava with its seat in Ston, the traditional capital of Hum. Peter had held this city early in the second decade of the thirteenth century, but presumably, after Stefan's campaign that led to Andrew's acquisition of the coast, Ston had gone to Andrew. Probably he still held it in 1219/20, making it easy for Stefan and Sava to install their bishop in Ston. Some scholars claim that Peter held Ston at this time; if so, he probably allowed the bishop's installation to avoid further friction with Stefan, which might result in Stefan expelling him from Ston. In any case, with its bishop installed in Ston, Raška could increase its influence in Hum, both binding tighter to Raška those parts of Hum already held by Raška and exerting its propaganda through the Church in the regions of Hum not under Raškan rule. In 1227 the Catholic bishop was allowed to return to Ston, and for a while the town had both a Catholic and a Serbian bishop.

Andrew of Hum disappears from the sources at about this time, unless he should turn out to be the Andrew referred to as Prince of Hum in the 1240s. Most probably, however, that individual was a second Andrew from a subsequent generation. Between 1222 and 1225 Peter is referred to as Prince of Hum (presumably the term still refers to western Hum, though possibly by the 1220s Peter had regained the coastal territory as far as Ston) at which time he was elected prince of the town of Split. Thomas the Archdeacon, historian of

Split, refers to Peter as a "heretic," though he never states the nature of Peter's heresy. Quite possibly this was merely a term of abuse directed at Peter because of his Orthodoxy and the support he gave to the Serbian Orthodox bishop in Ston. However, Thomas says, the townspeople of Split liked Peter and refused to listen to the Church and oust him. So, Peter remained in office until ca. 1225. For this disobedience the Catholic Church placed the whole town under interdict.

In the late 1230s Toljen (who died in 1239, according to Thomas), possibly Peter's nephew, was Prince of Hum; in addition he was active in the politics of Split, opposing the Šubići of Bribir who held Split as vassals of the King of Hungary. In the 1240s Toljen's successor Andrew, called Great Prince of Hum but clearly active only in western Hum, allied himself with Split and Ninoslav of Bosnia against the Hungarians' local supporters the Šubići and the town of Trogir. Andrew is last mentioned in 1249. He presumably died soon thereafter. Orbini says he was buried in an Orthodox church in Ston. Thus the holdings of these last rulers of western Hum seem also to have extended along the coast, beyond the Neretva, to and including Ston. How long the holders of western Hum had also controlled this coastal strip and Ston is not known. But, as noted, various scholars have claimed this control went back to Peter's reign, possibly as far back as 1219/20. When the second Andrew died his lands in Hum were divided among three sons, according to traditional Slavic inheritance custom, with the eldest, Radoslav, receiving the largest share.

Bosnia in the Second Quarter of the Thirteenth Century

After Ban Kulin disappears from the sources in 1204, Bosnia's history falls under a cloud of obscurity for a decade and a half. Possibly Kulin's son, who visited Hungary to confirm the Bolino Polje resolutions, succeeded in Bosnia. The Catholic Church in Bosnia, if we can believe later Ragusan chronicles, continued to recognize the Archbishop of Dubrovnik; it sent bishops to him for consecration and he toured Bosnia on occasion. Split and Hungary continued to complain about this relationship, but the Bosnians simply ignored the papal order to subordinate their Church to Split. Their policy seems to have succeeded temporarily, for sources from the 1210s no longer contain such complaints, and the Bosnians, remaining under Dubrovnik, were for a short while left in peace. Soon, however, Hungary was to change its line of attack and begin a campaign to subject the Church in Bosnia to Kalocsa, an archbishopric inside Hungary.

Meanwhile in the 1220s documents again refer to heretics in Bosnia and in the lands of the Kačići, a family of Dalmatian nobles based in Omiš and at the mouth of the Cetina River who was often involved in piracy. No source gives any details about what this heresy consisted of. A papal legate visited both regions in 1221 and 1222 but seems to have achieved little or nothing, for in 1225 the pope was calling on the Hungarians to launch a crusade to clean up Bosnia. At that time Hungary had too many internal difficulties to respond, so Bosnia was left in peace. Bosnia's Catholic Church continued to need reform; and in 1232 a papal letter described the Catholic Bishop of Bosnia as being illiterate, defending heretics (among whom was his own brother), having obtained his position through simony, being ignorant of the baptismal formula, not performing the mass, and not carrying out the sacraments in his own church. A papal legate removed this ignorant prelate, and in his place the pope appointed a German Dominican as Bishop of Bosnia. Thus for the first time a native Bosnian did not hold the bishop's post. Instead a foreigner was appointed, though it is not known whether the German ever actually set foot in Bosnia. What actually happened thereafter to the management of the Church in Bosnia is unknown; though presumably nothing in fact had changed, at least on paper the Bosnians had lost control of their Church hierarchy.

By this time the ruler of Bosnia was a ban named Ninoslav. In 1233, when the pope appointed the German Bishop of Bosnia, Ninoslav had renounced "heresy" (again, of unspecified character). But despite Ninoslav's renunciation, the pope in 1234 called on the Hungarians to crusade against heretics in Bosnia. This time the Hungarians willingly obliged. Thus either the Bosnians had not carried out their promises to reform and had simply continued to follow their own ways (possibly not knowing how to do otherwise), or else Hungary, now freed from its internal problems, wanted to use religion as an excuse to assert its authority over Bosnia, an authority that had become entirely nominal in the course of Kulin's reign and the following decades. Thus quite possibly the impetus for the crusade was Hungary's ambition to assert its authority in the southwestern Balkans, for which it gained papal endorsement by setting the pope up with alarming reports about conditions in Bosnia.

The campaign was actively carried out between 1235 and 1241. There is no evidence that Hungarian troops reached Bosnia proper (the Bosnian banate) before 1238; for in Slavonia and in various parts of greater Bosnia between the Sava and the northern borders of the banate there were said to be many heretics; and presumably the crusaders would have had to subdue these regions first before they could reach the Bosnian banate. Presumably the northerners would have resisted, and since theirs was a mountainous territory the crusaders' progress probably would have been slow. In any case, the first indication given of crusader success in Ninoslav's state comes from 1238. For in that year the Dominicans who followed in the wake of the crusaders were erecting a cathedral for Bosnia in Vrhbosna (modern Sarajevo). That they were erecting it here shows that the Hungarians controlled Vrhbosna; thus at least this part of Ninoslav's state had been occupied. However, it is clear that they had not conquered all his lands, for if they had one would expect the church to have been erected in the central part of his banate, in or around Visoko, rather than Vrhbosna, then a peripheral town. Also showing that Ninoslav was still in control of at least some of his territory is a charter of commercial privileges that, as Ban of Bosnia, he issued to Dubrovnik in 1240.

The Catholic Church in Bosnia was now placed in the hands of the Dominicans. The German bishop, who had never wanted the post, succeeded, after many requests, in having himself relieved of this office. The new bishop, the Dominican Ponsa, was also assigned "Hum." Whether this meant the Hungarians had also penetrated into Hum, between the Cetina and Neretva rivers, or whether this was simply a claim or plan is unknown. It is highly unlikely that the Hungarians penetrated into any of Serbian Hum; thus regardless of what the bishop's title may have been meant to claim, his actual jurisdiction at the most would have extended only to western Hum. Dominican sources also mention that some Bosnian heretics were burned at the stake. Yet despite the presence inside Bosnia of Hungarian clerics and troops who might have been in a position to discover some facts about the content of Bosnia's heresy, no source provides a single concrete fact about its nature.

Regardless of papal intent, the crusade had become a war of conquest for Hungary, and the Hungarians took advantage of it to occupy a large part of Ninoslav's banate (but not all of it, as the 1240 charter granted to Dubrovnik shows). Then in 1241 the Tatars, having conquered Kiev and south Russia, attacked Hungary. The Hungarians had to withdraw their troops from Bosnia to meet this threat. In a major battle on the Sajó River on 11 April 1241 the Tatars wiped out a major Hungarian army; among those killed was Koloman, brother of the Hungarian king, who had been the commander of the crusading forces in Bosnia. The Tatars then pursued King Bela of Hungary, who fled through Slavonia and Croatia to Dalmatia whence he took a ship to safety on an Adriatic island. The Tatars occupied themselves with plundering in both Croatia and Dalmatia—including some Serbian territory in southern Dalmatia—until news came of the death of the Great Khan in Karakorum. To be in on the action of electing a new khan, the Tatars turned back; they returned east via Zeta, Serbia, and Bulgaria, all of which they looted as they passed through, with the Bulgarians suffering the greatest damage. But though the Tatars proved a disaster for much of the Balkans, Bosnia benefited, for the Tatars forced the withdrawal of the Hungarian troops from Bosnia, and these troops were not to return. Thus Bosnia was able to reassert its independence and reoccupy the territories the Hungarians had taken.

In the mid-1240s, having failed to achieve his ends in Bosnia, the pope again called on the Hungarians to crusade in Bosnia. Thus this danger remained ever present. Ninoslav wrote the pope, insisting he was a good Catholic; he admitted associating with heretics but stated that he had only turned to them because he needed assistance in defending Bosnia from foreign invasion (i.e., the Hungarian crusade). The pope seems to have seen the logic of Ninoslav's argument, for in 1248 he ordered the Hungarians, who appeared ready to attack Bosnia, to take no action until the pope had had time to carry out his own investigation into the actual situation in Bosnia. The pope seems to have been interested in ascertaining the true facts, for this time he dispatched neither a Hungarian nor a Dominican but rather a Franciscan, together with a bishop from the coastal town of Senj, who should have had no ulterior motives to color their report. What they reported has not survived.

The Hungarians now changed their tack; once again they launched a polemical attack on Dubrovnik's archbishop and his inability to manage Bosnia's Church; once again the Hungarians called for the reassignment of Bosnia, but this time they sought Bosnia's subordination to Kalocsa, an archbishopric within Hungary. After King Bela repeated this demand in several letters written to the pope between 1246 and 1252, and after various papal inquiries, the pope at last gave in and in 1252 assigned the Church of Bosnia to Kalocsa. However, in so doing, instead of gaining Bosnia or even influence inside Bosnia, the pope and Hungary lost Bosnia for Catholicism entirely. For from 1252 the Hungarian-appointed Bishop of Bosnia resided not in Bosnia but in Djakovo in Slavonia. He remained resident there for the rest of the Middle Ages. It is clear that the Bosnians, seeing him as a tool of their political enemies the Hungarians, would have nothing to do with him and would not let him reside in Bosnia. Thus this bishop, bearing a meaningless title and having no influence upon Bosnian affairs, remained in Slavonia and involved himself chiefly with Hungarian court affairs and with land disputes in Slavonia.

Early in the fourteenth century documents begin to mention in Bosnia an autonomous institution known as the Bosnian Church. The papacy and Hungarians called it heretical and by the mid-fifteenth century were at times suggesting it was neo-Manicheen or dualist, thus part of the same movement as the Bulgarian Bogomils and the French Cathars. Like the clerics who represented the Bosnian Catholics at Bolino Polje, the Bosnian Church clerics seem to have been monks. And both the Catholic monks in 1203 and the later Bosnian Church clerics called themselves "Christians." The Bosnian Catholic bishops early in the thirteenth century had frequently—or even regularly—been drawn from among these monks. Thus it is probable that, after 1234, when the German had been appointed bishop, and after 1235, when the crusade was launched, the Bosnians simply ignored the organizational changes that international Catholicism was trying to force upon them. They continued to follow their own clergy and elect their own bishops; presumably these bishops continued to be chosen from their own monks. And thus the Bosnians continued to administer their own Church affairs.

When the Hungarians appeared with troops and Dominicans and tried to re-establish a branch of the international Catholic Church there, their activities were limited to the areas they occupied, where they did a certain amount of church building. But after only three years they had had to withdraw; thus they were given far too little time to make much impact on the local population, who, we may suppose, was hostile from the start. The Hungarians were never able to return; thus their crusade had little or no lasting impact on the Bosnians, who in the years that followed continued to follow their own clerics and their own ways. There was no incentive for the Bosnians to alter matters, particularly after 1252 when Bosnia's official Church was subordinated to a Hungarian archbishop. Thus what may have started as a temporary expedient, after the "reform" of 1252, turned into a permanent state of affairs and led to the establishment of a separate Church institution. Thus the crusades led to the permanent separation of the Bosnian monastic order (and those Bosnians who followed the monks) from international Catholicism. These Hungarian actions also increased the Bosnians' hatred for the Hungarians, a sentiment which was to last and be an influential factor in Bosnian politics up to (and even contributing to) the Ottoman conquest of Bosnia in 1463.

Most scholars have depicted the Bosnian Church as dualist. And some of the dualists living along the Dalmatian coast may indeed have come to Bosnia. In fact, Catholic Church sources do mention "heretics" fleeing from Split and Zadar into Bosnia. Unfortunately none of these sources ever specifies what sort of heretics these refugees were. It is likely, however, that some or all were dualists. However, the domestic Bosnian monks at the turn of the century seem to have considered themselves Catholics, and there was nothing dualist about the errors they renounced in 1203. The main flaws in Bosnian Catholicism then and later seem to have resulted not from particular heretical influences or beliefs but rather from ignorance. This ignorance is well illustrated by the description of the native Catholic bishop removed from office for that reason in 1232. The surviving Bosnian and Ragusan documents about the Bosnian Church that do make specific references to its beliefs suggest the Bosnian Church continued to hold mainstream Christian beliefs throughout its existence. Thus it seems to me, and I have argued this point at length elsewhere,[8] that the Bosnian Church emerged primarily to assert local independence from foreign interference; perhaps there was a little heretical or dualist influence upon it, but such influence certainly did not form the core of its beliefs. The new Church was based on a Catholic monastic order whose beliefs provided the basis of Bosnian Church beliefs. There was no reason for these monks, when seceding from international Catholicism, to have suddenly changed in a major way their existing beliefs. To have done so would have been an extraordinary occurrence—and though a handful of angry individuals might have adopted a new religion out of spite in such a situation, a whole monastic order certainly would not have.

Thus the Bosnians seem simply to have seceded under their own native clergy, who through ignorance had been carrying out certain "incorrect" practices; after secession they no doubt continued these practices. But they also would have retained the other beliefs and practices they had followed up to this point, and these were basically Catholic. Such an origin and course of development has the characteristics of what anthropologists call a Nativistic Movement, a term I find very fitting for Bosnia's newly emerging Church. Though this Church can be documented only from the early fourteenth century, at which time it is found in full-fledged existence, the logical time for its creation would have been in the middle of the thirteenth, a period for which we have very few sources and none from Bosnia itself. We shall discuss this Church again, as it becomes relevant, in our discussion of Bosnia in the fourteenth and fifteenth centuries.

Though Bosnia's religious policy was an act of defiance against Hungary, the Hungarians were unable to alter the situation. Ninoslav was still the ruler of Bosnia in 1249 when he issued another charter to Dubrovnik, with which he continued to maintain good relations. Since the Ragusans had been losing influence in Bosnia's Catholic Church, owing to Hungarian action, one would expect Dubrovnik to have had considerable sympathy for the Bosnians. After all their mutual relations had always been cordial. Had Dubrovnik, with its flexible tolerance, been allowed to continue supervising Bosnia's Catholic Church, the Bosnian schism presumably would not have occurred. Ninoslav is not mentioned again in the sources; presumably he died soon thereafter. The name of his successor is not known.

A Hungarian campaign was launched against Bosnia in 1253; presumably its aim was to subdue the banate and its Church. There is no evidence that Hungarian armies reached the banate, and for a variety of reasons I have presented elsewhere, it is apparent that the Hungarians did not conquer the banate then.[9] After 1253, and for the remainder of the thirteenth century, there were to be no more known Hungarian campaigns against Bosnia. Scholars have often argued that Bosnia was directly controlled by Hungary in the second half of the thirteenth century. But, if the banate was not conquered in 1253 and if no other Hungarian attacks occurred, how did Hungary gain this control? These scholars have generally believed this domination is demonstrated by "Bosnia's" being ruled over by a cousin of Ninoslav named Prijezda, who was a Hungarian vassal. Prijezda was clearly a Hungarian vassal, but all the specific lands he is documented as holding lay well to the north of the Bosnian banate, and no evidence exists to suggest he held any lands in the banate itself.

The northern reaches of greater Bosnia were without question under Hungary; they were ruled in the 1280s by Prijezda as well as by various members of the Hungarian royal house who were assigned appanages there. But this picture of Hungarian domination through vassal bans seems to have been true only for the northern regions, for every concrete reference to a region under such control refers to a region in the north—Soli, Usora, Vrbas, Sana. There is no evidence of Hungarian control or even activity in any part of the central Bosnian banate. Had the Hungarians held that region, they certainly would have tried to assert themselves, by sending troops and re-establishing the Church organization they had tried to initiate under the Dominicans in 1238–41. However, there is no evidence of any such action, and all the existing documents about the activities of Hungarian Dominicans in the second half of the thirteenth century concern Hungary itself or other territory well north of the banate. In fact no documents exist about the banate itself in the second half of the thirteenth century. Thus, as I have argued elsewhere, the Bosnian banate probably continued to exist, as it had during the first half of the century, as a de facto independent entity under Ninoslav's successors, whose names have not survived.

Croatia in the Second Quarter of the Thirteenth Century

Croatia and Slavonia remained fairly decentralized under local nobles throughout the thirteenth century. When the Hungarian nobles revolted against King Andrew II and forced him to issue in 1222 a charter, known as the Golden Bull, defining the rights of the nobility, this charter affected only Slavonia (north of the Gvozd Mountain). However, the Croatian nobles south of that mountain already enjoyed most of the privileges that document granted. By 1255 under the Croatian duke, there existed two bans, one for Croatia and Dalmatia, the other for Slavonia.

In 1235 King Andrew died and was succeeded by his son Bela IV (1235–70). Bela did not come to Croatia for a second coronation, and thus the custom of two coronations ended at this time. But, the notion of a dual monarchy, uniting two kingdoms, Hungary and Croatia, in the person of one king bearing two titles, remained. (Some scholars claim that when he became king in 1205 Andrew did not have a Croatian coronation either and thus believe that the custom of a separate Croatian coronation had been dropped already. This issue cannot be settled because we have no documents on Andrew's coronation[s] at all.)

Bela was concerned with the power of the great nobles, which had been growing as a result of the privileges granted by Andrew; these had been either granted "voluntarily" to win the nobles' support during civil war or forced upon him and expressed in the Golden Bull. And the great families in Slavonia and Croatia had by way of land-grabbing and/or royal grants been enlarging their already sizeable territories. The Babonići rose to become the most powerful family in western Slavonia. They held a huge territory along the right bank of the Kupa, between modern Karlovac and Sisak, which they extended to include the region of Gorica as well as parts of the Kranj region.

In Croatia great power belonged to the Šubić family of Bribir. Its lands were divided among various branches of the family, among which one branch dominated. The elder of the dominant branch, who earlier bore the title župan but from the end of the twelfth century was entitled knez, always held the family seat of Bribir. The Kačići, an unruly family practicing piracy, dominated the region between the Cetina and Neretva rivers. They also held various Adriatic islands in the area. Their main town was Omiš.

Between the Kačići on the Cetina River and the Šubići of the county of Bribir lay the lands of a certain Domald. His family ties are unknown, though he may well have been a Kačić. Holding Šibenik and Klis, he was elected Prince of Split in 1209. That same year he took Zadar from Venice; it was a brief triumph, for Venice soon took it back again. Probably as a reward for regaining Zadar, King Andrew in 1210 awarded Domald the župa of Cetina. In the decade that followed, however, Domald's relations with both king and

Split cooled. In 1221 the citizens of Split expelled him, electing in his stead a member of the Šubić family, Višan of Zvonigrad. War followed between Domald and the Šubići that soon involved various other Croatian families in the area. With royal support, the Šubići emerged victorious by 1223, and the king granted his Šubić allies a substantial portion of Domald's lands. Victory did not bring peace, however, for the Šubić family elder, Prince Gregory of Bribir, was not happy to see his uncle Višan as Prince of Split. The two Šubići were soon at war and in the course of 1223 Gregory captured and executed his uncle; as a result he annexed his uncle's territory in Lika and united all the Šubić lands under his own authority. However, after the death of their prince, the citizens of Split, to avoid accepting his executioner, elected Peter of Hum as their prince. Also contributing to this action was Split's emerging hostility toward Hungary—Gregory's patron—a feeling reflected not only in its choice of prince but also in its efforts during this period to reject Hungarian candidates for its archbishop by turning directly to the pope.

Meanwhile, following his defeat at the hands of the Šubići, Domald, still in possession of Klis, remained ambitious to regain Split. He soon attacked but failed to take Split. Peter remained under attack, however, for Gregory Šubić, victorious over his uncle, then sought to acquire Split. Warfare between Gregory and Peter followed in 1224 and 1225; shortly thereafter Peter died and by 1227 Gregory Šubić was Prince of Split. Having a large territory to manage, Gregory installed a deputy in Split. At about the same time Gregory's younger brother Stjepan was elected Prince of Trogir. The two brothers co-operated, and under their rule the two towns, usually rivals, established peaceful relations.

In the course of further warfare the Šubići took Klis from Domald. To try to restore his lost position Domald then allied himself with the Kačići and resumed the war. During it, in 1229, Domald's partisans in Split expelled Gregory's deputy and re-elected Domald as Split's prince. In the fighting that followed, the King of Hungary threw his support to the Šubići and by 1231 Gregory was again Prince of Split. Shortly thereafter Gregory is found also as Prince of Šibenik, a town until then held by Domald. Gregory is mentioned as still being Prince of Split in 1234, after which he disappears from the sources. Since he was not young, it is probable that he died.

Domald took advantage of the new situation to re-assert himself. In 1235 he was again Prince of Split. His success was short-lasting, for the king's party in the town led an uprising in 1237 that again expelled him and elected in his place Gregory's son Marko. But Marko soon died, and leadership of the Šubić family fell to Stjepan's son Stjepan (usually called Stjepko). At this point the citizens of Split chose an Italian nobleman as their prince, but Stjepko inherited Trogir. Domald soon launched an attack against Trogir; the king sent aid to Stjepko and their combined forces soon defeated and captured Domald at Klis, which at some point he had regained.

Peace was not to follow, however, as the rivalry between Split and Trogir heated up. Trouble came to a head in 1242 when King Bela of Hungary granted to Trogir lands in the hinterland of Split, which Split had long claimed for itself. Having the support of King Bela and also of the Šubići, who were angry at Split's attempt to exclude them, Trogir at once went to war against Split. Isolated and thus weaker, Split acquired new allies: the Kačići, Andrew of Hum, and Ninoslav of Bosnia. And in 1244 Split elected Ninoslav as its prince. He launched an attack against Trogir; his men ravaged the environs of Trogir, causing particular damage to its vineyards, but were unable to take the town itself. Ninoslav then returned to Bosnia, leaving a relative as his deputy in Split. The King of Hungary, supported by a large number of leading Croatian nobles (including Stjepko Šubić and Daniel Šubić, who held Šibenik for the family), marched against Split. Having no hope to withstand such opposition, Split immediately surrendered. Yielding to the king's demands, it made peace with Trogir and accepted as its prince a Hungarian appointee.

Soon thereafter Bela IV came to the conclusion that to prevent further wars among the Dalmatian towns his Croatian-Dalmatian ban, rather than the towns themselves, should choose the governors of towns. In 1250 he implemented this policy in Trogir and Split and in the years that followed in his other Dalmatian towns. The Šubići were unhappy over this change, for throughout the wars of the second quarter of the thirteenth century they had loyally supported the king, and now they were rewarded for their pains by being removed as princes from the Dalmatian coastal towns. The ban, who at this time had himself assumed the title of prince of each of the various Dalmatian towns, was unable to administer them directly. Thus he appointed a deputy—called a podesta or potestas—in each town to represent him. These deputies generally served for a year's term. And on one occasion, in 1263, the ban did appoint Stjepko Šubić to be his podesta for Šibenik.

While the warfare flared up all around it, Zadar tried to free itself from Venetian rule by a revolt in 1242–43, but failed.

As a result of the Tartar invasion of 1241–42, which caused considerable destruction in Croatia and Dalmatia, Bela IV allowed the nobles to establish securer defenses: to build castles on their lands and to increase the size of their private armies. The result, naturally, was to increase the power of the great nobles who became to an even greater extent independent masters of their districts; some even became great robber barons. This caused difficulties for Bela, and in an attempt to counter the authority of the great nobles in Hungary (including Slavonia) and to maintain his own influence, he tried to increase the power of the court nobility by assigning fiefs or even straight patrimonial grants to various courtiers and thereby provide them with a landed base. He also tried to appoint as his bans and governors nobles whose loyalty he trusted.

However, this policy of granting land to court nobles could not succeed in the long run, for later on the grantees (or their heirs) came to consider themselves great local lords with their own local interests, and thus in time many of them came to be members of the provincial independence-seeking nobility. Furthermore, the bans in the Slavic lands often tended to become supporters of local interests and thus could not always be relied upon, except at moments of royal strength, to enforce the will of the monarch. The development of localist tendencies among newly endowed nobles and their successors was also to result when similar attempts were made by the Hungarian kings Charles Robert and Louis in the fourteenth century.

Bela also issued charters giving free-town status to various towns in the hope of separating them from the authority of the local nobles. The charters granted were based on Germanic models. Varaždin had already obtained such a charter in 1220 from Andrew II, who also issued charters to Vukovar in 1231 and Virovitica in 1234. Other Slavonian towns followed under Bela: Petrinja in 1240; Gradec, the fortified economic center for Zagreb (but not the cathedral chapter [kaptol], where the Zagreb bishop resided, under its own administration) in 1242; Samobor in 1242; Križevci in 1252; and Jastrebarsko in 1257. The towns elected their own councils and magistrates (usually by annual elections carried out as defined in their charters), ran their own administrations and law courts, collected their own taxes and dues, and managed their own economies and trade. Power to do so was embodied in the articles of their charters, supplemented by the decisions of their councils and magistrates. The towns also owed military service to the king and, being directly under the king, were removed from the jurisdiction of provincial officialdom.

In Church affairs, as noted, the Croatians of Slavonia were subject to the Archbishop of Kalocsa (in Hungary). The leading bishopric in Slavonia was that of Zagreb. The Dalmatians and Croatians south of Velebit were under the Archbishop of Split. Though much has been written about the retention of Slavonic written with the glagolitic alphabet by the Church in Croatia, it should be noted that for most of the Middle Ages glagolitic was used only in a limited area. In Slavonia, it seems to have been scarcely used; the earliest evidence we have of glagolitic in the region under the jurisdiction of Zagreb appears in the fifteenth century. The area in which glagolitic thrived was that of Lika, Gacka, Krbava, Vinodol, Modruš, and the islands in the Gulf of Kvarner. The decisions of various Church councils against Slavonic in the tenth and eleventh centuries do not seem to have been particularly effective in this region. The Catholic Church seems to have become more liberal toward diversity in the thirteenth century; in 1215 a Lateran council allowed for various differences in the service. This new attitude may have encouraged Philip, the Bishop of Senj, to ask Pope Innocent IV (1243–54) for permission to use glagolitic Slavonic in his diocese. Having explained to the pope that it was an ancient language dating back to Saint Jerome(!), Philip received the papal permission he sought. Thereafter glagolitic Slavonic was used with papal sanction in both church services and matters of daily life throughout this region. Latin predominated only in the larger towns; for example, in the town of Senj Latin was used by the Church and usually by its secular leaders, who from the 1250s were drawn from the Krk (later Frankapan) family.

In the thirteenth century the Templars, already based in Slavonia since the twelfth century and holding Senj from 1180, acquired territory in Croatia.

In order to participate in the crusade of 1217 Andrew II had had to borrow from the Templars. Unable to repay them he had granted them Gacka as compensation in 1219. The Templars may not have administered this territory themselves but merely have taken income from it, for in the 1250s a Krk prince is documented as being podesta of Senj. The Templars remained in possession of this Croatian territory until 1269 when Bela IV granted them the župa of Dubica in exchange for Gacka and Senj.

NOTES

1. Ducellier, *La façade maritime,* pp. 161–62.
2. The Serbs were, of course, not without legal order. Besides customary laws, from at least the time of Nemanja their rulers issued specific legal acts in the form of charters and grants of individual privilege.
3. The version chosen here is that adopted by Nicol, "The Fourth Crusade and the Greek and Latin Empires, 1204–61," which is chapter 7 of *Cambridge Medieval History,* vol. 4, pt. 1, 1966 ed., pp. 309–10. A second version that depicts the threatened Latin Empire opening negotiations with Asen—rather than having the initiative come from Asen—is often seen. For example, G. Ostrogorsky, *History of the Byzantine State,* rev. ed. (New Brunswick, N.J., 1969), pp. 435–36. The only difference between the two versions is the camp from which negotiations were opened. For it is evident that matters were never resolved between Latins and Bulgarians. And possibly the Latins, even if they had initiated matters, were not serious about concluding an agreement with Asen, but simply hoped to raise his hopes of getting influence in the city by treaty and thus split his alliance with Theodore and prevent him from providing troops for Theodore's attack.
4. Ducellier, *La façade maritime,* p. 166.
5. The great empire founded by Ghenghis Khan should strictly be called Mongol and the term *Tatar* becomes proper only in about 1242/43 when Batu Khan established a more or less independent khanate, known as the Golden Horde, in south Russia. Thereafter the term *Mongol* should still be used for the great khanate centered in Karakorum, while *Tatar* becomes appropriate for the khanate of Batu and his successors. However, since this same Batu and his followers were active in the Steppe area from the mid-1230s—though then as forces under orders from the Great Khan—I think it justified and in some ways less confusing to use *Tatar* for these Mongol armies active in the Steppes even in the mid- to late 1230s, rather than switch from *Mongol* to *Tatar* in mid-stream in the already complex enough 1240s.
6. I. Božilov, "La famille des Asen (1186–1460): Généalogie et prosopographie," *Bulgarian Historical Review,* 1981, nos. 1–2: 140.
7. St. Stanojević, *Borba za samostalnost katoličke crkve u Nemanjićkoj državi* (Beograd, 1912), pp. 154–56.
8. J. Fine, *The Bosnian Church: A New Interpretation,* East European Monographs, vol. 10, East European Quarterly, distributed by Columbia University Press (Boulder and New York, 1975).
9. J. Fine, "Was the Bosnian Banate Subjected to Hungary in the Second Half of the Thirteenth Century?" *East European Quarterly* 3, no. 3 (June 1969): 167–77.

CHAPTER 4

The Second Half of the Thirteenth Century

Bulgaria upon John Asen II's Death

John Asen's heir was his seven-year-old son Koloman. As had been the case previously, no apparatus existed to hold the state together. Bulgaria lacked a state-wide bureaucracy staffed by administrative and financial officials appointed by the central government and dispatched to the provinces. There was also no state-financed army raised by the state to serve under the command of state-appointed generals who owed their positions solely to state service. Instead the provinces were dominated by a provincial nobility; these nobles governed their localities, rendered to the state local taxes which they themselves collected, and dominated the army, which was to a large extent composed of local levies raised by and serving under these nobles themselves. Even when governors were sent out from the center, they found themselves unable to deprive the boyars of their local authority and thus served in co-operation with them. When a tsar like Asen proved himself a successful war chief, he won from the boyars, through their fear of punitive action or through their eagerness for booty, expressions of loyalty. Then, through these personal ties of allegiance, the localities commanded by the boyars became temporarily bound to Trnovo and the central government. Clearly such bonds could not bring lasting cohesion to a state.

Koloman's regents quarreled among themselves and the boyars split into squabbling factions. Peripheral territories seceded and neighbors were again able to wrest territories away from Bulgaria. The disintegration was facilitated by a new outside factor. Already in Asen's lifetime the Tatars had appeared in the Steppes northeast of the Danube on Bulgaria's border. In 1238–39 they had brought the loosely-held-together Cuman state, which stretched between the Volga and the Carpathians, under their control. Since the Cumans had normally enjoyed good relations with Bulgaria and regularly provided Bulgaria's armies with large numbers of troops, the collapse of this state was to considerably weaken Bulgaria militarily, particularly since the new Tatar khanate was not usually particularly friendly. Thus Bulgaria saw a friendly neighbor replaced by a powerful and dangerous one. Many of the Cumans remained in the Steppes and were absorbed into the Tatar state, strengthening its armies. Others fled to Hungary, the Latin Empire, Nicea, or Bulgaria. Asylum granted to various Cuman leaders seems to have been a cause of the major Tatar attack, discussed above, launched against Hungary in the spring of 1241.

On 6 December 1240 Kiev fell to the Tatars. And, as we shall see, Asen gave asylum to various Russian princes and boyars, some of whom were presumably from families who had aided him during his ten-year exile in Russia. This Tatar expansion brought the Tatar state to Bulgaria's border. It was to remain there for the next century, being particularly influential on Bulgarian developments during the next sixty years. Of all the Balkan states, Bulgaria, having the Tatars immediately on its borders, was to be the most subject to Tatar influence: of all Balkan states it suffered the largest number of raids, fell first and remained longest under Tatar suzerainty, and absorbed the largest number of Tatar settlers, and thus experienced a greater mixing of peoples.

The Hungarians and Bulgarians, faced with this new power on their borders, must have seen the need to patch up their lesser differences and plan a joint defense should the Tatars try to expand further west. And, as we saw in the last chapter, early in 1240 a Bulgarian envoy was well received in Hungary, after which their relations seem to have improved. Then in the spring of 1241, before John Asen II died, the Tatars, having conquered south Russia, invaded Hungary. Defeating the Hungarian king's armies in a pitched battle on the River Sajó on 11 April 1241, the Tatars pursued King Bela to the Dalmatian coast, where he found safety by sailing to an island. The Tatars plundered Dalmatia until word reached them of the death of the great khan in Karakorum. They turned back, swinging east across Zeta—plundering Kotor, Svač, and Drivast (Drisht)—and Serbia, causing more destruction; possibly the inability of Serbia's King Vladislav to stop them alienated his subjects and thus contributed to his overthrow the following year.

The Tatars then passed through Bulgaria, meeting little opposition and doing considerable damage. Before they crossed the Danube, they probably also imposed tribute upon the Bulgarians. Such tribute is documented in 1253 as already in existence. Since there were no further known major Tatar attacks in the interim, 1242 seems the most likely date for its imposition. Since in 1242 time was short, the Tatars took only booty and prisoners; they took no fortresses and occupied no territory. Bulgaria's main rival for Thrace, Nicea, escaped Tatar attack. Though a second wave of Mongols had hit Anatolia from the east, as we saw above, it too had withdrawn to attend the selection of a new khan before it reached the Nicean state. And by devastating the realm of the Seljuks to Nicea's east, the Mongols had improved Nicea's position; for they had eliminated for a time Nicea's need to worry about a second front on its eastern frontier. The devastations from this attack, coming at a moment of weakness at the center, set Bulgaria spinning into a rapid decline from which it never recovered.

In 1246 Koloman, who was the son of the wife Asen lost in 1237, died. Koloman was succeeded by Asen's son Michael, the offspring of Irene, Theodore's daughter whom Asen had married late in 1237. Michael was only about eight, so the problems associated with a minor as tsar and with regents continued. The cause of Koloman's early death is not known. Acropolites reports that some say he died of a natural illness while others say he was poisoned. Many scholars believe he was murdered and argue that supporters of little Michael and his mother Irene were responsible. They then argue that Irene became the leading regent for Michael. However, regardless of how Koloman died, it is almost certain that Irene did not become the regent for Michael. Recently Lazarov has published a convincing study which not only discredits the evidence supporting such a role for Irene, but also shows she was residing with her brother in Thessaloniki late in 1246; the context suggests she had been there for a while. She presumably had been exiled from Bulgaria early in Koloman's reign. Lazarov identifies Sevastocrator Peter, a son-in-law of Asen who is found in a high position on a charter to Dubrovnik, as the leading regent for Michael.

Nicea and Epirus, 1246–61

The new regency in Bulgaria, which had not yet had time to install itself in power and which probably was faced with opposition from those who had surrounded Koloman, seems to have had little authority in much of Bulgaria. Taking advantage of this weakness, in 1246 Vatatzes of Nicea immediately attacked Bulgaria and took its holdings in Thrace as far as the upper Marica River. His gains included Adrianople and its district. Then, moving beyond Thrace, Vatatzes took the region of the Rhodopes, Melnik, Velbužd, and Serres. He also acquired the Chalcidic peninsula (with Mount Athos); his rule provided better order and security for the monasteries. He also took eastern Macedonia at least up to the Vardar, acquiring Skopje, Veles, and Prosek. Some scholars have argued that he actually pressed beyond the Vardar as far as Prilep or even Pelagonia (modern Bitola). This enormously successful campaign took only three months. In the course of it he also regained Tzurulum and Bizya from the Latins. Michael II of Epirus also got into the act and occupied western Macedonia, including Ohrid; much of Albania also clearly belonged to him at this time. Though some historians believe he now acquired Durazzo, it seems he had actually held it from the 1230s. Other scholars have argued that Epirus also acquired Bitola and Prilep. These scholars place the Epirote-Nicean border along the Vardar. Those scholars, noted above, who credit Vatatzes with greater success draw the border between Nicea and Epirus established by the end of 1246 between Pelagonia and Ohrid. In any case Bulgaria lost all this territory.

Having successfully annexed this region south of the Balkan Mountains which Asen had previously gained, Vatatzes, from a position of strength, obtained a treaty from Bulgaria that not only recognized Nicean possession of this territory but also brought Bulgaria into an alliance with Nicea against the Latin Empire. And apparently in 1247 the Bulgarians participated in a common military action with Nicea that acquired for Vatatzes several fortresses in eastern Thrace and even briefly besieged (without success) Constantinople. Bulgaria may also have suffered losses in the northwest. For in the late 1240s Hungary is found in possession of Beograd and Braničevo. If Asen had in fact recovered these cities from the Hungarians, as various Bulgarian scholars have asserted, then the Hungarians retook them, quite possibly in the midst of Bulgaria's troubles in 1246. However, it is by no means certain that Asen had regained them; thus they may have been in Hungarian hands since 1232.

At the close of Vatatzes' remarkably successful 1246 campaign against Bulgaria, he was preparing to return home when a marvellous opportunity to acquire Thessaloniki presented itself. In 1244 Theodore's son John had died. He had been succeeded in Thessaloniki by Theodore's younger son Demetrius, an extravagant and reckless young man. He quickly provoked against himself so much unpopularity that many Thessalonians came to feel it would be best to rid themselves of him and submit to Nicea. This would, of course, also have brought them the advantage of joining what was now the strongest Greek state, which more and more non-Nicean Greeks were coming to see as the Roman (Byzantine) Empire. Some leading Thessalonians formed a conspiracy to turn the city over to Vatatzes and sent envoys to him. Vatatzes naturally gave the conspirators his full support. He marched his armies to the city and ordered Demetrius to present himself and pay homage. Demetrius, suspicious of a conspiracy, refused to come out and do obeisance. Then the conspirators opened a gate to Vatatzes. Demetrius was captured, deposed on the grounds of refusing homage, and imprisoned briefly before being given large estates in Anatolia as compensation. His blind but still dangerous father, Theodore, was exiled to estates in Voden (Edessa). Vatatzes installed as governor in Thessaloniki Andronicus Palaeologus, the father of the future emperor Michael VIII Palaeologus. Michael at the time was made military governor of the newly recovered regions of Melnik and Serres. Vatatzes left a garrison in Thessaloniki and then rapidly annexed, against little opposition, the territory surrounding Thessaloniki.

Already sharing a border with Michael of Epirus somewhere in central or western Macedonia, Vatatzes now found himself facing Michael along a second border to his south, for Michael held most of Thessaly as well. Vatatzes' conquest of Thessaloniki had had little or no effect upon Epirus, for Epirus had already become for all practical purposes independent of the state of Thessaloniki. Interested in Constantinople, Vatatzes hoped to avoid conflict with Epirus, so he concluded a treaty with Michael. It was sealed with an engagement between Vatatzes' granddaughter and Michael's son and heir Nicephorus. This peace was not to last, however. Theodore, dissatisfed with events, eventually persuaded Michael to break the treaty. Michael took some minor fortresses from Nicea, probably early in 1251. If it was not his already, he may also at the time have taken Prilep. Then, still in 1251, he moved against Thessaloniki.

At that moment Vatatzes was mobilizing to besiege Constantinople. Michael may well have directed his march against Thessaloniki at this time to prevent or disrupt that siege, for Michael seems to have had a long-range hope for Constantinople, and it would have been easier for him to take it from the weak Latins than from a dynasty of Greeks from Nicea. Fearing an attack on his rear during his siege, Vatatzes called off the operation and led his troops west against Michael, who wisely avoided an engagement and withdrew his armies into the mountains of Albania. Vatatzes took Kastoria, probably early in 1252, and then entered into negotiations with various Albanian chieftains. By winning the allegiance of Golem, the Albanian chieftain who held the mountain fortress of Kroja, Vatatzes broke the ice. Soon various other Albanian tribal leaders brought their tribes into his camp. Thus Nicea, through the declared loyalty of these chieftains, won suzerainty over much of southern and central Albania.

Michael, threatened with attack and seeing his hold over a large portion of his Albanian lands evaporating, sent envoys to conclude a truce. Soon, in 1253, this truce became a peace treaty. By its terms Michael not only had to cede the fortresses he had taken from Nicea in 1250 or 1251, but he also had to surrender various others that since 1246 had been his, not Nicea's. Some of these, like Kastoria, had already been taken by Vatatzes by the time of the treaty. Michael had clearly lost his Macedonian holdings, for after the treaty Vatatzes garrisoned the principal fortresses between Thessaloniki and Ohrid. Vatatzes also acquired suzerainty over part of the Albanian interior. Theodore, who had played a major role in stirring up this warfare, was captured and taken to a Nicean prison where soon thereafter he died. Theodore's last appanage, Voden, also went to Nicea. Michael's son Nicephorus, already engaged to Vatatzes' granddaughter, retained his marital hopes but was taken to Nicea, albeit with honor, but also as a hostage. He was awarded the title of despot. Having recognized Nicean suzerainty, Michael was also rewarded with the title despot; he, of course, was already using this title, having received it from Manuel of Thessaloniki in the 1230s.

Nicea now seemed in a strong position and, alone of all the former candidates, able to take Constantinople. Bulgaria was powerless to make an attempt for the city and by then had lost its Thracian lands; the Kingdom of Thessaloniki no longer existed; and Epirus was not only reduced in size but, deprived of its Macedonian holdings, was pushed back into northwest Greece, with its borders that much further from Constantinople. Having lost its Macedonian and some of its Albanian holdings, Epirus had also lost much potential manpower and was thus that much weaker militarily. Nicea's prospects for conquering Constantinople, moreover, appeared excellent. The city stood alone, completely surrounded by Nicean possessions, at considerable distance from all its allies, and weakly defended.

To prepare for his attack on Constantinople Vatatzes, on his return from his 1252–53 campaign, took action to solidify his hold over his Thracian possessions. To do this he re-established the former Byzantine soldier-farmer system of settling soldiers who owed service for them on small plots of land. He did this not only in Thrace, but also in Macedonia to strengthen his hold on this newly gained region. Those so settled included many Cumans, who were still in large numbers leaving the Steppes, recently occupied by the Tatars.

Then, in November 1254, Vatatzes died. He was succeeded by his son Theodore II Lascaris, a scholarly man of letters. In January 1255 the Bulgarians took advantage of the death of the great military leader to overrun Macedonia all the way to Albania. Their reconquest was facilitated by local actions; for many Bulgarians living in Macedonian towns preferred Bulgarian rule to Nicean. Furthermore, Nicea had left only small garrisons in many of these towns; these garrisons were ousted without much difficulty. Two costly campaigns in 1255 and 1256 were required for the Niceans to recover this territory; all of it had been regained by July 1256. Peace was then concluded, mediated by Michael of Bulgaria's new father-in-law, Rostislav of Mačva. His presence reflected a recent Bulgarian decision on foreign policy. Having decided, after Vatatzes' death, that Nicea was its main enemy and the recovery of the southern and western territory its top priority, and moreover realizing it could not afford to face a second major enemy, Bulgaria renounced its claims to its northwestern lands (Beograd and Braničevo) and concluded an alliance with Hungary. Bulgaria, thus free from any worry about Hungarian action that could have led to a two-front war, was then able to devote its full attention to the recovery of Macedonia which, as we saw, it briefly achieved in 1255.

The peace with Hungary was sealed when Tsar Michael of Bulgaria married the King of Hungary's granddaughter in 1255. She was the child of Bela IV's daughter Anna and a Russian prince named Rostislav, who had been assigned the post of Ban of Mačva by Bela. Mačva, originally centered around the Kolubara River, had by this time been expanded to include the territory from the lower Drina in the west, the lower Morava in the east, Serbia in the south, and Hungary, along the Sava and Danube rivers, in the north. By this time Mačva included Beograd and by 1256, if not earlier, Braničevo. Bulgaria's efforts to regain Macedonia from Nicea then, as noted, ended in failure. But Michael's new ally Rostislav was able to mediate the above-mentioned Bulgarian-Nicean peace in the summer of 1256. Once again, by this treaty, the upper Marica became the Bulgarian-Nicean frontier. And the defeated Bulgarians had to become Nicean allies. As this alliance soon drew the Bulgarians into supporting Nicea against Constantinople, it led to a worsening of Bulgarian-Latin relations.

Epirus, as noted, had lost considerable territory and potential manpower to Nicea in 1253. However, Epirus had not become a weak state. It still retained its core area of western Greece (Epirus), and it had regained Acarnania and Aetolia, presumably by occupation on the death of Theodore's brother Constantine who had governed these regions. It also still held most of Thessaly, a comparatively rich province, and the Albanian coast, including the strategic port of Durazzo. Its dynasty also enjoyed considerable local popularity. The campaign that had brought about Michael's submission to Nicea in 1253 had not engaged his army, which was still intact, and, since the Nicean troops had not operated in Thessaly or Epirus itself, the most productive regions of the state had not been damaged. Nicea's military occupation had affected only Macedonia and Albania; and the territory that Epirus was to lose in the end, also in these regions, was territory recently gained by Epirus from Bulgaria that had not yet become an integral part of its state. Thus the Epirote state, controlling most of northern Greece and uninvaded, was still economically strong and both able and willing to support its ruler, Michael.

When Nicea became involved in the 1255–56 war with Bulgaria, Michael of Epirus, either ambitious to take advantage of matters for his own ends or afraid that a victorious Nicea operating in Macedonia along his northern border might next attack his heartland, entered into an alliance against Nicea with Uroš, King of Serbia. At the same time agents from Michael, bearing promises and gifts, traveled about the mountains of Albania to regain the support of Albanian chieftains. Seeing what was happening, and expecting further trouble from Michael, Theodore Lascaris, after his victory over Bulgaria in the fall of 1256, ordered that the wedding between his daughter and Michael's son Nicephorus take place. Michael himself wisely did not attend the ceremony, but his wife, the groom's mother, did. She was not allowed to return to Epirus but was held as a hostage, with her return dependent on Michael's surrendering Durazzo and the fortress of Servia to Nicea. To obtain her release, Durazzo was yielded to Nicea. The Albanians from the environs of Durazzo seem to have disliked the change. Michael's resulting anger found relief in the spring of 1257 when the tribal chiefs of Albania, stirred up and co-ordinated by Epirote agents, rose up against Nicea. The Serbian and Epirote armies then went into action simultaneously. Michael rapidly regained most of Albania, most probably including Durazzo. Then Michael dispatched his troops into Macedonia and quickly reoccupied Kastoria and Prilep.

In this conflict between the two Greek states a number of great magnates, either local landholders or generals appointed to command garrisons in Macedonian fortresses, supported Epirus. The small military holdings established by Vatatzes had threatened their authority. By taking lands which the magnates aspired to own and by using these lands to support soldiers to man a state army independent of the magnates and loyal to the emperor, serving under commanders appointed by the emperor, this policy undermined the influence of the magnates in military affairs. For, as noted, previously the Nicean armies had largely been composed of private troops, belonging to the individual magnates, who followed their master to battle and served under his command. However, the small-holding policy could provide the emperor with an army to balance the forces of the magnates and give him the freedom to appoint commanders of his choice and to by-pass members of the great military and landed families. Finding themselves probably with less influence in the army (to the degree the policy succeeded) and threatened with further losses of influence, many magnates had become disgruntled. As a result the emperor accused various leading magnates of conspiring against him; several of these had been arrested. Thus when war broke out between Nicea and Epirus, various leading Nicean magnates decided to throw their support to Michael. This proved costly to Theodore Lascaris, especially when the magnates who defected were fortress commanders and opened their gates to Michael.

Thus through a combination of these various factors, in the course of 1257 Michael rapidly regained much of western Macedonia. With momentum on his side, Michael was marching toward Thessaloniki, when suddenly he was attacked in the rear—on the west coast of Epirus—by a new actor, Manfred of Sicily. Manfred had first occupied the major Ionian islands, including Corfu. Then he had landed on the Albanian coast and taken Durazzo, Berat, Valona (Avlona, Vlonë, Vlora), and their environs. Faced with war on two fronts, Michael decided to sacrifice the west for gains in the east, which he hoped might include Thessaloniki and Constantinople. He therefore sent envoys to Manfred to offer peace and an alliance. He agreed in June 1258 to recognize Manfred's Ionian and Albanian conquests in exchange for an alliance against Nicea. Manfred agreed and their treaty was sealed by Manfred's marrying Michael's daughter Helen; Manfred was awarded his conquests as her dowry. Thus Manfred ended up in legal possession of the Albanian coast from Cape Rodoni past Valona to Butrinti.

At roughly the same time, in August 1258, Theodore II Lascaris died, leaving a minor son, John IV Lascaris, under a regency composed of trusted adherents who had supported Theodore in his campaign to reduce the influence of the aristocracy. Needless to say the aristocrats wanted to take advantage of Theodore's demise to re-assert themselves; furthermore, they desired revenge against the regents. Within ten days, they had overthrown the regency and the aristocrat Michael Palaeologus became the leading regent. He had formerly been Vatatzes' military governor of Melnik and Serres. Shortly before Lascaris' death, he had been accused of plotting against Lascaris but, by a clever defense and personal oath, he had escaped punishment. As regent, he soon acquired the title despot and shortly thereafter was crowned co-emperor.

Michael of Epirus decided to take advantage of the turmoil in Nicea to construct a major coalition and march against Nicea. He had already enrolled Manfred of Sicily, who had promised to supply a German cavalry detachment of four hundred horsemen. He also had at the ready a large unit composed chiefly of Vlachs under his illegitimate son John, who had taken the surname

Ducas, to whom Michael, it seems, had assigned the government of Thessaly. John had solidified his position in that province by creating close ties with the local Vlachs, who dominated the mountainous regions of west-central Thessaly, by marrying the beautiful daughter of Taron, the leading Vlach chief of Thessaly. Michael had also sent envoys to acquire the support of William Villehardouin, an able warrior who had succeeded to the rule of the Morea on the death of his brother Geoffrey II in 1246. William agreed, and he sealed the alliance by marrying Anna, another of Michael's daughters. The Serbs also agreed to help, but they never gave the coalition any support and by the end of the campaign had joined the Niceans, providing them with a limited number of troops.

Upon learning what was happening, Michael Palaeologus sent envoys to Epirus, but Michael II refused to receive them. Palaeologus then decided that quick action was the only solution. He mobilized an army composed chiefly of Seljuk and Cuman mercenaries, supplemented by contingents sent from Serbia and Hungary, and dispatched it under the command of his brother John on a surprise attack into Macedonia. These forces, arriving before Michael's allies could send support, won a skirmish against an Epirote army near Kastoria in March 1259. Michael II quickly withdrew his troops into Albania to regroup and await the arrival of his allies. The Niceans in the meantime occupied most of Macedonia, penetrating as far west as Ohrid, which they captured. Michael II had at once appealed to his allies, including Manfred who, now seeing his Albanian lands threatened, immediately dispatched his cavalry unit. Villehardouin soon showed up leading his own troops as did John of Thessaly. This joint force then marched into Macedonia, reaching the plain of Pelagonia (modern Bitola) in June 1259. Michael's combined forces greatly outnumbered the Nicean troops; however, the Epirote army was composed of four different groups—Epirote Greeks, Vlachs, Germans (Manfred's cavalry), and Morean Franks, each under its own leader. There was thus no unified command, and each group displayed a strong disinclination to take orders from anyone else. The units were also accustomed to different methods of warfare; thus their commanders disagreed on the tactics to be employed. The Nicean army that now approached Pelagonia, though composed of different mercenary groups, enjoyed a much more unified command, for its mercenaries were willing and ready to obey John Palaeologus.

On the eve of the battle John of Thessaly quarrelled violently with Villehardouin, who, it seems, had been making eyes at John's beautiful Vlach wife. John stalked back to his own camp, rounded up his troops, and marched off with them to the Nicean camp. When they accepted his condition that he need not fight against the troops of his father (Michael), John joined the Niceans. Seeing this defection and concluding that it would assure a Nicean victory on the morrow, Michael of Epirus, in order to preserve intact his own forces, slipped away with them in the night toward Albania. In the morning, seeing the situation, the Niceans quickly moved in for the kill. The Germans and French, even though the prince in whose cause they were fighting had departed and though they had no stake in western Macedonia, decided to stand their ground and do battle anyway. The Niceans won an overwhelming victory. The Westerners suffered heavy casualties and Villehardouin was captured.

With momentum on their side, the Niceans solidified their control over all Macedonia, subduing any fortresses that might have resisted up to this point, and over central-southern Albania to the walls of Manfred's Durazzo. It is likely, but by no means certain, that the Niceans also took Durazzo. They then marched into Epirus itself, whose defenses Michael had not had time to prepare, and occupied much of it, including Michael's capital of Arta. The citizens of Vonitsa and Jannina (Ioannina, Joannina) held out, behind their walls, loyal to Michael. Nicea made no attempt to conquer any of Epirus' islands. Unwilling to risk the loss of his armies, Michael did not try to oppose the Niceans, but withdrew his army to an island, where he planned his return. Epirus seemed subdued, with all but two of its fortresses fallen, and those two under siege. At the same time other Nicean troops, accompanied by John of Thessaly, overran much of Thessaly. Thus, not surprisingly, the Battle of Pelagonia is usually depicted as a major event that decided the fate of the Greek world.

However, Donald Nicol argues that the battle's significance has been greatly exaggerated.[1] The conquest of Epirus was superficial. The population remained loyal to Michael, and Nicea did not have sufficient troops to occupy it thoroughly and put it under military rule. When the shock of the rapid occupation wore off, the Epirotes were to rally and fight back. Michael had kept his army intact. So had John of Thessaly, who by now had clearly lost whatever attachment he had had to the Niceans. Possibly they had not allowed him to retain his former role in Thessaly. John soon brought his army to Vonitsa and sent an embassy to his father; he apologized for withdrawing from the battle, saying he had not realized that his actions could have cost the family Epirus itself, and promised to support Michael's recovery of Epirus. Michael forgave him and they began planning a counter-offensive. At the same time Manfred, angry at the defeat of his cavalry and seeing his Albanian possessions in danger (if not already partly occupied), promised further aid. So Michael, returning with his forces to the mainland, joined with John's army; together they marched on Arta, whose inhabitants opened their gates to them, welcoming them back. Having established their administration there, they then marched north to Jannina and dispersed the Nicean troops besieging that city. Shortly thereafter they had expelled the Niceans from Epirus entirely. This success was the result of the regrouping of Epirote forces, the loyalty of its population to Michael, the failure of the Niceans to establish an effective administration in the conquered region, and, in the final stages, the Niceans' poor generalship. Considering the short duration of the Niceans' occupation, their limited manpower, and the hostility of the local population, their administrative failure was probably something that the Niceans could not have prevented, even if they had been aware of the problem.

In the spring of 1260 Michael sent his son Nicephorus at the head of an army into Thessaly. These troops defeated the Nicean army at Trikorifi and captured its commander, Alexius Strategopoulos. As a result of this campaign Nicephorus recovered most, if not all, of Thessaly. It is possible that part of the east coast of Thessaly near the Gulf of Volos remained in Nicean possession. However, since Nicephorus was to grant land to a monastery (Makrinitisa) in the Volos region in 1266, it is evident Epirus had recovered it by then; 1260 seems a reasonable time for this recovery to have occurred. Moreover, since Nicephorus was, in 1266, the one to be granting this land, it appears he was governing this territory. Thus probably in the 1260s Nicephorus had been awarded an appanage in Thessaly. Whether his half-brother John still had a role in that province is not known. John had been active in Thessaly prior to the Battle of Pelagonia. But whether before and during 1259 he governed all Thessaly for his father—as most scholars believe—or only had large estates there, is not really known. The Vlach troops he brought to battle, though usually depicted as an official force, could easily have been a private army raised on his own estates. John may well have returned to Thessaly after its recovery by Epirus, but this is not certain. Nicephorus clearly was responsible at that time for at least a small region in Thessaly, but he may well have managed a much wider area, possibly all Epirote Thessaly. We simply do not know how Thessaly was administered. Manfred also sent forces to regain his Albanian possessions. Between 1260 and 1262, according to Pachymeres, he conquered numerous places in "Illyria and New Epirus." Thus we may conclude he regained most, if not all, of his Albanian possessions.[2]

Though Pelagonia was an ephemeral victory and Michael did not suffer long-term losses (being back to his former strength within a year) it was still important insofar as the battle had not gone the other way. For had Nicea lost, the Epirote coalition could have marched east and possibly taken Thessaloniki and who knows how much more.

Thus Michael had quickly regained northern Greece. Furthermore he still posed a threat to Nicea's ambitions. He had a fairly strong army and still hoped to recover Thessaloniki. Manfred had sent him a new military unit, a company of Italian soldiers, and Nicea did not know how many more troops he might send. Thessaloniki might actually find itself in danger. The Niceans strengthened their garrison in Thessaloniki and renewed their alliance with Bulgaria. They also concluded in March 1261 an alliance with Genoa (the Treaty of Nymphaeum). However, its purpose was not defensive but rather to obtain naval support for the conquest of Constantinople. A fleet was essential for this task, and the Niceans needed assistance in this area. Furthermore, since Constantinople would be defended by the powerful Venetian Eastern fleet, it seemed a good move to bring their Genoese rivals into action. The Genoese, who had suffered from the Venetians' monopoly of Constantinopolitan trade under the Latin Empire, were promised a series of privileges that in essence would allow them to take over Venice's position there when the city fell.

The Nicean Recovery of Constantinople

The Genoese alliance proved unnecessary, for Constantinople was to fall without Genoese aid. But the treaty had already been signed and Genoa collected on the promises; so, after regaining Constantinople, the Greeks were to find themselves once again dependent upon Italians for commercial transport as well as for naval defense. The Italians regularly were to take naval action to prevent the Byzantines (as we again can call the Niceans) from rebuilding their navy. And through blackmail, by threatening attacks on Greek islands or coastal towns, the Italians steadily increased their privileges and through them their hold on commerce, to the disadvantage of Greek merchants.

But lest we get too far ahead of ourselves, the recovery of Constantinople was to be ridiculously simple. An elderly general, Alexius Strategopoulos, with no orders to go against Constantinople, was reconnoitering in the suburbs of the city on 25 July 1261. Discovering that the Frankish garrison was not present in the city, he brought on his own initiative a small number of troops to the walls, forced an entry through a narrow secret passage, overcame a puny guard, and opened a gate from inside to the rest of his troops. He and his men were warmly welcomed by the Greeks of the city. Hearing the news, Baldwin II took flight aboard a Venetian ship. Thus after fifty-seven years of Latin rule Constantinople was taken by accident, without a battle or even a plan.

Michael Palaeologus hurried to Constantinople, leaving the young legitimate emperor, John IV Lascaris, back in Nicea. Michael had himself, and himself alone, crowned in Hagia Sophia. Shortly thereafter, he had John blinded and deposed. Thereafter Michael ruled alone. He founded the dynasty that was to rule Byzantium from then until the Turkish conquest. But by this time Byzantium was hardly an empire any longer—despite its titles, rhetoric, and court ceremonial; it was just another petty state, holding, together with Constantinople, western Anatolia, Thrace, Thessaloniki, and Macedonia.

The Struggle between Franks and Byzantines
for the Morea

Michael VIII, as Michael Palaeologus can now be called, was ambitious to restore the empire's lost territory and glory. His main targets of re-conquest were in Greece: Epirus, Thessaly, and the Morea (Peloponnesus). The last, though most distant, seemed the easiest to recover. First, its rulers were Franks whom Michael hoped the Greek population would not support; second, in 1261 he still had the Morea's ruler, William Villehardouin, in his power as his prisoner, having captured him in the Battle of Pelagonia.

Michael had started negotiating with his captive immediately after the battle. At first he had demanded all the Morea back in exchange for his release. William had refused, saying, even if he wanted to agree, it was not his to give; the peninsula was held collectively by all eleven great barons (of which he was only one, albeit the most important). He could yield only his own two baronies; the rest could be surrendered only by the Great Council of Achaea. Michael, deciding to bide his time, put William back in prison, where, it seems, he was at least housed under comfortable and honorable conditions. Meanwhile, Michael recovered Constantinople, and the Morea had accepted as its bailiff, or acting prince, Guy de la Roche, the ruler of Athens and the most powerful baron in the area. It was clear that Guy would not agree to yield much of the Morea, so Michael had to reduce his demands. He decided to seek possession of certain powerful fortresses to give him a foothold in the area, from which, he hoped, when the time was ripe, he could expand Byzantine rule. So, he demanded three important fortresses: Mistra (near old Sparta, a powerful fortress completed by William Villehardouin in 1249 for defense against the unruly Melingi, a Slavic tribe in the vicinity), Monemvasia (in the southeastern Peloponnesus, on the Malea peninsula, the last Greek fortress to fall to the Franks, which William had captured in 1248 after a three-year siege), and Maina (on the Mani peninsula on the southern tip of the Peloponnesus). William said he would agree if the Council did. So Michael released one captive Frank to go to the Morea and place the proposal before the Council. Guy opposed yielding any territory; he had several reasons to stand fast. William's return would reduce Guy's authority; at present Guy was the dominant figure in the whole of Frankish Greece as well as in the Morea, a position he would lose once William returned. Furthermore, there was no love lost between the two individuals, for the close relations that had existed between Geoffrey I and Othon had not continued under their heirs.

However, Guy could not act alone. Captive along with William were various other barons whose wives were representing them on the Council and who wanted their husbands back. So, after arguing against the offer, Guy had to yield. Then Michael VIII, after taking two powerful Franks as hostages for William's good faith and after extracting an oath of loyalty from William, released William, who returned to the Morea late in 1261 and turned over the three forts. Michael installed garrisons in them at once. Monemvasia was particularly important; not only were its strong fortifications virtually impregnable, but as a port it provided a gateway through which the Byzantines could bring troops and supplies to the peninsula. Mistra, a strong fortress located in the center of the peninsula, was also to be a nuisance to the Franks. The Byzantine position here quickly became stronger as the neighboring Tzakonians—a distinct Greek group that preserved to a considerable extent an archaic dialect—declared their allegiance to Michael, as did the Slavs of the Taygetos Mountains. These groups became a force supporting Byzantine expansion from that center.

William clearly was unhappy with these losses, as was the pope, who immediately assured William that he was not bound by his oath to Michael since it had been extracted under duress. Thus both sides prepared for war, Michael expecting William to try to recover the three forts, and William expecting Michael to begin expansion. The Byzantines based there, with local help, had at once made gains. Not only had they assumed at least suzerainty over much of the area around Mistra, but also by 1263 the Byzantines had driven the Franks from Malea, on which lay Monemvasia, and from Mani, two of the three promontories on the southern Peloponnesus. Then, in the summer of 1263, a Byzantine army landed at Monemvasia and marched through Laconia into Arcadia, with its destination Villehardouin's capital of Andravida. The army was successful, acquiring various small fortresses, until the Franks defeated it in an open field battle near Andravida. The Greeks fled in panic back to Laconia (where their city of Mistra was located). Their flight gave William time to regroup his forces.

Meanwhile a second Greek army, also operating in Arcadia, had taken Kalavryta, whose Greek population welcomed it. The Byzantines dispatched a new force from Mistra through Arcadia in 1264, again with the intent of attacking Andravida. But ten miles from that town it was met by a Frankish army. In the small skirmish that ensued, the Greek commander John Cantacuzenus was killed. The Greeks again lost heart and retreated. After this failure, the Turkish mercenaries—who made up a large part of the Byzantine forces, whose pay was long in arrears, and who had come to have little expectation of Byzantine success—deserted the Byzantine cause and offered their services to William, who was happy to hire them. Then William's armies, supplemented by these Turks, marched into Laconia and defeated the remaining Greeks in a fierce battle at Nikli. The Greeks retreated to Mistra which, behind its strong fortifications, they still held. The Franks then attacked, but failed to take, Mistra. Finlay notes:

> The weakness of the two contending parties, and the rude nature of the military operations of the age, are depicted by the fact that the Prince of Achaia continued to retain possession of Lacedaemon for several years after the war had broken out, though it was only three miles distant from Misithra [Mistra] which served as headquarters of the Byzantine army.[3]

Mistra's population grew rapidly as many Greeks from the surrounding area migrated to it. An Orthodox metropolitan was established there. However, Monemvasia, a port through which troops and supplies could enter, became the main Byzantine operational center. The Byzantine governor (kephale) for the empire's Morean holdings resided in Monemvasia throughout the 1270s. However, in time he moved to Mistra. He is to be found residing there in 1289. By 1262 the Metropolitan of Monemvasia had been given the senior rank among the Peloponnesian bishops. The inhabitants of Monemvasia were also successful corsairs in the Aegean. They were especially inclined to prey on the Venetians.

Michael VIII's campaigns in 1263 and 1264 failed to expand the empire's territory, and an uneasy peace followed. However, the threat of a new Byzantine offensive, which Michael clearly wanted, remained. The Byzantines sent agents among the Greek population of the Morea and raided Frankish territory from their fortified bases. Various skirmishes occurred from time to time. These activities all had a negative effect on commerce and agriculture which, having enjoyed prosperity for over fifty years, now declined together with the security of the area. Now for the first time the Frankish Morea actually had an enemy on, and even within, its borders. The Franks began building more castles.

William, worrying about the prospect of a major Byzantine offensive, now concluded that his principality needed a powerful protector. He found one in Charles of Anjou, brother of King Louis IX of France. Charles, as we shall see, was at the time becoming a major enemy of Byzantium. William, in 1267, became Charles' vassal and agreed that upon his death his principality would be inherited directly by the Anjous. William's daughter Isabelle married Charles' younger son Philip and, according to Charles' plans, Philip would succeed William as Prince of Achaea. It was also agreed, however, that should William have a son, that son would get as a fief one-fifth of Achaea (the Morea in this context) as a vassal of the Anjous. William in exchange received a promise of military support from Charles.

By the end of the 1260s the Byzantines had been able to take Lacedaemonia and had asserted their control over much of Laconia. They then decided to extend their authority over Arcadia, making two serious attempts to conquer that region between 1270 and 1275. However, in both cases Charles of Anjou sent forces to aid William, and the Byzantines were repelled. This warfare, beginning in the 1260s, ended the period of prosperity for the Morea. Continuing over the next decades, the wars were fought chiefly with mercenaries on both sides; these professionals, who had no stake in the area, freely plundered it. The Latins found themselves at a distinct disadvantage. The local Greek and Slavic populations, the majority of the peninsula's population, tended to support the Byzantines. Many Frankish fiefs, being held by widows, provided no troops, and since the Principality of Achaea was on the defensive and there were few or no new fiefs to distribute, few knights from the West were interested in coming to the Morea. Even so, however, the Frankish knights still dominated whenever they met the Greeks in a pitched battle. Thus Greek success depended on avoiding major confrontations, staging coups in towns, and picking off poorly garrisoned towns. Most of the warfare initiated by the Greeks consisted of sieges of forts and ambushes of small Frankish units.

The Struggle for Northern Greece

While the struggle for the Morea was occurring, Michael of Epirus, miffed by Nicea's success and Michael VIII's coronation, resumed his attack upon

Nicean (now Byzantine) territory. The Byzantines sent troops against him, which forced him to agree to a treaty in 1264. However, once again Michael had managed to keep his armies out of battle, and the Byzantines had failed to occupy Epirus. Thus both Michael's state and army remained intact. However, Michael's prospects had deteriorated as he found himself becoming isolated, for his ally Manfred was now fighting for his very survival against Charles of Anjou and unable to provide any further aid. So the Byzantines were able to force this peace upon Michael that compelled him to surrender Jannina and also forced his son Nicephorus to marry Anna, a niece of Michael VIII. Nicephorus' wife, Theodore Lascaris' daughter, seems to have died previously. In 1265 the new marriage took place, and Michael VIII granted Nicephorus the despot's title.

Then on 26 February 1266 at the Battle of Benevento Charles decisively defeated Manfred, who was killed. Charles of Anjou now gained Sicily. When he received word of Manfred's death, Michael of Epirus marched through the coastal regions of northern Epirus and into Albania, recovering the lands that Manfred had taken from him.

How much of Albania Michael was able to recover is unknown. He attacked Kanina, held by Manfred's governor for Albania, Philip Chinardo. He succeeded in securing the assassination of Chinardo, but failed to take the city whose Italian garrison refused to surrender. The garrison remained in control of Kanina as did Chinardo's deputies in Berat and Valona, resisting both Epirotes and Angevins until 1271 or 1272 when the Latin leadership of all three cities finally submitted to the Angevins. Whether these failures led Michael to give up the idea of proceeding further into Albania or whether, by-passing these towns, he did acquire control of territory beyond Valona and Kanina is not known. The Byzantines also retained a presence in the mountains of north-central Albania, at least along the Mati (Mat) River, as is seen in an inscription from that region from about 1266 mentioning their kephale. The Byzantines also controlled access into the area through possession of most of Macedonia.

Michael II of Epirus then died in 1267 or 1268, and his lands were divided; his son Nicephorus acquired Epirus with its capital of Arta, while his illegitimate son John Ducas inherited Thessaly. Gregoras states that John's holding extended from Mount Olympus in the north to Mount Parnassus in the south, with the Achelous River serving as its western border. John's capital was at Neopatras near Lamia.

Byzantine sources do not make clear what preceded this division. One author implies John received Thessaly at this time. A second implies he was already there at the time. It is clear that John had been in Thessaly in 1259, though it is not known how much of the province he then held. However, Nicephorus had the major role in recovering Thessaly from the Niceans in 1260 and he alone is documented as in possession of part of Thessaly in the 1260s—making a grant to a monastery in 1266. Though John may well have held part of Thessaly after 1260 during Michael's lifetime, this cannot be documented.[4]

By the late 1260s the Byzantines had again established a foothold in eastern Thessaly. Very likely they had taken advantage of the instability produced by Michael of Epirus' death to achieve this. A grant to a monastery from August 1268 by the east Thessalian nobleman Nicholas Maliasinos states that Nicholas had submitted to the emperor. This nobleman, presumably in the previous year (1267–68), had married a niece of Michael VIII. By 1270 Michael VIII had issued charters to two monasteries in eastern Thessaly near the Gulf of Volos (Makrinitsa and Neopetra), showing he had acquired that region. From these years imperial grants of pronoias and of tax exemptions to various notables of east Thessaly begin appearing. Thus probably in 1267/68 the Byzantines regained some or all of Thessaly's east coast. They clearly had at least acquired the territory just north of the Gulf of Volos. Since various local nobles were receiving rewards, it seems likely that the Byzantine conquest, though it may well have been carried out by invading troops, owed its success at least partly to local nobles' switching sides to join the Byzantine camp. Despite these gains, however, John of Thessaly still possessed the lion's share of the region, holding all western and central Thessaly, and presumably intending to reassert his authority over the lands he had lost in the east along the coast. In the years that followed, he was to launch various raids into eastern Thessaly. And since the Byzantines were not satisfied with having just the east coast but wanted to regain all of this rich province, tensions between the two camps continued.

Charles of Anjou Enters into Greek Affairs

Meanwhile Charles of Anjou, having seized Sicily, concluded in 1267 a treaty at Viterbo with Baldwin II, the dispossessed Latin emperor who had fled West when the Greeks regained Constantinople. At Viterbo Baldwin ceded to Charles all suzerain rights over Greece and the Greek islands, except for Constantinople itself and the islands of Lesbos (Mytilene), Chios, Samos, and Kos. Baldwin's son Philip was then betrothed to Charles' daughter Beatrice. At the same time, as noted above, Charles gained an actual foothold in Greece by concluding, also at Viterbo, his agreement with William Villehardouin, becoming William's overlord as well as his heir for the Morea. Charles next was to set about creating a coalition to gain the parts of Greece he had title to as well as to regain Constantinople for Baldwin.

Bulgaria between Byzantium, Hungary, and the Tatars, 1256–77

Meanwhile in Bulgaria, late in 1256 (probably in December) a group of boyars decided to kill Tsar Michael and replace him with his first cousin Koloman, the son of John Asen II's brother Sevastocrator Alexander. The plotters attacked Michael, who died soon afterwards from his wounds.

Koloman's claims to the throne were strong, for he was the highest ranking male member of the dynasty still living. To further his claims he forcibly married Michael's widow, the daughter of Rostislav of Mačva. It seems Koloman actually grabbed power briefly, though possibly holding nothing more than Trnovo and environs; he was faced with strong opposition from the start, some of which came from part of the army. Thus he could not consolidate power and had to flee from Trnovo almost immediately. He was captured in flight and killed. Whether Koloman had been an initiator of the plot against Michael or merely the tool of a boyar faction is not known.

Shortly before his demise, as noted, Tsar Michael had married the daughter of Rostislav, son-in-law of the King of Hungary and since 1254 Ban of Mačva. Rostislav's banate bordered on the Bulgarian province of Vidin. To protect his daughter Rostislav now, early in 1257, invaded Bulgaria. It seems he was using her as an excuse to acquire the Bulgarian throne for himself, a plan the Hungarians favored, for by it Bulgaria would fall under Hungarian suzerainty. Rostislav appeared at the gates of Trnovo. Inside the city, a boyar faction seized control. It is not certain whether these boyars had already, prior to Rostislav's arrival, ousted Koloman and taken over, or whether at Rostislav's appearance, lacking confidence in Koloman's ability to defend the city, they had then turned against him. Though it is sometimes stated that Rostislav briefly obtained Trnovo only to meet so much opposition that he was forced to withdraw, it seems that he probably never actually gained possession of the city. No Byzantine source claims that Rostislav ever acquired Trnovo. Acropolites says only that Rostislav attacked Trnovo and recovered his daughter. She could well have been yielded on demand to forces still outside the city. The boyars should have had no objection to surrendering her. If Rostislav had taken the city, or installed himself within it, presumably Acropolites would have mentioned it.

Meanwhile, because hostilities had resumed between Bulgaria and the Latin Empire after Nicea forced Bulgaria back into an anti-Latin alliance in the summer of 1256, the Latin emperor, Baldwin II, decided to strike against the weakened Bulgarians in the midst of the chaos of 1257. Since there was no land border between the two states, his attack had to be by sea. He enlisted the Venetians, who had a fleet then in Constantinople, to direct a raid against Mesembria. They took the town, plundering it. However, they did not try to hold it but soon withdrew, leaving it to the Bulgarians, possibly to Bulgarians under a certain Mico, whom we shall meet shortly, who also was a claimant for the Bulgarian throne. However, one may wonder whether this raid had not been launched in support of Rostislav, the Hungarian-supported candidate who that year was besieging Trnovo and who alone among the possible candidates might have been expected to support the cause of the Latin Empire.

In any case, having failed to take Trnovo, Rostislav retreated to Vidin, where he established himself, taking the title of Tsar of Bulgaria. The Hungarians recognized him with this title. In this way this major northwestern province was separated from the Bulgarian state and fell under Hungarian suzerainty, through the person of Rostislav. This secession also made Hungary's hold on the disputed provinces of Braničevo and Beograd to the west of Vidin that much more secure, for, by losing Vidin, the Bulgarians had lost their province that bordered on Braničevo.

Meanwhile in southeastern Bulgaria, Mico (the name is a dimunitive of the name Dimitri), another relative of John Asen II and the husband of Tsar Michael's sister, was proclaimed tsar. He most probably never obtained Trnovo, however, but simply created his own principality, which he separated from the rest of Bulgaria, while he sought support to march on Trnovo to establish himself there as tsar.

Thus outside Trnovo there existed two claimants (Mico in the southeast and Rostislav in Vidin), each ambitious for Trnovo and each calling himself tsar, while the boyars held Trnovo, opposed to both claimants and prepared to fight both. The boyars next, still in 1257, elected one of their number, Constantine Tih, as tsar. Constantine had large estates near Sardika (modern Sofija) and was half Serbian, related through his mother to the Serbian dynasty. Having no connection to the Asen family, he sought one, at the same time seeking an alliance with Nicea by sending envoys to the Nicean court to ask for the hand of Irene, Theodore II Lascaris' daughter, whose mother was a daughter of John Asen. The negotiations were successful and the marriage took place in 1258. Acropolites informs us that Constantine already had a wife whom he had to divorce in order to marry Irene. Thus now Constantine's connection to the Asen dynasty was as strong as Mico's.

Scholars have long disputed over who actually ruled Bulgaria after Michael's murder; thus lists of Bulgarian tsars vary from study to study. The problem is complicated not only by the fact that a variety of individuals claimed the title of tsar, some of whom almost certainly never, not even briefly, held power in Trnovo, but also because our three sources do not agree. It is noteworthy, however, that none of them claims Rostislav was ever tsar in Trnovo. After Michael's murder, Acropolites reports, Koloman succeeded, only to be ousted; then after further disorders Constantine Tih was elected. Acropolites states specifically that there was no other person entitled tsar in Trnovo between the flight of Koloman and the election of Constantine Tih; a boyar faction had run Trnovo in the interim. Pachymeres has Constantine Tih directly succeeding Michael, having no other figure recognized as tsar in Trnovo. Thus to accept Pachymeres would mean that Koloman's supporters, having murdered Michael, were not able to place Koloman in power and Koloman had had to flee without becoming tsar. Gregoras states that Mico succeeded Michael in Trnovo only to be deposed for Constantine. Thus in describing Bulgaria after Michael's murder one source has Constantine emerging rapidly in Trnovo as successor, while the other sources have an interim ruler before Constantine, in one case the murderer Koloman, in the other Mico.

Since Acropolites is usually considered the best source, most scholars have accepted a brief reign by Koloman after Michael's demise. What about Mico? It is conceivable that Mico did rule Trnovo briefly in the midst of the disorders Acropolites mentioned, but that Acropolites failed to mention Mico's rule either because he did not know of it or because he felt it too brief or unstable to be worthy of mention. Thus we cannot reject the possibility that Mico, as Michael's brother-in-law, tried to seize power when Koloman was ousted and succeeded very briefly, only to be ousted in his turn and forced to flee by the boyar revolt that succeeded in winning Trnovo and eventually in establishing Constantine Tih as tsar.

In any case, if Mico ever had Trnovo, he had it only briefly and was soon driven out. He next appears holding a small principality in southeastern Bulgaria centered in the Black Sea port of Mesembria. What followed is not clear: it is not known whether Mico accepted his fate and concentrated on establishing himself as ruler of this small separate principality or whether he still plotted to gain Trnovo. It also is not known what actions, if any, Constantine took against him before the 1260s. It is possible that Constantine, concerned with the more dangerous threat from Rostislav and Hungary, was forced to ignore Mico for a time.

Faced with the threat from Rostislav and Hungary and also concerned about Mico (and wanting to prevent Mico from obtaining help from his Nicean neighbors), Constantine had every reason to forge closer ties with Nicea. The Niceans also could profit from an alliance with Bulgaria, since they wanted freedom of action to oppose the serious threat to them from Epirus as well as to try to recover Constantinople. Thus the two states created an alliance sealed by Constantine's marriage to Irene in 1258. Soon thereafter the Nicean official and historian Acropolites visited Trnovo, probably in January 1260, to confirm the alliance. It is sometimes stated that hostilities developed between the two states in 1260 when Michael VIII supposedly came to the aid of Mico, besieged in Mesembria by Constantine Tih. Though this statement is frequently found in scholarly works, recent scholarship argues persuasively that the events around Mesembria took place not in 1260 but in 1263.[5] Thus it seems accurate to conclude that a period of peace between Nicea and Bulgaria existed from 1258 to 1262. Had there been any warfare during these years between the two states Acropolites, whose history goes down to 1261 and who was interested in and well acquainted with Bulgarian affairs, would certainly have mentioned it.

This peace allowed Constantine to concentrate on Rostislav, who was a major danger owing to the support he had from the powerful Hungarian state. And Constantine found late 1260 an excellent time to take action to solve that problem. That year the Hungarians, having become involved in a war with Bohemia, were diverted from Balkan issues. Moreover, the Hungarians, having difficulties in this war, had to call upon Rostislav for help. In answer to this call, he had led a large portion of his troops off to Bohemia. His men are the "Bulgarians" referred to as fighting for the Hungarians in Bohemia in

Western sources, a reference that occasionally has been misinterpreted by scholars. Thus Rostislav's Vidin province became undermanned, and Rostislav himself was absent. Despite Rostislav's assistance, the Hungarians next suffered a defeat in Bohemia.

Thus the situation was ideal for Constantine. He attacked the token forces left behind in Vidin and regained not only the city but the whole province to the borders of the province of Braničevo. Letting his success go to his head, Constantine then sent his troops across the Danube to raid, and briefly hold, Hungary's Severin banate. This last act infuriated the Hungarians. So, as soon as they had concluded peace with the Bohemians in March 1261, they, led by Stephen V, co-king and heir to the throne, attacked Bulgaria. They first overran the Vidin province and forced Constantine to withdraw his troops from it. Then, having regained Vidin, the Hungarians continued into Bulgaria proper, soon reaching the walls of Trnovo. The Hungarians also besieged Lom, which lay east of Vidin, on the Danube, which it seems they had not held before. As far as we know, Constantine did not meet the Hungarians in a pitched battle. Thus he presumably kept his army intact and withdrew with it to Trnovo. Finally, at the end of the campaigning season, the Hungarians recalled their forces from Bulgaria. Though it is often stated that the Hungarian withdrawal from Bulgaria at the end of 1261 followed a treaty with Bulgaria, there is no evidence to prove this. As a result of Hungary's action, Rostislav was restored to the position he had held prior to Constantine's attack on him in 1260. Once again Rostislav was master of Vidin, bearing the title Tsar of Bulgaria. After the campaign Stephen V assumed, or was given, special responsibility for the southern lands of the Hungarian kingdom.

Bulgaria survived, though presumably badly plundered; moreover, it had lost once again the northwestern province of Vidin. Whether further Bulgarian territory east of Vidin (e.g., Lom) was taken by the Hungarians or Rostislav is not known. The weakening of Bulgarian central authority, which had allowed the separation of Vidin, was to continue in the years to come; frequently under one or another ruler (be he a native Bulgarian or a foreign puppet), Vidin was to break away from the central government in Trnovo, and in time its citizens seem to have come more and more to support this separatism. Thus from then on, up to the Turkish conquest, there were often to be two Bulgarian states, one centered in Trnovo and one centered in Vidin.

In July 1261, as noted, the Niceans recovered Constantinople, and we can call them again the Byzantines. Up to this time Constantine Tih had been allied to them. However, as we saw, only Michael VIII Palaeologus came to Constantinople, where he alone was re-crowned. John IV Lascaris was left behind in Nicea, where at the end of 1261 he was blinded and deposed. Constantine Tih's wife was the deposed boy's sister. Relations immediately deteriorated and sources have given Contantine's wife a major role in stirring him to action against Michael VIII and Byzantium. At the same time the Byzantines seem to have come into contact with Mico and to have been on the verge of supporting him. Whether this contact was begun in 1261 and thus was another cause for Constantine's actions, or whether this contact was a Byzantine response to Constantine's changed attitude, is not certain. In any case in 1262 the Bulgarians launched an attack against Byzantine Thrace and seem to have taken various fortresses, including Stanimaka and Philippopolis. At least we may assume the Bulgarians took them, for prior to 1262—ever since 1255—they had been Byzantine, and shortly thereafter, in 1263, sources state the Byzantines recovered them, an act that would have been necessary only if the Byzantines had lost them. Since Bulgaria and Nicea (Byzantium) were at peace through 1261, the loss of these cities almost certainly took place in 1262.

At the same time in 1262 major changes occurred in the Hungarians' southern Slavic provinces. First Rostislav died. His lands were divided between two sons; his part of Bosnia—in northern Bosnia near the lower Drina—went to his elder son Michael, while Mačva, including Beograd, and the Braničevo province went to his younger son Bela. The immediate fate of Vidin is not known. In the same year, King Bela IV of Hungary, having made these assignments to Rostislav's children, who were also his grandsons, decided also to make some further changes in his peripheral territories. He took Slavonia, Dalmatia, and Croatia, which until then had all been under his elder son and heir, Stephen V, and which by now had become the appanage, by right, for the heir to the throne, and assigned them to a younger son named Bela. Stephen V was infuriated and immediately revolted against his father. In the fighting that ensued in 1262, Stephen came out on top. The father and son then concluded a peace on 5 December 1262, but the father was not pacified. Their former cordial relations were a thing of the past and hereafter tensions marked their relationship. And the nobles, who had split during the warfare in 1262, remained divided, inciting their patrons to further action. The treaty of December 1262 allowed Stephen V to retain the territory north of the Danube along Bulgaria's border.

Meanwhile documents for the first time begin to mention in Bulgaria a certain Jacob (Jakov) Svetoslav. He was of Russian origin. John Asen II, during his long exile in Russia, had established cordial relations with various Russian princes and boyars. When he returned to Bulgaria to fight for his throne in 1218, his army included a retinue of Russians. Later, after the Tatars had overrun south Russia, Asen had encouraged some of these Russians (as well as various Cumans from this region) to settle in Bulgaria and had given them lands. One such Russian—or the son of one such Russian—was Jacob Svetoslav, a man of princely origin who by 1261 bore the title of despot. He presumably received this honor from a tsar in Trnovo, though it is not known which tsar had granted it to him. He had also been granted by a tsar a large appanage in the southwestern part of the state. His lands apparently lay just south of the Vidin province. He seems to have had considerable autonomy there. Bearing the title of despot, he was clearly both one of the leading boyars in Bulgaria and also a figure closely associated with the court, from which his title came. And he had fought loyally for Constantine in the 1261 war against the Hungarians. It seems that in 1262 he had also supported Constantine against Byzantium, for when in 1263 the Byzantines launched a new attack against Bulgaria, they also invaded the lands of Despot Jacob Svetoslav.

Meanwhile in late 1262 or early 1263 Constantine seems to have decided to eliminate Mico, for he marched into the latter's principality and besieged Mico's capital of Mesembria. Mico, who was inside the city, sought aid from the Byzantines, who presumably were already preparing to invade Bulgaria to avenge themselves for the 1262 attack and to regain their lost fortresses in Thrace. In any case, in 1263 the Byzantines launched a major two-pronged invasion. Their first army marched north along the Black Sea shore until it reached Mesembria. After driving away the besieging Bulgarians, the Byzantines negotiated with Mico the surrender of Mesembria to Byzantium, in exchange for which Mico was given lands in Asia Minor. It was also agreed that Mico's son John should marry Michael VIII's own daughter. These terms were realized, though the marriage was not carried out for several years. Thus the threat to Constantine posed by Mico from within was over, but at the expense of losing Mico's lands to Byzantium and of having to face the prospect that at some time in the future the Byzantines might advance Mico as a candidate for the Bulgarian throne. The Byzantine troops also took the important port of Anchialos and overran Sredna Gora. The Black Sea area, now lost, had been a particularly hard one for Bulgaria to control. It had a large Greek population, which may well have preferred imperial rule to Bulgarian, and it had shown its separatist tendencies by its support of Mico's rebellion. At about the time the Byzantine army was recovering this coastal territory, the Byzantines dispatched a fleet to the Danube mouth which conquered a strip of territory which was to be accessible to the empire only by sea. The most important place taken by this attack was the port of Vicina, where the Byzantines installed a Greek archbishop.

Meanwhile, the second Byzantine army marched into western Thrace and took Stanimaka and Philippopolis as well as various lesser forts in that region. At campaign's end, the Byzantines probably held in the Black Sea area all the coastal territory as far north as Mesembria[6] and as far inland as the Tundža River; and in western Thrace they probably held at least everything south of the Marica River. That Mico's surrender of Mesembria occurred in 1263, not in 1260, is supported by Pachymeres who states that the Byzantines took Philippopolis at the same time that Mico yielded Mesembria. This second Byzantine army, having achieved its successes in western Thrace, then continued on to overrun the lands of Jacob Svetoslav. Constantine Tih, faced with a major assault against his own fortresses, was in no position to help him, so Jacob Svetoslav turned to his northern neighbor, Stephen V of Hungary, for aid.

Loyal to Bulgaria until then, Jacob Svetoslav may already have been harboring ambitions for greater independence. Stephen V, on the other hand, was seeking a new protégé on the ground to represent Hungarian interests in the south and prevent Trnovo from regaining Vidin, which now seemed vulnerable in the power vacuum created by Rostislav's death. Free at the moment of warfare between Bela IV and Stephen V, the Hungarians sent aid, drove the Byzantines out of Jacob Svetoslav's lands, and then continued on south to raid Byzantine territory. When the dust had settled from this, Jacob Svetoslav had concluded a treaty with Hungary by which he was granted the Vidin province and accepted Hungarian suzerainty not only for that province but also for his own territory in southwestern Bulgaria. Thus Trnovo suffered the secession of further lands, this time those in the southwest. Vidin is clearly documented as Jacob Svetoslav's in 1265, but most scholars believe it had been granted to him in 1263.

His new relations with Hungary caused difficulties for Jacob Svetoslav from Trnovo, which had hoped to take advantage of Rostislav's death to regain Vidin for Bulgaria. Presumably only the Byzantine attack in 1263 had prevented Constantine from moving against Vidin in that year. And it is apparent that of his two ambitions, the war against Byzantium had assumed a higher priority than war against Hungary, possibly owing to Constantine's wife's strong desire for revenge against Michael VIII, the usurper. Thus the hurried assignment of Vidin to Jacob Svetoslav in 1263, in the course of the Byzantine war, seems to have prevented the Bulgarians from regaining Vidin after Rostislav's death. And Trnovo knew that an attempt to regain Vidin by displacing Jacob Svetoslav would lead to war with his Hungarian protectors. Thus Hungary was able to secure its retention of these southern lands.

Caught between its two enemies Byzantium and Hungary, each of which was stronger than Bulgaria, and becoming weaker as a result of the loss in 1263 of even further territory, Constantine had little choice but to turn to his Tatar overlords. He sought aid against the Byzantines whose campaign in 1263 had caused not only considerable damage but also had wrested away from Bulgaria fortresses in two areas, western Thrace and along the Black Sea.

The appeal to the Tatars came at a moment the Tatars had reason to intervene against Byzantium. A Seljuk sultan named 'Izz al-Dīn had been ousted in a palace coup with the backing of the Mongols. 'Izz al-Dīn had fled to Byzantium for asylum but also sought aid. Michael VIII, having by then formed an alliance with the Mongols in Iran—who were supporting 'Izz al-Dīn's rival—did not want to risk that alliance by helping 'Izz al-Dīn. Thus, though receiving 'Izz al-Dīn honorably, Michael VIII kept him more-or-less under house arrest. 'Izz al-Dīn, needless to say, was not satisfied with this and secretly sent an embassy to the Steppe Tatars (the Golden Horde) for help. So the Tatars, already preparing to rescue 'Izz al-Dīn, were responsive to the Bulgarian appeal. In the winter of 1264–65 they crossed the Danube into Bulgaria, from which, after being joined by Bulgarian troops, they poured into Thrace and into the Black Sea region, causing severe devastation to both areas. They then laid siege to the town of Ainos, where 'Izz al-Dīn was held. To save their town, the citizens willingly yielded 'Izz al-Dīn to the Tatar armies of Khan Berke, who may have been leading his troops in person. The Tatars, having achieved their aims, lifted the siege and returned home. Thus the Tatar aid had been of no lasting value to the Bulgarians other than giving them the satisfaction of revenge and plundering. The Tatars had withdrawn after their own object was attained and had not helped the Bulgarians in their aims, i.e., the recovery of their lost cities. At the end of the winter 1264–65 campaign all the major fortresses that had been lost to the Byzantines remained Byzantine. However, Constantine's position vis à vis the Byzantines was improved; he now seemed to have gained a deterrent, for should they again attack Bulgaria, the Byzantines might expect further military action against themselves from Bulgaria's Tatar suzerain.

In that same year, 1264, the Hungarian civil war between father (Bela IV) and son (Stephen V) broke out again. In the course of that year's actions, the father had gained the advantage. This caused Jacob Svetoslav worry, for Stephen V was his protector. Should Bela IV win, would he favor the continued rule of Vidin by his son's protégé? Furthermore, as the father-and-son war continued into 1265, Stephen V, occupied with fighting for his own survival, was in no position to aid Jacob Svetoslav should he be attacked. And Trnovo in 1265, no longer in danger from Byzantium, was now free to move against its disloyal former vassal and regain its seceded territory. And Jacob Svetoslav alone was no match for Trnovo's forces, which might even be supplemented with Tatar troops. Thus in 1265 Jacob Svetoslav quickly renegotiated his position. Whether, as seems likely, Jacob Svetoslav initiated negotiations to prevent attack or whether Constantine through threat of attack forced him to submit is not known. Jacob Svetoslav was allowed to retain his lands, but he now held them under Trnovo's suzerainty. Though this did not bring them back under direct Bulgarian rule, it at least separated these lands from Hungary; and Trnovo could expect now to raise troops from this territory, through its vassal, in the event of war. Hungary in 1265 was in no position to prevent this change. In fact it seems that in 1265 Bulgaria and Jacob Svetoslav jointly raided Hungarian lands across the Danube. Presumably this attack was Constantine's idea, for it would have forced Jacob Svetoslav into even worse relations with Hungary and thus have increased his dependence on Trnovo.

The Hungarians were not happy with developments. By late 1265 the tide was turning in the civil war, and Bela IV, doing badly, found it necessary to come to terms with Stephen. They concluded peace again in March 1266. Stephen regained his former position, including supervision of Hungary's southern lands. Free to do so, he immediately took action to reassert his former authority over the western Bulgarian lands. His forces took Vidin, after a short siege, by 23 June 1266. Ravaging that whole province, his forces soon reasserted Hungarian control over it. He even sent troops to plunder the lands of the Trnovo tsar. The Bulgarian army tried to resist but was defeated in the course of the attack, and its remnants retreated to various forts in the interior. A second Hungarian wave subdued a series of fortresses, including

Pleven, along the Danube. Jacob Svetoslav again had to submit to Hungary, which, despite his earlier defection, decided it was best to leave him in Vidin. Possibly the Hungarians believed he had enough local support to guarantee local loyalty in the event of an attack against Vidin by Trnovo. For whatever reason, Jacob Svetoslav was restored to his former position; in 1266 Hungarian documents begin referring to him as Tsar of the Bulgarians, the title previously held by Rostislav. Whether this title was granted simply to give his province greater prestige and to assert its independence from Trnovo, or whether it indicated an ambition—Jacob's or the Hungarians'—for him to take Trnovo and become tsar there is not certain.

In any case, the 1266 campaign restored to the Hungarians their western Bulgarian lands, weakening Trnovo by the same amount that the Hungarians gained, and established a separate "Bulgarian" state under a puppet tsar who had to lean on the Hungarians to maintain his independence in internal matters. And possibly the Hungarians intended him to provide a threat to Trnovo itself, if Jacob Svetoslav's title indicated a claim to his being *the* Tsar of Bulgaria. And, as it clearly was in Hungary's interests to make its protégé more dependent on it, what better way was there to do this than by encouraging tensions between Jacob Svetoslav and Trnovo by granting him such a provocative title? This state of affairs for Vidin was to last until the death of Stephen V in 1272. (Stephen became sole ruler of Hungary in 1270 when Bela IV died.)

Trnovo thus found itself weaker than ever after 1266. It had lost its western lands and Jacob Svetoslav was again a Hungarian vassal. It stood in danger of Byzantine attack if it took its armies north against Hungary, an action making little sense anyway because Hungary was stronger than Bulgaria. Relations with the Byzantines remained bad, and because that front retained top priority with Constantine, it made sense for him to accept his western losses and make peace with Hungary to keep himself free to move south against Byzantium. Furthermore, Bulgaria could no longer count to any extent on help against Hungary or Byzantium from the Tatars, for Khan Berke, Bulgaria's suzerain who seems to have felt an interest in protecting Constantine, had died in 1265.

Berke was succeeded by his son Mangu Timur, who was not able to maintain control over the array of tribes within the khanate; this led to a weakening of the khanate's central authority and considerable separatism on the part of smaller units across the Steppes. In the western lands bordering on Bulgaria a great general—a member of Ghengis Khan's family and a nephew of Berke—named Nogaj asserted increasing independence from Mangu Timur. After Mangu Timur's death in 1280/81 Nogaj was to become for all practical purposes the master of an independent state. In the period 1265–80 Nogaj, probably already stronger than the legitimate khan, was occupied in Steppe affairs and had little time, especially during the late 1260s when he was building up his own position in the Steppes, to intervene in Bulgarian affairs, other than to raid for booty from time to time. Furthermore, Nogaj would not have intervened to assist Bulgaria, because he was hostile to that state; for the Bulgarians owed and paid tribute to Mangu Timur, from whom Nogaj was seceding and for whom Nogaj had little love. Thus Bulgaria found itself on the side of the Steppe faction opposed to its immediate neighbor, Nogaj.

To further add to Bulgaria's woes, Constantine himself became incapacitated. In 1264 or 1265 he fell from a horse and, we are told, badly broke his leg. Clearly his injuries were more serious than that, for he became paralyzed from the waist down and had to be carried in a litter or wagon. Thus his own personal leadership of armies became next to impossible, with the result that his control over his kingdom declined. As the Nogajs continued their raiding for pleasure and profit and as Constantine became less and less able to oppose them, various localities, particularly in the north, came more and more to be responsible for their own defense.

The Byzantines, concerned with Charles of Anjou's threat, however, had an interest in improving relations with Bulgaria. Though they probably were not in danger of losing major fortresses to the Bulgarians, they obviously wanted to spare themselves from plundering raids. So in 1268 Michael VIII tendered a proposal to Bulgaria for peace. He offered Constantine Tih, now a widower, his own niece Maria as a bride and agreed that as her dowry she would bring back to Bulgaria the two recently lost Black Sea cities, Mesembria and Anchialos, whose loss was Bulgaria's main grievance against Byzantium. The wedding followed, it seems in 1269.

Whether or not the Byzantines ever intended to surrender to the Bulgarians these two towns (both of which were militarily and commercially important) is not certain. However, by the time delivery was due, the Byzantines were in a strong enough position to renege on their promise. Michael VIII had in the interim entered into two valuable alliances that enabled him to do this. First, he had concluded an alliance with Hungary, by which his son and heir Andronicus married the daughter of Stephen V. Second, he had made an alliance with Nogaj, who was given as a bride for his harem Michael's illegitimate daughter Evrosina. Thus when the time came to do it, Michael simply refused to surrender the towns. Angry, Constantine raided Thrace, probably in 1271. The Byzantines then called on their new ally, Nogaj, who, on his own and without consulting Mangu Timur, launched a massive raid across the Danube that severely plundered Bulgaria.

Bulgaria was now surrounded by enemies on all sides, and the two northern ones, the Hungarians and the Nogajs, were allied to the southern one, Byzantium. Furthermore, because Bulgaria's Tatar suzerain no longer controlled territory on Bulgaria's borders, but had his lands further east, and because he was also weaker than his rival Nogaj, Bulgaria could find no protection from that source. Thus Constantine had no choice but to yield and make peace with Byzantium. Not surprisingly, however, he joined Charles of Anjou's coalition when he had the chance, in 1272 or 1273. But, surrounded by allied enemies, Constantine had to remain passive, unable to take action to try to regain his lost lands, either those to the northwest (Vidin) or the southeast (Mesembria and Anchialos).

Meanwhile, on 1 August 1272, Stephen V of Hungary died. He was succeeded by his son Ladislas IV, who was only ten years old at the time. The boy's mother, Elizabeth, became regent. In that same year Rostislav's son Bela, who held Mačva with Beograd and Braničevo, was killed. The Hungarian regency asserted control over this territory, at least ousting any heir Bela might have had, and soon assigned it to a royally appointed ban. In December 1272 a certain John was Ban of Mačva. By that time Rostislav's other son, Michael, no longer held northern Bosnia. Michael, by supporting Bela IV against Stephen V, had won Stephen's enmity. As a result, in 1268, after Stephen had made peace with his father and regained his former position, he ousted Michael. By 1272 a Stephen was Ban of [northern] Bosnia. A certain Gregory then held Braničevo, which united with Kučevo was separated again from Mačva, and a certain Paul commanded the Severin province across the Danube from Vidin. Jacob Svetoslav continued to retain Vidin.

But this policy of replacing hereditary vassal rulers, who had local ties, with royally appointed governors, which presumably was intended to bind these areas more closely to the center, seems to have failed. This failure may be attributed chiefly to weakness at the center, for the regency could not provide sufficient support to these appointees for the regency to retain its control over these Slavic provinces. Difficulties with the magnates and with Bohemia soon arose and, it seems, local figures ousted the bans in the more easterly lands. After June 1273 there are no more references to Bans of Braničevo. In July 1273 Hungary suffered a defeat at the hands of the Bohemians. By the end of the decade—or in the early 1280s—two Bulgarian boyars, of Cuman origin, named Drman and Kudelin, were in control of Braničevo. Most scholars believe these two men had asserted their independence, presumably by acquiring local support and ousting the Hungarian-appointed ban, very early, possibly as early as mid-1273, when Hungary was distracted by its loss in Bohemia.

If the Hungarians were unable to retain Braničevo, they had even less chance of retaining influence over more distant Vidin; in fact, whenever they had lost Braničevo, they had lost their best base from which to launch troops to intervene in Vidin. Thus when this occurred—quite possibly in ca. 1273— Jacob Svetoslav found himself in a position to assert his independence from the Hungarians. Thus Hungary's policy of working through puppets could succeed only when Hungary was strong. In times when it was weak, there was nothing to stop the puppets from asserting their independence and taking their lands out of the Hungarian state. However, independence from Hungary had its dangers, for, not strong enough to stand alone, Jacob Svetoslav now had no prop to maintain his position should Trnovo try to oust him. Thus it was clear that once again he would have to reach some accommodation with Trnovo. His chances of achieving this were good, for owing to Trnovo's increasing weakness, Constantine may have doubted his ability to conquer

Vidin and thus probably was willing, should Jacob Svetoslav submit under acceptable terms, to allow Jacob's continued rule there. Moreover, Trnovo needed allies.

By then, as noted, Constantine was incapacitated and his ability to provide effective leadership had declined. His new wife, Maria, had borne him a son, Michael, whom she wanted to succeed him. Michael was crowned co-tsar in 1273. Owing to Constantine's paralysis, Maria took an ever increasing role in state affairs, and since she ruled by building factions, playing one group or individual off against another, she seems to have provoked considerable opposition against the regime. And as various boyars came to oppose her, or she suspected that they did, she began taking measures against them, arresting and executing real or suspected boyar opponents, which only increased boyar hostility to her. At the same time Nogaj raids increased, causing economic losses and also greater dissatisfaction with Constantine who was able to do nothing to stop them. Maria seems to have come to feel that the existence of the dynasty was threatened—be it by a coup against Constantine himself or one against her son in the event of Constantine's death.

The populace in the peripheral regions, which the central government was unable to manage or defend directly and which was becoming more and more dependent on local figures for defense, might well rally around a powerful alternative leader. One of the most logical candidates for that role was Jacob Svetoslav. Of good family, he was a relatively strong ruler and apparently popular with his subjects in the west; already entitled tsar, he had also connected himself with the Asen dynasty by marrying a granddaughter of the great John Asen. Thus he seemed dangerous, and Maria wanted to get rid of him or, failing that, to at least co-opt him to the side of the ruling house. Since Jacob might not have been able to withstand a major attack from Trnovo, it was also in his interests to reach some arrangement with Trnovo. Thus the two entered into negotiations, probably at her initiative, and with a sworn safe-conduct Jacob Svetoslav accepted her invitation to Trnovo. He was received with much ceremony and at a church service adopted by Maria as her second son, thus making him part of the Trnovo royal family. In the agreement Jacob Svetoslav probably recognized himself as second son, ranked after the baby Michael; in so doing he would have given Michael recognition as heir and promised not to try to overthrow him. At the same time Jacob Svetoslav was probably recognized as the heir to the throne in Trnovo in the event of Michael's death.

Thus Jacob Svetoslav was officially separated from Hungary—then in decline and unable to respond to these changes—and, though still autonomous, at least brought to recognize Trnovo's suzerainty. Moreover, he was sufficiently bound—by religious oaths—to Trnovo's dynasty to have become a supporter of it rather than a potential leader of opposition to it. This agreement should have given more security to both, to Maria for her rule in Trnovo and for her son's future, and to Jacob for his possession of Vidin. However, Maria still did not feel secure; after all, when Constantine died, what was there to stop Jacob Svetoslav from breaking his oath and overthrowing little Michael? Thus Maria, owing to her suspicious mind, probably never intended to keep the agreement but from the start and throughout was bent on Jacob Svetoslav's destruction, only using the adoption as a means to create closer ties between herself and Jacob Svetoslav in order to more easily bring about his murder. In any case, in 1275 or 1276/77, she had him poisoned.

The immediate fate of Vidin is not known. Maria clearly would have liked to annex it; and various scholars, possibly correctly, have asserted that this happened. In support of this view they point out that in 1278 the Sv"rlig (Svrljig) province between Požarevac and Niš—which is believed to have been part of Jacob Svetoslav's original domain—was Bulgarian. Though this says nothing about Vidin, it does suggest that Bulgaria had been able to assert its control over at least part of Jacob's lands. Moreover, a Byzantine court poet, Manuel Philes, speaking about events in 1277 and 1278, says that Ivajlo, a rebel against Constantine who briefly succeeded him and whom we shall meet shortly, acquired rule over Bulgaria and Vidin. However, Manuel Philes is, as has been shown, a dubious source.[7] And it is possible that Manuel Philes may have been advancing only a title that Ivajlo claimed, rather than a statement about his actual possessions. For, in fact, Ivajlo almost certainly was never able to assert his authority in Vidin. However, Ivajlo's problems subsequently do not rule out the possibility that Maria and Constantine may have acquired Vidin immediately after Jacob Svetoslav's death and prior to Ivajlo's rebellion.

Against the view that Maria annexed Vidin, it can be argued that Maria, faced at home with increasing opposition, which eventually (within a year or so or even a matter of months, depending on when Jacob Svetoslav was poisoned) culminated in Ivajlo's rebellion, could never have asserted Trnovo's authority over Vidin unless the town had voluntarily submitted. And one might assume that the local inhabitants would not have happily submitted to the murderess of their prince. Thus one might expect Vidin's population, accustomed to the independence which had been developing in that region, to have supported the local big-men in Vidin, who presumably would have been trying to acquire authority and assert their province's independence, as Drman and Kudelin had in Braničevo. Thus if Maria had not been strong enough to strike quickly and effectively to take advantage of any instability that might have followed Jacob Svetoslav's death (for example, rivalry between local boyars), then Vidin probably would have resisted behind its walls and thus remained separate under local control. And even if Maria had been successful, quite likely Vidin would then have slipped from Trnovo's grasp when Ivajlo launched his rebellion against Constantine in 1277.

Thus with Trnovo and Hungary both weak and in no position to take decisive action, we may assume that Vidin remained independent of its two major neighbors; ten years later a certain Šišman had established himself as ruler of a principality there. Unless he had ousted some earlier secessionist, it seems probable that he had established his authority there in the late 1270s, a period for which we have no sources about Vidin. It is possible he received outside support to assert himself, for example by allying with the two boyars who were ruling Braničevo or with Nogaj, who probably would have been willing to offer aid; after all Nogaj was hostile to Trnovo—a vassal of his rival Mangu Timur—and would not have wanted to see Trnovo become any stronger through the acquisition of this northwestern territory. Nogaj support of Vidin—by action or threat of action—is also suggested by the fact that later Šišman was to have close ties with the Nogajs, whose suzerainty he accepted and who provided units of Tatars for his armies. Thus one may postulate that Vidin either continued to remain independent throughout or else, had it fallen to Maria immediately after Jacob Svetoslav's death, it broke away again almost immediately thereafter, probably at the time of Ivajlo's rebellion. One may also postulate that it did so with the support of the Nogajs who probably were its suzerain protectors. However, Vidin's probable success in retaining its independence did not necessarily apply to Jacob Svetoslav's other lands, his original holding to the south of Vidin. And, as noted, at least part of this territory was regained by Bulgaria.

Hungary now found itself withdrawn from northwestern Bulgaria. It was to remain so until the 1360s. But its policies over the first three-quarters of the thirteenth century had contributed considerably, by encouraging and supporting secessionist movements in these peripheral territories of Bulgaria, to the weakening of Bulgaria.

Byzantium's Efforts to Defend itself against Charles of Anjou

The Threat from Charles

Meanwhile, Charles of Anjou, who by the agreement at Viterbo had obtained the rights to most of the Latin Empire, set about realizing his claims. Having acquired Corfu in 1267, he began negotiations with the Latins who had held Valona, Kanina, and Berat for Manfred and had then retained this territory after Manfred's demise. He made no progress for several years. Then in 1271 or 1272, according to Ducellier, Charles acquired the submission of all three cities, leaving Valona's holder in possession of his city as a vassal for the time being. Nicol doubts Valona yielded this early. Then in 1272 Charles landed on the Albanian coast and took Durazzo. Its conquest was facilitated by the destruction of its walls by a devastating earthquake. In fact, the Byzantine officials had already departed before his arrival. Ducellier dates the quake 1266/67. Nicol redates it to 1271, which would have given the empire little or no time for repairs before Charles' arrival. He soon was also in possession of the fortress of Kroja. Soon thereafter, in 1274, he was able to oust his vassal in Valona and take direct control of that city and its hinterland. Nicol believes 1274 marks Valona's initial submission to Charles. After he had established himself on the coast many of the Albanian chiefs rallied to him, accepting him as their suzerain, and thus he became overlord over much of coastal Albania with its hinterland. Durazzo became his center of operations, the capital of his Kingdom of Albania, and he gave himself the title of king. Charles, as noted, also had a Balkan ally in Villehardouin, with whom he had concluded in 1267 a treaty by which Charles became Villehardouin's suzerain as well as his heir to the Morea.

The Byzantines in the meantime tried to counter this emerging threat by creating alliances nearer home; they, as noted, had co-opted Bulgaria, but then, by reneging on the agreement to yield the Black Sea cities, had antagonized Constantine Tih, who in 1272 or 1273 gladly joined Charles' coalition. Earlier, back in 1268, the Byzantines had tried to enlist the Serbs, and a Byzantine proposal gained tentative agreement; according to its terms Michael VIII's niece Maria would marry King Uroš' second son, Milutin, who in turn would become Uroš' heir. However, for some reason the plan fell through, and shortly thereafter the young lady had married Constantine Tih. Milutin was then married to a daughter of John of Thessaly. John was hostile to Michael VIII, who sought to regain John's Thessaly for the empire; thus, not surprisingly, John too was drawn into Charles' coalition in 1273. That same year (if not already in 1272) the Serbs also concluded an alliance with Charles. Thus the Byzantine Empire seemed to be in desperate straits, for Charles, ambitious for its conquest, was already established in the Balkans and had linked to himself by treaty all the Balkan leaders whose lands bordered on Byzantine territory between Charles' Albania and Constantinople: the Albanian chiefs, Serbia, Thessaly, Bulgaria, and also the more distant Morea.

Meanwhile, Epirus was also drawn into Charles' coalition. When the Byzantines were campaigning in Albania in late 1274, they took the town of Butrinti. Nicephorus of Epirus believed this port was his by right; when the Byzantines refused to restore it to him, he turned to Charles of Anjou and in the summer of 1276 concluded a treaty with him. He also strengthened his ties with his half-brother John of Thessaly, another ally of Charles. Both strongly opposed, or at least enjoyed capitalizing on, Michael VIII's acceptance of the Union of Lyons, an event to be discussed shortly. Faced with this opposition, Michael VIII enticed Nicephorus' younger brother Demetrius, also called Michael, to Constantinople, where he gave him the despot's title and his own daughter as a bride. It seems he was laying plans to use him as a replacement for Nicephorus in Epirus, if the chance arose. And Demetrius/Michael was soon to be given an assignment in the western Balkans, where he actively participated in the defense of Berat against the Angevins. However, no opportunity arose to send him into Epirus. Meanwhile, under this pressure, Nicephorus felt compelled to move even closer to Charles. Thus in 1278, the same year that he had been able to take Butrinti from the Byzantines, Nicephorus, pressured by Charles, made a formal vassal submission to Charles. Not only did he accept vassal status, but he also had to yield to Charles the newly recovered Butrinti as well as the port of Sopot. He also had to recognize Charles as Manfred's heir, giving Charles the right to all the towns Michael II had awarded to Manfred as the dowry of Michael's daughter Helen. Thus Nicephorus also had to surrender to the Angevins the important port of Himara (Chimara). As a result Charles acquired the Adriatic coast from the Akrokeraunian promontory (below the Bay of Valona) down to Butrinti.

Negotiations with Rome

Michael VIII's only hope was to persuade the pope to prevent Charles from launching his campaign. To do this Michael dispatched an envoy to Rome to present a proposal to unite the Churches. The pope, not surprisingly, was receptive, for though Charles was promising the same thing upon the completion of his conquest, his union would again mean one forced on the Greeks by Western foreigners. That policy had been tried by the Latin Empire for fifty-seven years without lasting effect. The pope believed that a union effected by a Greek emperor offered more likelihood of lasting success. So, he ordered Charles not to proceed and in 1274 convoked a Church council at Lyons, at which Michael's delegation accepted the Union of the Churches.

At the council the Byzantine delegation accepted union on papal terms, agreeing to papal supremacy and *Filioque,* the controversial Latin addition to the Creed. Of course, these envoys accepted these points only in the emperor's name; they spoke for neither the Byzantine clergy nor the Byzantine populace. And until those groups accepted it, union could not in fact be achieved. And neither clergy nor populace, just thirteen years after Constantinople's recovery from fifty-seven years of Latin rule (during which the Latins had tried to force both union and Latin customs upon them), was in a mood to have any part of it. Michael VIII, enjoying the freedom given leaders in the days before mass media (when it was possible to tell different groups different stories with a chance of getting away with it), insisted in public addresses to his people that his agreement with the pope did not endanger their beliefs. Nothing, he affirmed, would change in the Greek Church. However, union was necessary to avert a greater danger: Latin attack and the restoration of Latin rule. Thus the emperor's motives had been purely political. His delegation had accepted papal primacy, but unless the pope were to visit Constantinople, a most unlikely event, that primacy was meaningless. To mention the pope's name in Church services was harmless. They had, Michael insisted, accepted no change in beliefs and practices and thus had rejected the use of unleavened bread for communion and *Filioque.* (This last statement was an utter falsehood.)

Most of the populace and clergy were not persuaded. They were not sure what had actually been promised and they were afraid concessions had been made to the Latins on *Filioque* and the communion wafer. Michael had the reputation of being tricky, and he had already shown his duplicity by violating his oath to the Lascaris family when he had blinded and seized the throne from little John Lascaris, an act which had stirred up considerable wrath against him. The average Byzantine probably also did not fully comprehend how dangerous the threat from Charles was. Moreover, even if Michael's subjects had understood, it might not have mattered, for most of them believed that the Virgin protected Constantinople. The city had fallen in 1204 for their sins. Through her favor they had recovered it in 1261. Her intercession was clearly shown by the ease with which it was recovered, seemingly by chance. If they kept their faith pure, the Virgin would save the city from any danger. The best way to lose it was to betray the true faith and accept the heresy of Rome. Hatred for the Latins and the Latin Church was too strong for any danger to cause the populace to make compromises concerning their faith with the Latins.

The opposition was led by Patriarch Joseph, a supporter of Michael who had been installed when Patriarch Arsenius refused to accept the deposition of John Lascaris. But union was more than Joseph could stomach. Michael soon deposed him for an even more pliable cleric, John Bekkos. (To do Bekkos justice, it should be added that his acceptance of the Unionist position seems to have reflected a sincere conversion.) The Greek Church went into schism. The Arsenite party rallied around Joseph in this moment of danger, and most of the population supported the opposition. The Anti-Unionists included many high aristocrats and were led by Michael's own sister Irene, who had become a nun under the name of Eulogia; she was the mother of Maria, Constantine Tih's wife. Eulogia was soon thrown into jail for her opposition. Stirred up by Eulogia's daughter, who in this matter had the support of the local clergy, Bulgaria became a center of opposition to Michael's heresy. Thessaly became a second center of opposition to Michael's religious policy.

At first Michael's response was mild, and he stuck to reasoning and persuasion, chiefly through speeches. Two years passed before he himself was to accept union in an official ceremony.

But though it stirred up enormous opposition at home at a critical time when the population needed to be united, the Union of Lyons at least bought Michael time, for the pope, while awaiting Michael's execution of the agreement, refused to let Charles go into action. While Charles was thus restrained, Michael mobilized his forces and in 1274 attacked Charles in Albania. Michael's forces had considerable success and by 1276 had occupied most, if not all, of Charles' holdings in the Albanian interior, including the important fortress of Berat. By the campaign's end Charles held only Durazzo—which Michael had besieged unsuccessfully—and Valona, and overland communications between these two towns had been cut off. Charles seemed on the verge of being expelled from Albania entirely. To retain these two fortresses, which were to be the dispatch points for the troops he soon hoped to send against the Byzantine Empire, Charles began transporting thither a steady flow of mercenaries. Having increased his forces, he then launched a major attack against Berat in 1279. The Byzantines zealously defended Berat, and Charles' siege dragged on unsuccessfully for over two years.

In 1275 Michael VIII also ordered military action against his Greek rival John of Thessaly. An attempt to redate this attack to 1271 has not been generally accepted. It is not known whether Michael was chiefly reacting to past raids carried out by John's Thessalians against the Byzantine coastal holdings along the Gulf of Volos, or whether he hoped to annex more of Thessaly. It seems that he dispatched a large expedition, though it is highly unlikely that the Byzantine forces contained the forty thousand men Gregoras claims. Michael's armies marched successfully through Thessaly, taking one fortress after another, until they finally besieged John in his main residence of Neopatras. Things looked grim for John, so he slipped out of the city and traveled to the Duchy of Athens, which would find itself threatened by the Byzantines should Thessaly fall. John de la Roche, who in 1263 had succeeded to the duchy on the death of his father, Guy, sent support to John after the two rulers concluded an agreement. By this treaty, John de la Roche's son William, who was to succeed to Athens on the death of his father in 1280, married Helen, the daughter of John of Thessaly. As her dowry Athens acquired the towns of Gravia, Siderokastron, Gardiki, and Lamia (or Zeitounion) in southern Thessaly.

Meanwhile the Byzantines had divided their forces; leaving a token force to besiege Neopatras where John was still believed to be, the other troops moved off to plunder and capture various lesser forts. At this point John, accompanied by a contingent of knights from Athens, made a surprise attack on the Byzantines. Taken completely by surprise, the Byzantines panicked and, after a contingent of Cuman mercenaries switched sides and joined John, the Byzantines suffered a serious defeat.

Euboea

Meanwhile Euboea had become a bone of contention between Byzantium and the Latins. The island had been given by Boniface in fief to three Lombard lords, who came to be known as the "triarchs." After Boniface's death and Emperor Henry's campaign of 1209 into Greece against Count Hubert of Biandrate, the Lombards of Euboea accepted the suzerainty of Henry. Subsequently, in 1236, after William Villehardouin provided aid to defend Constantinople at a critical moment, Emperor Baldwin II gave suzerainty over Euboea to the Prince of Achaea. William became interested in a more active role on the island when he married Carintana, the niece and heiress of one of the triarchs. Her inheritance may well have consisted of a sixth of the island. When she died in 1255, William laid claim to direct control over her lands. The Lombard barons were opposed to this, for control of this territory would then have passed from their families into that of a powerful foreigner. So they allied against him and assigned Carintana's share to Grapella of Verona, a member of a "triarch" family. Venice, meanwhile, had established a major commercial station on the island under the authority of a bailiff (bailo) resident in Negroponte (Khalkis, Chalkis), whose presence dated from between

1211 and 1216. Bury describes Negroponte as a sort of Venetian naval station and diplomatic bureau.[8] In the years that followed Venice had at various times been accepted as suzerain by certain triarchs. Venice had thus acquired considerable local authority and had no desire to see William Villehardouin obtain a direct role in the administration of any part of the island. So, in June 1256 Venice concluded a treaty with the local Lombard barons by which it also obtained rich concessions, including the right to all the island's customs receipts; in exchange the triarchs themselves were exempted from commercial duties and freed from the tribute that up to this date they had rendered to Venice.

In 1256 William invaded Euboea; he summoned the two leading triarchs, who were his vassals (and who did not dare ignore the summons) and took them prisoner. Then he and Venice engaged in a two-year struggle over Negroponte, not only the seat of the Venetian bailiff but also the capital of the island. The general residence of all the triarchs, Negroponte was commonly held by them all. The town was taken by William, recovered by Venice, re-recovered by William, and then besieged for thirteen months until Venice obtained its submission in early 1258. By that time William was involved in a quarrel with Guy of Athens, his hereditary vassal for Argos and Nauplia. For William was now demanding that Guy accept the Prince of Achaea as his suzerain for his Athens duchy as well. Guy refused, causing William to invade Guy's duchy. Guy was defeated in battle at Karydi; but the two barons agreed to let the King of France judge their dispute. William was then captured by Michael Palaeologus at the Battle of Pelagonia in 1259 and Guy of Athens became the acting bailiff for Achaea. Now Guy and, subsequently after his release, William, faced with a serious Byzantine challenge to the Morea itself, needed to improve relations with Venice. As a result in May 1262 William and Venice concluded a treaty by which William gave up his claim to direct possession of a portion of Euboea but was to continue to be recognized by the barons and by Venice as the suzerain of Euboea.

Meanwhile, after William's capture at Pelagonia Guy had released the two arrested triarchs. One of those released, Narzotto, along with William's rival the triarch Grapella, soon took up piracy in the Aegean, raiding as far afield as the coast of Anatolia. They maintained over a hundred ships and amassed a considerable amount of plunder.

Venice increasingly found itself caught in the middle between the Byzantines and the local Lombards. Venice did not want to see the Byzantines acquire Euboea; but it also had to worry about its major commercial rival, Genoa, which by the Treaty of Nymphaeum (1261) and the subsequent Byzantine recovery of Constantinople, had replaced Venice as the dominant commercial power in Constantinople. So, in 1265 Venice concluded a treaty with the empire, by which it was allowed to regain a commercial role in the empire. The treaty also recognized Venetian possession of Coron and Modon in the Peloponnesus. Thus these two Venetian towns would not be attacked by Byzantine forces in that region.

Meanwhile the piratical triarch Narzotto died. His heir, Marino II, was a minor; his inheritance was managed by his mother, Felisa. Felisa soon fell in love with an Italian adventurer of humble origins from Vicenza named Licario. Her family and the aristocracy of Negroponte, where all the triarchs and other leading barons lived, disapproved. The lovers soon contracted a secret marriage. Felisa's brothers learned of it and vowed to avenge themselves on Licario. However, he managed to escape to a very stout fortress, Anemopylai, near Karystos. Having strengthened its fortifications and assembled a band of retainers, Licario proceeded to plunder the neighboring countryside, lands of his Lombard opponents. Meanwhile the Byzantines, ambitious to recover Euboea and angered by a raid against various of their possessions in Asia Minor in 1269 by a Euboean Lombard fleet, retaliated by attacking Euboea; they defeated a Latin army, took many prisoners, and established a beachhead. The Byzantines stepped up this warfare in 1276 and found support from a considerable number of local Greeks. Meanwhile Licario, who had expected that his position of strength would force the triarchs to treat with him, found the barons still adamant in their refusal to do so. So Licario sent envoys to the Byzantines and soon concluded an agreement with the empire. Byzantine troops then entered his fortress of Anemopylai and warfare against the Lombards was stepped up, in the course of which many more local Greeks joined Licario's standard.

Meanwhile, after the victory in 1275 of John of Thessaly and John of Athens over the Byzantine invaders of Thessaly, the Lombards of Euboea thought to take advantage of the Byzantine defeat to attack a Byzantine fleet off Euboea. They launched a very successful surprise attack; however, the tide quickly turned when a large force of Byzantines, in retreat from their defeat in Thessaly, appeared in Euboea. The Byzantines defeated a large army of local Lombards, killing one triarch and capturing a second along with many other knights. The Byzantines immediately dispatched further troops to Euboea with the aim of taking the whole island. In 1276 Licario, as a Byzantine ally, took the major Euboean fortress of Karystos. Michael VIII, pleased by his success, awarded the whole island to Licario as a fief. In exchange Licario owed the emperor military service with two hundred knights. Licario, in order to win possession of his grant, now stepped up his activities and began reducing the forts of Euboea one after the other. He did not limit his activities to the land, but also commanded a fleet that in about 1278 took the islands of Lemnos and Skopelos.

By 1277 or 1278 Licario had taken all Euboea except for Negroponte. At this point he attacked Negroponte. A major battle occurred beneath its walls, which resulted in Licario's winning an overwhelming victory. Among Licario's prisoners were Gilbert of Verona, one of the triarchs, and John, Duke of Athens, who had been assisting the beleaguered Lombards. The city lay open before him, but for some reason Licario did not take it. Perhaps he feared Venetian anger and wanted to avoid future opposition from that quarter; or perhaps he feared intervention on behalf of Negroponte from John of Thessaly, flush from a second victory over the Byzantines in 1277 and free now to actively intervene in Euboea. In any case, Licario left Negroponte alone and satisfied his ambitions by ruling the rest of the island, which he did from the fortress of Filla. He sent John of Athens to Michael VIII as a gift. Later in that or the following year Michael released him under uncertain circumstances, but seemingly for a large ransom.

Licario also became admiral of a Greek fleet in the Aegean and followed up his terrestrial successes with naval ones, expelling the Venetians from various Aegean islands. As a result by 1280 most of the islands of the Archipelago were Byzantine. Venice, upset by this turn of events, agreed in July 1281 to support Charles of Anjou's crusade against Byzantium. And at roughly this time Licario ceases to be mentioned in the sources; we have no idea of what became of him.

Byzantium and Charles' Coalition, 1276–82

Meanwhile, in 1277 the Byzantines attacked Thessaly again but were stopped at Pharsalos (Farsala) by John. The frustrated Byzantines then called on their Nogaj Tatar allies, who plundered Thessaly and caused considerable damage. The Tatars then withdrew. The year in which the Nogaj raid occurred cannot be determined.

In 1276 a new pope, Innocent VI, took office. He was more hostile than his predecessor toward the Greeks and toward Michael. Suspicious of Michael's words, he demanded results, ordering the emperor and Greek Church leaders to proclaim union and chant the Creed with *Filioque* in the presence of his legates. Michael, of course, had been insisting to his subjects that *Filioque* had not been part of the agreement. In April 1277 Michael followed the pope's order semi-publicly—for he did so in a palace ceremony—and chanted the Creed with *Filioque*. His action brought no nearer the conversion of his subjects, who were horrified when rumors about the palace ceremony spread through the city. So, Michael next wrote the pope stating he hoped the pope was satisfied, for he had carried out his part. He then suggested that the pope drop his demand about *Filioque* and leave the Greek Creed intact. After all, he stated, *Filioque* was not really a major theological point, but its importance had become blown out of all proportion in the minds of the Greeks. In the interests of peace and union, why not cease trying to force it on the Greeks? Neither Innocent nor his successors, however, would accept this reasoning.

Up to this time (spring 1277) Michael had treated his opponents leniently, trying to reason with them. But with both Greek opposition to union and Michael's need to persuade the pope of his own good faith increasing through 1276 and 1277, Michael turned to persecution. At first he resorted to arrests, jailings, and exilings; among those jailed was his own sister Irene/Eulogia, the mother of the wives of the rulers of Bulgaria and Epirus. Then, as resistance continued, he turned to mutilations (blindings or the cutting out of tongues) and even executions. Persecution merely increased the opposition and caused large numbers of Anti-Unionists, both clerics and aristocrats, to emigrate from the empire. They fled chiefly to Thessaly, which was becoming a center for Anti-Unionists and for other opponents of Michael. Their presence gave Michael further cause to make war on Thessaly, though by 1277 the Thessalians had proved themselves equal to the task of resisting his attacks. In 1277 John Ducas held an ecclesiastical synod in Thessaly at which the bishops present declared John's political and religious enemy Michael VIII a heretic and condemned the Union of Lyons.

Meanwhile, persecutions reached Mount Athos. The monasteries had suffered considerably economically during the early thirteenth century. After Michael recovered Constantinople he had given the Church in general and Athos in particular many gifts and had spent much to repair various churches and monasteries there. These gifts were necessary politically because Michael had deposed, as noted, the popular and respected patriarch Arsenius, which had stirred up considerable opposition to him within the Church, particularly in monasteries. And Michael did not want Athos to become an Arsenite center against him. When he saw the danger from Charles developing back in 1273, Michael had approached the monks on Athos about the possibility of his seeking Church Union; the monks had strongly rejected the plan.

When the Council of Lyons was concluded, the monks on Athos rose up as defenders of Orthodoxy against Rome and declared Michael's action heretical. Trying to be conciliatory, Michael continued through 1277 to bestow gifts upon the Athonite monasteries. However, the monks were not to be won over to his views. Persecutions seem to have started on Athos in 1279. Unfortunately, we have no contemporary sources about these persecutions; later accounts (written in the fourteenth century) speak of them, however: the impious Latinizers, they say, sent troops in 1275 (probably the actual date, as we shall see, was 1280) who attacked several monasteries including the Zographou, the Bulgarian house, whose monks opposed Michael's religious policy. Twenty-six men (including twenty-two monks) were killed at the Zographou monastery. Its church and several other buildings were destroyed in a fire. Many manuscripts and vestments were lost in that fire or carried off in the looting. Michael's officials persuaded the Great Lavra to accept union and then turned their attention to the Vatopedi monastery. Its monks went into hiding, but were caught, and those who did not accept union were hanged. The Xeropotamou was bribed into accepting union; then an earthquake followed, killing many monks. Živojinović thinks this account—though elements of legend may have been mixed into it—is probably fairly accurate, particularly in its description of the actions taken against the Zographou monastery.[9] He notes that the Bulgarians had defeated the Byzantines in a battle in July 1280 and, postulating that the persecution on Athos occurred in that year, suggests the military defeat could well have led angry Greek officials to take their frustrations out on the Bulgarian monks who refused to accept union. Supporting his dating and reasoning is the fact that in the fall of

1280 the remnants of the defeated Byzantine army are known to have appeared in the vicinity of Athos. And it is evident that these soldiers were an undisciplined and violent bunch who carried out a certain amount of pillaging in the vicinity of Athos as well as on the mountain itself.

Thus Michael seems to have substituted civil war (plots and popular unrest that could easily grow into large-scale rioting or bring about his own overthrow, as well as increased opposition from and warfare with his Thessalian neighbor) for the threatened invasion. And in the event of an invasion Michael needed to have his population united behind him. At the same time, though Michael had delayed the invasion, the threat of it still hung over his head, for the pope was demanding greater results than Michael could deliver. And if the pope should come to the conclusion that Michael would be unable to realize his promises, then he might lose patience and cease restraining Charles. And, as we might guess, Charles was also putting considerable pressure on the pope to permit him to attack the empire and restore the Latin Empire, whose government—after restoration—would then impose Church Union in the regions Charles controlled. Thus Michael clearly had very little time.

William Villehardouin of the Morea died in 1278. Charles inherited his principality according to the agreement made at Viterbo. William had had no son to inherit the fifth allowed by that treaty; thus the male Villehardouin line became extinct. At first glance, Charles' acquisition of the Morea might appear to be a considerable gain for him. However, in fact it was not. William as a local lord had been quite popular; he had understood local customs and had worked hard to maintain good relations with his Greek subjects. Now the Morea had acquired an absentee ruler who had no ties with the region. The chances of maintaining a Villehardouin connection had collapsed for a time because Charles' son Philip, who had married William Villehardouin's daughter Isabelle and who might have become a fit governor for the Morea, had died in 1277 with no sons. So, instead of being ruled by a prince on the ground, the Morea was run by a bailiff and his associates, outsiders sent in from the Anjou court. The populace found these foreign officials unpleasant; having no ties to the area and no understanding of local customs, they administered according to the ways of Anjou. At the same time as the old families of the Morea now became extinct, their lands were assigned by the Anjous to knights brought from France and Italy. These newcomers also did not know local ways or speak Greek; arrogant and throwing their weight around in district affairs, they stirred up considerable hostility on the local level.

Meanwhile in Rome, Pope Nicholas III (1277–80), who had succeeded Innocent VI, understood Michael's difficulties and had continued to restrain Charles. However, in August 1280 Nicholas died. In February 1281 Charles' candidate, Martin IV, became pope. Asserting that Michael had not realized the Union of the Churches, Martin declared Michael a schismatic to be deposed and excommunicated him. Charles was given permission to carry out the sentence. Thus Charles, who by this time had added Venice to his coalition, was at last free to march. He planned his attack for early 1282. So, Michael was back to where he had started in 1274, facing invasion from a great coalition; in fact his position was now even weaker than it had been in 1274, because his unionist policy had earned him hatred and divided the Greek population.

However, suddenly on 31 March 1282 a rebellion broke out in Palermo, the capital of Angevin Sicily; this uprising is known as the Sicilian Vespers. The Sicilians had disliked Charles and, well financed by the gold distributed by Byzantine agents who had been actively involved in stirring up unrest in Sicily, rose up and overthrew Charles' officials. The Sicilians invited Peter of Aragon to be their prince. Charles thereby had to go to war against Peter to recover Sicily. This proved to be a long and costly war, and it ended in failure. Thus Charles' dreams of restoring the Latin Empire collapsed. How much credit should be given to Michael for bringing about the rebellion is much debated among scholars, though most give him some credit. In any case, since the activities of secret agents are not the sort of thing committed to paper, it is something we shall never know. Charles was hated in Sicily, and that hatred was clearly the major cause of the rebellion; for, if Charles had been popular the Byzantine agents could have done nothing. And, of course, once the rebellion broke out it became a mob action out of the control of any leaders. Michael not surprisingly made self-serving statements about his role in it, but they hardly constitute proof. Shortly thereafter, in December 1282, having seen his empire saved from disaster and perhaps having masterminded its salvation, Michael VIII died.

Michael, however, died hated at home. His son and successor Andronicus II (1282–1328) immediately repudiated the union—which, of course, had never been accepted by most Greeks—that had existed on paper for eight years. There was no reason to retain it, since the cause for it, preventing Charles' invasion, had been otherwise removed, and probably no one in the empire really wanted it. Once again, as in 1261 (upon Constantinople's recovery), Holy Water was sprinkled around Hagia Sophia and the other churches to purify them. Michael was denied the last rites of the Church and was buried on a distant mountainside with no church service at all. After the Union of Lyons was repudiated, the Greek Church in Thessaly and Epirus returned to communion with and obedience to the Patriarch of Constantinople. Thus from here on, despite the political independence of Thessaly and Epirus, the Church in these regions remained under the jursidiction of the Patriarch of Constantinople.

Soon thereafter, in the 1280s (most probably late in 1284) Andronicus II marched west and recovered for Byzantium the central Albanian lands the Angevins had taken, acquiring among other places Valona, Kroja, and Durazzo. The southern region centered around Valona was to remain Byzantine until the Serb conquest in the 1340s. The Angevins, however, were able to retain their possession of the coastal town of Butrinti as well as the island of Corfu.

Civil War in Bulgaria, 1278–84

As noted, Tatar raiding increased in Bulgaria from the mid-1270s. These actions were carried out by the followers of the semi-independent chieftain Nogaj. Since Bulgaria's Tatar suzerain Mangu Timur was weaker than Nogaj, he could not put a stop to these depredations. The fact that Bulgaria still paid Mangu Timur tribute may even have caused an increase in Nogaj's raiding. Furthermore, the Nogajs were Byzantine allies. Bulgaria's anti-Byzantine policy—its lining up with Charles, opposing Church Union, and giving asylum to Michael's enemies—was grounds for Michael to encourage Nogaj to raid Bulgaria, a profitable activity that would have suited Nogaj's own need for booty to retain or obtain additional followers. At the same time the Bulgarian tsar Constantine Tih, as a result of the injury which left him paralyzed from the waist down, was not an effective leader in repelling these raids. Thus communities near the Tatar border or along Tatar raiding routes had more and more to assume responsibility for their own defense. And various localities produced leaders who commanded local resistance. The most successful of these was a swineherd named Ivajlo or, as Pachymeres calls him, Lahana—a name derived from the Greek word for kale. Pigs were a major Balkan livestock product, making it possible for the possessor of a large herd to join the ranks of a district's rural elite. The famous Karadjordje, who led the First Serbian Uprising against the Turks in 1804, was also a pig-farmer.

Ivajlo had great success in leading local "minute men" or vigilantes against the Tatar raiders, and with his success his following grew. He also seems to have been a charismatic figure; according to Pachymeres he had visions which promised great things for him. Various signs portending this were seen and so interpreted. And he claimed to be in contact with heaven and the saints. His success against the Tatars confirmed these predictions, and many Bulgarians came to see him as a God-given savior from the Tatars. His activities occurred at a time when, as noted, more and more central government functions were falling into the hands of the Byzantine-born Queen Maria, a scandalous intriguer who, to secure the succession for her son Michael, was turning against many of the boyars. Besides poisoning Jacob Svetoslav, she had imprisoned or executed various other boyars. Thus opposition to her and to Constantine was growing.

As Ivajlo's reputation and following grew, the area from which his support came also expanded; among his followers were also to be found an increasing number of boyars. Presumably they were not court boyars but provincial ones, who probably depended on Ivajlo's army for the defense of their estates and who also had become disillusioned with the regime as it turned more and more to arbitrary actions against real or imagined opponents. With this growing following, Ivajlo's effectiveness against the Tatars grew. And Ivajlo's growing power coincided with the increasing ineffectiveness of Constantine and with the increasing opposition to Maria. Soon the swineherd-brigand, having through his own bravery built up a large following, proclaimed himself tsar.

Constantine grew worried; so, presumably carried in a litter or wagon, he led his armies out to meet Ivajlo. Deserted by many of his supporters, Constantine's troops were defeated and Constantine was killed. This battle occurred at the end of 1277. Then, while Maria continued to rule in Trnovo as regent for little Michael, Ivajlo captured a whole series of towns.

Meanwhile, the Byzantines, also concerned about Ivajlo, were in the process of beefing up their border fortresses; Michael VIII, moreover, detested Maria, who supported both her mother's opposition to his Church policy and Constantine's alliance with Charles of Anjou. So, Michael now decided to intervene and place his own candidate on the Bulgarian throne, the son of Mico, John Asen's son-in-law, who had accepted Byzantine asylum and estates in Anatolia. This son, called John Asen III, was proclaimed Tsar of Bulgaria. Having made him take an oath of loyalty to the empire, Michael VIII married John Asen III to his own daughter, Irene.

The Bulgarian boyars were called upon to desert Maria and support the legitimate Asenid tsar, and some were to do so. Then, accompanied by a Byzantine army, early in 1278, John Asen III appeared in Bulgaria. By this time Ivajlo was besieging Trnovo. Nogaj units had also got into the act, crossing the Danube and plundering Bulgaria as far as the gates of Trnovo. Maria found herself caught between one domestic and two major foreign enemies, Tatars and Byzantines, for even though she was a Byzantine she hated her uncle the emperor whom she believed a heretic. To save her situation, Maria, after negotiations, opened the gates of Trnovo to Ivajlo in the late spring of 1278. He became tsar and married her; thus she remained as tsarica. Presumably the little Michael continued, in theory, to be the heir to the throne.

Most Marxist scholars have depicted Ivajlo's movement as a social one. Nikov has presented a good case, however, that such an interpretation is exaggerated.[10] He insists there is no evidence Ivajlo's was a social movement; he even had boyars among his supporters. There is no sign that he or his followers protested against social injustices or sought any social reforms. The movement did not pit the people against the boyars or the people against tsarist authority; it was simply a movement against a particular incompetent tsar. Ivajlo's willingness to marry the hated Tsarica Maria also militates against the social movement interpretation.

Once in power, Ivajlo found himself in new company, that of his Byzantine wife and presumably of much of her court, as well as that of various high Trnovo aristocrats; thus surrounded, he almost certainly became isolated from many of his original supporters. If he had had any social reforms in mind, as modern scholars often claim, he seems to have done nothing to advance them; he can hardly be faulted for this considering the conditions of the country, where, despite the submission of many towns to him, his authority hardly reached beyond Trnovo, which soon was under Byzantine siege. But in any case, whatever his initial ambitions, Ivajlo seems to have become part of the establishment. Presumably this disillusioned many of his original followers, if for no other reason than that they failed to obtain sufficient rewards. Since Ivajlo was inexperienced in state affairs one may well imagine that the local establishment, or the faction then dominating it, would have been fairly successful in manipulating him and keeping power in its hands. The local boyars probably also scorned Ivajlo's low origins and saw him and his retinue as a threat to their positions and influence. Thus probably from the start they wanted and plotted his removal. And if Ivajlo's following became alienated and drifted away, and if Ivajlo was unable to secure his own authority over state affairs, members of the establishment would have come to have few reasons either to fear him or to continue to play along with him. Very likely the desire of the courtiers to rid themselves of him was behind their urging Ivajlo to leave Trnovo in the autumn of 1278 to campaign against the Tatars.

Thus Ivajlo in the spring of 1278 had acquired Trnovo. At first he had considerable popular support, including that of some boyars, though not necessarily the major ones of Trnovo. The Tatars were looting in the vicinity of the capital, while a Byzantine army, also with some boyar support, accompanied by John Asen III, moved on Trnovo and laid siege to it beginning in the fall of 1278. Some Bulgarian towns had declared for Ivajlo, while others had not. Thus Bulgaria was in anarchy, and Ivajlo, besieged in Trnovo and facing two enemy armies within Bulgaria, was in no position to assert his authority over those towns that accepted him, let alone over those that did not. Surely if Vidin had been regained by Bulgaria after Jacob Svetoslav's death, it seceded again at this time. Since the Byzantines were allied to the Nogajs, the purpose of the Nogajs' presence at the moment (other than to plunder) was nominally to support the candidacy of John Asen III. A Nogaj unit, under a certain Kasim beg, served in the Byzantine army besieging Trnovo.

This situation lasted through the fall of 1278; in the course of the fall Ivajlo slipped out of Trnovo, mobilized an army, and went off to fight the Tatars. Rumors soon were circulated, probably sown by Byzantine agents (for John Asen III did have support among certain Bulgarians, including boyars), that Ivajlo had been killed. Because the rumors were believed, some citizens of Trnovo, who presumably had no love for Maria, opened the gates of Trnovo in February 1279 to John Asen III, who was recognized as tsar. He entered the city accompanied by Byzantine troops, and they remained in Trnovo to maintain him in power. The Nogaj Kasim beg received the high court title protostrator. After this allied victory, the Tatars did not withdraw from Bulgaria, but went off to roam and plunder the countryside. Maria, then pregnant, was turned over to the Byzantine commander by the Trnovo leaders. She was sent to the Emperor Michael VIII, who was then keeping in touch with the campaign from his town of Adrianople. (This town, located near the border, seems to have been Byzantium's chief intelligence post as well as its base for mounting attacks against Bulgaria.) He jailed Maria in Adrianople.

After taking Trnovo, John Asen III and the Byzantines sent part of their armies north in pursuit of Ivajlo, who shut himself up in the fortress of Silistria. The Byzantine forces besieged him there for three months but failed to take the town. John Asen's supporters meanwhile were unable to establish him firmly in power or put an end to the anarchy. Most of the country did not recognize him, and there were plots against him in Trnovo itself. To try to broaden his base of support John Asen III gave his own sister to become the wife of George Terter, a boyar leader who was of Cuman origin. In accepting, George sent the lady who had been his wife, along with their son Theodore Svetoslav, to Constantinople. Soon Ivajlo reappeared with a large army and laid siege to Trnovo. With him now was Kasim beg, who had changed sides. Two Byzantine armies were sent from the empire to aid the besieged John Asen. Ivajlo defeated them both, the first, supposedly of ten thousand men, on 17 June 1279, and the second, of five thousand men, at Sredna Gora on 5 August 1279. Realizing his own unpopularity and fearing for his life (after all, bolstered as he was by foreign armies, he must have appeared to the Bulgarians as a foreign puppet), John Asen III, late in 1279, secretly slipped out of Trnovo and fled to Mesembria where he found a ship to take him to Constantinople. The boyars inside the city, opposed to Ivajlo or ambitious to put their own clique into power (for Ivajlo surely had his own followers to award prizes to), then elected, still late in 1279, one of their number, the influential boyar George Terter, as tsar.

While George Terter established himself in Trnovo, his erstwhile opponents planned to carry on the struggle and oust him. Ivajlo and Kasim beg crossed the Danube to seek the aid of the powerful Tatar leader Nogaj. The Byzantines did not wish to accept Terter either—probably considering him a turncoat, for he had previously concluded the marriage alliance with John Asen III's sister—and, still intriguing, sent John Asen III with rich gifts to Nogaj's court to seek his aid. Nogaj seems to have expressed interest in the issue, but made no commitments and kept the suitors cooling their heels for several months. Then one evening at a banquet Nogaj, quite drunk, ordered the executions of Ivajlo and Kasim beg, and they were duly murdered. He seems to have at least nominally carried out this act as a Byzantine ally, for, according to Pachymeres, when he ordered Ivajlo's execution, Nogaj called Ivajlo an enemy of "my father" (the father being his ally Michael VIII, who was "father" over other rulers according to the Byzantines' theoretical hierarchy of rulers). It seems John Asen III barely escaped a similar fate; he was happy to return alive to Constantinople and to forget about further Bulgarian adventures. He settled down and became a member of the Byzantine aristocracy.

The Byzantines kept up their hostility to George Terter and encouraged Nogaj to raid Bulgaria, which he did over the next few years. Nogaj by now was becoming more of an independent actor, and thus less bound to the wishes of his Byzantine allies. Probably seeing nothing in it for himself, he made no effort to support John Asen's candidacy once Terter had gained the throne. And though he continued to raid Bulgaria as Byzantium recommended, he probably did it primarily for the booty to be gained. In 1285 he even sent one of these raiding parties beyond Bulgaria to plunder Byzantine territory in Macedonia and Thrace. Their alliance was clearly on the wane.

The Byzantines justified their continued hostility to George Terter by blaming him for his alliances with their enemies Charles of Anjou and John of Thessaly. However, cause and effect are hard to determine. The Byzantines seem to have been opposed to George from the start; thus he may have reaffirmed these existing Bulgarian commitments (dating from Constantine Tih's time) in a search for allies to defend himself against Byzantium.

However, despite Bulgaria's grievances, it clearly was in George Terter's interests to make peace with Byzantium. After the Sicilian Vespers in 1282, Charles of Anjou was out of the picture, and thus George could not use his coattails to regain any of Bulgaria's lost territory along the Black Sea or in Thrace. Bulgaria clearly was too weak to regain these regions on its own, so there was no reason not to make peace. And if George was willing to recognize Byzantium's possession of the disputed territory, there was no reason for the empire not to make peace and recognize George as ruler of Bulgaria. Clearly the Byzantines had no chance of installing their candidate, John Asen III, without Nogaj's help, and probably they were less enthusiastic about John Asen after his flight from Trnovo where they had installed him. Thus in 1284 Michael's successor, Andronicus II, agreed to a treaty with Bulgaria. Andronicus recognized George Terter as Tsar of Bulgaria and gave him the Byzantine court title of despot. He also allowed George to exchange wives; the Byzantines took back George's second wife, the sister of John Asen III, married to George during the exciting days when John Asen and his Byzantine retinue held Trnovo, and they returned to George his first wife and their son Theodore Svetoslav.

Serbia under King Uroš, 1243–76

Uroš, who in 1243 succeeded Vladislav in Serbia, seems to have been the ablest of the three brothers. (Though it might be said in the other two's defense that Uroš had the advantage over them in having his reign coincide with the decline of Serbia's two formerly powerful neighbors, Thessaloniki-Epirus and Bulgaria.) Under Uroš Serbia became a significant Balkan power. Serbia's rise is attributable not only to the weakening of its neighbors but also to its rapid economic development associated with the opening of its mines. The mines were developed primarily by the Sasi, Saxons from Hungary, who had the technical know-how to extract the ore. Located at the sites of the mines, their communities from the start, and throughout the Middle Ages, enjoyed a very privileged status; they were self-governing under their own laws with the right to have and to worship at Catholic churches. The earliest reference to Saxons in Serbia, which shows them already established, is in 1253 or 1254. The first mine to be reported in the sources is Brskovo on the

Tara, mentioned in 1253 or 1254. Brskovo was Serbia's richest silver mine during the second half of the thirteenth century. An important mint was soon established there. Brskovo was soon followed by mines at Rudnik, several in the region of Kopaonik, and at what was destined to become Serbia's richest mine, Novo Brdo.

The silver, gold, lead, copper, and iron extracted from these mines attracted greater numbers of Dalmatian merchants to Serbia. These merchants, particularly those from Dubrovnik and Kotor, also established privileged colonies in Serbia's economic and mining centers. Their colonies—like those of the Saxons—enjoyed freedom for their Catholic religion (provided they did not proselytize among the Serbs) and the right to live under their own officials and laws. Quarrels with local Serbs were resolved by mixed courts, with an equal number of Serbs and of colonists on the jury. These Dalmatian merchants took over the financial management of the mines and, particularly those from Kotor, assumed the higher financial offices at the Serbian court. They also bought the right to collect taxes and tolls within Serbia. In this way at the time of purchase the ruler was paid the income he expected from a particular income source for the year (thus this sum was guaranteed for him), while the purchaser hoped to profit by collecting more than anticipated. At times this led to overtaxing the populace, and the burden presumably fell most heavily on those least able to afford it, since the powerful magnates frequently had been granted charters providing broad financial exemptions. Accompanying this development, coinage, begun in Serbia under Radoslav, came under Uroš to be issued in much larger quantities.

The mines and increased trade resulting from their exploitation greatly improved the Serbian ruler's economic position. They gave him the cash to hire mercenaries, which, by giving him a military force independent of the nobles, provided him with a means to control his nobles. Thus unlike Byzantium, where increased use of mercenaries reflected the weakening of the state, mercenaries produced the strengthening of the state in Serbia. In the fourteenth century these mercenaries tended to be foreigners, frequently Germans, which further guaranteed their independence from local interests. Whether the policy of recruiting foreign mercenaries dates back to Uroš' reign is not certain.

Uroš' two main foreign policy concerns, since his southern and eastern neighbors were no longer threats to him, were maintaining his control over eastern Hum and defending Serbia from Hungary. These two problems were related. Radoslav of Hum, who had succeeded Andrew in western Hum and the coast in 1249, maintained close relations with his coastal neighbor Dubrovnik. Radoslav also improved relations with the King of Hungary, who was overlord over Radoslav's Croatian neighbors to Hum's northwest beyond the Cetina River. Documents show Radoslav in 1254, declaring himself a loyal vassal of the Hungarian king, allied with Dubrovnik and Bulgaria against Serbia. Some scholars have postulated that western Hum had been subjugated by Hungary in its brief campaign against "Bosnia" in 1253, and thus Radoslav had been forced to accept this vassalage. However, it makes more sense to hypothesize that Radoslav had voluntarily accepted this position to gain Hungarian support in his projected war against Serbia, a closer and therefore more dangerous enemy. Whether this policy would have been defensive, to defend Hum against an attack he expected from Serbia, or offensive, to build up alliances to make it possible for him to expand his control into Serbia's eastern Hum, is not known.

This was a tense time in that area. In 1252 and 1253 Serbian and Ragusan forces had skirmished along their common border in southern Dalmatia. According to a later Ragusan chronicle, whose bias not surprisingly puts the blame on Uroš, the Serbian king sought to conquer Dubrovnik or at the very least force the town to drop Venetian suzerainty for Serbian. The Dubrovnik-Bar Church quarrel may also have been a factor in the war. In these wars Dubrovnik, which never was able to field effective land armies, usually got the worst of it, having its territory outside its walls plundered. This time, as usual, its walls held out, keeping the Serbs out of the city itself. By the time fighting broke out again in 1254, Dubrovnik had acquired as allies Bulgaria and Radoslav of Hum; little is known about how much fighting occurred that year by any of the parties or where it took place. It seems the Bulgarians carried out what was little more than a raid, reaching the Lim River and plundering the area around Bijelo Polje. Separate peace agreements were made with Serbia in the autumn of 1254, which seem to have restored matters in all cases to pre-war conditions.

In the 1250s the Orthodox bishop of Hum moved from Hum's capital Ston, on the coast, far inland to the Church of Saint Peter and Saint Paul, built by Prince Miroslav, on the Lim River near the Serbian border and within the part of Hum controlled by Serbia. From then on throughout the Middle Ages the bishop remained at this church. The move followed shortly after an earthquake in Ston. Since the Orthodox Church's landed possessions in Hum lay chiefly in the more fertile regions near the Lim, this move has usually been linked to financial needs. Some scholars, however, have tried to relate this move to pressure on the Orthodox from heretics around Ston. While this hypothesis cannot entirely be ruled out, very little evidence exists (and what we have is questionable) concerning heresy in the vicinity of Ston.

Recently, V. Gračev has presented a more convincing explanation for the move.[11] He visualizes an on-going struggle throughout the first half of the thirteenth century by Miroslav's successors (he includes Toljen, Andrew II, and Radoslav; possibly we should also add Peter), allied with the local nobles of Hum, against the Serbian state allied to Sava's Serbian Orthodox Church represented in western Hum by the Serbian-appointed bishop in Ston. The importance of this bishopric is illustrated by the fact that Uroš' brother Sava—the future Archbishop Sava II—was appointed to that post. The Serbs through the Church had a means to gain further influence in western Hum, which presumably they used; at the same time the descendants of Miroslav sought to retain their position in an independent western Hum and possibly even to regain the territory east of the Neretva, formerly held by Miroslav but annexed by Serbia. How accurately Gračev's model may fit the whole century cannot be established since the sources, particularly for the second half of the thirteenth century, are woefully sparse; however, his model certainly seems applicable to Radoslav's position vis à vis Serbia. And it is noteworthy that when Radoslav concluded his alliance against Serbia, the bishop moved from Ston to the Lim. Gračev reasonably links the two events and sees the move as a defeat for the Serbian party inside western Hum.

In the second half of the thirteenth century the scarce sources about Hum become even scarcer. Serbia retained the territory east of the Neretva throughout and also managed to extend its overlordship over part of western Hum. Much autonomy seems to have remained, however, in the hands of the local nobility, who seem to have been in frequent feuds and skirmishes with one another. This encouraged localism and hindered the development of feelings of loyalty to Hum as an entity. Presumably Serbia's expansion of its suzerainty over parts of western Hum resulted from these feuds, with Serbia supporting this or that noble against his neighbors or against the Prince of Hum and accepting submission for that aid, and with the nobleman finding it advantageous to lean on the powerful Serbian state for the achievement of his local aims. The position of Miroslav's descendants meanwhile declined to that of petty noblemen under Serbian suzerainty. By the early fourteenth century some leading families of Hum had become clients of Bosnia while others remained in the Serbian camp, most having made their alliances to better their own positions vis à vis their neighbors. This situation was finally brought to a close in 1326 when Bosnia, taking advantage of strife in Serbia, annexed most of Hum.

Despite Serbia's peace with Dubrovnik, necessary for both sides' economic health, tensions remained, leading to a new war between them breaking out between 1265 and 1268. Later Ragusan chronicles, as usual, blame it on Serbia. Other than Uroš' supposed ambition to conquer the city or make it drop its recognition of Venice as overlord, the chronicles provide a series of lesser grievances: Uroš accused Dubrovnik of seizing Serbian coastal territory, of granting asylum to Serbian deserters, and of maintaining ties with Venice (at a time Serbia was allied to Byzantium which was allied to Genoa against Venice). During the war Uroš' wife, despite her husband's policy, favored Dubrovnik and kept in secret contact with the town, promising to warn it if and when Uroš planned to dispatch troops to plunder its lands.

Peace was made in 1268. It was agreed that Dubrovnik was to pay two thousand perpera in tribute on Saint Demetrius' Day, for which Dubrovnik received the right to trade duty-free in Serbia and to enjoy the territory it claimed along the Serbian border (which Nemanja had recognized as Ragusan). The tribute was to be paid to the holder of Trebinje and Konavli. At this time, and through the reign of Stefan Dušan (1331–55), the recipient was to be the King of Serbia. Thus Dubrovnik basically ended up paying protection money to keep the peace and what amounted to rent for the disputed lands; it retained use of the land, but Serbia received an annual payment. This Saint Demetrius' Day tribute had nothing to do with suzerainty, for Dubrovnik remained after 1268 under Venetian suzerainty and the tribute was to continue after 1358 when Dubrovnik accepted Hungarian suzerainty. Serbia and Dubrovnik had a brief clash again in 1275 over a local issue—a quarrel between the two commercial towns of Kotor and Dubrovnik; because Kotor was considered part of Serbia, accepting Serbian suzerainty though it was self-governing with its own laws and town council, Uroš sent Kotor aid. This quarrel was quickly resolved and had no lasting impact.

Despite the probable existence of tensions between Serbia and Hungary, fighting between them seems not to have broken out until 1268. Though Radoslav of Hum, at war with Serbia, accepted Hungarian suzerainty, there is no sign of any Hungarian participation in his war with Serbia. Presumably the border between Serbia and Hungary remained north of the West Morava River near Ravno (Ćuprije). Relations between the two states became belligerent in 1268. Uroš seems to have initiated the fighting; perhaps he sought to push his border northward, or perhaps he simply wanted plunder. In any case, in 1268 he led Serbian troops to plunder Mačva, then held for Hungary by Rostislav's widow Anna as regent for their son Bela. The Serbs did considerable damage before Hungarian help came. The Hungarians then managed to capture Uroš himself. Uroš was forced to purchase his release. Some scholars believe that the agreement concluded between the two states resulting in Uroš' release also resulted in the marriage between Uroš' eldest son Stefan Dragutin and Katherine, granddaughter of King Bela IV and daughter of his eldest son Stephen V. Other scholars believe the couple had been married prior to 1268.

Seeking to centralize his realm, Uroš tried to stamp out regional differences by dropping references to them. He dropped from his title separate references to Zahumlje (Hum), Trebinje, and Duklja (Zeta) and called himself simply "King of all Serbian land and the Coast." In Serbian Hum, as noted, Miroslav's descendants dropped to the level of other local nobles. The official representatives of the Serbian ruler there were drawn from other families. In Zeta the status of Vukan's descendants declined; in fact his descendants disappear from the sources after George's generation. "King" George (referred to as king by the Ulcinj bishop in the 1240s) is not heard of further. His brother Stefan built the monastery of Morača in 1252, quite possibly on his own lands. He was remembered as king by a seventeenth-century painter who redid the monastery's frescoes. The third brother, Dmitri, bore the lesser title župan, and soon became a monk. Thereafter nothing more is heard of any descendant of Vukan in Zeta. However, Milica, who was to be Knez Lazar's wife in Serbia in the second half of the fourteenth century, claimed descent from Vukan.

Thus if Vukan's descendants had retained significant positions in Zeta prior to Uroš' consolidation of power, which is not certain, they do not seem to have maintained them under Uroš. Under Uroš' successor Dragutin, Zeta was to become part of the appanage awarded, inside his own family, to his mother, Uroš' widow.

Uroš, seeking to centralize his state, did not create appanges for any son. Dragutin, his eldest son, lived at court. A Byzantine envoy who visited Serbia in about 1268 to negotiate a marriage that did not materialize owing to Serbian opposition (whose account may thus be somewhat biased) described the Serbian court as follows: "The Great King, as he is called [Uroš], lives a simple life in a way that would be a disgrace for a middling official in Constantinople; the king's Hungarian daughter-in-law [Dragutin's wife] works at her spinning wheel in a cheap dress; the household eats like a pack of hunters or sheep stealers." The envoy also stressed the insecurity of the highways.

Dragutin wanted an appanage, and his Hungarian in-laws seem to have exerted pressure for this too. Uroš resisted, and some scholars believe he even considered replacing Dragutin as heir with his younger son, Milutin. Finally in 1276 Dragutin demanded to share power. Uroš was furious at the suggestion and refused. Fearing for his life, Dragutin rebelled, receiving military help from his Hungarian father-in-law. Scholars disagree as to what set off Dragutin's rebellion. Dinić depicts it as being caused by the heir Dragutin's ambition and desire for a greater role in the state.[12] Mavromatis argues that Uroš had by 1276 selected his younger son Milutin to be his successor over Dragutin. Thus Mavromatis believes that decision caused Dragutin to rebel.[13] The Hungarian king, clearly wanting his son-in-law to succeed, threw his support behind Dragutin. Their joint armies defeated Uroš in battle near Gacko (in modern Hercegovina). Uroš abdicated and became a monk, dying in about 1277 at Sopoćani, the beautiful monastery he had built. Uroš throughout his reign had maintained close ties to the Church, which he also seems to have tightly controlled. He built the Preobraženje chapel at Hilandar on Athos. He also appointed his own brother Sava, until then Bishop of Hum, Archbishop of Serbia in 1263 and subsequently appointed as Serbia's archbishop Joanikije, a former Athonite monk and disciple of Sava II who prior to his appointment had been the abbot of Studenica. Joanikije was so closely associated with Uroš' cause that he left office when Uroš was overthrown. It is unknown whether he resigned in protest or whether he was seen by Dragutin as a partisan of Uroš who might plot against the new regime and thus had to be removed.

Hungary and Croatia

When King Stephen V of Hungary died in 1272 his minor son Ladislas IV succeeded. He was greatly under the influence of his mother, who not only was regent but also managed large appanages in the north of Bosnia and in Srem. Joachim Peter, the Ban of Slavonia, had considerable influence as well. The presence of a young scatter-brained king and a weak court led the nobles to assert themselves further. The situation became particularly critical in

Slavonia, leading to warfare between the ban and the most important noble family there, the Babonići. In the course of the warfare in 1277 Ban Joachim Peter was killed. The rise of the nobles is also reflected in the balance of power within the administrative system. As noted, Slavonia was subjected to an administrative system similar to that of Hungary. Thus Slavonia under its ban was divided up into large administrative districts called županijas. Originally it had three great districts, centered in Križevci, Zagreb, and Varaždin, each managed by a royal appointee called a župan (count). This župan was based in his fortified capital and was the region's military commander. His other main duties were to collect taxes, raise and maintain the local army, and direct the regional law court. Eventually these districts were to be subdivided and restructured, and then Slavonia found itself divided into fourteen županijas. Within the županijas were the so-to-speak natural counties arising from geography or from the family holdings of the local Croatian nobles. These smaller (natural) counties were also called županijas (or župas). To make things simpler when discussing Slavonia, I shall call the larger imposed administrative districts under the king's appointees županijas, and the smaller districts župas. Croatia south of the Gvozd Mountain was not divided into županijas. It had only the family territories or župas, dominated by the hereditary lords of the counties.

In the thirteenth century the županija system in Slavonia began to break down. This was owing to the increased power of the great nobles achieved as a result of the general privileges received from the Golden Bull and of huge individual royal grants, greatly increasing their landed power base. The recipients of these grants and privileges were freed from the royally appointed župan's authority and were directly subject to the king. This created a parallel administrative system, because the great noble ran his own county and its court, and the župan was not allowed to enter his territories (unless to put down a rebellion). Such a parallel system of administration that gave the župan jurisdiction over only part of his region could only weaken his authority, as did the increased strength of the great nobles backed by their private armies of retainers. Furthermore, the Church held huge estates, also separated from the authority of the župan, and owed service (including military service) directly to the king. Finally, the free towns too were separated from the župan's jurisdiction and also stood directly under the king.

In the thirteenth century councils or assemblies of nobles became more active; for example, a major council was held in Zagreb in 1273. We find the župans there, but their authority was clearly limited and they were dependent to a considerable extent upon the decisions of the council; thus the župans came more and more to represent the collective will of the nobility rather than the wishes of the more distant king who had appointed them. The Ban of Slavonia, like the župans under him, also found himself more and more representing the will of the Slavonian nobility rather than that of the king. In Croatia, more distant from Hungary, the ban found himself in a similar situation, and there, too, frequent assemblies of the nobility settled issues that affected the general welfare. In such a situation, with the nobles holding whole counties, administering them themselves, and presiding over the local courts and enforcing court decisions, the peasants found themselves entirely separated from any "state" organization. The peasants paid taxes for the state, but a nobleman collected the taxes from most of them, and if they were recruited into the army, they were mobilized by the noble and went to battle under him as part of his retinue.

The weakening of royal authority under the young king allowed the Šubići to regain their former role in Dalmatia. The Croatian ban lost authority and thus could not assert his right to appoint his own men as town podestas in Dalmatia. And in the early 1270s we find him yielding to the local balance of power and appointing members of the Šubić family as his deputies in various Dalmatian towns. In 1272 Stjepko Šubić's eldest son Paul is documented as podesta of Trogir, and in the following year Paul's responsibilities increased as did his title; at that time he is found as Prince of Split and Trogir. In 1274 Paul's brother George (Juraj) is found as podesta of Šibenik. In that year Stjepko died and Paul I Šubić succeeded as the family elder. Soon the young king, recognizing the balance of power in Dalmatia, named Paul as Ban of Croatia and Dalmatia. He was briefly removed from this post when he became too strong a partisan of Šibenik—supported by Split—which sought to free its Church from the jurisdiction of the Bishop of Trogir. But by 1278 (with the issue of the Church of Šibenik still unresolved) Paul had been re-appointed Ban of Dalmatia and Croatia, and his brothers were princes of the leading Dalmatian towns, Mladen of Split, and George of Trogir and Šibenik.

Venice, long annoyed by Kačić piracy against its ships and possessions in the Adriatic, took advantage of the weakness of that family's Hungarian overlord to strike the Kačići's coastal holdings, centered around Omiš, in 1279. In 1280 Venice took Omiš. The Venetian campaign, for all practical purposes, wiped out the Kačići, and they ceased to play a major role in Dalmatian affairs. Ban Paul, however, moved in at once to share in the spoils, and when the dust had settled Venice held of the former Kačić possessions only the citadel of Omiš and the islands of Brač and Hvar. For Paul had seized all the mainland holdings between the Neretva and Cetina rivers, including the lower town of Omiš. And in 1287 Paul was to take the castle of Omiš by force.

Meanwhile, the princely family of the island of Krk (whom I shall call the "Frankapans" even though they did not officially take that name until the early fifteenth century) was assuming an ever increasing role in Croatia. It has usually been stated that members of this family had long been active on the mainland, receiving from the King of Hungary the župa of Modruš in 1193 and the župa of Vinodol in 1225. Nada Klaić argues, however, that the charters providing evidence for this belief are later forgeries. The first firm evidence for the activities of this family on the mainland dates from the 1240s and 1250s. At that time two family members, Bartol and Vid, for some reason did not receive a share of Krk; going to the mainland, they entered the service of the King of Hungary. As a result of subsequent service in the 1250s one of Vid's sons was named podesta of Split, while a second one became podesta of Senj. Shortly thereafter, in 1257, a reliable document refers to a family member for the first time as Count of Modruš and Vinodol. Presumably this individual, whose name was Frederick, had been granted the two counties at about that time by Bela IV for faithful service. Klaić argues that the subsequent forgeries, pushing possession of these counties back several decades, were carried out to provide evidence that a particular branch of the family had a right to these counties and that this right dated back to grants so specifying from 1193 and 1225 respectively.[14]

The region held by Frederick was not particularly fertile; as a result many of its inhabitants were pastoralists and in the absence of large estates many of those engaged in agriculture were not enserfed. The inhabitants of Vinodol were soon quarrelling with their prince; they objected to his and other noblemen's enserfing free peasants and to his imposing various new financial and service obligations on the inhabitants. Finally, in 1288, a council, attended by representatives of the nine towns and districts of Vinodol, met with the prince and drew up a statute of seventy-seven articles, which defined the region's obligations to the prince as well as his functions, authority, and rights. To a considerable extent this statute upheld local customs. It also discussed crimes and their punishment and to a certain extent touched on private law by defining how quarrels between subjects should be settled. The Vinodol Statute of 1288 was the earliest legal code, written in Croatian, though already the towns on the Dalmatian coast, starting with Korčula probably in 1214, Split around 1240, and Dubrovnik in 1272, had begun codifying their town laws.[15] In many cases these Dalmatian codes, which were in Latin, were drawn up to protect the local laws and customs of these urban communities against possible violations or alterations by their princes who were often foreigners.

King Ladislas IV died in 1290 leaving no sons. The Hungarian nobles immediately elected as his successor Andrew III, the son of Bela IV's younger brother Stephen. Andrew came to Hungary and was crowned by the Archbishop of Esztergom (Ostrogon). The pope opposed the choice of Andrew and claimed that since the year 1000, when the papacy had granted a crown to Saint Stephen, it was the pope's right to make the choice. The pope favored a rival candidate, Charles Martel, the son of Charles II and Maria, the Angevin rulers of Naples. Queen Maria was the sister of Ladislas IV. Accepting her claim that she (i.e., her son) was the legal heir to the Hungarian throne, the pope by means of a legate crowned Charles Martel in 1292. Most Hungarian nobles rallied around Andrew, but a large number of Croatian nobles—including the Ban of Slavonia, the Šubići, Kurjak of Krbava, the Krk princes (the future Frankapans), and all the Babonići—supported the Naples candidate. Andrew marched into Slavonia, achieving considerable success, but on his return march he was captured by hostile Croatians and released only after a large ransom was paid. At this juncture the leading

Slavonian family, the Babonići, came out for Andrew; their reward came quickly when a Babonić was named Ban of Slavonia.

In response, Charles II of Naples awarded (on paper) all Slavonia to Dragutin's son Vladislav. And to revive his son's failing fortunes and to retain Croatian support, Charles (in the name of his son) awarded all Croatia from the Gvozd Mountain to the Neretva mouth hereditarily to Paul Šubić of Bribir, who had been holding the office of Ban of Croatia and Dalmatia from the time of Ladislas. Thus Charles converted Paul's personal position as ban into a hereditary one for the Šubić family. All other nobles in this vast region, he declared, were to be vassals of Paul Šubić. The most prominent nobles so assigned were Kurjak, the holder of Krbava, and George (Juraj) Isanov, the holder of Knin and progenitor of the Nelipčić (or Nelipić) family. To Paul's north lay the lands of the "Frankapans" who also were supporters of Naples.

To meet this challenge, Andrew III in 1293 also issued a charter naming Paul Šubić hereditary Ban of Croatia and Dalmatia (i.e., the very same position Charles II had given him). Whereas the Naples party had until then predominated in the Croatian interior, various towns along the Dalmatian coast had recognized Andrew on the ground that he alone had been crowned in Hungary. Andrew's efforts may have briefly won Paul over; however, if they did, Paul was clearly back in the Naples camp by 1295. As a result of this bidding for support and of the fact that in the course of the civil war no central power existed to restrain them, the already strong Šubići became the most powerful family in Croatia.

In 1295, the fighting became particularly violent in Zagreb, where the bishop's town supported Charles Martel and the free town (Gradec) supported Andrew. Then suddenly, in 1295, Charles Martel died in Naples of the plague. His "rights" to Hungary were left to his son Charles Robert.

Peace was briefly concluded at home between the two sides, and Andrew III was accepted as king. But when in 1299 the childless Andrew named his mother's brother as his heir, a new revolt on behalf of Charles Robert erupted. The papacy again threw its support to Naples, replacing as Archbishop of Split a partisan of Andrew with a court chaplain from Naples. The papal endorsement seems to have brought the Šubići back to active support of Naples. And George Šubić, Ban Paul's brother, went to Italy, visiting the pope and the Naples court. While at Rome he won papal approval for a long-standing Šubić aim, the removal of Šibenik's Church from the jurisdiction of the Bishop of Trogir and the creation of a bishopric for Šibenik which was to be directly under the Archbishop of Split. In August 1300 George returned to Split, bringing Charles Robert with him. Charles Robert was thus on the ground, so to speak, when Andrew III died in January 1301.

Andrew III's death brought the Arpad dynasty to an end. Ban Paul accompanied Charles Robert to Zagreb, where he was recognized as king; they then proceeded to Esztergom, where in 1301 the Archbishop of Esztergom crowned him King of Hungary and Croatia. The new king was only twelve years old. Trogir, presumably angry over Naples' support for the independence of the diocese of Šibenik, tried to refuse Charles Robert recognition. However, the town's resistance was short-lived and by 1303 all the towns of Dalmatia had recognized Charles Robert. For their services on his behalf the Šubići were confirmed in the privileges granted them by both sides during the civil war, in particular the hereditary banship of Croatia and Dalmatia. This was well deserved, for the Šubići, especially George, had played the dominant role in gaining the throne for Charles Robert. And the "Frankapans," also loyal to Naples throughout, were granted the župa of Gacka by the new king. Soon thereafter Charles Robert granted them Požega as well.

But though the Croatians all recognized the new king, the Hungarian nobles were divided, with a majority coming to support Wenceslas III, the King of Bohemia. Wenceslas was brought to Alba Regalis (Stolni Biograd, Székesfehérvár), then the main capital of Hungary, where he was crowned, also in 1301, King of Hungary. He took the name Ladislas V. Civil war followed. However, it did not touch Croatia, which remained loyal to Charles Robert and under the firm authority of Paul Šubić. Finally, in 1304, Pope Boniface VIII intervened and Wenceslas agreed to leave Hungary.

The Hungarian opposition, however, still refused to accept Charles Robert and now gave its support to Otto of Bavaria, whom it crowned in 1304. By 1308 Otto's support was already dwindling, when he was captured and jailed by supporters of Charles Robert. Offered his release if he would abandon his claim to the throne, Otto agreed, was released, and departed. A brief attempt to advance the candidacy of Vladislav, son of Stefan Dragutin of Serbia and Katherine, Stephen V's daughter, attracted few supporters. At this point one of the leaders of the anti-Naples party, Paul Garai (Gorjanski) declared himself for Charles Robert, and with his defection the remaining members of the opposition became more willing to negotiate. Papal envoys came to mediate peace; the Hungarian nobles said they would accept the papal candidate, Charles Robert, if the pope would renounce his claim that the papacy had the right to select the King of Hungary. The pope acquiesced, recognizing the nobles' right to choose their own king; then the nobles acknowledged Charles Robert as hereditary king. He was crowned in Buda in June 1309. And, shortly thereafter in August 1310, after he had received back from Otto the official Crown of Saint Stephen, he was given a new coronation with it in Alba Regalis. Thus the civil war was over. Various Hungarian nobles were to sporadically exhibit signs of insubordination against him for another decade. But the Croatian nobles all recognized him; however, even they continued to act independently in local affairs, greatly to the new king's irritation.

Meanwhile Paul Šubić, Ban of Croatia and Dalmatia, became "Lord of Bosnia" as well in 1299. No source provides any information on how this happened. It is doubtful that he really held all Bosnia, though he may well have been overlord over much of it. He also ruled directly or indirectly all Croatia and Dalmatia from the Gvozd Mountain down to the Neretva mouth, except for Zadar. He continued to delegate authority to various family members. He assigned whatever parts of Bosnia he held to his brother Mladen I, who had been Prince of Split from 1278 to 1301; by 1302 Mladen bore the title Ban of Bosnia. His brother George retained special responsibility for Dalmatia, with the title Prince of the Coastal Towns. When George died in 1303, he was succeeded in Dalmatia by Paul's son George (Juraj) II. In 1304 Ban Mladen I of Bosnia was killed fighting "Bosnian heretics." Paul seems then to have carried out a campaign against the Bosnians which evidently brought more of Bosnia under his rule, for Paul referred to himself in a 1305 charter as "lord of *all* Bosnia." At about this time Paul appointed his second son, Mladen II, Ban of Bosnia, and in 1305 his third son, Paul II, was elected Prince of Split. During these years many of Ban Paul Šubić's charters, awarding lands and titles, made no reference to the Hungarian king, showing that Paul was for all practical purposes an independent ruler within his banate.

The only thorn in his side was the Venetians' possession of Zadar, which seems to have bothered the citizens of Zadar as much as it did Paul. Finally a chance to liberate Zadar arose. In 1308 Venice and the papacy became engaged in a heated quarrel over the city of Ferrara, which led the pope in 1309 to put the city of Venice under interdict. Venice's involvement in Italy and the papal encouragement of Catholics to resist Venice, exhibited by the interdict, spurred Paul to action. Early in 1310 he brought his forces to the walls of Zadar. The Venetian garrison held out through that year, but in 1311 after much careful planning, an uprising against Venice broke out inside the city. The rebels arrested the Venetian authorities and took control of the town. The Venetians quickly dispatched a fleet to Zadar, besieging the town from the sea. Paul Šubić's troops actively participated in the city's defense. Meanwhile the town sent envoys to Charles Robert, offering him its submission and seeking his confirmation of all the town's traditional privileges, including the right to elect its own prince. The king graciously received the town's submission and confirmed the requested privileges. The town's citizens then elected as their prince Paul Šubić's son Mladen II, who was actively defending the town at the time. The situation soon reached a stalemate: the Venetian fleet could not take the town and the combined forces of Šubić and Zadar— receiving no re-enforcements from the king—were not strong enough to drive the Venetians off. In the midst of this stalemate, in May 1312, Paul I Šubić died. He was succeeded as Ban of Croatia and Dalmatia by his son Mladen II. He at once shared out his cities among his brothers. Gregory received Šibenik and Bribir, Paul II Skradin and Trogir, and George II Omiš, Nin, and Klis. Various podestas were appointed to supervise the towns.

Mladen immediately found himself in difficulties, however. Venice made peace with the pope, causing the papal interdict to be lifted; this allowed Venice to concentrate greater attention on Zadar. Alarmed by this prospect and suffering commercially from the Venetian blockade, some in Zadar began thinking of an accommodation with Venice and dispatched envoys to Venice for discussions. Mladen was able to hold the loyalty of sufficient citizens to retain the town through 1312. However, in September 1313, after it became apparent that the King of Hungary was not going to provide any relief, the citizens of Zadar finally submitted to Venice. Mladen's prestige among the Croatians suffered greatly from this defeat; moreover, his and his family's support of the Zadar rebels brought upon Mladen Venice's enmity.

During the next decade Mladen was faced with various revolts; in 1315 or 1316 Trogir attempted unsuccessfully to secede from his control, and in 1316 and 1317 Mladen was forced to defend his position against a coalition of Croatian princes—Budislav Kurjaković of Krbava, Nelipac (son of George Isanov) of Knin, the sons of Hrvatin of the Donji Kraji, and the Mihovilovići of Livno—who sought to assert their independence from the Šubić over-lordship imposed upon them by the Hungarian king at the time of the dynastic warfare. The Babonići of Slavonia, surely with the king's blessing, soon joined the coalition. In the course of this warfare Nelipac gained in strength and emerged as the leader of the coalition and the leading rival of the Šubići for hegemony. During this struggle Mladen maintained correct relations with King Charles Robert and supported him in his war against Milutin of Serbia in 1318 and 1319. In that campaign Mladen seems to have been active in Bosnia, and when the dust settled Stjepan Kotromanić had become Ban of Bosnia. Perhaps Mladen's activities in the Bosnian area were responsible for installing Kotromanić in power. In any case, Kotromanić appears as a Šubić vassal in 1318, when Mladen is found asking the pope to give special dispensation for a marriage Kotromanić sought. And in the fighting that ensued in the early 1320s Kotromanić remained lined up with the Šubići against Nelipac.

In the midst of the Serbian war the Šubić podesta for Šibenik seceded, seeking the help of Venice. Mladen marched against the town in 1319 or 1320; he succeeded in capturing the podesta during a skirmish but was unable to take the town itself, which was determined to continue its secession. Venice, hoping to increase its influence in Šibenik, stepped forward as a defender of Dalmatian urban autonomy and privileges, by providing aid to the besieged city. Then Šibenik, presumably with Venetian consent, accepted Mladen's opponent Budislav Kurjaković as its podesta. The following year, 1321, Trogir expelled its Šubić-appointed podesta. Venice, clearly by this time out to ruin its former enemy, urged the two towns, which had long been hostile to one another, to make an alliance against Mladen. The towns made peace and concluded the alliance, which included Venice, in January 1322. Mladen attacked both towns, devastating their lands beyond their walls, but he was unable to take either of them. Venetian ships participated in the defense of the two towns, both of which accepted Venetian suzerainty in the course of that year.

Mladen's loss of the towns was also a loss for the King of Hungary, who held ultimate suzerainty over all Mladen's territory. The king was displeased and encouraged joint Croatian action against Venice. As a result Mladen called a council meeting to discuss the recovery of the lost towns. It was attended not only by Mladen's supporters but also by the leading Croatian nobles, who had formed the coalition against him. Not surprisingly, the meeting was a tense one; Mladen accused the nobles of disloyalty toward him and of encouraging the towns' secession. After charges and countercharges were flung back and forth, the nobles stormed out of the meeting—which came to no decision on action over Šibenik and Trogir—and reaffirmed their alliance against Mladen. Thus all Croatia—excluding the Šubić lands—was in revolt against Mladen, the Croatian ban. The rebels then attacked Mladen's territory.

Mladen seems to have defended his lands well until he suffered a major betrayal. In April 1322 his brother Paul II, who until then seems to have supported him loyally, switched sides and joined the coalition. Paul's town of Trogir had been lost; possibly he had not received compensation from Mladen, or perhaps he hoped by this action to become the Croatian ban himself. Paul, in that month, concluded an alliance with the rebellious town of Trogir against Mladen. The third brother, George II, holding Nin, Klis, and Omiš, remained faithful and as Prince of Split was able to hold that town's loyalty to Mladen. The King of Hungary then decided to intervene, sending John (Ivan) Babonić, the Ban of Slavonia, with a force to support the coalition. Considerable fighting took place during that summer in the vicinity of Skradin; then finally in August or September Mladen was defeated in a major battle at Bliska (or Blizna, exact location unknown, but near Klis). Mladen fled to Klis; there he held out behind its walls. The coalition then seems to have taken and devastated Skradin and Omiš.

At this point the King of Hungary personally intervened, arriving with a substantial force in Croatia in September 1322. Establishing himself at Knin, he convoked a council at which he obtained the submission of the Croatian coalition members. They presumably also leveled various accusations against Mladen. He, meanwhile, sent his brother George as his envoy to the king. The king seemed gracious toward Mladen and arrangements were made between him and George for Mladen's appearance at Knin. Mladen duly appeared, only to be seized. He disappears thereafter from the sources. Though his fate is unknown, various later accounts report that he died in prison in Hungary.

Mladen's capture marks the end of the Šubić family's dominant position in Croatia. The king did not appoint Paul II Šubić as ban. Instead he terminated the family's hereditary banship and appointed John Babonić as Ban of Croatia and Dalmatia. And Stjepan Kotromanić, the new Ban of Bosnia, whom we shall discuss in the next chapter, until then a Šubić vassal, was recognized as independent (i.e., independent of the Šubići and a direct vassal of the King of Hungary). The "Frankapans" who had supported the king against Mladen received in 1323 the county of Drežnik as their reward.

The Šubići's holdings were also reduced. And what they retained was split between Mladen's brothers George II and Paul II, who were already at logger-heads as a result of Paul's defection during the war. Paul, isolated for a time from the rest of the family, held Bribir and Ostrovica, while George held Klis, Skradin, and Omiš. These five towns constituted the family's remaining possessions. The family's position and influence elsewhere on the coast was also greatly reduced. Venice retained suzerainty over Trogir and Šibenik. And Split and Nin, which until then had accepted Šubići as princes, now chose as their princes members of other Croatian families.

Many Croatian nobles were unhappy with the results of the king's intervention. For he had sought and partially succeeded in increasing his control over the Croatian lands by appointing a non-local, the Slavonian John Babonić, as Ban of Croatia. After the decline of the Šubići, Nelipac had risen to become the dominant figure in the Croatian lands. Seeking hegemony among the Croatians, he also sought to re-assert Croatian autonomy. These two goals led him into conflict with certain other Croatians as well as with the king and his officials. When threatened with royal intervention most of the Croatians, including Nelipac's local rivals, usually rallied around him. In any case, soon after the king's return to Hungary, Nelipac seized the royal city of Knin, which prior to 1322 had almost certainly been his, but which the king had taken over in 1322. Babonić's inability to prevent Knin's fall led Charles Robert to remove him from his banship and appoint a Hungarian as Ban of Croatia and Dalmatia. A Hungarian army, led by the new Slavonian ban, Ban Mikac (1325–43), was then sent into Croatia in 1326. Nelipac defeated this army, so all of Croatia from Lika and Krbava south to the Cetina River was in fact outside the king's authority. Only the "Frankapans," lords of Krk, Modruš, Vinodol, Gacka, and Drežnik, and the nobility of Slavonia supported the king.

In the local fighting Nelipac's leading opponent was George Šubić. In 1324 Nelipac took him prisoner in the course of a battle and held him captive for two years, during which time George's wife managed George's lands. However, to face Ban Mikac's invasion in 1326, the two made peace and Nelipac released George, who participated in defending Croatia against Mikac.

Meanwhile, taking advantage of this warfare, of the decline in royal authority, and of the need of the local nobles to concentrate their forces on opposing the king, Venice asserted its suzerainty over Split in 1327 and Nin in 1329. Venice thus acquired most of the coast from the mouth of the Cetina north to the Zrmanja—with Omiš and Skradin under the Šubići excepted. At the same time, during the late 1320s, Ban Stjepan Kotromanić of Bosnia, as we shall see, annexed the territory between the mouths of the Cetina and Neretva rivers as well as the territory between Bosnia and the coast: Imotski, Duvno, Livno, and Glamoč, which came to be known as Završje (or the Western Lands, Zapadne Strane). The Hungarian king did not oppose Kotromanić in this matter since most of his gains had been made at the expense of the king's major enemy in the area, Nelipac—or of Nelipac's allies like Mihovilović, who had been the lord of Livno. Kotromanić in fact had become the king's leading ally in the region. In the inland territory north of the Cetina River Nelipac, based in Knin, remained the most powerful among the Croatian nobles. Nelipac continued to have tense relations and frequent skirmishes with the Šubići during the 1330s. George II Šubić died between 1328 and 1330 to be succeeded by his son Mladen III. Pressure from Nelipac, including his capture of Ostrovica and various lesser Šubić places, led Mladen III and his uncle Paul II to make peace so as to better resist Nelipac. Venice, unhappy with the growing strength of Nelipac which might threaten its position on the coast, intervened and mediated a peace between Nelipac and the Šubići that included the return of Ostrovica to Paul.

However, while these territorial losses were taking place in Croatia, Charles Robert was able to assert firmer control over Slavonia. There his ban, Mikac, was able to reduce the local power of the Babonići. He found an excuse to go against the sons of Stjepan Babonić and to confiscate their fortress of Steničnjak. Mikac kept it for himself, eventually giving them various lesser forts as compensation. However, they remained angry and in 1336 concluded an agreement to serve the Habsburgs; as a result they seceded from Hungary with their lands. However, other Babonići, in particular the sons of Radoslav Babonić, continued in the king's service and as a result increased their holdings. Still, by provoking fights with nobles he felt to be disloyal and then seizing their key forts, Ban Mikac was able to reduce the authority of various leading Slavonian magnates. In so doing, he kept many of the confiscated fortresses for himself, thus augmenting his own local power. He did not, however, take advantage of his increasing power to assert himself against the king.

Ban Mikac also made it his policy to win over from the great nobles many of the lesser nobles who until then had served as vassals in the retinues of these local leaders. As a result he reduced the armies of the great, to the profit of the crown. With this growing core of loyal servitors Mikac was able to establish a reformed županija organization and also to augment the garrisons of the royal castles in Slavonia. Some of these castles were newly acquired by the king. For in this period, supported effectively by Mikac, Charles Robert was claiming various important Slavonian fortresses, hitherto controlled by magnates, as royal ones. Moreover, to increase state authority Mikac was able to expand the authority of the ban's court, asserting its jurisdiction over those lesser nobles who until then had been subject to the jurisdiction of the great local nobles. Slavonia thereafter remained at peace and loyal to the king until Charles Robert's death in July 1342.

NOTES

1. Nicol, *The Despotate of Epirus.*
2. The fate of Durazzo in the 1260s is a mystery. Since in 1261 an Orthodox metropolitan loyal to the Ecumenical Patriarch in Nicea is found in Durazzo, it seems likely that Nicea acquired Durazzo also after the Battle of Pelagonia. Did Manfred then regain the town in ca. 1262? Supporting such a conclusion is an inscription from 1266

from northern Albania referring to a kephale there who governed in the time of several mentioned rulers, one of whom was Manfred in Durazzo. However, later, in 1266/67 (according to Ducellier) or in 1271 (according to Nicol), after Manfred's death, the same Orthodox metropolitan is still to be found in Durazzo. His presence suggests Nicean rule, unless Manfred, showing unusual tolerance for a Latin ruler of this time, allowed the Orthodox metropolitan to continue to exercise his authority after Manfred's recovery of Durazzo. A further argument to suggest that Manfred did not regain Durazzo is advanced by Ducellier (*La façade maritime,* pp. 177–80). When Manfred was killed, Michael II of Epirus invaded Albania to recover his former lands. His chief opponent was Manfred's governor for Albania, Philip Chinardo, who was in the process of trying to create his own principality in Albania. But what is important for us is that Chinardo did not reside in the major city of Durazzo but in the lesser fortress of Kanina. Ducellier reasonably concludes that this shows Manfred did not hold Durazzo at the time of his death. Ducellier then turns to Pachymeres' description of the major earthquake that struck Durazzo (he believes it occurred at the end of 1266 or early 1267, but Nicol dates it to 1271). Since this account mentions actions by no officials in the town except the Orthodox metropolitan, Ducellier concludes that Durazzo had no foreign lord at this time but was governed by its own citizenry. Though Ducellier may be right about self-rule, it seems to me that these citizens would certainly have had some leader or council that would have taken or failed to take action when the earthquake struck and that Pachymeres would equally have been expected to mention. Thus since clearly some civil government, be it local or foreign, existed in Durazzo, the argument from silence is inconclusive. Nicea (by then Byzantium) may well have held the city at the time of the earthquake. Whether the Byzantines had held it continually since Pelagonia, or whether Manfred had at some point briefly regained it—hence the inscription—only to lose it again, is unknown. Thus we must conclude that we do not know who (and the who may be in the plural) controlled Durazzo in the 1260s.

3. Finlay, *History of Greece,* vol. 4, p. 204.

4. The discussion of Thessaly in this and subsequent chapters owes much to B. Ferjančić, *Tesalija u XIII i XIV veku,* SAN, Vizantološki institut, Monograph no. 15 (Beograd, 1974).

5. P. Petrov, "B"lgaro-Vizantijskite otnošenija prez vtorata polovina na XIII v. otrazeni v poemata na Manuil Fil 'Za voennite podvizi na izvestnija čutoven protostrator,' " *Izvestija na Instituta za B"lgarska istorija* (BAN) 6 (1956): 545–72.

6. At about this time, presumably in the warfare of 1262 or 1263, the Byzantines re-established control over the Danube delta including the town of Vicina. They almost certainly won this region through a naval attack; thereafter they could maintain communications with it only by sea. To defend Vicina and environs from the Bulgarians and from Steppe raids, Michael VIII established here in the Dobrudja some Anatolian Turks who had been serving him as mercenaries and who disliked barracks life near Constantinople. They soon established two or three towns in the delta and took up their defensive role. In time some migrated to the Steppes and others returned to Anatolia, but enough of them remained to maintain their own ethnic identity. In the years before the Ottoman conquest those Dobrudja Turks who remained converted to Christianity. This community of Christian Turks in the Dobrudja, known as the Gagauz, has survived to the twentieth century and still speaks a recognizably Anatolian dialect of Turkish. On the Dobrudja Turks, see P. Wittek, "Yazijioghlu 'Ali on the Christian

Turks of the Dobruja," *Bulletin of the School of Oriental and African Studies* (University of London) 14 (1952): 639–68.

7. Petrov, "B"lgaro-Vizantijskite otnošenija."

8. J. B. Bury, "The Lombards and Venetians in Euboia," *Journal of Hellenic Studies* 7 (1886): 329.

9. M. Živojinović, "Sveta Gora i Lionska unija," *ZRVI* 18 (1978): 141–53.

10. P. Nikov, in "Vesti i ocenki," *Periodičesko spisanie* 70 (1909): 575–76.

11. V. Gračev, "Terminy 'župa' i 'župan' v Serbskih istočnikah XII–XIV vv. i traktovka ih v istoriografii," in *Istočniki i istoriografija Slavjanskogo srednevekov'ja*, AN SSSR (Moscow, 1967), pp. 33–34, 49–50.

12. M. Dinić, "Odnos izmedju Kraljeva Milutina i Dragutina," *ZRVI* 3 (1955): 49–82.

13. L. Mavromatis, *La fondation de l'Empire Serbe: Le Kralj Milutin* (Thessaloniki, 1978), pp. 19–20.

14. N. Klaić, *Povijest Hrvata u razvijenom srednjem vijeku* (Zagreb, 1976), pp. 370–86.

15. For a brief summary of the contents of Dubrovnik's Statutes, see N. Klaić, *Povijest Hrvata*, pp. 245–48.

CHAPTER 5

The Balkans in the Early Fourteenth Century

Serbia at the End of the Thirteenth Century

Stefan Dragutin, having overthrown his father Uroš, became King of Serbia in 1276. He immediately granted his mother, Helen (or Jelena), an enormous appanage that comprised Zeta, Trebinje, part of the coast including Konavli and Cavtat, and part of western Serbia including the source of the Ibar River and Plav on the upper Lim. His younger brother Milutin, married to a daughter of John of Thessaly, took up residence at his mother's court in Skadar. Thus Dragutin, unlike his father who eliminated appanages and centralized his state, re-established the appanage system. Evidently there existed considerable pressure for this from part of the nobility, and, in order to obtain its support in his conflict with his father, Dragutin had agreed to allow considerably more autonomy to the great nobles, who had provided his major source of support, and thus restored at least certain appanages. The creation of appanages seems to have increased the influence of the nobles holding lands within these outlying territories, whereas Uroš' centralizing policy had favored the nobility drawn from the royal court and from the central region of Raška. To bind Zeta and Trebinje to his state, Dragutin installed his mother over that appanage; she was to be a firm supporter of Dragutin in the years that followed.

In 1282 Dragutin fell from a horse and broke his leg. The sources imply that his injury was serious enough for his future to have been in doubt; possibly the wound became infected or gangrenous. So, a council was convoked at Deževo to resolve the situation. Unfortunately no text of the council's decisions survive. We have only later sources, biased Serbian ones and those from Byzantine authors who were writing at considerable distance from the events they described. They report that at the council Dragutin abdicated in favor of his brother Milutin. But these sources leave much unsaid. For, if Dragutin's health was the sole problem, why did the council not simply create a temporary regency? Thus most scholars believe there was more to the issue than Dragutin's health. They point out that Archbishop Danilo's account attributes the council's actions to the injury and to "serious troubles," a vague phrase which Danilo does not elaborate upon. And thus they have seen the leg as an excuse for the nobles to depose Dragutin, a deposition they wanted for political reasons. What these political reasons might have been, we can only guess. Milutin seems not to have been present at the council; thus probably the nobility (or part of the nobility), rather than he, was the moving force at Deževo. Possibly the nobles who controlled the meeting decided to place Milutin on the throne in the hope that they could dominate him. Milutin became king for life.

Mavromatis argues that the council created a division of the realm; thus its results should be seen more as a division than as an abdication.[1] In any case, regardless of which term we use, Dragutin gave up his rule over the central Serbian lands and probably also gave up the title king. In exchange he received a large appanage in northern and western Serbia, including the mining town of Rudnik, Arilje, the region of Dabar (on the lower Lim which included a bishop who resided at the monastery of Saint Nicholas), and Uskoplje near Trebinje. Their mother, Helen, kept Trebinje itself and Zeta.

There is considerable dispute among scholars as to the extent of the territory Dragutin was to hold. His richest Serbian territory (Rudnik, Arilje) lay just south of the Hungarian border and formed a compact unit. He also held, as noted, some territory on the Lim and near Trebinje. Were these last isolated holdings lying in the midst of Milutin's kingdom from which Dragutin received income, or did he hold a narrow strip of territory stretching from his northern lands, passing across the Lim and upper Drina, down through Gacko to Uskoplje in the region of Trebinje? At present it seems impossible to resolve this question.

Many of the great nobles then chose, and were allowed, to accompany Dragutin to his appanage. Does this indicate the nobility was divided about Milutin's succession? Did Dragutin's appanage consist of the lands of those great nobles who remained loyal to him? Or was his appanage assigned, after which his supporters followed him thither, receiving new lands? Or did the nobles in the lands assigned to Dragutin, regardless of their own political stances, have to submit to him? Did some nobles retain lands in both realms? Did many lands undergo transfers of ownership through sale or exchange at the time? The answers to these and a host of other questions are unknown.

Milutin, as noted, received the title king. He is the only Serbian ruler called king from here on in the Byzantine sources. Western sources, however, refer to both brothers as kings. Most scholars believe that the Council of Deževo also decreed that Dragutin's son Vladislav should succeed Milutin as Serbia's king. Mavromatis argues, however, that this claim was made only by later Byzantine sources which, he believes, were poorly informed. Mavromatis believes the question of who was to succeed Milutin was not decided at Deževo.

Dragutin was soon, in 1284, granted a second appanage by the Hungarian king, his father-in-law. This appanage consisted of Mačva (stretching between the Drina, Sava, and Morava rivers and the Serbian border), Srem, and part of northern Bosnia, including Usora and probably Soli (the region of modern Tuzla). The Mačva territory lay just north of the core-lands of Dragutin's Serbian appanage. Thus Dragutin held two appanages. But though they bordered on one another, they were not integrated into one state for one was held under Milutin's suzerainty and the other under the suzerainty of the Hungarian king.

Relations, as we shall see, between Dragutin and Milutin seem to have been friendly at first. The Serbian nobles desired to press south against Byzantium to obtain lands and booty. Possibly Dragutin's failure to carry out this policy had caused his overthrow. In any case, Milutin immediately joined Charles of Anjou's coalition against Byzantium and attacked the empire. Scholars have almost unanimously followed Cantacuzenus and Danilo who state that Milutin immediately captured the important city of Skopje on the Vardar in 1282. Mavromatis rejects this claim, believing conditions in Serbia must still have been too unstable for a major campaign in 1282. He casts some serious doubts on the two just-mentioned sources' information and concludes the main push south, including the capture of Skopje, occurred in the 1290s. Mavromatis makes a strong argument for his point of view, but, owing to the limitations of our sources, his evidence is chiefly circumstantial. And though he may be right, he cannot prove the point; thus the date of Skopje's fall to the Serbs must remain an open question.

In any case, the Serbs did attack Macedonia in 1282, and, though we cannot ascertain the extent of their gains, they did provoke the Byzantines into retaliating. The empire summoned its allies, the Nogaj Tatars, to raid Serbia. The Serbs repelled their attack, and then in 1283 Milutin, supported by Dragutin, pressed further into Macedonia, occupying more territory. Since this campaign preceded Dragutin's acquisition of his second, his Hungarian, appanage, it is apparent that his Serbian appanage was sufficiently large (i.e., able to provide manpower enough) to render significant help to Milutin. That year one Serbian army swept into eastern Macedonia along the Struma River, reaching the Aegean Sea at Kavalla (Christopolis), while a second army pressed westward to take Kičevo and Debar (Dibra).

In the years that followed the Serbs carried out numerous raids for plunder against the empire, which retaliated from time to time in the same way against the Serbs. In the 1290s, as these activities continued, the Serbs were able to wrest away some Macedonian territory from the empire. However, our sources do not provide sufficient concrete information to document this expansion. Finally in the late 1290s, probably 1296, the Serbs launched a major attack into Albania and took Durazzo, which they were to hold only briefly. (Durazzo is documented as Byzantine again in 1301 and it seems logical to date its restoration to the treaty of 1299.) The loss of Durazzo angered the Byzantines greatly, and in 1297 they launched a major attack on

Serbia. This attack was repelled without too much difficulty by the Serbs, so the Byzantines decided to make greater efforts for a peace treaty. By that time, they found Milutin, as we shall see, more ready to entertain this idea.

Though he supported his brother against Byzantium, Dragutin's chief area of operations was in the north. There he created for all practical purposes a second kingdom—with its own loyal nobility—and took on all the trappings of an independent king. He maintained his Western orientation and had regular dealings not only with Hungary but also with the papacy. He allowed the establishment of a Catholic bishopric in his city of Beograd and supported in the 1290s a Franciscan mission in his northern Bosnian lands. His mother, Helen, of Catholic and French origin, probably of the Valois family, also encouraged the Franciscans in her appanage. By 1283 Franciscan missions supported by Helen existed in Bar, Kotor, and Ulcinj. The Ulcinj mission (and possibly also the Kotor mission) became a full-fledged monastery in 1288. Another Franciscan monastery was established that year in her main residence of Skadar.

Dragutin soon came up against the two brothers (probably Bulgarians of Cuman origin), Drman and Kudelin, who by this time had asserted their control over the city and province of Braničevo and had achieved their independence from Hungary. The Serbian author Danilo writes that they were very independent-minded and afraid of no one. Using Tatar and Cuman troops they caused difficulties for their neighbors, including Mačva on their western border. Mačva, prior to its assignment to Dragutin, had been under Elizabeth, the Queen Mother of Hungary, and between 1282 and 1284 she had sent troops to try to recover Braničevo. The attack had failed and the brothers had then plundered Mačva in retaliation. The Hungarians still wanted Braničevo back, and they next enlisted the help of their new vassal Dragutin in Beograd against the brothers. Perhaps Mačva was assigned to Dragutin to put a stronger figure in Mačva to defend that province from the brothers and also with the hope of regaining Braničevo. However, Hungary's and Dragutin's joint action in 1285 failed to dislodge them. The brothers soon retaliated, ravaging Dragutin's lands. Dragutin then turned to Milutin for help; Milutin obliged and in roughly 1291 they jointly defeated Drman and Kudelin; Dragutin thereupon annexed Braničevo. For the first time, that province was in the hands of a Serb.

Shortly thereafter Šišman of Vidin attacked Serbia. This is the first mention in the sources of this figure, who by this time was ruling as an independent prince the province of Vidin. Thus clearly Vidin had again (or was still) separated from Trnovo. Šišman presumably was a local boyar from the Vidin region. He was well established in power by the 1290s when we first hear of him. Most scholars push his taking power back to well before that time, some dating it as far back as the late 1270s after Tsarica Maria effected Jacob Svetoslav's murder.

Šišman's attack on Serbia may have been in retaliation for something his new neighbor Dragutin had done to him, for by annexing Braničevo Dragutin extended his lands to the borders of Vidin. It is also quite possible that Šišman had been a close associate, ally or vassal, of Drman and Kudelin; thus Šišman's action against Serbia may have been in response to the Serbs' actions against them. Šišman clearly was a Nogaj vassal. Whether these Tatars had helped to install him, or merely agreed to accept him after he had taken power, is unknown. His close ties with the Nogajs are shown by the large numbers of Tatar troops in the armies he sent into Serbia. The invaders from Vidin took no territory but carried out considerable plundering and burned the monastery of Žiča. Milutin, angry, marched against Šišman and captured Vidin. Šišman fled across the Danube to his Nogaj overlords. Peace soon followed, and Šišman returned to Vidin. At times scholars have wondered why Milutin treated Šišman so mildly and did not annex his lands, as Dragutin had annexed Drman's and Kudelin's Braničevo. However, the reason seems clear enough; the Tatars were not pleased with Milutin's actions, so, to forestall a major Tatar attack, Milutin quickly came to terms with Šišman. Šišman regained the principality of Vidin, seemingly accepting Serbian suzerainty. Šišman also took the daughter of a high Serbian nobleman/official named Dragoš as his wife. Subsequently these bonds were strengthened when Šišman's son Michael married Milutin's daughter. This whole sequence of events concerning Vidin (except Michael's marriage) probably occurred in 1292.

However, Šišman's Nogaj overlords still were not happy with the turn of events, probably disliking both Milutin's impudence in attacking their vassal as well as his increased influence in what they saw as their sphere of influence. They threatened to attack Serbia. Milutin preserved the peace by sending the Nogajs many gifts and also his eldest son, Stefan Dečanski, as a hostage. Stefan remained at the Nogaj camp several years until 1299, when, as we shall see, the Golden Horde turned against the seceding Nogajs and destroyed them as a separate power; in the chaos that followed Dečanski escaped home.

Upon his return most scholars believe Milutin gave Dečanski Zeta as an appanage. Up to this point Dragutin's relations with Milutin appear to have been good, with Dragutin contributing to Milutin's expansion in Macedonia and Milutin to Dragutin's expansion along the Danube. However, now, in about 1299, relations between the two brothers became tense. If in fact Milutin had awarded Zeta to Dečanski, this award could explain the worsening of relations, for Dragutin may have seen Dečanski's receiving Zeta as a sign that Milutin intended Dečanski, and not Dragutin's son Vladislav, to succeed. Recently, however, on the basis of Ragusan documents that show Helen holding Zeta to 1306 and show Dubrovnik dealing with Dečanski there for the first time in 1309, Malović has argued that Dečanski was given Zeta only in late 1308 or 1309 in the course of the war between Dragutin and Milutin. Thus Malović argues that the assignment of Zeta to Dečanski should not be seen as a cause of that war.[2] If Malović is correct, the war's causes cease to be clear. But in any case and for whatever reason—though it presumably had something to do with the succession—relations between Dragutin and Milutin worsened.

As a result Milutin became more receptive to Byzantine peace feelers. For he clearly wanted his southern border secure from Byzantine attack in the event of a war with Dragutin. Andronicus II and Milutin reached agreement on where through Macedonia the Serbian-imperial border line should run, and the Byzantine emperor offered Milutin an imperial bride, his own sister Eudocia, the widow of the Emperor of Trebizon. Milutin, who was then divorced, or at least separated, from his third wife, Anna, the daughter of the former Bulgarian tsar George Terter, agreed. But Eudocia then absolutely refused to go to Serbia. Milutin, however, demanded, as a condition for the peace, that he receive a Byzantine princess as promised. The only available bride fitting the bill was Andronicus' five-year-old daughter Simonida. So, Andronicus offered her to Milutin. At this point the negotiations, already threatened by serious opposition in Serbia, acquired strong resistance from the Byzantine Church.

The Serbian nobles in Milutin's entourage, according to the Byzantine envoy Theodore Metohites, who made five trips back and forth between courts in the course of the peace discussions, opposed the treaty because they wanted to continue the war. They liked fighting, were in the habit of it, and wanted the booty from it. Metohites stresses their influence at Milutin's court and, throughout the negotiations, was afraid that they would prevail on King Milutin or else that he in the long run would not be able to overcome their opposition. The Byzantines, on the other hand, wanted peace, but the Byzantine Church felt the proposed marriage between Simonida and Milutin violated Church canons. Not only was she too young, but fourth marriages were completely forbidden by the Church, and she was about to become Milutin's fourth wife. The Byzantine court eventually overcame this objection with an elegant piece of sophistry. Since Milutin's first wife had been alive at the time he contracted marriages two and three, those two marriages were in fact not marriages at all. However, now in 1299, since by then wife number one had died, Simonida could go to Serbia and become the second wife of the lonely widower. This reasoning at least officially satisfied the Church, so the marriage was carried out and the peace concluded.

Milutin was allowed to keep much of the territory he had conquered during the previous seventeen years as her dowry. Thus Serbia received official recognition of its conquests in northern Macedonia, including Skopje, which had already become Milutin's main residence. The official border was drawn through the following fortified cities, which were all retained by the Byzantines: Strumica, Štip, Prosek, Prilep, and Ohrid. Since Byzantium is found holding Durazzo in 1301, presumably the Serbs restored it to the empire as part of the 1299 treaty. Thus Serbia had acquired considerable Macedonian territory. And, at peace, Milutin was now free to face whatever threat might develop from Dragutin.

Simonida and her entourage arrived in Serbia, and their presence, combined with Milutin's interest in making a policy-matter of it, brought about a great increase in the Byzantinization-Hellenization of the Serbian court. More Byzantine functional titles, as well as honorary ones, appeared, and various Serbian offices were re-named, as, for example, dijaks now became logo-thetes, etc. New Byzantine taxes were introduced, either bearing Greek names or literal Serbian translations of Byzantine terms. The manner of drawing up and issuing charters became even more like the Byzantine. This Byzantinization of the court was to remain in effect regardless of shifts in Serbian policy in the years to come, retained even when Serbia was at war with Byzantium. Hellenization in Serbia was furthered by the acquisition of Greek populations in the lands just annexed from the empire, and was to be further re-enforced by the conquest of additional Greek lands in the years ahead. In such annexed lands, most existing Byzantine institutions, customs, and laws were allowed to remain in force.

Also during the time of Milutin the pronoia system appeared in Serbia. By it sources of income, usually landed estates, were awarded for service (usually military). The new system was to exist side by side with the estab-lished family system of patrimonial estates held jointly by brothers. For despite the appearance of pronoias in Serbia, patrimonial estates remained common and still as late as the fifteenth century were, according to Naumov, to be the chief form of landholding.[3] In Serbia from the start pronoias were hereditary, with the inheritor retaining the original service obligation. How-ever, though Byzantine pronoias had started as being non-hereditary, revert-ing to the state for re-assignment at the death of their holders, by the early fourteenth century, they were more and more frequently becoming hereditary. Thus the Serbs probably simply took over the system as it existed at the time in Byzantium. The pronoia system was in existence in the Macedonian lands Milutin conquered from Byzantium. The first reference to a pronoia in Serbia, from 1299/1300, is to one near Skopje (village Rečica, province Polog), in territory recently conquered by Milutin. The estate had been a pronoia under Byzantium, and Milutin, according to Ostrogorsky's interpretation of the document, disposed of the estate in the same way. If Ostrogorsky is correct, then, Milutin seems to have simply continued the system in places where it existed. Then subsequently Milutin or his successors introduced the system into the lands of Serbia proper.

Naumov, however, questions Ostrogorsky's conclusions about the status of this estate under Milutin. He also points out that little can be said with certainty about Serbian pronoias before Stefan Dušan (1331–55). Why, he asks, did Serbia need pronoias? The Serbian nobility holding their patrimonial estates already owed military service. One might answer Naumov by suggest-ing that pronoias would have been assigned to others—newcomers, lesser nobles—to build up a more dependable service class. However, since such a policy cannot be documented, its creation can only be a matter for specula-tion. Naumov also points out that before Dušan we do not have references to pronoias in the old Serbian lands. Thus until the second quarter of the fourteenth century the few references to pronoias in Serbia all appear in lands recently acquired from Byzantium. On occasion, Naumov also believes, the term, when it appears in Serbian documents, does not even indicate a service estate. He argues that the Greek term was sometimes taken over by the Serbs to simply mean a "holding," as he believes was the case with the 1299/1300 "pronoia" in Rečica noted above. On other occasions, he admits, the term *pronoia* used in Serbian Macedonia may reflect the continuation under Serb rule of existing Byzantine land tenure relationships, with the Byzantine landholder being allowed to remain on his land on the same terms as before, but now owing loyalty and service to the Serbian ruler. Naumov emphasizes that we also do not know the tenure or status of the newly conquered Macedonian lands assigned by Milutin to his Serb followers. Though we cannot rule out the assignment of what had been Byzantine pronoias to Serbs on pronoia terms, it is quite possible that Milutin regularly assigned Serbs new lands in Macedonia as patrimonial estates. For we have no evidence that Milutin actually assigned pronoias to new people or distributed lands on these conditions. Moreover, we have, as noted, no evidence of pronoias in the older Serbian lands until Dušan's time. And even then, Naumov stresses, patrimonial estates continued to greatly outnumber pronoias. Thus, though Milutin may have assigned some new pronoias to Serbs, it cannot be proved.

Bulgaria at the End of the Thirteenth Century

The Byzantines had failed in their attempt to take over Bulgaria, ca. 1279. Their candidate John Asen III had panicked and Ivajlo had twice defeated their invading armies. Then, faced with the threat from Charles of Anjou, the empire had to take a less and less active role in Bulgarian affairs. But though the new tsar, George Terter, was spared Byzantine intervention, he found the Tatar problem greatly increased. In 1280 or 1281 Mangu Timur died, and Nogaj took advantage of the increased weakness at the center of the Golden Horde to make himself entirely independent. Thereafter there was nothing to prevent his intervention in Bulgaria whenever he chose. From ca. 1280 until Nogaj's demise in 1299, Bulgaria endured the period of greatest Tatar interference and plundering. For having become the most powerful figure in the Khanate of the Golden Horde, at times even its king-maker, Nogaj had no further serious worries about Steppe affairs and wars and thus could concentrate more on the Balkans. He asserted his suzerainty not only over Trnovo but also over Vidin, where in the early 1290s he is found as Šišman's overlord, and even, it seems, over the emerging principality of Braničevo under the brothers Drman and Kudelin.

George Terter, who emerged as tsar out of the chaos in late 1279, ruled a very weak state. Elected in Trnovo during a siege, he had no opportunity at first to extend his authority over any part of Bulgaria beyond Trnovo itself. When the Byzantines withdrew and Ivajlo in his turn did so too, only to be murdered at Nogaj's court, Terter found himself lacking power either to prevent Tatar raids or to retain his outlying provinces. Soon he held only the eastern part of Bulgaria, and not even all of that. For the Byzantines held what had been Bulgaria's lands along the Black Sea from Mesembria on south. Losses elsewhere were more extensive. The Byzantines had also taken western Thrace along the upper Marica. Various boyars, moreover, were breaking away to establish their own petty principalities; some of these were supported by the Nogajs. The two most important secessionist provinces were, as noted, Vidin and Braničevo. And with Nogaj asserting his protection over these two provinces, Terter was not free to try to regain control over them. It was evident that he had to reach an understanding with his powerful Tatar neighbor. This probably occurred in 1285 when, after a particularly devastating raid, he accepted Nogaj suzerainty and agreed to pay Nogaj tribute. In so doing he dropped his allegiance to the Khanate of the Golden Horde, to which Bulgaria had been tributary until then and which from the death of Berke in 1265 had been unable to protect Bulgaria from Nogaj. To seal his agreement with Nogaj, George Terter sent his daughter to become a wife in the harem of Nogaj's son Čaka. At the same time George Terter sent his son Theodore Svetoslav to Nogaj as a hostage. This young man, along with his mother, previously had had to live in Constantinople; they had been sent there when Terter, still a boyar, had been drawn into the Byzantine coalition and had accepted John Asen III's sister as his wife. When George Terter and Byzantium concluded peace in 1284, with Andronicus II recognizing George as ruler of Bulgaria and awarding him the court title of despot, his son had been returned to him. Now, within a year, the young man resumed his career as a hostage, this time at the Tatar court.

Terter's agreement with the Nogajs reduced the number of Tatar raids against Bulgaria, eliminating at least most of those under Nogaj control. These, of course, had been the major ones. However, peace with the Tatars and Byzantium still did not allow Terter to assert his authority over what remained of his state. In fact we soon learn of further secessionist principalities, though we cannot determine whether they emerged before or after 1285. In these cases, it seems, local boyars simply asserted their independence in their home regions. First the sources mention a boyar, Smilec, who asserted his independence in the region between Sredna Gora and the Balkan Mountains. His independence seems to have been supported by the Byzantines, which may be the reason George Terter seems to have taken no action to force him to obedience. Smilec's lands bordered on the territory the Byzantines had annexed from Bulgaria along the Black Sea. Furthermore, showing his close ties with the empire, Smilec married Emperor Andronicus' cousin, the daughter of Sebastocrator Constantine, a brother of Michael VIII. This marriage almost certainly occurred while Smilec was still a boyar, before he captured the Bulgarian throne. A second secessionist principality was established in the region west of Sliven (Kr"nska hora), between Sliven and Kopsis (or in modern terms, between Sliven and Kazanl"k or even Karlovo) under Terter's brother Eltimir. These were probably the family's lands. Thus perhaps George acquiesced or even supported the creation of this appanage. Unlike the other, it probably remained a true appanage, loyal to Trnovo and rendering its obligations. Thus his brother's rule, rather than being disruptive, probably served as a means to tie this more distant region to Trnovo.

In 1292, a year in which a major Tatar raid occurred, George Terter fled to Byzantium. And Smilec emerged as tsar. Since the sources report that the Byzantines hesitated to give him asylum for fear of antagonizing the Nogajs, it seems likely that the Nogajs effected this change. The existence of a Nogaj attack that year also supports this view. However, as Nikov has noted, there seems to have been no reason for the Nogajs to have taken this action. Terter seems to have been a loyal vassal, rendering his dues, with his son still a hostage at the Nogaj court. Could Terter have done something provocative we know nothing of? Though possible, this seems unlikely, for it is to be doubted that he would have dared to try any such thing. So, Nikov postulates that Terter was brought down by a boyar faction, which presumably had been intriguing against Terter at the Nogaj court and had in the end persuaded the Tatar chief to support its candidate.[4] Presumably Nogaj obtained something in return for his help, probably at least increased tribute. Thus since Nogaj troops most probably drove Terter from the country and installed Smilec, it is not surprising that Smilec is usually seen as puppet tsar for the Nogajs. The Byzantines accepted the change. Not only did they want to avoid a conflict with the Nogajs, but Smilec was also an imperial in-law. Eltimir fled from Bulgaria along with his brother George Terter, so we may suspect his appanage was re-absorbed by Trnovo. However, Smilec's principality in or near Sredna Gora remained in the hands of his two brothers Radoslav and Vojsil. Presumably he felt this a safe arrangement, tolerating it for the same reasons that Terter during his reign had tolerated the appanage of his brother Eltimir.

Throughout his reign Smilec maintained good relations with both Byzantines and Nogajs. He seems to have undertaken no foreign adventures and done nothing to aid Vidin in its above-mentioned difficulties with Milutin. Smilec died in 1298, and at once Trnovo again became a center of plots and violence. Smilec's widow, a Byzantine princess, tried to maintain power. Usually it is said she was acting for herself, but recently Božilov has demonstrated that she and Smilec did have a son.[5] Thus we can assume she was trying to hold the throne for his eventual succession. She clearly was under tremendous pressure, for Theodore Metohites, the Byzantine envoy then negotiating with Serbia to arrange the 1299 peace and the marriage of Milutin to a Byzantine princess, found his plans challenged by the Bulgarians. For on one of his five visits to Serbia, a delegation arrived from a recently widowed queen of Bulgaria, offering her own hand to Milutin. This was certainly Smilec's widow, seeking marriage with Milutin in order to obtain his armed support to bolster her tottering throne. As we saw, Milutin rejected this option and married the child Simonida to make peace with Byzantium. However, at some time Stefan Dečanski married the widow's (and Smilec's) daughter. Though scholars usually date that marriage later, a late date makes little sense, because the Smilec family had little significance after 1299. Malović is probably correct in dating Smilec's daughter's marriage (or at least betrothal) to Dečanski at this time, attributing the agreement to Milutin's desire to maintain good relations with the Bulgarians at a moment when he risked offending them by rejecting their queen's offer to become his wife. Smilec's widow briefly received support from an unexpected source. Eltimir, George Terter's brother who had fled into exile when Smilec seized the throne and had probably spent his exile with the Tatars, now returned. He soon concluded an alliance with the insecure widow, marrying one of her (and Smilec's) daughters. This marriage probably occurred in late 1298.

However, the force of events was stronger than the widowed queen. Since 1297 Nogaj had been at war with Tokta (Tokhta, Tokhtu, Tuqta'a) Khan, the new leader of the Golden Horde, who had in fact been installed by Nogaj. However, the two men had fallen out, and Tokta aimed now to restore the khanate to its former grandeur, which meant putting an end to Nogaj's separatism. At first the warfare had gone well for Nogaj, but by 1299 Tokta had defeated Nogaj in battle. Nogaj had been killed, and his following was dispersed over the Steppe. A large number of his men stuck by Nogaj's son Čaka, and they fled together across the Danube into Bulgaria from Tokta who was marching west to assert control over what had been Nogaj's lands.[6] With Čaka in this flight was his brother-in-law Theodore Svetoslav, the son of George Terter, sent to Nogaj as a hostage at the time his sister had married Čaka. Ambitious to acquire the Bulgarian throne and yet at the same time dependent on his companion Čaka, who controlled an army and was now seeking a new land to settle down in to rule, Theodore Svetoslav decided to be patient and to assume for the present the role of king-maker. He presumably also had a variety of scores to settle with those boyars who had supported Smilec. Thus he secretly negotiated with a number of boyars and, making rich bribes, organized a plot through which the gates of Trnovo were opened to Čaka and his army. Smilec's widow and her son fled, first to Eltimir in Kr"n, and then from there to Constantinople, where she was well received by her cousin, Emperor Andronicus. There her son assumed the Byzantine name, from his mother's family, of John Comnenus Ducas Angelus Branas Palaeologus and settled down as a Byzantine aristocrat. He was never to be advanced by Byzantium as a pretender for the Bulgarian throne and eventually became a monk, dying before 1330. Since he had briefly held the throne of Bulgaria, or at least it had been briefly held in his name, Božilov argues we should call him John IV Smilec.

Meanwhile in Trnovo, Čaka, the Tatar, took over as Tsar of Bulgaria. We may suspect he had little local popularity, and, because his troops were soon scattered around eastern Bulgaria, be it to assert control or to plunder, Theodore Svetoslav's position rapidly became stronger. He secretly forged ties with various powerful elements in Trnovo. Having organized their plans carefully, Theodore Svetoslav's conspirators then seized Čaka and threw him in jail, where he was duly strangled. The executioner, we are told, was a Jew.

The Patriarch of Trnovo, Joakim, was also executed, pitched over a cliff into the Jantra River in 1300. He was accused of treachery. It is not certain whom, if anyone, he was supporting. Possibly his treachery had occurred at the time Smilec overthrew George Terter.

Thus Theodore Svetoslav, son of George Terter, came to power in 1300. He quickly made peace with his uncle, Eltimir, who, restored to his Kr"n province through the help of Smilec's widow, was happy to change sides. He declared his support for his nephew and briefly contributed to his cause before settling down to an independent existence in his own province, allied to the Byzantines. Smilec's two brothers Radoslav and Vojsil, who had jointly ruled in Sredna Gora, fled to Byzantium for aid. Presumably they had been expelled by force, whether by Čaka's troops in 1299 or subsequently by Theodore Svetoslav's supporters. They received some help from the empire, and Radoslav marched into Bulgaria with Byzantine troops. His forces were met by Eltimir, who managed to capture and then blind Radoslav. Vojsil remained in Byzantium, urging further Byzantine action on behalf of his family.

Theodore Svetoslav found himself secure on his throne because the Nogajs no longer existed on his border to interfere. The Golden Horde, having wiped out the Nogajs, presumably had nothing against the Bulgarian ruler who had murdered the son of their enemy Nogaj. In fact Theodore Svetoslav seems to have immediately guaranteed himself on this front by submitting to Tokta. This freed his hands to face any Byzantine action that might follow and may even have gained him the military support of the Tatars. That he quickly submitted to the Golden Horde is confirmed by certain Eastern sources, one of which states that Theodore Svetoslav executed Čaka "by command of Tokta," suggesting Čaka had been held in prison by Theodore Svetoslav for a period before his execution was carried out. Possibly Tokta had been consulted in the interim. A second source reports Theodore Svetoslav sent Čaka's head to Tokta. Thus we may assume that Theodore Svetoslav at once negotiated an agreement with Tokta by which he submitted to him, presumably for tribute, and then enjoyed peaceful relations on that frontier.

The Horde not only did not interfere in Bulgaria, but it even seems to have supported Bulgaria's expansion. For Theodore Svetoslav was able, by 1314, to extend his rule over what is now southern Bessarabia as far as Akkerman (Cetatea Alba, formerly Maurocastron) on the Dnestr', territory that had formerly been under Nogaj. From these lands he was able to recruit many Tatars for his armies. Since this had been Nogaj territory, which we can assume had subsequently been taken over by Tokta, Nikov is probably right to suppose that Theodore Svetoslav received it as a grant from Tokta. It is hard to imagine Theodore seizing it and thereby risking war with the Tatars. Moreover, such grants were in keeping with Tokta's policy at the time. For Tokta was then making to certain of his leading followers various large grants, comprising former Nogaj territory he had occupied. If Nikov is correct that this Bessarabian territory was awarded to Theodore Svetoslav by Tokta,[7] then we can assume it was part of a negotiated settlement between the two leaders and can be taken as further evidence that Bulgaria had submitted again to the suzerainty of the Golden Horde.

Bulgaria does not seem to have retained this Bessarabian territory for long. Tokta Khan died in 1321 and was succeeded by Uzbek, who took greater interest in these western lands. Soon after, if not immediately upon, his succession he seems to have taken back the territory ceded to Bulgaria at the mouth of the Dnestr' as well as the lands between the Dnestr' and the Danube mouth that Bulgaria held. This threatened the Byzantine outpost at Vicina on the Danube mouth. And at some point, between 1332 and 1337, the Tatars occupied Vicina.

Since the Horde's overlordship in the fourteenth century was very loose, Bulgaria may well have gained more from the relationship than the Tatars. For it is likely that the Tatar troops obtained by the Bulgarians throughout much of the fourteenth century were worth more than the value of whatever tribute the Bulgarians paid to the khan. After the death of Uzbek Khan in 1342, the Khanate of the Golden Horde declined, and surely Bulgaria's vassal obligations soon disappeared. But this may well have been to Bulgaria's disadvantage, for at that time it could have used strong support from the Tatars to face the developing Ottoman threat.

In the period from 1300 Tatar raids did not cease entirely. But they were rarer and smaller in scale, aimed at plunder rather than political interference. The largest known raids occurred in 1319 against Bulgaria and Byzantine Thrace and in 1331 against Vidin.

The Byzantines were not happy with the turn of events in Bulgaria. After Radoslav's failure to install himself in power with the troops the empire gave him, the Byzantines made a second military effort against Bulgaria. On this occasion, their troops were sent on behalf of a new candidate, Michael, who was the son of Constantine Tih and Michael VIII's niece. This effort failed as well.

Theodore Svetoslav turned to rebuilding his shattered state, reincorporating the seceded areas he was able to subdue, like Sredna Gora, whose rulers had fled to Byzantium, and allying with the rulers of other semi-independent areas, such as his uncle Eltimir. He seems also to have asserted his authority over the independent-minded boyars of Trnovo. In any case the sources at least cease making references to boyar factions and intrigues for the duration of his reign.

Having achieved these successes, he was then able to turn to the Byzantine problem. Not only had the Byzantines been warring against him and trying to install others to rule Bulgaria, but they still held the Black Sea territory which Bulgaria believed to be its own. In 1304 he launched an attack into this area and defeated a Byzantine army. On this occasion he probably recovered Mesembria and Anchialos. If he did not acquire the two towns then, he must have done so in the following year. The Byzantines responded by attempting to woo Eltimir over as an ally, giving him a warm reception in

Constantinople. However, their efforts did not at this time detach him from his alliance with his nephew. The following year, 1305, Andronicus' son Michael IX, already crowned co-emperor, directed a new attack against Bulgaria. Smilec's brother Vojsil commanded one unit in it. After some smaller engagements, one of which was won by the Byzantines near Sozopolis, the Bulgarians won a victory that allowed them to break through Byzantine lines and plunder the region of Adrianople. Michael IX assembled with difficulty a new force which invaded the territory of Eltimir, who shut himself up in one of his fortresses; this event shows that he was still faithful to his nephew's cause. Soon thereafter Eltimir switched sides, possibly forced to do so by this Byzantine attack. As a result, when Theodore Svetoslav attacked Byzantium, probably late in 1305, he also overran the territory around Jambol that he had recently regained from Byzantium and had granted to Eltimir. Theodore Svetoslav took this territory back and also plundered Eltimir's original appanage.

The Byzantines, discouraged by the above-mentioned failures and weakened also by the Catalans (whom we shall discuss shortly), made peace with Theodore Svetoslav in 1307 and recognized his Black Sea conquests. Their agreement restored to Bulgaria not only the ports but also the whole hinterland west to the Tundža River that the Byzantines had taken before. It seems this territory had all been retaken by Theodore Svetoslav in 1304 or 1305, and the treaty simply recognized Bulgaria's ownership. Thus Bulgaria no longer had its border with Byzantium along the Tundža, but had recovered the whole region between that river and the Black Sea. Furthermore, as a result of the treaty Theodore Svetoslav acquired a wife; for shortly thereafter, probably in 1308, he married Theodora, the granddaughter of Andronicus II.

Through the ports he regained on the Black Sea, Theodore Svetoslav increased Bulgaria's foreign trade, particularly on Venetian and Genoese ships. Bulgaria chiefly exported agricultural products and imported luxury goods. Under Theodore Svetoslav Bulgarian coins, which had begun to be issued under John Asen II, came to be issued in far greater quantities, presumably necessitated by the increased trade with the Italians on the Black Sea.

Byzantium and Greece in the Early Fourteenth Century

The Byzantines, meanwhile, began to have serious difficulties with a new enemy appearing on their eastern border. In meeting the threat from the West by Charles of Anjou, Michael VIII had concentrated almost all his attention in that direction and had ignored a very serious situation developing in Anatolia. The Tataro-Mongol invasions, which hit Russia and then swept across Hungary, Serbia, and Bulgaria in 1241–42 and which had also at the time plundered eastern Anatolia, had driven many Turkish tribes out of Central Asia into Anatolia. These newcomers mingled with the Turks already settled there. And as matters continued to be unstable in Central Asia in the period that followed, many more Turks were to migrate into Anatolia, seeking grazing lands and booty, over the next half century. Since they tended to appear in relatively small groups with little or no central organization, Nicea had been able to hold its own against them. But then in 1261 Constantinople was recovered. Until that moment Anatolia had obviously enjoyed top priority for the Nicean/Byzantine state. But after the recovery of the capital, Europe rose to ever greater importance, particularly owing to the growing threat from Charles. As a result many soldiers were transferred from Anatolia to Europe. Thus soon after the 1261 conquest, the eastern frontier defenses, based on Vatatzes' military small-holdings, began to decline.

The empire's emphasis on Europe was a god-send to the Turks. By 1300 most of Anatolia was in the hands of one or another Turkish group. The Byzantines retained only certain fortified towns in that region. The Turks established there a number of small principalities or emirates. The most important one for the future lay in Bithynia, in northwestern Anatolia; it was ruled by a certain Osman whose followers came to be called the Osmanlis (or in English, the Ottomans). This emirate rapidly began to expand, bringing under its control a growing number of tribesmen in an ever widening area. As a result Anatolia, long the backbone of the empire for men, grain, and taxes, was lost forever. Soon the Osmanlis were to be threatening Europe.

Byzantium was in dire straits, faced on its frontiers by two enemies, the Osmanlis in the east and the Serbs in the west, each growing stronger and each already stronger than it was. It held only Constantinople, Thrace, and parts of Macedonia and of the Morea. And its Macedonian holdings were gradually being annexed by the Serbs. It differed from the other states in the Balkans only in prestige and pretensions.

Byzantium's aristocracy had suffered a brief setback under Vatatzes and Theodore II Lascaris. But under the Palaeologoi, a dynasty arising from the ranks of the high aristocracy and coming to power as a representative of aristocratic interests, the great nobility reasserted itself, converting its landed base into provincial rule. Supported by their own private armies, the great magnates became local governors of their own regions, acquiring ever increasing independence. More and more pronoia holders made their pronoias hereditary. Some even managed to convert these conditional holdings into patrimonial estates, severing the service obligation entirely. Having no state control over them to compel their loyalty and prevent secession, the emperor had to grant them an increasing number of privileges. These were awarded through immunity charters, many of which granted further tax exemptions freeing particular estates of various taxes or all estates of a particular tax. This led to a reduction of the state's income at a time when it needed cash desperately. It also meant that since budgetary needs were not reduced, the burden ever increasingly fell upon those least able to pay, the peasants. Borrowing from the rich to meet their tax bills or to keep their struggling farms functioning, more and more peasants found themselves being enserfed through foreclosure.

At the same time, with less cash available to pay salaries, the bureaucracy declined. More and more provincial functions were either not carried out or were executed by the local magnates. The shrinking of the bureaucracy as well as of the state armies, which earlier had garrisoned provincial cities, meant the state had ever fewer means to check the local actions of the magnates. To try to prevent these uncontrolled regions from breaking away, it came to be common practice to grant whole provinces as appanages to members of the dynasty, brothers and sons of the emperor; it was hoped they could assert authority over these regions and thereby keep them both loyal to the dynasty and part of the empire. This worked frequently, but at other times the princely governor became ambitious for the throne himself and used his province as a base for revolt, offering the local nobles greater privileges to support his efforts.

As the soldier-holdings declined again under the aristocratic emperors, Byzantium found itself relying not only on the private forces of the magnates but also increasingly on mercenaries. The empire's need for troops was enormous, but it lacked the cash to pay for as many mercenaries as it needed. In fact it lacked sufficient cash to pay for those already recruited. Thus mercenaries frequently deserted at key moments, sometimes even in the midst of battles and joined the enemy's forces. The size of the Byzantine army rapidly declined. It was all Andronicus II could do to maintain a standing army of two thousand men in Europe and one thousand in Asia. Small armies, it should be noted, were a general feature of the whole Balkans in the fourteenth century; battles were frequently fought by several hundred on each side. But this spelled disaster when a state was faced with a coalition or with the larger army of some outside invader. The Serbs, though seemingly strong, were not really a great power. They simply were able to mobilize larger and more effective small armies.

In this crisis, to face the Ottomans, the Byzantines in 1303 hired as mercenaries a corps of sixty-five hundred unemployed Catalans. Sent to Anatolia against the Ottomans, they did very well when they put their minds to their work. They even defeated the Ottomans in a couple of engagements. But soon they lost interest in the task for which they had been hired and went off plundering. Since their pay was in arrears, their behavior is understandable. Accusations of bad faith and breach of contract were made with some justification by both Catalans and Byzantines. To try to force payment and extract more the Catalans stepped up their looting. They soon crossed back to Europe and began recouping their debts from Byzantine territory there. As they plundered Byzantine Thrace, word of their successes reached colleagues back West and further Catalans came to join them. To settle matters the Byzantines tried to single out three thousand of them to pay and retain, while dismissing the rest. But all the Catalans were determined to stay, and, as group solidarity was strong, it was impossible for the Byzantines to split them up in that way. By then the Catalans were divided into three major companies, each out for itself, but none of which was willing to submit to the Byzantines at the expense of the other two; thus all three remained ready to come together to defend Catalan interests against the Byzantines.

The Byzantines then, probably in 1306, turned to deceit. Michael IX invited a group of Catalans and their leader, Roger de Flor, to a dinner under a safe conduct. At the dinner Roger was murdered by the captain of Michael's Alan mercenaries, whose son had previously been killed by the Catalans. Roger's escort of three hundred was then massacred. Since no effort was made by the Byzantines to punish the Alans, the Catalans held the Byzantines responsible. The infuriated Catalans plundered Thrace again for revenge and pleasure. An army led against them by the co-emperor and heir, Michael IX, was easily defeated and Michael was wounded. For the next two years they devastated the countryside of Thrace, plundering, taking and burning lesser towns and villages, chopping down orchards, and carting off captives to Gallipoli, which they had taken and made into a great slave market. They even sacked Mount Athos. In 1308 they tried to take Thessaloniki but failed. The Byzantines by then had occupied a major mountain pass between Kavalla and Philippi. So after their failure against Thessaloniki, instead of attempting to fight their way back to Thrace, the Catalans moved off into Thessaly. Soon they hired themselves out to Charles of Valois, to whom we shall turn in a moment. Their success with such small forces well illustrates the weakness of the Byzantine empire at the time. Their early successes against the Turks in Anatolia also show that as late as 1303 the Ottomans had not yet become a major power. Thus a relatively small but disciplined force, had there been one to make the concentrated effort, might still in the first decade of the fourteenth century have defeated them and restored imperial rule to western Anatolia.

Meanwhile a new scheme, similar to Charles of Anjou's, was drawn up to restore Latin rule over the Byzantine Empire. Its author and leader was Charles of Valois. Having married a lady descended from Baldwin II, he had in Western eyes acquired the rights to "Romania" (the empire). He began building a coalition of allies. In 1306 he obtained Venice's support, and in 1308 he obtained (but probably, as we shall see, only nominally) the backing of Milutin of Serbia. And, of more potential significance, in that year the Catalans also agreed to join him. The pope, still ambitious to reunite the Churches, also endorsed the venture. In 1308 Charles landed in western Greece. But the Catalans almost immediately deserted him to go off plundering on their own. They lived off the land for a year, then entered the service of the Duke of Athens, served him for about a year, and then, defeating him in battle, seized control of Athens and established a duchy under their own control lasting from 1311 to 1388. Again their success illustrates the weakness of military forces in the Balkans. In 1309 Charles' wife, the basis of his claims to "Romania," died. By then his coalition was deteriorating. The Catalans, who had been his chief muscle, had departed southward. The Serbs, who probably never were serious in their support of Charles, never did give him any aid. And Venice, which had done little to assist his cause, now, seeing that matters were becoming hopeless, concluded an alliance, for lucrative privileges, with Byzantium in 1310. Thus Charles' threat evaporated away entirely.

Meanwhile, from their base in Mistra the Byzantines had gradually been expanding their rule in the Morea against the governors sent out by the Anjous. Finally in 1289 Charles II of Anjou (his father, Byzantium's nemesis Charles I, having died in 1285), to better defend the province against further losses, decided to allow William Villehardouin's daughter Isabelle to return to the Morea. By then she had married a Belgian nobleman named Florent. Florent was appointed bailiff, and subsequently Charles endowed him with Villehardouin's former title, Prince of Achaea. This prince of course recognized Charles' suzerainty. It was also specified that if Isabelle became a widow and was still without male heir, she could not remarry without the consent of the Angevin King of Naples. To secure his lands, Florent in the year of his arrival, 1289 or 1290, concluded a seven-year truce with the Byzantines of Mistra. This allowed for both the economic recovery of the whole peninsula and increased trade. Many of the local Greeks, particularly those who possessed lands in both realms—in Frankish Greece and in the area recovered by Byzantium—appreciated the peace. The Byzantine emperor was also happy to conclude the armistice, for it allowed him, as we shall see, to devote his attention to affairs in Thessaly and Epirus.

Florent was a fair, efficient, and popular prince, and matters prospered in his and Isabelle's realm until his death in 1297. He was able to maintain peace, on the whole, with Byzantium despite the face that on one occasion he did send aid to Epirus against Byzantium. After her husband's death, Isabelle continued to govern her father's and her husband's state until 1301 when she decided to marry Philip of Savoy. Charles II violently disapproved of this marriage, for he felt that by it his family would lose its role in the Morea. By this time Charles had officially assigned suzerainty over Achaea to his second son Philip of Taranto (Tarentum). However, the pope approved Isabelle's marriage, and Charles, though he fumed, did nothing to stop it. Philip of Savoy arrived in Achaea, and it was apparent from the start that Isabelle had made a poor choice of husband. He ignored existing policy and his wife's advice and, supported by a retinue of Piedmont adventurers, set out to enrich himself. He soon clashed with the Morean establishment, including the Frankish families. He ruled there for four-and-a-half years, surrounded by scandals, extorting wealth from the locals, selling offices and fiefs, and skirmishing with local Greeks and any others who opposed him. He also increased taxes and revoked various exemptions and privileges granted to the local Greeks and to the Slavs of Skorta, causing them to revolt. The rebels acquired some help from the Byzantine garrison at Mistra, but the aid was insufficient and Philip put the revolt down with great brutality, devastating both Greek and Slavic villages. He then confiscated the lands of the rebels.

Meanwhile the Byzantines under Andronicus II were exerting greater influence in and bettering relations with northern Greece, which had remained independent and divided between the two sons of Michael II of Epirus, John in Thessaly and Nicephorus in Epirus. The great enmity between Thessaly and the empire had decreased after Andronicus officially dropped the policy of Church Union. In Epirus Nicephorus, rather a passive figure, was dominated by his wife Anna, a niece of Michael VIII and leader of a pro-Byzantine party in Epirus. After the Churches in Constantinople and Epirus had made peace, Anna visited her cousin Andronicus II in Constantinople, where she was drawn into a plot against John of Thessaly. The Byzantines of course hoped the plot would contribute to the elimination of his dynasty, enabling them eventually to acquire the rich province of Thessaly. Weakening John would also have benefited Anna and Nicephorus, if there was truth in the story given that John had ambitions toward Epirus. And we find hints in the sources that John had actually carried out hostilities against the territory of Epirus, including an attack upon Jannina. In any case, both Andronicus and Anna saw John's son Michael as a disruptive element and agreed on a scheme to kidnap him. In 1283 or 1284 Anna and Nicephorus offered their daughter to Michael as part of a plan to unite Greece. Michael took the bait, came at once to Epirus, was kidnapped, and sent to Constantinople where he languished many years in jail, until he finally died. The Byzantines then sent troops against Thessaly to finish the job; the campaign was a fiasco, however, and an epidemic of malaria wiped out most of the invading army.

In the following year, 1284 or 1285, John of Thessaly, too weak to attack Byzantium, gave vent to his anger by attacking Epirus, concentrating on Arta and its environs. His troops did considerable damage but then withdrew. Thus his invasion appears to have been a punitive raid; no permanent annexation of territory seems to have been planned. Though presumably relations between Epirus and Thessaly remained strained and though some further border skirmishes or raids may have followed, no further major confrontations occurred between John and the Epirotes. This may be owing to the fact that John died soon thereafter. Though no source gives the date of his death and though scholars have often given it as 1296, a monastic charter from March 1289 already refers to John as being deceased. At whatever point prior to March 1289 he died, he was succeeded by his son Constantine. Constantine's younger brother Theodore shared in the rule. In what way— whether holding his own appanage or managing the whole province jointly with his brother—is not known. In the years that followed they seem to have acted in common and we have no evidence of any quarreling between them.

On their accession John's widow, the young rulers' mother, was worried that an outside attack might oust them from their rule. So she at once sought an agreement with Byzantium, willingly accepting Byzantine suzerainty and obtaining thereby recognition of her sons' rule and security from Byzantine attack. By the treaty both sons received the title sebastocrator. Their father, John, at some time had also concluded a similar treaty with Byzantium and had received the same title. The vassal relationship between Thessaly and empire was to remain nominal, for, like their father, the sons soon asserted their independence and from then on acted freely without consultation with Constantinople. The sources do not tell us why the Byzantines accepted this agreement; for one might have expected them to take advantage of the situation to attempt the annexation of Thessaly.

Anna of Epirus, already involved with Byzantium and threatened by Thessaly, hoped to make Epirus' ties with Byzantium even closer by marrying her daughter Tamara to Andronicus' son and heir Michael. But these plans, which might have led to the union of Epirus with Byzantium after Nicephorus' death, as was proposed, did not materialize owing to the Patriarch of Constantinople's objections that the proposed couple were too closely related. Nicephorus' and Anna's only son and heir, Thomas, was compensated by receiving from Andronicus the title despot. Thomas, at this time (about 1290), was probably less than five years old.

Meanwhile, the anti-Byzantine faction in Epirus, alarmed by Anna's policy which they feared would lead to Byzantium's annexing Epirus, suggested that Tamara, unable to marry the Byzantine heir, should marry Philip of Taranto, the second son of Charles II of Anjou. Though Anna opposed it, Nicephorus was persuaded and negotiations with the Angevins were begun in 1291.

The Byzantines, until then allied to Epirus, were upset by these negotiations and launched an attack against Epirus that successfully occupied much of northern Epirus and laid siege to Jannina. At this point Epirus requested and obtained support from Charles II's and Philip's loyal vassal Florent of Achaea. Richard Orsini, Count of Cephalonia, also sent aid. The Count of Cephalonia was rewarded with Anna and Nicephorus' daughter Maria, who became the bride of his son and heir John Orsini. This marks the beginning of the Orsini family's involvement in the affairs of Epirus. Florent's and Richard's help in 1292 or 1293 contributed not only to preventing the Byzantines from penetrating further into Epirus but also in expelling them from Jannina and most, if not all, the parts of Epirus they had occupied. Then, with the warfare over, negotiations for Tamara's marriage were renewed with the Angevins.

After it was agreed that Philip of Taranto and Tamara, rather than Thomas, would inherit Epirus, and that Philip would respect the Orthodox faith of Tamara and of his Epirote subjects, the agreement, which had been urged by the anti-Byzantine faction at Arta, was concluded. And Epirus accepted Angevin suzerainty. The wedding took place in August 1294. Philip at once received four fortresses from Epirus, including Vonitsa, Vrachova (which Nicol identifies as Eulochos near modern Agrinion), Angelokastron, and the very important one of Naupaktos, as Tamara's dowry. Charles II of Anjou then granted to his son Philip the rights he had inherited from his own father, Charles I, to the Latin Empire and to Greece; these rights included suzerainty over the principality of Achaea, which Charles II had until then exercised himself. Charles also awarded to Philip the island of Corfu and the one remaining Angevin city on the Albanian mainland, Butrinti. The countryside between the four Angevin forts in the south of Epirus was also granted to Philip, who soon assigned much of it as fiefs to his supporters. As could be expected, this caused tensions between indigenous Greek landlords and the new Latin fief-holders.

Thessaly saw in these events an opportunity both to avenge Anna's kidnapping of Michael and to expand. Thessaly launched an attack against Epirus in the spring of 1295. The Thessalians struck at two fortresses belonging, as a result of Tamara's dowry, to Philip of Taranto, Angelokastron and Naupaktos. They also attacked Acheloos. If Acheloos is a misnaming of Vrachova, a possibility Nicol suggests, then it too was Philip's; otherwise it belonged to Nicephorus. The three fortresses had insufficient garrisons and fell to the invaders. The Thessalians presumably also took other towns belonging to Epirus itself. For we have no reason to believe they directed their efforts particularly at Philip's holdings unless they seem to have been more weakly held or Thessaly had particularly objected to the Angevins' acquiring a foothold on the mainland. The Thessalians thus occupied part of Epirus, and our limited information suggests they concentrated their attack on the southern part of the region. But they were unable to retain their gains. Ferjančić speculates that they feared a Byzantine attack against Thessaly from the east should they prolong their absence.

A peace was concluded in the summer of 1296, by which most of the taken fortresses were restored to their pre-war holders. Angelokastron, however, was restored to the Angevins only after a second skirmish in 1301. Thus by 1301 the Angevins had regained all Tamara's dowry. Shortly after the 1296 peace, between 3 September 1296 and 25 July 1298, Nicephorus died. His widow Anna took over as regent. Nicol has persuasively argued against attempts to advance the date of Nicephorus' death.[8] Soon after the 1301 skirmish and agreement (Ferjančić suggests in 1302), Thessaly attacked Epirus again. The course of the campaign and its results are unknown. In the fighting of 1301 and 1302 the local Angevin governor of Naupaktos and Vonitsa aided Anna. Though we know of only these two attacks on Epirus by Thessaly, possibly other small incidents occurred. Furthermore, tensions and expectations of new attacks remained. Thus the regent Anna suffered from considerable insecurity. But she managed to hold her own, possibly once again receiving help from Florent of Achaea during this period. Finally after Florent's death she reached the conclusion that it made more sense to follow her own preferences and rely on the empire. So in 1304 she turned back to Andronicus II to secure his aid in restraining Thessaly. She suggested a marriage between her son Thomas, the titular ruler of Epirus, and Anna Palaeologina, the daughter of Michael IX. The Byzantines were receptive and eventually the marriage took place. The marriage is usually dated to 1313, but Nicol redates it to 1307.

Meanwhile in Thessaly Constantine died in 1303. His brother Theodore had pre-deceased him, probably a year or so earlier. Constantine's heir John II was a minor. The nobles of Thessaly convoked a council at which they agreed to seek support from Athens.

In Athens, after William de la Roche's death in 1290, his widow Helen, daughter of John of Thessaly, had become regent for their minor son Guy II. As such she had maintained friendly relations with Thessaly. Guy came of age in 1294 and his suzerain, Charles II of Anjou, ordered him to submit to the Prince of Achaea, Florent. Helen, as regent, had long resisted this submission, but Guy acquiesced in it. Soon thereafter, in 1299, Isabelle Villehardouin, who at that moment was ruling Achaea in her own right, engaged her daughter Matilda to Guy. Under Guy's rule, the Duchy of Athens, still including Attica, Boeotia, and the northeastern corner of the Peloponnesus, probably reached its height. After Constantine's death in 1303, Guy soon took advantage of the role the nobles of Thessaly gave him to assert his influence over Thessaly. For having taken an oath to respect the rights of the heir and the nobility of Thessaly, Guy was invited by the nobles to become the guardian of Constantine's son, the infant John II. The Thessalians expected this arrangement to last until John reached his majority. Guy established a semi-protectorate over Thessaly, appointing one of his barons to be bailiff of Thessaly. The Thessalian nobles had made a sensible decision, for almost at once Anna of Epirus, angry at Thessaly's attacks on Epirus and thinking the time ideal for revenge, had attacked Thessaly and taken Phanarion (Fanari). Guy, with his own men and with the barons of Thessaly whom he mobilized, marched against the Epirotes and drove them out of Thessaly.

Guy of Athens was a very powerful prince in this own domain, far more autocratic a ruler than the Prince of Achaea, who had to rule with the consent of his council composed of the great barons. Compared to the barons of Achaea, Guy's vassals were nobles of relatively low rank. Thus Guy was less obliged to consult them. Moreover, the landed base, the fiefs, of the Athenian nobles was less extensive than that of the Morean barons. In fact, many of the Athenian fiefs were held by Guy's own relatives, and Guy himself held a far greater portion of the land in his duchy than did the Prince of Achaea in his. Furthermore much of the Athenian duchy was not assigned as fiefs at all, but was left in the hands of tax-paying Greeks; their taxes were partly used to hire mercenaries, whose presence made the Duke of Athens less dependent on the feudal knights and their demands. It also happened that in the duchy much of the land nearest the major towns had been left to the Greeks, while many of the fiefs had been assigned in more distant places; this further reduced the influence of the fief-holders on state policy. Moreover, though the Greeks were important in paying taxes and in holding land that might otherwise have fallen to knights, they did not become major actors in Athens. For the leading Greeks tended not to be landlords but clerks and merchants. As such they had a much smaller role in the Athenian duchy than did the Greeks in the Achaean state. Not only did Guy maintain a firm hand on the administration of his state, but he also was blessed with a prosperous region possessed of a strong economic base. Under his rule trade and industry flourished in the duchy.

In 1302 Charles II of Anjou named his son Philip of Taranto to directly rule Achaea. Thus he sought to oust the unpopular and ambitious Philip of Savoy and to replace indirect Angevin rule, through Savoy and Isabelle under the suzerainty of Philip of Taranto, with direct rule by his son. Despite the appointment, however, Philip of Savoy remained in the Morea, and Philip of Taranto for the time being made no attempt to go there. At the same time, in 1304, Charles, annoyed at Anna of Epirus' new negotiations with Byzantium and seeking to increase his son's power base, called on Anna to fulfill her agreement and allow Philip and Tamara to take over the rule of Epirus. For, he claimed, they, rather than Anna as regent for Thomas, should have received Epirus upon Nicephorus' death. Anna refused, claiming the Angevins had broken their agreements with her; she accused them of not respecting Tamara's Orthodox faith and putting pressure on her to accept Catholicism. Expecting further trouble, she immediately sought Byzantine help.

In 1304 Charles II sent troops against Epirus; they were repulsed. The Epirotes then seem to have gone on to the offensive against the Angevin possessions on the mainland. For Nicol argues that in the fall of 1304 or in 1305 they took Naupaktos, Vonitsa, and the port of Butrinti in the north. But though unsuccessful on the Epirote front, the Angevins had more success against Epirus' Byzantine allies. For in 1304 Philip of Taranto had possession of Durazzo, where he is found confirming the privileges of various Albanian nobles.[9] Philip still had Durazzo in 1306. Still ambitious for Epirus, Charles in 1305 called on Philip of Savoy, who had aided the previous year's unsuccessful attack, to help in a new campaign for Epirus. Knowing Charles was trying to force him out of the Morea, Philip of Savoy felt it would be ridiculous for him to absent himself from the principality he wanted to retain. Thus he refused to help. His refusal was made more pleasant by the bribes he received from Anna of Epirus to stay neutral and remain in the Morea.

This refusal was the last straw for Charles II, who now demanded that Philip of Savoy immediately leave the Morea and turn the peninsula over to Charles' son Philip of Taranto. Charles stated he had never agreed to Philip of Savoy's marriage to Isabelle (an agreement she had been bound to obtain). And marriage to Isabelle, of course, was the basis for Philip of Savoy's rule, because he had entered the Morea as her husband and not by Angevin appointment. Philip of Savoy began trying to mobilize local support, but, having already acquired too many enemies, he had little success. So after Charles rejected their final appeals and protests, Philip of Savoy and Isabelle departed from the Morea for good; they soon separated from each other. And Philip of Taranto in 1307 arrived to take over his new position as Prince of Achaea.

In the interim, in 1306, Philip of Taranto had launched a second attack against Epirus. Thomas and Anna were able to bring the fighting to a close by restoring to Philip two of the fortresses that had been granted to him in 1294,

Naupaktos and Vonitsa, as well as Butrinti. Since the Angevins still possessed the first two forts in summer 1304, Nicol plausibly argues that Thomas had taken them after that date. Thus the 1306 agreement restored the pre-war territorial status quo. The Angevins still had possession of at least Vonitsa in 1314. Soon thereafter, either late in that decade or early in the 1320s, Vonitsa was again in the hands of Epirus.

In the interim the Epirotes strengthened their ties with the empire; they shared a common border north of Jannina, and the empire controlled most of the major fortresses in southern and central Albania, including Berat, Spina-rizza, Kanina, and Valona. As noted, Despot Thomas married the Emperor Andronicus II's granddaughter, probably in 1307. Relations between the two states continued smoothly for the next few years until a conflict broke out between Epirus and the Byzantine commander in southern Albania. The causes for the clash are unknown. As a result Byzantine forces carried out a major plundering raid against Epirus in 1315 that penetrated as far south as Arta, which was plundered. Thomas objected and within a year had been declared a rebel by Emperor Andronicus II. In response, Thomas imprisoned his Byzantine wife. Thomas soon, in early 1318, turned to Philip of Taranto for help; but before he could re-orient Epirus' policy toward the Angevins again, Thomas was murdered—an event to which we shall return shortly.

Upon his arrival in the Morea in 1307 Philip of Taranto received homage from the locals, carried out a brief campaign against the Byzantines of Mistra that gained him a couple of fortresses, and tried to launch another attack on Epirus, which failed. He then lost interest in Greece and soon returned to Italy. The principality of Achaea, managed by bailiffs under his suzerainty, declined, and the Byzantines quickly regained the forts that Philip of Taranto had taken from them. The Byzantines then began a policy of steady and gradual expansion in that region. By 1316 they probably had in their hands half of the Peloponnesus. Their expansion was facilitated by the acceptance of imperial suzerainty by many Frankish lords who, when threatened by Byzantine forces, quickly submitted in order to retain their possessions. As the empire restored its rule over former Frankish territory, it re-established the Orthodox hierarchy under the direction of the Metropolitan of Monemvasia.

Meanwhile, in 1309 Philip repudiated his wife Tamara for adultery. She was thrown into prison, where soon thereafter she died. Philip, now free, in 1313 married Catherine of Valois, the titular Empress of the Latin Empire. She had been engaged at the time to the Duke of Burgundy, who was quite vexed at her marriage. To console the family Philip arranged a marriage, probably also in 1313, between the duke's brother Louis and Matilda, the daughter of Isabelle Villehardouin and Florent. Matilda was the widow of Guy II of Athens. And Philip graciously bestowed the Morea upon Louis. To obtain his new lands, Louis had to put down, with the help of the Greeks of Mistra, an attempted take-over of the Morea by Frederick of Majorca, the son-in-law of Matilda's aunt Margaret Villehardouin. Frederick had landed at Clarenza (Glarentza) and established a foothold on the peninsula, but he was killed in a battle there against Louis in the summer of 1316, ending that rival claim. But a month after Louis' victory, Louis too died, possibly, if rumor was accurate, the victim of a plot organized by the Orsinis of Cephalonia. For the Count of Cephalonia had been administering the Achaea as the Angevin bailiff and seems to have been unhappy at being replaced by Louis. The utilization of the Count of Cephalonia to administer the principality made sense since the island of Cephalonia lay right off Achaea's coast.

Matilda, by then in the Morea, found herself in possession of the principality; but she had only a life-interest, since succession to the principality belonged now to Burgundy, under the suzerainty of Philip of Taranto. Philip by this time wanted to revoke the right to hold Achaea that he had granted to the House of Burgundy. He decided to achieve this by marrying Matilda to his own younger brother John, Count of Gravina. So Philip next ordered Matilda to marry John. She refused, and in 1318 Philip expelled her from the Morea and appointed John to rule the principality under Philip's continued suzerainty. One story, probably apocryphal, claims that Matilda was dragged to a marriage ceremony with John by force and then jailed. In 1320 Eudes of Burgundy sold his family's rights to Achaea back to Philip of Taranto. Having failed to take Mistra in 1325, John of Gravina returned to Italy. By then John was under pressure to give up the Morea from Philip's wife, Catherine of Valois, who wanted to grant the principality of Achaea to her son by Philip, Robert of Taranto. Eventually, in 1332, John sold Achaea to Robert and in exchange was granted Durazzo by Catherine. But before his departure from the Morea John had introduced a new actor into the peninsula. For his attack on Mistra had been expensive, and to carry it out John had been forced to borrow money from the Florentine banking family of Acciajuoli (Acciaiuoli). Lacking the cash to repay the Florentines, before his departure he had had to grant the Florentine bankers some forts in the northwestern Morea that he had offered as security at the time he contracted his loan.

In 1308 Guy II of Athens had died, probably of cancer. He had no son. His first cousin Walter of Brienne (Gauthier de Brienne), whose mother had been the sister of Guy's father William, succeeded him. Walter had lived in Naples until then and was ignorant of local conditions. He was faced at once with two major problems. First, the Catalans, who had swept into Thessaly and had been plundering it during the period 1306–09 were now poised on the border of Athens. Second, in Thessaly Constantine's son John II, by now of age, wanted to assert his own rule at home. Walter did not want this and hoped to retain Athens' role as Thessaly's protector. To try to achieve his independence, which he saw Athens did not want to allow him, John seems to have turned to Byzantium for aid, accepting Byzantine suzerainty and taking as his bride Irene, an illegitimate daughter of Andronicus II. Though it is usually dated to this time, as we shall see, Ferjančić dates John's turning to Byzantium a few years later. In any case, John II declared his independence from Athens. To assert his authority over Thessaly, Walter now concluded an agreement with the Catalans by which he hired thirty-five hundred cavalrymen and three thousand infantrymen. They stepped up their ravages of Thessaly in 1310 and occupied a series of forts (Lamia, Domokos, Almiros, Demetriada [Demetrias], and thirty small forts), which, however, they garrisoned themselves and refused to turn over to Walter.

Walter realized that he was creating a major problem for himself. To solve it he decided to retain only five hundred Catalans to be his own guard, and to dismiss the rest. The Catalans refused dismissal and also announced that they would retain the castles they had taken in Thessaly. They stated they would be willing to hold these castles under his overlordship, but they would not yield a single one until he supplied their back pay. The Catalans at the time were concentrated on Walter's border and probably did not respect that border any more than they respected other borders they came across. Seeing the mounting danger, Walter decided to drive them out. But before he could act, in the winter of 1310–11, five thousand Catalans crossed into Walter's duchy and occupied part of Boeotia.

Walter marched out to meet them. But the Catalans had had time to entrench themselves in a defensive position of their choice before his arrival. Thus the Catalans selected both the battlefield and their placement on it and had chosen these key matters to suit their own tactics. The two armies met on the banks of the Kephissos River in March 1311; Walter's heavily armored knights fell into the prepared trap and were driven into a swamp created by the Catalans. The knights found themselves completely unable to maneuver. Walter was killed and the majority of his knights perished as well. As a result much of the upper class of the duchy was wiped out. The Catalans then took over Athens and the rest of the duchy, establishing their own rule. They divided up the fiefs of the slain, in many cases marrying the widows of the defeated knights. By taking possession of the scattered strongholds throughout the duchy, they made themselves into local strongmen. To make matters seem more respectable they sought a reputable outside suzerain, choosing one who would not interfere greatly with their activities, Frederick, the Aragonese King of Sicily. Frederick accepted, naming one of his sons the titular Duke of Athens. Thereafter he sent a vicar general to the duchy to oversee the Catalans.

The Catalans continued to plunder the lands of the duchy's neighbors. They also frequently squabbled amongst themselves. However, they were always ready to conclude truces on the spur of the moment and unite at times of danger to themselves, thereby preventing their own ouster from Athens. But, in time, as they settled down, they became less bellicose, and by the second generation the Catalans of Athens were clearly less war-like and less successful in battle than their fathers, the conquerors of the duchy, had been. The Athens they acquired seems still to have been prosperous. The historian of their order, Mutaner, speaks of the duchy's fertile land, possessing olives, almonds, fig trees, and vineyards, well watered by aqueducts and cisterns. Mutaner also mentions the existence of active commerce, particularly in textiles.

Walter's demise liberated John II of Thessaly from the control of Athens, but his province still suffered from the plundering of the Catalans; in addition, the Catalans still occupied various of his fortresses in southern Thessaly. At the same time, within his province the Thessalian magnates were increasing their already vast estates, coming more and more to dominate local government and making themselves more and more independent of the so-called central government of Thessaly. Some of these magnates had even entered into relations with Constantinople, which gave the Byzantines a foot in the door, if and when they should move against Thessaly. In fact, the nobles had asserted themselves to such an extent that in much of Thessaly John's authority was non-existent. Thus John's Thessaly was hardly what one would call a coherent state. Ferjančić believes it was at this point, after 1311 and probably nearer to 1315, that John, faced with this deteriorating situation, turned to Byzantium for aid, recognizing imperial suzerainty and marrying the Byzantine princess Irene. And the Byzantines, it seems, did give John some military help against the Catalans after 1311.

In 1318 John II of Thessaly died without an heir. At his death, Gregoras reports, some of the towns of Thessaly submitted to Andronicus II, some were conquered by the Catalans, and others fell under the control of their own nobility. The Catalans, led by their new (since 1317) Vicar General Alphonso Frederick (Fadrique), the illegitimate son of King Frederick II of Sicily, quickly penetrated further into southern Thessaly, adding to the fortresses they already held in that region. Their expansion in southern Thessaly was carried out over several years, between 1318 and 1325. We know they took Neopatras (in 1319), Lamia, Lidoriki, Siderokastron, Vitrinitsa, Domokos, Gardiki, and Pharsalos. The last three seem to have been held only briefly since they do not appear on lists of subsequent Catalan possessions. The Catalans divided their holdings in southern Thessaly into five communes, each under a captain. Part of this region also became the feudal domain of Alphonso Frederick, whose heirs settled down as feudal lords in the duchy. His domain was centered around six fortresses: the isle of Aegina, Salona (Amphissa), Lidoriki, Vitrinitsa, Lamia, and on Euboea, Karystos.

Euboea, conquered by Licario for Byzantium in the late 1270s, had not long remained Byzantine. The Lombard barons were not happy with the loss of their fiefs and the Venetians were also upset by Byzantine gains on Euboea and on other Aegean islands. Licario disappears from the sources in about 1280. In about 1281 Klisura on Euboea was surrendered to the Lombards by treachery. A series of other forts were recovered by the Lombards during the next fourteen years, most of them probably by 1285. However, the Byzantines retained a number of Euboean forts including Karystos, Larmena, and Metropyle until 1296. In that year Boniface of Verona, a younger son and relative of one of the original families of triarchs, decided to win a principality for himself. A favored knight of Guy of Athens, Boniface, through Guy's good offices, had married a noble Lombard lady named Agnes, who was the heiress to Karystos. Determined to obtain his wife's inheritance, Boniface launched a campaign that captured Karystos in 1296. He also captured various other forts on Euboea, which he kept even though they were not part of her inheritance; presumably he was allowed to retain them as fiefs from the relevant triarchs who held title to them. By the end of 1296 he had expelled the Byzantines entirely from Euboea and made himself into the most powerful figure on the island. His gains were facilitated by the fact that title to much of the island at the time was in the hands of women, for the triarchs (including some who could more accurately be called hexarchs) of the previous generation had all died without sons, leaving their holdings (or title to holdings) to daughters.

The Venetians were also able to strengthen their position on the island. They had aided the Lombards in their Euboean recoveries in the early 1280s and had asserted from the start suzerainty over these restored triarchs. The Venetians had also purchased various castles from their vassals and thus come to actually hold a larger part of the island than they had previously. Boniface was not happy with the Venetian presence and entered into relations with the roving Catalans. Despite these ties, however, he and the other triarchs supported Walter of Brienne at the Battle of Kephissos. Boniface and two triarchs were captured in the battle; but whereas the two triarchs were executed by the Catalan victors, the Catalans spared Boniface. He seems to have concluded some sort of agreement at the time with his captors; one may presume they agreed to work jointly to oust the Venetians from Euboea and to install Boniface as Duke of Euboea under Catalan suzerainty. Such an agreement would have benefited the Catalans, surrounded by hostile states and barons, as much as it would have served Boniface. Venice seems to have expected trouble from Boniface and/or the Catalans, for at once it began raising money to beef up its Euboean forts and fleet. However, no action seems to have been taken by either potential enemy until 1317.

Then, in that year, the new Catalan vicar Alphonso Frederick, having assumed control of his duchy, married Boniface's daughter Marulla. Despite the existence of a son, Thomas, Marulla was Boniface's heir. Her inheritance included various castles in the Athens duchy granted to Boniface previously by Guy of Athens, which the Catalans seem to have allowed him to retain, and also his possessions on Euboea, which may have included by this time a third of the island. Alphonso mobilized his Catalan forces and in late 1317, or more likely 1318, invaded Euboea. They presumably aimed to expel the Venetians and Lombard triarchs, excluding Boniface, who undoubtedly was to rule the island under Catalan overlordship. The threatened Lombards joined with Venice to resist. At this point Boniface died. Alphonso inherited his holdings and seems by this time to have planned to reduce the whole island. And he may very well have actually conquered it all, including Negroponte. The angry Venetians then complained to Alphonso's father, Frederick II of Sicily, who, not wanting trouble with Venice, ordered his son and the Catalans to evacuate the island. Alphonso refused to obey the order, but after his fleet was defeated by the Venetians the tide turned. Soon most of the Catalans returned to the mainland. Venice's role in ousting the Catalans further increased its authority on the island. And, probably at the end of 1318, the doge ordered Venetian troops installed in all towns and forts on the island. He ordered the triarchs to co-operate with this order, and they did. This order, of course, did not affect Alphonso's forts.

Meanwhile, in 1318, Walter II of Brienne, heir to Walter I and ambitious to launch a campaign to recover the Duchy of Athens from the Catalans, tried to persuade the Venetians to broaden their war against the Catalans, offering them in exchange great privileges in Attica (if and when he recovered it) and possession of all Euboea. However, the Venetians, concluding it was better to be at peace with the Catalans, avoided committing themselves and instead signed in 1319 a truce with them, renewed several times during the next decade. By this truce the Venetians renounced their claims to Karystos, Larmena, and possibly some other forts belonging to Marulla's inheritance, while the Catalans recognized Venice's suzerain rights to the rest of the island. Moreover the Catalans promised to renounce piracy and agreed to maintain no ships in the Saronic Gulf, though they were allowed to have ships in the Corinthian Gulf. This last clause guaranteed the security of Euboea for as long as the Catalans abided by the treaty.

Venice continued to dominate Euboea for the next decades, standing over and mediating quarrels among the various Lombard barons. On occasion certain of the triarchs tried to assert themselves against Venice, but in no case did these attempts succeed. Late in the 1320s Marulla's brother Thomas died. He had been holding Larmena, presumably with her agreement. Marulla claimed it as did Thomas' own heir, his daughter Agnes, married to the Duke of Naxos. Venice supported the duke's claims and feared a Catalan war might result. Though no full-scale war was to follow, Catalan pirates did plunder the Euboean coast, and Turks from Aydin, nominally allied to the Catalans, carried out large-scale raiding from 1328 to 1333, taking many Euboeans (allegedly twenty-five thousand in 1331) as slaves. Unhappy at the extent of Turkish plundering and wanting at that moment to restore good relations with Venice (for at the time Walter of Brienne was mobilizing an expedition to try to recover Attica from the Catalans), Alphonso in 1331 made peace with Venice. Once again each recognized the other's possessions and it seems the disputed region—Thomas' former property—was divided in 1333 between Marulla and Agnes. In 1334 the Venetians are found in possession of Larmena, presumably the result of purchase.

The Turkish raids continued and the Catalans, who also suffered from their ravages, came to join local coalitions for mutual defense; these activities made them into more respectable neighbors. Meanwhile, in strengthening its fortifications to defend Euboea from these raids, Venice found the stronger forts useful to control the local Euboeans as well. Needing Venetian support against the Turks, the triarchs became increasingly obedient to Venetian wishes, and after Alphonso's death in 1338 Venice had no rival on the island. Finally in 1365 Venice bought Karystos from Alphonso's heirs.

Venice's position improved still further in the 1380s. By then only two triarchs remained, and in that decade both died without heirs. The first, who held two-thirds of the island, died in 1383. Various claimants for his lands emerged and Venice was able to intervene, judge the claims, and grant his territories to the two claimants of its choice; the two were to basically become Venetian puppets. The other triarch died in 1390, also without issue; in this case he left his lands to Venice directly in his will. These inherited lands were distributed as many small fiefs to various Venetian candidates, most of whom had no relationship to the former triarchs. Thus by 1390 Euboea was completely under Venetian control.

Meanwhile, in 1318, the Byzantines moved into Thessaly from the north, sending troops from Thessaloniki under John Cantacuzenus. Bent on annexation, their claim to Thessaly was based on the fact that John II, who had just died, had left no heir other than his widow, Irene, Emperor Andronicus' daughter. Byzantine rule was accepted by most of the magnates in the north, though in fact this was often a nominal submission. These nobles in fact were to be as independent of any imperial authority as they had been of John II's. The territory to the south of what the Byzantines took, in roughly central Thessaly, remained in the hands of various major magnates who did not at first bother recognizing Byzantium at all. This central region broke up, more or less, into a series of small principalities, each under a major landlord.

Cantacuzenus had been ordered to establish imperial authority in the north and then to help the central regions defend themselves from the Catalans. It was hoped that the Byzantine presence in the center would not only prevent further Catalan expansion, but also get the Byzantines a foot in the door there. And it seems that Cantacuzenus did provide some limited aid to the nobles of central Thessaly.

However, as might be expected, the great magnates of central Thessaly soon began quarrelling among themselves and thus gave their ambitious neighbors to the north and south a chance to increase their influence. Some nobles, like the leaders of the Melissenos family, which held lands on the Gulf of Volos and also Kastri and Likonia, turned to the Catalans for support to secure their local position. Other nobles, like Stephen Gavrilopoulos in western Thessaly, who held Trikkala with lands stretching as far into southwestern Macedonia as Kastoria, turned to Byzantium for the same reason. Gavrilopoulos accepted Byzantine suzerainty and received the title sebastocrator. Thus the Byzantines gradually received nominal submission from certain nobles of central Thessaly while the Catalans received it from others.

The Venetians were not indifferent to Thessaly's fate either. They had long traded in Euboea, which was the center from which the agricultural and pastoral riches of Thessaly were exported. Their ships loaded with these goods were a frequent target for pirates, who during the reign of Michael VIII, the Venetians claimed, had been encouraged in their crimes by the emperor. The key Thessalian port for Venice was Pteleon, which lay opposite

Euboea and from which Thessaly's goods were shipped to Negroponte, which the Venetians, as noted, retained after Licario had driven the Latins from the rest of Euboea. At some point (some scholars place it as far back as 1204, though most recent scholars date it to the late thirteenth or even early fourteenth century) the Venetians took over the port of Pteleon on the Gulf of Volos directly to guarantee their link between Thessaly and Negroponte. They appointed a resident rector to govern the town. In the chaos following John II's death in 1318, Venice seems to have taken control of several other harbors on the Gulf of Volos as well.

Thus, after the death of John II in 1318, Thessaly (if we exclude the Venetian ports) found itself split into three: the southern part including the former capital of Neopatras being absorbed by the Catalans who were expanding north from their duchy in Athens; the central area, under Greek magnates who were carving out various small principalities; and the northern part, once again under Byzantium, but with its magnates enjoying considerable independence.

Thomas of Epirus, probably in 1307, married Anna, a sister of Andronicus III. His own sister Maria had married John I Orsini, Count of Cephalonia, back in 1294. In 1317 Nicholas Orsini, their son, succeeded John as the Count of Cephalonia. Ambitious for Epirus, and having in the island of Cephalonia, just off the coast of Epirus and Acarnania, a fine jumping off place for Epirus, Nicholas made his move in 1318 when he murdered his uncle Thomas of Epirus. Nicholas then married Thomas' Byzantine wife and took over Arta and much of Epirus. He even declared himself to be Orthodox. Though the Orsinis had long been Angevin vassals, the Naples court objected to the Orsinis' getting a foothold on the mainland, since they could threaten Angevin ambitions in Epirus. However, the Angevins took no action at first. The Byzantines, also unhappy with events, nevertheless saw them as a fine chance to expand their influence into this region. So, they moved into northern Epirus, occupying a sizeable portion of it including Jannina, whose citizens submitted voluntarily. Nicholas tried to expel the Byzantines from Jannina in 1321, but was repulsed. Thus despite his claim to rule Epirus, Nicholas in fact held only southern Epirus and Acarnania. In 1321 Anna, his new wife, died. Shortly thereafter, in 1323, Nicholas was murdered by his own brother John II Orsini, who took over the rule of Epirus. He was to rule there until 1335. The Angevins, taking advantage of John's having to devote his efforts to establishing his rule in Epirus, appropriated from the Orsini family the Ionian islands—Cephalonia, Ithaca, and probably Zakynthos (Zacynthus, Zante)—in 1325.

Hoping to secure his position, John II Orsini came to an arrangement with Byzantium. He accepted, probably in 1328, imperial suzerainty, and, on condition that he govern Epirus as an imperial estate, the emperor granted him the title despot. John had already, probably in 1324, married Anna, the daughter of Protovestiar Andronicus Palaeologus who held a Byzantine command in the north of Epirus. John also joined the Orthodox Church. The

Orsinis' willingness to adopt Orthodoxy stands in sharp contrast to the staunch Catholicism of the other Latin families ruling regions of Greece after 1204. John and Anna soon had a son, Nicephorus, and a daughter, Thomais. By the end of the 1320s John had also regained Jannina; since the town's citizens supported John, Emperor Andronicus III accepted the situation. However, to retain the empire's rights, Andronicus III depicted John as an imperial deputy for Jannina.

Soon, in 1331, John Orsini was attacked by the Angevins who were upset by their declining position in Albania and western Greece; presumably they hoped Orsini would lack support in Epirus. Philip of Taranto had granted the Angevin rights to "Romania" to his son-in-law (the husband of his and Tamara's daughter Beatrice), a second Walter of Brienne, who was the heir to the Burgundian Duchy of Athens taken over by the Catalans. In Greece Walter still retained Argos and Nauplia, which were managed for him by vassals. Walter, visualizing a major campaign against both Epirus and Attica-Boeotia, began operations in August 1331. The Attica-Boeotian efforts were a failure. The Catalans avoided battle and the local Greeks did not support him. Running out of money, Walter was soon forced to give up his attempt to recover the Athenian duchy.

His efforts against Epirus showed more promise. He based his claims to Epirus on the Angevin rights that dated back to the marriage agreement of the 1290s between Tamara of Epirus and Philip of Taranto. Walter landed in Naupaktos, still held by the Angevins, and began negotiating alliances with various local Albanians. He then moved on to take Vonitsa, a second fortress the Angevins had received title to in 1294—and which they had actually held from at least 1306 until some time after 1314. By 1331 Orsini held it and Walter had to take it from him. Walter also took the island of Leucas (Leucadia, Levkas, Santa Maura) off the coast from Vonitsa. Next Walter's armies besieged, and probably took, Arta, the capital city. Orsini, unhappy with these events, was forced briefly to accept Angevin suzerainty. And under that condition he soon recovered—if indeed he had ever lost it—Arta and whatever else in Epirus Walter had taken, excluding Leucas and Vonitsa. Walter's campaign thus petered out and soon he was back in Italy, left only with Argos, Nauplia, and his two conquests, all of which he retained under Angevin suzerainty. He appointed deputies—constables of castles—to rule these possessions. The Angevins retained Naupaktos.

Walter's cause was weakened by the death of Philip of Taranto on 26 December 1331. His widow Catherine and their son Robert received in his will title to "Romania" (the Latin Empire) and ultimate suzerainty over the Angevin possessions in Greece, including the Epirote fortresses and the principality of Achaea. Philip's brother John of Gravina, holder of Achaea under Philip's suzerainty, did not want to recognize Robert's overlordship. However, the two soon settled their differences and in 1332 John sold his rights to Achaea to Robert and Catherine and received in exchange the Angevin lands in Albania. By 1333 John was calling himself Duke of Durazzo and Lord of the Kingdom of Albania. But he was not able to do anything about realizing his wider ambitions in Albania. In fact he probably held little more than Durazzo, whose hinterland was controlled by various Albanian tribesmen.

Meanwhile in the Latin Peloponnesus, Patras became a more-or-less autonomous city-state under its archbishop. An Italian of the Frangipani family, he seceded from Achaea, ceasing to recognize Catherine's bailiff, and accepted papal suzerainty. The Byzantines were also continuing to expand gradually at the expense of Achaea. Thus that principality found itself shrinking. Lacking sufficient knights to defend its territory, Achaea became more and more dependent on mercenaries for its defense. This gave a greater role in Morean affairs to bankers, in particular to the Florentine banking family of Acciajuoli, the leading bankers for the Angevin kingdom. The head of that family, Niccolo, as noted, had already acquired from John of Gravina certain fortresses and land in the Morea as security for loans. Then in 1335 Niccolo Acciajuoli was knighted by the Angevins and given further large estates in Achaea. Through purchase he increased his holdings there still more and soon became the leading baron in Achaea, far more influential than the Angevin bailiff. His rise was facilitated by Catherine's support. Rumor had it that Niccolo was her lover. Runciman thinks there may have been truth in the rumor; Cheetham has his doubts about it.

Catherine died in 1346. All Angevin rights in Greece went to her son Robert, who was not to reside in Achaea, but left its administration to bailiffs, who did little to improve the Angevin position there. In 1358 Niccolo Acciajuoli was appointed governor of Corinth (including eight other dependent fortresses in its vicinity) because he could afford to repair its defenses. This he did. Soon many of his relatives arrived in Corinth, one of whom, Nerio, bought the whole coastline between Corinth and Patras. Not surprisingly, when the Latin See of Patras became vacant in 1360, Nerio's brother Giovanni became Archbishop of Patras. When he died soon thereafter, another brother, Angelo, became bishop. When Niccolo died in about 1365, he left Corinth to his son Angelo, not to be confused with the bishop. Soon thereafter this Angelo mortgaged Corinth to Nerio, who by then had acquired vast tracts of land around Corinth. Nerio took up residence in Corinth. Though legally holding Corinth only as security for a loan, Nerio was soon for all practical purposes ruler of the town. In his lands, as in those of his other relatives, the feudal system was increasingly breaking down; for the bankers had cash to hire troops and did so. Thus they supported themselves with armies recruited for cash rather than ones based on local feudatories.

Through the 1360s into the 1370s the principality of Achaea remained under the Angevins, who adminstered it through bailiffs. Robert was the nominal lord until his death in 1364. His widow Mary of Bourbon then claimed the title on behalf of Hugh de Lusignan, her son by a previous marriage. She was challenged by Robert's brother Philip. Most of the local barons supported Philip's cause. After some skirmishing in the Morea between their partisans, Hugh was persuaded in March 1370 by a considerable bribe to renounce his claims to the Morea. Later that year Mary died, and Philip thereafter held the title undisputed until he died in his turn in 1373.

In 1370 Philip appointed as his bailiff for the Morea Louis d'Enghien, one of several nephews of Walter II of Brienne who had inherited, upon Walter's death in 1356, shares of or claims to various Brienne lands. Louis hoped to use his appointment to recover the most attractive part of this inheritance, the Duchy of Athens, from the Catalans. Almost immediately after his arrival, Louis attacked Attica, plundered the region, and even took the lower city of Athens. However, he soon became ill and returned in 1371 to the Morea. Louis continued on as bailiff through the 1370s but never succeeded in launching a successful campaign against Attica.

During the fourteenth century, when little or no central authority existed to defend much of Greece, large-scale migration of Albanians from the mountains of Albania occurred. This migration, particularly heavy in Epirus and Thessaly, carried them all over Greece, and many came to settle in Attica and the Peloponnesus as well.

The Byzantine Civil War between Andronicus II and Andronicus III

In 1320 Andronicus II's son and heir, Co-emperor Michael IX, died. Michael's son Andronicus III, was declared the new heir. Young, attractive, and popular with his grandfather, he was crowned co-emperor. He was extravagant, however, which upset the old emperor, for the times were not such as to allow extravagance. The last straw came one night when Andronicus III and his cohorts decided to eliminate a rival for a girl's affections and by error killed Andronicus' younger brother, who had come to the girl's house looking for his brother. The grandfather, infuriated, excluded Andronicus III from his inheritance; his decision was made manifest when he summoned state officials and troops to take oaths to himself alone and to whomsoever he might choose as his heir.

The young heir did not take this lying down, and he had support from a variety of younger nobles who were both ambitious and opposed to the skinflint policies, as they saw them, of the old emperor. Thus in the warfare to follow the two sides were divided along clear generational lines. Two of these youthful supporters, John Cantacuzenus and Syrgiannes, bought governorships in Thrace, which shows that the sale of offices was still widespread. Finlay argues that Andronicus II was happy to appoint them to provincial posts in order to get them out of the capital, where they might have engineered a coup on behalf of his grandson. They, however, seem to have sought these posts to advance their plot, for they used them to mobilize men for a rebellion. Since the provinces were overtaxed, it was not hard for them to win support by making lavish promises of tax exemptions. One source, possibly exaggerated, has the rebel leaders promising to free all Thrace from taxes. On Easter

1321 Andronicus III came to Adrianople, where his friends and the armies they had raised were gathered. The revolt was launched immediately.

Andronicus II was at a disadvantage. It was far easier for those out of power, and seeking it, to make lavish promises. But in being responsible for the state and holding office, Andronicus II would have been expected to deliver on his promises at once. So, with the advantage of irresponsibility, the young emperor rapidly built up considerable support. However, in this phase and in subsequent phases of the civil war, both sides were forced to buy support. Thus gifts of land, conversions of normal pronoias to hereditary ones, and ever greater tax exemptions were issued widely by both sides. The magnates thus gained from the war ever increasing independence in their regions and reduced tax obligations, both of which were to weaken further the central government and the state that emerged from these wars.

Syrgiannes led a large army toward Constantinople. Andronicus II decided to negotiate, and it was agreed in July 1321 to divide the empire. Andronicus III was to receive Thrace from Selymbria, close to the capital, east to Kavalla and north to the Rhodopes. Adrianople became his capital. The young emperor poured money into his cities of Adrianople and Demotika which both prospered. To reward and retain his followers, he gave them whole towns and regions to administer, allowing them to appropriate the revenues for themselves. In theory only the grandfather, resident in Constantinople, could conduct foreign policy. Thus basically the treaty created a lucrative appanage rather than a true division of the empire into two states. However, this foreign policy restriction was not observed, and Andronicus III freely negotiated with his neighbors. Peace, however, did not last. The old emperor was still rankling at his grandson's behavior and wanted to find a way to back out of the agreement. At the same time jealousies arose between Andronicus III's two leading supporters, Syrgiannes and Cantacuzenus. To exacerbate the situation it also seems that Andronicus III tried to seduce Syrgiannes' wife. When Andronicus III took Cantacuzenus' side against Syrgiannes, the bitter Syrgiannes stormed off in December 1321 to join the old emperor in Constantinople and once there worked to stir up his anger toward his grandson.

By then Andronicus II may have been considering the appointment of his younger son Constantine as heir. At least Andronicus III, believing this to be the case, took his unfortunate uncle captive and imprisoned him for a while in a well in Demotika. Fighting followed briefly between grandson and grandfather but was to be ended in July 1322 by a new truce. When these tensions developed in 1322, the Bulgarians advanced into Thrace, taking Philippopolis. But then as noted in July the two Byzantine sides made peace, and soon thereafter, at the end of the year, Tsar George II Terter died, setting off a succession crisis in Bulgaria. As a result the Byzantines eventually recovered the town. In 1325, after further strains in their relations, a new agreement was made in which Andronicus II confirmed his grandson's appanage and again recognized him as heir to the throne in a coronation ceremony that made him once again co-emperor.

The destruction caused by the fighting and in particular the further reductions in taxes through new privileges were to have disastrous effects on the economy. Moreover, while the quarrel over the succession was taking place, others took advantage of it to further their own ambitions. First, a nephew of Andronicus II, John Palaeologus, who was governor of Thessaloniki, decided to secede. His attempt gave similar ideas to two sons of Theodore Metohites, the grand logothete, who were governing Serres and Melnik respectively. These two young men for a short time also seceded. Fearing retaliation from Andronicus II, John Palaeologus turned for support to the new Serbian king Stefan Dečanski. However, before a serious war between the empire and the Serbs could develop (though a certain amount of plundering along the Struma by both John's and Serbian troops did take place) John, having agreed to peace, died, and the empire was able to reassert its control over Thessaloniki.

The Turks, meanwhile, continued their pressure against those cities the Byzantines still retained in Anatolia, and the empire, involved with its European problems, could not effectively resist. In 1326 Bursa fell and became the new capital of the Osmanlis. Next, in 1327, warfare again broke out between Andronicus III and his grandfather. For support the old emperor turned to the Serbs. Not to be outdone, the grandson in May 1327 sought support from the Bulgarians, whose tsar, Michael Šišman, had dropped his Serbian wife and married in 1323 or 1324 the sister of Andronicus III. Andronicus III was in possession of Byzantine Thrace before the Serbs could take the field on behalf of the old emperor. Next, after a brief military campaign in early winter 1327–28, Macedonia declared for the young emperor. Then in January 1328 Thessaloniki recognized him. He then marched on Constantinople, whose gates were opened to him in May. Andronicus II abdicated and entered a monastery. The young emperor rewarded his leading supporters liberally. The region between Thessaloniki and the Struma was assigned to one of them, Synadenos, while a Latin, Guy Lusignan, residing in Serres, was given the region east of the Struma up to the strong fortress of Kavalla to govern.

However, in the course of this last phase of the war rivalry between Serbia and Bulgaria had increased. Šišman's divorcing and incarcerating his sister angered Dečanski, and both rulers were ambitious for and advanced claims to Macedonia. The likelihood of war between them was increasing, and clearly Byzantium was interested in seeing what it could gain from such a war. At the inception of this rivalry Byzantium, under the victorious Andronicus III, was lined up on the Bulgarian side.

Thessaly and Epirus under Andronicus III

The Byzantines soon had a chance to extend their influence in Thessaly. In 1332 their nominal vassal Stephen Gavrilopoulos, who had held western Thessaly with Trikkala and part of southwestern Macedonia including Kastoria, died. Not only did this lead to a power vacuum there, but his heirs began quarrelling among themselves. John II Orsini of Epirus immediately stepped in and took most of Stephen's former lands, including Stagi, Trikkala, Phanarion, Damasis, and Elasson. At once Andronicus III ordered his governor in Thessaloniki, Michael Monomachus, to intervene, and then, that fall, Andronicus III led an army into the area himself. In his history, Cantacuzenus reports that the empire extended its rule as far south as Volos on the Gulf of Volos. He also claims that this campaign expelled Orsini, restoring the old Thessaly-Epirote border, but now, with the Byzantines asserting their authority, it became the Byzantine-Epirote border. Ferjančić, however, argues that the Byzantines did not succeed in expelling Orsini but reasserted their control only over eastern Thessaly while expanding somewhat into central Thessaly. Andronicus III spent that winter, 1332–33, in Thessaly; while there he concluded agreements with the local Albanian chieftains, who lived not in towns but in the mountains, and came down into the valleys in the winter. They seem to have represented three tribes—the Malakasi, the Buji, and the Mesariti—containing twelve thousand Albanian tribesmen. Andronicus then returned to Constantinople, leaving Michael Monomachus to govern the territory the Byzantines had acquired in Thessaly as a result of their actions in 1318 and 1332. Monomachus remained in office for a decade, trying to extend Byzantine authority over a greater area and also to a greater extent over the nobles within the area that was officially Byzantine already.

Then in 1335 John II Orsini died unexpectedly (rumors had him poisoned by his wife), leaving his widow Anna regent for their young son Nicephorus II. Opposition emerged against her from the start of her regency, and Ferjančić argues that it was now that Monomachus, and once again Andronicus III himself, taking advantage of the Epirote instability, moved into western Thessaly, conquering it up to the old Epirote border. Ferjančić notes that it is only from 1336 that we have charters and privileges from Andronicus III to monasteries in the area of western Thessaly. Thus by the end of these campaigns (1332, 1335/36) the empire had gained most, if not all, of Thessaly to the Catalan and Epirote frontiers. Taking advantage of the instability in Epirus, Andronicus III was also able to regain Jannina for the empire.

After this Byzantine success, the Albanians from the regions of Valagrita and Kanina raided into northwestern Thessaly, south-central Albania, and northern Epirus. They plundered the Byzantine towns of Berat, Kanina, Skropai (Skreparion), Klisura, and Tomor (Timoron). So, in 1337 or 1338 Andronicus led an army, composed chiefly of Turkish mercenaries from Aydin, successfully, against the Albanians, killing many and taking many others prisoner. He marched all the way to the walls of Durazzo. Next, still in 1338, Andronicus, commanding this large army just to the north of Epirus, summoned Anna of Epirus to negotiate.

Anna expected to pay homage to the emperor, recognize Byzantine suzerainty, and then continue to rule in Epirus. However, Andronicus, deciding the time was at last ripe to annex Epirus, had other plans. He used his troops to install an imperial governor, Protostrator Synadenos, in Arta. Anna, her daughters, and Nicephorus were to be taken back to the empire and granted large estates in the vicinity of Thessaloniki. Nicephorus was then engaged to a daughter of Andronicus III's leading counsellor John Cantacuzenus. Thus Epirus, Aetolia, and Acarnania were finally restored to the empire. Andronicus then carried out his plans, suffering only one set-back. The anti-Byzantine faction, possibly with Anna's help, smuggled Nicephorus out of Epirus. Thus he did not accompany his mother and sister to Thessaloniki.

As a result, the transition was not to be smooth. Almost immediately, in 1339 or 1340, a revolt broke out in Epirus against imperial rule. After enjoying a long period of independence, marked by hostility toward the Byzantine Palaeologian dynasty, surely many Epirotes were unhappy with imperial annexation. At the same time the Angevins, holding titular claims to parts of Epirus which could be more easily realized at the expense of a weak independent Epirus than at that of the empire, decided to take action. Through the agency of his tutor Richard, Nicephorus had been smuggled out of Epirus and taken to Taranto. There he had been engaged to a daughter of Catherine of Valois, the "Empress of the Romans" and widow of Philip of Taranto. Through Alois Caracio, her deputy for Durazzo (did this mean the Angevins had regained Durazzo from the Serbs or did Alois merely hold an empty title?), Catherine next made contact with supporters of Nicephorus in Epirus. As a result plotters inside Epirus, led by a certain Nicephorus Basilitzes, staged an uprising in the capital of Arta. Seizing and jailing Synadenos, they took control of Arta. Certain other towns, including Rogoi and the port of Thomokastron (identified by Nicol as Risa—later Riniasa—on the coast north of Preveza), recognized the rebel leaders. However, various other towns, probably the majority, seemingly troubled by the role of the Latin Angevins, remained faithful to the empire. Nicephorus, having been brought by ship from Italy to Patras, was now dispatched by a second ship to Epirus, with an Angevin regiment. He was soon established in Thomokastron. This seems to have occurred in the middle of 1339.

At the end of 1339, or possibly not until 1340, Byzantine troops under Michael Monomachus and John Angelus arrived in Epirus, followed, clearly in 1340, by Andronicus III himself. The rebel forces, believing they could best hold out inside their walled towns, avoided a pitched battle with the Byzantines. However, inside their towns pro-Byzantine factions existed; and after a matter of months through negotiations the Byzantines regained Rogoi and then, though less easily, Arta. Nicephorus, supported by an Angevin force, was then besieged in Thomokastron. The town was well supplied, and the siege continued for a time until negotiations delivered to the empire, in November 1340, that town too. Thus by the end of 1340 Byzantium had regained Epirus and Acarnania. Nicephorus, given the honorary title panipersebast (a rank slightly below that of despot), was settled in Thessaloniki. John

Angelus was appointed governor of Epirus. The rebels were pardoned and allowed to retain their possessions.

Thus after these campaigns the Byzantines had extended their control over Epirus and all Thessaly down to the Catalan frontier. The Byzantines were also able to retain their forts in southern Albania: Berat, Valona, Kanina, and Spinarizza. However, though they were able to hold the walled towns, we may assume they had little control over the countryside which was in the hands of various Albanian tribes.

However, since throughout Thessaly the local nobles remained masters of their estates, the Byzantines were probably unable to establish an efficient military presence in that region. Thus when troops were withdrawn, matters presumably reverted to their former state, with the local nobles, on paper loyal to the empire, running their own regions independently and Byzantine suzerainty being only nominal. For example, in 1342 (granted, a moment of imperial weakness, right after the death of Andronicus III when a new civil war was breaking out) we find Michael Gavrilopoulos, a relative of Stephen, running the town of Phanarion. He issued charters to lesser local nobles in which no reference is made to the emperor in Constantinople, though the things he promised were prerogatives of the emperor. The nobles receiving charters owed Michael military service in exchange for which he promised both to reduce taxes and not to settle Albanians in the territory under his control.

The Albanians referred to in the charter were now migrating in considerable numbers into the region; and though they were good warriors, they threatened local landholding and were a force of disorder. Their raiding picked up considerably after the death of Andronicus III, who had been able to subdue some tribes and negotiate settlements with various others. In their migrations during the first half of the fourteenth century, many Albanians entered the service of local officials. Some seem to have served loyally in that capacity, being particularly effective in fighting the Catalans. The Venetian sources, on the other hand, depict all Albanians as more-or-less unruly elements out for themselves and fighting everyone in Thessaly. One suspects there is truth in both descriptions, with some tribes entering the service of local leaders and serving them loyally while others simply moved into regions to plunder or to try to establish themselves as lords of the surrounding countryside.

Serbia in the Early Fourteenth Century

The tensions that developed in 1299–1300 between King Milutin and Dragutin seem to have arisen over the question of the succession to the throne of Serbia. Threatened with a serious civil war in which Dragutin would have two appanages from which to raise troops, Milutin was probably more receptive to Byzantine peace feelers and thus, as noted, concluded peace in 1299 with

Byzantium. Thus freed from the danger of foreign invasion, Milutin could concentrate on the domestic problem. Ironically, peace with Byzantium seems to have lost him considerable support from the most important domestic element, the nobility, who, wanting to continue the war with Byzantium to acquire lands and booty, opposed the peace. As a result many of the nobles, according to Byzantine sources, gave their support to Dragutin, believing that he, having neither Byzantine alliance nor in-laws, would as ruler be more likely to resume the fighting in Macedonia.

However, despite their support, Dragutin almost immediately found himself faced with serious difficulties. In January 1301, upon the death of Andrew III of Hungary, the last member of the Arpad dynasty, civil war resumed in Hungary between the Angevin party supporting Charles Robert and the Hungarian opposition advancing the candidacy of Wenceslas III of Bohemia. This meant that Dragutin could not devote full attention to his Serbian war but had to concern himself also with Hungarian politics, so as not to risk losing his Hungarian lands. It also meant that should things go badly for Dragutin in Serbia, he could not count on re-enforcements from the Hungarians; they were too occupied with their own wars to spare men for Serbia. And to make matters worse for him, in 1308 or 1309, after Wenceslas and Otto of Bavaria had failed to defeat Charles Robert, Dragutin allowed the Hungarian opposition to advance his own son Vladislav as candidate for the throne against Charles Robert, whom Dragutin had supported up to this point. This last effort was a fiasco, and Charles Robert emerged victorious in 1309. As a result Dragutin found himself not only doing poorly in the last phases of his war with Milutin but also having tense relations with, and no possibilities of help from, a Hungary controlled by Charles Robert and the faction Dragutin had come to oppose.

Now let us turn to the limited information that exists on the fighting in Serbia. Dragutin in about 1300, according to Byzantine sources, was preparing to attack his brother; then the Byzantines sent aid to their new ally Milutin, and Dragutin thought better of it and did not attack. The truth of this Byzantine report is unknown. If Dragutin had actually meant to fight, could some Byzantine aid, provided at a moment of considerable Byzantine weakness, have been sufficient to deter Dragutin from carrying out his plans? Actual fighting between the brothers seems to have begun in 1301. At least in that year Dubrovnik recalled its merchants from Dragutin's lands because of the danger of war and reported it was impossible for its merchants to cross Milutin's lands. The latter statement implies that warfare had actually broken out in Milutin's lands. That fighting had taken place is also suggested by the fact that in 1302 Milutin held Rudnik, the major mine that had been part of Dragutin's Serbian appanage; for in that year Milutin gave the Ragusan merchants the right to trade at Rudnik. This town had last been documented as Dragutin's in 1296; and 1301–02 seems the most likely time for Milutin to have taken it. Though Dubrovnik refers to peace being concluded in late 1302, it was clearly short-lived, for fighting is reported again in 1303.

The war continued for over a decade. Most scholars date its end to 1312, which is probably accurate. Mavromatis advances arguments that it actually lasted until 1314. Presumably Serbia did not endure uninterrupted warfare throughout this whole period. Undoubtedly the fighting was interrupted by various armistices, followed by temporary periods of peace. Presumably the fighting consisted chiefly of skirmishing along borders and sieges of fortresses, rather than full-scale pitched battles. Though Dragutin evidently lost Rudnik and possibly other parts of his Serbian appanage as well, there is no evidence that Milutin ever took any action against Dragutin's Hungarian appanage further to the north.

In this warfare many (or most) of the nobles seem to have supported Dragutin. But Milutin's great edge in the war lay in his wealth. His initial wealth came from the mines; he developed them far more extensively than his predecessors had. As a result Milutin benefited from them and the increased trade associated with them. A Western traveler says that he had seven silver mines from which he took for himself one-tenth of the produce. During his reign Novo Brdo became the richest silver mine in the Balkans. From the produce of the mines Milutin minted money on an even larger scale than his father had. His coins imitated those of the Venetians, but it seems they had a poorer silver content. Venice regularly complained about the coins, and Dante gave Milutin a place in one of the circles of Hell for his deceptive coins. But the coins were spent to advance his interests. He hired large numbers of mercenaries to balance the independent-minded nobility, and when the nobles threw their support behind Dragutin, Milutin used his mercenaries and recruited more to oppose them and carry on the war.

His wealth had also allowed him to erect many churches. One source says he vowed, and honored his vow, to build one church for each year he reigned. Not surprisingly, the Church appreciated this, so when Milutin found himself in difficulties, he enjoyed its active support; perhaps it did so particularly actively because Milutin's opponent Dragutin had so many Catholic ties. Thus the Church, we are told, readily turned over its wealth to Milutin, who used it to purchase further mercenaries. Turkish (Oseti) mercenaries, purchased with Church money, seem to have been the key element in a major victory Milutin gained over Dragutin in about 1312, which gave him the edge in the war and enabled him to initiate peace negotiations on his own terms.

In March 1308, during his war with Dragutin, Milutin concluded a treaty with Charles of Valois. The two men also discussed a marriage between Charles' son and Milutin's daughter. Scholars have almost unanimously believed this indicates that Milutin had broken his agreement of 1299 with Byzantium and given his support to Charles' anti-Byzantine coalition.

However, Mavromatis argues plausibly that such an interpretation would not be correct. He shows that Milutin's relations with Andronicus remained cordial after March 1308. He finds that later in 1308 Andronicus gave gifts to a church in Skopje, within Milutin's realm. Mavromatis concludes that though Milutin's treaty with Charles was nominally against Byzantium,

Milutin did not intend it to be so. Rather it was a ploy to prevent Charles and his Western allies from supporting Milutin's Serbian rival, as they otherwise might have done, should their forces land in the Balkans; this was a clear and present danger to Milutin, for Dragutin had close ties with the papacy and was supported by their mother, Helen, probably of the Valois family herself. Milutin was clearly worried about the West. Earlier in the course of the war, Milutin had been in touch with various other Western figures, seeking support or testing the air. Around 1304 he met Ban Paul I Šubić through the mediation of Dubrovnik. He was also in communication with the pope, holding out the hope of Church Union. And an envoy of his, the Bishop of Skadar, concluded an agreement—contents unknown—with the Angevin Philip of Taranto, who at the time was calling himself Prince of Achaea, Despot of Romania, and Lord of the Kingdom of Albania. Thus Milutin's treaty with Charles of Valois seems to have been merely one of a series of initiatives by Milutin to prevent Western intervention in his war with Dragutin.

And small scale intervention from that direction, though reflecting local ambitions rather than support of Dragutin, did occur during the war. The activities of Paul Šubić, which we shall examine in a moment, illustrate the danger Milutin faced. Thus it was sensible of Milutin to involve himself diplomatically with these Western leaders.

Let us now turn to Šubić's activities. In the course of the war between Milutin and Dragutin, Paul Šubić of Bribir had taken advantage of Milutin's occupation elsewhere to expand not only into western Hum but also beyond the Neretva to take the region toward Nevesinje and also territory toward Ston. Soon, by 1312/13, "Hum" was added to the title of Mladen II Šubić, who succeeded Paul in 1312. At least part of Paul's conquests were granted to his vassal Constantine Nelipčić. In 1313 Milutin, supported by Dragutin with whom he had concluded peace in 1312, went to war against the Šubić family. In the war that followed Milutin took one of Mladen's brothers captive; to get him back Mladen had to agree to restore part of Hum to Milutin. One might speculate that after this agreement in 1313 the Neretva again became the border between Serbian and western (now Šubić) Hum.

Peace between the Serbian brothers was concluded, almost certainly in 1312, after Milutin's mercenaries won a major battle over Dragutin's forces. The Church seems to have played a role in mediating the peace. The text of their agreement, if it was written down, has not survived. Thus its terms are unknown. It seems reasonable to believe that matters reverted to their pre-war state. Dragutin seems to have regained his Serbian appanage, for by the end of 1312 he is again found holding Rudnik.

Though Dragutin received his territory back, the war represented a major victory for Milutin. To demonstrate this conclusion Mavromatis cites the elaborate reception given to Milutin's wife Simonida at Dragutin's court in Beograd, where Hungarian ambassadors came to visit her and behaved toward her as they would have had she been at her own court. Their behavior, of course, may also have been intended as a slap at Dragutin by the victorious

Hungarian king, Charles Robert, who probably had little affection for Dragutin. Mavromatis also draws attention to a charter to the Banjska monastery
signed by both rulers: Milutin as King and Master of the Serbian Lands and
Dragutin as the king's brother and former king. Thus Milutin remained King
of Serbia, with Dragutin subordinate to him for those Serbian lands he held
and clearly the weaker militarily. There is no evidence that Dragutin's son
Vladislav was considered heir to the throne any longer, if he had ever really
been so previously. But there is also no evidence that Stefan Dečanski was
considered the heir either. In fact, there is no evidence that Dečanski was ever
declared Milutin's heir. Even when he held Zeta—be it from ca. 1299 or from
1309 (when we can first document him there)—no document calls him heir
and he seems to have borne no special title. Ragusan records of the town's
dealings with him in Zeta, which show him as ruling Zeta between 1309 and
1314, simply refer to Dečanski as the king's son.

Milutin also maintained his good relations with Byzantium, despite his
treaty with Charles of Valois and despite a small border dispute in 1311/12,
for in 1312 or 1313 Milutin sent a cavalry unit of two thousand men to aid
Andronicus in Anatolia against the Turks.

After the conclusion of peace between them, relations remained tense
between the two brothers. When their mother, Helen, died on 8 February
1314 Dragutin, though close to her, did not attend the funeral. Scholars have
suspected he did not dare come to the funeral lest he be seized. At that time
Dragutin was found witnessing a charter for the King of Hungary; thus he
probably was also trying to patch up relations with the new dynasty there. It
seems he was successful in this, for Dragutin still held his Hungarian appanage when he died in 1316. Upon Helen's death Milutin absorbed her
appanage, which included Trebinje, Konavli, further coastal territory, and
probably the region of the upper Lim.

In 1314 Stefan Dečanski, still holding his appanage in Zeta, revolted
against Milutin. He seems to have been pushed into the rebellion by his nobles
there. According to Danilo, who may have been trying to take the blame away
from the young prince, the nobles had told Dečanski that if he did not revolt
they would desert him. Thus persuaded, he launched his rebellion. It is also
possible that he revolted to force Milutin to make him heir. For it seems
Milutin had as yet made no statement of his intention that Dečanski should
succeed to the throne. Milutin's charters from this time state that the grants he
made were binding on him and his sons and other relatives, as if no definite
heir had been decided upon. Danilo then tells us that many of his father's
nobles joined Dečanski's side. Possibly these included some of those who had
supported Dragutin in the previous war and who were still seeking a ruler
who would adopt the policy they desired of making war on Byzantium.

Milutin sent troops out against his son; they won a victory, forcing
Stefan to retreat beyond the Bojana River. Stefan then agreed to meet with his
father, came to the meeting, and was taken prisoner. Soon thereafter, according to Serbian sources, Milutin had his son blinded. In keeping with Byzan-

tine custom, this rendered the mutilated individual ineligible for the throne. Dečanski was then exiled to Constantinople with his family, including his son, the future ruler Stefan Dušan, who was then about seven years old. Dečanski and his family were allowed to return only in 1320. Whether he was actually blinded or not is a question we shall examine later; it may be noted here, however, that the Byzantine sources that comment on his stay in Constantinople make no reference to his being blind. The choice of Constantinople as his place of exile shows the continuing good relations between the two states and the fact that Milutin could trust the Byzantine emperor both to guard the royal captives well and not to use them to cause trouble for Serbia. In this way Dečanski and his family were kept away from any Serbian nobles who might have tried to use them for their own purposes.

Even after Dečanski's exile, Milutin made no statement about the succession. Dečanski, disgraced and perhaps blinded, was presumably out of the running as far as Milutin was concerned, and it is highly unlikely that Milutin would have been favorable toward Dragutin's son Vladislav. This left as the most likely candidate Milutin's younger son Constantine. At some time after Dečanski's removal in 1314, Milutin had assigned to Constantine Zeta and the coast, including Kotor. When he made this assignment is not known. In 1318 reference is made to a certain Ilija as Count of Zeta. Did Zeta in this case refer to the whole region, meaning Ilija was its holder? Or was Ilija count of the original, and smaller, Zeta county within the greater region of Zeta? The latter leaves open the possibility that in 1318 Constantine was present there, ruling the whole region and standing above Ilija who governed only a county within it. The second alternative is supported by a reference from 1321 to "Ylia kefalia." Assuming Ylia is our Ilija, then we find him called by the Greek equivalent of *župan,* which usually denoted the holder of a smaller county or župa. Moreover a kephale in Byzantium, and later in Serbia, was usually the head of a town—who generally administered the town's environs too—who was appointed by the ruler to represent him locally; he was a semi-military figure who was responsible for keeping order, managed the local garrison, and put down brigands. Thus Ilija's presence does not contradict the view that Constantine was assigned Zeta. For the two men could easily have co-existed in Zeta, with Constantine being Ilija's superior. Thus from whenever he received Zeta it seems probable that Constantine was Milutin's heir.

However, despite this likelihood, Milutin made no known statement as to Constantine's succession and took no steps to assure that succession. In fact Milutin was to die without a testament. This situation encouraged the Byzantine empress to seek the succession for one of her sons. Milutin seems to have done nothing to discourage her, though it is hardly likely that he thought well of the idea. One Byzantine prince actually visited Serbia but disliked it and left; thus the plan died a natural death, without Milutin's having to do anything to kill it.

In 1316 Dragutin died. He seems to have become very religious in his last years; we are told that to prepare himself for death he regularly slept in a coffin. He became a monk shortly before he died. Possibly he undertook this change of status only on his death-bed.

Dragutin, despite his Catholic ties and the privileges he allowed to Catholics in his Mačva banate, had himself remained faithful to the Serbian Church. He built Orthodox churches in Mačva and encouraged the Serbian clergy to proselytize there. He also allowed the Serbian Church to establish bishoprics in Mačva and Braničevo. Thus throughout his realm, in both his Serbian and Hungarian appanages, the Serbian Church was active; its clergy under the Archbishop of Serbia belonged to the same institution as the Serbs of Milutin's state. The Serbian Church, as already noted, thrived under Milutin. Receiving rich gifts of cash and lands from the king, its material status greatly improved. It expanded its activities not only northward up to the Danube, under Dragutin's sponsorship, but it also penetrated southward into the Macedonian lands that Milutin had annexed. Serbian bishops, under the Serbian archbishop, were installed in Skopje and Debar in Macedonia.

Upon his father's death Vladislav inherited his father's Serbian appanage. With the consent of the Hungarian king he also inherited Dragutin's Hungarian appanage. Immediately, however, in 1316 or 1317, Milutin took Vladislav captive and imprisoned him. How this capture was effected is not stated in the sources. Scholars have suggested he was seized at Dragutin's funeral, for Dragutin was buried back in Serbia at a monastery church in Ras. Then, without Vladislav to oppose him, Milutin seized and added to his own state Dragutin's Serbian lands.

Despite Hungary's title to Dragutin's territory in Mačva and its claim to Braničevo (which Bulgaria would have disputed), Milutin was determined to strike fast and add this territory to his own realm. He quickly occupied these lands in 1316 or 1317 and continued on an even larger scale Dragutin's policy of installing Serbian clergy in the towns there. Charles Robert, however, had no desire to permit this situation to stand; so having built up his forces, he commanded an assault that recovered Mačva for Hungary; this campaign, usually dated early to mid-1319, is now re-dated by Ćirković to winter 1317–18. Charles Robert then returned to Hungary with the bulk of his forces.

Milutin counterattacked, sending his troops to overrun the territory all the way up to the Sava. During August and September 1319 Charles Robert was back in full force and regained the Mačva-Srem territory for Hungary. The Hungarian king then re-established Mačva as a banate under a Hungarian appointee. And it seems that by the end of 1319, as a result of one of these two campaigns, the Hungarians had regained Beograd. However, Milutin was able to retain the province of Braničevo which, though formerly Hungarian, had for a long time been separated from Hungary, ever since it was conquered jointly by Dragutin and Milutin in about 1291. And thus Serbia remained extended to the Danube and bordering on Vidin, which still remained a Serbian client state. In fact Vidin's dependence on Serbia had greatly increased after 1299, when the Nogajs had been destroyed, leaving Šišman in Vidin with no other power to balance Serbian influence.

During his war with Milutin over Dragutin's northern lands, Charles Robert also tried to weaken Milutin by stirring up trouble elsewhere in his realm. It seems that he, his Angevin relative Philip of Taranto, and Pope John XXII all tried to incite various northern Albanian nobles to revolt against Milutin.[10] Serbia's expansion in the Albanian region seems to have been halted after the 1299 treaty with the Byzantines. At the time of the treaty Milutin had probably yielded Durazzo to Byzantium, which soon lost it to the Angevins. However, though it is not clear how much of the northern Albanian lands Milutin had been able to retain by the 1299 agreement, it seems reasonable to suppose he held the territory at least as far south as the Mati River. Thus he probably held lands the Angevins felt belonged to Durazzo, which would have been reason for Philip to seek an Albanian revolt against Milutin in 1318–19. And in 1318 or 1319 various nobles in Milutin's northern Albanian lands did revolt. However, there is no evidence that this unrest was the result of Charles Robert's agitation. In fact, the Albanians probably acted in their own interests. Moreover in that same year, 1319, the citizens of Durazzo staged a revolt against the Angevins. And Ducellier even argues that the rebels, who seem to have been Orthodox, submitted to Milutin. The Angevins eventually, probably in 1322, suppressed the revolt and regained control of the city. Since Dečanski is to be found holding for Serbia territory in Albania at least to the mouth of the Mati River in 1323, we may assume Milutin put down his Albanian rebels as well. If, in fact, Milutin did acquire control of— or suzerainty over—Durazzo in 1319, as Ducellier believes, we may conclude Milutin had suppressed his Albanian rebels rapidly and without much difficulty.

Disorders continued in his realm until Milutin was taken ill in 1321. He had fallen from a bed, lost the power to talk, and then lingered on a while until he died intestate on 29 October 1321. One may suppose from the description that he had had a stroke. At that time sources mention that bands of roving armed men were plaguing Serbia. Shortly before Milutin's illness and death, probably in 1320, Stefan Dečanski had been allowed to return home to Serbia. The Continuator of Danilo states that Dečanski had written Danilo to intervene with his father. Danilo, the great biographer, had been appointed Bishop of Hum in 1317 but had quickly become disenchanted over the see's poverty and had returned to Mount Athos to become abbot of Hilandar. Danilo, having received Dečanski's letter on Athos, wrote Archbishop Nicodemus of Serbia who spoke with Milutin and persuaded him to recall his son. Dečanski's other—and later—biographer, Gregory Camblak, a Bulgarian who became abbot of Dečanski's endowment Visoki Dečani some seventy years after Dečanski's death, credits the mediation not to Serbian clerics but to letters to Milutin from Emperor Andronicus II and some Byzantine clerics. On his return, Dečanski was given a small appanage, Budimlje (the region around modern Ivangrad). Dečanski's son Stefan Dušan was not allowed to accompany his father to Budimlje but had to remain at court with his grandfather.

Upon Milutin's death at the end of October 1321 civil war immediately erupted among his sons (Dečanski, who still held Budimlje, and Constantine, who had Zeta) and his nephew Vladislav, who had escaped from prison, presumably released by supporters in the confusion at Milutin's death. Each of the three had his own supporters and each acquired mercenaries who were willing to serve the highest bidder. Milutin's widow, Simonida, immediately fled to Constantinople. She had had no children by Milutin and clearly had been unhappy in Serbia. Once previously, when she had returned to Constantinople for her mother's funeral, she had tried to become a nun so she would not have to return to Serbia; her father, responding to Milutin's insistence, had, however, sent her back by force. Now in 1321 there was nothing to prevent her from realizing her ambition to enter a convent, and she thus did so.

Constantine was probably Milutin's intended heir. Though no formal statement to this effect had been made, the fresco depicting the Nemanjić family tree at Gračanica, carried out under Milutin's direction when Dečanski was in Constantinople, depicts Constantine alone after Milutin. He was proclaimed king in Zeta immediately and started coining money in Skadar. Freed from jail, Vladislav established himself with an army in some part of Dragutin's former lands in the north. And Dečanski, claiming, "Look and be amazed, I was blind and now I see," became the third claimant. The miracle of his regained sight is described in his saint's life written nearly a century after his death by Gregory Camblak. A hostile source, Guy Adam, Archbishop of Bar, writing in the 1330s, claims that he had not been totally blinded but had hidden the fact he could see until then. Danilo also says the blinding was not total, and therefore he always could see a little. Interestingly, as noted, no Byzantine source mentioning his exile in Constantinople comments on his being blind. The Church supported Dečanski and, according to Church sources, the population flocked to him owing to the miracle, which, of course, was seen as a sign of God's favor as well as of his renewed eligibility for the throne. On 6 January 1322 the Archbishop of Serbia, Nicodemus, crowned him king and his son Stefan Dušan, "young king." This is the first coronation for a "young king" (Mladi kralj) in Serbian history. Was it done to create a co-ruler owing to Dečanski's blindness? For Constantine had been claiming, in keeping with the Byzantine custom, that the blind had no right to rule. Or was that coronation an attempt to assure Dušan's subsequent succession?

According to the later saint's life of Dečanski written by Camblak, Constantine's uprising broke out only after Dečanski's coronation and after Constantine had refused Dečanski's offer of the second position in the state and a large appanage. This version is probably a considerable distortion of reality. Since Constantine probably was the intended heir, he almost certainly asserted his claim from the moment he learned of Milutin's death. He would have delayed action until after 6 January 1322 only if news of Milutin's death had been successfully kept from him, which is not an impossibility. Whether

Dečanski really offered to split the realm is unknown. If he felt his position was weak, he might have done so. Otherwise it may be a fiction invented by his clerical biographer to show Dečanski's generosity and to provide a moral tale showing how the greedy, in this case Constantine in turning down the offer, came to a bad end. In any event, warfare followed Constantine's refusal to submit to Dečanski. Dečanski's troops invaded Zeta, and in the ensuing battle Constantine was defeated and killed. According to the hostile Guy Adam, Dečanski had the captured Constantine nailed through the hands and feet to a board and then had him chopped through the middle. After the victory, Zeta was granted to Dušan as an appanage. In this case the assignment clearly indicated that Dušan was Dečanski's intended heir.

Vladislav, still at large and having mobilized local support, presumably in the north from the nobles of Dragutin's former Serbian appanage around Rudnik, called himself king, issued charters, and coined money. He also seems to have received support from the Hungarians and from Ban Stjepan Kotromanić of Bosnia, though it is not clear if the latter ever provided any concrete aid. Vladislav consolidated his control over his lands and prepared to do battle with Dečanski. Thus, as in the days of Dragutin and Milutin, Serbia was again divided between two independent rulers, each of whom controlled the region that his father had previously held. In 1322 and 1323 Ragusan merchants freely visited the lands of both rulers for commercial activities.

In 1323 war broke out between the two cousins. In the fall of 1323 Vladislav still held Rudnik, for Dubrovnik sent gifts to him there. By the end of 1323 the market of Rudnik was administered by officials of Dečanski, and Vladislav himself seems to have fled north. However, some of Vladislav's supporters from Rudnik, seemingly commanded by a leading Ragusan merchant named Menčet Menčetić, had retreated to the near-by fortress of Ostrovica, where they resisted the troops of Dečanski. Dečanski sent envoys to Dubrovnik to protest this Ragusan's support of his enemy. Dubrovnik rejected Dečanski's protest, claiming that neither the town nor its merchant was holding the fortress of Ostrovica but that a group of Serbs held it; furthermore, the Ragusan merchant had fled to Ostrovica in fear of his life. This answer did not satisfy Dečanski, and early in 1324 he rounded up all the Ragusan merchants he could find in Serbia, confiscated their property, and held them captive. Dubrovnik forbade any other merchants to enter Serbia. By the end of the year, after Ostrovica (which seems to have been Vladislav's last fortress in Serbia) had been surrendered to him, Dečanski repented and released the captive Ragusan merchants and restored their property to them. Thus Dečanski took control of what had been Dragutin's Serbian appanage. Tensions between Serbia and Dubrovnik continued, however, for Dečanski's vassal Vojvoda Vojin of Gacko plundered Dubrovnik's territory in August 1325. As a result and in response to a Ragusan appeal, Dubrovnik's overlord Venice also banned trade with Serbia. But peace soon followed. On 25 March 1326 Dubrovnik received a new charter from Stefan Dečanski that reaffirmed all the privileges the town had enjoyed under Milutin. Trouble, as we shall see, erupted almost at once again, later in 1326, when Dubrovnik and Bosnia took action against a family of Dečanski's vassals, the Branivojevići, who had been plundering the town's caravans. However, we shall turn to that event later.

In the warfare between the two claimants for the throne, however, Vladislav was defeated, probably late in 1324, and fled to Hungary where he eventually died. In the course of their warfare, Dečanski seems to have invaded lands far to the northwest of Serbia. In July 1323 he had added "Bosnia and Usora" to his title and then in the spring of 1324 "Soli" (the region of modern Tuzla), suggesting he had occupied these regions. He was not able to consolidate his rule here, and within a year these territories were under the Ban of Bosnia, presumably because the local nobles preferred the ban over Dečanski as their overlord.

The fate of the disputed territory of Mačva during these years is obscure. The traditional view, that of V. Klaić, holds that after Charles Robert conquered Mačva in 1319 the Hungarians retained the territory for the duration of the Serbian civil war and Dečanski's reign. Paul Garai was appointed Ban of Mačva in 1320. Klaić, allowing no role in the region at any time for Dragutin's son Vladislav, believes Garai remained the Ban of Mačva straight through until 1328. He also finds no evidence that Mačva was involved in any of the Serbian dynastic warfare or that Dečanski ever gained control of it. He sees Dušan's counterattack in 1335, to be discussed below, as the first challenge to Hungary's control of Mačva. Recently, however, Ćirković, by redating certain undated references in various Hungarian charters, has presented a new interpretation: He believes that Garai's governorship was short and that Charles Robert awarded Mačva to Vladislav by the end of 1321. Thus at that time Vladislav found himself in possession of both appanages that had belonged to his father, Dragutin, with the possible exception of Braničevo, whose holder in the early stages of the Serbian civil war is simply unknown. Thus, when Dečanski defeated Vladislav and pursued him into northern Bosnia (Soli and Usora), Ćirković believes, he did so after annexing Mačva. This annexation presumably occurred in about 1324. One may assume, however, that in taking Mačva, Dečanski did not acquire the strongly fortified city of Beograd. It seems, however, that Dečanski did not long retain Mačva. A Hungarian campaign against Serbia occurred, probably in 1329, that penetrated to the Obona (the Ub) River. Assuming the Hungarians retained what they occupied, we may conclude that the Hungarians reacquired Mačva by this campaign.[11]

By the spring of 1323, after his victory over Constantine, Dečanski also held most of northern Albania and the coast of Zeta, for he then informed Dubrovnik he would be visiting Bar, Ulcinj, and possibly the land at the mouth of the Mati River. His success in Zeta may have been partly owing to Župan or Kefalia Ilija. That Ilija supported Dečanski is suggested by the fact that Dečanski used him as an envoy to Dubrovnik in August 1322.

Dečanski, therefore, by 1325 had finally established his rule in Serbia.

However, taking advantage of Serbia's internal difficulties after Milutin's death and Dečanski's involvement in them, Hum and Vidin were able to assert their independence from Serbia.

Serbia Loses its Part of Hum

During the civil war after Milutin's death many Serbian nobles had taken sides, presumably usually doing so to better their own local authority and increase their own landholding. Not surprisingly, even after the war was over the squabbling among various Serbian nobles continued. This situation seems to have been particularly intense in Hum. By 1325 the Branivojević family had emerged as strongest in Hum. After the death of Milutin the Branivojevići (the four sons of a nobleman named Branivoj), based on the lower Neretva and holding Pelješac (Stonski Rat) with a major court in Ston, had asserted their authority over a large number of other nobles in Hum. Though the Branivojevići had taken advantage of Serbia's difficulties to assert considerable independence for themselves, on the whole they were willing to call themselves vassals and supporters of Serbia. Their unlicensed behavior, particularly in plundering caravans, had become a thorn in the side of the merchants of Dubrovnik, and not surprisingly, by their land-grabbing behavior, they had stirred up considerable opposition among other nobles in Hum. Orbini claims that by force the Branivojevići had ended up with most of Hum from the Cetina River to Kotor. Thus they had also been asserting their control over much or most of western Hum. They also, Orbini claims, had forced vassalage upon the former ruling family of Hum, represented by Peter, the son of Andrew of Hum, and Peter's sons Toljen and Nicholas (Nikola), who held Popovo Polje and the coastal lands bordering on Popovo Polje. And though nominal vassals of Serbia, Orbini states, the Branivojevići had treated Serbian interests very cavalierly. They had attacked the Serbian župan, Crep, the king's deputy for Trebinje and Gacko, and, having defeated Crep, had killed him and annexed his lands. This action seems to have occurred in, or just before, 1322, because Crep is referred to in Ragusan documents from 1319 and 1321 as alive and active and from 1322 as being deceased.

In 1326 some of these dispossessed and angry Hum nobles turned against Serbia. For though now, after his victory, Dečanski was in a position to take action in Hum, he had done nothing about it; thus the frustrated nobles viewed his failure to act as support of the Branivojevići. These alienated nobles then approached the other strong ruler in the area, Stjepan Kotromanić, the Ban of Bosnia, who in the preceding years had asserted his firm control over the Bosnian lands and made Bosnia into a strong state. Allying himself to various families of Hum and to Dubrovnik, the ban intervened in Hum, dispatching two armies thither and annexing most of it. Orbini states that two of the Branivojević brothers were killed in the fighting. Recent research has securely dated this campaign of annexation to April–June 1326. Bosnia acquired considerably more territory than the Branivojević holdings, because the Branivojevići's opponents, who supported the ban in this campaign, submitted to him in the course of it as did various other nobles of Hum who had grasped what the new balance of power in the area was to be.

Relations between Bosnia and Serbia were extremely tense in the years that followed. Certain members of the Branivojević family, including Branoje, fled to Serbia to seek aid and the release of their captured brethren, who were languishing in a Ragusan jail where unfed at least one, Brajko Branivojević, died of starvation. Dečanski, however, trying to establish his authority at home and more concerned with the growing power of Bulgaria to his east and with the Byzantine civil war, took no action other than to make an appeal to Dubrovnik that procured the release of Brajko's wife, the daughter of Vojin of Gacko, one of his vassals. In fact it even seems that Dečanski abandoned Branoje who had fled to his court. For through bribes Dubrovnik persuaded the Serbs to arrest him and jail him in near-by Kotor, far from his supporters who might have been able to release him. There in the fall of 1326 the Ragusans succeeded in having him "die." Though presumably Dečanski was unhappy about the loss of Hum, he probably had little affection for the Branivojevići. When Branoje fled to him, seeking troops to fight the Bosnian ban whose soldiers had killed two of his brothers, he emphasized to Dečanski that the lost land was Serbia's by right and he offered to submit to Dečanski once he regained it. Dečanski, however, according to Orbini, in response simply pointed out Branoje's past sins, his failure to behave as a vassal should when he had held Hum before, and cited in particular his killing of Crep. And then he had Branoje jailed in Kotor. Presumably Dečanski had taken no action against the Bosnians because he had judged his own strength insufficient to best them.

The elimination of the Branivojevići permitted the Draživojevići of Nevesinje, who by the 1330s were clearly vassals of the Bosnian ban, to become the leading family of Hum. They rapidly expanded their holding to the coast. We know of no actual fighting between Serbia and Bosnia after Bosnia's annexation of Hum, though a reference to an attack on the Saint Nicholas monastery in Dabar on the Lim in Serbia suggests there may have been some minor action. Possibly Bosnia had tried to extend its authority to the Lim. If Bosnia had had such an intention, it was not to be realized at this time. The eastern parts of what is now Hercegovina, including the region of the upper Drina and Lim rivers as well as Gacko, held by Dečanski's loyal vassal Vojvoda Vojin, and the territory bordering on Zeta all remained under the Serbian state, which thus still reached all the way to the Adriatic in southern Dalmatia.

At this time, not surprisingly, relations deteriorated once again between Serbia and Bosnia's ally Dubrovnik. For Dubrovnik not only had participated in the war but also had tried to annex the Branivojevići's coastal holdings, which included Ston and the Pelješac peninsula. Serbia did not want to recognize the loss of this territory and diplomatic negotiations followed. Dubrovnik hoped to maintain the privileges granted to it by Dečanski's March 1326 charter, but Dečanski now demanded a huge new tribute, more or less as rent for this newly taken territory. Dubrovnik, though objecting to this suggestion, tried to keep relations cordial and sent doctors to Dečanski when he needed medical help in 1326. Matters took a turn for the better and then for the worse in 1327 when for an alleged commerical violation Dubrovnik seized a ship belonging to its commercial rival Kotor, a town under Serbian suzerainty. Kotor demanded large damages which Dubrovnik refused. War followed between Serbia and Dubrovnik lasting from summer 1327 to early fall 1328. Its course and the contents of the agreement that ended it are unknown, though by October 1328 relations appear normal again. However, Dečanski still refused to recognize Dubrovnik's rule over Pelješac and Ston. It is also not clear which state or states held Ston and Pelješac between 1326 and 1333. But finally in 1333 the new King of Serbia, Stefan Dušan, concluding that Macedonia was of higher priority than these western lands, sold Pelješac and Ston to Dubrovnik for cash and an annual tribute.

Vidin in the First Quarter of the Fourteenth Century

The second region to loosen its ties to Serbia was Vidin. By 1313 Šišman of Vidin had died and was succeeded by his son Michael Šišman. Michael enjoyed good relations with the Serbs, having married Milutin's daughter (and Dečanski's sister) Anna. It seems he was also to a degree dependent on the Serbs, whose protection may have prevented Vidin from being conquered and annexed by the increasingly strong and ambitious Theodore Svetoslav. However, this dependence on Serbia probably rankled with Michael to some extent. To obtain more independence Michael Šišman appears to have tried to steer a middle course between his Serbian and Bulgarian neighbors. He seems to have been fairly successful at this. At least a Venetian source from about 1313 refers to Michael as Despot of Bulgaria and Lord of Vidin. This title was clearly derived from the Bulgarian tsar. For only a tsar (emperor) could have granted this title, and the Venetians make the Bulgarian origin explicit by saying he was a "Bulgarian" despot. To have been granted this honor suggests that Michael must have established good relations with Trnovo. Thus he seems to have succeeded in steering the middle course upon which Vidin's independence hinged. He also seems to have been able to maintain good relations with his Serbian overlord Milutin without being obliged to fight for him. For there is no evidence that Michael participated in any of the warfare over Mačva between Milutin and Charles Robert of Hungary. However, Serbia still benefited, for Vidin's neutrality at least protected the eastern border of Serbia's province of Braničevo from Hungarian or Bulgarian attack.

Then Milutin died, and chaos followed in Serbia making it impossible for the Serbs to interfere in any way in Vidin's affairs. Though a much later Serbian source, the *Tronoški Chronicle,* says Michael and Byzantium supported Constantine in the Serbian civil war, Nikov doubts its statement is accurate. This late chronicle is frequently unreliable. No other source suggests Vidin played any role in the war at all. There is also no evidence that Byzantium involved itself in the Serb struggle. Furthermore, other than sympathy for Constantine, which Michael may or may not have felt, how could Michael in Vidin, northeast of Serbia, have supported Constantine, whose activities took place in far away Zeta? Thus Nikov rejects the story completely and believes that Michael played no part in the war at all. Michael, however, was able to take advantage of Serbia's inability to intervene in his affairs to establish closer relations with Bulgaria (Trnovo). In fact he was now able to take an active role in Bulgarian councils and in the politics of the Trnovo state. In this way he became a leading actor in these internal affairs and, as a powerful boyar with a huge appanage, a man for the Trnovo boyars to look up to.

Bulgaria in the 1320s

Meanwhile Theodore Svetoslav died in the fall of 1322 and his son and successor George II Terter died late in 1322; as a result the Terter line died out. Skirmishes had taken place throughout 1322 between Byzantium and Bulgaria. Then during the interregnum after George II Terter's death Byzantium obtained by voluntary local submission a long strip of Bulgaria's southern territory between Sliven and Mesembria. The fact that much of this region's populace was Greek probably contributed to this submission. Philippopolis, just regained for Bulgaria by George II Terter, now, after his death, found itself besieged by Byzantine troops. Faced with this major threat from Byzantium, the boyars, some of whom had lands in the lost or threatened territory, turned to the strongest local figure they could find. Between the end of 1322 and June 1323 they elected as Tsar of Bulgaria Michael Šišman of Vidin. Michael's election united the two parts of Bulgaria into one state again. The Šišman dynasty was to rule Bulgaria until the Ottoman conquest.

Presumably the closer ties Michael had forged with Trnovo as a result of the freedom of action given him by the Serbian civil war contributed to his election. Serbia's involvement in its civil war also made it easier for Vidin to merge with Bulgaria. A healthy Milutin, still in power, might well have taken steps to prevent this union in order to preserve his influence in Vidin, cover the eastern approaches to his Braničevo, and prevent the strengthening of Bulgaria that was to occur when its size was increased by a third. After the unification, Michael's half-brother Belaur became governor of Vidin. He bore the title despot. Whether he ran it as an appanage or tried to bring about more integration between it and the rest of the state is unknown.

Michael immediately went to war against Byzantium, broke the siege of Philippopolis, and won back the lost southern territory, much of which had been ceded by the Byzantines to Smilec's disgruntled brother Vojsil, who was allied to Byzantium. A subsequent Byzantine attack obtained Philippopolis again for the empire.

Negotiations followed in 1323 or 1324 between Michael and the empire.

Michael agreed to divorce his Serbian wife, who along with their son John Stefan (who had been his co-ruler and heir but now was deprived of his rights) was imprisoned, and to marry Theodora, widow of Theodore Svetoslav and sister of Andronicus III of Byzantium. This agreement did not put an end to mutual raiding. In 1324 the Bulgarians raided the Berrhoia area and the Byzantines soon thereafter retaliated with an incursion into Bulgaria. Peace was renegotiated, probably in 1326, between Bulgaria and Andronicus III which remained in force until 1330. For most of the Byzantine civil war between Andronicus II and Andronicus III, discussed earlier, Michael supported Andronicus III, who eventually obtained Constantinople and became sole emperor in 1328. The Serbian civil war made it easier for Michael to divorce Anna and conclude this convenient treaty with Byzantium. Fighting Vladislav, Dečanski was in no position to make an effective protest. Possibly Michael's divorcing Dečanski's sister was the basis for the chronicle story that Michael was at this time opposed to Dečanski. Michael's subsequent behavior would certainly re-enforce this view.

In any case, Michael's relations with Serbia had deteriorated from the time of Milutin's death. His assertion of greater independence and union with Trnovo could not have pleased any Serbs. And should the *Tronoški Chronicle* be correct when it claims Michael supported Constantine against Dečanski, this would have been one further annoyance. Michael's divorcing and incarcerating Dečanski's sister did little to improve matters. Nor did Bulgaria's support of Andronicus III help their relations, for Serbia, with long ties to the elderly Andronicus II, father of Milutin's wife Simonida, supported him.

Serbia, Bulgaria, and Byzantium, 1324–32

In his relations with Byzantium, though Dečanski more often supported Andronicus II than otherwise, his policy certainly was not to be completely consistent. The Serbs throughout sought at any given moment the policy that would best serve their own interests. The inconsistency seen in Dečanski's sporadic desertions of his ally Andronicus II may also have reflected a struggle inside Serbia between Dečanski, probably more faithful to Andronicus II, and the nobility seeking any excuse to move south into Macedonia. In any case, Serbia's ties with Andronicus II were temporarily tightened when Dečanski, a widower, married, probably late in 1324, Maria Palaeologina, a cousin of Andronicus II. She was the daughter of Andronicus' nephew John. This marriage alliance soon pulled Dečanski to a third Byzantine side when his wife's father, John Palaeologus, governor of Thessaloniki, tried to separate his city and its territory from Byzantium in 1325. He sought and received Dečanski's support. His troops, supported by Serb units, ravaged along the Struma River in 1326. Serres seems to have been surrendered to them. It appears that John gained little, however, probably owing to a lack of local support; he soon agreed to peace with Andronicus II. Then early in 1327 John died at the Serbian court. Andronicus II, fearing new hostilities with his grandson, renegotiated peace with Dečanski, while Andronicus III tightened his alliance with Michael of Bulgaria.

When war between the two emperors broke out again, Andronicus II called on the Serbs for help. But Serbia, though it mobilized twelve divisions at the time, took no action. Its inactivity probably facilitated Andronicus III's final triumph in 1328. For in the last phase of the war, as Andronicus III marched through Byzantine Macedonia obtaining the surrender of fortresses held by his grandfather, Serb units were present in the area but avoided battle. The Serbs, making no attempt to defend it, even yielded Serres to Andronicus III's troops immediately when they appeared at its gates. Possibly by then the Serbs were certain that Andronicus III would triumph and did not want to antagonize him further by opposing him in what seemed a lost cause. And possibly the Serbs were holding back their troops for other purposes, such as fighting the war with Dubrovnik, then going on, or guarding their borders against a possible Bulgarian attack. In any case, it seems the Serbs did acquire Prosek for themselves during this last phase of the Byzantine civil war. Malović argues that they may well have also acquired Veles, Crešće, and Dobrun at this time. However, the *Life of Dečanski* says these three towns were obtained following the Battle of Velbužd in 1330. In any case, whenever the Serbs acquired them, the possession of these towns opened the routes toward three key Byzantine cities: Thessaloniki, Strumica, and Bitola.

But as Dečanski emerged as sole ruler he found himself faced with a stronger Bulgaria under Michael Šišman, whose ambitions in Macedonia clashed with those of the Serbian nobility. Their rivalry was also exacerbated by the fact that for much of the Byzantine civil war the two states had been lined up on opposite sides. A clash between them loomed. Andronicus III also had no reason to appreciate the Serbs who, until the end, had opposed him. He feared the Serbs as a threat to his Macedonia and saw them as a more dangerous one than Bulgaria. Thus after his triumph in 1328 he was willing to retain his Bulgarian alliance as a defense against Serbia. He and Bulgaria re-affirmed their alliance in October 1328.

Serbia meanwhile sent troops into western Macedonia, plundering the region around Ohrid in 1329. The Serbs also besieged without success Ohrid itself. Whether their ambitions were plunder or annexation is not certain. In any case, when Andronicus III sent troops into that region, the Serbs hastily withdrew.

Worried about Serbia and hostile to it, the two allies Andronicus III and Michael Šišman planned a joint attack on Serbia for 1330. Hearing of the planned invasion, Dečanski sought peace, but Michael refused to discuss it. The allied venture was badly co-ordinated and the Byzantine army did not appear. The Bulgarian army thus found itself alone at Velbužd on 28 July 1330 to face the Serbian forces that Dečanski, worried most about Bulgaria, had concentrated on the Bulgarian front. It seems there were about fifteen thousand on each side. Dušan later claimed the Serbs had fifteen thousand including a thousand experienced Spanish mercenaries. And Gregoras claims the Bulgarians had twelve thousand Bulgarians and three thousand Tatar mercenaries. The Bulgarians, though not expecting such a large Serbian resistance force, still refused peace. Cantacuzenus claims, however, that they agreed to a one-day armistice. Not expecting battle at once and possibly feeling secure owing to the truce (if Cantacuzenus is accurate), Michael allowed much of his army to go out foraging. The Serbs, seeing this happening, launched an attack at once. In the ensuing battle the Bulgarian army, in disarray from the start, was largely destroyed. Seeing defeat looming, Michael Šišman tried to flee, fell from his horse, and was killed. The Serb cavalry played a key role in the battle, and Dušan, who commanded a unit, also distinguished himself.

A delegation of Bulgarian nobles, led by Michael's half-brother Belaur, immediately sought out Dečanski for negotiations. Though the sources mention no territorial changes, many scholars believe the Serbs recovered Niš and its region at this time. Besides whatever territorial settlement may have occurred, Dečanski demanded the immediate return to power in Trnovo of his sister Anna and his nephew, Anna's and Michael's son John (Ivan) Stefan. The boyar delegation agreed to these terms and Serbian troops, free to accompany them to Trnovo after word came of a Byzantine withdrawal from Serbia's southern border, installed the pair in Trnovo in August or September 1330. Belaur, who had concluded the peace, remained a prominent figure, probably still governing in Vidin. Theodora and her children fled to Constantinople. Some Serbian troops remained in Trnovo to guard Anna and John Stefan and oversee matters there. It seems that the Golden Horde, if it had not already done so, at this time re-occupied Bessarabia and extended its control, directly or indirectly, down to the Danube. Thereafter the Danube was to remain Bulgaria's northern border.

Bulgaria was never to regain its former position. The battle resulted in the Serbs' gaining what was to be a permanent edge—at times even hegemony—over Bulgaria to last until Bulgaria fell to the Turks at the end of the century. It also meant that the Serbs, not the Bulgarians, would acquire the lion's share of Macedonia from the Byzantines. They were to dominate that region for the next half-century. The Byzantines, it seems, had not planned to support their allies. While the Bulgarians were facing the main Serbian army, the Byzantine forces were shilly-shallying around western Macedonia, nowhere near the location of the proposed junction with Bulgarian forces, recovering some minor fortresses Dečanski had taken in 1329. Thus they were simply taking advantage of Serbia's pre-occupation elsewhere.

The Serbs' new influence in Bulgaria did not please Byzantium, and the exile of Theodora gave Andronicus III an excuse to intervene against the weakened Bulgarians. Thus the Byzantines, who had sent no aid to Bulgaria, now dropped their alliance with Bulgaria altogether. Late to battle, possibly intentionally, they had waited on the sidelines. Then, upon learning of the Serbian victory, they had withdrawn from the Macedonian border, leaving only small garrisons in certain forts to defend them should the Serbs attack. Deciding now to attack the losers, from whom they could gain the most, the Byzantines invaded Bulgaria and again annexed the disputed region between the Tundža River and the Black Sea, including the towns of Mesembria, Anchialos, Aitos, and Jambol. The Byzantines also regained whatever territory Michael had recovered south of the Balkan Mountains. Anna's inability to defend this territory and the threat of further losses to Byzantium led a group of Trnovo boyars, headed by the protovestijar Raksin and the logothete Philip, early in 1331 to overthrow John Stefan for John (Ivan) Alexander (1331–71). John Alexander, who was Michael's nephew and the son of Stracimir and Michael's sister, had been governing the province of Loveč and probably was party to the plot. Anna and John Stefan fled to Serbia. Soon thereafter John Stefan emigrated to Byzantium.

Belaur opposed the change. In his northwestern province he raised a rebellion, but was defeated by an army of Tatar mercenaries in the hire of John Alexander. Belaur fled from Bulgaria and later died in exile. It is usually believed that Vidin was then incorporated into the Bulgarian state, remaining part of it until the 1350s when John Alexander made it into an appanage for his son John Stracimir. However, Polyvjannyj argues that Vidin continued to have some sort of special status during John Alexander's first years.[12] At that time in Vidin with the title despot is found Michael Šišman's son Michael, known as Michael Vidinski or Michael Bulgarian Great Prince. Presumably Michael had not participated in Belaur's revolt. Whether he simply took over when Belaur fled and John Alexander felt it the safest policy to leave him there and recognize him, or whether John Alexander installed him there, is not known. Possibly, as Polyvjannyj points out, the presence of this young prince was a way to rally supporters of that branch of the Šišman family in the Vidin area and prevent the return of more dangerous members of the family like Belaur.

Meanwhile, right after Velbužd, the Serbs had an excuse to go against Michael's Byzantine allies; but Dečanski chose not to, thereby alienating many nobles. By January or February 1331 Dečanski and Dušan were quarrelling. The pro-Dušan sources claim that evil advisors turned Dečanski against his son; as a result Dečanski decided to seize Dušan and exclude him from his inheritance. He sent an army into Zeta against Dušan. Reaching Skadar, these troops ravaged it and its environs. Dušan, however, fled in time across the Bojana. Anarchy followed in parts of Serbia and merchants found themselves plundered or forced to pay protection money to pass along various routes. Peace was negotiated between father and son in early spring, probably April, 1331. Shortly thereafter, about three months later, Dečanski ordered Dušan to come to him. Dušan feared for his life. His advisors persuaded him to resist. So Dušan marched from Skadar and surprised his father at Nerodimlje, where he besieged him. Dečanski fled with a small retinue, while Dušan captured his treasury and family. He then set off in pursuit of his father, catching up with him at Petrić. On 21 August 1331 Dečanski surrendered to him. On the advice, if not the insistence, of Dušan's advisors, Dečanski was imprisoned. Dušan was crowned king during the first week of September 1331.

Byzantine sources stress the support of Dušan by leading Serbian nobles. They wanted to campaign against Byzantium for lands and booty, but Dečanski had not approved. These nobles, according to Byzantine sources, were regularly a pressure-group for Serbian expansion south, and no ruler was safe who opposed them. Seeking a king to carry out their wishes, they were the moving force behind Dušan's revolt; at first Dušan was more-or-less their puppet, powerless to resist when they threw his father into prison in chains and then murdered him there on November 11. Dečanski, buried in Visoki Dečani, the beautiful monastery he built, was soon canonized by the Church, and his cult became popular.

A second factor that may have played a role in Dušan's revolt was Dečanski's second marriage to the Byzantine princess. She had given birth to a son, Symeon, and it is possible that Dušan feared Symeon's appearance might threaten his own succession. We can suspect that Byzantium would have pressed for the succession of the son of its princess; and if Dečanski wanted good relations with Byzantium, as his post-Velbužd behavior indicates he may have, then making Symeon his heir could advance this cause and might even have been a means to seal a peace. Whether there was any chance of a new heir's being selected or whether Dušan merely feared there was, we do not know. But Symeon's presence provided one more reason for the war-party to press Dušan to revolt to prevent such a peace with Byzantium, and for Dušan to be susceptible to its arguments.

The struggle between Dušan and Dečanski, culminating in Dečanski's overthrow, created sufficient instability in Serbia to prevent Serbian intervention in Bulgaria on behalf of Anna and John Stefan. John Alexander, however, aware of future danger from Serbia once things were again settled there, immediately sought peace with Dušan. Dušan and the Serbian nobles, wanting their hands free to move against richer Byzantium, agreed to peace and to the change on the Bulgarian throne. In December 1331 (or spring 1332) the two rulers concluded peace and agreed to an alliance. It was sealed by Dušan's marriage to John Alexander's sister Helen (Jelena). Good relations with Bulgaria continued throughout Dušan's reign. And though Bulgaria was weaker than Serbia, it did not suffer any legal dependence. It was simply an independent, less powerful, and generally allied state. Dušan never tried to subject it or weaken it further. This peace with Serbia enabled John Alexander to attack the Byzantines and regain the two Black Sea ports of Mesembria and Anchialos as well as the territory between the Tundža and the coast that the Byzantines had seized. Byzantium recognized his possession of them in a treaty of 1332.

Though there seems to have been some Serbian raiding into Macedonia in late 1331, the expected major Serbian attack on Byzantium was to be delayed; for in 1332 Dušan had to suppress a revolt in Zeta, where some nobles led by a certain Bogoje seem to have tried to secede and form their own principality. This revolt is often brought forward as evidence that a Zetan consciousness was still strong and that such feeling should be seen as the explanation for the frequency with which members of the Raškan dynasty were installed in Zeta to rule it. Though possibly this conclusion has some truth to it, Malović points out that the nobility of Zeta had just played a major role in supporting Dušan in his revolt, if not actually pushing him into it. Thus these nobles may well have believed that since he owed his throne to their support, they should reap great rewards after his coronation. However, in the course of the war, and even more so at its conclusion, many of Dečanski's leading courtiers and officials had come over to Dušan's side, possibly even being promised this or that reward to do so. Thus, quite possibly, with much of the old establishment surrounding Dušan at the revolt's end expecting to continue in its former roles, the provincial nobles from Zeta ended up with much less influence than they had hoped and expected. Thus bitterness at Dušan's ingratitude may well have been what triggered the Zetan revolt. It soon spread into northern Albania, whose independent-minded chiefs did not relish subordination by Serbia. The Albanian rebel leader was a chief named Demetrius Suma. In any case, Dušan succeeded in suppressing the rebellion and in reasserting his control over Zeta in the course of 1332. The revolt, and the support it received, however, do suggest that the seeds for the splintering of Serbia that occurred after Dušan's death were already present during his reign.

Bosnia from the 1280s to the 1320s

Before turning to the reigns of Stefan Dušan and John Alexander, it is necessary to return to pick up the history of Bosnia from the 1280s to the 1320s to establish in power there those two rulers' great contemporary, Ban Stjepan Kotromanić (ca. 1318–53).

In the third quarter of the thirteenth century, as seen in the last chapter, the Hungarians reasserted their authority over the territory north of the Bosnian banate, installing various rulers, often entitled ban, over such northern territories as Soli, Usora, Vrbas, Sana, and Mačva. In 1284 Stefan Dragutin, the son-in-law of the King of Hungary, was granted Mačva and possibly Usora in this way. The territory to the west of his grant belonged to a second loyal Hungarian vassal, Ban Prijezda. Their border may have lain along the Drina River, but possibly it lay further west along the Bosna. These two figures, it seems, held all the northern territory between them. It also seems that Kulin's Bosnian banate to the south remained independent under Ninoslav's heirs; but we know nothing of its history or the names of its rulers. Soon Prijezda's son Stjepan Kotroman married Dragutin's daughter and emerged after his father's death at some time between 1288 and 1290 as the major figure in the north.

But Kotroman was soon faced with a major threat to his position from the

Šubić family of Bribir, to his southwest, in the region between Bosnia and Dalmatia. The Šubići were soon pressing into northwestern Bosnia at the expense of Kotroman. In 1299 Paul I Šubić was called "Ban of Bosnia"—a title which probably referred at that date only to this northern territory. In 1302 Kotroman met the Šubići on the banks of the Drina. If a battle followed, its results are not known. In 1304 Mladen I Šubić was killed by "Bosnian heretics" (a label typically used when a source's author felt hostile to the Bosnians he was describing). Whether his death occurred in the north as a result of battling with Kotroman or further south in the central banate is not known. In 1305 Paul Šubić was called "Ban of All Bosnia," which if taken literally would suggest he governed the banate too.

Many of his acquisitions would seem, however, to have been at Kotroman's expense. Was Kotroman expelled from his lands? Or did he retain some or even all of his lands as a Šubić vassal? We do not know. Did the Šubići expand far enough east to threaten Dragutin's holdings? The time was promising since at the time Dragutin, involved elsewhere in his war with Milutin, was not in a position to protect his northwestern border. Again we do not know. Much of this action in Bosnia could be seen as occurring in conjunction with the Hungarian civil war, for the Šubići were allied to Charles Robert whereas Kotroman supported the Hungarian opposition. Thus the Šubići may have been urged by Charles Robert to take what they could in the north of Bosnia to win that area for his cause. In that case, we would expect that the Šubići would have tried to assert their control over as much of Kotroman's territory as they could. Possibly, however, faced with defeat, Kotroman found himself forced to submit and declare for Charles Robert.

Kotroman died between 1305 and 1315, leaving some sort of holding, though what it then consisted of and what its legal status was in relation to the Šubići are not known. At Kotroman's death (whenever it was) disorders broke out in his lands (wherever they then were), causing his widow and his son Stjepan Kotromanić to flee to Dubrovnik. This information is conveyed in a later history, from 1601, by Orbini. Whatever source he used has not survived; thus it is hard to judge how reliable this information is. Orbini tells us that the leading barons of the realm had risen up against Kotromanić. Later, Orbini reports, Kotromanić was allowed to return with the consent of the barons. What caused their change of heart is not known. Most scholars believe he was able to return because he agreed to accept the overlordship of the Šubići.

In about 1318 Kotromanić is documented as holding the central Bosnian banate (in the Visoko-Zenica area). Whether Kotroman had ever held any part of that territory is not known and may well be doubted. How Kotromanić acquired this territory also is not known. Was Kotroman, and thus also Kotromanić, a member of the family (Kulin and Ninoslav's) that had ruled this land previously? If so, possibly the local nobles had invited him there as a candidate with a family right. Or had the Šubići granted him this land? By then the Šubići, with Mladen II as the family head, were already, as noted in the last chapter, beginning their decline. They clearly recognized Kotromanić's rule over the banate, but it is not known whether they had had a role in his installation.

In 1318 through the offices of Mladen Šubić, who was calling himself Ban of Bosnia, Stjepan Kotromanić received special dispensation from the pope to marry a Catholic lady who was a cousin of some sort to him. Mladen's intervention shows that the earlier differences between the two families had been settled. Thus we can see his action as that of an overlord assisting his vassal. Their relations seem to have remained smooth until 1322 when civil war broke out within the Šubić family. Kotromanić was soon drawn into the war as an ally of the king against Mladen. By the end of the year Mladen was taken prisoner by King Charles Robert of Hungary and permanently removed from the political arena. This civil war, which split the Šubić family and divided the Šubić vassals, brought about that family's rapid decline. The family now lost whatever dominance it had once had over the Bosnian banate. This war also marks the beginning of a close association between Kotromanić and the Hungarian king Charles Robert, who were allies in the war against Mladen. Their close association lasted throughout the remainder of Charles Robert's reign (which lasted until 1342) and continued under his successor until Kotromanić died in 1353. Charles Robert still had many domestic difficulties to face. Kotromanić supported him consistently and received in return Hungarian blessing for his own activities in Bosnia. Thus Kotromanić could consolidate his state and his own rule over it without major foreign intervention.

Most scholars agree that Kotromanić's rise to a position of full authority followed the events of 1322. From then, with Šubić recognition of Kotromanić's right to govern his own state without consulting the Šubići or anyone else, he was free to initiate and execute his own policies. Though Hungarian and papal letters mention Hungarian suzerainty, this was clearly only nominal. Bosnia and Hungary were more like allies, and since Kotromanić was useful to Charles Robert, the king had no thought of trying to meddle in Kotromanić's affairs. Kotromanić supported the king against his rivals, and the king supported Kotromanić at a key moment, in 1337/38, when the pope was trying to initiate a crusade against Bosnia.

The papacy had remained concerned about "heresy" in Bosnia. As early as 1318–19 the pope had called on Mladen Šubić to take action against these heretics. But it was also clear that Kotromanić was no heretic and the pope could not have considered him one. If he had, he would not have agreed to Kotromanić's marriage with his Catholic cousin. Since Kotromanić later, in the 1340s, converted to Catholicism, it seems almost certain that originally he was Orthodox; after all his mother, Dragutin's daughter, was Orthodox.

In 1324 Kotromanić had added "Soli" and "Usora" to his title. This territory had previously belonged to his maternal grandfather, Dragutin. Whether Kotromanić obtained it by inheritance, conquest, or acceptance by the local nobles is not known. A year or so earlier Dečanski had moved into this area in his war against Dragutin's son Vladislav. Presumably Kotromanić's acquisition of these lands came as a result of Dečanski's expulsion; but whether Kotromanić himself expelled him or whether Kotromanić benefited from actions of the local nobility is unknown. How much actual authority Kotromanić was to acquire in this area is also unknown. In any case, Usora retained great autonomy under Bosnia. The dominant figure there was the Vojvoda of Usora. He was a local nobleman; his office was hereditary.[13]

Then, after 1322 and before 1325, the leading family of the Donji Kraji, the Hrvatinić-Stjepanić clan, submitted to Kotromanić. This family had previously been vassal to the Šubići. Its submission to Kotromanić reflects also the decline of the Šubići. For the rest of the fourteenth century, except for the early years of Tvrtko I immediately after Kotromanić's death in 1353, the Donji Kraji was to be nominally part of Bosnia, though in fact it was a more-or-less autonomous principality under the Hrvatinić family. Two charters from ca. 1324 exist showing the above and confirming the rights of certain local nobles to lands they already possessed, but asserting the ban's suzerainty over them, in Usora, Soli, and the Donji Kraji.

After the decline of the Šubići the balance of power between the different Croatian noble families of Dalmatia, the Krajina, and southwestern Croatia changed. Old alliances collapsed and new ones were made. Nelipac of Knin rose to prominence. To face the threat from these newcomers the Šubići, trying to retain at least their family lands of Bribir, turned for help to Kotromanić. In the warfare that followed, Kotromanić's Bosnia made tremendous gains to the west, obtaining territory all the way to the coast including the Krajina and Završje, which coincided with western Hum between the Cetina and Neretva rivers and included the towns and regions of Livno, Imotski, Duvno, and Glamoč. He also acquired the port of Makarska. At Makarska and Duvno Roman Catholic bishoprics existed, both subordinated to the Archbishop of Split.

This territory was to remain part of Bosnia from then on, except for part of it temporarily lost in the early years of Tvrtko I. Of course, it must be stressed that considerable local autonomy remained in the hands of the local nobles, who seem to have simply submitted to Kotromanić's suzerainty. In this area, regardless of other religious loyalties of various powerful figures in the banate, the Catholic Church continued to function unmolested. The area remained under the jurisdiction of the relevant bishops, subordinated to Split. No attempt was made to assign these lands to the nominal Bosnian bishop in Djakovo. And no effort was made to introduce the Bosnian Church here. And there is little evidence of that institution's being active here. There is also no sign that state officials were sent into this area by the bans. The local nobility continued to manage local affairs, simply rendering to the ban whatever obligations he demanded from the area.

We saw earlier how Kotromanić, allied with the Draživojevići and other nobles of Hum, sent troops in 1326 into Hum to oust the Branivojevići and annex most of Hum. The Branivojevići disappeared from Hum, either killed, chased out, or jailed. They were replaced as Hum's leading family by the ban's allies the Draživojevići of Nevesinje—soon to be known as the Sankovići. Other families who supported the ban's intervention also rose in prominence. On the whole, as in the western conquests, the local nobility continued to manage its own regions. However, at the lucrative customs stations along the Neretva, particularly at Drijeva (near modern Metković), Kotromanić did install his own officials to obtain the income for him. After this annexation Bosnia came to control the important Neretva valley trade route and reached the Adriatic at that river's mouth for the first time.

On the whole Hum remained loyal to Kotromanić thereafter. At some point Toljen of Hum's son Peter revolted, only to be captured and executed. However, the revolt seems not to have involved the whole family, and the ban maintained close ties with Peter's uncle Nicholas—the grandson of Andrew of Hum through Andrew's son Peter. The ban gave Nicholas his daughter Catherine to be his wife. And he allowed Nicholas to retain the family's hereditary holding of Popovo Polje. The pair had two sons. Their descendants were to compose the prominent Hum noble family of Nikolić. Orbini's account of this family is confirmed by documents in Dubrovnik and also by a gravestone inscription referring to Vladislav Nikolić as the nephew of Ban Stjepan. Thus the ban successfully co-opted the loyalty of Hum's former ruling family. The only evidence of disloyalty in Hum during Kotromanić's reign—besides Peter Toljenović's revolt—is provided by Orbini, who claims that a certain number of nobles from Hum, including the Nikolić brothers Vladislav and Bogiša, supported Dušan when he attacked Bosnia in 1350. When that war was over the Nikolići after some difficulties seem to have made peace with the ban and regained at least some of their former holdings. Dušan's war with Bosnia is to be discussed in the next chapter.

In Hum the overwhelming majority of the population was Orthodox. Once again no attempt was made to interfere with beliefs or Church administration. Thus Bosnia remained an area of separate communities. In the central region the Catholic organization seems to have died out, and those Bosnians there who had ties to any Church were probably associated with the local Bosnian Church until the Franciscan mission, established in the 1340s and to be discussed, won the adherence of some central Bosnians. Thereafter the two Churches—Catholic and Bosnian—co-existed in the central region, with each Church having particular areas of support. The Catholic Church did particularly well in towns. To the west and north of the central banate the Catholic Church was dominant. The Bosnian Church penetrated the Donji Kraji and lower Drina to some extent, but the majority of the population in those areas seems to have remained nominal Catholics even though there was a great scarcity of priests which left much of the population priestless. At the same time these various areas all remained under the administration of the local land-based nobility. Thus there was little or no central administration and almost no interference in local customs and way of life. At the same time the population seems to have remained in its own original localities, and thus, with little or no migration, the different religious faiths remained in their home areas and were not spread elsewhere. Thus sectionalism remained strong, strengthened by the separation between communities resulting from the mountainous geography and by the dominance of local big-men to whom the locals remained loyal.

Thus Kotromanić was in the process of establishing a large state in Bosnia. He had more than doubled its size before 1330 and had asserted its full de facto independence from its neighbors. However, the state was held together by the ban's own personal power and the personal ties he had been able to create. He had not created any sort of state bureaucracy to bind the outlying regions to the central state. He also had not created, or as far as we know even attempted to create, any sort of land-for-service (like the pronoia) system. The nobles in greater Bosnia and Hum were thus far more secure in their lands and independent in their localities than their Serbian and Bulgarian equivalents. As long as they provided the services the ban demanded, his state and armies were strong; but there was no state structure to force their obedience.

In the 1320s and 1330s the ban issued a series of charters to the great nobles. In two of these, and in three or four more in the century that followed, the Bosnian Church guaranteed the contents of the charter. Thus, for the first time we find evidence of this institution, which probably had arisen in the middle of the thirteenth century. Headed by a djed, literally a grandfather, its clergy (called *Krstjani,* "Christians") remained based in monasteries scattered throughout central Bosnia, generally in villages. As far as we can tell all its clerics were monks based in monasteries, which makes it likely that they were derived from the Catholic monastic order seen at Bolino Polje in 1203. There is no evidence of any secular clergy in the Bosnian Church and also no evidence that Bosnia was divided up under some sort of hierarchy with abbot-bishops responsible for particular territories. These charters, signed at a Bosnian Church monastery and witnessed by the djed, not only show the existence of the Church in the center of the Bosnian banate but also show the ban's approval of the organization, for he visited its monastery and allowed its head to witness and guarantee a state document. Though such Bosnian Church–witnessed charters are emphasized in many scholarly works, some of which attempt to depict this organization as a state Church, it should be pointed out that charters witnessed by this Church are only a tiny minority of Bosnian charters; most charters were witnessed only by secular figures.

Though tolerating the Bosnian Church, Kotromanić, as noted, seems to have been Orthodox. He maintained, however, good relations with the pope, who approved his marriage in 1318. These relations soured in 1337 when the pope called on Nelipac of Knin and the Šubići of Bribir to help the Franciscans in their work in Bosnia where, he said, the ban and nobles had been aiding "heretics." Despite this statement, it seems the Franciscans had not even tried to establish a mission in Bosnia by this time. It also seems unlikely that the Šubići would have been interested in this venture. They were then threatened by Nelipac, and Kotromanić was their most logical ally against Nelipac. In fact, at about this time a Šubić girl married Stjepan Kotromanić's brother Vladislav. One suspects Nelipac had written the pope to whet his interest in the crusading idea, so as to advance Nelipac's own ambitions along the coast and against Bosnia, and maybe even against the Šubići should they refuse to help. And in fact, this seems to have happened, since in 1338 Nelipac is found attacking the Šubić town of Klis.

In the face of this threat the ban took quick action to forestall the potential crusade. He went on the offensive himself, dispatching in 1338 his armies via Trogir against Klis, which was under attack from Nelipac. The Bishop of Trogir protested the passage of "heretics," but Trogir's town fathers (the merchants) permitted it and received a charter granting generous trade privileges from the ban. We hear of no further military action; thus the ban's quick action seems to have prevented the launching of a crusade. At the same time the ban was aided by the King of Hungary who, as noted, in this period had close and cordial relations with the Bosnian ban; the king forbade any attack upon Bosnia, an effective order since he was the overlord of the would-be crusaders. The following year, in 1340, the Hungarian king, assisted by Bosnian troops, was fighting in Croatia against some disloyal vassals of his. In 1346 Kotromanić sent more aid to the Hungarians to help them relieve Zadar, then under a siege from Venice. Their good relations culminated in a marriage between King Louis, Charles Robert's successor in Hungary, and Kotromanić's daughter Elizabeth, in 1353.

The pope needed a new scheme to oppose the Bosnian "heretics" or, perhaps more accurately, to advance Catholicism. He turned to the idea of a Franciscan mission. The General of the Franciscan order visited the Bosnian ban in 1339 or 1340 and was well received. The ban agreed to allow the Franciscans to establish a mission in his state and promised to co-operate fully with them. By 1342 the Franciscan Vicariat of Bosnia was established. Eventually its territory was to include all those parts of southeastern Europe where the Franciscans worked. By 1385 the Franciscans had four monasteries in Bosnia proper: in Olovo, Visoko, Kraljeva Sutjeska, and Lašva. Another dozen were to be built in the Bosnian state between 1385 and the Turkish conquest, which occurred in 1463. By 1347 Ban Stjepan Kotromanić had accepted Catholicism. From then on, all Bosnian rulers, except possibly Ostoja, were to be Catholics.

The Franciscan chronicles state that hundreds of Franciscans came to Bosnia and converted hundreds of thousands of Bosnians. This is greatly exaggerated. As far as we can tell, at any given moment in the fourteenth century there were in Bosnia only a handful of Franciscans. We also must note that the term *Bosnia* in a Franciscan context refers to the whole vicariat, which included a much greater region than the state of Bosnia. For most of the fourteenth century the Franciscan order limited the number of Franciscans allowed the vicariat to from sixty to eighty men. In 1385 the vicariat had thirty-five monasteries, and, as noted, only four of these were in the Bosnian state. Thus one could conclude that there were at most about fifteen Franciscans in the entire Bosnian state. Since they were required to reside in their monasteries, thus in only four places, we may suspect they had very limited success. However, as three of their four monasteries were concentrated near the center of the state, possibly they did achieve some success in converting, or at least baptizing, Bosnians in that area, the central triangle between Sutjeska, Lašva, and Visoko.

However, reducing the Franciscans' effectiveness as missionaries were three other factors. The first concerns the locations of two of their four residences. Olovo was a mining town having many Saxon miners and coastal merchants while Visoko, though Bosnia's main town, also had a relatively large merchant colony. The Catholics in these places surely supported the Franciscans and protected them, should there have been opposition to them from Bosnians—something for which we have no evidence. At the same time, however, since other Catholic clergy seem not to have been present in Bosnia, the religious needs of these foreign Catholic communities surely took up much of the Franciscans' time. Second, the Franciscans had serious financial problems. Immediately a quarrel over who had the right to collect Church tithes in Bosnia erupted between the Bishop of Bosnia (resident outside of Bosnia in Djakovo in Slavonia who only had title to Bosnia) and the Franciscans, who at least were working in Bosnia. The ban supported the Franciscans, but the pope decided in favor of the bishop. This quarrel and the financial problems of the Franciscans continued for the next century. In 1347 the newly converted Catholic, Ban Stjepan Kotromanić, wrote the pope requesting more Franciscans for Bosnia and asking that those sent know—or have the ability to learn—Slavic. This last remark highlights the third difficulty; for it suggests that at least some of those sent earlier—and the names of Bosnian Franciscans preserved in the sources from this period tend to be Italian—did not know Slavic. Thus the effectiveness of Bosnia's limited number of Franciscans would have been greatly reduced owing to the language barrier.

Kotromanić had very cordial relations with the first Franciscan vicar, Peregrin Saxon. And when in 1347 a vacancy arose for the Bosnian bishop, Kotromanić wrote the pope suggesting that Peregrin be named to the position. This was an ideal solution to the division of authority between Franciscans and bishop as well as a means to settle the quarrel between the two institutions. The pope wisely accepted the suggestion, and so from 1349 to 1354 Peregrin was bishop. He was the first Catholic bishop to be active in Bosnia since the middle of the thirteenth century. Thus briefly the Bosnian bishop became relevant to Bosnia again. However, after Peregrin died, instead of continuing this sensible new program, the pope selected a cleric in Djakovo, and once again the two institutions were divided and the bishop, returning to reside in Djakovo, ceased to play any role in Bosnia.

Until the fourteenth century Bosnia and Hum were economically backward, less developed than many of the other regions making up what is now Yugoslavia. But under Kotromanić Bosnia's mines, particularly silver and lead ones, were opened and thus paved the way for Bosnia's economic development and greatly increased its commercial contacts with the coast. Further mines were to be opened under his successor Tvrtko. Technical expertise was provided by the Sasi (Saxons, chiefly from Hungary) while Ragusans took over the mines' administration and financial operation. The laborers were local Bosnians. Dubrovnik soon acquired a monopoly on Bosnia's silver. The most important silver mining center was Srebrnica. In these mining towns Ragusans established colonies of merchants, mining administrators, and soon craftsmen. Dubrovnik appointed a consul to govern each Ragusan colony according to Ragusan law. The Sasi were also governed by their own law code. In time artisans settled in the commercial centers growing up around the mines. Many of the more skilled craftsmen came from the coast, but soon many locals were also becoming craftsmen.

The ruler of a town (the ban or a great nobleman on whose lands the town lay) appointed a knez to keep order and be the chief legal figure. The town knez tended to be a literate and astute financier. He was frequently a Ragusan merchant. If the town was fortified, then, since the knez often lacked military knowledge, a garrison commander was also appointed. By the end of the fourteenth century the Bosnians were gradually entering the crafts and becoming merchants. By the fifteenth century some Bosnians were trading widely around Bosnia and even on the coast and in Italy. However, the major merchants continued to be Ragusans. The Ragusans kept their monopoly on silver, though certain Bosnians became successful in the lead trade. Bosnia's prosperity grew rapidly because, by the mid fourteenth century, most of Europe's mines were in decline. Such was not true of the newly opened mines of Serbia and Bosnia. By 1422 Serbia and Bosnia together were producing over one-fifth of Europe's silver. This led to great urban prosperity. Certain merchants made great fortunes, and through customs revenues various nobles were also becoming very wealthy. All sorts of luxury textiles and metal products were imported into Bosnia. At the same time, certain Bosnian craftsmen achieved great skill in metal crafts; Bosnian silver-work—especially cups and belt buckles—was in demand on the coast.

The rulers in the twelfth and thirteenth century (at least Kulin and Ninoslav), wanting to encourage the circulation of more goods in Bosnia, had allowed Dubrovnik to trade duty-free. But when the mines opened, the prospect of increased revenue prompted a change in policy. Kotromanić began imposing customs duties. By the end of the century the great nobles were doing the same. Customs were of three types: export duties collected at the point of purchase (e.g., at the mine where the silver was bought for export), which seem to have been 10 percent of the purchase price in kind; import duties collected at the market where the imported goods were sold, which also seem to have been 10 percent in kind; and duties on passage, generally collected in cash at toll stations along the routes the merchants traveled. The nobles frequently tried to establish additional toll stations on roads crossing their lands, a practice Dubrovnik regularly, and sometimes successfully, protested. The major customs collections were farmed out to particularly rich merchants (usually Ragusans) who at the time of purchase paid to the ruler the sum expected for the year and then collected the actual customs revenues for themselves, hoping for a profit. Unless there was a war or major epidemic, they usually earned good profits, but since trade could be suspended in a crisis there was risk involved. On one occasion, in 1376, a wealthy Ragusan named Žore Bokšić, with two partners, purchased all the customs stations in Bosnia.

Besides the towns growing up around commercial enterprises like mines, others grew up at major crossroads. Important commercial routes ran through Bosnia from the coast to Serbia, Bulgaria, Constantinople, and Hungary. Some places on these routes became centers for selling local goods; for example, Foča became important for selling wax, sheepskins, and other pastoral products. The Vlachs, who wandered with their flocks, had horses. By the fifteenth century certain Vlachs, particularly those of Hum, acquired great wealth running merchant caravans. Other Vlachs—as well as various nobles and their retainers—enriched themselves by plundering the caravans.

Still other towns appeared initially not for commercial reasons, but as castles, erected by a great nobleman or the ban, to defend a region from attack or maintain order in it. Naturally such a defensive center was often chosen as a local market. Such markets tended to be held once a week. But if the castle's market became a thriving one, the area below the castle in time acquired shops in which craftsmen sold goods daily rather than only at the weekly market. The noble in control of the castle collected the market duties.

As a result of the profits from the mines and trade, we find (e.g., in lists of goods pawned in Dubrovnik), in the fifteenth century in particular, certain Bosnians with considerable wealth. Some nobles came to maintain sumptuous courts stocked with luxury textiles and metal-work from Italy and Western Europe. Actors and musicians frequently visited them to perform. These performers did not limit themselves to the courts of the nobility; documents show them playing in commercial towns as well.

Since the towns were chiefly connected to commercial enterprises, in many of them foreigners (Ragusans, other Dalmatians, Sasi) were the predominant element in the urban population, with Bosnian Slavs making up an urban minority but, of course, the great majority in the surrounding villages. Thus not surprisingly, with the Ragusans strongly supporting the Franciscans, the commercial towns that developed were Catholic in character. Documents on the towns rarely mention the presence of the Bosnian Church or its clerics.

Stjepan Kotromanić died in 1353 and was buried in the Franciscan monastery at Visoko, the town that was his main residence. During his lifetime mention is made of a son; but at his death we find no sign of him, suggesting that he pre-deceased his father. Stjepan's brother Vladislav was still alive, but instead of Vladislav, Vladislav's son Tvrtko, then only about fifteen years old, succeeded. No documentation has survived explaining why the succession went the way it did. Though at first the state broke apart, Tvrtko, as we shall see, eventually was able to reassemble it, extend its boundaries to their farthest limits, and become the greatest of Bosnia's medieval rulers.

NOTES

1. Mavromatis, *La fondation de l'Empire Serbe.*
2. M. Malović, "Stefan Dečanski i Zeta," *Istorijski zapisi* 41, no. 4 (1979): 5–69.
3. E. P. Naumov, "K istorii Vizantijskoj i Serbskoj pronii," *Vizantijskij vremennik* 34 (1973): 22–31.
4. P. Nikov, *Tataro-b"lgarski otnošenija pr"z sr"dnit v"kov' s"ogled' k"m caruvaneto na Smileca,* in *Godišnik na Sofijskija universitet* (Istoriko-filologičeski fakultet) 15–16 (1919–20).
5. I. Božilov, "Beležki v"rhu B"lgarskata istorija prez XIII vek," in *B"lgarsko srednovekovie,* Dujčev Festschrift (Sofija, 1980), pp. 78–81.
6. Other Nogajs, including various Alans, who had been subject to Nogaj, fled to Byzantium's port of Vicina at the Danube mouth. Entering Byzantine service, many were soon transferred to Thrace, where they fought for the empire against the Catalans.
7. P. Nikov, *Tataro-b"lgarski otnošenija.*
8. D. Nicol, *The Despotate of Epiros, 1267–1479* (Cambridge, 1984), pp. 37–49.
9. Philip of Taranto granted privileges to thirteen Albanian tribes, thus documenting their existence at this time: Albos, Spatos, Cotarucos, Bischesini, Aranitos, Lecenis, Turbaceos, Marchaseos, Scuras, Zenevias, Buccesseos, Logoreseos, Mateseos. Though not receiving grants from Philip, other Albanian families are also noted in this period: among these Gin Tanush of the Dukagjin family, who already in 1281 bore the title duke, and the Matarango family deserve particular attention. See M. Spremić, "Albanija od XIII do XV veka," in *Iz istorije Albanaca* (Beograd, 1969), p. 36.
10. For a list of the Albanian families with whom Pope John XXII was in communication, see *Istorija Crne Gore,* vol. 2, pt. 1 (Titograd, 1970), p. 63.
11. See V. Klaić, *Povijest Hrvata* (reprint, Zagreb, 1982), vol. 2, pp. 37–38; and S. Ćirković, "Beograd pod Kraljem Dušanom?" *Zbornik Istorijskog muzeja Srbije* 17–18 (1981): 42–45.
12. D. Polyvjannyj, "K istorii Vidinskogo despotstva v XIV veke," in *B"lgarsko srednovekovie,* Dujčev Festschrift (Sofija, 1980), pp. 93–98.
13. On Usora see P. Andjelić, "O Usorskim vojvodama i političkom statusu Usore u srednjem vijeku," in P. Andjelić, *Studije o teritorijalnopolitičkoj organizaciji srednjovjekovne Bosne* (Sarajevo, 1982), pp. 142–72.

CHAPTER 6

The Balkans in the Middle of the Fourteenth Century

Dušan and Byzantium to 1334

Stefan Dušan came to the throne in Serbia as a result of a revolution led by a segment of the Serbian nobility that had been dissatisfied by Stefan Dečanski's unwillingness to wage war against Byzantium to expand into Macedonia. All evidence suggests that Dušan started what was to be a glorious reign as a mere puppet of these nobles. This is stated not only in the Byzantine sources, but also in Ragusan records. For example, on one occasion the town's instructions to an envoy at the Serbian court reminded him that decisions did not depend just on the ruler but also on his entourage. Not surprisingly, considering the political goals of the nobility, Serbian troops raided into Macedonia in the late fall of 1331 immediately after Dušan's succession. They reached the Struma River. Probably on this occasion they captured the town of Strumica. Further large-scale action in Macedonia was then delayed because in 1332 Dušan needed to put down the revolt of Bogoje in Zeta and northern Albania.

Dušan suppressed this revolt in 1332. He then had two foreign policy areas calling for attention. Besides Macedonia, he was faced with problems in the west, for, as we have seen, in the 1320s Serbia had suffered serious losses in that direction when Bosnia had annexed most of Serbia's Hum, and Dubrovnik had taken Ston and the Pelješac peninsula. Presumably Serbia would have liked to re-assert its authority in these areas. However, it was not strong enough to campaign on two fronts and it is evident that the nobles, desiring action in Macedonia because it would bring them benefits (rather than simply obtaining the recognition of Serbian suzerainty from existing landlords, most of whom presumably would keep possession of their lands), were a strong pressure-group for the Macedonian option. So Dušan opted for offensives to his south. To carry out this policy, it made sense to reach a settlement with Dubrovnik. Such an agreement would benefit Serbia financially, not only by preventing ruptures in the commercial activities from which Serbia's ruler collected customs but also by obtaining a cash settlement for the lands Dubrovnik had annexed.

So in 1333 after negotiations Dušan sold Ston and its environs—including the Pelješac peninsula and the coastland between Ston and Dubrovnik—to Dubrovnik for eight thousand perpera in cash and an annual tribute of five hundred perpera to be paid each Easter. From 1348 on, by order of Dušan, this tribute was donated to the Monastery of the Archangels Michael and Gabriel in Jerusalem. Dubrovnik also had to guarantee freedom of worship for Orthodox believers in this territory. This last promise was not observed, for almost before the ink was dry on the treaty Dubrovnik sent Catholic clergy, particularly Franciscans, into this territory to proselytize on behalf of Catholicism. However, despite Dubrovnik's encouragement of the Catholic missionaries, for much of Dušan's lifetime Orthodox priests were tolerated in Ston. But after 1347 scholars have found no further references to Orthodox clergy in Ston. In 1334 Bosnia recognized the Serbian-Ragusan agreement. With this settlement Serbia, which had been the aggrieved party, could expect peace on its western frontier and thereby gain a free hand to carry on an active southern policy.

Since later, in the nineteenth and twentieth centuries, nationalism became so prevalent in the Balkans, many modern scholars have at times attributed nationalist feelings to leaders in the medieval Balkans. It is worth noting, in that context, that Dušan and the Serb nobles opted for an internationalist policy—expanding south into lands with large numbers of Greeks and Albanians rather than attempting to regain the lands to the west inhabited by fellow Serbo-Croatian speakers.

Though there seem to have been a certain number of raids to the south after Dušan's accession, major gains did not occur until 1334, when a great opportunity presented itself to the Serbs. In late 1333 a leading Byzantine general, Syrgiannes, governor of the western provinces (including western Macedonia and Albania), revolted against Andronicus III and sought Dušan's help. We have already met Syrgiannes, who was half Cuman and half Greek, during the civil war between Andronicus II and Andronicus III; Syrgiannes had played an active role in it, first supporting Andronicus III and later Andronicus II. After Andronicus III's succession, he restored himself to the new emperor's favor and received his governorship. However, disliking John Cantacuzenus, Andronicus' leading advisor, Syrgiannes seems to have joined the emperor's mother in a plot against Cantacuzenus. Some information about his activities was uncovered, causing him to be accused of plotting against Andronicus III; to avoid arrest he fled into Albania and soon showed up at the Serbian court.

The Serbs, not surprisingly, agreed to support him and in the spring of 1334 launched an attack into imperial Macedonia; the invaders benefited greatly from Syrgiannes' knowledge of Byzantine defenses, his ability as a strategist, and the fact that he had many friends and supporters in high positions in that area. Fortresses surrendered rapidly to the Serbs, who soon found themselves in possession of Ohrid, Prilep, and Strumica. Syrgiannes then directed the capture of Kastoria. After this the Serbs marched down the Vardar toward Thessaloniki, soon reaching that city's walls. The hard-pressed Byzantines responded by implementing a well-conceived plot. Frantz (Sphrantzes) Palaeologus, who commanded several fortresses in the vicinity of Kastoria, deserted to the Serbs, who received him warmly. Next a Byzantine army moved into the province of Thessaloniki and set up camp near the beleaguered city; the Serbs withdrew a short distance away to the mouth of the Vardar. While the two armies were thus camped, Palaeologus succeeded in enticing Syrgiannes away from the main camp by himself; at once he and some associates murdered him and succeeded in escaping after the deed to Thessaloniki.

Dušan's plans were now seriously upset, for his successes until then had chiefly been owing to Syrgiannes' strategic abilities, knowledge of the Byzantine opposition, and friends who surrendered fortresses to the Serbs. His death lost Dušan these advantages. Thus Dušan, not surprisingly, was receptive when Andronicus III offered a peace with generous terms. Furthering Dušan's willingness to negotiate was intelligence that the Byzantines had just repelled a major Turkish raiding party—freeing more Byzantine troops for the Thessaloniki front—and a report that the Hungarians, knowing of Serbia's involvement in the south, were mobilizing to attack Serbia from the north. Thus the Serbs agreed to peace on 26 August 1334. The Byzantines recognized a large number of Serbian gains, thereby officially surrendering title to a series of forts already taken by the Serbs. These included Ohrid, Prilep, Strumica, Siderokastron, Čemren, and Prosek. This made the Byzantine-Serbian border almost identical to the present Greek-Yugoslav border. There is debate over when certain of these fortresses were taken by the Serbs. Prosek had clearly been taken previously, in 1328, by Dečanski. And Ostrogorsky, following Gregoras, thinks Strumica was taken in 1331. The others seem to have been taken in the course of 1334 after Syrgiannes had joined the Serbs. By the treaty Kastoria reverted to Byzantium.

Dušan and Hungary

Dušan then marched north to face the Hungarians. They had received military support from Bosnia. Whereas this support probably reflects Kotromanić's alliance with Hungary more than any particular hostility toward Serbia, it still shows that Dušan could not entirely ignore his western neighbor. The Hungarians, not expecting any serious Serbian resistance, had already penetrated well into Serbia, reaching the neighborhood of the Žiča monastery. They now quickly withdrew their armies. The Byzantine sources claim that the empire's treaty with Serbia had promised Byzantine aid to Serbia against the Hungarians. Fulfilling this promise, Byzantine troops had marched north with Dušan and their presence had caused the Hungarians to withdraw. Most scholars reject this claim as fiction; it is doubtful that the Byzantines, threatened by Turkish raiders, could have afforded to spare many troops. Furthermore, it is unlikely that whatever limited aid the Byzantines could provide would have seemed fearsome to the Hungarians. Thus most scholars have concluded that Byzantine authors were simply bragging to bolster the empire's declining prestige at a moment when it had had to conclude a humiliating treaty with Serbia that recognized Serbian possession of a large part of what had been Byzantine Macedonia.

Thus the Hungarian invasion, which does not seem to have been seriously planned and may have been intended only as a raid, led to no territorial losses for Serbia. In fact some scholars believe that Dušan made use of his mobilized forces to go on the offensive against the Hungarian aggressors to regain part or all of Mačva and restore the Danube and Sava as the Serbian-Hungarian border. Ćirković argues that Dušan even took Beograd at this time but was unable to retain it, and that soon thereafter, probably in 1339, the Hungarians recovered Beograd.[1] Furthermore, if Dušan in 1335 did regain Mačva, which other scholars doubt, he may not have been able to retain it either. For in the period that followed, Bans of Mačva, appointed by and loyal to Hungary, including a Ban Nicholas between 1335 and 1340, are mentioned in the sources. Though it is possible Nicholas and his successors merely bore this title as an empty court honor, which may also be regarded as an official statement of Hungary's claims to this territory, most scholars believe that the existence of these Bans of Mačva reflects Hungary's possession of some, or even all, of Mačva. However, we must conclude that we lack sources to resolve this question. The Hungarian attack and Serbian response is usually dated as occurring in 1335; however, the warfare may have been initiated in late 1334.

No peace seems to have been concluded with the Hungarians; thus a state of semi-war marked by mutual raiding seems to have continued. These sorties, chiefly for plunder, seem to have brought about no territorial changes except for the possibility of Beograd's changing hands. We know of forays and skirmishes in 1338, 1339, and 1342. Finally, it seems in 1346, a peace was concluded; its terms are unknown. Interestingly enough, despite this long period of hostility between Serbia and Hungary (including the Hungarian raid deep into Serbia as far as Žiča in 1334/35 and the possible fighting over Mačva), the Hungarians seem to have made no attempt to dislodge the Serbs from the province of Braničevo. Despite its vulnerable location on the Hungarian border, Braničevo remained Serbian and, it seems, unattacked throughout Dušan's reign.

Dušan, the Empire, and Albania

Dušan, concerned with the south, clearly did not want to involve himself in a major confrontation with Hungary. But though he seems to have had a new war with Byzantium in mind, no warfare was to take place against the empire from 1334 until the death of Andronicus III in 1341. In the interim the rulers of the two states met in 1335, spending seven days together. At the time the Byzantines, needing their forces elsewhere, were worried that the Serbs intended to break the 1334 treaty. The discussions were fruitful, and the Serbs agreed to take no action in Macedonia, thus leaving Byzantium free to divert its forces to Anatolia and the Aegean islands.

While the Serbs were maintaining their peace with Byzantium, they turned their attention to Albania, presumably both to subdue various chieftains who were not observing their obligations to their Serb suzerains and also to extend Serbian influence. At Dušan's accession the Serbs held the Albanian lands north of the Mati River. In 1336 Dušan had limited successes in central Albania which included the acquisition from the Angevins of a major prize, Durazzo. At the time Durazzo seems to have been managed by a clique of local nobles who recognized Angevin suzerainty. Dušan seems to have done nothing more than negotiate with these locals and persuade them to recognize his suzerainty. His acquisition of Durazzo, which occurred by August 1336, was not to last, for soon the city is found once again under the Angevins. Observing his treaty with Byzantium, Dušan does not seem to have disturbed Byzantium's holdings in Albania. In 1337 Dušan was still active in the area; at roughly the same time Andronicus III was campaigning against certain Albanian tribes in southern Albania who had been raiding his subjects who lived in the plains. Andronicus seems to have been fairly successful in the warfare, taking many prisoners and acquiring the submission of certain tribes. His successes, though, do not seem to have been long-lasting, and the tribesmen soon reverted to their former activities. Though Dušan was operating in the vicinity at the same time, he seems neither to have clashed with Andronicus nor to have collaborated with him. Some scholars believe that in 1337 Dušan acquired Kanina and Valona; if this occurred, Andronicus presumably was not pleased. However, it seems more probable that Dušan's forces remained well to the north of these towns and that they became Serbian at some time between 1343 and 1345.

Dušan in 1340

While the Byzantines were putting down the 1339–40 revolt in Epirus, the Serbs pressed further into Albania and obtained the submission of further tribal chieftains. The Serbs at this time were clearly operating in the south of Albania; sources document them in the vicinity of Jannina. Dušan at this time added "Albania" to his title. The Byzantines in 1340 were in no position to oppose him, but various Albanians probably did. And the tribes of Thopia (Topia), which controlled much of the territory between the Shkumbi and Mati rivers, and of Musachi (Muzaki), holding much of the region between the Shkumbi and Valona, concluded treaties with the Angevins against the Serbs. The Albanian leaders agreed that after their uprising succeeded their territories would recognize Angevin suzerainty. Except for one battle at about this time, in which Andrew II Musachi defeated a Serb unit in the Peristeri Mountains (for which he received a medal from the Byzantines), we know of no action taken by any Albanians to oust the Serbs and realize the treaty with the Angevins. We also know of no Angevin or Byzantine aid against the Serbs to these or any other Albanian tribes. However, though Serb troops penetrated into southern Albania, it is not at all clear which towns they took or how much of this area they occupied or asserted their control over. Some scholars date their acquisition of various towns to these years, but others believe the Serbs obtained submission, possibly only nominal, from various tribes but did not take any central or southern Albanian towns until 1343–45.

In the course of 1340 Dušan fell seriously ill. Quite probably at that time a certain amount of jockeying for power took place among his nobles. At this critical time one of Dušan's leading commanders, Vojvoda Hrelja, possibly finding himself allied with a weaker faction, deserted to the Byzantines, taking his lands with him. He could do this because he possessed a large holding right on the Byzantine-Serbian border that included the region of the middle Struma River, with Strumica and two other strongly fortified castles near-by. Some scholars believe he held the river's course to its mouth on the Aegean. Thus Hrelja seems to have obtained a sizeable chunk of the territory Serbia gained from the empire in the early 1330s. The Byzantines allowed him to retain his lands and granted him the high court title of caesar. Dušan soon recovered, but he was not immediately able to take any action to regain this lost region. The ease with which Hrelja was able to secede shows how decentralized the Serbian state was. Lacking officials from the central government to administer it and lacking garrisons of troops under generals appointed by and loyal to the king, this Struma territory was more-or-less the private holding of Hrelja, who, supported by his own forces, administered and defended the region.

Turkish Activities in the Balkans

Besides the civil strife and the international violence among the southeastern European states and peoples, already described, the Turks were also disrupting parts of the Balkans in the 1330s. Two different Turkish emirates, both based in Anatolia, caused particular hardship for the Christians of southeastern Europe: that of the Ottomans based in Bithynia in northwestern Anatolia and that of Aydin centered in Smyrna on the west coast of Anatolia. Raiding by sea, they disrupted Greek and Latin shipping, raided islands and towns near the coast, and took large numbers of captives as well as plunder.

Mehmed, the Emir of Aydin, was persuaded to conclude a treaty with the Byzantines in 1329. From then until his death in 1334 his Turks concentrated their activities against the Latin areas of Greece. However, peace with Aydin did not relieve the Byzantines from Ottoman attacks. In 1329 the Ottomans raided into Europe, plundering Trajanopolis and Bera in Thrace before being expelled. And Turks, presumably Ottomans, raided Thrace, particularly along the coast, in 1331, 1332, and 1334. On all these occasions the Turks were driven back, but they procured considerable plunder and the efforts against them were costly, as the empire lost manpower that it could ill afford to lose in battles against them.

Meanwhile, the Turks of Aydin took to the Aegean as pirates and raided the Latin islands and the coastal regions of Frankish Greece. A particularly large campaign was carried out, most probably during 1332 and 1333, under the direction of Mehmed's son Umur. He attacked Euboea and was persuaded to leave only after the Venetian bailiff agreed to pay him tribute. At this time he also raided the islands forming the Dukedom of Naxos and allegedly took fifteen thousand captives from these islands. On the mainland both the small Duchy of Boudonitsa and the Peloponnesian coast suffered from his raids as well. In 1334 Mehmed died and was succeeded by Umur; the Latins retaliated against him by launching a raid against Smyrna, but the city held out. Undeterred, Umur was back raiding the Peloponnesus in 1335. (In fact 1335 was a particularly active year for Turkish pirates in the Aegean.) And as he did not feel bound by his father's agreements with the empire, he plundered Byzantine Thrace in 1336 as well. However, in the course of that year the Byzantines negotiated a new treaty with him. And thereafter he maintained friendly relations with the empire, and particularly with John Cantacuzenus who seems to have been the envoy who concluded the treaty with him. Thus when Cantacuzenus found himself in difficulties in the early 1340s, he was able to turn to Umur and find in him a loyal supporter against any and all opponents. Immediately after the treaty of 1336, Umur provided two thousand infantrymen archers to assist Andronicus III in his Albanian campaign of 1337.

Since the most active raiders of the 1330s and early 1340s, the Turks of Aydin, concentrated their activities against the Latins, the Latins in turn were forced to take measures against Aydin. After considerable planning, they were to mobilize a crusading effort against Umur's capital of Smyrna. In 1343 a major naval effort led by the knights of Rhodes and the King of Cyprus was to fail. However, a second attack in the fall of 1344 was to have considerable success.

The Byzantine Civil War between Cantacuzenus and the Constantinopolitan Regency

On 15 June 1341 the Byzantine emperor Andronicus III died unexpectedly. The Serbs immediately took advantage of his death to dispatch a raiding party that penetrated deeply into Macedonia and reached Kritskoselerije near Thessaloniki. It seems this was done on the spur of the moment; not having time to prepare a major offensive, the Serbs' goal was simply plunder. Albanian tribesmen in the regions of Pogonia and Livisda also rose up, plundering the Byzantine town of Berat and part of northern Epirus.[2] And Turkish pirates launched extensive raids against the coasts of Macedonia and Thrace.

At the same time the Bulgarians threatened the Byzantines with war.

Taking advantage of the weakness anticipated from Andronicus' death, John Alexander sent an embassy to demand the person of John Stefan, who had fled to Byzantium when John Alexander overthrew him in 1331. John Cantacuzenus, who received the envoys, not only refused to comply but threatened to send Umur of Aydin to raid the Bulgarian coast and spoke of the possibility of a Byzantine-Turkish expedition along the Danube that could attack Vidin and other Bulgarian cities from that river. And to add force to his threat he allowed Umur's fleet to pass through the Straits and the Bosphorus into the Black Sea. It arrived at the Danube mouth in July or August 1341. Under this pressure, John Alexander backed down from his demands.

Andronicus' heir was his son John V (1341–91) who then was about nine years old. In his will Andronicus III had appointed his best friend and long-time associate John Cantacuzenus to be the regent. He was an immensely rich landlord having vast estates in Thrace and a large number of animals: five thousand cows, one thousand oxen, twenty-five hundred mares, two hundred camels, three hundred mules, five hundred donkeys, fifty thousand pigs, and seventy thousand sheep. Cantacuzenus was greatly disliked by Andronicus' widow, Anna of Savoy. He was to be an active figure in Byzantine politics for the next fifteen years, eventually in 1347 becoming emperor himself. After his forced retirement, he wrote a history that devoted its attention to the turbulent events he participated in. Thus his work is also a memoir, and, like many memoirs, it is a very biased source that depicts its author in the best possible light. Considerable scepticism must therefore be used when one evaluates many of its statements, particularly statements concerning Cantacuzenus' motives, verbal agreements, and aims.

The regent Cantacuzenus immediately led an army out from the capital to meet the Serbs while at the same time dispatching envoys to Serbia to try to re-establish the 1334 peace treaty. His aim at the time seems to have been to conclude peace with the Serbs so he could concentrate his efforts on fighting the Franks in the Peloponnesus and restore Byzantine rule over that peninsula. His interest in the Peloponnesus was strong, for his family had been very active in that region, supplying several governors for the territory recovered by the empire. Furthermore, Cantacuzenus had what seemed a glorious opportunity to acquire the rest of the Peloponnesus. Threatened by Byzantium's gradual expansion from Mistra and from other Peloponnesian centers, a group of important Latin barons had decided that the best way to retain the lands they still held was to submit to Byzantine suzerainty provided that the empire was willing to confirm them in their lands, castles, and existing privileges. Envoys bearing this offer approached Cantacuzenus; he was very receptive to it and began planning a Peloponnesian campaign under his own leadership that would accept the submissions of these barons. However, before he could act upon this, a new blow struck him.

Cantacuzenus' enemies took advantage of his absence from Constantinople at the end of September 1341 to stage a coup against him. Declaring him an enemy of the young emperor, they deposed him as regent and established a new regency under Empress Mother Anna of Savoy, Patriarch John Kalekas, and Alexius Apocaucus. Though the first two were titularly the leading regents, the most powerful figure, who was to dominate the regency, was Apocaucus, who became governor of Constantinople; as more-or-less a military mayor, he controlled the capital very tightly. Many of Cantacuzenus' supporters in the capital were arrested. Cantacuzenus, who had left the capital to fight an enemy of the empire, was incensed. Having acquired considerable support from Byzantine Macedonia and Thrace, particularly from the great landlords, members of his own class, Cantacuzenus at Demotika on 26 October 1341 declared himself emperor (John VI), while insisting he was not acting against John V, whose rights he had sworn to protect. And for a time all Cantacuzenus' charters and pronouncements were written in both their names, with the little boy's name in first place. Thus his revolt was raised not against the heir, but against the usurpation of the new regency.

Thrace and what the empire still retained of Macedonia were regions dominated by the great magnates. Under their leadership these provinces were ready to support Cantacuzenus. Faced with this serious opposition, the regency government in Constantinople set about trying to undermine Cantacuzenus' support in these provinces. The best means to do this was to incite other groups to revolt against the magnates and thereby establish a new leadership loyal to the regency in these provinces or at least create sufficient disorder and strife in Byzantine Europe to prevent the magnates from mobilizing their men and marching on Constantinople. Imperial agents began stirring up merchants and townsmen of Adrianople against the aristocrats who, holding great estates outside the town, possessed large town houses and palaces from which they dominated local politics; they seem to have had little popularity among the urban populace. These agents were successful and the town population of Adrianople, led by Branos, an agricultural worker who lived by manual labor in the gardens of the magnates, rose up against the aristocracy.

Soon various other Thracian towns followed suit, revolting, expelling the rich aristocrats, and confiscating their property. Limpidarios, the rebel leader in Ainos whose movement jailed or exiled most of that town's magnates, had been a servant or serf of a certain Duke Nicephorus. Thus the regency succeeded in unleashing a social revolution that temporarily took over many Thracian towns, thereby bringing these towns into the regency's camp. Revolt also occurred in Demotika, but here the magnates won, forcing many townsmen to flee. This city was to remain loyal to Cantacuzenus and be, for the next few years, his center of operations. But almost all the other cities of Thrace entered the regency's camp, and a whole series of aristocrats joined the regency's side to retain their property and positions.

Cantacuzenus' campaigns in 1342, as we shall see, took him into western Thrace and Macedonia. In his absence the regency carried out its abovementioned take-over of eastern and central Thrace. Cantacuzenus' capital, Demotika, left in the hands of his wife, was a beleaguered island in the midst of regency territory. Cantacuzenus was unable to break through regency defenses to come to his wife's relief, and she underwent a desperate winter of 1342–43, in which she was not only threatened by the regency but also besieged by the Bulgarians. Somehow she managed to hold out until support came from Cantacuzenus' old allies the Turks from the Emirate of Aydin, with whom Cantacuzenus concluded a new alliance. The Turks sailed up the Marica with some three hundred ships and a large number of men—Cantacuzenus claims twenty-nine thousand while the Turkish source claims fifteen thousand—and drove off the Bulgarians.

In any case, while the Thracian events were about to occur, Cantacuzenus began his campaign early in 1342 with an attack upon Kavalla. Defeated, he had to withdraw. He next turned his attention to Thessaloniki, for the aristocrats of that town, led by Synadenos the town's governor, were preparing to open the town's gates to troops loyal to Cantacuzenus. But then a rebellion broke out there against the aristocrats and against Cantacuzenus' cause. The rebels not only refused to open the gates to the pro-Cantacuzenus army, but killed or exiled from the town his supporters and many of the town's rich and seized their property. Those expelled included Synadenos. Then in early summer 1342 the rebels in Thessaloniki established their own government in the town. Those who came to hold power in Thessaloniki have come to be known as the zealots. For a long time scholars depicted their rule as a clear case of social revolution, in which for a while the poor successfully opposed the rich and governed an independent city-republic of Thessaloniki.

Recently, however, it has been shown that certain important sources which supported this depiction were not written at the time, as was thought at first, but somewhat later. Furthermore, among the zealots, and particularly in positions of leadership, various magnates were to be found. Thus magnates stood on both sides. In fact some of the important magnates on the zealot side had close ties with Constantinople, in particular with the regency and the Palaeologus family. For example the leader of the zealots was a certain Michael Palaeologus; also active in Thessaloniki was John Apocaucus, the son of Alexius Apocaucus, the governor of Constantinople and the most powerful regent. Thus it makes sense to argue that these zealots participated in the rebellion, if they did not actually lead it from the start, for political reasons (i.e., to support the regency against Cantacuzenus) rather than for social ones. This is not to say that social issues were not important for many adherents of the movement; in fact these issues had been emphasized by zealot leaders to acquire and hold mob support. And the zealot leaders seem to have ridden to power through this policy.

And thus was set up the so-called city-state of Thessaloniki. However, it was not an independent state; it recognized John V and the regency in Constantinople, and the regency government there recognized the zealots. In fact, in the name of John V the regency sent to Thessaloniki a governor who participated in running the town. However, it is evident that the local council predominated in local affairs and the governor did not direct town affairs as imperial governors had in the past. However, through this mutual recognition and the town's acceptance of the imperial governor, Thessaloniki remained part of the empire. And it must be stressed that in broad matters of policy—foreign policy and attitude toward Cantacuzenus—there was no real difference between the zealots and the regency. And even in social matters they did not differ seriously; though the regency was not advocating social revolution in Constantinople, it had been encouraging such revolution throughout Thrace. The regency, therefore, would not have opposed the social-revolutionary stance of the Thessaloniki zealots, particularly since it too was focused against the partisans of Cantacuzenus. Thus the zealots and regency were in agreement with one another on the major issues of the time. And one should consider the Thessaloniki zealots, led by Apocaucus' son and by a member of the Palaeologus family, as part of the regency's campaign against Cantacuzenus. As part and parcel of the regency, zealot leaders simply played on social issues to gain support from the townsmen and deprive of influence the important group of Thessalonian magnates who supported Cantacuzenus.

Cantacuzenus had turned for support in late 1341 to his former colleague Michael Monomachus, who was then governing Thessaly. Michael hesitated to commit himself and then early in 1342 left, or was forced out of, Thessaly. He went to Serres and there joined Cantacuzenus' opponents, who held that town for the regency. In Thessaly the nobles were left to their own devices; among those rising to great power and filling the power vacuum was another Michael, the leader of the powerful Gavrilopoulos family. We saw in the last chapter that in 1342 he was issuing charters to lesser nobles, defining their military obligations and guaranteeing tax reductions to them; these charters made no reference to the emperor though such matters were imperial prerogatives. Thus Michael Gavrilopoulos was acting as a fully independent prince. His actions presumably reflect the situation in Thessaly—or in his part of Thessaly—which, not yet recognizing either side, simply asserted its own autonomy. Since Michael's surviving charters all come from 1342, after Andronicus' death and before Thessaly, later in 1342, accepted Cantacuzenus' appointee John Angelus as its governor, we can see Michael's actions and authority as reflecting an exceptional time and situation. However, Michael's ability to assert this role shows that in Thessaly the institutional structure based on the local nobles still existed and had been little changed by a decade of administration under the imperial governor Monomachus.

The Serbs Are Drawn into the Byzantine Civil War

At the first sign of trouble in the empire in the late fall of 1341 both the Bulgarians and Serbs raided south against the empire. Cantacuzenus found himself facing a grim situation. By mid-1342 his supporters were losing power throughout much of Thrace and imperial Macedonia. He thus needed new allies. Furthermore, the empire's Slavic neighbors were trying to take advantage of the empire's troubles to wrest away more imperial territory. And Cantacuzenus did not have sufficient forces to stop them, either. Thus Cantacuzenus decided to negotiate with the Serbs to limit their conquests and to try, by making them into allies, to channel their activities into supporting his cause. He first visited Hrelja, who was then in the process of re-establishing his ties with Serbia. Hrelja was friendly but, not wanting to make his own situation any more complicated, refused to involve himself in the matter. So, Cantacuzenus decided to go to Serbia himself.

With two thousand soldiers and his sons, John Cantacuzenus marched north along the Vardar. He was received honorably at Prosek (now Serbian) by its governor, a Byzantine deserter named Michael who had been given the command by his new sovereign. He continued on to Veles where he was met by a Serbian army under the Despot John Oliver, who held a large appanage in that region that included Veles. Cantacuzenus already knew Oliver; it seems that both men had participated in the discussions between Andronicus III and Dušan in 1334 and 1335. Probably at one of those two meetings Andronicus had granted Oliver his title despot, for that title could only have originated with an emperor and Oliver seems to have borne it already in 1341 several years before Dušan took the imperial title that gave him the right to grant such titles. Cantacuzenus assured John Oliver that his presence in Serbia with an army reflected no ill intentions toward Serbia. The two men then entered into discussions; as a result of them, Oliver agreed to support Cantacuzenus and, accompanied by his own troops, led Cantacuzenus' party further into Serbia, while dispatching couriers ahead to inform Dušan of Cantacuzenus' visit. The couriers found Dušan en route to visit his brother-in-law John Alexander in Bulgaria. Cantacuzenus' arrival was important enough to effect a change in plans, so, on Oliver's advice, Dušan returned to Priština whither Oliver led Cantacuzenus.

There in July 1342 Cantacuzenus met with Dušan, Queen Helen (Jelena), and twenty-four leading Serb nobles led by Oliver. According to Cantacuzenus, Helen and Oliver took the most active part in the discussions. Cantacuzenus sought Serbian support to oust the Byzantine regency. For their help the Serbs expected to be rewarded with imperial territory. Cantacuzenus says the Serbs demanded everything west of Kavalla or at least west of Thessaloniki. Cantacuzenus says he refused to yield any territory and claims it was finally agreed that the Serbs could retain any Byzantine cities they had held at the time Andronicus III had died; however, all Byzantine cities taken after his death, including those still to be taken, would go to Cantacuzenus. The only exception made to this arrangement was to be Melnik, then in the process of being taken by Hrelja. Hrelja was to be allowed to retain Melnik; and since he was then negotiating his return to Dušan—a return recognized in the Dušan-Cantacuzenus agreement—this city was to go to the Serbs. Cantacuzenus insists that this was the agreement they made, but that Dušan violated it later by keeping what he took. Since this self-serving statement is hard to believe, most scholars believe Gregoras, who claims that Cantacuzenus yielded to Serbian demands and agreed that each party could hold the fortresses it conquered.

Since the Serbs were to supply the bulk of the troops, this in effect meant that if the allies were to be successful in their campaign, the Serbs would make extensive gains. In fact, according to Gregoras, their agreement was to give Serbia all Macedonia west of Kavalla excluding Thessaloniki. The only hope Cantacuzenus had to obtain any of these cities was provided, according to Gregoras, by a clause in the agreement that allowed voluntarily surrendering—as opposed to forcibly conquered—Byzantine cities to submit to the ruler of their choice, whether Cantacuzenus or Dušan. In any case, and even if Gregoras is not entirely accurate, Cantacuzenus clearly agreed to the Serbs' making substantial gains. Otherwise, there was no reason for them to aid him.

The sources state that Dušan was hesitant to involve himself. However, the twenty-four nobles, led by Oliver and Helen, were unanimous that Serbia should take advantage of the opportunity. So, in the end, Dušan agreed. Once again it was the nobility, ambitious to expand south, that pressed for and made the decision, whereas the ruler was hesitant and passive. Cantacuzenus then reports that the peace was sealed by a marriage. According to him Oliver wanted Cantacuzenus' son Manuel to marry Oliver's daughter. Dušan pushed the proposal because, according to Cantacuzenus, he was afraid to oppose Oliver. Cantacuzenus then accepted this proposal and Manuel remained in Serbia, presumably more or less as a hostage for his father's good faith in fulfilling the treaty, though Cantacuzenus claims Manuel remained because he was Oliver's son-in-law to be. According to Gregoras the marriage proposal originated with Cantacuzenus. Regardless of which man suggested it, the proposal probably dated back to the three-day meeting between Oliver and Cantacuzenus at Veles, before Cantacuzenus met Dušan. The marriage may well have been Oliver's condition for arranging the meeting with and for using his influence on Dušan on behalf of Cantacuzenus. These marriage plans were dropped in 1343, when Dušan switched sides and came out for the regency.

Despot John Oliver

It is worth pausing briefly on Despot John (Jovan) Oliver, a major figure in his own right. Like Hrelja, he controlled a major territory, which he seems to have ruled more or less as an independent prince; he accepted Serbian suzerainty but did not suffer royal officials or troops in his realm. He seems to have supported the king faithfully insofar as he did not secede. But he also pressured the king to carry out the policies he wanted. A 1336 Ragusan document refers to him as Oliver Gherchinich (the Greek), suggesting he was of Greek origin. This supposition is strengthened by the fact that he knew Greek. According to Orbini (writing in 1601 on the basis of a lost source) he had married Karavida, the daughter of a certain Karavid who had been one of Dušan's supporters in Zeta against Dečanski. Thus quite likely Oliver had also supported Dušan in his revolt and, unlike some of the others (e.g., Bogoje) who felt slighted afterwards, had been well rewarded for his support of Dušan. He had fought actively in the 1334 war against Byzantium.

By 1336 his wife Karavida was dead and by 1340 he had evidently married Maria (in Serbian, Mara) Palaeologina, Dečanski's widow and Dušan's step-mother. For a 1340 charter issued by Dušan to Hilandar refers to his step-mother as "my mother Despotica." We may assume her unusual title was derived from her relationship to Despot John Oliver. Thus he clearly held the title of despot that early—probably, as we have said, receiving it from Andronicus III in 1334 or 1335—and had married Maria by 1340.[3] Most scholars date Oliver's marriage to Maria to 1336 or 1337. He was also a great landholder, and since his lands lay on a foreign border—on that with Byzantium—he could exercise great independence. Their size gave him a large economic and manpower base to support himself. And their location prevented action against him, since he could in such an event easily switch allegiance to the emperor.

Considerable controversy exists about Oliver's landholding, in particular over when and how he acquired certain places. The controversy arises owing to the scarcity of sources and the uncertain dating of various documents in which these places are mentioned. The questions debated are: Did Oliver have a large basic holding prior to Dušan's accession? Or, were most of his lands granted to him by Dušan? Or, as is often argued, were many of the lands he is found holding in 1340 originally granted as an appanage to Queen Mother Maria, coming to Oliver subsequently through his marriage with her? Radonić believes that Maria had held, and Oliver thus obtained through her, the province of Ovčepolje, with Kratovo, Kočane, and Veles, as well as the territory, including the Tikveš and Morihovo provinces, between the Vardar and Crna Reka (the Black River).[4] In any case by about 1340 Oliver held all this territory. At Kratovo he had a rich mine that provided him with the silver he eventually was to use to coin his own money, a sign of his great independence. Though it is not known when he began issuing money, he evidently began doing so during Dušan's lifetime, for among his coins are some that have his name and Dušan's picture.

Thus John Oliver was a powerful prince, more-or-less autonomous in his realm, who, through his own clout and influence on the rest of the nobility, was a figure able to exert great authority inside the Kingdom of Serbia, sufficient at times to influence, if not even to dominate, the king. For given his power, one may well wonder how Dušan could have favored Oliver's concluding an agreement to marry his daughter to Cantacuzenus' son, a young man who, if Cantacuzenus' venture succeeded, might eventually become the Byzantine emperor.

Oliver's power is further illustrated by the fate of Hrelja's lands. In the summer of 1342, at the same time that Cantacuzenus and Dušan met, Hrelja negotiated his return to Serbia, retaining all his lands and agreeing to accept Dušan's suzerainty. To his earlier holding he had added during his brief stay under Byzantine suzerainty more territory, including the important fortress of Melnik. According to Gregoras, Melnik had been surrendered to Hrelja by its Byzantine commander, a supporter of Cantacuzenus against the regency acting on the orders of Cantacuzenus. Cantacuzenus, not surprisingly, does not mention this; he simply says that in his discussion with Dušan he had raised objections to Hrelja's including Melnik as territory to be under Serbian suzerainty. Whether Cantacuzenus objected or not, there clearly was nothing he could have done about it, and in the end he agreed to it. Soon thereafter, probably late in 1342, Hrelja died and was to be buried in the famous Rila monastery, which he had spent considerable money on restoring. After his death his lands were immediately annexed by Serbia. They seem, however, to have been divided between Dušan and Oliver. That Oliver was able to expand his great holdings even further, which surely was not in Dušan's interests, shows the power he must have had inside Serbia. Thus by 1342/43 Oliver held in addition to the lands noted previously much of the region bordering on the Struma River, including the important towns of Velbužd, Štip, and Strumica. Thus he held much of the territory lying between the Struma and Vardar rivers.

In 1341 he, like the Serbian kings, completed a zadužbina (obligation), the Lesnovo monastery. After 1346 the Lesnovo monastery became the seat of a Bishop of Lesnovo. At that time Dušan gave the monastery additional villages and freed the peasants in them from state duties. They were put under the authority of the Bishop of Lesnovo. Since Oliver was the monastery's founder, he was granted the right to participate in the bishop's selection.

Serbian Participation in the Byzantine Civil War

Cantacuzenus spent the next ten months with Dušan either at his court or on campaign accompanied by Serbian troops. In the late summer or early fall of 1342 Cantacuzenus, supported by a Serbian contingent, attacked the major Byzantine fortified city of Serres and laid siege to it. A stout Byzantine defense held the attackers off; then the Serbian troops came down with violent diarrhoea, said to have been caused by drinking too-young wine, and had to withdraw. Dušan meanwhile led a second army into southwestern Macedonia and took Voden (Edessa). In the fall of 1342, as noted above, Hrelja negotiated his return, bringing his lands back with him. He then died at the end of the year; his lands were absorbed by Dušan and John Oliver. An heir of his (unnamed in the sources) had tried to retain Melnik, but early in 1343 Dušan sent troops against him which took Melnik for himself.

The regency, alarmed by Cantacuzenus' Serbian alliance, in the fall of 1342 sent envoys to Dušan to offer him an alliance against Cantacuzenus. The regency, according to the hostile source Cantacuzenus, offered Dušan all Macedonia west of Kavalla, excluding Thessaloniki, if he would turn Cantacuzenus over to it. Though Dušan clearly had no sincere interest in Cantacuzenus' cause and though each was clearly using the other for his own ambitions, Dušan refused, presumably still calculating he could gain more by supporting Cantacuzenus against the regency. Soulis speculates that Cantacuzenus may have offered Dušan even more to prevent his accepting the offer. Soulis also points out that since pronoias in Byzantine Macedonia were then held by regency supporters, it was in the interests of the pronoia-seeking Serb nobles to oppose the regency.[5]

Between 1343 and 1345 the Serbs campaigned actively in Macedonia and Albania. Owing to a lack of precision in our sources, scholars cannot be certain as to when during these three years certain cities and regions were conquered. Thus different scholars advance different dates, and there is considerable controversy over the chronology of Dušan's expansion. However, it is evident that by the end of 1345 Serbia had all Macedonia, except Thessaloniki and possibly Veria, and all Albania, except Durazzo which was again in Angevin hands. In 1343 we know the Serbs were back on the attack again and operating east of the Vardar, taking Melnik from Hrelja's heir and failing again against Serres. They also seem to have made extensive gains in what was left of Byzantine Macedonia, including Kastoria and Hlerin (Florina)—if these two cities had not already fallen in 1342. In 1343 Dušan added "Greeks" or "Greek lands" to the other territories included in this title. In his Greek language documents he wrote "Romans," according to Byzantine custom. The Serbs also seem to have made extensive gains in Albania. But it is not at all clear which Serbian gains in Albania had been made earlier during the late 1330s and in 1340 when Byzantium was tied down in Epirus, which acquisitions dated from 1343 and what, if anything, remained to be taken in 1344 and 1345. In any case, at roughly this time Serbia can be documented holding Berat, Kanina, Kroja, and Valona.[6] Many Albanians were incorporated into Dušan's armies. On the whole, after obtaining their submission, he left the Albanian chiefs in power as local leaders. Eventually he was to appoint a Serbian governor for the area. But even under him the tribes, under their own leaders, continued to follow their tribal, pastoral ways as they had until then.

In late 1342, as Cantacuzenus' position improved, he appeared as an increasingly viable candidate for the throne. It is not surprising, therefore, that he seemed attractive to the magnates of Thessaly who had remained outwardly neutral until then. After all Cantacuzenus, a great landlord himself, could be expected to support continued privileges to the magnates and in general to benefit them more than the regency, which through 1341 and 1342 had been stirring up social revolution and encouraging the townsmen to oppose the magnates. In the course of 1342, as Cantacuzenus became more active in pressing his cause, the magnates of Thessaly became more open in their sympathy for him, and that summer some had joined him while others had promised him their support. By the end of the year the magnates of Thessaly were formally negotiating with him. They had hoped that Cantacuzenus would come to Thessaly himself; but since he needed to be active in Thrace, this was impossible.

Eventually, probably at the very end of 1342, these negotiations ended in an agreement. Thessaly accepted Cantacuzenus as emperor, and he sent to Thessaly a deputy to govern. The deputy appointed, John Angelus, was a rich magnate, a relative (probably nephew) of Cantacuzenus, who had long association with Cantacuzenus and had been loyal to his cause throughout, being a member of the entourage that accompanied him to Serbia. Angelus was appointed governor of Thessaly for life. After taking an oath of loyalty to and recognizing the suzerainty of Cantacuzenus, Angelus went to Thessaly, which he administered as an autonomous province until his death from the plague in 1348. The magnates of Thessaly rallied around this decision. Soulis claims that Cantacuzenus also awarded Angelus the governorship of Epirus, Acarnania, and Aetolia. He had been appointed to govern these three western regions by Andronicus III in the end of 1340 and as far as we know had continued to hold that post until he chose to accompany Cantacuzenus to Serbia. Whether the regency had been able to install a successor to him in these western provinces during 1342 is unknown but also may be doubted.

Cantacuzenus' acquisition of Thessaly greatly improved his position and alarmed Dušan, who did not want to see a strong neighbor to his south. Cantacuzenus' successes in 1342 had been the result of Serbian support, which allowed the Serbs to control the disposition of conquered territory. But now Cantacuzenus was beginning to build his own independent support that might enable him to act independently of Serbian wishes. Furthermore, in early 1343 Dušan became angry with Cantacuzenus who, he felt, had cheated the Serbs out of Veria. While the Serbs were besieging the town, Cantacuzenus, whom Dušan until then had successfully kept from independent operations, had with his son slipped away and secretly opened negotiations with the defenders. After secretly entering the town, he won acceptance from its leaders, who then got the town to openly accept him in April 1343. The besieging Serbs, completely uninformed throughout, were caught by the fait accompli and, since Cantacuzenus was their ally, had to accept his coup and leave him in control of the town. Cantacuzenus then installed his son Manuel as governor of Veria. Several other forts in the vicinity, including Servia, followed suit and also accepted Cantacuzenus. This seriously threatened Serbia's plans for expansion into Macedonia.

So Dušan now in April 1343 sent an envoy to the regency in Constantinople to express his willingness to reach an arrangement with it. Their alliance was concluded in the summer of 1343 and sealed by the engagement of Dušan's son Uroš to a sister of John V. Dušan's new alliance enabled him to attack Veria and the other forts in its vicinity that he had wanted but that his erstwhile ally Cantacuzenus had in the meantime taken.

Cantacuzenus, fortunate to be elsewhere when Dušan reached his agreement with the regency and improving his own position in the empire, needed a new ally to replace the Serbs. And during the winter 1342–43 he had already found this ally in Umur, the Emir of Aydin. Cantacuzenus' center of operations continued to be Demotika. There Cantacuzenus had to face either (or both) supply or discipline problems with his men. For his soldiers based in Demotika plundered the neighboring villages. Cantacuzenus admitted that the acts were committed by his partisans but claimed they were obliged to loot because they lacked any other means of subsistence.

In the summer of 1343 Cantacuzenus tried to take Thessaloniki, but the zealots, re-enforced by troops from Constantinople (showing the close ties between regency and zealots), successfully resisted him. He then moved into Thrace to try to rebuild the shattered fortunes of his scattered allies, the Thracian magnates. For it was necessary for him to oust as leaders of the Thracian towns the townsmen allied to the regency and restore to power his allies the magnates. The acquisition of Thrace, bordering on the capital, was also vital if he hoped to acquire the capital. Controlling Thrace would enable him to recruit further men from it and allow him to march freely against Constantinople and place his forces wherever he required them without fear of an assault upon his rear during that attack.

Between 1343 and 1345 Cantacuzenus was successful in this effort, frequently acquiring towns through subversion by the magnates from within rather than military conquest from without. With the help of Umur's Turks he acquired a series of fortresses along Thrace's Aegean coast, including Kavalla. He also took the region in the interior behind the coast as far north as the Arda River. The western part of this territory from the Mesta (Nestos) River in the west roughly to Gratianou in the east was called Merope; the territory to Gratianou's east as far as Demotika was called Morrha. Local support brought more of the towns of Merope to submit to him than did military conquest. Cantacuzenus assigned Merope's government in late 1343 to Momčilo, a brigand chief who, commanding his own retinue, was probably already based in the area. He had joined Cantacuzenus in 1343 and received from him the title of sebastocrator. The government of Morrha Cantacuzenus assigned to John Asen, a Byzantine aristocrat closely related to his wife. During the winter 1343–44, at the time he was acquiring most of this territory, he also besieged but failed to take Merope's main port, Peritheorion (Anastasiopolis). Having gained the territory south of the Arda, his troops moved north of the river early in 1344 to briefly take Stanimaka and Tzepania. During this time Cantacuzenus' garrison suppressed a revolt of townsmen in his capital of Demotika. Many of the townsmen were then forced to flee the city. His Turkish allies, who had successfully driven off the Bulgarian attack early in 1343, defended Demotika from a regency attack in 1344. In the course of 1344 Cantacuzenus took Adrianople.

At the end of the spring of 1344 Umur returned to Aydin and then was detained there as the Latins were preparing to attack Smyrna. That attack came in the fall, and on 28 October 1344 a Latin coalition took the castle at the port of Smyrna. However, Umur successfully defended the town's main citadel. When the fighting ended the Latins were unable to move beyond the port fortifications; however, Umur was equally unable to dislodge them from the castle at the port.

The regency, faced with Cantacuzenus' successes, probably in mid-1344, after negotiations, won to its side John Alexander of Bulgaria. For his support he was granted the region of the upper Marica, with nine Thracian cities including Philippopolis, Stanimaka, and Tzepania. He quickly occupied this territory, taking the two last-mentioned cities from Cantacuzenus. This territory was to remain Bulgarian from then until the Ottoman conquest. In 1344 the regency also persuaded Momčilo to switch sides. Awarded the title of despot by the regents, he then attempted to persuade the cities placed under him by Cantacuzenus to switch their loyalty to the regency. He also plundered the cities in the area that were loyal to Cantacuzenus and skirmished with the small Turkish forces that remained with Cantacuzenus.

This eastern activity of Cantacuzenus had the effect of abandoning Macedonia and Albania to Dušan's armies, and, as noted, in the course of 1343 and 1344 the Serbs were very successful. Only once did they meet opposition. In 1344 a Serb army under Vojvoda Preljub lost a skirmish to Cantacuzenus' Aydin Turks somewhere near the Aegean. However, this was a small-scale encounter that did nothing to stop the Serbs' advance in Macedonia.

Thus while the Byzantines fought one another in Thrace, leaving almost no troops to defend Macedonia, Albania, and Epirus, the regency's new ally looked out for his own interests. In 1344 Dušan was active in Macedonia and probably Albania, acquiring whatever cities he had not taken before. By the end of the year he had all Macedonia except Thessaloniki, Serres, and possibly Veria. Whereas some scholars believe he gained Veria in 1344, Soulis argues that this town held out under Manuel Cantacuzenus until 1347, when the Serbs were finally to acquire it.

Early in the spring of 1345, after the Latins had been pushed back to the port castle of Smyrna and besieged there (and thus were unable to threaten further action against Smyrna), Umur returned to the Balkans with twenty thousand men to assist Cantacuzenus. Upon their arrival, probably in May and early June, they pillaged Bulgaria. Then they turned to the serious task of defeating the warlord Momčilo and regaining the territory that had gone over to the regency with him. In 1344 and 1345, nominally loyal to the regency but in effect an independent prince, Momčilo was trying to assert his control in the Rhodopes, in the Byzantine-Bulgarian-Serbian borderlands. He had as loyal retainers five thousand footsoldiers and three hundred cavalrymen drawn from different nationalities. This large figure for his armies, given by Cantacuzenus, is confirmed by Gregoras, who reports Momčilo had over four thousand armed men under him. His career was marked by raids against his neighbors and a willingness to form alliances and then shift sides at will; his policy was always founded on doing whatever would bring him the greatest profit at a given moment. As noted, in 1344 the regency had enlisted his support.

This was to be Momčilo's undoing, for Cantacuzenus' Turks attacked him and wiped out his army, killing Momčilo in the process, on 7 July 1345. This battle occurred outside the walls of Peritheorion. It is usually stated that

Momčilo held that city. If so, presumably the regency had granted it to him at the time he joined the regency. If indeed this had occurred, then Peritheorion's inhabitants evidently disliked Momčilo, for when he and his retinue sought to avoid battle with the more numerous Turks by fleeing to Peritheorion, its citizens locked the town's gates against Momčilo, leaving him and his men outside to be killed by the Turks. Lemerle, however, believes Momčilo had never held the city.[7] Momčilo's career provides one more good illustration of the process of creating and maintaining a secessionist principality in a border region. He also made sufficient impression on his contemporaries to become an important figure in the epic poetry of the region. After Momčilo's death Cantacuzenus regained all Merope.

In 1345 Dušan once again laid siege to Serres. Cantacuzenus sent an envoy to him ordering him to desist from the siege or else face an attack from him and his Turks. Dušan did not give up the siege, but Cantacuzenus for two reasons did not bring his Turks west. First, on 11 July 1345 Alexius Apocaucus was murdered in Constantinople, causing Cantacuzenus to hurry with his troops toward Constantinople in the hope that Apocaucus' death would create sufficient instability in the capital to allow him to obtain it.[8] His hopes were not realized. Second, any plans he might have had against the Serbs depended on his Turkish troops; and such plans had to be given up when Umur, the Turkish leader, had to return with most of his men to Anatolia to defend his own land from a possible attack.

For in August 1345, outside the walls of Constantinople, the commander of a Turkish unit allied to Umur took sick and died. This commander was the son of the Emir of Sarukhan, whose lands bordered on Aydin. Afraid that the father might misinterpret his son's death and use it as an excuse to attack Aydin in Umur's absence, Umur hurried back home with his forces. His departure eliminated any hope that Cantacuzenus might have had of bringing sufficient forces against Dušan to prevent the capture of Serres. The attack against Aydin from Sarukhan did not materialize; however, having reached home, Umur learned that the Latins were sending a new force to relieve the besieged port castle. Umur had to wait until the summer of 1346 for these forces to arrive; he defeated them with ease and forced them to retreat into the castle. However, continuing tense relations with Sarukhan prevented Umur from returning to the Balkans. Faced with the loss of his support from Aydin, Cantacuzenus turned to the Ottomans. In the summer (probably June) of 1346 he concluded an agreement with them, sealed by giving his daughter Theodora to the Ottoman ruler, Orkhan. Umur remained at home; later, in May 1348, in an attempt to dislodge the Latins from the port castle of Smyrna, Umur was killed by an arrow. The Hospitaler knights were to hold the port fortress until they were driven out in 1402 by Timur shortly after his victory at Ankara.

Meanwhile Dušan, wiping out the stain of earlier failures, on 25 September 1345 finally took Serres after a long siege that had finally reduced the town to the last extremities. Following the conquest many Greeks remained in high positions; in fact the town's first governor under Dušan was a Greek named Michael Avrambakes. Dušan then took Kavalla and Drama, the rest of Albania and Macedonia (getting whatever fortresses he had not been able to take previously), and occupied most of the Chalcidic peninsula, including Mount Athos. The only opposition he met came from small garrisons inside certain towns. Neither Byzantine side was in a position to send relief to any of the towns Dušan was attacking. Thus at the end of 1345 Dušan held everything between (and including) Kavalla and Albania, except Durazzo, Thessaloniki, the western part of the Chalcidic peninsula, the independent town of Anaktoropolis (modern Eleutheropolis), which was more or less an independent fief of a Greek pirate who had served Apocaucus at times, and possibly Veria. Kavalla was to remain the most easterly city in Dušan's realm.

Dušan sent his logothete in September 1345 to visit Mount Athos and negotiate with the monks. For both political and religious reasons Dušan sought the support of this major religious center. He wanted the monks to recognize him as their suzerain and include his name in their prayers. This would not only bring him the benefits of the prayers but also would contribute to his obtaining broader recognition and acceptance from the Greek population he was adding to his empire. His envoy, having agreed to the monks' condition that they be allowed to continue to also mention the Byzantine emperor's name in their prayers, received a promise from the monks to accept Dušan's suzerainty and to pray for him. After reporting to Dušan, the envoy returned to Athos in November 1345 with a charter from Dušan to all the monasteries on Athos. This charter allowed the Byzantine emperor's name to be commemorated in their prayers and to precede the name of the Serbian ruler. It promised that Athos should continue to be governed by its existing rules and customs. Dušan promised to restore various possessions on the Struma River to the monasteries and to exempt these properties from all taxes and obligations. He also gave the monasteries' boats the right to fish duty-free on the Struma River. The city of Hierissos would not be governed by a kephale but jointly by the Athonite monks and the town's bishop.

Shortly thereafter Dušan began issuing separate charters to the individual monasteries that confirmed the monasteries in their lands and privileges. Two such privileges from January 1346 have survived. To celebrate his coronation as tsar (emperor) in April 1346 Dušan issued more charters confirming various monasteries' lands and immunities and extending some of the latter. In order to gain the monks' support for his coronation he was most generous to them. Subsequently Dušan himself visited Mount Athos, spending four months there from the end of 1347 to early 1348. He took his wife and son along. And the monasteries, which had rules against the presence of women on their terrain, made a special exception to allow Dušan's wife to visit. The royal family visited all the monasteries, giving rich gifts to each. At this time Dušan granted many new lands to Hilandar, the Serbian monastery, and he settled a quarrel over land between Hilandar and the Bulgarian Zographou monastery. His decision favored Hilandar; however, he granted new villages to Zographou to compensate the Bulgarians for what they might have felt to be their loss. These charters gave certain monasteries tax-free status for some of their lands. In November 1348 he issued a general charter to all the Athonite monasteries granting them all total tax exemption as well as total liberty from any and all service obligations to the state.

Thus the monasteries received large new tracts of land and other gifts from the Serbian ruler and also acquired tax-free status. It is not surprising that Dušan has gone down in their histories as one of Athos' major patrons. Good relations followed between ruler and monks. He continued to give them gifts while they entered his name in their prayers—along with that of the Byzantine emperor—and, despite objections from the Byzantines, they supported Dušan's raising the Serbian archbishop to the rank of patriarch and his own status from king to emperor. However, the monks called him Emperor of the Serbs rather than Emperor of the Serbs and Romans, as he called himself. In this period many more Serbs entered monasteries on the mountain and some rose to high positions. Under Dušan for the first time a Serb came to hold the office of protos, the primary elder, of the mountain. His appointment may well have resulted from political pressure.

Cantacuzenus' Triumph

By 1345, supported by Thessaly and Umur's Turks, Cantacuzenus was gaining the upper hand in the Byzantine struggle. He made progress even though the regency, through its acquisition of powerful allies, might have appeared the stronger. This was owing to the fact that Cantacuzenus' Turks fought well for him, while the regency's allies were clearly out for themselves and did nothing to aid the regency against Cantacuzenus. The Turks fought in the key area of Thrace. But Dušan avoided that region and devoted his efforts to acquiring Macedonia and Albania for himself. And John Alexander of Bulgaria (enlisted as an ally, probably in 1344, for which he was given Philippopolis, the upper Marica, and a sister of John V as a bride), though he did operate in Thrace, avoided Cantacuzenus' troops and simply took for himself what Thracian towns he could. He could do this easily since he concentrated his efforts in western Thrace, whereas Cantacuzenus, interested in the capital, was by then concentrating his attention on eastern Thrace. Thus Cantacuzenus' forces never came into contact with the armies of the regency's powerful allies. Most of eastern Thrace by this time was in Cantacuzenus' hands, which ended the fighting there. However, despite the end of the actual warfare, all of Thrace continued to suffer from the plundering of Cantacuzenus' unruly Turkish mercenaries. In 1346 Cantacuzenus strengthened his position by allying with a second Turkish state, the Ottomans. This alliance prevented the Ottomans from aiding the regency, which might have spelled disaster for Cantacuzenus. From that time, owing to Umur of Aydin's occupation with domestic worries and then his death in 1348, Cantacuzenus was to turn increasingly to the Ottomans and to obtain from them ever increasing support.

While Cantacuzenus strengthened his position and became the master of most of Byzantine Thrace, the regency's position declined. Holding little more than Constantinople and its environs, the regency was weakened further by the murder of its ablest leader, Alexius Apocaucus, in July 1345. Immediately thereafter a quarrel erupted in Thessaloniki between two zealot leaders, Alexius' son John Apocaucus and Michael Palaeologus. Their split may well have been related to events occurring in Constantinople. The quarrel ended with Michael Palaeologus' murder and Apocaucus taking power in Thessaloniki. However, the murder of his father had broken the ties binding him and his regime in Thessaloniki to the capital, and John no longer exhibited much loyalty to the regency. Letters, now lost but probably not particularly friendly, were exchanged between John Apocaucus and Constantinople. Then, breaking with the regency, he summoned an assembly in Thessaloniki, to which the masses were not invited, that endorsed his opposition to the regency and agreed to surrender Thessaloniki to Cantacuzenus if Cantacuzenus would recognize Apocaucus as governor of Thessaloniki and recognize the municipality's privileges. Having thus declared for Cantacuzenus, the assembly awaited Cantacuzenus' response. But before Cantacuzenus could take any action and before John Apocaucus could do anything about rendering the city to him, a counter-movement within Thessaloniki, supported by the majority of the original zealots and led by another Palaeologus (Andrew, head of the mariners' guild), overthrew and butchered Apocaucus and his friends, most of whom were said to be rich. The city then continued on as a pro-regency, anti-Cantacuzenus "city-state."

But despite this setback, matters stood well for Cantacuzenus. Alexius Apocaucus' death made resistance to him less effective. He now had Ottoman allies who provided effective, even if unruly, troops. His successes during 1344–45, both before and, more especially, after Apocaucus' death, included Adrianople, most of eastern Thrace, and the Aegean and Black Sea coastal cities. By the end of 1345 the regency seems to have retained only Constantinople, Thessaloniki, Sozopolis, and Heraclea. Cantacuzenus next marched toward the capital, stopping at Adrianople, where he was crowned emperor by the Patriarch of Jerusalem in May 1346. Despite his strength almost a year passed before he acquired Constantinople; he explains this delay by claiming he wanted to gain the capital through diplomacy or through his supporters inside the city, rather than turn his Turks loose against the capital. Finally, on 3 February 1347, the gates of Constantinople were opened to him and he took over its government as Emperor John VI, retaining the young John V as co-emperor. To seal an alliance with John V he married John V to his daughter Helen. Cantacuzenus was crowned again in Constantinople in May 1347. Though John V received full honors, Cantacuzenus ran the state and continued to do so for the next seven years. To solidify his family's position and to prevent further Serbian expansion to the east, Cantacuzenus converted the western part of Byzantine Thrace, from the Serbian border at Kavalla east to Demotika, into a special appanage which he assigned to his son, Matthew. One might see this appanage, established right on the dangerous Serbian border, as a special frontier march. Now Dušan found himself faced with a tougher Byzantium, for it was no longer divided and involved in civil war, but united once again under an able emperor.

Cantacuzenus, however, did not receive acceptance from the whole empire. Even after he acquired the capital the zealots, his enemies who administered Thessaloniki, refused to accept him. This marked the first time that a so-called zealot government in Thessaloniki refused to recognize a regime in Constantinople. And only from this moment early in 1347—when Thessaloniki's leaders refused to accept the emperor recognized in Constantinople—is one justified in speaking of an independent city-state of Thessaloniki. Thessaloniki's existence as an independent city-state was to be short-lived. In 1350 Cantacuzenus marched against Thessaloniki. When they realized defeat was imminent, some zealot leaders wanted to surrender the city to the Serbs rather than allow Cantacuzenus to obtain it. However, they were unable to realize their plans, for Cantacuzenus arrived there first. And in October 1350 Cantacuzenus regained Thessaloniki, reuniting it to the empire. Those zealot leaders who could, fled, some of them ending up in Serbia.

Dušan's Coronation (April 1346)

By this time Dušan had changed his own title. In 1343 he had added "of the Romans (Greeks)" to his title of King of Serbia, Albania, and the coast. In late 1345 he began to call himself tsar, the Slavic equivalent of emperor. He used this title in charters to two Athonite monasteries, one from November 1345 and one from January 1346. At a council meeting held at his new city of Serres around Christmas 1345 he seems to have called himself Tsar of the Serbs and Romans (the latter rendered as Greeks in Serbian language documents). Then on 16 April 1346 (Easter) he convoked a huge assembly at Skopje, attended by the Archbishop of Serbia, the Archbishop of Ohrid, the Bulgarian Patriarch of Trnovo, and various leaders from Mount Athos. These clerics and the assembly agreed to, and then ceremonially performed, the raising of the Serbian archbishop to the rank of patriarch. From then on he was the Patriarch of Serbia, though one document calls him Patriarch of Serbs and Greeks. The patriarch's residence was to be in Peć. Then the new patriarch, Joanikije, crowned Dušan Emperor (Tsar) of the Serbs and Greeks. Dušan's minor son Uroš was crowned king and nominally given the Serbian lands—which until then had been held by a king—to rule. Dušan, the emperor, though in fact governing the whole state, had particular responsibility for "Romania," the Roman (i.e., Byzantine) or Greek lands.

After his coronation a further increase in the Byzantinization of Dušan's court followed, particularly in court ceremonial and court titles. For as emperor, Dušan was now able to grant various titles that could only originate with an emperor. Thus many high Serbs in the years that followed received high non-functional honorary court titles, long found at the Byzantine court. Dušan's half-brother Symeon and Dušan's wife's brother John Comnenus Asen each received the title despot. John Oliver, as noted, also had this title, but, though Ferjančić believes Dušan granted it to him, he probably held it prior to Dušan's coronation, having obtained it from Andronicus III in the 1330s. Dejan, the husband of Dušan's sister and also lord of Kumanovo, by 1354, and Branko of Ohrid, the father of the famous Vuk Branković, by 1365 had received the next highest title, sevastocrator, while two able generals (voj-vodas), Preljub in 1348 and Vojin, became caesars. Serbian Church figures benefited in the same way from the creation of a Serbian patriarch. For the creation of a patriarch allowed the elevation in title of various other bishops, who, like the Bishop of Skopje, became metropolitans.

Constantinople had opposed increasing the title of the Serbian archbishop. For that reason Dušan had brought together at his council an impressive array of foreign clerics to sanction this change. The Byzantines also strongly opposed Dušan's taking the imperial title. Cantacuzenus and Gregoras in their histories always refer to him only as king. And later the Byzantine patriarch was to excommunicate both the new Serbian emperor and the new Serbian patriarch. However, though scholars often state this excommunication followed at once upon the 1346 coronation, it is now evident the excommunication came in 1350.

Administration of Dušan's State

Dušan's state was becoming increasingly multi-ethnic. His gains in Macedonia had brought large numbers of Greeks under his rule, and, by annexing Albania, he had added to his state large numbers of Albanian tribesmen. These Albanians, having bound themselves to Dušan by oath and recognized his suzerainty, were then left under their tribal leaders, who ran their mountain districts as they had previously. However, excluding the Albanian regions, most of the state was inhabited by two main peoples: Serbs and Greeks. Serbs dominated the original Serbian heartland and northern regions. Then as one moved south into the newly conquered lands one passed through a mixed zone of Slavs and Greeks that became increasingly Greek as one got further south. The differences between the Serbian and Greek lands were retained after Dušan's coronation. Serbia retained its status as a kingdom, under King Uroš, while the Greek lands, "Romania," long under the Byzantine emperor, retained rule by an emperor, though now this emperor was a Serb. The support of the many Greeks added to his realm was important for the smooth functioning of his state and for what was to emerge as Dušan's new goal—the creation of a Greek-Serbian empire, to replace the existing Byzantine Empire, that ideally would some day be run from Constantinople, if and when Dušan should take that city.

In the beginning Dušan had carried out the policy of expansion to the south because he was pressed, or even forced, to do so by his nobility. And he benefited from existing circumstances—Syrgiannes' revolt and the Byzantine civil war—to achieve astounding successes. In time, however, with his accomplishments Dušan was able to gain in his own right the authority that frequently belongs to victorious war leaders who can offer booty to their followers. And as his expansionist policy came to be increasingly successful, and as the size of his state grew along with his own authority over it, Dušan, who does not seem to have been averse to this policy, was swept up by events and acquired new and greater ambitions, imperial ones.

To realize such ambitions and to maintain order in the regions he conquered, he needed to keep the loyalty of the Greeks. Thus he left much of the Byzantine administration in place, maintaining the existing offices and often even their office holders. Greek titles, both functional and honorary, also usually remained in force. Many Greek magnates, including Byzantine pronoia holders, if they now swore allegiance to Dušan and provided service to him, were left in possession of their estates. Dušan confirmed these landlords in possession of their lands in typical Byzantine-style charters written in Greek. Greek remained the official language for the Greek lands. In the Greek provinces the existing legal structure also remained almost unchanged. Thus Byzantine civil, criminal, and tax laws on the whole continued in effect. However, as might be expected, matters did not remain static. Just as Byzantine institutions had been penetrating Serbia from the time of Milutin, now under Serbian rule certain Serbian taxes and titles began appearing in the Greek lands under Dušan.[9]

The most important change that took place was the insertion of Serbs into the highest positions on a provincial or regional level. Over half of what Ostrogorsky calls the top positions in the Greek lands were assigned to Serbs. However, they filled offices that had existed under the Byzantine Empire and that continued to bear their Byzantine names. Serbs were also assigned deserted lands—lands of those who had been killed or had fled. However, the middling and lesser Byzantine nobility entered Dušan's service in considerable numbers, keeping its former titles and properties.

With Greeks retaining much of the landed property they had previously held, with existing laws continuing in effect, and with Greeks remaining as office holders (excluding the highest offices) anarchy was avoided and Dušan was able to manage a large territory and acquire for himself considerable loyalty from his new population. The use of Greeks in official positions benefited him; for it is doubtful, particularly if we consider the difference in language, that he had enough trained manpower from Serbia to administer these lands. Furthermore, the Serbs would not have known how the Greeks managed their towns. Thus to have given the management of towns over to Serbs would have caused friction and unrest. By leaving existing administrators in office to serve under traditional rules and regulations meant the functions of government could continue and provide the Serbian state with revenue from the region. Moreover, with the face of the state little changed, the population would have been less likely to resist. In a conquered town a Serb governor (usually called by the Greek title *kephale*) stood over an administration of Greek bureaucrats and a Serb garrison. In this way Greeks, who held most of the municipal administrative posts, and certainly the posts that required contact with the local citizens, dealt in the local language with the problems and obligations of local Greeks and managed the day-to-day functioning of the town and its administration. However, since Serb troops were present in the major towns as garrisons under Serb commanders, the Greek population was in no position to resist Dušan's orders.

In the Church Dušan also seems to have appointed Serbs to the most important episcopal positions. To do so he expelled some high Greek clerics and replaced them with Serbs. This occurred particularly at the metropolitan level. We find, for example, that Dušan's friend Jacob was made Metropolitan of Serres in 1353; he held that post until 1360 when a new Serb was appointed to succeed him. Also, it seems that Dušan sought greater influence on Mount Athos by placing his appointees in high positions there. It seems that in 1347 he forced out Niphon, the Protos of Athos. In 1348 the protos was a certain Anthony, the first protos to sign documents in Cyrillic. Thus probably he was a Serb. He was succeeded by a series of short-term protoi, several of whom were clearly Serbs. Then in 1356 Dorotheus of the Serbian monastery of Hilandar became protos, holding that office to 1366.

Ostrogorsky stresses that we should not see the appointment of Serbs to these high positions as a "nationalist" policy. Dušan placed Serbs in the top civil, military, and ecclesiastical positions not only to keep order and to have people of known loyalty to him at the top to bind the area to his rule, but also because his Serb nobles demanded rewards. They had pressed for a militaristic policy, wanting to expand south for the gains to be had for themselves. Thus they expected land and other material rewards, including positions of authority in the newly conquered area. So Dušan had to consider their wishes and reward them with the high offices they expected. Such appointments, however, were not against his own interests and were a means to keep better control over his conquests.

The wishes or demands of the high Serbs who had carried out the conquest, to obtain lands in the newly conquered regions also caused problems at times, when there was insufficient abandoned land. Thus cases did exist in which Greeks lost lands or pronoias—for example, when Hrelja acquired villages and lands of various Greek pronoia holders near Štip—which must have caused some local dissatisfaction. However, if we take the conquered Greek lands as a whole, we probably would be justified in concluding that in general the Greeks were able to keep a large portion of their lands and were able to continue to live very much as they had before under the Byzantine Empire.

In the Serb territories, which also included the Albanian lands and northern Macedonia down to Skopje and possibly a bit beyond, Dušan did not change matters either. He saw no reason to introduce a Byzantine administrative system here. If he had it probably would not have functioned properly, because there were not enough Serbs who understood how the system ought to work. Thus, as noted, he left the Albanians under their tribal chiefs to manage their mountain districts according to existing custom. Serbian remained the language of his Serbian lands. Serbs filled offices there, though in some places he had foreign—often German—mercenary garrisons, probably to control regions where the nobility was not considered trustworthy. His best-known mercenary unit was that of the German Palman who commanded three hundred Germans. The existing Serbian tax system was retained and usually so were the Serbian titles for offices (e.g., župan).

The existing legal structure also remained in force. Until Dušan's reign Serbia had functioned under its customary law, supplemented in the early thirteenth century by a Church canon law code, introduced by Sava, that also covered many matters of civil and family law as well. Beyond these laws, rulers issued special acts (edicts) to a region or even to the nation as a whole in response to particular needs. Rulers also granted special charters of privilege to individual noblemen or monasteries (whose contents were often repeated to other individuals) or to special communities of foreign merchants or miners that allowed them to manage their own affairs under their own leaders according to their own customs. Dušan, though, soon came to believe his Serbian lands needed a more general code, and in 1349 he issued a state law code dealing with general matters. By it he intended to bring uniformity to the Serbian regions of his state and meet particular pressing problems. This document, which we shall turn to in a moment, excluding the general legal efforts possibly carried out by Milutin, is the first code of Serbian public law. Recognizing the existing division of the empire, it was valid only for the Serbian lands. In his Greek lands, as noted, existing Byzantine laws continued to be in force, supplemented only by Dušan's particular edicts or charters.

Thus in theory the Serbian empire was split down the middle, with two legal systems and two rulers—an emperor for the Greek lands and a king for the Serbian lands. However, since the king was only ten years old, Dušan in fact managed the whole kingdom. Greek language, civil and military titles, institutions, and laws marked the south (and article 124 of Dušan's law code recognizes the Byzantine charters for former Byzantine towns were to remain in effect), while Serbian language, civil and military titles, institutions and laws were used in the north. Dušan had two chancelleries, each under a logothete, one to issue Slavic documents and one to issue Greek ones. The position of logothete of the Serbian chancellery was held for a while by the father of the future prince, Lazar Hrebljanović. The chief financial official responsible for the state treasury and its income was the protovestijar. This position was regularly held by a merchant from Kotor who understood financial management and bookkeeping. It was long held by Nikola Buća of Kotor. Both protovestijars and logothetes were at times used as diplomats, the protovestijars in particular being sent west, for as citizens of Kotor they knew Italian and Latin.

Dušan's Law Code

Dušan's law code was promulgated at a council in 1349. After it was applied for a few years, it was found to have various short-comings. So in 1353 or 1354 he issued a series of additional articles to it.[10] Dušan's compilation is usually said to be the first code of public law in Serbia. However, four articles (nos. 79, 123, 152, 153), touching on various subjects, refer to the authority of the "Law of the Sainted King" (i.e., Milutin), which suggests that Milutin had issued some sort of code whose text has not survived. Dušan's code thus seems to have been a supplement to Milutin's non-extant code as well as a supplement to the various Church law codes that also had legal authority in Serbia at the time; in particular we may recall Sava's version of the Byzantine Nomocanon which he translated and which was accepted by the Serbian Church council in 1221. Moreover, Serbia had the *Syntagma* of Matthew Blastares. This collection of legal decisions, touching on ecclesiastical but also civil law cases, was written in the Byzantine Empire in 1335 and had soon thereafter been translated into Serbian. This text clearly received legal authority in 1349. Whether it had been given that authority prior to 1349 is a matter of debate. For when we are dealing with translations of legal texts, it is difficult to determine whether they were simply translated for information or as guides or, as most scholars think in the case of the *Syntagma,* as documents with binding authority in Serbia. In any case the *Syntagma*'s articles influenced the text of Dušan's code. Dušan's code was throughout very heavily influenced by Byzantine law—nearly half of its articles reflect that influence to a greater or lesser degree, often modified to meet Serbia's needs. The code has many articles concerning the Church that reflect Byzantine Church law; Byzantine civil law codes, especially the late-ninth-century compilation by Basil I and Leo VI, also influenced the Serbian code.

Dušan's code was not a thorough or systematic work but rather addressed a series of individual issues. Since most early manuscripts of Dušan's code also contain two other texts, many scholars, led by A. Solovjev and Soulis, conclude that the Council of 1349 actually issued a three-part comprehensive legal document. The first part was a newly prepared abridgement of Blastares' *Syntagma,* a fuller version of which, as noted, may already have acquired legal authority in Serbia. The second part was the so-called "Law of Justinian" (actually an abridgement of *The Farmer's Law*). And then, always given as the third part, was Dušan's original code itself. If the three texts were actually promulgated together and all given the force of law (as seems probable), then this would explain the unsystematic nature of Dušan's code itself; for if it was only the third part of a larger codex, its purpose would have been to supplement the first two texts, by picking up items not covered in them, rather than to establish a comprehensive legal system.

Before turning to the original Serbian part of the codex, let us examine the first two parts. Part One was an abridgement in Slavic of the *Syntagma* of Matthew Blastares. The original Byzantine work was a legal collection of an encyclopedic nature, providing discussions under alphabetical subject headings. Its content was drawn, as noted, from ecclesiastical and secular law; ecclesiastical articles made up a majority of the articles of the Byzantine original. Dušan's new version—or at least the version found in manuscripts containing his law code—contained only a third of the original Greek version; it omitted most of the ecclesiastical material and contained mainly secular articles. This should not surprise us, for, after all, Serbia already had an ecclesiastical code in Sava's Nomocanon. The secular articles of the abridged Serbian version of the *Syntagma* were drawn chiefly from Basil I's law code and the novels (new laws) of emperors who succeeded him; they focused on laws governing contracts, loans, inheritance, marriage, dowries, etc. as well as on matters of criminal law (both violent crimes and moral violations). Part Two, the so-called "Law of Justinian," was actually a shortened version of the eighth-century *Farmer's Law,* a code discussed in my volume on the early medieval Balkans. It focused on settling problems and disputes among peasants within a village.

These two texts were followed by Dušan's original code. This document seems to have been intended as a supplement to the other two parts, picking up what was not covered in them and dealing with specific Serbian situations. Since many aspects of civil and criminal law were well covered in the first two parts, Dušan's articles were more concerned with public law and legal procedure. His code also provided more material on actual punishments; on this subject there can be detected a strong Byzantine influence, with executions and mutilations frequently replacing Serbia's traditional monetary fines. Since Dušan's law code is actually a Serbian work, I shall discuss its contents in some detail.

The code touched on crimes or insults and their punishment; settlement of civil suits (including ordeals and the selection and role of juries); court procedure and judicial jurisdictions (defining which cases were to be judged by which bodies among Church courts, the tsar's court, courts of the tsar's circuit judges, and judgment by a nobleman); and rights and obligations, including the right to freely carry out commerce (articles 120, 121), tax obligations (what was owed in taxes and the time of year to pay them), grazing rights and their violation, service obligations to the tsar, exemption from state dues (usually for the Church), obligations associated with land, and the obligation of the Church to perform charity. The code also defined the different types of landholding (specifying the various rights and obligations that went with various categories of land), the rights of inheritance, the position of slaves, and the position of serfs. It defined the labor dues serfs owed to their lords (article 68) but also gave them the right to lay plaint against their master before the tsar's court (article 139)—a right probably rarely if ever exercised. The code also noted the special privileges of foreign communities (e.g., the Sasi).

Many articles touched on the status of the Church, thus supplementing the existing canon law texts. On the whole the Church received a very privileged position, though it was given the duty of charity in no uncertain terms: "And in all churches the poor shall be fed . . . and should any one fail to feed them, be he Metropolitan, bishop, or abbot, he shall be deprived of his office" (article 28). The code also banned simony. In most matters a clear-cut separation of Church and state was established, allowing Church courts to judge the Church's people and prohibiting the nobility from interfering with Church property and Church matters. It is also worth noting that though Dušan (like his predecessors) was on the whole friendly to, and willing to respect the rights of, foreign Catholics (such as the Sasi and coastal merchants residing in his realm), his code did not look favorably upon the Catholic Church. Dušan refers to it as the "Latin heresy" and to its adherents as "half believers." He prohibited proselytism by Catholics among the Orthodox, Orthodox conversions to Catholicism, and mixed marriages between Catholics and Orthodox unless the Catholic converted to Orthodoxy. He also had articles strongly penalizing "heretics" (presumably referring to Bogomils). Only the Orthodox were called Christians.

The code defined and supported the existing class structure, allowing court procedure, jurisdictions, and punishment to depend upon the social class of the individual involved. Articles touched on the status in society and in court of churchmen, noblemen, commoners, serfs, slaves, Albanians and Vlachs (the last two differentiated legally more for their pastoral occupation, thus different life-style, than for ethnic reasons), and the foreign communities. The code was also concerned with guaranteeing the state's authority and income; thus it contained articles on such matters as taxes, obligations associated with land, and services (and hospitality) owed to the tsar and to his agents.

The code also supported the state's efforts to maintain law and order. In this it did not limit itself to articles against crime and insults but also, reflecting the state's inability to keep order throughout the realm, gave responsibility in this field to specific communities. Thus the code made—or, as probably was the case, recognized the existing custom that made—each locality responsible for keeping order in its territory and liable for failure to do so. For example, a border lord was responsible for defending his border. Article 49 says, "if any foreign army come and ravish the land of the Tsar, and again return through their land, those frontier lords shall pay all [the people] through whose territory they [the army] came." The control of brigands, a constant Balkan problem, also fell to localities. This issue was addressed in articles 126, 145, 146, 158, and 191. Perhaps article 145 is most explicit: "In whatsoever village a thief or brigand be found, that village shall be scattered and the brigand shall be hanged forthwith . . . and the headman of the village shall be brought before me [the tsar] and shall pay for all the brigand or thief hath done from the beginning and shall be punished as a thief and a brigand." And continuing, in article 146, "also prefects and lieutenants and bailiffs and reeves and headmen who administer villages and mountain hamlets. All these shall be punished in the manner written above [article 145] if any thief or brigand be found in them." And article 126 states, "If there be a robbery or theft on urban land around a town, let the neighborhood pay for it all." And finally article 158 requires that the localities bordering on an uninhabited hill jointly supervise that region and pay for damage from any robbery occurring there.

These articles demonstrate the weakness of the state in maintaining order in rural and border areas, which caused it to pass the responsibility on down to the local inhabitants. By threatening them with penalties, the state hoped to force the locality to assume this duty. A second reason for the strictness of the articles toward the locality was the belief, often correct, that a brigand could not survive without local support, shelter, and food. Thus the brigand was seen as a local figure, locally supported, preying on strangers. As a result, the locality, allegedly supporting the brigand, shared in his guilt and deserved to share the punishment. These strict articles were therefore intended to discourage a community from aiding brigands.

Articles like the ones just cited are also valuable sources on Serbian social history. However, they must be used with caution. For a series of laws is not the same type of source as a visitor's description of a society. A law code does not describe how things actually functioned but only how they ought to have functioned. In some cases articles may have been based on customary laws; in such cases the articles' contents were probably generally observed or practiced and thus can be taken as evidence about actual practices and conditions. However, an article could also reflect an innovation, a reform the ruler was trying to bring about through legislation. In this case it would not have reflected existing customs and we must then ask, was the ruler successful in realizing his reform or did it remain a dead letter? Thus a law code may at times more accurately depict an ideal than reality. And since certain—perhaps many—articles in Dušan's code may have been attempts to legislate change, attempts which may or may not have been successful (and even if successful in one place, possibly not in others), we must always be careful and avoid leaping to the conclusion that this or that article describes the way things were done in fourteenth-century Serbia.

Serbia's Peasants

Because Dušan's code is one of our few sources on the position of peasants, this may be a good place to briefly discuss the peasantry in medieval Serbia. First it should be stated that we know almost nothing about free peasants. This is not to say that they did not exist or even that they were a rare phenomenon; our knowledge depends upon what sources have survived, while our ignorance coincides with what surviving sources do not contain. The overwhelming majority of documents about peasants that have survived are from monasteries, particularly from those on Mount Athos; not surprisingly, they discuss the peasants on the monasteries' lands, listing these peasants' lands, status, and obligations. These peasants were, of course, dependent ones.

Even Dušan's code, to the degree it discusses peasants at all, focuses on dependent ones. This may result from the fact that his code is accompanied by the "Law of Justinian" (i.e., an abridgement of *The Farmer's Law*), which deals with village situations and treats them in a free village context. Thus Dušan may well have felt its articles sufficed for this subject. However, this document goes back to the eighth century, and though laws or customs governing many situations may have remained unchanged since that time, those governing others may not have. Thus it would be risky to use its contents to depict specific rural conditions in the fourteenth century. Moreover, since many of its articles could be applied to villages within an estate, the presence of this text cannot even be used to demonstrate the survival of many free villages into Dušan's reign.

Some monasteries had enormous landholdings. At one time Hilandar possessed 360 villages scattered around Serbia, while the monastery of Visoki Dečani had 2,097 houses of meropsi, 69 of sokalniki, and 266 of Vlachs. According to a Visoki Dečani charter a merop was a peasant who ploughed six units of land and a sokalnik, three; this definition of these terms pertains to this monastery's lands and should not be taken as a standard to define the two classes throughout Serbia. The monastery peasants were bound to the land, but they also had a hereditary right to their land. They paid taxes to the state, collected by the landlord. This lord might have tax exemptions. Monasteries had very broad exemptions, and, as noted, sometimes even total exemption from all state taxes. In such cases, the peasants were better off than they would have been under a secular landlord; however, even the secular lord often had some exemptions, which would have made his peasants better off vis à vis the state than independent peasants owning their own plots. Dependent peasants were under the jurisdiction of a lord, be it the monastery abbot or a secular nobleman. He judged their disputes and small-scale crimes. Major crimes—murder, arson, rape, treason—were judged by the state, though as time passed certain major monasteries received the right to judge people on their lands even for certain serious crimes. In fact throughout the Serbian and Greek lands, in the course of the thirteenth, fourteenth, and fifteenth centuries, there was a trend to ever increase the area of jurisdiction of Church courts.

In addition to their state obligations, usually paid in cash, the peasants had obligations to their landlord. In Serbia these obligations were required partially in cash/kind and partially in labor. Labor dues predominated in Serbia, and the Hilandar charter obliges peasants to work two days a week on the monastery's lands. Dušan's code also requires a serf to labor two days a week on his lord's lands. In addition to their regular weekly obligation, peasants owed a certain number of other days' labor at critical times of the year (e.g., at harvest time). Dušan's code stipulates one day a year for harvesting and one day a year in the lord's vineyard. The Vlachs, who tended flocks instead of farming land, owed work dues in transport as well as a donation of a certain number of animals a year, while peasants owed chickens or certain amounts of produce at set times of the year. Byzantine peasants tended to owe smaller labor dues and greater cash payments than their Serb equivalents, whose obligations tended to be in labor and services. Scholars relate this difference to the fact that in Byzantium money was far more stable and better established as the basis of the economy, whereas in Serbia it was less so and penetrated the countryside to a smaller extent.

The monastery or nobleman, if rich, held a number of villages. They might be scattered around Serbia. A monastery was more likely to have widely scattered holdings than a nobleman. At times a nobleman might own part of a village and a monastery the rest. When that occurred, then each judged and collected from its own lands and people. Within a monastery's village, or part of a village, the land was divided between the direct holdings of the peasants and the lands of the monastery. The monastery's direct holdings were worked partly by the peasants fulfilling their labor dues. Reference at times is made to landless peasants; they presumably provided a full-time labor force on the lord's lands, probably receiving a share of the crop in return.

The peasants tended to live in houses clustered together around a center with the land lying outside, usually surrounding the village. Besides the land held directly by the landlord, other village land was held by the peasants. The peasants' lands were of two types: communal and private. Communal lands belonged to the village as a collective and included pasture land and woodland. Private lands were held by a particular peasant household. The peasant had a right to hold these lands, but title of ownership belonged to the lord, allowing him to demand dues and services from his peasants. These private lands, consisting of the peasants' plots of farmland, vineyard, etc., tended to be in scattered long strips rather than in consolidated plots. The peasants worked these lands during the other four (or so) days of the week; and from them the peasants subsisted and met whatever cash tax they owed to the state and the kind and/or cash dues they owed to the landlord.

In and near Serbia's Dalmatian coastal territory more obligations were met in kind or cash (usually valued at one-tenth of the produce) than in labor. This is probably related not only to the fact that cash was more common in this region—for people having cash from the coastal towns could come to the local markets and buy for cash—but also to the fact that the land in this area was less fertile and estates tended to be smaller. Thus with less land needing to be worked, it was in the landlord's interest to let the peasants retain as large a piece as possible and render rents for it.

Dušan Conquers Thessaly and Epirus

Dušan's appetite for expansion was whetted by success, and he saw no reason to limit his expansion to Macedonia and Albania. He was helped by various new Byzantine difficulties, including the great plague epidemic of 1347 and 1348 which swept through Thessaly and Epirus, killing among others John Angelus, the warlord and Byzantine governor of Thessaly (and probably also of Epirus, Acarnania, and Aetolia). Taking advantage of the chaos caused by the plague and the death or flight of various local leaders, Dušan, supported by various Albanian chiefs and their tribesman, took—probably in 1347— Epirus (including Jannina and Arta), Acarnania, and Aetolia. Thus Epirus, recovered by Byzantium with such great difficulty, remained part of the empire for only seven years. As a result, Dušan acquired all the western Balkans south from Serbia's older holdings in southern Dalmatia down to the Gulf of Corinth. Only Durazzo, remaining under the Angevins, did not fall to him.

At roughly the same time—most likely in 1348—Dušan's able general Preljub attacked Thessaly, which had been particularly badly hit by the plague. Facing very little resistance, he took the whole province down to, but not including, Pteleon, which was still held by the Venetians. His conquests also included most of the Catalans' lands in Thessaly, though the Catalans were able to retain Neopatras and its environs. The conquest of Thessaly was completed by November 1348. Many towns and noblemen seem to have surrendered quickly after negotiating agreements that allowed them to keep their existing privileges and lands. Preljub's armies also contained considerable numbers of Albanians.

Epirus was turned over to Dušan's half-brother Symeon to govern. To solidify his position he married Anna of Epirus' daughter Thomais. Preljub was assigned Thessaly, which he ruled from Trikkala. Part, or possibly all, of central Albania, clearly including Berat and Valona, was given to Dušan's brother-in-law John Comnenus Asen, who married the widowed Anna of Epirus to increase his ties to the appanage granted him. Soulis suggests that John Comnenus Asen was given direct rule only over Berat, Kanina, and Valona, while the rest of Albania remained under local Albanian chiefs who submitted directly to Dušan and were allowed to continue managing their communities as previously. Soulis may well be right; however, surviving sources do not tell us how much of the hinterland went with the three named cities and thus we do not know how much of Albania was assigned to his appanage. In any case most of the countryside was in the hands of the tribesmen; thus the question is, were they nominally under Dušan directly or under him indirectly through a nominal submission to John Comnenus Asen?

Thus in seventeen years Dušan was able to double the size of his empire, while halving that of the Byzantines. And it should be noted that he achieved all this without a single pitched battle in an open field. His conquests were carried out by taking a region's towns one by one through sieges. As a result

Dušan's realm stretched from the Danube in the north to the Gulf of Corinth in the south and from the Adriatic in the west almost to the Mesta River, as far as Kavalla beyond the Struma, in the east.

The depopulation resulting from the 1348 plague left vacant lands which attracted further Albanian migration into and settlement in Greece. The plague, having devastated northern Greece, then moved on to the Albanian and Dalmatian coast where it continued its destructive work. We do not know whether it penetrated Serbia itself. However, at this time Albanian migration into Serbia also did take place. A charter of Dušan from 1348 refers to nine katuns of Albanians north of Prizren.

The Condition of the Byzantine Empire in the Middle of the Fourteenth Century

The Byzantine Empire was now reduced to Constantinople, Thrace, Thessaloniki (regained in 1350), Anaktoropolis, the western part of the Chalcidic peninsula, certain Aegean islands (chiefly in the northern Aegean), and roughly half the Peloponnesus. The civil wars, Turkish plundering, and Bulgarian raids had devastated much of Thrace, bringing its agriculture and economy to a standstill. There had been considerable depopulation in Thrace even before the 1348 plague, which of course made the situation that much worse. The survival of Constantinople and the other cities of Thrace, when they had to do without the produce of Thrace, depended on the Genoese transporting grain from the Crimea and to a lesser extent from Bulgaria, where Varna was becoming an important port for the export of Bulgarian grain. These grain shipments averted serious famine in the late 1340s.

The depopulation and devastation, by reducing agricultural productivity, also reduced the tax base of the empire's provinces. And the rich, the only ones who could pay anything worth mentioning, in the course of the civil wars had been bribed by so many exemptions that they paid only a tiny fraction of their share. They had little sense of duty and continually sought more exemptions and evaded paying even the little that they owed. Thus the two great strengths of the empire in its days of glory, namely, its administration and treasury, had collapsed. Its income was so greatly reduced that the treasury was nearly empty. At Cantacuzenus' coronation banquet in 1347 pottery and lead dishes replaced the former gold and silver service. Cantacuzenus discovered that the bureaucracy had broken down. Even near-by Thrace was controlled by the great nobles. Cantacuzenus now divided the shrinking empire further by making the Byzantine Morea in 1348 or 1349 into an autonomous despotate under his second son, Manuel. His eldest son, Matthew, as noted, had already received an appanage in Byzantine Thrace along the Serbian border; from that border near Kavalla (which was Serbian and which lay a little bit to the west of the Mesta River) his appanage extended possibly as far east as Demotika (according to Florinskij). Or, as others have argued, it stretched east beyond Xantheia but not as far east as Demotika.

These assignments were made for several reasons: (1) to keep the provinces from seceding under feudal lords like Momčilo, now that there was no longer any administrative apparatus to bind them to the capital; (2) to prevent in the Thracian case further Serbian annexations of imperial lands and in general to defend that region against the Serbs and Turks; and (3) to establish Cantacuzenus' personal control over these regions. By utilizing his own family Cantacuzenus acquired a stronger hold over these provinces to bind them to him against the legitimate Palaeologian dynasty. And some of his opponents believed the creation of these appanages was a first step toward ousting the Palaeologians entirely. With regard to the second reason, in 1347 Matthew did repel a Turkish raid under Suleyman, but in 1350 he was not strong enough to prevent the Turks from plundering his lands and from then crossing the Marica to plunder Bulgaria. During that campaign they took much booty and many prisoners.

Dušan, Byzantium, and Bosnia in 1350

Dušan, having acquired Thessaly and Epirus, began thinking more seriously of trying to obtain Constantinople. He realized that to acquire that city, he needed a fleet. The fleets from Serbia's southern Dalmatian towns, even combined with Dubrovnik's fleet (if he could have persuaded Dubrovnik to join such a venture), were far too small for the task. Thus Dušan opened negotiations with Venice, with which he maintained fairly good relations. Venice was polite, not wanting to antagonize him; but fearing a loss or reduction of its privileges in the empire if the stronger Serbs should replace the weaker Byzantines as masters of Constantinople, Venice found excuses to avoid a military alliance with him. Each state attempted to use the other; while Dušan sought Venetian support against Byzantium, Venice sought Serbian support in its struggle with Hungary over Dalmatia. However, whenever it sensed Serbian aid in Dalmatia might result in a Venetian obligation to Serbia, Venice politely turned down Dušan's offers of help.

In 1350 Dušan launched an attack upon Bosnia. It was undoubtedly directed primarily at Hum. The motives behind this invasion were probably two-fold: to regain Serbian Hum, annexed by Bosnia in 1326, and to put a stop to Bosnian raids against the tsar's tributaries in Konavli. Dušan had been complaining about attacks on Konavli and had received no satisfaction. In the summer of 1350 Venice had also tried, without success, to mediate a settlement. Venice had involved itself here in the hopes of settling the issue before Dušan took action, for it feared that if Dušan intervened successfully with his troops in Dalmatia, he might acquire new interests in that region and threaten Venice's position in Dalmatia. But, diplomacy failed. So in October 1350 Dušan invaded Hum with an army which Resti, probably with exaggeration, claimed numbered eighty thousand men. This force seems to have successfully occupied part of the disputed territory.

According to Orbini, prior to his attack on Bosnia-Hum Dušan had been in secret contact with various Bosnian nobles, offering them bribes to support him. And many nobles—presumably chiefly those from Hum—were ready to betray the Bosnian ban. These included the Nikolić brothers, who were major nobles in Hum and descendants of Miroslav. Instead of meeting Dušan's forces, the Bosnian ban avoided a major confrontation by retiring into the mountains and dispatching small hit-and-run actions against the Serbs. Most of Bosnia's fortresses held out, though some nobles did submit to Dušan. The Serbs ravaged much of the countryside: with one army they reached Duvno and the Cetina River, while a second one penetrated up to the Krka River—on which lay Knin—in Croatia, and a third, having taken Imotski and Novi (near Imotski), left garrisons in the two towns and then moved into Hum. From this position of strength, Dušan tried to negotiate a peace with the ban. He wanted it sealed by the marriage of his son Uroš to the ban's daughter Elizabeth, with Hum as her dowry, thereby bringing about the restoration of Hum to Serbia. The ban was not willing to consider this proposal. How much of Orbini's account is reliable is a subject of controversy; unfortunately we lack evidence to resolve it.

Dušan may also have intended the Bosnian campaign to provide aid for his sister. In 1347 she had married Mladen III Šubić, the lord of Omiš, Klis, and Skradin. After her husband's death from the plague in 1348, she had tried to maintain her rule over these cities for herself and for her minor son. But she soon found herself challenged by both the Hungarians and the Venetians, who sought to acquire her cities. Interest in helping her could explain why Serbian armies were dispatched into western Hum and into Croatia (if, in fact, Orbini's statement to this effect is true), for operations in this region were not likely to help Dušan obtain his own major goal of recovering Serbian Hum. However, before Dušan's armies managed to reach her cities, if indeed that was their destination, and before they could occupy all of what had been Serbian Hum, Dušan was recalled to put down trouble in the east. Dušan was not to forget his sister's plight; in 1355, just before he died, he was to send her troops to garrison Klis and Skradin against Hungary.

Cantacuzenus tried to take advantage of Dušan's absence (and of the removal of many of his troops from Macedonia and Thessaly to participate in the Bosnian campaign) to regain part of Macedonia and Thessaly. To support his efforts the Constantinopolitan patriarch, Kallistos, excommunicated the new Serbian patriarch and emperor, accusing them of usurping titles, deposing Greeks from their bishoprics and replacing them with Serbs, and transferring Greek sees from the jurisdiction of Greek metropolitans to that of the Serbian patriarch. Thus Dušan's conquests had also expanded the territory under the Serbian Church at the expense of the Greek hierarchy. The Greek bishoprics transferred in this way to the jurisdiction of the Patriarch of Peć were the Metropolitans of Melnik, Philippi, Serres, and Kavalla and the Archbishop of Drama. The excommunication seems to have been intended to discourage the Greek population in Dušan's Greek provinces from supporting the Serbian administration and thereby to assist Cantacuzenus' campaign to recover them. The excommunication did not stop the Athonite monks from dealing with Dušan. They also continued to address him as tsar, though calling him Tsar of the Serbs rather than Tsar of the Serbs and Greeks.

Cantacuzenus, then, with a small army, the best he could muster, took the Chalcidic peninsula with Mount Athos; he next took the fortresses of Veria and Voden. Veria was the richest town in the region of Botie; to hold Veria Dušan had removed many Greeks from the town and replaced them with Serbs, including a Serb garrison. However, this was not sufficient to secure the town; for the remaining local citizens were still able to open the gates to Cantacuzenus in 1350. Voden resisted Cantacuzenus but was taken by assault. Cantacuzenus also took various smaller places in the vicinity of these two towns. He then advanced toward Thessaly but was stopped at Servia by Preljub and a force of only five hundred men. Thus the Byzantine army was prevented from entering into Thessaly. The Byzantine force retired to Veria, while the Turks associated with it went off plundering; their forays went as far afield as Skopje. The small size of the Serbian defending army also demonstrates the weakness of the invading force; the Byzantine army must have been tiny, for if it had had any kind of numbers, even if it could not have taken Servia, it would not have thought twice about by-passing Servia and pressing on further into Thessaly. Having five hundred men at one's rear should not have seemed a serious danger to a normal army.

Word of the Byzantine attack upon his Greek lands reached Dušan in Hum. He quickly reassembled his forces from Bosnia and Hum and, abandoning that region, marched for Thessaly. His withdrawal led to the loss of whatever gains he had made in the west. It seems therefore that the local nobility had not seriously supported his invasion. He was not to move against Bosnia and Hum again; thus once again on behalf of his southern interests he wrote off what had been Serbia's lands to the west. Some seventeenth-century sources suggest Dušan attacked Bosnia a second time in 1351, while others describe a single campaign which they date to 1351. However, most scholars believe he carried out only one campaign which took place in 1350. Bosnia remained in possession of Hum; in fact after Dušan's death Bosnia was to expand further at Serbia's expense, acquiring the remaining parts of Serbian Hum and thereby extending its authority all the way to the Lim River.

When Dušan reached Macedonia, the Byzantines quickly withdrew to Thrace. Dušan took Voden after a short siege. His troops plundered the town. He soon also regained Veria and the other places Cantacuzenus had taken. Thus Cantacuzenus' attempt to regain the empire's lost lands from the Serbs was an utter failure. Cantacuzenus gives a long account of the alleged negotiations with Dušan that followed; he states that Dušan, afraid of Cantacuzenus' strength and readiness to fight, came close to accepting an agreement that would have restored considerable territory to the empire. Florinskij argues, plausibly, that this account is entirely fictitious, presented to depict Cantacuzenus in a better light. Cantacuzenus was to make no subsequent attempt to regain from the Serbs the empire's lost territory.

Weak vis-à-vis the Serbs and suffering from Turkish raids, Cantacuzenus tried to make an alliance, supposedly directed chiefly against the Turks, with the Bulgarians. John Alexander—possibly under Dušan's influence or possibly simply mistrustful of the Byzantines—rejected it. He then succeeded in the face of some opposition to persuade his council of boyars to agree to its rejection. Cantacuzenus' negotiations with John Alexander, however, may have prevented a Bulgarian attack on Byzantium; for the Bulgarians had been angrily blaming Byzantium for raids into Bulgaria launched by Turks from Byzantine Thrace. Cantacuzenus at least was able to persuade John Alexander that the empire was not behind the raids and was powerless to prevent them.

Civil War Again in Byzantium

By this time the young legitimate emperor, John V, was reaching his majority and becoming restless at being excluded from power by his father-in-law. To try to pacify him, and also to remove him from the capital, Cantacuzenus assigned him in late 1351 or 1352 an appanage in the western part of Byzantine Thrace and in the Rhodopes. Including the former Boleron theme and the territory to its east, it stretched eastward at least to Ainos and shortly thereafter was extended to Demotika. His son Matthew, who had held this territory, was removed from it and given a new appanage to John V's east, centered in Adrianople. The two princes were soon quarrelling over boundaries, and Matthew refused to recognize John V as the heir to the throne. Shortly after the territorial assignments, still in 1352, war broke out between the two princes. John V, having concluded a treaty with Venice, hired a large number of Turkish mercenaries. Then, having been promised support by the Thessalonians (long hostile to Cantacuzenus), he marched against Matthew's appanage. One after the other Matthew's towns, including Adrianople, quickly surrendered to the young Palaeologian emperor. Expecting serious retaliation from Cantacuzenus, John V sought and was promised help from both Serbia and Bulgaria. To obtain Serbia's help, John V had to send his brother Michael to the Serbian court as a hostage. Contrary to general Byzantine policy and attitudes, John V also recognized Dušan's title of Tsar of the Serbs. He seems to have recognized his title for the first time in 1352; he continued to do so thereafter for the duration of Dušan's life.

After acquiring more troops from his Ottoman allies, Cantacuzenus marched into Thrace to rescue his son Matthew. When the Ottoman troops retook cities that had surrendered to John, Cantacuzenus allowed the Turks to plunder them. Among those so plundered was Adrianople. Thus it seemed that Cantacuzenus was on the way to defeating the young emperor, who retreated west seeking Serbian help. Dušan obliged by sending him four thousand horsemen. Orkhan, however, provided Cantacuzenus with ten thousand horsemen. The Ottoman cavalry met the Serbs and possibly also a Bulgarian force—since after the battle Turkish forces plundered Bulgaria—in an open-field battle near Demotika in October 1352. Thus the fate of the

Byzantine Empire was to be decided by a battle between Turks and Serbs. The more numerous Ottomans crushed the Serbs, and Cantacuzenus was able to retain power and assign appanages as he chose. Young John V, however, refused to surrender and sailed off to the Venetian-held island of Tenedos to continue his war.

The battle near Demotika was the first major battle between Ottomans and Europeans in Europe and its results made Dušan realize that the Turks were a major threat to eastern Europe. This danger became more serious in 1354 when the Ottomans crossed the Dardanelles and occupied the important fortress of Gallipoli, whose walls had collapsed during an earthquake. The Turks quickly repaired the walls and refused to depart, despite Cantacuzenus' protests. The Turks then stepped up the number of their raids, taking tribute from some towns of eastern Thrace and occupying others including ones along the coast of Thrace as far west as Kypsela on the lower Marica, which they took. They then advanced eastward along the north shore of the Sea of Marmora and conquered Rodosto (Rhaedestus). By late 1354 they held most of the north shore of the Sea of Marmora from Gallipoli to the walls of Constantinople. By this time, as he became more alarmed by the Turks, Dušan was actively trying to create a coalition, including members from the West, to oppose the Turks and drive them from Europe. He corresponded with both Venice and the pope on this subject but had no success.

Meanwhile, after the Turkish victory over the Serbs fighting for John V and a subsequent failure by John V to seize Constantinople in March 1353 when Cantacuzenus was absent from the city, Cantacuzenus lost his temper with the young Palaeologian emperor and decided to remove him from the imperial succession. He had his own son Matthew proclaimed emperor in April 1353, after which John V's name was dropped from state documents. Thus Cantacuzenus considered John deposed and Matthew to be his heir. To re-enforce this decision he sought a formal coronation for Matthew. When Patriarch Kallistos protested, he was deposed. Kallistos then withdrew to Mount Athos. His replacement then carried out Matthew's coronation as emperor in February 1354.

John V, still at large, was not ready to give up; he went to Galata and sought aid from the Genoese. He soon concluded an agreement with a brawling Genoese sea captain who was more or less a pirate; John gave the captain his sister as a wife and the island of Lesbos in exchange for helping him get Constantinople. Meanwhile, Cantacuzenus' unpopularity in the capital was increasing; he was particularly blamed for bringing to Europe the Turks, a Muslim force that was plundering Byzantine territory and taking Christians as slaves. Anger was turning to fear as the Turks took and securely fortified Gallipoli and then occupied the north shore of the Sea of Marmora to the very walls of the capital, which was now threatened by them. Cantacuzenus, blamed for their presence, also seemed incapable of doing anything about removing them. Thus John V could count on support inside Constantinople. So, having been recognized by the Byzantine Aegean islands as emperor, and having Genoese ships, including those of his brother-in-law, in the waters around the capital, John V with a small force advanced on the capital in late November 1354. Constantinople's gates were opened to him.

John VI Cantacuzenus abdicated and became a monk. In retirement he wrote his history/memoirs, a basic but biased source for the chaotic events we have been relating. John V, now sole emperor in his own right, nevertheless still respected his father-in-law's brains; thus he frequently consulted him on state affairs. And as far as we know, Cantacuzenus never tried to depose him or regain the throne for himself or his sons. Cantacuzenus, as a monk, advisor, and historian, remained active until his death in 1383. He is often blamed for bringing the Ottomans to Europe. He clearly was the first to utilize them for European affairs. However, if he had not invited them, they certainly would have soon arrived on their own.

After John Cantacuzenus' deposition, his son Matthew held out in the Rhodopes. John V marched against him and a number of Matthew's towns rapidly surrendered to John. Under siege Matthew concluded a treaty with John, surrendering Thrace and agreeing to a partition of the empire. Matthew was to retain the possessions he still had until arrangements could be made to turn over to him his new lands. However, Matthew soon heard rumors, perhaps accurate ones, that John V had no intention of keeping the agreement but in fact was planning Matthew's assassination. Feeling deceived, Matthew, before the end of 1355, had resumed the war to regain his former position in Thrace. This war continued into the fall of 1356 when Matthew was captured by a Serb, Vojin, the Count of Drama. At first planning to release Matthew for ransom, Vojin soon learned that John V was willing to pay a far greater sum for the captive. Thus Vojin sold Matthew to the emperor. As John's captive, Matthew was forced to renounce both his territorial claims and his imperial title, in a court ceremony in December 1357. Then he was released. Eventually in 1361 he was allowed to go to the Peloponnesus to join his brother Manuel.

Manuel Cantacuzenus in the Morea

Matthew's younger brother, Manuel, had been appointed, at the age of twenty-six or twenty-seven, in 1348 or 1349 to an appanage that consisted of the Byzantine Morea. As an emperor's son, having great prestige and residing at so great a distance from Constantinople, he was able to behave as an independent ruler. This was facilitated by his father's making him a despot and declaring his appointment a lifetime one. Thus from the moment of Manuel's appointment one can start to speak of a Despotate of the Morea. His position was not an easy one. His territory was raided by Latins from the Principality of Achaea, by Catalans, and by Turkish pirates. Moreover, the local nobles were not interested in losing their local authority by submitting to any central government. Furthermore, some of these nobles may not have been Cantacuzenus' partisans. And we may suspect that Manuel, besides being the

Byzantine governor, was appointed to be a defender of Cantacuzenus interests. He soon initiated a tax to finance the creation of a fleet to defend the Morea. The local Greek nobles greeted this tax with a rebellion; they probably were fighting as much for their own independence against central authority as against the tax. They attacked Mistra, and Manuel defeated them with his own body-guard, a corps of Albanian mercenaries, and with the help of some local Latins. This ended the offensive phase of the rebellion, though a few rebels held out in the provinces. But when his mercenaries began to plunder the lands of these diehards, the last rebels came out of the strongholds, in which they had been holed up, and submitted.

Manuel's wife was a Latin, the daughter of the ruler of Cyprus, and he maintained friendly relations with the Frankish nobles of the Morea and also with the Catholic Church, which made it easier for the Catholic barons to accept his rule. Mistra, his capital, became a thriving cultural center, with a lively court, literate people, and excellent architects and artists; under Manuel's patronage palaces and churches with fine frescoes began to appear. Though building activities were centered in Mistra, new monasteries were erected throughout the Byzantine Morea in this period.

When John V came to power at the very end of 1354, he wanted to oust Manuel from the Morea. John appointed two of his own cousins—Michael and Andrew Asen—to rule the Morea. They arrived there late in 1355 and won support from various Greek archons, some of whom had participated in the earlier revolt against Manuel. Manuel retired behind the walls of Mistra. Meanwhile the two cousins, trying to win local support by distributing booty, raided Venetian land in the vicinity of Modon and Coron, stirring the ire of the Venetians. As a result the Venetians gave their support to Manuel, as did most of the populace of the Morea. The two Asens soon returned to Constantinople. And John V, seeing the difficulties, which were exacerbated by the Morea's distance from the rest of the empire, gave up his plan to oust Manuel and confirmed him in his position. The Venetians, who dominated commerce in the whole peninsula (including their own ports and those of the empire and the Principality of Achaea), were pleased by Manuel's victory.

When Matthew Cantacuzenus was captured and forced to renounce his imperial title, he retired to the Peloponnesus, hoping, since he was the elder brother, to take over the Morea. Manuel and the court at Mistra, however, were not interested in changing the status quo. Realizing he had no hope of ousting his brother, Matthew accepted the situation; the brothers settled their relations amicably and Manuel continued to rule. Matthew settled in the Morea, supporting Manuel, and the two, who were both intellectuals, were active patrons of art and learning. When Manuel died in 1380 with no sons, his brother Matthew succeeded to the Morea.

The Morea in this period was spared the large-scale Turkish raids that Thrace and Bulgaria suffered. Peloponnesian violence was on a smaller scale; it consisted of feuds between different archons, an occasional armed act of resistance by a few archons against the authorities in Mistra (always put down rapidly), and Turkish piracy along the coast, which though causing damage did not threaten the peninsula with conquest. Italians and Greeks were also active as pirates.

Needing to build up his army, Manuel recruited many Albanians who had migrated into the Peloponnesus. To obtain further recruits he seems to have encouraged more Albanians to migrate into and settle in his principality. They came and settled as tribes, still under their chiefs. Some scholars have argued that their settlement should be dated to, and after, the mid-1380s under Palaeologian despots. Though Albanian settlement then took place on what was clearly a larger scale, it certainly had been taking place during Manuel's reign as well.

Greek Landholding, Peasants, and Lords

When we turn to the subject of Greek peasants, we are faced with various problems, most of which are derived from the nature of our sources. Basically, what have survived are documents describing monastic lands, particularly the holdings of the Athonite monasteries. The monastery archives preserve a few such documents about secular holdings that depict the former status of certain lands acquired subsequently by a monastery from a secular landlord. But very few of such documents exist and one must wonder if one is entitled to generalize from these few examples about secular estates as a whole. One also wonders to what extent conditions on secular estates resembled those on monastic ones; for if they were very similar, then one could use documents about monastic estates to describe great estates in general. The few documents touching on secular estates that are preserved do show certain differences; but whether these differences were typical or idiosyncratic for these particular estates is unknown. Furthermore, monasteries had particularly broad immunities. Their exemptions presumably had significant impact upon peasant obligations. As for peasants not on estates but in free villages, paying their taxes directly to the state, we are completely in the dark; for no cadaster describing such a village has survived. The absence of source material about free peasants has led some scholars to say there were no free villages left. This conclusion surely goes too far, but probably as time passed there were ever fewer of them. And in fact Charanis, in examining legal disputes, has uncovered a few examples of free peasants and even free villages in the thirteenth century. For example, he found a case in which a monastery sued some villagers who had usurped and farmed certain deserted lands which the monastery claimed belonged to it. Charanis reasonably concludes these were free villagers, for if they had belonged to an estate, the monastery would have sued the villagers' landlord.[11]

In the previous volume, and earlier in this one, we discussed the growth of great estates, which became a serious problem for the Byzantine state in the tenth century. As the lands of free peasants and soldiers became absorbed by the magnates' estates, the state became increasingly dependent on the great magnates with their private retinues. As a result there arose in the eleventh century the pronoia system. Pronoias, as noted earlier, were grants of an income source (usually a landed estate) for service. The state retained title to the land, but the holder had the right to its income, generally collecting for himself from the peasants the taxes formerly owed to the state and thus reducing the income from taxes received by the state. In exchange for this income he owed service (usually military) to the state. The number of retainers he had to bring to battle depended on the size of his pronoia. Upon his death or upon failure to perform the required service, the state took back the land for re-assignment. In time, particularly from the late thirteenth century, pronoias tended to become hereditary, but the state still, in theory, retained title and could demand service from them.

Recent scholarship shows that pronoias were a more complex institution than had previously been thought. Whereas the earliest pronoias were distributed from state lands, by the fourteenth century, as state lands became scarce, other types of land were granted as pronoias. For example a pronoia might be the recipient's own patrimonial estate; in this case, in exchange for service the state granted him the right to keep the taxes he owed to the state— in other words, the state gave him a tax exemption for service. Or the pronoia could be a free village, in which case the peasants henceforth paid their state taxes to the grantee rather than to the state. Or it could even be the lands of a third person or institution (e.g., a monastery) in which case the pronoia holder received the taxes the third person had previously paid to the state. The pronoia holder was usually granted the right to judge peasants on the lands granted to him; but when a pronoia holder received income from the lands of a third person, the pronoia holder did not receive judicial privileges. In theory, a free village that became a pronoia remained free. It owed no feudal rents to the grantee and he received no judicial authority over the village. He was not granted the village's land but its tax income. But though a very clear legal distinction exists, documents show, as one might expect, that holders of free-village pronoias frequently tried—sometimes with success—to convert the pronoia into their own holding and demanded from it feudal dues from the peasants in addition to the state taxes.

On occasion a whole region was granted as a pronoia. Generally such a grant was made to a close relative of the emperor. Thus Michael VIII granted the islands of Rhodes and Lesbos to his brother John. In such a grant the status of private lands located in the region did not change. The property owners simply paid the taxes to the new grantee instead of to the imperial treasury.

By the ninth century a free peasant owed a hearth tax—a collective family tax rather than an individual head tax for each adult—as well as land taxes to the state; he also owed supplementary taxes on particular items like bee-hives or fruit trees as well as various service duties like road or bridge building. The village also owed men for military service. These obligations to the state, in theory, remained when a village was absorbed by a great estate, unless the state specifically granted the lord an immunity charter. Such charters usually exempted the estate from a particular duty, not from obligations in general. In addition to state duties, peasants *on estates* owed rents and gifts to the landlord.

The most common term for a peasant in the late empire was *paroikos* (plural, *paroikoi*). Scholars have long argued about the legal significance of this term. It seems probable the paroikos was not a full serf. Though dependent to the degree that he was tied to his land, he was legally free. And despite the obligations he had to the estate, he was free to buy and sell other lands. Moreover, a paroikos on an estate, once he was established on his land, could not be evicted. Thus he had a legal right to his land. He also seems to have had an obligation to remain on it and work it. However, cases do exist where a paroikos was allowed to go and work in a town and send back to the estate in cash the feudal dues (or their equivalent) he owed the landlord. The typical paroikos, in the surviving documents, lived on a monastic estate. And of course, we do not know how similar he was to a paroikos on a nobleman's estate. Indeed we cannot even say with certainty that the peasants documented on the lands in Thrace and Macedonia, owned by the rich monasteries of Mount Athos, most of which had total or nearly total exemptions, were typical of peasants living on the estates of other monasteries.

Professor Laiou has made a detailed study of late medieval Greek peasants and the discussion that follows is much indebted to her work.[12] She shows that the typical Thracian-Macedonian Athonite peasant lived in a nuclear household paying the hearth tax. In 1300 the average household consisted of four to six individuals. Between 1320 and 1348 this average fell to between three and five. The village (the geographical unit with a name) was a conglomerate of houses with its lands lying around the outside. The whole village could be free, or it could all be part of one estate, or it could be split between free lands and households and dependent lands and households; the dependent ones could all be members of one estate or they could be divided between dependents of more than one estate. Laiou has found that most households had a vineyard, fruit trees, and a garden plot; they owned these entirely by right. The village had common lands for pasturing sheep. Many peasants owned animals that were their own personal property: bees, pigs, sheep, goats, chickens, sometimes even a cow. A few had oxen and/or horses. The village also tended to be drawn from a very small number of different families; thus villagers were often related, with brothers remaining in the village, keeping a share of the land, bringing in wives from outside, and starting new households. In general families were patriarchal; however, Laiou has found cases of widows managing lands. If a man died leaving only a daughter, she was briefly the household head, until she found a husband willing to move to her farm; then as her husband he replaced her as household head. Sometimes village rights were contested by a monastery. These quarrels usually centered around fishing rights or rights to the village's common land.

The monastery, even though it had been granted the village, was not entitled to interfere with these rights and could not legally put the common land to other uses.

In general, Laiou shows, peasants produced what was cheap to cultivate. Few had arable land for grain. Thus on estates the arable grain-producing land generally belonged directly to the monastery. This situation arose because arable land required capital: seed and oxen for plowing. The monastery, which alone had the capital, could then demand from the peasants the feudal rents owed for their own holdings in the form of labor (corvée) on its arable land. Corvée duties for peasants varied from monastery to monastery. The number of days seems to have depended partly on local custom and partly on what the monastery could get away with demanding. In Thrace and Macedonia, unlike Serbia, corvée was set at so many days a year. Frequently twelve days was considered a standard, but Laiou has turned up cases in which twenty-four and even forty-eight days a year were demanded from an individual. Presumably these days were staggered among different peasant families throughout the agricultural season. Thus the monastery got its direct holdings worked as its rent.

A monastery could also rent its arable land directly to a peasant. And Laiou has discovered a surviving contract stating that if the peasant cultivated at his own expense the land he rented, he might keep two-thirds of the produce, rendering only one-third to the monastery. Presumably in other cases, when the peasant depended on the monastery to provide him with all or some of the seed, and possibly the oxen with which to plow the land, the division of the produce would have been nearer fifty-fifty. Thus the monastery either rented out its own direct domain for a share of the produce or else had its lands farmed by the corvée owed by its peasants.

Shares of produce were based on the productivity of the year; thus a peasant paid more or less depending on how much he produced. This was a fairer arrangement than the state taxes, which demanded so much per hearth/acre regardless of whether it was a good or bad year.

Professor Laiou has also studied inheritance patterns. A partible inheritance sytsem, giving each son an equal share, existed in Macedonia and Thrace. Equal shares meant an equal share of everything, including equal portions of each type of land. This system increased the scattered nature of village lands. For each son inherited a piece of vineyard, of first-quality land, of second-quality land, of orchard, etc. And with each generation, each piece tended to be increasingly divided. Thus after several generations dwarf holdings could develop, unless there was sufficient abandoned land or sufficient unspoken for woodland available to be converted into usable land. However, the system described above allowed a peasant who inherited a dwarf plot to survive. For in addition to the small plots he inherited, the peasant could rent additional land from the landlord's domain for a share of the produce.

Laiou also believes the status of paroikos did not pass to all sons, if they did not want it. And she has found cases where one son inherited the land and the other sons left. Since primogeniture was a violation of both Greek and Slavic custom, it is not likely that those departing were actually disinherited. The younger sons probably saw no economic future in the village and wanted to leave; they thus presumably agreed that one brother should have the lands and paroikos status, while they, in return for some sort of compensation, left to seek their fortunes. Charanis argues that paroikos status went to only one son. But Laiou convincingly argues that legally one did not inherit the status but land, and that status was tied to the land. Laiou also notes that in certain areas long held by the crusaders, particularly in parts of the Morea, the Western custom of primogeniture took root even among Greek villages. The younger sons from this region, though disinherited, generally remained in the village, working as serfs on the domain of the landlord.

When a family in a free village died out or its last member wanted to sell a farm, the system of pre-emption (priority buying), going back to the tenth century, was still in effect. Under this system, other relatives and then other villagers had the right of refusal before the land could be placed on the open market, where a magnate would usually acquire it. However, by the late empire magnates regularly had lands in the village already, giving them the fellow-villager priority status; this helped them to expand their own holdings.

In the mid-fourteenth century and thereafter there were shortages of labor. These can be attributed to the depopulation caused by the civil wars, Serbian-Byzantine wars, Turkish raids, and also the plague epidemics. Laiou, however, argues that since plagues tended to strike urban areas, they may have had less effect on village populations than one might at first think. Land grants were almost worthless without people on the lands to work them (unless, as occasionally might be the case, the recipient had an excess of labor on some other estate); thus lands were usually granted with people on them. To help solve the labor problem imperial grants of people alone were sometimes made, enabling the recipient to acquire manpower for his lands. Landlords also tried to acquire more people through enticement and kidnapping. If an enticed or stolen paroikos was found, the case could be taken to court; if it was won, then the paroikos was restored to the original estate. The usual category of people recruited by a landlord or granted by the state were the eleutheroi (literally, free men, but in this case meaning free of land, landless). Since dependence was based on land and since they did not have it, they were free of fiscal obligations. Many of them were probably younger sons of land-poor families, who had left to seek a better life. Others were surely run-away paroikoi who had fled from bad situations, ruthless landlords, or the proximity of enemy raiders. Thus the eleutheroi were a mobile element. When settled on an estate, some remained eleutheroi as share-croppers (renting domain land) or as the domain's labor force, but others were settled on plots of land and became paroikoi.

Because labor was short and conditions unstable, owing to the great amount of military activity and the many raids that dislocated the population and ravaged the lands of Thrace and Macedonia, demographic mobility increased greatly from the second half of the fourteenth century. Presumably there was a steady movement of population from villages on or near main routes to those further afield. Some villagers fortified their villages, others limited themselves to erecting stockades in village centers.

Laiou argues that early in the fourteenth century Macedonia was still widely populated, and she guesses the region then may have had half the population of modern Macedonia. She thinks earlier scholars have regularly underestimated the size of villages. For example, she notes, various scholars have based village population figures on a cadaster for a monastery's village holdings and have taken the cadaster's figures to be the village's entire population, not taking into account the possibility that the monastery may have had title to only a part of the village. She notes that around 1300 one could still find villages of five hundred to a thousand people. Again though, one may ask, would such a large village have been typical?

Dušan's Last Years and Death

Dušan continued to dream about marching against Constantinople, conquering it, and becoming its emperor. Having failed to recruit Venice and provide himself with a fleet for this enterprise, he seems to have done little more than dream. There is little evidence to suggest he was making active preparations for such an expedition.

In 1354 he was attacked by the Hungarians. They occupied part of northern Serbia. At this point Dušan began corresponding with the pope, stating he was even ready to recognize papal supremacy. Since there is no other evidence that Dušan was seriously attracted to Catholicism, one may regard his letters as a diplomatic ploy to better relations with the papacy while Serbia was endangered by Hungary. When the Hungarians retreated at the end of that year, Dušan did not continue the correspondence.

Dušan successfully repelled the invasion, preserving, if not even extending, his original borders in the north. Peace was concluded in May 1355. Kalić-Mijušković believes this peace recognized Dušan's success in driving the Hungarians beyond the Sava and Danube and thus awarded Dušan Mačva, though not including with it Beograd, behind its strong fortifications.[13] Thus during his reign Dušan was able to hold his own against the Hungarians and prevent their expansion south. However, his southern focus prevented him from taking the offensive against the Hungarians. And even though he may have recovered in the end (1355) much of the territory held by Dragutin in Mačva, he did not acquire Beograd. Furthermore, whatever gains he may have made in this region were to be short-lived, not lasting much beyond his death. Thus on this frontier, as on the Bosnian one in the west, he basically held his own and simply prevented the expansion of his neighbor. Dušan's major foreign policy achievements were the results of his southern focus which added to his Serbian state: Albania, the remaining parts of Macedonia, most of the Chalcidic peninsula, Thessaly, and Epirus.

Having repelled the Hungarian threat, Dušan was again free to think about Byzantium and to plan his attack on Constantinople. Most scholars believe that now he did begin seriously to plan for this venture and indeed was actually preparing to march in 1356 against Constantinople—some scholars even go so far as to state that he had actually set out on his march toward that city—when, in December 1355, he suddenly died of a stroke at the relatively young age of about 47.

Florinskij, however, back in 1882, expressed serious doubts that Dušan was in fact planning to attack Constantinople in 1356.[14] Strangely, the serious arguments Florinskij advanced have been ignored by subsequent scholars, who still tend to hold to the view that only Dušan's sudden death prevented his attack on the capital. Florinskij first points out that no contemporary source states that Dušan was preparing in 1355 for such an attack. Since Byzantium was interested in Serbian affairs and since the empire's intelligence service and foreign contacts were active, it seems unlikely that Dušan could have kept such preparations secret from the Byzantines; and if the Byzantines knew of his plans, it is very unlikely that their historians would not have mentioned them. Cantacuzenus and Gregoras, however, say simply that he died; they never suggest that he was on a campaign or preparing one.

If we exclude later epic poetry, some of which does portray Dušan as dying en route to attack Constantinople, there is only one source, a seventeenth-century one, Luccari (writing in 1605), that provides evidence for the popular theory: Luccari says that in 1356 (sic) Dušan, marching for Constantinople with eighty-five thousand men, had reached the village of Diapoli in Thrace when he suffered a stroke and died on 18 December. Orbini, writing in 1601, a few years before Luccari, confirms part of Luccari's information. Orbini states that Dušan suffered a stroke at Diavolopote in "Romania" (i.e., the Byzantine Empire) and died at the age of 45 in 1354. But Orbini says nothing about Dušan's being there en route to Constantinople. In fact Orbini does not explain what Dušan was doing in Thrace. However, the correspondence between his account and Luccari's suggests the two may have had a common source; this source may well have been an oral one. Orbini clearly was not certain about the circumstances of Dušan's death, for he adds that a second story has the tsar dying at Nerodimlje, in Serbia.

Contemporary documents show that Dušan was in his own realm in December 1355 when he died. These prove only that he was not actually on campaign; they do not rule out the possibility that he was planning a major campaign for the following year. These contemporary sources include his correspondence during much of December 1355 with the Hungarian king, with whom he was then at peace, about the Venetian threat to Skradin and Klis. Dušan's letters came from Prizren and Macedonia. Furthermore, he issued a charter to Dubrovnik on 2 December 1355; this document was probably issued at Serres, as Florinskij argues, though an earlier scholar, Pucić, had read the place of issue as "Bera," which, if Pucić was right, could have been Bera in Thrace. A later source, though earlier than Luccari and Orbini, the sixteenth-century Serbian *Tronoški Chronicle,* reports that Dušan died at his court at Prizren. The death site of Prizren is also given in some of the epics.

Florinskij believes that Dušan's long successful wars against the empire, combined with his taking the title tsar (emperor), were sufficient to make this great tsar into an epic opponent of the Byzantines. Epic singers would naturally have wanted both to increase the dramatic aspects of his career and also to explain why he did not conquer Constantinople or, in fact, even try to do so. A dramatic way to explain this failure would have been to have him die, tragically, on the eve of such a campaign. And this is certainly a plausible way for an epic story to have developed. Thus one should not assume in this case that the epics reflect reality. Florinskij also thinks the seventeenth-century Dalmatian historians based their accounts on oral sources.

Florinskij concludes that Dušan died in Serbia, ambitious for, and in his long-range plans probably pondering the conquest of, Constantinople, but not actually prepared to do anything about these dreams and certainly not on the verge of launching an attack against Constantinople. Florinskij points out that Dušan still was not ready for such a campaign. Dušan realized he needed a fleet for the task and he still had not acquired one; in fact no Dalmatian or Venetian source suggests he was even seeking one in 1354 or 1355. Florinskij also thinks the large Ottoman presence near Constantinople, which controlled the north shore of the Sea of Marmora up to the city's walls, would not have facilitated Dušan's task. The Turks probably would have attacked his besieging armies, possibly trapping them against the city walls. Dušan, knowing of the Turks' presence there, surely would have hesitated to attack Constantinople in such a situation. Thus I believe that Florinskij has made a strong, granted not air-tight, case that Dušan, despite ambitions and long-term dreams for Constantinople, was not at the time of his death doing anything in particular to realize his dreams.

Dušan is considered one of the greatest of medieval Balkan conquerors, for he doubled Serbia's size, acquiring the parts of Macedonia his predecessors had not annexed, Albania, Thessaly, Epirus, and most of the Chalcidic peninsula. However, his strength should not be exaggerated. He acquired some of these lands during a Byzantine civil war, when he was allied to one or the other Byzantine side and when few troops existed to defend them. At times certain Byzantine commanders surrendered to him (often on behalf of his Byzantine ally) rather than allow their forts to fall to the other Byzantine side. Other lands he won in the aftermath of a major plague epidemic that had killed or caused the flight of many of the Byzantine leaders. He won all this territory by taking the cities within it by siege, without a single open-field, pitched battle.

He rose, as we have seen, from a semi-puppet of his nobles to become a powerful military leader and their master. By following the nobles' policy of war against Byzantium, he won many of them to his standard; the booty and lands he won attracted many more. Having thus won many nobles to obedience, he was able to create a relatively large military force loyal to him personally; he supplemented these troops with mercenaries, whom he had in large numbers and whose loyalty he retained by prompt and generous payment. Those whose loyalty he thus won, plus the mercenaries and the Albanians he recruited, then provided sufficient muscle to cow any who might have remained recalcitrant. Thus he ended up with a powerful army for the Balkans of his day and the ability to control his state. Control of the state, of course, meant only that he retained the loyalty of his nobles to the extent that they did not secede, but rendered to him their service and financial obligations. He placed military governors and mercenary garrisons in various provincial towns to retain his control over them and to supervise the local nobles. These outsiders presumably exerted pressure on the nobles to fulfill their obligations to the state. But they were not sufficient to institutionalize state control over a province. And Dušan never truly asserted state control over his whole realm. He could not, as we saw above, control brigandage or even guard all his frontiers. And his failure to establish centralized institutions left the nobles with great authority in their counties; as a result, the basis for separatism remained. His empire was to diminish piece-meal during and after the reign of his son and successor Uroš (1356–71).

Hungary and Venice Struggle for Dalmatia

Hungary was willing to conclude peace with Serbia, possibly even yielding Mačva, because it, like Serbia, could not afford to involve itself in a two-front war; and at this time it decided Dalmatia should have higher priority.

At that time, as had been the case since the Fourth Crusade, Venice was the dominant outside power along the Dalmatian coast. And much of Dalmatia had come to recognize Venetian suzerainty: Zadar in 1202; Dubrovnik, through three treaties, in 1232, 1236, and 1252; the isles of Hvar and Brač in 1278; Šibenik and Trogir in 1322; Split in 1327; Nin in 1329; and by the reign of Dušan also Krk, Osor, Rab, and Cres. Most of these cities and islands continued to manage their own affairs, under their own councils and laws, while rendering Venice tribute, military help when summoned, and observing the commerical regulations imposed by Venice. A Venetian prince or count (commonly rendered in Slavic as knez) was usually resident in each town, representing Venetian suzerainty and interests. His role, generally a formal one, was defined in the treaty concluded between the town and Venice. Thus, for example, the Venetian knez of Dubrovnik was to be a Venetian of high birth to serve for a two-year term. He was not to interfere in the management of Dubrovnik's local affairs, for local governmental and judicial functions were to be exercised by local councils drawn from the Ragusan nobility. However, we may suspect that the Venetian knez did have a supervisory function to see that Venice's trade regulations were observed by the Dalmatian towns.

Venetian overlordship was imposed chiefly to advance Venice's commercial interests. It thus consisted chiefly of creating and maintaining in Venetian Dalmatia limited "staple rights." Staple rights meant that a vassal town could sell goods only at home (for domestic needs) or in Venice, and, moreover, that foreign merchants could not go to the vassal town but had to purchase that town's goods in Venice. Thus Venice made itself the middleman, able to collect taxes on its vassal's goods and to make sure the pricing of these goods did not interfere with the sale of Venetian goods. Thus its first goal, though one never fully realized, was to make Venice the central clearing house for its own goods and those of all its vassals; its second goal was to force its vassals to purchase foreign goods only through Venice, be it in Venice itself or at home, with the goods brought thither from their point of origin on a Venetian ship.

In the thirteenth and the first half of the fourteenth century, the Venetians did not realize these goals; thus the Dalmatians had more commercial freedom than the theoretical vassals described above. Thus we can say the Dalmatians under Venice were subjected to a modified staple system. They were able to trade directly with each other and also with Ancona and Apulia; they were also free to trade with the Balkan interior. In this period Dubrovnik dominated the trade with the Balkan interior. But Venice did try to impose a variety of petty restrictions upon its Dalmatian towns; and it regularly took advantage of its vassals' difficulties to tighten its influence. Thus in the 1320s when Dubrovnik was threatened with a war with Dečanski of Serbia, Venice gave support to Dubrovnik in exchange for various commercial benefits to itself.

Furthermore, the Dalmatian towns were not at liberty to trade with the ports on the northern Adriatic; all the northern Italian trade, according to Venetian regulations, had to go through Venice as middleman. This particular restriction had little impact on Dubrovnik, whose economy was based on trading with other partners, but it rankled particularly with Zadar, located in the north, which found its potential to expand commercially severely restricted by Venice's staple system and especially by Venice's northern monopoly. Not surprisingly, then, Zadar had a strong pro-Hungarian faction; it also staged a series of revolts, all suppressed, the most important of which occurred in 1242–43 and 1311–13. In the second of these revolts the town chose Mladen II Šubić as its prince, against Venice's wishes. However, he was not strong enough to defend Zadar against a Venetian recovery. As a result of Zadar's proven unreliability, Venice, after crushing each of its uprisings, imposed increasingly strict control over the town, including the installation of a Venetian garrison in the town in 1247.

Dubrovnik was much better off than Zadar, because it had achieved the position of being the major exporter of goods, including silver, from the Balkan interior, a region in which Venice itself did not play an active role; thus Dubrovnik found in Venice a ready market for these Balkan goods. And since Venice was not interested in becoming involved in the overland trade with Bosnia, Serbia, and Bulgaria—though Venice did carry on extensive trade with Bulgaria for grain through the Black Sea ports, especially Varna— and yet was interested in acquiring various Balkan products, it granted Dubrovnik a variety of customs exemptions in Venice. Moreover, Venice was able to provide Dubrovnik with some support or protection against Dubrovnik's powerful Slavic neighbors from the interior. Thus Dubrovnik was able to benefit from the relationship with Venice.

To maintain or advance its position, Venice had to retain the loyalty of its vassal towns; and in this goal it was hampered by Hungary, which was seeking to restore its lost position in Dalmatia. Thus it tried to build up pro-Hungarian parties in Venice's towns. Hungary also worked hard to keep its control over its Croatian vassals in the area, aiming not to lose suzerainty over them and to use them to regain the lost towns. These Croatian nobles, who were not the most loyal of Hungarian vassals and were always seeking greater independence, like the independent-minded Nelipac of Knin, held a few coastal towns and most of the hinterland. Thus, if they could be mobilized, these Croatians were in a position to launch an effective attack upon Venice's coastal towns. Aware of this, Venice devoted considerable effort to maintaining good relations with its towns, to trying to make allies of the Dalmatian towns not under its control, and to keeping up good relations with Serbia. It also maintained contacts with Hungary's Croatian vassals and was not above tampering with these nobles in order to woo them over to its side. Venice made a major effort in this direction in 1343; on that occasion it sent embassies to several towns and to various Croatian nobles. This effort, however, netted only Mladen III Šubić, Prince of Klis, Omiš, and Skradin, and Paul II Šubić of Ostrovica. The Hungarian king, by this time Louis I (1342–82), unhappy with this Venetian tampering and also hoping to reassert his own authority in the Cetina region by taking advantage of the death of Nelipac of Knin in June 1344, mobilized an army for a Dalmatian campaign in 1345. King Louis and part of this army stopped at Bihać, but the rest of the army under Ban Nicholas continued on to besiege Knin. Nelipac's widow Vladislava, acting on behalf of her minor son John (Ivan) Nelipčić, tried to defend the town. However, seeing that her long-range chances were poor, she decided to negotiate. She and her son made the trip to Louis at Bihać, where they submitted to him. Louis accepted their submission and confirmed young John Nelipčić in most of his father's possessions excluding Knin, which Vladislava surrendered to Louis and he chose to retain. However, despite the retention of most of their lands, including the Cetina župa, the Nelipčići lost for a period much of their independence and became de facto vassals of the Hungarian king.

The king's presence in the area encouraged the pro-Hungarian faction in Zadar to stage a new revolt against Venice in 1345. The king sent troops to the town and the rebels submitted to him; however, the Venetians were not willing to accept the loss of Zadar and sent forces thither. After a long siege and a victory in July 1346 over the Hungarian army (owing to its own carelessness), the Venetians in late 1346 or early 1347 regained the city, whose populace suffered severe punishment. Moreover, for future security Venice destroyed Zadar's sea walls, ordered its citizens to surrender all their weapons, and prohibited the town from keeping more than a four-month supply of food in town. The Venetians also confiscated a large number of ships belonging to citizens of Zadar and sent a Venetian to be the town's knez. He was accompanied by a number of Venetians who assumed major roles in administering the town.

Hungary, then becoming involved in the affairs of Naples, was not able to send further troops to Zadar to reverse this. In fact, King Louis accepted an eight-year peace with Venice in 1348.

However, the king did have sufficient troops to spare for action against the Šubići, who during the 1340s had been forging closer ties with Venice. The family had gone so far as to support Venice against the rebels in Zadar. It seems Paul II Šubić had not expected the Hungarians to take action in this affair; thus when they did send troops to support the rebels in 1346, Paul found himself in considerable danger. Venice's victory over the Hungarians in 1346 saved Paul from immediate disaster. But the next year found King Louis determined to assert his control over the Šubići. By that time his enemy Paul had died—probably in August 1346—and Paul's fortress of Ostrovica had been left to his minor son, George (Juraj) III, under the regency of Paul's brother Gregory. Gregory's task was made more difficult because shortly before Paul's death Paul's wife, Elizabeth, and their little son had gone to visit her brother, Dujam "Frankapan." Paul's death found them there and Dujam, as a loyal vassal of King Louis, did not allow them to return to Ostrovica. Dujam wanted them to negotiate peace with Louis even if it meant surrendering Ostrovica to him. Gregory, determined to retain Ostrovica, sought aid from Venice, expressing his willingness to accept Venetian suzerainty. However, Venetian support was not forthcoming and on 31 July 1347, through the mediation of Dujam "Frankapan," Gregory agreed to negotiate with Louis. As a result Gregory and George III submitted to the king and surrendered Ostrovica to him. As compensation, later the same day, King Louis granted George hereditary possession of the župa of Zrin in Slavonia. Louis' acquisition of Ostrovica, which he placed under a royally appointed commander, strengthened the king's position in the Dalmatian-Croatian area. It also placed him in a better position to launch a new attack against Venice's holdings along the Dalmatian coast. George Šubić's descendants retained possession of Zrin and became hereditary counts of that province, from which they took the name Zrinski. They were to become one of the leading families of Slavonia.

By transferring one branch of the Šubić family to Slavonia, the king succeeded in reducing the family's strength in Croatia. Thus he was content to leave Mladen III Šubić in possession of Klis, Omiš, and Skradin. However, angry at the Hungarians, Mladen sought outside alliances to enable him to resist Hungarian control. In 1347, hoping for support from Dušan who already had poor relations with Hungary, Mladen married Dušan's sister Helen (Jelena). At about the same time he arranged the marriage of his younger brother, Paul III, with a Venetian noble lady and set about aligning himself more closely with Venice. However, before the developing situation could come to a head, Mladen III became seriously ill and then died in May 1348. His weak brother, Paul III, and his widow, Helen, inherited Mladen's territory.

An uneasy peace between the Šubići and Hungary followed. However, upon the conclusion of its war with Serbia in 1355, Hungary decided to mobilize its Croatian vassals and settle affairs with the Šubići. Dušan, whose hostility to Hungary had been exacerbated by the Hungarian attack on Serbia in 1354, decided—despite the peace treaty he had just concluded with Hungary in 1355—to support his sister, who then held Klis and Skradin. Late in 1355 he sent her troops under two able commanders to garrison her two cities. To Klis he sent a unit under his German mercenary commander Palman, and to Skradin he sent a unit under the Zetan nobleman Djuraš Ilijić (or Ilić), surely the son of Ilija the kefalia who had been active in Zeta under Milutin. The two towns were too distant for Dušan to extend effective aid; Croatian vassals of Hungary took Klis between late 1355 and March 1356, and Serbian troops were not sufficient to hold Skradin, which surrendered to Venice in January 1356, after Dušan's death. One suspects it surrendered to the Venetians to prevent the Hungarians from acquiring it. Serbian involvement in this part of Dalmatia ceased for a time as Dušan's successors had too many other problems nearer home. Palman does not seem to have returned to Serbia. No documents mention him there subsequently, and in 1363 he is found in Dubrovnik as a beneficiary of a will.

Having made peace with Serbia in May 1355, Hungary was ready for a major effort against Venice. And it saw Venice's acquisition of Skradin as a violation of the Hungarian-Venetian peace agreement of 1348. Hungary launched a major attack against Dalmatia in 1356. Venice was caught by surprise, for Louis had nominally mobilized his forces for an attack on Serbia—a likely target in view of Dušan's aid to Klis and Skradin—and then had suddenly dispatched them against Dalmatia. The Venetians found themselves no match for the Hungarians, who immediately took Skradin and Omiš. Split and Trogir quickly submitted to Hungary, then the other towns rapidly followed. Venice, through its garrison in the town, was able to retain only Zadar, inside of which considerable fighting did occur. By early 1358 Hungary had regained Dalmatia; all the towns, except for those under Serbian suzerainty like Kotor and Bar, from the Gulf of Kvarner south to, but not including, the Angevin's Durazzo submitted to Hungary. Venice was forced to give up, concluding the Peace of Zadar in February 1358, by which it surrendered to the Hungarians title to all its Dalmatian possessions—including Zadar—between the Gulf of Kvarner and Durazzo.

The Venetian prince left Dubrovnik at the end of February 1358. Under Hungary Dubrovnik and the other towns continued to manage their own affairs, rendering only tribute and naval service, when demanded, to their suzerain. Hungary, not a commercial power, placed no commercial restrictions upon its new vassals. Its liberal attitude is seen in the charter the king granted to Dubrovnik in May 1358, which was brought to the town by his envoy in July. Dubrovnik owed its suzerain, the King of Hungary, a tribute of five hundred ducats annually; Dubrovnik was to enjoy full autonomy, free trade in Hungary, and the right to trade freely wherever it wished, including in Serbia, even in the event of a Hungarian-Serbian war. Thus Hungary, understanding that trade with Serbia was the cornerstone of Dubrovnik's economy, respected Dubrovnik's right to trade with Serbia even though Serbia was no friend of Hungary. However, Dubrovnik's acceptance of Hungarian suzerainty did create difficulties with its Serbian neighbors whenever Serbia and Hungary were at war. This in particular was to be the case, as we shall see, in the decade after Dušan's death, when Dubrovnik's neighbor Vojislav Vojinović, holder of Trebinje, Konavli, and various regions further inland, used the Hungarian relationship as an excuse to plunder Dubrovnik's lands when war broke out between his Serbian suzerain and Hungary.

Hungary's victory also completed the subjection of the Šubići. After the Hungarian acquisition of Klis, Skradin, and Omiš in 1356, Paul III retained only the city of Bribir and its župa. He died later that year and his heirs, never able to regain their lost possessions, had to be satisfied with the possession of Bribir alone. The family is last heard of there in 1456.

Moreover, in areas under the king's control, like Knin and its environs, the king established a županija organization under the authority of the Ban of Croatia and Dalmatia. It was supported by the lesser nobility whom the ban actively recruited and converted into an organized royal nobility now subject to the ban's authority. These nobles served in his forces and were also under the jurisdiction of his court of law. The king also recruited for his armies Vlach pastoralists from the districts of Knin and Lika. These Vlachs were bound to royal service through land grants.

In much of Dalmatia—both in the towns and on the islands—there took place in the fourteenth century a solidifying of class lines and an increase in the richer merchants' dominance over towns. Throughout the thirteenth and early fourteenth centuries, the rich had predominated; but on major issues that affected a whole town, large assemblies, in which all citizens participated, were held. Moreover, individuals from the middle and occasionally even from the lower classes who acquired wealth could join the nobility. By the second quarter of the fourteenth century, however, the rich were coming more and more to form a closed aristocracy—known as the patriciate—that increasingly came to monopolize the administration and judiciary of the towns. For example, on Hvar a law of 1334 banned from the town council anyone whose grandfather was not a member of the council. A similar law was issued on Korčula in 1356.

Such a closing of the patriciate's ranks, blocking social mobility and leaving the town's affairs in the hands of councils whose members came to be drawn only from the patriciate, was not pleasing to the general populace. And various popular uprisings occurred that often led to temporary expulsions of the nobles. None of these uprisings succeeded in the long run, for neighboring towns, and outside powers like Venice, regularly supported the nobles and, through mediation and even at times military help, brought about the restoration of the ousted elite. Thus often the pro-Venetian party in a Dalmatian town was drawn from the aristocracy. Such rebellions, often in conjunction with a larger war in the area, occurred in Split in 1334, Trogir in 1357, and Šibenik in 1358; and unrest was rampant in Split again between 1398 and 1402.

NOTES

1. Ćirković, "Beograd pod Kraljem Dušanom?" pp. 44–45.

2. Both of these regions lay north of Jannina and south of Berat. Though Pogonia is rarely mentioned in the sources, it was important enough to be an archbishopric at the time of Andronicus III.

3. B. Ferjančić (*Despoti u Vizantiji i južnoslovenskim zemljama*, pp. 159–66) argues against the position I have taken and believes John Oliver received the title despot only in 1347 and from Dušan. He is clearly documented with the title in 1347. The question centers around how much earlier he might have held it. Ferjančić's major argument against John Oliver's holding the title in 1340 is a good one: John Oliver called himself "great vojvoda" in an inscription he composed in 1341 for the monastery he built at Lesnovo. Ferjančić plausibly argues that if he then held the title despot, he would have used it in this inscription. My only reply, which I grant is weak, is that for some reason in 1341 John Oliver chose to describe himself by a functional domestic title rather than by the honorary title he had been granted by the foreign, Byzantine, ruler. Possibly the fact that Serbia was then plundering Byzantine territory and thus in a state of war with the empire led him to avoid using a title of Byzantine origin. However, the reason that I do not follow Ferjančić on this point but follow what prior to Ferjančić's book had been the standard view, is Dušan's charter from 1340 referring to his step-mother, John Oliver's wife, as despotica. Ferjančić, it seems to me, has failed to explain away this important piece of evidence.

4. J. Radonić, "O Despotu Jovanu Oliveru i njegovoj ženi Ani Mariji," *Glas* (SKA) 94 (1914): 74–108.

5. G. Soulis, *The Serbs and Byzantium during the Reign of Tsar Stephen Dušan (1331–1355) and his Successors* (Dumbarton Oaks Byzantine Institute, Washington, D.C., 1984).

6. Dinić believes the Serbs took Valona in 1343 (M. Dinić, "Za hronologiju Dušanovih osvajanja vizantiskih gradova," *ZRVI* 4 [1956]: 1–10). Others have argued that Valona and Kanina were Serbian as early as 1337, while Spremić limits Dušan's activities in 1343 to Macedonia and believes he conquered the Albanian cities of Valona, Berat, and Kanina in 1345 (M. Spremić, "Albanija od XIII do XV veka," p. 35). Ducellier accepts 1345/46 as the date Dušan acquired Valona, Kanina, and Berat, but dates the conquest of Kroja to spring 1343.

7. P. Lemerle, *L'Emirat d'Aydin, Byzance et l'occident: Recherches sur "La Geste d'Umur Pacha"* (Paris, 1957), p. 211.

8. Apocaucus' murder has traditionally been dated 11 June (following Gregoras). Lemerle (ibid., p. 210) persuasively argues that it occurred on 11 July.

9. On these changes, see Lj. Maksimović, "Karakter poreskog sistema u grčkim oblastima Srpskog Carstva," *ZRVI* 17 (1976): 101–23.

10. An English translation of Dušan's Law Code exists; "The Code of Stephan Dušan," ed. and trans. M. Burr, *Slavonic and East European Review* 28 (1949–50): 198–217, 516–39.

11. P. Charanis, "On the Social Structure and Economic Organization of the Byzantine Empire in the Thirteenth Century and Later," *Byzantinoslavica* 12 (1951): 94–153.

12. A. Laiou-Thomadakis, *Peasant Society in the Late Byzantine Empire: A Social and Demographic Study* (Princeton, N.J., 1977).

13. J. Kalić-Mijušković, *Beograd u srednjem veku* (Beograd, 1967), pp. 75–76.

14. T. Florinskij, *Južnye Slavjane i Vizantija vo vtoroj četverti XIV veka* (St. Petersburg, 1882), pt. 2, pp. 200–208.

CHAPTER 7

The Balkans from Dušan's Death
(1355) to the Eve of Kosovo (1389)

Initial Territorial Losses for the Serbian Empire
after Dušan's Death

During the last decade of Dušan's reign the magnates had remained at peace within Serbia, loyal to Dušan's authority. His death was a signal for the stirring of separatist activity. But though disintegration of his empire followed, it was to be a piece-meal affair taking place over a period of twenty years. Furthermore, when we contrast Dušan's empire and the separatism after his death, we should not exaggerate centralism under Dušan. Despite his power and the glorious court titles he granted, he stood over a loosely bound state. In much of his realm great local noblemen continued to dominate local affairs, merely rendering obligations to him. Thus in many or even most areas he had not replaced local rule by central appointees. Even during Dušan's reign cases of separatism had occurred—like Hrelja's secession in about 1340—and great independence from Dušan's authority was shown throughout his reign by Despot John Oliver. And Dušan's law code, for example, in its laws on brigandage that gave responsibility for order to local authorities, also showed the state's inability to control large portions of its far-flung territory. Thus separatism in and after 1356 simply reflects the utilization for greater independence of a social/administrative structure already existing before and during Dušan's reign.

Dušan's son and heir Uroš (1356–71), though by this time twenty years old, was weak, possibly feeble-minded, and unable to take forceful action against this separatist tendency. Immediately after Dušan's death two Greek magnates—Alexis and John Asen—revolted and liberated Anaktoropolis, Chrysopolis, and the rest of the Aegean coastal territory between the Struma and Mesta rivers. Also possessing the near-by island of Thasos, they soon recognized the suzerainty of the Byzantine emperor, John V. These lands were direct holdings of the Asens, who were descendants of the former ruling dynasty of Bulgaria. By 1365 they were also administering Kavalla for the emperor; this town, however, did not become part of their appanage. Scholars argue over the status of Kavalla prior to the mid-1360s. Most of them believe Dušan had acquired it in 1345 and retained it to his death, at which point Alexis and John took it; very likely they then quarreled with the emperor over it until a compromise was reached which allowed them to govern it while the emperor retained direct title for it. Other scholars have claimed that Dušan never took Kavalla, but that it remained imperial throughout this period under various governors, among whom were numbered Alexis and John from about 1365. The Asens' activity affected only the territory along the coast; the interior lands between the Struma and Mesta rivers remained Serbian.

In 1356 the Byzantine rebel Matthew Cantacuzenus, needing to build up his own power base and hoping that the Greek population residing in the interior territory conquered by Dušan between the Mesta and Struma rivers would prefer his rule to Uroš', tried to re-establish his former appanage along the Serbian-Byzantine border. With five thousand Turks he attacked this region. But he failed to take Serres and soon was defeated in battle in late 1356 or early 1357 by a Serb army under Vojvoda Vojin, the holder of Drama, a major fortress in the vicinity. The Serbs captured Matthew with the intention of releasing him when he had raised the large ransom they demanded. However, John V, who had rapidly moved in to occupy Matthew's lands, offered Vojin an even larger sum to turn Matthew over to the empire. And Vojin found it very profitable to oblige. John V, after briefly imprisoning Matthew and making him renounce his imperial title, then released him to go to the Morea, where he joined his brother Manuel who was ruling there.

Meanwhile in the province of Braničevo two leading families of Serbian magnates quarreled. The weaker of the two, about to be bested and having little hope of support from the weak Serbian ruler who was faced with far more serious dangers, turned to the Hungarians for support. The Hungarians jumped at the chance to regain their influence in the province of Braničevo and sent aid, probably in 1359, to the petitioner. Their intervention was successful and they soon installed the Rastislalić family in power in Braničevo province (with Kučevo attached to it). Though it cannot be proved, it was almost certainly the Rastislalići who had sought Hungarian intervention. (Matteo Villani, the source on the quarrel between the two nobles that led to Hungarian intervention, does not name them.) By 1361 the Rastislalići were ruling this province, seceded from Serbia, under Hungarian suzerainty. The Hungarians tried to move beyond this region and make further gains at the expense of Serbia, still early in 1359. They were initially successful in penetrating Serbia but failed to engage the Serbian army, which intentionally avoided battle. Realizing they could not hold these further gains, they withdrew, probably in July 1359.

Thessaly and Epirus

Meanwhile, almost immediately after Dušan's death Preljub, his governor for Thessaly, died. His widow Irene, who was a daughter of Dušan, hoped to preserve the province for herself and their minor son Tomo Preljubović. But taking advantage of the instability caused by Preljub's death and of the anarchy caused by the influx of Albanian tribesmen, Nicephorus II, the former ruler of Epirus, arrived in the spring of 1356 in Thessaly; he hoped to acquire support from the local Greeks to gain Thessaly and then use that province as a base to regain his inheritance of Epirus. At that time he had been the governor of Ainos, appointed to that post by his father-in-law, John Cantacuzenus, when Cantacuzenus had become emperor. Nicephorus acquired considerable support from the Greeks of Thessaly and soon drove Irene out and gained Thessaly. She returned to Serbia, where she was granted Preljub's hereditary lands on the Crna Reka (Black River). She soon married a Serb nobleman, Hlapen (or Radoslav Hlapen), who had been Dušan's governor for, and was still holding, Voden and Veria. Thus he held the territory that lay just north of Thessaly.

Meanwhile, as we saw in the last chapter, Dušan had installed as his governor of Epirus his half-brother Symeon—who was the son of Stefan Dečanski and his second wife, Maria Palaeologina. To improve his local position Symeon had married Thomais, the daughter of Anna of Epirus and the sister of Nicephorus II, the titular despot of Epirus who had now taken over Thessaly and had his sights set on Epirus. Symeon's neighbor to the north was John Comnenus Asen, the brother of Dušan's wife and of John Alexander of Bulgaria. He, as mentioned, had married Anna of Epirus, the mother of Nicephorus and Thomais, and ruled a portion, if not all, of Dušan's Albanian lands from Valona, where he had established a Byzantine-style court.

Nicephorus, having gained Thessaly, moved against Epirus. He acquired considerable local support. Symeon was expelled from the capital city of Arta, which submitted to Nicephorus, who soon made himself the ruler of Epirus and Aetolia. It probably would be more accurate to say he was the ruler of the towns of these two regions, for much of the countryside was in the hands of Albanian tribesmen.

Symeon, driven north to the region of Kastoria and having lost most of his lands, was faced with the choice of settling down to be a petty prince like Hlapen or of assembling an army to win himself a worthy realm. Choosing the latter option and realizing that Nicephorus had a firm hold on Epirus, Symeon now set his sights on Serbia. As Dušan's brother he had a good claim to the Serbian throne, and he probably felt he had a good chance to win it. If, as seems likely, Uroš was feeble-minded, Symeon's chances probably seemed excellent. So, in 1356, in a ceremony in his town of Kastoria, he had himself proclaimed Tsar of the Greeks, Serbs, and Albanians. He soon acquired the support of John Comnenus Asen of Valona. He then began assembling an army. Aware of Symeon's plans, the Serbian nobles held a council in April 1357 at Skopje and decided to observe Dušan's will and support Uroš. Presumably they preferred to have a weak tsar, which allowed them far greater independence in their own provinces. In the war that followed, as Naumov points out, the nobles joined for their own ends, more as allies than as dependent vassals. Having mobilized a force of Greeks, Serbs, and Albanians that numbered four to five thousand men, according to the Jannina chronicle, Symeon advanced on Zeta. The forces of the Serbian nobility met Symeon's near Skadar, probably in the summer of 1358, and forced him to retreat. Symeon returned to Kastoria and never tried to acquire Serbia again. For the next year he was in no position to consider doing so, as it was all he could do to maintain a small principality centered in Kastoria. Soon new opportunities presented themselves to him and he became thoroughly involved in increasing his holdings and authority in northern Greece. Though many scholars have stated that Symeon's primary ambition had been Serbia, we really are totally ignorant of his ambitions and preferences. He moved against Serbia only after he had lost most of his Greek lands. Had Nicephorus not driven him from Epirus, Symeon might well have been satisfied with being a ruler in Greece and never have made the attempt on Serbia.

However, despite his successes, Nicephorus' position was by no means secure; for to acquire the support of the local Greeks who had been his muscle to this point, he had had to support their interests. They had previously been dispossessed of much of their land by the Albanian tribesmen who, of course, threatened to take what the Greeks still held. Thus Nicephorus was driven to launch a campaign against the Albanians to prevent their further expansion and to drive them from the lands they had occupied. He hoped to restore the lands recovered to his Greek followers. In this he had some success, but his policy stirred the animosity of the Albanians against him. At the same time he faced the threat of an attack from his neighbor to the north, Hlapen, who aimed to restore his wife to Thessaly and expand his own authority over that rich province. Nicephorus also had to be concerned about Symeon, who, though down at the moment, could, with Albanian support, become a menace again. Nicephorus could at least be thankful that Hlapen detested Symeon, which prevented an alliance between those two.

Faced with these dangers, Nicephorus needed to negotiate with one of his enemies and, possibly to prevent Symeon's Albanian allies from supporting the Albanians already in Epirus, decided to negotiate with Symeon who, married to Thomais, was, of course, his brother-in-law. Their discussions seem to have gone smoothly and a second marriage alliance to bind Nicephorus and Symeon together was discussed. But before it could be fully negotiated, Nicephorus was back fighting the Albanians in a war that was to prove fatal to him.

This particular phase of the warfare with the Albanians seems to have emerged from other marriage negotiations. To seek allies and possibly to find a restraining influence on Hlapen, who throughout these events had retained his loyalty to Uroš, certain of Nicephorus' advisors recommended that he establish closer relations with Serbia. To do this they suggested that he drop his present wife, Maria Cantacuzena, and marry the sister of Dušan's widow. Maria was placed under guard in Arta while the negotiations with Serbia were carried out; an agreement was reached with the Serbs and it was decided that Maria should be handed over to the Serbs in exchange for the new wife. Maria seems to have been popular with much of the court at Arta, so it was not difficult for her to send a message to her brother Manuel, the ruler of the Morea, to ask him to rescue her. Friends at court effected her escape from the palace and got her to the shore, where a ship from Manuel landed, took her aboard, and carried her to safety at Manuel's court in the Morea.

Maria had also been popular with various Albanian tribesmen who had already submitted to Nicephorus. These tribesmen now threatened revolt if Nicephorus did not give up his plans for the Serbian marriage and recall Maria. Faced with revolt (and possibly also coming to his senses, for Maria seems to have been a wholly admirable woman who still seems to have been devoted to him), Nicephorus summoned her back. But at the same time he decided to crush the Albanians who had dared threaten rebellion to pressure him to alter his policy. He marched into the region where they had settled; they mobilized a large force to meet him. The battle occurred in the late spring of 1359 near Acheloos in Aetolia. Nicephorus was killed and the Albanians won the battle. Thessaly and Epirus were left without a ruler. Soon thereafter Maria left the Morea for Constantinople, where she became a nun.

Symeon moved rapidly to fill the power vacuum in Thessaly. Before Hlapen even knew that Nicephorus was dead, Symeon had marched into Thessaly, where he was greeted in summer 1359 by the local Greeks as emperor in the capital city of Trikkala. And it seems most of Thessaly followed suit. Symeon then left his wife to govern Thessaly and set out to recover his former holding of Epirus. The towns of Epirus were threatened by the Albanian tribesmen, so Nicephorus' cities of Arta and Jannina, as well as various lesser towns, quickly submitted to Symeon. Thus he rapidly restored his rule over at least the towns of Epirus. But then, while Symeon was absent in Epirus, Hlapen attacked and took Damasis in northern Thessaly. Symeon hurried back to Thessaly to face Hlapen, but instead of fighting the two decided to negotiate a settlement. Having agreed upon a marriage between their two families, they were able to reach a territorial settlement that satisfied Hlapen and he called off his campaign. By the settlement Tomo Preljubović, Hlapen's step-son, married Symeon's daughter Maria Angelina. Since Maria was then only about ten years old, it has been argued persuasively that the pair were at the time only betrothed, and that the marriage occurred a couple of years later. In any case, by the mid-1360s the two were married.

Symeon allowed Hlapen to keep Damasis and also granted to Hlapen the lands Symeon had held to the west of Hlapen's principality, including the important city of Kastoria. This territory was almost certainly to be held under Symeon's suzerainty. Tomo Preljubović then, with or without his bride, went to Hlapen's court at Voden; possibly Voden, which belonged to Hlapen, had been marked out by the treaty as an eventual appanage for Tomo. Thus Hlapen came into possession of the lands between Symeon and Uroš' Serbia, giving each of those rulers a buffer against attack from the other. Hlapen, who held his initial lands of Voden and Veria from Dušan, had remained loyal to Uroš up to this time; his agreement with Symeon did not lead to any change in this relationship. Thus Hlapen might be considered an ideal buffer in the event that friction should occur between Symeon and his nephew. However, and possibly Hlapen deserves some credit here, no friction did develop and the two Serb tsars seem to have ignored one another entirely from the time Symeon retreated from Zeta in 1358 until their deaths. But Symeon's secession and activities did mean the loss of this Greek territory for Serbia. After his treaty with Hlapen, Symeon settled down in the richer province of Thessaly which by then he clearly preferred to Epirus.

In the wake of Nicephorus' death and Symeon's departure from Epirus, the governors Symeon left behind found themselves unable to control Epirus. This enabled the Albanians to migrate into Epirus in ever greater numbers; soon they had settled throughout Epirus and taken over most of the towns as well, including Arta. Since Epirus was nominally Symeon's (at least the townsmen there, including those of Arta and Jannina, had hastened to submit to him after Nicephorus' death), he tried to maintain at least indirect control by recognizing in Epirus and Aetolia as deputies for himself certain powerful locals whom he considered friendly. The most active figures in Aetolia and Epirus were John (Ghin) Bova (or Buji) Spata and Peter Liosha (Losha). These two Albanian chieftains seem to have acquired most of these two regions in the course of the mid- to late 1350s. They soon succeeded in obtaining Symeon's blessing, or at least his acquiescence, for their activities, and each obtained the title of despot from him. Soon Symeon agreed to the division of Aetolia (including southern Epirus with Arta) between the two of them. Peter Liosha's half included Arta. Spata's main fort was Angelokastron. Thus one could accurately say Epirus was under Albanian rule.

However, owing to their tribal structure and the absence of any central Albanian authority over the tribes, the Albanians did not replace Greek or Serbian rule with any sort of Albanian state. The Albanians remained divided into tribes, each under its own chief. They regularly feuded with one another and newly arriving Albanian tribes pushed already settled ones from the lands they had occupied; thus the specific territory under a given tribe and the extent of territory controlled by a tribe were frequently changing. Furthermore, in these years the Albanians did not limit their control to the countryside but took over towns as well.

Thus we can conclude that the Albanians became the true rulers of Epirus, but owing to their tribal divisions and mutual quarrels that made them unable to create an effective state authority there, the term *anarchy* would best describe Epirus in this period. The Albanians have remained in this region in large numbers to the present. Their large-scale settlement, much of which occurred at this time, has been attributed by certain scholars to Symeon's departure from Epirus. However, this is an unwarranted conclusion. They were widely settled in Epirus by the time Symeon returned in 1359 after Nicephorus' death. He clearly was not strong enough to expel all these tribesmen or to have stopped from entering Epirus those tribes who moved in during the 1360s. Furthermore, whatever success he might have had (and the little evidence we have on Symeon's military abilities does not suggest he would have had much) would probably not have lasted beyond his death, when the flood of Albanians would have been free to flow again.

By late 1366 or 1367 it seems only one city in the region, Jannina, was holding out against the Albanians. Its townsmen sent a delegation to Symeon requesting a governor, and he sent them his son-in-law Tomo Preljubović, who until then had been living at the court of his step-father Hlapen in Voden. Under the suzerainty of Symeon, Preljubović, from Jannina, nominally held a considerable portion of Epirus; but in fact his authority probably did not extend much beyond the immediate environs of Jannina. In that limited region he did, however, retain various small fortresses. The Albanian tribesmen, whose activities kept matters in a state of flux in Epirus, prevented Preljubović from asserting his authority in most of the lands that were nominally his. They also frequently attacked Jannina, thus creating great insecurity for his capital. By these means the Albanians prevented the development of anything resembling central authority in Epirus.

The main source for Preljubović's reign is what is known as the *Chronicle of Jannina*, whose anonymous author hated Preljubović. Writing during the reign of his successor who quite possibly had been involved in Preljubović's murder, the chronicler may well have presented Preljubović as a tyrant in order to justify the murder. Thus we should take the chronicle's account with a grain of salt. It claims that Preljubović's rule in Jannina was unpopular. The cornerstone of his policy was to support the interests of his army, which had accompanied him from Voden to Jannina and was composed chiefly of Serbs. To satisfy these troops he confiscated lands from Greek magnates and from the Church. The chronicler also accuses him of increasing taxes, creating new taxes, and establishing monopolies on the sale of certain products to benefit himself and his followers. The chronicler describes various actions Tomo took against local nobles. However, he also reports various local rebellions and attempted coups against Tomo. Thus it is hard to determine whether Tomo's policy provoked those rebellions or whether ambitious locals consistently opposing him caused him to take action against them. Tomo Preljubović also quarreled with the Church leadership in Jannina, which led to the Metropolitan of Jannina's going into exile in 1367, first to Thessaly and later to Constantinople. Jannina remained without its bishop until 1381, when a new one, appointed by the Patriarch of Constantinople, appeared in town. Tomo chased him out almost immediately but agreed to his return the next year, since the Byzantines agreed to grant Tomo the title of despot and the bishop was needed to perform the ceremony.

Tomo also fought regularly against the Albanians in the area, particularly against the Malakasi, Liosha, Zenevisi, and Musachi tribes. Immediately on Tomo's succession, Peter Liosha launched an attack against Jannina which kept the city under siege for a good part of the next three years. Peace was finally made in 1369/70 when Tomo's infant daughter was betrothed to Peter's son, John. A five-year peace followed with Liosha. However, Tomo had various fracases with other tribesmen during those years. Then in 1373/74 Peter Liosha died of the plague. John Spata immediately took advantage of his death to conquer Arta and unite the two parts of Aetolia/southern Epirus. Soon Spata attacked Jannina, but Tomo managed to conclude peace with him, giving Spata his sister as a wife. But this agreement did not bring peace to Jannina, for almost immediately thereafter the Malakasi began attacking Jannina; Tomo won a decisive victory over them in 1377, which dispersed them for a while. The following year Tomo was allied with Spata against a Frankish attack upon Acarnania led by the Hospitaler Knights of Saint John then ruling Achaea. The allies won a major victory over the Franks, probably late in 1378, in which they took prisoner Grand Master John Fernandez de Heredia and a rich Florentine adventurer, Esau del Buondelmonti. The latter was brought back as a captive to Jannina and was to play a major role in the region's history several years later. Whatever territory the knights had occupied in Acarnania—including Naupaktos, taken from the Angevins by Spata in 1376 or 1377—was regained by Spata.

In February 1379 the Malakasi, supported by local Bulgarians and Vlachs, again attacked Jannina, only to be defeated once again by Tomo. That May his recent ally John Spata marched against Jannina, but Tomo defeated him too. Next a coup was planned by some local nobles. Tomo was tipped off and nipped it in the bud by arresting the leading conspirators, one of whom was blinded while the other was poisoned in jail. His problems with the local Albanians continued, so in 1380 he turned to the Ottomans for assistance against them. The Ottomans were willing, and with their help Tomo recovered a series of small forts in the vicinity of Jannina. Then he took the offensive into central Epirus. What gains, if any, Tomo made as a result of this offensive are not known. It also seems that his Turkish allies were at times operating on their own, picking off various fortresses which they retained for themselves. A Turkish leader named Timurtash even tried, but without success, to take Arta from Spata in 1384.

Meanwhile Symeon, calling himself Symeon Uroš Palaeologus, settled in Thessaly. At Trikkala he established his main court, which imitated the Byzantine court. Greeks were the most numerous element present and the Angelus family, relatives of his wife, played a dominant role. All of Symeon's surviving charters are in Greek. However, there was no discrimination against other groups, and Serbs and Albanians held prominent positions too. The Greek magnates of Thessaly continued to hold great estates, managing them and local affairs with great independence. In 1366 or 1367 Symeon founded the remarkable Meteora monasteries, perched on the high rock pinnacles that rise up from the great Meteora plain. Their development continued beyond Symeon's lifetime, and the monasteries reached the height of their prosperity in the 1370s and 1380s right after his death. Symeon is last heard of in Trikkala in 1369. Soon thereafter he was dead. His successor was his elder son John Uroš. He also had a second son, Stefan. If we can believe seventeenth-century sources like Orbini, Stefan acquired his own holding in southern Thessaly, including the town of Pharsalos. Whether Symeon ordered this division of his realm or whether Stefan seized this territory is not known.

Most of Thessaly, however, went to John Uroš, a peaceful, religious type. He turned its administration over to Alexius Angelus, who seems to have been a relative of his mother and who held large estates in Thessaly. Alexius bore the title caesar; it is not known whether he received it from Symeon or from John Uroš. After Tsar Uroš' death in Serbia in 1371, John Uroš became the last living male Nemanjić (insofar as we know neither the fate of Stefan nor whether he had issue). However, John Uroš had few secular interests and became a monk (probably in 1372 or 1373, in any case before 1381) under the name of Joasaf. After John Uroš' departure to a monastery, Caesar Alexius Angelus remained in power and became the ruler of Thessaly. We have references to him as Lord of Thessaly through the 1370s and 1380s. As a powerful local magnate, he had acquired a dominant position during John Uroš' reign. Finding himself in power when John Uroš abdicated, if he did not indeed force that abdication, he simply secured his hold further with the support of local magnates. He was married to Maria, a daughter of Hlapen. He eventually entered into close relations with Manuel Palaeologus, who was governor of Thessaloniki (1382–April 1387) for his father, John V, and accepted Manuel's—and therefore also Byzantine—suzerainty. We find several cases in which Manuel confirmed charters issued by Alexius. However, we also have a series of Alexius' judicial decisions that were issued in his own right. Thus Thessaly found itself back in the Byzantine sphere by the early 1380s.

The last certain evidence we have of Alexius Angelus' being alive is a charter he issued to the Meteora monasteries in August 1388; we have a reference to his successor, Manuel Angelus, almost certainly Alexius' son, in 1392. Thus Manuel probably succeeded his father as hereditary governor of Thessaly in about 1390. Manuel also bore the title caesar. Since it required an emperor to grant it, presumably the title came from John V and indicates that Manuel recognized Byzantine suzerainty, in return for which his position as governor of Thessaly was recognized by the emperor in Constantinople. Manuel was to be the last Christian ruler of Thessaly since, as we shall see, the Ottomans conquered the province and drove him out in 1394.

Meanwhile in Jannina, on 23 December 1384, Tomo Preljubović was murdered, victim of a court intrigue. The hostile Jannina chronicle says his throat was cut by some members of his own body-guard. The population of Jannina was overjoyed and at once declared allegiance to his widow, Maria Angelina. They urged her to invite her brother, the monk Joasaf (John Uroš), to come to advise her. He obliged and soon after his arrival suggested that she marry Esau del Buondelmonti. Esau, as noted, had formerly been a captive in

Jannina after his capture in 1378 and may well have made a good impression on the widow and her court. Maria thought this a good idea, offered her hand to him, and Esau returned and married her.

Chalcocondyles presents a very different point of view. He reports that Maria had made the prisoner Esau her lover and implies that Esau had not been released. This contradicts the Jannina chronicle, which indirectly says Esau had been released since it states he returned to Jannina to marry her. Chalcocondyles then claims that together they carried out the murder of Tomo, after which she took over the rule of Jannina and married her lover. Tomo's and her son then fled to the Turks to seek help: help against Esau we might assume, but Chalcocondyles says help against Carlos Tocco, the Count of Cephalonia who was expanding into Acarnania. However, the two statements need not be viewed as contradictory, for Esau and Carlo Tocco were related; Carlo's mother was a Buondelmonti. Thus Carlo may well have been supporting his kinsman. In any case, Sultan Murad was not interested in the quarrel. He simply arrested and blinded Tomo's son.

Whatever their disagreements, both the Jannina chronicle and Chalcocondyles have Maria in power after Tomo's murder and soon marrying Esau. It also seems that Maria's brother (John Uroš, the monk Joasaf) did arrive to help her. At the same time Alexius Angelus' wife, accompanied by the widow's other brother Stefan, appeared for a visit. Whether their presence reflected ambitions on the part of Alexius Angelus and/or Stefan to take over in Jannina is not clear. Then in January or possibly February 1385 Esau del Buondelmonti, who may well have been the candidate of the anti-Tomo party, married Maria and thus triumphed—if holding Jannina at this time is something one would judge a triumph. Esau then became governor of Jannina. He was a Florentine, related to the Acciajuoli of the Morea and Attica (through his mother Lapa Acciajuoli) and, as noted, to the Tocco family of Cephalonia.

Before continuing with our account of Esau's rule in Jannina, it is worth pausing to explain that the Tocco family had acquired control of this Ionian principality—Cephalonia, Zakynthos, and possibly Ithaca—in about 1357 when the Angevin Robert of Taranto granted the islands to Leonardo Tocco, one of his leading retainers. Carlo Tocco succeeded to these possessions on Leonardo's death, which occurred between 1375 and 1377. Leonardo, probably in the 1360s but certainly by 1373, had also seized the island of Leucas and Vonitsa in Epirus from John d'Enghien, Walter II of Brienne's heir. Thus Carlo also inherited a foothold on the Epirote mainland.

After Esau's assumption of power, the monk Joasaf soon departed for Meteora and spent the rest of his days as a monk either on Meteora or on Mount Athos until his death in 1422 or 1423. The *Chronicle of Jannina*, which is very favorable to Esau, says he immediately abolished Tomo's new taxes, recalled various exiled local nobles, restored to the local landholders the lands Tomo had confiscated, and arrested—jailing, exiling, or blinding—Tomo's leading councillors. Esau sought recognition from Byzantium, which sent an envoy to invest Esau as despot in 1385/86. His attempts to reach understandings with the Albanians failed. Early in 1385 John Spata attacked Jannina but soon withdrew when he saw he could not crack the defenses created by Esau. The two soon concluded a peace, whose terms are unknown; but soon again they were at war with one another. Faced with the Albanian threat, Esau, as Tomo had, began negotiating with the Turks for aid. In 1386 he visited Murad's court and paid homage. As a result he received Ottoman military help for his local defense.

But then, right after the Battle of Kosovo (June 1389), in which Murad lost his life, the Ottomans for several months were not able to provide assistance to Esau. This encouraged the Albanians to immediately rise up again against Esau. In the summer of 1389 Spata attacked Jannina, unsuccessfully, though he did plunder the environs. Directly on the heels of Spata's attack, the Malakasi launched a raid against Jannina's territory and soon concluded an alliance with Spata for a new effort against the town itself. Faced with this threat, Esau, still in 1389, made an alliance with the "caesar from Thessaly"—either Alexius Angelus or his successor Manuel—and their joint forces defeated some Albanian nobles (presumably Spata and the Malakasi) late in that year. Bayezid I, having rapidly secured his position as sultan, sent troops that winter which helped Esau repel Spata once again. Then Esau went to Bayezid's court, supposedly spending fourteen months there, where he concluded a new alliance with the Ottomans. He returned to Jannina in December 1390, accompanied by an Ottoman army led by the able general Evrenos beg. Their joint forces soon defeated the Albanian tribes in the neighborhood, forcing them to withdraw back into the mountains, and a short period of peace (1391–94) followed.

Maria then died in December 1394. Just as they differ on the causes of Tomo's death and Esau's succession, our two sources differ in their assessments of her. The Jannina chronicle depicts her as kind and pious. Chalcocondyles sees her as an unfaithful wife of generally dubious morality. The Albanians soon became active against Jannina again, and to try to bring about peace with at least some of them, Esau in 1396 married John Spata's daughter Irene. Though this may have led to peace with Spata, it did not pacify the other tribes in the area, in particular the Zenevisi, against whom Esau went to war in April 1399. Esau was defeated and taken prisoner. The Florentines, who had found Esau's presence in Jannina beneficial for their policy, soon paid a huge ransom to purchase his freedom, enabling him to return to Jannina in July 1400.

Soon thereafter, in October 1400, John Spata died. His brother, Sgouros Bova Spata, obtained Arta. Sgouros had troubles at once when a certain Vango of mixed ethnicity—he called himself a Serbo-Albano-Bulgaro-Vlach—expelled him from Arta. By the end of 1401 Vango had been driven out of Arta. However, Sgouros did not regain the town; instead, his nephew and also the late John's grandson, Maurice (Muriki) Spata, took over Arta;

Sgouros had to settle for Angelokastron as his residence. At this point the Jannina chronicle comes to an end and our main source of information on Jannina and Epirus dries up.

At the time, the Spata family was involved in civil war. Carlo Tocco, holder of Cephalonia, Leucas, and Vonitsa, joined in the fighting as an ally. Successful, he acquired for himself several fortresses. Sgouros Spata of Angelokastron died in 1403 from wounds suffered in this warfare. He left his lands to his son Paul, who seems to have been without much ability. Carlo Tocco then took the offensive for himself; as a result Paul turned to the Turks for help, soon ceding Angelokastron to them. (The Turks did not hold it long; in 1408 Angelokastron belonged to Tocco.) A relatively small contingent of Turks sent to aid Paul suffered a defeat, probably in 1406, outside the walls of Vonitsa; as a result the Turkish commander came to an understanding with Tocco. Paul, seeing little hope, retired to Naupaktos, still a Spata family possession. The next year, in 1407, he sold Naupaktos to Venice. As a result of Paul's withdrawal, Aetolia and Acarnania were divided between Maurice Spata and Carlo Tocco. Maurice Spata still retained Arta, having successfully beaten off an attack upon it by Tocco. Maurice and Carlo remained in a state of war.

Meanwhile in Jannina, probably in 1402, Esau divorced Irene Spata—who by a previous husband was the mother of Maurice Spata—and took a new wife, Eudocia Balšić, the sister of Constantine Balšić, a leading Ottoman vassal in northern Albania. They had a son, George, who was only seven when Esau died on 6 February 1411. Immediately his widow tried to take control of Jannina. However, the town leaders disliked her and agreed to reject her when they learned she was seeking a Serb to be her new husband. On 26 February the citizens of Jannina revolted, exiled her, and summoned Esau's nephew Carlo Tocco to be lord of Jannina. Carlo arrived in Jannina on 1 April 1411.

Maurice Spata, unhappy with Carlo's acquisition of Jannina, soon formed an alliance with John (Gjin) Zenevisi, the leader of the most powerful tribe in the vicinity of Jannina, against Carlo. However, despite winning a major open-field battle against Tocco's forces in 1412, the Albanian allies could not take Jannina. Tocco owed much of his success to his ability to mobilize local Greek support against the Albanians. In 1414 Maurice Spata died, and Arta went to his brother, who had become a Muslim and taken the name Yaqub. Yaqub in his turn died in 1416. Carlo brought his forces south; the people of Arta submitted to him, and he entered the town in October 1416. At the same time Rogoi surrendered to him. Carlo turned the rule of Arta over to his own brother Leonardo, who had long been his faithful colleague, while he himself returned to the north to rule Jannina. Leonardo died in 1418 or 1419, leaving a son, Carlo. Since the elder Carlo had no legitimate sons, this Carlo was already his uncle's recognized heir. It is often said that Carlo Tocco became master of Epirus. He did hold the two major cities—Arta and Jannina—and presumably various other towns as well. However, it must be stressed that much of Epirus, as always in this period, was under the domination of various Albanian tribes, over which Tocco almost certainly had no authority. But in any case, holding various towns, Tocco was the nominal lord of Epirus, Aetolia, and Acarnania from his victory in 1418 until his death in 1429. He also retained his family's hereditary possessions of Cephalonia, Zakynthos, and Ithaca.

Dušan's Albanian Lands

Meanwhile, John Comnenus Asen established his own independence to Jannina's northwest, in southern Albania, bearing the title of despot Dušan had granted him. Though he had good relations with Symeon and even supported his invasion of Serbia, he did not recognize his suzerainty. After Symeon's retreat back to Kastoria in 1358, John Comnenus continued to rule in his principality centered in Valona and Berat. As noted in the previous chapter, it is not known whether his Albanian holdings were limited to the region of these two towns or whether, as some scholars believe, he held a good portion of Albania. To secure his position he maintained close ties with Venice, which, despite its loss of the territory north of Durazzo to Hungary in 1358, continued to be a major commercial and naval force in the region south of Durazzo. Valona at this time became a major commercial port—particularly trading with Venice and Dubrovnik—that sold cattle, pepper, sugar, and other spices wholesale. John Comnenus ruled his principality until he died of the plague in 1363.

His successor was named Alexander; he was probably John's son. Alexander ruled until about 1368, the last year he is mentioned in the sources. At Alexander's court we find mention of Serbs, Greeks, Albanians, and Vlachs. Sources also mention in 1366 a Castriot as kephale (head) of Kanina (the acropolis fortress above Valona) who probably was an ancestor of John Castriot and Skanderbeg, who were to become so prominent in the following century. North of Valona, holding Myzeqeja, the region between the Shkumbi and Devolli rivers, an Albanian named Blasius (or Blaž) II Matarango (1358–67) asserted his independence and set up a short-lived principality; he bore the title of sevastocrator which Symeon, who recognized his rule over this territory, granted him. On Lake Ohrid a Serb named Mladen, granted the title caesar by Dušan and soon succeeded by his son Branko Mladenović, for all practical purposes ruled this Albanian-Slavic border territory independently, though the family at least nominally recognized Uroš' suzerainty. Then as we move further east, beyond Mladen's lands, we run into the lands of Hlapen, who held Kastoria and Voden. The territories of these petty princes formed a buffer between Epirus and Thessaly on the one hand and the state of Serbia on the other under Uroš and its great nobles who, regardless of how independent they were in fact, still recognized the suzerainty of the Serbian tsar.

The Lands that Remained Loyal to Uroš

While these southern conquests of Dušan seceded, the core of his state held together. This included most of Macedonia, the interior Struma-Mesta lands, and the Chalcidic peninsula. In this core area one might expect the strongest nobleman to have been John Oliver. He outlived Dušan, for coins of his with Uroš' name on them exist. However, no written source mentions him in these years, and it seems he died shortly after Uroš' succession. He left two sons, but somehow they did not acquire major positions in Serbia. It is not known why, but we may suspect they were thwarted by a coalition of strong nobles. Most of Oliver's lands went to John and Constantine, the sons of Sevastocrator Dejan of Kumanovo. Earlier scholars believed they were relatives of Oliver. This is no longer accepted. Oliver also left considerable land to Hilandar on Mount Athos.

The lands that remained Serbian can be divided into three main parts: the western territories, including Zeta, the central Serbian lands of Uroš, and the southern lands (including the eastern part of Macedonia, with Serres its capital). Because the leading nobles of these three regions usually expressed loyalty to Uroš, no legal separatism occurred.

The Western Nobles

The two leading western noble families were those of Vojislav Vojinović and the Balšić brothers. Vojislav, the strongest, was the son of a certain Vojin who had governed Hum for Stefan Dečanski. Vojislav held lands along Zeta's borders between the Drina and the coast, including Užice, Gacko, Popovo Polje, Konavli, and Trebinje.

The Balšići held Zeta. No surviving source refers to this family before 1360. If we can believe Orbini (writing in 1601) the family founder, Balša, had been a petty nobleman, holding only one village under Dušan. Thus he entered Uroš' reign with a small holding. In fact, at that time the family was less influential in Zeta than a second noble named Žarko who also is not mentioned in surviving sources from the period before Dušan's death. Right after Dušan's death, however, Žarko emerged as the leading nobleman of Zeta. He is referred to on the coast in June 1357 as a baron of the Raškan king (Uroš) who ruled Zeta, the region of the Bojana River, and the (southern) coast. The phrasing shows that Žarko recognized Uroš' suzerainty. Žarko disappears thereafter from the sources as rapidly and unexpectedly as he had appeared. He had probably taken advantage of a power vacuum to expand a small holding only to be pushed out in the same manner by a more efficient force, which presumably was the Balšić family. However, Žarko probably survived for a while, holding some of his lands on the Bojana. His son Mrkše Žarković was to emerge subsequently as a figure of middling significance, but chiefly owing to lands belonging to the woman he was to marry.

By 1360, when we first hear of them, the Balšići were already quite powerful, though we cannot be certain about their specific holdings. For in September of that year, when we hear of them for the first time in a charter issued by Uroš to Dubrovnik, the Balšići were listed on the same level as Vojislav and said to be holding the Zetan lands. The charter granted the merchants of Dubrovnik the right to trade freely in Uroš' lands and in those of these two leading barons. Orbini states that the father (Balša) first acquired Skadar, which was betrayed to him by its defenders, and then he (and probably here we should read "they" to include the sons who succeeded him) expanded to acquire the territory between Lake Skadar and the coast to, but not including, Kotor. Orbini reports that this expansion into Upper Zeta and into the lands of the Dukagjins south of Lake Skadar was carried out fairly violently by the sons. Djuraš Ilijić of Upper Zeta was killed and the Dukagjins were either killed or imprisoned. Other Dukagjins, we know, survived, for the family was not to lose its prominence, though it may have suffered some diminution in territory. Orbini also makes the comment that the Balšići carried out their expansion more by trickery and cleverness than by force of arms. The scholarly consensus attributes their success to concluding advantageous marriages, supporting Uroš against Symeon to earn his gratitude, and land-grabbing. Three brothers (Stracimir, George [Djuradj], and Balša) jointly succeeded their father. Orbini says that in terms of goodness and trustworthiness Stracimir was the best of the three; George was wise and very skilled in the use of arms; while Balša was brave and a fine horseman, but not very intelligent. George is soon documented as bearing the title of župan (count).

But though we know the Balšići were powerful and held much of Zeta by 1360 and can trace, to the degree Orbini was accurate, the order of their acquisitions, we are left in the dark about exact chronology, for Orbini provides no dates, other than to say these gains occurred after Dušan's death. By 1363 they clearly had Skadar and Drivast and probably Bar. They probably took Drivast in the spring of 1362. If Orbini is accurate, and most scholars do accept him here, they probably acquired Skadar, which he states was the first major town they obtained, in or before 1360.

In 1361 these two leading western noble families (Vojislav and the Balšići) split. For when Vojislav, supported by Uroš, attacked Dubrovnik, the Balšići supported the town. Their ability to act independently illustrates the weakness of Uroš' control over his state.

Vojislav's quarrel with Dubrovnik broke out in the fall of 1358, when the Serbs and Hungarians clashed along the Danube. Using Dubrovnik's vassalage to Hungary as an excuse—for Dubrovnik had not earned this enmity by any actual participation in the fighting—and a commercial dispute between Dubrovnik and Kotor as further cause for anger, Vojislav prepared for war. On this occasion war was avoided, and Dubrovnik sent Uroš his Saint Demetrius' Day tribute. But tensions increased the following year, 1359, when Hungary launched a larger effort against Serbia that included support of the Rastislalići in Braničevo. Having eliminated the local opponents of the

Rastislalići, the Hungarians secured Braničevo's independence from Serbia and then used this territory as a base to penetrate further into Serbian territory. The Serbian army retreated to avoid battle with the attackers and the Hungarians had to be satisfied with plundering. The Serb Vojislav then took out his frustrations on Hungary's vassal Dubrovnik by sending his men to plunder into the part of Konavli belonging to Dubrovnik.

It seems that Vojislav, who probably had sent troops to help defend central Serbia from the Hungarians, waited until the Hungarians withdrew from Serbia before he attacked Dubrovnik. For it seems the Hungarians withdrew in July 1359, and Vojislav's troops were plundering Konavli in August. Vojislav also had by then begun to call himself the Prince (knez) of Hum—a title, it seems, awarded to him by Uroš, although Vojislav actually held only a very small part of Hum. He now demanded that Dubrovnik turn over to him Ston, the traditional capital of Hum, which Dubrovnik had purchased from Dušan in 1333. He next seized a Ragusan merchant caravan that was passing through his lands; he said the seizure was carried out on the orders of Tsar Uroš. When Vojislav brought his troops to the very walls of Dubrovnik, the town gave in and bought a temporary respite from the fighting by paying him four thousand perpera. However, matters remained very difficult for Dubrovnik. The following year (1360) it sent envoys to Serbia to attend the wedding of Uroš and Anna (Anka, Anča), the daughter of Alexander Basarab, Vojvoda of Wallachia, and the half-sister of Wallachia's reigning ruler—a marriage probably intended to seal an alliance against Serbia's and Wallachia's common enemy Hungary. These envoys complained of a series of new toll and customs stations erected throughout Serbia by various Serbian nobles in the years after Dušan's death. Uroš, at least on paper, declared these new stations abolished and took Dubrovnik's caravans under his protection.

War between Vojislav and Dubrovnik broke out again in 1361. Vojislav had the support of Uroš, who ordered the seizure of all Ragusan merchants in his realm. Kotor, which until recently had enjoyed good relations with Dubrovnik, declared its support for Vojislav. Kotor probably did so because it saw Vojislav as a protector against the ambitious Balšići, who had expanded to the Gulf of Kotor and clearly had their eyes on the town of Kotor. Moreover, Kotor, under Serbian suzerainty since the time of Nemanja, traditionally supported the Serbian ruler, who on this occasion supported Vojislav. Orbini provides further details. Pointing out that the two towns had regularly been allies until 1361, Orbini reports that when Vojislav attacked it, Dubrovnik asked Kotor not to sell him salt. In the interests of its economy, Kotor refused. Dubrovnik then burned Kotor's salt works. Furious, Kotor then came out strongly for Vojislav and began to sell him arms. Vojislav mobilized his troops to attack both Dubrovnik and Ston. Dubrovnik, secure in its own defenses, worried about Ston. To pressure Vojislav's men into wanting peace, Dubrovnik stopped exporting salt into the interior. This caused hardship not only for Vojislav's subjects but also for the shepherds of Zeta and Albania who depended upon this salt. The town moreover attacked Kotor and created a naval blockade of the Gulf of Kotor. It also offered a reward to anyone who would burn Vojislav's granaries in Gacko and Sjenica. Some of Vojislav's men meanwhile plundered the environs of Dubrovnik while others attacked, but failed to take, Ston and Pelješac.

At this moment George and Stracimir Balšić, holders of western Zeta (possibly already including Bar and Skadar), sent word to Dubrovnik of their support, as did Budva. Interestingly enough Budva seems to have supported Vojislav in 1359. However, by 1362 this town under its head Površko had accepted Balšić overlordship. If his submission had occurred, as it may well have, by 1361, then it would have been natural for Budva to fall into line with Balšić policy. The Balšići's decision to involve themselves on behalf of Dubrovnik was probably owing to the fact that Dubrovnik was at war with Kotor; ambitious to obtain Kotor, they presumably decided to support Dubrovnik in the hope of achieving that goal.

The Balšići's entry into the war on Dubrovnik's side, in opposition to their overlord Tsar Uroš, shows that Uroš was unable to control his vassals. And, since the war seems to have been pushed by Vojislav, one might conclude that Uroš had in fact been dragged into a war that was being carried out chiefly to serve the interests of his vassal. It is quite likely that Uroš and his court were unhappy with the situation; thus it is not surprising that in the summer of 1361 Uroš sent envoys to Dubrovnik to seek peace. Though his efforts failed, as did those of Tvrtko of Bosnia, Uroš at least was able to get salt exports resumed for much of the interior. However, Dubrovnik's ban remained in effect for Kotor and for Vojislav's own lands. Finally in 1362 an armistice was signed through the mediation of Venice, which was angry at the naval blockade that impeded its commerce and infringed upon what it felt were its rights to trade freely on the Adriatic. A peace treaty that restored matters to their conditions under Dušan was signed in August 1362. At the very end of the year peace was also concluded between Dubrovnik and Kotor; each side released the other's merchants who had been arrested and restored all confiscated merchandise. Thus the war concluded indecisively.

Dubrovnik was spared further trouble when Vojislav died in September 1363, probably a victim of the plague that was then ravaging Dalmatia. By then his ambitions seem to have been increasing, for he was calling himself Stefan (the Serbian royal name) Vojislav, Grand Prince of the Serbs, Greeks, and the coastal lands. The subjects listed for himself and the manner in which they were listed were clearly in imitation of the title of the Serbian ruler. One may well wonder what his specific goals were. In any case in the early 1360s Vojislav was the most powerful figure in Serbia. His death was to permit the rise of others. Vojislav's lands went to his widow, Gojislava, who was soon attacked by Vojislav's nephew Nicholas (Nikola) Altomanović. For the next three years, as a result of a grant made to her by Uroš (renewing a grant Uroš had made to Vojislav in 1358), Dubrovnik paid the two thousand perpera Saint Demetrius' Day tribute to Gojislava.

During and after these coastal events the Balšići were active in their own interests. In the period 1360–63, if they had not already done so, they acquired Skadar and probably Bar. In the fall of 1362 they besieged but failed to take the port of Ulcinj, which, though managing its own affairs, had officially become the property of Dušan's widow Helen after his death. The Balšići finally succeeded in taking Ulcinj in 1368. During this period they also acquired the port of Budva. Most scholars date its acquisition to the period 1360–63. Those who oppose this conclusion point to the fact that Orbini reports Budva as independent under a nobleman named Površko in 1363. However, he may well have been a Balšić vassal, for Orbini states that Površko had bought Budva or, as some say, been granted it by the Balšići for some service. In 1364, Orbini says, Kotor attacked Budva, and in the fighting Površko was killed. Kotor was probably taking advantage of a war (to be discussed later) then going on between Budva's probable suzerain, George Balšić, and the Albanian Thopias. Despite Površko's death Budva held out against Kotor and soon thereafter the Balšići had come to Budva's aid. Thus Budva was saved from Kotor and the Balšići were soon thereafter in control of Budva, where they installed a new vojvoda, Nicholas Zakarija (Zaccaria), to administer the town.

Kotor now found itself isolated and in difficulties. The most powerful figure in the area, George Balšić, was at war against it. And Kotor could not seek help from the Serbian ruler, for George was closely associated with Vukašin, who was coming to be the most powerful and influential figure at court. In fact George had married Vukašin's daughter Olivera. Kotor's former protector Vojislav had died, and since his heir, his widow Gojislava, was trying to defend her lands against her nephew Nicholas Altomanović, she was in no position to help the town. Only after Nicholas' victory over his aunt in 1368 did the town again find in Nicholas a protector close by. And by then the town's dangers had decreased since Uroš and his court had cooled toward the Balšići.

To further their coastal ambitions, in 1368 or early 1369 the three Balšić brothers accepted Catholicism. However, this did not lead to any effort by them to encourage the Orthodox Christians in their lands to convert.

Vukašin

The death of Vojislav, who, though active in his own interests, had, as far as we can tell, remained loyal to Uroš, weakened Uroš' position and encouraged more separatist activity. Needing a new protector, Uroš decided, or was persuaded, to turn to Vukašin Mrnjavčević. Orbini says Vukašin's family originated in Hum; he himself was born in Livno, the son of a certain Mrnjava. Originally poor, Mrnjava and his sons—Vukašin and Uglješa—rose rapidly under Stefan Dušan. Possibly the family had supported his invasion of Bosnia/Hum in 1350. That they were from Hum is confirmed by the fact that a certain Mrnjan (or Mergnanus) was a treasurer (kaznac) in Trebinje in the

1280s serving Milutin's mother, Helen. The family could well have moved to Livno after the Bosnian conquest of Hum and then, having supported Dušan in his preparations for his invasion of Bosnia (1350) and fearing punishment, have emigrated to Serbia prior to that war. Noteworthily, the first reference we have to Vukašin in Serbia comes from March 1350 when we find Vukašin as Dušan's appointed Župan of Prilep. For the rest of Dušan's reign Vukašin is mentioned in documents as a high courtier and as the ruler's deputy in Prilep; he also came to possess considerable territory around Prilep in his own right. His brother Uglješa may well have also been in Dušan's service already before the Bosnian campaign; at least a baron of Dušan's named Uglješa is documented in Ragusan records from 1346.

Having in 1364 made Vukašin a despot, Tsar Uroš in August or September 1365 crowned him king, repeating in theory the situation that had existed when Dušan was tsar and Uroš king. However, there was one major distinction between the present and former situations. For formerly, at least in theory, Uroš had held the Serbian lands, and Dušan the "Roman." Now Vukašin and Uroš were co-rulers and there was no territorial division between them; both jointly ruled the same Serbian land. Moreover, the king, Vukašin, was to become the dominant figure. Scholars have often depicted Vukašin as a usurper. However, though Vukašin may have pressured Uroš into crowning him, at first Uroš' rights were respected; through 1366 they appeared together on coins and on wall-paintings, on both of which Uroš was portrayed in the senior position on the right. Moreover, because Uroš was weak, possibly even feeble-minded, he did need support. The epics depict Vukašin as Uroš' kum (God-father). Though no contemporary source confirms this, it offers a plausible explanation for Uroš' action. One in trouble would naturally have turned to one's kum for support. Thus quite possibly Vukašin's coronation was a mutually convenient act, executed voluntarily by Uroš. However, in time Vukašin came to act increasingly on his own. In 1367 Vukašin was corresponding with Dubrovnik in his own name alone and in 1370 he issued a charter to Dubrovnik without reference to Uroš. However, he never ousted Uroš.

Vukašin may have had plans to establish his own dynasty. He crowned his son Marko "young king." This was the title borne by Dušan during the reign of Dečanski which indicated his position as heir to the throne. But since Uroš was childless, a desire on the part of Vukašin to secure Marko's succession need not have threatened Uroš' position. Only Orbini, a late author (1601), on the basis of a non-extant and unknown source, suggests outright friction between them; he states that in 1368/69 Uroš joined a coalition against Vukašin which resulted in his briefly being imprisoned by Vukašin. Vukašin also did take advantage of his position to expand his personal holdings further into Macedonia and Kosovo, acquiring by 1366 Skopje and by 1370 the important cities of Prizren, Ohrid (taken somehow from Branko Mladenović or from his son Vuk Branković), and most probably Priština and the rich mining town of Novo Brdo. Vukašin's rise followed the death of

Vojislav, whose departure from the scene meant there was no possible check on Vukašin except possibly the Balšići; however, their territorial expansion and ambitions did not overlap with those of Vukašin, and Vukašin had rapidly made them into allies by giving his daughter to George as a wife. Vuk Branković and Lazar were not yet on this level of power. Their rises followed the Battle of Marica (1371), in which Vukašin was killed.

Uglješa and Serres

Upon Dušan's death his widow Helen inherited the southernmost lands that Serbia retained, including the Greek lands between the lower Vardar and the Mesta as well as the Chalcidic peninsula. She also held Ulcinj on the Adriatic coast. Though she became a nun, Helen continued to play an active political role. Cantacuzenus claims that when Uroš had to fight his uncle Symeon for his inheritance, his mother was unfaithful both to her son and to Symeon, taking for herself many towns and using her armies to hold power for herself, neither fighting against either nor helping either, while in Serbia the strong nobles drove out the weaker ones from their towns and forts and took them over for themselves. Cantacuzenus' description is applicable to various nobles like the Rastislalići and the Balšići. But, as far as we can tell, it does not fit Uroš' mother. No other medieval source even hints that she quarreled with Uroš. In fact he frequently resided at her court in Serres, where he was recognized, at least on paper, as Serres' overlord. Moreover, his name appears first in her charters, even though he probably had no actual authority in Serres or the rest of Helen's realm.

Vukašin's brother John Uglješa is found serving at Helen's court in Serres. He was, for example, her envoy to Emperor John V in 1358 when the emperor visited Kavalla. Uglješa was married to the daughter of Vojvoda (later Caesar) Vojin of Drama. Since Uglješa is later found holding Drama, we may assume he inherited it and the rest of Vojin's lands after Vojin died in ca. 1360. In 1365, when Vukašin was crowned king, Uglješa was crowned despot. By 1366 Uglješa was the de facto ruler of Serres. Helen's role declined, and she eventually died in November 1376. Uroš' name soon disappeared from official documents in Serres. And in 1369 we find Uglješa calling himself "autocrat." However, no secession occurred, for Uglješa and his brother Vukašin co-operated closely with each other. This was facilitated by the fact that Uglješa's lands extended north to border on the Serbian lands of Vukašin and Uroš. Thus the core of Dušan's state—the central Serbian and Macedonian lands—remained united. And since scholars have emphasized the break-up of the Serbian empire after 1356, it is worth noting here that the years following Dušan's death did not only see territorial losses for the Serbs. For Uglješa (or Helen) actually expanded the territory of the Serres "state" beyond the borders that had existed in Dušan's day. For we find Uglješa's holdings stretching beyond the former Mesta River frontier to include the towns of Xantheia, Polystylon, and Peritheorion.

From the documents preserved on Mount Athos we know a great deal about Uglješa's state in Serres.[1] Its population was a mixed one dominated by Greeks, Slavs (including Serbs and Bulgarians), and Vlachs. In the villages, beside the dominant element of the peasantry, lived artisans (blacksmiths, tailors, carpenters, etc.). Most of the peasants seem to have been bound to great estates, whether of secular landlords or of the Church. There was also a fairly large number of landless laborers who were hired to work the land of others, often in exchange for a share of the produce. In Serres, as in Serbia, mines were a major source of income.

After the death of Dušan the administration of Serres remained efficient, following the policies established by Dušan. Greek remained the official language of Church and state. However, Uglješa issued charters in either Greek or Slavic, depending on the grantee; he had two chancelleries, one for each language, to issue his documents. Court decisions and administrative acts were issued in Greek. The titles for offices also tended to be Greek.

Like many other towns, the town of Serres (and its environs) was under a kephale (headman). By this time the term *kephale* was equivalent to the Serbian term *župan,* which was coming to mean a figure appointed to govern a town, like Vukašin in Prilep in 1350, rather than indicating, as formerly, a hereditary lord of a county. The kephale was responsible for the administration of the town and its environs. In Serres the position was usually held by a Serb. When Dušan took Serres he had left the Greek holder of that position in office; however, from 1360 until the Byzantines recovered Serres all Serres' kephales were Serbs. And, as noted in the last chapter, throughout the Greek lands ruled by Dušan Serbs tended to hold the highest administrative positions while the Greeks tended to dominate the lesser ones. This policy was continued in the Serres state under Uglješa. However, we find many Greeks at Uglješa's court. Uglješa was very free in issuing them inflated honorary (as opposed to functional) titles. Thus Greeks were included among the highest nobility at Serres and they made up the major portion of the local aristocracy. On the whole they were loyal to him, serving in his army or administration, holding their pronoias from him, participating at his court, and in general playing an active role in the state. Some of these Greeks were of high Byzantine families, tied by blood or marriage to the first families of Constantinople. They remained at Serres after its conquest by Dušan, keeping and even enlarging their large estates. The policies of recognizing the titles and landholding of the Greeks, while making even further grants of both, and retaining Greeks in many administrative positions were ways to keep peace and order. It made the Greeks less prone to revolt against Serbian rule and it also meant that Serbian manpower was not spread too thin. Ostrogorsky's study of Serres shows that Greeks held the majority of honorary court titles while the bulk of important functional ones went to the Serbs. However, if one takes the nobility of Serres as a whole, more Greeks were to be found in its ranks than Serbs.

However, despite the presence of these Greeks in various official positions at court and in possession of large estates, the Serbian nobility expected to be rewarded for their part in the conquest of this region, and they were. They walked off with the highest positions in both Church and state. In fact, Serbs dominated high Church positions to an even greater extent than they did state ones. As noted, at the time of his conquest Dušan removed a certain number of Greek bishops, including the Metropolitan of Serres, and replaced them with Serbs. And throughout the period of Serbian rule, Serbs occupied the position of Metropolitan of Serres. It was similar in many other towns in that region, though there were cases where Greeks were retained in or even appointed to bishoprics. A glaring exception (though in Thessaly rather than Serres) was Anthony, the Metropolitan of Larissa, who remained in office from 1340 to 1363 through a whole series of changes: Andronicus III, the civil war between regency and Cantacuzenus, the rule of John Angelus, Dušan's conquest bringing Preljub's governorship, Nicephorus of Epirus' rule, and finally the rule of Symeon. In addition to changing the men holding sees, the Serbs had removed Serres and various other bishoprics in the area from the jurisdiction of the Constantinopolitan hierarchy and placed them under the jurisdiction of the Serbian Patriarch of Peć. On Mount Athos, though Greeks continued to hold many high positions, frequently a Serb held the top position of protos.

As noted, Dušan allowed the monasteries on Athos to retain their ties with Byzantium and even allowed them to mention the emperor in their prayers. This policy continued under Uglješa. In fact, the Serres state and Byzantium recognized each other; they exchanged embassies and the empire recognized the titles used in the Serres state, not hesitating to call Uglješa despot. On a non-official level Greeks and Serbs of Serres had ties with the empire, particularly with Thessaloniki, which many Serres subjects visited for pleasure or business. Commerce between Serres and Thessaloniki was very active.

Bulgaria

John Alexander of Bulgaria outlived Dušan. In the 1350s he abandoned his first wife, with whom he did not get along, according to Orbini, because she was not bright enough. He then married Theodora, a converted Jewess, whose intelligence impressed him. Under her influence he disinherited the son of his first marriage, John Stracimir, and declared his and Theodora's son John Šišman as his heir. As compensation for Stracimir, shortly before 1360 John Alexander granted him Vidin, thereby dividing the realm again and making Vidin a separate principality once more. In 1365 the Hungarians invaded the province of Vidin. John Stracimir shut himself up behind the walls of Vidin, awaiting help from his father. In four days, before any help could arrive, the Hungarians on 2 June 1365 took Vidin; over the following three months the Hungarians took the rest of the principality. They established a Hungarian banate of Vidin under a Hungarian-appointed ban. John Stracimir was taken prisoner with his family and spent a period of honorary captivity in a Croatian castle. The Hungarians also called in the Franciscans to try to convert the population to Catholicism. Having the Hungarians on their eastern border must have cramped the style of the Rastislalići of Braničevo, who, up to then, though Hungarian vassals, had more or less been able to behave as independent lords.

In 1370 John Stracimir recovered Vidin. It seems he was allowed to return by the Hungarians. Later Hungarian sources describe a Wallachian raid against the Vidin banate, in which the province was plundered and the lower town of Vidin taken and burned. The Wallachians then besieged Vidin's citadel, which forced King Louis to bestir himself to intervene and drive them out. Louis then allowed Stracimir to return as his vassal. We may assume he reasoned that Stracimir would have more local support and thus could defend the province more effectively than a Hungarian-appointed ban. To assure Stracimir's loyalty, Louis kept Stracimir's two daughters at the Hungarian court. One soon died but the other was married, through Hungarian negotiations, to Tvrtko of Bosnia in 1374. Stracimir's recognition of Hungarian suzerainty also enabled him to assert his independence from his father and subsequently to resist his brother, toward whom he felt great bitterness throughout his life. Exercizing the freedom this Hungarian support gave him, John Stracimir now assumed the title of tsar and removed his Church from the jurisdiction of the Patriarch of Trnovo and subjected it to the Patriarch of Constantinople. He also began coining his own money.

John Alexander's Trnovo state suffered other losses as well. In northeastern Bulgaria, based in the fortified town of Karbona (modern Balčik), a boyar named Balik had already—probably back in the middle 1340s—defected. For Balik is mentioned as sending one thousand troops under his brothers Dobrotica and Theodore to aid Anna of Savoy in the regency's war against Cantacuzenus. Balik was succeeded by his brother Dobrotica, for whom part of his holdings, the Dobrudja, received its name. (The name Dobrudja, by which the region is known today, is a Turkish form derived from his name that came into use in the Ottoman period.) He also held the Black Sea coast below the Dobrudja, including Varna, which was becoming a major port. To further assert his independence from Trnovo, Dobrotica, too, separated the Church in his lands from Trnovo, recognizing the jurisdiction of the Patriarch of Constantinople. He soon acquired even more of the Black Sea coast, coming to hold most of Bulgaria's northern coastline. He carried on considerable trade on the Black Sea, much of it on Venetian and Genoese vessels.

To make Trnovo's commercial situation worse, John Alexander lost his major southern Black Sea ports as well. In 1364 a war, whose causes are unknown, had broken out between Byzantium and Bulgaria. Though it did not last long, it lasted long enough for the Byzantines to take Anchialos. Then in 1366 Emperor John V visited Hungary; when he attempted to return home overland via Bulgaria, John Alexander, possibly still angry over the events of

1364, detained him. Amadeus of Savoy, the emperor's Latin cousin, came to the rescue by launching his fleet against the Bulgarian Black Sea coast. Without difficulty he took Mesembria and Sozopolis. His actions led to negotiations that brought about not only the release of the emperor but also the cession of the two ports to Byzantium. Bulgaria was never to regain these ports from the empire.

Thus the tsar in Trnovo suffered considerable losses in trade and income. The income loss and territorial fragmentation were disastrous because the Turkish offensive against the Balkans was under way.

Upon John Alexander's death on 17 February 1371 his eldest son by Theodora, John Šišman, received the bulk of his father's dominions with Trnovo. Stracimir immediately attempted to conquer all Bulgaria. He succeeded in seizing Sofija but was able to retain it for only a year or two. Thereafter, Vidin and Trnovo, under the rival half-brothers, remained hostile to one another, preventing the Bulgarians from achieving any sort of united front against the Ottoman danger.

Bosnia: The Early Years of Tvrtko's Reign

In Bosnia Stjepan Kotromanić died in 1353 and, as noted, was succeeded by his teen-age nephew, Tvrtko I (1353–91). Kotromanić had created for Bosnia a strong army, yet he had erected little state administrative apparatus, generally leaving his vassals in outlying regions to administer their own lands. Based on their own lands in the provinces they dominated, these nobles rendered their obigations and services to the state. Thus though Kotromanić's authority was strong, his state was not. His authority was personal, not institutional. Tvrtko was only fifteen years old when he began his rule, and few of these nobles felt obliged to serve him; not bound to the state by any force, the nobles were free to act as they chose. Thus the strong "state" of Kotromanić split into separate units and would have to be reassembled. The only way the new ban could reassert central authority, if the nobles defied him, was to send out punitive forces; but the bulk of the forces that had served Kotromanić for this purpose had come from these same nobles, many (or most) of whom now chose to sit on the sidelines. Tvrtko's chances for success, if he were to try a military solution, would have to rest on his personal army from his personal holding and on the retinues of any other nobles who chose to participate. Thus holding only his family lands and presumably compelling obedience chiefly from the lesser lords of his own central banate, he had the task of acquiring the loyalty of the other regions that were seceding from his state.

This situation gave the Hungarian king a great chance to meddle and to try to reassert his lost control over some or all of the banate. The king actively began to woo the northern nobles. The Hrvatinić family, the most powerful of these, who were the lords of the Donji Kraji, split, some for Tvrtko and some for Hungary. The weak and inexperienced Tvrtko was thus faced with what might have seemed a no-win situation. He could not stand up to the Hungarians until he had re-created his state. And the Hungarians were doing everything they could to encourage the independent-minded Bosnian nobles to abandon the ban. Thus Tvrtko had to rebuild the state slowly and cautiously so as to retain or regain the support of the major nobles. To do this it was often necessary to outbid the Hungarian king.

The Hungarian king, Louis, had married Kotromanić's daughter Elizabeth in June 1353, just before Kotromanić's death. Louis now demanded that Tvrtko surrender to him, as her dowry, most of western Hum: namely, Završje and the lands between the Cetina and Neretva rivers, down to, and including, the rich customs town of Drijeva. Since Tvrtko was not at first able to acquire sufficient support from his nobles, Louis was able to compel him to come to Hungary in 1357 and surrender this territory. Thus Louis finally regained all the Croatian lands his father had lost; for first in 1345 Louis had acquired submission for the Cetina župa lands from the Nelipčić family and now in 1357 he acquired the lands to the south that Kotromanić had annexed. Tvrtko, stripped of this substantial territory, was then, as a Hungarian vassal, confirmed as ruler over Bosnia and Usora. "Hum" and "the Donji Kraji" were dropped from the title Louis confirmed him with, since the Hungarians had walked off with parts of these regions and did not want Tvrtko's title to support any Bosnian claims to them. In this period the pope stepped up calls for action against heretics in Bosnia. This increased Tvrtko's danger even though he himself was—and was to remain throughout his life—a Catholic. For if he tried to cross the Hungarian king, the king could take up the pope's call and invade Bosnia on a religious pretext.

We have no sources on Bosnian internal affairs from 1357, when Tvrtko submitted to Louis, until 1363, when a war (whose causes are unknown) broke out with Hungary. The Hungarians struck the north of Bosnia in two waves. The first wave struck the Donji Kraji, whose lords were divided among themselves, some for Tvrtko and some for the Hungarian king. This attack would be the crucial test. Loyalties already promised were not firm commitments. Vlatko Vukoslavić, loyal until then to Tvrtko, surrendered the important fortress of Ključ to Louis. However, Tvrtko came out on top as Vlkac Hrvatinić successfully defended Sokograd in the Župa of Pliva, and the Hungarian army was forced to turn back. Vlkac was given the whole Plivska župa as a reward a couple of years later; presumably that had been his price. The second Hungarian attack came a month later; this one was directed at Usora. Once again the Bosnian defense was successful; this time the Hungarians were halted at the fortress of Srebrnik in Usora, which held out against a massive attack. Thus somehow between 1358 and 1363 Tvrtko had become powerful enough to resist a major Hungarian attack. The sources are silent on how he managed to do this.

Shortly thereafter in February 1366 various major Bosnian nobles revolted against Tvrtko, forcing him to flee to the Hungarian court. The Hungarian king welcomed his enemy of two-and-a-half years before. The rebel nobles placed Tvrtko's younger brother Vuk on the Bosnian throne. Whether he initiated the action or was merely a figure-head for others is not known, but once on the throne he took up his new role with enthusiasm. However, Tvrtko, having again recognized Hungarian suzerainty, received aid from Hungary—we may presume "aid" meant troops—and was back in Bosnia in March. By the end of that month he had regained some, but not all, of his state. He was supported by the lords of the Donji Kraji. A variety of nobles participated in this affair, shifting sides throughout as suited their own interests. The most important defector in this affair was Sanko Miltenović, the leading nobleman of Hum, who held most of Hum between Nevesinje and Konjic and the coast. In the second half of 1367 he came to terms with Tvrtko, and a peace was concluded; by it, Sanko retained his holdings but again recognized Tvrtko's overlordship over them.

By the end of 1367 Tvrtko had regained his banate and Vuk was in exile. From exile Vuk began to seek outside help, particularly from the pope, who had been calling for a crusade against Bosnia. However, nothing was to come of Vuk's or the pope's plans because the King of Hungary stood by Tvrtko. By 1374 Vuk was reconciled with Tvrtko; possibly the occasion for the reconciliation was the marriage between Tvrtko and Dorothy, the daughter of John Stracimir of Vidin. She had been living as an honored hostage at the Hungarian court and it seems that Louis arranged the marriage. In the years that followed Vuk remained in Bosnia as a junior ban; the only traces of his presence from these years are the charters he endorsed.

Despite Tvrtko's Catholicism, the Bosnian Church continued to survive under Tvrtko. And we shall find it flourishing in the years immediately following his reign, when it is mentioned in many sources. One hostile source tries to link Tvrtko himself to it, but all the other sources indicate that Tvrtko remained a Catholic all his life. However, like his predecessors, he tolerated all the local faiths. He also maintained cordial relations with the Orthodox Church. It seems the Bosnian Church played no secular role under him; at least no charters witnessed by it have survived from his reign. One such charter purporting to have been issued by Tvrtko exists; from time to time it is cited by scholars, but I am certain it is a forgery.[2]

By the early 1370s, re-established in power and with his northern lands loyal and secure again (with the lords of the Donji Kraji back in line), Tvrtko began to meddle in the feuds of the Serbian nobles to his southeast. In particular, he actively supported Lazar against Nicholas Altomanović and as a result made considerable territorial gains for Bosnia. We shall turn to this event later.

The Albanian Lands in the 1360s

In the 1360s considerable fighting occurred in the Albanian-Zetan border region. This caused difficulties for Dubrovnik, whose main trade route to Prizren (one of the three main markets the town traded at in Serbia) went along the lower Bojana and Drin rivers through Albania. Owing to brigands and the frequent fighting between nobles and tribesmen in the vicinity, the route lacked security.

Three main families—the Balšići, the Matarangos, and the Thopias—were struggling for the region between Lake Skadar and Durazzo. Blaž Matarango, as noted earlier, had extensive lands within the square between the coast (including the port of Karavasta), the Shkumbi River to the north, the Seman (Semeni) River to the south, and the Devolli River to the east. These borders are extremely approximate; tribal movements were constant. Surely part of this territory included the pasture lands of various other tribes, some of which might have been Matarango clients, and very likely the Matarangos spilled out beyond this region at times. To the Matarangos' south lay Berat, which belonged to Alexander, John Comnenus Asen's heir. And to their north lay the lands of our third family, the Thopias.

The Thopias became prominent in the second quarter of the fourteenth century when the pope granted Tanush Thopia the title of count and recognized him as the holder of the lands between the Mati and Shkumbi rivers. Thus the border between the Matarangos and Thopias lay roughly along the Shkumbi River. In 1338 Tanush married an illegitimate daughter of Robert, King of Naples, and also was recognized as a count by the Angevins. This marriage allowed his son Karlo to brag in his epitaph that he was descended from the Kings of France. The Thopias—particularly under Karlo, who succeeded when Tanush died in 1359—became more prominent in the late 1350s and early 1360s at the same time as the Balšići did. The Thopias rapidly expanded their territory, subduing various lesser nobles and tribes, whose members were incorporated into their forces and then used to subdue others. They acquired the important fortress of Kroja in 1363 and at roughly the same time came to dominate the region around Durazzo. Durazzo itself, however, still remained Angevin.

War broke out between the Thopias and the Balšići in 1363 and lasted into 1364. Since the Balšići had been expanding at the expense of the Dukagjins, who were based along the Drin, we may suspect that the Balšići had penetrated into the region beyond the Drin toward the Mati, while the Thopias, in their turn, were pressing beyond the Mati toward the Drin, and that they had clashed as a result. The issue may well have been more complicated, since in these lands lived various other tribes who were being forced into clientship and who presumably were regularly trying to break away from such relationships. Furthermore the recent collective history of Montenegro suggests that the Matarangos also had somehow come into possession of some lands to the north between the Bojana and Durazzo. This description is too vague and the lands included in this region overlap with those of too many other tribes and noblemen to make much sense. That same work then claims that the Matarangos seem to have accepted the suzerainty of the Serbian tsar for these northern lands, but it adds that in fact they were independent.

In the 1363–64 Balšić-Thopia war the Matarangos were allied to the

Balšići. One would expect the Balšići to be opposed to the Matarangos if, in fact, the Matarangos were trying to establish themselves in this northern region. Thus, if the Matarangos did indeed have both northern lands and an alliance with the Balšići, one might conclude they were clients or vassals of the Balšići for these lands. However, it makes more sense to see Matarango involvement in the war as resulting from a Matarango-Thopia quarrel to the south. This view is confirmed by the fact that the citizens of Durazzo supported the Thopias. Possibly Blaž Matarango had attempted to take that town and Karlo Thopia had gone to the defense of the Angevin city with which he was allied. In the spring of 1364 in the course of a skirmish Karlo Thopia took George Balšić prisoner and held him captive until 1366 when Dubrovnik mediated peace and procured his release. In 1367 Blaž Matarango died, and Karlo Thopia was able to occupy the bulk of his lands; one presumes this refers to the southern lands beyond the Shkumbi; a small portion of his lands seems to have been left to his son John.

After Blaž's death the Matarangos ceased to play a major role in the affairs of Albania. By the early 1370s the Matarango family has disappeared from the sources.

Some historians have claimed that the Balšići acquired most of the Matarango lands. This view is based on Orbini, who reports that the Matarangos' southern lands were seized by the Balšići after the Balšići had violated a safe-conduct given to Blaž and his son John and jailed them—the father dying in jail and the son being released only after seventeen years. However, the places Orbini claims the Balšići obtained in this way (Berat and Kanina) were not so acquired. Balša Balšić obtained these cities for his family as a dowry when he married John Comnenus Asen's daughter in 1372. And though the Matarangos had been active in the lands between Berat and Kanina, these cities seem never to have been theirs but had remained in the possession of John Comnenus Asen and his heirs. Orbini was obviously confused about these events; in fact he calls Balša's wife Kanina, which is the name of the fort. Thus he may well have attributed the acquisition of lands actually acquired by dowry to the seizure of the Matarangos. If there is any truth to Orbini's report that the Balšići seized the Matarangos, and if any land fell to them as a result, then we may assume the lands involved were the Matarangos' secondary, and presumably fairly small, holdings in the vicinity of the Bojana instead.

In 1368 the Balšići and Karlo Thopia seem to have been fighting again; at least in January of that year Dubrovnik reported that the three Balšić brothers were camped on the Mati River preparing for a campaign against Karlo Thopia, whose lands lay to the south of that river. If any fighting occurred, it was evidently on a small scale, since two months later Karlo's hands were sufficiently free for him to involve himself in the affairs of Durazzo. For in March 1368 Durazzo, which had long remained a lonely bastion of the Angevins, fell to Karlo Thopia. Possibly the capture had the consent of the citizens of Durazzo, who seem to have been recent allies of Karlo in his war against the Balšići and the Matarangos. Karlo entered into close relations with Venice, which granted him Venetian citizenship and called him "Prince of Albania." Soon, in either 1372 or, as most scholars believe, 1376, Karlo lost Durazzo to Louis of Evreux, whom we shall meet shortly; but Karlo was able to recover the city again in about 1383.

Civil War among the Serbs

Meanwhile inside Serbia a struggle erupted over the former lands of Vojislav Vojinović. His widow Gojislava and nephew Nicholas Altomanović were the main participants, but four others—Lazar Hrebljanović (whose rise began in this period), the Balšići, Vukašin, and Tvrtko of Bosnia—also got into the act.

The first figure to consider in this affair is Nicholas Altomanović. It is very difficult to present an accurate picture of his rights, motives, and ambitions. Since he eventually was to be the loser in the struggle, it is not surprising that he was portrayed as a villain; his reputation has not improved with time and he still tends to be depicted as ambitious, greedy, and unscrupulous. Nicholas was the son of Vojislav's brother Altoman. It is often stated that Altoman died in 1363, the same year that Vojislav did. However, the last reference we have to his being alive is from 1359. Scholars are now coming to believe his death occurred nearer to that date. His son Nicholas was in his middle teens at the time, and it seems that some or even most of Altoman's lands went to Altoman's brother Vojislav. Whether this was by a testament, whether Vojislav simply seized them for himself, or whether he was given control of them to preserve them from predation by others to turn over to Nicholas later is not known. And not knowing the conditions under which he acquired the land, we are ignorant of what his obligations toward his nephew were and whether he was making any effort to fulfill those obligations. In any case, Vojislav died and his widow inherited all his lands, including those that had once been Altoman's.

By the fall of 1367 Nicholas, entitled župan, was clearly in possession of his father's former main residence, the mining town of Rudnik. That year he attacked his aunt Gojislava and took much of her territory along the coast bordering on Dubrovnik, presumably including her part of Konavli. In 1368 Gojislava was still holding Trebinje. Soon thereafter she disappears from the sources,[3] and Nicholas is found holding Trebinje as well. Nicholas is usually depicted as an aggressor against his unfortunate aunt. This may well be an accurate description, but it does seem that prior to this warfare she was holding territory on the upper Drina and along the border of Zeta that had belonged to Altoman. Thus possibly Nicholas was fighting to regain his father's lands that Vojislav had taken and Gojislava had not wanted to return. Before long—if not from the start—Nicholas wanted her lands as well in order to re-create under his authority the major holding that Vojislav had ruled at the time of his death. And it appeared that he might well be able to do this. By the end of 1367 he not only had the coastal territory noted above but also the territory Vojislav had held along the borders of Zeta. However, Nicholas' activities in turn threw him into conflicts and diplomatic relations with a host of other Serbian nobles.

The first of these whom we must consider was Lazar Hrebljanović. His father, Pribac, had been a logothete (chancellor) for Dušan, and Lazar had held various court positions as well. Having married Milica, a lady descended from Nemanja's son Vukan of Zeta, Lazar had left the Serbian court after 1363 and retired to his lands on the Ibar, South Morava, and West Morava rivers. His main residence was at Kruševac. Some scholars have dated his departure from court to 1365 and associated it with Vukašin's coronation as king, an act they suggest Lazar opposed. However, we simply do not know whether he voluntarily departed or was forced to leave by Vukašin. Lazar had as a neighbor Nicholas Altomanović, the holder of Rudnik and Užice, who was probably not an easy neighbor to have.

However, if we can believe Orbini (writing in 1601), Lazar's dislike of Vukašin was stronger, and at first he allied with Nicholas against Vukašin. Their alliance probably dates from about 1369, in which year, if we can believe Orbini, Lazar and Nicholas, jealous of Vukašin, won Uroš over to their side against Vukašin. Confirming the possibility of a break between Uroš and Vukašin is the fact that at this time Vukašin was issuing state charters and carrying on negotiations with foreign powers entirely in his own name, without reference to Uroš. Furthermore there is a tradition in Dubrovnik, written down in 1403, that after Vojislav's widow died and Uroš resumed receiving the Saint Demetrius' Day tribute, Vukašin had sought it for himself; but Dubrovnik insisted on sending it to Uroš until his death, stating (in 1403), "when Uroš was in trouble, he lost all except the Dubrovnik tribute." Uroš' defection would have threatened Vukašin, for after all Uroš was the official source for Vukašin's royal power. Orbini then proceeds to report that the Raškan nobles Lazar, Altomanović, and Uroš clashed with Vukašin in battle at Kosovo in 1369. However, Lazar withdrew from the fighting at the start, leaving his allies to oppose Vukašin. Altomanović suffered a defeat while Uroš was captured and briefly imprisoned by Vukašin. Confirming this story— or at least Uroš' removal from office—is the fact that in 1370 Vukašin issued a charter to Dubrovnik with no mention of Uroš. That a new charter to the town was necessary—since there had been no quarrel between Dubrovnik and Serbia at the time—may indicate a change of administration, as it was customary for the town to procure a new charter of its commercial privileges each time there was a change on the Serbian throne.

Soon thereafter, in 1370, Lazar is found holding Altomanović's Rudnik. Presumably he obtained it after Nicholas' defeat at Kosovo. Lazar may have simply seized it from a weakened Nicholas, or, as has been suggested, he may have collected it from the victorious Vukašin as his price for remaining neutral in the battle. Interesting as Orbini's report is, we cannot pass judgment on its reliability, because we simply do not know what his source(s) for it is.

Nicholas' quarrels were not limited to those just described; he also started a row with Dubrovnik, something, when we consider the town's success in preserving records, that was not likely to help his reputation among posterity. With Gojislava's departure from her lands, as noted, Uroš resumed receiving the Saint Demetrius' Day tribute. In October 1367 Nicholas, since he held part of Vojislav's coastal lands, most probably including Konavli, demanded that Dubrovnik pay him this tribute. The town refused, claiming that it was Uroš' to dispose of and pointing out that it had been paid to Vojislav and then to his widow only because Uroš had so decreed it. Therefore the tribute was owed to the ruler of Serbia. Altomanović countered with the claim that the tribute was actually payment for the agricultural use Dubrovnik made of what was Serbian land along its borders. Thus the payment should be made to the actual holder of Trebinje and Konavli. And he argued that the custom of delivering the money to the Serbian ruler had arisen only because in former times the Serbian ruler had been the actual holder of these particular lands; however, since now the holder was a second figure, himself, the tribute was his by right. Dubrovnik ignored Nicholas' demands and sent the tribute to Uroš. However, it could expect trouble from Nicholas in the future. Its main cause for optimism was the fact that Nicholas had so many irons in the fire he might not have time or men to spare to attack the town.

The potential threat to the town increased when a second powerful neighbor, Sanko Miltenović-Draživojević, concluded an alliance with Nicholas, though once again the town could be thankful that other opponents had a higher priority for the new allies. Sanko was the leading noble of Hum, whose lands of Popovo Polje, Dabar (not to be confused with Dabar on the Lim), and Trusina bordered on Trebinje. In 1368 he revolted for a second time against his lord, Tvrtko of Bosnia. Needing allies to defend himself against Tvrtko, he concluded a pact with Nicholas. However, if the threat from Tvrtko should be dissipated, the town could expect trouble; for Nicholas surely had not offered his aid to Sanko for nothing, and a combination of Nicholas and Sanko would pit against the town the two most powerful military forces in the neighborhood. Dubrovnik could count only on the good relations it had frequently enjoyed with Sanko in the past, and it now exerted its full diplomatic talents to break his alliance with Nicholas and to mediate Sanko's differences with Tvrtko. The last task was difficult, for this was not Sanko's first defection from Bosnia. Furthermore, Sanko's defection had lost for Bosnia a great part of Hum. Not surprisingly Tvrtko was angry and was ready to join the Serbian opponents of Nicholas.

However, by 1370, because of Dubrovnik's efforts and/or the losses Nicholas took at Kosovo at the hands of Vukašin, Sanko had deserted Nicholas' cause and soon, if we can believe Orbini, was actually at war with Nicholas, taking some of Konavli from him. Thus, like Lazar, Sanko seems to have turned against his erstwhile ally when he was down in order to grab territory from him. We last hear of Sanko alive in mid-1370. He was clearly dead by 1372. According to Orbini, Sanko was killed in battle near Trebinje by some Trebinje hillsmen who seem to have been supporters of Nicholas. In any case in 1371 Nicholas again held Konavli. However, despite the fact that before his death Sanko broke with Nicholas and again submitted to Tvrtko, Tvrtko remained allied against Nicholas.

Nicholas, meanwhile, forced to fight over Konavli and thus concentrate his attention on the region around Dubrovnik, became more and more hostile toward the town. In 1370 when Dubrovnik once again refused him the tribute he demanded, he ravaged the outskirts of the town. Dubrovnik had to re-route its caravans destined for Serbia through the Balšići's lands.

Meanwhile in 1368, hoping to acquire suzerainty over the town, the Balšići had gone to war against Kotor, which, as a result of the warfare of the 1360s, had been suffering economic decline. The town realized that submission to the Balšići would do nothing to help it economically. And seeing that Bar's tribute of one hundred perpera under Serbia had gone up to two thousand ducats under the Balšići and expecting the same fate for itself, Kotor resisted. The town first sought an alliance with Nicholas, but after his loss at Kosovo he could provide little aid. So Kotor sought help from Uroš and from Venice. Neither of them provided any serious help. Venice, in fact, seemed only concerned that no warships other than its own be on the Adriatic. It wrote Uroš in 1368, objecting to Serbia's having armed ships in the Adriatic— citing Bar, Budva, and Ulcinj as having them—in violation of a Venetian-Serbian treaty, and threatened to treat such ships as pirate vessels. Uroš replied that the ships about which Venice complained were George Balšić's ships, which, if the ships were from the towns mentioned, would have been true. Clearly unhappy with George's actions (which presumably were directed against Kotor, a town under Uroš' suzerainty), Uroš called George a rebel. And he concluded that, since George was a rebel, the Serbian court bore no responsibility for any of his actions that might violate the treaty. Since Vukašin, at least previously, had been a strong supporter of George, did Uroš' letter reflect a change in Vukašin's position? Or did Uroš' reply reflect his own personal view, as distinct from Vukašin's, and indicate an attempt to oppose Vukašin, possibly as part of a policy to extricate himself from his tutelage? Or did Uroš' remarks have no significance as far as Serbian court policy was concerned but merely offered a plausible excuse for Serbia not to involve itself in a quarrel between Venice and George?

In 1369 George laid siege to Kotor. Not receiving any help from its suzerain Uroš, Kotor now turned to Hungary and recognized Hungarian suzerainty. This submission was probably ratified in 1370. The Hungarians sent a nobleman from Zadar to be Kotor's prince. If we stop to consider how small the Hungarian presence was in southern Dalmatia and thus how unlikely it was that Hungary might provide effective help to Kotor, we must conclude that Kotor's turning and submitting to Hungary made little sense. Not only did it bring the town no benefits, but it simply increased Kotor's difficulties. First, it meant that Kotor lost for a time its trade privileges in Serbia, thus causing it further economic decline. Second, it provided, in the name of Serbian rights, an excuse for Nicholas Altomanović, who until then had been sympathetic to

Kotor, to attack Kotor, which he did in 1370. By spring 1370, probably through Venetian mediation, George Balšić had made peace with Kotor. In fact by 1371 he was lined up on Vukašin's and Kotor's side against Altomanović, for in June 1371 George announced to Dubrovnik that Vukašin and his son Marko, with their armies, were in Skadar with George, together preparing to attack Altomanović. Since their efforts, he claimed, were in Dubrovnik's interests, he hoped Dubrovnik would assist their campaign by providing ships to transport men and supplies. Dubrovnik agreed to provide this assistance.

The campaign never took place, because Vukašin and Marko were then called east to participate in Uglješa's campaign against the Turks, which culminated in the disaster at Marica. The departure of Vukašin did not free Altomanović of enemies. Nicholas now found himself faced with a very real threat from Tvrtko and Lazar. Desperate for a strong ally, Altomanović opened negotiations with George Balšić. Most scholars feel that at the end of these discussions George concluded an agreement by which he acquired Dračevica, Konavli, and Trebinje from Nicholas. It is not certain whether George received this territory for promising support—support which in fact he was not to provide—or whether he received it simply as a bribe to remain neutral, which is what in fact he did. Other scholars, including Mihaljčić, follow Orbini's account and argue that George concluded no such agreement but simply seized these coastal territories after Altomanović was defeated and captured by Lazar in 1373.

But if we pause and look at the Serbia that was about to stand up to the Turks at Marica in 1371, we find it a far cry from the state Dušan had left at his death. Thessaly, Epirus, and Albania had seceded from Serbia entirely. Nicholas Altomanović had for all practical purposes made himself independent in Rudnik and in the lands that had belonged to his uncle Vojislav. The sons of the now deceased Branko Mladenović, headed by Vuk Branković, in Macedonia, the Balšići in Zeta, and Lazar Hrebljanović in northern Serbia, though nominally under Uroš' suzerainty, were all autonomous lords of their lands and involved themselves little with state affairs or with the policy and concerns of those at court. This is well illustrated by the fact that all these vassal lords were conspicuous by their absence at Marica. When the crunch came and the Serbian court decided it was imperative to stand up to the Turks, only Vukašin and Uglješa, who of course made that decision, took part in the campaign. And the court of Tsar Uroš, which Vukašin represented, no longer had the power to compel these others to come.

The Turkish Threat and Uglješa's Response to It

A far more serious problem for Serbia—and the whole Balkans—than these internal squabbles, however, was the appearance in Europe of the Ottoman Turks followed by their penetration into Thrace. In 1354, as noted, they acquired Gallipoli on the European side of the Dardanelles. From there they, or Turkish bands loyal to them, expanded into Thrace, taking Demotika from the Byzantines in 1360 or 1361, Philippopolis from the Bulgarians in 1363, and finally the major city of Adrianople in 1369. By 1370 Turks had occupied most of Thrace to the Rhodopes and to the Balkan Mountains. As they reached the Rhodopes they collided with Uglješa, who had extended his realm beyond the Mesta into this territory. Thus Uglješa found his lands bordering on those of the Ottomans (or various Turkish march lords associated with the Ottomans in a variety of differing client/vassal relationships). There were no fixed frontiers, and the Turks moved about as they pleased, penetrating to raid or graze their flocks in territory nominally Uglješa's. And in much of the land beyond his border the Turks were not in actual occupation; they had simply swept through it, plundering and receiving promises of tribute from the inhabitants they had not taken off as captives. But throughout the 1360s the number of Turks entering Thrace and plundering beyond it into the Rhodopes and into Bulgaria increased; thus the Turkish threat to the Balkans, and in particular to Bulgaria and to the Serres state of Uglješa whose borders they had now reached, had become extremely serious.

Uglješa well realized the seriousness of the danger and set about trying to create a grand coalition against the Turks. For he realized that it was necessary to go on the offensive and drive them out of Europe rather than wait and try to defend fixed fortresses. To obtain Byzantine support he tried to improve relations with the Byzantine Church, which had excommunicated the Serbs in 1350. However, though embassies were exchanged between the Byzantines and Serbs, the schism between the Serbian Church (headed by its patriarch in Peć) and the Patriarch of Constantinople was not healed. In 1363 Patriarch Kallistos, accused in Serbian sources of being the patriarch who had excommunicated the Serbs, visited Serbia. Discussions seem to have been congenial; but Kallistos took sick and died in Serbia, and negotiations were not resumed. However, though the Serbian Church as a whole remained in schism, Uglješa did succeed in ending the Church schism between the Greek Church and the Church in his own lands. He apologized for past Serbian actions, and the Patriarch of Constantinople proclaimed an end to their schism in 1368. Uglješa agreed to restore the Metropolitan of Drama and its suffragans to the jurisdiction of Constantinople. And the patriarch agreed not to remove from their positions those Serbs then holding Church offices in the transferred diocese. However, Uglješa refused to restore the Metropolitanate of Serres to Constantinople, and thus it remained Serbian, in theory under the Patriarch of Peć, but surely in reality under the personal authority of Uglješa.

Uglješa's general good will toward the empire and his ecclesiastical submission, however, were not sufficient inducements to bring the Byzantines into an active alliance against the Turks. The Bulgarians were not to participate either. The Hungarians accused the Bulgarians of treachery on the occasion of the 1371 conflict. This is probably unwarranted. John Alexander had died in February and his successor John Šišman, at war with his brother who was trying to oust him, had not yet had a chance to consolidate his authority in

Bulgaria. Thus he was not in a position to undertake a foreign adventure, particularly one which, if it failed, could well cause the Turks to direct a major assault on Bulgaria. In fact some scholars believe that immediately after John Alexander's death the Turks had exerted considerable pressure, possibly threatening an actual attack on Bulgaria, upon the new ruler, who was therefore doing everything he could to appease them. Thus, under the circumstances it probably is not surprising that Bulgaria did not join Uglješa's coalition.

So, when he was ready for action in 1371, Uglješa had enrolled in his coalition only his brother Vukašin. The leading Serbian nobles were independent enough to avoid having to participate and either failed to realize the extent of the Turkish danger or feared to leave their own regions lest hostile neighbors seize their lands. Some may have wondered what Altomanović might grab in their absence, and the Balšići may well have feared that Karlo Thopia would attack Zeta should they take their armies away. Furthermore, from jealousy or other reasons, many nobles seem to have disliked Vukašin. Thus some may not have wanted to participate in a coalition with him, and some may even have looked forward to possible gains for themselves should the crusade fail and Vukašin either not return or return with only a small remnant of his forces.

The Battle of Marica and its Aftermath

The offensive against the Turks was originally scheduled for early 1371, but for some reason it was delayed. Possibly Uglješa had been expecting Bulgarian participation and then, having his plans overturned by the death of John Alexander, postponed the attack to await Bulgarian developments in the hope that John Šišman would establish himself in power and provide some forces. Since the campaign was delayed, Vukašin and his son Marko in the summer of 1371 marched west to Zeta to join the Balšići in a planned coalition against Nicholas Altomanović. They were all together in Skadar preparing for action, when Uglješa summoned Vukašin and Marko. The two hurried east with their forces, joining up with Uglješa and his army, and then together they easily penetrated into what was supposedly Turkish territory; their easy advance shows that the Rhodope–western Thrace region was not yet efficiently administered or incorporated into any sort of Ottoman state. Their armies, which were large but probably nowhere near the sixty thousand claimed by the monk Isaiah, reached Černomen on the Marica River. There on 26 September 1371 they met the Turkish forces. The Serbian armies were annihilated, and both Uglješa and Vukašin were killed. A later source, Chalcocondyles, blames the Serbian defeat on the Serbs' not having their horses and weapons in readiness and allowing themselves to be surprised.

The Battle on the Marica was the Ottomans' greatest success to that time and was far more significant in opening up the Balkans to the Turks and in weakening Serbian resistance than the more famous Battle of Kosovo (1389).

Owing to its vast losses at Marica and the increasing separatism that followed it, Serbia became ripe for the picking. Uglješa's territory was thereafter lost to Serbia, and in Serbia proper the various regions—the south, the west, and the north—became increasingly independent. Thus Serbia ended up being reduced to half of what it had been before the battle. Uroš had not gone to the battle, but he died childless in December 1371, ending the Nemanjić dynasty on the male side. The only Nemanjić left alive was Symeon's religious son John Uroš in Thessaly, who was about to become a monk and who left no sons. No subsequent ruler of Serbia bore the title tsar. (Lazar, though called "tsar" in the epics, was actually entitled prince.) Vukašin's son Marko, who survived the battle, had already been crowned "young king" and after Vukašin's death was crowned king. However, he was neither from the recognized—Nemanjić—dynasty nor more powerful than the other leading nobles. Thus he could not assert his authority over Uroš' state. In fact, after Marica the Brankovići (the sons of Branko Mladenović) and the Balšići (until then friendly to the Mrnjavčević family) seized part of Marko's family's holdings. Marko, who had suffered heavy manpower losses at Marica, was in no position to resist these neighbors who, in sitting out the battle, had kept their forces intact.

Marko's troubles began right after the battle. George Balšić expelled his wife Olivera (Marko's sister) and immediately, still in 1371, took Prizren from Marko. At about the same time Lazar grabbed Priština. The Balšići gained Peć, probably in 1372, and thus Marko found himself stripped of most of his Kosovo holdings. Then in the course of the 1370s he found himself being pushed out of both eastern and western Macedonia. By 1377 Vuk Branković had Skopje and an Albanian named Andrew Gropa had Ohrid. It is possible, however, that Gropa was a vassal of Marko. However, Andrew Musachi, who was based in east-central Albania and took Kastoria from Marko, was clearly no vassal of his. As a result of the significant territorial losses Marko suffered, his ability to raise new armies (to replace the forces lost at Marica) was severely reduced. Thus he found himself in no position to assert his kingship over Serbia; in fact, weaker than the Balšići, Lazar, and probably by the end of the decade the Brankovići, it was all he could do to maintain his reduced principality around Prilep in central Macedonia. However, despite his unfortunate career, Marko has gone down in history, as a result of his role in the epics, as Serbia's epic hero par excellence. The Serbian epics call him Kraljević—the king's son. The title is incorrect, for he actually was crowned king, a fact reflected accurately in the Bulgarian and Macedonian epics, which call him Krali (King) Marko.

Since no figure of national unity existed, separatism increased, thus further reducing Serbian unity and potential resistance to the Turks. The Battle of Marica contributed to the ease with which the remainder of Serbia fell apart; for the central government (such as it was) lost the bulk of its forces at Marica, while the nobles who had not gone retained their forces unimpaired. Thus not only were they stronger than King Marko and able to grab his personal holdings, but they were also stronger than he was in his capacity as king and able to resist any attempts he might make to reassert a central Serbian authority. Free to ignore any orders or tax demands he might issue, they made it impossible for him or anyone else to think of restoring the Serbian state even to the strength and size it had maintained under Uroš and Vukašin. Thus the great nobles (Lazar, the Balšići, Altomanović, Vuk Branković) established their own separate states, each having its own individual interests. These nobles recognized no subordination to any central authority, as is reflected, for example, in Balšić charters: in 1379 Balša II Balšić wrote, "I, Lord Balša by the Grace of God," and in 1386 George II Balšić was calling himself "autocratic Lord George." Hostile to one another and involved in enriching themselves at the expense of their neighbors, the nobles were blind to the ever increasing seriousness of the Ottoman danger and unwilling to co-operate against it. And as they skirmished and fought among themselves, further manpower, sorely needed to resist the Turks, was lost.

After the Marica battle the territory held by Uglješa, who had no heirs, was grabbed by others; a good portion of it lost all connection with Serbia or Serbs. The Ottomans themselves acquired very little of it, probably taking little more than his lands east of the Mesta. Manuel Palaeologus, the son of Emperor John V and the Byzantine governor of Thessaloniki, recovered Serres (by November 1371) and the Chalcidic peninsula with Mount Athos for the empire. Most, or even all, of Manuel's acquisitions were added by John V to Manuel's governorship. Soon thereafter, in late 1371 or 1372, the Greeks beat off an Ottoman attack against Mount Athos. The region further up from the coast between the Vardar and Struma rivers (including Velbužd, Štip, and Strumica) more or less seceded from Serbian rule under two noblemen, Despot John and Constantine Dragaš, whose main seat was Kumanovo. They were the sons of a certain Dejan, who had married Dušan's sister Theodora and had received from his brother-in-law the title sevastocrator. As supporters of the Mrnjavčevići, the family had built up a strong holding during Vukašin's rule. It included a large part of John Oliver's former lands. Dejan had not held Strumica and Štip, so it seems that his sons acquired these cities and much of the surrounding area by moving in and filling the vacuum left by Uglješa's death immediately after the Battle of Marica. These two cities became their main residences in the late 1370s. The brothers seem to have managed their holdings jointly. John is last heard of in 1378; he probably died at about that time. His entire share went to his brother Constantine. Constantine continued to increase his holdings and by 1380 had acquired Vranje.

Vukašin's "state" also broke up. As his "state" we must include (1) his personal lands, which were left to Marko (their fate, resulting in Marko's being left with only a small holding in central Macedonia, was traced above) and (2) the royal/imperial lands of Uroš, which presumably had been managed by King Vukašin. Uroš died without an heir; the fate of these royal lands must have had an impact on the future of a Serbian kingdom, for they could have provided a core of support (income and men) for a would-be holder of the state against the separatists. Unfortunately, we do not know which lands Uroš still directly held in 1371 and which had fallen under Vukašin's control. Vukašin almost certainly had relieved Uroš of various lands in the region of Kosovo-Metohija. Marko, as noted, was not able to retain these; the Balšići grabbed some at once, but in the long run the Brankovići were to get the lion's share. The history of the royal/imperial lands in central Serbia is more of a puzzle. But regardless of what lands Vukašin may or may not have taken from Uroš in that region, Marko did not end up with them. And though Nicholas Altomanović may have briefly picked off some of them after the Battle of Marica, Prince Lazar, as we shall see, was to end up with the major part of these. Thus Marko, the would-be king, ended up with little or none of the royal/imperial lands and no territory in the center of his would-be kingdom. This deficiency made his task almost impossible. Pushed to the fringes of the kingdom and supported only by his reduced personal holding, Marko, less powerful than some of the great nobles, was in no position to turn his title into a reality. And so King Marko, unrecognized by the rest of the nobility, became a petty prince in Macedonia who watched his principality shrink through the 1370s as his neighbors wrested away a large portion of his cities. In fact, it seems that he even had to share the little territory he retained with his brother Andrew (Andrejaš). That Andrew received his own holding is suggested by the fact that he issued his own coins. And as the royal authority disappeared, the royal lands were grabbed by others, and much of Serbia's territory seceded under local lords who made themselves independent of any central authority. Serbia ceased to be a state.

Besides the separatism and the weakening of Serbian resistance following the battle, Marica led to the acceptance of Ottoman suzerainty by Marko and the Dejanovići (probably both in 1371), the Byzantine Empire (by 1373), and Bulgaria (probably in 1376). This submission meant that all these vassals owed tribute to the Ottomans and also were obliged to supply troops for Ottoman campaigns, commanded by a member of the ruling family, often the heir to the throne in the case of states and the family head in the case of the noblemen vassals.

Activities of the Independent Serbian Nobles

After the Battle of Marica the Balšići of Zeta marched east, where they clashed successfully with Marko, taking Prizren from him immediately after the battle and Peć, probably in 1372. Altomanović, whose ambitions also included the Kosovo region, was not pleased by the Balšići's success. He attacked, but failed to take, Prizren in 1372; soon, probably in the spring of 1373 (but in any case before the major warfare of 1373), Nicholas made peace with George Balšić.

Prizren, the object of all this interest, was one of Serbia's major trade centers where there were resident many Serbian merchants as well as traders from the coast. Dubrovnik's consul for all of Serbia resided there. In the years after 1371 Prizren began to decline to some extent, for now it was part of a smaller principality and separated from the major mines, which no longer lay under the same ruler as the town. After 1371 merchant colonies at individual mines, like Novo Brdo, grew in size and importance, and much of the trade between the mining centers and the coast was carried on directly rather than being filtered through Prizren. Under the autonomous rulers of the different small units, the production of the mines increased; whether this was owing to a greater interest in the mines on the part of the more local rulers or to technological improvements is not known. However, Dubrovnik's profits from this increased production were reduced as individual noblemen set up many new customs and toll stations in their own lands. In former days the Kings/Tsars of Serbia had issued orders prohibiting the establishment of most new toll stations. Now, there was no one to issue such orders. Thus Dubrovnik found the existence of many small principalities, each with its own customs regime, harder on its profits than the single state regime that had existed under Dušan.

The tendency to create small principalities was not limited to the nobility. The patriarchs in Peć treated that region and their far-flung estates as their own domain, by 1390 even coining their own money. Indeed, in the period after Marica many of the leading Serbian nobles began minting money. Vuk Branković even allowed his vassals to coin money, whereas Lazar did not allow the nobility living in the lands he directly held to do so. When they belonged to Vuk certain towns, like Prizren and Skopje, also issued coins.

The Balšići, having expanded into the Kosovo region, soon clashed with the Brankovići, a family that had begun its rapid rise after Marica. Under Dušan, this family's founder Mladen had been the tsar's deputy in Ohrid. His son Branko Mladenović had ruled a principality centered in western Macedonia, probably still including Ohrid; from there he had acquired further lands toward and into the Kosovo, including the region of Drenica. Under Vukašin, Branko's heir Vuk Branković lost Ohrid and found his possessions reduced to a small holding around Drenica. What else, if anything, Vuk then held is not known. However, after Marica, taking advantage of Marko's weakness, Vuk began rapidly to expand his authority over much of Kosovo and Macedonia. By 1376/77 Vuk had acquired Skopje and Priština (which right after Marica seems to have been grabbed briefly by Lazar). After the death of George Balšić in January 1379, Vuk acquired Prizren.

The Balšići, in addition to pressing east into the Kosovo, remained active on the coast, where they acquired all the territory between (but not including) Kotor and the Mati River. In 1372 they acquired Valona, Kanina, Berat, and Himara as the dowry of John Comnenus Asen's daughter when she married Balša Balšić. This soon led to further fighting in Albania with the Thopia family, whose lands lay between the Balšići's Zeta and their newly acquired Albanian possessions. Old rivals of the Balšići, the Thopia were not happy to see them acquire more territory in Albania.

The Thopias were then in a major struggle over Durazzo, which, according to a recent calculation, underwent a total of thirty-two changes of lordship between 992 and 1392. Karlo Thopia had taken Durazzo, quite possibly with the consent of its citizens, from the Angevins in 1368. Shortly thereafter Louis of Evreux, brother of King Charles XII of Navarre, had married an Angevin, Joanna, the granddaughter of John of Gravina. John had received title to Albania from Catherine of Valois when he turned Achaea over to her. Joanna had inherited these so-called rights to Albania through John. Interested in realizing these rights, Louis hired four companies of knights from Navarre, who are usually referred to as the Navarrese Company, and took Durazzo, probably in 1376. Shortly thereafter Louis died, probably still in 1376.[4] The company remained in Durazzo, bored. Louis' widow soon thereafter (probably in late 1377) remarried; since the knights had been in Louis' personal service, they regarded their contract as terminated and left Albania for adventures elsewhere. We shall soon meet some of these Navarrese in the Morea. The Angevins retained Durazzo for a time, for in 1379 Joanna's new husband, Robert of Artois, is found issuing to Dubrovnik a charter pertaining to Durazzo. Karlo Thopia, who held the territory both north and south of the city, soon, probably in 1383, regained possession of Durazzo.

The End of Nicholas Altomanović

As noted earlier, Lazar of Kruševac and Tvrtko of Bosnia formed an alliance against Nicholas Altomanović. The alliance seems to have been in effect in 1371; in any case it clearly existed in 1372. Faced with this threat, Nicholas Altomanović opened negotiations with George Balšić. It is not certain whether George promised Nicholas aid or simply neutrality, but in either case the promise seems to have been expensive and Nicholas probably had to turn over to Balšić his territory near the coast, including Dračevica, Konavli, and Trebinje.

Venice seems to have mediated this agreement. It expressed its willingness to see George get Durazzo and Kotor (the last town, of course, was under the suzerainty of its enemy, Hungary) and Nicholas, the nominal Prince of Hum, acquire Hum's coastal lands, the Pelješac peninsula with Ston, from Dubrovnik. Venice also seems to have hoped that the two noblemen would attack Dubrovnik. This information, which may not be accurate, comes from Dubrovnik. It is worth noting that these plans are not mentioned in any document preserved in the Venetian archive. Worried, Dubrovnik complained to its suzerain Hungary, which seems to have issued a warning to the two would-be allies. Orbini, who accepts the Ragusan version of the affair, says the Hungarian king threatened to attack the two noblemen. This warning seems to have ended the alliance, and no attack on Dubrovnik occurred. And in November 1373 George Balšić personally visited Dubrovnik, assuring the town (by oath, in fact) of his friendship. As a result Dubrovnik agreed to pay him the Saint Demetrius' Day tribute, which the year before, after Uroš' death, the town had finally agreed to pay, and in fact had paid in 1372, to Altomanović. There was no reason for the town not to have yielded on this issue; after all, Uroš was now dead, and there was no longer a Serbian tsar; and though Marko was a king by name, in fact he was just a petty prince in Macedonia. Thus the town might as well pay the tribute to the actual holder of the Serbian territory on its borders where it exercised its privileges. That Dubrovnik paid it to George in November 1373 shows that by then he was in possession of Dračevica, Konavli, and Trebinje. In the agreement Dubrovnik stated it would pay George this tribute as long as he held these lands and as long as Serbia had no tsar. George was to receive this tribute until 1378.

By November 1373, when George paid his visit to Dubrovnik, Nicholas Altomanović had been defeated. According to Orbini, Nicholas, upon regaining Rudnik after Marica, tried to have Lazar murdered but failed. If Nicholas really did try this, his motive may have been anger at Lazar's desertion at Kosovo (1369) and his seizure of Rudnik from the defeated Nicholas after the battle. Worried about Nicholas, Lazar established closer ties with Hungary, which was already hostile to Nicholas, and accepted Hungarian suzerainty. Then in 1373 Lazar and Tvrtko attacked Nicholas' lands from two sides, ravaging them. One may doubt the motives for Lazar's attack given by Orbini, for it seems to have been planned before Nicholas' alleged plot to murder Lazar. According to Orbini the Hungarians also contributed to the effort a cavalry of a thousand men under Nicholas Garai (Gorjanski), the Ban of Srem. Caught between these two powerful opponents, Altomanović, according to Orbini, retreated toward the coast. Finding little support in that direction, he doubled back and shut himself up in his fortress of Užice. Lazar's troops besieged him and eventually, still in 1373, forced him to surrender. According to Orbini, Lazar then handed him over to some nobles under the command of Stefan Mušić. They were supposed to be responsible for guarding him. However, hating Altomanović, they blinded him. He entered a monastery and soon disappears from history. According to Orbini, Mušić, who we know was a leading servitor of Lazar, had the secret permission of Lazar to carry out the blinding.

Orbini seems to have been relying mainly on a source written with the intention of clearing Lazar of any wrong-doing; this source depicted Lazar's attack on Nicholas as a response to Nicholas' attempt to murder him and then placed the responsibility for the blinding of Nicholas on subordinates. Orbini deserves credit for seeing through the tradition of hero-worship of Lazar and accepting a second report that admitted Lazar did order Nicholas' blinding.

Nicholas' lands were divided among the victors in the fall of 1373. Tvrtko obtained his western lands, the upper Drina, and the Lim region, with Prijepolje and the monastery of Mileševo which housed the relics of Saint Sava. He also seems to have acquired the districts of Onogošt (Nikšić) and

Gacko. Lazar took Altomanović's eastern lands, including Užice and the rich mining town of Rudnik. Vuk Branković picked up Sjenica and Zvečan, although it is not known whether he received them for participating in the alliance (about which we know nothing) or gained them by land-grabbing after Nicholas' defeat. And the Balšići, as noted, acquired some of Altomanović's territory near the coast. George Balšić had remained on the sidelines during the war. His only possible action would have followed Nicholas' defeat when, according to Orbini, he occupied Nicholas' coastal lands. Other scholars, however, as noted, believe George had received these from Nicholas by agreement prior to the warfare. Tvrtko was to obtain this coastal land in 1377 after some local nobles revolted against the Balšići and submitted to Tvrtko. And from about 1379, when Dubrovnik recognized that his possession was secure, the town paid Tvrtko the Saint Demetrius' Day tribute. In 1377 Tvrtko, descended from Nemanja through his grandmother (Dragutin's daughter), was crowned King of Serbia and Bosnia at Mileševo by its metropolitan; his kingship rights were derived from Serbia's. Despite his title, he never obtained a role in Serbia or ever tried to obtain such a role; and no Serbian nobleman outside of Tvrtko's realm regarded him as an overlord.

As a result of Marica and the defeat of Altomanović, three families made rapid advances in the early 1370s, both in asserting their independence and in expanding their territories: the Brankovići, the Balšići, and Lazar. We shall turn to the Brankovići later, but it makes sense here to pause and regard the other two.

The Balšići had come to hold a massive territory, larger than the early medieval Kingdom of Duklja; their lands stretched from Peć and Prizren in the Kosovo to the coast, where they extended from the Gulf of Kotor (without Kotor itself)—and briefly between 1373 and 1377 beyond this gulf north to the borders of Dubrovnik's territory—south to the Mati River. Holding most of what is now Montenegro and part of Albania, the family acquired through Balša's marriage the region of Berat and Valona in Albania's south. Though Balša clearly had these towns, it is not certain that he had much of their hinterland in which, we know, various tribes were active. Though the possibility cannot be ruled out that some tribes submitted to him, no documentation of such submissions exists.

In 1373 Stracimir, the eldest Balšić brother, died; however, George, the second brother, had long been the major figure in the family. George now shared power with the third and youngest brother, Balša II, and Stracimir's son George II. Though they held their territory as a family collective, it seems each also held within the larger territory an individual holding; for in a 1373 charter issued to Dubrovnik George promised he would not establish new customs stations "in my lands or [in] those of my brother Balša or in those of my nephew George." This suggests that each of these individuals had an individual appanage. Balša's lands probably were those he received as a dowry in 1372, south of Durazzo.

Lazar's Principality

Lazar, who now emerges as a major figure, took Altomanović's eastern lands, including Užice and the rich mining town of Rudnik. Since Lazar also held Novo Brdo, which he seems to have seized right after the Battle of Marica, Lazar held the richest mines in Serbia. They gave him the wealth that made it possible for him to become the major lord in Serbia. He also built up a power base from the local lesser nobility by being very generous with land grants to them. His becoming a Hungarian vassal during the war against Altomanović also made possible his expansion to the north. He actively campaigned in this area and clearly was not opposed by the Hungarians. Having consolidated his control along the Morava, he soon reached the Danube. There he held Mačva, which had probably been granted to him by King Louis when he became a Hungarian vassal. His possession of Mačva—or at least part of it—is seen in a grant made by Lazar in 1381 to his Ravanica monastery, which mentions a number of villages in Mačva. In 1379 he defeated the Rastislalići and acquired their holdings, including Braničevo and Kučevo. Orbini, making a general statement about Lazar's northward expansion, says that in acquiring this land Lazar jailed some of the local nobles, expelled others, and forced still others to submit to him. By 1382, when King Louis died, Lazar had become strong enough to shed his vassalage. That year he tried, but failed, to take Golubac and Beograd, two major fortresses on the Danube, from the Hungarians.

Lazar also benefited because his territory, of all the Serbian lands, lay furthest from Turkish centers. This spared his lands from the ravages of the Turks until the mid-1380s and also attracted to his region immigrants from Turkish-threatened areas. Thus he gained manpower both to work the land and to serve as soldiers. These migrations, the Turkish threat, and the Turkish suzerainty imposed on various Serbs to the south, combined with the fact that Lazar had become Serbia's strongest prince, had the effect of placing the center of Serbia considerably to the north of where it had been before.

Lazar built a large number of churches including the famous Monastery Ravanica, granted the Church much land, and helped, by building churches and encouraging missionary work, to spread Christianity in the northern regions, where, except for certain towns on the Danube, little evidence of earlier Christian penetration exists.

In 1375 Lazar negotiated peace with the Constantinopolitan patriarch by renouncing the right of the Serbs to hold the imperial title (of tsar or emperor); in return he received Byzantine recognition for the Serbian patriarch's title and also confirmation of the Serbian Church's autocephalous status. As we saw earlier, being autocephalous meant that the Serbian Church both managed its own affairs and also chose without reference to Constantinople its own patriarch and hierarchy. Lazar also promised that should the Serbs occupy Greek lands in the future, the Serbs would not expel bishops appointed by the Patriarch of Constantinople. The call for this settlement was initiated by a delegation to Lazar of Serbian monks from Athos who were upset by the frequent quarrels between Greeks and Serbs on Athos. Lazar delayed acting on this request until after the death of Patriarch Sava (1354–75), which occurred early in 1375. This delay suggests that Sava had been opposed to discussions with Constantinople; possibly he feared losing his title, or perhaps, since he had held the office from the time of Dušan, he was a hard-liner who opposed any compromise with the Byzantines, be it in Church or state questions. Upon Sava's death Lazar sent a Serb monk named Isaiah and a Greek cleric as delegates to Constantinople, where they worked out the compromise described above.

A council was then held at Prizren (or possibly Peć), attended also by a delegation from the Patriarch of Constantinople, that announced the settlement and installed Serbia's new patriarch, Jefrem, with the blessing of the Byzantine Church. George Balšić, who then held Prizren (and Peć too), played an active role at the council even though he had by now become a Catholic. That the council was held in Prizren (or in nearby Peć) and not in Lazar's lands seems odd. The explanation may be simple; since Peć was the seat of the patriarch, it may have been considered proper to hold the council near, if not at, the Church's capital. However, one senses an undercurrent of opposition to Lazar at this moment. Possibly Sava had been a hard-liner who had had considerable support among the clergy; if so, perhaps his followers saw Lazar as soft and too willing to compromise. In this case, a strong Church faction may well have opposed having the council in Lazar's principality, where Lazar might have been able to exert more influence, and thus have insisted that the council be held in a city in Kosovo, where the Church had its centers and where many of the great Serbian monasteries were located. There may also have been differences over who the new patriarch was to be. If there was opposition to Lazar's choice, as seems likely from evidence we shall examine in a moment, then it also made sense to hold the council in a more neutral location.

Jefrem, who was elected, was a Bulgarian of retiring, mystical disposition. He did not long remain in office. When George Balšić died in 1379, Jefrem left office. The *Life of Jefrem* states this was at his own request, for he wanted solitude to meditate. However, many scholars believe that he was George's candidate, whom Lazar disliked for some reason and ousted upon the death of his patron. This supposition is confirmed by the fact that after Lazar died (and upon the death of Jefrem's successor, Spiridon) Jefrem returned as patriarch. His *Life* says the Serbian bishops at that time could not agree on a new patriarch, so they decided to invite him back.

Jefrem's *Life*, unlike those of many Serbian Church figures, takes a strong pan-Orthodox rather than pro-Serb position. In so doing, it condemns Dušan's coronation, seeing that act as a usurpation and also an evil because it broke the unity of the Orthodox Church. This position was to be taken frequently in works written by Serbian monks in the fifteenth century, some of whose authors saw the immediate decline of the state after Dušan's death and the Turkish successes that followed as divine punishment for Dušan's pride and usurpation. The *Life of Jefrem* also glorifies, far more strongly than most Serbian works, the monastic life that exerted such a strong attraction—far stronger than holding an episcopal position—upon the Jefrem it depicts.

Regardless of undercurrents of suspicion possibly felt by some clerics toward Lazar, Lazar emerged with the good will of the Church and even its strong appreciation. After all, he had brought about an end to the schism with Constantinople and gained recognition of the position of the Serbian Church from the Byzantines. He also, as noted, did many other services for the Church in the way of land grants, church building, and support of missionaries. Thus the Church soon came to support Lazar strongly and in ca. 1378 gave him a Church coronation as prince. He was crowned with the title "Lord of the Serbs and the Danube, Stefan [the Serbian royal name] Prince Lazar, autocrat of all the Serbs." Though he did not call himself king or tsar, his title bore all the other elements to suggest that he saw himself as a successor to, and continuer of, the Nemanjić state.

Lazar's strength was increased also through the marriage alliances he contracted for his four daughters: (1) Mara in 1365/66 married Vuk Branković. (2) Helen (Jelena) married George II Stracimirović Balšić in 1386/87. The son of Stracimir Balšić, he succeeded Balša II as ruler of Zeta in 1385, ruling it to 1403. (3) Theodora in 1387/88 married Nicholas Garai, a powerful Hungarian count who was active in Balkan affairs. (4) His fourth daughter married Alexander, the son of John Šišman, Tsar of Bulgaria. By 1386, after Helen's marriage to George II, the two major Serbian lords beyond his borders, both of whom now were his sons-in-law (Vuk Branković and George II Balšić), had come to recognize Lazar's suzerainty. For example, one of Vuk's charters from 1387 refers to Lazar as his lord (gospodin); moreover, Vuk had previously added Lazar's name to his coins, which was a sign of submission. Suggesting George's submission is the fact that in 1387 or 1388, right after George's marrige to Helen, Lazar added "and the Coast" to his title.

The Balšići in the 1370s and 1380s

Lazar's position was also helped by the decline of the Balšići at the end of the 1370s. George I died in 1379. (Until recently scholars had dated his death to 1378.) His death freed Tvrtko of worry about counter-attacks from George and secured Bosnia's possession of what had been the Balšić territories bordering on Dubrovnik, annexed by Tvrtko in 1377. In fact at George's death Tvrtko had taken the remainder of Balšić coastal land between the Gulf of Kotor and the lands Tvrtko had taken in 1377. Vuk Branković quickly sent his forces into Kosovo and seized Prizren and the rest of the Balšić holdings in that region. Thus, as so often happened, the death of a strong leader led to immediate territorial losses for his heirs.

After divorcing Vukašin's daughter in 1371, George I had married Theodora, Dejan's daughter, who was the former wife of Žarko of Zeta. Scholars speculate that at that time she brought him further territory in Zeta, i.e., whatever Žarko had been able to retain. George and Theodora had a son, Constantine. He was a minor when George died, so George's brother Balša II had no trouble in succeeding George. Whether George I had expected Constantine to take over Zeta later or to at least obtain an appanage is unknown. In any case Balša ignored any rights Constantine may have had, and their relations became increasingly strained. Balša's relations may also have been tense with the other major surviving Balšić, his nephew George II, who had been sharing power with his two uncles before George I's death. Our only suggestion that their relationship deteriorated comes from Orbini, who, on the basis of unknown sources, claims the two immediately quarreled and that Balša captured his nephew. Angry at his disobedience and afraid his nephew might oust him, Balša locked George II up in his Durazzo fortress, where he remained until Balša died (1385). Then George II was released from jail, returned to Zeta, and was accepted as its lord.

Clearly there are problems with this account. First, Ragusan sources show George II dealing with Dubrovnik off and on between 1379 and 1385; thus clearly George was not imprisoned throughout this period. However, a brief imprisonment at some time within this period cannot be ruled out. Second, Balša obtained Durazzo only in 1385. Of course, George might have originally been held in a different fortress and been transferred to Durazzo in 1385. Or, he might initially have been jailed in Durazzo, but in 1385 rather than in 1379. However, we really do not know anything about the relations between uncle and nephew, for no contemporary source provides us with any information. Thus we have no basis to judge whether or not there is a kernel of truth in this particular report given by Orbini.

In 1372, as noted, Balša had married the daughter of John Comnenus Asen and had received as a dowry the Berat-Valona region of Albania. His interests were increasingly directed toward that region, particularly as he became more interested in the affairs of Durazzo. This meant that he was able to devote less attention to matters in Zeta itself. He made no attempt to recover the lands lost to the Brankovići. However, he did retain an interest in the Adriatic region, and we have charters issued by him to his towns of Bar and Alessio (Lješ). His Adriatic interests overlapped with Tvrtko of Bosnia's. He clearly was unhappy with Tvrtko's seizure of Dračevica, Konavli, and Trebinje; and in the 1380s (probably 1383) the two rulers clashed in indecisive skirmishes in Konavli and Trebinje. Further straining the two rulers' relations was the fact that both Balša and Tvrtko sought overlordship over Kotor. Their ambitions also overlapped along the border of Zeta in what had been Altomanović's land.

In 1385 Balša Balšić conquered Durazzo, presumably from Karlo Thopia. In a charter to Dubrovnik issued in April 1385 he called himself Duke of Durazzo. He was not to enjoy his prize long. That summer a Turkish raiding party for the first time penetrated to the Adriatic and Ionian coast.

Balša, if we can believe Orbini, rounded up one thousand men in Durazzo and, ignoring the advice of his more level-headed courtiers, raced out to take on the Turkish raiders. Not surprisingly, his small forces had little success, and Balša was killed near Berat in battle against the Turks on 18 September 1385. We can see why Orbini called Balša brave but stupid. Orbini reports that Marko's brother Ivaniš, then living with Balša, also died in this battle. Whether or not the circumstances of Balša's death were exactly as Orbini reports, we do know that Balša was killed in battle against the Turks at this time. He was succeeded by his nephew George II Balšić (1385–1403). By the end of the year Durazzo was back in the hands of Karlo Thopia, who probably had already accepted Ottoman suzerainty. However, Karlo Thopia died in 1387 or 1388. He was buried in a church he built near modern Elbasan. His epitaph was given in three languages—Greek, Latin, and Serbian. Under George Thopia, his son and heir, the family's power declined. This enabled various client tribes to assert themselves in central Albania.

The Albanian lands Balša had received through his marriage with John Comnenus Asen's daughter almost at once slipped away from Balšić control. Balša's widow and their daughter Rugina (or Rudina) remained in possession of the Valona-Berat-Himara holdings. Shortly therefore, in 1391, Rugina married Mrkše Žarković, the son of the Žarko who was found holding Zeta right after Dušan's death. Balša's widow seems to have been the Valona duchy's main ruler until her death in 1396. By this time the family of Musachi had gained control of Berat. Mrkše succeeded to the duchy, calling himself the Lord of Valona; he held the city until his own death in 1415. Rugina succeeded him and briefly held Valona until the Ottomans conquered it in 1417. At various critical times during their rule, these heirs of Balša offered Valona to Venice, which always refused the responsibility.

The Albanian regions to the south of the consolidated Balšić holding of Zeta also fell away. The Albanian family of Dukagjin, which had been forced to submit to the Balšići, seceded. Already in 1387 the brothers Lek and Paul Dukagjin were issuing trade privileges to Dubrovnik in their lands, which included the important town of Alessio and the territory along the left bank of the Drin, probably extending south to the Mati. This Lek Dukagjin, or possibly a second individual bearing the same name from the following century, is credited with compiling Albania's oral law code, which came to be known as the *Law of Lek*. Also in this region, centered at Danj (Dagno), further inland on the left bank of the Drin, and also asserting its independence from the Balšići, was the Jonima family. The Dukagjins and the Jonimas were involved in a struggle for the territory along both sides of the Drin. And soon the Castriots were to be challenging Dukagjin dominance between the Mati and the Drin.

It is a thankless task to determine who held what in this general region. For nothing remained stable; a family's holdings could and did change from year to year. Borders within this large area between the Mati and the Bojana rivers, where these leading families and their clients resided, in particular, underwent frequent fluctuations, as first one and then another family rose to dominance. At the same time the Balšići were not happy to see the territory in which these northern tribes lived slip from their grip. Thus they carried on a struggle with the Dukagjins for the region between the Drin and the Bojana rivers. Needless to say, the Balšić-Dukagjin border was particularly unstable.

Even the Balšići's Slavic lands were not secure. Nicholas Zakarija, who had commanded the castle of Budva for the Balšići for nearly twenty years, revolted, probably in 1386, and made himself the ruler of Budva. This secession did not last. George II was again in possession of Budva by 1389. At this time also the Crnojević family began to assert its independence in the mountains behind the Gulf of Kotor as well as in certain other scattered lands in Zeta. This family, whose origins are obscure, seems to have begun its rise holding only the village of Oblik on the Bojana and two or three villages on Lake Skadar.

Having lost all this territory and struggling to retain his hold over his remaining Slavic lands in Zeta while trying to somehow bring the Crnojevići back to obedience, George II Balšić faced an uphill fight. Holding securely only the land between Skadar and the coast, he established his major residence in Ulcinj and maintained other courts and garrisons at Drivast and Skadar. Despite his shrinking fortunes, he maintained an elaborate court and kept up the court titles and ceremonial that had existed at Dušan's court. He also began to coin money. In 1386 he married Lazar's daughter Helen. And it seems that he accepted Lazar's suzerainty. Possibly he hoped by this means to obtain Lazar's support to reassert his rule over the Crnojevići and various other Slavic nobles and tribesmen who were seeking an independent path. Moreover, he had to face the Turkish threat, a far more serious danger than local separatism. Under Turkish pressure George also accepted Ottoman suzerainty, either immediately on his succession in 1385 or during the extensive Ottoman raids that overran parts of Zeta the following year. In any case, documents clearly show him as an Ottoman vassal in 1388.

Tvrtko of Bosnia from the 1370s to 1391

As noted earlier, as a result of his and Lazar's victory over Altomanović, Tvrtko received a large chunk of the loser's land. He obtained his gains in three installments. First, in late 1373 or early 1374, right after his victory, he acquired a strip of Hum along the border of Zeta, through Gacko and Onogošt to the upper Drina and Lim rivers, that included the region of Prijepolje with the important Serbian monastery of Mileševo. This brought the Bosnian-Serbian border near to the present border between the Republics of Serbia and Montenegro. In 1377 he received the second installment. As a result of a local rebellion against George Balšić, who had initially received this part of Altomanović's holdings, Tvrtko gained the coastal territory near Dubrovnik of Dračevica, Konavli, and Trebinje. When added to the parts of Hum gained by Bosnia in 1326, this gave Bosnia nearly all the territory that had composed

Serbian Hum in the twelfth and thirteenth centuries, except for Ston and the Pelješac peninsula held by Dubrovnik. According to Orbini, Tvrtko's annexation of these coastal lands (which George considered to be his own) led George, at the moment allied with the Thopias, to plunder Bosnia as far into the interior as Nevesinje. The raiders then withdrew; the action was not repeated because George then died in January 1379. Tvrtko immediately took advantage of George's death to acquire the third installment, annexing from the Balšići the coastal territory lying between the lands he gained in 1377 and the Gulf of Kotor. Thus Tvrtko gained control of the coast between Kotor and Dubrovnik but not including either city itself.

Tvrtko's conquests, particularly those along the Drina and Lim, brought many more Orthodox clerics, monks, believers, and churches into the Bosnian state. However, as noted earlier, throughout the Middle Ages Bosnia retained a localized character. Thus we see little sign that the other religions of Bosnia—Catholicism and the Bosnian Church—played any role in this newly conquered area or that the Orthodox migrated to or influenced the non-Orthodox areas of Bosnia.

This acquisition of Serbian territory, including the important Serbian monastery of Mileševo, combined with the fact that Tvrtko was a Nemanjić (through his grandmother, Dragutin's daughter), gave Tvrtko the idea to have himself crowned King of Serbia. After all, the royal Nemanjić line had died out with Uroš in 1371 and one could not expect Tvrtko to place much stock in the claims of Marko, who, despite his coronation, was just a petty princeling in Macedonia without a drop of Nemanjić blood. So, in 1377 the Metropolitan of Mileševo crowned Tvrtko King of Serbia and Bosnia. We find no evidence that any of the Serbian princelings and noblemen objected to the coronation; in fact, Tvrtko's relations with Lazar remained cordial after 1377. But, though none objected, it is also certain that no Serbian nobleman outside the borders of Tvrtko's realm recognized Tvrtko as an overlord. From this time on until the fall of Bosnia in 1463, all Bosnian rulers called themselves kings rather than bans. And though the kingship had meaning for only Bosnia and Hum, because that kingship was derived from the Nemanjići, they all called themselves Kings of Serbia and Bosnia.

Having established himself so firmly on the coast down to the Gulf of Kotor, Tvrtko's hopes of acquiring that major port increased. And a situation arose that might have provided an opportunity for him to realize that ambition. In 1378 a war had broken out between Genoa and Venice. The Hungarians soon joined the Genoese side and tried to mobilize their Dalmatian towns against Venice. A large Genoese fleet appeared on the eastern side of the Adriatic; Trogir became its regular base. Needing a base to oppose the Genoese, the Venetians attacked and took Kotor on 13 August 1378. Considerable fear of Venice swept Dubrovnik, the Dalmatian town that had been most loyal to Venice's enemy Hungary over the past twenty years. Furthermore, Dubrovnik provided asylum to various anti-Venetians who had fled from Kotor.

Tvrtko tried to maintain correct relations with both towns, though Dubrovnik tried to pressure him to cease trading with Kotor as long as the Venetians were in occupation. The citizens of Kotor, meanwhile, fearing an attack from Genoa to expel the Venetians, tried to improve relations with Bosnia. In fact a faction in Kotor believed that the best solution for the town's difficulties would be to expel the Venetians and then at once submit to Tvrtko, an idea the Bosnian ruler encouraged. In June 1379 the Venetians suffered a major defeat at the hands of the Genoese near Pula in Istria; Kotor's fear of a Genoese attack increased. At this moment a rebellion erupted in Kotor, evicting the Venetian officials from the town and announcing the town's recognition of Hungarian suzerainty once again. Thus Tvrtko's hopes fell through. A certain number of Venetian soldiers managed to flee to the fortress of Kotor, where they were able to hold out while the rest of the town accepted the revolution. But though the town had re-accepted Hungarian suzerainty, the giving up of which had initially caused the break between it and Dubrovnik, the quarrel between the two towns continued. In fact it became more heated when a group of local citizens in May 1380 expelled Kotor's governing council, which had been dominated by the richer nobility. This act upset many of the coastal towns in which the rich patriciate dominated, especially Dubrovnik; relations remained strained between the two towns until the nobles of Kotor succeeded in regaining power in October or November 1381.

Unfortunately, almost nothing is known about the revolutionary regime in Kotor. Orbini's description is flawed. He mixes the war I have just described with earlier events that involved George I Balšić and Altomanović, both of whom by this time were in fact deceased. Orbini's report is as follows: The population of Kotor, led by a man called Medoj, expelled their magistrates for bringing Dubrovnik's and Balšić's raids upon the town. The expelled aristocratic magistrates fled to Dubrovnik and offered peace between the two towns in exchange for aid. After debate the Dubrovnik council, infected with fear that Kotor's example might influence the general populace of Dubrovnik against its patriciate, agreed to help them. Then Dubrovnik's leaders negotiated with the rebel leaders in Kotor; these negotiations resulted in peace and the return of the expelled magistrates both to their town and to their former positions of power. And so ends Orbini's account.

By the time Kotor's aristocrats had restored themselves to power, Venice and Genoa had concluded peace and the Venetian troops had evacuated Kotor's citadel. All Dalmatia was once again under Hungarian suzerainty. And Tvrtko had failed to capitalize on the war to gain Kotor for himself.

Having failed to acquire an existing port, Tvrtko decided the next best thing was to develop his own port on the Adriatic and in this way to make himself more independent of the existing commercial centers, especially of Dubrovnik. He began building a new town early in 1382 called Novi (literally, "New"; modern Herceg-Novi). Dubrovnik protested strongly, particularly insisting on its right to have a monopoly in selling salt to the Balkan interior. Kotor and the Italians welcomed the new town, hoping by trading there to increase their share of the Bosnian market, particularly in the sale of salt. Soon Dubrovnik established a blockade of Novi and, besides pressuring others not to trade there, seized foreign ships sailing to Novi. Tvrtko tried unsuccessfully to purchase ships from Venice to defend his harbor. Dubrovnik and Bosnia came close to war, but finally in December 1382 Tvrtko gave in to Dubrovnik and agreed in a treaty to recognize the monopolies Dubrovnik claimed. Novi then stagnated. Tvrtko's capitulation owed itself to his desire to have his hands free to involve himself in the civil war that was then breaking out in Hungary. However, despite the affair over Novi and lesser issues that popped up from time to time, Tvrtko's relations with Dubrovnik tended to be cordial. The town's merchants were very active in Bosnia; besides trading, they served Tvrtko actively as financial officials, chancellors, and diplomats. Dubrovnik established colonies at various newly opened mines and increased the size of its colonies at the older mines. During Tvrtko's reign mines at Olovo (opened under Stjepan Kotromanić), Srebrnica, and probably Fojnica developed rapidly. By the end of the century a Franciscan mission was established at each of these towns.

Hungarian Civil War

On 16 September 1382 King Louis of Hungary died. His death ended the male line of the Hungarian Angevins. Three women remained behind: Louis' widow (Stjepan Kotromanić's daughter) Elizabeth, and their two daughters, Maria and Hedwiga (or Jadviga). Maria was engaged to Sigismund of Luxemburg, the son of Charles IV, King of Bohemia and Emperor of Germany. On 17 September 1382 Maria, aged twelve, was crowned "King" of Hungary. Louis had hoped that after his death the union between Hungary and Poland would hold. The Poles, however, announced that if Maria wished to be ruler of Poland she would have to reside there. Maria refused, so the Poles chose her sister as their ruler and she departed for Poland. Meanwhile in Hungary Maria's mother, Elizabeth, assumed the role of regent; her leading advisor was Nicholas Garai. An assortment of Hungarian nobles found the rule of a woman objectionable.

The first to go into active opposition was John of Paližna (Paližina), the Prior of Vrana. He seems to have been chiefly opposed to the centralizing policy enforced during the reign of Maria's father and to have hoped, by opposing Maria, to reassert local independence. He sought support from Bosnia, for Tvrtko was then operating in the Dalmatian area, immediately taking advantage of Louis' death to recover the territories he lost to Louis in 1357. Bosnian help did not materialize in time. A Hungarian army, supporting Maria, appeared before the walls of Vrana. The town was surrendered to it, while John fled to Bosnia.

After a brief period of peace a new movement against Maria emerged in 1385. This was led by the Horvat brothers, who were the leaders of a great family from the Vukovska župa (the county just west of Srem between the

Sava and Danube rivers). John Horvat was Ban of Mačva⁵ while his brother Paul was Bishop of Zagreb. Their rebellion was far more serious than John of Pališna's, for not only were the Horvats more powerful figures with much greater support, but they also offered a new candidate for the throne, Charles of Naples, the closest male relative to the deceased King Louis. He was descended from another Maria, the daughter of Stephen V of Hungary, who had married Charles II of Naples. Soon John of Pališna had joined the Horvat rebellion on behalf of Charles; this united the supporters of the earlier rebellion to Charles' cause.

In the course of these Hungarian troubles after Louis' death Tvrtko quietly dropped his vassalage to Hungary, which since about 1370 had been only nominal in any case. He also, as noted, at this time regained the territory lost to Louis in 1357: Drijeva and western Hum between the Cetina and Neretva rivers with Završje. Tvrtko also had a major success in southern Dalmatia, finally replacing Hungary as overlord of Kotor. In late 1382, taking advantage of the quarrel between Tvrtko and Dubrovnik over Novi, Balša Balšić had attacked Kotor. Failing to take it, he placed the town under siege from the land. Dubrovnik, despite being on good terms with Balša, continued to send Kotor shipments of grain to help it endure the siege. Skirmishes soon followed in 1383 between Balša and Tvrtko in Konavli and Trebinje; presumably Balša was trying to regain these lands, which Tvrtko had taken from George I in 1377. Soon in 1384 (quite likely in July) Kotor, still under pressure from Balša, finally submitted to Tvrtko. The official date given for the event is August 1385, when Hungary, Kotor's previous overlord, recognized Tvrtko's suzerainty over the town. Most scholars believe that the hard-pressed Hungarian ruler Maria, who accepted this change, was recognizing a fait accompli and was further hoping, by recognizing Tvrtko's acquisition, to win Tvrtko's support or at least neutrality.

In 1385, on the advice of her counselors, Maria tried to break her engagement to Sigismund, so that she could marry the brother of the King of France. Angry at this slight, Sigismund attacked Hungary. The country was then in a state of semi-anarchy, with whole regions recognizing the Horvats' candidate Charles of Naples. When Maria found herself in these further difficulties arising from Sigismund's attack, the Horvats decided that Charles should now come to Hungary and claim his throne. In September 1385 he landed at Senj and then marched to Zagreb, the seat of Paul Horvat. Faced with this increasing danger from her main rival Charles, Maria submitted to Sigismund and married him. The two then entered into negotiations with the Naples faction inside Hungary; a peace was concluded, which evidently neither side intended to honor, that left Maria as the ruler and recognized Charles as "Governor of Hungary." What this title meant in terms of authority is not clear, but, considering what was to follow, it is also not important. Since Sigismund had returned to his affairs in Bohemia, Maria took over again as ruler with Nicholas Garai, restored as Count Palatine, the leading figure at court. Meanwhile, Charles was persuaded to come to Hungary itself. Plots were hatched on all sides and he, no more sincere about the agreement than Maria, planned to expel Maria and have himself crowned king.

Charles came to Buda. His followers engineered a coup that forced a renunciation of the throne from Maria, and Charles was then crowned king. However, he then stupidly accepted an invitation to visit Maria at one of her palaces; upon his arrival there on 7 February 1386 he was murdered by one of her henchmen. Charles' supporters immediately rose up in arms, and thus the civil war resumed. They were now campaigning on behalf of Charles' son Ladislas.

In late 1386 Maria and her mother, Elizabeth, paid a visit to Djakovo in Slavonia. After they departed, they were attacked on the road by the Horvats and their retainers. Nicholas Garai, who had accompanied them, was killed, and the two ladies were taken prisoner. They were taken off to a castle in Novigrad near Zadar. John of Paližna, who had been named Ban of Croatia by the murdered Charles, became their jailer. When rumors reached Novigrad that Sigismund was on his way to rescue his beloved bride, the guards strangled Elizabeth before her daughter's eyes. In the meantime armed supporters of both candidates moved around Croatia, engaging in considerable local fighting. Sigismund meanwhile, hearing of his wife's capture, hurried to Hungary from Bohemia. The nobles in Alba Regalis accepted him and crowned him King of Hungary on 31 March 1387. Sigismund, supported by Nicholas Garai's son (also named Nicholas), then set about procuring Maria's release. This clearly had to be done by force; a large army volunteered by John of the Krk princely family (the future Frankapans) besieged Novigrad and procured her release in the spring of 1387. With Sigismund present and Maria freed, the tide turned against the Naples party and the Horvats were forced to flee to Bosnia.

Meanwhile in the Donji Kraji the branch of the Hrvatinić family that had supported Tvrtko against Hungary in 1363 and had thereafter risen to dominance in the region as a result (namely, Vlkac and his son Hrvoje), still loyal to Tvrtko, joined, in about 1387, the Horvats against Sigismund. Presumably this alliance was concluded with Tvrtko's consent. It also occurred in the nick of time for the Naples faction, for just when it had lost in Hungary and was on the point of losing in Croatia, the Bosnians took up its cause. Soon Bosnian and Croatian troops were campaigning together on behalf of Naples in Croatia in the region around Zagreb. And by the end of the year, 1387, the Bosnians and their Croatian allies were in control of most of Croatia and Slavonia. The Horvats, who had sought refuge with Tvrtko, were now able to make their return to Croatia. Tvrtko himself also came out openly for Naples in the course of 1387. He sent his own armies into Hungarian Dalmatia, in particular into the strip of coastland between Zadar and Dubrovnik. Actively helped by John of Paližna and Hrvoje, Tvrtko established his suzerainty over all the towns between these two cities, though not including Zadar and Dubrovnik themselves; thus Split, Omiš, Trogir, Šibenik, and even several Adriatic islands submitted to Tvrtko. He issued charters confirming their existing privileges, including their rights to remain self-governing under their own town councils and existing law codes. Tvrtko evidently intended to retain these towns for Bosnia. John of Paližna had been named Ban of Croatia, Dalmatia, and Slavonia in 1385 by the ill-fated Charles of Naples. Tvrtko recognized John's title and appointed him to be his deputy for various Dalmatian towns that submitted to him.

Some of the towns seem to have been unhappy with the change, preferring as their suzerain the more distant Hungary to near-by Bosnia. Tvrtko never tried to force his rule upon either Zadar or Dubrovnik. Thus between 1387 and 1389 Tvrtko made himself overlord over a large part of Slavonia, Dalmatia, and Croatia south of Velebit—including Knin, Ostrovica, and Klis. On behalf of Naples his troops even passed through Slavonia into Srem. Though these actions were carried out in the name of Naples, it is evident that Tvrtko and his own vassal, Hrvoje, with whom he was closely associated in this venture, were acting for themselves and it was they who held the actual authority in much of this vast area. In 1390 Tvrtko began to call himself King of Croatia and Dalmatia. Though they owed their revived fortunes and their return to Croatia to Tvrtko and his Bosnians, one still may wonder how the Horvats felt about Tvrtko's successes and claims. Surely Tvrtko's ambitions clashed with their own.

It seems that Prince Lazar of Serbia briefly joined the Naples cause and may even have sent some troops to participate in the fighting around Beograd and in Srem. But as the Turkish threat increased and Sigismund's support in Hungary itself grew, Lazar made peace with Sigismund; this peace was sealed, probably at some point in 1387, when Lazar's daughter Theodora married Sigismund's loyal supporter Nicholas Garai.

Tvrtko died in February 1391. John of Paližna died a month later. The Hungarian civil war continued unabated. In Bosnia a struggle for power followed among various members of Tvrtko's family. Hrvoje Vukčić, however, was clearly the strongest local figure. He was to become more-or-less a king-maker for Bosnia, while he retained tight control over his own Donji Kraji. He also moved rapidly to replace Tvrtko as overlord over Dalmatia and parts of Croatia. Ladislas of Naples, hoping to retain both this territory and Hrvoje's support, gave his blessing to Hrvoje's ambitions and recognized him as his deputy for this region.

Attica, Boeotia, and the Peloponnesus

The Catalans continued to rule Attica and Boeotia. They had, however, lost most of their holdings in southern Thessaly to the Serbs in 1348. Of that region only Neopatras and its district remained in their possession. They remained under the suzerainty of the King of Sicily. He, though appointing a vicar general to manage the duchy and various other officials, was not able to impose his authority against the wishes of the local Catalans. Besides the vicar general, an outsider appointed to oversee the whole territory who resided in Thebes, the king appointed two vicars (verguers)—one in Athens and one in Livadia—and a captain in Neopatras. These appointees generally served for terms of three years; their appointments could be renewed.

All the territory of the duchy was divided among these four major leaders. The vicar general, though responsible for supervising the whole duchy, also had particular responsibility for the fourth of the duchy that fell under Thebes. The vicar, or captain in the case of Neopatras, was responsible for the local military forces as well as for civil and criminal justice. Beneath these four leaders were a series of castellans who commanded lesser castles throughout the duchy. Some of these castles were held as fiefs assigned by the Catalan Company (and confirmed by the king); the castle fiefs were usually hereditary. Other castles, particularly the more important ones, received royally appointed commanders; frequently however, these appointees were drawn from the company. Each vicar was responsible for supervising the castellans in his own territory. Each vicar and castellan had a military force under his command to keep order, put down brigands, and defend his fortress. The king also appointed a marshall who, as the chief military figure of the duchy, co-ordinated military campaigns and major defense efforts. The marshall was always a local Catalan; for fifty years the position was hereditary in the de Novelles family. The vicar general stood over the marshall. However, in theory their spheres of responsibility seem to have overlapped; and even if their responsibilities were more clearly defined than is apparent to us now, in practice they certainly would have overlapped.

The local Catalans themselves were a military caste. They formed a corporation that had its own council responsible for company matters; they elected various civil and military officials who co-existed with the royally appointed administrators. As holders of lesser fortresses, various Catalans participated in the royal administration and as a company they made (on both local and duchy-wide levels) policy decisions which they presented to the king in petitions. Thus the Catalan Company was a separate policy-making group that, having its own council and enjoying the loyalty of most of the local military forces (its members), was in a position to behave as it chose. If the king ignored the Catalans' wishes, they could revolt, as they did in 1362 when Roger de Lluria, a Catalan marshall, carried out a military coup and took power in Thebes. The vicar general, Peter de Pou, was killed and de Lluria was recognized by his followers (who seem to have included most of the local Catalans) as the new vicar general. De Lluria then assigned the command of various fortresses in the duchy to his men. Soon he had Neopatras; it is not certain, however, that he acquired control of Athens. The king did not want to accept him and appointed a new vicar general, who tried, but failed, to oust de Lluria in 1363. Having failed to remove him, the king had little choice but to accept him, which he did in 1366 when he named de Lluria vicar general. De Lluria remained in power until he died, at some point after November 1368, probably in 1369.

After his death matters seem to have become particularly chaotic. A whole series of charters of royal appointment to the duchy from the 1370s have survived, but it often is not known whether the appointees ever actually assumed their offices. There also seem to have been various splits within the ranks of the local Catalans; and between 1374 and 1378 (a more exact date cannot be determined) warfare broke out between the Catalans of Thebes and Livadia on the one hand and those of Athens on the other. Peace was concluded between the two sides before the end of 1378.

In 1377 Frederick III of Sicily died, ending the male line of the Sicilian house; his heir was his daughter Maria, whose succession was illegal, because succession by a female had been outlawed by a previous king, Frederick II. A serious quarrel followed in Sicily. Scholars have often stated that it carried over to the Duchy of Athens/Thebes and split the local Catalans. Setton takes this view. Loernetz, however, while recognizing that various divisions did exist among the local Catalans, has noted that these splits existed before Frederick III's death; he also points out that no direct evidence exists to demonstrate that the Sicilian succession was an issue that troubled the local Catalans or that any of them rejected Frederick's daughter.[6]

By the end of 1377 Peter IV of Aragon had triumphed over Maria; he assigned the rule of Sicily to his son Martin. However, he continued to take an interest in the affairs of both Sicily and the Catalan duchy. By 1379 he had added "Duke of Athens" to his title and had come to the conclusion that the House of Aragon should take a more active role in the duchy or at least in selecting the Catalans who managed the duchy's affairs. However, his desire to manage the affairs of the duchy backfired on occasion; for he frequently summoned his vicar generals back to Spain to report and receive orders. In their numerous absences, which sometimes coincided with unanticipated crises, the local Catalans were free to act as they chose.

During their years of rule, then, the Catalans were a small military minority that ran the duchy. Their government seems to have been inefficient. There was considerable lawlessness within the state—some of which Catalans surely participated in—and commerce suffered. To keep their control, the Catalans separated themselves from the Greek population. They banned intermarriage between Greeks and Catalans. (This law seems to have been violated with some frequency.) They also only to a limited extent armed the local Greeks for defense needs. Though this may have avoided revolt, it also meant that in the event of a foreign invasion their forces were smaller than they might otherwise have been. They chiefly supplemented their own forces with Albanian and Turkish mercenaries. The Albanians at this time were migrating beyond Thessaly and Epirus into Attica and Boeotia, and we know of one Albanian chief, Demetrius, who was considered a baron of the duchy. Holding a large fief, he commanded fifteen hundred horsemen. Peter of Aragon, presumably seeking them as soldiers for the duchy, offered a two-year tax exemption to any new Albanians who would come to settle in the duchy. The Albanian response to his offer is not known.

The local Greeks held middle-level administrative positions that required literacy; they dealt with civil affairs as notaries, scribes, record-keepers, and tax collectors. The role of local Greeks, though limited, was still greater under the Catalans, who had little interest in administrative tasks and therefore willingly left them to Greeks, than it had been under the Burgundians. The Catalans also profited from the slave trade, selling Greeks, among others, as slaves. The center for this trade was Thebes.

Meanwhile, after the death of Philip II of Taranto in 1373, most of the barons of Achaea recognized Joanna, the Angevin Queen of Naples, as their suzerain. In late 1376 or early 1377 Joanna, tied down with Italian affairs, leased her principality of Achaea (the Frankish Morea) for four thousand ducats a year on a five-year lease to the Hospitaler Knights of Saint John. The relatives of the late Philip disapproved of her action and advanced their own candidate to rule Achaea, Philip's nephew Jacques des Baux.

Meanwhile the Hospitaler Knights of Achaea decided to invade Epirus. Though the reasons for this venture are unknown, it is probable that they were seeking to regain the Epirote forts granted to the Angevins in 1294 that had subsequently been occupied by the Albanians. Led by their Grand Master (from 1377) John Fernandez de Heredia, the knights in 1378 moved against John (Ghin) Bova Spata, the Albanian who, as noted, controlled Arta and much of southern Epirus and Acarnania. He probably had brought this attack on himself by his conquest in 1376 or 1377 of Naupaktos, the last Angevin town in Epirus. The knights directed their first attack on Naupaktos, which they captured, and then in April 1378 they are found in occupation of Vonitsa in Acarnania. It seems Vonitsa had been made available to them by its holder, Carlo Tocco. With the knights was a company of Navarrese—another Spanish military company. The Navarrese, who had been campaigning for Louis of Evreux around Durazzo previously, had found themselves at loose ends after his death in 1376. Presumably the Hospitalers had hired them for the Epirote campaign. The campaign began to go badly after Spata took John Fernandez prisoner. (The Florentines ransomed him and he was back in Achaea, in Clarenza, in May 1379.) His capture seems to have ended the campaign against Spata, who in 1380 is again found as master of Naupaktos. Carlo Tocco retained possession of Vonitsa. The Navarrese were then hired by the Hospitalers for eight months' service in Achaea itself.

Once there the Navarrese company soon split. One group remained in the Morea as a force of disorder while a second group, under John de Urtubia, soon became allies, if not retainers, of Nerio Acciajuoli, the Florentine banker who held Corinth. Urtubia's Navarrese, probably in the service of Nerio, soon marched against the Catalans. Nerio certainly acquiesced in, if he did not outright encourage, their activities, allowing them passage through his lands, which, after his conquest—aided by the local citizens—of Megara in 1374 from the Catalans, bordered on and controlled access to the Catalan duchy.

The Catalans, who seem not to have expected this attack, did not put up an effective or co-ordinated defense against the Navarrese. Between January and May 1379 the Navarrese took Thebes, and in 1380, or possibly early

1381, they took Livadia. Thebes shortly thereafter is found in the hands of Nerio, so it seems Urtubia yielded it to him. Whether this shows that Urtubia had been in Nerio's service or whether Nerio simply bought the town from him is not known.[7] Livadia was soon recovered for the Catalan duchy.

Many of the Navarrese then proceeded to return to the Morea, where, joining up with those previously hired by the Hospitaler Knights, they set about plundering the northeastern part of the Peloponnesus. Then in 1381, after Joanna was overthrown in Naples, the Navarrese decided to support Jacques des Baux, who was now styling himself Despot of Romania and Prince of Taranto and Achaea. Thus the Navarrese came to oppose the Knights of Saint John who had originally employed at least some of them. The Navarrese were successful in conquering much of Messenia, taking the towns of Androusa and Kalamata, in the name of Jacques. But then Jacques died in July or August 1383, and the Navarrese recognized no further overlord; on their own, they now held this territory for themselves. The Knights of Saint John, who had never succeeded in asserting their control over much of Achaea, at the expiration of their five-year lease in 1383, departed. This made things even easier for the Navarrese, who, operating on their own without a suzerain, soon decided to proclaim their own leader Peter de San Superano as Prince of Achaea.

The Navarrese then set their sights on the rich town of Corinth, held by Nerio Acciajuoli, the Florentine banker. Needing allies to oppose them, Nerio approached and soon, in 1384 or 1385, concluded an alliance against the Navarrese with the Byzantine Despot of the Morea.

By this time the Palaeologus family had regained control of this appanage. Wanting to make the Morea into an appanage for his own son Theodore, the emperor, John V, sent his father-in-law John Cantacuzenus as an envoy to Mistra to persuade his son Matthew Cantacuzenus to turn the Morea over to Theodore. Matthew earlier had had to swear an oath of loyalty to the imperial house; though in his youth he had not taken such promises seriously, now, older and mellower, Matthew seems to have done so. Agreeing to accept Theodore as Despot of the Morea, Matthew remained in office awaiting Theodore's actual arrival to turn the insignia of government over to him. But though Matthew agreed to surrender his authority, his son Demetrius, who had hoped to succeed to the Morea, did not. Already given an appanage in the Morea by Matthew, Demetrius decided to use it as a base to resist. Procuring the support of some local Greek magnates, and hiring some "Latins" (probably Navarrese mercenaries) and some Turkish bands, he began to extend his rule over more of the Morea. When Theodore Palaeologus arrived in December 1382, Matthew at once turned Mistra over to him and retired. (Matthew died soon thereafter, in June 1383, and thus was not to influence Peloponnesian affairs further.) However, by the time Theodore had assumed office Demetrius held most of the Byzantine Peloponnesus, including many fortified centers.

Demetrius had no desire to submit, and thus the Byzantine province remained divided, with probably the larger part of the population supporting Demetrius. However, late in 1383 or early 1384 Demetrius suddenly died; his leading supporter Paul Mamonas of Monemvasia submitted grudgingly to Theodore, and the revolt fizzled out. But one should emphasize that Theodore's position was saved only by Demetrius' sudden death. And Theodore could expect difficulties ahead, for though they had submitted to him, many magnates were not happy to have Theodore as their governor.

The economic problems of the Morea had increased significantly in the second half of the fourteenth century, when Turks from the Anatolian emirates had begun large-scale raiding of the coastal towns and stepped up their attacks upon shipping. Particularly effective as a predator was Umur of Aydin, the son of Cantacuzenus' supporter of the same name. Under the name of Morbassan, this Umur had the reputation of being the bloodiest pirate in the East. Raiding the shores of Greece, he called himself "Sovereign master of Achaea and Scourge of the Christians." In addition to plundering and destroying, the Turks also carried off large numbers of people to sell as slaves. Their activities, combined with the numerous wars fought on the peninsula, contributed substantially to the depopulation and economic decline of the whole Peloponnesus.

Theodore, in 1382 about thirty years old, was to rule the Peloponnesus as an autonomous state under the suzerainty of the emperor. Though emperors occasionally interfered in Peloponnesian matters during the next sixty years, on the whole Theodore and his successors ruled independently rarely consulting Constantinople. However, after 1382, when the Morea came to be administered by members of the same family as that which held the imperial throne, the Morean despots came to have closer relations with the capital and worked more frequently on behalf of the same general policy interests. But the Morea did have financial and judicial autonomy; the despots appointed their own officials, collected their own taxes, and issued grants of land and of privileges including financial and judicial immunities. However, the authority of the despots was limited. They did not issue their own coins but used imperial money. Moreover, no traces of local law are found in the Morea. Byzantine Church canons, Byzantine law codes, and the novels of the Byzantine emperors were the law of the Morea. The despots, though they headed local courts, had no legislative authority. And though the despots issued commercial privileges and sent envoys to foreign states to discuss local problems, the emperor in Constantinople had to conclude, or at least confirm, any major treaty.

Once established in power, Theodore was also concerned about the Navarrese, who were a force of disorder for the whole peninsula. Thus he was receptive to Nerio's proposed alliance, and in 1385, to seal it, he married Nerio's eldest daughter, Bartholomaea. Nerio had no legitimate son and it was understood that Bartholomaea was to eventually inherit Corinth. Thus Theodore saw his marriage as a means to regain for the empire that important town.

Strengthened by this alliance, Nerio then decided to move decisively against the Duchy of Athens. Possibly he feared the Navarrese had designs upon the duchy, and thus, by anticipating them, he could prevent them from establishing a strong base on his northern border. He dispatched his troops into the duchy in 1385, and they quickly overran Attica and Boeotia, taking almost all of it. Athens alone held out, and it was placed under siege. The ease with which the Catalan state fell is astounding and is difficult to explain. It has been estimated, however, that at this time there were only five to six thousand Catalans in the duchy, of whom about three thousand were based in Athens. These now undertook its defense and did so effectively, holding out until 1388 when Nerio finally took it. He then moved against the Catalans' special captaincy of Neopatras and conquered it by 1390. (Neopatras was a short-term gain since the Ottomans were to take it in 1394.) Thus the whole Duchy of Athens and Thebes became the private holding of this Florentine banker.

He quickly dismantled the feudal structure and turned the administration over to salaried agents he hired; in general he hired Italians. However, he gave a considerable role to the local Greeks, for he needed their support against any of the military companies—Catalan or Navarrese—that might try to evict him. And we find many Greeks working side by side with his Italian bureaucrats. Greek became the official language of his chancellery and he allowed a Greek archbishop to return to Athens. However, the Greek bishop had to live in the lower town. The upper town, with the Acropolis and its great cathedral church (the Parthenon), was reserved for the Catholic archbishop with whom Nerio had close relations.

After Nerio's conquest a few groups of Catalans remained in the duchy, holding a few scattered castles. As outcasts, they basically lived as brigands holed up in individual strongholds.

NOTES

1. The discussion that follows is greatly indebted to G. Ostrogorski, *Serska oblast posle Dušanove smrti* (Beograd, 1965).

2. This point is argued in Fine, *The Bosnian Church*, pp. 106–07.

3. Gojislava's fate is unknown. Scholars reject the two variant but similar stories recorded by Orbini that Nicholas had her and her two sons thrown into prison, where they died, or that he ordered them all to be poisoned. Ćirković points out that neither fate could have occurred, at least not to Gojislava, because we know Dubrovnik aided her escape to Albania. After that we lose all traces of her.

4. Ducellier (*La façade maritime*, p. 479) dates the reconquest to 1372. An expedition was planned for that year, but it seems it was never actually launched (See E. Léonard, *Les Angevins de Naples* [Paris, 1954], p. 438). Thus a later date is probably warranted. The evidence presented by K. Setton (*Catalan Domination of Athens, 1311–1388* [Cambridge, Mass., 1948], pp. 125–26) for the 1376 date for both the capture of Durazzo and Louis' death rests on the following: Louis continued to actively recruit troops through 1375; through most of 1375 until the summer of 1376

documents mention troops as embarking for the campaign; and though no source mentions the capture, a document from the end of the year 1376 refers to Louis as Duke of Durazzo, suggesting his enterprise was successful. This same document also refers to Duke Louis as being dead. Thus his death occurred the same year, possibly even in connection with the campaign.

5. The title Ban of Mačva presents problems. In 1381 we know that Prince Lazar held some or possibly all of Mačva, for in that year he awarded the income from various villages in Mačva to support his monastery of Ravanica. That same year, 1381, John Horvat is referred to in documents as Ban of Mačva. We know that John at the time held the Vukovska župa. Radonić proposes that by this time the more prestigious title "Ban of Mačva" was given to the holder of the Vukovska župa, a territory that earlier had often been granted by the Hungarian king to the holder (ban) of Mačva. Though this theory cannot be proved, it was not unusual to grant noblemen titles to lands claimed, but not held, by a given state. Thus Horvat's title found in sources from 1381 and 1382 should not be taken to indicate that Lazar did not actually possess much of Mačva.

6. Setton, *Catalan Domination of Athens,* and R.-J. Loenertz, "Athènes et Néopatras," in Leonertz, *Byzantina et Franco-Graeca* (Rome, 1978), p. 227.

7. George Dennis ("The Capture of Thebes by the Navarrese [6 March 1378] and Other Chronological Notes in Two Paris Manuscripts," *Orientalia Christiana Periodica* 26 [1960]: 42–50) has discovered a fragment of a Byzantine chronicle that dates Urtubia's capture of Thebes to 6 March 1378. If this date is correct, as Dennis believes, then it seems Urtubia's company, possibly in Nerio's service, first attacked Thebes. Then subsequently, after taking it, the company entered into service with the Hospitalers for the Epirote campaign. And then after that campaign's end, when the Navarrese Company of Mahiot de Coquerel entered into Hospitaler service in Achaea, Urtubia's band returned to Thebes and Boeotia.

CHAPTER 8

The Balkans in the Late Fourteenth Century

The Turks and the Balkans after the Battle of Marica

The Turks stepped up their activities in the Balkans in the years following the Battle of Marica (1371). Most Turkish activity through the 1360s and well into the 1370s (including probably the Marica victory itself) was carried out by free-ranging Turkish bands, whose members were sometimes called "ghazis," under their own begs (chiefs). Though these begs frequently recognized the suzerainty of the Ottoman sultan, on the whole their activities were independent of his control. The term *ghazi* designates a warrior for the Muslim faith. However, though the term had romantic and propaganda value within the Ottoman realm, we probably should give it a more worldly meaning, for the Turkish bands themselves were probably motivated primarily by a quest for plunder and grazing lands. The Ottomans in Anatolia, finding their lands flooded by an increasing number of Turcoman nomads from Central Asia and not wanting them to disrupt life within the Ottoman state, encouraged these tribesmen to move on to Europe to plunder and occupy Christian lands. Such activities increased in the late 1360s; at that time a group of Turks (probably not Ottoman) took Adrianople in 1369. Until recently, scholars, making use of late sources, dated Adrianople's fall to the period 1361–63. However, a eulogy to Emperor John V, commissioned in late 1366 by Adrianople's Metropolitan Polycarp, shows Adrianople was still Byzantine that late; in that case it makes sense to accept the information of several short Greek chronicles, based on an early but now lost chronicle, that date the Turkish capture of Adrianople to 1369. Thus 1369 is coming to be accepted in recent scholarship. Thereafter Turkish raiding was stepped up against the Balkans, facilitated by the weakening of the Serbs' potential to resist after their defeat at Marica in 1371. Bulgaria's internal disturbances at the same time greatly reduced the effectiveness of Bulgarian resistance.

In the mid-1370s the Ottomans under Sultan Murad I became seriously involved in the Balkans. The Ottomans now began seizing the Balkan acquisitions of other Turkish military groups. In 1377 the Ottomans acquired

Adrianople for themselves. Though many scholars have stated that Adrianople became the Ottoman capital, we should stress that the word *capital* is misleading. The sultan traveled with a huge retinue that included his whole court, central state ministers, clerks, archives, treasury, and a large military force. Thus the capital was located wherever the sultan happened to be. When he was physically in Adrianople, then it could be called a capital. And because it was his major European city, he visited it frequently and issued many documents from it. However, since he was frequently there in connection with campaigns aimed to penetrate deeper into the Balkans, maybe the word *base-camp* better describes the city's function.

Many scholars have stated that Bulgaria became vassal to the Ottomans in 1372 or 1373 as a result of the Battle of Marica (1371). Most Ottomanists, however, prefer to date Ottoman suzerainty over Bulgaria to 1376. This later date corresponds to the time when the Ottomans themselves, as opposed to the various ghazi bands, became active in the Balkans. Vassalage, as noted, meant that the vassal had to pay tribute and supply troops for Ottoman campaigns, often led by a member of the ruler's family in person. At times it also meant that a Balkan Christian princess had to enter the sultan's harem. This was to be the fate of Tamara, the sister of Bulgaria's Tsar John Šišman. Since an anonymous chronicle discusses the "marriage" of Tamara right after it discusses the Battle of Marica and just before it mentions the Ottoman recovery of Gallipoli in 1376 (after the Turks had briefly lost it), most scholars date Tamara's "marriage" to the period 1371–76. Some date it to the first year, seeing John Šišman's compliance with Murad's demand as a desperate measure to avoid a threatened invasion from the victorious forces after Marica, while others associate it with Bulgaria's formal submission to Murad in 1376.

Vassalge did not stop Turkish raids for plunder, and raiding parties continued to sweep through Bulgaria from time to time. Nor did vassalage prevent the Ottomans from conquering towns belonging to their vassals. Thus in 1385 they took Sofija from John Šišman and Štip from Constantine Dejanović. These activities of the 1380s, which wrested much of Thrace from Byzantium (including Serres in 1383) and parts of southern Bulgaria, reflected the direct participation of the sultan, who was playing an ever greater role in them. In these years around the mid-1380s—though the exact dates are unknown—the Ottomans took Kavalla, Kastoria, Bitola, and Veria, though Veria may not have been retained for long. In April 1387, after a four-year siege, the Ottomans took Thessaloniki. Byzantine sources suggest the defenders were demoralized and its fall owed itself more to poor morale than to Ottoman strength.

In 1388, it seems, the Bulgarians tried to shed their vassal ties, but they succeeded only in provoking a major Ottoman attack that took Preslav, Šumen, and Silistria. John Šišman, besieged in Nikopolis, was forced to agree to a very disadvantageous peace. The Bulgarians became Ottoman vassals again and suffered a considerable loss of territory. Moreover, the Ottomans acquired the right to establish garrisons inside Bulgaria and to move

their troops freely through Bulgaria. The presence of the Ottomans on the
borders of the Principality of Vidin during this campaign seems to have
caused Vidin to submit to Ottoman suzerainty as well.

The Ottoman raids brought about great instability in the regions of the
Balkans they penetrated. As crops were destroyed and peasants carried off as
captives, agricultural production was disrupted. Moreover, the raids caused
large numbers of refugees from the countryside or small towns to flee to the
better-fortified towns, presenting the towns with the problem of feeding and
sheltering them at a time when they were having difficulty in providing food
for their own citizens. And, as so often had happened in previous eras when
rural life was disrupted, many destitute or uprooted peasants took up brigandage, disrupting commerce and in general making the roads unsafe for would-
be travelers.

Brigandage, always a Balkan problem, became an acute one in the years
of Turkish raids and conquest. Needing more armed men to guard routes and
passes, local rulers frequently recruited brigands, who had the skills, for this
assignment. In addition, underpaid guards were frequently tempted to loot the
rich caravans they had been hired to protect. Thus in this period, as was to be
true through much of the Ottoman period, there was a gray area between the
klephts (brigands) and armatoloi (highway guards). Moreover, many soldiers,
at loose ends at a campaign's end or angry at being poorly rewarded, deserted
from official ranks to take up brigandage. As Bartusis puts it, "Few threats to
society are as great as that presented by a significant group of unpaid, underpaid, or unemployed warriors." And he finds many examples of soldiers, or
ex-soldiers, taking to brigandage on their own or in the hire of powerful local
figures. And since soldiers often deserted as bands, possessing and skilled in
the use of weapons, they may well have been the element that provided the
most effective brigands.[1]

In the mid-1380s the Turks began to raid Lazar's region. In 1386 they
took Niš and possibly at this time forced Lazar to accept their suzerainty. In
1388 a Turkish raiding party penetrated into Hum. On this occasion the
Christians scored a triumph when Vlatko Vuković, a leading nobleman in
Hum, met them with his forces at Bileća and wiped them out. If Lazar had
actually accepted Turkish vassalage in 1386, he now in 1388 repudiated it;
otherwise, in that year he refused an initial Turkish demand that he accept
Ottoman suzerainty. His repudiation or refusal caused the Turks to mobilize
for a major campaign against Lazar. Serbia seemed ripe for the picking, and,
besides punishing Lazar's insolence, Murad wanted to avenge the defeat at
Bileća.

Kosovo

This then was the background for the most famous battle in Serbia's medieval
history, the Battle of Kosovo. The battle is the subject of the most important
Serbian epic cycle. Kosovo epics are documented as being sung in the six-

teenth and seventeenth centuries. We may assume that they date back to near the time of the battle. These epics influenced the Dalmatian historians who wrote about the battle in the seventeenth century. We should note that these historians also had access to written documents which have subsequently been lost. Some of the written sources they used seem to have had some reliable data, but without the original texts it is hard for us to evaluate the accuracy of their information. The epics are suspect since their early versions had propagandistic motives. Not only were they partisan on behalf of the Serbs and Christians against the Turks and Muslims, but they also supported certain Serbian families against others. Furthermore, the epics couched the battle in New Testament terms, having Lazar's experiences imitate Christ's. Thus many matters concerning the battle have remained controversial.

The Turks first demanded that Lazar accept, or re-accept, Turkish suzerainty and pay tribute. He refused and, realizing that he would be faced with an invasion, sought aid from his neighbors Tvrtko and Vuk Branković. Tvrtko sent a large contingent under the command of Vlatko Vuković, the commander who had defeated the Turkish force at Bileća. Vuk Branković came himself, leading his own men. Thus the Serbian army was composed of three contingents under these three leaders, none of whom was then a Turkish vassal.

According to Orbini, who at least to some extent was following the oral epics, there were dissensions in the Serbian camp. The leading Serbian warrior was a certain Miloš Obilić (or Kobilić) who, Orbini says, was from Tijentište. Previously his wife had quarreled with Vuk Branković's wife over the relative bravery of their husbands. One lady struck the other which brought their husbands into the quarrel and finally resulted in a duel on horseback. In the first charge Miloš unseated Vuk but was prevented from finishing him off by the intervention of other noblemen who were present. Though these nobles mediated a verbal agreement of peace between the two men, hatreds still seem to have remained. The relations between Lazar and Vuk have also attracted much attention from both scholars and epic singers. Until the late 1380s Lazar had maintained close and cordial relations with Vuk Branković, who had married Lazar's daughter and who recognized Lazar as his suzerain. Relations between them seem to have cooled somewhat after 1386/87 when Lazar married a second daughter to George II Balšić, a rival of Vuk's. At about this time Vuk dropped Lazar's name from his coins; scholars have suggested this was caused by Vuk's annoyance at Lazar's concluding that marriage.

The Turks advanced into Serbia in June 1389 and the Serb forces marched to meet them. The two armies camped at Kosovo Polje. Lazar commanded the Serbs and Sultan Murad I commanded in person the Ottoman troops. According to the epic, on the eve of the battle Lazar had a dream offering him either a heavenly or an earthly kingdom and, being a man of the fourteenth century, he chose the heavenly. Furthermore, it was prophesied that he would be betrayed in the battle. As the epic account was paralleling the

New Testament, a Judas was needed. Thus the presence of a traitor in the epic may have been entirely fictional, added to fulfill this function. However, the existence of a literary requirement does not give us grounds to reject the possibility that there might also have been actual treachery. When the prophecy was revealed, Miloš Obilić was accused of being the one who on the morrow would betray his master. Vuk Branković charged him with being in secret contact with the Turks. When Lazar faced Miloš with the charge, Miloš denied it, saying, "Tomorrow my deeds will show that I am faithful to my lord." To prove his loyalty, shortly before dawn on 28 June (the day on which the battle occurred) Miloš slipped out of the Serbian camp and announced himself to the Turkish sentries as a Serbian deserter. Taken to the sultan, he pulled out a knife he had secreted in his garments and stabbed Murad, fatally wounding him. We do not know whether there had actually been any accusations in the Serbian camp before the battle, but it is a fact that a Serb named Miloš Obilić (or Kobilić) did desert and murder the sultan.

The news of the murder was kept from the Turkish troops, who were commanded by Murad's son, who was to be the new sultan, Bayezid I. A wild battle between the two armies then followed which resulted in the bulk of both armies being wiped out. In the course of the battle Lazar was captured and, upon being taken to Bayezid, executed. The Bosnians fought well, as did Vuk Branković, depicted in the epics as the actual traitor. In fact it would be difficult to prove that any Serb was a traitor in the battle. At the end of the battle the remnants of the Turkish army held the field while the remnants of the Serbian (Lazar's and Branković's) and Bosnian (Vlatko Vuković's) troops withdrew. However, then the Turks withdrew as well, for Bayezid needed to hurry back east to secure his position as sultan against his brothers and, moreover, he did not have enough troops remaining to carry on an offensive against the Balkan Christians. Thus since the Turks also withdrew, one can conclude the battle was a draw.

Because of the Turkish retreat from Serbia, Vlatko Vuković claimed a Christian victory in his message to Tvrtko, and Tvrtko depicted it as such in a message he sent to Italy. Thus Tvrtko was hailed as a savior of Christendom in Italy and France. However, though the actual battle may have been a draw, a major difference between the two sides made the Turks the real victors.

In providing a massive army for the Balkans at the time (estimates vary from twelve to twenty thousand men), the Serbs had brought to Kosovo close to the total of their fighting strength. The Turks, though they lost a vast number of troops (from an army estimated at between twenty-seven and thirty thousand men), had many more troops in the east. Thus in the years that followed the Turks were able to return and raid. Small Turkish raiding parties actually appeared later in 1389; the Ottomans then directed a campaign through Serbia against Hungary in 1390, and they carried out larger raiding campaigns into Serbia in 1391 and 1392. Thus the Turks were able to continue their successful push into the Balkans, whereas the Serbs were left with too few men to resist successfully. Thus, though the Serbs did not lose the battle, in the long run, over the next two to three years, they lost the war because they were no longer able to resist the Turks effectively; and the losses they had suffered at Kosovo were, of course, the major reason they had so few men left to defend Serbia. Thus one can say the immediate result of Kosovo was a draw, but the long-term result was a Serbian loss. And this is shown by the fact that after Kosovo, as we shall see, Lazar's and the other Serbian principalities one after the other became Ottoman vassals.

Lazar was succeeded by his son Stefan Lazarević. He was still a minor, so his mother, Milica, became regent. Almost immediately, in November 1389, she was attacked by the Hungarians under Sigismund, who hoped to take advantage of Serbia's weakness after Kosovo to regain at least some of the territory, formerly belonging to Hungary, that lay south of the Danube. The Hungarians took a series of the Serbs' northern fortresses and penetrated as far south as Kragujevac. Scholars disagree on the results of this attack and of the further fighting that occurred between Hungary and Serbia in the ensuing years. Moreover, because the Ottomans intervened in 1390, it is possible that places taken by the Hungarians in 1389 were subsequently abandoned, allowing the Serbs to recover some of them.

Concrete information on Mačva and its environs in the 1390s is slight and, as we shall see, able to be interpreted in two ways; for a charter reference can refer to actual possession or it can have been inserted to claim what is seen as a legal right. Thus it is impossible for scholars to arrive at a firm conclusion. For example, to suggest Hungarian acquisitions in the area is the fact that Hungarian "Bans of Mačva" are found witnessing charters in the 1390s. However, as noted above, the presence of men bearing this title does not prove Hungarian possession of Mačva, because at various times in the past men with this title co-existed with Serbian possession of Mačva. On the other hand, to suggest Serbian retention is the fact that in 1395 Milica and Stefan Lazarević issued a charter, confirming an earlier grant by Lazar, to the Saint Panteleimon monastery on Mount Athos that, among other places, awarded to the monastery Dragobili in Deboš, which is located in Mačva. However, possession of this place does not demonstrate that Milica held all Mačva. Furthermore, it does not even prove that she held the place mentioned; she may have simply been confirming her agreement that the monastery had rights to the village. In spite of the fact that evidence about Mačva's fate in the 1390s is lacking, most scholars believe that Hungary regained some, if not most or even all, of Mačva in the 1390s. If we could settle the question simply on the basis of the relative strength of the two countries—without having to concern ourselves with Turkish actions—this conclusion would be warranted.

Thus the Serbs, weakened after Kosovo, found themselves caught between two aggressive foreign powers, Hungary and the Ottomans. Since the Serbs could not stand up to both, it was necessary to ally with one to oppose the other. Not surprisingly, opinions differed; and though, presumably, supporters of each viewpoint could be found in any given city, the pro-Ottoman faction triumphed in one part of Serbia while the pro-Hungarians predominated in another. Geography was decisive to explain the decisions Serbian leaders took on this question. Milica's lands lay to the north and bordered on Hungary, which had just attacked her; not surprisingly, she was particularly worried about Hungary. Thus she was inclined to reach an agreement with the Ottomans. Vuk Branković, on the other hand, possessed lands in the south; he had no border with Hungary and a large frontier with the Turks. Not surprisingly, he was more concerned about the Turks. Wanting to find allies to resist them, in July 1389 he opened negotiations with the Hungarians.

Vuk also seems to have become ambitious to head a greater Serbia and succeed to the Nemanjić heritage. With Lazar dead and his son a minor, there was no Serb leader strong enough to prevent or even challenge such an assertion. Vuk had presumably accepted Lazar's suzerainty earlier only because Lazar had been sufficiently strong for Vuk to fear crossing him. But after his death, Vuk freely acted as if Lazar had left no heirs, thereby enabling Vuk to assume Lazar's role. For example, in a charter he issued to Hilandar in late 1389 or early 1390 Vuk calls himself "Lord Stefan [the Serbian royal name] Vuk." He also sought, though without success, the Saint Demetrius' Day tribute from Dubrovnik after Tvrtko died in 1391. Vuk presumably also had ambitions to increase his own holdings. However, it is not known whether he actually took any territory from Milica.

As a result, Milica found herself caught between two ambitious enemies, the Hungarians and Vuk, who were now negotiating together and on the verge of forging an alliance. She may well have feared the partition of her principality between them. Thus it is hardly surprising that when Ottoman armies, moving toward Hungary, reached Milica's border in the summer of 1390, Milica, on the advice of the Church (as pro-Milica sources hasten to say to justify her action), submitted to them at once. She accepted Ottoman suzerainty and allowed the Turks free passage through her lands. One account says that Milica and her son then had to travel to Sivas, where the sultan was based at the time, to submit formally. The Serbian patriarch then held a Church council, which endorsed her decision. Now Lazar's (Stefan Lazarević's) state owed the Ottomans tribute and military service. Stefan Lazarević also had to send his sister Olivera to join Bayezid's harem. These obligations, of course, were not yet binding on Vuk, who had made no such submission; thus relations seem to have been broken between Milica's Kruševac and Vuk's Priština.

Then in 1391 the Ottomans launched major raids against Greece, Zeta, Albania, and Durazzo. That winter, 1391–92, Ottoman troops were active all around Vuk, who was forced to surrender Skopje to them on 6 January 1392. Soon Vuk sued for peace and accepted Ottoman vassal obligations, military service and tribute. These vassal ties are documented in a charter of November 1392, but surely they date from late winter or early spring 1392, to about the time, if not the very moment, of Skopje's surrender. Thus by the end of 1392 all the Serbian lands, except for Hum under Tvrtko, had accepted Ottoman suzerainty.

This quarrel between Vuk and Milica, though short-lasting and of limited significance (no battles were ever fought between them in this period), seems to have led Milica's partisans to unleash a propaganda campaign of slander that was to have an effect on the epics and even on the written historical tradition that was to follow. Orbini's history of the Slavs (1601) states that Vuk betrayed Lazar on the field of battle. Orbini's statement is the earliest written accusation against Vuk, and the way he phrases it suggests that he was not certain that the charge was fact: "Vuk saved himself with almost all his troops because beforehand (as some say) he had had secret negotiations with Sultan Murad to betray (as he indeed did) his father-in-law and procure" Lazar's state. The phrase "as some say" shows that Orbini is reporting hearsay and strongly suggests that his source for this item was oral. This claim of Vuk's treachery is also found in the epics. Though these songs were all collected long after Orbini's time, they surely went back to the fifteenth, if not the late fourteenth, century. While traveling through Serbia in 1530, Kuripešić crossed Kosovo, where, he reports, he heard the tale of a battle about which many today sing in Serbia. Thus most scholars have plausibly concluded that Orbini's source for this statement was an oral, and probably epic, one.

It is true that Vuk did leave the field of battle, but he left after the Bosnians and after it was clear that the battle could not be won. Turkish sources report that Vuk had commanded the Serbian right wing and had fought well during the heat of the battle, achieving considerable success against the Ottoman left wing. He had withdrawn only after the Bosnian left wing had collapsed and was retreating and the Serbian center was falling. It should also be noted that Vuk was the last Serb prince (excluding the Serb nobles under Tvrtko) to accept Ottoman suzerainty. Why then should he be called a traitor? Possibly the Serbs needed a scape-goat for their defeat—the Serbs had not lost a battle but had been betrayed. But, perhaps, one should seek the cause of Vuk's damnation not in what occurred during the battle but in what happened after it. Vuk had opposed the widow of the sainted Lazar— for Lazar was canonized in the 1390s very soon after the battle. One may hypothesize that the epics were created in Lazar's territory and thus were pro-Milica works designed to blacken the reputation of the man who became her opponent in the years immediately following the battle. Furthermore, the need for propaganda against Vuk did not end in 1392; thereafter he and his sons continued to be rivals of, and frequently at odds with, Lazar's son Stefan Lazarević. As a result Saint Lazar was made into the hero of an epic whose contents were made to parallel the New Testament, with Vuk cast into the role of Judas.[2]

Before leaving the matter, I think it proper to note that a circumstantial case has been advanced against Vuk. Besides the oral accounts and Orbini's written statement, scholars have noticed that Serbian historical writing from the fifteenth century ignores Vuk. The silence of certain early fifteenth-century works can be tied to the fact that they originated at Stefan Lazarević's court. However, even after Vuk's son George succeeded Stefan Lazarević as ruler of Serbia in 1427, Vuk continued to be ignored, even in George's charters. Some scholars have taken this as evidence that there was something shameful in Vuk's past, possibly something associated with Kosovo. Furthermore, though Orbini was the first to specifically name Vuk as a traitor, his work was not the first to suggest treachery at Kosovo. In the late fifteenth century Constantine of Ostrovica states that the Battle of Kosovo was lost because of unfaith, jealousy, and disagreements between bad and unfaithful people. Like Constantine, certain sixteenth-century writers also mention some sort of treachery at Kosovo without naming the traitor or traitors. Some scholars have argued that these statements should be taken to refer to Vuk. However, all the above arguments can be accepted and still not increase the evidence against Vuk one jot. If slander against Vuk was started in the 1390s when he and Milica were rivals, the slander could easily have entered the oral tradition and then come to be believed. Thus the above items may all reflect negative feelings about Vuk, but they cannot be used as proof against him. They only suggest that various people in the fifteenth and sixteenth centuries *believed* he behaved badly.

This relatively insignificant quarrel between Vuk and Milica that may have had such an impact on subsequent historiography also seems not to have lasted long. For we find Milica visiting Vuk and her daughter Mara, Vuk's wife, in Priština in August 1392. Though we do not know how Milica and Vuk felt toward one another, it at least shows they were not in a state of open hostility. It also could be taken as evidence, circumstantial of course, that Milica did not believe Vuk betrayed Lazar; for had she believed that, would she have accepted his hospitality? Soon thereafter, according to Mošin between 1392 and 1398, Vuk allowed Lazar's body to be taken from Priština to the Monastery of Ravanica, built in his own principality by Lazar. This act had to have occurred in the earlier part of that period, before Vuk lost Priština which occurred, as we shall see, in 1396 (according to Dinić) or by 1394 (according to Purković).

Albania and Zeta

The years following Kosovo were marked by an increase in Ottoman military activity, which directly annexed certain territories and imposed suzerainty upon various hitherto independent princes and tribes. In 1392 the Ottomans launched a major raid through southern Serbia into Bosnia and a second one through Macedonia that reached Zeta and the coast. As noted, this campaign forced Vuk Branković to accept Ottoman vassalage.

The divided Albanian tribesmen were unable to band together to create any sort of unified resistance. There were several major Albanian families (or tribes) at this time. If we take them from south to north, we find: The Spata were dominant in Epirus; to their north lay the city-state of Jannina. To the north of Jannina two major tribes had emerged: The Arianiti (Araniti) and

Musachi. The lands of the former extended from behind Valona in a north-easterly direction to Mokro on the west shore of Lake Ohrid. In this same south-central region the Musachi family held lands between, as well as on both, the Vijosë (Vjosa, Voyoussa, Aoos) and Shkumbi rivers; their lands extended east along the Devolli and Osumi rivers and beyond to the region of Kastoria. The Musachi lost the city of Kastoria itself to the Turks in about 1385. The family also held some estates near Durazzo, and the family head, Andrew III (1388–93), regularly resided in a house in Durazzo. Holding Valona itself, and maybe not much more, were Mrkše Žarković and his wife Rugina. As we move further north we come to the lands of the Thopias stretching roughly between the Shkumbi and Mati rivers. They also held the major fortified cities of Kroja and Durazzo. They were being challenged by the emerging Castriots and may already have been pushed away from the territory on the left bank of the Mati near that river's mouth. The Castriots' holdings between the upper Mati and upper Drin stretched east almost as far as Debar. The Castriots were pressing north beyond the Mati, where they came into collision with the Dukagjins, who, by then split into two branches, held much of the territory between the Mati and middle and lower Drin. The Dukagjin family seat remained the important town of Alessio; the family's lands extended to the northeast as far as Djakova (Djakovica) in Kosovo. The Dukagjins also pressed beyond the Drin, controlling considerable territory between it and the Bojana. In this area they came into conflict with their old rivals, the Balšići, who controlled Zeta and most of the lands north of the Bojana (excluding the territory that had seceded under the Crnojevići); the Balšići still sought to assert themselves south beyond the Bojana. In the territory between the Drin and Mati, the Jonima were also trying to assert themselves, but they were clearly smaller fry.

The so-called borders—which needless to say were rarely stable—given here are of the roughest nature. The tribes were mobile with their flocks; their routes passed over considerable distances and were not necessarily entirely under their constant control. Moreover, territories changed as certain tribes became more or less powerful, and tribes sometimes split in two, giving birth to new tribes. There also were many smaller families living within the broad territories I have outlined. Thus the great families did not necessarily control the whole region specified, although they may have frequently exerted some sort of dominance over the lesser tribes whom they had as neighbors. Further adding to our difficulty is the fact that certain tribal chiefs had houses in towns; these towns did not necessarily lie within their zones of pastoral activities. However, when documents are lacking, as they often are, one can easily arrive at a mistaken conclusion: for example, that because a chief lived in Kroja, the tribal lands must have lain around or near that city.

Unlike most of Serbia, whose economy was based on settled agriculture, with peasants residing in villages and farming fields, most of Zeta and Albania were mountainous and unsuited in many parts for agriculture. Stock-raising, particularly of sheep, dominated. Thus, families practiced transhumance; this practice indicates an annual migration by some or all of a family from the valleys where its members lived in the winter up to mountain pastures in the summer. In a region like Zeta political fragmentation was natural; for it was difficult for any governmental authorities to establish firm control over its inaccessible territory. Mobile pastoralists with horses are obviously harder to control than settled villagers. As conditions became more unsettled, as they did when the Turks began raiding into the area, larger numbers of people left the lowlands and foothills to find refuge in the wilder mountains. This caused greater instability, as the mountains could not support a larger population. Furthermore, the new arrivals had to support themselves on territory already claimed by the old-timers. In such unstable times the family became increasingly important, and to be part of a large family gave one advantages. Thus cousins banded together to secure control of their pastures and of their flocks' migration routes.

The central government of the Balšići—if we can call it that—had never been able to control what went on in the mountains, and as conditions became more chaotic owing to the Turkish raids and large-scale migrations, it became less and less able to do so. The decline of, or lack of, central government caused an increasing need for self-help, for a family could not call upon the Balšići to bring forces and provide justice for it against, say, the Crnojevići or Dukagjins. And if one needed to rely on one's own family, it became important to be part of a powerful and large family. Thus the institution of the tribe became increasingly important. And as tribes supplemented families, the larger and more powerful a tribe was, the better off were its members. Thus in the fourteenth and particularly in the fifteenth centuries throughout Zeta, parts of Hum, and northern Albania, the tribes became increasingly prominent. And we find increased mention of them in the sources.

Since the state apparatus could not guarantee order, the families became more self-reliant in enforcing their own rights; they themselves punished crimes committed against themselves or insults to their honor. Thus the institution of the blood feud increased in importance. In such a society, loyalty came to be felt toward the family, rather than toward a province or a state; and a strong "we-they" mentality developed that demanded a certain pattern of conduct toward members of the tribe and allowed a less honorable mode of conduct toward outsiders.

Since these mountainous regions were also economically poor, unable at the best of times to support their populations, they produced a "plunder" economy under which the tribesmen plundered their richer neighbors in the plains—an activity encouraged by, and in turn further encouraging, the "we-they" mentality. And we have previously noted various cases of Albanian tribesmen plundering settled Greek society in Epirus and Thessaly. Later, mutual raiding came to be the way of life for the tribesmen of Zeta (Montenegro) and Hum (Hercegovina). The tribesmen also could and did plunder the caravans of merchants passing through their lands. Brigandage was a regular Balkan institution, particularly in the mountains. Though always present, it increased whenever conditions became unsettled.

The tribes were composed of brotherhoods, one of which usually was the strongest and regularly tended to dominate the whole tribe. In such cases that brotherhood's leader was regularly the tribe's knez or vojvoda. Tribes settled their own affairs according to their own customs; important decisions often were made by tribal assemblies—one such assembly is documented in 1423 when the Paštrovići decided to submit to Venice. Thus Zeta, much of Hum, and northern Albania were dominated by these autonomous, often mobile, self-governing units. And a "central government" like that of the Balšić rulers dealt with the tribes through their chiefs. And when the Balšići, the Venetians, or later the Crnojevići obtained submission from a tribe, the overlord did not interfere with the internal affairs of the tribe, but simply extracted allegiance and an agreement as to what services were to be rendered. The leaders of the larger tribes became the major noblemen of an area. Thus the nobility in these regions differed greatly from the also family-oriented but settled nobility of the plains and agricultural areas like Thessaly, Serbia, or Bulgaria.

George II Balšić found it impossible to take advantage of the Battle of Kosovo to reassert his family's former position. At home the Crnojevići refused him obedience and were managing to extend their sway over an ever greater part of Zeta. Moreover, a major rival to George appeared within his own family: Constantine Balšić, his first cousin, the son of George I. Constantine's mother, Theodora, had remained active after George I's death and had continued to manage a fairly large territory between the Drin and Bojana rivers where she resided with her son. Constantine had been excluded from participating in the government of Zeta, first by his uncle Balša, and then by his cousin George II. Wanting his rightful inheritance and supported by his mother, Constantine in 1390 or more likely 1391 broke with his ruling cousin and visited the court of Bayezid I, where he became an Ottoman vassal. He did not limit himself to one alliance but also established good relations with Vuk Branković, a long-time rival of the Balšići in Zeta. He also had various powerful relatives. His mother's niece Helen had, most probably in 1392, married the new Byzantine emperor, Manuel II (1391–1425). His half-brother Mrkše Žarković, the son of his mother's earlier marriage with Žarko of Zeta, had by marrying Rugina, John Comnenus Asen's granddaughter and Balša II's daughter, acquired the city of Valona. Constantine maintained close relations with his half-brother, frequently residing at his court. He also performed a major service for Mrkše; through his cousin the Byzantine empress, he arranged to have the Patriarch of Constantinople sanction Mrkše's marriage to Rugina, which had violated canons and not been recognized by the Church because the couple were too closely related.

Meanwhile, immediately after Tvrtko's death, George II had brought his troops to the walls of Kotor and demanded that the town pay him tribute.

Since matters were then unstable in Bosnia, the town yielded and agreed to pay George tribute. The following year, 1392, George was at war with the Crnojevići. The Ottomans, wanting to discuss the quarrel with him, summoned him to a meeting with the Sanjak-beg of Skopje. When George answered the summons (in 1392), he was taken prisoner; the Ottomans demanded a number of towns from him as the price for his release. The Ottomans may well have seized George on behalf of Constantine, who seems to have hoped to obtain Skadar at this time. With George out of the picture, his Crnojević rival, Radič Crnojević, immediately brought his troops to the coast and took Budva (which George seems to have regained; at least he is documented as being in that town in 1389) and various towns held by George on the Gulf of Kotor. Radič then moved south and expelled the Dukagjins from Alessio. His occupation of that town was very temporary, however, for the Dukagjins regained it early in 1393.

Faced with the Ottoman threat, the seriousness of which was vividly illustrated by George's capture, and challenged by various domestic or neighboring opponents who had become Ottoman vassals to obtain support for their local ambitions, the other local rulers found themselves in severe difficulties. If they did not choose to submit to the Turks, they had only one alternative: Venice. Venice, however, was not an ideal protector. Lacking an army, it could only assume the role of protector with its fleet; this limited Venice's usefulness to coastal cities or the few river ports attainable from the sea. Moreover, in the process of establishing commercial relations with the Turks, Venice was often hesitant about assuming obligations to various cities or petty princes for fear of antagonizing the Turks and possibly losing the commercial privileges it was acquiring. Yet Venice also had strong ambitions to dominate the Adriatic, and thus usually, after debate in its senate, it agreed to assume control over the Adriatic ports that offered to submit to it. However, Venice's interests were always connected to its commerce; thus once established it immediately strove to increase its business activities in its new acquisitions. These activities often clashed with those of local, or neighboring Dalmatian, traders and, moreover, by increasing the volume of business and of circulating coinage, had an unsettling effect on the newly acquired towns and their hinterlands.[3]

In 1392 George Thopia, the weak and ill son of Karlo Thopia, surrendered Durazzo to the Venetians. They immediately set to work to improve Durazzo's already most impressive fortifications. (As early as the eleventh century its walls had been so thick that four horsemen could ride abreast on top of them.) The Venetians were to hold Durazzo until 1501. Later that year George Thopia died without issue. The bulk of his holdings, for he surrendered only Durazzo and environs to Venice, went to his sister Helen. (A small piece was left to his younger sister Vojsava, who was married to a patrician of Durazzo known as Lord [Kyr] Isaac. That couple continued to reside in Durazzo under the Venetians.) Helen was married to the Venetian patrician Mark Barbadigo, who became the actual ruler of Helen's lands. Usually residing in the strong fortress of Kroja, Mark for a time held his and Helen's possessions under Venetian suzerainty. Radič Crnojević also recognized Venetian suzerainty over his lands, concluding a treaty with Venice on 30 November 1392. In early 1393 the Dukagjin brothers regained Alessio from Radič and, realizing that they could not defend it against an Ottoman assault, surrendered it in May or June 1393 to Venice. In return for the town the Venetians granted them titles and an annual pension. The Dukagjins, however, retained all their inland territory, which Venice, lacking the means to defend, had little interest in.

Losing territory to the Crnojevići and threatened by his cousin, George II did not dare stay away from the action for long. He negotiated his freedom from Turkish captivity by submitting once again to Ottoman suzerainty, agreeing to pay an annual tribute, and by surrendering to the sultan the cities of Skadar, Drivast, and Sveti Srdj, an important market on the Bojana. George then returned to his major residence in Ulcinj, which he was allowed to retain.

Constantine Balšić had hoped to obtain Skadar upon the Ottomans' acquisition of it. Some scholars believe that he may have briefly held it. In any case, if he did, it was only very briefly, for in 1393 the town is found under the governorship of Šahin, the Ottoman commander who had received the town from George's commander. Thus it is reasonable to conclude that Skadar was immediately placed under Šahin. Constantine may have quarreled with the Ottomans over this, for he fled for a short time to an Adriatic island from which he corresponded with Venice.

Meanwhile, having occupied Skadar, the Ottomans set about strengthening their influence among the Albanian lords of the area. They won over Demetrius Jonima, who soon arranged a meeting between Ottoman officials and Mark Barbadigo of Kroja, who had recently been quarreling with the Venetians. Presumably Mark also found himself under threat of attack from the Ottomans unless he submitted. These negotiations resulted in Mark's accepting Ottoman suzerainty; he was allowed to retain Kroja and his other lands, which stretched all the way to Durazzo. Ceasing to regard himself as a Venetian deputy, as he had until then, he began plundering Venetian lands in the neighborhood of Durazzo. As a result the Venetians ordered Nikola (Niketas) Thopia, who had been governing Durazzo for them, to take measures. Thopia led his troops against Barbadigo and defeated him badly. Presumably the Ottomans were disappointed by Barbadigo's failure, for now—probably late in 1394—they installed their vassal Constantine Balšić as governor of Kroja. Barbadigo went into exile, seeking asylum at the court of George Balšić. Thus if a quarrel between Constantine Balsić and the Ottomans had taken place, it was a brief one. In 1395 Constantine was fighting for the Ottomans at the Battle of Rovine. The Venetians were incensed at the turn of events and approached Constantine to yield Kroja to them, but he refused. Constantine soon married Barbadigo's wife, Helen Thopia, who had the hereditary rights (such as they were) to Kroja. Constantine's mother, who by now had become a nun, joined him in Kroja, playing an active role at court. Soon Constantine was also in possession of the town of Danj (Dagno) with its lucrative customs house.

In 1395 George II Balšić, after repelling an attack that year—if not in the previous one—from the Dukagjins, secured his relations with Venice. He hoped thereby to smooth his relations with the Dukagjins, Venetian vassals. It also strengthened his own position. And with the Ottomans occupied elsewhere, he discarded his vassalage to them and in October 1395 mobilized his forces to regain his lost cities. In short order he recovered Skadar, Drivast, and Sveti Srdj from the small Turkish garrisons in residence. He also took Danj from his cousin Constantine. But knowing he could not hold his conquests against an Ottoman counter-attack, in 1396 he yielded to Venice Skadar, Drivast, Sveti Srdj, Danj, Lake Skadar and its islands, and the right bank of the Bojana River. (Danj did not actually go to Venice. By then it had fallen into the hands of a restless soldier of fortune, Koja Zakarija, who had become an Ottoman vassal and refused to yield it.) George retained for himself only Ulcinj and Bar with their districts. His borders with Venice now ran along the southern shore of Lake Skadar and the right bank of the Bojana; it was agreed that neither would fortify its bank of the Bojana. Skadar was to remain Venetian until 1479.

Thus Venice had strengthened its position in the southern Adriatic, acquiring direct rule over many of the coastal towns while asserting suzerainty over various Slavic or Albanian lords of other coastal towns and even of the interior. Expecting success from the Christian anti-Turkish crusade of 1396, Venice at that moment had less fear of the Turks and was willing to take a more active role in the area. Moreover, though Skadar on its lake might seem to the reader to be fairly far inland, it was approachable by ship since the Bojana River, running between Lake Skadar and the Adriatic, was navigable for large ships as far as Sveti Srdj. And when weather and water conditions were right smaller ships with shallower drafts could reach the lake itself.[4]

Meanwhile, when George was regaining his cities in the late fall of 1395, Radič Crnojević moved down to the Gulf of Kotor and took Grbalj, whose peasants were happy to escape from the control Kotor had asserted over them. He then laid siege to Kotor. He was unable to take the town, but its council agreed to pay him tribute and so, satisfied with a new source of income, he withdrew his troops. At the same time Radič obtained submission from the major tribe in that region, the Paštrovići, who occupied the mountains above the Gulf of Kotor. Other Orthodox families in the mountains above Kotor not only submitted to Radič but gave him military support. Whether their Orthodoxy was a factor in their supporting him against the Catholic Balšići, as has sometimes been suggested, is not known, but it seems doubtful to me. Venice tried to mediate a settlement of this growing quarrel between its two Slavic Zetan vassals, but without success. Then in May 1396, during a skirmish with George's army, Radič Crnojević was killed. George seems to have at once seized some of Radič's lands from his weaker brothers, Dobrovoj and

Stefan, but George was not strong enough to take much. He had lost much local support and was economically too poor to raise a large enough army to go on the offensive. His lands had suffered greatly from the plundering of Radič's men in 1395; moreover, in 1396 a major earthquake had severely damaged his coastal cities of Ulcinj and Bar.

George also had to face a new and more dangerous enemy than Radič had been. For Sandalj Hranić of Bosnia, successor to Vlatko Vuković and the leading nobleman of Hum, had acquired Tvrtko's coastal holdings which, including Novi, stretched to the north bank of the Gulf of Kotor. He looked upon the two Zetans' forcible assertion of suzerainty over Kotor as a usurpation of Bosnia's rights, for Kotor had been under Bosnian suzerainty since 1384 or 1385. Sandalj's tribute demands were smaller than those of the Zetans, so through diplomacy the town of Kotor accepted Sandalj as its suzerain. The death of Radič Crnojević made this submission less risky for the town. Sandalj also restored to Kotor its lordship over various towns and districts along the coast—in particular over the Svetomiholjska Metohija—that Radič had liberated from Kotor. Sandalj then took Budva. He soon had won over the Paštrovići, and thus probably briefly asserted his lordship over the mountain districts behind Kotor that had formerly accepted the Crnojevići. Sandalj's presence on the coast led to a quarrel with Dubrovnik over its salt monopoly, for, like Tvrtko before him, Sandalj imported salt from Italy into Budva and Novi. He also skirmished in the late 1390s with George Balšić, who still claimed this area. In these fights the Paštrovići split. Many ardently supported Sandalj, and when he was soon forced to retire from the coastal area, many Paštrovići retreated with him and received lands on the Neretva in Hum.

After the death of Radič, the Crnojević family, under his brothers Dobrovoj and Stefan, suffered a major decline. They not only suffered territorial losses to George and then, as seen, to Sandalj, but also to a second family, probably related to them, the Djuraševići, led by the brothers George and Lješ. They, though first referred to in sources in 1403, seem to have been actively supporting George Balšić against the Crnojevići already in the late 1390s. The Djuraševići played a major role in George Balšić's campaign that expelled Sandalj from Budva in 1403. As a reward George assigned Budva to them; he also awarded them the region of the Svetomiholjska Metohija, which was once again taken away from Kotor. In this period the Djuraševići also took advantage of Balšić support to win for themselves much Crnojević land in the mountains behind Kotor, some of which seems to have been briefly held by Sandalj. The Crnojevići, in decline, still retained three villages near Lake Skadar and possibly some interior territory.

After defeating the Christian crusaders at Nikopolis and expelling the Brankovići from their lands (events to be discussed below), the Ottomans resumed an active role in Zeta and Albania. Their raiding was resumed again, probably in 1398. At that time Progon, the Dukagjin family head and a Venetian vassal, was killed trying to oppose the Turks. Not surprisingly, one after the other, various Albanian and Slavic lords of the Albanian-Zetan interior had to accept Ottoman suzerainty. Those submitting included the Dukagjins—now led by Tanush Major—for their lands along the Drin. So as the fourteenth century came to a close, the Venetian presence came to be limited to possession of or suzerainty over just the towns along the Adriatic, the Bojana River, and Lake Skadar.

In the cities they controlled the Venetians, who took advantage of their rule to further their own commerce, carried out few measures to strengthen local defense, even though they taxed the local population heavily for that purpose. The indigenous local leaders, who had agreed to submit to Venice because they felt Venice better able to defend their towns from the Turks, became disgruntled. A large revolt broke out against Venice in 1399, continuing for two years, among the overtaxed villagers in the vicinity of Skadar and Drivast. And riots, including acts of arson, also took place inside Skadar itself. The Venetian troops were able to hold out in Skadar and Drivast themselves, while the surrounding countryside ceased to recognize Venetian officials. Disillusioned with Venice's policy in his former lands and with its trade monopoly policy that caused economic stagnation in the ports he still retained, George Balšić brought troops into the districts he had previously yielded to Venice. He captured a large quantity of salt at Sveti Srdj, which he then sold. The Venetians attributed to him a major role in initiating the uprising. It is not certain whether or not this judgment was accurate; it is possible that he simply took advantage of a situation that arose spontaneously. The Turks also sent raiding parties through these rebellious Venetian territories. The rebellion was finally put down in 1402 and peace was reestablished.

In 1402, when many Albanian vassals of the Ottomans—Koja Zakarija, Demetrius Jonima, John Castriot, and probably Tanush Major Dukagjin—led their retainers personally to support Bayezid against Timur at Ankara, Constantine Balšić remained in Albania. He promptly launched an attack against Venice's Durazzo. The attempt failed and he was captured. The Venetians tried and then executed him. His city of Kroja was quickly seized by Nikola Thopia, acting for himself. The Venetians, whom he had previously served loyally and well, soon acquiesced and, in 1404, recognized him as governor of Kroja.

The Ottoman Conquest of Bulgaria

During the winter of 1392–93 John Šišman of Bulgaria entered into secret negotiations with Hungary's King Sigismund, who was then planning a major expedition against the Ottomans (an expedition that in fact was not to occur until 1396). Presumably John Šišman saw Hungarian support as a means to shed the heavy vassalage the Ottomans had imposed upon Bulgaria. The Ottomans, learning of these talks, launched a major invasion against Bulgaria. The country was devastated. Trnovo fell, after heroically resisting a three-month siege, in July 1393. The Ottomans, then, decided to annex the country. Bulgaria was placed under direct Ottoman administration; it was to remain under Turkish rule for nearly five hundred years. The Turks sent in their administrators and settled their cavalry on military fiefs (timars), which provided the Turks with a strong and loyal force within Bulgaria. They quickly and effectively established such firm control over Bulgaria that Bulgaria remained Ottoman even after the Ottoman defeat at Ankara (1402) and throughout the Ottoman civil war (1403–13). Only Vidin was not conquered. John Stracimir reaffirmed his vassalage to the sultan and remained as ruler of Vidin a few years longer.

The only other piece of "Bulgarian" territory that did not fall in 1393 was the disputed region along the Black Sea coast; it survived the 1393 attack since at the time it was not under Bulgaria. After 1366/67 the "Bulgarian" Black Sea coast had been divided. The southern half with Mesembria, Anchialos, and Sozopolis had been returned to the Byzantine Empire, while the central and northern part—Emona, Varna, Kavarna, Kaliakra—remained as part of the Dobrudja state of Despot Dobrotica, who was succeeded in about 1385 by his son Ivanko. Ivanko concluded a treaty with Genoa that gave the Genoese broad privileges, in 1387. These relations may have been partially intended to pave the way for an alliance with Genoa against Trnovo, which then enjoyed good relations with Genoa's rival Venice. However, Ivanko was not able to maintain the independence of his state. Perhaps he died. In any case the Dobrudja state was annexed by Mircea of Wallachia in early 1390 and was held by him to mid-1391. At least, this possession is suggested by Mircea's charters from 1390–91 in which, in addition to his other titles, he calls himself "Despot of the land of Dobrotica." His charters from 1392 and later omit this title, indicating that by then he had ceased to hold this territory.

Soon these Black Sea lands were held by Emperor Manuel II's nephew John VII, who also held an appanage, centered in Selymbria, that stretched from the region of Mesembria along the Black Sea shore to very near Constantinople. John held his appanage under Ottoman suzerainty. This territory had been the base from which John in 1390 had briefly seized Constantinople from John V. After his succession Manuel was unhappy about John VII's appanage but could take no effective action since the sultan, playing divide and rule, placed John VII under his protection. Presumably the Dobrudja was acquired by John in 1391 or 1392, when the Ottomans were raiding in the area. We may suspect that either John took advantage of the raiders' presence and the general instability caused by the raids to seize the lands—obtaining Ottoman confirmation afterward—or else the Ottomans occupied them and, supporting John as a rival to Manuel, decided to strengthen his position by granting them to him. The Turks took the Dobrudja in 1395, but John was to continue to hold the rest of his appanage until the Ottomans took Selymbria in 1399. We may suspect that at that time they took the Black Sea cities lying to its north as well. The conclusions presented above are based on the research of Naumov, who persuasively argues against the view, which prevailed until recently, that the Ottomans took Mesembria and the other Black Sea towns in 1380, if not even earlier.[5]

The Battles of Rovine and Nikopolis and their Results

In 1395 the Ottomans attacked Wallachia to punish its ruler, Mircea, for raiding into Ottoman territory. At Rovine, where the Turks met the Wallachians (Vlachs) in battle on 17 May 1395, on the Turkish side, fulfilling their vassal obligations, were Stefan Lazarević, Vukašin's son Marko, and Constantine Dejanović. Constantine and Marko were both killed in the battle. After their deaths, the Ottomans annexed their lands. Marko's territory around Prilep and Constantine's around Kumanovo were combined into a single Ottoman province centered in Kjustendil (formerly Velbužd). Despite the role which history forced upon him, Marko (called Marko Kraljević, "the king's son") became in the epics the greatest Serbian opponent of the Turks. But though many of his actual military activities between 1372 and 1395 were in support of the Turks, Marko's heart does not seem to have been with them. Constantine the Philosopher reports that on the eve of the Battle of Rovine Marko said to Constantine Dejanović, "I pray God to help the Christians and that I will be among the first dead in this war." The Wallachians won at Rovine and were thus successful in preventing the Turkish occupation of their lands beyond the Danube. However, the campaign did result in the Turks annexing the Dobrudja. Thus by the end of 1395 the Ottomans had taken Bulgaria (except the Vidin province), eastern Macedonia, Thrace, and—as we shall see—Thessaly.

Mircea of Wallachia not only managed to survive the Ottoman attack of 1395, but he also was able to take advantage of Timur's (Tamerlane's) successful war against the Golden Horde, which resulted in the destruction of the Horde's capital of Sarai. Capitalizing upon the weakened Horde's preoccupation with this major crisis, Mircea seized Kilia, an important port at the mouth of the Danube where the Genoese had a major colony; Kilia in the second half of the fourteenth century had replaced Vicina as the major port at the mouth of the Danube.

In 1396 King Sigismund of Hungary, against whom the Ottomans seem to have been planning a campaign, organized a major Christian crusading venture. The bulk of the Christian troops were drawn from Hungary and from France. The Christian armies crossed the Danube and reached Nikopolis, where they were met in September by the advancing Turkish army. The Christian armies lacked co-ordination, and the French knights refused to follow the plans suggested by Sigismund, who at least knew Turkish battle strategy. The divided command plus Turkish skill led to a massive Turkish victory. Thousands of Christians were captured and held for ransom; some spent years in Turkish captivity. Sigismund, almost captured, managed to escape on a Christian ship. Since Stracimir of Vidin had supported this crusade, the Turks swept through his lands after their victory at Nikopolis. It did not take them long to conquer them, and the Vidin province, the last bit of independent Bulgaria, was annexed as well. The following year the Turks poured into Greece again, overran Attica, and raided into the Peloponnesus. During these years they also blockaded Constantinople. Lacking a fleet, they could not take the city. However, by 1399, when they took Selymbria, Constantinople was completely surrounded by territory directly under Ottoman control. Thus many felt that it was only a matter of time before it fell.

Serbian Affairs

Toward the middle of the 1390s the Ottomans became angry at Vuk Branković. They had at least two legitimate causes: Vuk had not attended the Serres meeting of Bayezid's vassals in the winter of 1393–94—to be discussed below—and in April 1394 he had concluded an alliance with Venice. Thus they attacked him and drove him from his lands. This attack was long believed to have occurred in 1398. Recently Dinić, with strong evidence, has advanced the date to 1396. Subsequently Purković has presented evidence to argue that Vuk lost his lands even earlier than Dinić believes. For Purković has discovered that Stefan Lazarević donated lands near Peć to the Athonite monastery of Saint Panteleimon in the split year 1394/95 (i.e., between 1 September 1394 and 31 August 1395). That Stefan could make this donation shows that Vuk no longer possessed the whole Peć region. Thus, if Vuk lost all his lands in one Turkish action (something we cannot be certain of), then this action, and the subsequent award of Vuk's lands to Stefan Lazarević, must have occurred before the date the Saint Panteleimon charter was issued.[6]

In any case, before his expulsion Vuk had succeeded in getting much of his money out to Dubrovnik, where he banked it. Accounts of his fate differ, though in all versions he does not seem to have lived long thereafter. Orbini gives two variant stories, both presumably from oral sources and neither of which was considered reliable by the seventeenth-century writer. In the first Milica had him poisoned. In the second, having been jailed by Bayezid's son Musa, Vuk escaped to the Balšići, who beheaded him for treason. Other stories or rumors have him fleeing north to die in Beograd, fleeing into Macedonia where he was poisoned by order of Bayezid, or being captured by the Turks and dying in captivity. Ćirković has accepted this last version.[7] A later Serbian chronicle dates his death 6 October 1398. Recent scholarship has corrected this and concludes he died 6 October 1397. His widow (Lazar's daughter Mara) and sons, still as Ottoman vassals, retained only a small portion of Vuk's Macedonian lands, Trepča and Drenica with environs.

The Turks directly took and installed garrisons in two of his fortified towns: Jeleč and Zvečan. The bulk of Vuk's Kosovo area holdings went to Stefan Lazarević, a loyal Ottoman vassal. The Ottomans seem to have installed further troops in certain towns assigned to Stefan Lazarević. Thus despite the large grant to Stefan, the Ottomans still acquired considerable new authority in this region. Stefan, who had reached his majority in 1393, was by this time by far the strongest Serbian lord. Stefan's loyalty to the sultan had gained him the sultan's support, enabling him to expand the lands under his control and to acquire greater authority over the remaining much-weakened Serbian nobles. It has been suggested that he, or his mother Milica, had a role in inciting the Turks to move against Vuk; however, there is no evidence— other than Stefan's acquisition of some of Vuk's territory at campaign's end—to support this supposition.

Stefan Lazarević's good relations with the Ottomans also eliminated any serious external threat to Serbia. The Ottomans seemed content to leave him be and the Hungarians, fearing the Turks, also left him in peace. This enabled Stefan to concentrate on domestic affairs; he was able to use his time and energy to subdue and subject to himself the various nobles within his state.

And Stefan Lazarević did have certain difficulties with his nobility. The most serious case occurred in 1398 when a group of nobles led by Novak Belocrkvić of Toplica and Nicholas (Nikola) Zojić, seeking greater independence, organized a plot against the young ruler. They contacted the sultan and accused Stefan of being in secret contact with the Hungarians. Hoping to shed their vassalage to Stefan, they sought Ottoman help to overthrow Stefan and expressed a desire to submit directly to the sultan. Stefan, who learned of the plot near its inception, thus found himself threatened by a local revolt and Ottoman action, should the Turks believe the accusation. Stefan acted quickly; luring Novak to his court, he seized and executed him. Learning of this, Nicholas Zojić fled to the fortress of Ostrovica near Rudnik. Pursued, he surrendered to Stefan, who spared his life on the condition that he become a monk. And thus the plot was put down before the Ottoman troops made their appearance. Whether they appeared in answer to the plotters' request and what, if anything, they actually did are not known. But since they soon withdrew and Stefan Lazarević seems to have remained in the sultan's good graces, it seems that he cleared himself of the charges against him. According to Constantine the Philosopher, Stefan was actually guilty of the charge; admitting it at once, he sought and gained the sultan's forgiveness.

Stefan thereafter remained loyal to Bayezid, who seems to have liked him; thus the sultan encouraged him to put down the unruly nobles. This was in the sultan's interests, for it meant that Serbia would be a stronger state with stronger armies able to provide more effective service to the sultan. And Stefan, fulfilling his vassal obligation to lead his own troops in person, led effective Serbian units in the Ottoman armies at the major battles of his time: Rovine (1395), Nikopolis (1396), and Ankara (1402).

Bayezid, however, at some point between 1398 and 1402, restored to Vuk's sons, Gregory and George, most, if not all, of the lands taken from Vuk in ca. 1396. The young men seem to have been forced to purchase the territory back with the wealth that Vuk had banked in Dubrovnik. It is clear that the territory had been returned to the Brankovići before the Battle of Ankara in July 1402. Some scholars believe the territory was restored in 1398 or 1399; they argue that at that time the sultan, suspicious of Stefan Lazarević's ties with the Hungarians, would have wanted to weaken him. Others argue that the restoration occurred just before the Ankara campaign, when Bayezid, mobilizing to fight Timur, needed all the help he could find and thus decided to give them back their lands. Unless their lands were returned in two installments, the latter dating is preferable, for Stefan Lazarević is found holding the important Branković city of Priština as late as March 1402. Having received their lands back, Gregory and George did fight for the sultan at Ankara. In the restoration the Turks retained the two towns they had taken direct control of in ca. 1396, Jeleč and Zvečan.

In the meantime, Dubrovnik began to feel threatened. The Ottomans were operating in the vicinity of the town, which sooner or later might be directly attacked; moreover, much of the territory the town traded in was being absorbed into the Ottoman Empire and thus lost to its trade. Thus it made sense for Dubrovnik to enter into relations with the Turks. Through the mediation of Stefan Lazarević, who had achieved an excellent rapport with the sultan, Dubrovnik in 1392 was able to conclude a trade treaty with the Ottomans. This treaty was followed by a new one, granting the town even more extensive privileges, in 1397.

Affairs in Greece

Meanwhile, as noted, in April 1387 Thessaloniki fell. Manuel Palaeologus, who had been holding it as his appanage, fled to Lesbos. He soon went to the Ottoman court and submitted to Murad I. It has been claimed by Loenertz that his submission was graciously accepted and that Murad granted Manuel as a fief Kavalla, which the Ottomans had taken in the summer of 1387.[8] If Manuel received Kavalla, it is not certain whether he retained it until the Serres meeting, which probably occurred in the winter 1393–94, or whether the Ottomans assumed direct control over it prior to that date, possibly in 1391, as Loenertz and Lemerle believe. In any case, Manuel, who until then had been the leading anti-Turkish hawk in the Palaeologus family, acquiesced in the new situation and remained a loyal vassal to the Turks from this point, probably late in 1387, until the Serres meeting in the winter of 1393–94. His brother Theodore, Despot of the Morea, also accepted this policy and remained a loyal Ottoman vassal until the Serres meeting as well. After the fall of Thessaloniki the Greek lords of Thessaly, with the prospect of impending doom before them, also submitted to Ottoman suzerainty.

At this time the Greek magnates of the Peloponnesus, seemingly never happy with Theodore's rule, or maybe better to say with any central authority, rose up in rebellion. Theodore, who along with Manuel had submitted to the Ottoman sultan, received aid from the Ottomans, who sent an army to assist him under the able commander Evrenos beg. These troops appeared in the fall of 1387 and ravaged much of the countryside while the rebel leaders holed themselves up in various fortresses. The Turks collected much booty and forced the rebels to submit once again. Theodore accepted their submission, but he clearly was not pleased with them. In the years that followed he confiscated the lands of several of these individuals. Those suffering confiscations included Paul Mamonas, the Lord of Monemvasia.

Meanwhile, Venice was acquiring a more active role in Greece. In 1386 it took Corfu from the Angevins. Then it decided to increase its holdings in the Peloponnesus, which until then had been limited to the two southern ports of Coron and Modon. In 1388 it purchased Argos and Nauplia from the Brienne family which had held these towns throughout the fourteenth century.[9] However, before Venice could occupy these towns the two allies Nerio Acciajuoli and Despot Theodore attacked them, Theodore taking Argos and Nerio Nauplia. The Venetians arrived and soon managed to expel Nerio and occupy Nauplia, but they could not take Argos. Angry, they allied with the Navarrese Company. They also broke off commercial relations with Nerio and blockaded the port of Athens. The Navarrese in 1389 took Nerio prisoner, by violating a safe-conduct they had offered him. They then linked his release to Theodore's surrendering Argos to Venice. Theodore saw no reason why he should be penalized for Nerio's stupidity in trusting the Navarrese and thereby falling into their trap, so he refused. Nerio was held captive for well over a year, until he was released in 1391 for a huge ransom and the surrender of Megara to Venice. The Venetians, it was agreed, were to hold Megara until they acquired Argos, at which point Nerio would regain Megara. Needless to say, Nerio was angry at Theodore's leaving him in captivity for so long; their relations cooled. Angry at Theodore, Venice encouraged his local Greek enemies, the disgruntled magnates. Venice provided both supplies and asylum for them.

Led by Paul Mamonas, several of the dissident magnates, who had lost their lands, sent complaints to Sultan Bayezid. Bayezid decided to hold a court to judge their complaints and also to settle various other Balkan issues. So, in the winter of 1393–94, he set up court at Serres and summoned all his Balkan vassals: the new Emperor Manuel II (1391–1425), who had recently succeeded after John V's death in 1391; Manuel's brother Despot Theodore of the Morea; Manuel's nephew John (VII), who then held an appanage centered in Selymbria; Constantine Dejanović, the lord of Kumanovo; Stefan Lazarević of Serbia; and various lesser figures. Our major sources do not provide a date for this meeting, and various scholars have argued that it actually occurred in the previous winter of 1392–93. Though the evidence is not conclusive, I feel the case made for 1393–94 is stronger. However, if it did occur the previous year, then the dates given for the Ottoman campaign that followed the meeting, described in the pages that follow, should be put back one year.

Mamonas laid his grievances before Bayezid, who, we are told, became furious at Manuel. Manuel subsequently claimed that Bayezid hatched the plan to murder all the assembled vassals, which probably would have resulted in the direct annexation of at least Macedonia and Serbia. However, according to one story, the servant responsible for murdering them in their beds failed, through conscience, to execute the order, and Bayezid, having repented of his order by morning, was pleased that the order had not been carried out.

At this meeting Bayezid had the chance to come to know Stefan Lazarević, and came to like him. Their association, as already noted, was to be friendly for the next decade; and Stefan was to provide effective military support for various Ottoman campaigns and Bayezid was to support Stefan against his nobles, enabling Stefan to restore Serbia as a relatively strong state. According to Constantine the Philosopher, Stefan's biographer, the sultan gave the young prince valuable advice: depend on a strong army, repress the nobles, rely on new retainers whom you have selected rather than the hereditary nobles, and keep power centralized in your own hands.

It is often stated by scholars that at Serres the marriage between Manuel II and Constantine Dejanović's daughter Helen was arranged. Loenertz, however, argues that this marriage was not concluded at Serres but had been carried out several years before. He claims that Manuel's son and heir, John VIII, was born of Helen prior to the Serres meeting. Barker concurs, dating the marriage to 1392.[10] Regardless of when concluded, Manuel's marriage to the daughter of a petty magnate of Macedonia illustrates the come-down of the Byzantine emperor's prestige. But in those years it was clear that the Byzantines and Serbs would have to create closer bonds and work together if they were to have any hope of extricating themselves from their predicament. Serbian-Byzantine ties were to remain friendly in the years that followed; and en route home after the Battle of Ankara in 1402, Stefan Lazarević paid a visit to Constantinople, where Manuel granted him the title despot. In any case Manuel's marriage to Helen was a successful one, and she bore him several children including two future emperors, John VIII and Constantine XI, the last Byzantine emperor.

The chief order of business, that we know of, at Serres was to address the complaints against Despot Theodore presented by the Peloponnesian archons. Bayezid demanded that Theodore turn over to him the various disputed fortresses in the Peloponnesus, including Monemvasia, so that he could decide their fate. Loenertz concludes that Bayezid regarded Theodore, Mamonas, and the other magnates simply as his own vassals. They all had submitted directly to him and thus their claims were all equal. Therefore the disputed lands should be given to him as their suzerain to dispose of as he saw fit. He compelled Theodore to sign over to him a series of fortresses, including Monemvasia. Thus Bayezid now had title to the disputed towns; he planned to occupy them, after which he could distribute them as he chose; presumably he also had the option, if he chose to exercise it, of retaining them. Theodore, having signed, was requested to remain with Bayezid, a request he was unable to refuse, while the other Balkan lords, having reaffirmed their vassal ties with the sultan, were allowed to depart.[11]

Meanwhile, Turkish envoys, bearing Theodore's letter and accompanied by a small force, appeared, probably in February 1394, before Monemvasia. The citizens of the town did not want to obey the order and, refusing to open their gates, secretly sent an embassy to the Venetian bailiff in Negroponte, offering the city to Venice. The Venetian senate debated the offer in March and, not wanting to involve Venice in a war with the Turks, refused the offer. Rebuffed by Venice, it seems the town then opened its gates and a small Turkish garrison was admitted. Though certain scholars claim Monemvasia did not ever submit at this time, Loenertz makes a strong case that it did admit this garrison, probably in late March or early April 1394.[12]

Meanwhile, Bayezid and his army, with Theodore accompanying them as an honorary captive, began marching through Thessaly. Theodore's release had been promised as soon as the sultan received word that Monemvasia had been turned over to his mission. Ottoman envoys were then dispatched ahead of the main force to the Morea, bearing Theodore's signed orders to the commanders of the various other forts, including Argos, to turn their forts over to the Ottoman representatives. Next, Theodore left the Ottoman retinue. It is not certain whether the sultan released him upon receiving word of Monemvasia's surrender, or whether he escaped. In any case Theodore hurried to the Peloponnesus, beating the Ottoman officials to Argos and the other forts due to be surrendered, and countermanded his earlier signed orders. He then quickly set about preparing for the defense of the Peloponnesus, beefing up key garrisons, deploying troops to guard the main routes into the Peloponnesus, and repairing walls and fortifications. He also was determined to recover Monemvasia. The Turks did not have many troops in or around Monemvasia, and the routes by which they might bring re-enforcements to the town were blocked, so Theodore led his forces thither and laid siege to Monemvasia.

Anticipating a major attack from the Turks, Theodore clearly also needed to improve his relations with Venice. So he made peace with the Venetians, concluding the Treaty of Modon, 27 May 1394, by which he turned over to them the disputed town of Argos. The Venetians then restored Megara to Nerio. Procedures for arbitrating disputes between Venice and the despot—and between citizens of their two states—were also established by the treaty. Theodore prolonged negotiations with Venice and finally in July 1394 persuaded the Venetians to take action to prevent the Turks from supplying the besieged in Monemvasia by sea. As a result, Monemvasia shortly thereafter surrendered to the despot.

The Ottomans meanwhile moved through Thessaly, which they occupied as far south as Neopatras, Livadia, and Lamia. This area was directly annexed by the Ottoman Empire. We have no sources that describe the conquest of Thessaly, but we can suspect there must have been considerable resistance from the Greek lords; otherwise it is hard to explain why the Ottomans' main army, which was already in Thessaly early in 1394, did not attack the Morea when the despot defied them and relieve the siege of Monemvasia. However, after Thessaly was conquered, the Ottomans were that much closer to the borders of the Morea and ready to take action. They also stood directly at the borders of Nerio's Duchy of Athens and Thebes. Not surprisingly, Nerio submitted at once, accepting Ottoman overlordship for his duchy. Meanwhile that same year, in September 1394, Nerio died after changing his will because of his anger at Theodore. Megara, Corinth, and his Peloponnesian possessions were left to his second daughter, Francesca, who was married to Carlo Tocco, the Duke of Cephalonia.

The Ottomans launched a massive raid into the Peloponnesus in 1395, which broke through Theodore's main defenses and took a great deal of booty. They came partly in answer to a request for aid from Carlo Tocco, who was being besieged in Corinth by Theodore, who had been led to understand at the time he married Nerio's other daughter that he would inherit Corinth. The Ottomans, led by Evrenos beg, defeated Theodore's army before Corinth and put an end to the siege. The Turks then proceeded on into the Peloponnesus to plunder a good part of it. The campaign was violent but brief, and the Ottoman forces, having taken no territory, were soon withdrawn. The campaign's purpose seems to have been entirely punitive. Presumably the main reason for their rapid withdrawal was that Evrenos and this troops were needed for the war against Mircea of Wallachia that culminated in the Battle of Rovine in May 1395. The Ottomans next found themselves faced with Sigismund's crusade, which prevented them from taking further action in Greece until that threat had been met; they duly handled the crusaders, but not until September 1396 when they achieved their victory at Nikopolis.

As soon as the Ottomans departed in early 1395 Theodore again besieged Corinth but failed to take it. However, Theodore's luck soon changed. In 1396 the commander of the Navarrese Company, Peter of San Superano (Pedro Bordo de San Superano), proclaimed himself Prince of Achaea. At about the same time Carlo Tocco, needing support against Theodore, entered into an alliance with the Navarrese. Shortly thereafter, still in 1396, Peter's Navarrese agreed to provide aid to some Greek subjects in rebellion against Theodore. Theodore met them in battle and won a decisive victory, capturing a large number of Greek rebels and also Peter. Theodore pardoned the Greeks and allowed them to go free; however, he retained Peter as a captive, demanding Corinth as well as a large cash settlement for his release. Through the mediation of Venice Peter's release was negotiated, allowing Theodore finally to acquire Corinth.

In 1397, the Ottomans returned to Greece to carry out a second major plundering expedition. First they pillaged the countryside of Boeotia and Attica, though they took no towns; then they moved into the Peloponnesus. Among the towns they broke into there was Venice's Argos, which in early June 1397 was badly sacked; many people were massacred. They also badly mangled the army Theodore sent out against them. Once again, the Ottomans withdrew at campaign's end. The Ottomans were probably not ready to take the Peloponnesus. They still did not have Attica and Boeotia, and the fortresses in the Peloponnesus were too numerous—Venetian sources state there were 150 strong castles in the Morea—to be taken all in one season, particularly since many of them were ports, easily supplied by Venice, which dominated the sea in that area. Theodore, however, felt it was only a matter of time before the Ottomans returned with the aim of conquest. So he tried to obtain further commitments from Venice. It seems that previously, during the Ottoman attack of 1397, Theodore had tried to turn Corinth over to the Venetians, but they, trying to avoid further conflicts with the Turks, had refused to take the town. It seems Theodore made several proposals to Venice again in 1400, offering either to surrender certain territory to Venice or to submit to Venetian suzerainty. But the Venetians, still not wanting to provoke a war with the Turks or to take on so large a commitment, particularly for territory not on the coast, refused.

Having no luck with Venice, Theodore turned to the Hospitaler Knights of Saint John. They had given up on the Morea earlier and, not interested in renewing their lease to Achaea after its expiration, had departed from the peninsula in 1383. Now, however, they were willing to give it another try. So in 1400, if not a year or so earlier, Theodore turned Corinth over to them. Then in May 1400 he turned Kalavryta over to them to have and defend. The population of Kalavryta was unhappy and attacked the Knights, trying to prevent them from occupying the city. Though Zakythinos claims the resistance was successful and the Knights were forced to retreat, most scholars—Loenertz and Cheetham included—believe the Knights actually took over the rule of Kalavryta.

The Knights then began demanding other towns, including Theodore's capital of Mistra. Theodore, hard-pressed, was ready to yield to some of these demands. In fact, it seems he was prepared to move his court to Monemvasia and surrender Mistra. However, the local population of Mistra rioted and began to prepare the town's defenses to resist the Knights. Loenertz thinks the Knights succeeded in occupying the citadel of Mistra after Theodore somehow managed to temporarily pacify the town's inhabitants. However, most other scholars believe the Knights did not take Mistra. In any case, the Knights were establishing for themselves a firm foothold in the Peloponnesus, winning acquiescence from Theodore but provoking considerable opposition from the local Greek population, which had no use for Catholicism or the Knights. The Knights began to fortify the Isthmus of Corinth.

The Ottomans objected to this and planned to take action about it. However, Bayezid realized he had to delay his reponse to the Knights' provocation in order to prepare for his impending war with Timur (Tamerlane). So, in 1401 Bayezid sent an envoy to try to arrange a peace with Theodore; the sultan hoped that by taking pressure off Theodore it might then be possible to separate Theodore from the Knights. After all, Bayezid understood very well that Theodore had no desire to see the Knights establish themselves in the Peloponnesus but acquiesced in their activities only because he saw the Knights as the lesser of two evils. Bayezid, preferring Theodore to the Knights, hoped to conclude an agreement with him. By it he hoped to at least prevent the

Knights from acquiring further territory and possibly to even get Theodore, once he felt freed from the Ottoman danger, to demand the restoration of certain of his cities. Such a demand, the sultan hoped, would lead to tensions, if not a major quarrel, between Theodore and his knightly allies. It seems they did conclude a treaty, in which Theodore agreed to try to oust the Knights from the Peloponnesus.

Meanwhile, in July 1402, the Ottomans were defeated at Ankara by Timur. It at once became clear that the Peloponnesus was to be spared further Ottoman ravages, for the near future at least. Since the Knights were no longer needed, Theodore and the Greek population wanted them out. Theodore, it seems, had legal grounds to recover his cities, for the initial agreement he made with the Knights had given him a right of re-purchase. He now sought to exercise this right. He and Emperor Manuel entered into negotiations with the Knights. Procuring their departure was facilitated by the fact that Timur, after defeating Bayezid, had moved west across Anatolia and among other places had sacked the Knights' Anatolian town of Smyrna. Needing cash to rebuild it, the Knights agreed to depart for a large cash payment, recompense for the money they had spent on Corinth's defenses plus an additional forty-three thousand ducats.

The Knights were slow to vacate, but it seems this resulted from the fact that Theodore, having trouble in raising the money, was slow to pay. Nevertheless, it seems that after their agreement the Knights allowed the Greeks to assume the administration of the towns the Knights held, while the Knights occupied only the citadels. Upon receiving payment, the Knights departed; the last fortresses they held, Corinth and probably Kalavryta, reverted to Theodore in June 1404. Now that Corinth was securely Greek again, the prestige of its metropolitan bishop, prior to 1204 the major prelate in the Peloponnesus, rose rapidly. He soon came to rival and then eclipse the metropolitan in Monemvasia. And when the Metropolitan of Corinth demanded that the suffragan bishoprics of Maina and Zemenos be taken from Monemvasia and restored to Corinth, which historically had stood over these sees, the emperor granted the request. Not surprisingly, tensions developed between the two sees, and the citizens of Monemvasia, loyal to their prelate, had one further reason to be annoyed at Theodore and the Byzantines.

Throughout this whole period Theodore continued to have trouble with the local nobles, whose loyalty remained dubious. In 1397 a Venetian envoy reported that the despot was hated by his lords (nobles) to the extent that they even aided his enemies. The aristocrats not only desired local independence from central officials and resisted new or increased taxes, but they also particularly resented the appearance of newcomers to the landed aristocracy. For when Theodore (and it was to be true for his successors as well) arrived from the court of Constantinople, he brought with him a considerable number of retainers from the capital, to whom he granted not only administrative and court posts but also large landed estates. And we may suspect that in local politics, at least in the early years of their tenure, these newcomers supported the despot against local independence. Finally, these newcomers would certainly have had more influence at court than the indigenous nobles.

In time the balance of power between despot and rebel nobles came increasingly to favor Theodore. Besides the settling in the Morea of numbers of his own retainers, he also benefited from the migration into the Peloponnesus of many Albanians; it has been estimated that in the late fourteenth century some ten thousand crossed the Isthmus and demanded the right to settle. The despot agreed and enrolled many in his armies, which gave him many additional troops to use against the rebels. The Albanians, who continued to migrate into the peninsula during the following decades, increased the population; and as numbers of them settled down as peasants and shepherds, they increased the productivity of the area. Albanians were found throughout the peninsula, with their largest settlements located in Arcadia.

Theodore continued to rule the Morean despotate until he took ill in 1407, became a monk, and died. Emperor Manuel then visited the Peloponnesus, awarding it to his second son, who was also named Theodore and was then about twelve years old. Manuel installed a group of efficient and loyal administrators, many of whom came from Constantinople, to administer the province and who could also be trusted to look out for Theodore's interests. We shall continue with the despotate's story from 1407 under Theodore II in the next chapter.

Achaea, by this time, was a narrow strip of land in the western Peloponnesus that also included Arcadia. Under its leader Peter of San Superano, who styled himself Prince of Achaea, the Navarrese Company continued to rule Achaea until 1402 when Peter died. His widow Maria Zaccaria, of the Genoese family that held Chios, tried to rule Achaea after his death. However, her nephew Centurione Zaccaria, who had obtained huge estates in Arcadia from his uncle, ousted her and took over in Achaea. He was to be the last Latin to rule on the peninsula as Prince of Achaea. He quickly obtained recognition, both for his possession of Achaea and for his title, from the King of Naples. Centurione held a very unstable, threatened realm. The Greek despotate did not leave him in peace, gradually annexing bits and pieces of his territory. And at the start of Centurione's reign Carlo Tocco of Cephalonia, having been expelled from Corinth, returned with an expeditionary force to the Morea. But instead of directing his attack against Theodore, who had taken Corinth, he used his men to seize most of Elis, which until then had been part of the Achaean principality. At various times Centurione's state was reduced to little or nothing more than his own personal lands in Arcadia. We shall also pick up the end of the Principality of Achaea in the next chapter.

Meanwhile, upon Nerio's death in September 1394 his heir, his brother Donato, inherited Attica and the title Duke of Athens. He received Athens except for its Acropolis, which was left to the Catholic Archbishop of Athens, to whom Nerio owed a huge debt for ransoming Nerio from the Navarrese. Just before his death Nerio had won recognition of his conquests in Attica and had been granted the title Duke of Athens by Ladislas of Naples. Meanwhile, not getting along with the new duke, the Greek Archbishop of Athens called on the Turks to end Latin rule in Athens. The Turks sent a small force to besiege the Acropolis. Donato, feeling himself too weak to resist, sent a messenger to the Venetian bailiff in Negroponte on Euboea to offer Athens to Venice. The Venetian bailiff sent a small force that was sufficient to break the Turkish siege; the Ottomans withdrew and the Euboean Venetians took over in Athens. When it learned of the Negroponte bailiff's action, the Venetian senate approved it. Promising to respect existing rights, Venice established its typical colonial administration in Athens under a podesta and garrisoned the Acropolis.

The Venetian protectorate was short-lived. Nerio's illegitimate son Anthony, who had inherited Boeotia with Thebes from his father, launched a surprise attack in 1402 against Attica, which he conquered easily including the lower town of Athens. He laid siege to the Venetian garrison in the Acropolis. The furious Venetians sent an army from Negroponte to break the siege. However, Anthony managed to ambush these troops and force their retreat back to Euboea. Finally, after a siege of seventeen months, the starved Venetian garrison surrendered to Anthony in January or February 1403. For a cash payment and recognition of Venetian suzerainty over Athens, Venice accepted the situation and recognized Anthony as Duke of Athens. Anthony held the whole duchy until his death in 1435, when it was passed on to his heirs, who continued to rule the duchy until the Ottoman conquest of Athens in 1456. Under Anthony Catalans were still to be found in Athens as mercenaries.

Anthony was half-Greek through his mother, and his wife Maria Melissene was also Greek. She was from a major aristocratic family that held lands all over Greece. Under Anthony Athens revived. He resided there regularly, rather than in the duchy's former capital of Thebes. Athens' economy improved, and the city became famous for its stud farms. The archons of Athens then included Chalcocondyles, the father of the well-known historian Laonikos.

Religion and Culture

The fourteenth century, despite its tragic political history, was a period of cultural flowering for Bulgaria. Bulgaria was part and parcel of the Byzantine "Palaeologian Renaissance," for in these years Orthodoxy was truly an international movement, with an international culture in which the different Churches cross-fertilized one another. In the thirteenth and fourteenth centuries fine Byzantine-style churches with Byzantine-style frescoes were built in Trnovo and other towns. Particularly splendid are the frescoes of the Bojana Church, outside Sofija, painted under Constantine Tih.

A large number of major churches and monasteries were erected in the Second Bulgarian Empire, particularly in the fourteenth century. Many were built under the patronage of the rulers and nobles. John Alexander (1331–71) was a particularly generous patron. Certain monasteries acquired the reputation of being educational and literary centers; many of these had been established through, and thereafter remained under, the tsar's patronage. Primary education—reading and writing—tended to take place at town churches or monasteries. Some monasteries also provided what may be called secondary education, which included more advanced grammar as well as the study of the Bible and theological texts. Many of these advanced monastic schools instructed only monks or would-be monks, but some educated laymen too. Some of them also taught Greek. When an individual had completed this course of advanced study, he was entitled to be called "gramatik." Some of the figures known to have held this title were laymen.

Trnovo on the Jantra River was built on two hills, Carevac (the site of a huge fortified enclosure containing the royal palace, patriarchal residence, cathedral church, and other related buildings) and Trapezica (containing the palaces of the leading nobles and many private chapels). Below the two hills lay the market quarter where merchants and artisans plied their trades. The lower town also contained the various quarters for local residents, foreigners (defined as Franks), and Jews respectively.

Trnovo became a major cultural center whose influence extended beyond Bulgaria to have impact on Slavic culture in general. Its cultural activities were strongly supported by the court, particularly during the reign of John Alexander, who was also a great patron of art and literature. An educated man himself, he knew Greek well and had a large and fine library. Under his patronage many earlier works were copied, and many new translations from the Greek as well as original compositions were carried out. The translations included not only religious works—liturgical works, writings of the early Church Fathers as well as of more contemporary Byzantine theologians, saints' lives, and accounts of Ecumenical councils—but also secular works including Byzantine chronicles, popular tales (e.g., the *Fall of Troy,* the medieval *Alexander*), legal works, and works on medicine and natural science subjects. The Bulgarians at this time also produced original works, some of which were secular in character, including chronicles, apocryphical tales, and lives of Bulgarian saints. John Alexander commissioned an encyclopedia, which had a heavy theological emphasis and was based to a considerable extent on Byzantine learning. He also had produced the famous London Gospel, which was beautifully illustrated with some 366 miniatures, showing both biblical subjects and portraits of the tsar and his family. In fact many Bulgarian texts of this period were illustrated with outstanding miniatures.

In the fourteenth century paper increasingly replaced parchment; at first, paper, imported through Varna, was expensive, but in the course of the century it became more plentiful and cheaper, resulting in an increasing number of books produced. Some figures—usually monks—made careers of copying books; one John of the Saint Athanasius monastery on Mount Athos copied sixteen known books, while his disciple Methodius copied twenty-one. The rulers of Vidin, particularly John Alexander's son John Stracimir and his wife Anna, were also patrons of literature and art. The famous Bdinski (Vidin) sbornik (compilation), under the patronage of Anna, included many saints' lives, thirteen of which were of women. A variety of Bulgarian works on medicine, focusing on the cure of disease, have survived from this period. Many were based on Byzantine medicine or were simply translations of the writings of Byzantine doctors. However, there were also works of a more popular sort that tended to be collections of herbal-plant recipes, or magical (utilizing spells), or both. Some of these too were translated from the Greek, while others were original. At this time, as in Byzantium, certain Bulgarian monasteries had hospitals in the monastery complex, run by monks.

The mystical movement of Hesychasm had an impact on certain Bulgarian monasteries. The ideas and practices of Hesychasm were centuries old and can be found in the writings and practices of John Climacus (died ca. 650) and Symeon the New Theologian (eleventh century). But in the fourteenth century they experienced a revival and acquired wider popularity. The catalyst was Gregory of Sinai (1290–1346) who left his monastery on Mount Sinai and traveled west visiting various Byzantine monasteries on the way, before settling for a while on Mount Athos. At each stop he taught the monks a mental prayer, which, when repeated with the proper breathing, might enable one to see a divine light. His teachings were received enthusiastically in various places, particularly on Mount Athos, which became the center of the movement.

Hesychasm's highest goal was to see the Divine Light. This was to be achieved through prayer and meditation during which one employed specific ascetic techniques. In solitude the Hesychast repeated the *Jesus Prayer,* "Lord Jesus Christ, Son of God, have mercy on me," again and again, blending the prayer with his breathing so that the full prayer coincided with one breath. The successful supplicant had to have already purified himself by conquering his passions and rising above all distractions through a long period of meditation. This purification enabled a Divine Energy that had entered into the man at his baptism to become visible. Thus the successful supplicant, through contemplation, proper breathing, and the repetition of this prayer, achieved a feeling of ecstacy and of seeing himself overwhelmed by rays of supernatural divine light. The Hesychasts believed this light was the same light as that seen by the disciples of Christ on Mount Tabor; this light, they believed, was permanently visible to those able to achieve its vision.

The Hesychasts' claim that this was a worthwhile way for monks to spend their time, as well as their explanation for the light, was opposed by Barlaam, a Greek monk from Calabria in Italy who had come to Constantinople. His attack on Hesychast ideas was countered vigorously by Gregory Palamas (born 1296), who was by 1333 a monk on Athos. Barlaam said it was impossible to see the Light of Tabor, for it was not eternal but temporary like all God's creations. If the monks believed it to be permanent, then they were claiming to see the God-head itself, which was impossible for That was invisible. Palamas replied that one must distinguish between the Divine Essence (Ousia) and Divine energies. These energies, he claimed, are active in the world and manifest themselves to man. They are not created but are emanated in an endless operation of God. This emanation is what is seen in the visions, for God's energies are manifested in many different ways, one of which was the light seen on Tabor, and this emanation is eternally visible to those mystically illumined. Hesychasm, by providing a means to see the light, was therefore a means to bridge the gulf between man and God.

In a council held in Constantinople in 1341 and presided over by Emperor Andronicus III, Hesychasm, championed by Palamas, won a victory. Barlaam, whose views were condemned, returned West in disgust. However, the emperor promptly died, and Hesychasm's opponents resumed their attack upon the movement. The patriarch, John Kalekas, who had been indifferent to the issue and had tried to avoid passing judgment on it, had been forced by the emperor to hold the 1341 council. He then had signed the decisions of the council. After the emperor's death, as we saw earlier, Cantacuzenus became regent, only to be ousted by the trio of Andronicus' widow Anna of Savoy, Apocaucus, and John Kalekas. Since Palamas was a close associate of the regency's opponent Cantacuzenus, the patriarch now became anti-Palamas and took an anti-Hesychast position. He pointed out that the council of 1341 had banned further discussion of the issue and criticized Palamas for continuing to write and speak about it. Palamas replied that he was only replying to the on-going attacks upon his views. However, Kalekas, ignoring the activities of Palamas' opponents, kept up his attacks on Palamas until he finally jailed him in 1343; then in January 1344 Kalekas held a synod of the Constantinopolitan clergy to excommunicate Palamas.

Popular works often make Hesychasm out to be an active ingredient in the Byzantine civil war. This interpretation is unwarranted. The Hesychasts played no role in the war as such. Moreover, the lines were not clear-cut; certain opponents of Hesychasm supported Cantacuzenus, while some supporters of the regency, including one of the regents, Empress Anna, had sympathy for Palamas' ideas. However, as a result of Kalekas' policy, Hesychasm suffered eclipse and disgrace during the regency years. Then in 1347, when Cantacuzenus was on the verge of triumphing, the empress released Palamas from jail; as a major figure and friend of Cantacuzenus, Palamas then played a role, as an individual, in mediating peace between the two sides, which resulted in Cantacuzenus' being accepted as emperor early in 1347.

Cantacuzenus' triumph led to a reversal of Hesychasm's fortunes. Patriarch John Kalekas was deposed and a Hesychast monk and friend of Palamas named Isidore became patriarch. He was to be succeeded by another Hesychast, Kallistos (1350–53, 1355–63). And Palamas was soon appointed Archbishop of Thessaloniki by Isidore. Then in 1351, under Patriarch Kallistos, a new council was held in Constantinople that recognized the orthodoxy of Palamas and excommunicated the leading opponents of the movement. Its decisions were confirmed for Bulgaria by a council held in

Trnovo in 1360. Opposition to the 1351 council's decisions continued in Russia and Antioch for a while longer, but by the end of the fourteenth century opposition died out and Hesychasm became officially accepted and approved by the whole Orthodox Church from then on. We should stress, however, approval meant the Orthodox Church accepted the idea and the theory behind it. The number of its actual practitioners remained small. Palamas died in 1357 and was canonized in 1368. After Saint Demetrius he became Thessaloniki's most popular saint. Hesychast ideas were not limited to Byzantium but spread to the Slavic lands, fertilized chiefly by the spread of these ideas around Mount Athos, where Hesychasm was popular and where the Bulgarians, Serbs, and Russians all had monasteries.

However, Bulgaria had a second major source for Hesychast ideas. For Gregory of Sinai, unhappy with "barbarian raids" on Athos, had settled in the Bulgarian monastery of Paroria, whose exact location is unknown but which lay near the Byzantine border in what was said to be a wild and remote place, making it ideal for meditation. There Gregory enjoyed the patronage of Tsar John Alexander. Gregory acquired a number of Bulgarian disciples. The most prominent of these was the monk Theodosius of Trnovo, who after residing in various monasteries had come to Paroria. Theodosius knew Greek well and translated various of Gregory's Hesychast works into Bulgarian, thereby making them accessible to the Slavs.

Gregory also had Serbian disciples. The *Life of Gregory,* written by Patriarch Kallistos of Constantinople, refers to one, a Serb named Jacob (Jakov) who returned to Serbia, subsequently to become a metropolitan there. He probably was the Jacob who is documented later as Metropolitan of Serres, after Dušan's conquest of that town. The likelihood of this identification is enhanced by the fact that Jacob of Serres sent several books to the Monastery of Mount Sinai in 1360. Ties between Serbia and Sinai had long existed. Milutin had financed the building on Sinai of a church dedicated to Saint Stephen and a fair number of Serbs resided in the Sinai monastery, some of whom after residing there a while later returned to Serbia. Thus in tracing the spread of ideas, we should not ignore direct ties between Sinai and Serbia, and the libraries of Mount Sinai still contain a few manuscripts in Old Church Slavonic.

Brigands frequently bothered Paroria, so John Alexander who had given many gifts to that monastery built fortifications around it. After Gregory died in 1346, his disciples traveled off to various places, especially Athos. Theodosius of Trnovo went first to Athos, then to Thessaloniki, then to Berrhoia, before returning to Bulgaria to establish on the mountain of Kefalarevo, far from Trnovo and other towns, a series of cells. His fame attracted other monks and soon about fifty monks were living on the mountain, changing the "desert" into a town. Certain of these disciples who knew Greek well were also active translators of Greek works into Slavic. These included Dionysius, who translated various writings of John Chrysostom, and a certain John, who translated John Climacus.

Theodosius, however, remained a restless figure, not liking to stay long in one place; furthermore he was highly interested in Church affairs in this world. So he soon returned to Trnovo, and the tsar then financed for Theodosius near Trnovo a new monastery, the Kilifarevski monastery, whose rule was based on one that Gregory of Sinai had brought from Sinai. Theodosius became its abbot. He remained there nearly a decade, frequently, it seems, advising the tsar, defending Orthodoxy, and refuting and suppressing various minor heresies. This monastery in the interior of Bulgaria, far from barbarian raids and brigands, became a new Hesychast and translating center.

Theodosius acquired many disciples, some of whom went off to convert other monasteries into Hesychast ones or to establish from scratch new Hesychast monasteries. Soon Hesychast monasteries were existing near Mesembria, Madara, and Červen. According to the *Life of Romylos,* one of Gregory's and Theodosius' disciples, the monasteries stressed obedience to the Hesychast master, with the monks spending specific days with the master and others in solitude. Hesychast ideas also continued to be brought to Bulgaria from Athos, as Bulgarian monks, many of whom—like Theodosius— were already Hesychasts when they went to Athos, passed to and fro between Athos and Bulgarian monasteries.

Theodosius visited Constantinople with several disciples in 1363. There he took ill and died. Then, illustrating the international character of Hesychasm, the Hesychast Byzantine patriarch, Kallistos, wrote a *Life* of Theodosius. This *Life* was soon translated into Bulgarian.

At present we have a Slavic text of a *Life* of Theodosius. For a long while it was believed to be the *Life* written by Kallistos. However, Kiselkov presents many reasons to support his plausible view that, though Kallistos wrote such a *Life,* the text we have is not his. Kiselkov argues that the surviving text has Kallistos' work as a core to which a great deal of other material has been added. He proposes that the surviving text is a fifteenth-century re-working by a Trnovo monk.[13]

The surviving *Life* devotes several chapters to Theodosius' work against heretics. These are odd chapters. First, they depict the Bulgarian patriarch as being so ineffectual that Theodosius had to leave his monastery to more-or-less run the councils summoned to put down error and defend Orthodoxy. However, as Kiselkov notes, this does not seem an accurate depiction of the contemporary patriarch. That individual was also named Theodosius. And Kiselkov wonders if the common name may not have led the later editor of the *Life of Theodosius* to add items about the patriarch of that name to the *Life* of the Hesychast. This second Theodosius became patriarch in 1348 and remained in office through 1360. He was interested in books, had studied at Zographou on Athos, and later sent that monastery various manuscripts. He was a forceful figure, strongly supporting the independence of the Bulgarian Church, over which he clashed with Kallistos. For Kallistos elsewhere accused him of not mentioning the names of the Patriarch of Constantinople and the other Eastern patriarchs in Bulgarian Church services and of not sending to Constantinople for holy oil but preparing his own. Patriarch Theodosius also strongly supported the independence of the Serbian patriarch, at whose installation Theodosius' predecessor Symeon had participated. Possibly, if the depiction of the patriarch belongs to the original core by Kallistos, Kallistos' dislike of him was responsible for the demeaning depiction.

The first heretic the monk Theodosius attacked was a certain Theodorit who had come to Trnovo from Constantinople. He was learned and a disciple of Barlaam and Akindynos (i.e., anti-Hesychast) and also practiced magic, effecting cures by magical means. He attracted many of the well-born to himself and soon had a large number of followers. Among other things, they bowed before an oak tree and sacrificed sheep. The second heretical group consisted of the adherents of a nun in Thessaloniki named Irene. She taught the Messalian heresy—in this period the term *Messalian* usually means Bogomilism—and attracted many followers. Her ideas, which seem to have been more mystical and individualistic than classical Bogomilism, soon spread to Athos, where unopposed they infected many over a three-year period. Finally in 1344 a Church council was held against these heretics, who were condemned and exiled from the Byzantine Empire.

Two of Irene's exiled followers, named Lazar and Kiril "Bosota," came to Trnovo. Lazar went crazy and ran around town naked with only a pumpkin leaf to cover his private parts. Some scholars assert he was not insane but an Adamite, seeking to return mankind to its paradisaical state. Bosota, however, was a more serious enemy; he attacked icons, the cross, clergy, marriage (encouraging divorce), and advocated, if we can believe the hostile source, giving in to the desires of the flesh because the body was the devil's creation. He attracted a number of disciples, including a priest named Stefan. Since the patriarch did nothing about these heretics, according to the *Life,* the monk Theodosius went to the tsar and, explaining to him the serious situation, persuaded him to summon a council. A major council was then held, attended by patriarch and clergy as well as the boyar council. Theodosius played a dominant role, making a major speech to defend Orthodoxy. Not surprisingly, he won the support of the council. Lazar repented, but the other two, Bosota and the priest Stefan, did not. They were branded on the face and exiled.

But heretics did not disappear from Bulgaria. Theodosius soon had to refute the teachings of an Adamite who advocated the shedding of one's clothes in imitation of the first man and, if we can believe the hostile source, encouraged group orgies among his followers. Next, the *Life* claims, certain Jewish heretics (presumably Judaising Christians), who seem to have had the support of some real Jews, began to attack various aspects of Christianity like icons, church buildings, the clerical class, and the institution of monks. The *Life* notes that John Alexander's second wife had been a Jew. And the reader senses in the text here a certain hostility toward her and also toward the Jews in general.

The tsar was again persuaded to call a council, this one is dated 1360. It was attended by the royal family, patriarch, bishops, and many monks. The council concentrated its efforts against the Judaisers and condemned the anti-Christian Judaising teachers. One converted, but the other two refused and suffered torture. This council also condemned Bogomilism and Barlaamism. This reference is to be the last we shall have to Bogomilism in Bulgaria. That the heresy was condemned suggests there still were a few who were Bogomil, or believed to be such, in Bulgaria, possibly in the vicinity of Trnovo, which made it worthwhile to add their condemnation to the decisions of the council. After all, some of Bosota's views, condemned at the previous council, had a Bogomil flavor, and he was said to be the disciple of a "Messalian" (surely meaning Bogomil) nun. However, after 1360 no document refers to Bogomilism in Bulgaria. Not one Turkish source from the years after the conquest mentions Bogomils either. Moreover, since these references from the *Life of Theodosius* are the only evidence of the existence of Bogomils in Bulgaria since the early thirteenth century, it seems reasonable to conclude that by this time whatever Bogomils remained in Bulgaria were part of a very small and weak sect.

The most prominent disciple of Theodosius was Euthymius, the last Patriarch of Trnovo (1375–93). He was born, ca. 1325, into a Trnovo boyar family. He entered Theodosius' Kilifarevski monastery shortly after its foundation, around 1350. Then subsequently, ca. 1362, he went to Constantinople with Theodosius, and after his mentor's death in 1363, entered the famous Studios monastery in Constantinople, where he studied for about a year before moving on to spend several years on Mount Athos. Returning to Bulgaria shortly after 1370, he founded the Trinity monastery, about three kilometers north of Trnovo, which he made into a major literary center modeled on Zographou on Athos. A famous religious writer, he turned out a series of important saints' lives, eulogies, and letters.

Euthymius was also concerned that Bulgarian Slavic texts lacked standardization and reflected localisms, local dialects, and popular speech. The texts also had variations in spelling and grammatical errors. Euthymius therefore devoted great effort to linguistic reform, both orthographic reform—standardized spelling—and the establishment of literary standards, stressing style and grammar.

To eliminate linguistic differences, Euthymius called for, and then presented, a model, standardized language. His ideal language was found not in the present-day language but in the past, in the Old Church Slavonic of Constantine (Cyril) and Methodius. Thus one should look back to their language for correct forms and model one's writing on theirs. His purified language thus stressed archaisms over contemporary speech. And in keeping with his international view of Orthodoxy and Orthodox culture, it also favored a general Slavic language—which Old Church Slavonic had been—over the specific spoken ones, Bulgarian or Serbian. Thus he sought to re-create a common literary language for the Orthodox Slavs differentiated from contemporary speech, and he regretted Slavonic's break-down into local forms—

Bulgarian Slavonic, Serbian Slavonic—that reflected regional vocabulary, grammar, or spelling based on local pronunciation. He also sought more exact translations of Greek terms, which at times led him to introduce new terms into Slavonic. He urged that texts be corrected by going back to the Greek originals and carrying out rigorous checking and comparisons. And he himself corrected and revised various liturgical and theological texts which had been inaccurately translated from the Greek.[14]

As patriarch he tried to prevent the appearance of new, corrupt texts by banning newly copied texts from use until they had received patriarchal approval. And he ordered that each new book manuscript copied in Bulgaria be sent to the patriarch for approval. He also tried to limit copying to those people who had had proper training. Tsar John Šišman supported him in these efforts, endorsing his edicts on texts.

Euthymius also battled against heresy, repressing some further Barlaamites, namely, one Piron, who had come from Constantinople to Trnovo, and his disciple Theodosius, a monk known as Fudul. However, these two went beyond criticizing Hesychasm; they also attacked honoring the higher clergy and icons and, if we can believe our hostile source, occupied themselves with magic and devilish thoughts. They influenced various people from the upper classes and even the clergy. Euthymius succeeded in having them expelled from Bulgaria. Euthymius was also an advocate of strict morals; he took a firm stand against divorce as well as against third and fourth marriages for widowers or widows. As a result, we are told, many Bulgarians who sought to carry out these acts went to Wallachia and Moldavia, where standards were more lax.

Euthymius and his disciples, like the intellectuals of the previous generation, were responsible both for translations from the Greek and original works. As should be clear from the above, many Bulgarian Church intellectuals in this period knew Greek well. And the traveling of educated monks from monastery to monastery, including monasteries across international borders—in Byzantium, Athos, Bulgaria, Serbia—facilitated the circulation of ideas. Migration from monastery to monastery seems to have been common at this time. At times it was caused by the desire to escape Turkish or brigand raids, but the monks seem also to have been restless individuals. The *Life* of Theodosius' disciple Romylos mentions ten different changes of monastery for its protagonist, and Theodosius himself seems to have lived in about as many different monasteries.

When Bulgaria fell to the Turks, the Turks originally sentenced Euthymius to death. However, they quickly commuted the sentence, and in 1394 he was exiled to the Bačkovo monastery—a major foundation built under John Alexander's patronage and in possession of a good library. There Euthymius began a new school, where he taught until he died, probably in 1402. The school continued after his death under the direction of Euthymius' pupil Andronicus. The latter's students included Constantine Kostenečki, better known as Constantine the Philosopher (Konstantin Filozof). Constantine remained a monk at Bačkovo until he moved to Serbia in 1411. There he achieved considerable prominence. We shall return to his career shortly.

Turkish raids and the eventual conquest of Bulgaria by the Turks in 1393 caused the emigration of many Bulgarian intellectuals to Serbia, Moldavia, Wallachia, and Russia, where they brought their talents and many texts. The above-mentioned Romylos had been residing on Mount Athos at the time of the Battle of Marica. Expecting the worst from the victorious Turks and also suffering from a famine then plaguing the Holy Mountain, Romylos joined the large-scale exodus of monks then taking place. He first went to Valona on the Albanian coast. Little known in the religious world, it seemed obscure enough to favor solitude. However, it proved an unhappy place to live. According to the *Life of Romylos,* the people of the region were ignorant and savage, accustomed to brigandage and murder. The governors of the region—presumably appointees of Balša Balšić, who obtained Valona in 1372—were very unjust, killing innocent men, while the monks were full of error and vindictiveness, and the priests ministered unworthily. As a result Romylos eventually moved on to Serbia, settling in the monastery Lazar had just completed in 1381, Ravanica, where Romylos remained until his death.

So many texts were brought to Russia after the fall of Bulgaria that scholars speak of a Second South Slavic Influence on Russia. These emigrant intellectuals often rose to high places as bishops and abbots in their new lands. They had a major impact on Serbian, Moldavian, Wallachian, and Russian letters, bringing to these lands not only Bulgarian culture, but also Byzantine and Hesychast ideas. Particularly important in this regard were the two Camblaks and Constantine the Philosopher. Cyprian Camblak became Metropolitan of All Russia from 1390 until 1406 and made major efforts to correct Russian liturgical texts, which contained many errors, and also to revise Russia's canon law.

His nephew Gregory Camblak was on Mount Athos when Bulgaria fell to the Turks. He then went to Constantinople and soon seems to have been sent to Moldavia as an envoy by the patriarch. After the Turkish defeat at the Battle of Ankara in 1402 took pressure off Serbia, Gregory went to Serbia, where he became abbot of the famous monastery Visoki Dečani. He found that though this monastery had been erected by a king subsequently canonized, there was neither a service nor a saint's life of him—for the *Life of Dečanski* by the Continuator of Danilo, written before Dečanski was canonized, was not couched in the form of a saint's life. Gregory rectified the situation. He also altered the viewpoint of the Continuator of Danilo's shorter *Life,* for the earlier work, possibly because it was written during Dušan's reign, did not glorify Dečanski but made him somewhat of a sinner against both his father, whom he rebelled against, and his son, whom he turned against, leading Dušan to revolt and overthrow him.

Gregory presents a different view, in both incidents supporting Dečanski and condemning Milutin and Dušan. His work, unlike the earlier biographies of rulers written by Serbs, moreover, does not have as a motive the glorification of Serbia and its dynasty. In fact, he condemns Dušan's coronation as tsar, seeing it as a usurpation. And throughout he expresses more interest in general Orthodoxy than in Serbia. Gregory's work, like a more typical saint's life, makes Dečanski into a martyr. Besides emphasizing Dečanski's martyrdom, Gregory also stresses miracles. For instance, when Dečanski was blind Saint Nicholas appeared to him in a dream, promising his sight would be restored, which in due time occurred. Gregory also stresses the miracles that occurred at the martyred king's grave, which brought in his time, and still brings in ours, a large number of the sick to the monastery seeking cures.

Eventually, like his uncle, Gregory too moved on to Russia, probably arriving in Kiev in about 1409. He soon, in 1415, became Metropolitan of Kiev, a town then belonging to the Lithuanian-Polish state. He was part of a delegation sent by the Lithuanian ruler to the Council of Constance, where he had a cordial meeting with the pope and is usually thought to have expressed an interest in Church Union. Muriel Heppell, however, has presented a strong case that Gregory was not willing to consider Union if it meant submitting to the papal position and has raised serious doubts as to whether the text of a conciliatory sermon, allegedly delivered by Gregory at Constance, really was his work.[15] Gregory died in 1419 or 1420.

A final major Bulgarian emigré figure was Constantine Kostenečki (so called because he was born in the Bulgarian town of Kostenec); he is better known as Constantine the Philosopher. Having studied at Bačkovo monastery, where he became a monk and resided for several years under Euthymius' disciple Andronicus, Constantine emigrated to Serbia in 1411. He took up residence at the court of the ruler, Stefan Lazarević, and soon became the major figure at Stefan's very culturally oriented court. Constantine knew Greek well and besides the Slavic languages also seems to have known some Rumanian and Turkish. He established a school in Beograd and also served Stefan Lazarević at times as a diplomat. His first major work, written during the reign of Stefan, was his famous *On Letters,* which advocated the linguistic reforms proposed and enforced by Euthymius, which Constantine actively propagated in Serbia. He also wrote a travelogue of the Holy Land and a cosmological-geographical work, of which only a few pages survive, that shows Constantine believed the world to be round. After his patron died in 1427 and the Hungarians re-occupied Beograd, Constantine left Beograd. He settled in the lands of a vojvoda holding Vranje, where in the 1430s he wrote his famous biography of Stefan Lazarević. Constantine died at some point after 1439.

Monasteries flourished in medieval Serbia as well; we have already discussed many of them, noting royal patronage and the practice for each ruler to build at least one major monastery for the salvation of his soul. Many of these monastery churches are architectural masterpieces and their frescoes are stunning. Particularly worthy of note (and major tourist attractions to visit) are: Studenica, Žiča, Sopoćani, Mileševo, Gračanica, Visoki Dečani, the Patriarchate (Patriaršija) at Peć, Manasija, and Ravanica.

In Serbia, as in Bulgaria, many if not most schools were probably located in monasteries. Besides this source of education, one could study with priests, if they were willing and qualified, or with private lay tutors. Ćirković points out that there is no way to tell which form of education was most common. He also stresses the absence of any regular school program (or curriculum) or even calendar.[16] One might still expect to find common elements in most programs—reading and writing, with an emphasis on religious texts. Length of study and subject matter were probably dictated by the individual instructor; sometimes they may have been decided on in an agreement between parent and teacher with the teacher contracting to teach such and such for so much pay. In some cases the instructor might hold a group class; at others, if his pupils were at different levels, he presumably treated them as individual tutees. There seems to have been no standard length of time to obtain an education; thus some individuals completed shorter and some longer terms of study, just as there was no standard curriculum, leading some to study more broadly and to cover more subjects than others.

Particular needs might also have influenced study. By the fourteenth century there were two writing styles—a good hand for copying manuscripts and a fast hand for legal documents. Unless the latter was learned only on the job, as may have been the case, we might expect young men seeking secular bureaucratic careers to have engaged a tutor beforehand to teach them the fast hand. Foreign languages might also have been part of special programs aimed for specific ambitions. However, diplomacy probably was not one of these, since most frequently individuals who were naturally bi-lingual were used on diplomatic missions. However, in Serbia as in Bulgaria, Greek was presumably a major subject of study at the schools held in the major monasteries.

Education reached a higher level on the coast than in the interior. But interestingly enough, as far as we know, only Kotor had a town school. It was founded in the thirteenth century.

The Jews in the Balkans

The Jews of Greece[17]

Benjamin of Tudela, who traveled through the Levant in 1168 visiting Jewish communities, noted large ones in Thebes, Corinth, Negroponte, Naupaktos, Patras, Krissa (modern Khrisa?), Ravennika, Lamia, Almiros, Thessaloniki, and Arta. I do not give his figures on community size since scholars dispute their accuracy as well as whether they referred to numbers of families or individuals. In the Byzantine world the Jews were more integrated into society as a whole than they were in Western Europe. Thus sometimes they were not restricted to special quarters, and even when such quarters existed Jews were often found outside of them. Moreover, cases have been found of Jews and Christians working together and even being members of the same guild.

The best known community over the years was that of Thessaloniki. Though Benjamin of Tudela said the Jews there were much oppressed, other sources suggest he may have been exaggerating or else criticizing a specific and temporary hardship. For instance, the letters of Eustatius, Bishop of Thessaloniki (ca. 1175–94), make it clear that the Jews of Thessaloniki were not confined to one quarter and were buying and renting houses from Christians (including some with holy pictures on the walls, which bothered the bishop). In a sermon Eustatius criticized the lack of charity shown by Christians to other Christians, comparing it to the tolerance the Christians showed to the Jews. And we know the Jews joined the Christians in defending the city against the Norman attack in 1185. Under Theodore of Epirus' rule the Jews of Thessaloniki did suffer disabilities; he confiscated much of their wealth and a later chronicle suggests he even issued an edict against the practice of Judaism in his realm. Whether this chronicle was accurate is not known, and, if it was accurate, it still is not known how widely the edict was enforced. In any case, Theodore was removed from the scene in 1230, a little more than six years after he took Thessaloniki. And it is clear that any general restrictions existing against the Jews were abrogated by Michael VIII Palaeologus (1261–82) soon after his accession.

A second Jewish community about which something is known is that of Negroponte on Euboea. The Jewish quarter of Negroponte, with its synagogue, lay outside the town walls, making it vulnerable to attack from pirates and brigands. As a result the Venetians allowed the Jews to rent homes and buildings inside the walled area. Thus many Jews came to live outside of the Jewish quarter. Though a protest seems to have been made about this in 1402, causing the Venetians to order the Jews back to the ghetto, the order seems not to have been enforced. The lack of enforcement suggests public opinion did not care where the Jews resided. In 1423 the Venetians again banned the Jews from owning land or buildings in the city of Negroponte or to have any property outside the ghetto. Yet a 1429 document mentions Jewish property inside the city. In 1425 the Jewish quarter, which had been suffering from thieves, was allowed to build a wall. In 1439/40 the Jewish community, which seems to have been growing, was allowed to expand the area of its quarter and at the same time to erect new walls to include the new part. At the time the Venetians recognized that the Jews were beneficial to the city, stating, "for it is largely they who carry on the trade and enhance our receipts."

Though scholars heatedly debate whether or not the Jews of Byzantium in this period had to pay a special tax, it is evident that the Jews of Negroponte did pay a collective tax. Its rate went up and down. The Jewish community also was given special duties, to annually produce the Venetian flag for the town, to pay a special galley tax, and to pay for guarding the clock-tower. From time to time the community was hit with a special tax, like that of 1304 when it had to finance the building of a gate for the Venetian compound. In 1410, owing to defense needs against the Turkish threat, the community's collective tax was doubled from five hundred to one thousand hyperpera. In 1429 a document confirming this doubled assessment was issued. The Jewish community was also responsible for supplying the town's executioner, an obligation it bore until abrogated in 1452. Furthermore, whereas the Venetians gave their own merchants the right to import and export goods duty-free, Jewish merchants of Negroponte had to pay 5 percent import and export duties. In 1318, as a reward for helping to defend Negroponte against the Catalans, this import-export duty was removed. However, it was restored in 1338 when the Venetians needed cash to heighten the wall around their own commune.

Besides the collective tax, other special obligations, and the laws (often not enforced) issued from time to time ordering Jews to live in the Jewish ghetto, the Jews were also denied the privilege of acquiring Venetian citizenship, a privilege extended to many other non-Venetians of Euboea. However, once again, though this denial was Venice's stated policy, exceptions were made; for special services certain prominent Jews did receive Venetian citizenship, including David Kalomiti, the head of the Jewish community, the individual responsible for representing the community in its dealings with the Venetian authorities. In 1267/68 he not only received Venetian citizenship, but also the right to pass it on to his heirs. David Kalomiti was not only a leading political figure, but also an important merchant for silks and dyes who had estates with serfs outside of town. He also was a learned man who built the community's synagogue and was a patron for various learned scholars, including some who came to Negroponte from Thebes and elsewhere.

Benjamin of Tudela mentions that some of the Jews of Krissa (modern Khrisa?) farmed their own land. Farming, a pursuit rarely followed by medieval Jews, is also documented for Patras, where Jews are found in both urban and rural occupations. Shortly before 1430 a Jewish money-lender is found leasing a farm to a second Jew. This arrangement continued, at least for a while, after the Byzantines regained Patras in 1430.

Turning to Jewish communities under Byzantium, we are faced with the question: did these communities owe a special tax? They clearly did under a law of 429. This law, however, disappeared from the books in the legal compilations of Basil I (867–86) and Leo VI (886–912). It is not certain that it was ever re-instituted on an empire-wide basis. However, communities in certain towns did owe such a collective tax. The Jews of Zična in Macedonia clearly owed it, for in 1333 Andronicus III assigned the money raised by this tax to a monastery. Stefan Dušan, who soon thereafter took Zična, continued this policy by confirming this income for the monastery in a charter of his own. We also know that when the Venetians took over Thessaloniki from the Byzantines in 1423 a collective tax on the local Jewish community was then in existence; it is not known how old it was. The Venetians maintained this tax, though reducing it from one thousand hyperpera to eight hundred in response to a community petition that stressed the community's inability to pay the original large sum owing to large-scale Jewish emigration, including that of many of its richest members, from Thessaloniki because of high taxes and the Turkish danger. However, though such collective taxes existed in certain Byzantine and non-Byzantine Balkan cities, they can be documented only for a small number of cities. No post-ninth-century law code or text ever suggests that an empire-wide law instituting such a tax existed. And documents like Andronicus III's charter of 1319 to Jannina's Jews stating they were to enjoy freedom and not be molested suggests they did not have such a tax burden. Thus it seems probable that for specific reasons certain communities acquired this tax obligation, but it happened on an individual basis.

It also seems that in the Greek world, in theory, the Jews should have been restricted to ghettos. However, it is evident that in various places, including Thessaloniki, this legal ideal was not enforced. For example, in the 1220s when Durazzo belonged to Epirus, the Metropolitan of Durazzo wrote his superior, the well-known canonist Demetrius Chomatianos, Archbishop of Ohrid. The Metropolitan asked if the Armenians (who had their own schismatic Church owing to their rejection of the Council of Chalcedon) should be allowed to build churches in the midst of Orthodox communities. The question gives us evidence that among its minorities Durazzo had an Armenian community. Demetrius replied that minority groups, including Jews and Muslims, should be permitted no more than a limited degree of freedom. And he stated that their houses of prayer should not be tolerated outside of the quarter assigned for their residence. This not only shows the ghetto principle but, in recognizing it, it also suggests that at roughly the same time Theodore was allegedly banning Judaism, Theodore's leading bishop was recognizing the religion's right to exist. Is this evidence that Theodore never issued such a ban, or, if he did, does it show that it was not supported or enforced by his leading adherents? Or was Demetrius' letter, recognizing the right of synagogues to exist in ghettos, written prior to Theodore's edict?

The Jewish community of Durazzo continued to exist after Theodore's reign, and it also survived a later edict, issued by Charles II of Naples, which banned the practice of Judaism in his kingdom, which included Durazzo. (However, no information exists as to whether or not an attempt was made to enforce the ban in Durazzo.) For when Venice acquired Durazzo in 1392, it found the town's Jewish community owed the town's suzerain over ten yards of luxurious velvet cloth annually. The community, owing to its alleged poverty, petitioned Venice in 1401 to be exempted from this burden. It is not known which of Durazzo's many rulers instituted this obligation. Nor is it known how Venice responded to the 1401 petition.

The Jews in Bulgaria and Macedonia

Already in the eleventh and twelfth centuries documents mention the existence of Jewish communities in Sofija, Silistria, and Nikopolis on the

Danube. Soon after the re-establishment of Bulgarian independence the rulers of the Asen dynasty, in order to stimulate commerce, began to encourage Jewish merchant families to settle in Bulgaria. It seems that under this stimulus the number of Jews in Bulgaria significantly increased. In this period the Bulgarians also ruled two towns in Macedonia, Kastoria and Ohrid, that were leading Jewish intellectual centers producing learned scholars. Among these figures was Rabbi Tobias ben Eliezer from Kastoria, who became the leader of the Rabbanite community among the Romaniote (Byzantine/Balkan) Jews at the end of the eleventh and the beginning of the twelfth century. He wrote an important commentary on the Pentatuch known as *Midrash Leqah Tob*. Much of this work's argument was directed against the Karaites, who were numerous in Constantinople and also present in Thessaloniki and Adrianople.[18] One of his pupils, Leo Mung, converted to Christianity and became Archbishop of Ohrid. A second leading scholar was Judah Leon Mosconi, born in Ohrid in 1328, who in the course of his studies traveled widely to such diverse places as Chios, Cyprus, Negroponte, Egypt, Morocco, Italy, and France. A philosopher and metaphysician, he also wrote commentaries on the Pentatuch and, like his Slavic contemporary Euthymius of Trnovo, was interested in grammar and believed incorrect interpretations of scripture often resulted from neglect of it. He left among his many works an unfinished treatise on grammar.

In the 1360s and 1370s the Jews were expelled from Hungary and Bavaria. Many came to Bulgaria and to Macedonia (then a battle ground among various Serbian nobles). One of the places where many of these immigrants settled was Kastoria. As Weinberger has discovered:

> Friction soon developed between the native Jewish settlers, followers of the Romaniote ritual, and the newcomers from the north, due, probably, to the differing Romaniote marriage and divorce customs, such as their refusal to accept the decree of Rabbenu Gershom b. Judah of Mainz (11th century) banning the practice of polygamy. To deal with this conflict a special assembly was called in 1376 to reinforce R. Gershom's ban on polygamy and to address the several issues in dispute by the two parties. It was probably at this time that one Bulgarian Jewish community, the Kastoreans, decided to publish their own prayer-book according to the ritual in use in their synagogues and thereby preserve the special character of their congregational life. A section of this prayer-book . . . has survived.[19]

At the same time in Bulgaria contact between Christian and Jewish communities resulted in conversions (for example the second wife of John Alexander was a Jewess who converted to Christianity) and a certain degree of Christian-Jewish syncretism among certain Christians, which was rejected as heretical by the Orthodox establishment. This is seen in the trial, discussed above, in 1360 in Trnovo of three Jewish heretics. After their views were condemned, one repented and accepted Orthodoxy, whereas the other two, who did not, were subjected to torture. The *Life of Theodosius,* our source for this event, states that the three had been actively preaching against certain Christian practices. Therefore, since it was their own activism that brought the Church authorities down upon them, we cannot conclude that this trial reflected anti-Jewish public opinion or state policy in Bulgaria. And we know that over the next two decades Bulgaria, like the provinces of Macedonia, received a large number of Jewish refugees from Bavaria and Hungary.

NOTES

1. M. Bartusis, "Brigandage in the Late Byzantine Empire," *Byzantion* 51 (1981): 386–409.
2. On the Battle of Kosovo and these related issues, see G. Škrivanić, *Kosovska bitka* (Cetinje, 1956).
3. On the ways commerce and coinage can disrupt a society not accustomed to them, see F. Braudel, *The Structures of Everyday Life* (New York, 1981), chap. 7, esp. pp. 436–40.
4. I. Božić, "Mlečani na reci Bojani," in I. Božić, *Nemirno Pomorje XV veka* (Beograd, 1979), p. 238.
5. E. P. Naumov, "Iz istorii Bolgarskogo Pričernomor'ja v konce XIV veka," *Bulgarian Historical Review,* 1976, no. 1: 47–59.
6. M. Purković, *Knez i Despot Stefan Lazarević* (Beograd, 1978), pp. 34–37. If Purković is correct in re-dating to before January 1394 a second document that refers to Stefan Lazarević's assigning a Priština kefalija—showing that at the time Stefan held Vuk's Priština—to investigate a land dispute for a second Athonite monastery, then it seems Vuk lost his lands before January 1394. If the Serres meeting (winter 1393–94) had occurred in late November or early December 1393, possibly Vuk's disobedience in not attending had brought upon him immediate punishment from Bayezid. However, though Purković makes a strong case for this document's being issued in January 1394, it is not entirely certain that the charter was issued that early.
7. In the collective work, *Istorija srpskog naroda* (Beograd, 1982), vol. 2, p. 58.
8. R.-J. Loenertz, "Pour l'histoire du Péloponèse au XIVᵉ siècle (1382–1404)," *Études Byzantines* 1 (1943): 167; article reprinted in R.-J. Loenertz, *Byzantina et Franco-Graeca* (Rome, 1970), p. 236.
9. On the death of Walter II of Brienne in 1356 his towns of Argos and Nauplia had been left to his nephew, Guy d'Enghien. Guy had administered the towns through bailiffs. Guy died shortly after October 1376, leaving his holding to his daughter Maria, under the guardianship of his brother Louis, who was then the Angevin bailiff in Achaea. In 1377 Louis arranged Maria's marriage to a Venetian, Peter Cornaro. The newlyweds then took up residence in the Argolid. Venice found the increased commercial opportunities, made possible through Cornaro's rule, advantageous and supported him actively until his death in 1388. By then Peter Cornaro had come to be considered by many as the lord of the Argolid, and Venice had come to have considerable interest in the two towns. Immediately after his death Maria, either uninterested in these possessions or possibly pressured by Venice, sold the two towns to Venice for an annual stipend.

10. Loenertz, "Pour l'histoire du Péloponèse," *Études Byzantines* 1 (1943): 180, or in *Byzantina et Franco-Graeca*, p. 248. J. Barker, *Manuel II Palaeologus (1391–1425): A Study in Late Byzantine Statesmanship* (New Brunswick, N.J., 1969), pp. 99–104.

11. Ćirković argues that after the Serres meeting, and probably because of the scare received at it, the positions of Serbian nobles became polarized. Whereas Stefan Lazarević, Constantine Balšić, Constantine Dejanović, and Marko remained loyal to Bayezid, others, having lost confidence in the sultan, went into opposition. These, Ćirković argues, were George II Balšić, who submitted to Venetian suzerainty early in 1394; Vuk Branković, whose lands were confiscated by Bayezid shortly thereafter; and Marko's brother Andrew, who in 1394 appeared in Dubrovnik and soon thereafter moved to Hungary. See S. Ćirković, "Poklad Kralja Vukašina," *Zbornik Filozofskog fakulteta* (Beogradski univerzitet) 14, no. 1 (1979): 159–61.

12. Loenertz, "Pour l'histoire du Péloponèse," *Études Byzantines* 1 (1943): 181–85, or in *Byzantina et Franco-Graeca*, pp. 249–53.

13. V. S. Kiselkov, *Žitieto na sv. Teodosij T"rnovski kato istoričeski pametnik* (Sofija, 1926), pp. i–iii.

14. Though certain scholars have claimed that Euthymius was the founder or initiator of the movement to standardize language on the basis of Old Slavonic, recent scholarship shows that this movement was afoot and reflected in certain texts dating back to the thirteenth century. However, though not its initiator, Euthymius certainly was its leading exponent, pushing the reform and having great impact on its spread and enforcement.

15. M. Heppell, *The Ecclesiastical Career of Gregory Camblak* (London, 1979), pp. 81–95.

16. S. Ćirković, "Pismenost i obrazovanje u srednjovekovnoj srpskoj državi," in *Istorija škola i obrazovanja kod Srba,* vol. 1 (Beograd, 1974), pp. 9–30.

17. This section is indebted to J. Starr, *Romania: The Jewries of the Levant after the Fourth Crusade* (Paris, 1949).

18. On Tobias' polemic against the Karaites, see Z. Ankori, "Some Aspects of Karaite-Rabbanite Relations in Byzantium on the Eve of the First Crusade," in *Medieval Jewish Life,* ed. R. Chazan (New York, 1976), pp. 187–93, 216–23.

19. L. Weinberger, *Bulgaria's Synagogue Poets: The Kastoreans* (University, Ala., 1983), p. 1.

CHAPTER 9

The Balkans in the Early Fifteenth Century

Bosnia after the Death of Tvrtko

Tvrtko died in 1391 and was succeeded by a cousin, Dabiša (1391–95). An obscure figure somehow related to Tvrtko, Dabiša was clearly elderly. He had been mentioned in diplomatic records as far back as 1358. According to the seventeenth-century writer Orbini, he was a first cousin of Tvrtko and had supported Tvrtko's brother Vuk in the rebellion against Tvrtko in 1366. Dabiša may well have been chosen as ruler because he was elderly and weak and thus could be made into a puppet by the nobles. A council of nobles now becomes prominent in the sources.

According to most Yugoslav scholars, at this time (1391) the Bosnian state not only did not fall apart, as had occurred after the death of Kotromanić, but remained united because by this time a feeling for a Bosnian entity had come into existence. This unity, they argue, is illustrated by the institution of a state council of nobles, which met frequently in the 1390s and the first two decades of the fifteenth century. The council actively involved itself in the selection of kings as well as in domestic and foreign affairs. I do not accept this interpretation. The council clearly did exist and play this dominant role; however, I think it reflects not unity but the weakness of the king and of the central state. Too weak to assert their authority, Dabiša and his successors had no choice but to summon the leading nobles to obtain their agreement on important matters and thereby assure themselves that a particular course of action was acceptable to the nobles and thus would obtain support and not provoke a revolt. The king could not enforce decisions of moment unless he had aid in enforcing them from at least one or two of the most powerful nobles.

The council does not seem to have been a regular institution, but came together when summoned rather than holding sessions according to an established schedule. And, though it is often claimed, it is not certain that the council had a set membership who attended by right. Generally, however, the same major figures were in attendance almost every time, for the king clearly needed agreement from those who were the most powerful. One scholar speaks of the council's having the right to elect and dethrone kings. However, this was not a question of right in any juridical sense but of the de facto balance of power. If two or three great nobles wanted to dethrone a king, they had sufficient power (their own supporters) to do so. Rights and contracts meant almost nothing, and raw power counted for everything; and this became particularly true in the Bosnian state after Tvrtko's death. There is little evidence of loyalty to such abstractions as "the Bosnian state." If it was in the nobles' interests to co-operate—for example, against a Hungarian threat—they did so, but if their policy advanced the interests of a Bosnian state it was purely coincidental.

So on Tvrtko's death, the Bosnian state did not fragment into small units as it had in the 1350s. It did not fragment because the nobles decided it was in their interests to co-operate and hold it together. Thus the Bosnian state seemed to remain united. But this unity and apparent strength were illusory, for the authority of the king (and his limited central apparatus) was not what held the separate counties together. If several nobles had wanted to secede with their counties, they would have succeeded unless the other nobles decided to unite against them. Thus it was the general and voluntary co-operation of the nobles that really held the state together.

However, separatism remained strong, and the great nobles took advantage of Dabiša's impotence to gain more autonomy for their regions. As noted, regionalism had been strong in Bosnia throughout the Middle Ages, aiding the nobles at times in their separatist aspirations and regularly preventing the development of a feeling for state unity. The ban (now king) was the ruler of the central county (or župa) of Bosnia, and though Kotromanić and Tvrtko had been able to assert their overlordship over the neighboring regions, as they generally had since the 1320s, and called their whole greater state "Bosnia," they had not integrated the outlying regions into the state. Each region retained its own traditions and dominant hereditary noble families, both of which had far more appeal to the region's inhabitants than any concept of Bosnian unity. The lesser nobles of a region remained far more loyal to their local lord (e.g., Hrvoje) than to the king. The mountainous geography aided this localism, as did Bosnia's different religions; for the existence of three faiths, generally only one of which was prominent in any given area, prevented the development of the kind of state Church that in other Balkan lands had been a force for unity. The Bosnian Church, though sometimes depicted as such, was certainly no state Church. And though certain nobles had ties to it there is also no evidence that it supported the political aspirations of particular nobles or the nobles as a group against the central state, as many scholars have claimed.

It is generally believed that Bosnia's banship (kingship) was limited to members of the royal family. Tvrtko had no legitimate sons. Tvrtko II, who was to rule subsequently, was almost certainly Tvrtko's illegitimate son, but he does not seem to have been a serious candidate in 1391. He was at the time most probably a minor, but that in itself should not have bothered the nobility, which seems to have been seeking a puppet ruler. In fact the nobles probably selected Dabiša because he was elderly and ineffective. We have no evidence on how the selection of Dabiša occurred. V. Klaić argues that it followed the traditional Slavic system of inheritance by which the right to property belonged to a family collective and the eldest member of that family succeeded. Though we cannot refute Klaić's view for this occasion, this principle does not seem to have been practiced on previous occasions, for Kotromanić and especially Tvrtko I were extremely young at the time of their succession. However, it seems the "system" for succession was vague, with possession of the throne by the particular family the only binding principle. This vagueness would have encouraged a struggle for succession among different candidates, which in fact was to follow (and was to continually take place until Bosnia's fall to the Turks), and allow the nobles, by supporting weaker figures, to acquire greater power and influence for themselves.

Thus from 1391 Bosnia had weak kings and powerful nobles, a handful of whom had massive lands that they were ever trying to increase. Several of them had holdings as large if not larger than those of the king and, consequently, stronger and larger armies than the king did. Thus the king's superior title and theoretical overlordship over the nobles did not count for much. And the great nobles should be seen as the rulers of semi-independent principalities which, by their agreement, were joined in a loose federation, the Bosnian state. They and the king ran this federated Bosnia as a collective through the council.

At this time Bosnia had three leading noble families. First were the Hrvatinići, led by Hrvoje Vukčić, the son of Vlkac Hrvatinić. In the 1390s the Hrvatinići were Bosnia's most powerful family; after Hrvoje's death in 1416, their role in state affairs declined, though they continued to be masters of the Donji Kraji. Hrvoje also had some territory west of the Neretva and dominated the nobles who held lands there or nearby. Before 1391 he had already been active in Dalmatia as Tvrtko's lieutenant, and when Tvrtko died actual control of Bosnia's Dalmatian holdings fell into his hands. After Tvrtko's death he became Ladislas of Naples' (Sigismund's rival for the Hungarian throne) deputy for Dalmatia and extended his authority and overlordship over still more Dalmatian towns, ending up as overlord of most of them. And like earlier Dalmatian overlords, he did not interfere in the towns' administration but left them under their own laws and councils. He established his main residence in the town of Jajce, where he built a major fortified castle, which later was to be the last capital of the Bosnian kingdom.

Second was the Kosača family, led by Vlatko Vuković until his death in 1392. Vlatko was succeeded first by his nephew Sandalj Hranić (1392–1435) and then by Sandalj's nephew Stefan Vukčić (1435–66). The Kosače at first controlled a district in Hum east of the Neretva and the territory of the upper Drina, Tara, and Piva rivers. The family began its expansion immediately after Tvrtko's death, taking advantage of a local crisis. For in 1392 Radič

Sanković, lord of Nevesinje, Popovo Polje, and Konavli (probably then the strongest nobleman in Hum), sold his part of Konavli to Dubrovnik. A council meeting was convoked by the king or by the nobles who objected to this sale. Vlatko Vuković and Paul (Pavle) Radenović, whom we shall meet in a moment, received the council's blessing to march against Radič. They captured Radič and occupied Konavli which, despite Ragusan protests, they then divided between themselves. Vlatko then died, to be succeeded by Sandalj. He continued the struggle with Radič Sanković, who regained his freedom in 1398. Sandalj again took him prisoner and, having blinded him, kept him in prison until he died in 1404. As a result Sandalj was able to acquire Radič's lands from Nevesinje to the coast. When the dust settled Sandalj had almost all Hum. He then expanded south down the coast toward Kotor, making various gains at the expense of the Balšići, as we saw in the last chapter. However, other priorities closer to home prevented him from establishing lasting control over the territory on the Gulf of Kotor. In this period Sandalj was closely associated with Hrvoje, whose niece Helen (Jelena) he married in 1396. After Hrvoje's death in 1416 Sandalj became the most powerful figure in Bosnia.

Third, Raden Jablanić (who was succeeded at about the time of Tvrtko's death by Paul Radenović, who after 1415 was in turn succeeded by his sons the Pavlovići) had a huge holding in eastern Bosnia between the Drina and Bosna rivers. The family's main seat was at Borač; it also held Vrhbosna (the future Sarajevo).

These great nobles had independent political-economic domains. Ruling their lands like kings, they exercised, as Ćirković points out, in their own lands all—and the same—powers that the king exercised in his. The nobles collected taxes from their populaces; farmed out the management of and collected dues from the mines in their territory; established customs and toll stations on routes through and at markets in their lands and collected these dues; and maintained their own law courts, settling quarrels between their subordinates and judging criminals. They also carried out their own foreign relations, concluding foreign alliances and issuing commercial treaties with foreign states independently and without consulting the king. As Ćirković has noted, Dubrovnik generally dealt with the king only on issues concerning his own direct holdings; when the town had a problem in a part of Bosnia that belonged to a nobleman, the town dealt with that nobleman, only turning to the king if it needed him as a mediator. Ragusan records speak of the "country" (contrata) of Sandalj just as they speak of the "contrata" of the king. And when they spoke thus of the king's contrata, they tended to refer only to the king's personal holdings in the central župa. Thus the king, though in theory the ruler of the whole kingdom, in fact fully ruled only his own direct holdings.

By the 1390s the king and the great nobles—the above-mentioned three families and, until their final elimination by 1404, the Sankovići—among themselves held all Bosnia. In fact, the Hrvatinići and, after the elimination of the Sankovići, the Kosače each possessed more territory than the king. All the other, and lesser, nobles found themselves and their lands on the territory of, and thus under the suzerainty of, the king or one of the great nobles. At times a powerful but lesser family would try to assert its full independence from the king or a great nobleman; though occasionally successful, these attempts were always short-lasting, and soon the family found itself back in a subordinate position. The great nobles had solidly established themselves and, as Ćirković notes, there was no room for newcomers in their ranks. The victory of the great nobles is reflected in the fact that by the early fifteenth century in Bosnia the title župan (count), held previously by the old-timer hereditary nobles holding a county, had disappeared. This happened because in the course of the fourteenth and early fifteenth centuries the kings and great nobles succeeded in removing the hereditary local county rulers from their positions as fortress commanders and replacing them with their own appointees, whom we find in the fifteenth century bearing the title knez and commanding the castles within the lands of the king and the great nobles. The king, of course, was able to do this only in his direct holdings. His appointees were not installed in the lands of the great independent nobles. Thus by the early fifteenth century, as noted, all the lesser nobles had become subjected to one or the other of the few great ones.

In the early 1390s King Sigismund had temporarily secured his position in Hungary and thus was prepared to take a more active role in subduing the recalcitrant Bosnian and Croatian nobles. They still supported Ladislas, though it is more accurate to say they were using his cause to advance their own interests. Sigismund's main ally in the area was John "Frankapan," who had assembled under his authority all the family lands, thus giving him control of Senj, Krk, and the regions of Vinodol, Gacka, and Modruš. In 1391 Sigismund appointed him Ban of Croatia and Slavonia, an appointment valid only in the areas that recognized Sigismund, and called on him to lead the counter-offensive. Though our knowledge of specific events is very limited, it seems this counter-offensive had considerable success, for in 1393 Hrvoje submitted to Sigismund. One may assume Hrvoje had been pressured to do this.

John "Frankapan" then died in 1393, and Sigismund appointed Butko Kurjaković as Ban of Croatia. Butko was Prince of Krbava; his appointment suggests Sigismund must have won that family and its region to his side. (In about 1390 some of the Kurjakovići had been supporting Ladislas.) John "Frankapan's" son Nicholas inherited all the "Frankapan" lands. In 1394 Sigismund improved his position still further by defeating the Horvats in battle at Dobor in Usora on the lower Bosna River. Sigismund captured the brothers. John was executed for treachery by being tied to a horse's tail and dragged to death, and Bishop Paul was imprisoned in a monastery, where he died the same year. This ended the Croatian uprising of the Horvats and it seems Croatia was now Sigismund's. With Croatia subdued, Sigismund found himself in a position to interfere more actively in Bosnia. So he summoned Dabiša to Dobor.

Unable to stand up to Sigismund, whose victorious army at the moment was in the north of Bosnia, Dabiša went to Dobor and made peace with Sigismund, recognizing him as his overlord. He also renounced the Croatian-Dalmatian kingship asserted by Tvrtko, and returned to Hungary the Dalmatian and Croatian territory Tvrtko had gained. And under very decided pressure, Dabiša made Sigismund his own heir for the Bosnian throne. Some scholars have suggested Dabiša may not have been entirely unhappy with this agreement, for Dabiša may have hoped to use Sigismund's support to assert himself against the nobility. In any case, we can be certain that the nobles were horrified at the agreement Dabiša concluded.

In 1395 Dabiša died. Sigismund, presumably hoping to collect his inheritance, appeared in near-by Srem with troops. The Bosnian nobles, unwilling to let this happen, convoked a council and elected Dabiša's widow Helen (Jelena)—also known as Gruba—as queen. She was of the Nikolić family of Hum. That family had acquired considerable influence in the state under Dabiša and had obtained from him in 1393 the right to collect the Ston tribute from Dubrovnik. Helen-Gruba was to be the nobles' puppet for the next three years. Sigismund, apprehensive about taking on the united nobility in a war, withdrew. Hrvoje, once again actively opposed to Sigismund and allied with his fellow nobles, took advantage of the situation to renounce his submission to Sigismund and proclaim again his support for Ladislas. Sigismund was not able to respond to this disobedience at once, for other difficulties had overwhelmed him. In 1394 or 1395 his wife, Maria, died. She was the foundation for his position in Hungary, where he still had many opponents. Thus he had to devote his efforts to retaining and consolidating his authority there. Seemingly successful in this by the end of 1395, he returned to his long-put-aside crusading plans. Then the following year, as noted, he was crushingly defeated by the Turks at Nikopolis. Taking heavy losses, he found himself in no position to attack Bosnia. Moreover, his defeat made him even more unpopular in Hungary. Thus once more it was necessary for him to concentrate his efforts on maintaining his rule there.

Sigismund's failure at Nikopolis also revived the hopes of Ladislas and his party. Ladislas now appointed Stjepan Lacković as his deputy for Croatia, and they began organizing in the hopes of resuming the warfare. To prevent this Sigismund called a council at Križevci to which Lacković was invited on a safe-conduct. At the gathering Lacković was murdered, which set off a new Croatian-Hungarian uprising in the name of Ladislas. This uprising was led by Hrvoje Vukčić, whom Ladislas soon named as his deputy to replace Lacković. Hrvoje took a very active role in Croatia and particularly in Dalmatia, where in Ladislas' name he was able to extend his own authority over much of Dalmatia.

Helen-Gruba continued to rule as a puppet of the nobles—with all her extant charters specifically noting that they had the agreement of the great nobles—until 1398, when she was deposed under uncertain circumstances. It is often said that she then departed for an exile in Dubrovnik. However, Živković has shown that she actually remained in Bosnia, treated with honor. Nevertheless, it seems that some of the leading Nikolići, her brothers and nephews, who opposed her deposition, did for a while have to seek asylum in Dubrovnik. By 1403 they are found back at home as vassals of Sandalj Hranić. Thus if, as seems likely, the Nikolići tried to take advantage of Dabiša's and Helen's support to raise themselves to the level of independent barons, the attempt failed. Possibly Helen's overthrow was a move to suppress the family to which she belonged and which through her favors was becoming strong enough to pose a threat to the monopoly of power held by the established barons.

Helen was replaced by Ostoja, a member of the ruling family, though it is not certain how he was related to it. He had not been mentioned in earlier sources. Ostoja's first reign was to last from 1398 to 1404. All the powerful nobles who had supported Helen remained around Ostoja, so it seems none had strongly opposed his election. Why some, or all, of them had wanted him as king, however, we cannot say. Like Hrvoje, Ostoja once in power declared his support for Ladislas. At about this time Radič Sanković regained his freedom and, closely associated with Ostoja, set about recovering the lands he had lost to the Kosače. Sigismund tried to take advantage of the situation to attack Bosnia in 1398, but he was repelled. Bosnia also suffered a Turkish raid that year.

In 1400 Ostoja and Hrvoje sent a complaint to Dubrovnik about the sale of slaves in that town, many of whom were Bosnians. According to town law, Catholics could not be sold as slaves there. Thus most of the slaves were presumably members of the Bosnian Church—or at least passed off as such. Both Hrvoje and Ostoja had close ties with the Bosnian Church. Hrvoje was a member of it, while keeping cordial relations with the Catholic Church, and Ostoja almost certainly was also a member of the Bosnian Church. Their protests may be seen, then, as an effort to help their co-religionists. In 1416 Dubrovnik was to ban entirely the sale of slaves in Dubrovnik.

In 1401 Ostoja and Hrvoje moved onto the offensive on behalf of Ladislas. In that year Zadar submitted to Hrvoje, while retaining its existing institutions and privileges. Hrvoje then moved to regain the other Dalmatian towns for Ladislas; presumably many had gone over to Sigismund in 1393 at the time Hrvoje had capitulated to him. Split, which had earlier been taken by Tvrtko, refused now to submit to Hrvoje and went so far as to attack and besiege Hrvoje's town of Omiš. Dubrovnik, though a vassal of Sigismund, also maintained good relations with Hrvoje and shipped grain to those besieged in Omiš. Hrvoje was allied to his brother-in-law Ivaniš Nelipčić, who controlled most of the Cetina župa; he seems to have mobilized his forces to help Hrvoje against Split. Seeing the threat against itself increased, Split gave up its resistance and submitted to Hrvoje by 1403.

Meanwhile, matters went from bad to worse for Sigismund. In 1401 a group of Hungarian nobles seized and jailed him in Buda. Nicholas Garai and Herman of Celje eventually succeeded in procuring his release by making peace with his captors. Sigismund then left for Bohemia to raise an army, leaving a very unstable situation in Hungary. As a result, during these years (1401–03) he lost, as we have seen, most of Dalmatia to Hrvoje and Nelipčić, while also suffering losses in Croatia and Slavonia. The most important defection in Croatia was that of John "Frankapan's" son and successor Nicholas, who held Senj, the župas of Vinodol, Modruš, and Gacka, and also some castles in the vicinity of Zagreb. Probably the strongest Croatian prince of the time, he declared for Ladislas in 1403. However, Sigismund was able to retain the loyalty of a number of powerful northern Croatian and Slavonian princes: the Kurjakovići of Krbava, the Berislavići of Požega, and the princes of Zrin and Blagaj. In 1401 even the pope, Boniface IX, declared his support for Ladislas. Finally, encouraged by Hrvoje and other supporters, in July 1403 Ladislas arrived in Zadar, declaring his intent to assume control of his lands and to campaign actively for the throne. His allies hoped and Sigismund feared that he would now march on Buda to claim his throne. Hrvoje, who came to Zadar to greet him, and a large number of other supporters urged him to act quickly, stressing Sigismund's numerous difficulties at the time and the great likelihood of success. However, Ladislas hesitated, seemingly afraid to go to Buda where his father had been murdered. Finally, after extracting oaths of loyalty from a large assortment of nobles and naming Hrvoje as his deputy for Dalmatia (granting Hrvoje the title Herceg of Split), Ladislas returned to Naples.

Ladislas' failure to act distressed his followers, who became less zealous in his cause, and gave Sigismund an opportunity to rally support. For in the face of Ladislas' passivity, many Hungarian and Croatian nobles came to the realization that sooner or later they would have to make peace with Sigismund. To facilitate this, the alert Sigismund now offered an amnesty to all those who had opposed him. And many Hungarian and Croatian nobles, concluding it was the time to do so, accepted and, deserting Ladislas, submitted to Sigismund in late 1403 and 1404. These included Nicholas "Frankapan" in 1404. It was chiefly the nobles in peripheral regions like Bosnia, freer of Sigismund's retaliation and preferring a lethargic and distant suzerain in Italy to a more interfering one in near-by Hungary, who stuck by Ladislas.

Dubrovnik, though throughout recognizing Sigismund, tried to maintain correct relations with Sigismund's Bosnian opponents, Hrvoje and Ostoja. However, this attempt met with severe difficulties both at home and abroad. First, the Bosnian leaders objected to the sale of slaves in Dubrovnik; and second, the town's merchants had grievances against various Bosnian nobles—particularly those in Hum, including Sandalj—who had been arbitrarily establishing new customs stations and raising the amounts of customs and tolls, which cut into the profits of these merchants. The merchants also suffered from attacks on their caravans by brigands in Bosnia and Hum, brigands whom the Bosnians could not or would not control; and the Bosnians were not interested in giving the merchants restitution for their losses. Ostoja further complained that Dubrovnik was granting asylum to Bosnian deserters. This issue became a critical one in 1403 when a member of the Bosnian royal family, Paul (Pavle) Radišić, fled from Bosnia to Dubrovnik. It seems he had been involved in an unsuccessful plot for the Bosnian throne. At least Ostoja suspected that he was. Ostoja wrote Dubrovnik and insisted that it expel Radišić. He also demanded that the town accept him, Ostoja, in place of Sigismund, as its overlord. If his demands were not met in fifteen days, Ostoja threatened to expel its merchants from Bosnia and attack the town.

The town was caught by surprise; throughout the Middle Ages, and often at great cost to itself, it had insisted on its right to grant political asylum to anyone who sought it. It was not about to compromise this principle. Dubrovnik immediately sent envoys to Ostoja and to a number of Bosnian nobles who, it was hoped, could exert some influence on Ostoja. Hrvoje seems to have been upset and apparently tried to intervene with Ostoja on Dubrovnik's behalf; at least Dubrovnik believed he did. Such intervention had no effect. In July 1403 Ostoja's armies attacked the territory of Dubrovnik, sending refugees from the hinterland flocking to the town. Radič Sanković, Dubrovnik's direct Bosnian neighbor, who had long had good relations with the town but who was closely allied to Ostoja, to further his own attempt to regain his lost lands from Sandalj, joined Ostoja's attack. Dubrovnik confiscated his house inside its walls. In September Ostoja sent envoys to Dubrovnik, but they could not reach any agreement. So the town wrote Hrvoje again, suggesting he overthrow Ostoja and put Radišić on the throne. Hrvoje at the time rejected the plan but assured the town he wanted it to have peace with Ostoja.

By this time Hrvoje was clearly angry at Ostoja. He was unhappy with the war. But also he must have been angry at Ostoja's forcing the flight and seizing the lands of Paul (Pavle) Klešić, the lord of Glamoč and Duvno, who had sought asylum in Dubrovnik in June 1403. The location of his lands makes it probable that he was Hrvoje's vassal. Ostoja seems to have felt threatened by Dubrovnik's negotiations with Hrvoje and with Sigismund, particularly since Hrvoje, miffed at Ostoja's behavior, had cooled in his attitude toward the Bosnian king. Moreover, Sigismund was well on the way to victory, having regained the allegiance of large numbers of nobles and having recovered Buda, Višegrad (Visegrad), and Esztergom in Hungary; soon he would be in a position to involve himself once again in Bosnian matters. Should Hrvoje join the ranks of the Hungarian and Croatian nobility flocking at the time to Sigismund's camp, it could spell the end for Ostoja. So at the end of 1403, to prevent such an alliance against himself, Ostoja opened negotiations with Sigismund and soon agreed to accept him as his overlord. This submission occurred just six months after Ostoja had gone to war with Dubrovnik, at least in part because the town recognized Sigismund as its suzerain.

Ostoja's recognition of Sigismund was surely opposed by many, if not most, of the Bosnian nobles. Opposition from them would explain the change of heart Ostoja now was to show toward Klešić. For in January 1404, after intervention on Klešić's behalf by members of the Bosnian Church including the djed, Ostoja allowed Klešić to return and regain his lands, which Ostoja had taken from him "illegally." This intervention also reflects the influence on Ostoja of the Bosnian Church. Such influence was probably limited to this period when Bosnia had a ruler who almost certainly was one of its members. The Bosnian kings who preceded and followed Ostoja were all Catholics. It is further possible that Ostoja was receptive to the djed's plea, not to please the djed but to placate the powerful Hrvoje, who was also probably supporting Klešić's cause.

It is worth pausing a moment here to examine the case of Klešić more closely. For it was declared when Klešić was restored to his lands that this was right because the king had taken his land "illegally." What triumphed here was the principle that regardless of one's fault (regardless of what Klešić had done to anger the king), his lands were inviolate. Thus the Bosnians were not going to allow anyone to connect their landholding with their relation to state authority. This attitude, which they staunchly defended, clearly made it extremely difficult for any king to carry out the policy attempted by Ostoja of confiscating land as a punitive measure. This meant it was also impossible for a king to tie landholding to state service as the Byzantines and Serbs had done under the pronoia system. As a result the Bosnian kings, unable to make such a connection and obtain military service through land, were to remain weaker militarily in general and weaker vis à vis their nobles in particular than their eastern neighbors. Landholding was to remain free and not tied to service until the end of the medieval Bosnian state.

In January 1404, at the same time that Ostoja, surely under pressure, was allowing Klešić to return, Hrvoje and Dubrovnik were in the midst of discussing the question of overthrowing Ostoja and replacing him with Paul Radišić. If Ostoja had any inkling of these discussions, it is easy to understand why he changed his policy on Klešić. Klešić's return seems to have done much to improve Ostoja's relations with his nobles, and tensions seem to have dissipated. In March 1404 Ostoja made peace with Hrvoje and even concluded a truce with Dubrovnik. And it seems that Hrvoje was even considering making peace with Sigismund. Had that happened, the last major issue separating Ostoja and Hrvoje would have been resolved. Then suddenly the pieces of the kaleidoscope radically formed a new pattern, seemingly the result of new disagreements that surfaced when discussions were initiated between Ostoja and Dubrovnik on the terms for a formal peace between them.

The town demanded the restoration of all territory seized by Ostoja. Ostoja was reluctant to agree to this. However, Hrvoje, supported by Sandalj Hranić and Paul Radenović, wanted him to accept this demand. Ostoja, seeking support to bolster his stand, then sent an envoy, authorized to offer privileges, off to Venice to seek an alliance there. Dubrovnik and Hrvoje, who was overlord over much of Dalmatia, seeing Venice as a dangerous rival, were both much opposed to this idea. At this point Hrvoje, having Sandalj with him, seems to have broken with Ostoja, for a draft charter offered to Dubrovnik by Ostoja in late March 1404 had neither Hrvoje nor Sandalj as a witness; moreover, neither nobleman attended a council meeting Ostoja held at Visoko in late April.

Shortly thereafter, at the very end of April or even May 1404, the Bosnian nobility convened a council that ousted Ostoja and put on the throne Tvrtko II, who was, according to Orbini, the illegitimate son of Tvrtko I. His election was almost certainly effected by Hrvoje supported by Sandalj. Tvrtko was clearly Hrvoje's puppet at first. In fact, in the beginning of his reign he was frequently found residing in Hrvoje's Sana province. And in the spring of 1405 Tvrtko granted to Hrvoje Bosnia's richest mining town, Srebrnica. We may assume this lucrative gift was not granted happily. As long as Hrvoje and Sandalj, the two strongest figures in Bosnia, remained united, Tvrtko would have no chance to assert his independence.

Sandalj immediately took advantage of the situation to attack Radič Sanković, who had been able to maintain himself, it seems, chiefly because of Ostoja's support. Sandalj quickly occupied the lands Radič had regained; he even managed to capture Radič whom he blinded and then jailed. Radič never emerged from prison again, and all his family's lands were taken by the Kosače, who from then on held almost all of Hum. One wonders if Sandalj's support of Tvrtko II's candidacy was not motivated by his desire to eliminate Radič's prop and thereby facilitate this massive land grab. Peace with Dubrovnik was finally concluded in June 1405. Its conclusion was delayed owning to a dispute between the town and Sandalj over certain villages.

The nobles in general had probably turned against Ostoja because he was head-strong and wanted to act independently of them and assert his authority, as was shown by his war with Dubrovnik, which, as far as we can tell, was desired by none of the nobles, with the possible exception of Radič. The nobles also disliked Ostoja's new ties with the hated Sigismund. Further, they must have disliked Ostoja's willingness to turn to foreign powers, even unpopular ones, to find allies to support his interests against those of his nobles, as he had done with Sigismund and then tried to do with Venice.

Ostoja, who had patched up his relations with Sigismund, avoided capture by his opponents and fled from Bobovac to the Hungarian court. He at once was promised Hungarian military support. In June 1404 two Hungarian armies struck Bosnia, the first hitting Usora and taking among other places the fortress of Usora, which the Hungarians retained for a period thereafter. The second army took the major royal residence of Bobovac. Faced by strong resistance from the nobles, the Hungarians could not advance deeper into Bosnia. But though they could not extend their conquest further, they were able to retain Bobovac. And there Ostoja remained, propped up by a Hungarian garrison and ruling as a puppet king for Sigismund, while almost all the nobility of Bosnia supported Tvrtko II. The only relatively major noble family that stood by Ostoja at this time were the Radivojevići of western Bosnia.

However, by 1406 they too were found in Tvrtko's camp. After that, we may suppose, Ostoja's kingdom consisted of little more than Bobovac itself.

However, Tvrtko was never able to oust him, and thus throughout Tvrtko's first reign (to 1409) Ostoja remained in Bobovac and, which was particularly galling to Tvrtko, in possession of the Bosnian crown. He was also more than simply a thorn in Tvrtko's side, for there was an ever-present danger that Ostoja's Hungarian allies might launch a major expedition to gain for him more, if not all, of Bosnia. The likelihood of this seemed strong, for not only had Sigismund declared his support for Ostoja, but Ostoja's major opponent Hrvoje was still working for Ladislas and had easily made his puppet Tvrtko take this position as well. Thus Sigismund had added reason to attack Bosnia and rid that neighboring land of Ladislas' followers. Thus Hrvoje's continued support of Ladislas made Sigismund take a more active role in Bosnian affairs, which was certainly not in Bosnia's interests, and the quarrel between Tvrtko/Hrvoje and Ostoja/Sigismund that continued until 1409 can be viewed as a phase of the broader civil war between Sigismund and Ladislas.

Hungary took almost annual military action against Bosnia, though generally it was not on a major scale. In August 1405 the Hungarians attacked Bihać in the north of Bosnia. Hrvoje was able to expel them, regaining the town while the Hungarians withdrew their forces to Krupa on the Una. In 1406 a Hungarian attack was launched along the Drina and seems to have taken Srebrnica, a logical target, for not only was it a rich town, but it was then possessed by their enemy, Hrvoje. In 1407 the Hungarians raided Hrvoje's own lands of the Donji Kraji and also raided along the Bosna River valley. Though they do not seem to have made lasting conquests, the Hungarians did carry out considerable destruction and carried off much booty. Thus they made life a constant hassle for Tvrtko. In 1407 Sigismund was able to briefly acquire the submission of Hrvoje's brother-in-law Ivaniš Nelipčić. This submission was rendered in a meeting arranged through the mediation of Nelipčić's neighbor, Nicholas "Frankapan."

By this time Sigismund had basically put an end to the unrest in Hungary and Croatia. His major allies in this effort had proved to be the counts of Celje (Cilli). Celje lay south of Maribor on the Savinja, a tributary running into the Sava, in present-day Slovenia. Herman II of Celje had bravely supported Sigismund during the battle of Nikopolis, and the two had escaped the battle on the same fishing boat and then taken the long trip back to Hungary together. On his return Sigismund rewarded Herman II with the district of Varaždin as well as various districts in Zagorje in the borderlands between Slovenia and Croatia. He remained loyal to Sigismund when Ladislas' faction resumed the war, and, when Sigismund was captured and imprisoned in 1401, Herman II had a major role in procuring his liberation, by threatening to invade Hungary if he were not released. Having regained his freedom, Sigismund became even closer to this loyal supporter. In 1405 Sigismund, as noted a widower, married Herman's daughter Barbara and awarded Herman vast tracts of land in Slavonia; soon, in 1406, Sigismund named Herman the combined Ban of Croatia, Dalmatia, and Slavonia. For his major contributions to the pacification of the Croatian nobles, Sigismund also granted Herman the right to mint money, exact tolls, and to receive the revenue from various mines. Thus the counts of Celje, now of Celje and Zagorje, rapidly rose to become the major family in the Croatian lands.

The skirmishing, which took place chiefly in the north of Bosnia, between the Bosnian nobility and Sigismund continued until early 1409. It finally culminated in a battle fought at Dobor in Usora in September 1408, when Sigismund won a great victory over the Bosnian nobility. Later sources say 170 Bosnian noblemen—but not any of the major figures—were captured and pitched to their deaths over the town's battlements. This statement may well be exaggerated, for the same source claims Tvrtko II was captured. That certainly was not the case, however, for Tvrtko is found seeking tribute from Dubrovnik in February 1409. By that time Sigismund had basically won the war; for in January 1409 it was announced in a letter from Sigismund to Trogir that Hrvoje had submitted to him.

By this time Ladislas was openly planning to sell Dalmatia to Venice, a sale he actually carried out shortly thereafter, in July 1409. Thus Hrvoje's submission was probably motivated by two considerations: Sigismund's increased power in the region of Bosnia after his victory at Dobor, and Hrvoje's desire to retain Dalmatia for himself. For if he submitted to Sigismund, he could do so on the condition that he retain his position in Dalmatia; moreover, by serving Sigismund, he could then ignore Ladislas' sale of Dalmatia to Venice, something he could not do if he was still Ladislas' deputy there. At the same time Hrvoje's conditions could benefit Sigismund, for Hrvoje's presence in Dalmatia could keep Venice from acquiring its purchases and thus keep this region at least nominally his. And, surely as Hrvoje anticipated, the agreement between the two stated that Sigismund would allow Hrvoje to retain his titles and lands including Dalmatia, simply stipulating that Hrvoje held the region from Sigismund and not from Ladislas. Hrvoje now became an honored nobleman at court and was made a member of the newly established Dragon Order.

This order had been established by Sigismund in December 1408 in the midst of colorful ceremonies. Its aim was to defend the Hungarian royal house (i.e., Sigismund) from domestic and foreign enemies, and the Catholic Church from pagans and heretics. That Hrvoje was a member of the Bosnian Church did not appear to bother anyone, a fact suggesting that that Church was not, as has been claimed, Bogomil or dualist. The order included foreigners as well as Hungarians; the Orthodox rulers of Serbia (Stefan Lazarević) and Wallachia were made members. As a footnote it is worth mentioning that in the Wallachian case membership went from father to son. The son, famous for his brutality and known as Vlad the Impaler, was also known as Vlad Dracul, the name Dracul (dragon) being derived from his membership in the Dragon Order. A whole series of tales about Dracula, based on the activities of Vlad the Impaler and all ending in impalements, circulated around Europe in the fifteenth and sixteenth centuries. Though these stories were not supernatural, their protagonist eventually became so when Bram Stoker converted him into a vampire, also mistakenly making him into a Transylvanian.

Hrvoje was to remain loyal to and on good terms with Sigismund, who, of course, provided him with a legal basis to hold Dalmatia against Venice's claims, until 1413. Most of the other Bosnian nobles soon came to accept Sigismund and/or Ostoja shortly thereafter. Nonetheless, Ostoja's position remained precarious until Tvrtko was deposed. In February 1409 Tvrtko sent an envoy for tribute to Dubrovnik; he is not heard of again until the very end of 1409, when he sent another envoy to Dubrovnik. Throughout that year Tvrtko, though losing support rapidly, seems to have remained in Bosnia, calling himself king. By the end of 1409 Ostoja was effectively back as King of Bosnia, clearly holding most of the country and accepted by all the nobles whom we have record of. Tvrtko is not mentioned in the sources again until 1414, when he is found living on some lands belonging to Paul Radenović, a day's trip from Dubrovnik. And Tvrtko seems to have played no further role in Bosnian affairs until about that time.

Venetian sources credit Sandalj with playing the major role in Ostoja's restoration. If this claim be true, we do not know why Sandalj supported Ostoja. However, since Radič Sanković was dead and his lands were safely in Sandalj's possession, Sandalj no longer had a major reason to oppose Ostoja. However, even though Ostoja by the end of 1409 was universally recognized as king, his position was still weak. In his state the great nobles retained their independence, giving their own personal interests top priority, and negotiated on their own with Sigismund. In fact some of them, like Hrvoje, submitted to Sigismund directly and not to the Hungarian king through Ostoja, the Bosnian ruler. This gave Hrvoje great freedom of action and the means to use Sigismund on his own behalf against Ostoja. This was particularly dangerous to the king because some, like Hrvoje, were clearly stronger than Ostoja was. At the same time, and adding to the confusion, certain nobles like Sandalj, who came in 1409 to accept Ostoja, still did not recognize Sigismund. Sandalj remained loyal to Ladislas, with whom he corresponded through the summer of 1409, until forced to submit to Sigismund in October 1410.

Ostoja remained hostile to Hrvoje and tried through grants to assign to other noblemen, in particular to the Radivojevići, lands belonging to Hrvoje or to his vassals. Seeing this feud developing, Sigismund, interested in maintaining good relations with the powerful Hrvoje, began to cool toward Ostoja. Threatened by these two and jealous of Hrvoje, whose presence prevented Ostoja from truly ruling Bosnia, Ostoja worked hard to improve his relations with the other barons, Paul Radenović and Sandalj Hranić. Ostoja's opposition to Hrvoje and his patching up relations with these two powerful noblemen, both of whom still supported Ladislas, led Sigismund and Hrvoje to go to war against Ostoja in 1410. Hrvoje had already, during 1409, expelled the Radivojevići from their newly granted lands, including the rich customs town of Drijeva. Now, in 1410, and allied to Hrvoje, Hungarian troops struck northeastern Bosnia, capturing several fortresses in that area, including Vranduk, Srebrnik in Usora, and Srebrnica. Then the allies took the important town of Visoko, forcing Ostoja to flee.

Sandalj, meanwhile, took advantage of this fighting to seize Drijeva for himself. This act pleased neither Hrvoje nor Sigismund. The latter, who had also hoped that the campaign would force Sandalj and Paul Radenović to give up their support of Ladislas and submit to him, now decided to direct his army's attention against these two nobles. By October 1410 he had forced both of them to capitulate to him. According to Dubrovnik's records, Sigismund's success led him to consider, in the fall of 1410, having himself crowned King of Bosnia, in place of Ostoja then in disfavor. It seems he even was able to force Sandalj and Paul to acquiesce in this plan. For some reason—presumably Hrvoje's opposition, or at least Hrvoje's persuading him that such an act might have undesirable consequences—Sigismund soon gave up the plan. In the winter 1410–11, Ostoja, finding himself without support, made a trip to Djakovo to meet Sigismund and submit to him. Sigismund recognized him as King of Bosnia, while Ostoja recognized Sigismund as his suzerain and yielded to him Soli and Usora. At that time these two regions were probably still under Hungarian occupation. Thus Ostoja was recognizing a fait accompli; however, his agreement gave up Bosnia's claim to the area. These two regions were then assigned to deputies chosen by Sigismund.

In the course of this warfare, as noted, in early 1410 Sigismund had seized the richest silver-mining town in Bosnia, Srebrnica on the Drina. Later, probably in 1411, Sigismund assigned Srebrnica to his loyal vassal Stefan Lazarević of Serbia, whose state lay just across the Drina from Srebrnica. For most of the rest of the fifteenth century—until the Turkish conquest—Srebrnica was to be Serbian, and Bosnian attempts to regain it were to cause several wars with Serbia.

In these years Hrvoje and Sandalj had each vastly increased his holdings and power; each clearly outstripped the king in lands and size of armies. A struggle between the two noblemen seemed likely; not only were they rivals for influence in state affairs, but Sandalj was probably unhappy with the closer ties between Bosnia and Sigismund that were developing as a result of Hrvoje's policies and which culminated in Sigismund's campaign against and victory over Sandalj himself in 1410. Had Hrvoje not gone over to Sigismund voluntarily and then become his active ally, Bosnia might well have retained greater independence from Hungary and have avoided the territorial losses in the north. In 1411 Sandalj divorced Hrvoje's niece and married Helen (Jelena), the widow of George II Balšić of Zeta and the sister of Stefan Lazarević. This marital change reflected both Sandalj's deteriorating relations with Hrvoje and his forging closer ties with Serbia. He was to send help, as we shall see, to Stefan Lazarević in the latter's war against the Ottoman pretender Musa in 1412 and 1413. Good relations between the Kosače and

Stefan's family were not new, for Sandalj's predecessor Vlatko Vuković had led the Bosnian forces that had fought for Lazar at Kosovo.

In 1412 peace seemed to reign in Bosnia. Sigismund held a major festival in Buda that year attended by among others the leading Bosnians, Ostoja, Hrvoje, Sandalj, and Paul Radenović. A Polish chronicler speaks of the prowess of the Bosnians in knightly games. Shortly thereafter, in the spring of 1413, Sigismund declared Hrvoje a rebel and accused him of dealing with the Turks. Hrvoje, he said, had attacked Sandalj's lands when Sandalj was absent from them, fighting the Turks (Musa) in Serbia. Živković, noting Hrvoje's anger at Sandalj's seizing Drijeva from him in 1410, believes the charge was true, though of course his treachery was primarily against Sandalj rather than Sigismund. However, since Sigismund was supporting the coalition against Musa, he did have cause for anger. As a result Sigismund withdrew the titles and authority he had granted Hrvoje in his realm. Sigismund's action had immediate effect in Dalmatia, for, beginning with Split, one after the other the Dalmatian towns ousted Hrvoje's representatives and declared their loyalty to Sigismund. Thus Hrvoje's rule seems to have been unpopular on the coast. Hrvoje pleaded in letters to Sigismund and to the Hungarian queen that the charges were unjust and that he was still loyal to Sigismund. His protests had no effect. In disgrace, Hrvoje now had no choice but to do what he was accused of; he turned to the Turks and received mercenaries from the Ottoman governor of Skopje. He was also joined by Tvrtko II, who reappeared as mysteriously as he had disappeared four years earlier.

Tvrtko at the time was living on lands belonging to Paul Radenović near Dubrovnik. The Turks decided to seriously involve themselves in the issue and in May 1414 launched a major expedition of thirty thousand troops, according to contemporary Venetian sources, against Bosnia. They concentrated on plundering the lands of Ostoja and Sandalj, Hrvoje's major enemies at the time. The Ottomans also proclaimed Tvrtko II as King of Bosnia. Thus they seem to have hoped to weaken Bosnia by provoking a civil war for the throne. At once Paul Radenović and his son Peter Pavlović declared their support for Tvrtko, with whom they seem to have maintained good relations, allowing him to reside on their lands. After a major plundering expedition, the Ottomans withdrew, leaving Bosnia divided with two kings present in the land. Most of the nobles, headed by Sandalj, seem to have remained loyal to Ostoja. Paul Radenović was the leading—and in fact only known—powerful local supporter of Tvrtko. Though it would have been logical for Hrvoje to have supported Tvrtko too (since Hrvoje was hostile to Sandalj and since his allies the Turks were supporting Tvrtko), we have no documentation that Hrvoje really did so.

In February 1415 Sigismund sent troops into Bosnia. We may presume they were directed against the lands of Hrvoje. Soon the Ottomans were back, raiding Ostoja's lands. These foreign armies soon met in battle. Hrvoje and the Turks of Ishak beg (governor of Skopje, 1415–39) won a major victory over the Hungarians in August 1415. The battle, generally said to have taken place at Doboj, probably actually took place near Lašva. As a result Hrvoje regained Usora, which Sigismund had taken early in 1411. Many Hungarian prisoners were taken, including some high nobles. A Hungarian chronicler depicts Hrvoje's magnanimity as a victor as well as his sense of humor: Among the Hungarian prisoners was a nobleman who had amused the Hungarian court by mocking Hrvoje's stocky stature and hoarse voice by imitating a bull whenever Hrvoje entered a room he was in. Hrvoje now had this nobleman sewn into an ox hide and said to him, "If you bellowed like a bull when in human shape, now you have the shape of an ox with which to bellow." He then had him, still sewn inside the hide, thrown into a river to drown.

The Turkish victory marked the end of Sigismund's influence in Bosnia and the beginning of an active Turkish role in Bosnian politics. Sandalj and Ostoja quickly made peace with Hrvoje. In their triumph Hrvoje and the Turks forgot about Tvrtko II, who had supported them in the war, and confirmed their recent opponent, Ostoja, as king. Why they did so is not known. After their victory, the Ottoman troops raided into Croatia for the first time, plundering all the way to Celje, the hereditary lands of one of Sigismund's closest supporters. For the next twenty years Ottoman soldiers, usually supplied by Ishak beg, were to be active in Bosnia as mercenaries in various Bosnian civil wars.

In late August 1415, Ostoja and Sandalj, still closely associated, convoked a council at Sutjeska and invited various nobles including the powerful Paul Radenović. He came with his son Peter, leaving his other son Radoslav at home. After their arrival, the hosts suggested a pleasant ride in the country. Radenović and his son accepted. Shortly into the ride, the king, Sandalj, and their retainers turned on the pair. Paul Radenović was killed, allegedly for trying to escape, and Peter was taken prisoner. Sandalj, it was reported, planned to blind Peter; however, for some reason he did not carry out this act. Sandalj later told a Ragusan ambassador that this action had been necessary because the pair were traitors. What their treachery consisted in was not stated, though it seems probable it was their recent—and possibly still ongoing—association with ex-king Tvrtko II. Paul's son Radoslav, still at large, immediately went to war to avenge the murder and also to prevent the division of his lands between Sandalj and Ostoja, which seems to have been planned and had been the fate that met Radič Sanković's lands earlier. Radoslav's enemies grabbed what they could; his losses included the rich mining town of Olovo, which was taken by Sandalj's ally, the second-level nobleman Vukmir Zlatonosović. Radoslav procured a Turkish contingent and, joined by his brother Peter, who had either escaped or been released, regained his lost lands. Then he and the Turks proceeded to ravage Sandalj's lands.

Hrvoje played no part in this. He had not even attended the Sutjeska gathering. He died in 1416. His death ended the enormous influence of the Hrvatinići in Bosnian affairs. He was succeeded by a very weak son, but authority soon passed to a more dynamic nephew, George (Juraj) Vojsalić, who, though able, was still no Hrvoje. George, though he was to have much less influence in general Bosnian affairs, did obtain a dominant role in the Donji Kraji. His reduced influence was partly owing to the considerable loss of territory that immediately followed Hrvoje's death. Omiš and the Krajina were grabbed by Ivaniš Nelipčić, Hrvoje's brother-in-law. Furthermore, right after Hrvoje's death Ostoja divorced his own wife to marry Hrvoje's widow, who brought with her considerable territory, including Jajce which was to be the last Bosnian capital. Ostoja's divorced wife was also a relative of the murdered Paul Radenović—further reason for him to rid himself of her at this time. Sigismund acquired Hrvoje's Korčula, Brač, and Hvar. His possession of these islands was brief, as Venice took them in 1420.

Ostoja's increased strength from his acquisition of these extensive lands that had formerly belonged to Hrvoje alarmed the sultan, who did not like Ostoja and certainly did not want to see anyone in Bosnia becoming too powerful. He ordered a council meeting, which was attended by both Sandalj and Radoslav. The council was clearly designed against Ostoja, who did not attend and who was assigned the blame for Paul Radenović's murder. Since Paul's alliance with Tvrtko II had chiefly threatened Ostoja, this verdict may well have been true. Under Ottoman pressure Sandalj and Radoslav did conclude a truce, but it was not to last; the two had too many grievances against one another for it to work. Among Ostoja's many enemies at this meeting—if we can believe Orbini—was his son Stefan Ostojić, who was then angry at his father for divorcing his mother, Kujava, to marry Hrvoje's widow. Ostoja, severely threatened, fled to the lands of the Radivojevići, who through his various ups and downs had probably been his most consistent supporters.

In the months that followed, Ostoja somehow extricated himself from this major crisis. Probably playing upon the differences between the new, but still hostile, allies Sandalj and Radoslav, he somehow made peace with Paul Radenović's sons, the Pavlovići, and joined them in their new war, which resumed in 1417, against Sandalj, Ostoja's former ally who had helped him destroy their father. Their combined forces, ably supported by Turkish troops, pushed Sandalj back toward the sea and occupied much of his land. Ostoja acquired Blagaj, a major Kosača fortress, and also the key customs town of Drijeva on the lower Neretva. Once in possession of the latter he banned the sale of slaves there. Then suddenly in 1418 Ostoja died. His son Stefan Ostojić (1418–21) succeeded him. Sandalj and his allies the Zlatonosovići refused to recognize him. However, Sandalj's other major vassals, the Nikolići, probably hoping to assert their own independence again, did support Stefan Ostojić.

In 1419 Sandalj, needing cash for his war, sold to Dubrovnik his—the eastern—part of Konavli that he had seized back in 1392 when Sanković had tried to sell Konavli to Dubrovnik. Dubrovnik had protested Sandalj's and Radenović-Pavlović's possession of the two parts of Konavli ever since that time. (Radoslav still retained his—the western—half; he eventually was to sell it with Cavtat to Dubrovnik in late 1426 or 1427. As a result of the sales, the two noblemen and their heirs were to receive an annual tribute thereafter.) The new king confirmed Sandalj's sale. At this point he and Sandalj concluded a truce—and confirmation of the sale was probably a condition for it—but it was not to last. For Stefan Ostojić entered into negotiations for an alliance with Venice that was partially directed against the Balšići, with whom Sandalj then had good relations. So Sandalj broke his truce and in 1420 procured Turkish help to launch a counter-offensive against the lands of the Pavlovići and of the new king. Tvrtko II was with the Turks now, and they clearly had under consideration his restoration. Sandalj immediately occupied the Pavlović half of Konavli, which the Ragusans tried to persuade Sandalj to sell to them, while the Pavlovići protested violently. Sandalj did not oblige the town, as he felt it was then more important to work out a peace with the Pavlovići. For each was able to see that all this fighting would profit no one but the Turks, whose goals were booty and the weakening of Bosnia. Thus in late spring 1420 a peace conference was convened, attended by the Pavlovići, Sandalj, and Ishak beg, the commander of Sandalj's Turks. In the course of the discussions Ishak beg killed Peter Pavlović. As Sandalj later explained it, Ishak took this action because Peter had been faithless to the sultan. Needless to say the conference broke up. As a result of this murder and Sandalj's continued alliance with Ishak beg, Sandalj was able to regain most of the territory he had lost to Ostoja and the Pavlovići in the earlier phase of the war.

Realizing the strength of the force mobilized against him, in early 1420 Stefan Ostojić tried to make peace with Sandalj, but it was too late. In July 1420 Stefan was ousted from power, through the action of Sandalj. The ex-king fled to the coast; there he entered into various intrigues to regain his throne. These were ineffective and soon he found himself ignored by the Bosnians. He was dead before April 1422. His supporters, the Nikolići, also had to flee to Dubrovnik. The town mediated a peace between them and Sandalj, enabling them to return to their lands in Hum. Thereafter, as far as we know, they remained loyal vassals of the Kosače.

Tvrtko II, always ready, and now having Ottoman support, became king again. He established himself in Visoko, surrounded by the leading Bosnian nobles except for Radoslav Pavlović, whose name is conspicuously absent from the charters issued by Tvrtko that summer. Presumably Radoslav still supported Stefan Ostojić. In October 1420 Radoslav finally agreed to peace with Sandalj; in doing so he also agreed to accept Tvrtko II as king. Radoslav's hesitancy in recognizing Tvrtko provides confirmation for the view that Tvrtko was Sandalj's candidate. To seal their peace, in 1421 Radoslav married Sandalj's niece Theodora; she was the sister of Stefan Vukčić, who was to be Sandalj's successor. Their agreement did not lead to a permanent peace; the two were fighting again briefly in 1422 or 1423, after which a new peace was concluded.

Tvrtko, having received a formal coronation at a council meeting in August 1421, ruled through the early 1420s without serious challenge. The narrative that follows of Tvrtko's second reign relies heavily on the recent reconstruction of events by Živković.[1] Involved elsewhere, the Turks bothered Bosnia less until 1426, giving Bosnia about five years to enjoy greater independence and to improve its economic situation. Bosnia's mines reached the height of their activity in this period under Tvrtko. And the number of Ragusan merchants in Bosnia increased considerably in the 1420s. Moreover, in December 1422 Tvrtko concluded a trade treaty with Venice that increased Venetian commercial activity in Bosnia. Dubrovnik was unhappy, but Bosnia benefited from the competition, especially by acquiring cheaper salt. More Bosnian goods also found their way to Venice. This new association with Venice alarmed the Turks, who were struggling with Venice over the Albanian-Zetan region, and prompted an Ottoman raid against Bosnia in the early spring of 1424. It was not a major raid, and Tvrtko was able to repel it, but the message was clear to Tvrtko: do not associate too closely with Venice. And since Venice was in no position to help Tvrtko defend his lands against Turkish attack, Tvrtko had to take the message to heart. Thereafter his relations with Venice became less close and the two states gave up various plans—then being discussed—for joint Bosnian-Venetian action on the Dalmatian coast.

Dubrovnik was pleased with the cooling of these relations; however, it was not to enjoy improved relations with Tvrtko because in 1424, following its traditional policy, it granted asylum to a member of the ruling family named Vuk Banić who had fled from Bosnia after an unsuccessful plot to seize the throne. Events in 1425 made these relations worse. In that year, Tvrtko took advantage of a Turkish raid against Serbia to direct an attack on the rich, and formerly Bosnian, mining town of Srebrnica. The Serbian garrison received assistance in defending the town from the local Ragusan merchants; they held out until the Turkish raiders withdrew from Serbia, enabling Stefan Lazarević to bring his main forces to Srebrnica and drive the Bosnians away. The victorious Serbian troops then pursued the retreating Bosnians, plundering Bosnian territory.

Needing an ally in the event of further Ottoman attacks and seeing that Venice was useless in this respect, Tvrtko decided to patch up his relations with the Hungarians; their renewed relations were sealed by a treaty in 1425 or 1426. Construing this treaty as an act of defiance against them, the Ottomans launched damaging raids against Bosnia, causing particular harm to Usora, including the lands of the Zlatonosovići there. This action caused Tvrtko to submit to the Ottomans; he accepted their suzerainty and agreed to pay an annual tribute. After his submission the Ottoman forces withdrew. Ragusan records indicate they had departed from Bosnia by August 1426.

Tvrtko was back to square one. He still had no protector against the Turks, and his submission to them was no guarantee against future raids. The only serious choice he had was Hungary. The Hungarians, seeing his desperate plight, upped their terms. They insisted that Tvrtko, who had no children, should make Herman II, Count of Celje, his heir. Herman could be considered a member of the Bosnian royal family because his father, Herman I, had married Catherine, the daughter of Stjepan Kotromanić, in 1361. Hearing of this demand, the Bosnian nobles became most unhappy. They had no desire to see Hungary acquire a stronger role in Bosnia, which it certainly would get should this Hungarian count become their king. The nobles wanted to control the Bosnian succession and, in fact, saw the election of Bosnia's kings as their right. They also feared that the creation of such close links with Hungary would provoke a major Turkish attack. And finally, they feared that if this plan were realized, Tvrtko could use Herman and the Hungarians as props to assert himself and reduce the power and privileges of the nobility. The nobles began discussions among themselves about ways to oppose this scheme. The leading opponents of Herman's succession were Sandalj and his allies the Zlatonosovići. Soon Radoslav Pavlović, who also opposed the plan, made peace with Sandalj.

Learning of their concern, the exiled plotter Vuk Banić, who as a member of the royal family was also eligible for the Bosnian throne, contacted the dissident nobles from his Dubrovnik exile. Realizing that opposition was building up against himself, Tvrtko felt it necessary to tighten his Hungarian ties to gain assurance of Hungarian support in the event of a revolt. He agreed in the fall of 1427 to the succession of Herman and then in 1428 married Dorothy, the daughter of the prominent Hungarian nobleman John Garai (Gorjanski). Sandalj, Radoslav, and Paul Zlatonosović showed their opposition by not attending Tvrtko's wedding with Dorothy. As a result Tvrtko found himself in effect under two suzerainties; he again had accepted Hungarian overlordship, while still paying tribute to the Ottomans.

Tvrtko was able, somehow, to come to an accommodation with Sandalj, though on what terms is not known; for shortly after his wedding Tvrtko visited Sandalj at Sandalj's Blagaj court. We may conclude that Paul Zlatonosović remained obdurate, for in 1430 Tvrtko marched against him. Tvrtko won a resounding victory after which the Zlatonosović family disappears from the sources. Presumably Tvrtko annexed their lands. Interestingly enough, Paul's overlord and long-time ally Sandalj did not come to his defense and in fact took no action against Tvrtko for this attack other than to complain that Tvrtko had acted without consulting the council.

Meanwhile, in late 1429 a quarrel broke out between Radoslav Pavlović and Dubrovnik. He believed the town owed him money, and it refused to pay. So, Radoslav collected his debt by seizing the goods of a Ragusan merchant caravan. As the quarrel heated up, he declared he had changed his mind over the sale of Konavli and wanted it back. Then in 1430 he attacked Konavli, which, as a result of his and Sandalj's sales, was now entirely the property of Dubrovnik. Dubrovnik, not prepared for war, sent envoys to Tvrtko, Sigismund, the sultan, and Sandalj. Though sympathy was expressed for the town, no one took any action, except for Sandalj, who took advantage of the situation to grab some land from Radoslav. However, he sent no aid to help Dubrovnik defend itself. All he did was to propose a league to be composed of himself, Tvrtko, and Dubrovnik to oppose Radoslav. However, after Bosnian

Church clerics visited both noblemen's courts, talk of such a league ceased. The Church may well have been instrumental in quenching the growing quarrel between Radoslav and Sandalj, two of its adherents.

Threatened by Tvrtko's opposition to his policies, Radoslav in late 1430 came up with a plan to depose Tvrtko and replace him with Radivoj, a son of Ostoja. With the proposal for the league dropped, Radoslav was soon in contact with Sandalj to discuss this plan. Envoys from George Branković, the new ruler of Serbia, also visited Sandalj's court to discuss it. Alarmed by these discussions, Tvrtko, probably in the summer of 1431, made peace with Radoslav, who soon, in late 1432 or early 1433, ended his war with Dubrovnik. However, Sandalj remained interested in Radivoj's candidacy, be it for the possibilities of utilizing him as a puppet or be it from anger at Tvrtko's relations with Hungary and/or at his destruction of the Zlatonosovići. Until late 1430 Radivoj had been living at the Ottoman court. Now in 1431 the Ottomans, at the moment angry at Tvrtko for turning down an Ottoman offer to mediate Radoslav's quarrel with Dubrovnik but surely even more so for his agreements with Hungary, decided to let Radivoj press his candidacy. Given some military support, Radivoj entered Bosnia where Sandalj welcomed him, promising him his support as well. He settled down at Sandalj's court, calling himself king and sending envoys to Dubrovnik to collect the tribute the town owed Bosnia. Needless to say, the town refused to pay it.

Tvrtko was disturbed, particularly by the Serbian envoys at Sandalj's court. Tvrtko and George Branković had bad relations over Srebrnica, and Tvrtko seems to have feared that George might provide military support for Radivoj. His fears were serious enough for him in October 1431 to ban the transit of Ragusan merchants across Bosnia to Srebrnica. The prohibition was soon lifted, but in the summer of 1432 Tvrtko is found at war against George on Bosnian territory near the Drina. At the time George received support from Sandalj, who, as noted, had maintained cordial relations with the Serbian court over the previous twenty years and was married to Stefan Lazarević's sister. Since Radoslav had by then made peace with Tvrtko, he was drawn into the fighting; his men were soon clashing with Sandalj's along their common border. Tvrtko, if we exclude Radoslav, found himself increasingly isolated. His Hungarian allies would provide him no aid because they sought to maintain good relations with George Branković, also a vassal of theirs. Furthermore, the Turks, supporting Radivoj, were opposed to Tvrtko and at that moment also favorable toward George. In fact, they launched a raid against Bosnia early in 1432; however, it seems to have been aimed for plunder rather than to realize any particular political objective, for the raiders soon withdrew.

The forces against Tvrtko did well. After a lull in the fighting over the winter 1432–33, George Branković was back in action on the Bosnian side of the Drina in the spring of 1433. In the course of this campaign he occupied the former territory of the Zlatonosovići from Zvornik to the Spreča. The Turks also launched a raid for plunder into Bosnia in August 1433. Since Tvrtko was clearly doing badly, his ally Radoslav saw no advantage in sticking to his cause, particularly if the campaign was to result in Tvrtko's being ousted by Radivoj. So, he made peace with Sandalj in April 1433 and with George Branković late that summer. This left Tvrtko completely isolated, except for the limited support provided to him by Hrvoje's nephew and successor George Vojsalić and, it seems, by the Radivojevići. Tvrtko retreated to Visoko. However, the fates were then good to him. Sandalj took sick in September 1433 and dropped out of the action, and George Branković, having annexed the Zlatonosović lands, decided he was satisfied and withdrew from the warfare. Presumably he feared, if indeed he had not been explicitly informed, that Sigismund disapproved of any further action against his vassal Tvrtko.

However, Bosnia itself was now divided. Tvrtko held much of central Bosnia, and the lands to his north and northwest were loyal to him. However, Radivoj resided at Sandalj's court and was recognized by Sandalj and Radoslav; as a result eastern Bosnia and Hum were lost to Tvrtko. Moreover, as a result of the fighting Sandalj was in possession of part of Tvrtko's own personal lands, including the important town of Kreševo. And most important, the Turks still were declared for Radivoj. And they, under Ishak beg, seem to have been present inside Bosnia, for a Ragusan report of September 1433 says that Tvrtko was shut up inside the fortress of Visoko, awaiting Hungarian help. Many scholars claim that Tvrtko, faced with this massive opposition, actually fled to Hungary in late 1433 only to return in 1435. However, Živković has found documentation that Tvrtko was still inside Bosnia in late 1433 and through 1434. The Ottomans continued their campaigning in Bosnia on behalf of Radivoj through late 1433 and early 1434, even taking, we are told, the fortress in which the Bosnian crown was then kept. If the crown was still housed in its traditional location, it can be concluded Bobovac was sacked.

Though worried about provoking the Turks against themselves, the Hungarians finally realized that they had to come to the rescue of their beleaguered vassal. In the middle of 1434 Hungarian troops finally entered Bosnia in support of Tvrtko and recovered, or at least occupied, for him: Jajce, Vranduk, Bočac, Hodidjed (the fortress for Vrhbosna), and Komotin. Clearly, Živković shows, Tvrtko had remained in Bosnia, awaiting this aid and then participating alongside the Hungarians in their campaign. In the course of 1434 Sandalj tried to extend his territory into western Hum across the Neretva at the expense of Tvrtko's ally George Vojsalić; but George repelled him. However, excluding Vojsalić's success, 1434 was not a good year for Tvrtko. For his cause depended on the presence of Hungarian troops; and when at the end of the campaigning season of 1434 they withdrew, Tvrtko seems to have felt unable to retain what they had gained. So, it seems, he went to Hungary with the withdrawing forces. In any case, at the beginning of 1435 he is found at the Hungarian court.

However, as Živković notices, even though Tvrtko seems to have departed, Radivoj remained based at Sandalj's court. He did not try to establish his residence in the royal lands at the center of the kingdom. Thus one may conclude that a significant part of that region's population was opposed to him and loyal to Tvrtko. But despite the likelihood of such local support, Tvrtko had still felt it necessary to withdraw; presumably he had felt incapable of resisting an attack from the outside, particularly one from the Turks in support of Radivoj. This central region presumably was left under deputies appointed by Tvrtko. Possibly some of them were expelled by Sandalj's forces, which may have occupied some of central Bosnia. Meanwhile in Hungary Tvrtko met with Geroge Branković and through Sigismund's mediation they concluded a peace. This peace seems to have allowed George to retain the territory he had taken in Usora. Possession of Usora would have provided greater security for George's Srebrnica.

Meanwhile Sandalj died in March 1435. The early historian Junius Resti (1669–1735), who on the basis of local records compiled an excellent chronicle on medieval Dubrovnik, provides the following apt but brief obituary for Sandalj:

> He was a prince with lively spirit, with great intelligence and with much delicacy [!], who was always able to penetrate the heart of the matter with great facility, whose memory would have been immortal, if his life had not been stained and his fame obscured with the error of schism and the Patarin [Bosnian Church] rite in which he was born and in which he died.[2]

Sandalj was succeeded by his nephew Stefan Vukčić, who inherited a vast direct holding from the lower Neretva to the upper reaches of that river at Konjic, and from Onogošt (Nikšić) in "Montenegro" and the upper Drina and Lim rivers to the "Montenegrin" coast. Stefan continued the policy of supporting Radivoj, who remained in residence at his court.

Meanwhile, having again accepted Hungarian suzerainty and sworn fealty to Sigismund, Tvrtko returned to Bosnia in April 1435, accompanied by Hungarian troops. With Sandalj dead and the Turks occupied with suppressing a rebellion at the time in Albania, Tvrtko found himself in a position to reverse his fortunes. Supported by Hungarian troops and George Vojsalić, Tvrtko's troops moved along the Neretva. They immediately obtained the support of the Radivojevići, a major family of that region, who had been forced against their will to join Sandalj in the earlier warfare. The Radivojevići, it seems, recognized Sigismund's suzerainty, hoping to become independent of any figure inside Bosnia. Sigismund surely encouraged them in this, if, indeed, he did not pressure them into it, for it seems he hoped that this campaign, which he ordered to concentrate on Hum, would result in Hungary's acquisition of Hum.

Since the Ottomans were temporarily out of the picture and since Tvrtko had support from the Hungarians, Radoslav saw a chance to regain some of his lost lands from the Kosače, if not to grab some of their lands as well. So he dropped his alliance with the Kosače, divorced his wife (who was Stefan Vukčić's sister), allied himself with Tvrtko, and attacked Stefan Vukčić's lands. Radoslav and Stefan were actively fighting by April 1435. Tvrtko, evidently in the meantime, quickly regained whatever lands he had lost in central Bosnia over the winter. His losses may have been few, for, as Živković argues persuasively, throughout all the warfare these lands had been loyal to him. And with the lords to his west, north, and now—with the Pavlovići—to his east supporting him, Tvrtko found himself by mid-1435 master of all Bosnia, except for the large territory under Stefan Vukčić.

Faced with this large coalition against him, Stefan sought aid from the Turks, who by late summer 1435 were able to, and did, send him troops. Until their arrival, Stefan had found it difficult to hold his fortresses and had suffered various losses. Fifteen hundred Turks arrived to help Stefan in July; they plundered the lands of Stefan's opponents and of those who had defected from his cause in Hum. More Turks followed, sufficient to defeat a Hungarian unit in Hum in August and force the Hungarians out of all the parts of Hum they had occupied. By the year's end, Tvrtko did not hold a single fort in Hum. With the Turks again active in Bosnia, Tvrtko again that winter (1435–36) left Bosnia to reside at the Hungarian court. There, as we shall see, he had to defend himself against charges made by the Franciscan vicar Jacob de Marchia that he was a heretic. He succeeded in defending himself before the Hungarian Diet but had to agree to support the Franciscans in their work, which included support of various reforms Jacob sought to impose and Tvrtko opposed.

In March 1436 the Turks and Stefan Vukčić carried their raids up to Croatia. Meanwhile, it had become clear to Tvrtko that Hungarian help would not be sufficient to regain his throne. He would have to change sides and accept Ottoman suzerainty once more. To realize this would not be easy, for it required persuading the Turks to drop Radivoj's cause and accept him. Furthermore, he would have to carry on the negotiations with the Turks secretly while still a guest at the Hungarian court, which would not have favored any contact between him and the Turks.

The Hungarians could provide him with no aid that year because their troops were needed to defend the Banat from a major Ottoman raid. Tvrtko, still opposed by the Turks and Stefan Vukčić, thus could not return to Bosnia. Nevertheless, still residing at the Hungarian court, Tvrtko somehow managed to secretly dispatch envoys to effect his changing sides. These envoys were successful, and in mid-1436 Tvrtko was able, with the agreement of the Ottomans, to return to Bosnia as king. He again became a tribute-paying Ottoman vassal. He also made peace with Stefan Vukčić in June 1436 and became his ally against Hungary. In return, Stefan gave up his support of Radivoj's candidacy for the throne. Presumably all these alliances had been agreed upon before Tvrtko actually made his return. Thus once again the Ottomans—and a pro-Ottoman orientation in Bosnia—had triumphed, and the policy of dependence upon Hungary was dropped. Tvrtko's peace with Stefan Vukčić did not result in lasting peace between Stefan and Radoslav, however. There were too many disputes and grievances between them. Though they did make peace early in 1436, they were again at war in the second half of the year. When their war resumed, Tvrtko threw his support behind his new ally Stefan Vukčić. As long as that alliance held, Tvrtko had no reason to worry about the anti-king, Radivoj. And since Tvrtko had again become a tribute-paying vassal of the Ottomans, they ceased their raids against his lands for the remainder of 1436 and 1437. Though this new orientation could have led to trouble with Hungary, it did not; for the Hungarians were occupied in 1436 and 1437 with other problems. In fact to deal with these concerns, Sigismund wanted to be at peace with his Bosnian neighbors and even made peace with Stefan Vukčić, recognizing Kosača rule of Hum. Then Sigismund died in late 1437. Both Tvrtko and Stefan Vukčić recognized the suzerainty of his successor, King Albert. But their recognition was only words; both were active tribute-paying vassals of the Turks.

Sigismund was followed by a weak successor, Albert, who then died in 1439, setting off a civil war in Hungary. Despite the many difficulties Sigismund had caused the Balkan peoples during his reign, his death was to hurt the Balkan states of Serbia and Bosnia. For now Hungary was less able to intervene in Balkan affairs. At earlier periods this would have been seen as a blessing, but the Turkish threat altered everything. Sigismund had seen himself to some extent as a protector of the Balkans, if for no other reason than that he wanted to have a buffer between himself and the Turks. Moreover, seeing himself as the suzerain of Bosnia and Serbia, at times he did come to their assistance. Now these states were to be deprived for a time of significant aid from Hungary. This meant an increased Ottoman presence; moreover, since the Ottomans knew they would not be faced with serious Hungarian opposition, they could carry out further direct annexations of territory. That in fact was to be the fate of Serbia, the bulk of which, as we shall see, was to be conquered by the Turks in 1439.

It thus came as no surprise that the Turks were back raiding in Bosnia again in 1438. These raids were stepped up at the very end of the 1430s and in the early 1440s. During this period the Ottomans were again frequently supporting the claims of Radivoj. However, though they declared support for him, their attacks consisted of raids for plunder; they directed no campaign against Tvrtko himself with the aim of actually effecting his deposition. Thus in the years after 1436 Radivoj was primarily a threat held over Tvrtko's head and a way for the Turks to extract increased tribute from Tvrtko, rather than an actual danger. Neither the Turks nor Stefan Vukčić, who again came to declare support for Radivoj in December 1439, were ever to go to war against Tvrtko with the purpose of expelling him in favor of Radivoj. The Ottomans' increased raiding in Bosnia came about, in part, naturally, for after their conquest of Serbia in 1439 their territory came to border on Bosnia. But though the number of Ottoman raids increased, the Turks took no Bosnian towns in the 1430s, other than various towns along the Drina itself, some of which had actually been in Serbian possession at the moment of their conquest. This point is worth stressing since scholars have frequently claimed that various Bosnian towns, including Vrhbosna (Sarajevo), were taken in 1436. Recent scholarship, however, has shown that these eastern Bosnian towns fell between 1448 and 1451.[3]

Stefan Vukčić, still at war with Radoslav, took advantage of the 1438 Ottoman raids that plundered Radoslav's lands to take Jeleč (on the Čeotina near where it enters the Drina) and Trebinje from him—towns Radoslav had seized on the death of Sandalj. Having made peace with the Turks and seen their withdrawal, Radoslav resumed his war with Stefan. Tvrtko, having made peace with Radoslav in April 1438, remained on the sidelines this time. In early 1439 the Turks again raided Tvrtko's lands in central Bosnia. Finally in May or June 1439 Radoslav and Stefan Vukčić concluded peace, and Radoslav agreed to take his wife back. The Ottomans were active in Bosnia for much of that year, plundering; by the end of the year, in December, presumably as a result of Ottoman pressure, Stefan Vukčić again was recognizing Radivoj, the Ottomans' declared candidate. However, since they could clearly have installed him, had they wanted to, we may conclude they were not committed to his cause but were actually just using him to divide and weaken Bosnia for their own benefit later. By recognizing Radivoj, Stefan effected a general improvement in his relations with the Turks. But, not surprisingly, his recognition of Radivoj annoyed Tvrtko. So, when fighting again erupted between Stefan Vukčić and Radoslav in 1440, Tvrtko sent aid to Radoslav. By this time the Ottomans, having conquered Serbia, had become a major factor in Bosnian events. They had a much greater role in mediating Bosnian quarrels than King Tvrtko. Not only were the nobles increasingly taking their grievances to the Turks, but even Dubrovnik had come to seek Ottoman guarantees for trade matters inside Bosnia.

In November 1441 Radoslav Pavlović died and was succeeded by his son Ivaniš Pavlović. Ivaniš was not the equal of his father, and thus Radoslav's death had the effect of greatly increasing the relative strength of Stefan Vukčić, who also at the time had of all the Bosnian leaders the best relations with the Turks. Radoslav's demise meant that Tvrtko no longer had a strong possible ally inside Bosnia against Stefan's pretensions. Ivaniš had a brief quarrel with Stefan Vukčić, but Stefan soon agreed to peace, for he was then far more interested in expanding into Zeta toward the coast. For after the fall of Serbia, the interior of Zeta, in the hands of various often feuding nobles and tribesmen, seemed up for grabs. So Stefan advanced into Zeta, reaching Lake Skadar and then the coast. There he clashed with Venice, taking Bar and threatening Budva. In 1443 Tvrtko tried to take advantage of Stefan's absence in Zeta and of the Ottoman concern with the Christian crusade of that year to attack Stefan's lands. This forced Stefan to withdraw from Zeta to defend his own territory. Consequently Tvrtko was unable to achieve anything by this attack. Dubrovnik soon mediated peace between the two. The only beneficiary from this warfare was Venice, which after Stefan's withdrawal regained what Stefan had taken from it.

The decentralized nature of Bosnia, which was basically a federation of autonomous units, is well illustrated by a Ragusan report from 1441 that discusses the activities of a Bosnian Church cleric (Gost Gojisav) who administered a border post–customs station for Stefan Vukčić on his border with the Pavlovići. This report shows that Ragusan merchants—and presumably anyone else as well—had to present to this official a safe-conduct or passport to cross the border from the territory of one Bosnian noble to that of the other. Without proper documentation, their goods were confiscated.

Many scholars, Ćirković notes, have accused the Bosnian nobles of selfishness and of having no feeling for general Bosnian interests. Ćirković would modify this charge. Their council and the fact that the great nobles remained members of it, and thus remained Bosnians, rather than entirely seceding, shows that they had some idea of a general Bosnian interest. One might argue against this that if they had seceded entirely and thus lost their other Bosnian allies, whom they retained through joint membership in the council, they would have been quickly swallowed up by more powerful neighbors like Hungary, Serbia, or the Ottomans; thus it was still a particular, rather than general, interest that bound them to Bosnia and its council. But Ćirković insists the issue was not separatism, but the constitution of the state. The nobles, he argues, wanted Bosnia to be a loose federation; and this they had succeeded in creating at Tvrtko I's death in 1391. Thus they had a feeling for Bosnia, but it was a Bosnia along these particular lines. And in fighting for their rights, they opposed any move to centralize the state or concentrate more power in the king's hands. This did, of course, have the effect of producing a weaker state to oppose the Ottomans, and it also provided the Ottomans with chances to intervene in Bosnian quarrels to advance Ottoman interests. And, moreover, all the resulting warfare did cause further losses of manpower and economic resources and thus contributed to weakening Bosnia even more. But all this, Ćirković argues, was a result of the existing constitution of the state, which the nobles fought to preserve. Given their desire for independence, the concept they held of Bosnia and their maintenance of this loose federation still gave Bosnia more power to resist than the region would have produced had a Bosnian idea not held them and had they separated entirely as, for example, the Dejanovići did from Serbia.

Though there is truth in this view, the warfare between the nobles was not always or even usually over constitutional interests. Wars were frequently fought between two nobles trying to wrest territory from one another, as in the endless Pavlović-Kosača wars. Fighting over such issues with the Ottomans at the gates, if not actually participating in the fighting, can only be described as selfish and detrimental to the general interest. Such warfare cannot by any stretch of the imagination be said to have been fought over any constitutional principle. And the nobles' acceptance at various times of Ottoman support and vassalage to advance their own interests against king or neighboring noble certainly cannot be seen as advancing any sort of Bosnian interest.

Tvrtko died in November 1443. He, however, was not succeeded by Radivoj. Nor was there any question of Herman II of Celje succeeding, for not only were matters in Hungary too unstable for any sort of Hungarian intervention, but Herman had pre-deceased Tvrtko. Tvrtko's successor was a second son of Ostoja, Radivoj's brother Stefan Tomaš (1443–61) who already was holding power in Bosnia in December 1443. Tvrtko, detesting Radivoj, had probably designated Stefan Tomaš as his successor. At least that is what Stefan Tomaš subsequently claimed in a charter. The succession went relatively smoothly inside Bosnia. Thus Tvrtko had probably prepared the way for him before his death. Radivoj, still a claimant, found support only from Stefan Vukčić. Thus Stefan Tomaš began his reign without Stefan Vukčić's recognition.

Religion and Culture inside Bosnia

In earlier chapters we have encountered the Bosnian Church, an institution that grew out of a Catholic monastic order which broke, probably in the middle of the thirteenth century, with international Catholicism. Its existence as a specific institution, however, can be documented only from the early fourteenth century. Documentation from that century and especially from the fifteenth, when we have more sources, shows the Bosnian Church, under its own bishop called a djed (literally, grandfather), to be a monastic institution. No sources suggest that any change of theology occurred at the time it broke with Rome and almost all later local and Ragusan sources on the Bosnian Church suggest it was mainstream Christian in its theology throughout its existence. Thus the Bosnian Church most probably retained the beliefs and practices it had held up to its schism with Rome. But though it retained its "Catholic" theology, its peasant composition and the absence of any educated elite surely led to various errors in practice.[4]

Throughout its history, the Bosnian Church retained both its more-or-less Catholic theology—though it used the Slavic language—and its monastic character. Its clergy (except for a few resident at royal or aristocratic courts) resided in monasteries called hiže (sing. hiža, meaning house). The clergymen bore the title of Christians (krstjani)—usually rendered as Patarini in Ragusan Latin language sources. The head of a monastery (hiža) was often called a gost. The djed and his council of twelve strojnici, chiefly composed of gosts, provided what overall supervision there was. Their monasteries were not found throughout Bosnia but were clustered in the center of the state, extending east to the Drina and south toward and beyond the Neretva, with a few on the lands of the Kosača family in what is now Hercegovina. Some of their monasteries served as hostels for travelers and were used by Ragusan merchants. The Bosnian Church never established a secular clergy or any sort of territorial organization. Thus calling it a "Church"—even though they themselves did—may be somewhat misleading. The institution seems to have consisted only of a series of scattered monastic houses, usually in villages, each having a relatively small number of monks. Probably peasants could go to these monasteries for services. Gravestone inscriptions at least show that krstjani participated in the burials of laymen.

The Bosnian Church was tolerated by the state even after the 1340s when a Franciscan mission was established inside Bosnia and the rulers became Catholic. The tolerance, or indifference, of Bosnian rulers and nobility regarding religious issues is a prominent feature of medieval Bosnia. The Bosnian Church did not play a major role in the state and was not a state Church, though various scholars have said so. For most of its existence—other than occasionally allowing its hierarchs to witness charters—it had no political role in the state. In fact a political role can be shown chiefly in the early fifteenth century—particularly between 1403 and 1405—when the djed was an influential advisor at court. His influence then was probably owing to the particular sympathy for his Church on the part of King Ostoja, who most probably was an adherent of the Bosnian Church and the only post-1340 ruler who was not a Catholic. This djed's influence may also have been owing to his particular qualities as an individual. Since Bosnia's rulers from the 1340s—except Ostoja—were all Catholics, it is not surprising that the Bosnian Church was not a major state institution.

Though some scholars have argued that an alliance existed between the Bosnian Church and the nobility, this statement too is greatly exaggerated. Connections between the Bosnian Church and specific noblemen can be shown for fewer than ten families, and all these documented ties fall into the last seventy years of the state. The Church's supporters, however, did include the major nobles; Hrvoje Vukčić, the Radenović-Pavlovići, Sandalj Hranić and Stefan Vukčić, and Paul Klešić were among its adherents. However, we find in the sources that for most of these nobles the services performed for them by the krstjani were entirely religious. For only a very small number is the Bosnian Church found providing political or secular services; in those cases the krstjani usually served as diplomats or mediators in quarrels. And for only two families—the Kosače and Radenović-Pavlovići—did these ties last longer than one generation. Documents from the 1430s show that by then most of the nobility, including Paul Klešić's and Hrvoje's successors, were Catholics. Moreover, no document shows any Church figure supporting the nobility against the state or working to advance decentralized interests. And the close ties between the Church and King Ostoja, who as king was the main representative of centralization, cast strong doubts on the theory that the Church favored or supported the nobility against the king or against centralization by the state. The evidence strongly supports the view, which I have argued at length elsewhere, that the Church's political or secular role was minimal.

Few Bosnian Church texts survive. Of these, most important are the surviving pages of Gospel manuscripts. Some are beautifully illustrated: the Radosav Ritual, the Hval Gospel, Tepčija Batalo's Gospel. These Gospels are completely Orthodox in character, and one Gospel even has the words "beginning" and "end" in the margins through the text in the very spots that readings begin and end in the Orthodox service. Certain other surviving Bosnian Gospels may also have been from Bosnian Church circles, but proof is lacking. The last will and testament from 1466 of Gost Radin—a Bosnian Church leader and important diplomat, first for the Pavlovići and later for Stefan Vukčić—survives; it testifies not only to Radin's great wealth but also to the orthodoxy of his religious beliefs. A letter written by the djed in 1404, concerning the dispute between the king and the nobleman Paul Klešić, also provides some information on the Church.

Many scholars have depicted the Bosnian Church as dualist (Bogomil). Domestic sources about the Church (Bosnian and Ragusan) do not suggest this. They show that the Bosnian Church, unlike the Bogomils, accepted an omnipotent God, the Trinity, church buildings, the cross, the cult of saints, religious art, and at least part of the Old Testament. Radin's will, for example, begins with a cross, refers to his patron saint, and leaves money to build a church at his grave. He also left money to the Catholic Church in Dubrovnik and sought its prayers for his soul. The Bosnian Church Gospels are not iconoclastic, but are beautifully illustrated and even depict favorably John the Baptist, rejected by dualists. Furthermore, the cordial relations, shown in the sources, between Bosnian Churchmen and both Catholic officials (from Dubrovnik and zealously Catholic Hungary) and Orthodox clerics could not have occurred had these Bosnians been neo-Manichees: Sandalj was invited to Catholic Church services in Dubrovnik; Patarin diplomats to Dubrovnik were well received by the town and showered with gifts; King Matthew (Matthias) Corvinus of Hungary gave Gost Radin a luxurious robe (mentioned in his will); Alphonso of Naples made Stefan Vukčić a member of the Virgin's Order; and Hrvoje was enrolled by Sigismund in his Dragon's Order, one of whose aims was to defend the Catholic Church from heretics. Hrvoje also stood God-father to a daughter of Sigismund. The Bosnians, just mentioned, were all members of the Bosnian Church.

The only contemporary sources describing dualists in Bosnia are foreign (chiefly Italian). They come from the inquisition or the papacy. The papal sources date almost entirely after the late 1440s. Most of these sources simply call the Bosnian dualists they describe "Bosnian heretics." Moreover, most of these sources do not state or even imply that these dualist "Bosnian heretics" were members of the body known as the Bosnian Church. To the degree that they are accurate, these sources probably refer to a separate and small dualist current also existing in Bosnia that was derived from a Dalmatian dualist Church (Ecclesia Sclavonia), some of whose members fled to Bosnia at the time of Ban Kulin. This heresy, attracting few followers but seemingly surviving in Bosnia until the end of the Middle Ages, throughout remained a separate institution, distinct from the Bosnian Church.

One of Bosnia's main differences from other Balkan lands lay in the fact that no Church had a central role in the life of the state or of the nobles. Noblemen were distributed among all three faiths: Bosnian, Catholic, Orthodox. Excluding Albania, which in medieval times never became a unified state, Bosnia was the only country in the Balkans where membership in the community was not dependent on a common religion. And formal religion does not seem to have been important to the Bosnian nobles. They freely changed faiths and freely associated and allied with figures of different faiths. Religious institutions simply were not a central part of Bosnian life. And thus tolerance, or rather indifference, marked Bosnian religious issues until the very end of the state, when papal pressure finally forced, as we shall see, King Stefan Tomaš to turn to persecutions.

The Catholic Church in Bosnia was represented solely by a limited number of Franciscans, who were also limited, at least from the time of Jacob de Marchia's reforms in the 1430s, to a small number of monasteries. And though Catholicism became important to the last two kings and to a few nobles, the Catholic Church, too, never became a major institution in the state. The Catholics also had no territorial organization in Bosnia. The Catholic bishop, the titular Bishop of Bosnia, resided outside the state in Djakovo in Slavonia and played no role in Bosnia, possessing only theoretical authority there. And like the Bosnian clerics, the Franciscans were based in monasteries, though theirs tended to be in, or on the outskirts of, towns. Catholic clerics also played a very limited role in the Bosnian state, witnessing charters and serving as diplomats, but little more.

The Orthodox Church, existing in Hum and the region west of the Drina, possibly as far west as Vrhbosna, was not a major institution in Bosnia either. The Orthodox did have a major bishop, a metropolitan, at Mileševo, a famous Orthodox monastic center which presumably had considerable influence upon the population of the Lim region. Moreover, Mileševo, housing Saint Sava's relics, which were believed to work miracles, was a major shrine that attracted Christians of all faiths, and even Jews, for its cures. Excluding the Kosače, the overwhelming majority of noblemen in Hum were Orthodox. And those who lived toward the east, particularly the nobility in the regions annexed late by Tvrtko, in the 1370s, did considerable church building, as did Sandalj and Stefan Vukčić; these two Kosače at one time or another had Orthodox wives who took an interest in their Church. Orthodox clerics tended to be found alongside Bosnian ones at the Kosača court. However, the influence of the Orthodox was limited to these regions. Orthodox clerics were not found at the royal court or in most of Bosnia. And the number of Orthodox clerics in Hum and the Drina region, as a whole, does not seem to have been large.

The existence of three faiths in Bosnia prevented the development of a national Church and blocked any Church institution from acquiring a major role in the state. And since none of the Churches became strong it also meant that few Bosnians became firm Christians. Both the Bosnian and Catholic

Churches had few clergymen in Bosnia—there were clearly fewer than a hundred Franciscans in all of Bosnia—and since they were monastery based, it meant that the few they did have were clustered. The Orthodox do not seem to have had a large number of clergy present either, though that Church did have priests in addition to monks. Since the number of clerics and churches was small, we may assume that many Bosnians rarely saw a priest of any faith and thus had little understanding of Christian doctrine or practice and little or no sense of being members of a Christian community. Given the weak religious institutions and the conditions that resulted from them, it is not strange that many Bosnians were to convert to Islam after the Ottoman conquest. In fact, the only two Balkan regions where large-scale conversions to Islam occurred were Bosnia and Albania; and Albania, with its many mountains and poor communications, also had few priests and a very weak Church organization in the interior.

In the 1430s the Franciscans became more active in Bosnia, building several new monasteries. In this work they received considerable impetus from Jacob de Marchia (later a saint) who was special visitor to the Bosnian vicariat in 1432–33 and then its vicar from 1435 to 1439. Jacob tried to establish discipline among the local Franciscans and also struggled against heresy. Much of his anti-heretical work was carried out in Srem and regions north of Bosnia against the Hussites. He also fought with Tvrtko II over disciplining the Franciscans in the Bosnian kingdom. Jacob often found them living not in monasteries, but in private homes, and earning incomes rather than living on alms. Horrified, Jacob expelled the guilty Franciscans from Jajce. Tvrtko ordered them to return. Though his actions encouraged the local Franciscans to violate their rule, still, considering Bosnian conditions, Tvrtko's actions made sense. If the Franciscans had to live in monasteries, then they could not work in Jajce and various other places where monasteries did not yet exist. Thus to insist that the Franciscans live in the handful of monasteries then existing in Bosnia meant that they would have much less success in teaching the "heathen." And since the Franciscans had very little support from Bosnians who, whether they were Catholic or belonged to other faiths, were indifferent to formal religion and thus would not be generous in their alms to the friars, one wonders how Jacob expected them to live. Tvrtko's letters show him to be a faithful Catholic, interested in the Franciscans' work and anxious that the work be carried out effectively under the conditions then existing in Bosnia.

However, in 1433, after Tvrtko recalled the errant Franciscans to Jajce, Jacob stormed out of Bosnia and went to Hungary, where he made all sorts of accusations against Tvrtko, including the charge that he was a heretic. And in the general Franciscan sources, supporting Jacob, Tvrtko is depicted as an evil man; he is said to have sent a magician against Jacob who by incantations was to kill him or cause him to go mad. However, Jacob confounded the magician by striking him dumb for life. Then Tvrtko's queen, who is depicted as being every bit as evil as Tvrtko if not more so, ordered robbers to ambush

Jacob. But the saint made them completely rigid, until he thought it safe to restore their mobility. They then begged their forgiveness from him. The evil queen, it should be noted, was also a loyal Catholic, namely, Dorothy Garai, of Hungarian origin, whom Tvrtko was allowed to marry only after he had convinced the pope of his own Catholicism. This depiction of the royal pair was entirely owing to their resistance to Jacob's reform efforts, in which they defended the local Franciscans. In the years after Jacob's return to Bosnia as vicar in 1435, he had complete freedom of action. For Tvrtko, as we have seen, as a supplicant for Hungarian help, had had to agree in the winter of 1435–36 to support the Franciscans, which entailed supporting Jacob's reforms.

In these years from the mid-1430s to the fall of the Bosnian state, Catholicism made great gains. Considerable Catholic church building took place and many nobles accepted Catholicism. We find, for example, Vladislav Klešić and George Vojsalić—the successors of Paul Klešić and Hrvoje, who had both been members of the Bosnian Church—becoming Catholics. The towns in which the Franciscans were active, a high percentage of whose populations were Catholic merchants from the coast, appear as essentially Catholic. Despite Catholic gains, however, the Bosnian Church—whose monasteries were chiefly rural—continued to be tolerated. The Orthodox Church maintained its dominance in Hum (though Sandalj and Stefan Vukčić supported the Bosnian Church) and had some following in Bosnia near the Drina.

The Franciscans were also active in bringing about the conversions of Orthodox believers in the region of Konavli, which Dubrovnik purchased from Sandalj and Radoslav Pavlović in 1419 and 1426/27 respectively. The town dispatched the Franciscans into the newly acquired region and in the course of the 1430s seized most of the property belonging to the Orthodox Church, which it then turned over to the Franciscans. In this way the Orthodox priests, though legally able to remain and preach, lost the basis for their support. In 1426 there had been about fifty Orthodox churches in the district of Konavli. One by one in the years that followed they were taken over by Latin rite clergy. As a result no Orthodox clergy can be found in the sources about Konavli from the 1450s.

Bosnia and Hercegovina (roughly, Hum) are now famous for their enormous medieval gravestones (particularly those from the fourteenth to sixteenth centuries) known as stećci. They are sometimes called "Bogomil Tombstones." This label is derived from the belief that the Bosnian Church was Bogomil and the further belief that since these stones seem to have been idiosyncratic to Bosnia and since the Bosnians had their own local Church, the stones must be related to that Church. However, this view has not held up under more serious examination. First, the stones are found in a broader area of Yugoslavia than that in which the Bosnian Church had been active. Secondly, the inscriptions on them indicate that they were in fact erected by wealthy people of all faiths, Catholic, Orthodox, and Bosnian. Thus they reflect a regional cultural phenomenon and should not be tied to membership in a particular faith. The stones were carved into various shapes such as great sarcophagi (though these were solid blocks having the deceased buried beneath them), standing slabs, and great crosses. Though the majority are unmarked, some have carved motifs. These vary from simple geometrical designs (e.g., spirals, rosettes, crosses) to elaborate scenes (e.g., tournaments, hunting scenes, round dances, etc.). Some of their creators were excellent artists. The most elaborate and interesting motifs are found on stones erected by Vlachs, especially in the area of Stolac. Particularly famous are the stones of the Orthodox Vlach family of Miloradović at Radimlja.[5]

Bosnia was studded with imposing stone fortresses. Certain of the palaces (e.g., the king's at Bobovac) were not only impressive architecturally, but were also decorated with excellent stone reliefs and frescoes. Bosnia also had many medieval churches. In general they were small and do not compare favorably with the handsome Catholic churches along the coast or the Orthodox monastery churches in near-by Serbia. That Bosnian patrons invested less in their churches probably reflects the indifference of the Bosnian nobles to formal religion. It is often stated that the Bosnian Church rejected church buildings, thus the ruined churches found in Bosnia must be Catholic or Orthodox. This statement almost certainly is false. We know Gost Radin left money in his will to build a church. Furthermore, church ruins occur beside medieval cemeteries that contain tombstones belonging to Bosnian Church clerics, and ruined churches show up in villages where Bosnian Church hižas are mentioned in the medieval sources. Thus it is almost certain that some, and possibly even many, of these ruined medieval churches were Bosnian Church buildings.

In addition to stone-carvers and stone-masons, Bosnia also had fine metal-workers. Though most of its known goldsmiths came from Dubrovnik, Bosnians themselves worked in silver. And as noted earlier, certain silver products in the Bosnian style were in demand on the coast. Bosnia was also the first inland Balkan country to produce fire-arms and cannons. It seems the original masters of this trade were Germans working in Bosnia. Bosnian textile products never were comparable to those produced by the coastal cities; however, we suspect that quite early the different regions of Bosnia already had the elaborately embroidered home-made folk-costumes for which Bosnia later became famous. Bosnians also, as noted, produced several surviving Gospel manuscripts, some of which had exquisite miniatures.

Mining was a major Bosnian industry. In the beginning, the technical/engineering side was dominated by Sasi (Saxons) whereas the commercial and business side was run by Ragusans. Bosnians provided the labor. As time went on more Bosnians came to be involved in the technical side. The most lucrative were the silver mines, which lay in the king's lands, except for the richest of all, Srebrnica, which had passed into Serbian hands. Dubrovnik soon procured a monopoly on the silver trade. Individual Ragusans (or a group as partners) "farmed" the mines, rendering a set sum of money to the king and then managing the mine for a term (usually a year) in the hopes of earning a handsome profit. The major non-royal mine was found at Olovo. As its name indicates, it was a lead mine. During most of the late fourteenth and fifteenth centuries, the Radenović-Pavlović family owned Olovo. Lead was less important than silver, so there was only a small Ragusan colony there. However, the Franciscans did set up a monastery at Olovo, so it became a Catholic center. Furthermore, lead never became a Ragusan monopoly like silver. Thus the domestic, Bosnian element acquired a major role in the lead trade.

Dalmatia

We saw in the last chapter Venice's acquisition of various southern Adriatic towns on the Albanian and Zetan coasts in the 1390s. We shall discuss Venice's further activity in this region below when we continue our treatment of the Balšići and Zeta. In the discussion of Bosnia, given above, we traced the shifting fortunes during the Hungarian civil war of the northern Dalmatian towns, all belonging to Hungary after the 1358 treaty between Hungary and Venice. We saw how, willingly or not, the different towns found themselves under vassals of Sigismund or Ladislas. These vassals were frequently Bosnians, and for a time Tvrtko and then after his death Hrvoje actually exercised royal authority in Dalmatia. Hrvoje dominated Dalmatia for much of the 1390s and throughout most of the first decade of the fifteenth century. For most of this time he acted in the name of Ladislas. After his submission to Sigismund in 1409 he exercised his authority in the name of Sigismund. Though he issued charters, allowing the towns to retain their existing privileges of self-government, his rule seems to have been unpopular. And in an effort to escape him, or possibly to avoid the warfare in connection with the Hungarian civil war that also was occurring in and around Dalmatia at the time, various Dalmatian towns in the period 1401–03 decided the best way out was to seek Venetian suzerainty. Venice had not yet shown the dominating policy it was soon to show in that area. Venice at this moment was hesitant to become involved in Dalmatian affairs.

However, by 1408, as Ladislas' fortunes went from bad to worse (though in name Dalmatia was still his since Hrvoje, who directed the region, was his nominal vassal), he sought support from Venice for what had become a half-hearted war. Venice, which until then had been neutral in the war, saw a grand opportunity. It began discussions with Ladislas to purchase Dalmatia from him. Meanwhile, Sigismund defeated the Bosnians at the Battle of Doboj (or Lašva). Under pressure from the victorious Sigismund and knowing that he would lose the legal basis for his position in Dalmatia should Ladislas sell Dalmatia to Venice, Hrvoje switched sides in 1409 and submitted to Sigismund. In his agreement with Sigismund, Hrvoje retained all his titles and territory, including Dalmatia. Thus, by switching overlords, Hrvoje was able to carry on as before. Of the major coastal towns, only Zadar objected to the new arrangement and refused to accept Sigismund.

Then in July 1409 Ladislas carried out his sale to Venice of his only actual possessions—namely, Zadar, Vrana, Novigrad, and the isle of Pag (all of which Venice assumed control of at the time)—and of his "rights" to the rest of Dalmatia. These "rights" came from his claim to be King of Hungary. As Venice sent ships into Dalmatia to conclude treaties with Zadar and its new possessions, the populations of the town of Nin and the islands of Rab and Cres, and then shortly thereafter of the towns of Skradin and Ostrovica, all sent envoys to Venice to submit. Venice accepted their submissions, basing its right of overlordship on its purchase of Dalmatia from the man who it claimed was the legitimate King of Hungary. With these successes, Venice increased its presence along the Dalmatian coast, directing its ships to sail into the towns' harbors to seek submission. In this way it asserted itself over much of northern Dalmatia. It also gained all the islands north of Zadar, except for Krk, held by its hereditary princes the "Frankapans". In this process Venice took advantage of the break in 1413 between Hrvoje and Sigismund. For when Sigismund deprived Hrvoje of his "rights" in Dalmatia and urged the towns to expel his officials, many towns, disliking Hrvoje, did just that. They then had to decide whether to submit to Venice, which had an active presence in the area and could provide actual help should Hrvoje direct a counter-offensive into the area, or to Sigismund. Within the towns, pro-Venetian and pro-Sigismund factions quarreled, at times coming to blows. Overall the pro-Venetian factions tended to be the stronger, and thus frequently the Venetians actually received invitations to take suzerainty over various towns.

King Sigismund protested Venice's actions, but he was ignored. Finally in 1411 Venice attacked the town of Šibenik, which had remained loyal to Sigismund. This attack finally caused Sigismund, who of course never recognized Ladislas' sale of Dalmatia and saw the region as an integral part of his kingdom, to declare war on Venice. Sigismund does not seem to have been able to take effective action in the area; his most active supporter, Nicholas "Frankapan," had already lost Rab to the Venetians and clearly was no match for the Venetian navy, which immediately established an effective blockade of Senj, the "Frankapans' " main port. Afraid of losing Krk, whose position was very vulnerable, "Frankapan" seems to have remained fairly passive. In the course of 1412 the besieged town of Šibenik fell to Venice. And soon Sigismund, not being successful and fearing to lose what he still possessed, agreed to a five-year peace with Venice that he hoped would secure his remaining possessions. He agreed to sell to Venice the cities it then held, but Venice was to leave the other towns alone. Venice signed the peace; however, wanting all Dalmatia, it was not satisfied. Its appetite was whetted and it realized that the balance of power in the area now favored it over Hungary.

In the meanwhile the two strongest Croatian nobles in the Dalmatian region, Ivaniš Nelipčić and Nicholas "Frankapan," made an alliance. Nelipčić, without sons, agreed to the marriage of his eldest daughter, Catherine, whom he declared to be his heir, to Nicholas "Frankapan's" eldest son, John. Thus upon the death of Nelipčić the "Frankapans," already holding the counties of Vinodol, Modruš, and Gacka with the port of Senj and the isle of Krk, would greatly expand south of Velebit by inheriting the extensive Nelipčić lands including the Cetina Župa and much of the Krajina. In 1412 Sigismund both approved the marriage and renounced the rights he had claimed to these lands in the event Nelipčić had no male heir. The marriage took place amidst elaborate ceremonies in 1416.

Venice, meanwhile, ambitious to re-open its Dalmatian campaign and extend its authority over the rest of the region, took advantage of the expiration of the five-year peace with Sigismund to resume its naval action. Most probably in 1418, though Živković claims it was actually in 1419, the Venetians sent their ships to various ports to request submission. Venice rapidly acquired in this way the islands of Korčula, Brač, and Hvar. But when it sent its ships into the harbors of Trogir and Split, it met with strong resistance. Eventually, however, since no Hungarian aid was sent to them, these two towns had no choice but to open their gates to Venice. Pro-Venetian parties existed in each of these towns; they were led by members of the elite. Tensions, not surprisingly, existed between the aristocracy and the general populace. And in the end it was the aristocracy that brought about the towns' submission to Venice. In both cases, Venice won considerable support among aristocrats, by promising to support their desire to keep the patriciate a closed corporation barred to new members. Venice was to follow this policy of alliance with the nobility, supporting its social and class ambitions, throughout Dalmatia. Upon assuming power in Trogir and Split, Venice allowed the leaders of the anti-Venetian faction to depart in peace. Hungary soon declared war on Venice; but it was far too slow in mobilizing and fought even less effectively in this war than in the previous one.

The Venetians next attacked Omiš and the region of Poljica, two former possessions of Hrvoje that had been taken over by his brother-in-law Ivaniš Nelipčić when Hrvoje died in 1416. Ivaniš strongly resisted, and the attack failed. Venice soon opened negotiations with Bosnia's new king, Tvrtko II, to try to create an alliance against Nelipčić. These discussions, as noted, did result in Tvrtko's granting broad trade privileges to Venice in Bosnia—followed by increased Venetian trade in that land—and considerable talk about an alliance against Nelipčić. This alliance would have given Venice the coastal towns and Tvrtko the hinterland behind the coast, Nelipčić's Krajina holdings. However, as noted, before a treaty could be concluded and any action taken, the Turks in 1424 attacked Bosnia, and Tvrtko, made aware of Ottoman opposition to his co-operation with Venice, dropped all plans for the alliance.

However, well before this, in 1420, the Venetian-Hungarian war had come to an end. By then Venice was in possession of most of Dalmatia, the northern part taken from Hungary by purchase, submission, and conquest, and the southern—Zetan and Albanian—part through surrender from local nobles, unable to resist the Ottomans. In the middle of its possessions stood Dubrovnik, independent under Hungarian—i.e., Sigismund's—suzerainty. Venice had made no attempt to attack Dubrovnik. The only other coastal territories not held by Venice were those in the direct possession of the powerful Croatian nobles, who having been present, had been able to command effective defenses. These territories included Ivaniš Nelipčić's town of Omiš and the region of Poljica, which Venice had tried and failed to take, and the "Frankapan" possessions including the town of Senj, the Vinodol coast, and the isle of Krk, which as far as we know the Venetians had not even considered attacking this time.

To briefly look ahead: Omiš and Poljica remained in the Nelipčić family until Ivaniš Nelipčić died in 1434. The fate of Nelipčić's territory then became the subject of a major dispute, resulting in warfare and the eventual assignment in 1436 of his whole principality, including Poljica and Omiš, to the Croatian ban appointed by Sigismund, the region's overlord. Then, in the course of the warfare between Stefan Vukčić and Hungary, Stefan took much of that region, including Nelipčić's former coastal lands. Stefan's holding of them can be documented in 1440. In 1444 Venice was finally able to acquire Poljica and Omiš. From that time Venice held all northern-central Dalmatia from Zadar to the mouth of the Neretva, as well as the towns noted earlier in the southern coastal region. With its conquest of Bar in 1443, Venice acquired the whole Zetan coast. The Frankapans held on to their coastal holdings longer; but in 1469 the King of Hungary was to seize Senj and Vinodol and put them under his direct control. Venice was to finally acquire Krk in 1481.

In the second half of the fourteenth century, fire-arms—in particular, cannons of various sizes and later, as we move into the fifteenth century, harquebuses—were added to the weaponry of Balkan, and especially Dalmatian, warfare. The earliest references to cannons on the coast, one for Dubrovnik and one for Zadar, come from 1351. Over the next decades Dubrovnik became a center for the firearms industry, producing cannons of all sizes. Generally these cannons fired stone cannon balls. The early craftsmen tended to be Italians, but Hungarians, Germans, and locals were also found producing these guns in Dubrovnik. Dubrovnik soon became a major exporter of these weapons, selling them and gunpowder along the Dalmatian coast and in the Balkan interior to those states with which it was at peace. The earliest surviving record of such a sale is an order from Tvrtko I of Bosnia in 1378. Tvrtko seems to have had a small number of cannons and to have put them to only limited use. However, the number of cannons bought and used increased greatly in Bosnia in the fifteenth century; then we find the great nobles as well as the king purchasing them in Dubrovnik. By the mid-fifteenth century Bosnia was producing fine cannons itself; then even Dubrovnik turned to Bosnia to find cannon-makers. Zeta followed quickly on the heels of Bosnia; it is documented for the first time importing these weapons in 1379.

Serbia's situation is less clear. Orbini, writing in 1601, claims Lazar used cannons in his victory over Nicholas Altomanović in 1373. Since this is not documented in any earlier source, some scholars have rejected this testimony. In any case, in 1386 Lazar can be documented ordering craftsmen from Dubrovnik to construct cannons. One Turkish chronicler, though from the late fifteenth or the early sixteenth century rather than a contemporary, claims cannons were used in the Battle of Kosovo (1389). Scholars are not agreed on whether or not to accept this testimony. However, it is clear that cannons were used in the Serbian-Bosnian wars over Srebrnica in the mid-1420s and by both sides in the Turks' successful attack on Smederevo in 1439.

Despite their availability, cannons are not documented as being employed in Dubrovnik's wars in the fourteenth century. The first reference to their use by Dubrovnik—though almost certainly it was not the first time they were actually used in urban defense—comes in August 1402, when Dubrovnik, worried about a possible attack on Ston from King Ostoja of Bosnia, ordered the installation of cannons on Ston's walls. We may presume that in the warfare that followed, Dubrovnik also had cannons placed on its own walls. There is no evidence that the Bosnians employed cannons for their attacks upon Dubrovnik during this war. When warfare broke out between Dubrovnik and Radoslav Pavlović in 1430, Dubrovnik offered cannons to Sandalj, presumably for use against Radoslav. In the war, to be discussed below, between Stefan Vukčić and Dubrovnik between 1451 and 1454, both sides used firearms.

Dubrovnik seems to have usually kept its guns in arsenals, bringing them out to the walls only when needed. The city also stock-piled gunpowder, which exploded on a couple of occasions (1435 and 1463), causing considerable damage and serious fires. Dubrovnik and Serbia were both in the habit of christening their largest cannons with pet names. By the second quarter of the fifteenth century, the best harquebuses were produced in Senj; Dubrovnik and even various Italian cities imported them from Senj.[6]

Effects of Venetian Rule[7]

The Dalmatian town we have the most information about is Dubrovnik. But the other towns were similarly administered, each having its own written statute, town council, and knez (prince or mayor). And we have seen that each town through the fourteenth century kept its own autonomy regardless of changing overlords, whether the overlord was Byzantium, Croatia, Bosnia, Serbia, Hungary, or, despite a few restrictions, even Venice. But things were now to change. As we have seen, at the end of the fourteenth and during the early fifteenth century, Venice extended its suzerainty over most of the towns on the Dalmatian coast. Though in theory the towns were still to be allowed their autonomy and rights, Venice now demanded to examine and confirm all statutes. As a result certain articles were dropped from the law codes and some new Venetian laws were added to them. Furthermore, some of the existing laws that were confirmed remained dead letters. The indigenous nobles, who had dominated local administration up until then, rapidly or gradually lost their prerogatives and ended up with advisory roles. They were kept occupied, struggling for their class privileges and economic interests, while the Venetians walked off with the power to make political decisions.

The chief town figure, the knez, was no longer a local. Now he and his major assistant, the treasurer, were sent from Venice. The locals had no role in their selection. The knez was responsible to Venice, not to a local council. The knez chaired the town council meetings, which could be held only when he summoned them or agreed to their being held. All council debate had to be in Italian, for the presiding knez usually did not know Slavic and had to understand the debate. Though in many cases the Dalmatian nobles knew Italian well, this excluded from debate all who did not. The knez had to approve all the council's decisions; he also ran the civil and criminal courts. Moreover, he named the elders of villages within the territory of the town. No local control over the knez existed. The knez was in charge of internal and external security. He supervised the state of fortifications, was responsible for their being in good repair, and also commanded the garrison. In some major towns, like Zadar, a separate kapetan commanded the garrison; however, he too was sent from Venice. The garrisons were small—fifty to three hundred men, depending on the town. But they were not recruited from the town in which they served. The Venetians raised levies of Dalmatians for garrison duty, sent the recruits to Venice, and then sent them back to Dalmatia to serve wherever the Venetians required them. Needless to say, they were not as-signed to their own towns.

Furthermore, prior to Venetian rule each town had its own autonomy. Venice now introduced a certain degree of centralization, dividing Dalmatia into ten great regions, each centered around a major town. Each of these ten towns had a knez and a bishop. All other towns found themselves assigned to one of these ten regions and thus under the knez of one of the ten large towns. As a result the lesser towns lost their autonomy and were subordinated to the larger ones. This, not surprisingly, was resented by the smaller towns, which sought, without success, to regain their autonomy and be subjected directly to Venice under their own local knez.

The former Great Council of Nobles, now meeting only when the knez called or permitted it to meet, was a closed corporation of the nobility. From it the local functionaries (now those holding the second level positions, since Venetians held the major posts) were drawn. The social position of this council, its limited membership, and the status of its members were confirmed in each town by Venice, which in this way gained the loyalty of and acquired a hold over these local nobles. For the nobles were afraid to oppose Venetian political power for fear that Venice might turn to the middle or lower classes. The nobles wanted to keep the ranks of the nobility closed, and from the beginning of its rule Venice usually supported this desire. However, Venice was very clever in playing off one faction of the nobility against another. Venice throughout was harsh toward any opposition, and when on occasion local nobles did involve themselves in plots against Venetian rule, they were usually punished by exile and the confiscation of their property.

Taxes were increased, for Venice's needs were far greater than the earlier and limited needs of the individual towns. Part of Venice's demands for revenue may have actually been necessary for meeting the Ottoman threat. Venice did to some extent use local taxes for local needs, but it also tended to raise a tax income in excess of these; the excess was sent back to Venice. When still more income was needed the Venetians sold offices, frequently farming out local tax collection. But the most serious abuses carried out by Venice concerned local commercial activities; and the fears that had led many Dalmatian merchants to prefer Hungarian rule to that of Venice, a commercial rival, now became a reality. For now Venice told the towns to whom they could sell goods and what they could sell. If Venice was at war with Hungary, then the Dalmatian merchants could not trade with Hungary. If Venice sought a monopoly on a particular product (either a general monopoly or a monopoly on a product for a particular region), then it banned its export from Dalmatian towns. Thus the Dalmatian merchants found themselves greatly hindered in their commerce. And when war broke out with Hungary between 1418 and 1420 Venice banned trade with Hungary; this ban included all commerce with Sigismund's Croatian vassals. As a result the Dalmatian towns were blocked from trading with their own hinterlands. Thus the commerce of all the towns was damaged in the name of what was for them a foreign war. Furthermore, if Venice sought a particular product, the towns had to send it to Venice rather than market it where it would receive the best price. Moreover, Venice could set the product's price; and Venice, of course, was then free to re-export it at the price it chose. Thus the free Dalmatian market that had existed up to this time was eliminated.

In the 1430s the Venetians began to limit the towns' imports to internal needs and forbade the towns to re-export goods. At times Venice also insisted that the carrying trade from a given town's harbor be limited to that town's ships and those of Venice. Thus by the 1450s few foreign ships were to be found in Dalmatian harbors. Not only did Venice actively oppose the presence of foreign ships, but by then there was little for them to buy in Dalmatia. Protests by the towns occasionally resulted in mitigation of particularly onerous laws, but the changes were usually short-lasting and the restrictions were soon re-imposed.

Up to this point (ca. 1400, with the exact date depending on the town) the Dalmatian towns had been growing in size, the town government institutions had been thriving, and their trade had been increasing. The towns had been carrying on their own foreign affairs, concluding treaties according to their own interests, and trading whatever goods with whomever they wanted. Now under Venetian rule, this all ceased. Local activities and commerce became subordinated to Venice's interests, much to the detriment of the Dalmatian economy but of course to the benefit of Venetian profits. Thus in the fifteenth century there took place a marked decline in the trade and prosperity of the Dalmatian towns. Dalmatian merchants had fewer sales and thus became economically poorer; the local artisans had fewer buyers for their goods, and thus local productivity and industry also declined. In fact local industry became reduced to what was necessary for domestic needs.

Dubrovnik was not affected by this decline, for, remaining under Hungary, it escaped Venetian dominance. Thus while the rest of Dalmatia declined, Dubrovnik prospered. In fact the decline of its neighbors aided Dubrovnik's economic development. However, the Venetian presence did negatively effect Dubrovnik at times. For once Venice obtained control of the Albanian ports, it insisted that all their grain be shipped to Italy, thus depriving Dubrovnik of what had been a major source of relatively inexpensive grain.

Croatia

Meanwhile, in the interior of Croatia, two families struggled for hegemony. First were the Frankapans, headed by Nicholas, the first to take the name Frankapan (which was recognized by the pope in 1430); he held the family seat of Krk, the town of Senj, and the counties of Vinodol, Modruš, and Gacka, as well as Lika in Croatia and Cetin, Slunj, and Ozalj in Slavonia. Sigismund appointed him Ban of Croatia in 1426, an office he held until his death in 1432. In the year of his appointment Nicholas made a huge loan to Sigismund, for which he received as security the royal fortresses of Bihać, Knin, Lapac grad, Vrlika, Ostrovica (near Bribir), Skradin, Sokograd, Ripač, Čoka, Rmanj, Lab, and the Lučka county (between the Krka River and the Zrmanja). As a result he held just about all of Croatia—excluding, of course, Croatian Slavonia—except for Krbava, held by the Kurjakovići, and the large Nelipčić holdings to the south, to which, as noted, his son John, married to Catherine Nelipčić, was heir. The second family struggling for hegemony was that of Herman II of Celje, who was Ban of Slavonia. The father-in-law of Sigismund, he held, as we noted earlier, much of Slovenia and Zagorje while possessing enormous tracts of land in Slavonia.

A marriage was contracted between the two families in about 1405 when Nicholas' daughter Elizabeth married Herman's son Frederick. A huge cash dowry was agreed upon, but since Nicholas lacked the cash at the time he gave Frederick as security half the island of Krk and three fortresses in Vinodol. Thus Frederick took possession of certain castles (and their income) within the Frankapans' lands. His father, Herman, then granted Frederick Kranj and certain castles in Slavonia. Frederick settled down with Elizabeth, and in about 1406 a son, Ulrich, was born. All went well until about 1414 when Frederick met the luscious Veronica; leaving Elizabeth, Frederick took up housekeeping with her. Both fathers were distressed and pressured Frederick in every way possible to go back to Elizabeth, for there was the dowry at issue. Finally in 1422 Frederick knuckled under to the pressure and returned to Elizabeth; in the morning, it seems after his first night back, Elizabeth was found murdered in her bed.

Furious, Nicholas Frankapan seized the dowry castles within his lands and then invaded Frederick's holdings, sending troops into both Slavonia and Kranj. Frederick fled to the Hungarian court to seek asylum with his sister Barbara, Sigismund's wife. Shortly thereafter Elizabeth's brother John appeared at court and, accusing Frederick of murdering his sister, challenged him to a duel. The king prevented the duel from taking place. John accused Frederick of cowardice in getting royal intervention rather than fighting, and laid his accusations against Frederick before the Hungarian court. Through the influence of Barbara, Frederick was allowed to leave the court; he returned to Slavonia and married his beloved Veronica. The Frankapans were pressuring Sigismund to take action, and Frederick's father, Herman II, was also furious at Frederick for marrying Veronica; so, when Sigismund finally responded to the complaints and sentenced Frederick to death in absentia, his father seized him, incidentally saving his life, and put him in a dungeon, where he remained until 1429. Herman's anger against Veronica simmered for a while until, unable to repress it, he brought her to trial as a witch; found guilty, she was drowned in a fishing pond under the castle of Celje. But though Sigismund was able to prevent a major war between his two vassals, bad feeling remained strong between the two families.

In 1432 Nicholas Frankapan died, leaving nine sons. With seniority going to John, the eldest, the nine ruled the lands jointly, each residing in a different castle. John was soon appointed to replace his father as Ban of Croatia; the appointment probably came almost immediately in 1432, though some have argued that he did not receive the appointment until 1434. He also retained the royal fortresses his father had held as security for the large loan to Sigismund.

In 1434 Ivaniš Nelipčić died, and, as noted, since he had no sons his lands were left to his daughter Catherine, the wife of John Frankapan. The Nelipčić inheritance was enormous, including roughly all Croatia between Velebit and the Cetina River. John moved south to reside in his new holdings, living usually in Klis or Omiš, leaving his brothers to manage the family's holdings in the north. Sigismund, fearing the increase in power these lands would give the Frankapans, now forbade the carrying out of Ivaniš' testament and, on the basis of a law that awarded to the king the property of holders dying without male heir, demanded the Nelipčić inheritance for himself. John and Catherine, in possession of a charter from 1412 signed by Sigismund himself, in which he agreed to the arrangement, refused. So, Sigismund declared John Frankapan a rebel to be deprived of all lands and titles. Since John still refused to submit, Sigismund called upon Matko Talovac, who had been appointed Ban of Slavonia upon the death of Herman II of Celje in 1435, to enforce his wishes. Making Matko also Ban of Croatia to replace the rebel

John, Sigismund told Matko that his family could keep whatever lands he took from John.

Fierce fighting followed in 1436, but it seems Matko was able to take only one town, Sinj, on the Cetina River. That winter he was back in Zagreb, and in his absence John recovered Sinj. But then at the end of 1436 John died, leaving a widow and an infant son. Encouraged by the new situation, Matko began preparing for another campaign. Feeling incapable of resistance, Catherine, through a mediator, entered into negotiations with Matko and in 1437 ended up agreeing to a treaty that surrendered her whole inheritance to Sigismund. She and her son then sought refuge in the Frankapan castle of Rmanj on the Una.

The behavior of John's eight brothers during these events is not known; there is no evidence that they participated in the warfare during 1436 and there is no sign that they tried to stick up for their sister-in-law when she was left a widow. The eldest remaining brother, Stjepan, throughout these events in 1436–37, was clearly in Sigismund's good graces, for he was frequently at court witnessing charters. And shortly thereafter Stjepan, still a favorite, received large grants in Kranj and Slovenia, including Ljubljana. Thus one suspects that to stay in the king's good graces the other Frankapans simply left Catherine to her fate.

The victorious king then assigned the Nelipčić inheritance to Matko Talovac and his three brothers. The Talovac family also greatly expanded its holdings in the north, for it received from Sigismund large grants in the Drava region as well as in Slavonia. When the Nelipčić problem had been success-fully settled, Sigismund thought it best to split the banships of Slavonia and Croatia. Leaving Matko as Ban of Slavonia, a post he held until his death in 1444, he appointed Matko's brother Peter Ban of Croatia in 1438. Peter remained in that office until he died in 1453. However, though greatly favoring the Talovac family, Sigismund seems to have worried that it might be-come too strong. He evidently sought a balance between the Talovac family and the Frankapans, who had now been cut down to size. And we find a letter from 1437 by Sigismund forbidding Matko Talovac to interfere in the affairs of the county of Bužane and the town of Potogan, for they had been assigned to the Frankapans. The Frankapans soon increased their lands further; in the late 1430s one of the brothers, Martin, married Helen (Jelena) Mučina of Lipovac. When her father died in 1442, Martin inherited his lands, including the major market town of Jastrebarsko between the Sava and Kupa, and also his two fortresses in the county of Dubica.

Meanwhile, to defend the approaches to Croatia from Ottoman and Ve-netian attacks, Sigismund in 1432 (with additional reforms in 1435) formed three military marches based on owed military service from the local nobles and on forts with garrisons. The three were: (a) Croatia, directed toward the Adriatic with responsibility falling on the Croatian ban, Dubrovnik, and the Krbava (Kurjakovići), Cetina (Nelipčić, then Talovac), and Senj (Frankapan) princes; (b) Slavonia to the Una, with responsibility falling on the Ban of Slavonia, the Prince of Blagaj on the Una, the Prior of Vrana, and the Bishop of Zagreb; and (c) Usora, supported by the nobles of lower Slavonia and southern Hungary.[8]

Croatian-Hungarian affairs became more complex after Sigismund's death in 1437 and that of his successor Albert of Habsburg, who was married to Sigismund's daughter Elizabeth. Albert died in 1439, leaving a pregnant widow. She tried to take over as ruler, hoping to secure the inheritance for her yet unborn child. She based her claim upon her parentage, for after all Albert had acquired Hungary as Sigismund's son-in-law, and upon some powerful supporters, including certain of the Frankapans, Prince Nicholas Iločki, and the Counts of Celje, Frederick and his son Ulrich. Ulrich had more or less run the affairs of the family from the time of his grandfather's death in 1435. His father, Frederick, seems not to have minded and lived a life of retirement in a Slavonian castle.

Despite Elizabeth's assets, however, the majority of Croatian and Hungarian nobles, led by Ladislas Garai, Ban of Mačva, opposed her. In 1440 these nobles held a council at Buda that elected Vladislav Jagiellon, the King of Poland, as their king. He was the son of Louis the Great's daughter Hedwiga. Envoys were sent to bring him the good news, while Elizabeth gave birth to her baby, a son named Ladislas, known as Ladislas Posthumous. His mother immediately crowned him in Alba Regalis (Székesfehérvár). Vladislav was thrilled at the chance to add Hungary to his rule and to participate in a new Hungarian civil war that could provide him with excitement for years to come. He appeared in Buda, still in 1440, with an army. The presence of his forces caused most of Elizabeth's supporters to change sides and recognize him, though Ulrich of Celje remained faithful to her. For safety Elizabeth sent her little son and the Hungarian crown to the court of Frederick III, her Habsburg brother-in-law.

While these struggles were occurring, the Turkish sultan sought to take advantage of them by attacking Beograd. However, the city was ably defended by John Talovac, Matko's and Peter's brother, and after a six-month siege Murad II gave up and withdrew his forces.

Elizabeth, still supported by Ulrich, now acquired German help from the Habsburgs, and civil war erupted in Croatia and Hungary. However, in the face of the Turkish threat, the war was finally ended through the mediation of the Church; Cardinal Cesarini played a major role in the negotiations. The two sides agreed to accept Vladislav as King of Hungary on the condition that his heir for Hungary be Ladislas Posthumous. Elizabeth then died unexpectedly in 1443.

While this fighting was going on, as noted, Stefan Vukčić of Hum took advantage of Hungary's preoccupation with its dynastic struggle to occupy most of the region between the Neretva and Cetina rivers. And though Venice was to grab Omiš and Poljica from him in 1444, Stefan Vukčić was able to retain the Krajina, the interior area behind this strip of coast.

The Battle of Ankara

We have by now brought Byzantium and Serbia down to 1402, the year of the Battle of Ankara. We have traced the Ottomans' extensive expansion into Europe. The Ottomans during the same period had also been extending their control over western and much of central Anatolia. As they pressed east there, they expelled various Turkish, and Muslim, emirs who had been ruling in that territory. The displaced emirs complained to the great Tatar conqueror Timur (Tamerlane), who controlled a vast empire in Central Asia. Timur wrote Sultan Bayezid, demanding tribute. Bayezid refused this demand in an arrogant reply. Timur, then, having mobilized a huge force of Turks and Mongols, marched into Anatolia in 1402. Bayezid assembled a large army to oppose him, containing contingents under his sons and under his various European vassals, including Stefan Lazarević and George Branković.

The two armies met outside of Ankara on 28 July 1402. The battle has been described by my colleague Rudi Lindner as the equivalent of the college football all-stars against the professional football league champions, for Bayezid's talented and able troops, fighting as separate units, were far less coordinated and disciplined than the polished machine of the professional Timur. The battle ended in a rout for Timur. His victory was owing not only 'o the superiority of his forces and his superior qualities as a leader, but also to the fact that, even before the battle's results were assured, the sultan's sons, fearing defeat, deserted with their armies, hoping to keep them intact to fight for their own advancement in the post-Bayezid world.

The largest of these deserting forces were those of Suleyman, who returned with his troops to Ottoman Europe. Bayezid was captured and, according to tradition, put in a large cage, where he remained for about a year until he died. According to Stefan Lazarević's biographer, Constantine the Philosopher, the Serbian ruler fought bravely. After Bayezid was surrounded, three times Stefan entered the struggle to try to free him, but without success. After the battle Timur penetrated to the Aegean, ousting not only the Ottoman governors but also the Hospitaler knights from Smyrna. He then restored the displaced emirs to their thrones, under his suzerainty. His plan for the restoration of legitimate rulers included the Ottomans, but he limited them to a smaller territory in northwestern Anatolia. There he confirmed Bayezid's son Mehemmed as sultan. Having settled affairs in Anatolia according to what he felt was the principle of legitimacy, he returned to his own Central Asian realm, where he died shortly thereafter.

This battle at first sight would seem to have been a massive defeat for the Ottomans, for they did lose much of Anatolia. However, they still held northwestern Anatolia; moreover their European possessions were still intact under an unimpaired military occupation that maintained firm control over the Ottoman European provinces. The elite of the army, the feudal cavalry, were established on service estates (timars) within the various provinces, which they managed. These fief-holders had also assumed a major role in local administration. Moreover, the Ottoman governors, administrative officials, and religious judges were still ensconced in their offices when Suleyman returned to Europe with much of his army intact. Thus the whole system was functioning smoothly on his return and he, at first unchallenged in Europe, quickly took control of the European army and administration, whose leaders all recognized him. Thus there was little or no chance for the Christians of Bulgaria and Macedonia to take advantage of the Ottoman defeat to rise up and regain their independence.

But we must also stress that the Ottomans were still weakened; they had lost over half their lands in central Anatolia, they had taken large manpower losses at Ankara, and their remaining forces almost immediately were to become divided among the surviving brothers, who at once became rivals for the throne of their father. At first the empire was split into two parts, with Mehemmed holding Anatolia and its armies, and Suleyman Europe. Soon the two were to be at war, which led to further losses in manpower. But, except for some peripheral European territories surrendered to Byzantium by Suleyman to gain allies, the Ottomans—represented by Suleyman—were to retain intact the bulk of Bayezid's European holdings. However, as Ottoman forces came to be divided and involved in a civil war for the next decade, Ottoman expansion was to be halted until the civil war was over. The war was concluded in 1413, and then the victor, Mehemmed, was to need nearly another decade, to 1421, to consolidate his control over his lands before a new wave of expansionist activity could be launched. Thus the unconquered Balkans— Serbia, what remained of Byzantium, including Constantinople, and the Balkan lands, like Bosnia, lying beyond them—received a breather that allowed them to survive longer. The Byzantine empire, thus, was to last, in its reduced size, for another fifty years.

Serbia after Ankara

Stefan Lazarević, who had been a loyal Ottoman vassal and had fought well at Ankara, survived the battle along with a good portion of his troops. He stopped at Constantinople on his way home. He was well received by the emperor, who granted him the title of despot, by which he was to be known from then on and by which his successors were also to be known.

On his return to Serbia, Stefan immediately faced opposition from his nephew George Branković. As we recall, George's mother was Stefan's sister. George had no love for Stefan, who may well have had a role in inciting the Ottomans to expel George's father, Vuk, from his lands between 1394 and 1396. In any case Stefan had ended up with the lion's share of these lands at the time, and it was only later, probably on the eve of the Battle of Ankara, that George and his brother were restored to the bulk of these lands by the sultan. Who bore the responsibility for the new dispute that erupted in 1402 is not certain. Our sources are generally late and leave much to be desired. The basic surviving story claims that after Ankara George at once concluded an agreement with Suleyman. What they agreed upon is not stated. But Stefan feared that George, with his new ally's help, planned to attack Stefan and seize his realm. So, Stefan tried to persuade the Byzantines to seize George when he returned from the battle through their territory. According to Orbini's version, the Byzantines obliged and actually jailed George, who then escaped and fled to the Turks (presumably to Suleyman) who gave him troops with which he returned home. Dinić doubts this account, which at least partially tries to justify Stefan. Dinić believes that Stefan was the aggressor, and that he incited the Byzantines to jail George so that he himself could take advantage of George's absence to regain the Branković lands, which he had acquired between 1394 and 1396 but which had been restored by Bayezid to the Brankovići shortly before Ankara. In any case, George got home safely and soon was at war with Stefan.

At first Stefan's policy seems to have been to take advantage of Ankara to shed Ottoman vassalage and to assert Serbia's independence. George Branković, however, seems from the start to have been bent on increasing his strength by relying on Ottoman support. At once he established close ties with Suleyman, recognizing his suzerainty and maintaining close relations with the Ottoman governor in Skopje. Moreover, after Ankara the Ottomans retained garrisons in the two Branković towns they had directly taken between 1394 and 1396. As a result they had an active presence inside George's lands and a means to compel him to toe the line. Thus possibly George's relations with the Ottomans (i.e., Suleyman) were not entirely by choice.

The tensions between Stefan and George soon led to actual warfare. This brought about strained relations between Stefan and the neighboring Turkish leader, Branković's suzerain Suleyman. Not surprisingly, Stefan was receptive when Sigismund of Hungary approached him for an alliance.

At this time Sigismund of Hungary was in difficulties. In 1401, as noted, a group of nobles in his capital had revolted and briefly imprisoned him. This encouraged the Naples party to step up its activities. At the same time Pope Boniface IX had recognized Ladislas. Upon his release from prison, Sigismund had gone to Bohemia to raise an army. In Hungary the nobles remained divided and his partisans continued to fight those of Ladislas. Much of 1402 was spent by Sigismund in winning support from Austria, which he won by promising that Albert of Austria would be his heir if he died without male issue. The Naples party was successful in the southern and western lands, and Hrvoje, who dominated in this region, was urging Ladislas to come to Dalmatia so that together they could march on Buda to install Ladislas there as king.

In these difficulties, it is not surprising that Sigismund sought allies. It seems that it was he, with an alliance in mind, who initiated negotiations with Stefan Lazarević, probably still in 1402. Stefan, probably still at war with George Branković, was not averse to good relations with his neighbor to the north, assuming, of course, that Sigismund did recover his position in Hungary. Sigismund was very generous in his terms; he offered Stefan Lazarević

Mačva, including Beograd, for Stefan's life-time if he would accept Hungarian suzerainty for it. Since it seems Ladislas had some support in Mačva, turning the region over to a Serb ally could actually strengthen Sigismund's position; after all in 1402 he was in no position to take any sort of action toward asserting himself in Mačva. And by granting Stefan Mačva, Serbia's territorial ambition, he could prevent Stefan from allying at some point with Hrvoje and reviving the former anti-Sigismund coalition that briefly existed at the time of Tvrtko and Lazar. Moreover, putting Mačva in friendly hands would allow Sigismund to concentrate on Bosnia and Croatia, without fear of a revolt in his rear. Stefan, finding a way to regain Mačva bloodlessly, agreed. It is not certain whether their treaty was concluded in late 1402, or, as is more likely, early in 1403. It clearly was signed before April 1404, when Sigismund wrote to the Duke of Burgundy that Stefan had submitted to him.

In the interim, in November 1402, Stefan defeated Branković's forces (which included troops from Suleyman) at Tripolje, ending for a time their warfare. Peace was concluded a few months later between Stefan on the one hand and George and Suleyman on the other. Thus for a time Stefan found himself secure in his Serbian lands, to which was added for his life-time Mačva with Beograd; and for the newly granted lands he had accepted Hungarian suzerainty. This suzerainty could also be useful if and when an Ottoman victor emerged to resume pressure on Serbia. Moreover, the Hungarian alliance and suzerainty gave him greater freedom in dealing with Suleyman. At this time Stefan also acquired from Sigismund the important fortress of Golubac on the Danube.

Stefan decided to make Beograd his capital. It had the advantage of being distant from both the Ottomans and the Brankovići and was a strong fortress. He repaired and added to its fortifications, making them even stronger. This was to be the first time that Beograd was a capital for the Serbs. Its being made into a capital also illustrates the process by which the center of Serbia was ever withdrawing further to the north. The city had fine fortifications, an impressive palace, several churches, an active market, and even a hospital, located at the Church of Saint Nicholas beyond its walls.

Stefan, as a result, also became more involved in northern matters, in particular in the on-going Hungarian squabbles. As an ally of Sigismund, he soon found himself at war against Sigismund's Bosnian opponents across the Drina from Serbia. Because of his support, in 1411 Sigismund awarded him the rich mining town of Srebrnica, taken from the Bosnians, on the Bosnian side of the Drina. Sigismund's motives were probably as much to weaken the Bosnians as to reward the Serbs. The income from the Srebrnica mine at the time has been estimated at thirty thousand ducats annually. The town, and its mine, was to be a constant source of conflict between Bosnia and Serbia for the next forty years, weakening both to the Ottomans' advantage. Neither Slavic state could yield on the issue, for both needed the income from the mine—particularly later, in the 1420s and thereafter, when the Ottomans had regained their strength and demanded large tribute from both countries. Thus the rivalry over this mine was to keep the two states divided and prevent them from uniting against the Ottomans, who threatened both.

The Ottoman Civil War

The main event of the decade 1403–13 was the civil war between the three sons of Bayezid, each of whom wanted the Ottoman throne. At first it was fought between Suleyman, who held Europe, and Mehemmed, residing in Bursa, who held Ottoman Anatolia. In the early phases of the war the third brother, Musa, was residing in Anatolia and supporting Mehemmed. He soon was to become an independent actor out for himself. However, before we turn to the war, it cannot be stressed too much (particularly since many works fail to explain it) that though the Ottomans were involved in a civil war, they, represented by Suleyman, still firmly held their European provinces. There was no way for the Balkan people under Ottoman rule to rise up successfully against the Ottomans. The Ottomans controlled the cities and kept garrisons in them. The spahis, their feudal cavalry, remained inside the provinces, holding feudal estates that collectively included a large portion of the agricultural land and villages. Thus the Ottoman structure was hardly altered by Ankara and the civil strife that followed. Furthermore, the forces of Suleyman alone were not only sufficient to put down an uprising but were also larger and stronger than the armies of any one of his independent neighbors, be it Byzantium or Serbia. What would have helped the Balkan Christians would have been a split within the Ottoman forces of Europe. However, at first this did not happen. The European provinces remained united under Suleyman. Furthermore, in the first years there was no fighting between the brothers in Europe itself, which might have weakened Suleyman's position there.

The only hope, then, would have been for all the Christian neighbors to form a coalition and march against Ottoman Europe. But, this was not to happen. Whether it was even seriously considered is not known. However, Suleyman, either fearing such a possibility or else simply needing to acquire allies against his brother, at once approached various neighboring Balkan leaders and offered them in certain cases good terms to become allies. Thus by drawing them into his affairs, Suleyman prevented them from working out among themselves independent policies that might have threatened him.

Suleyman immediately, in 1403, concluded a treaty with Byzantium; it terminated Byzantine vassalage to the Ottomans, ending both tribute and required military service. He offered better commercial terms to Greek merchants. He returned all the Christian prisoners he had to the empire. And finally he restored considerable peripheral territory to the empire: Thessaloniki and its environs, including the littoral of the Thermaic Gulf at whose head Thessaloniki lies, the Chalcidic peninsula, and the Thracian coast from that peninsula probably to the mouth of the Struma, the north shore of the Sea of Marmora from Panidos to the capital, the Black Sea coast from the capital up to Mesembria, and various Aegean islands. It is not certain how much of the Thracian coast was restored. The Ottomans clearly retained Kavalla and its hinterland with Serres. Thus I have followed Lemerle's conclusion that the Struma River mouth became the new border, with the Byzantines holding the territory to its west and the Ottomans the coast east of it. Ducas claims the restored Black Sea coastal territory went beyond Mesembria, including the coast as far north as Varna. Most scholars, however, have rejected this claim and have accepted the contemporary Venetian report, which includes what alleges to be an Italian translation of the treaty text; this text gives Mesembria as the furthermost Black Sea city restored.

It also seems that Suleyman came to some sort of arrangement with Stefan Lazarević. It is sometimes said that Suleyman, probably in 1403, concluded a treaty with Stefan and released him from all vassal obligations and returned to him a limited amount of territory which, it is often claimed, included the important town of Niš and its district. The Venetian text, however, gives no such generous terms but reports that Suleyman recognized Stefan's authority only over his existing state (the lands he held from the time of Bayezid) and expected him to continue with his existing obligations, tribute and military service. Thus Serbia in theory remained a vassal of the Ottomans. However, for much of this period Stefan behaved as if he were a free agent and not under any Ottoman overlord.

Thus the Byzantines were released from their vassal status to become, as they did at first, Suleyman's allies. However, as such they were drawn into the Ottoman civil war on the side of one Ottoman faction and thus prevented from becoming active against the Ottomans in general. And any successes they were to have, which were at the expense of their own manpower, benefited one or the other Ottoman side, rather than themselves. Thus throughout their civil war, the Turks, whether one side or the other, continued to hold their European lands, with no loosening of this hold—except for the peripheral lands they restored to the empire. The issue at stake was not whether the Turks were to be or not to be, but which Turk was to emerge as victor. And though the civil war was to last for ten years, no subjected Balkan Christians, except those in the territories surrendered in 1403 by Suleyman, were able to extricate themselves from Turkish rule.

In fact, the civil war tended to weaken the Balkan peoples further, since the leading Balkan rulers were drawn into the Ottoman strife, supporting one side or another and thereby suffering the loss of many of their own troops. And it is hard to see how they could have failed to be drawn in, since the armies of either Ottoman claimant were stronger than those of any individual Balkan state. Thus the Christian rulers seem to have felt fortunate to become Ottoman allies. And though Manuel II seems to have hoped at times to play one Ottoman side off against the other, the chance to do so and thus gain some major advantages for the empire never arose. Manuel might have been able to do this at the very start in 1402–03, but at the time he was in the West, seeking aid for the empire, whose demise, in the days before the Battle of Ankara, had seemed imminent. By the time he returned home the chance had been lost. His nephew John VII, who had ruled in his absence, had already concluded the treaty with Suleyman, and the empire was committed to an alliance and involvement in the Ottoman civil war.

By 1407 things were prospering for Suleyman. He marched into Anatolia and seized Bursa. However, Mehemmed's ally Musa soon outflanked Suleyman, sailing across the Black Sea for Wallachia, where he acquired the Vlachs as allies. Mircea of Wallachia had taken advantage of the Ottomans' difficulties after Ankara to take over the Dobrudja as well as the important fortress of Silistria on the Danube. Since Suleyman, possessor of the rest of Bulgaria, could be expected to try to regain these lands, it made sense for Mircea to support Suleyman's rival. Having assembled his army in Wallachia, Musa soon crossed the Danube into Bulgaria, thereby attacking Suleyman's rear. This forced Suleyman to return to Europe. And Mehemmed regained Bursa and soon had again solidified his hold on western Anatolia. By 1409 Suleyman found himself in a serious struggle to retain his Balkan possessions against Musa. In 1409 Suleyman visited Constantinople to confirm his treaty of friendship with the empire and to seek aid.

While this was occurring, Stefan Lazarević of Serbia defected from Suleyman's camp and agreed to support Musa's campaign. With this defection, Suleyman, seeking allies and wanting to reduce the support Stefan could provide for Musa, entered into negotiations with Stefan's brother Vuk. He encouraged him to revolt against Stefan. Vuk was ambitious and at the time hurt by his brother's treatment of him. Orbini says Stefan was not treating Vuk like a brother and refused to give him a share of their father's state. So Vuk departed to Suleyman accompanied by many nobles who were in his service. Suleyman gave him many honors and lands in his realm. Constantine the Philosopher, Stefan's biographer, gives a somewhat different version. According to him, Vuk initiated the crisis by concluding an alliance with George Branković and then, on the strength of that, demanding an appanage from Stefan. When Stefan refused his demand, in late 1408 or early 1409, Vuk revolted, acquiring troops from both Suleyman and Branković. After an initial military failure, Vuk returned for a second attempt, still supported by his allies; it was successful and he established a principality in the south of Serbia. Orbini claims that Suleyman provided him with the unbelievable number of thirty thousand troops. His troops and those of his allies were said to have plundered Raška (presumably meaning the territory under Stefan) for six months. It clearly was in Suleyman's interest to encourage Vuk's attempt, since it would weaken Stefan, who had by then joined Musa's camp. In the course of this warfare, in 1409, Sigismund of Hungary gave some aid to Stefan against Vuk. It is not certain how much territory Vuk seized. Orbini reports that Vuk forced a territorial settlement on his brother; however, the division Orbini presents makes no sense. Radonić thinks Vuk took a truly substantial area, possibly all of Serbia itself, leaving Stefan only the Mačva lands he had received from Sigismund after Ankara. Vuk's lands were held under Ottoman (Suleyman's) suzerainty.

In 1410 Musa, still supported by Mircea of Wallachia and Stefan Lazarević, launched a two-pronged attack on Suleyman's Bulgarian lands. In February 1410 their forces defeated Suleyman's beglerbeg. Then they marched toward Constantinople, where near its walls they met Suleyman's own forces, which had Byzantine support. Byzantine envoys secretly approached Stefan to try to detach him from his alliance with Musa. They failed. In the ensuing battle, Suleyman emerged victorious and Musa fled. Pursued, Musa was defeated a second time but once again escaped. Then with a small force Musa took to the mountains and carried on a guerrilla war against Suleyman.

In the course of this action, Musa maintained close ties with Stefan, at one point even seeking asylum at his court. Musa also put an end to Vuk's principality. Vuk, it seems, had briefly switched sides, also joining Musa. But then, on the eve of the first 1410 battle near Constantinople, he had deserted Musa and returned to Suleyman. Suleyman, as we have seen, won that battle. Stefan, who had been on Musa's side, fled. Vuk, then, with Suleyman's blessing and a small retinue, hurriedly set off for Serbia to take over the lands still retained by Stefan after the events of 1409. Suleyman had agreed that Vuk could have all Stefan's lands. While he was en route to Serbia, some of Musa's men captured him. They took him to Musa, who then beheaded him, probably in July 1410. Though some of the details given above, drawn from Orbini, may not be exact, it is certain that Vuk did fall into Musa's hands and, as a result, was executed.

The liquidation of Vuk allowed Stefan to recover his lost lands. In June 1411 in a charter to Hilandar Stefan calls himself "lord of all Serbia, having united all of it after the death of Vuk."

Suleyman did not follow up his advantage and pursue Musa further. He allowed his advantage to deteriorate and fell, we are told, into lethargy and debauch. This enabled Musa to regroup his forces. He was also able to win support from many of Suleyman's former followers. Wittek believes he was able to do this by playing upon ghazi ideology, since many ghazis (warriors for the Islamic faith) allegedly were unhappy with Suleyman's tolerance of and alliance with Christians. This seems far-fetched, for alliance with Christians had been general Ottoman policy for decades and, furthermore, Musa too was allied with Christians. But regardless of their motivation—possibly Musa was simply a more inspiring and successful war leader, offering more opportunities for booty—Musa was able to rebuild his armies, partly through the winning over of many of Suleyman's former supporters. This gave him the advantage in the next round. In 1411 he returned to action, and as he marched through Bulgaria large numbers of Suleyman's followers deserted and went over to him. Suleyman was captured near Adrianople; taken to Musa, he was strangled in February 1411. George Branković, who had remained loyal to Suleyman throughout, now submitted to Musa.

Musa by this time was no longer campaigning for Mehemmed but clearly was out for himself. Furthermore, he now posed a threat for Stefan, who at the very end of the warfare, probably early in 1411, switched sides again and rejoined Suleyman. Musa, having eliminated his brother, immediately turned against the neighboring Christian states that had not supported him, Serbia (which had deserted his cause) and Byzantium. Attacking Serbia, he took Pirot and its district. Faced with this threat, Stefan strengthened his ties with Sigismund, visiting him in July 1411 in Buda. It seems on this occasion—if he had not already done so in 1409 when he received aid from Sigismund against Vuk and Suleyman—he accepted Hungarian suzerainty for all of Serbia. At least, it has been plausibly argued that the suzerainty he accepted in 1403 was only for the nominally Hungarian lands of Mačva (with Beograd), which he then was granted, while that agreement left him as an independent ruler over his other lands. However, if he now in 1411 wanted Hungarian aid to defend his original Serbian lands, then he had to accept that suzerainty for the whole kingdom which would then obligate Hungary to take an interest in this other territory as well. Their relations, already cordial, became even more so at this point, and in 1411, as noted, Sigismund granted Stefan the rich mining town of Srebrnica, which Hungary had just captured from the Bosnians.

Musa continued to apply pressure to his Christian opponents, laying siege late in 1411 or in 1412 to Byzantium's Thessaloniki and Constantinople and to Serbia's Novo Brdo. He failed to obtain any of the three, and the Ragusan merchant colony played an active and important role in the defense of Novo Brdo. However, Musa did succeed in sacking Stefan's town of Vranje. Faced with this threat, Emperor Manuel II tried to build up support among the Turks for a new candidate, Suleyman's son Orkhan, whom he provided with troops and hoped might become a Byzantine puppet. However, Orkhan was betrayed to Musa and executed. So for help Manuel turned to a stronger figure, whom at first he probably had hoped to avoid strengthening, Mehemmed in Anatolia. Manuel offered him an alliance against Musa, who, now acting for himself, had replaced the late Suleyman as Mehemmed's main enemy. Mehemmed agreed to the alliance and his armies were ferried to Europe from Anatolia on Byzantine ships. An insufficient number were brought over, for in the first engagement, in July 1412, Musa's forces won.

That fall Stefan, having earlier (possibly even in 1411) lined up with Mehemmed against Musa, patched up his differences with George Branković through the mediation of George's mother, who was Stefan's sister. This time their peace was to be a lasting one. In fact George was eventually to become Stefan's heir. As a result, George also joined the coalition against Musa.

That winter, 1412–13, Stefan also encouraged a Turkish border-lord, Hamsa, who had been serving Musa on the upper Timok, to desert from Musa. Learning of this defection, Musa in March 1413 had Hamsa seized and executed. And then, using Stefan's tampering with his vassals as an excuse, he attacked Serbia shortly thereafter, taking Bolvan (or Bovan, between modern Soko-Banja and Aleksinac), Lipovac (below Ozren), Stalać (on the Morava), and Koprijan (near Niš). Expecting further action against himself,

Stefan set out to build up a major coalition against Musa, including George Branković and Sandalj Hranić of Bosnia, who in late 1411 had married Stefan's sister (also George II Balšić's widow), Helen. He also negotiated with his suzerain, Sigismund, and with Mircea of Wallachia. Sigismund was just then in the process of concluding a five-year treaty with Venice, which would free him for Balkan involvement. Meanwhile, in April 1413 Mehemmed's armies returned to Europe, once again ferried on Byzantine ships. These forces joined up with those of the Slavic coalition, Stefan's, Sandalj's, Branković's, and those provided by Sigismund, led by John Maroti, titular Ban of Mačva. At this moment, the trend among the Turks was to desert Musa for Mehemmed, supposedly owing to Musa's cruelty and arbitrariness. The final battle occurred on the upper Iskar, below Vitoša, in July 1413. Musa was defeated, captured, and strangled.

Mehemmed thus triumphed and found himself the master of all the Ottoman Empire, including now its European provinces. Musa, as Musa Kesedjie of the three hearts, was to become the epic enemy of Marko Kraljević (the Serb epic hero who, as noted, died in 1395). The choice is interesting, for, like Marko, Musa was a relatively minor figure. Possibly his days as a brigand guerrilla leader made him easier to identify with and thus more appealing to Balkan imaginations.

Mehemmed kept his agreement with Byzantium throughout the remainder of his reign, 1413–21. He recognized Byzantium's rule over the territory restored to it by Suleyman in the 1403 treaty. In fact, a new peace was signed between him and the empire to this effect. He also issued a charter to Stefan Lazarević for his services that either awarded to him, or confirmed his possession of, Niš and environs and the region of Znepolje, lying east of Vranje. As a result Stefan's territory stretched all the way to, but did not include, Sofija. Mehemmed kept peace with Stefan too for the duration of his reign. Mehemmed's policy was to be one of consolidating his control over his expanded empire and gaining the loyalty of the Turkish servitors; presumably a special effort was needed to secure the loyalty of the European-based leaders and cavalry men who had for a decade fought for Mehemmed's opponents. Thus working to unite his new European possessions to his Asiatic lands, he did not try to expand Ottoman territory beyond its existing borders. However, both the Byzantines and Ottomans realized that the peace could be only temporary.

And thus the Turks emerged from their civil war in 1413 with most of their European holdings intact, and the Balkan subjects residing in them had no further chance, if they had ever had one, to liberate themselves. The sole survivor of the internecine feud, Mehemmed I, ruled from then until his death in 1421. By 1421 he had succeeded in solidifying his authority over the former territories of Suleyman in the Balkans. He also, probably in 1417, recovered most, if not all, of the Dobrudja, which had been taken by Mircea of Wallachia after the Battle of Ankara.[9] During this period he also restored the Ottomans to their former position of power in Anatolia, where he recovered a large portion of the territory Timur had returned to the various emirs in 1402. His reign, by restoring the empire to roughly the position it had enjoyed in 1402 prior to the Battle of Ankara, laid the foundations for a new period of expansion under his successors.

Stefan Lazarević and Hungary

From their treaty in 1402 or 1403 Stefan Lazarević had maintained cordial relations with Sigismund, who clearly regarded Stefan as one of his most reliable supporters. In 1408 when Sigismund created his Dragon Order to defend the Hungarian realm from internal and foreign enemies, Stefan was one of the first foreign members to be enrolled. After Stefan accepted Hungarian suzerainty for his whole kingdom in 1411, Sigismund began to grant Stefan lands within Hungary. In fact, Stefan soon became one of the largest landowners in Hungary.

Sigismund's treatment of Stefan differed from his treatment of other nobles in greater Hungary—i.e., nobles in lands officially under Hungary but not in Hungary proper—like his Bosnian supporters or the Garais. These, though granted territory, received their grants in peripheral regions that Hungary was claiming and trying to retain. However, they did not receive lands in Hungary itself. Stefan, in contrast, after his visit to Buda in July 1411, was granted not only Srebrnica in Bosnia but also other mining sites within Hungary, Szatmar, Németi, Nagybánya, and Felsöbánya, the last also having a mint. He not only obtained the Szatmar mine but the whole county of Szatmar as well as Debreczen, the seat of the Hajduk county. In 1414 he was to obtain most of the Torontal county in the western Banat, whither Stefan Lazarević sent a deputy to govern, seated at Arács. Though Stefan held this Hungarian territory from Sigismund, it was Stefan who named the officials and collected the customs, tolls, and judicial levies. In 1417 his representatives were found in the county of Ung and also in Temes and Krassó counties. A letter by Sigismund from 1421 shows Stefan as his financial representative in Szatmar. He also owned a palace in Buda. For these territories Stefan established his own Latin chancellery.

One may suspect that these grants were resented by the Hungarian nobility, but possibly Sigismund felt them necessary to keep Stefan as an ally against the Turks. Or perhaps he felt Stefan was more to be trusted than the Hungarians, and thus Stefan could secure the loyalty of these areas to Sigismund's rule. We may also suspect that various Serbs would have disliked the close ties formed between Stefan and Catholic Hungary. Though the great land grants had not been awarded to him that early, Stefan had already back in 1408 become a member of the Dragon Order; thus Radonić wonders if Stefan's Hungarian ties may not have caused some Serbs to support Vuk against him in 1409–10.

Stefan also regularly attended the annual diet of Hungarian nobles. At the diet of 1423 Stefan was listed first among the nobles present. At these diets Stefan often participated in knightly tournaments, excelling in them. On one occasion he bested all the Hungarians only to be defeated by another Serb.

Constantine the Philosopher's biography stresses Stefan's knightly prowess and ability as a military leader over all his other qualities. He fought, as has been seen, in a considerable number of major battles; his armies did well and, even in defeat, never suffered devastating losses. Like his contemporaries Stefan also held tournaments at his own court, and knightly poetry and tales were popular there. But Constantine the Philosopher notes that, despite this lively knightly side to his character and despite his active patronage of art and literature, Stefan's court was modest and puritanical. The despot would tolerate no rowdy behavior, raucous laughter, stamping, and shouting. He also disliked popular music, considering it to be somewhat immoral; he banned it from his court, allowing only martial music when needed for battle order. He also, his biographer informs us, did not pursue women.

In this context it may be worth while to turn to Constantine's description of the character of Stefan's subjects, the Serbs. We should keep in mind that to some degree this may be an idealized picture, but at least it should stress the values Serbs admired:

> The Serbs are quick to obey but slow to speak; in bodily cleanliness they surpass other peoples; they are charitable and sociable; when one is poor, the others all help him; they do not live basely or against nature; they pray to God more than twice a day; they greet their lords with doffing their caps; the son stands before his father as obedient as a servant; this one sees not only among the rich but also among the most rude and poor.

Albania and Zeta after Ankara

After the Battle of Ankara various Ottoman vassals in Zeta and Albania gave up their vassalage to the Ottomans and submitted to Venice. Among these was Koja Zakarija who had been closely associated with, if not subordinate to, Constantine Balšić. He held several small fortresses in the vicinity of Kroja. Having fought for the Ottomans at Ankara and returned to discover that the Venetians had eliminated Constantine, Koja submitted to Venice. Demetrius Jonima and various members of the Dukagjin family also substituted Venetian for Ottoman suzerainty after the Battle of Ankara. In 1403 Tanush Major's brother George Dukagjin, in submitting to Venice, received two villages on the right side of the Drin, north of Alessio, as a pronoia for which he owed forty horsemen and one hundred footmen in local Venetian military campaigns. It should also be noted that though Tanush Major had submitted to the Turks in 1398, bringing many members of the family with him, some other Dukagjins had remained in Venetian service thereafter. And, in fact, throughout the many changing alliances and submissions made by the family chiefs, various Dukagjins were regularly found as Venetian citizens resident in

Skadar. The Ottoman defeat and Constantine Balšić's death allowed the Venetians to regain Kroja, which they allowed Nikola Thopia to govern as their vassal. Nikola soon asserted himself and by 1410 was holding for Venice most of the territory between Kroja and the lower Shkumbi River. With control over this territory, whose inhabitants probably preferred him to Venice, Nikola was probably, as Ducellier puts it, more an ally of than a deputy for Venice.[10]

As the Venetians became active on the Albanian coast, followed by the establishment in the early 1390s of Venetian regimes in various coastal cities, Albanians began settling in Venice itself. From the middle of the fourteenth century Albanians had been taken in fairly large numbers and sold as slaves in Italy. Subsequently, after the Venetians established themselves on the coast, others began emigrating voluntarily. Ottoman pressure at the turn of the century caused increasing numbers of Albanians to emigrate to Italy, and, since Venice was actively involved in Albania, naturally many turned up in Venice. There they tended to take up the lower occupational positions generally occupied by immigrants breaking into a new society: domestic servants, couriers, night watchmen, custodians. Others became artisans, in particular barbers and bakers. In the fifteenth century Albanians were regularly hired as military retainers (bravos) in Italy. A few through military service, where they had the chance to demonstrate their ability, reached higher ranks. For example, we find an Albanian as castellan of Bassano. The Albanians soon established their own quarter in Venice, where newly arrived Albanians tended to settle. They had their own church and priest, John of Drivast. Large-scale emigration of Albanian peasants to Italy—in this case chiefly to southern Italy—came only at the end of the fifteenth century. Though this migration occurred after the Ottoman conquest, economic motives—the seeking of a more prosperous life—seem to have had more influence than political ones.

George II Balšić died in April 1403. He was succeeded by his son Balša III, who was then about seventeen years old. His mother, Stefan Lazarević's sister Helen (Jelena), played an active role in Zeta's affairs under Balša. Strongly pro-Serb, she wanted closer relations with Serbia and had strongly disapproved of her late husband's pro-Venetian policy, including his sale of Skadar and the other towns to Venice. She disliked Venice's interference with the Orthodox Church in its Zetan territory; she complained that Venice hindered contacts between the Orthodox Metropolitan of Zeta and the Serbian Patriarch of Peć and that it deprived the Orthodox churches around Skadar of their rightful income. She also objected to Venice's monopolistic trade policy, which lost Zeta considerable income. Helen had brought Balša up to hold her views. And he gave up the Catholicism of his predecessors and returned to the Serbian Church.

In early 1405 a revolt against Venice broke out in the region of Skadar. Though Venice was able to retain Skadar itself, the rebels expelled many Venetian officials from the outlying area. Balša sent troops into the rebellious area and soon, though only briefly, took Drivast; the Venetians were back in possession of that town in August. He also seems for a time to have held the lower town of Skadar, though not its citadel. It is not certain whether he had encouraged the revolt from the start or whether he simply moved in to take advantage of an existing situation. However, the angry Venetians responded actively along the Zetan coast and soon captured Balša's three main ports: Bar, Ulcinj, and Budva. Since his potential Serbian allies had become embroiled in the Ottoman civil war and thus could not come to his aid, and since he was threatened not only by Venice but also by Sandalj Hranić, who wanted to regain control over the Gulf of Kotor, Balša sent envoys in 1405 to Suleyman, the holder of Ottoman Europe, and accepted Ottoman vassalage again, agreeing to pay tribute. From time to time, when there was a lull in the Ottoman war, Suleyman was to send Balša troops, which then were to plunder Venetian Zeta.

Both Balša and the Venetians worked hard to win the support of the local nobles, who shifted sides for their own advantage during the whole war, which was to last eight years. The Djuraševići remained faithful to Balša throughout; however, if Venice had given them their long-sought goal of Budva, they probably would have joined the Venetian side. Koja Zakarija and Demetrius Jonima supported Venice. The Dukagjins, on the whole, remained neutral. Though Venice held the advantage along the coast, inland, where many of the nobles supported him, Balša had considerable strength. Balša had little tolerance for the loose loyalty of many of these nobles, however, and took strong measures against those who had deserted him whenever he was able to capture them; many of these suffered mutilations, by which they lost their noses and/or limbs.

Early in 1407 Balša married the daughter of Nikola Thopia, a Venetian vassal. From that moment on, often with Nikola as a mediator, active negotiations between Balša's representatives and Venice accompanied the fighting. When it was believed that Venice might return Bar to Balša, many local citizens objected; they had welcomed the Venetians back in 1405 and greatly feared Balša's revenge. As negotiations dragged on fruitlessly and the Ottoman civil war prevented both Turks and Serbs from giving Balša sufficient help to restore his authority along the coast, Helen herself went to Venice to negotiate. She remained there from July to October 1409 and then returned with a draft treaty. However, its clauses had not been observed during the truce then in effect, so Balša launched new attacks on Venetian territory early in 1410. And so matters continued until December 1410, when Balša's mother married Sandalj Hranić, transforming Balša's serious enemy into a strong ally. After the marriage Balša's negotiators ceased seeking compromises and began making demands. Finally in 1412 Sandalj himself became the mediator and demanded that the borders be restored to where they had been at the time of George II's death in 1403. The Venetians did not want to return the three ports, so Balša besieged Bar and began seizing Venetian merchants and merchandise along the coast. As a result, the Venetians finally on 26 November 1412 agreed to Sandalj's terms: each would hold the territory it had held before the war began—thus Balša would regain his three ports—and Venice would again pay tribute to Balša for Skadar and for the other towns surrendered to it by George II. And Balša had to promise amnesty to the inhabitants of his regained towns who had supported the Venetians during the war. Sandalj, the guarantor of the treaty, was responsible for seeing to its execution. Balša ratified the treaty on 30 January 1413, and so the long war was over.

Having regained the three ports, Balša made Bar his main residence. It is worth noting that under the Balšići, and subsequently under the Serbian despot, the traditional political autonomy of Bar, Ulcinj, and the other ports continued. Even though the Balšići had a palace in Bar that frequently served as their main residence, and though later the despot's vojvoda (or deputy for Zeta) was to have his residence in Bar, both were careful to respect the town's rights. Neither thought to interfere with the autonomous organization of the town commune or to interfere in how the town collected and used its income. The Balšići and Serb vojvodas simply collected the income due them from the town.

From his residence in Bar Balša now successfully devoted his attention to asserting his control over the interior regions of Zeta. He sent his vojvodas to defend the self-governing coastal towns and to supervise the hereditary chieftains who controlled the rural areas. He seems to have completed the subjugation of the Crnojevići, though their relatives the Djuraševići rose in rank and power and came to dominate the Paštrovići and the other tribes in the mountains above Kotor and Budva. The Djuraševići held the most honored position at court and their names appeared first among witness-guarantors of charters. Balša's new step-father, Sandalj, remained a firm ally, and under Sandalj's pressure Kotor resumed its annual tribute payments; these were now split between Sandalj and Balša. However, Sandalj, as we have seen, was soon involved in a series of major wars in Bosnia that prevented him from providing anything more than diplomatic support for Balša.

Balša strove to develop close relations with his neighbors, except for Venice, for which he retained his hatred. He divorced his wife, the daughter of Nikola Thopia. Nikola had ceased to be a worthwhile ally because Theodore Musachi had captured him in a skirmish, probably in late 1411, and retained him as a prisoner. In late 1412 or early 1413, Balša married the daughter of Koja Zakarija, who had already given another daughter to one of the Djuraševići. Balša gave Koja Budva to administer. Released from jail in July 1413, Nikola Thopia returned to Kroja, which he again administered for the Venetians; but very soon thereafter, certainly by early 1415, he died.

Whereas Mehemmed I respected his treaties with Byzantium and Serbia and did not resume attacks on them, he considered the Albanian-Zetan region fair game. Seeking to restore the Ottomans to their former strong position in the area, he launched a large attack thither in 1415. His forces took Kroja and several lesser forts in the area. Under this threat, Balša reaffirmed his vassalage to the sultan, and the other nobles in the area, including the Dukagjins, set about establishing good relations with the local Turkish commanders.

By this time, as the Balšić and Thopia families declined (the latter especially after the death of Nikola), two other families rose in importance. The Arianiti (Araniti), dominating the interior behind Valona, became the major family in the south. And the Castriots, led by John Castriot, had already begun their rise that was to make them by about 1420 the major family in northern Albania. In the 1390s the Castriots, holding territory between the upper Mati and upper Drin, had begun pressing to the north where they came into conflict with the Dukagjins. By 1415 John Castriot held Tirane and the territory north of that town to the Mati, if not beyond it, and controlled, or had suzerainty over tribes controlling, lands almost as far east as Prizren. How much of the lower Mati he then held is not known. It is likely that he gained its mouth and access to the sea only between 1417 and 1420.

It is possible that John Castriot also accepted Ottoman suzerainty in 1415, though Ducellier dates his submission to 1417. For in 1417 the Ottomans were again active in Albania. Mrkše Žarković had died in 1415, leaving the administration of Valona to his widow, Rugina. She was not to hold it long. The Ottomans took Valona in 1417, including its citadel of Kanina. The same campaign also gave the Ottomans Berat and Pirg. Rugina sought asylum with Balša, who soon—by 1419—gave her Budva to rule.

Meanwhile, probably between 1417 and 1420, John Castriot, capitalizing on his good relations with his Ottoman suzerain, expanded down the Mati to the coast and took control of the territory between the mouth of the Mati and the Erzen River. Besides apparent Turkish approval to do this, he was able to take advantage of a power vacuum in this area. The Thopia family, once dominant there, had declined greatly after the death of the energetic Nikola Thopia in about 1415. Moreover, the Jonima family, which also had been active in the region of the Mati mouth but was already greatly weakened by the end of the fourteenth century, disappears from the sources, and possibly from a role in the area, after 1409. Thus John Castriot was able to move coastward. Possibly he acquired some of the Jonima lands shortly after 1409; however, John's major gains along the coast seem to have come after the death of Nikola Thopia and after his own submission to the Turks.

Now that John Castriot's lands reached the sea, new economic possibilities emerged; for the first time he was in a position to market the timber he had in abundance. In 1420 he issued a charter to Dubrovnik, allowing that town's merchants to trade in his lands, which stretched from Suffada, on the coast between the Mati and Erzen rivers, inland as far as Prizren. Some scholars believe that he also occupied the Cape of Rodoni at this time. Ducellier, however, rejects this view. He argues that the territory north of Durazzo up to and including that Cape traditionally belonged to Durazzo; taken by Venice along with Durazzo in 1392, the Cape was retained by Venice, according to Ducellier, until the later Castriot leader Skanderbeg took it in about

1450. John Castriot, who did his best to maintain good relations with Venice, had accepted Venetian suzerainty and citizenship in 1413 and was doing his best to retain these cordial ties after he had had to become a Turkish vassal between 1415 and 1417; he was not likely to have endangered these relations by trying to seize the Cape from Venice.

By 1421, if not a year or so earlier, the Ottomans had acquired direct control over central Albania. They set about assigning much of this territory as military fiefs (timars) to their supporters. A 1431 census shows that about 80 percent of these timars were awarded to Turkish colonists from Anatolia and about 20 percent to native Albanians. Throughout the 1420s Turkish authorities in this newly conquered region had to face considerable resistance from the local Albanians. To the north of this annexed territory the Castriots, Thopias, and Dukagjins were able to retain most of their lands by accepting Ottoman suzerainty. The Musachi family, much of whose land lay in the conquered territory, suffered considerable eclipse.

Balša's differences with Venice continued. Neither side believed the other was observing all the clauses of the 1412/13 peace treaty; each felt the other owed reparations for destruction carried out during the war, and Venice seems to have continued to interfere with the rights and privileges of the Orthodox Church in the Skadar region. Then a new issue emerged. The Hoti, a large Albanian tribe living north of Skadar, quarreled with the neighboring Mataguzi tribe over pasture lands. Balša, called on to judge the dispute, found for the Mataguzi. The Hoti, ignoring his judgment, then seized the disputed lands. The Mataguzi, with the permission of Balša, attacked the Hoti, killing four Hoti tribesmen in the fracas. When Balša ignored Hoti complaints about the Mataguzi attack, the Hoti leaders went to the Venetian governor in Skadar and offered to serve him. In the agreement the Hoti promised the Venetians that in return for a stipend they would provide three hundred warriors, eighty of whom would be mounted, for Venetian campaigns in the area. This in effect lost Balša control over the territory in the Skadar border region controlled by the Hoti that until then had nominally been his. Balša complained to Venice, which by treaty was bound to return any deserters to him. The Venetians ignored Balša's complaints and a few skirmishes followed. After launching a large raid into Venetian territory in December 1417, Balša began planning a major campaign to restore his authority over the Hoti by force, while they prepared to resist. Trade issues exacerbated the quarrel with Venice, and Balša began laying plans to seize all Venetian merchants in his lands. Tensions and small-scale fighting continued through 1418.

Finally in March 1419 Balša launched a major attack that overran the Skadar district and laid siege to Drivast; that town fell in May and its citadel was starved into surrendering in August. Involved at that time in serious warfare against Hungary and the towns that had remained loyal to Hungary in northern Dalmatia, Venice had few troops available for a campaign in Zeta. The Venetians offered a large award to anyone who would assassinate Balša. They also tried, it seems without success, through bribes to persuade the

Dukagjins and Castriots to go to war against Balša. Balša meanwhile moved along the Bojana, taking Sveti Srdj while a couple of his ships took up positions on the Bojana and closed off all movement along the river. Balša's success was short-lasting. He was already seriously ill. A surgeon from Dubrovnik visited him from April to the end of June 1420. Also in the spring of 1420 Kotor, which for years, to escape the demands of its greedy neighbors, had been attempting to submit to Venice (always to be rebuffed), renewed the offer. This time Venice agreed. Sandalj, at war in Bosnia, could do no more than protest. Moreover, the Venetians, by then having been successful in their northern Dalmatian campaign (securing their control over Split and Trogir), now had ships available for the south. These sailed into the Bojana and soon opened that river for traffic again. Warfare along the river heated up. The Venetians also sent a naval squadron into the habor of Budva. Rugina surrendered the town to them at once, making no attempt to resist. She then departed (with the town's treasury) for Dubrovnik. Kotor, with Venetian blessing, then actively began to assert its control over various villages on the Gulf of Kotor. Balša, occupied with the fighting on the Bojana, was not able to respond to the threat to his lands on the Gulf of Kotor until the winter of 1420–21. At that point he and the Djuraševići arrived there in force. Their appearance caused the villagers of Grbalj to rise up against Kotor. The rebels burned property in villages remaining loyal to Kotor.

But Balša was in no position to lead a major campaign. He was much sicker and, realizing that death was approaching, was concerned with his succession. His one son had died as an infant. His eldest daughter—who was to marry Sandalj's nephew Stefan Vukčić in 1424—was then only about thirteen. So, while his officials were carrying on unsuccessful negotiations with Venice, Balša, extremely ill, took a rigorous trip to visit his uncle Stefan Lazarević, in Serbia. Realizing that only Stefan would be strong enough to defend Zeta against Venice, which now seems to have been confident that it was about to obtain control over the whole Zetan coast, Balša offered his state to Stefan. Then on 28 April 1421, shortly after his arrival at the Serbian court, Balša died.

The Venetians immediately stepped up their efforts and in May 1421 they took Drivast, Ulcinj, and, it seems, Bar. The Zetan commanders seem to have yielded these cities quickly, offering little or no resistance. The most powerful local figures, the Djuraševići, took advantage of Balša's death without an heir on the ground to take over various interior lands and villages belonging to the Balšići and to press into Upper Zeta. And soon thereafter they also moved into the Gulf of Kotor and took over Grbalj and the Svetomiholjska Metohija, both of which Kotor claimed for itself. Balša's widow, a daughter of Koja Zakarija, unable to resist these seizures, returned to her family in Danj.

Since the Venetians did not recognize Stefan Lazarević's inheritance and were holding onto the Zetan coast and much of Balša's former territory on the Bojana, including Drivast, Stefan had to take action. In August 1421 he led his armies into Zeta. Unlike Byzantium, which, on Mehemmed I's death in 1421, had tried to support a pretender to the Ottoman throne against Murad II, Stefan had immediately recognized Murad and thus for a while continued to enjoy peaceful relations with the Turks. Stefan immediately took Sveti Srdj and Drivast; he then moved to the coast and took Bar in November. Leaving deputies to administer and defend his Zetan possessions, Stefan, after also concluding a truce with Venice, returned to Serbia. As a result of this campaign Venice found itself holding in Zeta only the towns of Skadar, Ulcinj, and Budva—plus Kotor, which though it had submitted was autonomous—with most of the countryside around these towns supporting the Serbs. And there seems to have been considerable unrest inside the town of Skadar. Stefan sent an envoy to Venice to demand the surrender of these coastal towns to him. When Venice in early 1422 refused, war resumed.

Stefan's troops returned to Zeta, probably in June 1422, and besieged Skadar. And by blockading the Bojana, his troops prevented Venice from shipping troops or supplies to Skadar. Venice retained its possessions through that year, though it seemed only a matter of time until they would be lost. But then, assisted by some local Albanians, the Venetians defeated the Serbs in battle at Skadar in December 1422; this victory broke the Serbian siege. Next, in January 1423, through bribes and deals the Venetians won over the Pamaliot tribe on the Bojana River. Thus Venice's position in this part of Zeta greatly improved. Soon thereafter Venice through more bribes won over a series of tribal leaders in or near Zeta who until then had been loyal to the despot: namely, the local Paštrovići, John Castriot (who by now had extended his dominance to the outskirts of Alessio), the Dukagjins, and Koja Zakarija. Though none of these figures actually mobilized to help Venice militarily, their men were removed from the ranks of Stefan's forces and thus became a potential danger to the despot.

The Paštrovići held an assembly (zbor) in April 1423 that accepted the terms offered by Venice and ratified a treaty. The tribe agreed to defend, without pay, the Kotor region and lands as far south as Bar and its hinterland. If called upon to fight in the Skadar region, the Paštrovići were obliged to serve free for only eight days, after which they were to be paid for this service. Accepting Venetian suzerainty, they also agreed to pay one perpera per hearth to Venice. In exchange Venice promised it would continue to respect the tribe's existing customary institutions. For example, each year the tribe held an assembly by which it chose from its midst an elder, entitled a vojvoda, who kept order, exercised tribal and local judicial functions, and led the tribe in battle. These institutions—the tribal assembly and elected vojvoda—were to be allowed to continue, and Venice promised to confirm the vojvoda the tribe elected. The tribe's present lands were guaranteed and this guarantee was extended to include lands formerly held by the tribe but now lost, should the tribe regain them. Thus Venice recognized the tribe's rights to all the land it had held at the time of Balša's death. Venice also recognized the tribe's right to retain pronoias held from the last two Balšići in the vicinity of

Budva. Finally, Venice granted tribesmen the right of asylum in Venetian territory.

Excepted from the treaty were the lands of those Paštrovići who remained loyal to the despot. Thus the treaty did not recognize the tribal land as a permanent unit but endorsed its division. The annual tribal assembly (zbor) was to be held in Venetian territory and therefore the vojvoda it elected had binding authority only over the Paštrovići in Venetian territory (i.e., in the lands of the Paštrovići who had submitted to Venice and who thereby had converted their personal lands into Venetian territory). The leader of the pro-Venetian faction, Radič Grubačević, was elected vojvoda in 1423; he was re-elected each year into the early 1430s. By the late 1420s he headed what had clearly become the most powerful clan within the tribe. He received as vojvoda a monthly salary from Venice (or from Kotor, which, of course, had by then accepted Venetian suzerainty).

Though recognized as traditional, the tribally elected vojvoda was actually a recent innovation. Dušan and the Balšići, the previous overlords of the area, had sent a kefalia or vojvoda into the region to oversee the tribesmen. This outside overseer had presided over a court/council of elders/judges drawn from the local chiefs. When central authority declined subsequently, the tribesmen became in fact independent and started electing their own vojvoda to be the regional tribal and military leader. The Venetians were never to try to impose a governor over them but allowed this recent innovation to continue.

There were twelve recognized Paštrović clans who attended the zbor. Presumably there were more than twelve families, but the other families, not recognized as noble council clans, had to affiliate themselves as clients to one of the twelve main clans. Each clan had a headman—a chief—who usually represented his clan at the zbor, which was attended by one member of each clan. In addition to the vojvoda, the zbor elected four judges who also served for a year until the next zbor. By the end of the fifteenth century the tribe had come to have two vojvodas, each elected, still for a year, by the assembly. Presumably this second vojvoda emerged as a compromise to prevent the walk-out of a dissident faction within the tribe. Major quarrels and quarrels between clans tended to be settled by the assembly rather than by the vojvoda.

The Paštrovići had no urban centers in their land, though they had at least two forts. They were peasants and shepherds, holding small plots of not very fertile land. They were also fine warriors. And since they had little wealth and were able to provide fine soldiers to Venice, which was always short of manpower in the Zetan-Albanian region where few Italians wanted to serve, the Venetians were willing to leave the tribesmen to their own customs. However, it seems the Venetians did all they could to support Grubačević and the pro-Venetian faction within the Paštrovići to help it retain its dominance over the tribe.[11]

Having strengthened their position, the Venetians then in the spring of 1423 took Sveti Srdj. With the tide turning somewhat in Venice's favor, the despot, who had spent large sums of money on the war without achieving much success, became willing to negotiate. Venice also wanted to end the war. Not only had it spent a lot on the war, but, by preventing trade, the warfare had cost it much commercial income. Moreover, the Ottoman civil war between Murad II and the pretender Mustafa was over, which meant that Murad could now provide aid against Venice to his loyal vassal Stefan, who had supported Murad against Mustafa. Stefan, meanwhile, delegated his ally George Branković to manage the Zetan war, including negotiations, for him. George appeared in Zeta for this purpose with eight thousand horsemen. To strengthen his position George assigned a large portion of his troops to the Bojana, where they were in a position to cut off supplies and Venetian access to Skadar.

In August 1423 George and the Venetians concluded a treaty—the Peace of Sveti Srdj, where the final negotiations occurred—which put an end to the fighting. Noticeable among George's witnesses were two Turkish officials. The treaty allowed Venice to keep Skadar, Ulcinj, and Kotor. Stefan Lazarević was allowed to keep Drivast and Bar. Venice also promised to turn over to Serbia the Grbalj region, which the Venetians seem to have retaken, and Budva. Thus Serbia would again reach the Adriatic. The Venetians also agreed to pay to Stefan the thousand ducat annual payment for Skadar which they had regularly made to the Balšići. The two sides agreed on a prisoner exchange and to henceforth return to the other fleeing criminals. The Bojana River remained Venetian. The Serbs were to have no rights on the river and could not build forts along it. Both sides, moreover, promised to raze their existing forts on the river. It was also agreed that after the territorial settlement, vassals of one state who found they had land in the other's territory should be able to keep and make use of such land.

Various other issues were left up in the air, such as establishing the borders between Serbia and Venice in various places—in particular, how much territory beyond the walls was to go with the above-mentioned towns and how much territory held by tribesmen was therefore to be recognized as belonging to the state holding suzerainty over them. Venice was especially concerned about the lands near Skadar taken by a certain Andrew (Andrej) of Hum. Since he was loyal to the despot, his—and through him Serbia's—possession of these lands seemed a threat to Venice's hold on Skadar. On the other hand, how much of the Paštrovići's land was to go to Venice? (This was a touchy matter since their defection had given Venice considerable territory above the Gulf of Kotor that Stefan had no desire to lose.) Furthermore, Stefan insisted that Kotor, despite its defection, still owed the Balšić tribute, which should now be paid to him. Sandalj, too, since April 1422, had been objecting to Kotor's defection and demanding its return to his overlordship. When the town and Venice ignored his complaints, Sandalj banned his Vlachs from trading in Kotor, which considerably damaged the town's economic position. However, under pressure from Bosnia's King Tvrtko II, who was trying to improve his relations with Venice, Sandalj gave in and concluded in

November 1423 a treaty with Venice in which he renounced his claim to Kotor. However, Stefan Lazarević had no intention of yielding on this issue.

Though no further fighting broke out, the Venetians and Serbs continued to quarrel over these various unresolved issues. In addition certain items they had agreed upon were not carried out. For example, Venice did not turn Budva and Grbalj over to Serbia. Finally a major conference was held, resulting in a new treaty that was signed on 22 July 1426. Serbia was again represented by George Branković. Orbini claims that Stefan had actually granted Serbia's part of Zeta to George in 1425. We have no confirmation of this statement in any contemporary document. However, it is a fact that George was extremely active in the region; he had been Serbia's representative in Zeta and in the negotiations about it since 1423. By this new treaty Grbalj was given to Kotor. Kotor remained Venetian and was no longer obliged to pay the "Balšić tribute" to any Slavic ruler. Budva was now to be yielded to the despot. Most of the tribal lands under dispute near Skadar were to go to Venice to secure the town's defense. Most of the Paštrović land was to become Venetian—though the land of those Paštrovići who had remained loyal to the despot after the 1423 zbor was to remain Serbian. And most of the disputed territory around Bar was to go to the despot.

A further clarification was negotiated in November 1426 by which the two sides defined the territorial borders around the towns of Skadar, Drivast, Ulcinj, Kotor, Budva, and the Paštrović lands. By it Venice was recognized as holding all of Lake Skadar and all of the islands on the lake. The Venetians also promised to recognize the Serbian Metropolitan of Zeta's authority over Orthodox bishops and over believers in their Zetan cities and to respect the rights of the Orthodox. The Serbs promised to respect the rights of Catholics in their Zetan cities and to recognize the Archbishop of Bar's authority over them. The Serbs also agreed to turn over to Venice income taken by them since the 1423 treaty from the lands assigned by that treaty to Venice but retained beyond 1423 by the Serbs, and Venice was to begin at once to pay the Skadar tribute. As a result Serbia held the whole coast from, but not including, Kotor to the Bojana, except for Ulcinj and the Paštrović lands.

The Orthodox Metropolitan of Zeta, whose residence lay in a monastery at Prevlaka on the Gulf of Kotor, clearly had had considerable difficulty in maintaining himself in this territory under the authority of Venice's Kotor. Evidence exists that Catholic propaganda and proselytism were encouraged among the local Orthodox, and various Orthodox priests were expelled from their communities; as a result certain Orthodox churches and some Orthodox Church lands were taken over by the Catholics. These acts were allegedly carried out not as attacks upon Orthodoxy but as measures against political opponents of the Venetian-supported government of Kotor. The atmosphere clearly was not conducive for the metropolitan to maintain his residence there; thus, it is not surprising that shortly after Budva was restored to the Serbs in 1426, the metropolitan took up residence there.

This 1426 treaty was observed; so for a short time merchants from

Venice, Dubrovnik, Kotor, and the other coastal towns were able to move freely around and to trade in this area and also to pass through it into Serbia. As a result the economy of the whole region briefly improved. However, needless to say, many of the new treaty's provisions were not observed. The Venetian governor in Skadar refused to pay the Skadar tribute. The sale of salt soon became a major cause of dispute. The population of Grbalj objected to being placed under Kotor and staged a revolt. And certain Paštrović clans which had agreed to submit to Venice in 1423 now were no longer willing to do so. In fact, a pro-Serb faction emerged among the so-called Venetian Paštrovići and actively opposed the general tribal policy agreed upon at the tribal assemblies (zbors) of 1430 and 1431. Radič Crnac, the leader of the pro-Serb faction, was in fact seized and sent to a jail in Kotor during the meeting of the 1431 assembly. Pressure from his supporters led to his release after twenty-five days, but he was not allowed to leave the town of Kotor for some time. Eventually peace was mediated between the two factions within the Paštrovići, and Grubačević remained as vojvoda, pushing a pro-Venetian policy. These issues dividing the Serbs and Venetians, though at times causing fracases, did not lead to war. Further negotiations between Venice and Serbia followed, resulting in another agreement in 1435 between George Branković, by then the ruler of Serbia, and Venice. In this agreement the Serbs gave in to Venice on most issues, but the Venetians did recognize that Serbia's town of Budva was to have extensive rights to trade in salt.

Despite Venice's gains, most of Zeta, in particular the interior regions— excluding the territory around Skadar and along the Bojana—was now legally Serbian. Moreover, most of the nobles and tribesmen in Zeta—led by the Djuraševići—were willing to submit to the ruler of Serbia. Yet owing to Zeta's distance from Serbia and owing to the fact that the Branković lands lay between Stefan's realm and Zeta, Serbia's control over Zeta was very loose and the local nobles managed their own affairs. This led to increased power and independence for the Djuraševići, under the family head George (Djuradj), who, as noted, nominally expressed his loyalty to Stefan. George's policies paved the way for the family's even greater success under his son Stefan, who, as we shall see, revived the name Crnojević.

Stefan Lazarević's control over Zeta was not threatened by any of Zeta's neighbors. Stefan now had good relations with George Branković, who was soon, in 1427, to succeed him. He also had good relations with Sandalj, his brother-in-law, who held the lands to the north of Zeta. None of the Albanian lords to the south were prepared to challenge Serbia's overlordship over Zeta. And though Serbia and Venice had many differences over Zetan issues, Venice did not threaten Serbia's position in the interior of Zeta. Thus the only serious threat to Serbia's position in Zeta was to come from the Turks.

The Turks, meanwhile, in 1423, directed a major offensive into Albania. If he had not already done so earlier, John Castriot now accepted Ottoman suzerainty; so did the Arianiti in the south. Both sent their sons to Adrianople as hostages. One of these young men was to rise to great prominence in later life. This was John Castriot's son George, born in about 1404, who, soon after his arrival in Adrianople in 1423, became a Muslim, taking the name Iskendar and becoming known later as Skanderbeg. He quickly won the favor of the sultan and served him loyally in campaigns both in Europe and Asia. He did well and rose rapidly to become a high-ranking Ottoman military commander.

Stefan Lazarević's Last Years in Serbia

Faced with so many actual and potential foreign threats, Stefan took measures to beef up the defense of his state. He divided the territory of Serbia into a series of military districts, each called an authority (vlast) under a governor, bearing the title vojvoda, who was a military commander. The local inhabitants were mobilized as a militia, with the obligation to appear armed on call. A series of new fortresses were erected, and new taxes were instituted to support these defense efforts.

This military districting reform was put into effect throughout Stefan Lazarević's realm except, as Dinić has shown, for the territory that made up the Branković holding in Kosovo.[12] The Ottomans, already in possession of two fortresses in that territory and maintaining an active presence there—to keep the route open between their center in Skopje and Bosnia—almost certainly would not have permitted the establishment in Kosovo of a more effective Serbian military system. Zeta was placed under a single vojvoda, resident in Bar, who, in effect, was the despot's governor for that region.

As a result of these reforms the vojvodas became the dominant figures in the major towns and soon had usurped many of the functions of the kefalias who until then had governed the towns. The kefalias, many of whom had previously exercised both civil and military authority, were now increasingly limited to civil functions and, as the military took precedence, had to act in accordance with the wishes of the vojvoda. Not surprisingly, the importance of the kefalias declined and in some places the office died out altogether.

Moreover, in need of cash, the state awarded fewer immunity grants to the estates of monasteries and the nobility, and some of the immunities previously awarded were reduced. It was now regularly expected that all villages and estates, including those of monasteries, would supply manpower to serve in the army.

After 1413 Stefan skillfully managed to avoid conflict with his powerful Turkish and Hungarian neighbors by submitting to the suzerainty of both. And until 1425 neither overlord seems to have made serious objections to his submission to the other. However, in 1425 the Ottomans seem to have become suspicious of Stefan's increasingly close ties with Sigismund. As a result they launched an attack upon Serbia that pillaged the territory between Niš and Kruševac. The Hungarians sent troops to Stefan's support; as a result he was able to negotiate with the Turks to procure their withdrawal.

Taking advantage of this Ottoman raid into Serbia, the Bosnians attacked

Srebrnica in 1425. However, when the Turks quickly withdrew, Stefan was able to take his army and drive the Bosnians away from Srebrnica, which until his arrival had been defended not only by a Serb garrison but also by the Ragusan colonists there. Having driven off the Bosnians, the Serbs then raided into Bosnian territory.

According to Stefan's biographer Constantine the Philosopher, Stefan, who by 1426 was about fifty years old, had long suffered from an illness in the leg. When it grew worse he became worried about the succession, for he had no children. Constantine then describes his decision to make George Branković his successor, the recognition of this decision by a council at Srebrnica, his successful repulse of a Turkish attack through diplomacy and of a Bosnian attack on Srebrnica through military action, and then his death. In addition to Constantine's brief account we have two slightly different texts from the sixteenth century of an agreement made between Stefan and Sigismund at Tati (Totis) in Hungary. No contemporary source or any later narrative source mentions an agreement between the two rulers near the end of Stefan's reign. However, the contents of the agreement—as written in the sixteenth-century copies—are reasonable; and since Sigismund was Stefan's overlord and since Stefan had cordial relations with Sigismund, it made sense for Stefan to obtain confirmation from Sigismund for his succession plans. Thus most scholars believe that the Tati meeting and agreement occurred, though it is possible that the surviving document is not a verbatim text.

Moreover, the sequence of events occurring in Stefan's last years (1426–27) is not certain. Did the events occur in the sequence in which Constantine gave them, as they are listed above? If so, and if the Tati meeting did take place, then where in that sequence does it belong? Did Stefan go to Hungary with his plans and, having obtained Sigismund's approval, then present them to the Serbian council in Srebrnica, which we know met in July 1426, as Radonić believes? Or did the Tati meeting follow the Serbian council and reflect Sigismund's confirmation of what the Serbs had already agreed to?

In the absence of further information from the sources, it is impossible to resolve the problem. Thus, relying on probability, I shall follow Radonić and hypothesize that the Tati meeting preceded the Srebrnica council.[13] Since Stefan had cordial relations with Sigismund and there was no reason for Sigismund to oppose Stefan's plans, in the interest of realizing these plans, it made sense diplomatically to clear them first with his overlord, a touchy individual, rather than face him with a fait accompli which might have caused Sigismund to oppose Branković upon Stefan's death.

Thus we can postulate the following sequence of events: Since Stefan had no son or obvious heir, a struggle for succession could have occurred in Serbia. Fearing Turkish meddling in such an event, he wanted to ensure a quick, smooth succession. Having decided on his nephew George Branković, he wanted to prevent the development of any opposition to his choice. (And such opposition might reasonably be expected; after all, before their peace in 1411, there had been twenty years of enmity between Stefan's and George's families, and many of Stefan's nobles might still have felt hostility toward Branković.) Besides the choice of his successor and paving the way for his succession, Stefan had to face territorial issues, which could not be decided without Sigismund's agreement. His lands were in two parts: his Mačva lands, with Beograd, received from Sigismund for his own lifetime and his patrimonial lands of Serbia. From the time of reception the former, and from about 1411 the latter, had been held under Hungarian suzerainty. Stefan also had large landholdings inside of Hungary that he obviously could not dispose of without Sigismund's agreement. So—following the text of the Tati agreement and Radonić's reconstruction of events—Stefan left George to administer Serbia and went to Tati in May 1426 where he met Sigismund. After discussions they drew up an agreement that (1) recognized the vassal status of Raška (Serbia) to Hungary, (2) recognized George Branković as heir to Raška and admitted him to the ranks of the high Hungarian nobility, the barons, (3) agreed that the lands of Mačva, with the fortresses of Beograd and Golubac, were to revert to Sigismund for his disposition, and (4) promised that George would take on the obligations of a Hungarian vassal (e.g., attendance at the annual diet, military aid to his lord, etc.) that had been borne by Stefan. No reference was made in the sixteenth-century text to Stefan's properties in Hungary. Possibly they had been mentioned in the original, but later Hungarian copiers omitted reference to them so as not to give support to any Branković family claims to particular lands in Hungary at that time.

Stefan then returned to Serbia, and, strangely enough, chose an insecure border town, Srebrnica, to hold a great Serbian council of the nobility and clergy. Possibly this site was chosen to emphasize the Serbian character of this disputed town. At this council Stefan obtained Serbian recognition of George Branković's succession. No mention is made of Mačva and Beograd in Constantine's brief account of this meeting. Thus we have no evidence that the Serbs accepted the surrender of this northern territory to Hungary. Whether Stefan, chiefly concerned with winning approval for George, decided to ignore this issue or whether he tried but failed to obtain Serbian agreement to its surrender is not known.

Next comes the issue of the two military events mentioned by Constantine the Philosopher: the Turkish attack on Serbia and the Bosnian attack on Srebrnica. If we follow Constantine's chronology, these two events followed the July 1426 Srebrnica council meeting. However, some scholars, like Radonić, want to place one or both of these military actions earlier, prior to the Srebrnica meeting. The Turks were active in the area during this whole period, raiding Bosnia during the summer of 1426 and departing from that country by early August. They could well have hit Serbia on their return east, though we have no source stating that they actually did so then. The Turks had every reason to be angry at Stefan Lazarević at the time for his agreement with Sigismund—assuming, of course, that the Tati meeting preceded the Srebrnica council. Thus it seems likely that Constantine is right in dating the threatened Turkish attack after the Srebrnica council meeting. According to Constantine, Stefan defused this threat by diplomacy.

Meanwhile in the spring of 1427 the miners of Srebrnica revolted against Stefan's town governor, killing him in the process. The other inhabitants of the town immediately joined in the rebellion. Whether this reflected their general dislike of Serbian rule or whether they were unhappy at particular Serbian policies of the moment is not known. Stefan immediately sent forces thither that brutally suppressed the rebellion.

Constantine the Philosopher's text, meanwhile, lists after Stefan's above-mentioned success against the Turks a military defense of Srebrnica against the Bosnians. If his list is intended to be in chronological order, then this "attack" occurred between the fall of 1426 and July 1427 when Stefan died. Is mention of this "attack" a misleading reference to the local rebellion? Or did the Bosnians send troops, whose appearance was omitted in other sources, to support the rebels? Or is this a misplaced reference to the Bosnian attack on Srebrnica made previously in 1425? Since we lack the sources to provide answers to these questions, we must admit that we do not know whether there was a single Bosnian attack on Srebrnica in these years, occurring in 1425 before Tati and the Srebrnica council, or whether there were actually two Bosnian attempts directed at Srebrnica, with the second one occurring in late 1426 or early 1427, most probably in the spring of 1427 at the time of the local uprising. In any case the Bosnians failed to take Srebrnica. Then in July 1427 Stefan Lazarević died.

Constantine the Philosopher describes the wild grief and great mourning of the Serbian population at the death of Stefan.

Besides his political role, Stefan had been very active culturally. He built several monasteries including the spectacular fortified monastery of Resava (Manasija). The monastery, begun in 1407, according to Constantine, was built specifically as a center for the Hesychasts, showing the ruler held them in great honor. He endowed Resava generously with books and icons. Kašanin points out that Resava has frequently been called the cultural center of Serbia during this period by scholars, who use the term *Resava School* for literary and artistic works of this period. Kašanin sees this as a misnomer; other than housing the usual activity of translating and copying religious manuscripts, Resava was not a major literary center. And since its literary efforts were narrow and traditional, it certainly was not a representative center for this period, which was important for having a greater variety of literary genres than any earlier period in Serbian history. The center of Serbian culture at this time, where original creativity could be found, was the new capital, Beograd.[14]

During Stefan's reign Serbia enjoyed a literary revival, spurred on by various Bulgarian and Greek emigrés who had fled their homelands after Ottoman occupation. This revival produced both translations from the Greek and original works. The leading literary figure, Constantine the Philosopher, who wrote, as we have seen, tracts on language and orthography as well as his famous biography of Stefan Lazarević, was of Bulgarian origin. Stefan Lazarević was both a participant in and a patron of literature. In fact he himself carried out translations from the Greek as well as original compositions. Two of his works, a panegyric poem to his father Knez Lazar and a complex poem on love full of literary devices and acrostics, survive. Under him we find, in comparison to other reigns, the largest number of active writers and the most translations carried out. We also find variety. In addition to the usual works on theology, we find original chronicles, annals, and travelogues, as well as translations of popular romances, knightly tales, and poems. And like other rich and cultured rulers of his time, Stefan commissioned a major anthology.[15]

That Marko and Vuk Branković were rivals of Lazar's dynasty and that the literary figures who produced the surviving chronicles were affiliated with Stefan's court probably explains why the chronicle tradition slights Marko's and the Brankovići's careers. The literati's and the Church's support of Lazar's dynasty in building Lazar's cult also created the popular tradition making Kosovo more significant than Marica, the battle that in fact was more significant and in which Marko's father and uncle died. The chronicles at this time also created genealogical myths to support the legitimacy of Stefan Lazarević's dynasty. Earlier genealogical works, written during the reigns of various Nemanjići, had simply begun their genealogies with Nemanja, the founding figure. Now chronicles argued that Constantine the Great's rival Licinius was a Serb who married Constantine's sister, and from a truncated tree they made Nemanja a descendant of that union, thereby linking him to the Roman Empire. Having transformed Nemanja into a figure of universal history, they then made Lazar's wife and Stefan Lazarević's mother, Milica, a descendant of Nemanja through his son Vukan, and thereby connected Stefan Lazarević to the Nemanjić dynasty. Associated with the cult of Lazar as well, Stefan had the best of both possible worlds and a strong ideological foundation to advance against any would-be usurpers like the Brankovići.

George Branković's Succession

After Stefan's death, George Branković succeeded to the Serbian throne. He did not at once succeed to the despot's title. For the first two years of his reign, he simply called himself lord (gospodin). Then in May 1429 a Byzantine envoy, bringing him the proper insignia, installed him as despot.

George's succession was greeted by several major complications. First, the Turks were to attack him. Second, he, or his advisors, was unhappy about restoring Serbia's recent capital, Beograd, to Sigismund; this caused Sigismund to come with his army to Beograd. Sigismund arrived there a little over a month after Stefan's death, suggesting that he did not trust George to carry out the Tati agreement. To avoid a confrontation and bad relations, Sigismund made it seem that his concern was to prevent the Turks from acquiring this key fortress. For, taking advantage of Stefan's death, they had already invaded Serbia. Sigismund's acquisition of his fortress clearly was not easy. Constantine the Philosopher says the commander of the fortress refused to let anyone into the town until George himself arrived. And Sigismund's dated documents from this period, from 17 September to 30 October 1427, are dated "near Beograd" (i.e., at his camp). Only on 31 October is a document dated *in* Beograd. At the same time that Sigismund was impatiently waiting outside of Beograd, the Turks were actively plundering the Serbian countryside and besieging Novo Brdo, Kruševac, and several other fortified towns.

George arrived at Beograd at some point in October. Even so, it seems the town was still not surrendered to Sigismund. Instead a council meeting was held to discuss what answer to give Sigismund. According to a monk named Radoslav from a monastery near Golubac, the council was attended by clerics. Radonić believes, therefore, that the Orthodox clergy was particularly opposed to turning the city over to the Catholic Hungarians. However, with the Turks in the land, it seemed sensible not to antagonize one's strongest possible ally. So more practical heads prevailed, and with the consent of the council George ordered the surrender of Beograd to Sigismund.

The Hungarian historian Turosci says that in exchange for Beograd George received from Sigismund various towns and settlements in Hungary, some of which had previously been held by Stefan and some of which were newly granted to him by Sigismund. Sigismund then extracted an oath of loyalty from George and recognized him as the ruler of Serbia. Thus it seems that George was willing to surrender Beograd only as part of a deal, and Sigismund, knowing the Turks were in the vicinity and wanting to regain Beograd, a fortress vitally important for the defense of Hungary's southern border, was willing to make all sorts of concessions to get it as quickly as possible. Golubac was also to be returned to Hungary. However, its commander refused to turn it over and soon thereafter surrendered it to the Turks.

Since George is thereafter documented holding parts of Mačva and appointing officials there, its disposition is a matter of scholarly controversy. Did Sigismund take back both Beograd and Mačva and then re-grant Mačva to George? Or by this time was Mačva divided, with part reverting to Sigismund and part being retained by George? For we have no way to be certain that the term "Mačva" in the fifteenth century referred to the exact same extensive territory that it had referred to in the thirteenth. Dinić argued that despite the Tati agreement all Mačva remained under the Brankovići. He also thought it likely that this retention of Mačva had Sigismund's agreement. And subsequently Spremić has provided sufficient documentary evidence of Serbian activity in Mačva, including its northernmost parts, to demonstrate conclusively that Serbia held Mačva until the Turks conquered it in 1439.[16]

The Ottomans continued their offensive against Serbia in 1428, acquiring in that year Niš, Kruševac, and Golubac. Despite their other successes, the Turks could not take the rich mining town of Novo Brdo, which resisted a siege of nearly a year. Sigismund led his forces to try to recover Golubac. He was defeated, however, and forced to retreat. As a result of the 1428 campaign George had to accept Ottoman suzerainty, owing both an annual tribute of fifty thousand ducats and military service, with the stipulation that he had to lead his troops in person.

Zeta and Albania, 1427–30

While the Ottomans were raiding Serbia in 1427 and 1428, it seems the Djuraševići of Zeta took advantage of Serbia's difficulties to more-or-less declare their independence. At about this time they revived the old name of Crnojević, from the broader family of which they seem to have been a part. This name had fallen into disfavor at the beginning of the century when Radič Crnojević had clashed with the Balšići.

In 1429, though at peace with Serbia, the Ottomans supported an attack upon Zeta. Supplied with some Turkish troops, the attack was led by a Stefan Balšić, probably a son of Constantine Balšić, who was seeking to acquire his family's former lands. He quickly obtained military support from Koja Zakarija of Danj, who was angry at Serbia for pressuring Ragusan merchants to use a new trade route that by-passed Danj, where Koja had his customs station. Tanush Minor Dukagjin also joined Balšić's offensive, and the invaders took the town of Drivast, though the Serbian garrison was able to retain the citadel. Venice, realizing that its Zetan possessions were threatened also, wanted to make an alliance with Branković against Balšić.

The following year, 1430, after Thessaloniki fell, the sultan decided to take advantage of the newly re-opened route to Greece to concentrate on Epirus, whose ruler Carlo Tocco had just died. But Murad also had sufficient troops to spare for an attack upon Epirus' neighbor Albania. Ottoman troops under Ishak beg, governor of Skopje, marched through Albania to besiege Durazzo. Durazzo, held by the Venetians, withstood the attack, but the countryside surrounding it was plundered. George Branković, having made peace with the Turks, had no interest in risking his position by making any sort of alliance with the Venetians, against whom the Turks were now directing their offensive. The Turks at the same time occupied the bulk of John Castriot's lands, installing garrisons in at least two of his former fortresses while razing the rest. The Ottomans were angry at him, for, despite submitting to Ottoman suzerainty, he had retained close relations with Venice. Giving up Stefan Balšić's cause, the Turks also turned against his allies. They took Danj, expelling Koja Zakarija. Nothing more is heard of him. They also occupied much or even most of the Dukagjins' lands; the Dukagjin chiefs, Tanush Major and Nicholas, fled to Skadar. Enjoying at the moment good relations with Branković, the Turks allowed the Serbian garrison to regain control of Drivast for Serbia. As a result of the improvement in Branković's fortunes and of the fact the Turks were supporting him, the Djuraševići-Crnojevići submitted again to Branković. We can be sure this submission was only nominal. Not only did they exhibit no interest in Branković's affairs, but there was no way he could exercise actual authority in the mountains of Zeta.

Serbia in the 1430s

George Branković erected the great fortress of Smederevo at the junction of the Morava and Danube rivers, which became Serbia's last capital. This fortress was built rapidly, as might be expected with the Ottoman threat ever present. It was erected by forced levies at the expense of considerable suffering. The initial fortress was completed in 1430, with further walls erected later in the decade. His wife Irina (Jerina in Serbian) Cantacuzena, whom he had married in 1414, may well have had a major role in this undertaking. This would explain why she became known as the Cursed (Prokleta) Jerina in the Serbian epics. A lively market developed in Smederevo. A Ragusan colony quickly appeared, and a mint was also established there.

Many Greeks, associates of George's Greek wife, including her brothers Thomas and George Cantacuzenus, who also lived at court, came thither in the 1430s and had considerable impact on Serbian court life and culture. Thus despite the death of Stefan Lazarević and the loss of Beograd to Hungary, Serbian culture did not suffer an eclipse. Smederevo and Novo Brdo—the latter had also been active culturally under Stefan—were centers of culture. And literati continued to turn out translations and new literary efforts of various genres: Church literature, chronicles, and anthologies containing a varied assortment of texts or fragments from texts. George Branković was an active patron and possessed a large library that in addition to Slavic works had Latin and Greek books as well; George knew both these languages and seems also to have had an understanding of Hungarian and Turkish. Unlike his predecessor, he liked music and supported an outstanding Church choir at Smederevo. He, however, was not a church builder, though he donated money to existing churches and also interested himself in their repair and renovation. His major building efforts, a sign of the times, were fortifications.

When Constantinople fell in 1453, many more Greeks came to Serbia. In fact George was to ransom from Turkish slavery large numbers of Greeks, both noblemen and Church figures, whom he welcomed to Smederevo. His court and its officials reflected the increasingly international character of Serbia, as it acquired emigrés from the neighboring lands falling under the Turks. At Novo Brdo his military commander was an Albanian, and his official representative in charge of customs was a Byzantine of the Cantacuzenus family. That representative's son, Demetrius Cantacuzenus, remained in Novo Brdo after its fall to the Turks and in the 1460s and 1470s was a prominent cultural figure. Demetrius was to build churches, expand an already large library—containing works of and on Church fathers, religious topics, Greek classics, history, geography, natural science, and medicine—and be a significant Serbian-language writer on religious and moralistic subjects. In Smederevo, George's finance minister was from Dubrovnik and his chancellor was a native of Kotor who also had a large library in Smederevo that among its collection contained many works by Italian humanists. George also had Hungarians and even some Turks in his service.

George, as noted in our discussion on Bosnia, became involved in Bosnian affairs in the early 1430s, as a result of which his armies took a large chunk of Bosnian territory in Usora, including Zvornik and Teočak, along the Drina. These acquisitions served as a buffer between Srebrnica and the Bosnian kingdom and thus provided additional security for Srebrnica's defense.

The Ottomans, meanwhile, beefed up the fortifications of Kruševac on the new Serbian border. That fortress became the center from which Ottoman raids were dispatched against Serbia. Under continual Ottoman pressure George finally, in 1433, had to agree to the marriage of his daughter Mara to Sultan Murad II. The marriage took place in Adrianople in September 1435. As her dowry the sultan received the districts of Toplica and Dubočica. These regions were most probably surrendered to Murad in 1433 at the time Mara's engagement was concluded. Despite this marriage Ottoman raids continued, and by the late 1430s the Turks were occupying large chunks of territory. In 1437 Braničevo fell. And in 1438 the Ottomans took Ravanica, Borač, and Serbia's Ostrovica.

During the 1430s George Branković tried to steer a middle course between the Turks and Hungarians. At the same time that he married Mara to Murad II, he married his other daughter, Catherine (also known as Cantacuzina), to Ulrich of Celje, one of Hungary's leading noblemen. By 1439 Serbia, owing to the Ottoman annexations of 1437 and 1438, was greatly reduced in size. As a result, Sigismund's successor Albert began putting pressure on George to yield Smederevo to Hungary, arguing that Hungary could defend it better against the Turks than George could. George may well have felt unable to defend it and have agreed to yield it. For, according to one account, he exchanged it for more property in Hungary, including Világosvár (Világos) and one hundred and ten villages. Smederevo fell to the Ottomans anyway, after a three-month siege, in August 1439.

Orbini gives a second, but similar, account of Smederevo's fall. George went to Hungary to seek aid, leaving his son Gregory (Grgur) to defend it. No Hungarian help was forthcoming. The Turks attacked, and, despite the fortress's strong walls, Gregory was forced to surrender the town because it lacked supplies to feed the garrison. Presumably relying on an oral tradition hostile to George's wife Jerina, Orbini blames the lack of supplies on her; for wanting cash, she had sold the town's grain reserves. Murad received Gregory kindly and granted him the former Branković lands in southern Serbia as a fief. Orbini states that Gregory was to share the rule of these lands with his brother Stefan, who had been living for some time at the Ottoman court as a hostage. Whether or not this was the way that Gregory acquired this appanage, we do know he was holding it the following year. In the course of 1439 the Ottomans also took Srebrnica and Mačva. At the end of the Ottoman campaign of 1439 the Serbs retained only Novo Brdo, which again that year had withstood an Ottoman attack, and their territory in Zeta. The Turks were back in 1440. For six months they laid siege to Hungarian-held Beograd, but failed to take it.

Zeta in the Late 1430s and Early 1440s

Faced with the end of Serbia and holding only Novo Brdo, George Branković was still at least the suzerain of Zeta. In addition, the Turks had allowed his son Gregory, as their vassal, to govern the former Branković lands in southern Serbia. During the winter of 1440–41 George traveled through his son's province to Zeta, whose territory the Turks had as yet made no attempt to annex, to try to organize some sort of resistance to save Serbia.

At this time the Djurašević, once again known as the Crnojević, were still the major family in Zeta. The older generation of this family seems to have died out, for the brothers George and Lješ are not heard of after 1435. George Djurašević had left four sons; the eldest and family leader was Stefan, who had played an active military and political role under his father for several decades. Stefan was married to Mara, the daughter of John Castriot and sister of Skanderbeg. By this time, with Serbia collapsing, the Crnojević had for all practical purposes become the independent rulers of a good part of Zeta. However, they had not yet broken with George Branković. They received him cordially, even though they did not fall in with his plans. At the same time, foreseeing the end of Serbia, Stefan Vukčić Kosača of Bosnia laid plans to move against Zeta and annex as much of it as possible to his growing realm. Stefan Vukčić was already by this time negotiating with various nobles in Zeta. He was to be the greatest impediment to the creation of an independent state in Zeta under the Crnojević.

Meanwhile in April 1441, accusing him—probably justly—of plotting against the sultan, the Ottomans removed Gregory Branković from his governorship. In May 1441, on the orders of the sultan, they blinded him and his brother Stefan for treason. Nothing was to come of their father's efforts to raise resistance either. In June 1441 the last Serbian city, Novo Brdo, fell to the Turks. George Branković, on the coast at the time, still trying to organize some sort of resistance, soon moved to Hungary, where he took up residence on his lands there. Serbia, annexed by the Ottomans, disappeared as a state. Orbini provides a story which cannot be confirmed in the contemporary documents: He states that George was visiting Bar, when the Ottomans opened negotiations with the citizens of Bar to hand him over. Forced to flee, he went to Budva, where he found things no better. The Crnojević, operating in the area, turned against him and planned to capture him. To avoid this George made a hasty escape on a Ragusan ship.

The fall of Serbia resulted in the interior of Zeta becoming independent under its various noblemen and tribesmen. For without a power base in Serbia to provide troops, George Branković had no means to assert his suzerainty over or to try to establish himself as the ruler of even a small part of Zeta. The Crnojevići set about trying to win over or subdue the other nobles of the land without losing the loyalty of those who had already submitted to them. They also had to prepare to defend their territory against attack from Stefan Vukčić, from an extension of Venetian authority in the coastal regions, and also sooner or later from the Turks.

By this time Zeta was coming more and more to be called Crna Gora (Black Mountain or Montenegro), the name by which the region has been known from that time to the present. Though this name is associated with the state—if such a loose federation of tribesmen can be called a state—created by the Crnojevići, the name is older and was originally associated with the Paštrovići. In the late fourteenth century, the mountain system, including Lovćen, behind the Gulf of Kotor was coming to be called the Black Mountain. Much of this region in the early fifteenth century was dominated by the large Paštrović tribe, and soon the term came to refer to the territory that the tribe controlled. Early in the fifteenth century George Djurašević became active in this area as well, at times controlling much of it. Presumably his association with this region caused the name to become attached to the territory he controlled; then as his family extended its sway over a large part of Zeta, the name Crna Gora came more and more to replace the previous name, Zeta.

In 1441, after negotiations with various nobles of Zeta, Stefan Vukčić of Bosnia marched with his army into Upper Zeta, reaching the Morača River. Stefan Crnojević, who presumably had been unable to raise sufficient support to resist the Bosnians, seems to have decided to make the best of the situation. He came forward to treat with Stefan Vukčić. Crnojević, caught between Stefan Vukčić and Venice, may also have submitted to the former as the lesser of two evils. Stefan Vukčić was then occupying a region including five katuns; for Crnojević's submission this region was restored to the Crnojević brothers, with two katuns going to Stefan and one each to each of the other three brothers. Stefan Crnojević's son John was then handed over to Stefan Vukčić as a hostage. He spent the next decade at the Kosača court. Fear for the welfare of his son seems to have played a major role in Stefan Crnojević's policy thereafter.

Stefan Vukčić continued his march through Zeta, following a policy of extracting submissions from the Zetan nobles and tribesmen and then leaving them in possession of their lands. Among the many he won over in this way were the Albanian Mataguzi and the Bjelopavlić tribe. He soon temporarily won over most of the Paštrović clans. Their long-time vojvoda, Radič Grubačević, disapproved of this and with his brothers remained faithful to Venice, where he went into exile, enjoying a large Venetian pension. His popularity seems to have declined. In the previous year, 1440, he had had to flee to Kotor when his clan had become involved in a blood feud. His return had been made possible by a tribal assembly that ended the feud through a mutual exchange of kumstvos (God-fatherships). The Knez of Kotor also had a role in pacifying the feuding tribesmen, for the final peace had been signed in his palace.

Stefan Vukčić rapidly extended his territory down to the north shore of Lake Skadar; in much of this newly acquired territory he simply extracted homage and left the local nobles to rule. Once there Stefan Vukčić became ambitious to acquire the nominal coastal possessions of the Serbian despot: Bar, Budva, and Drivast. Venice had the same aim. Drivast had remained in the hands of the commander placed over the town by George Branković. This commander was still loyal to George. Budva had been turned over, prior to Serbia's fall, to the Metropolitan of Zeta, who managed the city and supported himself on the income raised from the Svetomiholjska Metohija on the Gulf of Kotor. Bar was still nominally held by George, but it seems to have remained independent under its town council.

In March 1442, after wintering at home, Stefan Vukčić returned to Zeta and, accompanied by Stefan Crnojević, took Bar. He then moved to the district of Budva, which presumably was next on his agenda. Threatened by Stefan Vukčić's alliance with Stefan Crnojević, which presumably would result in the Gulf of Kotor region's being granted to Crnojević as a Kosača vassal, the Paštrovići began to resist Stefan Vukčić. They soon joined the Venetian camp. The Venetians, seeing their own ambitions in danger, stepped up their response. In the summer of 1442 they sent their fleet into the threatened area and opened up a major diplomatic offensive. These efforts soon won over the three younger Crnojević brothers, who seem to have believed their elder brother was becoming a puppet of Stefan Vukčić and thereby forfeiting the family's dominant role in Zeta. As a result of the younger brothers' defection, the two Stefans confiscated their lands in Upper Zeta. The three younger brothers merely strengthened their ties with Venice. Next, faced with the Venetian fleet, the Metropolitan of Zeta surrendered Budva to Venice in August 1442. The Venetians were to hold Budva until 1797. Kotor at once dispatched its forces to reassert itself along the gulf and seized the Svetomiholjska Metohija, the major source of income for the metropolitan. Venice next attacked and took, still in August 1442, Drivast. Winning over the local Pamaliot tribe, the Venetians established a strong position along the Bojana River. They began planning their attack upon Bar.

Stefan Vukčić, who had returned to Bosnia to defend his lands there against an attack from King Tvrtko II, hurried back to Zeta. He dispatched his troops through Venice's Skadar territory, which they plundered. And once again he secured submissions from his supporters in the region between Onogošt (Nikšić) and Lake Skadar. Venice did not back down, however; it continued to woo the local nobles, agreeing to their retention of any territory Stefan Vukčić had previously awarded them. In this way it soon won over the Bjelopavlići. Various other tribal chiefs followed suit. In the late spring of 1443 Venice took Bar, which it was to hold until 1571. With this conquest the

Venetians took possession of the whole Zetan coast. And Stefan Vukčić found himself pushed back to his interior possessions in Upper Zeta. He was unable to turn to his Ottoman suzerain for aid, because the Ottomans were occupied with the Christian Crusade of 1443. This crusade, as we shall see, resulted in George Branković's return to Serbia. The treaty concluded between crusaders and sultan at the campaign's end in 1444 restored Serbia—defined as twenty-four named fortresses—as a state and recognized George as its ruler. George immediately accepted the sultan's suzerainty again. The sultan recognized him not only as ruler of Serbia but also of Srebrnica and Zeta.

Stefan Vukčić, who had been operating partially in Branković's name and also as a vassal of the sultan, had to go along with the sultan's decision. Stefan Vukčić renounced his Zetan ambitions and surrendered Upper Zeta with Medun to George. Stefan even supported George militarily in his war for Srebrnica against the King of Bosnia. Most of the nobles of Upper Zeta soon submitted to George, though many of them may have done so only nominally; those submitting included Stefan Crnojević. However, faced with Stefan Vukčić's withdrawal and the opposition of Venice, which was allied to his three brothers, Stefan Crnojević made peace with Venice in March 1444 and soon thereafter with his brothers. However, his peace with his brothers was an uneasy one, and tensions remained among them. But even so, the Crnojevići, headed by Stefan, remained the most powerful local family. The renunciation of his Zetan ambitions made it possible for Stefan Vukčić to conclude peace with Venice as well. After reaching agreement in 1444, Stefan Vukčić and the Venetians signed a treaty in 1445.

The fall of his protector, Serbia, and Venice's acquisition of Budva in 1442 led to new difficulties for the Orthodox Metropolitan of Zeta. Kotor stepped up its action against the Orthodox, ignoring Venice's advice to work gradually. Kotor expelled Orthodox priests from the towns and villages along its gulf and by 1452 had turned over almost all, if not all, of the Orthodox churches of this region to Catholic clerics. By 1455 the last Serbian monk had been expelled from the Gulf of Kotor. Lands belonging to Orthodox monasteries and the Orthodox Church met the same fate. Thus the Serbian Church had almost no sources of income along the coast. The Venetians allowed the harassed metropolitan to move from Budva in 1442 to a monastery on Lake Skadar, which was under direct Venetian authority. But his tenure there was to be of short duration. In 1452 he was to be driven from his monastery and replaced by a Greek monk who had accepted the Union of the Churches proclaimed at Florence. The Venetians recognized this Uniate as the Metropolitan of Zeta and ordered that all Orthodox Church financial dues go to him. The protests of Orthodox clergy and believers were ignored. The deposed Orthodox metropolitan withdrew into the mountains of Zeta, moving from one village to another, existing almost without income, and in no position to maintain ties with his clergy or defend his embattled Church, until finally, supported by the Crnojevići, he established himself in 1485 at Cetinje, which was to become the permanent seat of the Metropolitan of Zeta.

Albania in the 1430s

Meanwhile, the Albanians suffered severe losses to the Turks as a result of the Ottoman campaigns of 1430 and 1431. Particularly hard hit were the Dukag-jins and Castriots, who lost most of their lands in the vicinity of the Mati River. The full extent of their losses is not known, but it seems probable that the Turks took over most of the fortresses as far north as Danj and the Drin River. Thus both families suffered considerable eclipse. As they had a decade earlier in central Albania, the Turks began registering these new lands and assigning a good portion of them as fiefs (timars). Once again most of the timars were assigned to Ottoman servitors from Anatolia, while about a quarter of the known timars were assigned to submissive members of the Albanian elite, some of whom accepted Islam. As a result of the assignment of these fiefs, many members of the Albanian elite were dispossessed. Conse-quently, already in 1431 various mountain regions (for example, Tepelene) resisted the cadastral surveys. Thus much of the territory surrounding the fortresses taken in 1430 was in fact not subdued, for the inhabitants had taken up armed resistance against the establishment of these timars.

In 1432 Andrew Thopia revolted against his Ottoman overlords and defeated a small Ottoman detachment in the mountains of central Albania. His success inspired other Albanian chiefs, in particular George Arianite (Araniti) who held lands along the middle course of the Shkumbi River. Hearing—falsely, as it turned out—that Murad II had died, Arianite raised a large rebellion of his own tribesmen in 1433. The revolt rapidly spread throughout Albania from the region of Valona up to Skadar. The rebels defeated three major Ottoman offensives between 1433 and 1436, including a large force led in 1434 by Ishak beg, the Ottoman governor of Skopje. Nicholas Dukagjin took advantage of the rebellion to return to his family's former lands; in taking them over, he submitted to Venetian suzerainty. He also took Danj, which he soon yielded to Venice. However, the Venetians, learning that Murad was still alive and fearing to provoke the Turks, repudiated Dukagjin and broke off all relations with him. To show their good faith, the Venetians returned Danj to the Turks by 1435. At this time, though summoned home by his relatives back in Albania, Skanderbeg did nothing; he remained in the east, loyal to the sultan, serving actively in Asia Minor. In 1436 the Ottomans sent a massive army into Albania that finally put down the revolt; the campaign was savage, marked by massacres and the erection of pyramids of skulls. The Ottoman troops also devastated parts of northern Epirus. George Arianite, who had probably been the most successful rebel commander, escaped and took to the mountains with a small group of followers; from there he continued his resistance as a guerrilla. He was not to be subdued and was still active when the major revolt of 1443 broke out. He was to participate actively in that rebellion as well.

After his triumph in 1436, the sultan left those Albanian chiefs who had submitted to him in possession of a considerable portion of their lands and with considerable autonomy; however, he also took more of their sons off east as hostages. The sultan remained angry at the Dukagjins and forbade Tanush Major Dukagjin to return to Albania. Tanush briefly served as vojvoda for Venice's Skadar district, but then he was suspected by the Venetians of treason and arrested. He was soon sent to Italy. His guilt was not proved and so he was released from confinement; but, fearing he might in revenge take actions against Venice's interests, the Venetians forced him to live thereafter in Italy. He lived in exile, on a Venetian pension, in Padua, never to return to his native region.

Byzantium and the Turks after Mehemmed I's Death (1421)

The Byzantines maintained good relations with Mehemmed I (1413–21), the candidate they had supported to gain the Ottoman sultanate, through his reign. Having won the throne and then having had to devote his attention to consolidating his position, Mehemmed had not tried to wrest territory away from the empire. Matters changed after his death and the Byzantines were responsible for provoking the troubles that befell them. For, at the death of Mehemmed, the empire supported a pretender against Mehemmed's legitimate successor, Murad II (1421–51), a ploy that failed. This policy had the effect of stirring Murad's wrath against the empire and of giving him an excuse to terminate existing agreements with Byzantium and to resume the Ottoman offensive against the empire. However, one should not exaggerate the importance of Byzantium's misfired policy; for we can be sure that even if the empire had greeted Murad II with timbrels and dancing, sooner or later the Ottomans would have resumed their offensive against its territory.

Murad II besieged Constantinople in 1421 and then unleashed a raid through Greece that ravaged the Peloponnesus in 1423. This militant policy threatened Thessaloniki, which the empire felt unable to defend against a major assault; so, it assigned the city to Venice in 1423. The empire soon knuckled under to Ottoman pressure, becoming a tribute-paying vassal of the Ottomans again in 1424. However, this submission did not stop Ottoman raids; for the Ottomans had many excuses, like the surrender of Thessaloniki to Venice, to continue their raids. Pressure was kept up against Thessaloniki until the Ottomans took it by assault in 1430.

In desperate straits, the new emperor John VIII (1425–48), Manuel's son and successor, reached the conclusion that salvation for the empire could come only from the West. However, to obtain Western support, the empire needed to approach the pope; and the pope would give his blessing to aid only if the Byzantines accepted Church Union. Needless to say, as we have seen in earlier attempts to effect Union, the Byzantine populace strongly opposed it; at least, the Greeks opposed Union on papal terms, and the pope would accept no others. John VIII initiated negotiations with Rome anyway, and in November 1437 he, his patriarch, and a large assemblage of bishops set off for Rome.

Their arrival in Italy created enormous protocol problems. For though it was accepted that the pope had honorary precedence over the patriarch, the two parties held different views on how the pope stood vis à vis the emperor. Bickering over ceremonial matters began at the very start, when Patriarch Joseph, though willing to admit papal primacy in precedence, was not willing to kiss the pope's foot. Pope Eugene IV backed down on this issue and agreed to a more equal embrace, though he insisted this greeting should occur in a private audience and not in public. A host of questions about seating followed. Both sides agreed the pope should sit higher than the patriarch, but disagreed over the placement of the emperor's seat. On this issue the pope won out; for the Greeks were at a distinct disadvantage in being in Italy as supplicants, with the further disadvantage of being maintained (fed and housed) by the pope.

In early 1438 the council to effect Church Union opened in Ferrara and shortly thereafter moved to Florence—it is known by the name of either city. The Roman side had many advantages: the council was meeting in its territory; in hosting the aid-seeking Greeks, the Roman Church was literally feeding the Greek guests; and the Roman side was united. Each Roman debater advanced the same theology. The Greek party, on the other hand, was divided between those interested in compromise and those bent on arguing the Greek position. Within these two categories all sorts of individual positions on particular points existed. To make discussion more difficult, the council did not address issues directly. Thus it did not ask: is *Filioque* (the double descent of the Holy Spirit from the Father *and the Son*) correct doctrine or not? Instead, the question was debated indirectly through argument as to whether or not it was permitted to add to the creed. For the Greeks claimed, correctly, that *Filioque* was an addition to the Nicene Creed. The debate went on endlessly, and single speakers could and did ramble on for several days at a stretch.

After interminable discussions the council finally promulgated its edict of Union in July 1439. The Greeks were allowed to keep their own rite, service, and language of service. They were also allowed to retain leavened bread—rather than the Latin unleavened bread—in the communion wafer. But they had to recognize papal primacy—in terms only slightly modified from the original papal position—and accept the Latin position on all disputed theological points, including the major issue of *Filioque*. Thus the Greek delegation accepted the Latin belief that the Holy Spirit descends from the Father and the Son, rather than from the Father alone as the Greek Church believed. The Latins had throughout insisted on their position and had strongly rejected a compromise advanced by some Greeks that the Holy Spirit descended from the Father *through* the Son.

John VIII, his patriarch, and his bishops—except for Mark Eugenius, the Bishop of Ephesus—accepted the Union. However, the results of the council were not as dramatic as they might seem. First, other than one major crusading effort, which was to have initial successes in 1443, little Western help was to follow. Furthermore, since most Byzantines detested the West, the papacy, and all the variant beliefs and practices of the Roman Church, the Byzantine people refused to accept Union. A slogan was heard in Constantinople that it would be far better to see the Turkish turban in the city than the Latin tiara. Thus the council divided the population at a critical moment when the empire needed a unified populace to face the Turkish threat. The Union was also very bad for popular morale, particularly since it contributed to defeatism among the Greeks. For most Byzantines seem to have believed that imperial decline was a result of their sins; to commit the further sin of selling out to the heretical Latins would surely lose God's favor completely and bring about the fall of the empire. Thus the great majority of the population remained Anti-Union and avoided Unionist churches.

The lone dissenter who had attended the Council of Florence, Mark Eugenius, became an instant hero and led the Anti-Unionist party. At his death George Gennadius Scholarius, one of the most learned men of his time, became the leader of the Anti-Unionists. Interestingly enough, George Scholarius was much taken with Catholic theology and read Thomas Aquinas with great interest and approval. But though he had sympathy for much in Catholicism, he detested the papacy's pretensions; believing the pope had no right to dictate to the whole Church or to meddle in dioceses other than his own, Scholarius strongly upheld the Greek belief that disputes must be settled by Church councils, not by papal fiat. The Anti-Unionists had most of the population behind them and wrangled with the smaller number of Unionists—most of whom were unhappy with the Union theologically but had accepted it as a necessary evil in order to obtain aid against the greater evil of the Turks. The wrangling continued until the fall of the empire.

The Council of Florence also cost the Greek Church considerable prestige in the broader Orthodox world. The Patriarchs of Antioch, Alexandria, and Jerusalem—the other three ancient and great patriarchs besides Constantinople and Rome—all condemned it, as did the Muscovites who saw Florence as a betrayal of the true faith. However, it should be noted that for the empire's survival in this world, this loss of prestige among the Orthodox was unimportant. The other three Eastern patriarchs all resided in Turkish territory, and thus were useless in supplying aid for the defense of the empire, and Moscow, though independent, was too distant and too weak to provide help against the Turkish threat.

The Morea and Non-Turkish Greece

In this period the emperor continued the policy of granting appanages to high family members, to his brothers and sons. The Peloponnesus (Morea) was always so assigned, sometimes to one family member and sometimes divided between two or even three relatives. The holder or holders bore the title of despot. Through the 1430s when there was more than one despot, the individuals tended to co-operate. Later on, multiple despots frequently quarreled, undermining the unity, and therefore the defense, of the peninsula and giving the Ottomans, who at times provided troops for one side or the other, a foothold in the area. Until it was ceded to Venice, Thessaloniki had frequently been assigned to an imperial family member. In 1414 it had been assigned to Manuel's son Andronicus. Selymbria on the Sea of Marmora was also regularly assigned as an appanage.

In the last chapter we discussed the despotate of the Morea (Peloponnesus) down to 1407, when Manuel's brother Theodore died and Manuel installed his minor son Theodore (II) as despot in the Morea under a regency. The Morea at this time enjoyed considerable peace. It was distant from the Ottoman civil war then occurring in the east-central Balkans. Thus the Morea suffered no Ottoman raids from the Battle of Ankara (1402) until 1423. Furthermore, the Morea was now stronger than the Latin principalities in the Peloponnesus. Thus the despotate was not threatened by the Latins; it was usually the initiator of confrontations with them and usually fought with success. Thus it gradually obtained further territory from the declining Latin state of Achaea. Freedom from outside invasion also allowed the Peloponnesus to prosper agriculturally and economically: metals were mined, and silk and cotton were produced, along with wine, wheat, wax, and honey. In fact the Morea seems to have been self-sufficient agriculturally.

A certain amount of disruption was caused by further Albanian migration and settlement, but this had benefits as well. Albanians, settled in deserted and mountainous regions, added to the number of farmers and shepherds and thus contributed to increased agricultural production and tax income. The Albanians also provided further, and excellent, soldiers. However, the Albanians were also a source of disorder and brigandage. For though their settlement at times took place on vacant lands, at others it resulted in the ousting of already settled agriculturalists. And since many Albanians were shepherds and continued to be so, a portion of Morean farm land went out of crop production to become pasture land.

In March 1415 Emperor Manuel arrived in the Morea, investing his son Theodore, who was now of age, with full authority. For defense Manuel decided to construct a fortification across the Isthmus of Corinth, the famous Hexamilion. Its construction was extremely rapid—taking only thirty-five days in April and May—but it stirred up local opposition, for it required higher taxes to finance it and levies of peasants to build and later to man it. As a result there was, as we shall see, a certain amount of unrest among the local nobility (resulting in a small rebellion in July 1415, which Manuel put down) and enough dissatisfaction among the peasants for many to abandon their lands and migrate to Venetian territory. The Venetians still held the cities and environs of Modon, Coron, Argos, and Nauplia on the peninsula. Despite Theodore's and Manuel's demands, the Venetians refused to send these peasants back. Feeling threatened by the increasing strength of the despotate and by Manuel's presence, the Prince of Achaea, Centurione Zaccaria, hurried to Mistra to pay homage to Manuel and to accept him as his suzerain.

Shortly after Manuel's return to Constantinople, he sent a second son, John, the future emperor, to assist Theodore in the Peloponnesus. They took further action in 1416 against the remnants of Achaea, which since 1407 had been under Venetian protection. It is often stated that this protection—exerted diplomatically by Venice—saved the remnants of Achaea from the despotate's successful 1416 campaign that brought the bulk of the Peloponnesus under the authority of the despotate. After that campaign the Latins—excluding Venice—retained only Patras and the regions of Arcadia and Elis.

In this period of economic prosperity and no major warfare, considerable building took place, particularly in the Morean capital of Mistra. Many beautiful churches were erected and adorned with fine frescoes. A lively Byzantine-style court was maintained, where a variety of leading literary figures, including philosophers and theologians, participated and wrote. Theodore II was an active participant in these activities and was considered one of the best mathematicians of his time. He was also a literary patron and had considerable interest in theology. Influenced by these Orthodox theologians, and possibly also by political realities, many Latins living in the territory recovered by the Byzantines accepted Orthodoxy. Many of these converts seem to have been gasmoules, the children of mixed Latin-Greek marriages.

The leading figure in the intellectual life at court was George Gemistos Plethon, who had come to Mistra after the death of Theodore I to tutor Theodore II. A philosopher and follower of Plato, he revived Plato's thought and wrote a work on laws. Under the influence of Classical Greek thought rather than the tradition of multi-national empire that had dominated Greek political thinking for the preceding thousand years, Plethon advocated the idea of Hellenism. The term *Hellene* had for centuries had a bad odor within the Christian empire because it connoted a pagan. But Plethon proudly used the term and urged the Greeks to concentrate on a Greek state based on a more homogeneous population and upon the compact and more defensible territory of mainland Greece, rather than to dream of a far-flung, multi-ethnic Roman Empire. Thus Hellenic particularism should replace Roman universalism. He wanted this state—small, consolidated, not over-extended, and based on Hellenism—to be centered in the Peloponnesus, which he believed was readily defensible. Plethon is often seen as the first exponent of Greek nationalism. Plethon wrote prolifically to advance his ideas. He also proposed various legal reforms, including a new law code, and a reordering of society in the Morea.[17] His works, as noted, were highly influenced by Plato. However, as interesting a figure as he was, he had little impact on policy, for the leading political figures were wedded to the preservation of the empire and were not inclined to listen to such proposals. In any case, Mistra was a second center of Greek life, comparable to Constantinople but on a smaller scale. And far from the major warfare involving the Turks, it was a region where Greek life could exist for a while longer with security.

The years of peace came to an abrupt end in 1423 when the Ottomans, as noted, launched a major raid against the Peloponnesus. The raiders broke through the undermanned Hexamilion in May and caused considerable damage before they withdrew with considerable plunder. On this occasion the Turks annexed no territory. The Greeks defeated one Turkish detachment, but an Albanian army that opposed the Turks at Davia near Tripolis in Arcadia was routed. The Turks left a pyramid of eight hundred Albanian heads on the battlefield. The Turks were to return in 1431 with a second major and devastating raid.

Though most works on Byzantine civilization stress the positive side of Morean life in this period up to ca. 1430—excluding the 1423 attack—and emphasize the flowering of culture with its literary, architectural, and artistic achievements, life in the Peloponnesus at this time was not always a bed of roses. Zakythinos argues that, excluding the elite, the general educational level was low.[18] Possibly owing to the presence of large numbers of foreigners, the Greek spoken there was poor. Its culture seems to have been centered in one place, Mistra. There an elite was advancing Greek culture, but it was a narrow, privileged group. The rest of the Peloponnesus, Zakythinos claims, had little high culture; morals and life-style were in general rude. The Turkish raids of 1423 and 1431—and then others in the years to follow—caused devastation.

The nobles, as seen, also caused considerable unrest. The major nobles, some of whom had enormous estates, were for all practical purposes independent rulers of their own lands. The mountainous geography helped them to preserve this independence. Yet it should be stressed that when we speak of the nobles (archons) as local rulers, it means only that they managed their own estates, collecting the state taxes from their peasants and rendering them to the despot—and, of course, ignoring all such taxes and obligations when they could. But they collectively had no general provincial (Morean-wide) authority. They did not form any sort of council to participate in local legislation or in decisions touching on taxes. Those decisions were made by the despots, advised by their own courtiers. And the despots' courtiers tended to consist more of dependents coming from Constantinople than of nobles of local origin. Thus many nobles probably did see the court and despots as foreigners. However, though historians have tended to condemn the nobles and sympathize with the despots, Finlay does note, "it must not be forgotten that what the historian feels compelled to call [their] anarchy, contemporaries dignified with the name of liberty."[19]

A large number of rebellions by the nobility against the empire (or the despots, the imperial representatives on the ground) did occur. In fact in the 1390s, as noted, certain nobles—in particular Paul Mamonas, expelled from Monemvasia—had sought and received Sultan Bayezid's intervention, leading to the Serres meeting. The nobles' independent-mindedness and desire to separate and establish "their own tyrannies" (as one pro-despot source says) continued into the 1420s. Each attempt to raise taxes provoked unrest or even out-and-out rebellion, as we saw in 1415 when Manuel raised taxes to build the Hexamilion. The nobles, after 1402 believing they had little to worry about from the Ottomans and thus little or no need to establish a defense against the Turks, continued thereafter to resist each tax increase or attempt by the despot to centralize political authority or even to centralize the military defense. This resistance, resulting in actual small-scale fighting at times, continued in the years after 1415. These clashes caused a certain amount of destruction and some loss of manpower, thereby weakening the area vis à vis the Turks. Venice, trying to retain its cities in the Morea and wanting to prevent the development of a strong Greek state in the area that might threaten its possessions, encouraged the independence of the magnates.

Life for peasants on estates in the Peloponnesus must have been hard, for we hear of widespread flights of peasants to Venetian territory. The Venetians, needing labor, were happy to receive them. Thus they refused to return them, despite the fact they were obliged to do so under an article in the treaty they had concluded with Manuel. Plethon might dream that the Morea could be the core of a Greek state, but even Greek unity was lacking. And to expect such unity is probably anachronistic, for the fifteenth century fell in a pre-nationalist period, when feelings of community followed religious rather than ethnic lines. Moreover, in this so-called Greek heartland, we find many Latins, gasmoules (who were often Catholics in religion and attached to many Western values), and large numbers of Albanian warrior-tribesmen who were in the process of settling the area. Many of these Albanians did not immediately settle permanently in a particular place but continued to move around the area, providing an unstable element that was not always averse to plundering. Thus the Albanians were a factor contributing to anarchy; however, as noted, they also had a very positive aspect, providing able soldiers for the despot's army.

Cydones was able to say of the Peloponnesus: "Towns and laws disappeared here." An Italian humanist who spent seven years in Greece states that in the Peloponnesus there remained nothing worthy of praise. Stressing barbarian attacks and the laziness of the inhabitants of the region, he states that the Peloponnesus was then deprived of its former wealth and worthy men. The author of a satire speaks of the cruelty of the barbarians and then adds that "the local populace, forgetting God and no longer recognizing the law, cannot even speak Greek properly." And he too stresses the disloyalty of the population to its lord (the despot).

These two pictures, though they clash, are not necessarily contradictory. Prosperity and hardship can co-exist at any given moment in any given place. And when we try to examine a region about which broad generalizations are made, great differences are found between different areas, different classes of the population, and different years. Moreover, large agricultural yields, though signs of prosperity, may encourage heavier taxation, leaving the producers not as wealthy as their yields might suggest and entirely breaking those farmers whose farm production did not fit the general pattern of a year, owing to one misfortune or another. And the high culture of Mistra, though it may have filtered down to some extent to other towns—we know, for example, that George Cantacuzenus had a fine library at Kalavryta—may well have borne little resemblance to the semi-literacy and poor spoken Greek of much of the region's populace. Thus the historians should try to steer a middle course and recognize that both pictures contain elements of the truth.

Throughout the 1420s Theodore was able to hold his own against his Latin neighbors. He drove out Anthony Acciajuoli of Athens when Anthony tried in 1423–24 to conquer Corinth, the former seat of his family. Theodore also did well in various skirmishes against Centurione Zaccaria of Achaea, who was supported by Navarrese troops. Theodore and his brothers also expelled Carlo Tocco from the Morea entirely.

In the last chapter we met Carlo Tocco, Count of Cephalonia, Leukas, Zakynthos, and Ithaca, whose wife Francesca had inherited Corinth from her father, Nerio Acciajuoli. Carlo had tried to establish himself there but had eventually been expelled by Theodore I. Ambitious for holdings in the Peloponnesus but not wanting to challenge Theodore further, he returned to the peninsula shortly after 1402 and seized Elis from Centurione Zaccaria, the Prince of Achaea. Soon Carlo inherited Jannina from his uncle Esau, in 1411. Becoming interested in Epirus, he concentrated his attention against the Albanians who held most of Epirus. By the end of 1416 he had acquired almost all Epirus, including Arta. He was assisted by the local Greeks, who were sick of the anarchy existing under the Albanians. He was also helped by the lack of unity among the different Albanian tribes. Thus Carlo managed to create a large but scattered principality in Greece.

Theodore was unhappy with the foothold that Tocco had gained in the Peloponnesus. Meanwhile Emperor Manuel II died and was succeeded by his son, John VIII (1425–48). John decided to divide the Morea, assigning an appanage there to his and Theodore's younger brother Constantine. As his appanage Constantine received the southwestern Morea. Thus his lands bordered on Centurione Zaccaria's Arcadia and Carlo Tocco's Elis. Theodore does not seem to have objected to Constantine's arrival, and the two brothers co-operated. Deciding on a more aggressive policy, they determined on an offensive to eliminate Tocco's rule in Elis. In 1427 the troops of the two despots, supported by others from Emperor John VIII, took Tocco's main city, the port of Clarenza. The surrender was made to the future well-known historian George Sphrantzes, a native of Monemvasia. The following year, supported by their third brother Thomas, Constantine attacked Elis again and, defeating Carlo's troops, obtained Carlo's niece as a bride with all Elis as her dowry. Thus the Tocco family was expelled from the Peloponnesus and Constantine was able to expand his appanage. A slightly variant account, but one having the same result, was given by the eye-witness Sphrantzes. He claims that in 1427 the two forces met in battle. Defeated and realizing he had no future there, Tocco agreed to the marriage of his niece to Constantine and the surrender of all his Morean forts, including Clarenza. Sphrantzes thus claims that Constantine occupied Clarenza after and as a result of the treaty. Though the first version is probably seen more often, the second, written by Sphrantzes, who was present, probably should be accepted.

Carlo I Tocco then died in Jannina in July 1429. Having no legitimate children, he left his lands to his nephew Carlo II Tocco (1429–48). However, Carlo I's illegitimate sons, who held lands in the region of the Achelous in Aetolia, appealed to the Turks that Carlo II had usurped the lands Carlo I had intended for them. The Ottomans found this a fine excuse to intervene; in October 1430 Ottoman armies appeared before Jannina. The city—represented, it seems, by the local nobility rather than by Tocco or a deputy of his—surrendered on demand and received a charter of privilege from the Ottoman conquerors giving Jannina autonomy, the right to collect and deliver its own taxes, and religious liberty. The Ottomans were to observe this treaty for several centuries thereafter. In 1431 the Ottomans returned to conquer almost all Epirus and Aetolia. Annexing most of it, they allowed Carlo II to hold Arta as an Ottoman vassal. He ruled Arta and its district until he died in 1448. Then, in 1449, the Ottomans expelled his successor Leonardo and directly annexed Arta and the rest of Epirus, excluding Venice's possessions there. The Venetians continued to hold on to Naupaktos (Lepanto) on the north shore of the Gulf of Corinth, which they had acquired in 1407 from the Albanian chief Paul Spata.

Having eliminated the Tocco holdings, Constantine in 1429 turned against Patras, the major Latin city in the Morea, still administered by its Catholic archbishop who recognized only the suzerainty of the pope. Constantine had relatively little difficulty in taking the city, though its citadel held out until May 1430. Theodore was worried about this conquest, fearing that either or both the Venetians and Ottomans might object and decide to take action against the Peloponnesus. These two powers, and the pope also, made verbal objections. However, none of them took any action over it, and the Greeks retained Patras. At the same time Thomas, the third brother, attacked the remnants of Achaea. The Venetians, to whom the elderly Prince of Achaea, Centurione Zaccaria, appealed, refused him aid, so the prince decided to surrender. He offered his daughter Catherine, his only legitimate child, to Thomas and most of his domains as her dowry. Centurione sought to keep only part of Arcadia and the town of Kyparissia for himself for his lifetime, for which he was willing to accept Byzantine suzerainty. After Thomas agreed, a treaty to this effect was signed in September 1429, and Thomas married Catherine in January 1430. Thus Thomas acquired a territorial holding of his own in the Morea. Centurione then died in 1432, and Thomas took Kyparissia and whatever parts of Arcadia Centurione had retained. This put an end to the Principality of Achaea. All the Peloponnesus, except for the four previously noted Venetian towns, was now Greek again. But life was not to be smooth, for already the Ottomans had begun to raid the peninsula again, having carried out a very destructive raid in 1431. At this time the Ottomans were out for plunder and to soften up the area. They were not yet conquering towns or annexing any territory. But the earlier fate of Thessaly and that of most of Epirus in 1430–31 should have been a clear message to the Morea that its days were numbered.

The Byzantine Morea thus found itself divided among the three brothers, with each ruling his own specified territory. After Thomas' new acquisitions in 1432 the boundaries of the Morean territories were readjusted. Thomas, also holding, since 1430, the title of despot, received what had been Constantine's lands in the southwest (with Androusa) and also Constantine's northwestern acquisitions (Elis with Clarenza), while keeping his own Arcadian lands. Constantine took the region north of Arcadia with Kalavryta as well as the northeastern part with Corinth. He also retained Patras. Thus he held the northern and northeastern parts of the peninsula. Theodore retained the southeast with the traditional capital of Mistra. Theodore was given no authority over his brothers, but he did keep an honorary precedence.

Meanwhile Anthony Acciajuoli died in 1435. Having no sons, he left his Attican-Boeotian duchy to Nerio and Anthony, two sons of a cousin. However, Anthony's widow, Maria Melissena, tried to seize power for herself. A Greek, she had considerable local Greek support. Thus her attempt was a threat to local Latin interests. She also sent envoys to try to obtain recognition for her rule from the sultan. Constantine, the Morean despot whose lands bordered on Attica, decided to take advantage of the struggle to see if he could not grab the duchy. He dispatched his troops, still in 1435, across the Isthmus of Corinth into Attica. It is not entirely certain whether he was acting on his own or whether perhaps Maria had sought his support against domestic Latin opponents. Though he occupied parts of Attica for a brief time, Constantine was unable to take any major towns.

Meanwhile, the Latin aristocracy suspected that if Maria found herself in greater difficulties, she would certainly try to turn the duchy over to her fellow Greek, Constantine; this, the aristocrats believed, would result in the duchy's being annexed by the despotate and cost them their lands and positions. Sphrantzes, in fact, claims that Maria did try to effect this, offering Constantine Athens in exchange for other lands in the Morea. To forestall this danger, the Latin nobles rose up and overthrew her, establishing young Nerio II as the duke in Athens. Thus Constantine's attempt failed, and he soon withdrew, leaving the Athenian duchy to the victor in the local succession struggle, Nerio II. Nerio quickly agreed to accept Ottoman suzerainty and ruled over the duchy until 1451—except for the years 1439–41, when he was briefly ousted by his brother Anthony II.

On the whole the three brothers in the Morea co-operated, but tensions developed between Theodore and Constantine in the mid-1430s. In those years it became apparent to Theodore that his brother, Emperor John VIII, who had no sons, had begun to favor Constantine as his heir over Theodore, even though Theodore was the elder. Constantine found himself opposed by both Theodore and Thomas in various small local issues, and Sphrantzes says that small-scale fighting actually occurred before imperial ambassadors brought about peace. Then in 1437, when John VIII went west to the Council of Ferrara-Florence, he turned the empire and Constantinople over to Constantine to rule as regent. Theodore was assigned temporary rule over Constantine's lands in the Morea. Theodore was not happy with the favor shown Constantine on this occasion.

The Council of Florence increased family tensions. For Constantine and Thomas supported John's decision to accept Church Union. Theodore, the scholarly brother who had long been interested in theology and was much more strongly Orthodox in his beliefs, adamantly opposed the Union on theological grounds. The youngest brother, Demetrius, who then held the Selymbria appanage, was Anti-Union too. In 1442 or 1443 John VIII, distrusting Demetrius, became worried over his holding an appanage so close to Constantinople, from which, should he obtain Ottoman support, he might try to seize the capital. So, John decided to re-assign appanages. He ordered Demetrius to the Peloponnesus and offered the Selymbria-Mesembria appanage to Constantine. Demetrius revolted and with a Turkish retinue ravaged the suburbs of Constantinople. Peace was soon concluded, and Constantine assumed control of the Selymbria appanage for a short time. Then deciding on a new plan, John sent him back to the Morea. John now gave the Selymbria appanage to the more level-headed Theodore, who occupied it in March 1444.

In the Morea Constantine received the senior appanage that Theodore had held, which included Laconia and was centered in Mistra. He also acquired the appanage in the northern Morea, including Patras and Corinth, that he had held prior to his transfer to Selymbria. Thomas continued to hold his appanage in the west. Demetrius, presumably in disfavor, received no appanage at the time. Theodore remained in Selymbria until he died in the summer of 1448, a few months before the death of his imperial brother. Constantine during this period maintained cordial relations with his brother Thomas. Constantine also made various concessions to the local nobles, trying to infringe less upon their rule over their own lands and assigning important Morean governorships to certain important local aristocrats. As a result of these concessions, Constantine won their agreement to certain special levies he wanted for defense and, as we shall see in the next chapter, in 1443 for offense.

NOTES

1. P. Živković, *Tvrtko II Tvrtković* (Sarajevo, 1981).

2. Resti, *Chronica Ragusina*, p. 264.

3. H. Šabanović, "Pitanje turske vlasti u Bosni do pohoda Mehmeda II 1463 g.," *Godišnjak Društva istoričara Bosne i Hercegovine* 7 (1955): 37–51.

4. On the Bosnian Church, see Fine, *The Bosnian Church*.

5. On the stećci, see M. Wenzel, *Ukrasni motivi na stećcima* (Sarajevo, 1965), and M. Wenzel, "Bosnian and Herzegovinian Tombstones—Who Made Them and Why," *Südost-Forschungen* 21 (1962): 102–43.

6. M. Dinić, "Prilozi za istoriju vatrenog oružja u Dubrovniku i susednim zemljama," *Glas* (SKA) 161 (1934): 57–97.

7. This section is much indebted to M. Šunjić, *Dalmacija u XV stoljeću* (Sarajevo, 1967).

8. A detailed description of the military marches and their defense responsibilities can be found in R. Petar, "Poslednje godine balkanske politike Kralja Žigmunda (1435–1437)," *Godišnjak Filozofskog fakulteta* (Novi Sad) 12, no. 1 (1969): 89–90. Petar also notes that at this time Sigismund borrowed vast sums of money from his vassals and as security gave them lands in Croatia and southern Hungary in areas often struck by Turkish raids. In this way he forced his vassals to assume broader defense responsibilities.

9. Kilia at the mouth of the Danube alone held out. And though it fell to the Turks in 1420, the Moldavians occupied it in about 1424. The port then held out in the hands of one or the other of the Rumanian principalities or in those of Hungary until the Turks finally conquered it in 1484.

10. A. Ducellier, "La façade maritime de la principauté des Kastriote de la fin du XIVᵉ siècle à la mort de Skanderbeg," *Studia Albanica,* 1968, no. 1:119–36.

11. On the Paštrovići, see I. Božić, "Srednjovekovni Paštrovići," *Istorijski časopis* 9–10 (1959): 151–85.

12. M. Dinić, "Vlasti za vreme despotovine," *Zbornik Filozofskog fakulteta* (Beogradski univerzitet) 10, no. 1 (1968): 237–44.

13. On Tati and contemporary political issues, see J. Radonić, "Sporazum u Tati 1426 i Srpsko-Ugarski odnosi od XIII–XVI veka," *Glas* (SKA) 187 (1941): 117–232.

14. M. Kašanin, *Srpska književnost u srednjem veku* (Beograd, 1975), pp. 371–72.

15. Ibid., pp. 349–66.

16. M. Spremić, "Despot Djuradj Branković i Mačvanska banovina," *Istorijski časopis* 23 (1976): 23–36.

17. The reforms suggested by Plethon are summarized in W. Miller, *The Latins in the Levant: A History of Frankish Greece (1204–1566)* (London, 1908), pp. 380–83.

18. D. Zakythinos, *Le Despotat Grec de Morée* (Athens, 1953), vol. 2, p. 310.

19. Finlay, *History of Greece,* vol. 4, p. 224.

CHAPTER 10

The Balkans for the Remainder of the Fifteenth Century

The Crusade of Varna 1443–44

In 1443 the Union of Florence bore the fruit for which the Greeks had accepted it: a papally-sponsored crusade. Twenty-five thousand soldiers were mobilized under three leaders: Vladislav III, the Polish king who had recently also become King of Hungary; John (Janos) Hunyadi; and George Branković. Hunyadi, a major figure at the Hungarian court, governed Transylvania for Hungary and had had previous successes in fighting the Turks. George Branković had been living in Hungary since the Ottomans had evicted him from his realm. He led a force of Serbs who had also fled to Hungary.

In 1443 the Ottoman sultan, Murad II, was occupied in Anatolia suppressing a large rebellion of the Karamanlis. The crusaders crossed the Danube, captured Smederevo, and then marched south through Serbia. They won a victory over the Ottoman governor of Niš near that town and as a result took Niš. They then moved on and captured Sofija. Thus they liberated all the towns along the main route through Serbia between the Danube and Sofija. It should be stressed, however, that the crusaders' victories were against the armies assigned to garrison the towns and fortresses along this route. They had not yet seen the major Ottoman army. The crusaders' successes inspired two other major revolts, both of which we shall discuss later: the revolt of Skanderbeg in Albania and a temporarily successful attempt to liberate Ottoman-occupied areas of central Greece by Despot Constantine of the Morea, who took advantage of Ottoman difficulties to bring his troops across the Isthmus of Corinth into central Greece.

As they withdrew the Ottoman troops burned the environs of Sofija and the lands along the route east, to hinder the crusaders in finding provisions. The sultan hurried to Europe in order to establish defenses along this route to prevent the crusaders from reaching Adrianople. The crusaders made it a policy to convert mosques in the towns they took into churches. Many local Bulgarians actively assisted the crusaders, especially in supplying provisions. The crusaders soon continued their march east from Sofija toward Adrianople, but along the route, at Zlatica, they met a strong and well-placed Ottoman defense force. After a period of facing each other, including it seems a couple of skirmishes (about which our few sources contradict one another on details and outcome), the crusaders retreated to Sofija; soon most of them had withdrawn into Serbia or even out of the Balkans entirely. Since the Ottomans seem to have taken no immediate action on a large scale to reassert themselves in this territory, it seems some sort of truce was in existence.

Faced with this critical situation in Europe and still occupied with the Karamanli revolt in Anatolia, Sultan Murad II declared himself ready to treat with the crusaders. First, in March or April 1444, he sent envoys to George Branković, offering him peace on generous terms that allowed Serbia to be restored as a state under Branković. Branković, happy to regain his state, quickly agreed to the peace. On 15 August 1444 the formal agreement between Murad and Branković was signed. By it, the territory of the reborn Serbia was defined. Serbia acquired twenty-four major fortresses, including Smederevo, Golubac, Braničevo, Novo Brdo, Ostrovica, Zvornik, and Srebrnica. This last town, in the meantime, had been picked off by Stefan Tomaš of Bosnia, who had taken advantage of the Ottomans' troubles with the crusaders to seize it. George Branković also agreed to accept Ottoman suzerainty and pay the sultan a tribute of sixty thousand ducats. And finally, the sultan agreed to restore to him his two blinded sons. The Ottomans, it seems, retained the important fortress of Kruševac. Thus the reborn state included Serbia north of the West Morava River, Mačva, and Usora (or at least part of it) on the Bosnian side of the Drina. Already by 22 August George was found in Smederevo, assuming the rule of his regained state.

In the meantime, on the sultan's invitation, envoys from the crusade's leaders came to meet with the sultan in Adrianople (Edirne) in June 1444. The sultan quickly agreed to a ten-year truce, which would leave the crusaders in possession of what they had taken. After the sultan agreed to these terms he sent his own envoys to Szegedin in Hungary to obtain King Vladislav's ratification of the agreement. The sultan, then, having apparently secured matters in Europe, returned to Anatolia to resume his actions against the Karamanlis. In July 1444 Vladislav ratified the treaty.

At times various scholars, particularly Poles, have denied that Vladislav actually agreed to the treaty; their motive seems to have been to make the Polish king look better by denying that he broke his oath when the crusaders shortly thereafter violated the agreement and resumed the war against the Ottomans. Most scholars, however, have found this scholarly attempt unconvincing and believe the evidence makes it clear that Vladislav did in fact ratify the treaty. At the moment of Branković's and Vladislav's ratification matters seemed promising for the Balkan Christian cause: Serbia had re-appeared as a state and the Christians in the western and central Balkans had before them the prospect of an entire decade of peace during which they could reconstitute themselves.

Meanwhile, the papacy was very disappointed when it learned of the treaty the crusaders had concluded with Murad. Rome felt that the Christians had momentum on their side and thus had a chance to drive the Turks from Europe entirely. Furthermore, and unknown to those who had signed the peace, a Western fleet had been dispatched eastward to support the crusaders. Thus the papacy was confident this expulsion could be achieved and believed that compliance with the treaty would let a great chance slip away. The papacy does not seem to have taken into consideration the important facts that the crusaders' successes thus far had been against garrisons and that the crusaders had not yet seen the full Ottoman army, which throughout 1443 had been involved in Anatolia. Thus the pope was determined to proceed with the crusade. He sent east a leading "hawk," Cardinal Cesarini, who quickly persuaded Vladislav to fall in with papal plans and absolved him from his oath. Then, ignoring the treaty they had just concluded, Vladislav, Hunyadi, and Cesarini began re-mobilizing the Christian forces. By September 1444 the crusaders were again on the march. But this time their armies were considerably smaller. The original force had been disbanded after the treaty was concluded and it had not been possible to re-assemble all the dispersed soldiers. Moreover, in this second round the crusaders were without the not small support of Branković and the Serbs.

Branković was satisfied with the treaty, for it had realized his goals. He also had the most to lose, for should the new crusade fail, Serbia, in the most vulnerable position, would most likely be re-occupied by the Turks. Thus he declared his neutrality and refused to participate. In fact, to secure Serbia's future, he even, it seems, sent envoys to re-affirm Serbia's vassal ties to the sultan and to warn Murad of the impending attack from the crusaders. Since the Serbs refused to participate and also refused the crusaders passage through Serbia, the crusaders crossed the Danube into Bulgaria and marched toward the Black Sea.

Having learned of the treaty's violation, Murad rapidly mobilized his forces and in record time brought a massive army from Asia Minor to Europe. A contemporary Burgundian account accuses the Genoese of ferrying the Ottoman troops across the Bosphorus. This accusation is repeated in various later sources. It was in Genoa's interests to aid the Turks and thereby preserve its Black Sea monopoly. However, it is worth mentioning that contemporary sources from Byzantium, Dubrovnik, and Genoa's rival Venice do not make this accusation. The two armies met at Varna on 10 November 1444, and the Ottomans won an overwhelming victory. The Christian army was nearly wiped out, and the dead included King Vladislav and Cardinal Cesarini. The Varna crusade, as it has come to be called, was to be the last concerted Christian offensive against the Turks. The Serbian ruler, George Branković, who had wisely remained neutral, re-affirmed his vassal ties to the Turks and remained on good terms with Sultan Murad II for some time thereafter. For the next few years the Serbs occupied themselves with trying to regain parts of Zeta from Venice. In 1445, seeing the balance of power shift from Hungary to the Ottomans, Wallachia submitted to Murad and accepted Ottoman suzerainty.

Hungary and Croatia after Varna

Vladislav was succeeded, as stipulated in the 1442 treaty, by Ladislas Posthumous, now Ladislas V (1445–57). Like his father Albert of Habsburg, Ladislas V was King of Austria and Hungary. Since Ladislas was only five years old, the brilliant general and Vojvoda of Transylvania John Hunyadi was appointed regent, assuming, in 1446, the title of governor. Hunyadi at first ruled Hungary alone, for the Habsburgs under Frederick III, Albert's brother and Ladislas' uncle, fearing for Ladislas' safety, did not allow him to return to Austria or Hungary. Finally in 1452 a revolt, particularly vigorous in Austria, broke out. Frederick III, besieged by the rebels, backed down and allowed Ladislas V, then twelve years old, to take up residence in his domains. Thereafter he usually resided in Vienna. Even after his return his Hungarian lands remained under the control of Hunyadi.

At the start of his regency Hunyadi was faced by a major crisis in Croatia. For early in 1445 Matko Talovac, Ban of Slavonia and holder of vast territories south of the Drava, died. Frederick and his son Ulrich, the Counts of Celje, immediately marched into Slavonia, seizing a large portion of Matko's lands and claiming the banship of Slavonia. In the fighting Matko's brother John, who probably had succeeded Matko as Slavonian ban and who had been the Prior of Vrana, was killed. Having taken over the whole district of Zagreb, Ulrich appointed a new bishop for Zagreb.

Hunyadi, who at the start of this crisis had been involved in a quarrel with the ruler of Wallachia and thus unable to intervene, was infuriated. Freeing himself from other affairs, he held a council that condemned Ulrich's actions and then sent an army against Croatia. His forces plundered large areas of Croatia and forced the Counts of Celje to relinquish the towns and lands they had seized. However, the Counts of Celje still claimed the banship of Slavonia. And Hunyadi, having many other affairs that demanded his attention, eventually recognized Frederick of Celje as Ban of Slavonia; however, to try to retain some control over the Celje counts, Hunyadi appointed John Szekely, a Hungarian, to a newly created position of Vice Ban of Dalmatia, Croatia, and Slavonia.

The third Talovac brother, Peter, who held the Talovac lands (the former Nelipčić lands) south of Velebit and had been appointed Ban of Croatia by Sigismund, was having so much difficulty in retaining his lands—fighting a holding action and suffering various losses against Stefan Vukčić and Venice—that he could play little or no part in defending his family's lands in Slavonia.

To the north of Peter Talovac's banate in southern Croatia, the Frankapans remained the great landlords.[1] They had tried their best to ignore, and remain neutral in, the civil war between Hunyadi/Talovac and the Counts of Celje. In 1449 the eight surviving Frankapan brothers held a family council that divided the family lands into eight parts, one for each brother. To try to keep the family somewhat united and thus in possession of the influence it had enjoyed when it jointly held its vast territory, the brothers agreed that after the partition the two most important towns, Krk (on the island of Krk) and Senj, would be held jointly and the two towns' income shared by the eight brothers. Each of the eight regions was to pass on to the son of its recipient. Should any of the eight brothers die without an heir, then the family was to hold a new council to divide the deceased's share among the surviving brothers. This decision was reached by the family on its own; it neither consulted the king nor did it seek a charter of confirmation from him. And thus were formed the eight branches, each holding its own hereditary lands, of the Frankapan family.

Family dissensions, which had caused the 1449 division, however, did not cease after the partition council. At least one brother, John, felt he had received a poor deal. Ambitious to obtain the island of Krk, he established cordial relations with Venice to realize his ambition. After further bickering with his brothers, John obtained their consent that he relinquish all his mainland holdings in exchange for the whole island of Krk. John then accepted Venetian protection for his island and thereafter more or less broke with his brothers, ceasing to participate in family councils or affairs. Despite John's Venetian ties, Krk remained officially under Hungarian suzerainty.

Frederick of Celje remained as Ban of Slavonia, though we may assume that his son Ulrich actually wielded the authority. When Frederick died in 1454, Ulrich became Ban of Slavonia. Shortly before Frederick's death, in 1453, the Ban of Croatia, Peter Talovac, died. Frederick immediately claimed his title too. And the Celje counts dispatched their armies against Peter's former lands, succeeding in acquiring a large portion of them. Thus the Celje family found itself holding also most of Croatia south of Velebit, except for the Frankapan lands and Klis. To maintain themselves against retaliation from Hunyadi, the Counts of Celje made an alliance with Stefan Vukčić Kosača. Hunyadi, needless to say, opposed the advance of the Celje counts into Croatia. Hunyadi appointed his own son Ladislas as Ban of Croatia. The Celje family, not surprisingly, ignored this appointment. However, soon a major attack on Beograd by Sultan Mehemmed II in 1456 (to be discussed below) led to a truce in March 1456 between the feuding parties to enable both sides to participate in the city's defense.

Hunyadi successfully resisted the Turkish attack, but soon after the Turkish withdrawal he died of the plague. His son Ladislas (or Laszlo) assumed the command of the fortress. At that moment, in November 1456, Ulrich of Celje, who had not been present at the defense, appeared at the walls of Beograd accompanied by the young king, Ladislas V, with whom he had created close ties. These ties greatly worried the Hunyadi faction, which saw them as a threat to its position in the state. Ulrich seems to have expected young Hunyadi to turn command of the fortress over to him. Ladislas Hunyadi granted Ulrich a safe-conduct and allowed him and the king, but not their troops, to enter the city. On the following day Hunyadi summoned Ulrich alone, without the king, to a meeting. At it the two men quarreled, and Hunyadi's men leaped into the fray and murdered Ulrich of Celje. His death ended the powerful Celje family. Ladislas V had not been present and was furious, but, since he was in the hands of Hunyadi's men, he had to avoid showing his displeasure. He was held as an honorary prisoner for several weeks; then after being pressured to take an oath not to retaliate against Ladislas Hunyadi, the king was allowed to depart. Ladislas V awaited his opportunity; it was not long in coming, and in March 1457 he, in violation of his oath, seized and executed Ladislas Hunyadi. Ladislas Hunyadi's younger brother, Matthew Corvinus, was also seized, but he was sent off to Prague as a prisoner.

Later that year, in November 1457, Ladislas V died without an heir. Matthew Corvinus' uncle Michael Szilagyi, who had been in rebellion against Ladislas V since March, when the king had executed Ladislas Hunyadi, then appeared in Pest with fourteen thousand armed retainers. He convened a council of nobles, which elected Matthew Corvinus Hunyadi as king. At the time Matthew was still imprisoned and only fifteen years old. He was immediately released and, after being crowned, took up his royal duties. However, various Croatian and Hungarian nobles did not want to recognize him. The opposition, led by Ladislas Garai and Nicholas Iločki, looked for support from Frederick III Habsburg of Germany. Since 1440, when little Ladislas Posthumous had been sent to him for safety, Frederick had had in his possession the official Hungarian crown. This meant that many Hungarians did not, or had an excuse not to, recognize Matthew's coronation. Eventually, after considerable intriguing and some skirmishing, peace was concluded between Matthew and the opposition nobles and then between Matthew and Frederick III. It was agreed in 1463 that Matthew should be King of Hungary, but if he had no heir, then Frederick or a son of Frederick should succeed to the Hungarian throne. Then in March 1464 Matthew received a formal coronation with the true Hungarian crown, which Frederick returned. This official date notwithstanding, Matthew had actually been ruler of, and in control of, most of his realm since the end of 1458.

Meanwhile, upon Ulrich of Celje's death his widow, Catherine, the daughter of George Branković, succeeded to his lands. Immediately various other claimants appeared, the most important of whom was Frederick III Habsburg, who claimed all Ulrich's lands in Styria, Carinthia, and Carniola. Ladislas V, whom Ulrich had intended to be his eventual heir, showed considerable sympathy to Catherine and by March 1457 had appointed one of Ulrich's leading associates, Vitovec, to be the new Ban of Slavonia. Vitovec was able to repel an attack by Frederick's forces in April. But after this promising start Catherine's affairs crumbled. Ladislas V died in November 1457; having lost her main prop, she agreed to negotiate with Frederick. They concluded a treaty on 15 December 1457 by which Frederick obtained all the Celje castles in Carinthia, Styria, and Carniola, while she retained the family castles in Hungary and Croatia. But even this arrangement was not to last. Vitovec soon made peace with Frederick and entered his service. With the defection of her leading supporter to Frederick, and presumably under considerable pressure from Frederick and Vitovec, Catherine in 1460 sold to Vitovec all but one of her castles. She then retired to Dubrovnik, living off the income of the one castle she retained. And thus was ended the "state" and power of the Celje counts.

After this summary of Hungarian and Croatian events, we may now turn back to Serbia and its relations with the Hungarians after the Varna defeat (1444) in which Serbia had been neutral.

Serbia after Varna

The years that followed Varna were marked by growing tensions between Serbia and Hungary. Branković's non-participation in 1444 had angered the Hungarians, and Branković continued to follow his policy of avoiding conflict with the Turks in the ensuing years. He consistently refused to support any of the smaller crusading efforts John Hunyadi mobilized during the years after 1444 and even refused to allow Hunyadi to march with his troops through Serbia. While so doing, Branković found himself constantly under pressure from Hungary to support wars against the Turks. Yet Branković knew that Hungary was not strong enough to truly defeat the Turks and provide real salvation for Serbia. And thus Serbian involvement could only result in Serbia's conquest by the Turks. Knowing that even to allow Hungarian troops to pass through Serbia would endanger his delicate relations with the Turks, he consistently resisted the Hungarians when they attempted to send their troops through Serbia against the Ottomans. As a result relations deteriorated between Serbia and Hungary.

In 1448 John Hunyadi again demanded Serbian participation in a new crusade. After being again refused, he demanded passage for his troops through Serbia. Again rebuffed, Hunyadi then, according to later chroniclers, warned George Branković that if he defeated the Turks he would seize George's realm and grant it to one worthier. Then he led his armies through Serbia anyway, plundering Serbia like an enemy land. George, angry and concerned for Serbia's future, seems to have again sent envoys to warn Murad of the Hungarian attack and to explain that the Hungarians' passage through Serbia was by force and against his wishes. Hostile sources, whose remarks are recorded by Orbini, even say George passed on to the Turks information on the size of the Hungarian force and offered strategic advice to the sultan, which was followed and was responsible for the Turkish victory over Hunyadi after three days of fighting on the battlefield of Kosovo in 1448.

The defeated Hungarians fled from the battlefield in all directions, and George ordered that all Hungarian soldiers found in Serbia after the battle be taken to his authorities. In this way George was able to seize Hunyadi himself. He held Hunyadi in prison for a time, demanding a huge ransom to compensate for the damage done by the Hungarians on their way to Kosovo. Eventually Hunyadi was released on the promise of a ransom payment, which was never to be made. Needless to say this incident made relations even worse between the two sides. And it seems to have caused the Hungarians to launch a raid to plunder Serbia in the following year. Serbian-Hungarian tensions were also exacerbated by the fact that in the civil war in Bosnia, to be discussed, Hunyadi supported King Stefan Tomaš whereas George Branković retained Serbia's long-standing alliance with the Kosača family and supported Stefan Vukčić. As a result of these quarrels and differences, Hunyadi confiscated most of Branković's property in Hungary.

But while Branković's relations deteriorated with Hungary, he maintained close ties with Orthodox Byzantium. In 1446 his son Lazar married Helen, the daughter of Thomas Palaeologus of the Morea. And an inscription from the fortifications of Constantinople shows that in 1448 George had funded the repair of one of the towers of Constantinople's walls.

In this period, to maintain itself, Serbia had to maintain close ties with the Turks. It seems the Turks also exercised far more influence inside of Serbia than they had prior to Serbia's conquest by the Turks in 1439–41. For example, in about 1445 Branković turned down a Ragusan request for commercial privileges in the Serbian town of Priština, because, as he himself states, he was powerless to do anything about the request because the Ottomans controlled matters there.

In accordance with the 1444 treaty restoring Serbia as a state, the sultan had recognized Branković's possession of much of Serbia proper (defined as twenty-four named fortresses), Srebrnica, and Zeta. As noted, Stefan Tomaš of Bosnia had seized Srebrnica early in 1444, preventing its transfer to Serbia. In April 1445 George is found in possession of Srebrnica; how he acquired the town is not known. He briefly lost it to the Bosnians again in late summer 1446. At the end of that year the Serbs and Bosnians reached an agreement by which the two states were to split the income from the town's mine. Officials from both states operated in the town, whose coins had one ruler's name on one side and the other ruler's name on the other. Warfare broke out over the town again in the fall of 1448. The Serbs defeated a Bosnian force and not only took the town but the whole left bank of the Drina as far south as Višegrad. Stefan Vukčić supported the Serbs on this occasion. The Bosnians, refusing to yield on the issue, were again in possession of Srebrnica by early 1449. However, they could not retain it; threatened by a new Serbian attack, which had the sultan's blessing if not his military support behind it, the Bosnians agreed to let the Ragusans mediate a peace. By the resulting treaty, in July 1451, the Serbs regained sole possession of the town.

The interior of Zeta—Upper Zeta, the region between Serbia and Bosnia/Hum and Lake Skadar—seems to have quickly submitted to Branković. As noted earlier, Stefan Vukčić restored the territory he held in this region to George when the sultan restored George to rule over Serbia. George established his own vojvoda in Upper Zeta, whose seat was located at Podgorica. Branković soon made peace with the most powerful family in the area, the Crnojevići, whose main fortress at the time was in Žabljak. Thus Branković soon was overlord—but surely in a very loose sense—over the territory from Serbia to Lake Skadar. He does not seem to have minded that the Crnojevići also maintained close ties with Venice; presumably trying to re-assert himself in Zeta, George was in no position to object. Thus the Crnojevići were openly serving two masters. In the coastal area, Lower Zeta, George regained nothing, as Venice refused to restore the former lands of George that it held, which included Bar, Budva, and Drivast.

Skanderbeg's Revolt in Albania

Between 1437 and 1440 the Albanian nobleman and Ottoman vassal John Castriot died; the sultan, instead of allowing the family to continue to control its holdings, ordered the Ottoman governor of Kroja, Hasan beg, to take control of all the forts in the Castriots' lands.

Shortly thereafter, in 1443, the Christian crusade was launched. John Castriot's son, long converted to Islam under the name of Skanderbeg and at the time in active Ottoman service, became infuriated at what was happening to his family's lands. Seeing that the sultan was involved with the crusaders as well as with the Karamanlis, Skanderbeg decided to revolt. The sultan evidently had had no misgivings about Skanderbeg's loyalty, for he had sent him west with an army at the time to join the Ottoman forces opposing the crusaders at Niš. Skanderbeg, however, chose the time of the battle to desert with three hundred loyal Albanian horsemen. He arrived at Kroja with a forged document, allegedly from the sultan to Hasan beg, ordering Hasan to turn Kroja over to Skanderbeg, who was to be the new Ottoman governor of the town. Hasan beg duly turned Kroja over to him. Skanderbeg then announced that he was again a Christian and began to take action against the Islamization that had been occurring around Kroja. Those who refused to accept Christianity, including the Ottoman officials he had seized, among whom was Hasan beg, were impaled. Next Skanderbeg recovered all the former Castriot fortresses taken by the Turks. Taking advantage of the events around Kroja, and the problems the Ottomans faced elsewhere in their empire, the Arianiti in southern Albania again revolted, acquiring considerable support in that region. The Arianiti concluded an alliance with Naples, but it was not to bring them any actual aid. The Arianiti also allied with the Castriots; each promised the other aid, and Skanderbeg married Andronike, George Arianite's daughter.

Having liberated his own family's lands, Skanderbeg set about trying to unite all the Albanian chiefs into a league to resist the Turks. In March 1444 he called a congress at Alessio, a town then held by the Venetians, who also were invited to the meeting. He received considerable support and was made head of the league and also commander of the Albanian armies. All were aware of the imminent danger of Ottoman attack, and the tribesmen willingly provided soldiers and even submitted to central discipline in the armies. Thus, for the first time, Albania was united under an Albanian leader, and Skanderbeg, as head of the league, stood over the numerous tribal chiefs who continued to manage their own regions. Skanderbeg immediately set about repairing fortifications in Albania, in particular those of Kroja.

In the spring of 1444 the Ottomans attacked. Skanderbeg's spies sent him advance word of the invasion and its planned route. This knowledge, combined with the rugged mountainous terrain that was ideal for a smaller army to ambush a larger one, resulted in the Albanians' defeating the invaders in June 1444.

Meanwhile, shortly after the Albanians' victory over the Turks, Nicholas Dukagjin killed Lek Zakarija, the Albanian lord of Danj, in a blood feud. Venice quickly sent a force into Danj and received support from Lek's mother and the local populace, who preferred Venice to any of the local Albanians who all supported Skanderbeg's league. The town's hostility to the Albanian league was presumably owing to the Dukagjins' membership in the league. Venice also took over Zakarija's other towns of Sati, Gladri, and Dušmani, with the agreement of Lek's mother. Skanderbeg demanded that Venice restore to him these towns and also Drivast. Venice refused. The Albanian league then sent envoys to its Serbian neighbors Crnojević and George Branković. George expressed his willingness to help against Venice, from which he was still trying to regain the parts of Zeta left to Serbia by the last Balšić in 1421. However, George made it clear that he would assist the Albanians only against Venice and not against the Turks.

Leaving four thousand armed men to guard his frontier in the event of a new Ottoman invasion, Skanderbeg then ordered the rest of his troops against Danj in 1447. The Venetians, more concerned about this town than the anti-Ottoman war, offered an award to anyone who would assassinate Skanderbeg. The Venetians also sent envoys to the Ottomans to urge them to attack Albania again. Receiving word that the Venetians were sending a large force to the relief of Danj, Skanderbeg left a small force to carry on the siege of Danj and marched from the town to meet the arriving Venetians. The two armies met on the Drin at some point in 1448, and the Albanians annihilated the Venetian force. After this victory the Venetian presence was reduced to small garrisons within a number of walled cities, including Danj. Except for these towns and their Albanian residents, all Albania accepted Skanderbeg's leadership, including the leaders of the powerful Dukagjins who had been with him at least from the time of the Alessio congress, which had been attended by two Dukagjin chiefs. A few members of this family, particularly some residing in Skadar, remained loyal to Venice, however.

Later in 1448 the Ottomans attacked Debar, causing considerable devastation. Skanderbeg, leaving part of his army to carry on the siege of Danj, met the Turks in battle in September 1448 and routed them, causing them again to withdraw. At roughly the same time, the Ottomans severely defeated Hunyadi at the second battle of Kosovo. Since Hunyadi was not soon to be able to mobilize a serious new force to attack the Turks, the Ottomans were now free to concentrate their attention on Albania. Aware of this danger, Skanderbeg at the end of 1448 concluded a peace with Venice, leaving the Venetians in possession of the disputed towns.

In 1449 and 1450 the Ottomans launched major attacks on Albania. In both years Murad II led his forces in person. They achieved a few temporary successes in 1449, including the conquest of Svetigrad after a siege. Moreover, in the course of the 1449 campaign Skanderbeg was briefly forced to submit to Ottoman suzerainty and to agree to pay six thousand ducats a year as tribute. However, it seems that he never paid it, and within a year he had again ceased to recognize this suzerainty. The Venetians, despite their peace with Skanderbeg, profited from the fighting by selling supplies to the Ottomans.[2]

In 1450 Murad II and his son, the future Mehemmed II the Conqueror, moved against Kroja, supposedly with one hundred thousand troops. Skanderbeg left a loyal commander in Kroja and departed with an army to the mountains. From there he launched hit-and-run attacks upon the besieging Ottoman forces. These forays were successful, and the Ottomans sustained heavy losses from them while the walls of Kroja and their defenders held out. At the end of the 1450 campaigning season, the Ottomans with heavy losses were forced to retire.

Receiving no help from Venice and believing that without outside help sooner or later the Ottomans must defeat the Albanians, Skanderbeg in 1451 turned to Alphonso of Naples and accepted his suzerainty. In fact, however, Skanderbeg remained the independent ruler of his lands. A small number of soldiers, it seems, were sent from Naples to support Skanderbeg. And in 1452 the Albanians defeated in the mountains a new Ottoman force sent against Albania.

Meanwhile, tensions were developing between Skanderbeg and the Dukagjins. They were already skirmishing in a small way by 1450; and in that year some members of the Dukagjin family seem to have supported the Ottoman campaign, as a result of which they increased their own territorial holdings. It also seems that some family members remained vassals of Venice and/or residents of Venetian Skadar throughout this period. Thus one should not see the Dukagjins as a united family. In 1452 the Catholic Church began urging a peace between Skanderbeg and the rebellious Dukagjins; this peace was concluded by 1454. During this time the Ottomans, under the new sultan, Mehemmed II (1451–81), were focusing their attention on ending the Byzantine Empire. Thus the Turks were to leave Albania in peace for a few years.

George Branković and Zeta

We have seen that in 1447 Skanderbeg had launched an attack against Venetian-held Danj. At the time he had also moved against various other Venetian possessions in that region including Durazzo and Ulcinj. He took none of these major towns, but his men carried out considerable plundering. These activities were particularly hard on the Ulcinj area, which had suffered a major earthquake in 1444 and still had not recovered. Some Venetians seem to have believed that Skanderbeg's attack on Ulcinj was carried out at the request of, and was even financed by, George Branković. And we know from Venetian sources that George Branković in 1447 had received Skanderbeg's envoys cordially and had expressed his willingness to see the Albanians take Danj. Whether Ulcinj was discussed on that occasion is not stated.

A second and later Venetian source—a chronicle—states that Skanderbeg attacked Ulcinj in his own interests. Upon acquiring Kroja, the chronicle states, Skanderbeg declared himself the heir of the Balšići and declared his intention to recover his inheritance. As a result, he plundered the region of Bar and Ulcinj. In this action he was supported by the Dukagjins and various other local Albanians. Fearing Skanderbeg, the Venetians began offering rewards for his assassination.

Whether George Branković was behind, or even supporting, this 1447 campaign against Ulcinj is unknown. But one may at least conclude that the raid helped soften up the area for subsequent action by Branković to restore to Serbia some of its former possessions that were then in Venetian hands. In June 1448 the despot's army of seven thousand marched into Zeta, reaching the Gulf of Kotor. This force was immediately joined by the Crnojevići, who presumably had participated in the planning of the campaign. The villagers of Grbalj, as usual, took this as an excuse to rise up against their hated master, the town of Kotor. The Paštrovići also supported Serbia again, going against the established policy and wishes of the family leader, Grubačević, who once again remained faithful to Venice. The Serbs announced that they intended only to regain the former Serbian towns and had no ill intentions toward any of the Venetian possessions. However, by this time Venice considered the former Serbian towns to be Venetian. Having picked up support from most of the Paštrovići, the despot's armies marched against Bar, where they met a defeat.

Expecting a new attack (though one actually did not occur for a while), the Venetians began to mend fences, in particular with Stefan Crnojević. By 1451 Venice proposed that if he submitted to Venice and broke relations with Serbia, Venice would give him a large annual stipend of five hundred ducats and recognize him as Great Vojvoda of Zeta. The negotiations dragged on for almost a year, during which Stefan had a major quarrel with his brothers, the cause of which is unknown; perhaps the brothers remained loyal to Serbia and objected to Stefan's negotiations with Venice. Stefan triumphed over them, taking most, if not all, of their lands. After this the brothers do not appear any longer in the sources, and Stefan emerged as the sole major figure in Zeta, prominent in both Upper and Lower Zeta. The agreement between him and Venice was finally concluded on the above-mentioned terms in late 1451 or 1452 and included an alliance against the Serbian despot. From here on one can speak of the Crnojevići as the actual rulers of Zeta. But though Stefan Crnojević dominated Zeta, his actual landholdings, which remained scattered, were never massive, consisting of a handful of villages on Lake Skadar, at least one village on the Bojana, the five villages he received from Stefan Vukčić in Upper Zeta, Žabljak, and the territory he acquired above the Gulf of Kotor that included Mount Lovčen.

As part of his agreement with Venice, Stefan Crnojević was obliged to help Kotor suppress the Grbalj rebels, which he did brutally in 1452. The rebel leaders were wiped out, though Kotor was probably responsible for the actual executions of the leaders at the rebellion's end.

Late in 1452 George Branković's troops again marched into Upper Zeta, proof that the agreement with Stefan was concluded in the nick of time for Venice. Stefan Crnojević defeated them, preventing them from reaching the coast. Crnojević then went on the offensive and drove the despot's officials out of part of Upper Zeta. However, Branković's officials seem to have remained in the region between Podgorica and Cetinje. The despot's men also managed on this occasion to take, and temporarily retain, Žabljak, the major fortress of the Crnojevići. In September 1452 a second Serbian invasion was launched into Zeta, this one led by Branković's brother-in-law Thomas Cantacuzenus. Stefan Crnojević defeated this army as well, almost taking Thomas prisoner. Stefan then moved on to the offensive himself and drove the Serbs from Upper Zeta as far as the mouth of the Zeta where it flows into the Morača. A series of tribes, including the Bjelopavlići, now agreed to accept Venetian suzerainty. As a recent history of Montenegro points out, this suzerainty was symbolic, but it did mean real overlordship for Venice's deputy, Stefan Crnojević.[3] After this triumph the Venetians awarded Stefan by obtaining through negotiations the restoration of his son, John (Ivan), who had been held as a hostage for ten years by Stefan Vukčić Kosača.

Shortly thereafter, probably early in 1453, the Serbs made a final attempt to regain their position in Zeta. Once again Stefan Crnojević defeated the Serbian army. Then he went onto the offensive along the Zeta and Morača rivers and took all Upper Zeta, except for the fortress of Medun, which refused to submit. Among the fortresses he captured were Podgorica, the despot's local capital, and Žabljak, the Crnojević family fortress recently taken by the Serbs. The Serbs could do nothing about reversing matters, for in 1453 they had to support the sultan's troops against Constantinople. And then, despite their loyalty to the sultan on this campaign, the Serbs' turn came next. In 1454 the Turks were already raiding against Serbia. A major campaign followed in 1455. It took Novo Brdo in June and whatever remained of the former Branković family lands in the south. Shortly thereafter, in late 1455 or early 1456, the Ottomans captured Medun. The despot no longer held any territory in Zeta. Almost all of Zeta was now under the rule or overlordship of Stefan Crnojević, who stood as suzerain over the various tribesmen and nobles of the area. But Zeta too had been reduced by the Ottoman campaign of 1455; for the Ottomans had extended their authority over all the territory of Zeta as far west as the Morača River, which now became the Ottoman-Zetan border.

Venice now extended its suzerainty, until then limited to the coast (Lower Zeta), to what remained of Upper Zeta as well. The Venetian over-lordship was nominal and Crnojević was the de facto master of the area. A new treaty, reaffirming his position and confirmed by a Zetan assembly of fifty-one counties or military brotherhoods, was issued by Venice in September 1455. The document states that the nobles of Zeta were to serve the Great Vojvoda of Zeta, owing Venice the same service they had previously owed to the Balšići. The nobles were obliged to serve only as far away from home as the Drin River and Alessio. Liking the system of a major local figure standing over the various local princes and chieftains, Venice in the following year established a new and similar "great vojvoda" for the region south of Zeta between Skadar and Durazzo. George Arianite was awarded this honor. He was not able to benefit from the position to the extent that Crnojević was able, since there were other powerful figures including Skanderbeg—who clearly was not going to submit to Arianite—within his theoretical vojvodate. The two vojvodas, similarly tied to Venice, established close relations, how-ever, and Stefan Crnojević's son and heir married a daughter of George Arianite.

Zeta between the coast and the Morača was to suffer from small plunder-ing raids by Ottoman troops based in Medun off and on during the late 1450s. And mutual raiding, necessary to maintain the plunder economy, occurred along the Zetan-Kosača border. By 1459 some of the Zetan tribesmen had dropped their allegiance to Venice and had accepted Ottoman suzerainty. And thus matters continued until Stefan Crnojević died in late 1464 or early 1465. He was succeeded by his son John.

Affairs in Greece from 1443

While the Ottomans were occupied with the crusaders in 1443, Despot Con-stantine Palaeologus of the Morea marched across the Isthmus of Corinth into Attica. Faced with this large army, Nerio II, the Florentine Duke of Athens, at once initiated negotiations. Constantine agreed to leave Nerio in possession of his duchy if he accepted Byzantine suzerainty and paid the despot the tribute he had formerly paid to the sultan. Having obtained Nerio's submission in early 1444, the despot then pressed north into Ottoman territory, restoring Greek rule over Thessaly up to Mount Olympus by the end of 1445. The Albanians and Vlachs of the Pindus Mountains, on Thessaly's western bor-ders, recognized his suzerainty. Moreover, various Albanian tribes also rose up against the Turks in parts of Epirus.

However, these successes were not to last. The Ottomans defeated the crusaders at Varna in November 1444. The Byzantines and the Morean despot were not present at this battle. This victory freed the sultan to turn his atten-tion to Greece, where his hold was beginning to unravel. In 1446 the sultan launched a major invasion into central Greece and quickly recovered Thessaly. Nerio hastened to recognize the sultan's suzerainty again over Attica and Boeotia. The despot's troops withdrew to the Isthmus of Corinth, thereby withdrawing from all their acquisitions of 1443–45. Constantine prepared his troops to defend the Hexamilion, which he had repaired in 1444. The Ottomans arrived at the Isthmus in November 1446. Constantine sent envoys to the sultan, who refused to listen to any of Constantine's proposals but demanded the destruction of the Hexamilion. Constantine refused, so the sultan attacked the fortifications with cannons, breaking through the Hexamilion on 10 December 1446.

The Ottoman army was then divided into two forces, one sent to ravage Achaea—the geographical region of Achaea in the northwest of the peninsula—and the other, the region of Mistra. Many cities fell and were looted. The whole region was devastated, and many people were massacred or carried off as slaves. Sixty thousand were taken as slaves, according to both the Venetian and Greek sources. Then, in early 1447, the Ottomans received unconditional submission from the two despots Constantine and Thomas, who agreed to vassalage and a huge annual tribute. The two rulers also promised not to rebuild the Hexamilion. The Ottoman troops then withdrew. The despots probably escaped more lightly than they otherwise might have, since the sultan was then more concerned about the threats to his empire from Hunyadi and Skanderbeg.

In October 1448 the Byzantine emperor, John VIII, died; Constantine was his designated successor. Constantine was crowned emperor in January 1449 in Mistra by an Orthodox bishop. The manner of the coronation was chosen to win support in Constantinople, whose populace would have objected to his being crowned by the Unionist patriarch. Constantine then divided the Morea into two appanages, each under one of his brothers, each of whom bore the title despot. The western part of the peninsula from the southern tip of Messenia and Kalamata to Kalavryta and Patras in the north— including Messenia, Elis, Achaea, and most of Arcadia—went to Thomas. The young Demetrius, who formerly held the Black Sea appanage and had shown himself to be highly ambitious, having a history of intriguing with the Ottomans for his own interests, was given the eastern parts of the peninsula from the Isthmus of Corinth, with Corinth, in the north to the tip of the Malea peninsula in the south—including the Argolid and Laconia with Mistra, Maina, and Karytania.

At his investiture each despot swore to respect the rights of the other. But as soon as Constantine left for Constantinople the two began to quarrel and intrigue against each other. They quarreled over territory and religion. Thomas was a Unionist, Demetrius an Anti-Unionist. They also quarreled with Venice about the four Morean cities Venice held, at a time when both needed Venice as an ally against the Turks. Soon Thomas tried to seize the district of Skorta that belonged to Demetrius. Demetrius declared war on his brother and sought support from Turakhan beg, the Ottoman governor of Thessaly. The intervention of Ottoman troops brought about peace talks, and under Ottoman pressure Thomas was forced to surrender to Demetrius the important town of Kalamata as compensation for Skorta, which Thomas was allowed to keep. Presumably the Ottomans hoped to make Kalamata into a bone of contention between the two brothers. The brothers then swore before the Ottoman commander that they would live in peace and respect the new arrangement.

Meanwhile a small remnant of Epirus, including Arta, still remained in the hands of Carlo II Tocco, who had accepted Ottoman suzerainty for it. He died in 1448, leaving his lands to his minor son Leonardo. The Ottomans in 1449 launched an assault against his lands, taking Arta and the bulk of southern Epirus, except for three isolated fortresses. Of these the Turks took Angelokastron in 1460 and Vonitsa, the last, in 1479. His islands, including Zakynthos where he usually resided, were not secure either; in late summer 1479 the Turks captured them all.

In 1451 Murad II died and was succeeded by Mehemmed II. The new sultan at once began planning to take Constantinople. He built two large fortresses above the city on either side of the Bosphorus, Rumeli and Anaduli Hisari. Constantine XI, realizing the magnitude of the threat, sought Western aid, adding substance to his request by again proclaiming the Union of the Churches, which, of course, stirred up violent opposition from the local Greeks. Having lost everything else, the Greeks strongly clung to their faith.

Mehemmed planned his assault on Constantinople for 1453. As a diversion, and to prevent Peloponnesian aid to Constantinople, Mehemmed launched a major plundering raid into the Morea in 1452. The Greeks of the Morea fought well, even defeating one large unit of these forces. But the diversion worked. The Morea could send no aid to Constantinople, and the two despots had to reaffirm their status as Ottoman vassals. In 1453 Mehemmed II slowly moved toward Constantinople. On the way he conquered Anchialos and Mesembria on the Black Sea coast. He stopped at Selymbria, but it resisted; so, leaving it blockaded (it was taken later that year), he marched on to Constantinople. On 7 April 1453 Mehemmed began the siege of Constantinople. A small Greek army of only a couple of thousand and a Genoese force of seven hundred constituted the defenders of the capital. The city's hopes depended on its magnificent walls. However, the Ottomans had a vast number of well-disciplined troops as well as cannons to use against these walls.

The city fell to a major assault on the night of 29–30 May. Constantine XI died fighting. The Ottomans plundered the city for three days, and then Mehemmed entered the city, which he now made into the capital of his empire. Hagia Sophia was converted into a mosque. Mehemmed left most of the churches intact, however, and made a strong effort to win the support of his Greek subjects. He granted them freedom of religion under their patriarch. Moreover, to gain the Greeks' support, he installed as patriarch the leader of the Anti-Unionist party, George Gennadius Scholarius, thereby supporting the Greek religion against Catholicism and Church Union. Thus the Union of

Florence died. Few Greeks regretted its passing, and most of those intellectuals who did emigrated to the West. The fall of the city is traditionally seen as the end of the Byzantine Empire.

Meanwhile the Palaeologus family still ruled the Morea. The two despots there were not popular with their numerous Albanian subjects. And in 1453 these Albanians, angry over a tax increase, rose up in a major rebellion. The initiator seems to have been a chieftain named Peter Bova. He also was able to win the support of various Greek archons there, including Manuel Cantacuzenus, a grandson of John VI Cantacuzenus' son Matthew. This Manuel Cantacuzenus had previously been appointed by Constantine as governor of Mani. Manuel soon rose to become the leader of the rebels against Demetrius. Many of Manuel's supporters called him despot with the hopes of installing him as the ruler of the Morea. At roughly the same time John Asen Centurione Zaccaria, a bastard son of Centurione Zaccaria, the last Prince of Achaea, and of a Byzantine woman descended from the Bulgarian and subsequently Byzantine family of Asen, escaped from Despot Thomas' jail where he had been imprisoned for an earlier revolt. Supported by a major Greek magnate named Nicephorus Loukanis, John Asen Centurione Zaccaria began to call himself Prince of Achaea and set about trying to revive his father's former principality. He soon came to lead the rebels in Thomas' lands.

The leaders of both rebellions sought recognition from the sultan. Thomas and Demetrius, finding themselves overwhelmed, shut themselves up in strongholds—Thomas in Patras and Demetrius in Mistra—and also sought aid from the sultan. Facing enough trouble from the Albanians of Skanderbeg, the sultan did not want to see a new Albanian state established and thus sent a major force into the Peloponnesus in December 1453. By the late summer or early fall of 1454 the Ottoman troops had suppressed both rebellions. In the course of their work they severely plundered the lands of the rebels. Centurione fled to Venice, while Manuel Cantacuzenus fled to Dubrovnik, which he later left to take up residence in Hungary. The Ottomans decided to pardon Peter Bova and left him as the chief of his tribe. The Albanians, having submitted, were to benefit from the further depopulation resulting from the rebellion and from Ottoman intervention; the Albanians not only expanded their landholding but also converted considerable farm land into pasture land.

The despots were then re-invested in their offices by the Turks, with the obligation to pay an even higher tribute. At the same time certain major archons sought to become direct vassals of the sultan. Seeing this as a means to play "divide and rule" more effectively, Mehemmed accepted their request. Thus certain lands of the Morea, though remaining in Greek hands, became independent of the despots and came to be held directly from the sultan. This also had the effect of reducing the size of the despots' armies and of reducing their tax income, which was needed both for defense and for their ever-increasing tribute payments. As various other magnates, in theory under the despots, also failed to pay the taxes they owed, the despots were faced with a major financial problem. By 1458 the despots' tribute was three years in arrears.

Seeing the Ottoman threat to their lands increasing, the brothers took different approaches. Demetrius became more and more subservient to the Turks in the hopes of retaining his position, whereas Thomas sought to defend his lands by acquiring support from the West. To achieve this Thomas clung to a Unionist position. In 1458, provoked by the arrears in tribute and Thomas' negotiations with the West, Mehemmed II sent a large force into the Peloponnesus. Though it attacked the lands of both brothers, it concentrated its efforts against the less-subservient Thomas, whose lands suffered particularly severe ravages. The towns the Ottomans attacked resisted strongly; thus the Ottoman acquisition of towns was slow. But by the end of the summer, according to Kritovoulos, the Turks had gained about a third of the Peloponnesus, including Patras and Vostitsa (Aiegion). The despots then had to submit to a new treaty, allowing the sultan to retain what he had taken. However, according to Sphrantzes, Patras, Kalavryta, and Greveno were not taken but were surrendered by the 1458 treaty. Demetrius also had to accept the permanent loss of Corinth, which had finally been starved into surrender after a siege lasting the whole summer. Both despots had to agree to increased tribute, something that their territorial (and therefore revenue) losses were to make an impossibility to obtain. Then, in October 1458, the sultan's armies withdrew with many captives. However, an Ottoman governor, Omar Pasha, remained in the Peloponnesus, based in Corinth, to govern the territories annexed by the Turks. And Turkish garrisons were placed in the Turkish towns.

Demetrius decided it was best to accept the situation. However, Thomas, bitter at the loss of Patras, acquired some Western mercenaries and attacked Patras. This effort failed, but, according to Sphrantzes, his forces did recover Kalavryta. Next, Thomas attacked Demetrius and seized various forts. Presumably he was angry at Demetrius' failure to support his Patras campaign and at Demetrius' policy of accommodating the Turks. Thomas probably also was jealous because Demetrius had lost less territory to the Turks than he had and had thus come out better in the 1458 settlement with the Turks. Presumably, Thomas hoped to rectify the situation by grabbing some of Demetrius' lands. Demetrius was taken by surprise and sought aid from the sultan. The sultan ordered Thomas to withdraw from Demetrius' lands and to restore to Demetrius the forts he had taken. It seems that Thomas did not return all the forts, for Demetrius next attacked Thomas' land. Occupied elsewhere, the sultan could only send a unit of troops based in Thessaly to pillage Thomas' Arcadia. Then, struck down by the plague, these Turkish forces were withdrawn. Expecting a new intervention by the Turks, the two brothers then met and concluded a peace. But it was soon broken, and the two were again skirmishing and pillaging each other's lands in the winter of 1459–60. Kritovoulos blames the Peloponnesian magnates for inciting the brothers against each other, hoping, Kritovoulos claims, to expand their own possessions with lands taken in civil warfare.

Next, a rebellion broke out in Demetrius' territory, during which, Kritovoulos reports, many Albanians deserted Demetrius' lands for Thomas'. Forced by the rebels to flee to Monemvasia, Demetrius again appealed to the sultan. Occupied elsewhere, he could not at once send troops. But he did order Thomas to restore to Demetrius the forts he had taken from him, to pay an increased tribute to the Ottomans, and to report in person to the sultan within twenty days. Thomas, it seems, was ready to obey these orders, but his nobles refused to yield various of the forts in question (which they had assumed possession of) and to render the money necessary for this tribute. Thus negotiations broke down, and anarchy increased in the peninsula. The Albanians took advantage of the strife to plunder Greeks of both sides, laying waste villages and farms to create more pasture land. And, it seems, the Ottoman garrisons in the Turkish-held towns also moved into Greek territory to enrich themselves by plundering villages.

On the Albanians Sphrantzes reports:

> Then the base and most useless race of the Albanians took advantage of the present situation, which was suitable to their reputation and thievish disposition. What did they neglect to do, what crime did they not commit? For they broke faith sometimes twice on the same Sabbath and were always deserting one lord for the other. They demanded, in their own tongue, castles for their estates; if they were denied by one lord they would run to the other despot, while the rest would then approach the first despot in a similar way. In the meantime, if they found anything belonging to the unfortunate Romans [Greeks] and even to the Albanians, to their relatives and dependents, they would plunder and destroy it. Who could provide an adequate lamentation over such great misfortunes?[4]

Mehemmed saw the time was ripe to finish off Greek rule in the Peloponnesus; he also wanted to secure the province before Pope Pius II could mobilize the new crusade he was planning. Though such a crusade was called for by Pius in 1459 and actively pursued as a policy goal, nothing in fact was ever to come of it. Moreover, Mehemmed was angry at Thomas for not reporting to him and not obeying his other orders. He probably was also annoyed at Demetrius, who, though more submissive than Thomas, was not rendering all the tribute he owed either.

So, the sultan attacked the Peloponnesus with a major force in the spring of 1460. Demetrius surrendered Mistra to him on 30 May 1460. Mehemmed then proceeded to conquer the rest of the peninsula. Two towns, Gardiki and Kastritsi (Kastrion), resisted and were taken by storm. The inhabitants of these two towns, including six thousand at Gardiki, were massacred. Thomas tried to submit, but he could not raise the vast tribute the sultan demanded. So the Ottoman campaign continued. The massacres led Greek town commanders to resist more strongly; but this merely prolonged the campaign. The Ottomans pressed on, taking the various Morean forts one by one. By the end of 1460 the Ottomans had conquered all the Greek Peloponnesus except for Monemvasia and Salmenikon; Salmenikon held out heroically under siege for a full year until it finally fell in July 1461. With its fall all the mainland territories that had been part of the Byzantine Empire—except Monemvasia—were conquered, and the Ottomans had annexed all the Byzantine Morea. Many Peloponnesians were carted off to Constantinople to help repopulate that city. Mehemmed repaired and garrisoned what he felt to be the key fortresses and leveled the rest.

Thomas did not even stay to participate in the attempted defense of his lands; instead he fled via Venice's Modon to Corfu and then to Italy, where he lived on a papal pension until his death in 1465. Demetrius, who had surrendered his person to the Turks when summoned early in the campaign in 1460, was received by the sultan with honors and promised an appanage in Thrace. He soon thereafter received it; it included Imbros, Lemnos, parts of Thasos and Samothrace, and the Thracian town of Ainos. He lived in Ainos for seven years until he was disgraced in 1467, allegedly for being involved in cheating the Ottomans of income from a local salt monopoly. He was moved to Demotika and then to Adrianople. Kept under close supervision, he died in a monastery in Adrianople in 1470. His death followed by a year that of his daughter Helen, who had been designated for Mehemmed's harem. However, the sultan had then thought better of it, fearing she would poison him. Having rejected her, he banned her from ever marrying; so, she died a spinster.

After the fall of Salmenikon in 1461, all the Peloponnesus except for the four Venetian towns, Monemvasia, and the mountains of the Maniot peninsula was Ottoman. In 1464 Monemvasia accepted Venetian rule, and a podesta was installed. The Ottomans took Argos from Venice, most probably in 1462, though Kritovoulos dates it 1463.

Kritovoulos claims that after the Ottoman governor of the Peloponnesus launched a damaging raid against Venetian Naupaktos, the Venetians in 1463 retaliated with an expedition that landed on the Isthmus of Corinth. They immediately started to restore the former wall across the Isthmus. Their presence encouraged various subjugated Greek towns to revolt. Lemnos and certain Aegean islands in the Cyclades, according to Pius II, followed suit and "threw off the Turkish yoke and deserted to the Venetians." But then Ottoman troops from north of the Isthmus attacked the Venetians at the same time as the Ottoman Peloponnesian forces struck them from the south. Those Venetians who could, escaped to their ships. The Turks then marched on Argos, which, seeing the impossibility of holding out, surrendered on demand. A large portion of its populace was transferred elsewhere and its fortifications were destroyed. Then the Turks easily subdued the last Greek rebels.

In 1470 the Ottomans took from Venice Euboea, including Negroponte.

568   *Late Medieval Balkans*

And they took Vonitsa from the Toccos in 1479. Modon, Coron, and also Naupaktos (Lepanto)—on the northern shore of the Gulf of Corinth—were surrendered by Venice to the Turks in 1500. Monemvasia and the last of the four original Venetian towns, Nauplia, were ceded, still unconquered, by the Venetians to the Turks in 1540 after a disastrous war in which the Ottomans severely bested the Venetians.

Meanwhile, the Ottomans also ended the Florentine Duchy of Athens and Thebes. In 1451 Nerio II died. His son Francesco was a minor. Nerio's young widow, Chiara, had a lover, a Venetian, Bartholomeo Contarini, whose father commanded the Venetian town of Nauplia. Bartholomeo was already married to a lady in Venice. Wanting to marry Chiara, he escaped the sin of bigamy by murdering his Venetian wife. Then he married Chiara and, as guardian for Francesco, took over the governorship of the duchy. He seems to have been an arbitrary ruler who stirred up much opposition among the local Greeks. They complained to the sultan, who had not been happy to see a Venetian ruling the duchy. The sultan summoned Bartholomeo to his court; Bartholomeo, upon obeying the summons, was thrown into jail.

Francesco's cousin Franco—the son of Anthony II, who had briefly ruled Athens, 1439–41—was then installed as regent by the sultan. Ambitious to take over the duchy in his own right, Franco in 1456 jailed and then murdered Chiara, Nerio's widow and his own aunt. The murder upset the local populace, who saw it as the first step toward Franco's deposing the rightful heir, Francesco. This provided an excuse for the sultan to intervene, and in June 1456 he attacked the duchy. He quickly took Athens. By the surrender agreement Franco was allowed to go to Thebes, from which he ruled all Boeotia as a fief from the sultan. Attica was immediately annexed by the sultan in 1456. Franco did not rule Boeotia long. In 1460, on a campaign in the service of the Ottomans, he was strangled on the orders of the sultan, and Boeotia too was placed under direct Ottoman rule. The Ottomans expelled all the remaining Latin clergy from Attica and Boeotia, while confirming the Greek clergy in possession of all the local churches, except for those that were made into mosques. Among the latter was Athens' great Church to the Virgin, the Parthenon.

The Fall of Serbia

The Ottomans tolerated the existence of George Branković's Serbia during the reign of Murad II. However, Murad's successor Mehemmed II intended to annex Serbia, and, having taken Constantinople, decided Serbia's turn had come. The Serbs, who had faithfully fulfilled their vassal obligations to the sultan (including providing troops for the attack on Constantinople), tried to renew their peace treaty with the Ottomans, which had just lapsed, but the sultan refused. In 1454 the Ottomans launched a raid against Serbia that plundered extensive regions and may have picked off a few lesser forts. Ostrovica may well have fallen in this campaign. The Turks also besieged

Smederevo, but without success. They took many captives, some of whom were utilized in the repopulation of the new Ottoman capital of Constantinople.

Then in 1455 the Ottomans directed a major assault against Serbia. Southern Serbia, the Kosovo region (including all the direct holdings of the Branković family), and the richest mine, Novo Brdo, fell. It is estimated that at the time of its capture Novo Brdo yielded an income of 120,000 ducats annually. After the 1455 campaign Branković retained only the territory north of the West Morava River. These new boundaries were specified in an agreement signed between him and the Ottomans in late 1455 or early 1456. Among Serbia's losses in 1455 was Peć, the seat of the Serbian patriarch. Not wanting the head of his Church to reside in Ottoman territory, Branković, after receiving confirmation of Serbia's right to its own patriarch from the Patriarch of Constantinople, appointed a new patriarch for Serbia. This bishop, presumably residing in Smederevo, had jurisdiction only over the dioceses lying in the territory Branković retained. The Archbishop of Ohrid, who possessed a long memory, quickly moved in and re-asserted his jurisdiction over the Serbian lands conquered by the Turks that had belonged to Ohrid prior to 1219. After Serbia's fall in 1459 the dioceses that had been under Peć remained divided between Ohrid and a Serbian hierarch (whose title and residence seem frequently to have changed) until the re-establishment of the Patriarchate of Peć in 1557.

In 1456 Hungarian-held Beograd underwent a full-scale siege. The city was heroically defended by John Hunyadi and Cardinal Capistrano. After the Christians won a battle against the attackers and Beograd was hit by an outbreak of the plague, the Ottomans withdrew, still in 1456. Thus the defense succeeded, and Beograd was to hold out under Hungary until 1521. However, its defense had been costly, for the plague struck down many of its defenders, including both Hunyadi and Capistrano. The loss of Hunyadi was particularly distressing to the Christian cause, for he was one of Christianity's two most successful commanders—the other being Skanderbeg—against the Turks. Furthermore, civil war then ensued in Hungary, first a conflict between Hunyadi's family and Ulrich of Celje that culminated in Ulrich's murder in November 1456, and then, after Ladislas V's death in November 1457, between the partisans of Matthew Corvinus Hunyadi and those of Frederick III Habsburg. Though Matthew had by early 1458 assumed control over most of Hungary, tensions continued between him and Frederick until 1463. These internal struggles temporarily weakened Hungary at this key moment and also limited the action Hungary could take in the defense of Serbia.

Meanwhile, on 24 December 1456, after the Ottoman campaign against Beograd that had plundered Serbia as it marched to and returned from Beograd, George Branković died. He was an elderly man by then, most probably in his eighties. The circumstances of his death are not entirely certain. Later sources, including Orbini, state that George died from the after-effects of a clash with Michael Szilagyi, the Hungarian governor of Beograd.

According to this story, which evidently takes place after the Ottoman withdrawal from Beograd, some Hungarians had been killed in a skirmish with some of Branković's Serbs. Quite possibly the two sides had clashed as a result of Ladislas Hunyadi's murder of Ulrich of Celje. For Michael Szilagyi was Ladislas Hunyadi's uncle and a leading figure in the Hunyadi party, while George Branković had been allied to Ulrich, who had been married to George's daughter Catherine. In any case, after the just-mentioned skirmish Szilagyi sought revenge and ambushed George Branković and his entourage. In the ensuing scuffle Branković was wounded—losing two fingers from his right hand—and taken prisoner, being held for ransom. That he was captured by Szilagyi and held for ransom is confirmed by the contemporary, Kritovoulos. Kritovoulos adds that George's son and heir, Lazar, had a bad spirit toward his parents and had not wanted to pay the ransom. However, he had finally paid over thirty thousand pieces of gold, albeit grudgingly and against his will, after being urgently pressed to do so by his mother. His release procured, George returned home. According to Orbini, his wound festered and eventually proved fatal. Kritovoulos says simply that George was worn out by grief and a severe disease.

George was succeeded by his youngest son, Lazar—who, as noted, had become the heir because the Turks had blinded his two older brothers. Desperate to save his lands, Lazar submitted to the sultan in January 1457, promising to pay an annual tribute of forty thousand ducats. Lazar had no choice in this, because Serbia was unable to resist the Turks alone, and Lazar was in no position to obtain aid from Hungary. For Hungary then seemed to be in the hands of the Hunyadi faction that in the previous two months had murdered Lazar's brother-in-law Ulrich of Celje and had attacked Lazar's father, in the process wounding him if not causing his death. Two months later, however, new possibilities opened for Lazar, for in the middle of March 1457 Ladislas V, as noted, seized and executed Ladislas Hunyadi. This set off further civil strife in Hungary as Ladislas Hunyadi's uncle, Michael Szilagyi, mobilized to resist the young king.

Lazar immediately in April 1457 attacked the Banat and took the district of Kovin which belonged to the Hunyadis. This district, lying across the Danube from Smederevo, stretched from the Danube to the Temes River. In May Lazar's forces were defeated on the Temes River by Michael Szilagyi's troops, and Lazar was forced to give up his offensive, though for the time he retained the Kovin district. It is not known whether Lazar had simply taken advantage of the Hungarian strife to avenge himself on the Hunyadis and make gains at Hungary's expense or whether he moved against the Hunyadis after negotiations with, and as an ally of, the young Hungarian king. Had there been no such agreement, Lazar would have been inviting retaliation from the Hungarians as soon as they had concluded their strife. Yet to have made a compact with the Hungarian king would have invited trouble from the Ottomans. And would the Hungarian king have acquiesced in Lazar's taking the Kovin district? In the light of such questions we must emphasize that we do not know whether or not Lazar had in fact entered into a compact with the Hungarian king. However, various scholars have argued that he did and have seen this alleged agreement as the cause of the quarrel that occurred at this time within the Branković family.

In this quarrel Lazar seems to have been opposed by his brother Gregory, sister Mara, mother Jerina, and uncle Thomas Cantacuzenus. But whether they were opposed to him owing to their advocacy of maintaining close ties with the Turks and of doing nothing to provoke them or for some other reason is not certain. They may equally well have been squabbling over a succession question. Lazar had only one child, a daughter, Helen (Jelena), whom he may well have wanted to be his heir. After all through her marriage, particularly if she were heiress to Serbia, Lazar might be able to win an ally from a neighboring state. And we know that, at least after Lazar's death, Lazar's wife, also named Helen, was actively working for this daughter's succession. However, there was a second Branković who had strong claims to the succession. This was Gregory's illegitimate son, Vuk. Vuk was not only a male, but his father Gregory was George Branković's eldest son. And Gregory, as noted, had been George's heir until 1441, when his blinding at the hands of the Turks had disqualified him. Furthermore, we note that in the line-up of figures in this dispute Lazar and Gregory were on opposite sides. Unfortunately we can only speculate, for the sources on the Branković family quarrel are as vague as they can be.

Kritovoulos states that after his succession Lazar clashed with his mother, Jerina Cantacuzena. He refused her a share in the government and injured her in many ways, constantly bothering her by seeking a share of his inheritance and the treasure she had accumulated and hidden. She, unable to bear Lazar's insults any longer, fled. Lazar pursued her. Being old and sick, she could not flee far; she died, after which Lazar recovered the treasure. Orbini states that after George's death, Lazar's position inside Serbia was challenged by his mother, Jerina, to whom George's testament had assigned a major role in Serbia's government. Wanting to rule alone, Lazar murdered her by poisoning her salad. This act horrified many Serbian nobles, who turned against him. Mehemmed II decided the time was ripe to conquer Serbia. Realizing the helplessness of his position, Lazar took ill and died, leaving no male heir.

It is impossible to confirm either account, both of which stress a quarrel between son and mother, though one has them bickering over wealth and the other over power. Many scholars do think, however, that there had at least been some sort of power struggle within the family and that quite possibly Lazar and his mother had been on opposite sides. In any case he was in Smederevo when she, residing separately in Rudnik, died, naturally or otherwise, on 3 May 1457.

Sphrantzes and the sixteenth-century Serbian annals report that immediately on her death Lazar's older brother, the blind Gregory, his sister Mara, and his uncle Thomas Cantacuzenus fled to the Turks, taking considerable treasure with them. Kritovoulos confirms the flight of the three to the Turks, though he has it precede Jerina's death. If true, their flight might indicate that they feared action against themselves from Lazar. In any case, regardless of whether or not there was a struggle for power within Serbia during 1457, Lazar, faced with the likelihood of a new Turkish attack, did die on 20 January 1458. Rumor said he was poisoned by some of his nobles. Michael Szilagyi, the commander of Beograd (who had retained control of Beograd throughout the chaos of 1457), shortly thereafter regained the Kovin district for Hungary. The Bosnians also attacked and retook Srebrnica, probably also in 1458, and eleven other lesser towns, including Zvornik, along the Drina. Thus the Drina again became the border between Serbia and Bosnia.

Lazar's widow Helen, the daughter of Thomas Palaeologus of the Morea who had married Lazar in December 1446, and Lazar's other blind brother, Stefan, tried to assume power in Serbia. Their position, to say the least, was insecure. The leading Serbs seem to have been divided as to whether Serbia should seek to retain what it still had by submitting completely to and co-operating with the Turks or whether Serbia should try to improve its position by seeking an alliance with the Hungarians. And following Lazar's death, representatives of these two view-points seem to have clashed, with the result that two weeks to a month—depending on which source one accepts—passed before Serbia had any kind of government. This government, chosen at some time in February 1458, apparently by a council of some sort, was a collective affair that had Vojvoda Michael Andjelović (Angelus), the leader of the pro-Turkish faction, as its primary figure. However, he had to share power with Lazar's widow Helen and Lazar's brother Stefan. The Hungarians were in no position to oppose Michael's installation, for at this critical moment they were struggling over Matthew Corvinus' establishment as King of Hungary.

Members of the Angelus family of Thessaly, Michael and his brother had been living in exile in Novo Brdo when the Ottomans attacked that town in 1427. The brothers fled separately; Michael escaped to George Branković, who housed him at his court, while the other brother was captured by the Turks. The latter soon converted to Islam and rose rapidly in the Ottoman military establishment, becoming Mahmud Pasha, Beglerbeg of Rumeli (roughly Ottoman Bulgaria). The brothers seem to have maintained cordial ties. Meanwhile Michael, who had been appointed by Lazar to the position of great vojvoda, the highest military office in Serbia, wanted to maintain Serbia's existence by closely tying its fortunes to the Turks and by opposing the Hungarians. Not surprisingly, when he rose to the position of first man in the ruling collective, Helen felt frustrated and, not at all interested in sharing power, set about increasing her contacts with the Hungarians in the hope that they would help her oust Michael.

Michael, meanwhile, had no intention of relinquishing his position, and rumors circulated that he was ambitious to become Despot of Serbia and hoped the Ottomans would assist him to realize this ambition. And it is reported that soon townsmen in Smederevo were calling him despot. At the same time opposition to him was growing, presumably incited by Helen. And eight thousand Hungarian soldiers under Michael Szilagyi gathered on the Danube. So, Michael received a unit of Turkish troops to beef up his garrison in Smederevo. He clearly intended to use them to advance his own cause and saw them as allies. Upon their arrival, in March 1458, these Turks promptly raised the Turkish flag over the battlements of Smederevo. Whether this signified their intention to ignore Michael's cause and seize the town for the sultan is not certain. In any case this proved to be more than the local Serbian citizens could take, and they staged a spontaneous uprising that killed many Turks and took Michael prisoner. Possibly the presence of the Hungarian troops a short distance up the river provided the rebels with the courage to carry out the revolt. This uprising enabled Helen, who had already opened up serious negotiations with the Hungarians (through Michael Szilagyi, the commander of Beograd), to take power in Serbia. Thus the pro-Hungarian faction, to which she belonged, won the local struggle.

However, the jailing of Michael—and diplomatic sources mention him as still being a prisoner in Smederevo in the fall of 1458—and the policy orientation of the victors were not pleasing to the Turks, particularly not to Mahmud Pasha, Michael's brother. The Turks decided to attack Serbia and mobilized their forces. They entered Serbian territory in early April, if not at the very end of March. The Turkish forces, led by Mahmud Pasha himself, seem to have been large. Thus Helen's Hungarian allies were in no position to support her. Matthew Corvinus, still faced with much opposition at home, had to concentrate his attention on dealing with internal enemies and consolidating his own position. He was able to provide his uncle, Michael Szilagyi, in Beograd with only eight thousand men. As they were far too few in number to intervene and oppose the Turks in Serbia, Michael based them along the Danube frontier to prevent the Turks from attempting to cross the river into Hungary.

Accompanying the Turkish forces was Gregory, Lazar's blind brother, who was to be advanced as a pretender to the throne. Whether he had been with the Ottomans from the time of his flight during Lazar's lifetime or whether he had returned to Serbia upon Lazar's death only to fail in an attempted coup and flee again to the Turks—as Hungarian sources state—is not entirely certain.

Kritovoulos confirms none of the above. He simply states that Lazar had refused to pay the tribute owed, so the sultan became angry and decided to attack Serbia. When he learned of Lazar's death, he ordered an immediate invasion.

Whatever the truth in the story of Michael Andjelović, Helen soon after taking power entered into new discussions with the Hungarians. The Hungarians, seeing the end of Serbia in sight, tried to persuade Helen and Stefan to turn over what was left of Serbia, including Smederevo, to Hungary in exchange for lands within Hungary. Some, or possibly all, of the lands offered them in Hungary seem to have been lands that previously belonged to the Branković family but which had been confiscated by the angry John

Hunyadi in 1450. These negotiations did not go smoothly. Later sources say that Helen wanted to yield only Golubac for these lands, while keeping Smederevo. Furthermore, it was claimed, John Hunyadi's widow, who seems to have acquired many of the former Branković estates, did not want to give them up.

At some time between Lazar's death (20 January 1458) and the arrival of Turkish forces in Serbia (late March–early April 1458), Hungarian sources state, Gregory Branković, the other blinded Branković brother, accompanied by his twenty-year-old illegitimate son Vuk, tried to take power in Serbia. If this statement is true, then Gregory, who had sought asylum with the Turks in May 1457, must have left Ottoman territory to stage this rebellion. To have been able to do this suggests he had the Turks' blessings for his attempt. Hungarian sources then claim that Gregory and Vuk were defeated in Srem. They soon, in April 1458, were to be found back in the Turkish camp, which later authors claim was located at Kruševac. Thus it seems the Branković family was divided into two factions, each seeking power, with one enlisting the help of the Hungarians and the other that of the Turks.

In any case, regardless of the actual background for it, by April 1458 the Turks were preparing for an assault and Gregory Branković was present in their ranks. The Turks were actively on the warpath again inside Serbia in May 1458. In the course of that spring they took Resava, Žrnov (Avala), Bela Stena, and Višesav. In August they took Golubac, which seems not to have been turned over to the Hungarians. When this campaign was completed, Serbia consisted of little more than Smederevo itself. Smederevo seems to have escaped the coup de grâce in 1458 because Mahmud and a portion of his forces had to be withdrawn in the course of the summer to join a major Turkish campaign in the Peloponnesus ordered by Mehemmed II.

Nevertheless, Helen was well aware that Smederevo could expect a new attack the following year. Her negotiations with Hungary had not brought Serbia any Hungarian help during the disasters of 1458, so she needed a new ally. (In all fairness to Hungary, it must be repeated that Matthew Corvinus in 1458 had had to devote his energies to securing his own authority at home against considerable opposition.) So, Helen now tried to arrange a marriage that would procure Bosnian aid for Serbia. She offered her daughter Helen (Jelena), then about eleven years old, as a bride for Stefan Tomašević, the eldest son and heir of the Bosnian king. The Bosnians were interested, for such a marriage agreement would secure their possession of Srebrnica against future Serbian attack. However, the Bosnians would enter into the arrangement only if it did not bring them into conflict with Hungary. In January 1459, at a council meeting of the Hungarian nobility, taking place after Bosnia had again agreed to accept Hungarian suzerainty, King Matthew Corvinus of Hungary agreed to the marriage and to Stefan Tomašević's taking over as ruler of Smederevo. Matthew seems to have seen this as a means to draw Bosnia into the struggle against the Turks; he may also have dreamed that a union between Bosnia and Serbia would result, creating a buffer state between the Turks and Hungary.

Angry at their vassal Bosnia's lining up with Hungary, the Turks were already raiding Bosnia in March 1459. Stefan Tomašević arrived in Smederevo and took over command of its fortress, also in March. To guarantee a smooth take-over Michael Szilagyi appeared with a Hungarian force to supervise the transition. Stefan Tomašević's wedding to Helen, who upon her marriage took the name Maria, took place in April. The title "despot"—held by Stefan Lazarević, George Branković, and even Lazar, who during his father's lifetime had received it from a Byzantine envoy—somehow went with Smederevo to Stefan Tomašević. Perhaps Lazar's widow, as a Byzantine princess of the Palaeologus family and in the absence of a Byzantine emperor after the fall of Constantinople, felt she had the right to grant the title. A week after the wedding, on 8 April, the new regime in Smederevo exiled Stefan Branković from Serbia.

The Ottomans then launched a major assault against Smederevo, taking it on 20 June 1459. Serbia again disappeared as a state. This time Ottoman control was to last until the nineteenth century. Stefan Tomašević and his new bride fled to Bosnia. The Hungarians eventually attacked and recovered in 1476 the region of Šabac in Serbia; they held it until the major Ottoman campaign of 1521, which not only reconquered the Šabac province but also took Beograd.

After the fall of Smederevo, Matthew Corvinus accused Stefan Tomašević and the Bosnians of selling out to the Turks. He also seems to have placed some blame on the Brankovići, or at least used the fall of Smederevo as an excuse to do so, for he took from the Branković family the town of Tokai and its district, a major possession of the family within Hungary.

Matthew's accusations were at once taken up by the papacy, and Pope Pius II, writing at about that time in his diaries, later published as the *Commentaries,* states,

A few months after he [Stefan Tomašević] entered it [Smederevo], he called in the Turks and sold them the town for a great weight of gold. This was as crushing a blow to the spirits of the Hungarians as the loss of Constantinople had been. For Senderovia [Smederevo] is, as it were, the gate from Rascia [Serbia] to Wallachia, a most convenient base for making war against the Hungarians. . . . The Bosnian envoys, however, had left Mantua before the betrayal was generally known and it was reported first to the Hungarian ambassadors.[5]

Pius makes his source for this information clear, stating that it was reported to, and we may conclude circulated thereafter by, Hungarian ambassadors. Confirmation for the substance of this accusation is found only in Hungarian sources or in sources derived from them. No Turkish source suggests a betrayal. Most modern scholars believe the accusation to be slander and have concluded that the Bosnian prince, unable to resist the superior strength of the Turks, was forced to surrender the town. The pope soon dispatched an envoy to look into the charges; he found the Bosnian king conciliatory. In fact Pius states, "The King of Bosnia, to atone for having surrendered Senderovia to the Turks and to give proof of his religious faith . . . forced the Manichees . . . to be baptised or to emigrate. . . ." Suggesting Bosnian innocence of the Hungarian charge is the fact that Pius simply uses the neutral expression "surrendered Senderovia" rather than a more loaded term like "sold" or "betrayed." Also suggesting Bosnian innocence is the friendliness subsequently regularly shown by Pius to Stefan Tomašević when he succeeded to the Bosnian throne in 1461. Pius would hardly have been so supportive of the young man if he had actually sold the fortress to the Turks. Thus we may conclude that Pius at first believed and thus recorded the Hungarian accusation but soon, as a result of his own investigation, found the charges unfounded. He therefore did not repeat them. However, he failed to go back and correct the statement he had made earlier in his text.

Bosnian innocence of the charge of betraying Smederevo is also confirmed by Chalcocondyles, who states that the Smederevo Serbs ("Raškans"), unhappy with Bosnian rule and believing they could not resist the Turks, went out to meet the sultan, turning over to him the keys of the city of Smederevo. Constantine Mihailović, the Janissary chronicler, supports this view of events, insofar as he writes that the Smederevo Serbs, unhappy with Bosnian rule, preferred the Turks to the Hungarians. Given the context, Constantine's remarks imply this Serbian attitude played a role in the city's surrender.

As a postscript to this discussion of Smederevo and the Serbs it should be noted that the Turks soon thereafter, in the course of a small skirmish, took Michael Szilagyi prisoner. The Turks took him to Constantinople, where they beheaded him in 1461.

The long years of Ottoman raiding followed by the Turks' eventual conquest of Serbia caused large-scale migrations of Serbs from Serbia. The refugees ended up in one or the other of three regions: (1) the highland regions of Hercegovina or Zeta, where Ottoman control was always to be less direct and heavy; (2) Bosnia (from which some of them moved to the coast or up to Croatia, when Bosnia in its turn fell; as a result of this migration Orthodox populations appeared in parts of Bosnia where they had not been found at all previously, particularly in Lika and in the Krajina); and (3) Hungary, in particular in the region that came to be known as the Vojvodina. The Vojvodina, which had had no Serbs to speak of before the fifteenth century, acquired a large Serbian population that came to be the majority in many of its southern reaches along the border with the Turks. Many of these Serbs were to play an important role in defending the Hungarian frontier from Ottoman attack and in raiding the border lands of the Ottoman Empire. In the centuries that followed more Serbs were to emigrate from the Ottoman Empire to settle in this region.

Moreover, the raids and warfare drove many peasants settled on lands near main routes into more out-of-the-way places, particularly into the hills and mountains. This resulted not only in demographic change within the Balkans but also in a change of livelihood. The mountains were more conducive to stock rearing than agriculture. Moreover, in the event of an attack one's fields were vulnerable, whereas one might hope to escape with some or all of one's animals. Thus, these years were marked by an increase in the number of mobile pastorialists with flocks and a decline in the number engaged in agriculture.

Bosnia from 1443[6]

In the last chapter we brought Bosnia's story down to the death of King Tvrtko II and the succession of Stefan Tomaš (1443–61). Stefan Vukčić Kosača in Hum did not participate in the new king's election and immediately refused to recognize him. He announced his support of the new king's brother Radivoj, the long-time anti-king frequently supported by the Turks, who was then residing at the Kosača court. At this time, 1443, the papacy was trying to create a great counter-offensive against the Turks and sent envoys to both the king and to Stefan Vukčić about it, but neither could consider participation in any sort of league because civil war had quickly broken out between them. It is often stated that the Bosnians did not participate in the 1443 crusade at all. Recently, however, Živković has found that one of the major second-level nobles of eastern Bosnia, Peter Kovač Dinjičić, was a participant, leading six to seven hundred men.[7]

While this major confrontation between Christians and Turks took place to their east, the Bosnian rivals also went to war. Ivaniš Pavlović joined the king's side and the pair attacked Stefan Vukčić. Doing poorly, and further threatened since John Hunyadi also recognized the new king, Stefan Vukčić sought outside support from Alphonso of Naples. Alphonso accepted Stefan Vukčić as a vassal and admitted him to his knightly order of the Virgin.[8] But he sent no troops, so Stefan Vukčić's position remained precarious.

Once the Turks had defeated the crusaders, Stefan Vukčić, whose relations with the Ottomans were usually cordial, found his difficulties at an end. He received help from them and also from another Ottoman vassal, the restored George Branković, who also had had good relations with the Kosača family. Hunyadi, though recognizing Stefan Tomaš, sent the king no troops. Thus strengthened, Stefan Vukčić rapidly recovered the lands he had lost the previous year. The Bosnian civil war continued into 1446. By that time, as papal correspondence shows, the king had become a Roman Catholic; presumably until that time he had been a member of the Bosnian Church to which his father, Ostoja, had adhered.

Early in 1446 Stefan Vukčić and Stefan Tomaš finally made peace;

Stefan Vukčić agreed to recognize Stefan Tomaš as king, and the pre-war borders were restored. The peace was sealed by a marriage between the king and Stefan Vukčić's daughter Catherine, who had to become a Catholic in order to marry the king. In this period many Bosnian nobles were becoming, or are found in the sources already as, Catholics. Vladislav Klešić and George Vojsalić had become Catholics. Ivaniš Pavlović became a Catholic in 1446, though he returned to the Bosnian Church in 1449. Even Stefan Vukčić expressed interest in becoming a Catholic, though he did not do so. A considerable number of Catholic churches, including a couple built by the king and several new Franciscan monasteries, were erected at this time. There were both political and cultural reasons to accept Catholicism in these years. When the Bosnians wanted to create alliances with Western figures, either for internal reasons or against the Ottomans, the Westerners exerted considerable pressure on the Bosnians to become Catholics. At the same time Western cultural influences—musical, artistic, architectural, dress styles, etc.—that were closely intertwined with the Catholic faith were penetrating Bosnia from the Catholic coast.

The peace concluded between Stefan Vukčić and the king was not pleasing to the Turks, whose aim was to encourage divisions within Bosnia. George Branković, quarreling with Stefan Tomaš over Srebrnica, was also displeased. Thus in 1448, when the Turks sent an expedition to plunder the king's lands, they sent troops to plunder Stefan Vukčić's as well. Stefan Vukčić sent envoys to George Branković to try to improve his relations with Serbia; possibly he also hoped that George would intervene on his behalf with his Ottoman suzerain. And in 1448—possibly to bolster his case with the Ottomans—Stefan Vukčić declared his separation from Bosnia by dropping his title Vojvoda of Bosnia (which his predecessors Vlatko Vuković and Sandalj Hranić had also borne) which indicated the holder's subordination to the King of Bosnia. He assumed a title suggesting his own independence: Herceg (Duke) of Hum and the Coast. A year later he changed his title to Herceg of Saint Sava, calling himself after the famous Serbian saint whose relics lay in the monastery of Mileševo, which stood in the eastern part of Stefan Vukčić's principality.

This second title had considerable public relations value because Sava's relics were considered miracle-working by people of all Christian faiths, who flocked to Mileševo for cures. The Serbian connotations of the title may also have reflected the restoration of good relations between Stefan Vukčić and George Branković. The improvement in their relations is seen by the fact that when in 1448 or 1449 a Serbian-Bosnian war broke out over Srebrnica, Stefan Vukčić supported the Serbian side against Stefan Tomaš. He and his successors were to call themselves hercegs until the Ottoman conquest. From this title his lands became known as Hercegovina (the herceg's lands), a name that stuck throughout the Ottoman period and has lasted to the present.

At the time Serbia fell to the Turks for the first time (1439–41), the Serbs had held Srebrnica. In 1439 or 1440 the Turks took that city, retaining it until the crusaders' invasion of 1443. The Bosnians seem to have taken advantage of the Turks' and Serbs' occupation with that event to seize Srebrnica. Meanwhile, in the treaty of 1444 that restored Serbia as a state, the sultan recognized Srebrnica as belonging to the resurrected Serbia. The Serbs were back in possession of the town in April 1445. The Bosnians were not happy with this and, in late summer 1446, immediately following the peace concluded between the king and Stefan Vukčić, attacked and took the town back. Before the year ended the Serbs and Bosnians had concluded an agreement to administer the town jointly and to split its income. Neither side was happy with this arrangement and after a year or so each was trying to oust the other from the town. This led to further fighting in 1448 or 1449. After three years of sporadic fighting Serbia, which enjoyed the support of the Ottomans, gained in 1450 or 1451 sole possession of the town. Since Herceg Stefan supported the Serbs in this dispute, fighting also occurred between him and the king in 1449 and 1450.

While this warfare went on, the Ottomans stepped up their attacks on Bosnia. And now they began to annex parts of eastern Bosnia. Their gains were chiefly at the expense of the Pavlovići, whose main territories lay just west of the Drina. Ivaniš Pavlović died in 1450. The following year the Ottomans took Vrhbosna. Vrhbosna, under its new name Sarajevo, was to develop rapidly under the Ottomans to become the major city in Bosnia during the Turkish period. Greatly weakened by territorial losses, Ivaniš' brother and successor Peter became a vassal of Herceg Stefan. Thus the Pavlovići ceased to be numbered among the great nobles and joined the ranks of the second-level vassal nobility.

Meanwhile the Ottoman tribute owed by the king and herceg was regularly increased, particularly after the fall of Constantinople in 1453. Funds were also needed by both men to maintain the luxury of their courts and to finance their frequent wars. With several mines on his lands, the king was in a better financial position than the herceg, whose lands had no mines. Yet even so, the king had insufficient funds for his needs. His financial difficulties were the root cause for the frequent wars over the rich Srebrnica mine. Ćirković has calculated that between 1453 and 1457 the king had to turn over to the sultan 160,000 ducats in tribute, a sum that constituted the bulk of Bosnia's silver production from all its mines during those years.

The herceg, dependent on tolls and customs levies, was in a weaker financial position. So in the late 1440s he began trying to develop Novi and make it into a major port. The reader may recall that Tvrtko I, after he had acquired territory on the southern Dalmatian coast, had established Novi and had tried to develop its port facilities. His efforts had not succeeded, chiefly owing to the opposition of Dubrovnik. The herceg now made a new attempt, and Novi came to be called, as it still is, Herceg-Novi. He created ties with southern Italy, whence he imported weavers to establish a weaving industry. Then he tried to market salt, challenging Dubrovnik's near monopoly on selling salt to land-locked Bosnia and Serbia. To support this effort the herceg forbade his Vlachs to buy salt in Dubrovnik. Dubrovnik and Kotor—which to a lesser extent was also a marketer of salt—complained. Dubrovnik also accused the herceg of interfering with the activities of its merchants in Hercegovina. The herceg replied that everyone should look out for his own interests and asserted that he was free to do what he liked in his own lands. Tensions increased, and in protest Dubrovnik banned its merchants from Hercegovina. In June 1451 Herceg Stefan, having received permission from the sultan to make war on Dubrovnik, invaded Konavli. He met little opposition, for Dubrovnik was never able to field an army of any size or quality. The Serbian despot did not like this turn of events, and Herceg Stefan's relations with him grew strained.

Meanwhile tensions were also developing inside the herceg's own family. Some merchants, knowing that the herceg's eldest son, Vladislav, sought a bride, brought a girl of low reputation but great beauty from Siena to the herceg's court. Hoping to be richly rewarded, they claimed she was of noble birth. Vladislav was much impressed with her, but immediately his father made her his mistress. Angry words followed between father and son, resulting in the herceg's locking up Vladislav. Vladislav was quickly released by some nobles. He and his mother, who was jealous over the Sienese girl, then left court. They were soon—in August 1451—approached by envoys from Dubrovnik, which hoped to capitalize on this family feud. Vladislav readily agreed to enter the war against his father. Treachery was, in fact, operating in both directions. For in 1451 Dubrovnik instructed envoys to Hercegovina to discover who, in violation of the town's laws, was smuggling firearms to Herceg Stefan from Dubrovnik. As far as we know the culprit was never discovered. In November 1451 the King of Bosnia also agreed to aid Dubrovnik. However, two of his nobles, Vladislav Klešić and George Vojsalić, did not want to attack the herceg and instead attacked the king's lands. Next, and illustrating the growing authority of the Catholic Church in Bosnia, a papal legate was sent to Bosnia who persuaded the two dissident noblemen to make peace with their king. This mediation occurred by April 1452, for in that month they joined the king in his invasion of Hercegovina.

The previous month Vladislav Kosača had launched his well-planned revolt. Immediately a series of the herceg's fortresses, including some major ones like Blagaj, surrendered to him. By April Vladislav held all western Hum and the lower Neretva except for the region of Ljubuški. The herceg's position deteriorated further when in April the Bosnian king and his nobles invaded Hum.

The herceg received some temporary relief when the Ottomans launched a major raid through Bosnia, causing the Bosnian invaders to return home to defend their own lands. The herceg also concluded an alliance with Venice. Shortly thereafter the region of the Krajina revolted against its new master, Vladislav, and declared its loyalty to Venice. Venetian ships, in support of the herceg, then appeared in the mouth of the Neretva River and temporarily occupied the customs town of Drijeva. By this time the Ottoman raiders had withdrawn from Bosnia, enabling the Bosnian king to resume his invasion of Hercegovina. Stefan Tomaš marched on Drijeva and expelled the Venetians, claiming that from then on the town was to be his. Then, to reassert Bosnian control over Hercegovina, which, as noted, had more-or-less completely separated itself from Bosnia in the course of the 1440s, the king laid claim to Blagaj. Vladislav, who held it, however, refused to turn it over to the king. The king then offered to confirm Vladislav as ruler of all the land from the Čemerno Mountains to the sea in exchange for Blagaj. Vladislav wisely retained Blagaj, pointing out to the king that the whole region, which the king was so generously offering, was still held by Herceg Stefan. The king then threatened to abandon Vladislav's cause and return to Bosnia.

The war continued with considerable destruction of villages and crops until July 1453. At that time the herceg, through the mediation of Bosnian Church clerics, made peace with his wife and son. Their treaty stipulated that matters were to be restored to their pre-war condition. Pre-war conditions seem to have included the herceg's continued liaison with his Sienese mistress, for later documents continue to refer to her as living at his court and receiving gifts from Ragusan embassies. In concluding his peace, Vladislav left his ally Dubrovnik, still at war with the herceg, to make its peace as best it could. The town finally obtained peace in April 1454 after long negotiations with the herceg's ambassador Gost Radin, who clearly was in it for himself, mediating the peace efficiently but also receiving enormous bribes from the town in the process. However, since this peace also simply restored matters to their pre-war condition, all the causes of tension—Novi, the salt monopoly, etc.—remained. The herceg's wife died at the end of 1453; his mistress remained at his side.

In 1456 the Ottomans demanded that King Stefan Tomaš surrender four major towns to them. After he refused, Ottoman attacks on Bosnia became more frequent. The king also continued to squabble with Serbia and Herceg Stefan; occasionally their quarrels flared up into minor skirmishes. In late 1458 or early 1459, after the deaths of George Branković and his successor Despot Lazar, King Stefan Tomaš took advantage of Serbia's weakness to seize eleven towns along the Drina, including Srebrnica. Very shortly thereafter he made peace with Lazar's widow, the weak ruler of Serbia; as a result his son Stefan Tomašević married Lazar's daughter Helen/Maria. As a dowry Stefan Tomašević, now bearing the title despot, received Smederevo. He took control of Smederevo in March 1459. On 20 June 1459 the Turks took the city, thus absorbing all Serbia again—this time for keeps. The Hungarians accused the Bosnians of selling the fortress to the Turks, which did little to help Bosnian-Hungarian relations at this critical time. As noted earlier, it seems this accusation was unfounded.

As the Ottoman threat increased, Stefan Tomaš sought papal aid. The pope, however, stated he would provide help only if action were taken against the Bosnian Church. So, the king agreed to initiate a forceful policy. He may also have been accommodating to papal wishes in order to reduce the effect of the Hungarian accusation that the Bosnians were not good Christians and therefore had surrendered Smederevo to the Turks. Thus, now, for the first time, a Bosnian ruler adopted the policy, long demanded by international Catholicism, of persecution. It is worth emphasizing this, for until the last four years of the kingdom Bosnia's rulers, most of whom were Catholics, had abstained from persecutions and had remained tolerant of—or perhaps it is more accurate to say indifferent to—the religious beliefs of their subjects. In 1459 the king gave Bosnian Churchmen—most probably meaning the Bosnian Church clergy—the choice of conversion or exile.

Pope Pius II reports that some two thousand chose conversion, whereas only forty chose exile. This suggests that by that time morale had become very poor within the Church. The exiles emigrated to Hercegovina where, protected by Herceg Stefan, they were not persecuted. At the same time the king confiscated considerable land belonging to the Bosnian Church monasteries, which surely made this action more attractive for him. He also sent three heretics to Italy; taken before the inquisition, they, not surprisingly, converted to Catholicism. The inquisition documents depict the three as dualists. No evidence exists to show that the three belonged to the Bosnian Church. If the description of their beliefs is accurate, which is doubtful, the three could well have been adherents of the small dualist current that seems to have co-existed with the Bosnian Church.

The persecutions were successful. This is not surprising when we take into consideration the Church's low morale. Furthermore, the Bosnian Church seems to have simply been a monastic order. For no evidence exists that it had a secular or preaching clergy. Thus its clerics, excluding those few resident at secular courts, were restricted to monastic communities. Such a clustering would have made it easier for the king to seek the clerics out and face them with his ultimatum and to seize their buildings and land. Thus the elimination of the Bosnian Church as an institution could have been quickly effected. Furthermore, there were extensive regions of Bosnia and Hercegovina where Bosnian Church monasteries do not seem to have existed; in such regions the Church probably had little or no following. Thus a large portion of Bosnia's peasantry had probably rarely or even never seen a Bosnian Church cleric. Thus the peasants were probably even more indifferent to formal religion than Bosnia's nobility and thus also indifferent to the royal attack on the Bosnian Churchmen. And since the majority of the Church's clerics chose conversion over exile, showing their morale was not high, it is likely that such clerics had not instilled strong faith even in those peasants living near their monasteries. Thus after the conversion of most of its clergy and the exile of the handful who felt strongly about the Church, the Bosnian Church's lay adherents were left without leaders or any sort of clergy. The result, then, was the undermining, if not the destruction, of the Bosnian Church in Bosnia between 1459 and 1463, even before the arrival of the Turks. It is not surprising that it was to disappear completely soon after the Ottoman conquest, as its members were absorbed by Islam, Orthodoxy, and

Catholicism. It is also worth stressing that despite the Bosnian king's submission to papal demands, no papal aid was to be forthcoming.

In July 1461 Stefan Tomaš died. He was succeeded by his son Stefan Tomašević (1461–63). The new king immediately sent to Pope Pius II two envoys, described by the pope as tall and dignified old men. The text of Stefan Tomašević's long letter is given in Pius' *Commentaries*.[9] The king first sought a crown from the pope, noting that his father had been offered a papal crown but had been afraid to accept it, fearing such action would provoke the anger of the Turks. Stefan Tomašević stated that he himself, however, having been baptized as a boy and, having learned early the faith and Latin, did not fear being crowned. He also sought bishops. The plural is worth stressing, for Bosnia at the time had only one bishop, still residing outside the kingdom in Djakovo. Thus it seems that Stefan Tomašević wanted new ones created, presumably to be installed within Bosnia, to bring about a more efficient Church organization to Catholicize his country.

The king also told the pope that he had been informed that the Turks planned to invade Bosnia the following summer. Since Bosnia was not in a position to withstand such an attack alone, the king sought aid from the pope, saying that if he received substantial help, then the Turks might change their minds; and if the Turks still went through with their plans, then this aid might give the Bosnians more hope to fight more bravely. And if morale was high, Bosnia might be able to hold out. After all, it had numerous almost impregnable fortresses. He also pointed out that during the reign of his father the pope had given orders that arms should be collected in Venetian-controlled Dalmatia to be sent to Bosnia, but that the Venetian senate had countermanded these orders. Could the pope not bid the Venetians to allow these arms to be sent to him? He also asked the pope to send an envoy to Hungary to commend Bosnia's cause to the King of Hungary and urge him to join arms with Bosnia. He then stated:

> The Turks have built a number of fortifications in my kingdom and are showing a kindly disposition toward peasants. They promise that all who desert to them shall be free and they welcome them graciously. The inexperienced rustics do not understand their wiles and think their liberty will last forever. The people will be easily induced by such tricks to desert me unless they see me fortified by your aid, and the nobles, if they are deserted by the peasants, will not hold out long in their fortresses.

There was truth to the king's statement, for the peasants could see that in Ottoman Serbia and in occupied parts of Bosnia the peasants did pay lower taxes. And taxes in the Kingdom of Bosnia, both to prepare the land's defense and to meet the ever-increasing tribute demanded by the Turks, were extremely high.

Stefan Tomašević's letter then went on to say that it was in the papacy's interests to take action now, for the Turks had no intention of stopping with

Bosnia, but next would move against Croatia, Dalmatia, Hungary, Venice, Italy, and Rome itself. He concluded:

> Such are the enemy's plans. I tell you what I have learned that you may not one day say you were not warned and accuse me of negligence. My father predicted to your predecessor and the Venetians the fall of Constantinople. He was not believed. Christianity to its great hurt lost a royal city and a patriarchal see and the prop of Greece. Now I prophesy about myself. If you trust and aid me I shall be saved; if not, I shall perish and many will be ruined with me.

The pope promised to fulfill the king's requests, stating only that since Bosnia was vassal to Hungary, permission had to be obtained from the King of Hungary before he could send a crown to the Bosnian ruler. If the Hungarian king did not object, the pope would promptly send the crown, which was ready, to Stefan Tomašević by an ambassador. The pope also urged the Bosnian king to do everything he could to conciliate the powerful Matthew Corvinus, whose support Bosnia needed if it wished to resist the Turks. Having dismissed the embassy with encouraging words, the pope then sent envoys to Hungary and Venice. In November 1461 Stefan Tomašević received his crown from the hands of a papal legate.

Bosnia's fate was, in fact, as inevitable as matters can be in history. It was merely a question of when. In 1462, a decade after his first revolt against Herceg Stefan, his son Vladislav sought an appanage from his father. When his request was rejected, he revolted again. Unable to capitalize on an existing war as he had in 1452, he sought aid from the willing Turks. Besides this Hercegovinian invitation, Bosnia too may have provoked Turkish action. For, after the fact, Pius II placed some of the responsibility for the Turkish attack upon Stefan Tomašević himself, claiming that the king, "relying no one knows on what hope," had refused tribute to the Turks. Furthermore, Stefan Tomašević's close ties with the papacy surely were in themselves also a contributing factor to the Ottoman invasion.

The Turks launched massive attacks on Bosnia and Hercegovina in 1463. They cleverly concealed their plans by making it appear as though the army being assembled were intended for Hungary, and then re-directing their troops against Bosnia in a surprise attack at the last moment. Despite the fact they were partially responding to Vladislav's call, this time they came in their own interests. They were clearly bent on putting an end to Bosnian independence. Bosnian fortresses fell rapidly one after the other. The king fled from Jajce up toward the Donji Kraji, while the queen fled to the coast. The Turks, in hot pursuit, caught up with the king at the fortress of Ključ on the Sana. They persuaded him to surrender the fortress on condition that he would be allowed to escape. They immediately broke their promise and took him as a prisoner back to the sultan who was then staying at Jajce. There, still believing his life would be spared, he was made to issue an order for the surrender of all

Bosnia's fortresses. Then he was beheaded. The Ulema, the Turkish religious authorities, justified the broken promise by stating that the general who had issued the safe-conduct did so without the knowledge of the sultan, and therefore the promise was not binding. The late king's written instructions were then sent to the Bosnian commanders of the various citadels that were holding out. They all obeyed the orders, and Pius claims that seventy strong fortresses were surrendered in eight days and over a million ducats fell into Turkish hands.

Most of Bosnia fell in a matter of weeks. The speed with which it fell, despite its inaccessible mountain fortresses, surprised everyone. Predictably, charges of treason were bandied about in the aftermath. However, it is hard to document treason. To explain the Turks' success we may, however, note the fact that the Turks, having succeeded in making their attack a surprise one, exhibited great speed of movement and military efficiency. We may also stress the lack of organization and co-ordination among the Bosnians, as well as the numerous surrenders following the capture of King Stefan Tomašević. Moreover, Bosnian morale seems to have been low. Presumably many Bosnians believed it was just a matter of time before their country fell and thus were defeatist. Many scholars have presented the religious issue (of forced conversions to Catholicism) as another reason for poor morale. Though this may have been a factor in some cases, we cannot document it as such, and since most Bosnians, about whom we do have documentation, seem to have been indifferent about religious matters, we certainly should not over-emphasize religion in explanations of Bosnia's rapid fall.

Many Bosnians seem to have felt it was inevitable that Bosnia would fall to the Turks or to the Hungarians and to have preferred the Ottomans to their long-time enemies the Hungarians. That this was a Bosnian attitude is shown by the fact that after the conquest a delegation of lesser nobles went to Venice to seek aid from Venice and to offer the kingdom to Venice. The delegates stated that if Venice would not help they would prefer to remain under the Turks. For under no circumstances would they accept being under the Hungarians.

The Ottoman attack also struck Hercegovina. The herceg retreated with his armies to the coast, while the Turks occupied his lands. At the end of the invasion, the main Ottoman forces withdrew, leaving behind garrisons in certain major fortresses. Their withdrawal allowed for the partial recovery of the conquered lands. The herceg, who had withdrawn to the coast to keep his armies intact, now marched back into Hercegovina and quickly regained most of the fortresses that had fallen. Vladislav, making peace with his father, participated in the recovery and received his own appanage that included the region of the Lim River. Thus Hercegovina was restored as a state, and in name it was to remain independent until 1481. However, the date 1481 marks only the fall of Hercegovina's last fortress. For in the period 1465–81 the Turks made numerous attacks on Hercegovina, usually seizing territory; thus it was to be steadily reduced in size.

While Herceg Stefan was restoring his state at the end of 1463, the Hungarians, who had remained inactive until the main Ottoman armies were withdrawn, stormed into Bosnia from the north and recovered a large portion of northern Bosnia including Jajce, Sana, and Usora. They also pressed down from Jajce into the region of western Hum toward the Neretva. And, assisted by Herceg Stefan and Vladislav, who had by this time made their peace, they recovered the Krajina and Završje. The Krajina was granted by the Hungarians to the herceg, on this occasion their ally, on condition that he retain it under Hungarian suzerainty. Završje including Rama (with Prozor), Uskoplje (with Vesela Straža), and Livno were granted to Vladislav by King Matthew.

The northern territory taken by the Hungarians—not including the Krajina and Završje—was made into a new Bosnian banate under Hungarian control and Hungarian governors (bans). In 1464 the Turks laid siege to Jajce, but despite two vigorous assaults they were unable this time to take the city. During the late 1460s the Turks were able to pick off other Hungarian fortresses in northern Bosnia.

The Turks returned in 1465 with a large force that took the Lim region, thereby eliminating the appanage Vladislav had received from his father. In the spring of 1466 Vladislav still held Livno. But before the summer was over the noble family of Vlatković possessed Livno. That August Ivaniš Vlatković was calling himself Count of Vratar and Vojvoda of the Land of Hum and Livno. Vladislav moved to the coast and soon emigrated to Hungary.

Upon seeing the size of the Ottoman force that attacked Vladislav's appanage, Herceg Stefan sought help from the Hungarians. He invited them to assume control of a series of his fortresses and promised that he would pay for the maintenance of their garrisons. However, the Turks succeeded in taking all the forts he had offered the Hungarians—including Samobor—before the Hungarians had time to respond. By September 1465 the Turks, having taken the Lim region, Gacko, and Ljubomir, had reached the coast and occupied Popovo Polje. The herceg's territory seems to have been reduced to the two walled ports of Risan and Novi (Herceg-novi), the Neretva valley plus the Krajina (lying between the Neretva and Cetina rivers), and a few other fortresses lying in the midst of Turkish regions that had resisted assault. Expecting the Turks to attack the Krajina also, the herceg offered that region to Venice. The Venetian Prince of Split responded immediately and that fall occupied the Krajina, the mouth of the Neretva, and the important customs station of Drijeva on the Neretva.

The Hungarians were not happy with these Venetian gains, for the Krajina had been held by the herceg under Hungarian suzerainty and now it had passed completely out of Hungarian control. The Hungarians seem to have been determined to take a more active role in the region and to establish their own forces there. As a result they pressed talks to allow them to assume garrison duty in various Hercegovinian forts. The herceg gave in (whether willingly or not is uncertain), and in the fall of 1465 five thousand Hungarian soldiers arrived to occupy the forts the herceg held along the Neretva, including Počitelj. By May 1466, when the herceg died, more than half of his lands, including almost everything east of the Neretva, found itself again in Ottoman hands. Most of his remaining lands were being defended by Hungarians or Venetians, and thus for all practical purposes out of his control. His direct holdings were reduced to a small strip of land with the two ports along and near the coast, and a few scattered forts inside the Turkish zone.

Though it is often stated that everything east of the Neretva was annexed by the Turks in 1465, this is not completely true. Ključ and Blagaj held out until 1468. Shortly thereafter, in 1468 or 1469, the Turks carried out a survey of their territories in this region; certain areas east of the Neretva do not appear in the cadaster (defter) created on this occasion. Their absence indicates that the Ottomans did not have, or at least did not hold firmly, those few places. Moreover, we know that Herceg Stefan's successor Herceg Vlatko still held Klobuk in 1469. By 1477 Klobuk was to be in Ottoman hands.

Herceg Stefan was succeeded by his second son, Vlatko, who also bore the title herceg. Vlatko's succession should surprise no one. The peace made between Herceg Stefan and Vladislav had been based on mutual need to face the crisis of the Ottoman invasion. To seal it, the herceg had had to award Vladislav a principality of his own. His anger at Vladislav, who had caused him so many difficulties, had continued, and he seems to have felt that that appanage fulfilled his obligations to Vladislav and to have from that time on planned to leave the lands he retained to Vlatko. Then after 1465, when the Turks conquered Vladislav's lands, depriving Vladislav of his power base, the herceg had had no further worries about him as a danger, and he certainly felt no sympathy for his position. The disinherited Vladislav departed for Hungary, where he was soon granted lands in Slavonia by King Matthew. Thus all that remained of Herceg Stefan's principality went to Vlatko.

Vlatko also inherited the obligation to maintain the service of the Hungarian troops garrisoning his Neretva fortresses. Having lost much of the economic base that might have enabled him to finance this service, Vlatko sought to avoid payment, which caused tensions between him and the Hungarian king. In order to secure the money, the Hungarians ordered their vassal Dubrovnik not to deliver to Vlatko the money Herceg Stefan had deposited in Dubrovnik for safe-keeping and which he had left to Vlatko in his will. The quarrel over this money led to a deterioration in the relations between Vlatko and Hungary. Hungary began to ponder the possibility of restoring Vladislav to rule in Hercegovina and worked to create and maintain good relations with the leading family of the local nobility, the Vlatkovići.

As a result, in 1470—at some point prior to July of that year—Vlatko turned to the Turks, concluding a treaty with them by which he accepted Ottoman suzerainty and agreed to pay tribute. The sultan seems to have been agreeable to this, for he was concerned with the Hungarian presence in Hum and interested in separating Vlatko from his Hungarian alliance. As a reward the sultan returned to Vlatko, either in 1470 or early 1471, Trebinje and Popovo Polje. He probably also granted him Bijela; for in March 1471 Vlatko is found in possession of it. Moreover, with the Ottomans standing behind him and intervening diplomatically, Vlatko was now able to obtain his money from Dubrovnik. And in the summer of 1470 Dubrovnik turned the money over to Vlatko. Vlatko by his submission presumably also sought to safeguard the territory he still held. For in the preceding years, particularly in 1468, the Ottomans had been campaigning in and around Hum, taking Blagaj and Ključ from him. They also at that time had attacked Završje via Bosnia and taken, probably from the Vlatkovići, most of that region.

Almost immediately after Vlatko's submission to the Turks, Žarko Vlatković, a Hungarian vassal who surely used Vlatko's new allegiance as an excuse, seized Vrgorac near Makarska from Vlatko. The Turks now intervened and in 1471 launched a major attack on those forts of Hum, including Počitelj, held by Hungarian troops. Počitelj fell to the Turks in September 1471. Shortly thereafter Žarko Vlatković submitted to the Turks, though his brother Ivaniš managed to avoid doing so. By campaign's end the Turks had taken all the fortresses along the Neretva and had eliminated the Hungarian presence from the Neretva region, except for a couple of forts at the river's mouth that the Hungarians may have retained. The Christians were pushed back toward the Cetina River; in the region on the left bank of the Cetina, the Vlatkovići still retained some lands, and the Hungarians were drawing up plans to create a strong defense along that river to prevent the Ottomans from expanding across it into the territory on and beyond its right bank. However, even if they created such a defense, the Cetina region was still vulnerable to attack from Ottoman-held Bosnia.

Vlatko clearly was not happy with the course of events, for it seemed likely that all his lands, and probably sooner rather than later, were going to be annexed by the Turks. Therefore he had been careful to maintain his relations with Venice throughout. It seems these ties annoyed the sultan and possibly caused a cooling in his attitude toward Vlatko. In any case, in 1473, the sultan took back Trebinje and Popovo Polje from Vlatko; in 1476 the sultan granted the two regions to Herak Vraneš, a Vlach from the Lim region.

It seems that in their 1471 campaign the Turks did not attack the territory held by the Venetians in the Krajina, the inland territory just behind the coast between the Neretva and Cetina rivers. And most of it, including the region around Imotski, remained Christian until the Turks conquered it along with the Makarska coast in 1492 or 1493. Šabanović believed the Venetians retained control of this territory until its fall. Recently Atanasovski has argued that the Hungarians encouraged their vassals the Vlatkovići to oppose the Venetians; this, he believes, resulted in the Vlatkovići's taking control of part of the Krajina, including part of the Imotski region.

In response to the 1471 disaster, that fall Matthew Corvinus convoked a council to re-organize the defense of his Bosnian and Croatian lands. Having settled his differences with the powerful nobleman Nicholas Iločki, Matthew made him governor of Bosnia, and, to increase the prestige of his shrinking region of Bosnia, he increased the governor's title from ban to king. Nicholas remained "King" of Bosnia until his death in 1477. Blaž the Magyar, who at that moment—and since early 1470—had been joint Ban of Croatia, Dalmatia, Slavonia, and Bosnia, did not attend the congress; it seems that he had already joined a group of Hungarian and Croatian nobles who were trying to organize a revolt against Matthew Corvinus. At this moment, however, it seems Blaž lost only Bosnia; but soon thereafter, probably early 1472, Nicholas Iločki seems to have been made Ban of Slavonia, Croatia, and Dalmatia as well. This appointment apparently indicates that Blaž had gone into rebellion by that time. This additional assignment to Iločki could have been intended to serve two purposes: to retain his loyalty to Matthew at this critical time and to co-ordinate more effectively the defense of this whole region should the Turks attack again in 1472.

Nicholas Iločki did not retain his joint positions for long, however. Damian Horvat had been from mid-1471 a junior colleague of Blaž, bearing the title ban and having responsibilities in Slavonia. Horvat, it seems, had retained this function in Slavonia under Iločki, which had allowed Iločki to concentrate his attention on the critical frontier region of Bosnia. Now, before the end of 1472, Horvat was appointed Ban of Slavonia, Croatia, and Dalmatia; Iločki was left with only Bosnia. In November 1473 Horvat's region was divided between two bans, with Horvat retaining Croatia and Dalmatia and a new actor named Ernušt being assigned the banship over Slavonia. Despite these reforms and appointments, the Turks succeeded in conquering most of the Bosnian banate (now "kingdom") in the 1470s.

In 1481, upon news of the death of Mehemmed II, King Matthew sent armies into Bosnia with the aim of major recoveries. His troops reached Vrhbosna (Sarajevo). Their gains were only temporary, however, and within a year the Turks were again in control of whatever the Hungarians had occupied. The Hungarian Kingdom of Bosnia after the 1470s consisted of only a handful of fortresses; Ottoman campaigns continued to reduce its size until, in the third decade of the sixteenth century, it had been reduced to a strip of territory just south of the Sava and the fortress of Jajce itself. Then in 1527—the year after the Turkish victory over the Hungarians at Mohacs—the Turks took Jajce and put an end to the Hungarian province of Bosnia. All Bosnia was now Ottoman and was to remain so until the Austrian occupation after the Treaty of Berlin (1878).

Despite Bosnia's years of hostility with the Turks, many Bosnians entered Ottoman service. As we have seen, various Bosnians had long been allying themselves to the Turks in the course of their mutual domestic warfare, and as shaky Christians probably many were not bothered by the Turks' Islam. We find for example that the third son of Herceg Stefan, also named Stefan, went to Constantinople in about 1473 and soon converted to Islam, taking the name of Ahmed. Known as Ahmed Hercegović, he rose to high rank in the Ottoman administration and twice—from 1503 to 1506 and from 1510 to 1514—was to serve as Grand Vizier under Sultan Selim the Grim. These were extremely long stretches of time to have held that position under that sultan, and, unlike many other Grand Viziers of Selim, Ahmed was not executed, but died a natural death in 1519. A young son of Stefan Tomaš and the herceg's daughter Catherine, named Sigismund, was captured as a teenager by the Turks in 1463 and taken to Constantinople. He also converted to Islam and in 1487 is found serving as a sanjak-beg in Karasi in Asia Minor. These examples are only two among many Bosnian cases.

The preceding remarks should not be taken as idealizing matters. For the Ottoman conquest was bloody; many Bosnians were carried off as captives or killed, including many executed after the conquest. The executed included the king and members of the greatest families. The members of the Bosnian nobility who were allowed to submit and keep their lands tended to be from second-level families. The great nobles who sought and were accepted into Ottoman service were usually removed from Bosnia and given lands and posts in Anatolia.

Croatia after 1463

After the fall of Bosnia in 1463 Turkish raiding parties began with some regularity to penetrate into Croatia. Already in 1463 they had plundered Krbava and the Frankapans' province of Modruš. And in 1468 and 1469 they carried out major incursions through Krbava and Modruš to the coast. Each raiding party returned with large numbers of captives—sometimes as many as several thousand. Unable to successfully defend their lands and seeing that King Matthew Corvinus was involved in too many other affairs to defend Croatia effectively, the Frankapans opened discussions with the Habsburgs—who, holding Slovenia, were also threatened by the Ottomans—and then turned to Venice for help. Fearing the latter negotiations would lead to Venice's acquisition of the important port of Senj, Matthew sent against the Frankapans a large army under a brutal but able general, Blaž the Magyar, that captured Senj for Matthew in 1469. This loss was bitterly resented by the Frankapan family, most of whose members now became enemies of King Matthew. Matthew, faced with their enmity and worried about Venice, next procured for himself most of the northern Adriatic coast from Senj to Trieste. The Frankapans retained Novigrad and a couple of other ports. King Matthew also annexed most of the province of Vinodol. To further these efforts, Matthew in early 1470 appointed Blaž the Magyar, who was directing the campaign against the Frankapans, as Ban of Croatia, Dalmatia, and Slavonia. And to concentrate on subduing the Frankapans, the new ban took up residence in the town of Senj, recently taken from them. Since Blaž's efforts were directed at Croatia, in mid-1471 he was given a junior colleague, also with the title ban, to be responsible for Slavonia.

In the 1470s the Turks regained much of the Bosnian territory the Hungarians had retaken late in 1463. Then the Turks stepped up their action against Croatia. Particularly hard hit were Lika, Krbava, and northern Dalmatia. The raids penetrated even as far as the region of Kranj in Slovenia.

In 1479 Martin Frankapan became seriously ill. His brother John, holder of Krk, who since 1451 had been a loner, avoiding the family assemblies and maintaining close ties with Venice, landed in Martin's lands and took Novigrad and Bribir. Martin ordered him to leave, but John paid no attention to his brother's wishes. Matthew Corvinus, interpreting John's action as a Venetian plot to acquire Senj, ordered Blaž the Magyar (no longer ban) to expel John from the mainland. In late 1479, after Martin's death in October, Blaž drove John back to Krk and captured the mainland forts that John had taken from Martin. Blaž then decided to finish John off by taking the island of Krk, whose populace included many people dissatisfied with John's rule. He procured ships from Senj, transported his army to the island, and laid siege to the fortress of Krk.

In response to John's call for help, Venice sent ships to Krk's waters. The Venetians tried to obtain Blaž's withdrawal through negotiations, but the general refused even to discuss the matter. There was a strong pro-Venetian party in the fortress of Krk, and Venice would not have had much difficulty in gaining the fortress by a coup. However, the island was legally Hungary's, as John Frankapan was holding it under Hungarian suzerainty. And since Blaž's troops were there to punish a rebel against Hungary, Venice, which had no desire for a war with Hungary, had no legal basis to assist John. The Venetians explained to John that they could not help him as matters then stood; however, if he would voluntarily surrender the island to Venice, then the Venetians could take action. John, faced with a hopeless situation (besieged by a strong Hungarian force and not trusting the loyalty of his own subjects, many of whom disliked him), had little choice but to accept the Venetian plan. As a result—and without even consulting the Croatians at his court— John surrendered Krk to Venice in February 1480. A Venetian then took command of the local garrison.

As a large portion of the island's population supported the Venetians and as a Venetian fleet now sailed into the harbor of Krk, Blaž realized he could not take Krk. He tried through negotiations to obtain Venice's recognition of Hungary's possession of those parts of the island he then occupied; however, the Venetians refused, demanding that he totally evacuate the island. Blaž finally gave in, surrendering the fort of Omišalj, which he held, and his prisoners, and the Venetians helped transport his soldiers back to the mainland.

John Frankapan expected at this point to resume the rule of his island. And it is quite possible that the Venetians, in the negotiations that led to his surrender of the island to them, had promised to install him as the island's governor after the Hungarian threat was over. However, if they had made such a promise, they certainly had no intention of keeping it. And shortly thereafter John and various of his Croatian courtiers, who were considered unreliable, were sent off to Venice, where they could not cause trouble. The island, though Catholic, had, in the face of opposition from the international Church hierarchy, long been a center for Slavic language books and services.

In 1481 the Venetians chased out the Slavic monks and declared Latin to be the language of all churches and monasteries on the island.

Meanwhile the Hungarians were furious at Venice's acquisition of the isle of Krk. However, lacking a navy of any quality, they could do little about it. But, the angry Blaž occupied the rest of the lands of the late Martin Frankapan, including the rest of Vinodol. Thus the Frankapan family, though left much of Martin's land in his will, received none of it and was more or less eliminated from the Adriatic coast. The family retained little more than Modruš and the territory east of it to a little beyond the Glina River, including Cetin. After these Hungarian successes the Frankapan family was sufficiently weakened for Matthew Corvinus to have no further worries about it. And since he was concerned about defending Croatia against the Turks and since the family had considerable popularity among the local populace, in March 1481 Matthew restored a portion of the family's lost lands to Stjepan, the Frankapan brother who had been the most loyal to the Hungarian king. He issued a charter granting Stjepan the eighth of the Frankapan lands—including much of Modruš—Stjepan had received at the 1449 assembly as well as various new towns, some of which lay in the family's former province of Vinodol and some of which lay in the region of Zagreb. When Stjepan died later that year his son Bernard inherited all of his father's holding.

In 1490 Matthew Corvinus died. Many Hungarian and Croatian nobles disliked his policies of centralization and taxation—for Matthew had violated many tax privileges and attempted to raise extensive money from the nobility for warfare against the Turks. Thus these nobles refused to accept as king Ivanis, his only son, whose cause was further weakened by the fact that he was illegitimate. A council of nobles met at Pest and elected Vladislav II of Bohemia as king. Supported by few major figures other than Lovro Iločki, Ivanis accepted the decision and received the position of hereditary Duke of Slavonia. Soon, to enable him to better co-ordinate his defensive responsibilities, Ivanis was also named Ban of Croatia and Dalmatia. He eventually married Beatrice, a Frankapan, and established his main residence at Bihać, where he remained until his death in 1504.

However, Hungary found itself faced with a new crisis, for Vladislav's election violated the 1463 treaty between Frederick III Habsburg and Matthew that stipulated that if Matthew had no son, a Habsburg should succeed to the Hungarian throne. Maximillian of the Habsburgs now claimed the Hungarian throne as his right and attacked Hungary. He found many allies inside Hungary; Lovro Iločki had never been happy with the choice of Vladislav and immediately agreed to support him. Maximillian also was able to mobilize support from various disgruntled Frankapans, in particular from John and Nicholas, and from the Talovac family. The free city district of Zagreb (Gradec) also declared for Maximillian, though the bishop's district remained loyal to Vladislav. However, various other Croatian nobles and the overwhelming majority of Hungarian nobles, including Ivanis, remained loyal to Vladislav. Seeing that the strength of the opposition was sufficient to thwart his ambition, Maximillian agreed to a new treaty in 1491; it declared that should Vladislav have no son the Habsburgs would succeed him as King of Hungary. The treaty also provided amnesty for those who had supported the Habsburg cause.

A council met in Buda in 1492 at which the nobility expressed much opposition to any eventual Habsburg succession. But in the end the council accepted the treaty. The nobles, however, took advantage of the situation and Vladislav's weakness to assert themselves at the council to reduce taxes and eliminate various hated tax measures established by Matthew. The Franka-pans also tried to take advantage of the dynastic crisis to recover Senj. They failed, and then, when they found themselves faced with a large Ottoman attack in 1493, they made peace with the king. This Ottoman incursion, which ravaged not only Croatia but Slovenia as well, was a massive raiding party. The king decided to oppose it on its return; his forces and those of the Frankapans met the returning Turks at Krbava Polje (modern Udbina) in September 1493 and suffered a massive defeat. Thereafter Ottoman incur-sions into Croatia increased; furthermore, Croatia suffered many smaller raids for plunder from the Muslim inhabitants of Bosnia. By 1494 certain Croatian noblemen—including the Blagajski, Kurjaković, and Zrinski families—were paying tribute to the Turks, in exchange for which their lands were guaran-teed. These families were also obliged to allow the Turkish raiders passage through their lands into the non-tributary parts of Croatia.

Believing that King Vladislav was doing little to prevent these incur-sions, Lovro Iločki, the ruler of Srem and the Vukovska župa, led a move-ment in 1494 to overthrow Vladislav. It failed, and Lovro was forced back into obedience in 1495. Opposition to Vladislav and to his treaty of 1491 with the Habsburgs remained and enabled the rising Zapolja family of Tran-sylvania to convoke an assembly in 1505 that issued a law stating that no foreigner could occupy the Hungarian throne, thereby renouncing the treaty between Vladislav and the Habsburgs. Before the Habsburgs could respond, Vladislav had a son, thus delaying the relevance of this law. However, faced with the Ottoman threat and not wanting the Habsburgs as enemies, Vladislav defied his opponents and concluded a new treaty with Maximillian, affirming the earlier agreement and stating that whenever his line died out the Habsburgs were to succeed. And to strengthen their relationship, he married his daughter to a grandson of Maximillian.

Ottoman raids continued to be frequent; however, until about 1520 they were carried out for plunder and captives, and no Croatian territory—exclud-ing the area between the Neretva and Cetina rivers—was annexed. However, after one major raid into Modruš and into the Kupa region in 1511 and another that reached as far as Skradin in 1512, various Croatian towns became alarmed. The district of Poljica rapidly dropped Venetian suzerainty and accepted Turkish suzerainty with tribute. In 1515 Skradin began to pay tribute to the Turks.

King Vladislav died in 1516, to be succeeded by his ten-year-old son

Louis (1516–26). Vladislav has been accused by scholars of doing little against the Ottoman threat. In his defense, it has been pointed out that he spent a quarter of his state income on the defense of Croatia; yet even so, his major project in this theatre was the hiring and financing of fourteen hundred professional soldiers who were then divided among various forts along the Croatian border. This was clearly a drop in the bucket compared to the forces that were needed.

King Louis was surrounded by a circle of corrupt advisors, so a struggle soon emerged between the court and an opposition led by John Zapolja. The Ottomans stepped up their incursions. Kamengrad between the Sana and the Japra became the center from which many attacks were dispatched. All of Bosnia except the very northern regions and Jajce itself fell. The Ban of Croatia, Peter Berislavić, responsible for the defense of Croatia, worked heroically but with limited success until he himself was killed battling the Turks on the Una in 1520. The Turks then began to annex significant chunks of Croatia, including major cities. Having taken Beograd and Šabac in 1521, thereby opening the route to Pannonia, the Turks took part of Srem and then moved against Croatia from the east, at first just plundering eastern Slavonia. They did not forget the region to the west of Bosnia, either. In 1522 they captured Knin and Skradin as well as the region of the Cetina River, except for Klis and Obrovac. In 1523 they conquered Ostrovica on the Una River. (This Ostrovica, mentioned here for the first time, should not be confused with the Ostrovica near Bribir.) And that winter, 1523–24, they pressed on from there to raid the region of the Kupa.

Then in 1526 they launched a major attack, which, having taken Petrovaradin, moved along the Sava, taking eastern Slavonia with Osijek and Djakovo. As a result the Turks came to possess almost all of Srem and the plains of Slavonia. Having made these gains in Slavonia, the Turks then swung north along the Danube and met the Hungarians and Croatians in a massive battle at Mohacs, on 29 August 1526. The Turks gained an overwhelming victory over their Christian opponents. King Louis was killed in the battle. The following year the Turks captured Jajce, Obrovac, and Udbina. They then completed the conquest of Krbava. In 1528 they took Lika along with the northern Bosnian territory just south of the Sava, including the courses of the lower Una, Vrbas, Ukrina, and Bosna rivers. As a result all of Bosnia was Ottoman. By 1528, after these annexations, the Turks held southern Croatia up to a line slightly south of Senj, Karlovac, Sisak, and Bjelovar. Along that line the Hungarians established a Croatian Military Frontier March; its history belongs to the period that was to follow.

The Turks did not stop their expansion with these successes. In 1536, operating beyond the Sava, they took the region of Požega. And finally in 1537 they captured the fortress of Klis in the west, which had long eluded them. After that they began putting more pressure on Hungary itself, conquering a large portion of Hungary, including Budapest, in 1541.

Dubrovnik had managed to save itself from conquest by accepting Ottoman suzerainty in 1483. Thereafter the town worked hard to keep itself secure by maintaining good relations with the Turks; to do this it readily sold and shipped to the Turks whatever goods they required. The other Dalmatian towns had unwittingly saved themselves by falling to Venice. Thus their independence from the Turks was guaranteed as long as Venice maintained correct relations with the Turks. These towns were also fortunate to lie at considerable distance from Ottoman centers. Thus when Ottoman-Venetian wars occurred, the Ottomans concentrated their attention on the Venetian possessions nearer to Constantinople, the Greek islands and the Venetian ports on the Greek mainland.

Meanwhile, after the death of King Louis at Mohacs, the Hungarian nobility split over whether the new king should be Ferdinand of the house of Habsburg, who was the legal heir to the throne according to several treaties, or whether it should be the nobleman and leader of the anti-Habsburg party John Zapolja, Duke of Transylvania. The Croatians too were divided. Those south of of the Kupa, north of which lay the Habsburgs' Slovenia, believed that the Habsburgs would provide serious aid in order to prevent the Ottomans from expanding up to their own border; so, in general they supported Ferdinand. The Croatians of Slavonia, however, were chiefly for Zapolja, who was elected king by a Hungarian assembly in November 1526. Slavonia immediately accepted Zapolja's rule. On 31 December 1526, however, an assembly held by the Frankapans at their town of Cetin elected Ferdinand King of Croatia. By 1528 Ferdinand had also acquired what remained of Slavonia, including Zagreb. After Ferdinand's election and his acquisition of the non-Turkish parts of Slavonia, the Croatian lands that went to him—like the neighboring lands, fallen or about to fall to the Turks—entered a new period. Thus this is a good moment to bring our account of medieval Croatian history to a close.

Albania and Zeta after 1455

Albania to the Late 1470s

In the fall of 1455, after the completion of that year's Serbian campaign, the Ottomans launched raids through parts of Albania, causing much destruction and taking many prisoners. Some of the captives were made into slaves while the rest were massacred. A major assault directed at Berat failed to take the town and cost the Turks five to six thousand men. Skanderbeg's heroics were becoming widely known in Europe and various Westerners came on their own to support him. For example, in 1456 a French knight with fifty retainers enrolled to serve Skanderbeg for a year. And that same year among the defenders of Kroja, besides the Albanians, were to be found Germans and Serbs.

In 1456 a new Ottoman attack led by an Albanian renegade was defeated by Skanderbeg. The defeated leader sought and obtained forgiveness from

Skanderbeg, receiving back his lands that had been confiscated. A second Ottoman force that year defeated the armies of the Arianiti near Berat. As a result the Arianiti accepted Venetian suzerainty and the family chief became the Venetian captain for his lands—as well as the theoretical Great Vojvoda of Albania—until he died in 1470. Treason continued to frustrate Skanderbeg in 1457. In that year a fortress was sold to the Turks by its Albanian commander, and Skanderbeg's own nephew (the son of his deceased older brother), jealous of his uncle and believing that, since he was the heir of the elder brother, he should head the family and the Albanian league, went over to the Turks.

In the fall of 1457 a large Ottoman army, said to have had sixty thousand men, occupied the plains of Albania up to the borders of Venice's Alessio. The Albanians, avoiding battle, took to the mountains and harassed the Ottomans when they marched through the mountains with guerrilla hit-and-run raids. The Ottomans besieged but failed to take Kroja; however, they did cause considerable damage to its region and again took many prisoners. Finally that fall the Albanians won a substantial victory over a large Ottoman force at Albulena. Mehemmed II then proposed an armistice, but Skanderbeg, his hopes raised by papal plans for a crusade (which, of course, was not to materialize), refused to negotiate. In 1458 Skanderbeg repelled a new Ottoman invasion, despite further treason in his ranks; this time Lek Dukagjin went over to the Ottomans.

Lek had already since 1456 been fighting with Venice over Danj and its district. In 1456 he had seized the town, but Venice had attacked him and regained it in August 1457. Lek's desertion to the Turks may well have resulted from this struggle with Venice. He officially made peace with Venice in 1459, presumably recognizing Venice's possession of Danj, but he remained unhappy, for his territorial ambitions still clashed with Venice's. Thus efforts in the early 1460s to persuade him to break with the Turks failed. However, in 1463 the Venetians, after long efforts to avoid clashing with the Turks, finally were drawn into a Turkish war. They began now to make every effort to bring about peace between Skanderbeg and the Dukagjins (Lek and Nicholas) and to mobilize the Dukagjins against the Turks. The archbishop of Venice's Durazzo took an active role in this effort and mediated peace between Lek and Skanderbeg in 1464. Thereafter the Dukagjins again took an active role against the Turks as allies of Skanderbeg.

This Lek Dukagjin is often credited with compiling the Albanian tribes' traditional oral law code known as the *Law of Lek*. As noted, sometimes his namesake from the 1390s is also credited with the compilation. However, the code is clearly a traditional work, surely far older than either Dukagjin, and Božić points out that there is no solid evidence to connect either Lek Dukagjin with the oral code.[10]

The Turks attacked Albania again in 1462; this time they dispatched two armies, one from the north and one from the south, that were intended to effect a junction. Skanderbeg managed to defeat the first before the junction was made and then hurried through the mountains to defeat the second force. After this, he and Mehemmed II finally agreed to a peace, which was signed in April 1463. Gegaj believes Skanderbeg was now willing to conclude such an armistice because he realized a Western crusade was not going to occur; thus, it made sense to conclude a truce immediately after a victory when he could gain the best terms.[11] He presumably realized he could not defend Albania forever, and thus it made sense to obtain Ottoman recognition of the status quo, at a propitious moment when there were few, if any, Turks in occupation of Albanian castles and when the Albanians were united behind him.

Venice, then at war with the Turks and desperately trying to defend its eastern possessions, in particular the isle of Lesbos, from Ottoman attack, tried unsuccessfully to prevent Skanderbeg from concluding peace with the Ottomans. However, the treaty with the Turks did not last long. It is not known who broke it. Skanderbeg, seeking to capitalize on Ottoman involvement in the war with Venice, may well have violated the truce by some action against a Turkish position. Thus the Ottoman attack of 1464, the first violation of the truce appearing in extant sources, may well have been in response to some act of Skanderbeg rather than the initial act that broke the peace. In any case, in 1464 another renegade Albanian led an Ottoman army against Albania that carried out considerable destruction as well as much violence against the population. So, when Skanderbeg finally defeated this force late in the year, he massacred without pity the Ottoman troops who surrendered. The renegade leader escaped and returned in 1465 with a second army, which Skanderbeg defeated handily.

The resumption of war with the Turks led Skanderbeg to enter into closer relations with Venice. In 1464 he concluded a treaty with Venice that provided him with a pension, the right of asylum in Venice, and a guarantee that any Venetian treaty with the Turks would include a guarantee of Albanian independence. Venice also promised that, as a deterrent, each year from April to June its fleet would cruise off the Albanian coast. This pact differed from Skanderbeg's earlier treaty with Naples, for then Skanderbeg declared himself a vassal, whereas now Skanderbeg stood as an ally and independent ruler.

Meanwhile Mehemmed II, the conqueror of Constantinople, Serbia, and the Morea, was becoming infuriated at his failure to subdue little Albania. Moreover, he dreamed of acquiring a port on the central Adriatic, on the Albanian coast, to threaten Italy. The annexation of the interior would facilitate that goal and also provide such a port with security after he obtained it. In 1466 the sultan led in person a massive army, said by the sources to have contained from two hundred to three hundred thousand men, against Kroja. Skanderbeg left a small garrison in the city under a member of the Thopia family, while he and his main forces retreated into the mountains above Kroja. In June 1466 the Ottomans arrived, devastating the lands and villages through which they passed. Fourteen ship-loads of Albanians fled to Italy at their approach. The Ottomans reached Kroja without difficulty and commenced their siege. Skanderbeg and his men directed hit-and-run forays against the besiegers. After several weeks it became clear to Mehemmed that the walls were strong, the defenders well supplied, and no one inside could be persuaded to betray the city. At the same time Skanderbeg's forays were causing the Ottomans severe losses. So, late that year Mehemmed raised the siege and returned to Constantinople.

Inalcik believes, however, that on his withdrawal the sultan left troops to garrison the forts along the route between Kroja and Macedonia. Thus from this time, late 1466, Skanderbeg no longer controlled most of the territory east of Kroja. Moreover, Mehemmed did not give up his goal. He returned the following year, once again leading his forces in person. This time instead of Kroja he had as his aim the towns along the Albanian coast. Should he conquer the coast, then Kroja would be cut off from the sea and from the supplies it received from Italy. Thus he hoped to bring about Kroja's fall by isolating it from outside help. He took various small castles along his route; he left small garrisons in these. Finally reaching the coast, he laid siege to Durazzo. This siege failed, as did a second brief siege of Kroja itself. Skanderbeg mounted a strong opposition, defeating an Ottoman army led by Balaban beg. However, when Mehemmed withdrew, he again left garrisons in the lesser forts he had taken. Thus he had a stronger foothold inside Albania than he had had previously. The 1467 campaign also resulted in many more Albanians being taken prisoner by the Turks or fleeing to Italy to escape them. Then in January 1468 Skanderbeg died.

He had been a brilliant military leader and became a heroic figure for both the Albanians and for the Christian anti-Turkish cause. But dramatic as his victories were, one should not lose sight of the fact that the numerous invasions Albania suffered caused enormous destruction. They greatly reduced the population and destroyed flocks and crops. At the same time, though Albania could hold its own, there was no way, short of surrender, that Skanderbeg could put a stop to these invasions. For his manpower and economic base were insufficient to expand the war and drive the Turks from his borders. Thus Albania was doomed to face an unending series of attacks until it should eventually fall. Its only hope lay in a successful foreign crusade to drive the Turks back from its borders. Foreign aid given merely to bolster the defenses of Albania could not solve the long-term problem. Thus the grants received from the papacy, Dubrovnik, Venice, and Naples were nowhere near sufficient to meet the huge defense needs Albania had.

Thus Skanderbeg, assisted by the rugged mountainous terrain, had been able to defend a limited territory. But he could only delay the final conquest. After his death Albanian unity was to weaken. Feuds resumed, including a major one within the Dukagjin family, between Nicholas and Lek. As a result, Lek was once again to briefly join the Turks until a new peace was brought about between the two brothers, who then both submitted to Venice.

Skanderbeg's son John succeeded to leadership of the Albanian league. He immediately sought and gained Venetian protection. Venice soon assumed responsibility for the defense of Kroja. John, however, had luck on his side for a time. For the Ottomans were to be diverted through much of the 1470s by a war with Venice. The Ottomans directed their attention against Venice's Greek possessions—particularly the island ones. By the end, as noted, the Turks had acquired Euboea with Negroponte as well as various islands. Then once again, in 1477–79, they were to turn their attention to Kroja. But before we can turn to this major Ottoman offensive, it is necessary to go back and pick up the story of Zeta to that point, since the Ottoman campaigns were to be directed against that region as well as against Albania.

Zeta in the Decade before the Ottoman Onslaught of 1477

John (Ivan) Crnojević, married to Gojisava, the daughter of George Arianite of Albania, succeeded to the rule of Zeta after the death of his father. His main residence was in Žabljak. He opened his rule in 1465 by quarreling with Kotor; when Venice announced its support of Kotor, John marched to the Gulf of Kotor. He immediately received support, as usual, from the villagers of Grbalj and from the Paštrovići. Venice put a price on John's head, but after a few skirmishes peace was concluded in 1466.

By this time the Ottomans had weakened his Kosača neighbor, Stefan Vukčić. For, as we saw, the Turks launched major attacks against the Kosača lands in 1463 and 1465 that resulted in Ottoman occupation of most of them. In 1466 Stefan Vukčić died, to be succeeded by his second son, Vlatko. The removal of Stefan Vukčić made it possible for John Crnojević to make peace with the Kosače. This was promptly done, and for the next decade John and Vlatko maintained close and cordial ties. After Gojisava died, John in July 1469 married Vlatko's sister Mara. In 1470, under pressure from the Turks, Vlatko accepted Ottoman suzerainty; early the following year John Crnojević followed suit.

In 1474 the Ottomans directed a major attack against both Zeta and the Venetian Zetan lands around Skadar. To meet this threat Venice and Crnojević concluded an alliance. The Turks first took Danj, held by Venice at the time, by storm. The Ottomans did not try to retain it, being content to demolish its fortifications. The Ottomans then besieged Skadar. After a major assault failed, the defenders erupted from the city and defeated the Ottoman attackers, causing the Ottomans to withdraw. But though the Turks failed to wrest away any of Venice's territory, they occupied another large chunk of Zeta, taking the lands between the Morača and Zeta rivers. Expecting the Ottomans to resume their offensive in the near future, John sought from the Venetians munitions and money to repair defenses and to enable him to launch a counter-offensive to recover some of his losses. Afraid that such efforts would only provoke the Turks to further action, the Venetians refused.

Not giving up his plan, John then turned to Vlatko Kosača, who was also looking for a chance to recover lost lands. The two then, in 1476, jointly attacked the Turks. They achieved some limited successes along the former

Zetan-Kosača border. Then for some reason—probably over the division of their limited spoils—the two quarreled. John withdrew his troops, and the Turks who had been garrisoning various fortresses in the area were able to put together an army and easily recover everything the two Slavic lords had taken. Vlatko immediately sought peace and forgiveness from the sultan, who, seeing John as the initiator of the previous attack and the more dangerous of the two, owing to his ties with Venice, accepted Vlatko's homage at the end of 1476 and encouraged him to attack John. The sultan offered to support Vlatko in this and promised to allow him to keep whatever he was able to take.

The Ottoman Offensive of 1477–79 against Albania and Zeta and of 1481 against Hercegovina

However, before Vlatko could go into action (if he really planned to do so), the Ottomans in 1477 launched a massive two-pronged assault into the western Balkans. The first wave, directed at the Venetian holdings in Albania and Zeta, had Kroja as its first objective. Kroja underwent a year's siege; finally in June 1478, owing to shortages in supplies and mismanagement by its commanders, Kroja fell. The Ottomans massacred all the males of the city and carted off the women as slaves. They then continued the offensive, taking Drivast in September 1478 and Alessio shortly thereafter. Most of the town of Alessio was burned. The Turks converted the cathedral of Alessio into a mosque. Thus Venice lost three of its major towns. The Ottomans then attacked, but again failed to take, Skadar. Of Venice's interior territory, Skadar, now alone, held out. And the sultan had gained for himself a firm foothold in northern Albania. The fall of the remainder of the region was just a matter of time. Lek and Nicholas Dukagjin fled to Italy.

The second Ottoman wave of 1477 overran much of Zeta, taking Žabljak and then late in 1477 or early 1478 meeting and defeating John Crnojević's main army. The Ottomans then concentrated their forces at Skadar, which finally surrendered to them in March 1479. The Ottomans established a sanjak-beg in Skadar. By the agreement, the Ottomans allowed those inhabitants of Skadar who wished to depart to do so unmolested. Many did, appearing as refugees in Bar and Ulcinj. Soon many of these refugees emigrated to Italy. Then in 1480/81 a peace was concluded that left Venice in possession of a strip of coastal territory that included Ulcinj, Bar, Budva, and Kotor. The region of the Paštrovići was also recognized as Venetian and was to remain Venetian until 1797. The Venetians tried to include John Crnojević in the treaty as a Venetian subject. However, the Ottomans refused to recognize him with that status, seeing him as an Ottoman subject who had defected and ceased to pay tribute. Therefore, since the Ottoman-Venetian treaty did not discuss Zeta, the Ottoman campaign continued against John until it had completed the conquest of his lands. He fled to the coast, and his state came to an end. Thus, all that remained of what we might consider Zeta was the above-mentioned coastal strip that Venice was allowed to retain by the treaty.

Vlatko of Hercegovina, who had made peace with the sultan in 1476, was spared the Ottoman invasion of 1477–79. However, his downfall was soon to come, and he brought it down upon himself. In 1481 when Sultan Mehemmed II died, Vlatko decided to take advantage of the Turks' momentary difficulties to expand his rump state. His forces were driven back by local Turkish garrisons. But his actions annoyed the new sultan, Bayezid II, who dispatched Ottoman forces into what remained of Hercegovina. These troops defeated Vlatko's army in June of that year. Having no hope of resistance, Vlatko fled to his coastal territory and took refuge in his fort of Novi (Herceg-novi). He sought help from the Hungarians, which was dispatched. However, the Turks took Novi before the Hungarians arrived in September 1481. With Novi's fall, Hercegovina disappeared as a state.

After having to surrender Novi to the Turks, in the fall of 1481, Vlatko received, probably as part of the terms of the surrender, a small piece of land back from the sultan. However, as Atanasovski emphasizes, it was purely for his economic support and for his lifetime only. Since the sultan held title to it, the territory was the sultan's; thus Vlatko was no longer really a ruler. Soon thereafter, in 1486 or 1487, Vlatko fell into some sort of difficulty with the Turks. Fleeing from Ottoman territory, he sought sanctuary with Venice. He took up residence on the Venetian island of Rab, where he died before March 1489.

Novi had been the last town held by Vlatko. However, a few odds and ends of Hercegovinian territory in the hands of other Christian commanders—local nobles or representatives of foreign states—held out a bit longer. In the 1480s Augustin Vlatković, as an Ottoman vassal, still retained the districts of Vrgorac and Ljubuški. The fortress of Koš (modern Opuzen), on the Neretva, about fifteen miles up-river from its mouth, was still held by a Hungarian garrison in 1488. The Ottomans took Koš in 1490 or shortly thereafter. The Makarska coast and the Krajina with Imotski seem at this time to have still been holding out. It has generally been believed that these regions were still under Venetian control. Atanasovski argues, however, that part of the Krajina, including part of the region of Imotski, was by this time held by certain Vlatkovići as Hungarian vassals. In any case, and regardless of how much besides Markarska Venice held and how much the Vlatkovići may or may not have acquired, in 1492 or 1493 the Ottomans took possession of it all.

Albania after 1479

The Albanians, however, were not ready to quit. Taking advantage of the death of Sultan Mehemmed II in 1481, a revolt, led by Skanderbeg's son John Castriot and supported by the Himariot tribesmen, broke out, liberating much of the territory of central Albania and putting to rout an Ottoman army sent out against them. Both Dukagjin brothers returned from Italy to take an active role in the rebellion. By 1488 the revolt was in full swing, with tribesmen from the territory between Kroja and Valona participating in it and defeating the Ottoman detachments sent out against them. However, finally in 1488 the Ottomans sent their fleet into the harbor of Valona; at the same time Western help promised to the rebels failed to materialize. As a result the tide turned, and soon thereafter the revolt was suppressed. In 1501 the Ottomans finally took Durazzo. The Venetians, however, were able to hold onto Bar and Ulcinj until 1571 when the Ottomans finally took those two towns. Budva remained Venetian until 1797.

This warfare led to a great deal of Albanian emigration to Italy. A particularly large number departed during the decade after Skanderbeg's death in 1468 and settled as farmers in southern Italy. A large exodus also occurred in 1481 as hundreds of Albanians sought to escape the Ottoman armies sent against the rebels in that year. Another large exodus occurred in 1492.

But it should be stressed that though Albania was conquered, it remained a tribal land; thus it was very difficult for the Ottomans to administer it or even to treat it as a unified province. Soon many tribes were breaking away, refusing to pay tribute. This forced a cost-accounting administrative decision, for the large losses sustained in campaigns against the Albanians were more costly than the value of the tribute this poor land could render. And the religious situation was to make such a decision palatable.

For many tribesmen in the north had early on come to accept Islam. This fact allowed the Ottomans thereafter to leave them to their own devices as long as they did not disrupt the smooth functioning of the machinery of state; thus to keep the Albanians peaceful, the Ottomans granted them tribal autonomy, including the right to bear arms, in exchange for a minimal tribute. At times this tribute was not delivered, and frequently the Ottoman authorities rather than force the issue chose to ignore these lapses. In time these northern tribesmen came to be numbered among the most loyal servitors of the sultan, proud of their privileges and the right to bear arms. They flocked to the sultan's armies and even provided a special body-guard corps for the sultan.

Zeta after 1479

When John Crnojević fled to the coast in 1479, he dreamed of regaining his lands. Venice made no effort to help him, fearing to jeopardize the peace it had concluded with the Turks. John's chance came in 1481. Taking advantage of the death of Mehemmed II and the Albanian revolt that followed, he returned from Italy to the Zetan coast. Venice still showed no interest in his plans. So, he began recruiting Montenegrin tribesmen in the inland region behind the Gulf of Kotor. Having created an effective force, he established himself in the village of Obod. Next, in late 1481 or early 1482, he sent envoys to the new sultan, Bayezid II, offering his submission and requesting a restoration of the conditions existing in 1471, when John had submitted to Mehemmed II and been allowed to hold Zeta for an annual tribute.

Bayezid, trying to establish himself in power, concerned with the Albanian revolt, and wanting to avoid a similar manifestation in Zeta/Montenegro, was receptive and recognized John as the ruler of a small vassal principality. John, owing tribute, was to have complete autonomy at home but was not to have independence in foreign affairs. No Ottoman officials were to reside in his small Montenegrin principality, which lay between the coast and the Zeta River and then extended down to Lake Skadar. John soon moved his capital to the town of Cetinje below Mount Lovčen. The move to Cetinje was made before 1489. To secure John's obedience, Bayezid in 1485 took John's youngest son Staniša to reside at his court as a hostage. The young man soon converted to Islam, taking the name Skanderbeg.

The Orthodox Church had suffered many disabilities during the previous decades from Venetian rule and from Kotor, whose bishop carried out a policy of converting Orthodox villagers in the vicinity of Kotor to Catholicism. Now under John the Orthodox Church had a chance to revive, and John Crnojević strongly supported its efforts. The Metropolitan of Zeta moved to Obod. Soon John was financing the building of a Metropolitan church and monastery in Cetinje, which was completed in 1484 or 1485. Then the metropolitan (the vladika) moved to Cetinje.

George (Djuradj), John's eldest son, was his heir. By 1489, still in John's lifetime, George had already come to be the de facto ruler of Montenegro. George was tall, brave, a fine horseman, and a lover of books. When John died, early in July 1490, George officially became the ruler, soon thereafter receiving official recognition from the sultan. George is most famous for the printing press he established; it was the first Cyrillic printing press to be established among the South Slavs. Modeled on presses existing in Italy, the machine and the letters were actually made in Montenegro. Its products were of the highest quality, in particular aesthetically. Church books made up the bulk of its products. George also produced a text of Dušan's law code, which seems to have been recognized as the law in Montenegro.

George's reign was to be brief. King Charles VIII of France was trying to create an anti-Turkish league to carry out a new crusade. The venture was widely advertised in Italy and soon drew into its fold Constantine Arianite, who had taken the surname Comnenus. Constantine was the brother of Gojisava, John Crnojević's first wife, and thus the uncle of George. Constantine set about planning a new Albanian uprising, which he duly launched. The French king had promised him aid once his venture was under way. Needless to say this help never materialized. It seems that George was drawn into Constantine's plans. At least it was rumored that he supported the venture. Bayezid, faced with this new outbreak in Albania and hearing that George was involved, decided to prevent any Montenegrin support of the revolt by putting an end to Montenegrin independence and ridding the region of the Crnojevići. In 1496 he gave George three days to report to the sultan or else get out of Montenegro. George chose to get out. Taking as much treasure as he could carry and accompanied by some Cetinje monks with the treasures of the Cetinje church, George left for Budva, whence he took a boat to Venice, arriving there in December 1496. George's brother Stefan, who had played only a minor role in Montenegro up to this time—at least, his name appears as a witness on a few charters—hoped to succeed George. However, Bayezid ignored him and re-absorbed Montenegro into the regular Ottoman administration. Subsequently, in 1513, one of its governors was to be Skanderbeg–Staniša Crnojević.

Explanation for the Ottoman Success

The last chapters have traced the Ottoman conquest of southeastern Europe. We have seen what happened, but we have not seriously paused to address the question: How could what began as such a small emirate in northwestern Anatolia have achieved such great success?

The first point to emphasize is the weakness of the Ottomans' opponents. The Byzantine Empire was no longer an empire and after Dušan's death neither was Serbia. And we have traced the territorial fragmentation of Serbia, Bulgaria, and the Greek lands. As a result these regions became split into a number of petty principalities in the hands of nobles who fought for their own independence and expansion. Not only did they refuse to co-operate with one another, but they were also frequently at war with one another. We have also noted the general military decline of all the Balkan states. None had large armies, and in their wars usually only hundreds, rather than thousands, were to be found on a given side. The Turks were able to participate in these wars, at first as mercenaries. From their participation they could see the weakness of the Balkan armies and also learn the techniques and strategies of warfare in the Balkans. After the death of Dušan, no state in southeastern Europe was strong enough to prevent the expansion into the Balkans of a state with a large army.

How did the Ottomans obtain large and strong armies? Probably their geographical position was most responsible. The Ottomans happened to hold the principality nearest to Constantinople.

In the first half of the thirteenth century Muslim states had dominated eastern and central Anatolia, but they had not been able to gain control of the western regions. However, toward mid-century the Mongol invasions dislocated large numbers of Turks from Central Asia and eastern Anatolia. Looking for booty and lands upon which to graze their flocks and settle, many migrated into Anatolia. The Byzantine Empire, after the transfer of its capital to Nicea in 1204, had given Anatolian affairs top priority and had been able to defend its borders in central Anatolia. However, in 1261 the Byzantines regained Constantinople; priorities shifted, and, fearing an attack from Charles of Anjou, the Byzantines became much more concerned with the

West. To obtain sufficient troops for their European needs, they denuded their eastern frontier. This enabled the Ottomans—and other emirates—to establish themselves in western Anatolia and to expand. The Ottomans consolidated their position in northwestern Anatolia, and as the Byzantines became involved in foreign and long-term domestic wars in their European provinces, they lost sight of Anatolia and lost it.

By 1300 much of Anatolia—apart from the nominally Seljuk territories under Ilkhanid rule in the central and eastern parts of the peninsula—was in the hands of one or another of these Turkish emirates. The emirates' populations were swelling owing to the influx of refugees from Central Asia. These refugees, many of whom were nomads, were difficult to control and caused considerable domestic disorder. Most of the emirates were led by warriors and lacked educated people to administer their territories. To survive they needed ever new conquests and booty. When expansion and booty ceased, they were unable to create efficient financial administrations to raise domestic taxes, and most crumbled from within. Best situated were those emirates in a position to fight Christian states—i.e., Aydin (until the Hospitalers took Smyrna in the middle of the 1340s) and the Ottoman emirate in northwestern Anatolia. And these two states attracted large numbers of would-be ghazis (Muslim warriors for the faith). We need not exaggerate the religious side—fighting for faith and paradise—as a motive. For there was also a strong worldly side to it; one who fought against other Muslims was in theory restricted in the extent he could loot. When one fought against infidels one could loot freely, within the rules governing the division of spoils within the army. Thus many were certainly attracted to the Ottomans for the chance to fight infidels and freely enrich themselves. And whenever I speak of ghazis this materialistic aspect is to be understood.

The emirate of Osman in northwestern Anatolia had the advantage of bordering on Byzantium, which was Christian territory and, as such, attracted large numbers of these would-be ghazis. Osman's principality also lay on major trade routes between Byzantium on the one hand and Central Asia or Syria on the other, allowing the Ottomans to rob or tax the caravans passing along this route. Thus its location produced considerable wealth. Being the only emirate that bordered on Byzantium not only put the Ottomans in the best position to fight Christians but also meant that they were the Turks most frequently hired as mercenaries in the Balkans by the Byzantines to fight in their domestic and foreign wars from the mid-1340s. The position of the Ottomans improved further from this time as a result of three events: the fall of their rival Aydin to the Hospitalers in the mid-1340s; their absorption of Karasi, giving them control of the southern shore of the Dardanelles, in 1345; and their acquisition in 1354 of Gallipoli on the European side of the Dardanelles, giving them control of the Straits. The Ottomans now had free access to Europe, and from then on the Ottoman emirate became a magnet for thousands of Turcoman nomads who, finding no open pastures in Anatolia, saw marauding in Europe as the best means to alleviate their lot. Thus wars in or against Europe attracted many such nomads and the Osmanli emirate was the point of departure for such activities.

And so, thousands came to the Ottoman emirate and either joined its armies or else, having expressed loyalty to the Ottoman emir (later sultan), passed on to Europe under their own warlords. In the beginning of their conquests these Turcoman refugees and nomads pushed out on their own against the Christian Balkans. Many of the Turkish conquests in the Balkans into the 1370s were actually carried out by various warlords, often leading bands of these Turcomans. Thus instead of causing domestic problems, they plundered and weakened Balkan territories and eventually even conquered some of these lands.

Then subsequently the Ottoman sultan could move in with a larger force and take over the conquests carried out by these warlords and their bands. Thus the Ottomans were able to escape population pressure from these nomads, whose numbers regularly grew from new arrivals, by sending them away from the state to settle the lands of their Christian neighbors and thus keep them busy at something useful to the Ottomans. During the later 1370s and after, the Ottomans were able to consolidate their hold not only over the territories taken by these bands but also, by the end of the fourteenth century, to assert their control over the warlords themselves. The Ottomans did so by diluting, and in some cases replacing, the warlords with a new service class, the devşirme, raised from Christian children levied in the Balkan lands, forcibly converted to Islam, educated, and then enrolled in Ottoman service. For an intelligent elite this service meant posts in the administration; for the rest, assignment in the army as Janissaries. The Janissaries came to balance the older Turkish cavalry and in time came to supersede it as they eventually acquired fire-arms. And the soldiers and administrators from the devşirme, totally dependent upon the sultan, were able to balance the power of the old Turkish aristocracy for the benefit of the sultan.

Thus we may conclude the following: Geography gave the Ottomans access to the Balkans, which, being potentially exploitable and Christian, attracted to their state a large amount of manpower. The other ghazi emirates that lacked Christian neighbors declined when they no longer had proper enemies to keep remunerative warfare going and to keep their states expanding. Without such wars, they had no way to defuse the restless nomads, who became major internal forces of disorder and thereby weakened these states. The Ottomans, however, by dispatching these excessive nomads across the Dardanelles into Europe, were able to keep them engaged in activities useful to their state and outside of the state, thereby preventing them from carrying out internal disturbances.

A second problem of the other ghazi states that were led by warriors was the lack of educated people to administer their lands. The Ottomans mastered this problem. Fighting against stubborn resistance from fortresses between 1330 and 1360, Ottoman conquests were relatively slow, making it easier for them to incorporate new conquests into their state. The sultans were also intelligent enough to see the need for experienced, literate administrators, and thus they attracted to their state educated Muslims from the former Seljuk centers in Anatolia. The sultans respected their learning and wisely gave these educated Muslims influence and state positions. The Muslim educated class, known as the ulema, established schools, brought administrative techniques, and also advanced the old Islamic ideal that people of the Book, Christians and Jews, should be allowed to keep their faith if they paid a special tax for this privilege. Thus the Ottoman sultans followed a policy of toleration toward their subjects who belonged to other faiths. And since this policy was practiced, Christians became more willing to surrender to the Ottomans when they found themselves hard pressed. That the Ottoman rulers were receptive to the ulema's teachings made them more respectful of civilization; it also made them see the need to establish efficient administrative institutions.

The quality of the sultans and their talent for organization also contributed heavily to Ottoman success. The sultan was a clearly recognized leader. The Ottomans were able to overcome the Balkan tendency toward feudal fragmentation and jealousies of the "if I can't lead, I won't follow" type. Though certain warlords and border lords of the mid- to late-fourteenth century manifested symptoms of this tendency, the sultans were able to suppress them and eliminate this problem. The sultans for the first two and a half centuries were all capable leaders and most of them enjoyed long reigns. The sultans also—with the possible exception of Bayezid I—were not hot-heads, but were willing to move gradually, annex a small region, consolidate their hold on it, and then move on further. In this way, they could effectively absorb a small region, establish the ulema, administrators, and cavalry on fiefs, and truly make it part of the state before expanding further. Moreover, they did not spread their elite too thin, but annexed at a given moment only as much territory as they could effectively absorb. All the early sultans were also able generals. Successful in their campaigns, they amassed considerable booty and thus attracted many followers to their standard. They then were successful in establishing discipline over their followers, which resulted in effective armies.

Furthermore, the Ottomans effectively incorporated new territories into their state because they carried out their conquest in stages. The gradualness of conquest made the Balkan people less likely to resist as strongly as they might have otherwise. At first the Ottomans merely established contact with the Balkan states. Then they began to play upon disorders within these states. They provided mercenaries in civil wars who at times retained the fortresses they had taken; they encouraged these civil wars and local rivalries, giving support to one or the other side in a quarrel in exchange for submission. They offered advantages to pro-Turkish parties and built up such factions within countries by supporting the leaders of such factions. Even before they reduced a state to vassalage they often had certain local nobles already under their suzerainty. For example, in Bosnia various nobles submitted years before

King Tvrtko II did. The Ottomans' position was helped further by the fact that the small Balkan states were also faced with a threat from Hungary. Thus certain Balkan leaders saw no chance for permanent or even long-term independence and realized they would have to reach an accommodation with one or the other of these outside powers. To many the Ottomans seemed the better choice. Orthodox Christians, who knew of Ottoman religious tolerance, often came to prefer the Turks to the intolerant Hungarians who were likely to force Catholicism upon them. And many Bosnians, after a long history of wars in which the Hungarians tried to assert their authority over Bosnia, clearly preferred the Turks to the Hungarians, as was shown in the statement of the Bosnian delegation to Venice in 1463.

Next in the process of conquest came the vassal stage. For the Ottomans usually did not immediately conquer or annex a region, but left a local prince in office—be it the existing prince or a newly installed member of the ruling family whose loyalty they counted on—who accepted the sultan's suzerainty and promised tribute and military service. In this way the Ottomans bettered their own economic position while weakening that of the tribute-paying state. By this means they also increased the size of their own armies. And by leaving a Christian prince to rule the region, they did not spread their own limited pool of educated administrators too thin. Thus they could collect wealth from the region without having to maintain the bureaucracy necessary to collect that wealth. Moreover, the continued rule of the native prince made revolts—at least those that could endanger the Ottoman position—less likely. And because of the Ottomans' willingness to accept vassal submissions, a Christian prince, when faced with the Ottoman armies, usually was not presented with the either/or situation that if he did not fight to the finish he would lose everything. Instead of being faced with total losses, he was given the opportunity to remain in power and submit to only limited disabilities. The degree of the disabilities—i.e., the amount of tribute—tended to be small at first, increasing with time as Ottoman power grew. At times accepting Ottoman suzerainty even enabled a native prince to increase his own strength vis à vis his neighbors or his own nobility, for the Ottomans could and often did provide him with troops. And we saw how Stefan Lazarević of Serbia, by leaning on the Ottomans against his own nobility, was able to consolidate his state and again make Serbia into a relatively large and strong state.

As a vassal state the country was weakened and the population became used to the Turks. Frequently during this phase the Ottomans also acquired footholds within the vassal state by establishing garrisons in certain of its fortresses, as they did in the lands of the Brankovići and in Bulgaria. And the Ottomans frequently weakened the state further by seizing from time to time portions of its territory. Moreover, as time passed, the Ottomans regularly upped their tribute demands, forcing the rulers to constantly increase taxes, the burden of which fell on the peasants. Thus life became harder for the peasants, both from the increased native taxes and also from the regular Ottoman raids that were launched against vassal states on one pretext or another. These raids caused destruction and lowered morale. Thus the position of the peasantry deteriorated. Next came Ottoman propaganda promising to a region that accepted direct Ottoman rule the benefits of lower taxation—Stefan Tomašević's letter showed the Turks were promising this to his peasants—and an end to warfare and raids. According to Stefan Tomašević's letter, the peasantry was receptive to such propaganda. This enabled the Ottomans to initiate the next, and final, stage, direct annexation, which meant the removal of the native dynasty and the incorporation of the state under Ottoman administration.

This step was clearly necessary since the vassal system did not provide permanence; there was always a question of a vassal's loyalty, and when the chance presented itself—crusades, Hungarian promises, etc.—various vassals had shed their vassalage, on occasion at critical moments, and joined the enemy. Thus the Turks needed to carry out frequent campaigns to enforce obedience. Since the Ottomans had not had the strength to absorb the whole Balkans rapidly, the vassal stage had been a fine temporary expedient. But it made sense, once the states were softened up, to gradually put them under direct rule. And Bayezid I (1389–1402) began carrying out a policy of direct annexation, absorbing into his growing empire much of northern Greece, Bulgaria, and the lands of Marko and the Dejanovići. However, Bayezid made the mistake of annexing the lands of various Muslim emirates in Anatolia as well, which brought upon himself Timur's attack. Bayezid's loss at Ankara, followed by civil war, set back the Ottoman time-table for annexation. But after recovery and a new period of consolidation, Murad II (1421–51) and Mehemmed II (1451–81) again launched a policy of replacing the vassal system with direct rule. And during their reigns most of the until then unannexed parts of the Balkans were incorporated into the empire.

At this stage the native dynasty was eliminated. And by this time, when it did make sense for the Christian prince to fight to the finish, his state had been weakened sufficiently to make effective resistance impossible.

The experience of the vassal stage made the subsequent process of annexation easier for both ruling Turks and subjugated Christians. Moreover, making the pill easier to swallow for those absorbed were the policies the Ottomans at first applied to their new populations. First, as noted, they tolerated Christianity. Second, they provided for a time occupational opportunities for those with talent and energy. For through the fourteenth, and much of the fifteenth, century, after incorporating a region, the Ottomans, in order to maintain large armies, allowed Christians from that region to enter military service and on many occasions even awarded fiefs (timars) to Christians. And as they absorbed new territories, they also permitted Christians to serve in administrative positions; thus they could avoid spreading their own administrative talent too thin and at the same time, by leaving former administrators in office, avoid the local unrest caused by changing the way administrative tasks were carried out. In this way, at the time of annexation, the Ottomans co-opted part of the Christian military and administrative elite. And whole vassal contingents—often of Vlachs—as well as thousands of individual Ottoman soldiers, officers, administrators, advisors, and wives were to serve and remain Christian or Jewish. And allowing Christians honors and positions even made annexation attractive to some of them.

But annexation from the start also meant the establishment of Ottoman institutions and personnel. For it was this that guaranteed the permanence of Ottoman control. The region's lands were divided among the Ottoman establishment, and the Ottoman cavalry was settled on fiefs inside the conquered region, giving the Ottomans a loyal, landed power base within the locality. Ottoman administrators were sent to serve in the cities, who at once carried out a cadastral survey and soon efficiently set about collecting the region's wealth in taxes. Garrisons were established in key fortresses, and the others were razed so they could not become centers of resistance. And though Christians were co-opted to serve in these tasks and even at times given fiefs, they were still a small minority in the ruling institutions; thus they benefited as individuals but were no threat to Ottoman interests.

In time, after Ottoman success was achieved, policy changed. With most of the Balkans conquered, there was less need to attract Christians in newly annexed or unannexed regions, and the devşirme provided sufficient Muslim soldiers and administrators for the empire's needs. So, the Ottomans no longer had to utilize infidels in the military or administration. Thus late in the fifteenth century—after most of the conquests were completed—Islam became a requirement in most cases for membership in the Ottoman army or administration. (There were exceptions in specific situations; for example small local units to oppose brigands and maintain law and order.) Moreover, those Christians who now (from the mid- to late-fifteenth century) entered Ottoman service, besides having to convert, with far greater regularity were sent to serve in far away provinces, usually Anatolia, where they had no personal ties. The members of the pre-conquest elite who did not enter Ottoman service or flee tended to be eliminated. Thus the conquered people were deprived of their natural leaders. And the Christians now found themselves not only in a Muslim state, but also in one almost entirely staffed by Muslims.

The Islamicization of government and army, thus, was also carried out gradually through stages; first the state co-opted and utilized Christian talent and then subsequently, when control was firmly established and the services of Christians no longer needed, excluded participation by infidels. The gradualness of establishing Ottoman control, from vassal arrangements to direct annexation (but at first utilizing local Christians in running things) to a fully Muslim-run administration, facilitated the establishment of an efficient regime and thereby contributed greatly to the long-range success of the Ottomans.

However, many Ottomans and Balkan Christians would have explained Ottoman success more simply, seeing it as resulting from the will of God, be it divine favor toward the Ottomans or divine anger at the Christians for their sins. This belief surely contributed to Ottoman success, for it gave to their troops confidence, an intangible, but important, factor in the winning of battles. Having won the Balkans and firmly established their state apparatus in the manner described, the Ottomans were then able to retain the Balkans under their rule far more successfully than any of their predecessors. Thus when a strong sultan died, the empire's hold on its peripheral territories did not falter as had been the experience of the various Balkan empires and even of Byzantium. However, the history of the Balkans under Ottoman rule, which includes the manner in which the Ottomans were able to retain their conquests, is a subject for a book itself; it goes well beyond the task that I have undertaken of surveying the medieval Balkans.

NOTES

1. On the Frankapans, see V. Klaić, *Krčki knezovi Frankapani* (Zagreb, 1901).

2. Venice's failure to support Skanderbeg and its conflict with him at this critical time have led scholars to condemn the Republic. However, in addition to the actual towns of contention between them, Skanderbeg's activities put Venice in a very difficult situation. Venice wanted to maintain peace with the Turks in order to safeguard its extensive commercial interests in the East. Thus Venice was in no position to support Skanderbeg actively. Moreover, the Albanian coast was of secondary importance to Venice as compared to the Aegean. Thus the sultan's good will was far more important to it than whether or not Albania resisted the Turks. Thiriet goes so far as to say that a spheres of influence understanding was in effect in the 1450s between the Ottomans and Venetians, with the Venetians willing to see the Ottomans hold Albania in exchange for Ottoman recognition of Venice's position on Crete and Euboea (F. Thiriet, "Quelques réflexions sur la politique Vénitienne à l'égard de Georges Skanderbeg," *Studia Albanica,* 1968, no. 1: 87–93).

3. *Istorija Crne Gore,* vol. 2, pt. 2, p. 228.

4. George Sphrantzes, *The Fall of the Byzantine Empire,* trans. and ed. M. Philippides (Amherst, Mass., 1980), pp. 78–79.

5. The *Commentaries* of Pius II have been translated by F. Gragg and provided with introduction and notes by L. Gabel. They were serialized with consecutive pagination in *Smith College Studies in History* 22, nos. 1–2 (1936–37); 25, nos. 1–4 (1939–40); 30 (1947); 35 (1951); 43 (1957). I have utilized Gragg's translation in all my citations. The reference to the specific passage cited here is vol. 35, p. 201.

6. This section on Bosnia, and in particular on Stefan Vukčić Kosača, is heavily indebted to S. Ćirković, *Stefan Vukčić-Kosača i njegovo doba,* SAN, posebna izdanja, 376) (Beograd, 1964). The reader is also referred for Bosnian matters to Ćirković's *Istorija srednjovekovne bosanske države* (Beograd, 1964).

7. P. Živković, *Tvrtko II Tvrtković,* p. 207.

8. It is worth pausing to examine this event; for Stefan Vukčić was a leading supporter of the Bosnian Church, and one of that Church's leaders, Gost Radin, was more-or-less his foreign secretary and resided at his court. His wife was Orthodox. And now, having sent a Ragusan Catholic abbot as his envoy to Alphonso, Stefan was admitted to a Catholic knightly order. These alliances strongly suggest that the Bosnian Church could not have been a heretical, neo-Manichean institution.

9. Pius II, *Commentaries, Smith College Studies* 43 (1957): 740–42.

10. I. Božić, "O Dukadjinima," *Zbornik Filozofskog fakulteta* (Beogradski uni-verzitet) 8, no. 2 (1964):424.

11. A. Gegaj, *L'Albanie et l'invasion Turque au XVe siècle* (Paris, 1937).

Medieval Rulers

Byzantine Emperors from 1143 to 1453

1143–80	Manuel I Comnenus
1180–83	Alexius II Comnenus
1183–85	Andronicus I Comnenus
1185–95	Isaac II Angelus
1195–1203	Alexius III Angelus
1203–04	Isaac II (again) and Alexius IV Angeli
1204	Alexius V Murtzuphlus

(Resident in Nicea)

1204–22	Theodore I Lascaris
1222–54	John III Vatatzes
1254–58	Theodore II Lascaris
1258–61	John IV Lascaris (with Michael Palaeologus regent co-emperor)

(Resident again in Constantinople)

1261–82	Michael VIII Palaeologus
1282–1328	Andronicus II Palaeologus
1328–41	Andronicus III Palaeologus
1341–91	John V Palaeologus (with Anna of Savoy, Apocaucus regency, 1341–47, and John VI Cantacuzenus ruling co-emperor, 1347–54)
1391–1425	Manuel II Palaeologus
1425–48	John VIII Palaeologus
1448–53	Constantine XI Palaeologus

Latin Emperors of Constantinople

1204–05	Baldwin I of Flanders
1206–16	Henry of Flanders
1217	Peter of Courtenay
1217–19	Yolande
1221–28	Robert of Courtenay
1228–61	Baldwin II (with John of Brienne regent co-emperor, 1231–37)

Rulers of Epirus

1204–15	Michael I
1215–24	Theodore

(With conquest of Thessaloniki state continues as Kingdom of Thessaloniki)

1224–30	Theodore (same as above)
1230–37	Manuel
1237–44	John (in association with Theodore)
1244–46	Demetrius

(Epirus re-emerges as separate state)

ca. 1231–67/68	Michael II
1267/68–96/98	Nicephorus I
1296/98–1318	Thomas
1318–23	Nicholas Orsini
1323–35	John Orsini
1335–40	Nicephorus II

(Thessaly as separate state within the family)

1267/68–ca. 1289	John I
ca. 1289–1303	Constantine
1303–1318	John II

Rulers of the Morea

(Frankish Princes of Achaea)

1205–08	William of Champlitte

1209–28	Geoffrey I of Villehardouin
1228–46	Geoffrey II of Villehardouin
1246–78	William of Villehardouin
1278–85	bailiffs for Charles I of Anjou
1285–89	bailiffs for Charles II of Anjou
1289–1307	Isabelle of Villehardouin (married to Florent of Hainaut, 1289–97, and to Philip of Savoy, 1301–07)
1307–13	Philip I of Taranto and bailiffs for him
1313–16	Louis of Burgundy
1316–18	Matilda of Villehardouin
1318–32	John of Gravina and bailiffs for him
1332–64	bailiffs for Robert of Taranto
1364–70	bailiffs for Mary of Bourbon
1370–73	bailiffs for Philip II of Taranto
1373–76/77	bailiffs for Joanna of Naples
1376/77–83	Hospitaler Knights of Saint John (leasing principality from Joanna)
1383–1402	Peter of San Superano (of the Navarrese Company) with title Prince of Achaea from 1396
1402	Maria Zaccaria
1402–32	Centurione Zaccaria

Greek Despots of the Morea

1348–80	Manuel Cantacuzenus
1380–82	Matthew Cantacuzenus
1383–1407	Theodore I Palaeologus
1407–43	Theodore II Palaeologus (ruling alone until 1428, then sharing rule with his brothers Thomas and Constantine, 1428–43)
1443–49	Constantine and Thomas Palaeologus
1449–60	Thomas and Demetrius Palaeologus

Latin Rulers of Athens and Thebes

1204–25	Othon de la Roche
1225–63	Guy I de la Roche

1263–80	John de la Roche
1280–90	William de la Roche
1290–1308	Guy II de la Roche
1308–11	Walter of Brienne
1311–88	Catalan Company under suzerainty of the Aragonese Kings of Sicily
1388–94	Nerio I Acciajuoli
1394–1402	Athens: Donato Acciajuoli, followed by rule of a bailiff from the Euboea Venetians Thebes: Anthony I Acciajuoli
1402–35	Athens and Thebes: Anthony I Acciajuoli
1435–39	Nerio II Acciajuoli
1439–41	Anthony II Acciajuoli
1441–51	Nerio II Acciajuoli (again)
1451–56	Various regents for Francesco Acciajuoli

Bulgarian Tsars

1185/86–96	Asen I
1196–97	Peter
1197–1207	Kalojan
1207–18	Boril
1218–41	John Asen II
1241–46	Koloman
1246–56	Michael
1257–77	Constantine Tih
1278–79	Ivajlo
1279	John Asen III
1279–92	George I Terter
1292–98	Smilec
1298–99	Regency for Smilec's son by his widow
1299–1300	Čaka
1300–22	Theodore Svetoslav
1322	George II Terter
1323–30	Michael Šišman
1330–31	John Stefan

1331–71	John Alexander
1371–93	John Šišman

Rulers of Serbia
Titles are given in parentheses after name

ca. 1167–96	Stefan Nemanja (Grand župan)
1196–1227	Stefan the First-Crowned (Grand župan until crowned king in 1217)
1227–34	Stefan Radoslav (king)
1234–43	Stefan Vladislav (king)
1243–76	Stefan Uroš I (king)
1276–82	Stefan Dragutin (king)
1282–1321	Stefan Uroš II Milutin (king)
1321–31	Stefan Uroš III Dečanski (king)
1331–55	Stefan Uroš IV Dušan (king to 1346; tsar from 1346)
1355–71	Stefan Uroš V (Tsar Uroš)
1371–89	Lazar (prince)
1389–1427	Stefan Lazarević (prince/lord to 1402; despot from 1402)
1427–56	George Branković (lord to 1429; despot from 1429)
1456–58	Lazar Branković (despot)
1458–59	Regency for Lazar's daughter Helen
1459	Stefan Tomašević of Bosnia (despot)

Rulers of Zeta

ca. 1360	Balša
ca. 1360–79	George I Balšić (sharing rule with his brothers Stracimir [died 1373] and Balša II)
1379–85	Balša II Balšić (sharing rule with his nephew George II Stracimirović Balšić)
1385–1403	George II Stracimirović Balšić
1403–21	Balša III Balšić

Rulers of Bosnia
Bearing title of ban to 1377, thereafter king

ca. 1180–ca. 1204	Kulin
ca. 1204–ca. 1232	unknown
ca. 1232–ca. 1250	Ninoslav
ca. 1250–ca. 1314	unknown (various bans referred to, but quite possibly none of them ruled the central banate)
ca. 1314–53	Stjepan Kotromanić
1353–91	Tvrtko I
1391–95	Stefan Dabiša
1395–98	Helen/Gruba
1398–1404	Stefan Ostoja
1404–09	Stefan Tvrtko II Tvrtković
1409–18	Stefan Ostoja (again)
1418–21	Stefan Ostojić
1421–43	Stefan Tvrtko II Tvrtković (again)
1443–61	Stefan Tomaš
1461–63	Stefan Tomašević

The Kosača Rulers of Hum/Hercegovina

?–1392	Vlatko Vuković
1392–1435	Sandalj Hranić
1435–66	Stefan Vukčić (Herceg Stefan)
1466–81	Vlatko (herceg)

Kings of Hungary

1172–96	Bela III
1196–1204	Imre
1204–05	Ladislas III
1205–35	Andrew II
1235–70	Bela IV
1270–72	Stephen V
1272–90	Ladislas IV
1290–1301	Andrew III

1301–42	Charles Robert
1342–82	Louis I
1382–87	Maria alone
1387–95	Maria and Sigismund of Luxemburg
1395–1437	Sigismund of Luxemburg
1437–39	Albert of Austria (Habsburg)
1439–40	Elizabeth on behalf of Ladislas Posthumous
1440–44	Vladislav I
1444–57	Ladislas V ("Posthumous")
1458–90	Matthew Corvinus
1490–1516	Vladislav II of Bohemia
1516–26	Louis II

Ottoman Sultans

1299–1326	Osman I
1326–60	Orkhan
1360–89	Murad I
1389–1402	Bayezid I
1402–13	Civil war among Bayezid's sons
1413–21	Mehemmed I
1421–51	Murad II
1451–81	Mehemmed II
1481–1512	Bayezid II
1512–20	Selim I
1520–66	Suleyman I

Glossary of Terms

Adamite: Member of a heretical religious current that sought to return mankind to Adam's original state in paradise.

Appanage: A large land grant by a ruler to a member of his family. Usually not hereditary. Holder usually had rights of internal administration and local tax revenue but owed military service to his superior and was allowed no independence in foreign affairs.

Archdeacon: A high Catholic Church official, serving more-or-less as executive secretary to a bishop.

Archon: A leader; term used in a variety of ways. In this volume it particularly pertains to the Greek landed nobility.

Armatoloi (or Martolozi): During the Ottoman period, Christians of a locality mobilized and armed to serve under one of their number (a captain) to keep local order.

Assize: Term used by the Franks for a session of a legislative body or court, and also for decisions reached at such a session.

Autocephalous: Self-headed, autonomous. Used to describe a branch of the Orthodox Church (e.g., the Serbian Church) that could, while remaining in communion with Constantinople, elect its own bishop and administer itself; such a Church, however, did not have the power to alter doctrine.

Bailiff (or bailie, bailo): An official who administered a territory for a superior lord. Thus the Angevins sent bailiffs to administer their lands in the Morea.

Ban: A ruler or governor of a large province, usually a subordinate of the King of Hungary (or historically so). The title was used in the western Balkans in Bosnia, Croatia, Slavonia, and Mačva. On occasion a banship became hereditary. Sometimes bans were able to achieve considerable, if not complete, independence.

Banate (or Banovina): The territory ruled by a ban.

Beg (or bey): A Turkish lord. In the thirteenth and fourteenth centuries often a tribal or territorial chief. Also, from the late fourteenth century, a governor of an Ottoman province (e.g., a sanjak beg). Later on the title was borne by a large landholder.

Beglerbeg: The military governor of a major Ottoman province (or beglerbeglik).

Bogomil: A member of a dualistic, heretical sect that arose in Bulgaria in the mid-tenth century and spread beyond Bulgaria into the Byzantine Empire, and from there along the Mediterranean to the south of Western Europe. (For details, see Fine, *Early Medieval Balkans*, pp. 171–79.)

Bosnian Church: An independent Church in Bosnia, often called heretical, but probably only in schism from Rome. It existed from the mid- to late thirteenth century until the late fifteenth century.

Boyar (bojar): A member of the military landed aristocracy in Bulgaria. The term was also used in Russia.

Cadaster: A tax register listing population on, ownership of, and extent of land.

Caesar: The second title (after emperor) in the Byzantine Empire until the late eleventh century. Then it was eclipsed by new titles, first by sebastocrator and then by despot, and thus fell to fourth place.

Canon law: Ecclesiastical law. A canon is a particular article of such law. A canonist is a specialist in canon law.

Castellan: A captain of a castle. For example, a Catalan castellan commanded/held a castle of second rank.

Cathars: Dualist heretics found in the later Middle Ages in southern France.

Chartophylax: Keeper of archives and/or general secretary (or chancellor) of a bishop in the Orthodox Church.

Corvée: Labor owed by a serf to his landowner.

Count palatine: In Hungary, the highest court official after the king, who served in place of an absent king.

Cumans (also called Polovtsy): A Turkish people who appeared in the Steppes in the eleventh century after the decline of the Pechenegs. They were a problem for the eastern Balkans for the next two centuries owing to their raids. However, others settled in Bulgaria and comprised a valuable portion of the armies of the Second Bulgarian Empire.

Cyrillic: The alphabet used for the Slavic languages of the Orthodox Slavs: e.g., the Bulgarians, Serbs (including Montenegrins), Macedonians, and Russians. It was named for Saint Cyril (Constantine), one of the two apostles to the Slavs who created in the ninth century the first Slavic literary language (what we now call Old Church Slavonic).

Despot: An honorary court title of the Byzantine Empire, introduced in the twelfth century as the second highest title after that of emperor. It was an honorary title in the court hierarchy, and though on occasions it was given to the holder of a territory, the title still reflected the holder's position in the Byzantine court rather than his position as ruler of his holding. Thus the term *despotate* for such a territory is often inappropriate.

Devşirme: The Ottoman levy of Christian children for future service in the Ottoman state. The term is also used for those so levied.

Dijak: Slavic for a secretary or scribe.

Djed: Title borne by the head of the Bosnian Church; it literally means "grandfather."

Doge: The title borne by the ruler of Venice.

Država: Serbian for state, derived from the verb *to hold*.

Dualist: Religiously, one who believes in two opposing gods or principles: generally, good vs. evil (or spirit vs. matter). Under this heading one finds the Manichees, the medieval Bogomils, and their Western off-shoots (Patarins, Cathars, etc.).

Eleutheroi: In the Byzantine Empire, term used for rural persons not bound to the soil. Literally, "a free man."

Emir: A prince or ruler of an Islamic territory, or emirate.

Filioque: "And the Son." An addition to the Nicene Creed by which the Holy Spirit descends from the Father *and the Son.* Arising in Spain in the sixth century, it had by the ninth century become regular usage in the Western (Catholic) Church.

After the 1054 break it became the major theological point of difference between the Orthodox and Catholic Churches.

Franciscan: A member of the Catholic Order founded by Saint Francis.

Gasmoule: An individual of mixed Frank (Latin) and Greek parentage.

Ghazi: A Turkish warrior for the (Islamic) faith.

Ghegs: Members of the Albanian ethnic group to which the tribesmen of northern Albania belong.

Glagolitic: The first alphabet worked out by Cyril and Methodius for Slavic. It was soon replaced in most places by the Cyrillic alphabet. However, Glagolitic survived for many centuries in Croatia.

Gospodin: Slavic for a lord. At times borne by the ruler of a state (e.g., George Branković for the first years he ruled Serbia).

Gost: The second highest title in the Bosnian Church, often held by clerics who headed Bosnian Church religious houses.

Gramatik: Among the South Slavs, the title earned by one who had successfully completed a prolonged course in literary study.

Grand župan: Literally, "Grand Count." The title held by the ruler of Raška/Serbia until Stefan Prvovenčani assumed the royal title in 1217.

Grof: German for a count.

Hajduk: Serbian term for a brigand, often possessing positive—social bandit—connotations.

Hellene: Literally, "a Greek." The name was rejected by Greeks through most of the Middle Ages since it connoted a pagan.

Herceg (in German, Herzog): A duke; the title was assumed by various rulers in the western Balkans in the fifteenth century.

Hesychasm: A mystical movement whose members, called Hesychasts, through special practices achieved a vision of the Divine Light. Though the ideas and practices were much older, the term is often used specifically for the movement that achieved prominence in the fourteenth century.

Hexamilion: The wall built across the Isthmus of Corinth to stop would-be invaders of the Peloponnesus.

Hiža: Literally, "a house"; a residence for Bosnian Church clerics.

Hospitalers: The Knights of Saint John of Jerusalem. A Catholic military order.

Hussites: The followers of John Hus; considered heretics by the Catholic Church. Though their center was in Bohemia, some of them were to be found in the northern Balkans, particularly in Srem.

Janissary: Derived from Yeni çeri, literally, the "new corps"; a member of a very effective Turkish infantry corps, armed with fire-arms. Its members were originally drawn from the devşirme (the child) levy.

Kapetan: A military commander; term used at times for garrison commanders or for leaders of small independent bands of soldiers. In the Ottoman period used in the Slavic Balkans for a fortress commander responsible for keeping order in a region.

Karaites: Members of a Jewish sect that rejected the Talmudic interpretations of the Bible. Going directly back to the Bible, they came up with their own interpretations; thus their customs differed considerably from those of the mainstream—Rabbinical—Jews.

Katun: A settlement of Balkan pastoralists, in particular the settlements of Vlachs, Albanians, and Montenegrins.

Kaznac: In Slavic, a treasurer.

Kephale (in Slavic, kefalia): Literally, "a head." A Byzantine town commander who combined military and civil functions. The term came to be used subsequently in regions under the Serbs.

Khan: Turkish title for a supreme chief, used by the Tatars.

Klepht: Greek term for a brigand, having often the same positive connotations as the Serbian term *hajduk*.

Knez (in Serbian or Croatian; knjaz in Bulgarian): Prince. At times, however, the term was used for leaders with lesser roles: e.g., the mayor of a Dalmatian city, the military leader (and family head) of a major—Montenegrin, Hercegovinian, or Vlach—tribe, or a fortress commander in Bosnia.

Krstjanin (plural, krstjani): A Bosnian Church religious.

Ktitor (in Slavic, from Greek ktistes or ktetor): A founder. Used in our text for monastery founders.

Kum/kumstvo: A God-father/God-fathership.

Lavra: By the later Middle Ages, a major monastery.

Legate: An ecclesiastic appointed to represent the pope.

Logothete: In the Middle and Late Byzantine period, a high Byzantine court secretary standing at the head of a bureaucratic department. The term spread to the Serbs and Bulgarians among whom logothetes tended to be secretaries responsible for drawing up documents.

Manichee: A member of a dualistic religion (opposing light against darkness) based on the teaching of a third-century Persian named Mani. Damned as a heresy by the Christian Church. The term was frequently used for later medieval dualists and generally as a term of abuse.

Megaduke: Grand admiral of the Byzantine navy.

Merop (pl. meropsi): A category of dependent peasant in Serbia.

Messalians (Massalians): Members of an enthusiastic early Christian sect. The sect had died out long before the period this volume covers. However, the name was revived as a term of abuse for Bogomils.

Metropolitan: A major bishop, standing over a major diocese, ranking below the patriarch and above the archbishops.

Midrash: Verse by verse exegesis of the Old Testament by Jewish teachers over the centuries. Many volumes of such have been published.

Nomocanon: A legal compilation combining secular and Church law for the use of Church courts. The secular items tended to focus on matters coming before Church courts, like marriage, inheritance, etc. Long used in Byzantium, the Nomocanon appeared in Serbian and Bulgarian editions—based on Byzantine texts—in the thirteenth century.

Orthodox: Correct belief. A term used for the mainstream Church in East and West until the Church split. Subsequently the term came to refer to the Eastern Churches in communion with Constantinople, while the term Catholic, also originally used to refer to the Church both in the East and West, came to refer solely to the Church of Rome.

Ousia: A Greek word meaning essence/substance. The divine ousia was frequently a matter of theological discussion and debate. In the fourteenth century Hesychasts defended their visions by insisting what they saw was a divine energy and not the divine ousia, which is invisible and unknowable.

Panipersebast: A Byzantine court title just below that of caesar.

Paroikos (pl. paroikoi): The Greek term used for dependent peasants in the Later Byzantine Empire.

Patarin: A name first used for certain Church reformers in Milan allied to Pope Gregory VII. Later the term came to be applied to dualist heretics in Italy who were part of the Cathar movement. The name then came to be used by Italians and Dalmatians, when writing in Latin, to describe members of the Bosnian Church, even though those Churchmen do not seem to have been dualists.

Patriarch: A major bishop who was the independent head of a major diocese. In the Early Church (from the mid-fifth century) there were five recognized patriarchates: Rome, Constantinople, Alexandria, Antioch, and Jerusalem. After they became autocephalous the Bulgarian and Serbian Churches sought and at times unilaterally assumed this title for the heads of their Churches. At times through pressure they even received recognition for their patriarchal titles from the Constantinopolitan patriarch.

Patriciate: The collective, often closed, group of elite merchant families who controlled the affairs of many Dalmatian towns.

Paulicians: Member of a religious sect, seen as heretical by the Orthodox Church, arising in Armenia and eastern Anatolia. Long considered to be dualist, the Paulicians have recently been shown to have been Adoptionists. After being defeated by the Byzantines, many Paulicians were transferred to Thrace and the Rhodopes to defend the border with Bulgaria, where (centered in Philippopolis) many continued to retain their beliefs and practices.

Podesta (potestas): A deputy appointed to govern a town or community by a superior, e.g., in the 1250s the Hungarian Ban of Dalmatia appointed a podesta in each town to represent him.

Praitor: Governor of the late-twelfth-century combined theme of central Greece and the Peloponnesus. By then the office had become chiefly a civil one. The holders were often absentees.

Praktor: A high financial official responsible for assessing and collecting taxes in the late twelfth century in the combined Greek theme. The praktor acted as governor in the absence of the praitor.

Pronoia: In the Byzantine Empire (and later in Bulgaria and Serbia) a grant of an income source (usually land) given in exchange for service (usually military) to the state. The pronoia reverted to the state when the holder died or ceased to perform the services for which it had been assigned. In time the grants tended to become hereditary, but the service obligations remained.

Pronoiar: The holder of a pronoia.

Protos of Mount Athos: The chief elder or first monk on Mount Athos.

Protostrator: A high Byzantine court title which occasionally was granted to foreign leaders. Choniates, writing in the early thirteenth century, equates it with the Latin title of Marshall.

Protovestiar: The title of a Byzantine palace official in charge of the imperial wardrobe. The title was taken over by the South Slavs. Though it is not certain what the functions of the Slavic protovestiars were, they seem to have been some sort of financial official.

Romania: Western term for the Byzantine (and also the Latin) Empire or its territory.

Romaniote Jews: Members of the Greek-speaking Jewish communities of the Byzantine Empire.

Sabor: Slavic for a council.

Sanjak: An Ottoman province, a subdivision of a beglerbeglik.

Sasi (Saxons): Germans from Saxony; many migrated to Hungary, however, where some became active as miners. Between the thirteenth and fifteenth centuries some came from Hungary to various Balkan regions, where they provided technological know-how for the mining; they were known as Sasi.

Sbornik (Zbornik): A collection of texts.

Sebastocrator (Sevastocrator): Second title after emperor, above caesar and below despot.

Sevast: Title borne by town governors appointed by Strez in Macedonia early in the thirteenth century.

Shaman: A healer-priest who communicates with the spirit world, often in a trance. Such priests were found among medieval Balkan Vlachs.

Sokalnik: A category of dependent peasant in medieval Serbia.

Spahi (Sipahi): An Ottoman cavalryman who provided his service in exchange for a fief (a timar).

Stećak (pl. stećci): Scholars' term for the unusual medieval gravestones found throughout Bosnia and Hercegovina. This term is preferable to the frequently used term *Bogomil gravestone;* for there is nothing Bogomil about the stones, which were erected by members of all denominations: Orthodox, Catholic, and Bosnian Church.

Strategos (pl. strategoi): Greek for general; from the seventh century used specifically for the military commander of a theme (a military province). The strategos not only commanded the local troops but was also more-or-less the governor of the province.

Strojnik (pl. strojnici): Member of the council that guided the djed, the leader of the Bosnian Church.

Subinfeudation: A Western feudal practice by which a vassal of a superior lord could also have vassals of his own. In contrast, in the Orthodox lands all fiefs were held from the crown and all service was owed the ruler.

Suffragan bishop: A lesser bishop subordinate to a greater one.

Sultan: Title of the Ottoman sovereign.

Syncretism: A combining of differing beliefs from two or more religions.

Synod: A Church council.

Synodik: A text presenting the decisions of a synod.

Talmud: Collection of ancient Rabbinic writings constituting the basic religious authority for traditional Judaism.

Tepčija: A high official at the medieval Bosnian and Serbian courts. Neither the meaning of the title nor the functions carried out by its holder are known.

Theme: Originally a Greek term for an army corps, it came in the seventh century also to refer to a Byzantine military province defended by that corps. Soon thereafter the whole Byzantine Empire was divided into these military provinces, each under the direction of a strategos.

Timar: An Ottoman fief assigned to a spahi—or other serviceman—for military service.

Tosks: The members of the ethnic group to which most Albanians of southern Albania belong.

Transhumance: A pastoral life-style, in which shepherds carry out a regular seasonal migration with their animals, wintering in the valleys and moving up into the mountains in the summer.

Triarch: The island of Euboea was divided among three great fief-holding barons; each was called a triarch.

Tsar: Slavic equivalent of the Greek *basileus,* emperor. The Slavs used it for the Byzantine emperor, and in time when Slavic rulers—i.e., the rulers of the Second Bulgarian Empire and Dušan of Serbia—claimed for themselves the imperial title, they called themselves tsars.

Turcoman: Turkic nomadic tribesmen from Central Asia who began pouring into Anatolia in the eleventh century. Their migrations continued over the following centuries. Many became associated with the Ottomans and provided much of the manpower for the Ottomans' extensive conquests.

Typikon: Literally, "a rule;" used for the foundation charter of a monastery; it laid down the rules by which the monastery would be run.

Ulema: The doctors of Muslim religious law, tradition, and theology.

Uniate: An Orthodox believer who has accepted Church Union with Rome and submitted to the pope; in most cases the popes allowed the Uniates to retain their own services.

Vicariat of Bosnia: The territory of southeastern Europe in which the Franciscans carried out a mission to win the populace to Catholicism; the mission was headed by a vicar.

Vlachs: A pastoral people, related to the Rumanians and presumably descended from the Dacians, found in large numbers in certain parts of the Balkans, particularly in Thessaly, Macedonia, Bulgaria (where they played an important role in creating the Second Bulgarian Empire), northeastern Serbia, and Hercegovina.

Vlast: Stefan Lazarević divided Serbia into military districts, each called a vlast (meaning an authority); each was under a governor who was also a military commander and bore the title vojvoda.

Vojvoda: A military commander. Also used to denote the chief of a Montenegrin tribe. At times used for a subordinate territorial ruler (e.g., Stefan Vukčić, prior to assuming the title herceg, bore the title Vojvoda of Bosnia).

Zadužbina: An obligation for one's soul; each Nemanjić ruler of Serbia built a monastery as his zadužbina.

Zbor: A tribal assembly.

Župa (županija): A territorial unit (roughly equivalent to a county) in Croatia, Bosnia, and Serbia.

Župan: The lord of a county—a count.

Sources and Authors of Sources Referred to in the Text

Acropolites, George (1217–82): Byzantine (and Nicean) statesman and diplomat who wrote a chronicle covering the period 1203–61. (A. Heisenberg, ed., *Georgii Acropolitae opera*, vol. 1 [Leipzig, 1903].)

Benjamin of Tudela: Jewish traveler who wrote an account of the Jewish communities he visited in 1168 in the Byzantine Empire (including many in Greece). (English translation in *Jewish Quarterly Review* 16–18 [1904–06].)

Blastares, Matthew: compiled in 1335 a syntagma (an encyclopedic compilation of ecclesiastical and secular legal decisions) that, soon translated into Serbian, had considerable impact on Serbian law.

Camblak, Gregory (ca. 1365–ca. 1419): Bulgarian-born cleric, abbot of monastery of Dečani, and later a bishop in Russia, who wrote a saint's life of King Stefan Dečanski.

Cantacuzenus, John: Byzantine emperor, 1347–54, who after his forced retirement wrote a detailed history (and memoir) of his times covering the period 1320–62. (Bonn corpus, 3 vols., 1828–32.)

Chalcocondyles, Laonikos: Byzantine historian who in the 1480s wrote a world history from ancient times to 1463, important for his coverage of the period from the 1360s. (J. Darko, ed., *Laonici Chalcocondylae historiarum demonstrationes*, 2 vols. [Budapest, 1922–27]. Also older Bonn edition.)

Choniates, Michael: Brother of Niketas and Archbishop of Athens (1182–1204) whose letters are a major source on Athens at that time.

Choniates, Niketas (died 1210): Byzantine court secretary and historian whose history deals with the period from the death of Alexius Comnenus in 1118 to 1206. (Greek text: J.-L. van Dieten, ed., in *Corpus fontium historiae byzantinae*, vol. 11, pts. 1–2, series Berolinesis [Berlin, 1975]. Also Bonn edition. English translation: H. Magoulias, ed. and trans., *O City of Byzantium, Annals of Niketas Choniates* [Detroit, 1984].)

Constantine the Philosopher (Konstantin Filozof, Konstantin Kostenečki): Bulgarian-born scholar and writer who came to Serbia in 1411, was active at the court of Stefan Lazarević, and wrote a biography of Stefan Lazarević in about 1431.

Cydones, Demetrius (died 1410): Byzantine statesman and author whose treatises and numerous surviving letters provide important data, particularly about ecclesiastical affairs, Thessaloniki, and the Peloponnesus in the second half of the fourteenth and early fifteenth centuries.

Danilo (ca. 1270–1337): Serbian monk, active in court and Church politics. Archbishop of Serbia from 1323. Author of *The Lives of the Serbian Kings and Archbishops* (in medieval Serbian) containing biographies of the Serbian kings from Uroš I through Milutin and of the eight contemporary archbishops.

Danilo Continuatus: An anonymous Serbian cleric who continued the work of Danilo, writing biographies of Dečanski and Dušan to 1335 as well as of four heads of the Serbian Church including Danilo.

Domentian (ca. 1210–ca. 1265): Serbian monk on Hilandar who wrote biographies of Saints Sava and Simeon (Nemanja).

Ducas: First name unknown. Fifteenth-century Byzantine historian who chronicled the fall of the empire in a work covering the period 1341–1462. (Greek text: V. Grecu, ed., *Ducas, Istoria turco-bizantina (1341–1462)* [Bucharest (Romanian Academy of Sciences), 1958]. English translation: H. Magoulias, trans., *Decline and Fall of Byzantium to the Ottoman Turks by Doukas* [Detroit, 1975].)

Dušan's Law Code: Stefan Dušan, ruler of Serbia (1331–55), issued a law code in two installments in 1349 and 1354. (English translation: M. Burr, ed. and trans., "The Code of Stephan Dušan," *Slavonic and East European Review* 28 (1949–50): 198–217, 516–39.)

Gregoras, Nicephorus (1290/91–1360): Byzantine scholar and historian whose history covers the years 1204–1359. (Greek text: Bonn Corpus, 2 vols., 1829–30.)

Jannina, Chronicle of: An anonymous chronicle, written in Greek in Jannina early in the fifteenth century, covering the years 1357–1400.

Kritovoulos: A Greek from Imbros in the service of the Ottomans, who wrote a history of the fall of the empire, covering the period 1451–67. (Greek text: V. Grecu, ed., *Critobuli Imbriotae De rebus per annos 1451–1467 a Mechemete II gestis* [Bucharest (Romanian Academy), 1963]. English translation: C. T. Riggs, ed. and trans., *History of Mehmed the Conquerer* by Kritovoulos [Princeton, N.J., 1954].)

Luccari, Jacob: Renaissance historian who published in 1605 a history of Dubrovnik, including much material on the Slavic interior, entitled *Copioso ristretto degli annali di Ragusa di Giacomo di Pietro Luccari.* He made use of the Dubrovnik archives and the works of various earlier historians. Some of the material from them is no longer extant.

Metohites, Theodore: Byzantine statesman and diplomat who left an account of his embassy to the Serbian court of Milutin in 1298/99.

Morea, Chronicle of: Written in the first quarter of the fourteenth century by a Hellenized Frank, it survives in French, Italian, Aragonese, and two Greek versions. It covers the period of Frankish rule. (For the different editions, see G. Ostrogorsky, *History of the Byzantine State* [New Brunswick, N.J., 1969], p. 419 n. 2.)

Mutaner: Catalan who participated in the Catalan Company's expedition to Byzantium and Greece at the beginning of the fourteenth century and wrote an account of it.

Orbini, Mavro (ca. 1550–1611): Historian who published in 1601 *Il Regno degli Slavi,* an important history of the South Slavs that makes use of many earlier sources no longer extant.

Pachymeres, George (1242–1310): Byzantine scholar and historian whose important history covers the years 1255–1308. (Greek text: Bonn Corpus, 2 vols., 1835.)

Philes, Manuel: Byzantine poet whose panegyrics to high state and military officials contain some important, but sometimes difficult to interpret, material.

Pius II, Pope (Enea Silvio de Piccolomini, 1405–64, pope 1458–64): His major work in thirteen books, a combination memoir (based on diaries) and history of his times known in English as the *Commentaries,* contains much material on Hungary and Bosnia. (See bibliography for English translation and specific references.)

Resti, Junius (1669–1735): Wrote a chronicle of Dubrovnik (including material on the Slavic interior) from the town's origins to 1451. Basing his chronicle on Dubrovnik's archives, Resti had access to many documents no longer extant.

Sava, Saint (1175–1235): Son of Stefan Nemanja. Tonsured as a monk in the early 1190s, and Archbishop of Serbia (1219–33), he wrote a life of Saint Simeon (Nemanja).

Sphrantzes, George (1401–77): Byzantine official and historian close to the imperial family. He wrote a chronicle covering the period 1413–77. His actual work is what is now known as the *Short Chronicle (Chronicon minus).* The long version formerly attributed to him is actually an expansion of his work done in the sixteenth century. (Greek text: V. Grecu, ed., *Chronicon minus* [Bucharest, 1966]. English translation of the short version: M. Philippides, ed. and trans., *The Fall of the Byzantine Empire: A Chronicle by George Sphrantzes, 1401–1477* [Amherst, Mass., 1980].)

Stefan Prvovenčani ("The First-Crowned"): Son of Stefan Nemanja, King of Serbia (1196–1227), and author of a life of Nemanja.

Theodosius of Hilandar: A Serbian monk on Hilandar who in the second half of the thirteenth century wrote a life of Saint Sava based on the earlier *Life of Sava* by Domentian.

Theodosius of Trnovo, Life of: The surviving Bulgarian text is probably a fifteenth-century re-working of the no-longer-extant *Life of Theodosius* written in Greek by Kallistos, Patriarch of Constantinople (1350–54, 1355–63). The text has much material on the Hesychast movement in Bulgaria and Bulgarian Church history.

Thomas the Archdeacon of Split (died 1268): Author of a history of Split (*Historia Salonitana*) covering the period from the seventh century to his own time. An expanded version of his work from the sixteenth century, known as *Historia Salonitana maior,* also exists. (N. Klaić has recently published critical editions of both texts.)

Turosci, John: Hungarian historian, active in the late fifteenth century, author of *Chronicon regnum Hungariae.*

Villehardouin, Geoffrey de (died 1213): Participant on the Fourth Crusade whose chronicle on the crusade and its aftermath is probably the best single source on that major event. He was the uncle of the Geoffrey de Villehardouin who created the principality in the Morea. (The original is in French; several English translations exist.)

Selected Bibliography

(Slavic Ć, Č, Š, and Ž are treated as Ch, Ch, Sh, and Zh, respectively.)

Anastasijević, D. N. *Otac Nemanjin.* Beograd, 1914.

Andjelić, P. "Barones regni i državno vijeće srednjovjekovne Bosne." *Prilozi Instituta za istoriju u Sarajevu* 11–12 (1975–76): 29–48.

———. "O Usorskim vojvodama i političkom statusu Usore u srednjem vijeku." In P. Andjelić, *Studije o teritorijalnopolitičkoj organizaciji srednjovjekovne Bosne.* Sarajevo, 1982. Pp. 142–72.

———. *Studije o teritorijalnopolitičkoj organizaciji srednjovjekovne Bosne.* Sarajevo, 1982.

Ankori, Z. "Some Aspects of Karaite-Rabbanite Relations in Byzantium on the Eve of the First Crusade." In *Medieval Jewish Life,* edited by R. Chazan. New York, 1976. Pp. 169–232.

Asdracha, C. *La region des Rhodopes aux XIIIe et XIVe siècles: Etude de geographie historique.* Texte und Forschungen zur byzantinisch-neugriechischen Philologie. Beihefte der "Byzantinisch-neugriechischen Jahrbücher," no. 49. Athens, 1976.

Atanasovski, V. [= Trpković, V.] *Pad Hercegovine.* Beograd, n.d. (ca. 1981).

Babić, A. *Iz istorije srednjovjekovne Bosne.* Sarajevo, 1972.

Barišić, F., and Ferjančić, B. "Vesti Dimitrija Homatijana o 'vlasti Druguvita.'" *Zbornik radova Vizantološkog instituta* (Serbian Academy of Sciences) 20 (1981): 41–55.

Barker, J. *Manuel II Palaeologus (1391–1425): A Study in Late Byzantine Statesmanship.* New Brunswick, N.J., 1969.

Bartusis, M. "Brigandage in the Late Byzantine Empire." *Byzantion* 51 (1981): 386–409.

———. "Chrelja and Momčilo: Occasional Servants of Byzantium in 14th Century Macedonia." *Byzantinoslavica* 41 (1980): 201–21.

Benac, A., et al. *Kulturna istorija Bosne i Hercegovine od najstarijih vremena do početka turske vladavine.* Sarajevo, 1966.

Birnbaum, H. "Serbian Models in the Language and Literature of Medieval Russia." In H. Birnbaum, *Essays in Early Slavic Civilization.* Munich, 1981. Pp. 99–111.

Bowman, S., *The Jews of Byzantium, 1204–1453.* University, Ala., 1985.

Božić, I. "Gospodin Kojčin." *Gjürmimet Albanologjike* 1 (1968): 117–28.

———. "Katuni Crne Gore." *Zbornik Filozofskog fakulteta* (Beogradski univerzitet) 10, no. 1 (1968): 245–49.

———. "Mlečani na reci Bojani." In I. Božić, *Nemirno Pomorje XV veka*. Beograd, 1979. Pp. 218–40.

———. *Nemirno Pomorje XV veka*. Beograd, 1979.

———. "O Dukadjinima." *Zbornik Filozofskog fakulteta* (Beogradski univerzitet) 8, no. 2 (1964): 385–427.

———. "O jurisdikciji Kotorske dijeceze u srednjevekovnoj Srbiji." *Spomenik* (Serbian Academy of Sciences) 103 (1953): 11–16.

———. "O položaju Zete u državi Nemanjića." *Istoriski glasnik,* 1950, nos. 1–2: 97–122.

———. "O propasti monastira sv. Mihaila na Prevalici." *Anali Filološkog fakulteta* (Beogradski univerzitet) 7 (1967): 75–81.

———. "Promene u društvenoj strukturi srpskih zapadnih oblasti uoči turskog osvajanja." *Jugoslovenski istorijski časopis* 1 (1964): 3–12.

———. "Srednjovekovni Paštrovići." *Istorijski časopis* 9–10 (1959): 151–85.

———. "Le systeme foncier en 'Albanie Venitienne' au XVᵉ siècle." *Bollettino dell' Istituto di Storia della societa e della stato* 5–6 (1964): 65–140. Translated into Serbo-Croatian in I. Božić, *Nemirno Pomorje XV veka*. Beograd, 1979. Pp. 259–331.

———. "Zetske vojvode pod despotima." *Glasnik Društva za nauku i umjetnost Crne Gore* 2 (1975): 5–24.

Božilov, I. "Beležki v"rhu b"lgarskata istorija prez XIII vek." In *B"lgarsko srednovekovie*. Dujčev Festschrift. Sofija, 1980. Pp. 78–81.

———. "La famille des Asen (1186–1460): Généalogie et prosopographie." *Bulgarian Historical Review,* 1981, nos. 1–2: 135–56.

Brand, C. *Byzantium Confronts the West, 1180–1204*. Cambridge, Mass., 1968.

Bratianu, G. I. *La Mer Noire: Des origines à la conquête Ottomane*. Acta Historica, vol. 9. Societas Academica Dacoromana. Monachi, 1969.

———. *Recherches sur le commerce Génois dans la Mer Noire au XIIIᵉ siècle*. Paris, 1929.

Braudel, F. *The Structures of Everyday Life*. New York, 1981.

Burmov, A. "Istorija na B"lgarija prez vremeto na Šišmanovci (1323–96)." *Godišnik na Sofijskija universitet* (Istoriko-filologičeski fakultet) 42 (1946–47), fasc. 1, pp. 1–58; fasc. 2, pp. 1–22.

Bury, J. B. "The Lombards and Venetians in Euboia." *Journal of Hellenic Studies* 7 (1886): 309–52; 8 (1887): 194–213; 9 (1888): 91–117.

Cambridge Medieval History. Vol. 4, pt. 1. Edited by J. Hussey. Cambridge, 1966.

Cankova-Petkova, G. "Vosstanovlenie bolgarskogo patriaršestva v 1235 g. i meždunarodnoe položenie bolgarskogo gosudarstva." *Vizantijskij vremennik* 28 (1968): 136–50.

Charanis, P. "On the Social Structure and Economic Organization of the Byzantine Empire in the Thirteenth Century and Later." *Byzantinoslavica* 12 (1951): 94–153.

Cheetham, N. *Mediaeval Greece*. New Haven, 1981.

Ćirković, S. "Beograd pod Kraljem Dušanom?" *Zbornik Istorijskog muzeja Srbije* 17–18 (1981): 37–45.

———. *Istorija srednjovekovne bosanske države*. Beograd, 1964.

———. "Pismenost i obrazovanje u srednjovekovnoj srpskoj državi." In *Istorija škola i obrazovanja kod Srba,* vol. 1. Beograd, 1974. Pp. 9–30.

————. "Poklad Kralja Vukašina." *Zbornik Filozofskog fakulteta* (Beogradski univerzitet) 14, no. 1 (1979): 153–63.

————. "Rusaška gospoda." *Istorijski časopis* 21 (1974): 5–17.

————. *Stefan Vukčić-Kosača i njegovo doba.* Serbian Academy of Sciences, posebna izdanja, 376. Beograd, 1964.

Choniates, Niketas. *O City of Byzantium, Annals of Niketas Choniates.* Edited and translated by H. Magoulias. Detroit, 1984.

Ćorović, V. *Historija Bosne.* Serbian Royal Academy, posebna izdanja, 129. Beograd, 1940.

————. *Kralj Tvrtko I Kotromanić.* Serbian Royal Academy, posebna izdanja, 56. Beograd, 1925.

————. "Motivi u predanju o ubistvu Cara Uroša." *Prilozi za književnost, jezik, istoriju i folklor* 1 (1921): 190–95.

————. "Podela vlasti izmedju Kraljeva Dragutina i Milutina, 1282–1284 godine." *Glas* (Serbian Royal Academy) 136 (1929): 5–12.

Ćurčić, S. *Gračanica: King Milutin's Church and its Place in Late Byzantine Architecture.* University Park, Pa., 1979.

————. "The Nemanjić Family Tree in the Light of the Ancestral Cult in the Church of Joachim and Anna at Studenica." *Zbornik radova Vizantološkog instituta* (Serbian Academy of Sciences) 14–15 (1973): 191–95.

Clement-Simon, F. "Une grand famille en Europe Centrale au XVᵉ siècle: Les Comtes de Cilli." *Revue d'histoire diplomatique* (Paris) 44 (1930): 1–19.

Cvetkova, B. "Analyse des principales sources Ottomanes du XVᵉ siècle sur les campagnes de Vladislav le Varnenien et Jean Hunyadi en 1443–1444." *Studia Albanica,* 1968, no. 1: 137–58.

Dančeva-Vasileva, A. "B"lgarija i Latinskata Imperija, 1207–1218." *Istoričeski pregled* 33, no. 1 (1977): 35–51.

Dennis, G. "The Byzantine-Turkish Treaty of 1403." *Orientalia Christiana Periodica* 33 (1967): 72–88. Also included in Dennis, *Byzantium and the Franks.*

————. *Byzantium and the Franks, 1350–1420.* Variorum reprint. London, 1982.

————. "The Capture of Thebes by the Navarrese (6 March 1378) and Other Chronological Notes in Two Paris Manuscripts." *Orientalia Christiana Periodica* 26 (1960): 42–50. Also included in Dennis, *Byzantium and the Franks.*

Dinić, M. *Humsko-Trebinjska vlastela.* Serbian Academy of Sciences, posebna izdanja, 397. Beograd, 1967.

————. "Nešto o Palmanu." *Prilozi za književnost, jezik, istoriju i folklor* 13 (1933): 76.

————. *O Nikoli Altomanoviću.* Serbian Royal Academy, posebna izdanja, 90. Beograd, 1932.

————. "Odnos izmedju Kraljeva Milutina i Dragutina." *Zbornik radova Vizantološkog instituta* (Serbian Academy of Sciences) 3 (1955): 49–82.

————. "Prilozi za istoriju vatrenog oružja u Dubrovniku i susednim zemljama." *Glas* (Serbian Royal Academy) 161 (1934): 57–97.

————. *Srpske zemlje u srednjem veku.* Beograd, 1978.

————. "Vlasti za vreme despotovine." *Zbornik Filozofskog fakulteta* (Beogradski univerzitet) 10, no. 1 (1968): 237–44.

————. "Za hronologiju Dušanovih osvajanja vizantiskih gradova." *Zbornik radova Vizantološkog instituta* (Serbian Academy of Sciences) 4 (1956): 1–10.

————. *Za istoriju rudarstva u srednjovekovnoj Srbiji i Bosni.* 2 vols. Serbian Academy of Sciences, posebna izdanja, 240, 355. Beograd, 1955, 1962.

Dinić-Knežević, D. "Prilog proučavanju sveštenstva u srednjovekovnoj Srbiji." *Godišnjak Filozofskog fakulteta u Novom Sadu* 11, no. 1 (1968): 51–61.

Ducas [Doukas]. *Decline and Fall of Byzantium to the Ottoman Turks by Doukas.* Edited and translated by H. Magoulias. Detroit, 1975.

Ducellier, A. *La façade maritime de l'Albanie au moyen âge: Durazzo et Valona du XIᵉ au XVᵉ siècle.* Thessaloniki (Institute for Balkan Studies), 1981.

————. "La façade maritime de la principauté des Kastriote de la fin du XIVᵉ siècle à la mort de Skanderbeg." *Studia Albanica,* 1968, no. 1: 119–36.

Dujčev, I. *B"lgarsko srednovekovie.* Sofija, 1972.

————. "Le Mont Athos et les Slaves au moyen âge." In *Le Millénaire du Mont Athos 963–1963: Études et Mélanges,* vol. 2. Venezia-Chevetogne, 1964. Pp. 121–43.

————. "Ot Černomen do Kosovo Polje." In I. Dujčev, *B"lgarsko srednovekovie.* Sofija, 1972, Pp. 546–87.

————. "Prinos k"m istorijata na Ivan Asen II." In I. Dujčev, *B"lgarsko srednovekovie.* Sofija, 1972. Pp. 289–321.

————. "V"stanieto v 1185 g. i negovata hronologija." *Izvestija na Instituta za b"lgarska istorija* (Bulgarian Academy of Sciences) 6 (1956): 327–56.

Dušan, Stefan. "The Code of Stephan Dušan." Edited and translated by M. Burr. *Slavonic and East European Review* 28 (1949–50): 198–217, 516–39.

Ferjančić, B. *Despoti u Vizantiji i južnoslovenskim zemljama.* Serbian Academy of Sciences, posebna izdanja, 336. Beograd, 1960.

————. *Tesalija u XIII i XIV veku.* Serbian Academy of Sciences, Vizantološki institut, Monograph no. 15. Beograd, 1974.

Fine, J. *The Bosnian Church: A New Interpretation.* East European Monographs, vol. 10, East European Quarterly, distributed by Columbia University Press. Boulder and New York, 1975.

————. *The Early Medieval Balkans: A Critical Survey from the Sixth to the Late Twelfth Century.* Ann Arbor, Mich., 1983.

————. "Mid–Fifteenth Century Sources on the Bosnian Church: Their Problems and Significance." *Medievalia et Humanistica,* n.s., 12 (1984): 17–31.

————. "Uloga Bosanske Crkve u javnom životu srednjovekovne Bosne." *Godišnjak Društva istoričara Bosne i Hercegovine 19 (1970–71).* Sarajevo, 1973. Pp. 19–29.

————. "Was the Bosnian Banate Subjected to Hungary in the Second Half of the Thirteenth Century?" *East European Quarterly* 3, no. 3 (June 1969): 167–77.

Finlay, G. *A History of Greece from its Conquest by the Romans to the Present Time,* B.C. *146 to* A.D. *1864.* Rev. ed. Vols. 3 and 4. Oxford, 1877.

Florinskij, T. *Južnye Slavjane i Vizantija vo vtoroj četverti XIV veka.* 2 vols. St. Petersburg, 1882.

Foretić, V. "Ugovor Dubrovnika sa Srpskim Velikim županom Stefanom Nemanjom i stara Dubrovačka djedina." *Rad* (Jugoslavenska akademija, Zagreb) 283 (1951): 51–118.

Geanakoplos, D. *Emperor Michael Palaeologus and the West.* Cambridge, Mass., 1959.

Gegaj, A. *L'Albanie et l'invasion Turque au XVᵉ siècle.* Paris, 1937.

Gjuzelev, V. "La Bulgare, Venise et l'Empire Latin de Constantinople au milieu du XIIIᵉ siècle." *Bulgarian Historical Review*, 1975, no. 4: 28–49.

————. *Duhovnata kultura na srednovekovna B"lgarija prez XIII–XIV v.* Sofija, 1977.

————. "La guerre Bulgaro-Hongroise au printemps de 1365 et des documents nouveaux sur la domination hongroise du royaume de Vidin, 1365–1369." *Byzantinobulgarica* 6 (1980): 153–72.

Gračev, V. "Terminy 'župa' i 'župan' v serbskih istočnikah XII–XIV vv. i traktovka ih v istoriografii." In *Istočniki i istoriografija Slavjanskogo srednevekov'ja* (Academy of Sciences of the USSR). Moscow, 1967. Pp. 3–52.

Gruber, D. "O Dukljanskoj i Dubrovačkoj nadbiskupiji do polovice XIII stoljeća." *Vjesnik Kr. Hrvatsko-Slavonsko-Dalmatinskoga Zemaljskog Arkiva* 14 (1912): 1–42, 121–77; 15 (1913): 104–46.

Heppell, M. *The Ecclesiastical Career of Gregory Camblak.* London, 1979.

————. "The Hesychast Movement in Bulgaria: The Turnovo School and its Relations with Constantinople." *Eastern Churches Review* 7 (1975): 9–20.

Herrin, J. "Realities of Byzantine Provincial Government: Hellas and Peloponnesos, 1180–1205." *Dumbarton Oaks Papers* 29 (1975): 255–84.

Historija naroda Jugoslavije. Vol. 1. Zagreb, 1953. A collective work.

Inalcik, H. "Ottoman Methods of Conquest." *Studia Islamica* 2 (1954): 103–30.

————. "Les regions de Kruje et de la Dibra autour de 1467 (après les documents Ottomans)." *Studia Albanica,* 1968, no. 2: 89–104.

Istorija Crne Gore. Vol. 2, pts. 1–2. Titograd, 1970. A collective work. Vol. 2 covers the period from the end of the twelfth to the end of the fifteenth century.

Istorija srpskog naroda. Vols. 1–2. Beograd, 1981–82. A collective work published by the Srpska književna zadruga.

Iz istorije Albanaca. Beograd, 1969. A collective work published by the Društvo istoričara Srbije.

Jacoby, D. "Les archontes grecs et la féodalité en Morée franque." *Travaux et mémoires* 2 (1967): 421–81.

————. "The Encounter of Two Societies: Western Conquerors and Byzantines in the Peloponnesus after the Fourth Crusade." *American Historical Review* 78 (1973): 873–906.

Jireček, K. *Istorija na B"lgarite.* 1876. Reprint. Sofija, 1978.

————. *Istorija Srba.* Translated into Serbo-Croatian and updated by J. Radonić. 2 vols. Beograd, 1952.

————. "Položaj i prošlost grada Drača." *Glasnik Srpskog geografskog društva* 2, no. 2 (September 1912): 182–91.

————. "Srpski Car Uroš, Kralj Vukašin i Dubrovnik." In *Zbornik Konstantina Jirečeka,* vol. 1. Serbian Academy of Sciences, posebna izdanja, 326. Beograd, 1959. Pp. 339–86.

————. "Toljen sin Kneza Miroslava Humskog." In *Zbornik Konstantina Jirečeka,* vol. 1. Serbian Academy of Sciences, posebna izdanja, 326. Beograd, 1959. Pp. 433–42.

————. "Trgovački putevi i rudnici Srbije i Bosne u srednjem vijeku." In *Zbornik Konstantina Jirečeka,* vol. 1. Serbian Academy of Sciences, posebna izdanja, 326. Beograd, 1959. Pp. 205–304.

————. *Zbornik Konstantina Jirečeka*. Vol. 1. Serbian Academy of Sciences, posebna izdanja, 326. Beograd, 1959.

Kalić-Mijušković, J. [= Mijušković, J.] *Beograd u srednjem veku*. Beograd, 1967.

Karpozilos, A. D. *The Ecclesiastical Controversy between the Kingdom of Nicea and the Principality of Epirus (1217–33)*. Thessaloniki, 1973.

Kašanin, M. *Srpska književnost u srednjem veku*. Beograd, 1975.

Každan, A. "La date de la rupture entre Pierre et Asen (vers 1193)." *Byzantion* 35 (1965): 167–74.

Kiselkov, V. S. *Žitieto na sv. Teodosij T"rnovski kato istoričeski pametnik*. Sofija, 1926. Includes Bulgarian translation of the text.

Klaić, N. *Povijest Hrvata u razvijenom srednjem vijeku*. Zagreb, 1976.

Klaić, V. *Bribirski knezovi od plemena Šubić do god 1347*. Zagreb, 1897.

————. "Hrvatska plemena od XII do XVI stoljeća." *Rad* (Jugoslavenska akademija, Zagreb) 130 (1897): 1–85.

————. *Krčki knezovi Frankapani*. Zagreb, 1901.

————. *Poviest Bosne*. Zagreb, 1882.

————. *Povijest Hrvata*. 5 vols. 1899–1911. Reprint. Zagreb, 1982.

Kovačević-Kojić, D. [= Kovačević, D.] *Gradska naselja srednjovjekovne bosanske države*. Sarajevo, 1978.

————. "O knezovima u gradskim naseljima srednjovjekovne Bosne." *Radovi* (Filozofski fakultet, Sarajevo) 6 (1970–71): 333–44.

————. "Prilog pitanju ranih bosansko-turskih odnosa." *Godišnjak Društva istoričara Bosne i Hercegovine* 11 (1961): 257–63.

————. "Razvoj i organizacija carina u srednjevjekovnoj Bosni." *Godišnjak Istoriskog društva Bosne i Hercegovine* (subsequently *Godišnjak Društva istoričara Bosne i Hercegovine*) 6 (1954): 229–48.

————. "Žore Bokšić, dubrovački trgovac i protovestijar bosanskih kraljeva." *Godišnjak Društva istoričara Bosne i Hercegovine* 13 (1962): 289–309.

Kovačević, Lj. "Nekoliko hronoloških ispravka u srpskoj istoriji." *Godišnjica Nikole Čupića* 3 (1879): 387–96.

————. "Nekoliko pitanja o Stefanu Nemanjiću." *Glas* (Serbian Royal Academy) 58 (1900): 1–108.

Krekić, B. *Dubrovnik in the Fourteenth and Fifteenth Centuries: A City between East and West*. Norman, Okla., 1972.

————. "O ratu Dubrovnika i Srbije, 1327–1328." *Zbornik radova Vizantološkog instituta* (Serbian Academy of Sciences) 11 (1968): 193–203.

Kritovoulos, *History of Mehmed the Conqueror*. Edited and translated by C. Riggs. Princeton, N.J., 1954.

Laiou-Thomadakis, A. *Peasant Society in the Late Byzantine Empire: A Social and Demographic Study*. Princeton, N.J., 1977.

Lascaris, M. "Influences byzantines dans la diplomatique Bulgare, Serbe et Slavo-Roumane." *Byzantinoslavica* 3 (1931): 500–510.

[Lazar, Knez.] *O Knezu Lazaru*. Papers from the Kruševac symposium on Knez Lazar. Beograd, 1975.

Lazarov, I. "Upravlenieto na Mihail II Asen i Irina Komnina (1246–1256)." *Vekove*, 1984, no. 2: 12–19.

Lemerle, P. *L'Emirat d'Aydin, Byzance et l'occident: Recherches sur "La Geste d'Umur Pacha."* Paris, 1957.

————. *Philippes et la Macédoine orientale*. Paris, 1945.

Léonard, E. *Les Angevins de Naples*. Paris, 1954.

Lišev, S. *B"lgarskijat srednovekoven grad*. Bulgarian Academy of Sciences, Institute for History. Sofija, 1970.

Loenertz, R.-J. "Athènes et Néopatras." 2 pts. In *Byzantina et Franco-Graeca*. Rome, 1978. Pp. 183–293.

———. "Aux origines du despotat d'Epire et la principauté d'Achaie." *Byzantion* 43 (1973): 360–94.

———. *Byzantina et Franco-Graeca*. 2 vols. of collected articles. Rome, 1970, 1978.

———. "Une page de Jérôme Zurita relative aux Duchés Catalans de Grèce." *Revue des Études Byzantines* 14 (1956): 158–68.

———. "Pour l'histoire du Péloponèse au XIVᵉ siècle (1382–1404)." *Études Byzantines* 1 (1943): 152–96.

Longnon, J. "Problèmes de l'histoire de la principauté de Morée." *Journal des savants*, 1946, pp. 77–93, 147–61.

Luce, S. B. "Modon—A Venetian Station in Medieval Greece." In *Classical and Medieval Studies in Honor of E. K. Rand*. New York, 1938. Pp. 195–208.

Luttrell, A. *Latin Greece, the Hospitallers, and the Crusades, 1291–1440*. Variorum reprint. London, 1982.

———. "The Latins of Argos and Nauplia." *Papers of the British School at Rome* 34 (n.s. 21) (1966): 34–55. Also included in Luttrell, *Latin Greece, the Hospitallers, and the Crusades*.

———. "Vonitza in Epirus and its Lords: 1306–1377." *Rivista di Studi Bizantini e Neoellenici* 11 (n.s. 1) (1964): 131–41. Also included in Luttrell, *Latin Greece, the Hospitallers, and the Crusades*.

Maksimović, Lj. "Karakter poreskog sistema u grčkim oblastima Srpskog carstva." *Zbornik radova Vizantološkog instituta* 17 (1976): 101–23.

Malović, M. "Stefan Dečanski i Zeta." *Istorijski zapisi* (Titograd) 41, no. 4 (1979): 5–69.

Marković, I. *Dukljansko-barska metropolija*. Zagreb, 1902.

Mavromatis, L. *La fondation de l'Empire Serbe: Le Kralj Milutin*. Thessaloniki, 1978.

Meyendorff, J. *A Study of Gregory Palamas*. London, 1962.

Mihaljčić, R. *Kraj Srpskog Carstva*. Beograd, 1975.

Mijušković, J. [= Kalić-Mijušković, J.] "Humska vlasteoska porodica Sankovići." *Istorijski časopis* 11 (1960): 17–54.

Miller, W. *Essays on the Latin Orient*. Cambridge, 1921.

———. *The Latins in the Levant: A History of Frankish Greece (1204–1566)*. London, 1908.

Mirković, L. "Mrnjavčevići." *Starinar*, n.s., 3 (1924–25): 11–41.

Mošin, V. "Vizantiski uticaj u Srbiji u XIV v." *Jugoslovenski istoriski časopis* 3 (1937): 147–60.

Mutafčiev, P. *Istorija na b"lgarskija narod*. Completed by I. Dujčev. Pt. 2. Sofija, 1944.

———. *Izbrani proizvedenija*. 2 vols. Sofija, 1973.

———. "Proizhod"t na Asenovci." In P. Mutafčiev, *Izbrani proizvedenija*, vol. 2. Sofija, 1973. Pp. 150–94.

———. "Vladetelite na Prosek." In P. Mutafčiev, *Izbrani proizvedenija*, vol. 1. Sofija, 1973. Pp. 172–285.

"Napredak." *Poviest hrvatskih zemalja Bosne i Hercegovine.* Sarajevo, 1942.

Naumov, E. P. "Feudalniot separatizam i politikata na Dušan vo 1342–1355 godina." *Istorija* (Skopje), 1968, no. 2: 63–76.

_____. *Gospodstvujuščij klass i gosudarstvennaja vlast v Serbii XIII–XV vv.* Moscow, 1975.

_____. "Iz istorii bolgarskogo Pričernomor'ja v konce XIV veka." *Bulgarian Historical Review*, 1976, no. 1: 47–59.

_____. "K istorii vizantijskoj i serbskoj pronii." *Vizantijskij vremennik* 34 (1973): 22–31.

Nicol, D. *The Byzantine Family of Kantakouzenos.* Dumbarton Oaks Studies, vol. 11. Washington, D.C., 1968.

_____. *The Despotate of Epirus.* Oxford, 1957.

_____. *The Despotate of Epiros, 1267–1479.* Cambridge, 1984.

_____. "The Fourth Crusade and the Greek and Latin Empires, 1204–61." Chapter 7 of *Cambridge Medieval History*, vol. 4, pt. 1. Cambridge, 1966. Pp. 275–330.

_____. *The Last Centuries of Byzantium, 1261–1453.* New York, 1972.

_____. "The Relations of Charles of Anjou with Nikephoros of Epiros." *Byzantinische Forschungen* 4 (1972): 170–94.

Nikov, P. "Beležki za jugoiztočna B"lgarija prez" epohata na Terterovci." *Periodičesko spisanie* 70 (1909): 563–88.

_____. "B"lgari i Tatari v" srednite vekove." *B"lgarska istoričeska biblioteka* 2, no. 3 (1929): 97–141.

_____. *B"lgaro-ungarski otnošenija ot 1257 do 1277.* In *Sbornik* (Bulgarian Academy of Sciences) 11. Sofija, 1920.

_____. "Car Boril pod svetlinata na edin nov pametnik." *Spisanie* (Bulgarian Academy of Sciences) 3 (1912): 121–34.

_____. *Istorija na Vidinskoto knjažestvo do 1323 godina.* In *Godišnik na Sofijskija universitet* (Istoriko-filologičeski fakultet) 18, no. 8. Sofija, 1922.

_____. "Izpravki k"m b"lgarskata istorija." *Izvestija na Istoričeskoto društvo v Sofija* 5 (1922): 57–84.

_____. "K"m istorijat na severozapadnite B"lgarski zemi." *Spisanie* (Bulgarian Academy of Sciences) 16, no. 9 (1918): 43–64.

_____. *Tataro-b"lgarski otnošenija pr"z sr"dnit v"kov s"ogled k"m caruvaneto na Smileca.* In *Godišnik na Sofijskija universitet* (Istoriko-filologičeski fakultet) 15–16. Sofija, 1920.

_____. "S"dbata na severozapadnite B"lgarski zemi prez srednite vekove." *B"lgarska istoričeska biblioteka* 3, no. 1 (1930): 96–153.

Novaković, R. "Oko natpisa na crkvi Sv. Luke u Kotor." Zbornik za likove umetnosti 5 (1969): 15–21.

Novaković, S. "Poslednji Brankovići u istoriji i narodnom pevanju 1456–1502." *Letopis Matice srpske* 146 (1886): 1–47; 147 (1886): 1–32; 148 (1886): 1–70.

Orbini, M. *Kraljevstvo Slovena.* Edited by S. Ćirković. Beograd, 1968.

Ostrogorsky, G. [= Ostrogorski, G.] "Étienne Dušan et la noblesse serbe dans la lutte contre Byzance." *Byzantion* 22 (1952–53): 151–59.

_____. *History of the Byzantine State.* 3d ed. New Brunswick, N.J., 1969.

_____. *Pour l'histoire de la féodalité Byzantine.* Brussels, 1954.

_____. *Serska oblast posle Dušanove smrti.* Serbian Academy of Sciences, Vizantološki institut, Monograph no. 9. Beograd, 1965.

Petar, R. "Poslednje godine balkanske politike Kralja Žigmunda (1435–1437)." *Godišnjak Filozofskog fakulteta* (Novi Sad) 12, no. 1 (1969): 89–108.

Petrov, B. "B"lgaro-vizantijskite otnošenija prez vtorata polovina na XIII v. otrazeni v poemata na Manuil Fil 'Za voennite podvizi na izvestnija čutoven protostrator.'" *Izvestija na Instituta za B"lgarska istorija* (Bulgarian Academy of Sciences) 6 (1956): 545–72.

Pius II. *Commentaries*. Introduction and notes by L. Gabel. Translated by F. Gragg. Serialized in *Smith College Studies in History*, vol. 22, nos. 1–2 (1936–37); vol. 25, nos. 1–4 (1939–40); vol. 30 (1947); vol. 35 (1951); vol. 43 (1957).

Polyvjannyj, D. "K istorii Vidinskogo despotstva v XIV veke." In *B"lgarsko srednovekovie*. Dujčev Festschrift. Sofija, 1980. Pp. 93–98.

Pulaha, S. "Sur les causes des insurrections des années '30 du XVe siècle en Albanie." *Studia Albanica*, 1967, no. 2: 31–42.

Purković, M. *Knez i Despot Stefan Lazarević*. Beograd, 1978.

Radonić, J. "O Despotu Jovanu Oliveru i njegovoj ženi Ani Mariji." *Glas* (Serbian Royal Academy) 94 (1914): 74–108.

————. "Der Grossvojvode von Bosnien Sandalj Hranić Kosača." *Archiv für slavische Philologie* 19 (1897): 387–456.

————. "O Knezu Pavlu Radenoviću—priložak istoriji Bosne krajem XIV i početkom XV veka." *Letopis Matice srpske* 211 (1902): 39–62; 212 (1902): 34–61.

————. "Sporazum u Tati 1426 i Srpsko-Ugarski odnosi od XIII–XVI veka." *Glas* (Serbian Royal Academy) 187 (1941): 117–232.

————. *Zapadna Evropa i balkanski narodi prema Turcima u prvoj polovini XV veka*. Novi Sad, 1905.

Resti, J. *Chronica Ragusina ab origine urbis usque ad annum 1451*. Edited by S. Nodilo. Jugoslavenska akademija, Zagreb. Monumenta spectantia historiam Slavorum Meridionalium 25, Scriptores 2. Zagreb, 1893.

Rozov, V. "Sinajci v Serbii v XIV v." *Byzantinoslavica* 1 (1929): 16–21.

Runciman, S. *Mistra: Byzantine Capital of the Peloponnese*. London, 1980.

Russel, J. "Late Medieval Balkan and Asia Minor Populations." *Journal of the Economic and Social History of the Orient* 3 (1960): 265–74.

Ruvarac, I. "Vukan, najstariji sin Stevana Nemanje, i Vukanovići." *Godišnjica Nikole Čupića* 10 (1888): 1–9.

Savčeva, E. "Sevastokrator Strez." *Godišnik na Sofijskija universitet* (Istoričeski fakultet) 68 (1974): 67–97.

Setton, K. "Athens in the Later Twelfth Century." *Speculum* 19 (1944): 179–207.

————. *Catalan Domination of Athens, 1311–1388*. Cambridge, Mass., 1948.

————. "The Latins in Greece and the Aegean from the Fourth Crusade to the End of the Middle Ages." Chapter 9 of *Cambridge Medieval History*, vol. 4, pt. 1. Cambridge, 1966. Pp. 389–430.

Šabanović, H. *Bosanski pašaluk*. Naučno društvo Bosne i Hercegovine, Djela, 14. Sarajevo, 1959.

————. "Pitanje turske vlasti u Bosni do pohoda Mehmeda II 1463 g." *Godišnjak Društva istoričara Bosne i Hercegovine* 7 (1955): 37–51.

Šišić, F. *Pregled povijesti hrvatskoga naroda*. 1920. Reprint. Zagreb, 1975.

————. *Vojvoda Hrvoje Vukčić-Hrvatinić i njegovo doba*. Zagreb, 1902.

Škrivanić, G. *Kosovska bitka*. Cetinje, 1956.

Šmaus, A. "Kuripešićev izveštaj o Kosovskom boju." *Prilozi za književnost, jezik, istoriju i folklor* 18 (1938): 509–18.

Šufflay, M. "Povjest Sjevernih Arbanasa." *Arhiv za Arbanašku starinu, jezik i etnologiju* (Beograd) 2, no. 2 (1924): 193–242.

———. *Srbi i Arbanasi.* Beograd, 1925.

Šunjić, M. *Dalmacija u XV stoljeću.* Sarajevo, 1967.

Soulis, G. *The Serbs and Byzantium during the Reign of Tsar Stephen Dušan (1331–1355) and his Successors.* Dumbarton Oaks Byzantine Institute, Washington, D.C., 1984.

Sphrantzes, G. *The Fall of the Byzantine Empire.* Edited and translated by M. Philippides. Amherst, Mass., 1980.

Spremić, M. "Albanija od XIII do XV veka." In *Iz istorije Albanaca.* Collective work published by Društva istoričara Srbije. Beograd, 1969. Pp. 33–44.

———. "Despot Djuradj Branković i Mačvanska banovina." *Istorijski časopis* 23 (1976): 23–36.

———. "Sveti Srdj pod mletačkom vlašću 1396–1479." *Zbornik Filozofskog fakulteta* (Beogradski univerzitet) 7, no. 1 (1963): 295–312.

Stanojević, St. *Borba o nasledstvo Baošino.* Sremski Karlovci, 1902.

———. *Borba za samostalnost katoličke crkve u Nemanjičkoj državi.* Serbian Royal Academy, posebna izdanja, 38. Beograd, 1912.

———. "Dogadjaji 1253 i 1254 god." *Glas* (Serbian Royal Academy) 164 (1935): 191–98.

———. "Hronologija borbe izmedju Stevana i Vukana." *Glas* (Serbian Royal Academy) 153 (1933): 93–101.

———. "Nemanja." *Godišnjica Nikole Čupića* 42 (1933): 93–132.

———. "O napadu ugarskog Kralja Andrije II na Srbiju zbog proglas kraljevstva." *Glas* (Serbian Royal Academy) 161 (1934): 109–30.

Starr, J. *Romania: The Jewries of the Levant after the Fourth Crusade.* Paris, 1949.

Stiernon, L. "Les origines du Despotat d'Epire." *Revue des Études Byzantines* 17 (1959): 90–126.

Stracimirović, Dj. "O prošlosti i neimarstvu Boke Kotorske." *Spomenik* (Serbian Royal Academy) 28 (1895): 11–13.

Thiriet, F. "Quelques réflexions sur la politique Vénitienne à l'égard de Georges Skanderbeg." *Studia Albanica,* 1968, no. 1: 87–93.

Topping, P. *Feudal Institutions as Revealed in the Assizes of Romania, the Law Code of Frankish Greece.* Philadelphia, 1949.

———. *Studies on Latin Greece:* A.D. *1205–1715.* Variorum Reprint. London, 1977.

Trpković, V. [= Atanasovski, V.] "Branivojevići." *Istoriski glasnik,* 1960, nos. 1–2: 55–84.

———. "Humska zemlja." *Zbornik Filozofskog fakulteta* (Beogradski univerzitet) 8 (1964): 225–59.

———. "Tursko-ugarski sukobi do 1402." *Istoriski glasnik,* 1959, nos. 1–2: 93–120.

Vacalopoulos, A. *Origins of the Greek Nation: The Byzantine Period, 1204–1461.* New Brunswick, N.J., 1970.

Vasil'evskij, V. "O pervyh Nemanićah." Appendix 3 of his "Sojuz dvuh imperij." In V. Vasil'evskij, *Trudy,* vol. 4. Leningrad, 1930. Pp. 91–102.

Vego, M. *Iz historije srednjovjekovne Bosne i Hercegovine.* Sarajevo, 1980.

———. *Naselja bosanske srednjevjekovne države.* Sarajevo, 1957.

Villehardouin, Geoffrey de. "Chronicle of the Fourth Crusade and the Conquest of Constantinople." In *Memoirs of the Crusades by Villehardouin and de Joinville*, edited and translated by F. Marzials. New York, 1958.

Weinberger, L. *Bulgaria's Synagogue Poets: The Kastoreans*. University, Ala., 1983.

Wenzel, M. "Bosnian and Herzegovinian Tombstones—Who Made Them and Why." *Südost-Forschungen* 21 (1962): 102–43.

———. *Ukrasni motivi na stećima*. Sarajevo, 1965.

Wittek, P. "Yazijioghlu 'Ali on the Christian Turks of the Dobruja." *Bulletin of the School of Oriental and African Studies* (University of London) 14 (1952): 639–68.

Wolff, R. L. "The Organization of the Latin Patriarchate of Constantinople, 1204–1261: Social and Administrative Consequences of the Latin Conquest." *Traditio* 6 (1948): 33–60. Also included in Wolff, *Studies in the Latin Empire*.

———. "The Second Bulgarian Empire: Its Origin and History to 1204." *Speculum* 24 (1949): 167–206. Also included in Wolff, *Studies in the Latin Empire*.

———. *Studies in the Latin Empire of Constantinople*. Variorum Reprint. London, 1976.

Wratislaw, A. "History of the County of Cilly." *Transactions of the Royal Historical Society* 5 (1877): 327–38.

Zachariadou, E. "The Conquest of Adrianople by the Turks." *Studi Veneziani* 12 (1970): 211–17.

———. "The First Serbian Campaigns of Mehemmed II (1454–1455)." *Anali Istituto Universitario Orientale di Napoli*, n.s., 14 (1964): 837–40.

Zakythinos, D. *Le Despotat Grec de Morée*. 2 vols. Athens, 1932, 1953.

Živković, P. *Tvrtko II Tvrtković*. Sarajevo, 1981.

Živojinović, M. "Sveta Gora i Lionska unija." *Zbornik radova Vizantološkog instituta* (Serbian Academy of Sciences) 18 (1978): 141–53.

———. "Sveta Gora u doba Latinskog carstva." *Zbornik radova Vizantološkog instituta* (Serbian Academy of Sciences) 17 (1976): 77–90.

Zlatarski, V. *Istorija na b"lgarskata d"ržava prez srednite vekove*. Vol. 3. Sofija, 1940.

Index

For major topics, see the Contents. Since Ć and Č, Š, and Ž are the equivalents of Ch, Sh, and Zh, words using these letters are alphabetized as if they were written Ch, Sh, and Zh. Italicized numbers in the index refer to items referred to, but not by name (e.g., Constantinople being referred to as "the capital," Helen being referred to as "Dušan's wife"). The limited number of topical headings are not complete; they are intended to pick up more sustained discussions and do not attempt to include all passing references. In the Later Middle Ages family names are coming into existence for much of the high nobility; unfortunately no agreement has been reached as to whether such people should be indexed under first or last names. Thus Geoffrey I Villehardouin may be found under either Geoffrey or Villehardouin. As a general rule, when all things are equal and a particular name is not by tradition listed under a first name, I have chosen family names to list individuals. In the case of women, since frequently they were married more than once, I have chosen to list them under the families they were born into. Since the index is too long to cross-list all such individuals, however, the reader, not finding an individual under one name, should then seek him/her under the other.

Čemren (town), 288
Čeotina River, 479
Černomen (village, site of Marica Battle), 379
Červen (town), 440
Chiara (wife of Nerio II), 568
Chinardo, Philip (Manfred's governor for Albania), 169, 215 n
Chios (island), 36, 170, 434, 450
Ćirković, S. (scholar), 261, 265, 289, 404 n, 425, 446, 452 n, 456, 457, 480, 579
Čoka (fortress), 495
Chomatianos, Demetrius (Archbishop of Ohrid), 79, 113–16, 119–20, 127–28, 136, 449
Choniates, Michael (Archbishop of Athens), 34, 36–37, 64
Choniates, Niketas (Byzantine historian), 4–5, 10–11, 13, 25–26, 29, 31, 34, 81, 85, 95
Christopher (Bishop of Ancyra), 127
Chrysopolis (town), 345
Chrysos, Dobromir (Vlach brigand chief), 29–30, 32–33, 37, 86–87, 95
Church Law, 39, 91, 115, 117–19, 314–15
Church Union, issue of, 56, 60–63, 67, 75–80, 83, 107, 185–87, 191–95, 233, 235, 258, 445, 534, 536–38, 546, 562–65. *See also* Anti-Unionists; Florence, Council/Union of; Lyons, Council/Union of
Cistercians, 65
Clarenza [Glarentza], 240, 401, 543–45
Clement V, Pope, 142
Coinage (and cash economy), 22, 200, 230, 257, 263, 264, 299, 319, 358, 363, 367, 382, 383, 389, 392, 403, 409, 418, 451 n, 465, 555
Commerce (and merchants), 9, 19–20, 23, 51, 60–62, 65, 68, 71, 125, 128, 141–42, 145, 164–65, 189, 200, 202, 230, 246–47, 256, 264, 273, 279, 281–84, 315, 328, 337–38, 341–42, 357, 359–61, 366–67, 370, 383, 391, 394–95, 418, 422, 427, 436, 447–48, 450, 451 n, 456, 460–61, 472, 474, 479–80, 487–88, 490–92, 494–95, 503, 511, 514–15, 519–21, 579–81, 611 n
Comnenus dynasty/family, 9, 60. *See also* Alexius II, Andronicus I, *and* Manuel I Comnenus
Comnenus, Isaac (son-in-law of Alexius III Angelus), 28
Constance, Council of, 445
Constantine I (Byzantine Emperor), 526

Constantine XI Palaeologus (Morean despot, then Byzantine emperor), 429, 543–46, 548, 561–64
Constantine (brother of Theodore of Epirus), 128, 133, 160
Constantine (of Thessaly, son of John I of Thessaly), 235, 237, 238, 241
Constantine Bodin (ruler of Zeta), 2
Constantine Mihailović of Ostrovica (Janissary chronicler), 414, 576
Constantine Nemanjić (son of Milutin), 260, 263–65, 268–70
Constantine the Philosopher (Kostenečki), 424, 426, 429, 443–45, 499, 505, 510, 523–27
Constantine Tih (Tsar of Bulgaria), 172–83, 185, 187, 195, 196, 199, 435
Constantinople (city), 6–7, 9, 12, 14–15, 25, 27–29, 32–38, 51, 55–56, 60–66, 68–69, 71, 76, 78, 80, 82–88, 90–91, 98–99, 105, 112–13, 115, 120, 122–26, 128–35, 157–59, 161, 164–66, 170–71, 173–74, 185–89, *191,* 192, 194, 198, 204, 215 n, 225, 227, 230–31, 235–36, 243, *250,* 251–53, 255, 260, 263, 270, 272, 284, 293–96, 302–03, 305, *307,* 308–10, 321–22, *325,* 326–27, 334–36, 349, 351, 353, 365–67, 378, 387–89, 403, 423, 425, 429, 433–34, 437–44, 450, 500, *503,* 505–07, 529, 536, 538, 540–41, 546, 555, 560, 562–64, 567–69, 575–76, 579, 584, 589–90, 595, 597–98, 604
Constantinople, Church/diocese/Patriarch of: Greek (including Patriarch in Nicea, 1208–61), 68, 78, 80, 90–91, 114–16, 119–21, 127, 129–31, 194, 214 n, 366–67, 378, 387–88, 417, 444, 536–38, 563, 569; Latin (1204–61), 56, 62–63, 76, 78, 80, 114; Council of (1341), 438; Council of (1351), 438–39. *See also* Greek Church
Contarini, Bartholomeo (Venetian nobleman), 568
Corfu [Kerkira, Corcyra] (island), 7, 9, 68, 126, 128, 161, 184, 194, 236, 428, 567
Corinth (town), 36–37, 64–65, 90, 249, 401–03, 431–34, 446, 543, 545–46, 562, 565; Archbishop of (Greek), 433; Archbishop of (Latin), 90; Gulf of, 36, 65–66, 245, 320–21, 544, 568; Isthmus of, 37, 64, 432, 434, 539, 545, 548, 561–62, 567
Cornaro, Peter (Venetian nobleman), 451 n
Coron [Korone] (town), 71, 189, 328, 428, 539, 568

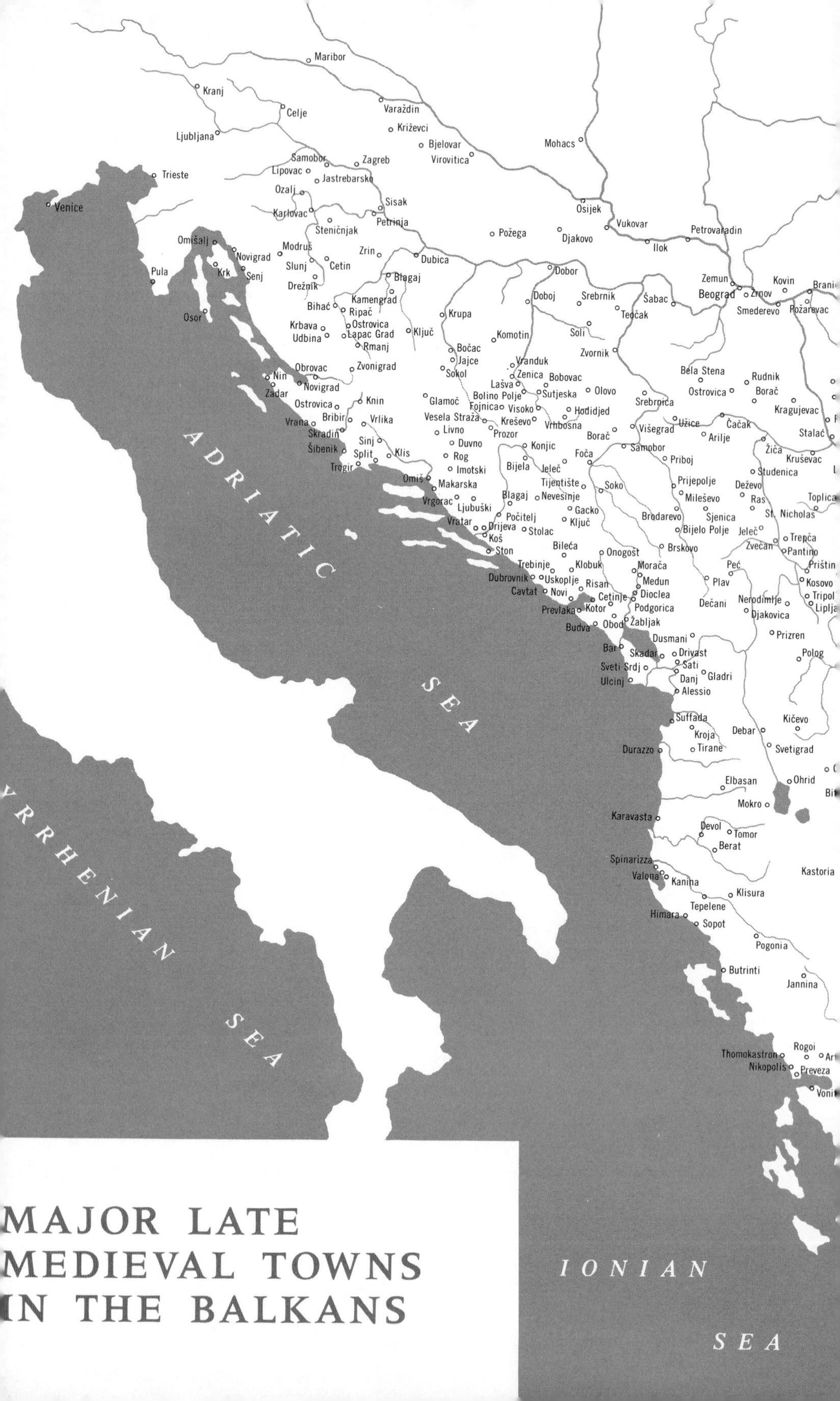

MAJOR LATE
MEDIEVAL TOWNS
IN THE BALKANS

CARINTHIA

STYRIA

Savinja R

SLOVENIA

ZAGORJE

PANNONIA

Danube R

CARNIOLA

KRANJ

Krka R

CROATIA

Kupa R

GORICA

Glina R

Gvozd Mt

MODRUŠ

ISTRIA

VINODOL

Krk

Cres

Rab

GACKA

BUŽANE

Drava R

VOJVODINA

BANAT

SLAVONIA

Sava R

VUKOVSKA ŽUPA

SREM

Una R

DUBICA

Vrbas R

Japra R

Ukrina R

USORA

Spreča R

MAČVA

ŠUMADIJA

Gulf of Kvarner

Pag

Mt Velebit

LIKA

KRBAVA

Sana R

DONJI KRAJ

Zrmanja R

LUČKA ŽUPA

Krka R

ČETINA

BRIBIR

Cetina R

DALMATIA

Brač

Vis

Hvar

Korčula

Pelješac

PLIVA

ZAVRŠJE

LIVNO

POLJICA

IMOTSKI

KRAJINA

DINARIC RANGE

USKOPLJE

RAMA

Nerewa R

DUVNO

HUM

TREBINJE

LJUBOMIR

POPOVO

KONAVLI

B O S N I A

Bosna R

Vrbas R

Drina R

LAŠVA

DABAR

TRUSINA

Zeta R

Moraća R

Piva R

Tara R

Ub R

SOLI

SERBIA

Kolubara R

Morava

W Morava

Čemerno Mts

KOPAONIK

Lim R

Č.cetina R

BUDIMLJE

Mt Rogozna

Ibar R

Ibar R

Toplica

DRENICA

Drenica

HVOSNO

KOSOVO

Sitnica

LIM

POLOG

POREČ

PEĆ

Gulf of Kotor

GRBALJ

UPPER ZETA

Lovćen Mt

ZETA

L. Skadar

LOWER ZETA

Drin

PILOT

Bojana R

Mati R

Erzen R

Cape Rodoni

ALBANIA

MYZEGEJA

Shkumbi R

Devolli R

L. Ohrid

Seman R

Osumi R

Mt Tomor

Akrokeraunian
Promontory

Vijose R

PI

Corfu

EPIRUS

TYRRHENIAN SEA

ADRIATIC SEA

Gulf of Arta

Leucas

ACA

Ithaca

Cephalc

IONIAN ISLANDS

Zakyr

IONIAN SEA

LATE MEDIEVAL
BALKAN REGIONS